STEREOTYPES
AND PREJUDICE

Key Readings in Social Psychology

General Editor: ARIE W. KRUGLANSKI, University of Maryland at College Park

The aim of this series is to make key articles in each area of social psychology available to senior undergraduate and graduate students in an attractive, user-friendly format. Many professors want to encourage their students to engage directly in research in their fields, yet this can often be daunting for students coming to detailed study of a topic for the first time. Moreover, declining library budgets mean that articles are not always readily available, and course packs can be expensive and time-consuming to produce. **Key Readings in Social Psychology** aims to address this need by providing comprehensive volumes, each one of which will be edited by a senior and active researcher in the field. Articles will be carefully chosen to illustrate the way the field has developed historically as well as current issues and research directions. Each volume will have a similar structure, which will include:

- An overview chapter, as well as introductions to sections and articles,
- Questions for class discussion,
- Annotated bibliographies,
- Full author and subject indexes.

Published Titles

The Self in Social Psychology	Roy F. Baumeister
Stereotypes and Prejudice	Charles Stangor

Titles in Preparation

Social Psychology	Arie W. Kruglanski and E. Tory Higgins
Social Cognition	David Hamilton
Motivation and Cognition	E. Tory Higgins and Arie W. Kruglanski
Close Relationships	Harry Reis and Caryl Rusbult
Group Processes	John Levine and Richard Moreland
Intergroup Relations	Michael Hogg and Dominic Abrams
Language and Communication	Gün R. Semin
Attitudes and Persuasion	Richard E. Petty, Shelly Chaiken, and Russell Fazio
Social Psychology of Emotions	W. Gerrod Parrott
Social Psychology of Culture	Hazel Markus and Shinobu Kitayama
Social Psychology of Health	Peter Salovey and Alexander J. Rothman

STEREOTYPES AND PREJUDICE:
Essential Readings

Edited by

Charles Stangor
University of Maryland
College Park, MD

USA	Publishing Office:	PSYCHOLOGY PRESS *A member of the Taylor & Francis Group* 325 Chestnut Street Philadelphia, PA 19106 Tel: (215) 625-8900 Fax: (215) 625-2940
	Distribution Center:	PSYCHOLOGY PRESS *A member of the Taylor & Francis Group* 47 Runway Road, Suite G Levittown, PA 19057-4700 Tel: (215) 269-0400 Fax: (215) 269-0363
UK		PSYCHOLOGY PRESS *A member of the Taylor & Francis Group* 27 Church Road Hove E. Sussex, BN3 2FA Tel: +44 (0)1273 207411 Fax: +44 (0)1273 205612

STEREOTYPES AND PREJUDICE: Essential Readings

2 3 4 5 6 7 8 9 0

Printed by Edwards Brothers, Ann Arbor, MI, 2000.
Cover design by Ellen Seguin.

A CIP catalog record for this book is available from the British Library.
∞The paper in this publication meets the requirements of the ANSI Standard Z39.48-1984 (Permanence of Paper).

Library of Congress Cataloging-in-Publication Data

Stereotypes and prejudice : essential readings / [edited by] Charles Stangor.
    p. cm.— (Key readings in social psychology)
    Includes bibliographical references and index.
    ISBN 0-86377-588-8 (alk. paper) — ISBN 0-86377-589-6 (pbk. : alk. paper)
    1. Stereotype (Psychology) 2. Prejudices. I. Stangor, Charles. II. Series

BF323.S63 S735 2000
303.3'85—dc21   99-056936

ISBN: 0-86377-588-8 (case)
ISBN: 0-86377-589-6 (paper)

Contents

About the Editor   ix
Acknowledgments   xi

Volume Overview   1
    Charles Stangor

P A R T   1
Conceptualizing Stereotypes and Prejudice   17

READING 1
The Nature of Prejudice   20
    Gordon W. Allport

READING 2
Social Categorization: Cognitions, Values and Groups   49
    Henri Tajfel and Joseph P. Forgas

READING 3
Stereotypes as Individual and Collective Representations   64
    Charles Stangor and Mark Schaller

P A R T   2
Measuring Stereotypes and Prejudice   83

READING 4
Are Racial Stereotypes *Really* Fading?
The Princeton Trilogy Revisited   86
    Patricia G. Devine and Andrew J. Elliott

READING 5

Racial Ambivalence and American Value Conflict:
Correlational and Priming Studies of Dual Cognitive Structures   100

Irwin Katz and R. Glen Hass

READING 6

Category and Stereotype Activation: Is Prejudice Inevitable?   119

Lorella Lepore and Rupert Brown

PART 3

How do Stereoypes Develop?   139

READING 7

Gender Stereotypes Stem From the Distribution
of Women and Men Into Social Roles   142

Alice H. Eagly and Valerie J. Steffen

READING 8

Illusory Correlation in Interpersonal Perception:
A Cognitive Basis of Stereotypic Judgments   161

David L. Hamilton and Robert K. Gifford

READING 9

Prejudice as Self-Image Maintenance:
Affirming the Self Through Derogating Others   172

Steven Fein and Steven J. Spencer

READING 10

Language Use in Intergroup Contexts:
The Linguistic Intergroup Bias   191

Anne Maass, Daniela Salvi, Luciano Arcuri, and Gün Semin

PART 4

Why Are Stereotypes Maintained Even When They Are Inaccurate?   209

READING 11

A Hypothesis-Confirming Bias in Labeling Effects   212

John M. Darley and Paget H. Gross

READING 12

The Nonverbal Mediation of Self-Fulfilling Prophecies
in Interracial Interaction   226

Carl O. Word, Mark P. Zanna, and Joel Cooper

READING 13

Compensating for Stigma: Obese and Nonobese
Women's Reactions to Being Visible   234

Carol T. Miller, Esther D. Rothblum, Diane Felicio, and Pamela Brand

P A R T   5
When Do We Use Stereotypes and Prejudice?   251

READING 14

Stereotypes as Judgmental Heuristics:
Evidence of Circadian Variations in Discrimination   254

Galen V. Bodenhausen

READING 15

Social Dominance Orientation: A Personality Variable
Predicting Social and Political Attitudes   259

Felicia Pratto, Jim Sidanius, Lisa M. Stallworth, and Bertram F. Malle

READING 16

The Aversive Form of Racism   289

Samuel L. Gaertner and John F. Dovidio

READING 17

Self-Directed Versus Other-Directed Affect as a Consequence of Prejudice-
Related Discrepancies   305

Margo J. Monteith, Patricia G. Devine, and Julia R. Zuwerink

P A R T   6
The Impact of Stereotypes and Prejudice   323

READING 18

Perceived Intragroup Homogeneity in Minority–Majority Contexts   326

Bernd Simon and Rupert Brown

READING 19

Social Science Research on Trial: Use of Sex Stereotyping
Research in *Price Waterhouse v. Hopkins*   338

Susan T. Fiske, Donald N. Bersoff, Eugene Borgida, Kay Deaux, and Madeline E. Heilman

READING 20

Social Stigma: The Affective Consequences
of Attributional Ambiguity   353

Jennifer Crocker, Kristin Voelkl, Maria Testa, and Brenda Major

READING 21

Stereotype Threat and the Intellectual Test Performance
of African Americans   369

Claude M. Steele and Joshua Aronson

PART 7
Improving Intergroup Perceptions and Behavior   391

READING 22

Contact and Categorization: Social Psychological
Interventions to Change Intergroup Relations   394

Miles Hewstone

READING 23

Social Categorization and Behavioral Episodes:
A Cognitive Analysis of the Effects of Intergroup Contact   419

Myron Rothbart and Oliver P. John

READING 24

How Does Cooperation Reduce Intergroup Bias?   435

Samuel L. Gaertner, Jeffrey A. Mann, John F. Dovidio, Audrey J. Murrell, and Marina Pomare

References   451

Appendix: How to Read a Journal Article in Social Psychology   457

Christian H. Jordan and Mark P. Zanna

Author Index   467

Subject Index   481

About the Editor

Charles Stangor is an Associate Professor of Psychology at the University of Maryland, College Park. His research interests concern the development and maintenance of stereotypes and prejudice, and their influence on the targets of prejudice. He has published 6 books and over 30 research articles and currently serves as an associate editor of the *European Journal of Social Psychology*.

Acknowledgments

The Authors and Publishers are grateful to the following for permission to reproduce the articles in this book:

Reading 1: G. W. Allport, The Nature of Prejudice. Chapters 1–4. Cambridge, MA: Perseus Books Publishers. Copyright ©1988 by Perseus Books Publishers. Reprinted with permission.

Reading 2: Social Categorization: Cognitions, Values and Groups by H. Tajfel and J. P. Forgas from Social Cognition, 113-140, copyright © 1981 by Academic Press, reprinted by permission of the publisher.

Reading 3: C. Stangor and M. Schaller, Stereotypes as Individual and Collective Representations. In C. Macrae, C. Stangor, & M. Hewstone (Eds.), Stereotypes and Stereotyping, 3-40. New York: The Guilford Press. Copyright ©1996 by The Guilford Press. Reprinted with permission.

Reading 4: P. Devine and A. Elliot, Are Racial Stereotypes Really Fading? The Princeton Trilogy Revisited. Personality and Social Psychology Bulletin, 22, 22-37. Copyright © 1995 by Sage Publications. Reprinted with permission.

Reading 5: I. Katz and R. Hass, Racial Ambivalence and American Value Conflict: Correlational and Priming Studies of Dual Cognitive Structures. Journal of Personality and Social Psychology, 55, 893-905. Copyright © 1988 by the American Psychological Association. Reprinted with permission.

Reading 6: L. Lepore and R. Brown, Category and Stereotype Activation: Is Prejudice Inevitable? Journal of Personality and Social Psychology, 72, 275-287. Copyright © 1997 by the American Psychological Association. Reprinted with permission.

Reading 7: A. Eagly and V. Steffen, Gender Stereotypes Stem from the Distribution of Women and Men into Social Roles. Journal of Personality and Social Psychology, 46, 735-754. Copyright © 1984 by the American Psychological Association. Reprinted with permission.

Reading 8: Illusory Correlation in Interpersonal Perception: A Cognitive Basis of Stereotypic Judgements by D. Hamilton and R. Gifford from Journal of Experimental Social Psychology, Vol. 12, 392-407, copyright © 1976 by Academic Press, reprinted by permission of the publisher.

Reading 9: S. Fein and S. Spencer, Prejudice as Self-Image Maintenance: Affirming the Self through Derogating Others. Journal of Personality and Social Psychology, 73, 31-44. Copyright © 1997 by the American Psychological Association. Reprinted with permission.

Reading 10: A. Maass, D. Salvi, L. Arcuri, & G. Semin, Language Use in Intergroup Contexts: The Linguistic Intergroup Bias. Journal of Personality and Social Psychology, 57, 981-993. Copyright © 1989 by the American Psychological Association. Reprinted with permission.

Reading 11: J. Darley and P. Gross, A Hypothesis-Confirming Bias in Labeling Effects. Journal of Personality and Social Psychology, 44, 20-33. Copyright © 1983 by the American Psychological Association. Reprinted with permission.

Reading 12: The Nonverbal Mediation of Self-fulfilling Prophecies in Interracial Interaction by C. Word, M. Zanna & J. Cooper from Journal of Experimental Social Psychology, Vol. 10, 109-120, copyright © 1974 by Academic Press, reprinted by permission of the publisher.

Reading 13: C. Miller, E. Rothblum, D. Felicio, & P. Brand, Compensating for Stigma: Obese and Nonobese

Volume Overview

Charles Stangor

There is perhaps no topic that has so engaged the interest of social psychologists as that of stereotypes, prejudice, and discrimination. Researchers have studied stereotypes and prejudice toward African Americans (Gaertner & Dovidio, 1986), women (Deaux & Major, 1987; Eagly & Mladinic, 1989), the elderly (Brewer, Dull, & Lui, 1981), the mentally ill, fat people (Crandall & Biernat, 1990), homosexuals (Herek, 1987), the physically handicapped (Kleck, Ono, & Hastorf, 1966), and individuals with AIDS (Pryer, Reeder, & McManus, 1991), to name just a few.

Interest in studying stereotyping and prejudice comes in part from its immense practical importance. Many societies are becoming increasingly ethically diverse (Jackson & Ruderman, 1995), and technological advances are increasing global interactions, such that people from different cultures are coming into greater contact with each other. These increased contacts between individuals from different ethnic groups, both within and across societies, are bringing with them increased opportunities for the expression of stereotypes and prejudice, and these contacts may in some cases even be accompanied by outright hostility between and among cultures, races, and ethnic groups.

Social psychologists are thus interested in stereotyping and prejudice because these beliefs can have negative outcomes both for the individuals who are the targets of prejudice (Crocker & Major, 1989; Jones, 1996; Steele & Aronson, 1994; J. T. Swim & Stangor, 1998) and for society at large. However, researchers are also interested in studying these topics because stereotyping and prejudice represent a basic part of a more central interest in social psychology: understanding how people make sense of and react to each other. Stereotyping and prejudice are integrally related to the most central topics in psychology, including attitudes, social cognition, person perception, conformity, group behavior, and aggression.

The goal of this volume is to introduce you to some classic readings on stereotypes, stereotyping, and prejudice. *Stereotypes* are beliefs about the characteristics of groups of individuals (for instance, that women are emotional or that college professors are absent-minded), and *stereotyping* is the application of these stereotypes when we interact with people from a given social group. *Prejudice* is a negative feeling or negative attitude toward the members of a group. These readings are *empirical*, in the sense that they rely upon the measurement of the thoughts, feelings, and behaviors of individuals to draw their conclusions about stereotyping and prejudice. This introductory section provides an overview of the field of stereotyping and prejudice. We will first consider the process of social categorization, which forms the basis of stereotyping and prejudice, and then discuss some

1

of the important questions about stereotypes that have been the topics of inquiry in social psychology.

Social Categorization

Imagine that you are walking home alone to your house or dorm room late at night, after returning from a movie. As you continue, you realize that you are a bit nervous because no one else is around, and it's very late. You start to walk a bit faster, when suddenly you see a figure standing on the street corner ahead. It's too late to turn around and take a different route, so you cross the street and begin walking even faster. In a minute, you realize that the figure is a man, and that he is actually not standing still, but now seems to be moving toward you. Your heart beats faster and a sense of dread overcomes you. Suddenly, under the streetlight you capture a glimpse of something shiny on the man. Your first thought is that it is a gun, and you begin to shake uncontrollably. But then you suddenly realize that the figure is that of a policeman and it is his badge that is glimmering in the light. You remember now that the campus has hired some new police officers to patrol at night. With a great sigh of relief, you turn into your building, closing and locking the door behind you.

Stereotypes and prejudice are the result of *social categorization*. Social categorization occurs when, rather than thinking about another person as a unique individual, we instead think of the person as a member of a group of people, for instance, on the basis of their physical characteristics (such as skin color, gender, or age) or other types of categories (as an alcoholic, a policeman, or a schizophrenic). And once we categorize someone, thoughts and feelings about the categorized person are also quickly activated (Brewer, 1988; Fiske, 1982, 1998). In our example, for instance, you didn't really care about the name of the person you saw on the street, whether he had blue eyes or brown, or even if he was a nice guy. Just the thought that he was a criminal was enough to scare you, and discovering that he was a policeman was enough to provide relief. In fact, in this case we can probably say that your reaction to the figure on the street was determined entirely by your social categorization of the person.

Spontaneous Categorization

Social categorization is a natural phenomenon, and it is unlikely that we could do without it. We categorize people, just as we categorize houses (split levels and ranches), television shows (soap operas and documentaries), and furniture (chairs and sofas). In one well-known experiment, Shelley Taylor and her colleagues (S. E. Taylor, Fiske, Etcoff, & Ruderman, 1978) demonstrated how easily social categorization occurs. They showed some college students a slide show presenting the pictures of other college students who were discussing how they should publicize a play that they were putting on. There were three men and three women in the discussion group, who were each seen making some suggestions about the topic under discussion. Furthermore, the statements were controlled so that, across all of the research participants, the statements that the men made were not any better or worse in terms of their quality than the ones the women made.

The research participants were simply told to pay attention to the information as they watched it. After they had seen and heard the discussion, the participants were given a pop quiz: They were given a list of all of the suggestions, along with pictures of the three men and three women, and asked to indicate which person had made which statement. The participants weren't very accurate at making these judgments, but—more importantly to the research—the errors they made were very systematic. They confused the men with other men and the women with other women much more frequently than they confused men with women or women with men. Taylor and her colleagues concluded that these confusions occurred because people had engaged in social categorization. They had spontaneously associated the statements of the individuals with the gender of the person who made them, even though they had not been given any instructions to do so. In fact, it turned out that these research participants, who were given no particular instructions about how to view the slide show, made just as many within-gender errors as another set of participants who were given explicit instructions to categorize the speakers according to their gender.

Categorization and Individuation

The results of the research by Taylor and her colleagues (S. E. Taylor et al., 1978) are important because they show that social categorization occurs easily and frequently, and suggest that people are not even aware they are doing it. Fortunately, however, people don't always only categorize each other. Rather, although we may normally begin with social categorization when we first meet someone, we may, at least in some cases (and hopefully most often!), go beyond this initial step. Whether or not we do so will depend upon our current relationship with the other person as well as our goals for further relationships with him or her. If we find the person interesting or relevant enough, or if we are dependent upon them for some reason, then we are likely to go beyond social categorization to learn more about the person (Brewer, 1988; Fiske & Neuberg, 1990).

In one relevant study (Neuberg & Fiske, 1987), research participants played a game with another person who was described as being a recovered mental patient (an "ex-schizophenic"). In some cases the participants were dependent upon the other person for rewards, in the sense that they had to work together with the other person to win a prize. In another experimental condition, the research participants worked in the same room with the other person, but each person was competing on their own for the prize. Neuberg and Fiske found that the participants paid much more attention to information about the person when they were dependent upon him to win the prize, causing them to learn more about him—and particularly to find out his positive characteristics (things that they had not expected to be true of ex-schizophrenics). The participants who worked individually on the task to gain their own prizes, however, didn't pay much attention to the other person, categorized him as a schizophrenic, and (although they had seen information that should have disconfirmed this expectation) perceived him negatively.

One potential outcome that can occur when we continue to learn about someone is known as *subtyping*. Subtyping occurs when the individual recategorizes the individual into a lower level social category (a subtype). Subtyping involves combining information from two or more categories together to form our judgment of the person. For instance, although we may first think of a person as an African American, we may later subtype him as an African-American businessman or an African-American nurse if we later learn this information about him. In this case a second category (his profession) has combined with the first category (ethnicity), and our judgments about the person may change. Because subtypes provide even more meaningful information about the person than do broader social categories, they are likely to be used routinely when we think about people (Devine & Baker, 1991; Stangor, Lynch, Duan, & Glass, 1992).

In still other cases, it may not be possible to classify the individual into a subtype, and *individuation* or *personalization* may occur (Brewer, 1988; Fiske & Neuberg, 1990). In this case, rather than using a person's social category or categories as a basis of judgment, we consider them instead in terms of their own unique personality—that they are friendly, courteous, and like to play tennis, for instance. Individuation is likely to occur when there is no social category that seems relevant, or when the person behaves so inconsistently with the category that it no longer seems relevant. In this case the category membership of the person becomes only one small part of the information that we use to make sense of the person.

In short, the extent to which we categorize or individuate an individual can vary substantially depending upon how much time and interest we have in learning about the person. We may base our judgments almost exclusively on a person's social category memberships when the category is all that we know about the person (for instance, if we are viewing a picture of a stranger who is known to be a member of a campus fraternity; Brodt & Ross, 1998). In other cases when we know the individual very well (such as how grade-school teachers know their own students; Madon et al., 1998) we may ignore stereotypes almost completely and base our judgments exclusively on the individual qualities of the person.

Why Categorize Others?

Given that social categorization seems to occur with great frequency in everyday life, there are probably good reasons for it. In some cases, we might think about others in terms of their social category memberships because we believe that categorization is informative, in the sense that we believe it provides information about the characteristics of the other person (Jussim, Lee, & McCauley, 1995; Oakes & Turner, 1990; Turner, 1987). For instance, if you found yourself lost in a city, you might look for a police officer or a taxi driver to help you find your way. In this case, social categorization would probably be useful, because a policeman or a taxi driver would be particularly likely to know the city streets. Of course, using social categories will only be informative to the extent that our beliefs about the category are accurate. If policemen didn't actually know much about the city layout, then using this particular social categorization wouldn't work.

Although we may sometimes categorize others to learn something about them, another reason for doing so is because we may not have time to do anything more thorough. Thus, using our stereotypes to size up another person might simply make our life easier (Allport, 1954; Bodenhausen, 1990; Macrae, Hewstone, & Griffiths, 1993; van Knippenberg, van Twuyver, & Pepels, 1994). In this case thinking about other people in terms of their social category memberships is a functional way of dealing with the world: Things are complicated, and we reduce complexity by categorizing others.

In still other cases the function of social categorization is to help us feel better about ourselves. People have an underlying need to be part of social groups and to be accepted by others (Baumeister & Leary, 1995). We value other people in the groups that we belong to, and this makes us feel good about ourselves. The positive feelings that we gain from being a part of important and respected groups is known as *social identity* (Hogg & Abrams, 1990; Turner, 1975). Judging the groups that we are members of (that is, our *in-groups*) more favorably than we do other groups (*out-groups*) is known as *in-group favoritism*, and it occurs routinely for many different types of people, in many different settings, and on many different dimensions (Hogg & Abrams, 1988; Howard & Rothbart, 1980; Jetten, Spears, & Manstead, 1996; Tajfel, 1970; Tajfel, Billig, Bundy, & Flament, 1971; D. M. Taylor & Jaggi, 1974; Turner, 1987). Thus we routinely categorize others in terms of in-group and out-group memberships because being part of a relevant in-group, and feeling that our group is better than other groups, provides social identity and makes us feel good about ourselves (Fein & Spencer, 1997).

Which Categories Do We Use?

Because people are members of many different social categories, and because any one of these categories can be used to judge the person, it becomes important to attempt to understand which categories are used by which people under which circumstances to categorize others. Most generally, there is a two-part answer to this question: Which categories we use is determined in part by the characteristics of the person being categorized, and in part by the characteristics of the person doing the categorizing.

Category Salience

Research suggests that social categories are likely to be used to the extent that they are highly *salient*, meaning that they are immediately apparent when we see someone. For instance, it is frequently found that social categorization occurs on the basis of a person's physical attractiveness, their gender, their race or ethnicity, and their age, at least in part because these features are immediately physically apparent to us when we first meet someone (Asch, 1952; Brewer, 1988; McArthur & Baron, 1983; Stangor, et al., 1992). On the other hand, categories such as a person's religion or sexual orientation might be important and informative social categories, but they might nevertheless be less likely to be used, at least in initial impression formation, because they are not so immediately visible.

In addition to differences in the overall salience among different categories, any one social category can also become salient depending upon the social context in which the individual is observed. For instance, Shelly Taylor and her colleagues (S. E. Taylor & Fiske, 1978) found that a woman was more likely to be categorized as a woman in a group in which she was the only woman, in comparison to groups that contained some men and some women. When individuals are unusual, infrequent, or "token" members of their social categories, that category becomes contextually salient and the members of the category become particularly likely to be thought about in terms of their category membership (Cota & Dion, 1986; Kanter, 1977; Oakes, Turner, & Haslam, 1991; S. E. Taylor & Crocker, 1981).

Category Accessibility

Although which categories are used to think about another person is determined in part by the salience of the categories, the characteristics of the individual who is doing the categorizing are also important. People vary in the categories that they find important to use when judging others such that some are more highly *accessible* (that is, more likely to be used in information processing) than are others. For instance, members of minority groups (such as African Americans) might find ethnicity to be a more important category than members of majority groups (European Americans) and, because it is highly accessible, these individuals might be particularly likely to think about others in terms of their ethnicity. Similarly, highly prejudiced people may also be particularly likely to categorize by race (Stangor et al., 1992), and women who are active in the feminist movement might be particularly likely to think about people in terms of gender (Bem, 1981; Pinel, 1999).

Stereotypes

There would be no particular reason to categorize each other if we didn't think that social categories were informative. Rather, we categorize as a result of our *stereotypes*: beliefs about the characteristics of groups of individuals (Ashmore & Del Boca, 1981; Fiske, 1998; Hamilton & Sherman, 1994; Stangor & Lange, 1994). Many of us have stereotypes that, for instance, car salesmen are dishonest, librarians are introverted, and skinheads are violent. We also have stereotypes about occupations (think of your own stereotypes about lawyers, construction workers, and college professors). And we have stereotypes about gender, nationality, race, and ethnicity. Although we might not like to admit it, we might agree that, by and large, Italians are romantic, Russians like to drink, Germans are punctual, and women are compassionate.

The term "stereotype" was coined by the American journalist Walter Lippman in his 1922 book entitled *Public Opinion*. Lippman was interested in how individuals reacted to people from different countries and different races, and he thought of stereotypes as the "pictures in our heads" of the people in the social groups around us. Lippman's first use of the term was followed by many others over the following years, and the study of stereotyping is now a central concern of social psychologists.

Stereotypes as Cognitive Representations

Stereotypes can be thought of as the characteristics that are mentally associated with a social category label in long-term, semantic memory (Stangor & Lange, 1994). As we learn about groups, stereotypes become a part of our memory, just like any other concept or category that we learn. Stereotypes are stored in memory in cognitive representations, frequently called *prototypes* or *schemata*, that contain linkages between a social category and the traits associated with it (Dovidio, Evans, & Tyler, 1986; Perdue, Dovidio, Gurtman, & Tyler, 1990; S. E. Taylor & Crocker, 1981). We also remember our experiences with particular individuals from social categories, known as *exemplars* (Bodenhausen, Schwarz, Bless, & Wanke, 1995; Smith & Zarate, 1990), and our stereotypes are driven in part by these memories. More current models of stereotypes have considered them as types of cognitive, neural networks (Kunda & Thagard, 1996).

One potential cognitive representation of a person's beliefs about college professors is shown in Figure 1.1. This person has several stereotypes (for instance, "absent-minded") that are associated with the concept of college professors in memory, and an exemplar (Professor Fox, pictured) is also associated with the category label. Because stereotypes are linked to the social category, when a person perceives another person as a member of a social category (in this case, as a college professor), the stereotypes associated with the category are quickly activated, and the new individual may be compared with Dr. Fox. This activation may even be *automatic*, meaning that it occurs quickly and without awareness, takes little effort, and is difficult to stop (Bargh, 1994, 1999).

Cultural and Individual Stereotypes

Many of our stereotypes are shared with other individuals in our culture (Haslam, Oakes, Reynolds, & Turner, 1999; Haslam et al., 1998; Ruscher, Hammer, & Hammer, 1996;

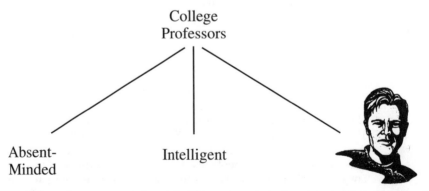

FIGURE 1.1 ■ **A cognitive representation of a social category, including stereotypes and an exemplar.**

Schaller & Latane, 1996; Stangor & Schaller, 1996). Other stereotypes are more individual in the sense that they are only held by one or a few people within a society. Cultural stereotypes have a broader impact than individual stereotypes, particularly because members of groups that are likely to be stereotyped may realize that they are seen in similar (frequently negative), stereotypical ways by many other people. As a result, people from groups that are routinely stereotyped may expect to be stereotyped, not only by some or a few people, but by a whole culture of people. In Western societies, for instance, people who are overweight are constantly aware that they are the targets of stereotypes about the obese (e.g., that they are undisciplined because they cannot control their weight) and that many, if not most, people hold these stereotypes. Knowledge that one is stereotyped can influence both self-perceptions (Crocker & Major, 1989; Crocker, Major & Steele, 1998) and behavior (Steele & Aronson, 1994).

Agreement about stereotypes of groups comes in part from the fact that the people who live in the same culture have similar contacts with members of other social groups (Haslam et al., 1996). Because people's beliefs are based in part on their common perceptions of social behavior, they should have common stereotypes (Gardner, 1994). But people also communicate their individual stereotypes with each other (Harasty, 1997; Ruscher et al., 1996; Schaller & Latane, 1996), and this communication may turn individual beliefs into cultural stereotypes. However, although there is consensus on many stereotypes, no stereotype is held by 100 percent of the people in a culture. There are still differences among individuals within a culture both in the stereotypes that they hold and in the strength with which they hold them.

Stereotype Accuracy

Stereotypes would probably not continue to exist if they were completely inaccurate. In fact, cultural stereotypes about many social groups appear to have at least some "kernel of truth" (R. B. Clarke & Campbell, 1955; Judd, Ryan, & Park, 1991; Jussim et al., 1995; McCauley & Stitt, 1978; J. K. Swim, 1994). In some cases the kernel of truth is a result of the social roles that individuals from different categories play in society (Hoffman & Hurst, 1990). For instance, the stereotype that women are "nurturant" and that men are "dominant" may occur in part because, on average, men are more likely to be in occupations of high status, whereas women are more likely to play the role of homemakers and child-care workers (Eagly, 1987; Eagly & Steffen, 1984). Thus the stereotypes are at least partly "true" for many of the members of the social category, because the individuals express the characteristics when they fulfil the roles, although the characteristics might not be due to real personality differences between the groups (Schaller, 1992). But not all stereotypes are accurate. Some studies have found that people are very wrong about what stereotypes are true of a given group, and people are also willing to express stereotypes about groups of which they have never met a single member, and even to express stereotypes about groups that do not exist (D. Katz & Braly, 1933).

Furthermore, even if they are in part accurate, stereotypes are frequently *overgeneralized* or exaggerated. When we ascribe stereotypes to groups as a whole (for instance, saying that all college professors are absent-minded), this is necessarily inaccurate because there are at least a few who are not. And when we use beliefs about a group to judge an individual group member, there is a strong potential for inaccuracy. Using stereotypes is unfair to the individuals being judged, because since no stereotype is true of all of the category members, it may not be true of this individual (Stangor, 1995). When a man decides that a woman is not likely to be a good sales manager because he thinks that women are "emotional," this decision can be harmful to the female job candidate, even if there is at least some truth to his stereotype (Fiske, Bersoff, Borgida, Deaux, & Heilman, 1991).

Prejudice

While it is likely that almost everyone has at least some stereotypes about many important social groups, and it may well be the case that many of us routinely categorize each other, having stereotypes does not necessarily mean that we are prejudiced. *Prejudice* goes farther than stereotypes, in the sense that it involves a negative feeling or attitude toward the members of a group (Allport, 1954). In contrast to stereotypes, which involve thoughts or beliefs about the group, prejudice has an emotional component as well. Prejudice involves negative feelings toward group members, including likes and dislikes, anger, fear, disgust, discomfort, and even hatred. When applied to specific groups, prejudice can be called something more specific (for instance, *racism* is racial prejudice and *sexism* is prejudice based on gender).

Prejudice takes many different forms in contemporary society, ranging from direct and traditional hatred ("I hate Jews and Blacks") to more modern and subtle forms. *Modern prejudice* involves beliefs that out-groups (such as African Americans and women) are no longer handicapped by racial or gender discrimination, and therefore should not be offered special treatment, coupled with negative feelings about the group. For example, some European Americans may simultaneously believe that African Americans have equal rights and that they contribute to the society, even while believing that Blacks are nevertheless different than Whites in a way that makes them a problem for contemporary society (I. Katz & Hass, 1988). For instance, the Modern Racism scale (McConahay, 1986) contains items such as "African Americans are getting too demanding in their push for equal rights," and "African Americans should not push themselves where they are not wanted."

As with stereotypes, one of the characteristics that makes prejudice so insidious is that it often occurs quickly and without our awareness. It has even been argued that everyone (even those who do not think that they are) is prejudiced, at least in the sense that they favor their own group over others and know the cultural stereotypes about other groups. This argument proposes that we must all work to attempt to control our prejudices, and that doing so is not always that easy (Devine, 1989; Fiske, 1989). Prejudice has also been conceptualized as a tendency to believe that one is acting more negatively toward out-group members than one thinks one should, despite efforts to avoid these negative behaviors (Monteith, Devine, & Zuwerink, 1993).

Measuring Stereotypes and Prejudice

Because our knowledge about stereotypes and prejudice, and about their effects upon social behavior, is determined through empirical research, we must have a way of measuring them empirically. There are a number of useful methods for doing so, and we can divide these approaches into two major types: *direct measures* and *indirect measures*. In direct measures, people are simply asked to self-report on their stereotypes or prejudices, whereas indirect measures attempt to assess these beliefs without directly asking about them.

DIRECT MEASURES

Most researchers have taken the direct approach. For instance, some researchers who studied stereotyping (Gilbert, 1951; Karlins, Coffman, & Waiters, 1969; D. Katz & Braly, 1933) simply gave people a list of social categories and a list of traits that might be perceived as stereotypical of each. The research participants were asked to indicate, by checking them off, which traits they thought were true of which groups. This became known as the *checklist approach* to stereotype measurement. Another common technique is the *percentage approach*, in which people are given a list of social categories and traits and asked to indicate what percentage of the group has each of the traits; for instance, "what percentage of Italians do you think are *romantic*?" (Gardner, 1973). The checklist and percentage approaches also have the advantage of allowing the researchers to assess the extent to which stereotypes about social groups are shared among the people that are tested (that is, to see if they are cultural or individual stereotypes), and also, because they have been used for many years, to study how stereotypes have (or have not) changed over time.

Other researchers have argued that providing individuals with the traits that might be seen as stereotypical is not a good idea because it limits stereotyping to those traits that are perceived as relevant by the researcher—the participant may have other, very different, stereotypes in mind. In the *open-ended approach* to stereotype measurement, the participants are given only the social category name (for instance, "women") and asked to freely list the traits that they see as typical of the group (Eagly & Mladinic, 1989; Ford & Stangor, 1992). The researcher then studies the traits that are listed by the individual to see what stereotypes are being used. In addition to allowing the participant to determine the stereotypes, the open-ended approach has the advantage of allowing us to directly measure the association of a stereotype with a category in memory (see Figure 1.1). Traits that are strongly associated with the category should come to mind quickly and thus be listed first.

Prejudice can also be measured using direct measures, for instance, by asking people how much they like the members of a given group, or how much they would like to have them as friends. Prejudice sometimes shows up in agreement with strong statements such as "I hate blacks" or "Jews make me sick," but it is more likely to take more subtle, "modern" forms. Sometimes prejudice is conceptualized as in-group favoritism, a tendency to favor in-groups over out-groups, even when the out-groups are not evaluated all that negatively.

INDIRECT MEASURES

Although free-response measures are designed in part to measure the extent to which stereotypes are activated when one thinks about a social group, *indirect measures* are based explicitly on the idea that, because category labels and stereotypes are connected in memory through associative links, the associated stereotypes should be quickly, or even automatically, activated upon exposure to the group label. Thus, perceiving a member of a category or thinking about the category should quickly activate associated stereotypes and even prejudicial attitudes, and we should be able to use subtle cognitive measures to determine whether a stereotype or a negative feeling has been activated (Banaji & Hardin, 1996; Bargh, 1999; Devine, 1989; Dovidio et al., 1986; Fazio, Jackson, Dunton, & Williams, 1995; Sigall & Page, 1971; Wittenbrink, Judd, & Park, 1997). When a stereotype or other cognitive construct has been activated so that it is currently accessible, we say that it has been *primed*. Thus, the goal of indirect measures is to present a social category, and then to assess the extent to which the associated stereotypes or the associated attitudes are primed.

The indirect measurement approach has a particular advantage because it reduces the potential for *self-presentation*. Self-presentation occurs when the research participants attempt to present themselves in a favorable light. When we measure stereotypes or prejudice directly, participants might not be willing to admit that they hold negative beliefs. However, indirect measures bypass this problem, because once the category label is presented, the associated traits and beliefs should quickly become accessible, and the participant should be unable to prevent the activation of related stereotypes, even if he or she should desire to.

In one important study, Dovidio et al. (1986) presented college students with category labels (the terms BLACK and WHITE) on a computer screen, followed immediately by trait terms that were known through pretesting to be perceived as stereotypical of the groups ("ambitious," "musical") as well as other terms that were not traits ("drafty," "metallic").

The participants were given the goal of stating as quickly as possible whether the characteristic could ever be true of the group (e.g., "Could musical ever be true of Blacks?"). Supporting the idea that the group label quickly activated the associated stereotypes, participants were significantly faster in saying "yes" to stereotypical traits than they were to saying "yes" to nonstereotypical traits. Other more recent studies have also measured stereotypes by assessing their activation upon exposure to category members, and have found support for the idea that stereotypes are spontaneously activated upon exposure to social categories (Banaji & Hardin, 1996; Gaertner & McLaughlin, 1983; Perdue & Gurtman, 1990).

It is also possible to measure prejudice indirectly. For instance, in one study Fazio and his colleagues (1995) presented faces of Black and White college students to European-American students, followed quickly by positive and negative words (such as "wonderful" and "annoying") and measured how quickly the participants could judge each word as being "good" or "bad." They found that White participants were faster at judging negative than positive words after they had just seen a Black face and that Black participants were faster at judging negative than positive words after they had just seen a White face. They concluded that prejudice (in the sense of favoring in-groups over out-groups) was automatically activated in responses to the faces. Prejudice can also be measured using indirect measures of behavior, in which the participants are not aware that their behavior is being observed (Crosby, Bromley, & Saxe, 1980).

There is at this point conflicting evidence about the comparability of direct and indirect measures of stereotyping and prejudice. Because indirect measures are assumed to avoid self-presentation, whereas direct measures are not, one possibility is that direct and indirect measures will be more highly related for high-prejudice individuals (who are willing to admit their negative beliefs publicly) than for low-prejudice individuals (who are assumed to have the beliefs, but to be unwilling to admit them on direct measures; Fazio et al., 1995; Monteith et al., 1993; Wittenbrink et al., 1997).

The Origins of Stereotypes and Prejudice

One thing that is clear about stereotypes is that they are learned early in life. If you ask a 4- or 5-year-old child who can be a race car driver, they will tell you that "men can" and if you ask them who can bake cookies they will say that "women can" (Brown, 1995; Liben & Signorella, 1980; Mackie, Hamilton, Susskind, & Rosselli, 1996; Ruble & Martin, 1998). Young children easily classify each other according to gender and race (Aboud, 1988; Brown, 1995), and in some cases may even display prejudice. Even very young European-American children have been found to prefer White dolls to Black dolls (K. Clark & Clark, 1947), suggesting that they favor their in-group. (Evidence about whether African-American children favor Black over White dolls is less clear.) But where exactly do stereotypes and prejudice come from? Unfortunately, there are many sources of stereotypes and prejudice, ranging from direct experience with members of the stereotyped groups to messages we hear from those around us. In short, stereotypes and prejudice are *overdetermined*, and this makes them very easy to develop and very difficult to change (Ashmore & DelBoca, 1976; Bar-Tal, 1997; Mackie et al., 1996; Stroebe & Insko, 1989).

Communication and Conformity

Stereotypes are learned in part from our communication with relevant others, for instance from our parents and our peers (Aboud & Doyle, 1996) as well as from the media (Brown, 1995). It has been shown that the racial attitudes of children are similar to those of their parents (Epstein & Komorita, 1966). And individuals, particularly adolescents, tend to learn and to conform to the attitudes held by their peers. In many cases, learning about group beliefs comes indirectly from observing how others who are important to us behave toward members of other groups, rather than through direct verbal statements from them. For instance, a parent may cross the street or tighten a grip on a child's hand when a member of a different ethnic group walks by, or an adolescent may see that no members of his peer group associate with Hispanics. Often these communications are rather subtle; for example, people may simply talk differently than members of other groups (DePaulo & Coleman, 1986; C. T. Miller, Clarke, Malcarne, Lobato, et al., 1991).

Illusory Correlations

Stereotypes may also be learned from perceptions of the world around us. As an example, some stereotypes are formed because people incorrectly estimate the frequency with which individuals from different groups perform positive versus negative behaviors (Fiedler, 1991; Hamilton, Dugan, & Trolier, 1985; Hamilton & Gifford, 1976; Hamilton & Sherman, 1996). The problem is that both negative behaviors and minority group members are particularly easy to remember, because there are fewer of them. And when they are well remembered, we tend to overestimate the number of times they have occurred. This phenomenon, known as *illusory correlation*, predicts that stereotypes about minority group members will frequently be negative, simply because of the natural distribution of positive and negative behaviors. As an example, because there are fewer Hispanics than Whites in California, and also relatively few homicides, overall, individuals may erroneously associate aggressiveness with Hispanics, even if the proportion of homicides committed by Whites and by Hispanics does not actually differ. Illusory correlations have been studied in hundreds of research articles, and it has proved to be very easy to create them (Mullen & Johnson, 1990).

Outcomes of Social Categorization

There would be no particular reason to be concerned about social categorization if it did not have such important outcomes for the individuals we categorize and stereotype, and who are the targets of our prejudices.

Discrimination

Perhaps the most straightforward negative outcome of social categorization occurs because, once another person has been categorized, stereotypes of and prejudicial feelings about the category may also be activated. It is known that stereotypes frequently color our perceptions and judgments of others (Cantor & Mischel, 1977; Duncan, 1976; Sagar & Schofield, 1980; Secord, Bevan, & Katz, 1956), even though we may have no idea that they are doing so. For instance, individuals who are asked to act as jurors in mock courtroom trials give harsher judgments to perpetrators who are members of a group for which the crime is stereotypical rather than nonstereotypical (Bodenhausen & Lichtenstein, 1987; Ugwuegbu, 1979), and stereotypes also influence hiring decisions (Fiske et al., 1991; Glick, Zion, & Nelson, 1988). When stereotypes or prejudice produce negative behaviors toward others, the behavior is called *discrimination*.

Although in some cases the stereotypes that are used to make the judgment might actually be true of the individual being judged, in many other cases they are not. Thus stereotyping is problematic when the stereotypes held about a social group are inaccurate, or when they do not apply to the individual who is being judged (Bargh, 1999; Stangor, 1995). Although it may be difficult, people who wish to not be prejudiced or to not use their stereotypes may be able to do so (Fiske, 1989; Lepore & Brown, 1997; Monteith et al., 1993). But in many cases the person who is doing the judging may not even realize that he or she is being influenced by stereotypes. This occurs because stereotypes are frequently activated without our conscious awareness, and so we are unable to adjust for them. In one interesting study, Greenwald and Schuh (1994) found that Jewish researchers were more likely to include references to papers written by other Jews in their research reports than were non-Jewish researchers, suggesting that they favored other Jewish researchers, although it is unlikely that they had any idea they were doing so.

Perceptual Accentuation

Another outcome of social categorization is the tendency to perceive individuals from the same social group as more similar to each other than they really are and to perceive members of different social groups as very different from each other (Ashton & Esses, 1999; Ford & Stangor, 1992; Rothbart, Davis-Stitt, & Hill, 1997; Tajfel, 1970, 1978; Tajfel & Wilkes, 1963). These mistaken impressions seem to occur in part because they allow us to make clearer (although potentially erroneous) distinctions between the members of different out-groups.

The most avidly researched outcome of perceptual accentuation is the tendency to see members of the same group as more similar (or *homogeneous*) to each other than they really are. Although it would be expected that we would see members of almost all social groups as homogeneous, it turns out that this tendency is particularly strong for out-groups, and this phenomenon is called perceived *out-group homogeneity* (Judd & Park, 1988; Linville, Salovey, & Fischer, 1986; Ostrom & Sedikides, 1992; Park & Judd, 1990; Park, Judd, & Ryan, 1991; Park & Rothbart, 1982; Park, Ryan, & Judd, 1992; Simon & Brown, 1987). Research has shown, for instance, that men tend to see women as more similar to each other than women see each other, and women also tend to see men as homogeneous.

In some cases perceived out-group homogeneity probably occurs because people (for instance, Americans) don't have as much contact with out-group members (for instance, Russians) as they do with in-group members (Linville et al., 1986), and thus they cannot learn about the real differences among individuals from the out-group. But although this might explain the effect for members of some social groups, it does not appear to explain it entirely, since men and women have been found to perceive out-group homogeneity in the opposite gender group (a case in which it does not seem likely that there is less social interaction) and even for artificial groups created in the laboratory that have had no interaction with each other at all. Another possibility is that, because individuals routinely categorize out-group members, they never get a chance to individuate them and learn about their individual characteristics. Therefore, when we think about out-groups, we tend to think about them as groups—comparing them to our in-groups—rather than as individuals.

Although research suggests that there is a general tendency toward perceived out-group homogeneity (Ostrom & Sedikides, 1992), there are also cases in which in-groups are seen as more homogeneous than out-groups. This occurs particularly when the size of the in-group is small in relationship to the out-group (Simon & Brown, 1987), and when the in-group is particularly organized or the members are highly identified as group members. In these cases the members of the group stereotype themselves, as extreme, unified, and therefore similar, in relationship to the larger (and hence more diverse) comparison group (Simon & Hamilton, 1994).

In-group Favoritism

In addition to allowing us to differentiate out-groups from each other, stereotypes also serve another particularly important function: that of differentiating "us" (in-groups) from "them" (out-groups). And this distinction generally occurs in a particular direction, such that the in-group as a whole, as well as individual members of the in-group, are seen as having particularly positive characteristics, whereas the members of out-groups are seen to have relatively less positive or more negative characteristics. As we have seen, this process is called in-group favoritism.

In-group favoritism is a robust phenomenon that can occur even in cases where the characteristic that forms the basis of in-groups and out-groups is arbitrary or minimal. In one well-known study (Tajfel, 1970; Tajfel et al., 1971), high school students were told that they had been divided into two groups ostensibly on the basis of their preference for paintings by two abstract artists (the group who preferred paintings by Kandinsky and the group who preferred paintings by Klee). But actually the groups were formed on a random basis. As part of the experiment, the children were then asked to allocate rewards, in the form of "points," to other members of their own group as well as to members of the other group. The children were found to assign a significantly greater number of points to other members of their own group than they did to members of the other group, even though they were never allowed to assign any points to themselves. This phenomenon is called the *minimal intergroup effect* because it occurs in groupings that are minimal (for instance, when the grouping is perceived to be on the basis of a trivial dimension such as painting preference) and because there is no apparent advantage to the individual for making such biased assignments.

Although there are a number of explanations for in-group favoritism (Brewer, 1979; Cadinu & Rothbart, 1996; Diehl, 1990) many of which probably simultaneously determine its occurrence, two primary reasons seem to be most important. For one, people perceive themselves positively, and because they are themselves part of their in-group, these positive perceptions may generalize to the group as a whole (Cadinu & Rothbart, 1996; Smith & Henry, 1996). Second, in-group favoritism occurs at least in part to provide a feeling of positive esteem and social identity to the self (Jetten et al., 1996; Oakes & Turner, 1980; Rubin & Hewstone, 1998; Turner, 1975). In short, people can feel good about themselves because they are members of valued groups, and perceiving our in-groups as better than out-groups contributes to this positive feeling (Fein & Spencer, 1997; Lemyre & Smith, 1985; Rubin & Hewstone, 1998).

Stereotype Maintenance

One of the fundamental characteristics of stereotypes is that they are difficult to change once they become established. Of course, some stereotypes do change, at least in some cases, but they may not change as fast as they should given the new information that we learn about group members. In part, this resistance to change can be due to the use of the stereotypes themselves—once stereotypes are activated, they tend to become self-maintaining.

Biased Information Search and Interpretation

In some cases individuals may respond to members of stereotyped categories as if they already knew what they were like, and so they don't bother to attempt to individuate them. If individuation doesn't occur, then the group stereotype cannot be changed. For instance, Trope and Thompson (1997) found that in mock interviews individuals addressed fewer questions to individuals who were members of groups about which they had strong stereotypes, and the questions that they did ask were likely to confirm the stereotypes they already had (Johnston & Macrae, 1994). Furthermore, once information is obtained, stereotypes may color how that information is interpreted. Ambiguous information is likely to be interpreted in ways that are consistent with existing stereotypes (Duncan, 1976; Sagar & Schofield, 1980).

Biased Memory

In other cases stereotypes are maintained, not because information is differentially collected, but rather because the collected information is differentially remembered. Because stereotypes are stored in cognitive representations (schemas or prototypes), information that fits with the representation is easier to remember, and later easier to retrieve, in comparison to information that is inconsistent with the stereotype. Thus people, including children, are better able to learn associations among stereotypical than nonstereotypical characteristics (Albert & Porter, 1983; Martin & Halverson, 1981), and also better recall information that is consistent, rather than inconsistent, with their group stereotypes (Fyock & Stangor, 1994; Liben & Signorella, 1980; Sagar & Schofield, 1980; Snyder & Uranowitz, 1978; Stangor & Ruble, 1989; Van Knippenberg & Dijksterhuis, 1996).

Communication and Stereotypes

Stereotypes are also likely to be maintained through communication with others. When people describe the positive behavior of members of in-groups, they use broad trait terms ("we are generous and friendly") but they describe negative in-group behaviors in terms of low-level, specific behaviors ("Bill hit someone"). On the other hand, out-groups are described as having broad negative traits ("they are aggressive"), while positive out-group behaviors are described in terms of specific behaviors ("Bill was friendly to her"). This differential communication pattern, known as the *linguistic intergroup bias* (Maas & Arcuri, 1996; Maas et al., 1989; von Hippel, Sekaquaptewa, & Vargas, 1997) helps maintain differential beliefs about in-groups and out-groups through communication.

Self-Fulfilling Prophecies

Finally, and perhaps most damaging of all, stereotypes may result in behavior toward the stereotyped group members that actually make the stereotypes come true. Such behaviors, known as *behavioral conformation effects or self-fulfilling prophecies* (Darley & Fazio, 1980; Hilton & Darley, 1985; Jussim, 1989; Jussim & Fleming, 1996; Merton, 1948; D. T. Miller & Turnbull, 1986; Snyder, 1981; Word, Zanna, & Cooper, 1974), occur when individuals' expectations, either consciously or unconsciously, change the behavior of the person who is being stereotyped such that they end up acting in accord with the stereotypes.

One type of self-fulfilling prophecy occurs when people conform to the expectations of others in order to gain rewards or respect from them. Zanna and Pack (1975) found that women who expected their male interviewers to have traditional sex role beliefs arrived at a job interview wearing more traditional dress and more makeup than did women who did not think their interviewers had strong gender stereotypes. You can see that this behavior, while potentially useful for getting the job, is likely to leave the interviewer's stereotypes about women intact—in essence, making them come true.

In other cases, the behavior of one individual can influence the behavior of another, not as a result of motivations to be perceived positively, but simply as a result of stereotypes. In one study, Rosenthal and Jacobson (1966) informed some elementary school teachers that they had identified that some of the students in their classes were "late bloomers." According to the researchers, these students could be expected to show sudden and dramatic increases in IQ over the course of the school year. In fact, these students had been selected at random. When the researchers measured the achievement of the students at the end of the year, they found that, especially for younger children, the "late bloomers" had actually gained more in IQ than the other students, even though there was nothing genuinely special about them. Somehow, the teachers' expectations about the children influenced how they behaved toward them, and this made their expectations come true.

A substantial amount of research has demonstrated self-fulfilling prophecies based on social categories such as ethnicity, gender, social class, and physical attractiveness, in both laboratory situations and everyday life (Jussim, 1989, 1991; Jussim & Fleming, 1996; M. C. Taylor, 1979). Although the extent of many self-fulfilling prophecies is not large, over a long period of time they may have a substantial effect on individuals. On the other hand, they can be prevented if the individuals who are interacting are aware that they might occur and take steps to prevent them (C. T. Miller, Rothblum, Felicio, & Brand, 1995; Neuberg, 1989; Swann & Hill, 1982).

Changing Stereotypes

It will naturally be difficult to change stereotypes and prejudice, because such change will need to overcome all of the cognitive processes, such as biased information search, interpretation, and memory and behavioral confirmation, as well as social processes, such as pressures to conform to the beliefs of others, all of which work to maintain stereotypes intact. Nevertheless, social psychologists have developed numerous theories about when and why stereotypes will or will not change, and some interventions have been effective at changing stereotypes (Bar-Tal, 1989; Brewer & Miller, 1984; Hewstone, 1996; Johnston & Macrae, 1994; Weber & Crocker, 1983; Worchel & Rothgerber, 1996).

In general, there are three types of change in beliefs that can help reduce negative intergroup encounters. Perhaps the most obvious change involves creating more positive perceptions of the group as a whole. When we reduce an individual's level of prejudice or change his or her stereotypes to be more positive, we have produced this type of change. But change does not always have to involve becoming more positive about the group. If we change the perceptions of the variability of a group such that the individual no longer believes that all of the group members are the same, we have also reduced stereotyping, even if the beliefs have not become more positive overall. Finally, we will have been successful if we have been able to reduce the tendency for an individual to use social categories when judging others, with the result that they are more likely to individuate others instead.

The Contact Hypothesis

The most common approach to changing stereotypes is to provide individuals with information that their stereotypes are false. For instance, we might have them interact with members of the other group, with the hope that they will directly perceive that their beliefs are mistaken. The *contact hypothesis* proposes that contact between different groups, such as in schools or the workplace, will increase positive relations between them (Allport, 1954; Amir, 1969; Brewer & Miller, 1984; Cook, 1978, 1984; Gaertner, Rust, Dovidio, Bachman & Anastasio, 1994; Hewstone & Brown, 1986; Stephan, 1987). As an example, part of the idea of busing children to integrated schools, introduced in the United States in the 1960s, was to produce intergroup contact and thus reduce stereotypes (Stephan, 1978, 1985, 1987). In support of this hypothesis, analyses of social programs that have attempted to effect stereotype change through intergroup contact have suggested that when the contact occurs under conditions of egalitarian norms, and true social integration, they do have a positive impact upon attitudes toward members of the groups that are encountered

(Hewstone, 1996; Stephan, 1985). Such change is particularly likely to occur when the contact is personalized or individuated, such that the individuals from the different groups get a chance to know each other as individuals (Cook, 1984; N. Miller, Brewer, & Edwards, 1985).

However, despite the empirical evidence to support it, intergroup contact does have some substantial limitations in its ability to create stereotype change. For one, stereotypes and prejudice will only change to be more positive when the contact is itself positive. Negative intergroup interactions, such as those that are themselves based upon unequal status, un-equal opportunities, or hostility may actually *increase* rather than decrease the extent of prejudice and stereotyping. Another limitation in producing belief change through contact is that, although change in beliefs toward the individuals with whom contact occurs is most effective when the individuals think of each other as individuals rather than as members of social categories, this perception ironically makes it less likely that change at the individual level will generalize to the group as a whole. Thus, when a White child gets to know a Black child as a person, he may develop positive feelings toward this specific child. But because this child is more likely to be individuated, and less likely to be categorized as an African American, attitudes toward the group as a whole may not follow (Hewstone & Brown, 1986). As a result, it is not necessarily beneficial to attempt to stop social categorization entirely; rather the individuals with whom one has contact must be seen as individuals, but simultaneously as members of the out-group (Rothbart & John, 1985).

Indirect Change

Direct contact with individuals from different social groups is only one way that stereotypes are changed. Alternatively, beliefs might change through learning about the beliefs of others, and perhaps through learning that prejudice is socially inappropriate. In this sense, stereotype change might result from persuasive arguments against intolerance and discrimination, or from learning that other in-group members are not prejudiced (Bar-Tal, 1989). Societal approaches, such as affirmative action and educational programs, and even legal approaches, such as equal opportunity housing and employment laws, can also be effective in changing stereotypes and prejudice because, once behavior is changed, more positive attitudes may follow.

Organization of the Readings

OK. You've heard enough from me. Now let's turn to what other researchers have said about stereotypes and prejudice, and the research they have conducted. I have organized the readings into seven sections, each containing several articles, and each designed to review one of the most fundamental topics concerning stereotyping and prejudice. I have tried to choose a balance between more "classic" (i.e., older) articles and more contemporary ones in each case. I hope you'll find the papers informative.

Conceptualizing Stereotypes and Prejudice

Prejudice and stereotyping are not new phenomena. Indeed social categorization, from which stereotyping and prejudice emerge, is such a basic process that it has always has been—and likely always will be—an integral part of human existence. Yet the formal empirical study of stereotyping and prejudice has only begun in the 20th century, as an outgrowth of the increased interest in the study of social behavior, particularly in the field of psychology. The goal of this first set of readings is to provide a basic understanding of stereotypes and prejudice, as viewed by researchers writing both earlier and later in the century. As you read these texts, you will see that the ways that psychologists conceptualize and measure stereotypes and prejudice have become more sophisticated, and yet the fundamental assumptions about their nature and function have remained essentially the same.

Although there are many notable books on stereotyping and prejudice, perhaps the most well known and important was written by the Harvard professor Gordon Allport in 1954. Allport simply called his book *The Nature of Prejudice*. This book is still as relevant today as it was when first published in 1954, although some of the examples that Allport uses may seem out of date to you (of course, this points out that prejudice—at least in some respects—does change!). Although Allport was primarily a theorist, and less of an empiricist, he had profound insight into the nature of social categorization, stereotyping, and prejudice, and his analysis has guided 50 years of empirical research by social psychologists. As you will see, Allport's analysis of prejudice was based upon principles of social categorization, or, as he calls it "overcategorization." Allport felt that, although social categorization is a normal part of everyday life, it can easily develop into unwarranted prejudice, and he argues that people and societies must work together to stop it.

Notice that Allport's definition of prejudice assumes that it is irrational; he described it as "thinking ill of others without sufficient warrant" and says that it is based on an "absence of fact." Furthermore, he notes that what makes prejudice irrational is in part that it is resistant to change. As he puts it, prejudices are beliefs that are "not reversible when exposed to new knowledge." Allport's final definition of prejudice, found on p. 23 of this volume, represents a classic definition, in the sense that it argues that prejudice is both erroneous and inaccurate.

In Chapter 2, Allport considers how and when social categories are activated to help us make judgments about others, and this chapter provides perhaps the first scientific argument that stereotypes serve to simplify our social worlds and to make them comprehensible. Allport also argues that there is normally (but not always) a relationship between stereotypes (beliefs) and prejudice (attitude). He also deals with other important topics, including the fact that prejudice is frequently spread throughout a culture and that prejudice serves other functions for the individual, such as making them feel better about themselves.

Allport expands his discussion of prejudice in Chapters 3 and 4 to take into consideration its negative outcomes on members of stigmatized groups. He frames his discussion around some of the social events that were shaping life in the United States in 1954, such as racial segregation. At this time, prejudice was still very much condoned within U.S. society and was assessed with such measures as the social distance scale of Bogardus. Allport also considers the important question of whether favoring one's in-group is a natural and therefore acceptable process, and how in-group favoritism relates to prejudice against out-groups.

The reading by Tajfel and Forgas, written during the 1980s, considers the process of social categorization in more detail and from a somewhat more current perspective. This is a classic reading, because it was Henri Tajfel himself who conducted the first studies demonstrating that in-group favoritism could occur even in "minimal" groups in which there was no rational basis to favor one's own group. In this chapter, Tajfel and Forgas consider the processes of social categorization from a cognitive perspective, but they also point out the importance of the "value" dimensions of categorizations (for instance, "we are better than they are"). Categorizing people as in-group or out-group members may help individuals create a positive social identity and thus feel good about themselves, but it is also a fundamental cause of prejudice. Note that Tajfel and Forgas also consider the importance of shared social beliefs as fundamental to stereotyping.

The reading by Stangor and Schaller was designed to summarize the state of thinking about stereotypes in 1996, as an introductory reading to a book on this topic. Note that this reading is more specific about the ways that stereotypes are mentally represented (as *schemas*, *prototypes*, and *exemplars*) than Tajfel and Forgas were, and this reflects the substantial amount of research on social categorization, much of it based on principles of cognitive psychology, that occurred during the 1980s and 1990s. As did Tajfel and Forgas, Stangor and Schaller consider the stereotypes held by both individuals and groups and argue that there are similar functions for each.

Perhaps the most important theme of these three readings is that stereotypes and prejudice are *functional*, meaning that they meet some need, desire, or goal for the individuals who have or use them. People hold their stereotypes and their prejudices because these beliefs help them make sense of the world around them and make them feel better about themselves. Holding these beliefs also—because they are part of our society—allows us to fit in with and be accepted by others.

Discussion Questions

1. What are prejudice, stereotyping, and discrimination, and how are they related to social categorization?
2. In what ways have race relationships in the U.S. changed since Allport wrote his book in 1954? In what ways have they remained the same?
3. Summarize the functions that stereotypes and prejudice serve, both for individuals and for societies.
4. What are schemas, prototypes, and exemplars, and why are they important for studying stereotyping?

Suggested Readings

Fiske, S. T., & Neuberg, S. L. (1990). A continuum of impression formation, from category based to individuating processes: Influences of information and motivation on attention and interpretation. In M. P. Zanna (Ed.), *Advances in Experimental Social Psychology* (Vol. 23, pp. 1–74). New York: Academic Press. This paper is perhaps the most important ever written about social categorization, and it outlines its causes and outcomes.

Lee, Y. T., Jussim, L. J., & McCauley, C. R. (1995). *Stereotype accuracy: Toward appreciating group differences.* Washington, DC: American Psychological Association. Are stereotypes accurate? This book attempts to answer the question.

Leyens, J. P., Yzerbyt, V. Y., & Schadron, G. H. (1994). *Stereotypes and social cognition.* London: Sage. A current review of stereotyping, from the perspective of social identity theory.

Macrae, C. N., & Bodenhausen, G. V. (in press). Social cognition: Thinking categorically about others. *Annual Review of Psychology.* A current review of theories and data about social categorization.

Macrae, C. N., Stangor, C., & Hewstone, M. (1996). *Stereotypes and stereotyping.* New York: The Guilford Press. A book summarizing some important current approaches to stereotyping.

The Nature of Prejudice

Gordon W. Allport • Harvard University

Chapter 1. What Is the Problem?

For myself, earth-bound and fettered to the scene of my activities, I confess that I do feel the differences of mankind, national and individual. . . . I am, in plainer words, a bundle of prejudices—made up of likings and dislikings—the veriest thrall to sympathies, apathies, antipathies.

CHARLES LAMB

In Rhodesia a white truck driver passed a group of idle natives and muttered, "They're lazy brutes." A few hours later he saw natives heaving two-hundred pound sacks of grain onto a truck, singing in rhythm to their work. "Savages," he grumbled. "What do you expect?"

In one of the West Indies it was customary at one time for natives to hold their noses conspicuously whenever they passed an American on the street. And in England, during the war, it was said, "The only trouble with the Yanks is that they are over-paid, over-sexed, and over here."

Polish people often called the Ukrainians "reptiles" to express their contempt for a group they regarded as ungrateful, revengeful, wily, and treacherous. At the same time Germans called their neighbors to the east "Polish cattle." The Poles retaliated with "Prussian swine"—a jibe at the presumed uncouthness and lack of honor of the Germans.

In South Africa, the English, it is said, are against the Afrikaner; both are against the Jews; all three are opposed to the Indians; while all four conspire against the native black.

In Boston, a dignitary of the Roman Catholic Church was driving along a lonesome road on the outskirts of the city. Seeing a small Negro boy trudging along the dignitary told his chauffeur to stop and give the boy a lift. Seated together in the back of the limousine, the cleric, to make conversation, asked, "Little Boy, are you a Catholic?" Wide-eyed with alarm, the boy replied, "No sir, it's bad enough being colored without being one of those things."

Pressed to tell what Chinese people really think of Americans, a Chinese student reluctantly replied, "Well, we think they are the best of the foreign devils." This incident occurred before the Communist revolution in China. Today's youth in China are trained to think of Americans as the worst of the foreign devils.

In Hungary, the saying is, "An anti-Semite is a person who hates the Jews more than is absolutely necessary."

No corner of the world is free from group scorn. Being fettered to our respective cultures, we, like Charles Lamb, are bundles of prejudice.

Two Cases

An anthropologist in his middle thirties had two young children, Susan and Tom. His work required him to live for a year with a tribe of American Indians in the home of a hospitable Indian family. He insisted, however, that his own family live in a community of white people several miles distant from the Indian reservation. Seldom would he allow Tom and Susan to come to the tribal village, though they pleaded for the privilege. And on rare occasions when they made the visit, he sternly refused to allow them to play with the friendly Indian children.

Some people, including a few of the Indians, complained that the anthropologist was untrue to the code of his profession—that he was displaying race prejudice.

The truth is otherwise. This scientist knew that tuberculosis was rife in the tribal village, and that four of the children in the household where he lived had already died of the disease. The probability of infection for his own children, if they came much in contact with the natives, was high. His better judgment told him that he should not take the risk. In this case, his ethnic avoidance was based on rational and realistic grounds. There was no feeling of antagonism involved. The anthropologist had no generally negative attitude toward the Indians. In fact he liked them very much.

Since this case fails to illustrate what we mean by racial or ethnic prejudice, let us turn to another.

In the early summer season two Toronto newspapers carried between them holiday advertisements from approximately 100 different resorts. A Canadian social scientist, S. L. Wax (1948), undertook an interesting experiment. To each of these hotels and resorts he wrote two letters, mailing them at the same time, and asking for room reservations for exactly the same dates. One letter he signed with the name "Mr. Greenberg;" the other with the name "Mr. Lockwood." Here are the results:

To "Mr. Greenberg":
52 percent of the resorts replied;
36 percent offered him accommodations.
To "Mr. Lockwood":
95 percent of the resorts replied;
93 percent offered him accommodations.

Thus, nearly all of the resorts in question welcomed Mr. Lockwood as a correspondent and as a guest; but nearly half of them failed to give Mr. Greenberg the courtesy of a reply, and only slightly more than a third were willing to receive him as a guest.

None of the hotels knew "Mr. Lockwood" or "Mr. Greenberg." For all they knew "Mr. Greenberg" might be a quiet, orderly gentleman, and "Mr. Lockwood" rowdy and drunk. The decision was obviously made not on the merits of the individual, but on "Mr. Greenberg's" supposed membership in a group.

Unlike our first case, this incident contains the two essential ingredients of ethnic prejudice. (1) There is definite hostility and rejection. The majority of the hotels wanted nothing to do with "Mr. Greenberg." (2) The basis of the rejection was categorical. "Mr. Greenberg" was not evaluated as an individual. Rather, he was condemned on the basis of his presumed group membership.

A close reasoner might at this point ask the question: What basic difference exists between the cases of the anthropologist and the hotels in the matter of "categorical rejection"? Did not the anthropologist reason from the high probability of infection that it would be safer not to risk contact between his children and the Indians? And did not the hotelkeepers reason from a high probability that Mr. Greenberg's ethnic membership would in fact bring them an undesirable guest? The anthropologist knew that tubercular contagion was rampant; did not the innkeepers know that "Jewish vices" were rampant and not to be risked?

This question is legitimate. If the innkeepers were basing their rejection on facts (more accurately, on a high probability that a given Jew will have undesirable traits), their action would be as rational and defensible as the anthropologist's. But we can be sure that such is not the case.

Some managers may never have had any unpleasant experiences with Jewish guests—a situation that seems likely in view of the fact that in many cases Jewish guests had never been admitted to the hotels. Or, if they have had such experiences, they have not kept a record of their frequency in comparison with objectionable non-Jewish guests. Certainly they have not consulted scientific studies concerning the relative frequency of desirable and undesirable traits in Jews and non-Jews. If they sought such evidence, they would, as we shall learn in Chapter 6, find no support for their policy of rejection.

It is, of course, possible that the manager himself was free from personal prejudice, but, if so, he was reflecting the anti-Semitism of his gentile guests. In either event our point is made (Wax, 1948).

Definition

The word *prejudice*, derived from the Latin noun *praejudicium*, has, like most words, undergone a change of meaning since classical times. There are three stages in the transformation (cf. Murray, 1909).

1. To the ancients, *praejudicium* meant a *precedent*—a judgment based on previous decisions and experiences.
2. Later, the term, in English, acquired the meaning of a judgment formed before due examination and consideration of the facts—a premature or hasty judgment.
3. Finally the term acquired also its present emotional flavor of favorableness or unfavorableness that accompanies such a prior and unsupported judgment.

Perhaps the briefest of all definitions of prejudice is: *thinking ill of others without sufficient warrant.*[1]) This crisp phrasing contains the two essential ingredients of all definitions—reference to unfounded judgment and to a feeling-tone. It is, however, too brief for complete clarity.

In the first place, it refers only to *negative* prejudice. People may be prejudiced in favor of others; they may think *well* of them without sufficient warrant. The wording offered by the *New English Dictionary* (Murray, 1909) recognizes positive as well as negative prejudice:

> *A feeling, favorable or unfavorable, toward a person or thing, prior to, or not based on, actual experience.*

While it is important to bear in mind that biases may be *pro* as well as *con*, it is none the less true that ethnic prejudice is mostly negative. A group of students was asked to describe their attitudes toward ethnic groups. No suggestion was made that might lead them toward negative reports. Even so, they reported eight times as many antagonistic attitudes as favorable attitudes. In this volume, accordingly, we shall be concerned chiefly with prejudice *against*, not with prejudice *in favor of*, ethnic groups.

The phrase "thinking ill of others" is obviously an elliptical expression that must be understood to include feelings of scorn or dislike, of fear and aversion, as well as various forms of antipathetic conduct: such as talking against people, discriminating against them, or attacking them with violence.

Similarly, we need to expand the phrase "without sufficient warrant." A judgment is unwarranted whenever it lacks basis in fact. A wit defined prejudice as "being down on something you're not up on."

It is not easy to say how much fact is required in order to justify a judgment. A prejudiced person will almost certainly claim that he has sufficient warrant for his views. He will tell of bitter experiences he has had with refugees, Catholics, or Orientals. But, in most cases, it is evident that his facts are scanty and strained. He resorts to a selective sorting of his own few memories, mixes them up with hearsay, and overgeneralizes. No one can possibly know *all* refugees, Catholics, or Orientals. Hence any negative judgment of these groups *as a whole* is, strictly speaking, an instance of thinking ill without sufficient warrant.

Sometimes, the ill-thinker has no first-hand experience on which to base his judgment. A few years ago most Americans thought exceedingly ill of Turks—but very few had ever seen a Turk nor did they know any person who had seen one. Their warrant lay exclusively in what they had heard of the Armenian massacres and of the legendary crusades. On such evidence they presumed to condemn all members of a nation.

Ordinarily, prejudice manifests itself in dealing with individual members of rejected groups. But in avoiding a Negro neighbor, or in answering "Mr. Greenberg's" application for a room, we frame our action to accord with our categorical generalization of the group as a whole. We pay little or no attention to individual differences, and overlook the important fact that Negro X, our neighbor, is not Negro Y, whom we dislike for good and sufficient reason; that Mr. Greenberg, who may be a fine gentleman, is not Mr. Bloom, whom we have good reason to dislike.

So common is this process that we might define prejudice as:

> an avertive or hostile attitude toward a person who belongs to a group, simply because he belongs to that group, and is therefore presumed to have the objectionable qualities ascribed to the group.

This definition stresses the fact that while ethnic prejudice in daily life is ordinarily a matter of dealing with individual people it also entails an unwarranted idea concerning a group as a whole.

We can never hope to draw a hard and fast line

---

[1]This definition is derived from the Thomistic moralists who regard prejudice as "rash judgment." The author is indebted to the Rev. J. H. Fichter, S. J., for calling this treatment to his attention. The definition is more fully discussed in LaFarge (1945, 174ff).

between "sufficient" and "insufficient" warrant. For this reason we cannot always be sure whether we are dealing with a case of prejudice or nonprejudice. Yet no one will deny that often we form judgments on the basis of scant, even nonexistent, probabilities.

Overcategorization is perhaps the commonest trick of the human mind. Given a thimbleful of facts we rush to make generalizations as large as a tub. One young boy developed the idea that all Norwegians were giants because he was impressed by the gigantic stature of Ymir in the saga, and for years was fearful lest he meet a living Norwegian. A certain man happened to know three Englishmen personally and proceeded to declare that the whole English race had the common attributes that he observed in these three.

There is a natural basis for this tendency. Life is so short, and the demands upon us for practical adjustments so great, that we cannot let our ignorance detain us in our daily transactions. We have to decide whether objects are good or bad by classes. We cannot weigh each object in the world by itself. Rough and ready rubrics, however coarse and broad, have to suffice.

Not every overblown generalization is a prejudice. Some are simply *misconceptions*, wherein we organize wrong information. One child had the idea that all people living in Minneapolis were "monopolists." And from his father he had learned that monopolists were evil folk. When in later years he discovered the confusion, his dislike of dwellers in Minneapolis vanished.

Here we have the test to help us distinguish between ordinary errors of prejudgment and prejudice. If a person is capable of rectifying his erroneous judgments in the light of new evidence he is not prejudiced. *Prejudgments become prejudices only if they are not reversible when exposed to new knowledge.* A prejudice, unlike a simple misconception, is actively resistant to all evidence that would unseat it. We tend to grow emotional when a prejudice is threatened with contradiction. Thus the difference between ordinary prejudgments and prejudice is that one can discuss and rectify a prejudgment without emotional resistance.

Taking these various considerations into account, we may now attempt a final definition of negative ethnic prejudice—one that will serve us throughout this book. Each phrase in the definition represents a considerable condensation of the points we have been discussing:

Ethnic prejudice is an antipathy based upon a faulty and inflexible generalization. It may be felt or expressed. It may be directed toward a group as a whole, or toward an individual because he is a member of that group.

The net effect of prejudice, thus defined, is to place the object of prejudice at some disadvantage not merited by his own misconduct.

Is Prejudice a Value Concept?

Some authors have introduced an additional ingredient into their definitions of prejudice. They claim that attitudes are prejudiced only if they violate some important norms or values accepted in a culture (Dyer, 1945, pp. 219–224; Williams, 1947, p. 37) . They insist that prejudice is only that type of prejudgment that is ethically disapproved in a society.

If we use the term in this sense we should have to say that the older caste system in India—which is now breaking down—involved no prejudice. It was simply a convenient stratification in the social structure, acceptable to nearly all citizens because it clarified the division of labor and defined social prerogatives. It was for centuries acceptable even to the untouchables because the religious doctrine of reincarnation made the arrangement seem entirely just. An untouchable was ostracized because in previous existences he failed to merit promotions to a higher caste or to a supermortal existence. He now has his just deserts and likewise an opportunity through an obedient and spiritually directed life to win advancement in future reincarnations. Assuming that this account of a happy caste system really marked Hindu society at one time, was there then no question of prejudice?

Or take the Ghetto system. Through long stretches of history Jews have been segregated in certain residential zones, sometimes with a chain around the region. Only inside were they allowed to move freely. The method had the merit of preventing unpleasant conflict, and the Jew, knowing his place, could plan his life with a certain definiteness and comfort. It could be argued that his lot was much more secure and predictable than in the modern world. There were periods in history when neither the Jew nor gentile felt particularly outraged by the system. Was prejudice then absent?

Even today, in certain states, a *modus vivendi* has been worked out between white and colored people. A ritual of relations is established, and most people abide unthinkingly by the realities of social structure. Since they merely follow the folkways they deny that they are prejudiced. The Negro simply knows his place, and white people know theirs. Shall we then say, as some writers have, that prejudice exists only when actions are *more* condescending, *more* negative, than the accepted culture itself prescribes? Is prejudice to be regarded merely as deviance from common practice?[2]

What shall we say about this line of argument? It has impressed some critics so much that they hold the whole problem of prejudice to be nothing more than a value-judgment invented by "liberal intellectuals."

These critics, it would seem, confuse two separate and distinct problems. Prejudice in the simple psychological sense of negative, overgeneralized judgment exists just as surely in caste societies, slave societies, or countries believing in witchcraft as in ethically more sensitive societies. The second problem—whether prejudice is or is not attended by a sense of moral outrage—is a separate issue altogether.

There is not the slightest justification for confusing the objective facts of prejudice with cultural or ethical judgment of these facts. The unpleasant flavor of a word should not mislead us into believing that it stands only for a value-judgment. Take the word *epidemic*. It suggests something disagreeable. No doubt Pasteur, the great conqueror of epidemics, hated them. But his value-judgment did not affect in the slightest degree the objective facts with which he dealt so successfully. *Syphilis* is a term flavored with opprobrium in our culture. But the emotional tinge has no bearing whatever upon the operations of the spirochete within the human frame.

Some cultures, like our own, abjure prejudice; some do not; but the fundamental psychological analysis of prejudice is the same whether we are talking about Hindus, Navahos, the Greeks of an-tiquity, or Middletown, U.S.A. Whenever a negative attitude toward persons is sustained by a spurious overgeneralization we encounter the syndrome of prejudice. It is not essential that people deplore this syndrome. It has existed in all ages in every country. It constitutes a bona fide psychological problem. The degree of moral indignation engendered is irrelevant.

Functional Significance

Certain definitions of prejudice include one additional ingredient. The following is an example:

> Prejudice is a pattern of hostility in interpersonal relations which is directed against an entire group, or against its individual members; it fulfills a specific irrational function for its bearer. (Ackerman & Jahoda, 1950, p. 4)

The final phrase of this definition implies that negative attitudes are not prejudices unless they serve a private, self-gratifying purpose for the person who has them.

It will become abundantly clear in later chapters that much prejudice is indeed fashioned and sustained by self-gratifying considerations. In most cases prejudice seems to have some "functional significance" for the bearer. Yet this is not always the case. Much prejudice is a matter of blind conformity with prevailing folkways. Some of it, as Chapter 17 will show, has no important relation to the life-economy of the individual. For this reason it seems unwise to insist that the "irrational function" of prejudice be included in our basic definition.

Attitudes and Beliefs

We have said that an adequate definition of prejudice contains two essential ingredients. There must be an *attitude* of favor or disfavor; and it must be related to an overgeneralized (and therefore erroneous) *belief*. Prejudiced statements some times express the attitudinal factor, sometimes the belief factor. In the following series the first item expresses attitude, the second, belief:

> I can't abide Negroes.
> Negroes are smelly.

> I wouldn't live in an apartment house with Jews. There are a few exceptions, but in general all Jews are pretty much alike.

---

[2]The following definition is written from this relativistic point of view: "A prejudice is a generalized anti-attitude, and/or and anti-action toward any distinct category or group of people, when either the attitude or the action or both are judged by the community in which they are found to be less favorable to the given people than the normally accepted standard of that community" (Black & Atkins, 1959).

I don't want Japanese-Americans in my town. Japanese-Americans are sly and tricky.

Is it important to distinguish between the attitudinal and belief aspects of prejudice? For some purposes, no. When we find one, we usually find the other. Without some generalized beliefs concerning a group as a whole, a hostile attitude could not long be sustained. In modern researches it turns out that people who express a high degree of antagonistic attitudes on a test for prejudice, also show that they believe to a high degree that the groups they are prejudiced against have a large number of objectionable qualities.[3]

But for some purposes it is useful to distinguish attitude from belief. For example, we shall see in Chapter 30 that certain programs designed to reduce prejudice succeed in altering beliefs but not in changing attitudes. Beliefs, to some extent, can be rationally attacked and altered. Usually, however, they have the slippery propensity of accommodating themselves somehow to the negative attitude which is much harder to change. The following dialogue illustrates the point:

Mr. X: The trouble with the Jews is that they only take care of their own group.

Mr. Y: But the record of the Community Chest campaign shows that they give more generously, in proportion to their numbers, to the general charities of the community, than do non-Jews.

Mr. X: That shows they are always trying to buy favor and intrude into Christian affairs. They think of nothing but money; that is why there are so many Jewish bankers.

Mr. Y: But a recent study shows that the percentage of Jews in the banking business is negligible, far smaller than the percentage of non-Jews.

Mr. X: That's just it; they don't go in for respectable business; they are only in the movie business or run night clubs.

Thus the belief system has a way of slithering around to justify the more permanent attitude. The process is one of *rationalization*—of the accommodation of beliefs to attitudes.

It is well to keep these two aspects of prejudice in mind, for in our subsequent discussions we shall have occasion to make use of the distinction. But wherever the term *prejudice* is used without specifying these aspects, the reader may assume that both attitude and belief are intended.

Acting Out Prejudice

What people actually do in relation to groups they dislike is not always directly related to what they think or feel about them. Two employers, for example, may dislike Jews to an equal degree. One may keep his feelings to himself and may hire Jews on the same basis as any workers—perhaps because he wants to gain goodwill for his factory or store in the Jewish community. The other may translate his dislike into his employment policy, and refuse to hire Jews. Both men are prejudiced, but only one of them practices *discrimination*.

It is true that any negative attitude tends somehow, some where, to express itself in action. Few people keep their antipathies entirely to themselves. The more intense the attitude, the more likely it is to result in vigorously hostile action.

We may venture to distinguish certain degrees of negative action from the least energetic to the most.

1. *Antilocution.* Most people who have prejudices talk about them, With like-minded friends, occasionally with strangers, they may express their antagonism freely. But many people never go beyond this mild degree of anti-pathetic action.
2. *Avoidance.* If the prejudice is more intense, it leads the individual to avoid members of the disliked group, even perhaps at the cost of considerable inconvenience. In this case, the bearer of prejudice does not directly inflict harm upon the group he dislikes. He takes the burden of accommodation and withdrawal entirely upon himself.
3. *Discrimination.* Here the prejudiced person makes detrimental distinctions of an active sort. He undertakes to exclude all members of the group in question from certain types of employment, from residential housing, political rights, educational or recreational opportunities, churches, hospitals, or from some other social privileges. Segregation is an institutionalized

---

[3]Not all scales for measuring prejudice include items that reflect both attitudes and beliefs. Those that do so report correlations between the two types of the order of .80. Cf. Samelson (1945) and Rose (1947).

form of discrimination, enforced legally or by common custom.[4]

4. *Physical attack.* Under conditions of heightened emotion prejudice may lead to acts of violence or semiviolence. An unwanted Negro family may be forcibly ejected from a neighborhood, or so severely threatened that it leaves in fear. Gravestones in Jewish cemeteries may be desecrated. The Northside's Italian gang may lie in wait for the Southside's Irish gang.

5. *Extermination.* Lynchings, pogroms, massacres, and the Hitlerian program of genocide mark the ultimate degree of violent expression of prejudice.

This five-point scale is not mathematically constructed, but it serves to call attention to the enormous range of activities that may issue from prejudiced attitudes and beliefs. While many people would never move from antilocution to avoidance, or from avoidance to active discrimination, or higher on the scale, still it is true that activity on one level makes transition to a more intense level easier. It was Hitler's antilocution that led Germans to avoid their Jewish neighbors and erstwhile friends. This preparation made it easier to enact the Nürnberg laws of discrimination which, in turn, made the subsequent burning of synagogues and street attacks upon Jews seem natural. The final step in the macabre progression was the ovens at Auschwitz.

From the point of view of social consequences much "polite prejudice" is harmless enough—being confined to idle chatter. But unfortunately, the fateful progression is, in this century, growing in frequency. And as the peoples of the earth grow ever more interdependent, they can tolerate less well the mounting friction.

Chapter 2. The Normality of Prejudgment

Why do human beings slip so easily into ethnic prejudice? They do so because the two essential ingredients that we have discussed—*erroneous generalization* and *hostility*—are natural and common capacities of the human mind. For the time

being we shall leave hostility and its related problems out of account. Let us consider only those basic conditions of human living and thinking that lead naturally to the formation of erroneous and categorical prejudgment—and which therefore deposit us on the very threshold of ethnic and group antagonism.

The reader is warned that the full story of prejudice cannot be told in this—or in any other—single chapter of this book. Each chapter, taken by itself, is one-sided. This is the inevitable defect of any *analytical* treatment of the subject.

The Separation of Human Groups

Everywhere on earth we find a condition of separateness among groups. People mate with their own kind. They eat, play, reside in homogeneous clusters. They visit with their own kind, and prefer to worship together. Much of this automatic cohesion is due to nothing more than convenience. There is no need to turn to out-groups for companionship. With plenty of people at hand to choose from, why create for ourselves the trouble of adjusting to new languages, new foods, new cultures, or to people of a different educational level?

Thus most of the business of life can go on with less effort if we stick together with our own kind. Foreigners are a strain. So too are people of a higher or lower social and economic class than our own. We don't play bridge with the janitor. Why? Perhaps he prefers poker; almost certainly he would not grasp the type of jests and chatter that we and our friends enjoy; there would be a certain awkwardness in blending our differing manners. It is not that we have class prejudice, but only that we find comfort and ease in our own class. And normally there are plenty of people of our own class, or race, or religion to play, live, and eat with, and to marry.

It is not always the dominant majority that forces minority groups to remain separate. They often prefer to keep their identity, so that they need not strain to speak a foreign language or to watch their manners. Like the old grads at a college reunion, they can "let down" with those who share their traditions and presuppositions.

One enlightening study shows that high school students representing American minorities display even greater ethnocentrism than do native white

---

[4]Aware of the world-wide problem of discrimination, the Commission on Human Rights of the United Nations has prepared a thorough analysis of *The Main Types and Causes of Discrimination* (1949).

Americans. Negro, Chinese, and Japanese young people, for example, are much more insistent upon choosing their friends, their work companions, and their "dates" from their own group than are white students. It is true that they do not select "leaders" from their own group, but prefer the non-Jewish white majority. But while agreeing that class leaders should come from the dominant group, they then seek the greater comfort of confining their intimate relations to their own kind. (Lundberg & Dickson, 1952)

The initial fact, therefore, is that human groups tend to stay apart. We need not ascribe this tendency to a gregarious instinct, to a "consciousness of kind," or to prejudice. The fact is adequately explained by the principles of ease, least effort, congeniality, and pride in one's own culture.

Once this separatism exists, however, the ground is laid for all sorts of psychological elaboration. People who stay separate have few channels of communication. They easily exaggerate the degree of difference between groups, and readily misunderstand the grounds for it. And, perhaps most important of all, the separateness may lead to genuine conflicts of interests, as well as to many imaginary conflicts.

The Process of Categorization

The human mind must think with the aid of categories (the term is equivalent here to generalizations). Once formed, categories are the basis for normal prejudgment. We cannot possibly avoid this process. Orderly living depends upon it.

We may say that the process of categorization has five important characteristics.

1. *It forms large classes and clusters for guiding our daily adjustments.* We spend most of our waking life calling upon preformed categories for this purpose. When the sky darkens and the barometer falls we prejudge that rain will fall. We adjust to this cluster of happenings by taking along an umbrella. When an angry looking dog charges down the street, we categorize him as a "mad dog" and avoid him. When we go to a physician with an ailment we expect him to behave in a certain way toward us. On these, and countless other occasions, we "type" a single event, place it within a familiar rubric, and act accordingly. Sometimes we are mistaken: the event does not fit the category. It does not rain; the dog is not mad; the physician

behaves unprofessionally. Yet our behavior was rational. It was based on high probability. Though we used the wrong category, we did the best we could.

What all this means is that our experience in life tends to form itself into clusters (concepts, categories), and while we may call on the right cluster at the wrong time, or the wrong cluster at the right time, still the process in question dominates our entire mental life. A million events befall us every day. We cannot handle so many events. If we think of them at all, we type them.

Open-mindedness is considered to be a virtue. But, strictly speaking, it cannot occur. A new experience *must* be redacted into old categories. We cannot handle each event freshly in its own right. If we did so, of what use would past experience be? Bertrand Russell, the philosopher, has summed up the matter in a phrase, "a mind perpetually open will be a mind perpetually vacant."

2. *Categorization assimilates as much as it can to the cluster.* There is a curious inertia in our thinking. We like to solve problems easily. We can do so best if we can fit them rapidly into a satisfactory category and use this category as a means of prejudging the solution. The story is told of the pharmacist's mate in the Navy who had only two categories into which he fitted every ailment that came to his attention on sick call: if you can *see* it put iodine on it; if you *can't*, give the patient a dose of salts. Life was simple for this pharmacist's mate; he ran his whole professional life with the aid of only two categories.

The point may be stated in this way: the mind tends to categorize environmental events in the "grossest" manner compatible with the need for action. If the pharmacist's mate in our story were called to task for his overcrude practice of medicine, he might then mend his ways and learn to employ more discriminated categories. But so long as we can "get away" with coarse overgeneralizations we tend to do so. (Why? Well, it takes less effort, and effort, except in the area of our most intense interests, is disagreeable.)

The bearing of this tendency on our problem is clear. It costs the Anglo employer less effort to guide his daily behavior by the generalization "Mexicans are lazy," than to individualize his workmen and learn the real reasons for their conduct. If I can lump thirteen million of my fellow citizens under a simple formula, "Negroes are stupid, dirty, and inferior," I simplify my life enormously. I simply avoid them one and all. What could be easier?

3. *The category enables us quickly to identify a related object.* Every event has certain marks that serve as a cue to bring the category of prejudgment into action. Wen we see a red-breasted bird, we say to ourselves "robin." When we see a crazily swaying automobile, we think, "drunken driver," and act accordingly. A person with dark brown skin will activate whatever concept of Negro is dominant in our mind. If the dominant category is one composed of negative attitudes and beliefs we will automatically avoid him, or adopt whichever habit of rejection (Chapter 1) is most available to us.

Thus categories have a close and immediate tie with what we see, how we judge, and what we do. In fact, their whole purpose seems to be to facilitate perception and conduct—in other words, to make our adjustment to life speedy, smooth, and consistent. This principle holds even though we often make mistakes in fitting events to categories and thus get ourselves into trouble.

4. *The category saturates all that it contains with the same ideational and emotional flavor.* Some categories are almost purely intellectual. Such categories we call concepts. *Tree* is a concept made up of our experience with hundreds of kinds of trees and with thousands of individual trees, and yet it has essentially one ideational meaning. But many of our concepts (even *tree*) have in addition to a "meaning" also a characteristic "feeling." We not only know what *tree* is but we *like* trees. And so it is with ethnic categories. Not only do we know what Chinese, Mexican, Londoner mean, but we may have a feeling tone of favor or disfavor accompanying the concept.

5. *Categories may be more or less rational.* We have said that generally a category starts to grow up from a "kernel of truth." A rational category does so, and enlarges and solidifies itself through the increment of relevant experience. Scientific laws are examples of rational categories. They are backed up by experience. Every event to which they pertain turns out in a certain way. Even if the laws are not 100 percent perfect, we consider them rational if they have a high probability of predicting a happening.

Some of our ethnic categories are quite rational. It is probable a Negro will have dark skin (though this is not always true). It is probable that a Frenchman will speak French better than German (though here, too, are exceptions). But is it true that the Negro will be superstitious, or that the Frenchman will be morally lax?

To make a rational prejudgment of members of a group requires considerable knowledge of the characteristics of the group. It is unlikely that anyone has sound evidence that Scots are more penurious than Norwegians, or that Orientals are more wily than Caucasians, yet these beliefs grow as readily as do more rational beliefs.

In a certain Guatemalan community there is fierce hatred of the Jews. No resident has ever seen a Jew. How did the Jew-is-to-be-hated category grow up? In the first place, the community was strongly Catholic. Teachers had told the residents that the Jews were Christ-killers. It also so happened that in the local culture was an old pagan myth about a devil who killed a god. Thus two powerfully emotional ideas converged and created a hostile prejudgment of Jews.

We have said that irrational categories are formed as easily as rational categories. Probably they are formed *more* easily, for intense emotional feelings have a property of acting like sponges. Ideas, engulfed by an overpowering emotion, are more likely to conform to the emotion than to objective evidence.

There is a story of an Oxford student who once remarked, "I despise all Americans, but have never met one I didn't like." In this case the categorization went against even his firsthand experience. Holding to a prejudgment when we know better is one of the strangest features of prejudice. Theologians tell us that in prejudgments based on ignorance there is no question of sin; but that in prejudgments held in deliberate disregard of evidence, sin is involved.

When Categories Conflict with Evidence

For our purposes it is important to understand what happens when categories conflict with evidence. It is a striking fact that in most instances categories are stubborn and resist change. After all, we have fashioned our generalizations as we have because they have worked fairly well. Why change them to accommodate every new bit of evidence? If we are accustomed to one make of automobile and are satisfied, why admit the merits of another make? To do so would only disturb our satisfactory set of habits.

We selectively admit new evidence to a category if it confirms us in our previous belief. A Scotsman who is penurious delights us because he vindicates our prejudgment. It is pleasant to say, "I told you so." But if we find evidence that is contradictory to our preconception, we are likely to grow resistant.

There is a common mental device that permits people to hold to prejudgments even in the face of much contradictory evidence. It is the device of admitting exceptions. "There are nice Negroes but . . . " or "Some of my best friends are Jews but. . . . " This is a disarming device. By excluding a few favored cases, the negative rubric is kept intact for all other cases. In short, contrary evidence is not admitted and allowed to modify the generalization; rather it is perfunctorily acknowledged but excluded.

Let us call this the "re-fencing" device. When a fact cannot fit into a mental field, the exception is acknowledged, but the field is hastily fenced in again and not allowed to remain dangerously open.

A curious instance of re-fencing takes place in many discussions concerning the Negro. When a person with a strong anti-Negro bias is confronted with evidence favorable to the Negro he frequently pops up with the well-known matrimonial question: "Would you want your sister to many a Negro?" This re-fencing is adroit. As soon as the interlocutor says, "No," or hesitates in his reply, the biased person can say in effect, "See, there just *is* something different and impossible about the Negro," or, "I was right all along—for the Negro has an objectionable essence in his nature."

There are two conditions under which a person will not strive to re-fence his mental field in such a way as to maintain the generalization. The first of these is the somewhat rare condition of *habitual open-mindedness*. There are people who seem to go through life with relatively little of the rubricizing tendency. They are suspicious of all labels, of categories, of sweeping statements. They habitually insist on knowing the evidence for each and every broad generalization. Realizing the complexity and variety in human nature, they are especially chary of ethnic generalizations. If they hold to any at all it is in a highly tentative way, and every contrary experience is allowed to modify the pre-existing ethnic concept.

The other occasion that makes for modification of concepts is plain *self-interest*. A person may learn from bitter failure that his categories are erroneous and must be revised. For example, he may not have known the right classification for edible mushrooms and thus find himself poisoned by toadstools. He will not make the same mistake again: his category will be corrected. Or he may think that Italians are primitive, ignorant, and loud until he falls in love with an Italian girl of a cultured family. Then he finds it greatly to his self-interest to modify his previous generalization and act thereafter on the more correct assumption that there are many, many kinds of Italians.

Personal Values as Categories

We have been arguing that rubrics are essential to mental life, and that their operation results inevitably in prejudgments which in turn may shade into prejudice.

The most important categories a man has are his own personal set of values. He lives by and for his values. Seldom does he think about them or weigh them; rather he feels, affirms, and defends them. So important are the value categories that evidence and reason are ordinarily forced to conform to them. A farmer in a dusty area of the country listened to a visitor complain against the dustbowl character of the region. The farmer evaded this attack on the place he loved by saying, "You know I like the dust; it sort of purifies the air." His reasoning was poor, but it served to defend his values.

As partisans of our own way of life we cannot help thinking in a partisan manner. Only a small portion of our reasoning is what psychologists have called "directed thinking," that is, controlled exclusively by outer evidence and focused upon the solution of objective problems. Whenever feeling, sentiment, values enter we are prone to engage in "free," "wishful," or "fantasy" thinking.[5] Such partisan thinking is entirely natural, for our job in

---

[5] In the science of psychology the processes of "directed thinking" and "free thinking" have in the past been kept quite separate. The "experimentalists," traditionally so-called, have studied the former, and the "dynamic psychologists" (e.g., the Freudians) the latter. A readable book in the former tradition is Humphrey (1948); in the latter tradition, Freud (1914).

this world is to live in an integrated way as value-seekers. Prejudgments stemming from these values enable us to do so.

Personal Values and Prejudice

It is obvious, then, that the very act of affirming our way of life often leads us to the brink of prejudice. The philosopher Spinoza has defined what he calls "love-prejudice." It consists, he says, "in feeling about anyone through love more than is right." The lover overgeneralizes the virtues of his beloved. Her every act is seen as perfect. The partisan of a church, a club, a nation may also feel about these objects "through love more than is right."

Now there is a good reason to believe that this love-prejudice is far more basic to human life than is its opposite, hate-prejudice (which Spinoza says "consists in feeling about anyone through hate less than is right"). One must first overestimate the things one loves before one can underestimate their contraries. Fences are built primarily for the protection of what we cherish.

Positive attachments are essential to life. The young child could not exist without his dependent relationship on a nurturant person. He must love and identify himself with someone or something before he can learn what to hate. Young children must have family and friendship circles before they can define the "out-groups" which are a menace to them. (See Allport, 1950; Ashley-Montagu, 1950.)

Why is it that we hear so little about love-prejudice—the tendency to overgeneralize our categories of attachment and affection? One reason is that prejudices of this sort create no social problem. If I am grossly partisan toward my own children, no one will object—unless at the same time it leads me, as it sometimes does, to manifest antagonism toward the neighbor's children. When a person is defending a categorical value of his own, he may do so at the expense of other people's interests or safety. If so, then we note his hate-prejudice, not realizing that it springs from a reciprocal love-prejudice underneath.

A student in Massachusetts, an avowed apostle of tolerance—so he thought—wrote, "The Negro question will never be solved until those dumb white Southerners get something through their ivory skulls." The student's positive values were idealistic. But ironically enough, his militant "tolerance" brought about a prejudiced condemnation of a portion of the population which he perceived as a threat to his tolerance-value.

Somewhat similar is the case of the lady who said, "Of course I have no prejudice. I had a dear old colored mammy for a nurse. Having grown up in the South and having lived here all my life I understand the problem. The Negroes are much happier if they are just allowed to stay in their place. Northern troublemakers just don't understand the Negro." This lady in her little speech was (psychologically speaking) defending her own privileges, her position, and her cosy way of life. It was not so much that she disliked Negroes or northerners, but she loved the status quo.

It is convenient to believe, if one can, that all of one category is good, all of the other evil. A popular workman in a factory was offered a job in the office by the management of the company. A union official said to him, "Don't take a management job or you'll become a bastard like all the rest of them." Only two classes existed in this official's mind: the workmen and the "bastards."

These instances argue that negative prejudice is a reflex of one's own system of values. We prize our own mode of existence and correspondingly underprize (or actively attack) what seems to us to threaten it. The thought has been expressed by Sigmund Freud: "In the undisguised antipathies and aversion which people feel towards strangers with whom they have to do, we recognize the expression of self-love, of narcissism."

The process is especially clear in time of war. When an enemy threatens all or nearly all of our positive values we stiffen our resistance and exaggerate the merits of our cause. We feel—and this is an instance of overgeneralization—that we are wholly right. (If we did not believe this we could not marshal all our energies for our defense.) And if we are wholly right then the enemy must be wholly wrong. Since he is wholly wrong, we should not hesitate to exterminate him. But even in this wartime example it is clear that our basic love-prejudice is primary and that the hate-prejudice is a derivative phenomenon.

Summary

This chapter has argued that man has a propensity to prejudice. This propensity lies in his normal and natural tendency to form generalizations, concepts, categories, whose content represents an oversimplification of his world of experience. His rational categories keep close to first-hand experience, but he is able to form irrational categories just as readily. In these even a kernel of truth may be lacking, for they can be composed wholly of hearsay evidence, emotional projections, and fantasy.

One type of categorization that predisposes us especially to make unwarranted prejudgments is our personal values. These values, the basis of all human existence, lead easily to love-prejudices. Hate-prejudices are secondary developments, but they may, and often do, arise as a reflex of positive values.

In order to understand better the nature of love-prejudice, which at bottom is responsible for hate-prejudice, we turn our attention next to the formation of in-group loyalties.

Chapter 3. Formation of In-Groups

The proverb *familiarity breeds contempt* contains considerably less than a half-truth. While we sometimes do become bored with our daily routine of living and with some of our customary companions, yet the very values that sustain our lives depend for their force upon their familiarity. What is more, what is familiar tends to become a value. We come to like the style of cooking, the customs, the people, we have grown up with.

Psychologically, the crux of the matter is that the familiar provides the indispensable basis of our existence. Since existence is good, its accompanying groundwork seems good and desirable. A child's parents, neighborhood, region, nation are given to him—so too his religion, race, and social traditions. To him all these affiliations are taken for granted. Since he is part of them, and they are part of him, they are *good*.

As early as the age of five, a child is capable of understanding that he is a member of various groups. He is capable, for example, of a sense of ethnic identification. Until he is nine or ten he will not be able to understand just what his membership signifies—how, for example, Jews differ from gentiles, or Quakers from Methodists, but he does not wait for this understanding before he develops fierce in-group loyalties.

Some psychologists say that the child is "rewarded" by virtue of his memberships, and that

this reward creates the loyalty. That is to say, his family feeds and cares for him, he obtains pleasure from the gifts and attentions received from neighbors and compatriots. Hence he learns to love them. His loyalties are acquired on the basis of such rewards. We may doubt that this explanation is sufficient. A colored child is seldom or never rewarded for being a Negro—usually just the opposite, and yet he normally grows up with a loyalty to his racial group. Thoughts of Indiana arouse a glow in the breast of a native Hoosier—not necessarily because he passed a happy childhood there, but simply because he *came* from there. It is still, in part, the ground of his existence.

Rewards may, of course, help the process. A child who has plenty of fun at a family reunion may be more attached there after to his own clan because of the experience. But normally he would be attached to his clan anyway, simply because it is an inescapable part of his life.

This principle of the *ground* in human learning is important. We do not need to postulate a "gregarious instinct" to explain why people like to be with people: they have simply found people lock-stitched into the very fabric of their existence. Since they affirm their own existence as good, they will affirm social living as good. Nor do we need to postulate a "consciousness of kind" to explain why people adhere to their own families, clans, ethnic groups. The self could not be itself without them.

Scarcely anyone ever wants to be anybody else. However handicapped or unhappy he feels himself, he would not change places with other more fortunate mortals. He grumbles over his misfortunes and wants his lot improved; but it is *his* lot and *his* personality that he wants bettered. This attachment to one's own being is basic to human life. I may say that I envy *you*. But I do not want to *be* you; I only want to have for myself some of your attributes or possessions. And along with this beloved self go all of the person's basic memberships. Since he cannot alter his family stock, its traditions, his nationality, or his native language, he does well to accept them. Their accent dwells in the heart as well as on the tongue.

What Is an In-Group?

There is one law—universal in all human societies—that assists us in making an important prediction. *In every society on earth the child is regarded as a member of his parents' groups.* He belongs to the same race, stock, family tradition, religion, caste, and occupational status. To be sure, in our society, he may when he grows older escape certain of these memberships, but not all. The child is ordinarily expected to acquire his parents' loyalties and prejudices; and if the parent because of his group-membership is an object of prejudice, the child too is automatically victimized.

It is difficult to define an in-group precisely. Perhaps the best that can be done is to say that members of an in-group all use the term *we* with the same essential significance. Members of a family do so, likewise schoolmates, members of a lodge, labor union, club, city, state, nation. In a vaguer way members of international bodies may do the same. Some we-organizations are transitory (e.g., an evening party), some are permanent (e.g., a family or clan).

> Sam, a middle-aged man of only average sociability, listed his own in-group memberships as follows:
>
> > his paternal relatives
> > his maternal relatives
> > family of orientation (in which he grew up)
> > family of procreation (his wife and children)
> > his boyhood circle (now a dim memory)
> > his grammar school (in memory only)
> > his high school (in memory only)
> > his college as a whole (sometimes revisited)
> > his college class (reinforced by reunions)
> > his present church membership (shifted when he was 20)
> > his profession (strongly organized and firmly knit)
> > his firm (but especially the department in which he works)
> > a "bunch" (group of four couples who take a good deal of recreation together)
> > surviving members of a World War I company of infantry (growing dim)
> > state where he was born (a fairly trivial membership)
> > town where he now lives (a lively civic spirit)
> > New England (a regional loyalty)
> > United States (an average amount of patriotism)
> > United Nations (in principle firmly believed in but psychologically loose because he is not clear concerning the "we" in this case)
> > Scotch-Irish stock (a vague feeling of kinship with others who have this lineage)
> > Republican party (he registers Republican in the primaries but has little additional sense of belonging)

Sam's list is probably not complete—but from it we can reconstruct fairly well the membership ground on which he lives.

In his list Sam referred to a boyhood circle. He recalls that at one time this in-group was of desperate importance to him. When he moved to a new neighborhood at the age of 10 he had no one of his own age to pal with, and he much desired companionship. The other boys were curious and suspicious. Would they admit him? Was Sam's style compatible with the gang's style? There was the usual ordeal by fistfight, set in motion at some slight pretext. This ritual—as is customary in boys' gangs—is designed to provide a swift and acceptable test of the stranger's manners and morale. Will he keep within the limits set by the gang, and show just enough boldness, toughness, and self-control to suit the other boys?

Thus some in-group memberships have to be fought for. But many are conferred automatically by birth and by family tradition. In terms of modern social science the former memberships reflect *achieved* status; the latter, *ascribed* status.

Sex as an In-Group

Sam did not mention his membership (ascribed status) in the male sex. Probably at one time it was consciously important to him—and may still be so.

The in-group of sex makes an interesting case study. A child of two normally makes no distinction in his companionships: a little girl or a little boy is all the same to him. Even in the first grade the awareness of sex-groups is relatively slight. Asked whom they would choose to play with, first-grade children on the average choose opposite-sexed children at least a quarter of the time. By the time the fourth grade is reached these cross-sexed choices virtually disappear: only two percent of the children want to play with someone of the opposite sex. When the eighth grade is reached friendships between boys and girls begin to re-emerge, but even then only eight percent extend their choices across the set boundary (Moreno, 1934).[6]

For some people—misogynists among them—

---

[6]These data are somewhat old. At the present time there are grounds for believing that the sex boundary is not so important among children as formerly.

the sex-grouping remains important throughout their lives. Women are viewed as a wholly different species from men, usually an inferior species. Such primary and secondary sex differences as exist are greatly exaggerated and are inflated into imaginary distinctions that justify discrimination. With half of mankind (his own sex) the male may feel an in-group solidarity, with the other half, an irreconcilable conflict. Lord Chesterfield, who in his letters often admonished his son to guide his life by reason rather than by prejudice, nevertheless has this to say about women:

> Women, then, are only children of a larger growth; they have an entertaining tattle, and sometimes wit; but for solid reasoning, good sense, I never knew in my life one that had it or who reasoned or acted consequentially for four and twenty hours together. . . .
> A man of sense only trifles with them, plays with them, humors and flatters them, as he does a sprightly, forward child; but he neither consults them about, nor trusts them with serious matters; though he often makes them believe that he does both; which is the thing in the world that they are most proud of. . . . (Strachey, 1925, p. 261)
> Women are much more like each other than men; they have in truth but two passions, vanity and love: these are their universal characteristics. (Strachey, 1925, p. 5)

Such antifeminism reflects the two basic ingredients of prejudice—denigration and gross overgeneralization. This famous man of intellect neither allows for individual differences among women, nor asks whether their alleged attributes are in fact more common in the female than in the male sex.

What is instructive about this antifeminism is the fact that it implies security and contentment with one's own sex membership. To Chesterfield the cleavage between male and female was a cleavage between accepted in-group and rejected out-group. But for many people this "war of the sexes" seems totally unreal. They do not find in it a ground for prejudice.

The Shifting Nature of In-Groups

Although each individual has his own conception of in-groups important to himself, he is not unaffected by the temper of the times. During the past century, national and racial memberships have risen in importance, while family and religious memberships have declined (though they are still exceedingly prominent). The fierce loyalties and rivalries between Scottish clans is almost a thing of the past—but the conception of a "master race" has grown to threatening proportions. The fact that women in Western countries have assumed roles once reserved for men makes the antifeminism of Chesterfield seem old-fashioned indeed.

A change in the conception of the national in-group is seen in the shifting American attitude toward immigration. The native American nowadays seldom takes an idealistic view of immigration. He does not feel it a duty and privilege to offer a home to oppressed people—to include them in his in-group. The legend on the Statue of Liberty, engraved eighty years ago, already seems out of date:

> Give me your tired, your poor,
> Your huddled masses yearning to breathe free,
> The wretched refuse of your teeming shore.
> Send these, the homeless, the tempest-tossed to me.
> I lift my lamp beside the golden door.

The lamp was virtually extinguished by the anti-immigration laws passed in the period 1918–1924. The lingering sentiment was not strong enough to relax the bars appreciably following the Second World War when there were more homeless and tempest-tossed than ever before crying for admission. From the standpoint of both economics and humanitarianism there were strong arguments for relaxing the restrictions; but people had grown fearful. Many conservatives feared the importation of radical ideas; many Protestants felt their own precarious majority might be further reduced; some Catholics dreaded the arrival of Communists; anti-Semites wanted no more Jews; some labor-union members feared that jobs would not be created to absorb the newcomers and that their own security would suffer.

During the 124 years for which data are available, approximately 40,000,000 immigrants came to America, as many as 1,000,000 in a single year. Of the total immigration 85 percent came from Europe. Until a generation ago, few objections were heard. But today nearly all applicants are refused admission, and few champions of "displaced persons" are heard. Times have changed, and whenever they change for the worse, as they have, in-group boundaries tend to tighten. The stranger is suspect and excluded.

The following amusing passage from H. G. Wells' (1905) *A Modern Utopia* depicts a snob—a person whose group loyalties are narrow. But even a snob, it appears, must have a certain flexibility, for he finds it convenient to identify himself sometimes with one in-group and sometimes with another.

The passage illustrates an important point: in-group memberships are not permanently fixed. For certain purposes an individual may affirm one category of membership, for other purposes a slightly larger category. It depends on his need for self-enhancement.

Wells is describing the loyalties of a certain botanist:

> He has a strong feeling for systematic botanists as against plant physiologists, whom he regards as lewd and evil scoundrels in this relation; but he has a strong feeling for all botanists and indeed all biologists, as against physicists, and those who profess the exact sciences, all of whom he regards as dull, mechanical, ugly-minded scoundrels in this relation; but he has a strong feeling for all who profess what he calls Science, as against psychologists, sociologists, philosophers, and literary men, whom he regards as wild, foolish, immoral scoundrels in this relation; but he has a strong feeling for all educated men as against the working man, whom he regards as a cheating, lying, loafing, drunken, thievish, dirty scoundrel in this relation; but as soon as the working man is comprehended together with these others, as *Englishmen* . . . he holds them superior to all sorts of Europeans, whom he regards. . . . (Wells, 1905, p. 322)

Thus the sense of belonging is a highly personal matter. Even two members of the same actual in-group may view its composition in widely divergent ways. Take, for instance, the definition that two Americans might give to their own national in-group (see Figure 1.1).

The narrowed perception of Individual A is the product of an arbitrary categorization, one that he finds convenient (functionally significant) to hold. The larger range of perception on the part of Individual B creates a wholly different conception of the national in-group. It is misleading to say that both belong to the same in-group. Psychologically, they do not.

In-Groups and Reference Groups

We have broadly defined an in-group as any cluster of people who can use the term "we" with the

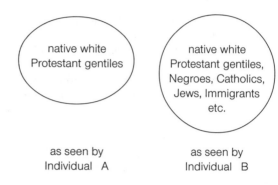

as seen by
Individual A

as seen by
Individual B

FIGURE 1.1 ■ The national in-group as perceived by two Americans.

same significance. But the reader has noted that individuals may hold all manner of views concerning their membership in in-groups. A first-generation American may regard his Italian background and culture as more important than do his children, who are second-generation Italian-Americans. Adolescents may view their neighborhood gang as a far more important in-group than their school. In some instances an individual may actively repudiate an in-group, even though he cannot escape membership in it.

In order to clarify this situation, modern social science has introduced the concept of reference group. Sherif and Sherif have defined reference groups as "those groups to which the individual relates himself as a part, or to which he aspires to relate himself psychologically" (Sherif & Sherif, 1953, p. 161). Thus a reference group is an in-group that is warmly accepted, or a group in which the individual wishes to be included.

Now usually an in-group is also a reference group, but not always. A Negro may wish to relate himself to the white majority in his community. He would like to partake of the privileges of this majority, and be considered one of its members. He may feel so intensely about the matter that he repudiates his own in-group. He develops a condition that Kurt Lewin has called "self-hate" (i.e., hatred for his own in-group). Yet the customs of the community force him to live with, work with, and be classified with the Negro group. In such a case his in-group membership is not the same as his reference group.

Or take the case of a clergyman of Armenian descent ministering in a small New England town. His name is foreign. Townsmen classify him as an Armenian. Yet he himself seldom thinks of his ancestry, though he does not actively reject his background. His reference groups (his main interests) are his church, his family, and the community in which he lives. Unfortunately for him, his fellow townsmen persist in regarding him as an Armenian; they regard this ethnic in-group as far more important than he himself does.

The Negro and the Armenian cleric occupy *marginal* roles in the community. They have difficulty relating themselves to their reference groups because the pressures of the community force them always to tie to in-groups of small psychological importance to them.

The concepts of in-group and reference group help us to distinguish two levels of belongingness. The former indicates the sheer fact of membership; the latter tells us whether the individual prizes that membership or whether he seeks to relate himself with another group. In many cases, as we have said, there is a virtual identity between in-groups and reference groups; but it is not always so. Some individuals, through necessity or by choice, continually compare themselves with groups which for them are not in-groups.

Social Distance

The distinction between in-group and reference group is well brought out in studies of social distance. This familiar technique, invented by E. S. Bogardus (1928), asks respondents to indicate to which steps on the following scale they would admit members of various ethnic and national groups:

1. to close kinship by marriage
2. to my club as personal chums
3. to my street as neighbors
4. to employment in my occupation
5. to citizenship in my country
6. as visitors only to my country
7. would exclude from my country

Now the most striking finding from this procedure is that a similar pattern of preference is found across the country, varying little with income, region, education, occupation, or even with ethnic group. Most people, whoever they are, find the English and Canadians acceptable as citizens, as neighbors, as social equals, and as kinsmen. These ethnic stocks have the least social distance. At the other extreme come Hindus, Turks, Negroes. The ordering—with a few minor shifts—stays substan-

tially constant. The order found by Bogardus (1928) was found essentially unchanged by Hartley (1946), and again by Spoerl (1951).

From such results we are forced to conclude that the member of an ethnic minority tends to fashion his attitudes as does the dominant majority. In other words, the dominant majority is for him a *reference group*. It exerts a strong pull upon him, forcing attitudinal conformity. The conformity, however, rarely extends to the point of repudiating his own in-group. A Negro, or Jew, or Mexican will ordinarily assert the acceptability of his own in-group, but in other respects he will decide as does his larger reference group. Thus, both in-group and reference group are important in the formation of attitudes.

The Group-Norm Theory of Prejudice

We are now in a position to understand and appreciate a major theory of prejudice. It holds that all groups (whether in-groups or reference groups) develop a way of living with characteristic codes and beliefs, standards and "enemies" to suit their own adaptive needs. The theory holds also that both gross and subtle pressures keep every individual member in line. The in-group's preferences must be his preference, its enemies his enemies. The Sherifs (1953), who advance this theory, write:

> Ordinarily the factors leading individuals to form attitudes of prejudice are not piecemeal. Rather, their formation is functionally related to becoming a group member—to adopting the group and its values (norms) as the main anchorage in regulating experience and behavior. (p. 218)

A strong argument in favor of this view is the relative ineffectiveness of attempts to change attitudes through influencing individuals. Suppose the child attends a lesson in intercultural education in the classroom. The chances are this lesson will be smothered by the more embracing norms of his family, gang, or neighborhood. To change the child's attitudes it would be necessary to alter the cultural equilibrium of these, to him, more important groups. It would be necessary for the family, the gang, or the neighborhood to sanction tolerance before he as an individual could practice it.

This line of thought has led to the dictum, "It is easier to change group attitudes than individual attitudes." Recent research lends some support to the view. In certain studies whole communities, whole housing projects, whole factories, or whole school systems have been made the target of change. By involving the leaders, the policies, the rank and file, new norms are created, and when this is accomplished, it is found that individual attitudes tend to conform to the new group norm. Among the studies of this type we may refer especially to Morrow and French (1945), Lippitt (1949), Wormser and Selltiz (1951), and Lewin (1947).

While we cannot doubt the results, there is something unnecessarily "collectivistic" about the theory. Prejudice is by no means exclusively a mass phenomenon. Let the reader ask himself whether his own social attitudes do in fact conform closely to those of his family, social class, occupational group, or church associates. Perhaps the answer is yes; but more likely the reader may reply that the prevailing prejudices of his various reference groups are so contradictory that he cannot, and does not, "share" them all. He may also decide that his pattern of prejudice is unique, conforming to none of his membership groups.

Realizing this individual play of attitudes, the proponents of the theory speak of a "range of tolerable behavior," admitting thereby that only approximate conformity is demanded within any system of group norms. People may deviate in their attitudes to some extent, but not too much.

As soon as we allow, however, for a "range of tolerable behavior" we are moving toward a more individualistic point of view. We do not need to deny the existence of group norms and group pressure in order to insist that each person is uniquely organized. Some of us are avid conformists to what we believe the group requirement to be. Others of us are passive conformists. Still others are nonconformists. Such conformism as we show is the product of individual learning, individual needs, and individual style of life.

In dealing with problems of attitude formation it is always difficult to strike a proper balance between the collective approach and the individual approach. This volume maintains that prejudice is ultimately a problem of personality formation and development; no two cases of prejudice are precisely the same. No individual would mirror his group's attitude unless he had a personal need, or personal habit, that leads him to do so. But it likewise maintains that one of the frequent sources, perhaps the most frequent source, of prejudice lies in the needs and habits that reflect the influence of in-group memberships upon the development of the individual personality. It is possible to hold the individualistic type of theory without denying that the major influences upon the individual may be collective.

Can There Be an In-Group without an Out-Group?

Every line, fence, or boundary marks off an inside from an outside. Therefore, in strict logic, an in-group always implies the existence of some corresponding out-group. But this logical statement by itself is of little significance. What we need to know is whether one's loyalty to the in-group automatically implies disloyalty, or hostility, or other forms of negativism, toward out-groups.

The French biologist, Felix le Dantec, insisted that every social unit from the family to the nation could exist only by virtue of having some "common enemy." The family unit fights many threatening forces that menace each person who belongs to the unit. The exclusive club, the American Legion, the nation itself, exists to defeat the common enemies of its members. In favor of Le Dantec's view is the well-known Machiavellian trick of creating a common enemy in order to cement an in-group. Hitler created the Jewish menace not so much to demolish the Jews as to cement the Nazi hold over Germany. School spirit is never so strong as when the time for an athletic contest with the traditional "enemy" approaches. Instances are so numerous that one is tempted to accept the doctrine. Studying the effect of strangers entering a group of nursery school children, Susan Isaacs (1933) reports, "The existence of an outsider is in the beginning an essential condition of any warmth or togetherness within the group" (p. 250).

Now there is no denying that the presence of a threatening common enemy will cement the in-group sense of any organized aggregate of people. A family (if it is not already badly disrupted) will grow cohesive in the face of adversity, and a nation is never so unified as in time of war. But the psychological emphasis must be placed primarily on the desire for security, not on hostility itself.

One's own family is an in-group; and by definition all other families on the street are out-groups; but seldom do they clash. A hundred ethnic groups compose America, and while serious conflict occasionally occurs, the majority rub along in peace. One knows that one's lodge has distinctive characteristics that mark it off from all others, but one does not necessarily despise the others.

The situation, it seems, can best be stated as follows: although we could not perceive our own in-groups excepting as they contrast to out-groups, still the in-groups are psychologically primary. We live in them, by them, and, sometimes, for them. Hostility toward out-groups helps strengthen our sense of belonging, but it is not required.

Because of their basic importance to our own survival and self-esteem we tend to develop a partisanship and ethnocentrism in respect to our in-groups. Seven-year-old children in one town were asked, "Which are better, the children in this town or in Smithfield (a neighboring town)?" Almost all replied, "The children in this town." When asked why, the children usually replied, "I don't know the kids in Smithfield." This incident puts the initial in-group and out-group situation in perspective. The familiar is *preferred*. What is alien is regarded as somehow inferior, less "good," but there is not necessarily hostility against it.

Can Humanity Constitute an In-Group?

One's family ordinarily constitutes the smallest and the firmest of one's in-groups. It is probably for this reason that we usually think of in-groups growing weaker and weaker the larger their circle of inclusion. Figure 1.2 expresses the common feeling that the potency of the membership becomes less as the distance from personal contact grows larger. Only a few sample memberships are included in the diagram in order not to complicate the point at issue.

Such an image implies that a world-loyalty is the most difficult to achieve. In part the implication is correct. There seems to be special difficulty in fashioning an in-group out of an entity as embracing as mankind. Even the ardent believer in One World has trouble. Suppose a diplomat is dealing at a conference table with representatives of other countries whose language, manners, and ideology differ from his own. Even if this diplomat believes ardently in One World, still he cannot escape a sense of strangeness in his encounters. His own model of propriety and rightness is his own culture. Other languages and customs inevitably seem outlandish and, if not inferior, at least slightly absurd and unnecessary.

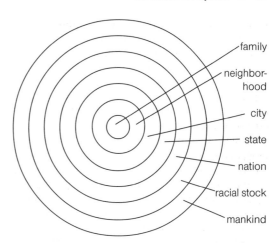

FIGURE 1.2 ■ Hypothetical lessening of in-group potency as membership becomes more inclusive.

Such almost reflex preference for the familiar grips us all. To be sure, a well-traveled person, or one who is endowed with cosmopolitan tastes, is relatively more hospitable to other nations. He can see that differences in culture do not necessarily mean inferiority. But for persons neither imaginative nor well-traveled artificial props are needed. They require *symbols*—today almost lacking—in order to make the human in-group seem real. Nations have flags, parks, schools, capitol buildings, currency, newspapers, holidays, armies, historical documents. Only gradually and with small publicity are a few of these symbols of unity evolving on an international scale. They are greatly needed in order to provide mental anchorage points around which the idea of world-loyalty may develop.

There is no intrinsic reason why the outermost circle of membership needs to be the weakest. In fact, race itself has become the dominant loyalty among many people, especially among fanatic advocates of "Aryanism" and among certain members of oppressed races. It seems today that the clash between the idea of race and of One World (the two outermost circles) is shaping into an issue that may well be the most decisive in human history. The important question is, Can a loyalty to mankind be fashioned before interracial warfare breaks out?

Theoretically it can, for there is a saving psychological principle that may be invoked if we can learn how to do so in time. The principle states that *concentric loyalties need not clash*. To be devoted to a large circle does not imply the destruction of one's attachment to a smaller circle.[7] *The loyalties that clash are almost invariably those of identical scope.* A bigamist who has founded two families of procreation is in fatal trouble with himself and with society. A traitor who serves two nations (one nominally and one actually) is mentally a mess and socially a felon. Few people can acknowledge more than one alma mater, one religion, or one fraternity. On the other hand, a world-federalist can be a devoted family man, an ardent alumnus, and a sincere patriot. The fact that some fanatic nationalists would challenge the compatibility of world-loyalty with patriotism does not change the psychological law. Wendell Willkie and Franklin Roosevelt were no less patriots because they envisioned a United Nations in One World.

Concentric loyalties take time to develop, and often, of course, they fail completely to do so. In an interesting study of Swiss children Piaget and Weil discovered the resistance of young children to the idea that one loyalty can be included within another. The following record of a seven-year-old is typical of that age:

Have you heard of Switzerland? *Yes.* What is it? *A canton.* And what is Geneva? *A town.* Where is Geneva? *In Switzerland.* (But the child draws two circles side by side.) Are you Swiss? *No, I'm Genevese.*

At a later stage (eight to ten) children grasp the idea that Geneva is enclosed spatially in Switzerland and draw their relationship as one circle enclosing the other. But the idea of concentric loyalty is still elusive.

---

[7]This spatial metaphor has its limitations. The reader may ask, What really is the innermost circle of loyalty? It is by no means always the family, as Figure 2 implies. May not the core be the primordial self-love we discussed in Chapter 2? If we regard self as the central circle, then the broadening loyalties are, psychologically speaking, simply extensions of the self. But as the self widens, it may also *recenter* itself, so that what is at first an outer circle may become psychologically the focus. Thus a religious person, for example, may believe that man is made in God's image: therefore his own love of God and man may, for him, lie in the innermost circle. Both loyalties and prejudices are features of personality organization, and in the last analysis each organization is unique. While this criticism is entirely valid, still for our present purposes Figure 2 can stand as an approximate representation of the fact that for many people the larger the social system the less easily do they encompass it in their span of understanding and affection.

What is your nationality? *I'm Swiss.* How is that? *Because I live in Switzerland.* You're Genevese too? *No, I can't be.* Why not? *I'm Swiss now and can't be Genevese as well.*

By the age of ten or eleven the child can straighten the matter out.

What is your nationality? *I'm Swiss.* How is that? *Because my parents are Swiss.* Are you Genevese as well? *Naturally, because Geneva is in Switzerland.*

Likewise by the age of ten or eleven the child has an emotional evaluation of his national circle.

I like Switzerland because it is a free country.
I like Switzerland because it's the Red Cross country.
In Switzerland our neutrality makes us charitable.

It is evident that these emotional valuations are learned from teachers and parents, and are adopted ready-made. The mode of teaching ordinarily stops the process of enlargement at this point. Beyond the borders of the native land there is only the domain of "foreigners"—not of fellow men. Michel, aged nine and one-half, answered the interviewer as follows:

Have you ever heard of such people as foreigners? *Yes, the French, the Americans, the Russians, the English.* Quite right. Are there differences between all these people? *Oh yes, they don't speak the same language.* And what else? Try to tell me as much as possible. *The French are not very serious, they don't worry about anything, and it's dirty there.* And what do you think of the Americans? *They're ever so rich and clever. They've discovered the atom bomb.* And what do you think of the Russians? *They're bad, they're always wanting to make war.* Now look, how did you come to know all you've told me? *I don't know . . . I've heard it . . . that's what people say.*

Most children never enlarge their sense of belonging beyond the ties of family, city, nation. The reason seems to be that those with whom the child lives, and whose judgment he mirrors, do not do so. Piaget and Weil (1951) write, "Everything suggests that, on discovering the values accepted in his immediate circle, the child feels bound to accept the circle's opinions of all other national groups" (p. 570).

While the national orbit is the largest circle of loyalty that most children learn, there is no necessity for the process to stop there.

In summary, in-group memberships are vitally important to individual survival. These memberships constitute a web of habits. When we encounter an outsider who follows different customs we unconsciously say, "He breaks my habits." Habit-breaking is unpleasant. We prefer the familiar. We cannot help but feel a bit on guard when other people seem to threaten or even question our habits. Attitudes partial to the in-group, or to the reference group, do not necessarily require that attitudes toward other groups be antagonistic—even though hostility often helps to intensify the in-group cohesion. Narrow circles can, without conflict, be supplemented by larger circles of loyalty. This happy condition is not often achieved, but it remains from the psychological point of view a hopeful possibility.

Chapter 4. Rejection of Out-Groups

We have seen that in-group loyalty does not necessarily imply hostility toward out-groups. It may not even imply any awareness of the existence of corresponding out-groups.

In one unpublished study a large number of adults were interviewed. They were asked to name all the groups they could think of to which they belonged. There resulted for each adult a long list of memberships. Family came first in frequency and intensity of mention. Then followed the specification of geographical region, occupational groups, social (club and friendship) groups, religious, ethnic, and ideological memberships.

When the list was complete the subjects were asked to name "any groups which you feel appear in direct contrast to, or as a threat to, one of the groups you are identified with." In response to this direct invitation only 21 percent of the subjects responded by mentioning out-groups. Seventy-nine percent were unable to name any. Those who did identify out-groups named chiefly ethnic, religious, and ideological groups.

The out-groups mentioned took a diversity of forms. One woman from the South named New Englanders, non-university people, colored people, foreigners, Midwesterners, and Catholics as uncongenial out-groups. A general librarian declared that specialty librarians were an out-group. An employee of a nutritional laboratory felt that the hematologists in the upstairs laboratory were alien and unwelcome.

Thus it is apparent that our loyalties may, but do not necessarily, involve hostile attitudes toward contrasting groups. In Chapter 2 we argued that love-prejudice (especially when frustrated) prepares the way for reciprocal hate-prejudice. But though this line of reasoning is sound, it is evident that positive partisanship does not necessarily breed negative prejudice.

Yet many people do define their loyalties in terms of the other side of the fence. They think a great deal about out-groups, worry about them, and feel under strain. To reject out-groups is for them a salient need. For them an ethnocentric orientation is important.

People with salient attitudes toward out-groups may express them with all degrees of intensity. In Chapter 1 we suggested a scale of intensity resulting in five types of rejective behavior:

1. Antilocution
2. Avoidance
3. Discrimination
4. Physical attack
5. Extermination

In the present chapter we shall examine the gradations of rejection of out-groups in some detail, simplifying the five steps into three:[8]

1. Verbal rejection (antilocution)
2. Discrimination (including segregation)
3. Physical attack (of all degrees of intensity)

Verbal Rejection

Words betraying antagonism come easily.

Two cultivated middle-aged women were discussing the high cost of cut flowers. One spoke of a lavish floral display at a certain Jewish wedding, and added, "I don't see how they afford it. They must doctor their income tax returns." The other replied, "Yes, they must."

In this snatch of trivial gossip three important psychological facts are present. (1) The first speaker made a spontaneous reference to Jews not called for by the topic of conversation. Her preju-

---

[8]Without doubt, this simple three-step scale would have a high "coefficient of reproducibility," according to Guttman's criterion for an acceptable attitude scale (scalogram). No person would take part in physical attack without also manifesting discriminatory and verbal rejection. The higher steps in the scale presuppose the lower. Cf. Stouffer (1951).

dice was so salient that it intruded itself into the discussion. Her dislike of this out-group was pressing for release. Probably she obtained a somewhat pleasant catharsis from speaking her mind. (2) The conversation itself was wholly secondary to the maintenance of good relations between the ladies. They were trying to sustain a friendly acquaintanceship. To do so their agreement on every topic was desirable. To cement this two-person in-group it helped for the members to name and disparage an out-group. As we have just seen, hostility to out-groups, though not necessary for in-group solidarity, can serve to strengthen it. (3) Both speakers reflected the attitudes of their class. They were thus showing a certain class-solidarity. It was as though each admonished the other to be a good upper middle-class gentile and adhere to the outlook and ways of the class. Needless to say, none of these psychological functions was consciously present in their minds. What is more, neither lady was intensely anti-Semitic. Both had many Jewish friends. Neither would countenance active discrimination, certainly not violence. Theirs was the lowest degree of prejudice (antilocution). But even the lowest degree betrays some of the complexities of the problem.

More intense hostility is reflected in the antilocution of name-calling. Epithets like "kike" "nigger," "wop" generally issue from deep and long-standing hostility. There are two marked exceptions. Children often use these pert terms innocently, realizing vaguely that they have "power," but not knowing clearly to what they apply. Also such epithets may mean much less when used by people in the "lower" classes than when used by people in the "higher" classes whose vocabulary is flexible enough to avoid them—if they wish to do so.

As noted previously, the more spontaneous and irrelevant the antilocution, the stronger the hostility that lies behind it.

A visitor to a Maine village was chatting with his barber about the local poultry industry. Wishing to learn something about this type of farming, the visitor innocently asked how long, on the average, the farmers kept their hens for laying purposes. Gesturing with a vicious jab of the scissors, the barber replied, "Until the Jews get them."

The barber's emotional outburst was sudden, irrelevant, and intense. The only rational connection lay in the fact that some Jewish dealers came into the vicinity to buy poultry for the market. No farmer needed to sell to a Jewish dealer unless he wanted to. The reply had little bearing on the question asked.

Such sudden inruptions of prejudice into irrelevant contexts is a measure of the intensity and salience of a hostile attitude. In such cases it appears that a complex against out-groups presses hard upon the individual's mental life. He does not wait for some relevant occasion to express his hostility. The attitude is so dynamically charged that it explodes even under the influence of remote associations.

When antilocution reaches a high degree of intensity, the chances are considerable that it will be positively related to open and active discrimination, possibly to violence. A certain senator spoke on the floor of Congress against a federal bill to subsidize school lunches. In the course of his remarks he shouted, "Of course we will starve to death before we will strike down the bars and let whites and blacks go to school together" (*New Republic*, 1946). Strong antilocution of this order is almost certain to be backed up by discriminatory action.

Discrimination

We often separate ourselves from people whom we find uncongenial. It is not discrimination when we do so, so long as it is *we* who move away from them. *Discrimination comes about only when we deny to individuals or groups of people equality of treatment which they may wish* (Commission on Human Rights, 1949, p. 2). It occurs when we take steps to exclude members of an out-group from our neighborhood, school, occupation, or country. Restrictive covenants, boycotts, neighborhood pressure, legal segregation in certain states, "gentlemen's agreements," are all devices for discrimination.

Our definition of discrimination must be further amplified. A criminal, a psychotic, a filthy person may desire "equality of treatment" and we may without compunction deny it to him. Differential treatment based on *individual* qualities probably should not be classed as discrimination. Here we are interested only in differential treatment that is based on ethnic categorization. An official memorandum of the United Nations defines the issue: "Discrimination includes any conduct based on a distinction made on grounds of natural or social categories, which have no relation either to individual capacities or merits, or to the concrete behavior of the individual person" (Commission on Human Rights, 1949, p. 9). It is a detrimental distinction which does not take account of the particular characteristics of an individual as such.

Among the forms of discrimination *officially* practiced in various parts of the world, the United Nations lists the following:

unequal recognition before the law (general denial of rights to particular groups)

inequality of personal security (interference, arrest, disparagement because of group membership)

inequality in freedom of movement and residence (ghettoes, forbidden travel, prohibited areas, curfew restrictions)

inequality in protection of freedom of thought, conscience, religion

inequality in the enjoyment of free communication

inequality in the right of peaceful association

inequality in treatment of those born out of wedlock

inequality in the enjoyment of the right to marry and found a family

inequality in the enjoyment of free choice of employment

inequality in the regulation and treatment of ownership

inequality in the protection of authorship

inequality of opportunity for education or the development of ability or talent

inequality of opportunity for sharing the benefits of culture

inequality in services rendered (health protection, recreational facilities, housing)

inequality in the enjoyment of the right to nationality

inequality in the right to participate in government

inequality in access to public office

forced labor, slavery, special taxes, the forced wearing of distinguishing marks, sumptuary laws, and public libel of groups

In addition to these public and official indignities the list of acts that may be indulged in by private individuals is long. Opportunities for employment, promotion, or credit may be discriminative. Denial of residence opportunities or equal housing facilities is common, likewise exclusion from hotels, cafes, restaurants, theaters, or other places of entertainment. In the media of communication differential treatment of news concerning groups sometimes occurs. Refusal to offer equal educa-

tional opportunities or to associate with members of an out-group in churches, clubs, or social organizations is common. The catalogue could be greatly extended (Commission on Human Rights, 1949, pp. 28–42).

Segregation is a form of discrimination that sets up spatial boundaries of some sort to accentuate the disadvantage of members of an out-group.

A certain Negro girl applied for a job in a federal office in Washington. At each stage in the process she encountered attempts to discriminate against her: she was told by one officer that the job had been filled, by another that she would not be happy in a white office. But by persistence she finally "landed" the job. When she went to work the supervisor placed her in a corner of the office and placed a screen around her desk. She had won out over various attempts to discriminate against her, but had run headfirst into *segregation*.[9]

Discrimination in housing is especially widespread. It is the rule in American cities to find Negroes living in segregated regions. The reason is not that they wish to or that rents are cheaper where they live. Customarily people in "white districts" pay less rent for equal or better accommodations. The social pressures that keep Negroes from spreading are reflected in restrictive covenants. Nor are Negroes the only people affected. Deeds sometimes contain such phrases as the following:

. . . And furthermore, no lot shall be sold or leased to, or occupied by, any person excepting of the Caucasian race.

. . . Provided further, that the grantee shall not sell to Negroes or permit use or occupation by them, except as domestic servants.

. . . shall not permit occupation by Negroes, Hindus, Syrians, Greeks, or any corporations controlled by same.

. . . No part of the area may be owned or occupied by any person of Negro blood or by any person who is more than one-fourth of the Semitic race ... including Armenians, Jews, Hebrews, Turks, Persians, Syrians and Arabians. . . . (Gertz, 1947)

In a historic decision of 1948 the Supreme Court of the United States ruled that such covenants may not be enforced by the courts of the land. But there

---

[9]This episode is reported in Lohman (1949). The report is a complete account of segregation in the city of Washington in respect to housing, jobs, health services, education, and access to public places.

is nothing to prevent their being adhered to by "gentlemen's agreement." They often are. Various studies by public opinion polling methods indicate that roughly three-quarters of the white population would object to having Negroes live in their immediate neighborhoods. Hence there is widespread discrimination by common consent.

Discrimination in education is, like many forms of discrimination, usually a clandestine affair. This is not true, of course, in certain southern states where, in spite of the Supreme Court ruling of 1954, many schools and colleges (the number is decreasing) openly practice 100 percent segregation. In northern states, the process is more subtle and variable. A great many institutions, especially those that are tax supported, admit students without regard to race, color, religion, or national origin. Others sometimes limit the admission of certain groups to a stated fraction of the total enrollment, and still others exclude them altogether (Stetler, 1949).

Occupational discrimination is also a subtle matter. One method of studying the practice is to count the number of out-group exclusions in "Help Wanted" advertisements in daily newspapers: "Gentiles only," "Protestant preferred," "Opening for Christians," "no colored," and the like. One study of this sort suggests that over a period of 65 years the trend is for discriminative advertisements to rise with the increased proportion of a minority group in the total population. Other studies indicate that this barometer is a sensitive reflection of the times: rising in periods of depression with general fear of outsiders, subsiding when the general state of tension is less (Cohen, 1938; Severson, 1939; Strong, 1941). It is unlikely, however, that this ingenious barometer can be used by social science analysts in the future. Some newspapers voluntarily ban discriminatory advertising, and an increasing number of states are passing laws against it.

It is not necessary to summarize here the story of occupational discrimination in America. It has been told by Myrdal, Davie, Saenger, and others; see, especially, Davie (1949), Myrdal (1944), and Saenger (1953). The uneconomic aspects of discrimination have many times been disclosed. Many firms will not hire the best man for a job if his skin is dark, or if he happens to be Jewish, Catholic, foreign born. Sometimes such a person is twice as efficient and productive as his white competitor for the job, but he is not hired. It is equally

uneconomical to maintain two sets of schools, waiting rooms, hospitals, when one would serve; or to keep whole groups of the population so economically depressed that they cannot buy goods and thus stimulate production. It is probably not an accident that the states with the greatest discrimination have the lowest standards of living, and the states of greatest tolerance the highest standards.[10]

Discrimination leads to all sorts of curious patterns. As a traveler I may sit willingly next to a Jew and, if I am a Northerner, next to a Negro; but I may draw the line on living next door to either one. As an employer I may admit the Jew but not the Negro to my office; but at home I may welcome a Negro to work in my kitchen, but not a Jew. However, a Jew but not a Negro may sit in my parlor. At school I may welcome all groups, but try to prevent some from attending school dances.

The Red Cross is an organization oriented to humanitarian service with the aid of scientific knowledge. Yet during World War II the Red Cross in many places segregated the blood given by Negro donors from that given by white donors. Science could not tell the blood apart, but social mythology could. Rightly or wrongly, certain offices of the Red Cross felt it better in wartime to respect the mythology and to shelve science and efficiency in deference to prejudice ("Actions Lie," 1942).

As common as discrimination is in its many forms, it is not as common as antilocution. Two examples will show how people's bark (antilocution) is often sharper than their bite (actual discrimination). One common instance is the experience of many employers who fear to introduce Negroes or other minority members into their factory, store, or office because the employees protest bitterly. But when, perhaps through legal necessity (Fair Employment Practices legislation), they do so—opposition evaporates. Over and over again it has been predicted that if discrimination is stopped dire consequences will follow—perhaps strikes or riots. Very seldom do they follow. What happens is that the verbal protest is greater than the demand for actual discrimination.

One instance of low discrimination but high verbal rejection comes from the cleverly conceived

---

[10]The economic costs of prejudice are discussed in Cohen (1946).

study of La Piere (1934, pp. 230–237). This American investigator traveled widely in the United States with a Chinese couple. Together they stopped at 66 sleeping places and 184 eating places and were refused service only once. Afterwards, the proprietors of these places received through the mail questionnaires asking whether they would take "members of the Chinese race as guests in your establishment." Ninety-three percent of the restaurants and 92 percent of the hotels said they would not serve Chinese people. A control group of places which had not been visited gave similar questionnaire results. To raise the question which of these two sets of behavior was an expression of their "true" attitude is, of course, foolish. The outstanding contribution of La Piere's study design consists in showing that both are "true" attitudes, fitted to two different situations. The "verbal" situation aroused more hostility than the actual situation. People who threaten to discriminate may not do so.

La Piere's findings have been confirmed by Kutner, Wilkins, and Yarrow (1952). These investigators arranged for visits to eleven restaurants and taverns in a fashionable suburb of New York. Two white girls entered first and obtained a table for three. Shortly afterward a colored girl entered and said she was joining the party. In no case was service refused and in no case was it unsatisfactory. At a later date the proprietors of each eating place received a letter asking for reservations for dinner; the letter included the phrase "since some guests are colored, I wonder whether you would object to their coming." None of the proprietors answered the letter. When follow-up phone calls were made eight denied receiving the letter, and all temporized in such a way as to avoid making the desired reservations.

We may venture the following generalization: Where clear conflict exists, with law and conscience on the one side, and with custom and prejudice on the other, discrimination is practiced chiefly in covert and indirect ways, and not primarily in face-to-face situations where embarrassment would result.

Conditions of Physical Attack

Violence is always an outgrowth of milder states of mind. Although most barking (antilocution) does not lead to biting, yet there is never a bite without previous barking. Fully seventy years of political anti-Semitism of the verbal order preceded the discriminatory Nürnberg Laws passed by the Hitler regime. Soon after these Laws were passed the violent program of extermination began (Massing, 1949). Here we see the not infrequent progression: antilocution → discrimination → physical violence. Verbal attacks in the time of Bismarck were relatively mild. Under Hitler they had become ferocious: the Jews were loudly and officially blamed for every conceivable crime from sex perversion to world conspiracy.

But even the sponsors of verbal aggression in Germany were apparently astonished at the final consequences of their campaign. At the Nürnberg trials both Rosenberg and Streicher (the philosophers and publicists of the Nazi movement) disclaimed responsibility for the extermination of two and a half million Jews at Auschwitz because they "had no idea" that their preachment could issue into such action. Yet the Nazi officer in charge of the mass murders at Auschwitz, Colonel Hoess, made it clear that it was precisely this incessant verbal indoctrination that convinced him and his fellow executioners that the Jews were in fact to blame for everything and that they ought to be exterminated (Gilbert, 1947). It is apparent, therefore, that under certain circumstances there will be stepwise progression from verbal aggression to violence, from rumor to riot, from gossip to genocide.

In cases where violence breaks out we can be fairly certain that the following steps have prepared the way.

1. There has been a long period of categorical prejudgment. The victim group has long been typed. People have begun to lose the power to think of the members of an out-group as individuals.
2. There has been a long period of verbal complaint against the victimized minority. The habits of suspicion and blaming have become firmly rooted.
3. There has been growing discrimination (e.g., the Nürnberg Laws).
4. There has been some outside strain upon members of the in-group. They have for a long time suffered from economic privation, a sense of low-status, irritation due to political developments—such as wartime restrictions, or fear of unemployment.
5. People have grown tired of their own inhibi-

tions, and are reaching a state of explosion. They no longer feel that they can or should put up with unemployment, rising prices, humiliations, and bewilderment. Irrationalism comes to have a strong appeal. People distrust science, democracy, freedom. They agree that "he who increaseth knowledge increaseth sorrow." Down with intellectuals! Down with the minorities!

6. Organized movements have attracted these discontented individuals. They join the Nazi party, the Ku Klux Klan, or Black Shirts. Or a less formal organization—a mob—may serve their purpose in case no formal organization exists.

7. From such a formal or informal social organization the individual derives courage and support. He sees that his irritation and his wrath are socially sanctioned. His impulses to violence are thus justified by the standards of his group—or so he thinks.

8. Some precipitating incident occurs. What previously might have been passed over as a trivial provocation now causes an explosion. The incident may be wholly imaginary, or it may be exaggerated through rumor. (For many people who participated in the Detroit race riot, the precipitating incident seems to have been a wildly circulating rumor to the effect that a Negro had seized a white woman's baby and tossed it into the Detroit River.)

9. When violence actually breaks out, the operation of "social facilitation" becomes important in sustaining the destructive activity. To see other equally excited persons in a condition of mob frenzy augments one's own level of excitement and behavior. One ordinarily finds his personal impulses heightened and his private inhibitions lessened.

These are the conditions required to remove the normal brakes that exist between verbal aggression and overt violence. They are likely to be fulfilled in regions where the two opposing groups are thrown into close contact: for example, at bathing beaches, in public parks, or at boundaries of residential districts. At such meeting points the precipitating incident is most likely to occur.

Hot weather favors violence, both because it increases bodily discomfort and irritability, and because it brings people out of doors where contact and conflict can occur. Add the idleness of a Sunday afternoon, and the stage is well set. Disas-

trous riots do, in fact, seem to start most frequently on Sunday afternoons in hot weather. The peak of lynchings is in the summer months ("Lynchings," 1931; see also Davie, 1949).

The fact that verbal hostility may, in the above circumstances, lead to violence raises an issue concerning freedom of speech. Where freedom of speech is highly prized, as in the United States, it is commonly agreed by legal authorities that it is unwise and impracticable to attempt to control spoken or even printed slander against any outgroup. To do so would imply a restriction of people's right to criticize. The American principle is to allow complete freedom of speech up to the point where there is a "clear and present" danger to public safety through an actual incitement to violence. But this legal line is hard to draw. If conditions are ripe, then even a relatively mild verbal attack may start an unimpeded progression toward violence. In "normal" times a good deal more antilocution can be tolerated, for its aggressive thrusts meet with counter-arguments and with inner inhibitions to action. Most people normally pay little attention to slanderous remarks about outgroups. Normally too, as we have seen, persons who make them would usually stop short of active discrimination, certainly of violence. But in strained circumstances the principle of progression operates. This fact has led a few states, for example New Jersey and Massachusetts, to enact laws against "racial libel"—but to date they have been found hard to apply, and their constitutionality is not clearly established.[11]

The participants in fist fights, gang fights, vandalism, riots, lynchings, pogroms, it has been noted, are predominantly youthful (Doob, 1952). It seems unlikely that young people are more frustrated in their lives than older people, but presumably they do have a thinner layer of socialized habit between impulses and their release. It is relatively easier for a youth to regress to the tantrum stage of infant wrath and, lacking long years of social inhibition, to find a fierce joy in this release. Youth too has the agility, the energy, and the risk-taking proclivity required for violence.

In America the two most serious forms of eth-

---

[11]The President's Committee on Civil Rights decided that this remedy was too dangerous to endorse, since censorship, once started, might threaten the expression of all disapproved opinion. See the Committee's report, *To Secure These Rights* (The President's Committee, 1947).

nic conflict are riots and lynching. The chief difference between them is that in a riot the victims of attack fight back; in a lynching the victim cannot do so.

Riots and Lynching

Most riots occur where there has been some rapid change in the prevailing social situation. There has been an "invasion" of a residential district by Negroes, or members of a certain ethnic group have been imported as strikebreakers in a region of industrial unrest, or there has been a rapid rise in immigrant population in an unstable region. None of these conditions alone produces riots. There must also be a prepared ground of previous hostility and well-formed ideas concerning the "menace" of the particular group that is attacked. And, as we have said, prolonged and intense verbal hostility always precedes a riot.

It has been noted that rioters are usually drawn from lower socio-economic classes, as well as from the youthful age level. To some extent this fact may be due to the lesser degree of discipline (self-control) taught in families of these classes. To some extent it may be due to the lower educational level which prevents people from perceiving correctly the true causes of their miserable conditions of living. Certainly the crowdedness, insecurity, and deprivations of existence act as direct irritants. In general, rioters are marginal men.

A riot—like any form of ethnic conflict—may conceivably be based on a realistic clash of interest. When a large number of impoverished Negroes and equally impoverished whites are competing for a limited number of jobs, it is easy to see that rivalry is genuine. Insecurity and fear make the individuals both irritable and angry. But even in so realistic a situation we note the essential illogicality of regarding only the man of the *other* race as a threat. One white man takes a job away from another white man as surely as does a Negro. The chances are, therefore, that the conflict of interests between ethnic groups in the same vicinity is not wholly realistic. There must be also a previous sense of in-group and out-group rivalry before the lines of competition can be perceived as ethnic, rather than individual, rivalry.

The origins of a riot, therefore, lie in the prior existence of prejudice strengthened and released by the chain of circumstances reviewed in this chapter.[12] After a riot has broken out the resulting pandemonium has no logic. In the Harlem riot of 1943 the precipitating incident was apparently an "unfair" arrest of a Negro by a white policeman. The racial protest, however, took a nonracial form. Hot, tense, rebellious Negroes went wild. They looted, burned, destroyed stores owned by Negroes, and damaged Negro property as well as property owned by whites. Of all the forms of physical hostility a riot is the least directed, the least consistent, and therefore least logical. It can be likened only to the blind temper tantrum of an angry child.

Lynchings occur chiefly when discrimination and segregation are firmly entrenched and where they are customarily enforced by severe intimidation. There is an additional essential condition—a low level of law enforcement in the community. The fact that lynchings are not prevented, that lynchers, even when known, are seldom apprehended, and almost never punished, reflects the silent acquiescence of police officials and courts. The entire process, therefore, partakes of a "social norm"—and cannot be explained entirely in terms of the mental life of the lynchers.

This whole macabre practice depends to a considerable extent upon cultural custom. Among marginal and uneducated men of certain localities there has existed the tradition of a manhunt (not unlike the tradition of the coon hunt). To "get your nigger" has been a permissible sport, virtually a duty. Toward this tradition law-enforcement authorities, as we have said, sometimes show a lenient or permissive attitude. When excitement grows high in the course of a lynching it is taken for granted that there will be looting and destruction of Negro homes and businesses. Not infrequently furniture from Negro homes is used as firewood for burning the victim's body. It seems like a sound idea to teach *all* the niggers a lesson at the same time.

The frequency of lynching has markedly declined. During the decade of the 1890s there was an annual average of 154 lynchings; during the 1920s an annual average of 31; during the 1940s only two or three per year. See Berry (1951) for a good, brief summary of the facts concerning lynching.

---

[12]A comparable list of circumstances leading to riots, with a somewhat more historical and sociological emphasis, is given by Dahlke (1952).

The Essential Role of Rumor

We may state as a dependable law that no riot or lynching ever occurs without the aid of rumor. Rumor is found to enter into the pattern of violence at one or all of four stages.[13]

1. The gradual building up of animosity preceding a violent outbreak is assisted by stories of the misdeeds of the hated out-group. One hears particularly that the minority in question is itself conspiring, plotting, saving up guns and ammunition. Also the customary run of ethnic rumors takes a spurt, thus reflecting the mounting strain. One of the best barometers of tension is the collection and analysis of ethnic rumors in a community.
2. After preliminary rumors have done their work, new rumors may serve as a call to rioting or lynching parties. They act like a bugle to assemble the forces. "Something is going to happen tonight by the river." "They'll catch that nigger tonight and whale the life out of him." If alert to the situation the police may use these "marshalling rumors" to forestall violence. During the summer of 1943 in Washington, D.C., rumor had it that large numbers of Negroes were planning an organized uprising on the occasion of their parade scheduled for a certain day. Such a rumor was almost certain to bring out an opposing army of hostile whites. But by taking a firm public stand in advance of the event, and by providing adequate protection for the Negro marchers, the police were able to forestall the threatened clash.
3. Not infrequently a rumor is the spark that ignites the powder keg. Some inflammatory story flies down the street, becoming sharpened and distorted at each telling. The Harlem riot was spread by means of an exaggerated story to the effect that a white policeman had shot a Negro in the back (the truth of the episode was much milder). A dozen wild rumors bruited around Detroit were the immediate touch on the trigger of overcharged passions. But for months before the fateful Sunday, Detroit had been fed on racial rumors. One tale to the effect that carloads of armed Negroes were heading for

Detroit from Chicago had even been broadcast over the radio (Lee & Humphrey, 1943).

4. During the heat of the riot rumors sustain the excitement. Particularly puzzling are the stories that appear based on hallucination. Lee and Humphrey tell how at the peak of the violence in Detroit, police received a telephone report from a woman who claimed to have witnessed with her own eyes the killing of a white man by a mob of Negroes. When the squad car reached the scene the police found a group of girls playing hopscotch and could find no trace of violence nor any support for the woman's story. Other citizens, as excited as she, no doubt believed the tale and spread it.

Let us turn back for a moment to the suggestion that rumor provides a good barometer of group tension. In themselves, of course, rumors are mere antilocutions, expressions of verbal hostility. One hears them directed against Catholics, Negroes, refugees, government officials, big business, labor unions, the armed services, Jews, radicals, various foreign governments, and many other outgroups. The rumors without exception express hostility and give a reason for the hostility by featuring some objectionable trait.

Anti-Semitic rumors were collected in great quantities during the war. Many of them took some such form as the following:

> West Coast draft boards have refused to draft any more men until the Jewish boys in New York, Philadelphia, and Washington, deferred by Jewish draft boards, are drafted.

> All the officers at Westover are Jews. It is almost impossible for gentiles to get any of the higher offices in that air field.

> The Associated Press and the United Press are both controlled by Jews and therefore we cannot believe anything pertaining to Germany or Hitler who really knows what ought to be done to the Jews.

Stories derogatory to Negroes are somewhat less numerous. Of 1000 rumors collected and analyzed in the war year 1942, 10 percent were anti-Semitic, 3 percent anti-Negro, 7 percent anti-British, and about 2 percent each against business and against labor. The armed forces accounted for 20 percent, and the administration for 20 percent. About two-thirds of all rumors were directed against some

---

[13]The account here is condensed from Allport and Postman (1947).

out-group. Most of the others expressed deep-seated fears concerning the course of the war (Allport & Postman, 1947).

Thus rumor seems to offer a sensitive index for the state of group hostility. The discrediting of rumors may provide one means—probably a minor one—of controlling group hostility. During the war "rumor clinics" in newspapers attempted this service, and probably did succeed in making people aware of some of the dangers involved in rumor-mongering. It is doubtful, however, that the mere exposure of a rumor changes any deeply rooted prejudices. What it does at most is to warn those of mild or negligible prejudice that wedge-driving rumors in wartime or in peacetime are not in the best interests of the nation.

REFERENCES

Ackerman, N. W., & Jahoda, M. (1950). *Anti-Semitism and emotional disorder.* New York: Harper.

Actions lie louder than words—The Red Cross's policy in regard to the blood bank. (1942). *Commonweal, 35,* 404–405.

Allport, G. W. (1950). A psychological approach to love and hate. In P. A. Sorokin (Ed.), *Explorations in altruistic love and behavior.* Boston: Beacon Press.

Allport, G. W., & Postman, L. (1947). *The psychology of rumor.* New York: Henry Holt.

Ashley-Montagu, M. F. (1950). *On being human.* New York: Henry Schumann.

Berry, B. (1951). *Race relations: The interaction of ethnic and racial groups.* Boston: Houghton Mifflin.

Black, P., & Atkins, R. D. (1950). Conformity versus prejudice as exemplified in white–Negro relations in the South: Some methodological considerations. *Journal of Psychology, 30,* 109–121.

Bogardus, E. S. (1928). *Immigration and race attitudes.* Boston: D. C. Heath.

Cohen, F. S. (1946). The people vs. discrimination. *Commentary, 1,* 17–22.

Cohen, J. X. (1938). *Toward fair play for Jewish workers.* New York: American Jewish Congress.

Commission on Human Rights. (1949). *The main types and causes of discrimination.* United Nations Publication XIV. New York: United Nations. Commission on Human Rights.

Dahlke, O. H. (1952). Race and minority riots—a study in the typology of violence. *Social Forces, 30,* 419–425.

Davie, M. R. (1949). *Negroes in America society.* New York: McGraw-Hill.

Doob, L. W. (1952). *Social psychology.* New York: Henry Holt.

Dyer, H. S. (1945). The usability of the concept of "Prejudice." *Psychometrika, 10,* 219–224.

Gertz, E. (1947). American Ghettos. *Jewish Affairs, II*(1).

Gilbert, G. M. (1947). *Nüremberg Diary.* New York: Farrar, Straus.

Freud, S. (1914). *The psychopathology of everyday life.* New York: Macmillan.

Hartley, E. L. (1946). *Problems in prejudice.* New York: Kings Crown Press.

Humphrey, G. (1948). *Directed thinking.* New York: Dodd, Mead.

Isaacs, S. (1933). *Social development in young children.* New York: Harcourt, Brace.

Kutner, B., Wilkins, C., & Yarrow P. R. (1952). Verbal attitudes and overt behavior involving racial prejudice. *Journal of Abnormal and Social Psychology, 47,* 649–652.

LaFarge, J. (1945). *The race question and the Negro.* New York: Longmans, Green.

La Piere, R. T. (1934). Attitudes versus actions. *Social Forces, 13,* 230–237.

Lee, A. M., & Humphrey, N. D. (1943). *Race riot.* New York: Dryden.

Lewin, K. (1947). Group decision and social change. In T. M. Newcomb & E. L. Hartley (Eds.), *Readings in social psychology.* New York: Holt.

Lippitt, R. (1949). *Training in community relations.* New York: Harper.

Lohman, J. D. (1949). *Segregation in the nation's capital.* Chicago: National Committee on Segregation in the Nation's Capital.

Lundberg, A., & Dickson, L. (1952). Selective association among ethnic groups in a high school population. *American Sociological Review, 17,* 23–24.

Lynchings and What They Mean. (1931). Atlanta: Southern Commission on the Study of Lynching.

Massing, P. E. (1949). *Rehearsal for destruction: A study of political anti-Semitism in imperial Germany.* New York: Harper.

Moreno, J. L. (1934). *Who shall survive?* Washington, DC: Nervous and Mental Disease Publishing Co.

Morrow, A., & French, J. (1945). Changing a stereotype in industry. *Journal of Social Issues, 1,* 33–37.

Murray, A. H. (Ed.). (1909). *A new English dictionary.* Oxford: Clarendon Press.

Myrdal, G. (1944). *An American dilemma: The Negro problem and modern democracy* (Vols. 1 and 2). New York: Harper.

New Republic (1946, March 4).

Piaget, J., & Weil, A.-M. (1951). The development in children of the idea of the homeland and of relations with other countries. *International Social Science Bulletin, 3,* 570.

The President's Committee on Civil Rights. (1947). *To secure these rights.* Washington, DC: U.S. Government Printing Office.

Rose, A. (1947). *Studies in reduction of prejudice* (Mimeograph). Chicago: American Council on Race Relations.

Saenger, G. (1953). *The social psychology of prejudice.* New York: Harper.

Samuelson, B. (1945). *The patterning of attitudes and beliefs regarding the American Negro.* Unpublished manuscript, Radcliffe College Library, Cambridge, MA.

Severson, A. L. (1939). Nationality and religious preferences as reflected in newspaper advertisements. *American Journal of Sociology, 44,* 540–545.

Sherif, M., & Sherif, C. W. (1953). *Groups in harmony and tension.* New York: Harper.

Spoerl, D. T. (1951). Some aspects of prejudice as effected by religion and education. *Journal of Social Psychology, 33,* 69–76.

Stetler, H. G. (1949). *Summary and conclusions of college*

admission practices with respect to race, religion, and national origin of Connecticut high school graduates. Hartford: Connecticut State Interacial Commission.

Stouffer, A. (1951). Scaling concepts and scaling theory. In M. Jahoda, M. Deutsch, & S. W. Cox (Eds.), *Research Methods in Social Relations* (Vol. 2). New York: Dryden.

Strachey, C. (Ed.). (1925). *The letters of the Earl of Chesterfield to his son* (Vols. 1 and 2). New York: G. P. Putnam.

Strong, D. (1941). *Organized anti-Semitism in America: The rise of group prejudice during the decade 1930–40.* Washington: American Council on Public Affairs.

Wax, S. L. (1948). A survey of restrictive advertising and discrimination by summer resorts in the Province of Ontario. *Canadian Jewish Congress: Information and comment, 7,* 10–13.

Wells, H. G. (1905). *A modern utopia.* London: Chapman & Hall.

Williams, R. M., Jr. (1947). *The reduction of intergroup tensions.* New York: Social Science Research Council.

Wormser, M. H., & Selttiz, C. (1951). *How to conduct a community self-survey of civil rights.* New York: Association Press.

Social Categorization: Cognitions, Values and Groups

Henri Tajfel • University of Bristol
Joseph P. Forgas • University of New South Wales

Introduction

The aim of this chapter is to review and discuss the role of categorization in social behaviour. For our purposes, categorization will be understood as the process of ordering the environment in terms of categories, i.e., through grouping persons, objects, and events as being similar or equivalent to one another in their relevance to an individual's actions, intentions, or attitudes. The principal function of categorization resides in its role as a tool in the systematization of the environment for the purpose of action. The segmentation of the environment in terms of groupings which are equivalent to one another for given purposes is a *sine quo non* condition of survival. The categorization of incoming information is thus a basic human characteristic. As Bruner (1958) pointed out long ago, "the most self-evident point . . . is that perceiving or registering an object or an event in the environment involves an act of categorization" (p. 92). We categorize information partly as a reflection of the fact that objects in the natural world themselves display coherent and non-random patterning of features; they form "natural" object categories (Rosch, Mervis, Gray, Johnson, & Boyes-Bream, 1976). They are also active constructions imposed on the environment, which affect our perception and interpretation of incoming informa-

tion. It is this second feature of categorization which is of major importance for this discussion.

In this paper, we would like to argue that social categorization entails much more than the cognitive classification of events, objects, or people. It is a process impregnated by values, culture, and social representations (cf. Moscovici, 1981), which goes beyond the purely analytic classification of information. Although interest in categories, prototypes, and scripts (Rosch, 1975; Rosch & Lloyd, 1978; Cantor & Mischel, 1979; Bower, Black, & Turner, 1979) is one of the major themes in contemporary social cognition research, the uniquely normative nature of social categorization has been largely disregarded. Much of the work has been oriented towards formulating laws or relationships of a general cognitive nature and extending or applying them to social behaviour and experience. Some of these extensions and applications have undoubtedly proven useful. But just as it is important to take note of the continuities between the non-social and the social processes in cognition, so it is essential to be clearly aware of the specifically social character of many of the phenomena which are involved (cf. Forgas, 1979; Krauss, 1980).

Social categorization lies at the heart of commonsense, everyday knowledge, and understanding. The way an individual or a culture identifies similarities and differences between persons and groups in their milieu is the foundation on which everyday social intercourse is based. Social categorization is thus much more than a purely cognitive task: it is central to social life, and as such, it is subject to the pressures and distortions of the rich and variegated culture within which it arises. It is this complex, normative aspect of social categorization as it manifests itself in everyday social life, that we are concerned with here.

To achieve this objective, we shall begin by briefly considering some general aspects of categorization: its functions, the origins of relevant research, and the continuities between social and non-social categorization. In the second part of the chapter, we aim to present an argument for the normative nature of social categorization. In particular, the role of individual and cultural values, and of social identity in categorization will be considered. In the third and final part of the chapter, some particularly important applied areas of social categorization will be discussed: the use of person prototypes, stereotyping, and the ideologizing of collective actions.

Some General Aspects of Categorization

Functions and Origins of Categorization

The effects of cognitive categories or "schemata" on various aspects of information processing have been well recognized at least since Bartlett's (1932) early work on memory. The traditional view in cognitive psychology about category membership is that it is "a digital, or all-or-none phenomenon" (Rosch & Mervis, 1975, p. 573). However, such exclusive and non-overlapping categories are comparatively rare in everyday life. Natural categories are more likely to be characterized by a particular constellation or pattern of nonexclusive features. A good example is the varied combination of several characteristics, none of them exclusive to the group, which nevertheless allows members of a family to be identified as belonging to the same category.

Such patterns of "family resemblances" (Wittgenstein, 1953; Rosch & Mervis, 1975) or "fuzzy sets" (Zadeh, 1965) may differ in the extent to which they represent the ideal or "prototypical" pattern within that category (Rosch, 1975). It is this more relativistic view of cognitive cat-

egorization, and subsequent cognitive research which has stimulated recent social psychological work on categorization. This is perhaps not surprising. Very few objects in the social world can be unambiguously assigned into exclusive categories. However, nearly all people, events or groups that we come into contact with can be, and are, categorized in terms of their particular patterns of nonexclusive characteristics. As we shall argue later, the relative ambiguity and fluidity of the perceived characteristics in terms of which social categories are identified means that motivational, normative, and value biases play a much more important role in social than in non-social categorization.

Non-Social and Social Categorization

Before discussing the modes of categorization which are specifically social, the implications of the general process of categorization need to be reviewed. They are of two kinds, which correspond to the "inductive" and "deductive" aspects of the act of categorizing respectively (Tajfel, 1962).

The first of these is basically concerned with assigning an object or an event to a category on the basis of insufficient information (Bruner & Potter, 1964; Hershenson & Haber, 1965). For example, in the Bruner and Potter study, subjects were shown a familiar object projected out of focus; the clarity of the projection was then slowly and progressively increased. It was found that the misidentification of the object occurring in the earlier and unclear stages prevented correct identification in the later and clearer stages during which normally no mistakes would have been made.

Hershenson and Haber (1965) reported that when English and Turkish words were flashed several times on a screen, the rate of correct identification for Turkish words (unfamiliar to their subjects) was slightly faster than the rate for English words, which were presumably more easily *mis*identified in the earlier stages of the task. This kind of misidentification (i.e., assignment to the wrong category on the basis of insufficient or ambiguous information) of course occurs very frequently in the course of social categorization. In the studies just mentioned, the relatively slow achievement of the correct response was presumably due to the blocking of the search process by the persistence of incorrect assumptions about the nature of the stimuli (cf. Bruner, 1957). This is *a fortiori* the case in the interpretation of much that happens in the social environment.

These "inductive" continuities between non-social and social categorizing have their parallel in the "deductive" aspects of categorization. This consists of drawing inferences about the nature of an object or an event on the basis of the properties of a category. This can again be exemplified by reference to an experimental study (Tajfel & Wilkes, 1963). Three groups of subjects were presented with a series of eight lines which differed in length from each other by a constant ratio. They were asked to estimate the length of each line in turn. For one group, the four shorter lines were labelled A, the four longer ones, B. For the second group, the labels A and B were attached each to half of the lines, but in a random relation to length. The third group had the lines presented without any labels. As a result of these arrangements, the first group, which experienced a fully predictable relationship between the labels and the length of lines, exaggerated the differences between the two categories considerably more than did the two control groups. There was also some evidence (though much less clear-cut) that lines *within* each of the two categories were judged as more similar to each other than was the case in the control groups. Similar results using different types of stimuli were obtained in several other experiments (e.g., Campbell, 1956; Davidon, 1962; Lilli, 1970; Marchand, 1970).

The relevance of these findings to social categorization is fairly straight-forward. The implication of the experimental findings is that people belonging to different categories will be judged *in certain respects* as more different from each other than they would have been if their category membership was not known, and people in the same category would be judged as more similar to one another than would have been the case had they not been identified as belonging to the same category. The inductive and deductive biases in categorizing objects are likely to be accentuated in the case of social targets. There are several reasons for this. In the case of judgements applying to the physical environment, it is likely that shifts leading to erroneous and maladaptive responses will be quickly eliminated due to the potential availability of objective, reliable feedback about physical objects. In the case of the social environ-

ment, the information received (about, for example, the personal characteristics of people) is generally much more ambiguous to interpret and lacking in clear-cut criteria for its validity. Less information than is the case for physical categories will be needed to confirm these judgements, and considerably more to disconfirm them in the face of what appears to fit in with consensual social "reality" (cf. Moscovici, 1981).

Secondly, when a social categorization into groups is endowed with a strong value differential, encounters with negative or disconfirming instances would not just require a change in the interpretation. Much more importantly, the acceptance of such disconfirming instances threatens the value system on which the category differentiation is based. For Allport (1954), the cognitive process in prejudice consisted of "selecting, accentuating and interpreting" the information obtained from the environment. It is in this way that the process of categorization fulfills its function of protecting the value system which underlies the division of the surrounding social world. There are thus important continuities, but also crucial differences between non-social and social categorization. Perhaps the most notable difference is that social categorization is often value-based and normative; it is this issue that we shall turn to next.

Normative and Value Aspects of Social Categorization

We shall be concerned with "values" in the context of social categorization: (i) when a term which has a value connotation (such as "good" or "bad," "liked" or "disliked," "beautiful" or "ugly," "beneficial" or "harmful," etc., is *readily* applicable to a social category that an individual is using; and (ii) when two or more categories differ from one another with regard to one or more sets of value connotations. The expression "readily applicable" was used above because value connotations can, in principle, be applied to practically anything in the world (Osgood, Suci, & Tannenbaum, 1957). It is, however, a fair assumption that value connotations are more widely, readily, and emphatically applicable in the context of social interaction than they are in situations which do not involve people or groups of people or social events (cf. Zajonc, 1980).

Values and Cognition

The role of values in perceptual and cognitive provinces has been well recognized for several decades. Bruner and Goodman's (1947) study, showing that children overestimated the size of coins as compared with "neutral" discs, and that "poor" children did it a little more than children who were not so poor, illustrated the general principle that perception must be understood as an active interaction between the human organism and its environment, and that therefore "values and needs" could be shown to intervene in this process.

In the heyday of the "New Look" in the study of perceptual processes, the overestimation of the magnitude of the stimuli which had some "value" relevance to the individual was considered well established (cf. Bruner, 1973). In an important paper, Bruner and Rodrigues (1953) drew attention to the possibility that what appeared to be a simple "overestimation" may have been in fact a *relative* increase in the perceived subjective differences between stimuli (such as coins). This notion was elaborated and developed a few years later (Tajfel, 1957) and confirmed in a number of subsequent experiments (see Eiser & Stroebe, 1972 for a general review). A major implication was that the increased accentuation of judged differences may also apply to social categorizations of people into differing groups (cf. Doise, 1978; Eiser & Stroebe, 1972; Tajfel, 1959, 1963). This early research paved the way for numerous empirical studies exploring the role of values in the formation, maintenance, and accentuation of social categories (cf. Tajfel, 1979; Tajfel & Turner, 1979).

Values and the Formation of Social Categories

Categorizations of people, groups of people, and social events in terms of value differentials are probably one of the earliest and most basic forms of social categorization. Cognitive egocentrism of the young child and anthropomorphism can both be considered as categorical projections onto the outside world of experiences which begin in the small private social world of the individual. In the case of egocentrism as the term is understood by Piaget, we are dealing with an inability to *conceive* a situation from a point of view other than one's own. This applies to cognitive as well as to moral development (Piaget, 1927). In this sense, egocentrism represents a projection of the first primitive conception of social relations onto the first small social world that the child encounters outside his family. Anthropomorphism can be seen as a similar process pushed one stage further. It is, as it were, the egocentrism of the species, the projection of human motives and intentions from the interpersonal world to the physical world at large.

These two projections represent fairly simple stages of categorizing the social and the physical environment in terms of their values for the individual. No doubt, these value differentiations remain of permanent importance in the later, more abstract stages of conceptualization. However, they are tempered by the capacity for more "objective" forms of analysis which transcend subjective connotations. For all these reasons, differentiations in terms of values represent one of the early and basic forms of social categorization.

There is as yet little experimental evidence to support this view, but we may illustrate it with a study which is, at best, suggestive (Tajfel & Jahoda, 1966). In a study of the development of national attitudes in children, each child was asked to estimate the relative sizes of America, France, Germany, and Russia. In another test, his preferences for the same four countries were elicited. There was more consensus among children of the age between six and seven that they "preferred" America and France to Germany and Russia than that *both* America and Russia are larger in size than *both* France and Germany. What is important is the priority of ordering in terms of *preferences* over ordering in terms of even the simplest *factual* criteria (Zajonc, 1980). There is thus a good reason to believe that young children categorize the social world in terms of values, often self-oriented, before more objective classificatory schemes are mastered. The role of normative variables such as interpersonal empathy and cooperation in early cognitive development is only beginning to be recognized (cf. Bruner & Sherwood, 1981; Doise & Mackie, 1981). More extensive empirical research is badly needed in this area.

Values and the Preservation of Social Categories

Values play a role not only in the formation, but more importantly, in the maintenance and preservation of existing social categories. Of course, it has been well recognized by social psychologists for some time that cognitive categories, once established, have a biasing and filtering effect on our perceptions. George Kelly (1955) suggested that information is likely to be selectively reinterpreted to conform to the existing construct systems. More recently, Snyder and his co-workers showed in a series of studies that our recent notion of man as the scientist and the hypothesis tester (Heider, 1958) is seriously limited. According to the hypothesis-testing metaphor, "individuals in the course of their quests for understanding of the events of their lives, are engaged in the systematic testing of hypotheses about the nature of their social worlds" (Snyder & Gangestad, 1981, p. 40).

In fact, human beings appear to be strongly and consistently biased towards confirming rather than rejecting hypotheses about the social world: "It seemed to matter not at all to participants in this series of investigations where their hypotheses originated, how likely it was that their hypotheses would prove accurate or inaccurate, whether the hypotheses defined both confirming and disconfirming attributes, or whether substantial incentives for accurate hypothesis testing were offered" (Snyder & Campbell, 1980; Snyder & Swann, 1978). In each case, they planned to preferentially solicit ". . . evidence that would tend to confirm their hypotheses" (Snyder & Gangestad, 1981, p. 14). Such normative biases would clearly operate in favour of the preservation and maintenance, rather than the change of the existing systems of social categorization.

Values also clearly affect the kind of mistake that an individual is prepared to commit in his identification of social category memberships. In general, two types of mistakes are possible: to be wrong because an item which was not a member of a given category was included in it; and to be wrong because an item which was a member of a given category was excluded from it. The greater the difference in value between social categories, the more likely it is that errors of assignment into a negatively valued category will be in the direction of overinclusion, and errors of assignment into a positively valued category will be in the direction of overexclusion. Real-like examples of both kinds abound. For the first case, the search for "impure" specimens in racist societies provides an instance; for the second, the close scrutiny of the characteristics of a candidate to a membership of

an exclusive club. A similar reasoning underlies the analysis of some aspects of category and concept formation undertaken years ago by Bruner, Goodman, and Austin (1956, pp. 216–230).

The case of overinclusion into negatively valued categories is well represented in a group of studies on the recognition of Jews which were conducted in the United States (cf. Tajfel, 1969b, for a detailed review). A prediction could be made from our previous discussion that anti-semitic subjects would include relatively more of the facial photographs of persons into the category "Jews" since the categorization had a greater value-loading for them than for non-antisemites. This is indeed the conclusion that can be drawn from a survey of the findings. An interesting experiment conducted in South Africa by Pettigrew, Allport, and Barnett (1958) resulted in similar findings: Afrikaner subjects tended to assign ambiguous faces to the extremes of "European" and "African" with a less frequent identification as "Coloured" or "Indian." Lent (1970) repeated the study in Texas, using Whites, Mexicans, light-skinned Negroes, and dark-skinned Negroes. He failed to replicate many of the previous findings; but he did report that there was a difference between various groups of White subjects. As Lent pointed out, the experimental analysis of these phenomena cannot succeed

> through the use of "individual" psychological variables alone. Such an analysis should be complemented with the relevant situational—especially interactional—variables. For example: (a) the *subjectively* perceived situation of one's own group in society . . . (b) the *subjectively* perceived relation of the individual to his ethnic group . . . (c) the *objectively* perceived relation of ethnic group to the larger society as specified by demographic variables. (p. 531)

This conclusion is generally valid for studying how a system of social categories is associated with values. The problem is important both theoretically and socially. It is important theoretically, because it touches upon one of the basic aspects of the cognitive organization of the social environment. Socially, it is important because it reflects the normative structure of a society or of a social group in the kind of information about others that its members seek and in the use that they make of the information.

The above studies offer a rather undramatic illustration of this process. It must not be thought that the "value" aspects of the functioning of social categorization remain equally undramatic in periods of high stress, social tensions, and acute intergroup conflicts (cf. Billig, 1978).

The Clarity and Distinctiveness of Social Categories

Values not only play a role in the assignment to social categories, as we have seen above, but also in preserving and enhancing the clarity and distinctiveness of existing social categories. A good example of this process can be found in an early experiment by Secord, Bevans, & Katz (1956), in which prejudiced subjects tended to accentuate more differences in personality traits (inferred from a set of facial photographs), as well as differences in skin colour and other physical characteristics between blacks and whites than did nonprejudiced subjects. This accentuation of differences is by no means, however, confined to situations connected with race. It finds its way, for example, into the mutual comprehension and acceptance by interacting groups of their languages and dialects. As Fishman (1963) wrote

> Divisiveness is an ideological position and it can magnify minor differences; indeed, it can manufacture differences in languages as in other matters almost as easily as it can capitalize on more obvious differences. Similarly, unification is also an ideologized position and it can minimize seemingly major differences or ignore them entirely, whether these be in the realm of languages, religion, culture, race or any other basis of differentiation. (p. 45)

Fishman's "ideologized positions" are positions in which similarities or differences which could *in principle* be entirely "neutral" (e.g., between languages, landscapes, flags, anthems, postage stamps, football teams, and almost anything else), become endowed with emotional significance. But despite all the indications that the resulting value-loaded system of categories tends "to magnify minor differences" or minimize seemingly major differences," this aspect of categorization received less than its due share of attention in recent years.

General Conclusions About Values

Several general conclusions can be drawn from our discussion of the role of values in the formation and the preservation of social categories:

(a) Differentiations in terms of values tend to be more widespread, frequent, and emphatic in categories applying to social interaction than they are in categorizations of a non-social nature.

(b) It is likely that the criteria for the establishment of social categories, at least in the simpler and earlier stages of the formation of these categories, are primarily based on considerations of value.

(c) A system of categories which is associated with a system of values tends towards self-preservation. This is achieved in at least two ways:

 (i) Through the selection and/or modification of information received from the social environment in a manner which is consonant with the existing value differentiations.

 (ii) Through processes which tend towards an increased clarity of the categories associated with values and an increased distinctiveness between these categories.

(d) When a system of categories is associated with values in such a way that there is a *conflict* between the different values which are relevant to the distinctions between the categories, a compromise will be achieved. This compromise will tend to favour those value considerations which are more general, more important or more relevant to social action. It follows that, in some cases, conflicts of values will determine changes in a system of social categories.

Social Categorization and Social Identity

The concept of identity has had a long and controversial history in psychology, defying easy definitions. For our present limited purposes, we may define social identity as an individual's "knowledge that he belongs to a certain social group together with some emotional and value significance of his membership" (Tajfel, 1978b, pp. 66–67). In other words, an individual's self-image and self-concept may be thought of as, to some extent, dependent on his group memberships, and in particular, on the differentiation which exists between his own group and others.

It is this comparative perspective which links social categorization with social identity. In Festinger's (1954) theory of social comparison processes, it is hypothesized that there exists, in human beings, a drive to evaluate their opinions and abilities, and that such evaluations are accomplished by reference to the opinions and abilities of others to the extent that objective means are unavailable. The theory was primarily addressed at the *within-group* effects of the processes of social comparison (such as pressures towards uniformity in a group) while comparisons with members of a different status group, either higher or lower, may sometimes be made on a phantasy level, but very rarely in reality. Though Festinger qualifies this statement by adding that comparisons between groups that differ are not completely eliminated, the focus of his discussion remains on individuals comparing themselves with other individuals. We would like to argue, on the basis of extensive experimental evidence, that social comparison processes play a very important role in between-group discrimination and in the creation and maintenance of positive social identities (cf. Tajfel, 1979; Tajfel & Turner, 1979): "we are what we are because *they* are not what we are." An important expression of these attempts at achieving positive identity through differential categorization can be found in the social myths, group actions, and social movements which aim at the creation or preservation of a "positive distinctiveness" of one's own group from others. This appears to be one of the processes accounting for the importance of "differentials" in a large number of social and industrial conflicts. This is not to deny the primary importance of the "objective" socio-economic factors which are involved. But we have by now enough evidence, originating from dozens of experimental studies and several studies in "natural" conditions, that an analysis of the "objective" factors in such situations does not tell us the whole story (cf. Brewer, 1979; Tajfel, 1978b, 1979; Tajfel & Turner, 1979; for some of the recent reviews).

The psychological aspects and consequences of group membership are capable of any kind of a definition only because of their insertion into a multi-group structure. A social group will therefore be capable of preserving its contribution to an individual's social identity only if it manages to keep its positively valued distinctiveness from other groups. This establishment of distinctiveness through attributing positive characteristics to one's own group in comparison with other groups is particularly salient in situations of intergroup conflict. Many such cases have to do with the forging of positively valued identity by underprivileged groups. The hammering out by the American Blacks of a group distinctiveness in which they can feel pride is a case in point. Another example can be found in the attempts to establish a new and distinctive national identity in many new nations.

There is also some experimental evidence showing that conflict or competition are *not* necessary conditions for creating positive ingroup evaluations (Rabbie & Horwitz, 1969; Rabbie & Wilkens, 1971). In evaluating their own groups, the subjects in these experiments behaved as if even a transient and relatively unimportant social categorization required the establishment of a distinct and positively valued social identity. In experiments by Tajfel, Flament, Billig, and Bundy (1971), it was shown that social categorization based on flimsy criteria of arbitrary division into groups, can *by itself* lead to discrimination in favour of one's own group. In these studies, previous hostility between the groups was not possible, and discriminatory responses towards the outgroup had no relation to the individual subjects' self-interest; the only variable accounting for the results was an act of explicit social categorization into two groups.

We are not, however, concerned here with the implications of these studies for problems of intergroup relations, but with their relevance to social categorization and social identity. These studies created an "empty" and almost Kafkaesque experimental condition which had to be infused (as all experimental situations must be) with some kind of meaning by the subjects. This meaning was found by them in the adoption of a strategy for action based on the *establishment*, through action, of a distinctiveness between their own "group" and the other, between two social categories in a truly minimal "social system." Distinction from the "other" category provided *ipso facto* an identity for their own group, and thus gave some kind of meaning to an otherwise empty situation.

We propose thus that social categorization insofar as it affects group differences, is intricately related to an individual's social identity. Far from being a purely rational analytic process, it is closely affected by our need to achieve moral worth and distinctiveness (cf. Harré, 1981), and is partly a reflection of the dominant values and representations in our society (cf. Moscovici, 1981). Of course, not *all* categorizations are as value-loaded, or as closely tied to social identity as those pertaining to group membership. However, we would want to argue that *no* social domain of any importance is classified in a completely value-free manner, as currently prevalent cognitive-individualistic research would lead us to believe. In the next section, we shall look at some examples which further illustrate this point.

Some Everyday Examples of Social Categorization

In previous sections, we have already referred to the numerous real-life examples illustrating the normative use of social categories. We shall now briefly consider three domains where interpersonal and intergroup categorization offer particularly salient illustrations of the processes we described above.

Person Prototypes

Just as individuals differentiate between social groups in terms of their values and identities, they tend to judge other individuals in terms of their pre-existing category system of the "types" of people known to them. The study of this kind of interpersonal rather than inter-group categorization has long historical roots in social psychology. Asch's (1946) Gestalt view of person perception emphasized the notion that certain traits, characteristics or prototypes are more "central" and important in organizing our perceptions of other people than are other traits. He did not, however, proceed to speculate about the functional significance of such central traits. After a long spell of atomistic research on person perception, which conceived of impression formation as little more than the simplistic addition or averaging of essentially constant-value traits (Anderson, 1974), in recent years, interest in person perception prototypes has once again come to the fore. It has been suggested that we form impressions of, and remember others differently, depending on whether the target is consistent or inconsistent with already established person prototypes (Cantor & Mischel, 1979).

In terms of our earlier arguments regarding the normative nature of social categorization, it would seem that impression formation is unlikely to be reducible to a simple, cognitive information-processing model. When we categorize somebody in terms of our existing person prototypes as a "typical radical feminist" or a "keen young academic," these categories are normatively loaded by our pre-existing implicit theories about people, which may result in two completely different information-processing strategies being adopted about persons belonging to these categories. What is at issue here is the implicit assumption of normative equivalence between person prototypes in the recent literature, and the corollary belief that a single information-processing model may be sufficient to explain person perception processes.

In two recent studies (Forgas, 1980), we tried to explore this issue more fully. The first study was designed to elicit and collect a sample of naturally used person prototypes in a subcultural milieu (students) and to construct a quantified taxonomy of these person prototypes. One-hundred and eighty students listed a total of more than 1200 often overlapping "types" of people known to them; the most frequently nominated 20 types were subjected to a multidimensional scaling analysis, resulting in a three-dimensional prototype space. The three underlying dimensions, academic performance, sociability, and radicalism clearly have normative-evaluative connotations. The similarity of these dimensions and the dimensions underlying implicit perceptions of personality traits (Rosenberg & Sedlak, 1972), and jargon terms denoting student types (Friendly & Glucksberg, 1970) supports the idea that cognitive categories used to organize our perceptions of others form a consistent hierarchical structure. Within such a scheme, person prototypes may be thought of as "natural" middle-level categories most readily reported by judges, representing an optimum compromise between inclusiveness and abstraction (Rosch & Mervis, 1975). It is necessary to elicit and quantify such natural categories of people before meaningful tests of impression formation strategies become feasible.

In the second study, subjects were asked to read descriptions of eight characters, four of whom were consistent with a single prototype, while four characters were inconsistent, containing elements from four different prototypes. The normative content of the prototypes was factorially varied within these conditions, so that within each of the above groups, two characters contained highly salient, and two contained low-salient prototypes (salience was defined in terms of extremity in the prototype space). Subjects were asked to form impressions of, recall, and predict each of the characters. Result showed a significant interaction between prototype consistency and salience, suggesting that schema models of information-processing best accounted for how the subjects formed impressions about highly salient characters, but depth of processing models (Craik & Lockhart, 1977) were a better approximation of the perception of low-salient characters. In other words, person prototypes which were important and endowed with some normative significance for this group of subjects, were used as cognitive schemata to which other information was assimilated, but for low-salient, and presumably normatively neutral characters, prototype-inconsistent information had a disproportionate effect on judgements. These results help to reconcile the apparently contradictory findings by Cantor and Mischel (1977, 1979) reporting "schema" effects, and Hastie and Kumar's (1979) results showing contrast effects in impression formation. It appears that both models may be right, the former applying to salient and normatively loaded prototypes, while the latter is more appropriate for explaining how we use low-salient prototypes in impression formation.

These two studies show that: (a) the collection of natural, middle-level person prototypes is essential if a realistic model of impression formation is to be developed; and (b) the salience and normative importance of the prototype has a profound effect on judgements, so much so that different information-processing models are needed to explain judgements of high and low salient characters. This study is of course suggestive rather than definitive; it only represents the first hesitant step towards working out the exact role of normative factors in impression formation. One of us is currently engaged in further studies in this field. The situation is quite different in the case of stereotypes, a much more extensively studied domain of social categorization to which we shall turn next.

Stereotypes

Stereotypes are perhaps the most extensively studied examples of social categorization. They may be defined as "an oversimplified mental image of . . . some category of person, institution or event which is shared . . . by large numbers of people . . . Stereotypes are commonly, but not necessarily accompanied by prejudice . . . "

(Stallybrass, 1977, p. 601). The essential feature of this definition is that it emphasizes the shared collective and often group-specific nature of stereotypes. This is indeed the traditional social psychological approach to the study of this important domain. It is all the more surprising to find, once again, that the renewed interest in stereotypes in the past few years is characterized by an implicit assumption that stereotypes are individual rather than social products, and can be explained in terms of biases in information-processing strategies alone, without recourse either to normative, or to collective phenomena. A few examples may serve to illustrate this point:

> . . . there is no theoretical or empirical reason to assume that forming generalizations about the ethnic groups is radically different from forming generalizations about other categories of objects. (S. E. Taylor, Fiske, Etcoff, & Ruderman, 1978, p. 778)

> Stereotypes are not a unique structure or process but exist and operate in the same manner as cognitive processes in general. (D. M. Taylor & Aboud, 1973, p. 330)

> Differential perception of majority and minority groups would result *solely* from the cognitive mechanisms involved in processing information about stimulus events that differ in their frequencies of co-occurrence. (Hamilton & Gifford, 1976, p. 392, italics ours)

On the following pages we shall briefly consider *both* the cognitive and the normative aspects of stereotyping.

Cognitive Aspects of Stereotyping. The recent work of Rothbart and his colleagues, as well as that of Hamilton (1976, 1979; Hamilton & Gifford, 1976), once again drew attention to some cognitive aspects of social stereotyping. Foremost among these is the subjective inflation or exaggeration of the significance of social events which either occur or co-occur with low frequency in the social environment. Impressions of *groups* of people are affected by "the way in which data on some individual members of these groups are organized in memory" (Rothbart, Fulero, Jensen, Howard, & Birrell, 1978, p. 237). Extreme events or extreme individuals are more accessible to memory retrieval than are more average instances. Rothbart et al., following Tversky and Kahnemann (1973), argue that those instances from a class of events which are the most available for retrieval serve as a cue for judging the frequency of their general occurrence. Thus, *negative* behaviours of members of *minority* groups are likely to be over-represented in memory and judgement. The attitudinal aspects of these interactions between social categorizations and memory have recently been studied by Eiser, Van der Plight, and Mossop (1979).

There is some similarity between this research and the work on "illusory correlations" reported in Hamilton (1979) and Hamilton and Gifford (1976). The concept of "illusory correlation" was introduced by Chapman (1967) who defined it as "the report by observers of a correlation between two classes of events which in reality, (a) are not correlated, or (b) are correlated to a lesser extent than reported" (Hamilton & Gifford, 1976, p. 151). Experiments showed that this kind of processing of information, associating, as in Rothbart's views, "infrequent" events with "infrequent" people, is directly related to the formation of stereotypes about minority groups. A careful reading of Brunswik's (1947) classic work on the uses of "representative design," and his reports of the studies in which he applied these concepts to the perception of people, shows that very similar ideas served already as his point of departure. Over thirty years ago, Brunswik was able to show how "illusory correlations" function and how they can be made to disappear in certain conditions. In all, there exists a long and reputable tradition of work showing that the formation and use of social stereotypes cannot be properly understood without a careful analysis of the cognitive functions they serve. We must now turn to the second major function of stereotypes: the role they play in the preservation of an individual's system of values.

Values and Stereotypes. There is considerable evidence for the value-based origins and accentuation of stereotypes, some of which we considered earlier. A typical way to test this hypothesis has been to compare the ratings of the personal attributes of people belonging to two different social categories by subjects who are differentially prejudiced against the targets. The results usually showed that the prejudiced group judged the differences between the members of the two categories to be larger than the non-prejudiced group (cf. Doise, 1978, for a recent review).

The second line of evidence indicates the biasing role of values in the identification in ambiguous conditions of members of disliked social categories (Bruner et al., 1956). As we saw earlier, the risks in such judgements are that a "bad" person could be assigned to a "good" category or a "good" person to a "bad" one. If this happens too often, it could threaten or even invalidate the value differential. From the empirical evidence we have, it looks as if the former of these two kinds of errors is avoided more persistently than the latter. Here again, it appears that value differentials guide the use made of ambiguous information. The maintenance of a system of social categories acquires an importance which goes far beyond the simple function of ordering and systematizing the environment. It represents a powerful protection of the existing system of social values, and any "mistakes" made are mistakes to the extent that they endanger that system. Such value-based categorization plays a particularly important role in the ideologization of various forms of collective action.

Collective Action and Social Categorization

We shall now turn to a discussion of the specific functions of social stereotypes in justifying certain types of collective actions. This domain was largely left to sociologists and social anthropologists in the past, and there is very little work in social psychology concerned with such examples of collective action, as for example, witchhunts. Tens of thousands of "witches" were tortured and killed in Europe in the sixteenth and seventeenth centuries. As Thomas (1971) wrote:

> It was the popular fear of *maleficium* which provided the moral driving-force behind witch prosecution, not any lawyer-led campaign from above. (Thomas, 1973, p. 548)

In his early functionalist analysis of witchcraft, Kluckhohn (1944) characterized witches as being generally "outsiders." It is interesting to note that the social psychological parallels to functionalist views in social anthropology have mainly stressed the *individual* motivational processes rather than their social equivalents. Social psychologists have largely ignored the study of collective conditions under which intergroup stereotypes become more active, intense, or extreme. Some of the more important issues relevant here may be summarized as follows:

Why, when and how is a social categorization salient or not salient? What kind of shared constructions of social reality, mediated through social
categorizations, lead to a social climate in which
large masses of people feel that they are in long-
term conflict with other large masses? What, for
example, are the *psychological* transitions from a
stable to an unstable social system? (Tajfel, 1979,
p. 188)

In answer to some of these questions, we shall
propose a rough and preliminary classification of
the psychological functions that stereotypes can
serve for social groups; we shall follow by pointing to some potential developments which could
provide a theoretical and research articulation for
these functions.

From general evidence in social psychology,
social history, and social anthropology it appears
that outgroup social stereotypes tend to be created
and widely diffused in conditions which require:
(i) a search for the understanding of complex, and
usually distressful, large-scale social events; (ii)
justification of actions, committed or planned,
against outgroups; (iii) a positive differentiation
of the ingroup from selected outgroups at a time
when such differentiation is perceived as becoming insecure and eroded.

We shall refer to these three functions as, respectively, those of *social causality, justification,*
and *differentiation*. We can do no more here than
give a brief selection of examples in order to illustrate the nature of each of these categories. To start
with causality: something was "needed" in the
seventeenth century to explain the plague, but as
Thomas (1971) writes, its incidence

> was too indiscriminate to be plausibly explained
> in personal terms . . . the Scots were accused to
> have poisoned the wells of Newcastle in 1639,
> Catholic sorcery was held responsible for an out-
> break of gaol fever in Oxford in 1577 and the lo-
> cal Independent congregation was blamed for an
> outbreak of plague in Barnstaple in 1646. (Tho-
> mas, 1973, pp. 667–668)

An even clearer example can be found in anti-
Semitism. This is carefully and brilliantly traced
in Norman Cohn's (1967) description of the persistence of the myth about the Protocols of the
Elders of Zion. As Billig (1978) wrote:

> The emotional ferocity of the crudest anti-
> Semitism makes it easy to forget that anti-
> Semitism can provide an extensive cognitive in-
> terpretation of the world. Above all, crude

anti-Semitism is based upon a belief that Jews have
immense powers of evil in the world. Modern anti-
Semitic dogma asserts that Jews control both communism and capitalism and that they aim to dominate the world in a regime which will destroy
Western civilization. All facts are explained in
terms of this perverse belief. (p. 132)

The *justification* principle is well illustrated by
the development of European attitudes towards the
outside world in the imperial age, when the con-
quest of African and Asian peoples was "ideologized" as Europe's mission to bring "human rights"
and "civilization" to the savages (Kiernan 1972).
The *"differentiation"* principle could be considered as a part of the general syndrome of ethnocentrism understood in Sumner's (1906) sense of
the term. The creation or maintenance of differentiation, or of a "positive distinctiveness" of one's
own group from others which are relevant to the
group's self-image seems to be, judging from the
accounts of social anthropologists, a widespread
phenomenon in many cultures. As this intergroup
differentiation has been discussed recently and
extensively elsewhere (cf. Tajfel, 1974, 1978b,
1979; Tajfel & Turner, 1979; Turner, 1975), we
shall simply note it here as the third of the major
group functions served by stereotyping.

From the foregoing discussion it should be clear
that social stereotypes cannot be understood without a consideration of the functions they serve in
the competitive and power relationships between
the groups concerned. This functional perspective
would be a significant advance upon both the earlier, "descriptive" tradition, and the more recent
information-processing research on stereotyping.
A related point could be made about the links between the group functions of stereotyping and the
individual functions discussed in the preceding
sections. It seems that the analytic sequence should
start from the group functions and then relate the
individual functions to them. As we argued above,
an individual uses stereotypes as an aid in the cognitive structuring of his social environment as well
as for the protection of his system of values. As
Berger and Luckman (1967) so cogently argued
some years ago, social reality is not "out there" to
be comprehended or assimilated. It is constructed
by individuals from the raw materials provided to
them by the social context in which they live. If
this were not the case, the selection and contents
of social categorizations and social stereotypes
would have to be conceived of as arbitrary and

random occurrences, capriciously varying from one society to another, from one historical period to another. As it is, the restricted variety of the combination and recombination of their common elements can be attributed to the limited number of the major group functions that they generally serve. Future research in social psychology may clarify the relationship between group and individual functions of stereotypes. Two recent research initiatives seem particularly promising.

The first of these relates an individual's self-respect or self-concept (or his "social identity") to the relative position of his group on a number of dimensions in a multi-group social system, as described earlier. It is not possible to review here, even briefly, the substantial amount of recent research on this subject. The most recent reviews can be found in e.g., Tajfel (1978b) and Tajfel and Turner (1979). An apt one sentence summary has been provided by Commins and Lockwood (1979):

> The social group is seen to function as a provider of positive social identity for its members through comparing itself and distinguishing itself, from other comparison groups, along salient dimensions which have a clear value differential. (p. 282)

The second of the two initiatives mentioned above concerns "justification" and consists of some recent attempts to argue for a more "social" rather than individualistic approach to attribution theory (cf. Apfelbaum & Herzlich, 1971; Deschamps, 1977, 1978; Duncan, 1976; Hamilton, 1978; Hewstone & Jaspars, 1981; Mann & Taylor, 1974; Stephan, 1977; D. M. Taylor & Jaggi, 1974). Accordingly, attributions are dependent not only on the characteristics of individuals, but also on the social and group context (cf. Forgas, 1981b). For example, following Buss (1978), Hewstone and Jaspars suggest that "reasons" would tend to be used to explain the behaviour of ingroup members and "causes" would apply to outgroup members. This dichotomy would also be strongly affected by the positive or negative evaluations of the behaviour. Some results by D. M. Taylor and Jaggi (1974) are not too far removed from the "reason–causes" dichotomy. The static, stable consensus implied by descriptive studies of stereotypes is replaced here by the shifting perspectives closely related to the individual's evaluation of the changing social situations, which are perceived *in terms of the nature of the relations between the groups involved*. It is in this way that the potential devel-

opment of social attribution theory provides the second of our links between the group and the individual functions of stereotyping.

Conclusions

Social categorizations serve the need to reduce the complexity of the social environment. In achieving everyday understanding, perhaps of greatest importance are the individual's ideas about the "causal nexus" of the social environment (cf. Heider, 1958). Large scale social events (such as inflation, unemployment, wars, social conflicts, etc.) which affect directly the life of an individual *require* him to build systems of social causation. These are his "naive theories" of social action. But (as in the case of systems of social categories) the events are much too complex to be easily encompassed. A royal road towards simplification and a form of understanding is through the attribution of collective traits and intentions to various social groups. Such attributions are moulded by the individual's values and social identity, which are reflected in the social categories which are at his disposal. There is considerable evidence for the normative nature of social categorization. We only have to look as far as the first street corner where long hair, a police uniform, or skin colour warrant quick assignment to a category from which further inferences can then be drawn. There is no reason why the normative functions of social categorization could not be submitted to a systematic theoretical and experimental inquiry.

Indeed it is rather remarkable that the current interest in the role of categorization in social behaviour owes more to recent developments in cognitive psychology (Rosch & Lloyd, 1978; Schank & Abelson, 1977) than to the long tradition of research on social categories. In at least two ways, recent research on social categorization represents a retreat from earlier work. In its emphasis on purely cognitive variables, it neglects the uniquely normative and value-based attributes of social categorization. Secondly, the prevalent tendency to study individual processes bypasses the essentially collective, social nature of categorization (cf. Krauss, 1980; Moscovici, 1981).

In this chapter we have moved from basic processes of social categorization through values and social identity to reach finally the role of categorization in everyday social action. If there was an underlying theme in this chapter, it had to do with the analysis of the role of values and meaning in social cognition. In a sense, the segmentation of the social environment through the construction of a system of categories applying to it is one of the basic forms of meaning with which social situations are always invested. We need at present more studies on the role of values and meaning in various aspects of social experience and behaviour, and more attempts at theoretical integration. We also need more theoretical and research links between our systems of explanation and the more recent information-processing approaches to the study of social categorization.

REFERENCES

Allport, G. W. (1954). *The nature of prejudice*. Cambridge, MA: Addison-Wesley.

Anderson, N. (1974). Cognitive algebra: Integration theory applied to social attribution. In L. Berkowitz (Ed.), *Advances in experimental social psychology*. New York and London: Academic Press.

Apfelbaum, E., & Herzlich, C. (1971). Le théorie de l'attribution en psychologie sociale. *Bulletin de psychologie, 44*, 961–976.

Asch, S. E. (1946). Forming impressions of personality. *Journal of social psychology, 41*, 258–290.

Bartlett, F. C. (1932). *Remembering*. Cambridge, England: Cambridge University Press.

Berger, P., & Luckman, T. (1967). *The social construction of reality*. London: Allen Lane.

Billig, M. (1978). *Fascists*. London and New York: Academic Press.

Bower, C. H., Black, J. B., & Turner, T. J. (1979). Scripts in memory for text. *Cognitive Psychology, 11*, 177–220.

Brewer, M. (1979). Ingroup bias in the minimal intergroup situation. *Psychological Bulletin, 86*(2), 307–324.

Bruner, J. S. (1957). On perceptual readiness. *Psychological Review, 64*, 123–152.

Bruner, J. S. (1958). Social psychology and perception. In E. E. Maccoby, T. M. Newcomb, & E. L. Hartley (Eds.), *Readings in social psychology*. New York: Holt Rinehart & Winston.

Bruner, J. S. (1973). *Beyond the information given*. New York: Norton.

Bruner, J. S., & Goodman, C. C. (1947). Value and need as organizing factors in perception. *Journal of Abnormal and Social Psychology, 42*, 33–44.

Bruner, J. S., Goodnow, J. J., & Austin, G. A. (1956). *A study of thinking*. New York: Wiley.

Bruner, J. S., & Potter, M. C. (1964). Interference in visual recognition. *Science, 144*, 424–425.

Bruner, J. S., & Rodrigues, J. S. (1953). Some determinants of apparent size. *Journal of Abnormal and Social Psychology, 48*, 585–592.

Bruner, J. S., & Sherwood, (1981). In J. P. Forgas (Ed.), *Social cognition*. London: Academic Press.

Brunswik, E. (1947). *Systematic and representative design of psychological experiments with results in physical and social perception*. Berkeley, CA: University of California Press.

Buss, A. R. (1973). Causes and reasons in attribution theory. *Journal of Personality and Social Psychology, 36*, 1311–1321.

Campbell, D. T. (1956). Enhancement of contrast as a composite habit. *Journal of Abnormal and Social Psychology, 53*, 350–355.

Cantor, N., & Mischel, W. (1977). Traits as prototypes: Effects on recognition memory. *Journal of Personality and Social Psychology, 35*, 38–48.

Cantor, N., & Mischel, W. (1979). Prototypes in person perception. In L. Berkowitz (Ed.), *Advances in experimental social psychology*. New York and London: Academic Press.

Chapman, L. J. (1967). Illusory correlations in observational report. *Journal of Verbal Learning and Verbal Behaviour, 6*, 151–155.

Cohn, N. (1967). *Warrant for genocide*. New York: Harper.

Commins, B., & Lockwood, J. (1979). The effects of status differences, favoured treatment and equity on intergroup comparisons. *European Journal of Social Psychology, 9*, 281–289.

Craik, F. I. M., & Lockhart, R. S. (1977). Levels of processing. *Journal of Verbal Learning and Verbal Behaviour, 11*, 671–684.

Davidon, R. S. (1962). Relevance and category scales of judgement. *British Journal of Psychology, 53*, 373–380.

Deschamps, J. C. (1977). *L'attribution et la categorisation sociale*. Bern: Peter Lang.

Deschamps, J. C. (1978). La perception des causes du comportement. In W. Doise, J. C. Deschamps, & G. Mugny (Eds.), *Psychologie sociale expermentale*. Paris: Armand Colin.

Doise, W. (1978). *Groups and individuals*. Cambridge: Cambridge University Press.

Doise, W., & Mackie, D. (1981). In J. P. Forgas (Ed.), *Social cognition*. New York: Academic Press.

Duncan, B. L. (1976). Differential social perception and attribution of intergroup violence. *Journal of Personality and Social Psychology, 34*, 590–598.

Eiser, J. R., & Stroebe, W. (1972). *Categorization and social judgement*. London and New York: Academic Press.

Eiser, J. R., Van der Pligt, J., & Mossop, M. R. (1979). Categorisation, attitude and memory for the source of attitude statements. *European Journal of Social Psychology, 9*, 243–251.

Festinger, L. (1954). A theory of social comparison processes. *Human Relations, 7*, 117–140.

Fishman, J. A. (1963). Nationality-nationalism and nation-nationalism. In J. A. Fishman, C. A. Ferguson, & J. D. Gupta (Eds.), *Language problems in developing countries*. New York: Wiley.

Forgas, J. P. (1979). *Social episodes: The study of interaction routines*. London and New York: Academic Press.

Forgas, J. P. (1980). *Person prototypes in impression formation*. Sydney: University of New South Wales.

Forgas, J. P. (1981a). Group milieu and episode perception. *British Journal of Social and Clinical Psychology*.

Forgas, J. P. (1981b). Responsibility attribution by groups and individuals: The effects of the interaction episode. *European Journal of Social Psychology, 11*, 87–99.

Friendly, M. L., & Glucksberg, S. (1970). On the description of subcultural lexicons. *Journal of Personality and Social Psychology, 14,* 55–65.

Hamilton, D. L. (1976). Cognitive biases in the perception of social groups. In J. S. Carroll & J. W. Payne (Eds.), *Cognition and Social Behaviour.* Hillsdale, N.J.: Erlbaum.

Hamilton, D. L. (1978). Who is responsible? *Social Psychology, 41,* 316–328.

Hamilton, D. L. (1979). A cognitive-attributional analysis of stereotyping. In L. Berkowitz (Ed.), *Advances in experimental social psychology.* New York and London: Academic Press.

Hamilton, D. L., & Gifford, R. K. (1976). Illusory correlations in interpersonal perception. *Journal of Experimental Social Psychology, 14,* 392–407.

Harré, R. (1981). In J. P. Forgas (Ed.), *Social cognition.* London: Academic Press.

Hastie, R., & Kumar, P. A. (1979). Person memory: Personality traits as organising principles in memory for behaviours. *Journal of Personality and Social Psychology, 37,* 25–98.

Heider, F. (1958). *The psychology of interpersonal relations.* New York: Wiley.

Hershenson, M., & Haber, R. N. (1965). The role of meaning in the perception of briefly exposed words. *Canadian Journal of Psychology, 19,* 42–46.

Hewstone, M., & Jaspars, J. (1981). Intergroup relations and attribution processes (to be published).

Jones, E. G., & Gerard, H. B. (1967). *Foundations of social psychology.* New York: Wiley.

Kelly, G. A. (1955). *A theory of personality.* New York: Norton.

Kiernan, V. G. (1972). *The lords of human kind.* Harmondsworth: Penguin Books.

Kluckhohn, C. (1944). *Navaho witchcraft.* Harvard University, Peabody Museum Papers, Vol. 22, No. 2.

Krauss, R. M. (1980). *Cognition and communication.* Paper presented at the Society for Experimental Social Psychology Meeting, Stanford.

Lent, R. H. (1970). Binocular resolution and perception of race in the United States. *British Journal of Psychology, 61,* 521–533.

Lilli, W. (1970). Das Zustandekommen von Stereotypen über einfache und complexe Sachverhalte. *Zeitschrift fur Sozialpsychologie, 1,* 57-59.

Mann, J. F., & Taylor, D. M. (1974). Attribution of causality. *Journal of Social Psychology, 94,* 3–13.

Marchand, B. (1970). Answirkung einer emotional wertvollen und einer emotional neutralen Klassifikation auf die Schatzung einer Stimulusserie. *Zeitschrift fur Sozialpsychologie, 1,* 264–274.

Moscovia, S. (1981). On social representations. In J. P. Forgas (Ed.), *Social cognition* (pp. 181–209). London: Academic Press.

Osgood, C. E., Suci, G. J., & Tannenbaum, P. H. (1957). *The measurement of meaning.* Urbana: University of Illinois Press.

Piaget, J. (1927). *Le jugement moral de l'enfant.* Paris: Alcan.

Pettigrew, T. F., Allport, G. W., & Barnett, E. V. (1958). Binocular resolution and perception of race in South Africa. *British Journal of Psychology, 49,* 265–278.

Rabbie, J. M., & Horwitz, M. (1969). Arousal of intergroup bias by a chance win or loss. *Journal of Personality and Social Psychology, 13,* 269–277.

Rabbie, J. M., & Wilkens, G. (1971). Intergroup competition and its effect on intra- and intergroup relations. *European Journal of Social Psychology, 1,* 215–234.

Rosch, E. (1975). Cognitive reference points. *Cognitive Psychology, 7,* 532–547.

Rosch, E., & Lloyd, B. B. (1978). *Cognition and categorization.* Hillsdale, NJ: Erlbaum.

Rosch, E., & Mervis, C. B. (1975). Family resemblances: Studies in the internal structure of categories. *Cognitive Psychology, 7,* 573–605.

Rosch, E., Mervis, C. B., Gray, W. D., Johnson, D. M., & Boyes-Bream, P. (1976). Basic objects in natural categories. *Cognitive Psychology, 8,* 332–339.

Rosenberg, S., & Sedlak, A. (1972). Structural representations of implicit personality theory. In L. Berkowitz (Ed.), *Advances in experimental social psychology, 6,* 235–297.

Rothbart, M., Fulero, S., Jensen, C., Howard, J., & Birrell, P. (1978). From individual to group perspectives. *Journal of Experimental Social Psychology, 14,* 237–255.

Schank, R., & Abelson, R. P. (1977). *Scripts, plans, goals and understanding.* Hillsdale, NJ: Erlbaum.

Secord, P. F., Bevans, W., & Katz, B. (1956). The Negro stereotype and perceptual accentuation. *Journal of Abnormal and Social Psychology, 53,* 78–83.

Snyder, M., & Campbell, B. H. (1980). Testing hypotheses about other people. *Personality and Social Psychology Bulletin, 6,* 421–426.

Snyder, M., & Gangestad, S. (1981). Hypothesis-testing processes. In J. H. Harvey, W. J., Ickes, & R. F. Kidd (Eds.), *New directions in attribution research* (Vol. 3.). Hillsdale, NJ: Erlbaum.

Snyder, M., & Swann, W. B., Jr. (1978). Hypothesis-testing processes in social interaction. *Journal of Personality and Social Psychology, 36,* 1202–1212.

Stallybrass, O. (1977). Stereotype. In A. Bullock & O. Stallybrass (Eds.), *The Fontana dictionary of modern thought.* London: Fontana/Collins.

Stephan, W. (1977). Stereotyping. *Journal of Social Psychology, 101,* 255–266.

Sumner, G. A. (1906). *Folkways.* New York: Ginn.

Tajfel, H. (1957). Value and the perceptual judgement of magnitude. *Psychological Review, 64,* 192–204.

Tajfel, H. (1959). Quantitative judgment in social perception. *British Journal of Psychology, 50,* 16–29.

Tajfel, H. (1962). Social perception. In G. Humphrey & M. Argyle (Eds.), *Social psychology through experiment.* London: Methuen.

Tajfel, H. (1963). Stereotypes. *Race, V,* 3–14.

Tajfel, H. (1969a). Cognitive aspects of prejudice. *Journal of Biosocial Sciences, 1,* Suppl. Mon. No. 1, *Biosocial Aspects of Race,* 173–191.

Tajfel, H. (1969b). Social and cultural factors in perception. In G. Lindzey & A. Aronson (Eds.), *The handbook of social psychology* (2nd ed., Vol. III.). Reading, MA: Addison-Wesley.

Tajfel, H. (1974). Social identity and intergroup behaviour. *Social Science Information, 13*(2), 66–93.

Tajfel, H. (1978a). The structure of our views about society. In H. Tajfel & C. Fraser (Eds.), *Introducing social psychology.* Harmondsworth: Penguin Books.

Tajfel, H. (Ed.). (1978b). *Differentiation between social groups. European monographs in social psychology,* No. 14. London and New York: Academic Press.

Tajfel, H. (1978c). *The social psychology of minorities.* London: Minority Rights Group.

Tajfel, H. (1979). Individuals and groups in social psychology. *British Journal of Social and Clinical Psychology, 18,* 183–190.

Tajfel, H., Flament, C., Billig, M. G., & Bundy, R. P. (1971). Social categorization and intergroup behaviour. *European Journal of Social Psychology, 1,* 149–178.

Tajfel, H., & Jahoda, G. (1966). The development in children of concepts and attitudes about their own and other nations. *Proceedings of the XVIIIth International Congress of Psychology Moscow,* Symposium 36, 17–33.

Tajfel, H., & Turner, J. C. (1979). An integrative theory of intergroup conflict. In W. G. Austin & S. Worchel (Eds.), *The social psychology of intergroup relations.* Monterey, California: Brooks/Cole.

Tajfel, H., & Wilkes, A. L. (1963). Classification and quantitative judgment. *British Journal of Psychology, 54,* 101–114.

Tajfel, H., & Wilkes, A. L. (1964). Salience of attributes and commitment to extreme judgment in the perception of people. *British Journal of Social and Clinical Psychology, 2,* 40–49.

Taylor, D. M., & Aboud, F. E. (1973). Ethnic stereotypes. *Canadian Psychologist, 14,* 330–338.

Taylor, D. M., & Jaggi, V. (1974). Ethnocentrism and causal attribution in a South Indian context. *Journal of Cross-Cultural Psychology, 5,* 162–171.

Taylor, S. E., Fiske, S. T., Etcoff, N. L., & Ruderman, A. (1978). Categorical and contextual bases of person memory and stereotyping. *Journal of Personality and Social Psychology, 36,* 773–793.

Thomas, K. (1971). *Religion and the decline of magic.* London: Weidenfeld & Nicholson. Reprinted in 1973, Penguin Books.

Turner, J. C. (1975). Social comparison and social identity. *European Journal of Social Psychology,* 5–34.

Tversky, A., & Kahneman, D. (1973). Availability. *Cognitive Psychology, 5,* 207–232.

Wittgenstein, L. (1953). *Philosophical investigations.* Oxford, England: Blackwell.

Zadeh, L. A. (1965). Fuzzy sets. *Information and Control, 8,* 338–353.

Zajonc, R. (1980). Feeling and thinking: Preferences need no inferences. *American Psychologist, 35,* 151–175.

Stereotypes as Individual and Collective Representations

Charles Stangor and Mark Schaller • University of Maryland

Stop for a moment and think about one of the many social groups that make up a diverse geographic area such as Europe or the United States. You'll easily (perhaps you think too easily!) conjure up a portrait of what the people in the group are like. You may generate an oversimplified impression of the characteristics of the group as a whole—that Greeks are fun-loving, that the Irish drink too much, or that African Americans are boisterous. Or perhaps you will retrieve particular instances of people from the group—maybe an image of Marcello Mastroianni appears, reminding you that Italian men are good-looking.

This type of thought process reflects the most traditional conceptualization of stereotypes within social psychology, in which stereotypes are considered to be the "pictures in the head" of individuals looking out into their social worlds (e.g., Lippmann, 1922). But stereotypes also exist from the point of view of the person who is being stereotyped. Consider the African American man who is repeatedly denied employment because the white employers in his neighborhood have decided that blacks are lazy and ignorant. Or the frustration of a Catholic woman in Northern Ireland who is denied admission to a major university because of her religion. In these cases, the effects of stereotyping are much more than the simple "picture in the head" would indicate. Certainly the discriminating individuals in these scenarios have negative beliefs about the targets of their discrimina-

tion, but the real problem for the individual being stereotyped is that in each case the individuals who are making the decisions have the *same* pictures in their heads. If stereotyping were only an individual problem, the person could go to another company and speak to a different employment officer, or enroll in a different university. But when stereotypes are consensually shared within a society, their consequences become much more pernicious, because they affect entire groups of people in a common way. As Gardner (1973, p. 134) put it, an ethnic group member "may be somewhat chagrined to find that a few individuals in the larger community have beliefs about the characteristics of the group of which he is a member, but it has major implications . . . when such beliefs are relatively widespread in the community."

The basic theme of this chapter is that stereotypes can be conceptualized from two complementary perspectives, and that a full understanding of the stereotyping process involves looking at both types of approaches. From one perspective stereotypes are represented within the mind of the individual person. From the other perspective, stereotypes are represented as part of the social fabric of a society, shared by the people within that culture. We will consider the implications of thinking about stereotypes in these different ways upon the important questions that researchers ask about stereotypes, including what stereotypes are and how they should be measured. In doing so, we will consider how stereotypes are represented (i.e., stored for future use) at both individual and collective levels.

Individual and Collective Approaches: History and Overview

The idea that stereotypes are both individual and cultural phenomena is not a new one. Indeed, individual and collective approaches to the study of social psychological issues more generally have long traditions within psychology, as does the distinction between the two. Wundt (1900) made a clear distinction between individual and collective psychology, and this distinction was maintained by McDougall (1920) on the collective side, and Allport (1924) on the individual side.

Historically, these theorists were concerned about whether "social reality" exists at the level of the individual or at the level of the group (as a "group mind"). That question is less relevant now; there is no longer a question that all beliefs, including social beliefs such as stereotypes, exist in the minds of individual persons (cf. Asch, 1952). Rather, the pivotal point of distinction between individual and collective approaches lies in the assumed importance of shared social beliefs, above and beyond that of individual beliefs, as determinants of social behavior. This distinction is particularly important for a complete understanding of stereotypes and stereotyping.

Individual approaches have not been particularly concerned about stereotype consensus, focusing instead on the meaning of the stereotype to the individual. According to this perspective, "neither the definition nor the measurement of stereotypes should be constrained by the necessity of consensual agreement" (Hamilton, Stroessner, & Driscoll, 1994, p. 297). To theorists within the cultural approach, on the other hand, societal consensus is paramount. Because group values and group behavior provide the underlying foundation of stereotyping, stereotypes only have meaning (indeed stereotypes are only stereotypes!) to the extent they are culturally shared (Gardner, Kirby, & Findlay, 1973; D. Katz & Braly, 1933; Moscovici, 1981; Tajfel, 1981; Tajfel & Forgas, 1981). Moscovici observed that "any reduction to cognitive patterns and constructs, by eliminating the extraordinary richness of collective thought . . . converts an im-

portant problem into a mere academic exercise" (p. 208). Let us turn now to a more detailed exploration of the individual and collective approaches to stereotype representation.

Stereotype Representation

Stereotypes as Individual Beliefs: A Social Cognitive Perspective

The individual approach to stereotyping has primarily been associated with the dominant social cognitive tradition within North America (cf. Fiske & Taylor, 1991; Markus & Zajonc, 1985). The basic assumption of this approach is that, over time, people develop beliefs about the characteristics of the important social groups in their environment, and this knowledge influences their responses toward subsequently encountered individual members of those groups. Thus stereotypes (as one type of knowledge about the social world), develop as the individual perceives his or her environment. The perceived information about social groups is interpreted, encoded in memory, and subsequently retrieved for use in guiding responses. Furthermore, each of these processes is potentially subject to biases due to the assimilative effects of existing knowledge on information processing.

As mental representations of the world, stereotypes influence what information is sought out (Johnston & Macrae, 1994; Rothbart, 1981; Snyder, 1981), attended to (Belmore & Hubbard, 1987), and remembered (Fyock & Stangor, 1994) about members of social groups, as well as influencing social behavior (cf. Jussim & Fleming, 1996). Indeed the effectiveness of a given model of stereotype representation at the individual level is judged in terms of its ability to account for these basic processes. Stereotype development (Hamilton & Gifford, 1976; Jussim, 1991; Schaller & O'Brien, 1992; Stangor & Duan, 1991), maintenance (Hamilton & Rose, 1980; Stangor & McMillan, 1992), and change (Hewstone & Brown, 1986; Weber & Crocker, 1983) have all been addressed from this perspective (cf. Hamilton & Sherman, 1994; Stangor & Lange, 1993).

An interest with individual-level beliefs and interpersonal interactions has led researchers within the social cognitive tradition to focus upon the "bottom-up" determinants of stereotypes. It has been assumed within this approach that stereotypes are learned, and potentially changed, primarily through the information that individuals acquire through direct contact with members of other social groups.[1] Hypothesized, data-driven mechanisms through which stereotypes may be acquired involve attention to information (Langer & Imber, 1980; McArthur & Post, 1977), recall of information (Fyock & Stangor, 1994; Hamilton & Gifford, 1976), and integration of information (Schaller & O'Brien, 1992). Given the role of information in stereotype formation, information acquired through intergroup contact is expected to offer the best means of change (Hewstone & Brown, 1986). Although the possibility that stereotypes may also be learned and changed through indirect sources (from leaders, parents, peers, the mass media) is not explicitly denied by the individual approach, little research has focused on this possibility (but see Park & Hastie, 1987).

Three general approaches as to how information about social groups is represented within memory have been proposed. These are *group schemas, group prototypes,* and *exemplars.* Because each of these approaches is framed at a different level of specificity and makes different assumptions about how group beliefs are represented, each is thus differentially effective at answering important questions about stereotype development and its subsequent impact on social responses. In addition, each of the different approaches has implications for how stereotypes should be measured.

GROUP SCHEMAS

The most traditional approach to stereotyping within the individual approach is based on the cognitive schema (Fiske & Linville, 1980; Taylor & Crocker, 1981). Schemas are abstract knowledge structures that specify the defining features and relevant attributes of a given concept. Schemas give meaning to social information and promote parsimonious and effective information processing (Fiske & Taylor, 1991; Markus & Zajonc, 1985). As representations of social groups, *group schemas* are collections of beliefs about the characteristics of a social group.

Once developed within memory, schemas have broad influences upon person perception, including attention, perception, interpretation, and storage of social information, as well as judgments of and behavior toward others. At the attentional stage, schemas allow the individual to ignore what are perceived to be unrelated and unimportant details of a situation and thus reduce informational complexity; rendering more elaborative processing unnecessary (cf. Barlett, 1932). At the storage stage, schemas result in better memory for stereotype-confirming (in comparison to disconfirming) information, because this information is more easily assimilated into the schema. Schemas also provide a basis for making judgments about others—inferences beyond the information given (Bruner, 1957). These schema-based inferences include social responses, and particularly guessing in the direction of schema consistency when unsure (Locksley, Stangor, Hepburn, Grosovsky, & Hochstrasser, 1984; Markus & Zajonc, 1985; Stangor, 1988). Schemas also guide behavior through activation of relevant behavioral "scripts" (Schank & Abelson, 1977). In addition to knowledge about stereotypic traits of social groups, schemas may also contain affective information (Fiske, 1982; Fiske & Pavelchak, 1986).

The schema concept has had great heuristic value for the study of stereotyping because "schematic processing" provides an underlying mechanism to account for stereotype maintenance and use. Because the schema concept is so broad, however, it is difficult to use it to make specific predictions about stereotyping. In some cases the schema notion overpredicts, and thus becomes nonfalsifiable. For instance, both faster and slower reaction times for schema-relevant decisions have been taken as evidence for schematic processing (Bem, 1981; Markus, Crane, Bernstein, & Sidali, 1982). In other cases, the schema concept underpredicts. Schema models have difficulty accounting for better memory for scheme-inconsistent versus schema-consistent information, a common finding in the literature on person perception. One particular limitation of the schema approach is that it does not make clear predictions about how one should measure stereotypes independently of the schematic effects themselves. Although diverse measures, including biased memory (Fyock & Stangor, 1994: Stangor & McMillan, 1992), clustering in recall (Noseworthy & Lott, 1984), reaction times (Bem, 1981; Markus et al.,

---

[1]In this sense, the individual approach has implicitly assumed that there is at least a kernel of truth to most stereotypes, although that kernel may be subsequently exaggerated through information processing biases.

1982), and release from proactive interference (Mills & Tyrrell, 1983) have been used as measures of schematic processing, there is no well established method of validating the existence of the schema independently of its outcomes. As a result the concept often becomes circular, because there is a tendency to attribute any type of information-processing bias to "schematic" processing.

GROUP PROTOTYPES

Because one of the primary goals of the cognitive approach has been to "get specific" about how information is mentally represented, researchers have recently turned away from the schema and its inherent ambiguity toward a conceptualization of stereotypes in terms of more clearly articulated models of mental representation. One popular concept in this regard is the *group prototype*. Group prototypes are mental representations consisting of a collection of associations between group labels (e.g., Italians) and the features that are assumed to be true of the group (e.g., a feature of Italians might be "romantic").[2] Thus, prototypes are mental representations of social groups, similar to group schemas, but at a lower and more specific level of representation.

One advantage of a feature-based prototype approach is that it makes more explicit predictions about the activation and measurement of social stereotypes than do schema models. Because stereotypes are defined as mental associations between category labels and trait terms, stereotypes can be measured by the extent to which these traits are activated upon exposure to category labels; that is, if the trait "romantic" is stereotypic of Italians, then when thinking about Italians, "romantic" should quickly come to mind through spreading activation (Collins & Loftus, 1975). One approach in this regard is to use reaction time methodology (Diehl & Jonas, 1991; Dovidio, Evans, & Tyler, 1986; Gilbert & Hixon, 1991) to assess stereotypes. When presented with a target label (e.g., "Italians"), subjects should be quicker at identifying stereotypic versus nonstereotypic traits as words. Alternatively, free-response formats may be used in which those attributes generated frequently, or early in a protocol, are considered stereotypic because they are activated in response to the category label.

A second advantage of the prototype approach is that it makes explicit predictions concerning memory for group-relevant information. On the basis of prototype models, one can predict that either stereotype-consistent or stereotype-inconsistent information may be well remembered, depending on any number of factors that determine the development of associative links between category labels and associated stereotypes (cf. Srull & Wyer, 1989; Stangor & McMillan, 1992). Nevertheless, there is a clear memory advantage for expectancy-confirming information about existing social groups (Fyock & Stangor, 1994).

Despite their greater theoretical specificity, prototype models are more limited in scope in comparison to schema approaches, and cannot account for the diverse effects that schemas have been used to understand. For instance, it is not clear how behavior and affect would be linked to the stereotyping process within prototype models.

EXEMPLARS

A final approach to conceptualizing stereotype representation is based on the commonsense notion that, in addition to abstract representations of social groups, people also have memories for specific individuals (exemplars) whom they have previously encountered (Smith & Zárate, 1992). And these memories may influence responses when these memories are activated through encounters with others who are similar to the stored memories (cf. Lewicki, 1985). The exemplar approach has been given impetus by the recent interest in understanding how variability among group members is represented in memory, and (although it is possible for prototype models to account for variability judgments) it appears that such information is stored at least partially through memory for exemplars (Linville, Salovey, & Fischer, 1986; Park & Judd, 1990).

Exemplar models have the ability to account for many of the same phenomena as do schemas and prototype models (cf. Smith & Zárate, 1992). Zebrowitz (1996), for instance, presents an exemplar-based approach that can account for many important stereotyping effects, including activation of affect and behavioral responses. However, it is known that stereotyping is a heuristic device, occurring more often when the capacity or moti-

---

[2]Prototypes may also be conceptualized as containing the average, most typical, or idealized value of group members (Italians are, on average, more romantic than other groups).

vation to process individuating information is reduced (cf. Bodenhausen, 1993). The notion of activating an abstract prototype or schema from
memory, which serves as a simplifying summary
judgment, seems well suited to account for these results. People also possess stereotypes about groups
of which they have had little or no direct contact
(Hartley, 1946), suggesting that stereotyping occurs in the absence of exemplar-based processing.
Finally, in contrast to the prototype approach, the
exemplar approach has not yet dealt explicitly with
the issue of stereotype development, including the
important questions of how stereotypic characteristics become associated with individual exemplars
in memory, and which of the many possible stereotypes of a person might be so linked.

Stereotypes as Collective Belief Systems: A Cultural Perspective

The individual approach to stereotype representation is framed at a micro-analytic level, delineat-
ing the cognitive systems that allow individuals to
efficiently store and retrieve stereotypes. Although
these models range to some extent in generality
from the breadth of group schemas to the narrow-
ness of individual exemplars, they are all intra-
personal in orientation. The cultural approach is
broader in scope, transcending the intraindividual
perspective. Cultural models consider society itself to be the basis of stored knowledge, and stereotypes as public information about social groups
that is shared among the individuals within a culture. In this approach, although stereotypes exist
"in the head of the society's perceivers," they exist
also in the "fabric of the society" itself.

Consensual stereotypes represent one aspect of
the entire collective knowledge of a society. This
knowledge includes the society's customs, myths,
ideas, religions, and sciences (Boster, 1991;
Duveen & Lloyd, 1990; Farr & Moscovici, 1984).
Because such concepts are traditionally more sociological or anthropological than psychological
in nature, their study has not been the traditional
focus of experimental social psychologists. And
yet, as Tajfel (1981) argued, because cultural stereotypes represent one part of an individual's social knowledge, and because these beliefs have
important effects on social behavior, their consideration is essential for a full understanding of stereotypes and stereotyping.

In addition to considering stereotypes from a

different level of analysis, cultural approaches also
differ from individual models in terms of the assumed sources of stereotype development and
change. Whereas the individual approach has focused on how stereotypes are learned through direct interaction with others, cultural approaches
consider the ways that stereotypes are learned,
transmitted, and changed through indirect
sources—information gained from parents, peers,
teachers, political and religious leaders, and the
mass media. For this reason, cultural approaches
focus explicitly on language as a representation
of social groups.

LANGUAGE

"There is no completely non-verbal social stereotyping," wrote Fishman (1956, p. 48). Indeed, a
cultural approach to stereotyping emphasizes that
stereotypes are learned, maintained, and potentially changed through the language and communication of a culture. Language transcends the individual and offers a means of storing stereotypic
beliefs at a collective, consensual level.

Particularly central to language acquisition are
the processes of naming, labeling, and categorizing (Anglin, 1977). Thus it is no surprise that language provides a basic mechanism by which individuals are categorized into groups, and by which
stereotypes are shared with others (Allport, 1954;
Fishman, 1956; Moscovici, 1981). It is well known
that stereotypes are learned through communication. Correlations between the stereotypes and
prejudices of parents and children are commonly
observed (Epstein & Komorita, 1966; Fagot,
Leinbach, & O'Boyle, 1992). Furthermore, stereotype change occurs through education (Stephan &
Stephan, 1984), which must involve some degree
of communication.

Study of the role of language in stereotyping
leads to an explicit focus on the content of the category labels and the stereotypes. Within the individual approach, the tendency has been to study
generic category labels, such as "women" or
"Blacks." But the flexibility of language suggests
that these standard labels do not capture the full
flavor of stereotypes (cf. Devine & Baker, 1991).
The same social groups can be labeled in different
ways, ranging from the benign and politically correct ("Black," "homosexual," "woman") to the
derogatory ("nigger," "faggot," or "bitch").

Whereas benign labels connote mere category
membership, the derogatory slurs connote the fla-

vor of the stereotype itself. This is evident when one recognizes that slurs are typically not applied indiscriminately to all members of the social category, but primarily to those members who fit a certain stereotypic profile. Users of the word "nigger," for instance, often claim that not all Blacks are "niggers," only some of them. So just as other slang terms often convey a more negative experience or expectation than conveyed by the simple descriptive noun, derogatory group labels convey a particular negative stereotype to a greater degree than less offensive descriptive terms. It is in these labels, then, that the stereotype is most purely and powerfully signified in the transpersonal storage system of language.

In addition to its influence on the representation of category labels, language also affects the nature of the stereotypes themselves. One commonly observed effect concerns the tendency to relabel traits in ways that signify the valence of the preferred belief (cf. Saenger & Flowerman, 1954). Of course, language interacts with stereotyping in other ways as well, for instance when it becomes a category itself, or determines which categories are activated (cf. Giles & Saint-Jacques, 1979).

Despite the clear importance of language as a basis of stereotyping, empirical research has not been as abundant, or as integrated into other approaches to stereotyping, as it might be. The study of derogatory labels, or "ethnophaulisms," has received some research attention. Palmore (1962) observed a relationship between the degree of prejudice directed toward a particular ethnic group and the number of derogatory nicknames that exist for that group in the common language. More recently, Mullen and Johnson (1993) observed a correlation between the size of the ethnic group and the number of nicknames. In both cases, the data were based upon collective repositories of cultural beliefs (e.g., dictionaries of slang).

The content of everyday discourse has also been analyzed as it relates to the transmission and reproduction of stereotypes and prejudice (cf. Giles, 1977; van Dijk, 1987). Although language is transpersonal, language users are individuals. And research has examined the individual use of stereotypic language (see Greenberg & Pyszczynski, 1985; Maass & Arcuri, 1996).

THE MEDIA

In modern society, the form by which most stereotypes are transmitted is through the mass media—literature, television, movies, newspapers, E-mail, leaflets, and bumper stickers. The tangible artifacts of consumable mass media thus comprise an "information highway" for the transmission of social stereotypes. These representations of stereotypes are bought, sold, traded, checked out, and otherwise shared by millions, even billions of people across boundaries of distance and time untraveled by ordinary interpersonal communication.

That the mass media are an important collective repository for group stereotypes is recognized explicitly by individuals who attend to the way that groups and group members are portrayed in the media, and by researchers who codify these representations. Many studies have used qualitative data-analytic techniques to describe the manifestations of stereotypes in such diverse media as television shows (e.g., Hartmann & Husband, 1974; Wilson & Gutierrez, 1985), advertising (e.g., Bell, 1992; Pasadeos, 1987), and children's school texts (e.g., Dixon, 1977; Stinton, 1980; Zimet, 1976). Although these studies typically involve descriptive, qualitative methods of coding content, these measurement schemes are amenable to hypothesis-testing contexts as well. For instance, a number of researchers (e.g., Pasadeos, 1987; Weigel, Loomis, & Soja, 1980) have used such methods to study changes in cultural stereotypes over time. Again, although this type of study is typically out of the realm of the everyday life of the experimental social psychologist, the development of comprehensive models of stereotyping will require the ability to understand and assess stereotype development and transmission at both individual and collective levels.

SOCIAL NORMS AND ROLES

The language of a social group is explicitly bound up in the norms and the roles of the individual members of those groups (cf. Crandall, Thompson, Sakalli, & Schiffhauer, 1995). Thus, cultural norms are more than simply contributors to individual beliefs about groups; they are a social system through which stereotypes are represented and perpetuated across individuals, across generations, and across time (cf. Sherif, 1936).

Allport (1954) was well aware of the extent to which stereotypes developed through conformity to prevailing norms. On the basis of stereotypes of American soldiers during the Second World War (Stouffer, Suchman, DeVinney, Star, & Williams, 1949), he calculated that "about half of all prejudiced attitudes are based only on the need to conform to custom" (p. 272). Pettigrew (1958, 1959) found that those people who adhered most strongly to norms were also the most prejudiced against out-groups. Recent theoretical analyses of gender stereotypes also implicate social customs and norms—at least in the form of traditional gender roles—in the formation of gender stereotypes (Eagly, 1987; Hoffman & Hurst, 1990). Indeed, measures of gender-specific norms typically evolved from other measures designed to assess prevailing stereotypic beliefs (e.g., Bem, 1974; Spence, Helmreich, & Stapp, 1975).

The social psychological importance of shared group beliefs is clearly demonstrated by examining the power of consensual stereotypes to influence normative behaviors. Once group stereotypes exist in a culture, expected patterns of behavior for those group members follow, and these expectations determine both responses to group members and the behavior of the group members themselves. Consider the influence of traditional gender roles on the behavior of men and women. The power of these norms is twofold: First, men and women feel pressure to comply with the appropriate gender-based social norms rather than risk the collective derogation attendant on norm violation. When group members willingly (or unwillingly) act in stereotypic ways, their behavior justifies and perpetuates the stereotype. Second, even if particular group members wish to act in ways inconsistent with the norm, their ability to do so may be constrained by the norm-based expectations of others via behavioral confirmation effects (see Jussim & Fleming, 1996).

One example of the power of cultural stereotypes to influence behavior is demonstrated in recent work by Steele and his colleagues (Spencer & Steele, 1992; Steele, 1992; Steele & Aronson, 1995) concerning the effects of culturally-held stereotypes about women and about African Americans on scholastic achievement. Steele and Spencer argue that there is a consensual stereotype within American culture that women are poor at math in comparison to men, and that African Americans are poor in academic tasks more generally. Because women and Blacks are aware of these shared beliefs, they recognize that failure in relevant academic tasks will perpetuate the damaging stereotype. As a result, they experience extra pressure to defy the stereotype and succeed. But the extra pressure itself may be so great as to

sabotage those efforts, ironically diminishing the likelihood of performing well. Steele's analysis is provocative, because it uses the stereotype concept to account for behavioral outcomes in a way that individual-level analyses cannot. The influence of stereotypes on performance exists only because stereotypes are consensual, and members of stereotyped groups are themselves intensely aware of these culturally shared beliefs.

Points of Contrast

The approaches to understanding stereotype representation reviewed earlier vary substantially in terms of both level of analysis and basic underlying assumptions. In the next sections we compare the emphases of the individual and collective approaches, noting the strengths and weaknesses of each. Then we turn to a discussion of ways in which the two approaches might be integrated.

Individual Approaches

The individual approach to stereotyping has recently defined how stereotypes are understood within contemporary social psychology (cf. Hamilton & Sherman, 1994; Stangor & Lange, 1993), at least in part because it has provided a unifying theoretical perspective for the study of the stereotyping process. In addition to providing specific answers to the basic questions of how central tendency and variability information about social groups are mentally represented, this approach has unified the study of how stereotypes develop (e.g., Hamilton & Gifford, 1976; Schaller & O'Brien, 1992; Stangor & Ford, 1992; see Mackie, Hamilton, Susskind, & Rosselli, 1996), influence judgments of others (e.g., Brewer, 1988; Fiske & Neuberg, 1990), and change, particularly when the individual encounters stereotype-disconfirming behaviors (e.g., Rothbart & Lewis, 1988; Weber & Crocker, 1983; see Hewstone, 1996; Eberhardt & Fiske, 1996). The individual approach makes it clear that these central questions are all conceptually interrelated. The same basic cognitive processes that are part of stereotype formation also underlie stereotype maintenance and change.

A second advantage of the individual approach is that it provides a conceptual foundation for uniting the study of stereotypes with social knowledge more generally, through the language of mental representation. For instance, conceptualizing stereotypes as the cognitive (belief) component of prejudice provides a way of studying stereotypes within the broader literature on attitudes (Eagly & Chaiken, 1993; Fazio, 1990), and provides a means of linking stereotypes to the study of discriminatory behavior (see Dovidio, Brigham, Johnson, & Gaertner, 1996).[3] And the links between stereotyping and the self-concept become clear when self-stereotypes are considered in terms of their positive (Turner, 1975) or negative (Jacobs & Eccles, 1985; Spencer & Steele, 1992) effects on the self.

The individual representational approach also provides a mechanism to account for the often-observed flexibility of stereotyping. Despite possessing stereotype knowledge, people do not always make use of these stereotypes (see Brewer, 1996). The individual approach explains stereotype flexibility through the concepts of construct accessibility (Higgins & King, 1981; Oakes & Turner, 1990; Stangor, 1988) and spreading activation (Collins & Loftus, 1975). As with any type of mental representation, both stereotype representations (schemas; prototypes) and the contents of those representations (the stereotypical beliefs) may be differentially accessible across individuals and across contexts (Stangor & Lange, 1993). Thus, stereotypes may or may not be used as a basis of judgment, depending upon how the target person is categorized (Stangor, Lynch, Duan, & Glass, 1992), the fit between the target individual and the perceiver's expectations about the group to which he or she belongs (Lord, Lepper, & Mackie, 1984; Turner, 1987, Chapter 6), the strength of association between the stereotype and the category label (Dovidio et al., 1986), the contextual demands of the situation (Bodenhausen & Lichtenstein, 1987), as well as individual differences in stereotype accessibility (Bem, 1981; Markus et al., 1982; Stangor, 1988; Stangor et al., 1992).

Despite these important contributions toward understanding stereotyping, the individual approach has overemphasized the role of individual perception and direct contact with target group members as determinants of stereotypes. People

do form stereotypes about groups with whom they have had no direct contact (Hartley, 1946)—stereotypes that may be quite rich and well developed. And, despite the basic assumption that stereotypes will change through direct contact with members of other groups, contact has only small effects on stereotypes (Hewstone & Brown, 1986; Rothbart & John, 1992). Furthermore, the individual approach often overlooks the socially important outcomes of stereotyping that do not occur at a purely individual level.

Despite the laudable goal of being specific about how information is mentally represented, there is inherent ambiguity in this process, and it is not clear that more specificity necessarily provides a better understanding of stereotyping. Not only is it virtually impossible to distinguish representational formats at the level of specificity that some researchers have claimed (e.g., Barsalou, 1990, has argued that it may be impossible to distinguish exemplar from prototype representations), but it also may not matter from a practical perspective exactly how social information is stored. The important issues concern what information is activated under what conditions, and how and when stereotypes influence social behavior. More macroanalytic investigations may provide greater insights into these questions.

Collective Approaches

In contrast to the emphasis on cognitive representations within the individual approach, the collective approach emphasizes the transmission and reproduction of stereotypes across individuals and generations, and the social outcomes of stereotyping. One concomitant of this broader social approach is an explicit concern with *content* of stereotypes, in comparison to the emphasis on process that has driven the individual approach (Tajfel, 1981). When a common set of beliefs are internalized within a group, these beliefs begin to influence the group's collective behavior. Indeed, it is the stereotype content, consensually shared across a culture, that makes stereotypes particularly problematic. It *matters* that the stereotypes of Blacks include "lazy," "athletic," and "musical," rather than some other set of traits, both because these beliefs are involved in determining the social status of Blacks within a society and because these beliefs are determined *by* the social position of Blacks.

---

[3]In fact, if stereotypes are purely the belief component of attitude, with no other social significance, the concept becomes redundant with that of belief (cf. Gardner, 1973).

Furthermore, the collective approach makes it clear that it is consensual, and not individual, stereotypes that lead to the outcomes that make stereotypes of interest in the first place. These include both the negative consequences of behavioral confirmation, biased interpretation of events, and discrimination, and the positive effects of stereotyping on self-esteem (Crocker & Major, 1989; Crocker, Voelkl, Testa, & Major, 1991; Turner, 1975). Indeed, arguments that stereotypes do not need to be consensual disregard the fundamental requirement that influences of stereotypes at a group level are based upon interindividual consensus.

Because group consensus is such a central part of the collective approach, it is at first blush problematic that stereotypes often demonstrate a significant degree of cross-individual inconsistency (Katz & Braly, 1933; Stangor & Lange, 1993). For instance, in their classic study of ethnic stereotypes, Katz and Braly found that less than 40% of their subjects considered such putatively central traits as "ignorant" and "musical" to describe "Negroes." And for 5 out of their 10 target groups, there was not a single trait that was considered centrally stereotypic by more than half of their subjects. This lack of consensus is partly what led individual level analyses to ignore it.

Yet, it would naturally be expected that the consensus of group beliefs would vary, both between in-groups and out-groups (Linville et al., 1986), across different cultures, and even in subgroups within a single society (cf. Boster, 1991). Thus, treating consensus as a variable can provide important information about the process of stereotyping. Indeed, consensus in group beliefs is a common dependent measure within cognitive anthropology (cf. Boster & d'Andrade, 1989), and sophisticated approaches to such measurement have been developed (cf. Gardner, Kirby, Gorospe, & Villamin, 1972, for an example within social psychology).

As one example, interindividual consensus could be used to assess whether the development of a given stereotype is determined by top-down or bottom-up processes. To the extent that stereotypes are culturally transmitted through norms and language, individuals who communicate more often (e.g., within families, jobs, or peer groups) should develop stronger stereotype consensus. On the other hand, if consensus is determined by bottom-up factors, then stereotypes should be based

on the number and quality of direct or indirect interactions with out-group members, independently of communication with in-groups.

The collective approach also offers a unique perspective on the question of how to change stereotypes. Because cultural models are based on the assumption that many stereotypes are learned and modified through indirect sources, the role of intergroup contact as a source of attitude change is not emphasized. Rather, the collective approach focuses on stereotype change that occurs through institutional changes (Reicher, 1986), leadership (Bar Tal, 1989), and education (P. A. Katz & Zalk, 1978; Stephan & Stephan, 1984).

Indeed, educational intervention represents a mechanism of stereotype change that implicitly integrates individual with collective approaches. Educational interventions may take many forms, including exposure to stereotype-disconfirming information about groups, structured cooperative interactions between members of different groups, and instruction to be more tolerant of others' differences. Such interventions are individualistic in that they are directed toward changing the cognitions of individual minds, rather than changing the cultural institutions that maintain stereotypes. But these interventions are collective in that they are administered to large groups of people at a time. They are also collective in that they often draw on collective values (e.g., cultural values emphasizing cooperation or tolerance). And they are collective in that, if successful in changing the cognitions of individual minds, they may indeed effect changes in the cultural institutions that maintain stereotypes—such as language use and contents of the mass media.

Stereotype change also occurs through the efforts of groups to redefine and relabel themselves. The labels "Negro" and "colored" have fallen out of favor, with the labels "Black," "Afro-American," and finally "African American" replacing them. Similar changes have occurred through the work of those who have struggled to change cultural stereotypes about the roles and stereotypes of women. In this sense, a consensual stereotype may also have positive effects when it motivates a group to band together to overcome it—to create or change its own stereotype. These types of top-down change, which occur without changes in the amount or quality of intergroup contact, have been understudied within social psychology.

Yet, there are fundamental weaknesses to collective approaches as well. Most important there is not yet a unified theoretical or empirical tradition in the area of culturally determined stereotypes. Although these approaches argue that social values and norms are the important determinants of stereotyping, there is little hard evidence to support these hypotheses. Furthermore, the approaches often rely on individual-level measures of perceptual distortion and bias, without being specific about the underlying cognitive mechanisms that produce them.

Points of Contact: Functional Determinants of Stereotype Representation

Despite fundamental differences underlying individual and collective approaches to the study of stereotyping, there is an even greater set of commonalities. In addition to sharing the basic goals of understanding the development, stability, and change of group beliefs, as well as their influence on judgment and behavior, both the individual and collective approaches have adopted an underlying functionalist perspective, based on the fundamental supposition that the format in which stereotypes are represented (as is all knowledge) is determined not only by objective reality, but also by the extent to which that knowledge meets important goals. This assumption dates from earlier formulations of stereotyping (Allport, 1954; Erhlich, 1973; Fishman, 1956; Harding, Proshansky, Kutner, & Chein, 1969) and runs through contemporary theorizing in both individual (Fiske & Neuberg, 1990; Snyder & Miene, 1994; Stangor & Ford, 1992) and collective (Jost & Banaji, 1994; Tajfel, 1981; Turner, 1975, 1987) approaches.

The few theorists who have addressed both individual and collective functions of stereotypes have emphasized the differences between underlying functions at the two levels. For instance, Tajfel (1981; Tajfel & Forgas, 1981) noted that stereotypes serve an individual function by systematizing and simplifying information available to a perceiver, and protecting that perceiver's value structure. At a collective level, Tajfel suggested that stereotypes serve groups by offering culturally accepted explanations for events, by justifying group actions, and by providing a means for groups to differentiate themselves positively from other groups. These two sets of functions are separate enough in perspective that Tajfel (1981) openly

doubted whether an all-encompassing theory binding them together would even be possible.

Superficially, the underlying functions implied by the two approaches seem different, and it is true that they are again driven by the respective interests in bottom-up versus top-down processing. In the case of individual beliefs, the focus is on individual perceivers interacting with their environment. This approach has emphasized reliance on stereotypes as cognitive tools to satisfy basic needs for environmental understanding and for self-protection. Within the cultural approach, the focus is more top-down, concerning the influence of motivations to accept and transmit culturally shared values or knowledge upon perception and behavior. In this sense, stereotypes function to meet the needs of the culture, its political or religious structures, and the *zeitgeist* more generally.

But this distinction may be more apparent than real. Despite his pessimism, Tajfel (1981) did hint at theoretical initiatives that may relate individual and collective functions together, essentially suggesting that collective needs inform and guide individual needs. We offer a related, but somewhat different perspective. We argue that, just as both approaches are based upon the same underlying set of cognitive mechanisms (categorization, accentuation, and perceptual biases), they are also founded on a similar set of underlying motivational needs. Furthermore, individual and collective needs are inherently intertwined. Just as many individual-level concerns require a collective context (e.g., social acceptance by others requires that the individual be located within a phenomenologically relevant culture), so culturally shared values and beliefs are meaningless if not for the fact that individuals translate those values into specific actions.

Here, then, we encounter a fundamental point of rapprochement between the individual and collective perspectives—a set of overlapping and symbiotic motivations. In this section, we focus on two fundamental human needs (explanation and prediction of the social world, and esteem maintenance) and review evidence highlighting the role of these needs in the development of both individual and culturally shared stereotypes.

Epistemic Functions of Stereotypes

A basic human motive is that of knowing, understanding, and predicting others (cf. Heider, 1958; Kelley, 1967; Kruglanski, 1989), and one of the more basic functions of stereotypes is to provide useful information about others (cf. Oakes & Turner, 1990). At an individual level, stereotypes are useful for making both inductive and deductive judgments (Diehl & Jonas, 1991). People constantly meet new individuals about whom they have little information except their social category memberships, and they use this knowledge in an adaptive manner to draw dispositional inferences about the person. At other times, individuals view the behavior of an individual, using this knowledge in conjunction with his or her stereotypes to predict category memberships ("Is she Jewish?"; "Is he gay?"; cf. Gardner et al., 1973).

The prevailing goal of making informed judgments about individuals suggests that stereotypes will develop in a way that enhances the ability to perform this task. Stereotype representations have informational value to the extent that they maximize "meta-contrast" (Turner, 1987; see also Ashmore & Del Boca, 1981; McCauley, Stitt, & Segal, 1980), such that between-group differences are large and within-group differences are small. For instance, based on the assumptions of Tajfel's accentuation theory, Ford and Stangor (1992) hypothesized and found that stereotypes would develop more strongly to the extent that they maximized group differentiation, regardless of whether that differentiation was the result of high between-group distinctiveness or low within-group variability.

Just as individuals use their beliefs about social groups to help them understand and explain individual behavior, stereotypes also develop at the collective level as a basis for rendering social events more tangible (Hewstone, 1989; Tajfel, 1981; Tajfel & Forgas, 1981). These explanations provide information and structure where formerly there was ignorance and confusion. For instance, in the absence of theories about germs and contagion, European communities in the 16th and 17th centuries reacted to outbreaks of bubonic plague by developing plausible (but deeply misguided) explanations for the fever that ravaged their population. The people in Newcastle believed the Scots had poisoned their wells; Barnstaple residents believed it was the work of a local Independent congregation; and in Oxford they blamed it on the sorcery of the Catholic church (Thomas, 1971, cited in Tajfel & Forgas, 1981). Across communities, explanations differed; but within communities, explanations were consensual, satisfying a

collective need to understand the community misfortune.

Predicting and adequately responding to others requires not only sufficient information, but also some means of simplifying or structuring the over complex and often contradictory data that are manifest in the environment (Kruglanski, 1989; Neuberg & Newsom, 1993). Thus, just as stereotypes sometimes supplement an information-impoverished environment, at other times they may reduce the complexity of an information-rich environment. Research amply demonstrates that the use of social stereotypes increases in cognitively demanding situations (see Bodenhausen & Macrae, 1996), and also develop more strongly when needs for structure or coherence are enhanced (cf. Kruglanski & Freund, 1983; Stangor & Duan, 1991).

But individual motives for closure or simplification extend beyond use of categories to include needs to bring beliefs about diverse social categories into cognitive consonance. One of the original explanations for stereotypes is that they served to justify the negative attitudes that are held about others (Allport, 1954; Fishman, 1956; Myrdal, 1944; Ryan, 1971). Consistent with this notion is evidence demonstrating the relationship between prejudice and stereotypes (see Dovidio et al., 1996). Furthermore, just as individuals attempt to justify negative events that befall other individuals (Lerner & Miller, 1978; Milgram, 1974), people may develop stereotypes about categories of victimized others. Research suggests that just such a justification process operates in the formation of negative stereotypes about the survivors of sexual assault (Mazelan, 1980).

Just as stereotypes function to clarify individual cognitive representations of the world, they also act to simplify communication at the social level, allowing people to enjoy an economy of words when speaking about and to others. A speaker can convey an abundance of information by simply labeling a person as a "Jew," "nigger," or "feminist." The reason that verbal exchange is simplified is, of course, the implicit assurance that the category label will convey information to the recipient of the communication through shared group beliefs. Thus, whereas the surface features of the communication may be simple, the level of interpersonal understanding is rich with implied meaning. Moreover, the stereotype label does not merely imply extensive information, but also extensive information that is evaluatively coherent as well, making the communication both simple and compelling (cf. Graumann & Wintermantel, 1989; van Dijk, 1987).

Needs to simplify and structure understanding may be heightened within societies during times of crisis, such as wars, economic recessions, and natural disasters. During these times, leaders use stereotypes of the enemy to reduce potential ambiguity, stifle dissent, and to provide a clear set of behavioral norms. Thus, dehumanizing stereotypes of Japanese, Koreans, and Vietnamese developed in the United States during prominent wars of the 20th century. Even outside of crisis, stereotypes are promoted by collectives to rationalize or justify existing economic or political conditions. Just as individuals justify the pain suffered by others by derogating them, collectives justify actions toward others groups of people that would otherwise be considered unfair or reprehensible through stereotypes. Demeaning stereotypes of African Americans and Native Americans can be attributed at least partially to the need within the White American community to justify the slavery and genocide that victimized those populations.

Stereotypes not only allow societies to justify collective actions, but also to justify collective inaction as well. Stereotypes serve the status quo. Advantaged groups who feel they are unjustly advantaged by a system that favorably allocates rewards to them may rationalize their advantaged state by blaming the failure of others on their inherent personality weaknesses (Pettigrew, 1979). If disenfranchised, downtrodden, and oppressed populations are viewed in terms of negative stereotypes, these beliefs may justify a collective lack of concern by those responsible for the oppression.

Esteem-Related Functions of Stereotypes

Whereas needs for understanding and simplifying the social environment seem more "coldly" functional, stereotypes also serve "hotter" ego-relevant functions at both the individual and the collective level. In order to function capably, people need to feel good about both themselves (Solomon, Greenberg, & Pyszczynski, 1991; Steele, 1988; Tesser, 1988) and the groups to which they belong (Cialdini et al., 1976; Crocker & Luhtanen, 1990; Greenberg et al., 1990; Turner, 1975). Thus, stereotyping and prejudice have traditionally been

considered in terms of their relations with the need to maintain self-esteem or self-valuation.

At the individual level, it has been predicted that those who are chronically low in self-esteem would develop stronger stereotypes as a means of regaining positive regard (e.g., Ehrlich, 1973; Wills, 1981). Nevertheless, research support for this hypothesis is weak (Crocker & Schwartz, 1985), and the validity of the expected theoretical relationship has also been questioned (Abrams & Hogg, 1988; Crocker & Schwartz, 1985). After all, to the extent that derogating out-groups successfully enhances self-esteem, then the expected negative relationship between self-esteem and prejudice would be weakened.

On the other hand, there is evidence that temporary threats to self-esteem cause individuals to make more stereotypic and prejudicial responses (e.g., Brown, Collins, & Schmidt, 1988). These studies lead to the more specific hypothesis that stereotypes will develop more strongly when they satisfy basic motivations for self enhancement. Indeed, in a recent study, Ford (1992) found that subjects who were led to believe that they were a member of a social group that had some negative and some positive characteristics in comparison to a relevant out-group developed stronger stereotypes (as assessed through reaction-time measures) about the dimension upon which they compared favorably with the other group.

The relation between self-valuation and stereotyping cannot be understood from a purely individual perspective; it is necessary to consider group- or collective-level variables (Tajfel, 1981). Several different theoretical perspectives explicitly link self-valuation to stereotyping processes through the mediating link of collective-level variables. One theoretical model suggests that by derogating out-groups or favoring in-groups, one implicitly enhances the relative status of one's in-group, which in turn enhances one's view of oneself (Turner, 1975, 1987). Another model suggests that by derogating out-groups or favoring in-groups, the individual may implicitly uphold the standards of one's own culture, which is alleged to be a fundamental source of self-valuation (Solomon et al., 1991). Both perspectives are consistent with the more general notion that individuals' feelings about themselves are not independent of "group-esteem" (Hinkle, Taylor, & Fox-Cardamone, 1989) or "collective self-esteem" (Luhtanen & Crocker, 1992), or other collective-level values. Collective self-esteem is related to the shared aspects of group identity that group members use to enhance their self perceptions (e.g., "Black is Beautiful"), and appears to have an important effect on in-group bias (Crocker & Luhtanen, 1990).

Because a group's collective self-esteem would be expected to be closely related to its perceived status within a society, it might be expected that the tendency to develop and use stereotypes would be greater for groups with low social status—particularly minority groups. Indeed, there is research showing that, within a minimal group design, members of a minority group expressed greater in-group favoritism than did members of a majority group (Gerard & Hoyt, 1974). However, other work that examines more directly the role of status in intergroup perception indicates that greater prejudice is exhibited by groups of higher status (Sachdev & Bourhis, 1987, 1991). In retrospect, this finding represents an interesting parallel with work on individual self-esteem, which has also demonstrated unexpected relationships in this regard.

Parallel to research on individual self-esteem, there is the suggestion that temporary threats to the collective esteem of a high status group might lead to increased incidence of prejudice. For instance, Hovland and Sears (1940; see also Hepworth & West, 1988) found that the rate of race-related lynchings in the American South appeared to be influenced by regional economic threat—which may operate as a temporary threat to the self-valuation of the people in that region. Other analyses also reveal that societal threat is positively related to both attitudes and behavior toward out-group members (Doty, Peterson, & Winter, 1991).

Finally, it is important to recognize that another means of obtaining positive self-regard is through acceptance by significant others. Thus, the need for social acceptance is another powerful motivation underlying both individual and collective behavior (Crowne & Marlowe, 1964; Hill, 1987). By developing and expressing consensual stereotypes of out-groups, individuals may be more readily accepted by other in-group members. Indeed, "any individual who does *not* know the stereotypes of thought and feeling . . . may be said to be a stranger to [a] culture" (Hayakawa, 1950, p. 209). The expression of stereotypes within language "serves as a peculiarly potent symbol of the social soli-

darity of those who speak the language" (Sapir, 1933, p. 159). Furthermore, by acting towards out-group members in stereotypical ways, a person symbolically expresses his or her group identifications, and thus may be more likely to reap the rewards of social acceptance from his or her own group (cf. La Violette & Silvert, 1951; Turner, 1987).

Concluding Remarks

If you were to ask a biologist, "Where does life come from?" you might get one of two different answers. The biologist might tell you how organic life arose in the first place, emerging in the form of some string of nucleotides from a primordial soup. Or the biologist might give you a very different answer, describing how every generation of animal life is reproduced from that before it, through coupling of sperm and egg and recombination of DNA. Although these two answers are very different, they are entirely compatible, representing two complementary perspectives on organic life.

Similarly, the study of group stereotypes can be approached from two different, yet complementary perspectives. The individual approach to stereotyping emphasizes the "beginnings" of stereotypes, focusing on the individual cognitive-motivational processes that account for the fact that stereotypes have to begin somewhere (see Mackie et al., 1996). Yet, once a stereotype has emerged within a culture, it takes on a life of its own and influences social behavior in ways beyond that of the actions of any individual. At this point, stereotypes depend not so much on direct perception (and misperception) of the social environment as on the existing manifestations of those stereotypes in the behavior and language of the society (Hartman & Husband, 1974). The collective approach to stereotyping has emphasized the "reproduction" of stereotypes, focusing on the means through which stereotypes are transmitted and maintained, and on the ways in which stereotypes serve culturally shared values.

Throughout the short history of the scientific study of stereotypes, the relative popularity of consensual and individual approaches has changed. This is evident both in the manner in which stereotypes are measured by researchers and in the questions researchers ask about stereotypes and their consequences. Before the cognitive revolution in social psychology, techniques such as those used by Katz and Braly (1993) were prevalent, assessing consensus in cultural beliefs about various ethnic groups (Brigham, 1971). Since then, stereotype measurement techniques have been decidedly individual, assessing the manner in which individual beliefs are cognitively represented (e.g., Devine & Baker, 1991; Dovidio et al., 1986; Ford & Stangor, 1992; Martin, 1987; McCauley & Stitt, 1978; Park & Judd, 1990).

In addition, just as the two perspectives on organic life suggest two rather different sets of questions to be answered, and at different levels, the individual and collective perspectives toward stereotypes also promote different types of inquiry. Because the collective approach attends to the specific *content* of stereotypic beliefs, researchers working within this approach have typically dealt directly with meaningful real-world categories. But this perspective has offered limited insight into the underlying, individual-level stereotyping *processes* through which stereotypes exert their effects. In contrast, the individualistic perspective on stereotype representation has focused directly on the *processes* of stereotype development and change, offering insights into these processes that could not have emerged in the absence of such a perspective. Of course, researchers working within this perspective have often relied on studies using artificial social groups (e.g., alien beings from other planets, or members of group "A") or real groups of limited social relevance ("Nobel Prize winners").

Complementary lines of inquiry are fine, but an integrated perspective may yield insights that are unlikely to emerge from any single line of inquiry. That the time is ripe for a synthesis is suggested by the recent interest in socially shared cognition (e.g., Levine, Resnick, & Higgins, 1993; Resnick, Levine, & Teasley, 1991; Wegner, 1987), and by concentrated attempts to locate individual cognitions about groups within a broader social context (Oakes, Haslam, & Turner, 1994; Turner, 1991). We do not suppose to identify the form that synthesis will or should take. However, one area of inquiry is suggested by the question of whether cultural consensus is an important part of a stereotype. Rather than debate this question as a matter of definition, it might be more fruitful to treat "consensualness" as an important variable. Some stereotypes are more consensually held than oth-

ers. What consequences might this variable have on important stereotyping phenomena? This variable might have implications for the development and cognitive representation of stereotypes. Perhaps consensual stereotypes are more likely to be represented as abstractions and schemata, and less likely to be represented as prototypes and exemplars. Because of their relevance to needs for social acceptance, perhaps consensual stereotypes are associated more closely in memory with other socially relevant knowledge structures. Perhaps they are more closely tied to one's self-concept. Consensualness might also have implications for the accessibility of stereotypes, the strength of their effects on judgment, and the conditions under which they might exert those effects. Finally, consensualness of stereotypes may have important consequences for understanding change and revision of stereotypic beliefs. Consensual and nonconsensual stereotypes may be differentially vulnerable to the effects of different interventions.

Whether or not these sketchy speculations are accurate, they do highlight the value of considering multiple levels of inquiry into stereotypes and stereotyping processes. A complete understanding of organic life demands consideration of biological processes that operate at several different levels. A full understanding of stereotypes demands, at the very least, some simultaneous adoption of both individual and collective perspectives.

REFERENCES

Abrams, D., & Hogg, M. A. (1988). Comments on the motivational status of self-esteem in social identity and intergroup discrimination. *European Journal of Social Psychology, 18*, 317–334.

Allport, F. H. (1924). *Social psychology*. New York: Houghton Mifflin.

Allport, G. W. (1954). *The nature of prejudice*. Reading, MA: Addison-Wesley.

Anglin, J. (1977). *Word, object, and conceptual development*. New York: Norton.

Asch, S. (1952). *Social psychology*. New York: Prentice-Hall.

Ashmore, R. D., & Del Boca, F. K. (1981). Conceptual approaches to stereotypes and stereotyping. In D. L. Hamilton (Ed.), *Cognitive processes in stereotyping and intergroup behavior* (pp. 1–35). Hillsdale, NJ: Erlbaum.

Barsalou, L. W. (1990). On the indistinguishability of exemplar memory and abstraction in category representation. In T. K. Srull & R. S. Wyer, Jr. (Eds.), *Advances in social cognition* (Vol. 3, pp. 61–88). Hillsdale, NJ: Erlbaum.

Bartlett, F. C. (1932). *Remembering*. Cambridge, UK: Cambridge University Press.

Bar-Tal, Y. (1989). Can leaders change followers' stereotypes? In D. Bar-Tal, C. F. Graumann, A. W. Kruglanski, & W.

Stroebe (Eds.), *Stereotyping and prejudice: Changing conceptions* (pp. 225–242). New York: Springer-Verlag.

Bell, J. (1992). In search of a discourse on aging: The elderly on television. *Gerontologist, 32,* 305–311.

Belmore, S. M., & Hubbard, M. L. (1987). The role of advance expectancies in person memory. *Journal of Personality and Social Psychology, 53,* 61–70.

Bem, S. L. (1974). The measurement of psychological androgyny. *Journal of Consulting and Clinical Psychology, 42,* 155–162.

Bem, S. L. (1981). Gender schema theory: A cognitive account of sex typing. *Psychological Review, 88,* 354–364.

Bodenhausen, G. V. (1993). Emotions, arousal, and stereotypic judgments: A heuristic model of affect and stereotyping. In D. M. Mackie & D. L. Hamilton (Eds.), *Affect, cognition, and stereotyping: Interactive processes in group perception* (pp. 13–37). San Diego: Academic Press.

Bodenhausen, G. V., & Lichtenstein, M. (1987). Social stereotypes and information processing strategies: The impact of task complexity. *Journal of Personality and Social Psychology, 52,* 871–880.

Bodenhausen, G. V., & Macrae, C. N. (1996). The self-regulation of intergroup perception: Mechanisms and consequeces of stereotype suppression. In C. N. Macrae, C. Stangor, & M. Hewstone (Eds.), *Stereotypes and stereotyping* (pp. 227–253). New York: Guilford Press.

Boster, J. S. (1991). The information economy model applied to biological similarity judgment. In L. B. Resnick, J. M. Levine, & S. D. Teasley (Eds.), *Perspectives on socially shared cognition* (pp. 203–225). Washington, DC: American Psychological Association.

Boster, J. S., &. D'Andrade, R. G. (1989). Natural and human sources of cross-cultural agreement in ornithological classification. *American Anthropologist, 91,* 132–142.

Brewer, M. B. (1988). A dual process model of impression formation. In T. K. Srull & R. S. Wyer (Eds.), *Advances in social cognition* (Vol. 1, pp. 1–36). Hillsdale, NJ: Erlbaum.

Brewer, M. B. (1996). When stereotypes lead to stereotyping: The use of stereotypes in person perception. In C. N. Macrae, C. Stangor, & M. Hewstone (Eds.), *Stereotypes and stereotyping* (pp. 254–275. New York: Guilford Press.

Brigham, J. C. (1971). Ethnic stereotypes. *Psychological Bulletin, 76,* 15–33.

Brown, J. D., Collins, R. L., & Schmidt, G. W. (1988). Self-esteem and direct versus indirect forms of self-enhancement. *Journal of Personality and Social Psychology, 55,* 445–453.

Bruner, J. S. (1957). On perceptual readiness. *Psychological Review, 64,* 123–152.

Cialdini, R. B., Borden, R. J., Thorne, A., Walker, M. R., Freeman, S., & Sloane, L. R. (1976). Basking in reflected glory: Three (football) field studies. *Journal of Personality and Social Psychology, 34,* 406–415.

Clark, M. S., & Fiske, S. T. (1982). *Affect and cognition.* Hillsdale, NJ: Erlbaum.

Collins, A. M., & Loftus, E. F (1975). A spreading-activation theory of semantic processing. *Psychological Review, 82,* 407–428.

Crandall, C. S., Thompson, E. A., Sakalli, N., & Schiffhauer K. L. (1995). *Creating hostile environments: Name-calling and social norms.* Unpublished manuscript, University of Kansas at Lawrence.

Crocker, J., & Luhtanen, R. (1990). Collective self-esteem

and ingroup bias. *Journal of Personality and Social Psychology, 58,* 60–67.

Crocker, J., & Major, B. (1989). Social stigma and self-esteem: The self-protective properties of stigma. *Psychological Review, 96,* 608–630.

Crocker, J., & Schwartz, I. (1985). Prejudice and intergroup favoritism in a minimal intergroup situation: Effects of self-esteem. *Personality and Social Psychology Bulletin, 11,* 379–386.

Crocker, J., Voelkl, K., Testa, M. & Major, B. (1991). Social stigma: The affective consequences of attributional ambiguity. *Journal of Personality and Social Psychology, 60,* 218–228.

Crowne, D. P., & Marlowe, D. (1964). *The approval motive.* New York: Wiley.

Devine, P. G., & Baker, S. M. (1991). Measurement of racial stereotype subtyping. *Personality and Social Psychology Bulletin, 27,* 44–50.

Diehl, M., & Jonas, K. (1991). Measures of national stereotypes as predictors of the latencies of inductive versus deductive stereotypic judgments. *European Journal of Social Psychology, 21,* 317–330.

Dixon, R. (1977). *Catching them young. I. Sex, race, and class in children's fiction.* London: Pluto Press.

Doty, R. M., Peterson, B. E., & Winter, D. G. (1991). Threat and authoritarianism in the United States, 1978–1987. *Journal of Personality and Social Psychology, 61,* 629–640.

Dovidio, J. F., Brigham, J. C., Johnson, B. T., & Gaertner, S. L. (1996). Stereotyping, prejudice, and discrimination: Another look. In C. N. Macrae, C. Stangor, & M. Hewstone (Eds.), *Stereotypes and stereotyping* (pp. 276–322). New York: Guilford Press.

Dovidio, J. F, Evans, N. E., & Tyler, R. B. (1986). Racial stereotypes: The contents of their cognitive representations. *Journal of Experimental Social Psychology, 22,* 22–37.

Duveen, G., & Lloyd, B. (1990). *Social representations and the development of knowledge.* Cambridge, UK: Cambridge University Press.

Eberhard, J., & Fiske, S. T. (1996). Motivating individuals to change: What is a target to do? In C. N. Macrae, C. Stangor, & M. Hewstone (Eds.), *Stereotypes and stereotyping* (pp. 369–415). New York: Guilford Press.

Eagly, A. H. (1987). *Sex differences in social behavior: A social-role interpretation.* Hillsdale, NJ: Erlbaum.

Eagly, A. H., & Chaiken, S. (1993). *The psychology of attitudes.* Fort Worth, TX: Harcourt Brace Jovanovich.

Eagly, A. H., Makhijani, M. G., & Klonsky, B. G. (1992). Gender and evaluation of leaders: A meta-analysis. *Psychological Bulletin, 111,* 3–22.

Ehrlich, H. J. (1973). *The social psychology of prejudice.* New York: Wiley.

Epstein, R., & Komorita, S. S. (1966). Prejudice among Negro children as related to parental ethnocentrism. *Journal of Personality and Social Psychology, 4,* 643–647.

Fagot, B. I., Leinbach, M. D., & O'Boyle, C. (1992). Gender labeling, gender stereotyping, and parenting behaviors. *Developmental Psychology, 28,* 225–230.

Farr, R. M., & Moscovici, S. (1984). *Social representations.* Cambridge, UK: Cambridge University Press.

Fazio, R. H. (1990). The MODE model as an integrative framework. *Advances in Experimental Social Psychology, 23,* 75–109.

Fishman, J. A. (1956). An examination of the process and

function of social stereotyping. *Journal of Social Psychology, 43,* 27–64.

Fiske, S. T. (1982). Schema-triggered affect: Applications to social perception. In M. S. Clark & S. T. Fiske (Eds.), *Affect and cognition: The 17th Annual Carnegie Symposium on Cognition* (pp. 55-78). Hillsdale, NJ: Erlbaum.

Fiske, S. T., & Linville, P. W. (1980). What does the schema concept buy us? *Personality and Social Psychology Bulletin, 6,* 543–557.

Fiske, S. T., & Neuberg, S. L. (1990). A continuum of impression formation, from category-based to individuating processes: Influences of information and motivation on attention and interpretation. *Advances in Experimental Social Psychology, 23,* 1–74.

Fiske, S. T., & Pavelchak, M. A. (1986). Category-based versus piecemeal-based affective responses: Developments in schema-triggered affect. In R. M. Sorrentino & E. T. Higgins (Eds.), *Handbook of motivation and cognition: Foundations of social behavior* (Vol. 1, pp. 167–203). New York: Guilford Press.

Fiske, S. T., & Taylor, S. E. (1991). *Social cognition* (2nd ed.). New York: McGraw-Hill.

Ford, T. E. (1992). *The effect of motivation and attribute diagnosticity on stereotype formation.* Unpublished doctoral dissertation, University of Maryland at College Park.

Ford, T. E., & Stangor, C. (1992). The role of diagnosticity in stereotype formation: Perceiving group means and variances. *Journal of Personality and Social Psychology, 63,* 356–367.

Fyock, J., & Stangor, C. (1994). The role of memory biases in stereotype maintenance. *British Journal of Social Psychology, 33,* 331–344.

Gardner, R. C. (1973). Ethnic stereotypes: The traditional approach, a new look. *Canadian Psychologist, 14,* 133–148.

Gardner, R. C., Kirby, D. M., & Findlay, J. C. (1973). Ethnic stereotypes: The significance of consensus. *Canadian Journal of Behavioral Science, 5,* 4–12.

Gardner, R. C., Kirby, D. M., Gorospe, F. H., & Villamin, A. C. (1972). Ethnic stereotypes: An alternative assessment technique, the stereotype differential. *Journal of Social Psychology, 87,* 259–267.

Gerard, H. B., & Hoyt, M. F. (1974). Distinctiveness of social categorization and attitude toward ingroup members. *Journal of Personality and Social Psychology, 29,* 836–842.

Gilbert, D. T., & Hixon, J. G. (1991). The trouble of thinking: Activation and application of stereotypic beliefs. *Journal of Personality and Social Psychology, 60,* 509–517.

Giles, H. (1977). *Language, ethnicity, and intergroup relations.* New York: Academic Press.

Giles, H., & Saint-Jacques, B. (1979). *Language and ethnic relations.* Oxford: Pergamon Press.

Graumann, C. F., & Wintermantel, M. (1989). Discriminatory speech acts: A functional approach. In D. Bar-Tal, C. F. Graumann, A. W. Kruglanski, & W. Stroebe (Eds.), *Stereotyping and prejudice: Changing conceptions* (pp. 183–204). New York: Springer-Verlag.

Greenberg, J., & Pyszczynski, T. (1985). The effects of an overheard ethnic slur on evaluations of the target: How to spread a social disease. *Journal of Experimental Social Psychology, 21,* 61–72.

Greenberg, J., Pyszczynski, T., Solomon, S., Rosenblatt, A., Veeder, M., Kirkland, S., & Lyon, D. (1990). Evidence for terror management theory II: The effects of mortality salience on reactions to those who threaten or bolster the cultural worldview. *Journal of Personality and Social Psychology, 58,* 308–318.

Hamilton, D. L., & Gifford, R. K. (1976). Illusory correlation in interpersonal perception: A cognitive basis of stereotypic judgments. *Journal of Experimental Social Psychology, 12,* 392–407.

Hamilton, D. L., & Rose, T. L. (1980). Illusory correlation and the maintenance of stereotypic beliefs. *Journal of Personality and Social Psychology, 39,* 832–845.

Hamilton, D. L., & Sherman, J. W. (1994). Stereotypes. In R. S. Wyer, Jr., & T. K. Srull (Eds.), *Handbook of social cognition* (2nd ed., Vol. 2, pp. 1–68). Hillsdale, NJ: Erlbaum.

Hamilton, D. L., Stroessner, S. J., & Driscoll, D. M. (1994). Social cognition and the study of stereotyping. In P. G. Devine, D. L. Hamilton, & T. M. Ostrom (Eds.), *Social cognition: Contributions to classic issues in social psychology* (pp. 291–321). New York: Springer-Verlag.

Harding, J., Proshansky, H., Kutner, B., & Chein, I. (1969). Prejudice and ethnic relations. In G. Lindzey & E. Aronson (Eds.), *Handbook of social psychology* (2nd ed., Vol. 5, pp. 1–76). Reading, MA: Addison-Wesley.

Hartley, E. L. (1946). *Problems in prejudice.* New York: King's Crown Press.

Hartmann, P., & Husband, C. (1974). *Racism and the mass media.* London: Davis-Poynter.

Hayakawa, S. I. (1950). Recognizing stereotypes as substitutes for thought. *Etc.: Review of General Semantics, 7,* 208–210.

Heider, F. (1958). *The psychology of interpersonal relations.* Hillsdale, NJ: Erlbaum.

Hepworth, J. T., & West, S. G. (1988). Lynchings and the economy: A time-series reanalysis of Hovland and Sears (1940). *Journal of Personality and Social Psychology, 55,* 239–247.

Hewstone, M. (1989). *Causal attribution: From cognitive processes to cognitive beliefs.* Oxford: Blackwell.

Hewstone, M. (1996). Contact and categorization: Social psychological interventions to change intergroup relations. In C. N. Macrae, C. Stangor, & M. Hewstone (Eds.), *Stereotypes and stereotyping* (pp. 323–368). New York: Guilford Press.

Hewstone, M., & Brown, R. (1986). Contact is not enough: An intergroup perspective on the 'Contact Hypothesis'. In M. Hewstone & R. J. Brown (Eds.), *Contact and conflict in intergroup encounters* (pp. 1–44). London: Blackwell.

Higgins, E. T., & King, G. (1981). Accessibility of social constructs: Information-processing consequences of individual and contextual variability. In N. Cantor & J. F. Kihlstrom (Eds.), *Personality, cognition and social interaction* (pp. 69–121). Hillsdale, NJ: Erlbaum.

Hill, C. A. (1987). Affiliation motivation: People who need people ... but in different ways. *Journal of Personality and Social Psychology, 52,* 1008–1018.

Hinkle, S., Taylor, L. A., & Fox-Cardamone, D. L. (1989). Intragroup identification and intergroup differentiation: A multicomponent approach. *British Journal of Social Psychology, 28,* 305–317.

Hoffman, C., & Hurst, N. (1990). Gender stereotypes: Perception or rationalization. *Journal of Personality and Social Psychology, 58,* 197–208.

Hovland, C. I., & Sears, R. (1940). Minor studies of aggression: Correlation of lynching with economic indices. *Journal of Psychology, 9,* 301–310.

Jacobs, J., & Eccles, J. S. (1985). Gender differences in math ability: The impact of media reports on parents. *Educational Researcher, 14,* 20–25.

Johnston, L., & Macrae, C. N. (1994). Changing social stereotypes: The case of the information seeker. *European Journal of Social Psychology, 24,* 237–266.

Jost, J. T, & Banaji, M. R. (1994). The role of stereotyping in system-justification and the production of false consciousness. *British Journal of Social Psychology, 33,* 1–27.

Jussim, L. (1991). Social perception and social reality: A reflection-construction model. *Psychological Review, 98,* 54–73.

Jussim, L., & Fleming, C. (1996). Self-fulfilling prophecies and the maintenance of social stereotypes: The role of dyadic interactions and social forces. In C. N. Macrae, C. Stangor, & M. Hewstone (Eds.), *Stereotypes and stereotyping* (pp. 161–192). New York: Guilford Press.

Katz, D., & Braly, K. (1933). Racial stereotypes in one hundred college students. *Journal of Abnormal and Social Psychology, 28,* 280–290.

Katz, P. A., & Zalk, S. R. (1978). Modification of children's racial attitudes. *Developmental Psychology, 14,* 447–461.

Kelley, H. H. (1967). Attribution theory in social psychology. In D. Levine (Ed.), *Nebraska Symposium on Motivation* (Vol. 15, pp. 192–238). Lincoln: University of Nebraska Press.

Kruglanski, A. W. (1989). *Lay epistemics and human knowledge.* New York: Plenum.

Kruglanski, A. W., & Freund, T. (1983). The freezing and unfreezing of lay inferences: Effects on impressional primacy, ethnic stereotyping, and numerical anchoring. *Journal of Experimental Social Psychology, 19,* 448–468.

La Violette, F., & Silvert, K. H. (1951). A theory of stereotypes. *Social Forces, 29,* 237–257.

Langer, E. J., & Imber, L. (1980). Role of mindlessness in the perception of deviance. *Journal of Personality and Social Psychology, 39,* 360–367.

Lerner, M. J., & Miller, D. T. (1978). Just world research and the attribution process: Looking back and ahead. *Psychological Bulletin, 85,* 1030–1051.

Levine, J. M., Resnick, L. B., & Higgins, E. T. (1993). Social foundations of cognition. *Annual Review of Psychology, 44,* 585–612.

Lewicki, P. (1985). Nonconscious biasing effects of single instances on subsequent judgments. *Journal of Personality and Social Psychology, 48,* 563–574.

Linville, P. W., Salovey, P., & Fischer, G. W. (1986). Stereotyping and perceived distributions of social characteristics: An application to ingroup-out-group perception. In J. E Dovidio & S. L. Gaertner (Eds.), *Prejudice, discrimination, and racism* (pp. 165–208). Orlando, FL: Academic Press.

Lippman, W. (1922). *Public opinion.* New York: Harcourt Brace.

Locksley, A., Stangor, C., Hepburn, C., Grosovsky, E., & Hochstrasser, M. (1984). The ambiguity of recognition memory tests of schema theories. *Cognitive Psychology, 16,* 421–448.

Lord, C. G., Lepper, M. R., & Mackie, D. (1984). Attitude prototypes as determinants of attitude-behavior consistency. *Journal of Personality and Social Psychology, 46,* 1254–1266.

Luhtanen, R., & Crocker, J. (1992). A collective self-esteem scale: Self-evaluation of one's social identity. *Personality and Social Psychology Bulletin, 18,* 302–318.

Maass, & Arcuri, (1996). Language and stereotyping. In C. N. Macrae, C. Stangor, & M. Hewstone (Eds.), *Stereotypes and stereotyping* (pp. 193–226). New York: Guilford Press.

Mackie, D., Hamilton, D. L., Susskind, & Rosselli (1996). Social psychological foundations of stereotype formation. In C. N. Macrae, C. Stangor, & M. Hewstone (Eds.), *Stereotypes and stereotyping* (pp. 41–78). New York Guilford Press.

Markus, H., Crane, M., Bernstein, S., & Sidali, M. (1982). Self-schemas and gender. *Journal of Personality and Social Psychology, 42,* 38–50.

Markus, H., & Zajonc, R. B. (1985). The cognitive perspective in social psychology. In G. Lindzey & E. Aronson (Eds.), *The handbook of social psychology* (3rd ed., Vol. 1, pp. 137–230). New York: Random House.

Martin, C. L. (1987). A ratio measure of sex stereotyping. *Journal of Personality and Social Psychology, 52,* 489–499.

Mazelan, P. M. (1980). Stereotypes and perceptions of the victims of rape. *Victimology, 5,* 121–132.

McArthur, L. Z., & Post, D. L. (1977). Figural emphasis and person perception. *Journal of Experimental Social Psychology, 13,* 520–535.

McCauley, C., & Tyrrell, D. J. (1983). An individual and quantitative measure of stereotypes. *Journal of Personality and Social Psychology, 36,* 929–940.

McCauley, C., & Stitt, C. L. (1978). An individual and quantitative measure of stereotypes. *Journal of Personality and Social Psychology, 36,* 929–940.

McCauley, C., Stitt, C. L., & Segal, M. (1980). Stereotyping: From prejudice to prediction. *Psychological Bulletin, 87,* 195–208.

McDougall, W. (1920). *The group mind.* Cambridge, UK: Cambridge University Press.

Milgram, S. (1974). *Obedience to authority.* New York: Harper & Row.

Mills, C. J., & Tyrrell, D. J. (1983). Sex-stereotypic encoding and release from proactive interference. *Journal of Personality and Social Psychology, 45,* 772–781.

Moscovici, S. (1981). On social representations. In J. Forgas (Ed.), *Social cognition* (pp. 181–209). London: Academic Press.

Mullen, B., & Johnson, C. (1993). Cognitive representation in ethnophaulisms as a function of group size: The phenomenology of being in a group. *Personality and Social Psychology Bulletin, 19,* 296–304.

Myrdal, G. (1944). *An American dilemma: The Negro problem and modern democracy.* New York: Harper.

Neuberg, S. L., & Newsom, J. T. (1993). Personal need for structure: Individual differences in chronic motivation to simplify. *Journal of Personality and Social Psychology, 65,* 113–131.

Noseworthy, C. M., & Lott, A. J. (1984). The cognitive organization of gender-stereotypic categories. *Personality and Social Psychology Bulletin, 10,* 474–481.

Oakes, P. J., Haslam, S. A., & Turner, J. C. (1994). *Stereotyping and social reality.* Oxford: Blackwell.

Oakes, P. J., & Turner, J. C. (1990). Is limited information processing capacity the cause of social stereotyping? In W.

Stroebe & M. Hewstone (Eds.), *European review of social psychology* (Vol. 1, pp. 1 11-135). Chichester, UK: Wiley.

Palmore, E. B. (1962). Ethnophaulisms and ethnocentrism. *American Journal of Sociology, 67,* 442–445.

Park, B., & Hastie, R. (1987). Perception of variability in category development: Instance- versus abstraction-based stereotypes. *Journal of Personality and Social Psychology, 59,* 621–635.

Park, B., & Judd, C. M. (1990). Measures and models of perceived group variability. *Journal of Personality and Social Psychology, 59,* 173–191.

Pasadeos, Y. (1987). Changes in television newscast advertising, 1974–1985. *Communication Research Reports, 4,* 43–46.

Pettigrew, T. F. (1958). Personality and sociocultural factors in intergroup attitudes: A cross-national comparison. *Journal of Conflict Resolution, 2,* 29–42.

Pettigrew, T. F. (1959). Regional differences in anti-Negro prejudice. *Journal of Abnormal and Social Psychology, 59,* 28–36.

Pettigrew, T. F. (1979). The ultimate attribution error: Extending Allport's cognitive analysis of prejudice. *Personality and Social Psychology Bulletin, 5,* 461–476.

Reicher, S. (1986). Contact, action and racialization: Some British evidence. In M. Hewstone & R. Brown (Eds.), *Contact and conflict in intergroup encounters* (pp. 152–168). London: Blackwell.

Resnick, L. B., Levine, J. M., & Teasley, S. D. (1991). *Perspectives on socially shared cognition.* Washington, DC: American Psychological Association.

Rothbart, M. (1981). Memory processes and social beliefs. In D. L. Hamilton (Ed.), *Cognitive processes in stereotyping and intergroup behavior* (pp. 145–181). Hillsdale, NJ: Erlbaum.

Rothbart, M., & John, 0. (1992). Intergroup relations and stereotype change: A social-cognitive analysis and some longitudinal findings. In P. M. Sniderman & P. E. Tetlock (Eds.), *Prejudice, politics and race in America.* Stanford CA: Stanford University Press.

Rothbart, M., & Lewis, S. (1988). Inferring category attributes from exemplar attributes: Geometric shapes and social categories. *Journal of Personality and Social Psychology, 55,* 861–872.

Ryan, W. (1971). *Blaming the victim.* New York: Random House.

Sachdev, I., & Bourhis, R. Y. (1987). Status differentials and intergroup behavior. *European Journal of Social Psychology, 17,* 277–293.

Sachdev, I., & Bourhis, R. Y. (1991). Power and status differentials in minority and majority group relations. *European Journal of Social Psychology, 21,* 1–24.

Saenger, G., & Flowerman, S. (1954). Stereotypes and prejudicial attitudes. *Human Relations, 7,* 217–238.

Sapir, E. (1933). Language. *Encyclopedia of the Social Sciences, 9,* 55–169.

Schaller, M., & O'Brien, M. (1992). "Intuitive analysis of covariance" and group stereotype formation. *Personality and Social Psychology Bulletin, 18,* 776–785.

Schank, R. C., & Abelson, R. P. (1977). *Scripts, plans, goals, and understanding: An inquiry into human knowledge structures.* Hillsdale, NJ: Erlbaum.

Sherif, M. (1936). *The psychology of social norms.* New York: Harper & Row.

Smith, E. R., & Zárate, M. A. (1992). Exemplar-based model

of social judgment. *Psychological Review, 99,* 3–21.

Snyder, M. (1981). On the self-perpetuating nature of social stereotypes. In D. L. Hamilton (Ed.), *Cognitive processes in stereotyping and intergroup behavior* (pp. 183–212). Hillsdale, NJ: Erlbaum.

Snyder, M., & Miene, P. (1994). On the function of stereotypes and prejudice. In M. Zanna & J. M. Olson (Eds.), *The psychology of prejudice: The Ontario Symposium* (Vol. 7, pp. 33–54). Hillsdale, NJ: Erlbaum.

Solomon, S., Greenberg, J., & Pyszczynski, T. (1991). A terror management theory of social behavior: The psychological consequences of self-esteem and cultural worldviews. *Advances in Experimental Social Psychology, 24,* 93–159.

Spence, J. T., Helmreich, R. L., & Stapp, J. (1975). Ratings of self and peers on sex-role attributes and their relations to self-esteem and conceptions of masculinity and femininity. *Journal of Personality and Social Psychology, 32,* 29–39.

Spencer, S. J., & Steele, C. M. (1992, August). *The effect of stereotype vulnerability on women's math performance.* Paper presented at the 100th Annual Convention of the American Psychological Association, Washington, DC.

Srull, T. K., & Wyer, R. S. (1989). Person memory and judgment. *Psychological Review, 96,* 58–83.

Stangor, C. (1988). Stereotype accessibility and information processing. *Personality and Social Psychology Bulletin, 14,* 694–708.

Stangor, C., & Duan, C. (1991). Effects of multiple task demands upon memory for information about social groups. *Journal of Experimental Social Psychology, 27,* 357–378.

Stangor, C., & Ford, T. E. (1992). Accuracy and expectancy-confirming processing orientations and the development of stereotypes and prejudice. *European Review of Social Psychology, 3,* 57–89.

Stangor, C., & Lange, J. (1993). Cognitive representations of social groups: Advances in conceptualizing stereotypes and stereotyping. *Advances in Experimental Social Psychology, 26,* 357–416.

Stangor, C., Lynch, L., Duan, C., & Glass, B. (1992). Categorization of individuals on the basis of multiple social features. *Journal of Personality and Social Psychology, 62,* 207–281.

Stangor, C., & McMillan, D. (1992). Memory for expectancy-congruent and expectancy-incongruent information: A review of the social and social developmental literatures. *Psychological Bulletin, 111,* 42–61.

Steele, C. M. (1988). The psychology of self-affirmation: Sustaining the integrity of the self. *Advances in Experimental Social Psychology, 21,* 261–302.

Steele, C. M. (1992). Race and the schooling of black Americans. *Atlantic Monthly, 269*(4), 68–78.

Steele, C. M., & Aronson, J. (1995). Stereotype threat and the intellectual test performance of African Americans. *Journal of Personality and Social Psychology, 69,* 797–811.

Stephan, W. G., & Stephan, C. (1984). The role of ignorance in intergroup relations. In N. Miller & M. B. Brewer (Eds.), *Groups in contact: The psychology of desegregation* (pp. 229–257). Orlando, FL: Academic Press.

Stinton, J. (1980). *Racism and sexism in children's books.* London: Writers & Readers.

Stouffer, S. A., Suchman, E. A., DeVinney, L. C., Star, S. A., & Williams, R. M., Jr. (1949). *The American soldier: Vol. 1. Adjustment during army life.* Princeton, NJ: Princeton University Press.

Tajfel, H. (1981). Social stereotypes and social groups. In J. C. Turner & H. Giles (Eds.), *Intergroup behavior* (pp. 144–167). Chicago: University of Chicago Press.

Tajfel, H., & Forgas, J. P. (1981). Social categorization: Cognitions, values, and groups. In J. P. Forgas (Ed.), *Social cognition: Perspectives on everyday understanding* (pp. 113–140). London & New York: Academic Press.

Taylor, S. E., & Crocker, J. (1981). Schematic bases of social information processing. In E. T. Higgins, C. P. Herman, & M. P. Zanna (Eds.), *Social cognition: The Ontario symposium* (Vol. 1, pp. 89–134). Hillsdale, NJ: Erlbaum.

Tesser, A. (1988). Toward a self-evaluation maintenance model of social behavior. *Advances in Experimental Social Psychology, 21,* 181–227.

Thomas, K. (1971). *Religion and the decline of magic.* London: Weidenfeld & Nicholson.

Turner, J. C. (1975). Social comparison and social identity; Some prospects for intergroup behavior. *European Journal of Social Psychology, 5,* 5–34.

Turner, J. C. (1987). *Rediscovering the social group: A self-categorization theory.* Oxford: Blackwell.

Turner, J. C. (1991). *Social influence.* Milton Keynes, UK: Open University Press.

van Dijk, T, A. (1987). *Communicating racism.* Newbury Park, CA: Sage.

Weber, R., & Crocker, J. (1983). Cognitive processes in the revision of stereotypic beliefs. *Journal of Personality and Social Psychology, 45,* 961–977.

Wegner, D. M. (1987). Transactive memory: A contemporary analysis of the group mind. In B. Mullen & G. R. Goethals (Eds.), *Theories of group behavior* (pp. 185–208). New York: Springer-Verlag.

Weigel, R., Loomis, J., & Soja, M. (1980). Race relations on prime time television. *Journal of Personality and Social Psychology, 39,* 884–893.

Wills, T. A. (1981). Downward social comparison principles in social psychology. *Psychological Bulletin, 90,* 245–271.

Wilson, C. C., & Guiterrez, F. (1985). *Minorities and the media.* Beverly Hills, CA, & London: Sage.

Wundt, W. (1900). Voelkerpsychologie. Leipzig: Engelmann.

Zebrowitz, L. (1996). Physical appearance as a basis of stereotyping. In C. N. Macrae, C. Stangor, & M. Hewstone (Eds.), *Stereotypes and stereotyping* (pp. 79–120). New York: Guilford Press.

Zimet, S. (1976). *Print and prejudice.* London: Hodder & Stroughton.

Measuring Stereotypes and Prejudice

Because social psychology is an empirical science, we must have a way of measuring the ideas that we are interested in studying. The unifying theme of the readings in this section concerns the measurement of stereotypes and prejudice. There are a number of possibilities for doing so, and in this section we consider some of the most important ones.

Perhaps the most direct approach to measuring stereotypes is to simply ask research participants to indicate, from a large list of provided traits, those that they think are most typical of a group. Devine and Elliot take this approach in Reading 4. In addition to being very straightforward, this "checklist" approach has been used by many researchers over a number of years. As a result, it has been possible to study the extent to which stereotypes about some social groups have changed over time. Devine and Elliot compare their data, collected in the 1990s to similar measures collected in the 1930s, 1950s, 1960s, and 1980s. The checklist approach used by these researchers also has the advantage of allowing them to assess the extent to which stereotypes about social groups are shared among the people that are tested (that is, to see if they are cultural or individual stereotypes).

Devine and Elliot add to this prior research not only by assessing the stereotypes held by college students in the 1990s, but also by pointing out that there has been substantial changes in the stereotypes held about African Americans over the past decades. In addition, this paper argues that it is important to differentiate one's knowledge of the cultural stereotype (what I think that other people think) from one's own *personal beliefs* (what I personally think). In the end, Devine and Elliot conclude that there has been at least some change in the stereotypes that

European Americans hold about African Americans over the past few decades. On the other hand, many of the beliefs are unfortunately still the same.

Katz and Hass, in Reading 5, argue that the beliefs that European Americans hold about African Americans are *ambivalent*. Rather than being a simple positive or negative feeling about the group, these researchers argue that the beliefs that European Americans hold about African Americans include both positive feelings (those based upon humanism and empathy, and concern for the group's social difficulties) and negative feelings (those based upon perceptions that African Americans violate the protestant work ethic by not contributing enough to society). Katz and Hass test the important hypothesis that how European Americans judge and behave toward African Americans depends upon which set of beliefs (the positive ones or the negative ones) are accessible (that is, ready to be used) at the time of the judgment or behavior.

The theoretical approach of Katz and Hass, based on the idea of ambivalence, is similar to other current theories of prejudice. For instance, the theory of "modern racism" (McConahay, 1986) suggests that racist beliefs have fundamentally changed in the United States, particularly since the civil rights movement of the 1960s. These approaches assume that although there are still some "traditional" or "red-necked" racists, most White Americans do not currently harbor hatred or antipathy toward Blacks, but their beliefs about them are more subtle. Modern prejudice thus involves beliefs that Blacks, as a group, have some positive characteristics, and yet that they nevertheless are different than Whites in a way that makes them less positive and that threatens current social norms. A similar analysis of "modern sexism" has

also been proposed (Glick & Fiske, 1996; Swim, Aikin, Hall, & Hunter, 1995).

One difficulty with direct self-report measures of stereotypes and prejudice, such as those used in the prior article in this section, is that they are likely to be influenced by faking—a problem technically known as *self-presentation*. People may not tell the truth about their stereotypes or prejudices on these measures, either because they don't want the researcher to know that they are prejudiced or (perhaps even more importantly) because they don't want to think of themselves as being prejudiced or having stereotypes. As a result, contemporary researchers have created measures of stereotyping and prejudice that bypass direct responding from the participant, and thus that get around the difficulties of self-presentation (Sigall and Page, 1971; Crosby et al., 1980). The idea is that, if we activate (or *prime*) a category label (say, African Americans), the stereotypes that are part of the cognitive representation of that group should be quickly (and possibly *automatically*) activated. Lepore and Brown take this approach to measuring prejudice in Reading 6. Their goal is to prime the category label and look for effects of that category on judgments. The participants cannot fake their responses because the category is primed entirely out of their awareness.

Lepore and Brown also address an important issue regarding the differences between high- and low-prejudice individuals. The question concerns whether these individuals differ in the content of their stereotypes (their personal beliefs), or whether high- and low-prejudice individuals both hold the same personal beliefs, but differ only in terms of their desires to avoid using their negative stereotypes. As you will see, Lepore and Brown use a complex and yet clever procedure to answer this question.

Discussion Questions

1. What methods have been used to measure stereotypes and prejudice, and what are the advantages and disadvantages of each?
2. Considering the research reported by Devine and Elliot (Reading 4), would you say that stereotypes are changing or staying the same? What makes you think so?
3. Why do Katz and Hass (Reading 5) believe that racial attitudes are "ambivalent?" Do you think that African Americans also have ambivalent attitudes about European Americans?
4. According to Lepore and Brown (Reading 6), what are the differences between high- and low-prejudice individuals in terms of their cognitive representations of stereotypes?

Suggested Readings

Biernat, M., & Crandall, C. S. (1999). Racial attitudes. In J. P. Robinson, P. R. Shaver, & L. S. Wrightsman (Eds.), *Measures of political attitudes* (pp. 297–411). San Diego: Academic Press. A current review of a wide variety of self-report measures of stereotyping and prejudice.

Crosby, F., Bromley, S., & Saxe, L. (1980). Recent unobtrusive studies of black and white discrimation and prejudice: A literature review. *Psychological Bulletin, 87,* 546–563. Crosby and colleagues consider a wide variety of interesting behavioral measures designed to avoid self-presentation problems.

Glick, P., & Fiske, S. (1996). The Ambivalent Sexism Inventory: Differentiating hostile and benevolent sexism. *Journal of Personality and Social Psychology, 70,* 491–512. An application of the attitude ambivalence approach to perceptions of women.

McConahay, J. B. (1986). Modern racism, ambivalence, and the modern racism scale. In S. Gaertner & J. Dovidio (Eds.), *Prejudice, discrimination, and racism* (pp. 91–126). Orlando, FL: Academic. An introduction to the concept of modern racism.

Swim, J., Aikin, K., Hall, W., & Hunter, B. A. (1995). Sexism and racism: Old-fashioned and modern prejudices. *Journal of Personality and Social Psychology, 68,* 199–214. A measure of modern attitudes toward women.

Are Racial Stereotypes *Really* Fading?
The Princeton Trilogy Revisited

Patricia G. Devine • University of Wisconsin–Madison
Andrew J. Elliott • University of Rochester

In this article, the authors identify three methodological shortcomings of the classic Princeton trilogy studies: (a) ambiguity of the instructions given to respondents, (b) no assessment of respondents' level of prejudice, and (c) use of an outdated list of adjectives. These shortcomings are addressed in the authors' assessment of the stereotype and personal beliefs of a sample of University of Wisconsin students. In contrast to the commonly espoused *fading stereotype* proposition, data suggest that there exists a consistent and negative contemporary stereotype of Blacks. Comparing the data from the Princeton trilogy studies with those of the present study, the authors conclude that the Princeton trilogy studies actually measured the respondents' personal beliefs, not (as typically assumed) their knowledge of the Black stereotype. Consistent with Devine's model, high- and low-prejudiced individuals did not differ in their knowledge of the stereotype of Blacks but diverged sharply in their endorsement of the stereotype.

During the past 50 years, there have been dramatic shifts in the social and political climate in America that have made racial discrimination illegal and overt expressions of racial prejudice socially taboo. In the wake of these macro-level changes, many social scientists have been interested in the extent to which individual-level social stereotype change has followed suit. These considerations are important in intergroup relations research, as stereotype change is commonly considered a prerequisite to prejudice reduction and more amicable intergroup interactions. Based on data from the adjective checklist procedure, the classic stereotype assessment technique developed by Katz and Braly (1933), many researchers have concluded that individual racial stereotypes in America have generally faded over the years. In the present research, we offer a critique of Katz and Braly's procedure, guided by the question, Are individual racial stereotypes in America *really* fading?

In Katz and Braly's (1933) adjective checklist procedure, respondents are provided with a list of 84 trait adjectives and instructed "to read through the list of words and select those which seem to you typical of (target group)" (p. 283). Respondents are encouraged to select as many adjectives as necessary to capture the target group adequately and are encouraged to add their own adjectives as needed. Respondents are then asked to identify the five words in the list that seem to them most typical of members of the target group. The content of the stereotype of a group is defined as the set of adjectives that respondents most frequently assign to the group.

In their seminal study, Katz and Braly (1933) found a high level of consistency in the adjectives respondents associated with the Black stereotype. In addition, the majority of the adjectives selected were fairly negative (e.g., superstitious, lazy, ignorant). Several studies have replicated Katz and Braly's procedure in efforts to examine the amount of stability or change in stereotypes. Two of the studies (Gilbert, 1951; Karlins, Coffman, & Walters, 1969), together with Katz and Braly's study, have been referred to as the Princeton trilogy, because they assessed stereotypes held by three generations of Princeton students. The two later studies in the Princeton trilogy used the same procedure and the same set of adjectives employed in Katz and Braly's initial investigation. Many years later, Dovidio and Gaertner (1986), although not studying Princeton students, reported another investigation of the Black stereotype that followed Katz and Braly's procedures exactly.[1]

In summarizing the pattern of findings for the Black stereotype, Dovidio and Gaertner (1991) stated that "adjective checklist studies, in which respondents are asked to select traits that are the most typical of particular racial or ethnic categories, indicate that negative stereotypes are consistently fading" (p. 202; see also Gilbert, 1951, and Karlins et al., 1969). That is, over time, respondents have selected a different set of traits to represent the Black stereotype, they have displayed less consistency in the adjectives selected, and the traits they have chosen have been less negatively valenced. These findings could be interpreted as very encouraging for intergroup relations. They suggest that stereotype change is possible and that White Americans are becoming more positive in their perceptions of Blacks. Changes in the social and political climate, then, do appear to be associated with individual-level changes. However, we believe that there is some ambiguity in exactly what has changed over time. In reviewing this literature, we found that Katz and Braly's (1933)

adjective checklist procedure as it has been traditionally implemented suffers from several shortcomings that make conclusions about stereotype persistence or change tenuous at best. In what follows, we outline these shortcomings and report a study designed to address each of the shortcomings in an effort to document the nature of Whites' representations of Black Americans as a social group.

The methodological shortcomings of the adjective checklist procedure fall into three general categories: (a) ambiguity of the instructions given to respondents, (b) no assessment of respondents' level of racial prejudice, and (c) use of an outdated list of adjectives. In addition to these methodological shortcomings, there has been a conspicuous absence of attention to theoretical and conceptual considerations in employing Katz and Braly's (1933) procedure and in stereotype assessment research more generally (Ashmore & Del Boca, 1981). In the following section, we briefly review Devine's (1989) model of automatic and controlled processes in stereotyping and prejudice, which highlights a conceptual distinction in need of consideration in the stereotype assessment literature.

The Distinction Between Stereotypes and Personal Beliefs

Devine (1989), in her model of automatic and controlled processes in prejudice, argued that stereotypes and personal beliefs are conceptually distinct cognitive structures and that each structure represents only part of an individual's entire knowledge base of a particular group. Devine suggested that a stereotype is a well-learned set of associations that link a set of characteristics with a group label (see also Dovidio, Evans, & Tyler, 1986). Through the socialization process, all individuals learn a variety of cultural stereotypes that become part of their associative network (Ehrlich, 1973). Although everyone possesses knowledge of numerous stereotypes, not all possess personal beliefs that are congruent with these stereotypes. Devine argued that beliefs are propositions that are endorsed and accepted as true. Therefore, whereas most White Americans possess knowledge of the Black stereotype (i.e., the stereotype exists within their associative network), only a subset of these individuals actually endorse the stereotype

---

[1]Dovidio and Gaertner (1986) reported their stereotype assessment data in a chapter and only provided a comparison of the traits most frequently selected by their respondents with those most frequently selected in the Princeton trilogy studies. Details about the number of respondents that participated in the study, the percentage of respondents who refused to complete the task, and so forth are not provided in their chapter.

and believe it is veracious (for a comparable argument in the attitude theory literature, see Pratkanis, 1989; Zanna & Rempel, 1988). For high-prejudiced individuals, their knowledge of the Black stereotype and their personal beliefs about Blacks are highly congruent, whereas low-prejudiced individuals have rejected the stereotype and adopted a distinctly different set of personal beliefs about Blacks. Importantly, however, rejection of the Black stereotype by low-prejudiced individuals does not immediately eradicate the stereotype from their associative network. On the contrary, the stereotype often remains a well-organized, frequently activated knowledge structure (see Devine, 1989, Study 2; Jamieson & Zanna, 1989; Klinger & Beall, 1992; Kruglanski & Freund, 1983; Sherman & Gorkin, 1980).

Devine (1989, Study 1) provided direct empirical evidence that both high- and low-prejudiced respondents possess equivalent knowledge of the Black stereotype. In a free-response task, respondents were instructed to list the components of the Black stereotype. Respondents were informed that the researchers were not interested in their personal beliefs about Blacks but only their knowledge of the Black stereotype. Comparisons of the trait ascriptions generated by high- and low-prejudiced respondents failed to yield any significant differences. Indirect support for the proposition that high- and low-prejudiced individuals possess different personal beliefs toward Blacks was obtained in a subsequent study (Devine, 1989, Study 3). Under conditions emphasizing anonymity, respondents were instructed to list their thoughts about Black Americans as a social group. Analysis of these free-response data yielded clear differences between high- and low-prejudiced respondents: Those high in prejudice listed more negative traits than did those low in prejudice. In general, low-prejudiced respondents' thoughts reflected themes of equality and negation of the stereotype. Together, these studies support the conceptual distinction between stereotypes and personal beliefs.

Shortcomings of the Princeton Trilogy Studies

The stereotype/personal-belief distinction is especially relevant to the first methodological shortcoming of the Princeton trilogy—the ambiguity of instructions. Both Gilbert (1951) and Karlins

et al. (1969) reported that many of their respondents found Katz and Braly's (1933) task confusing. From their written comments about the task (which respondents were encouraged to provide), it appears that some respondents thought the instructions asked for them to list their knowledge of the stereotype, whereas others thought they were being instructed to list their personal beliefs. Given the ambiguity of the instructions, it is difficult to know precisely what it is that respondents reported—their knowledge of the stereotype or their personal beliefs. Clearly, before claims about stereotype change can be made from the Princeton trilogy data, it is important to ascertain whether respondents indeed reported their knowledge of the stereotype. An equally plausible possibility, from Devine's (1989) perspective, is that the stereotype has remained stable through the years (in consistency and valence, not necessarily in specific content), whereas personal beliefs have undergone a revision. In the present research, we sought to eliminate ambiguity by providing respondents with clear instructions concerning whether they should list their knowledge of the Black stereotype or their personal beliefs about Blacks. In fact, all respondents completed both stereotype and personal beliefs measures so that respondents' knowledge of the stereotype could be compared with their personal beliefs.

Our second methodological criticism of the Princeton trilogy is also driven by a consideration of the stereotype/personal-belief distinction. In none of the studies in the Princeton trilogy was there any independent assessment of respondents' level of prejudice toward the target group. From Devine's (1989) perspective, the assessment of prejudice is of fundamental importance, given that high- and low-prejudiced individuals are equally knowledgeable of the Black stereotype but diverge in their endorsement of the stereotype. Consideration of prejudice level, therefore, can afford a much more precise analysis of respondents' representation of the target group. Karlins et al. (1969) recognized the value of employing an independent indicator of prejudice in research on stereotypes and attitudes, and actually called for future research to attend more closely to differences between high- and low-prejudiced individuals. In the present research, we heeded the call of Karlins et al. by assessing prejudice with McConahay, Hardee, and Batts's (1981) Modern Racism Scale (MRS).

Our third criticism of the Princeton trilogy studies is that they all employed the same list of 84 adjectives used in Katz and Braly's (1933) initial assessment. Karlins et al. (1969) expressed concern over the adequacy of the 1933 list for capturing the then current stereotype: "We suspect that a comprehensive list for today would have to include several terms not found in the 1933 version, terms which might have been widely subscribed to by our subjects" (p. 14). Although respondents were encouraged to add traits to the list, Karlins et al. argued that the constraints of a provided list are strong and that typically few respondents depart from the list. Devine's (1989, Study 1) stereotype assessment study validated the concerns of Karlins et al., as many of the characteristics most frequently generated by respondents to capture the stereotype of Blacks (e.g., poor, criminal, athletic) were not included on the original Katz and Braly list.

Karlins et al. (1969) argued that the reason they used the outdated list of adjectives (and the same set of instructions) was to ensure comparability across the studies (their study being the third in the trilogy). They wanted to ensure that any differences found in the pattern of trait selection were not due to changes in the task. However, change in a stereotype may involve the addition, as well as deletion, of traits from the original characterization of Blacks suggested in Katz and Braly's (1933) study. Therefore, in the present research, we expanded the list of adjectives provided to respondents to include the traits frequently listed by Devine's respondents (1989, Study 1) that were not included in the original Katz and Braly list.[2]

In summary, the primary goal of the present research was to assess the contemporary stereotype of Blacks and the personal beliefs about Blacks among a sample of University of Wisconsin undergraduates, using a revised Katz and Braly procedure, one that addressed the previously discussed methodological shortcomings. In so doing, we hoped to provide evidence attesting to the veracity of our methodological critique and to offer a reevaluation of the *fading stereotype* proposition currently being espoused on the basis of the Princeton trilogy data. Given the presumed implications of stereotype change for the nature of intergroup relations, it is important to develop a clear analysis of exactly what has and has not changed over time (and for whom). In addition, the present study allowed us to replicate Devine's (1989) stereotype assessment study and, more important, to directly test the proposition that high- and low-prejudiced respondents would report differential personal beliefs, despite their possessing equivalent knowledge of the stereotype.

Method

Respondents and Design

Respondents were 147 White University of Wisconsin–Madison undergraduates who received extra credit in their introductory psychology class in return for their participation. All respondents completed both the stereotype and the personal beliefs assessments. Half the respondents completed the stereotype assessment first and then the personal beliefs assessment, whereas the other half completed the tasks in the reverse order. Respondents were randomly assigned to one of the two orders. A nonreactive measure of anti-Black attitudes was administered at the end of the session, and respondents were assigned to a high-prejudice ($n = 74$) or a low-prejudice ($n = 73$) group based on a median split of the scores obtained in the sample.

Procedure

Respondents first read and signed a consent form stating that the purpose of the research was to understand people's knowledge of and reactions to various social groups and that in the present study, the focus was on Blacks. They were told that all their responses would be kept anonymous and that their participation was voluntary. After providing respondents with a booklet containing the materials and instructions, the experimenter left the room. The instructions asked respondents not to write their names or any other identifying information in the booklet. Respondents were informed that at the completion of the study, each respondent would

---

[2]We also conducted a pilot study in which we gave 50 respondents the Katz and Braly (1933) list of adjectives and very clear instructions to consider whether the list was adequate to capture the contemporary cultural stereotype of Blacks. Respondents were specifically instructed to think about the cultural stereotype and not their personal beliefs. They were further instructed to add any traits they thought would be necessary to capture the cultural stereotype. The types of traits added to the original list of traits overlapped almost completely with the traits frequently listed by respondents in Devine's (1989) free-response stereotype assessment task (e.g., athletic, poor, rhythmic, uneducated, criminal, low in intelligence).

place the booklet into an unmarked envelope that would be deposited in a drop box. This procedure was designed to assure respondents that responses could not be associated with any particular individual. Respondents then completed the stereotype and personal beliefs assessments (a full description is given below). Finally, an independent assessment of respondents' prejudice level was obtained. Upon completion of their booklet, respondents were debriefed, presented with an extra-credit card, and dismissed.

Measures

Stereotype assessment. The stereotype assessment instructions were designed to eliminate the ambiguity present in Katz and Braly's (1933) instructions (cf. Gilbert, 1951; Karlins et al., 1969) by explicitly stating that we were interested in respondents' knowledge of the cultural stereotype of Blacks. The instructions read as follows:

> On the back of this page you will find a list of adjectives and on the page next to that a series of blank lines. Please read through the list carefully and identify those adjectives that *make up the cultural stereotype of Blacks*. Note, these characteristics may or may not reflect your personal beliefs. So, select those adjectives that you know to be part of the cultural stereotype whether or not you believe the stereotype to be true. Please list them in the blanks. If you do not find all the necessary adjectives in the list (i.e., the list is incomplete), you may add any other information that you think is necessary to represent the *cultural stereotype*. Use as many or as few blanks as you need.

After respondents selected adjectives and turned the page, they read the following instruction:

> What we would like you to do now is to go back to the set of adjectives you selected and listed as making up the cultural stereotype. Please mark with a star the *five words* that seem to you to be the most typical of Blacks according to the cultural stereotype.

Personal beliefs assessment. The personal beliefs instructions were designed to make it clear that we were interested in respondents' personal beliefs about Blacks. Again, our concern was to be unambiguous about what we were asking respondents to report. The instructions read as follows:

> On the back of this page you will find a list of adjectives and on the page next to that a series of

blank lines. Please read through the list carefully and identify those adjectives that you *personally believe* characterize Blacks. Please list them in the blanks. If you do not find all the necessary adjectives (i.e., the list is incomplete), you may add any other information you think is necessary to represent your *personal beliefs* about Blacks. Use as many or as few blanks as you need.

After respondents completed the personal beliefs assessment, they were asked to go back to the list they had generated and mark with a star the five words that seemed most typical of Blacks according to their personal beliefs.

Adjective List. Respondents were presented with a list of 93 adjectives. This list included the 84 original Katz and Braly (1933) adjectives as well as 9 characteristics that were strongly suggested to be part of the cultural stereotype of Blacks in a free-response task (see Devine, 1989, Study 1). The characteristics added were athletic, criminal, hostile, low in intelligence, poor, rhythmic, sexually perverse, uneducated, and violent. The 93 characteristics were randomly ordered and presented on the page in three columns.

Prejudice Assessment. The 7-item version of the Modern Racism Scale (MRS) was employed to assess respondents' level of prejudice toward Blacks. This assessment device was designed to be a nonreactive measure of anti-Black attitudes and has been useful in predicting a variety of responses, including voting patterns (Sears & Kinder, 1971) and reactions to busing (Sears & McConahay, 1973). Previous research has attested to the reliability and validity of the scale (see McConahay, 1986), and the scale proved reliable in the present study (Cronbach's alpha = .85).

The MRS items were embedded in a series of other social and political questions, and respondents indicated their agreement with each of the items (e.g., "It is easy to understand the anger of Black people in America") on a 9-point scale that ranged from –4 (*Disagree strongly*) to +4 (*Agree strongly*). Although the possible range of total MRS scores was –28 (low prejudiced) to +28 (high prejudiced), the observed range of scores in the present sample was –28 to +9. It is common in college samples for the distribution of MRS scores to be positively skewed, and we have observed this pattern in University of Wisconsin samples during the last several years. However, despite the restriction in range in MRS scores, the scale has been sensitive to even subtle differences between those who score extreme in the low end of the continuum and those who score in the middle to high ranges of the scale (e.g., Zuwerink, Monteith, Devine, & Cook, 1996).

Results

Preliminary Analyses

Preliminary analyses tested for effects of the order of stereotype and personal beliefs assessments. No order effects were found in any of these analyses; thus all results reported below are collapsed across the order variable.

Knowledge of Cultural Stereotype

In comparing the content of the Black stereotype across the Princeton trilogy studies, researchers have commonly adopted the frequency of trait selections in the *five-starred-traits* task as their unit of analysis. Table 4.1 presents these data for the Princeton trilogy studies, the 1982 Dovidio and Gaertner investigation (cited in Dovidio &

TABLE 4.1. Frequency of Trait Selection (in Percentage of Respondents Who Selected the Trait) in the Five-Starred-Traits Task of the Present Study and Four Previous Studies

Trait	Katz and Braly (1933)	Gilbert (1951)	Karlins, Coffman, and Walters (1969)	The 1982 Dovidio and Gaertner Study (cited in Dovidio & Gaertner, 1986)	The Present Study
Superstitious	84	41	13	6	0
Lazy	75	31	26	12	45
Happy-go-lucky	38	17	27	15	3
Ignorant	38	17	11	10	14
Musical	26	33	47	29	11
Ostentatious	26	11	25	5	0
Very religious	24	17	8	23	11
Stupid	22	10	4	1	11
Physically dirty	17	–	3	0	9
Naive	14	–	4	4	0
Slovenly	13	–	5	2	0
Unreliable	12	–	6	2	6
Pleasure loving[a]	–	19	26	20	1
Sensitive[b]	–	–	17	13	0
Gregarious[b]	–	–	17	4	0
Talkative[b]	–	–	14	5	5
Imitative[b]	–	–	13	9	0
Aggressive[c]	–	–	–	19	5
Materialistic[c]	–	–	–	19	0
Loyal to family[c]	–	–	–	39	11
Arrogant[c]	–	–	–	14	3
Ambitious[c]	–	–	–	13	0
Tradition loving[c]	–	–	–	13	0
Athletic[d]	–	–	–	–	74
Rhythmic[d]	–	–	–	–	57
Low in intelligence[d]	–	–	–	–	46
Poor[d]	–	–	–	–	45
Criminal[d]	–	–	–	–	35
Hostile[d]	–	–	–	–	25
Loud	–	–	–	–	40

Note: The 10 most frequently selected traits in each study are in bold (9 or 11 traits are bolded in the case of incomplete information or ties). Unknown values, because of selective reporting in some of the studies, are indicated with a dash.
[a]Additional trait reported by Gilbert (1951).
[b]Traits needed by Karlins et al. (1969) to account for the 10 most frequent selections.
[c]Traits added by Dovidio and Gaertner in 1982 (Davidio & Gaertner, 1986).
[d]Traits needed to account for the 10 most frequent selections in the present study.

Gaertner, 1986), and the present study. In keeping with tradition (see Karlins et al., 1969), this table presents (a) the 12 traits most frequently selected in Katz and Braly's 1933 study, (b) the additional trait reported by Gilbert in 1951 (marked with a superscript "a"), (c) the traits needed by Karlins et al. in 1969 to account for the 10 most frequent selections (marked with a superscript "b"), (d) the traits added by Dovidio and Gaertner in 1982 (marked with a superscript "c"), and (d) the traits needed to account for the 10 most frequent selections in the present study (marked with a superscript "d"). Unknown values, because of selective reporting in some of the studies, are indicated with a dash. The 10 most frequently selected traits in each study are in bold (9 or 11 traits are bolded in the case of incomplete information or ties).

Perhaps the most striking feature of the data in Table 1 is the fact that 6 of the 10 most frequently selected adjectives in the present study were new additions to Katz and Braly's (1933) list. These 6 adjectives were added because they were found to be an integral part of the contemporary Black stereotype in a recent free-response assessment (Devine, 1989, Study 1). Katz and Braly's list was also based on then-recent free-response data; therefore, it is highly probable that their results accurately and somewhat comprehensively captured the then-contemporary stereotype of Blacks. In comparing the present data with those obtained by Katz and Braly,[3] it is clear that the content of the Black stereotype has indeed undergone revision over the years, and it is possible to delineate the precise nature of this content change. Subsequent Princeton trilogy studies (and the 1982 Dovidio and Gaertner study, cited in Dovidio & Gaertner, 1986) were not based on then-recent free-response data; these investigations merely employed the same list of 84 adjectives used in the initial Katz and Braly assessment. Therefore, although the data from these studies clearly demonstrated a change in stereotype content, the precise nature of this change remains an open question. That is, it is likely that traits representing the then-contemporary stereotype were not present on Katz and

Braly's list, forcing respondents to select from an incomplete offering of adjectives.

Stereotype consistency is commonly represented by a stereotype uniformity index, which is indicated by the smallest number of traits needed to account for 50% of the total number of trait selections. The stereotype uniformity indexes for the Princeton trilogy studies and for the present investigation are reported in Table 4.2. Although the second and third Princeton trilogy studies appear to support the proposition that the stereotype was becoming less consistent over the years, the present uniformity index is nearly exactly that obtained in the original Princeton trilogy study. In light of this new data point, it is possible to offer an alternative to the fading stereotype proposition. It may be that despite the change in stereotype *content* over the years, there has remained a coherent, consistent stereotype of Blacks. Providing respondents an outdated, inadequate list of adjectives in the second and third Princeton trilogy studies may have spuriously elevated the uniformity indexes, thereby ostensibly representing fading (decreased consistency). Specifically, faced with an incomplete set of adjectives from which to choose, respondents may have resorted to selecting synonyms or simply less adequate traits, resulting in a less reliable assessment and an increase in the uniformity index.

Favorability ratings (in standard deviation units) were obtained from Rothbart and Park's (1986) comprehensive summary of several characteristics of a large list of trait adjectives. Based on these ratings, favorability indexes were computed for each sample that reflected the average degree of favorability of the most frequently selected traits.[4] Table 4.2 displays the favorability indexes for the

---

[3]Despite the fact that the present sample, like Dovidio and Gaertner's (1986), was not drawn from Princeton University, we believe that students at the University of Wisconsin and Princeton University are similar enough in the attributes relevant to racial attitudes to warrant the comparisons offered in this section.

[4]Rothbart and Park (1986) did not report favorability ratings for several of the adjectives that were added to Katz and Braly's (1933) list in the present study (e.g., athletic, criminal, poor, rhythmic). To obtain favorability ratings for these traits, we repeated Rothbart and Park's procedure for assessing the favorability of traits for the new words and for a random subset of 20 of Katz and Braly's traits. A total of 25 respondents completed the favorability rating task. Our results for Katz and Braly's traits replicated Rothbart and Park's findings, in both the direction and the magnitude of the favorability scores. Moreover, the favorability ratings for the new words also appeared to be consistent with Rothbart and Park's findings in terms of both direction (e.g., athletic and rhythmic were positive, whereas poor and criminal were negative) and magnitude (e.g., criminal was rated as more negative than poor).

TABLE 4.2. Uniformity and Favorability Indexes for the Various Stereotype Assessment Studies

Study	Uniformity	Favorability
Katz and Braly (1933)	4.6	−.60
Gilbert (1951)	12.0	−.36
Karlins, Coffman, and Walters (1969)	12.3	+.02
The 1982 Dovidio and Gaertner study (cited in Dovidio & Gaertner, 1986)	NA	+.21
The present study	4.5	−.64

Note: NA = not available.

Princeton trilogy studies, the 1982 Dovidio and Gaertner investigation (cited in Dovidio & Gaertner, 1986), and the present study. These data appear to represent a peculiar pattern; it seems that the stereotype becomes progressively less negative over the years until the present study, at which time the favorability index reverts back to the negativity of the 1933 sample.

We believe this pattern is only peculiar if one assumes that the previous studies were measuring (as they purport) the Black stereotype. Although the ambiguity of instructions given to respondents precludes any definitive statements, if the previous stereotype assessment studies actually represent (primarily) the measurement of respondents personal beliefs about Blacks, the data are no longer peculiar. The present study, in this scenario, is the only one of the assessments under consideration that explicitly measured the Black stereotype, and the data from our study suggest the existence of a consistent and highly negative contemporary stereotype of Blacks. We now turn to the personal beliefs data to determine if these data are congruent with an interpretation of the previous studies as (primarily) personal beliefs assessments.

Personal Beliefs Assessment

Although none of our respondents refused to complete the stereotype assessment task, 21% (all but one of whom were low prejudiced) declined the request to fill out the personal beliefs task. Interestingly, both Gilbert (1951) and Karlins et al. (1969) also reported that a number of their respondents refused to complete the task presented to them. Respondents in our study who refused to complete the personal beliefs assessment gave reasons that were very similar to those expressed by

the respondents in the studies of Gilbert and Karlins et al. (e.g., "I don't think you can characterize a whole group of people with a list of traits–everyone is an individual") . This differential pattern of *refusniks* for the stereotype and personal beliefs assessments lends credence to our argument that the Princeton trilogy studies primarily assessed personal beliefs.

As with the stereotype assessment results, our initial consideration will be an examination of the frequency of traits chosen to represent respondents' personal beliefs and the consistency with which these traits were selected. As with the stereotype assessment, a substantial number of the most frequently selected traits (4 of 10) were new additions to Katz and Braly's (1933) list (e.g., athletic, rhythmic, poor). These data underscore the importance of providing respondents with an updated and comprehensive list when assessing their representations of social groups. Computation of a personal beliefs uniformity index further attests to the importance of a complete set of adjectives. The personal beliefs uniformity index was 4.6, suggesting that respondents' personal beliefs about Blacks were consistent in their organization.

Of central importance in determining whether the previous assessments measured stereotypes or personal beliefs is the personal beliefs favorability index. Computation of this index from Rothbart and Park's (1986) ratings yielded a value of +.22. Juxtaposing the present favorability index with those from previous studies (see Table 4.2) strongly suggests that the previous studies were primarily assessing personal beliefs, not stereotypes. Adopting this interpretation enables one to conclude that personal beliefs toward Blacks have progressively become more favorable over the years, to the point that they are, at present, predominately positive.[5] Therefore, it appears that the Princeton trilogy is relatively silent on the issue of stereotype fading but speaks clearly, and somewhat optimistically, to the issue of personal belief change.

High- Versus Low-Prejudiced Individuals

In addition to making interstudy comparisons, we also sought to examine the effects of respondents'

---

[5]The personal beliefs favorability index obtained in the present study is most likely a conservative value, given that ratings from the refusniks (who presumably possessed predominantly positive personal beliefs) could not be incorporated into the computation of the index.

prejudice level on their knowledge of and belief in the Black stereotype. The total number of traits selected by respondents was submitted to a mixed-model analysis of variance (ANOVA), with prejudice level (high vs. low) as the between-subjects variable and type of assessment (stereotype vs. personal beliefs) as the within-subjects variable. This analysis yielded a type of assessment main effect, $F(1, 112) = 26.69$, $p < .001$, indicating that respondents selected more traits during the stereotype ($M = 19.96$) than during the personal beliefs ($M = 15.29$) assessment.

Columns 2 and 3 of Table 4.3 display the traits most frequently selected by low- and high-prejudiced respondents to characterize the Black stereotype; columns 4 and 5 display the comparable frequency data for respondents' personal beliefs. The 10 most frequently selected traits within each column are in bold print (11 in the case of ties). For each trait in Table 4.3, the percentage of respondents selecting that trait was submitted to a Prejudice Level × Type of Assessment mixed-model ANOVA. As indicated in the table, 15 of the 24 interactions (which test the effect of central interest) were significant ($p < .05$), and another 4 attained a marginal level of significance ($p < .10$). Decomposition of the 19 significant and marginally significant interactions revealed that high-prejudiced respondents' personal beliefs significantly ($p < .05$) diverged from their knowledge of the stereotype for only 9 of the 19 traits, whereas the personal beliefs and knowledge of the stereotype for low-prejudiced respondents differed significantly ($p < .05$) for all 19 of the traits considered (see Table 4.3).[6] All of these effects were in the anticipated direction (i.e., the percentage for negatively valenced traits was greater in the stereotype than in the personal beliefs assessment and vice versa for positively valenced traits). A second set of comparisons probed for prejudice-level differences within assessment type. These analyses revealed no significant differences for the stereotype assessment, whereas all 19 prejudice-level comparisons for the personal beliefs assessment attained significance ($p < .05$). Again, all these effects were in the anticipated direction (i.e., low-prejudiced respondents reported a greater percent-

---

[6]Despite the large number of comparisons, we deemed corrections for alpha inflation unnecessary given the fact that we intended to amalgamate the set of comparisons to test (heuristically) a single hypothesis.

TABLE 4.3. The Most Frequently Selected Traits (in Percentage of Respondents Who Selected the Trait) for the Stereotype and Personal Beliefs Assessments as a Function of Prejudice Level

Trait	Stereotype Assessment		Beliefs Assessment	
	Low Prejudice	High Prejudice	Low Prejudice	High Prejudice
Lazy	78_{aA}	82_{aA}	6_{aB}	72_{bA}
Ignorant	74_{aA}	67_{aA}	2_{aB}	65_{bA}
Musical	60	56	57	58
Stupid	77_{aA}	66_{aA}	2_{aB}	25_{bB}
Unreliable	80_{aA}	59_{aA}	0_{aB}	10_{bB}
Loud	68_{aA}	64_{aA}	30_{aB}	71_{bA}
Aggressive	58_{aA}	59_{aA}	23_{aB}	57_{bA}
Athletic	85	90	80	90
Rhythmic	77	82	52	76
Low in intelligence	88_{aA}	82_{aA}	8_{aB}	56_{bB}
Poor	87_{aA}	80_{aA}	20_{aB}	72_{bA}
Criminal	78_{aA}	84_{aA}	0_{aB}	44_{bB}
Hostile	78_{aA}	71_{aA}	5_{aB}	75_{bA}
Uneducated	81_{aA}	80_{aA}	16_{aB}	43_{bB}
Sexually perverse	81_{aA}	80_{aA}	0_{aB}	12_{bB}
Rude	46_{aA}	55_{aA}	2_{aA}	71_{bA}
Sensitive	1	3	43	25
Loyal to family	42	33	39	46
Artistic	7_{aA}	3_{aA}	39_{aB}	9_{bA}
Honest	0_{aA}	1_{aA}	76_{aB}	4_{bA}
Intelligent	0_{aA}	1_{aA}	50_{aB}	8_{bB}
Kind	1_{aA}	6_{aA}	86_{aB}	13_{bB}
Sportsmanlike	12_{aA}	18_{aA}	39_{aB}	17_{bA}
Straightforward	3_{aA}	8_{aA}	60_{aB}	22_{bB}

Note: The 10 most frequently selected traits for each column are in bold. Two types of mean comparisons were conducted: tests for prejudice-level differences within each assessment type and tests for assessment type within each prejudice level. Within assessment type, percentages that significantly differed ($p < .05$) by prejudice level are indicated by different lowercase subscripts. Within prejudice level, percentages that significantly differed ($p < .05$) by assessment type are indicated by different uppercase subscripts. Comparisons were only conducted for trait percentages that yielded a significant ($p < .05$) or marginally significant ($p < .10$) Prejudice Level × Type of Assessment interaction.

age than high-prejudiced respondents for the positive traits and vice versa for the negative traits). Together, these comparisons clearly support Devine's (1989) hypothesis that high- and low-prejudiced individuals both possess the same stereotype of Blacks but that the stereotype is only endorsed by the former group of individuals.

Respondents' average favorability scores were analyzed in a Prejudice Level × Type of Assessment mixed-model ANOVA. This analysis yielded a main effect for prejudice level, $F(1, 112) = 50.90$, $p < .001$, indicating that across assessments, high-prejudiced respondents' trait selections were less favorable ($M = -.11$) than those for low-prejudiced respondents ($M = -.03$). A type of assessment main effect, $F(1, 112) = 228.16$, $p < .001$, was also obtained, such that respondents' overall trait selections were less favorable for the stereotype ($M = -.15$) than for the personal beliefs ($M = +.01$) assessment. Importantly, both of these main effects were qualified by a significant Prejudice Level x Type of Assessment interaction, $F(1, 112) = 58.18$, $p < .001$. The means clearly show that high- and low-prejudiced respondents did not select differentially valenced traits for the stereotype (both $Ms = -.15$), whereas the two prejudice levels diverged sharply on the personal beliefs assessment ($Ms = -.07$ and $+.09$ for high- and low-prejudiced respondents, respectively, $p < .001$). Analyses employing the number of negative and positive traits selected in the two assessments both yielded results identical to those for the average favorability scores (i.e., the same two main effects and interactions were significant) and highly comparable patterns of means.

Discussion

It is often argued that stereotype change is an important precursor to prejudice reduction and the amelioration of intergroup relations. As such, it is important to carefully evaluate the techniques used to assess the nature and extent of such change. Classic stereotype assessment studies were found to be lacking in several ways that encourage caution with regard to statements concerning stereotype stability or change. First, historically, stereotype assessment research has been guided more by methodological factors than theoretical and conceptual considerations (Ashmore & Del Boca, 1981). In the present study, we applied Devine's (1989) conceptual distinction between stereotypes and personal beliefs to the classic Princeton trilogy studies in the interest of reevaluating the oft-espoused claim that the Black stereotype is changing in content, consistency, and valence (Brehm & Kassin, 1990; Dovidio & Gaertner, 1986). Second, we addressed several methodological shortcomings of the classic adjective checklist procedure that prevented clear conclusions about

stereotype change. By disambiguating the instructions provided to respondents, attaining an independent assessment of prejudice, and presenting respondents with an up-to-date and comprehensive list of trait adjectives, we were able to obtain a precise snapshot of our respondents' representations of Black Americans as a social group. This picture leads us to the conclusion that the Black stereotype is not fading among Whites; rather, personal beliefs about Blacks are undergoing a revision.

Results from our stereotype assessment suggest that there is a clear, consistent contemporary stereotype of Blacks and that this stereotype is highly negative in nature. Our personal beliefs data, however, indicate that there is an equally consistent set of beliefs about Blacks that, in stark contrast to the contemporary stereotype, is positively valenced. The Princeton trilogy assessments did not distinguish between stereotypes and personal beliefs but merely asked respondents to select traits that seemed typical of Blacks. From the comments respondents provided Gilbert (1951) and Karlins et al. (1969), it is clear that some construed the task as a stereotype assessment, whereas others thought their personal beliefs were being assessed. This variability in task construal makes it difficult to make definitive statements about the Princeton trilogy data.

In spite of this interpretational obstacle, we believe that a comparison of the data pattern from the Princeton trilogy studies (and the 1982 Dovidio and Gaertner study, cited in Dovidio & Gaertner, 1986) to that obtained in the present investigation strongly suggests that the previous studies primarily assessed respondents' personal beliefs. The favorability ratings across the previous studies display a clear trend from highly negative scores in the 1933 sample ($-.60$) to a more positive value in Dovidio and Gaertner's sample ($+.21$). Interestingly, the favorability index for personal beliefs in the present study ($+.22$) fits nicely into the temporal trend observed in the previous investigations, whereas the favorability ratings for the stereotype ($-.64$) matches that of the initial Katz and Braly (1933) assessment. We believe these data indicate that respondents primarily reported their personal beliefs in the traditional Katz and Braly task, beliefs that were predominantly negative (and, presumably, highly congruent with the then-contemporary stereotype) in 1933 and progressively became more positive as a result of changes in the fabric of American society (see Dovidio & Gaertner, 1986; Schuman, Steeth, & Bobo, 1985, for reviews). This interpretation is bolstered by the fact that none of Katz and Braly's respondents refused to complete the task (as with our stereotype assessment), whereas a number of respondents refused to complete the task in the later Princeton trilogy studies (as with our personal beliefs assessment). Thus reevaluating the Princeton trilogy studies in light of the present investigation impels us to conclude that the classic stereotype assessment studies are not stereotype assessment studies at all; rather, these studies assessed personal beliefs, which may (in Katz & Braly, 1933) or may not (in all the subsequent studies) be congruent with the stereotype.

Our inclusion of an independent measure of prejudice, like our independent assessments of the stereotype and personal beliefs, enabled us to obtain a more precise understanding of respondents' representations of Black Americans. Both high- and low-prejudiced respondents apparently possess the same stereotypic knowledge in their associative network, as the two groups did not differ in their reports of the content or valence of the Black stereotype. In contrast, high- and low-prejudiced respondents diverged sharply in reports of their personal beliefs. High-prejudiced respondents endorsed beliefs that overlapped considerably with their knowledge of the Black stereotype, whereas the beliefs of low-prejudiced respondents were highly discrepant from their knowledge of the stereotype. These data provide strong support for Devine's (1989) proposition that high- and low-prejudiced individuals alike possess equivalent knowledge of the Black stereotype; it is in their endorsement of the stereotype that they diverge. Thus the present study not only replicates Devine's stereotype assessment findings but also provides the first direct evidence in support of the personal beliefs aspect of Devine's model. More important, assessing both the stereotype and personal beliefs in the same study enabled us to empirically validate the stereotype/personal-beliefs distinction in compelling fashion—by treating type of assessment as a within-subjects variable.

It is interesting to note that the low-prejudiced respondents in our sample may be divided into two types: those who agreed to complete the stereotype but not the personal beliefs assessment and those who agreed to complete both tasks. Those in the first group apparently perceived the very

process of ascribing traits to Blacks when reporting personal beliefs as an unacceptable activity and refused to engage in the task. Those in the second group agreed to complete the task but resorted to selecting positive, often counterstereotypic traits (e.g., intelligent, honest) to represent their personal beliefs. Thus, although they differed in strategy, both types of low-prejudiced respondents were unwilling to endorse negative stereotypic generalizations about Blacks.[7] High-prejudiced respondents, in contrast, reported personal beliefs that overlapped considerably with their knowledge of the stereotype.

Consideration of the stereotype/personal-beliefs distinction is essential in attempting to understand the social psychological experience of the low-prejudiced individual. The coexistence of a rejected yet enduring negative stereotype of Blacks and a positive set of beliefs about Blacks places the low-prejudiced social perceiver in a precarious position. A considerable amount of research indicates that stereotypes can be automatically activated by the perception of social stimuli (e.g., exemplars of the group, group labels), resulting in prejudice-like feelings, thoughts, and behaviors for high- and low-prejudiced individuals alike (Devine, 1989; Klinger & Beall, 1992). It is only when low-prejudiced individuals possess the time and cognitive capacity necessary to engage in controlled processing that they are able to inhibit the automatically activated stereotype and respond based on their personal beliefs (Devine, 1989; Klinger & Beall, 1992). Functional eradication of the stereotype from the low-prejudiced individual's associative network is possible (Monteith, 1993) but is likely to represent an arduous and prolonged task (Devine & Monteith, 1993). In the process of "breaking the prejudice habit," the low-prejudiced individual is susceptible to negative self-directed

---

[7]Although the refusal of a large portion of our low-prejudice respondents to complete the personal beliefs task would typically make comparisons involving prejudice level and/or the personal beliefs assessment tenuous, in the present study this attrition actually made for a more conservative set of analyses. Low-prejudiced respondents who agreed to complete the personal beliefs assessment primarily selected positive traits to characterize their personal beliefs about Blacks. It is almost certain that those who refused to complete the personal beliefs assessment would have adopted a comparable, and perhaps even more extreme, version of this strategy. Therefore, the absence of these respondents actually has the effect of minimizing the probability that we would find prejudice-level differences in our analyses.

affect (Devine, Monteith, Zuwerink, & Elliot, 1991) when their feelings, thoughts, or behaviors prove discrepant from their internalized personal beliefs or standards (Monteith, Devine, & Zuwerink, 1993).

Our critique of the stereotype assessment literature in the present study focused on Katz and Braly's (1933) technique because it has been the workhorse of stereotype measurement over the years. Many of the alternative stereotype assessment devices that have been developed possess the same weaknesses that we have identified in Katz and Braly's procedure, the most important being the failure to clearly distinguish between stereotypes and personal beliefs (e.g., Brigham, 1971; Gardner, Lalonde, Nero, & Young, 1988; McCauley & Stitt, 1978). Only those measures that assess stereotypic associations nonreactively (e.g., Dovidio et al., 1986; Gaertner & McLaughlin, 1983) appear to be beyond the scope of our critique. Despite their many positive qualities, however, nonreactive measures are somewhat limited in their use, as they cannot be employed to assess controlled processes such as personal beliefs (see Klinger & Beall, 1992).

Besides our own interpretation of the Princeton trilogy data, there is an additional explanation that deserves comment. Some have suggested that changes in the pattern of traits selected in assessment studies over the years simply reflect respondents' increasing sensitivity to nonprejudiced social norms rather than true stereotype or belief change (Crosby, Bromley, & Saxe, 1980; Dovidio & Gaertner, 1991; Sigall & Page, 1971). Clearly, this social desirability argument is not applicable to our stereotype assessment data, because these data revealed the existence of a contemporary stereotype that is highly consistent and negative in valence. High-prejudiced respondents' reports of their personal beliefs overlapped considerably with their knowledge of the stereotype; therefore, their pattern of trait selection cannot be attributable to social desirability concerns either. Thus a social desirability interpretation of the present data requires the assumption that low-prejudiced respondents—the only group that reported predominantly positive personal beliefs about Blacks—are more sensitive to social desirability demands than their high-prejudiced counterparts.

Although we cannot definitively rule out the possibility that our results for low-prejudiced respondents reflect social desirability demands, we think it is highly unlikely for the following three reasons. First, our procedure was carefully designed to minimize social desirability concerns; all respondents completed both the stereotype and the personal beliefs assessments under conditions that highlighted anonymity. Second, research by Monteith (1993) has demonstrated that behavior discrepant from the personal standards of low-prejudiced respondents creates negative self-directed affect and activates prejudice reduction processes in these individuals. Third, in related research, we have found that for those who report low-prejudiced attitudes toward Blacks, responding to Blacks in a nonprejudiced manner is a highly important, internalized aspect of their self-conceptions (Devine et al., 1991; Zuwerink et al., 1996). This research has further suggested that it is high-prejudiced, rather than low-prejudiced, respondents who are highly sensitive to social desirability cues (see Devine et al., 1991, Study 3).

Results from the present study validate our methodological critique of the traditional Katz and Braly (1933) procedure and provide a clearer picture of the complex nature of Whites' representations of Blacks. We recommend that researchers interested in employing this assessment procedure in future research (a) provide respondents with unambiguous instructions that indicate whether they should select traits based on their knowledge of the stereotype or based on their personal beliefs about the target group, (b) include an independent assessment of prejudice if respondents' personal beliefs about the target group are of interest, and (c) provide respondents with a list of adjectives that has the potential to comprehensively capture all aspects of the contemporary stereotype and/or set of beliefs about the target group (this requires that the adjective list be based on recent free-response data). Implementing these modifications in the present study yielded a data set that provided us with a clear picture of respondents' cognitive representations of Blacks. Therefore, in spite of our critique of Katz and Braly's procedure, we believe that it can, in modified form, be an effective tool in contemporary stereotype and prejudice research.

Our data suggest an apparent paradox between considerable belief change (at least among some respondents) and stereotype persistence. If stereotypes are ceasing to represent what people believe about a social group, why do they persist? A number of individual-level cognitive and sociocultural factors contribute to the persistence of stereotypes. First, it is important to recognize that individual-level changes in one's beliefs (i.e., renouncing prejudice and stereotypes) does not lead to the immediate elimination of stereotypes from memory (Devine, 1989; Higgins & King, 1981). Moreover, during the process of prejudice reduction, stereotype-based responses are highly accessible and serve as rivals to belief-based responses (Devine, 1989; Jamieson & Zanna, 1989; Kruglanski & Fruend, 1983). Thus change at the individual level is not all-or-none; overcoming stereotyped-based responding requires a great deal of personal motivation and effort (Devine, 1989; Monteith, 1993). An additional challenge to such efforts is suggested by recent evidence that efforts to suppress stereotypes may even heighten their accessibility (Macrae, Bodenhausen, Milne, & Jetten, 1994).

One of the main impediments to the fading of racial stereotypes is that they remain deeply embedded in the cultural fabric of our nation (Ehrlich, 1973; Jones, 1972). Despite a shift in social norms regarding overt expressions of prejudice and discrimination, stereotypic images of Blacks persist in the dominant media (e.g., television, newspapers), and Blacks continue to be underrepresented in traditional positions of power (e.g., education and industry; Schuman et al., 1985). As a result, stereotypes are perpetuated within the culture in subtle, yet highly effectual, ways. Although efforts such as affirmative action and increased sensitivity to media portrayals of Blacks may ultimately have positive effects and facilitate the fading of cultural racial stereotypes, it is likely that such changes will take place over a protracted period of time. We, optimistically, believe that change will eventually take place; our analysis of stereotypes simply leads us to the conclusion that this change, at both the macro (societal) and micro (individual) levels, takes time to unfold.

REFERENCES

Ashmore, R. D., & Del Boca, F. K. (1981). Conceptual approaches to stereotypes and stereotyping. In D. L. Hamilton (Ed.), *Cognitive processes in stereotyping and intergroup behavior* (pp. 1–35). Hillsdale, NJ: Erlbaum.

Brehm, S. S., & Kassin, S. M. (1990). *Social psychology.* Boston: Houghton Mifflin.

Brigham, J. C. (1971). Ethnic stereotypes. *Psychological Bulletin, 76,* 15–33.

Crosby, F., Bromley, S., & Saxe, L. (1980). Recent unobtrusive studies of Black and White discrimination and prejudice: A literature review. *Psychological Bulletin, 87,* 546–563.

Devine, P. G. (1989). Stereotypes and prejudice: Their automatic and controlled components. *Journal of Personality and Social Psychology, 60,* 5–18.

Devine, P. G., & Monteith, M. J. (1993). The role of discrepancy-associated affect in prejudice reduction. In D. M. Mackie & D. L. Hamilton (Eds.), *Affect, cognition, and stereotyping: Interactive processes in intergroup perception* (pp. 317–344). San Diego: Academic Press.

Devine, P. G., Monteith, M. J., Zuwerink, J. R., & Elliot, A. J. (1991). Prejudice with and without compunction. *Journal of Personality and Social Psychology, 60,* 817–830.

Dovidio, J. F., Evans, N. E., & Tyler, R. B. (1986). Racial stereotypes: The contents of their cognitive representations. *Journal of Experimental Social Psychology, 22,* 22–37.

Dovidio, J. F., & Gaertner, S. L. (1986). Prejudice, discrimination, and racism: Historical trends and contemporary approaches. In J. F. Dovidio & S. L. Gaertner (Eds.), *Prejudice, discrimination, and racism* (pp. 1–34). New York: Academic Press.

Dovidio, J. F., & Gaertner, S. L. (1991). Changes in the expression of racial prejudice. In H. Knopke, J. Norrell, & R. Rogers (Eds.), *Opening doors: An appraisal of race relations in contemporary America.* Tuscaloosa: University of Alabama Press.

Ehrlich, H. J. (1973). *The social psychology of prejudice.* New York: Wiley.

Gaertner, S. L., & McLaughlin, J. P. (1983). Racial stereotypes: Associations and ascriptions of positive and negative characteristics. *Social Psychology Quarterly, 46,* 23–30.

Gardner, R. C., Lalonde, R. N., Nero, A. M., & Young, M. Y. (1988). Ethnic stereotypes: Implications of measurement strategy. *Social Cognition, 6,* 40–60.

Gilbert, G. M. (1951). Stereotype persistence and change among college students. *Journal of Personality and Social Psychology, 46,* 245–254.

Higgins, E. T., & King, G. (1981). Accessibility of social constructs: Information processing consequences of individual and contextual variability. In N. Cantor & J. F. Kihlstrom (Eds.), *Personality and social interaction* (pp. 69–121). Hillsdale, NJ: Lawrence Erlbaum.

Jamieson, D. W., & Zanna, M. P. (1989). Need for structure in attitude formation and expression. In A. R. Pratkanis, S. J. Breckler, & A. G. Greenwald (Eds.), *Attitude structure and function* (pp. 383–406). Hillsdale, NJ: Lawrence Erlbaum.

Jones, J. M. (1972). *Prejudice and racism.* New York: Random House.

Karlins, M., Coffman, T. L., & Walters, G. (1969) . On the fading of social stereotypes: Studies in three generations of college students. *Journal of Personality and Social Psychology, 13,* 1–16.

Katz, D., & Bray, K. (1953). Racial stereotypes in one hundred college students. *Journal of Abnormal and Social Psychology, 28,* 280–290.

Klinger, M., & Beall, P. (1992, May). *Conscious ad unconscious effects of stereotype activation.* Paper presented at the 64th annual meeting of the Midwestern Psychological Association, Chicago.

Kruglanski, A. W., & Freund, T. (1983). The freezing and unfreezing of lay inferences: Effects of impressional primacy, ethnic stereotyping, and numerical anchoring. *Journal of Experimental Social Psychology, 19,* 448–468.

Macrae, C. N., Bodenhausen, C. V., Milne, A. B., & Jetten, J. (1994). Out of mind but back in sight: Stereotypes on the rebound. *Journal of Personality and Social Psychology, 67,* 808–817.

McCauley, C., & Stitt, C. (1978). An individual and quantitative measure of stereotypes. *Journal of Personality and Social Psychology, 36,* 929–940.

McConahay, J. G. (1986). Modern racism, ambivalence, and the Modern Racism Scale. In J. F. Dovidio & S. L. Gaertner (Eds.), *Prejudice, discrimination, and racism* (pp. 91–125). New York: Academic Press.

McConahay, J. G., Hardee, B. B., & Batts, V. (1981). Has racism declined? It depends on who's asking and what is asked. *Journal of Conflict Resolution, 25,* 563–579.

Monteith, M. J. (1993). Self-regulation of prejudiced responses: Implications for progress in prejudice reduction efforts. *Journal of Personality and Social Psychology, 65,* 469–485.

Monteith, M. J., Devine, P. G., & Zuwerink, J. R. (1993). Self-directed and other-directed affect as a consequence of prejudice-related discrepancies. *Journal of Personality and Social Psychology, 64,* 198–210.

Pratkanis, A. R. (1989). The cognitive representation of attitudes. In A. R. Pratkanis, S. J. Breckler, & A. G. Greenwald (Eds.), *Attitude structure and function* (pp. 71–98). Hillsdale, NJ: Erlbaum.

Rothbart, M., & Park, B. (1986). On the confirmability and disconfirmability of trait concepts. *Journal of Personality and Social Psychology, 50,* 131–141.

Schuman, H., Steeth, C., & Bobo, L. (1985). *Racial attitudes in America: Trends and interpretation.* Cambridge, MA: Harvard University Press.

Sears, D. O., & Kinder, D. R. (1971). Racial tensions and voting in Los Angeles. In W. Z. Hirsch (Ed.), *Los Angeles: Viability and prospects for metropolitan leadership* (pp. 51–88). New York: Praeger.

Sears, D. O., & McConahay, J. B. (1973). *The politics of violence: The new urban Blacks and the Watts riot.* Boston: Houghton Mifflin.

Sherman, S. J., & Gorkin, L. (1980). Attitude bolstering when behavior is inconsistent with central attitudes. *Journal of Experimental Social Psychology, 16,* 388–403.

Sigall, H., & Page, R. (1971). Current stereotypes: A little fading, a little faking. *Journal of Personality and Social Psychology, 18,* 247–255.

Zanna, M. P., & Rempel, J. K. (1988). Attitudes: A new look at an old concept. In D. Bar-Tal & A. W. Kruglanski (Eds.), *The social psychology of knowledge* (pp. 315–334). New York: Cambridge University Press.

Zuwerink, J. R., Monteith, M. J., Devine, P. G., & Cook, D. (1996). Prejudice toward Blacks: With or without compunction? *Basic and Applied Social Psychology, 18,* 131–150.

READING 5

Racial Ambivalence and American Value Conflict: Correlational and Priming Studies of Dual Cognitive Structures

Irwin Katz • City University of New York
R. Glen Hass • Brooklyn College

Whites' racial attitudes have become complex, with feelings of friendliness and rejection toward Black people often existing side by side. We believe these conflicting sentiments are rooted in two largely independent, core value orientations of American culture, humanitarianism–egalitarianism and the Protestant work ethic. We devised four scales, Pro-Black, Anti-Black, Protestant Ethic (PE), and Humanitarianism–Egalitarianism (HE). In Study I, the scales were given to White students at eight colleges. As predicted, significant positive correlations were usually found between pro-Black and HE scores and between Anti-Black and PE scores, whereas other correlations tended to be much lower. In Study 2, we used a priming technique with White students to test for causality. As predicted, priming a given value raised scores on the theoretically corresponding attitude but did not affect scores on the other attitude; priming a single attitude influenced scores on the corresponding value, but not on the other value. Implications are discussed.

The main finding from 40 years of survey research is that racial attitudes currently expressed by White Americans are far more liberal than the views they once held (Lipset & Schneider, 1978; Schuman, Steeh, & Bobo, 1985; T. W. Smith & Sheatsley, 1984). Public opinion has shifted from widespread acceptance of segregation and discrimination in the 1940s to a broad national consensus in support of racial equality and integration. The favorable temporal trends are more apparent for survey items that deal with civil rights principles than for items about concrete policies for implementing the principles. Nonetheless,

many important remedies have received popular support.

Some experts take the position that White people's opposition to policies such as mandatory school busing and use of job quotas is proof that their commitment to change in the status quo is superficial and conceals a fundamental prejudice against Blacks (see, e.g., Feagin, 1980; Hsu, 1972; Jackman, 1978; F. C. Jones, 1977; J. M. Jones, 1972). A similar perspective is implied in the theory of symbolic racism proposed by Sears and others (e.g., McConahay, 1986; Sears & Allen, 1984). However, Schuman et al. (1985) have pointed out that the mounting endorsement of integration principles and policies accords with observable changes in White people's public behavior toward Blacks and with the substantial progress in race relations that has taken place since World War II, so that even allowing for some faking of opinions on the part of respondents, it is reasonable to conclude that most White adults now have a genuine commitment to many civil rights goals.

On the other hand, one should not infer that discriminatory attitudes are rare. Support for residential integration, for example, tends to be ambiguous. Furthermore, anti-Black feelings have been revealed in social psychological experiments involving unobtrusive measures of intergroup affect and preference (reviewed by Crosby, Bromley, & Saxe, 1980). Although these studies have used relatively small samples (usually college students), the findings suggest that, at least at an unconscious level, some amount of racial bias is still commonplace.

Present Research Aims

Reasoning from evidence such as the foregoing, Katz and associates (cf I. Katz, 1981) have concluded that ambivalence is a pervasive feature of White America's racial attitudes. They have incorporated this notion in a theory used to predict Whites' extreme behavior, both favorable and unfavorable, toward Black individuals in certain types of interactions. Supposedly, if there are cues present that activate the conflicted attitude, the White actor will experience psychological tension and discomfort. Efforts at tension reduction may polarize reactions to members of the target group.

As yet, the assumption that the cross-racial polarization phenomenon is mediated by ambivalence has not been adequately tested. An important aim of this research was to facilitate this task by identifying and scaling connecting components of racial attitude that (a) are prevalent among White college students, (b) appear to be of some importance, and (c) are largely unrelated, so that an index of ambivalence could be derived from the component scores. These scales could then be used in future investigations of the relation between individual differences in one type of racial ambivalence and extremity of reactions to Blacks.

Previous studies using factor analysis have documented the multidimensionality of racial attitudes. Most notably, the authors of the Multifactor Racial Attitude Inventory (Brigham, Woodmansee, & Cook, 1976; Woodmansee & Cook, 1967) have devised 13 subscales that measure distinctive pro and anti dimensions. However, the subscales tend to be substantially intercorrelated (rs above .30). Our aim is to construct two countervailing scales with the empirical property of virtual independence.

Assumptions About Pro and Anti Attitudes

If Whites appear to have conflicted attitudes about Blacks, what might be the specific content of important pro and anti components that are only weakly or not at all related? Part of the answer, we believe, resides in the fact that Blacks, having a history of exclusion from the main society, are often perceived by the majority as both *deviant* in the sense of possessing certain disqualifying attributes of mind or body and *disadvantaged*, either by the attributes themselves or by the social and economic discrimination that having them entails. The dual perception of deviance and disadvantage likely generates in the observer conflicted feelings of aversion and sympathy. Accordingly, anti-Black attitudes would include beliefs about deviant characteristics and associated negative affect, and pro-Black attitudes would reflect sympathetic beliefs and feelings about the minority group as underdog.

Today, relatively few Whites openly express the old racist belief that Blacks are inherently inferior (cf T. W. Smith & Sheatsley, 1984). However, Blacks are often criticized for not doing enough to help themselves. In a survey conducted some years ago, Campbell (1971) observed that many of the same White respondents who felt there was job discrimination in their communities and favored enactment of laws to abolish it were ready to blame the economic woes of Blacks on their own "lack of ambition, laziness, and failure to take advantage of opportunities" (p. 14). More than half of the sample voiced this judgment. More recently, the National Opinion Research Center (NORC) reported 59 percent of a nationwide sample agreeing with the statement that Blacks are worse off economically than Whites because most of them just "don't have the motivation or will power to pull themselves out of poverty" (cited in Lipset, 1987, p. 5).

At the same time, however, Blacks apparently are often perceived sympathetically. After reviewing the research literature, Lipset and Schneider (1978) concluded that most Americans "view race as a categorical disability deserving of special aid. . . . Blacks should be helped because they have been down so long" (p. 41). Surveys conducted in the 1980s by NORC show substantial majorities expressing the view that Blacks continue to be held back by Whites, that further progress toward complete equality is necessary (*Public Opinion,* 1983; T. W. Smith & Sheatsley, 1984).

It seems, then, that Blacks are perceived as deserving help, yet as not doing enough to help themselves; and both attitudes may exist side by side within an individual. One is reminded of a conceptual distinction made by Brickman et al. (1982) between perceptions of responsibility for the origin of a problem involving deprivation or suffering (e.g., illness, addiction, poverty) and perceptions of responsibility for the solution of the problem. They noted that each type of responsibility can be assigned by observers either to the victims or to external factors beyond the control of victims, and that perceptions of causes and cures can be largely unrelated. The Brickman et al. perspective implies that having sympathy for Blacks as innocent targets of discrimination does not necessarily determine how one thinks about what Blacks can and should be doing to help themselves and how well they are doing it. Also relevant is Schuman's (1969) observation that a naive belief in free will, although rarely mentioned as such, seems to lead many Whites to blame Blacks for their disadvantages.

American Core Values

One can probably learn much about racial attitudes by studying their relation to the values that are held in common by members of the society. Our assumption is that values—conceived as generalized standards of the goals and goal-directed behaviors of human existence—are more central and fundamental components of a person's makeup than attitudes and, moreover are determinants of attitudes as well as behavior. This conception of values has been held by many theorists, including

Allport (1954), Lipset (1967), Parsons (1960), Rokeach (1973), and Williams (1979). Similarly, the functional approach to attitudes that was introduced by D. Katz (1968) and M. B. Smith, Bruner, and White (1956), and recently extended by Herek (1986), accords primary importance to the value-expressive function of attitudes.

A common theme in sociological descriptions of the American system is that there are two core value orientations: *individualism,* with its emphasis on personal freedom, self-reliance, devotion to work, and achievement; and *communalism,* which embraces egalitarian and humanitarian precepts (see, e.g., Hsu, 1972; Lipset, 1967; Williams, 1979). Drawing on historical, economic, political, and sociological sources, Williams (1979) described some 15 major American value themes, most of which clearly fall within the categories of individualism and communalism.

In our study, the focus with respect to the individualistic value orientation is on those components, embodied in the Protestant ethic (Weber, 1904–1905/1958), that emphasize devotion to work, individual achievement, and discipline. The Protestant ethic appears to be strongly implicated in people's judgments and feelings about some minority groups. Scores on the Mirels and Garrett (1971) Protestant Ethic Scale have been found to be related to conservatism and racial attitudes (Feather, 1984), attitudes toward the poor and public assistance programs (MacDonald, 1972), and reactions to equity norms in competition (Greenberg, 1978). Regarding our conception of communalism, we emphasize adherence to the democratic ideals of equality, social justice, and concern for the others' well-being. We refer to this orientation as *humanitarianism–egalitarianism.*

As to how the two value orientations are related as individual difference variables, we expect that they will prove to be largely independent of each other. This position is compatible with Kerlinger's (1984) finding that liberalism (made up largely of egalitarian and humanitarian attitudes) and conservatism (attitudes reflecting the Protestant ethic, and traditional beliefs about religion, authority, etc.) are essentially orthogonal dimensions.

Relations Between Values and Attitudes

Earlier we proposed that White people tend to regard Blacks as both deviant and disadvantaged.

We now suggest that the Protestant ethic outlook strengthens the perception of deviancy, whereas the humanitarian–egalitarian perspective strengthens the perception of disadvantage. Adherence to the Protestant ethic should sensitize the observer to behavior patterns that deviate from and thereby threaten its tenets. It is well known that Black rates of unemployment, welfare dependency, school failure, illegitimate births, and crime are higher than White rates. Given the element of Puritanism in the Protestant ethic, adherents should be inclined to attribute Blacks' problems to shortcomings of Blacks themselves—such as lack of drive and discipline—rather than to poor job opportunities and other external factors. On the other hand, people who have a humanitarian outlook should respond empathically to the needs and aspirations of Blacks, feel sympathy for them, and support public efforts to improve their lot. There should be a tendency to see the minority group in a favorable light, perhaps emphasizing the contributions it could make to the larger society if allowed. That is, the Protestant ethic outlook should be related to anti-Black attitude, and humanitarianism to pro-Black attitude. However, given our assumptions of low interdependence between the two value orientations and between the two types of attitude, associations should be relatively weak between the Protestant ethic variable and pro-Black attitude, and between humanitarianism and anti-Black attitude.

To summarize, we propose a theoretical model consisting of dual cognitive (i.e., value–attitude) structures. In the present research, we undertook to measure individual differences in the respective value orientations and attitudes, and then to investigate their linkages using both correlational and experimental methods.

Study 1

Method

CONSTRUCTION OF PRO-BLACK AND ANTI-BLACK SCALES

We made up 60 sentence stubs for the purpose of eliciting impressions concerning Black people in various domains such as work, education, family roles, and civil rights. A sample of 84 White college students in the New York City area completed the items. Content analysis of the responses revealed a number of themes that were favorable or unfavorable to Blacks. From this material we generated 40 statements, half intended to be pro-Black and consistent with the humanitarian–egalitarian outlook, and the other half anti-Black with a Protestant ethic flavor. We used a 6-point response format (*strongly agree* to *strongly disagree*, with no neutral point), and scored from 0 to 5. We administered the randomly ordered items to several samples of White college students in the New York City area, with ns ranging from 50 to 80. After each testing, we performed an item analysis, using two criteria of acceptability: An item had to show a significant correlation with the total score on other items of the same type, and a low or zero correlation with total score on items of the opposite type. Items that did not meet these criteria were either discarded or rewritten.

Thus, in selecting items our purpose was not to tap all important areas of racial attitude or to cover a theoretically or empirically defined domain completely, but rather to focus on two widely held, conflicting sets of beliefs that turn up repeatedly in opinion surveys of the past 20 years, keeping in mind conceptual linkages with two value orientations, and seeking to build in dimensional orthogonality. This procedure yielded 10 pro-Black and 10 anti-Black statements, with two of each type being keyed in reverse. The revised questionnaire was administered to 115 White students at Brooklyn College. (See Appendix for the items.)

The Pearson correlations between scores on individual Anti-Black Scale items and on all other Anti-Black items ranged from .27 to .66, all significant beyond the .01 level.[1] Correlations between individual Anti-Black items and the total Pro-Black Scale ranged from −.14 to .03, all nonsignificant. Cronbach's coefficient alpha for the Anti-Black Scale was .80.

Correlations between individual Pro-Black items and all other Pro-Black items combined ranged from .41 to .57 (ps < .01), except for the two reversal items (Pro-Black Items 4 ad 5 in the Appendix), which were not clearly related to the scale as a whole. Because these two items had functioned adequately in prior tryouts, we decided to retain them until further data were available. Correlations between individual Pro-Black items and

---

[1]All p levels reported in this article are two-tailed.

the total Anti-Black Scale ranged from .03 to −.22. Cronbach's coefficient alpha for the Pro-Black Scale was .73.

Next, we performed a principal-components factor analysis with varimax rotation on the sample's responses to the 20 attitude items. A three-factor solution accounted for 45% of the total explained variance. (We tried other factor solutions, but they did not provide additional interpretable information.) Using a loading criterion of .35 or higher, we found that all Pro-Black items, except the reversal items (Pro-Black Items 4 and 5), loaded on only one factor (Factor 2). The two exceptions loaded only on Factor 3. The Anti-Black items all loaded only on Factor 1, except for Anti-Black Item 8, which also loaded (negatively) on Factor 3. Thus, the factor loadings were consistent with the item-total correlations in showing that, except for Pro-Black Items 4 and 5, which stood by themselves as a separate factor, Pro- and Anti-Black items constituted two essentially unrelated dimensions.[2] The independence of the two scales was further indicated by their low, nonsignificant correlation, $r(113) = .12$. (As regards Pro-Black Items 4 and 5, in subsequent testing of six out of seven other college samples, scores on both items were significantly related to Pro-Black scale scores, $p < .05$, but not to Anti-Black Scale scores.)

To assess the influence on the racial attitude scores of a tendency to give socially desirable responses, a sample of 59 White undergraduates at Brooklyn College were given the racial attitude questionnaire and also the Marlowe-Crowne Social Desirability Scale (SDS). For the SDS and the Pro-Black Scale, $r(57) = .11$, and for the SDS and the Anti-Black Scale, $r(57) = .10$. Thus, social desirability apparently did not influence subjects' responses to the racial attitude items.

Next, the Pro-Black and Anti-Black scales were administered along with parts of the Woodmansee and Cook (1967; Brigham et al., 1976) Multifactor Racial Attitude Inventory (MRAI) to 59 White students at Lehman College (in New York City). Because of changes in Black–White relations over the past 20 years, many of the MRAI items seem less appropriate now for assessing racial attitudes than they were when constructed in the mid-1960s. However, two of the subscales, Derogatory Beliefs and Ease in Interracial Contacts, appear to be relevant for evaluating the construct validity of our scales.[3]

We expected the Anti-Black Scale and the Derogatory Beliefs subscale of the MRAI to correlate highly. Although some of the Anti-Black items refer to economic behavior, the scale as a whole reflects the broader view that Blacks lack the inner resources—such as self-respect, discipline, and concern for one another—needed to improve their lot. By comparison, the Derogatory Beliefs subscale depicts Blacks as deficient in self-control, pushy, hypersensitive to racial slights, and inclined to blame Whites for their problems. Thus, the two measures seem to tap a common set of beliefs that Blacks are unready to meet the moral responsibilities that go with full equality.

In addition, we expected to find a strong relation between the Pro-Black Scale and the MRAI's Ease in Interracial Contacts subscale, which is concerned with willingness to associate publicly with individual Blacks and to accept them in close relationships such as friendship and marriage. Our assumption was that the Pro-Black Scale measures not only egalitarianism on civil rights issues, but also empathic sympathy and liking for the minority group underdog, sentiments in accord with the social acceptance round in the Ease in Interracial Contacts subscale. Furthermore, if Pro-Black and Ease are similar measures, we should expect to see little if any relation between Anti-Black and Ease, inasmuch as we conceptualize the Pro-Black and Anti-Black scales as being only weakly related, if at all.

As predicted for Anti-Black and Derogatory Beliefs, $r(57) = .64$, $p < .001$, and for Anti-Black and Ease, $r(57) = -.02$ (ns). These correlations provide evidence of both convergent and discriminant validity for the Anti-Black Scale. Also as expected, for Pro-Black and Ease, $r(57) = .55$, $p < .001$, indicating convergent validity for the Pro-Black Scale.

Turning to the correlation to be expected between Pro-Black and Derogatory Beliefs, we note first that in the latter subscale there is, in addition to moral criticism, a tendency to minimize the extent to which Black people are still discriminated against. For example, one item reads, "The problem of racial prejudice has been greatly ex-

---

[2]A factor analysis with oblique rotation (three-factor solution) gave similar results. The factor intercorrelations were all close to zero.

[3]Schuman and Harding's (1963) measure of sympathetic identification with the minority underdog was also considered somewhat out-dated and therefore not used for validation.

aggerated by a few Black agitators." By contrast, the persistence of racism is a major theme in the Pro-Black Scale. Because Derogatory Beliefs contains the two elements, the obtained $r(57) = -.49$ between Pro-Black and Derogatory Beliefs is ambiguous as regards the convergent or discriminant validity of the Pro-Black Scale. In all, there are five Derogatory Beliefs items that explicitly minimize or defend the persistence of discrimination, stating that Blacks sometimes see discrimination where it does not exist, are too touchy and impatient about getting their rights, and should be more willing to accept exclusion. When these items were dropped from the 10-item scale the correlation between Pro-Black and the remaining Derogatory Beliefs items was nonsignificant ($r = -.18$). However, the correlation between Anti-Black and the shortened Derogatory Beliefs subscale remained virtually unchanged ($r = .63$). Thus, the new analysis supports the discriminant validity of the Pro-Black Scale without weakening the evidence of Anti-Black validity.

We then compared the racial attitude scores of Black and White students. Table 5.1 shows the results at Brooklyn College ($n = 115$ for Whites and 69 for Blacks) and at four other northern campuses: Carnegie-Mellon University, Iowa State University, Providence College, and Manhattanville College (located near New York City). We combined the latter four samples because of the small number of Black subjects (total $n = 484$ for Whites and 63 for Blacks). As expected, all four racial comparisons resulted in significant differences. Both at Brooklyn College and at the other northern colleges, Black students had higher Pro-Black scores than White students, and lower Anti-Black scores.

We also compared White regional samples, because it is known that southern Whites are less supportive of equality than nonsouthern whites (cf. Schuman et al., 1985). We compared attitude scores of White students at three southern state universities—Delaware, Georgia, and Texas A&M (total $n = 166$)—with those of students from the five northern institutions previously mentioned (total $n = 617$).[4] Pro-Black scores of the southern sample ($M = 27.01$) were significantly lower than

Table 5.1. Comparison of Racial Attitudes Scores of Black and White Subjects

Measure	White	Black	Difference	t	p
	Subjects				
	Brooklyn College				
Pro-Black Scale					
M	27.42	36.88	9.46	9.32	.001
SD	8.38	5.91			
Anti-Black Scale					
M	27.72	21.00	-6.72	5.74	.001
SD	8.59	7.50			
	Four other northern colleges				
Pro-Black Scale					
M	29.34	36.60	7.26	9.25	.001
SD	6.71	5.74			
Anti-Black Scale					
M	23.39	20.60	-2.79	2.70	.01
SD	7.40	7.61			

Note. For Brooklyn College, $n = 115$ for Whites and 69 for Blacks; at four other northern colleges, $n = 484$ for Whites and 63 for Blacks. The names of the other northern colleges and the *ns* for their respective White samples can be found in Table 5.2. The *ns* for Blacks at these institutions ranged from 12 to 20. Items were scored from 0 to 5, with 5 always representing high pro-Black or high anti-Black.

those of the northern sample ($M = 29.34$); $t(781) = 3.88, p < .001$.

However the two sample means for the Anti-Black Scale were not significantly different from one another ($Ms = 24.48$ in the South and 23.76 in the North). One possibility is that the beliefs tapped by the Anti-Black Scale are indeed similar in both regions, with the usual North–South differences in racial attitudes being confined to the kinds of favorable sentiments that are reflected in the Pro-Black items. However, one should note that the samples were not systematically selected to be representative of the two regions.

CONSTRUCTION OF VALUE SCALES

To measure the Protestant ethic value orientation we used 11 items from the 19-item Mirels and Garrett (1971) Protestant Ethic Scale. The short version had a correlation of .93 with the full scale (and an alpha coefficient of .76) in a sample of 59 students at Lehman College. Data supporting the validity of the Protestant Ethic Sale have been reported by Mirels and Garrett (1971), Feather (1984), and other investigators. In addition, we

---

[4]The U.S. Census lists Delaware as a southern state, and this designation is used by three major opinion survey originations: NORC, Gallup, and the Institute of Social Research at the University of Michigan.

obtained a nonsignificant correlation of .14 between the short version and the SDS in a sample of 50 undergraduates at Brooklyn College. (The 11 Protestant Ethic Scale items are presented in the Appendix.)

Next we generated 20 statements whose endorsement could be considered consistent with a humanitarian–egalitarian value outlook. Using a Likert 6-point response format, we administered the items to 75 students at Mercy College (located near New York City) and retained the 10 items showing the highest correlations with the total test. Coefficient alpha for the 10 items was .83. We combined these items in random order with the 11 items of the Protestant Ethic (PE) Scale, and administered them together with Rubin and Peplau's (1975) Just World Scale to another sample of Mercy College students ($n = 83$).

Discriminant validity for the Humanitarianism–Egalitarianism (HE) Scale would require that HE scores be largely independent of scores on both the PE and Just World scales. That is, to be conceptually distinctive, the humanitarian–egalitarian perspective would have to be more than just an inverse expression of the need to believe that people deserve their misfortunes (Just World), or that poverty and failure give proof of laziness and moral inadequacy (PE). Similarly, PE should not be closely related to Just World. As expected, the correlations were low: for HE and PE, $r(81) = .09$, ns; for HE and Just World, $r(81) = .16$, ns and for PE and Just World, $r(48) = .24$, $p < .10$. Also, HE scores were unrelated to score on the SDS, $r(39) = .13$, in a sample of Brooklyn College undergraduates.

Subsequent administrations of the value scales revealed some instability in correlations of four HE items with the PE Scale, which seemed attributable to ambiguous wording. These items were revised, and the new version of the value questionnaire was presented to 67 students at Manhattanville College. (The HE items are presented in the Appendix.) With one exception, all item–test correlations for the revised HE Scale were above .50. The alpha coefficients were .84 for the revised HE Scale and .70 for the PE Scale, indicating that both instruments had adequate internal consistency.

The value questionnaire was administered to additional samples, one of which—at Carnegie-Mellon University—was large enough ($n = 167$) for a factor analysis. We carried out a principal-

PRINCIPLE - Components factor analysis?

components factor analysis, using a four-factor solution with varimax rotation. It accounted for 46% of the total explained variance. (We tried other factor solutions, but they did not provide additional interpretable information.) With a cutoff value of .35 to determine loadings, 9 out of 10 HE items loaded on Factor 1, Factor 3, or both. HE items loading on Factor 1 seem primarily to advocate kindly concern for others, whereas HE items loading on Factor 3 generally invoke egalitarian principle. All PE items, but no HE items, loaded on Factors 2 or 4. Factor 2 items seem mainly to involve moral rejection of pleasure and the easy life, whereas Factor 4 items extol the work motive and emphasize its role in success. Three PE items loaded (negatively) on Factor 3; none loaded on Factor 1.[5]

✗ combine the two

PROCEDURE FOR TESTING RELATIONS

To assess value–attitude relations, the racial attitude and value questionnaires were administered to a total of 783 White undergraduates at eight campuses. In each sample, half the subjects received the value items first and the other half received the attitude items first. We found only a few scattered order effects, and these did not show any discernible pattern either within samples or across samples. Therefore, we disregarded order in analyzing the data.

Results

We predicted that relations between scales would be consistent with the notion of two largely independent cognitive structures, each having one value component and one attitude component. In Table 5.2 we present the relevant data. It is apparent that correlations from the three southern samples provided no consistent support for the model. In contrast, the northern campus correlations were mostly in line with the theoretical predictions. In all six northern samples, correlations between HE and Pro-Black scores and between PE and Anti-Black scores were significant, with most rs at or above .40. Cross-over correlations, on the other hand,

---

[5] A factor analysis with oblique rotation (four-factor solution) provided similar results, but with no overlap at all in the loadings of PE and HE items. Factor intercorrelations are close to zero, except for a correlation of .37 between the two factors on which PE items loaded.

generally were low and nonsignificant, with all but 2 of the 24 being below .30.

The bottom row in Table 5.2 consists of the pooled within-cell correlations for all samples to which the scales were administered. (Because pooling of correlations involving the HE Scale made use of data from the revised HE Scale only, the samples used for the pooled HE correlations were Carnegie-Mellon, Manhattanville, and Brooklyn 2.) It can be seen that the pooled correlations fit the theoretical model reasonably well (see Figure 5.1). The one exception is the correlation of −.28 between HE and Anti-Black scores, which is somewhat higher than expected. In accordance with the model, this correlation is significantly lower than the $r = .46$ for HE versus Pro-Black, $t(547) = 2.09$, $p < .03$. However, contrary to prediction the HE versus Anti-Black correlation is not significantly lower than the correlation of .40 between PE and Anti-Black.

Discussion

Study 1's results were consistent with our theoretical model of value–attitude relations, except for the southern data, suggesting that the theoretical model may be less appropriate in the South than in the North. (The deviation of the southern data from the model is discussed later in this article.)

Although there appears to be some content overlap between the value and attitude items, there is also a substantial amount of independence. The value items are statements about general moral precepts, preferred end states of life, and preferred instrumentalities, whereas the attitude items refer mainly to beliefs and judgments about a particular group. The obtained correlations with two MRAI subscales indicate that attitudes are more than mere extensions of the two value orientations into the domain of race. As yet, there exists no convergent or predictive validation for the HE Scale. However, extensive research on the PE Scale finds little if any evidence that it directly implies beliefs about Blacks' self-respect, community cohesion, family strength, or even parental attitudes toward education (Anti-Black Items 1, 2, 4, 7, and 9). In previous studies (e.g., Feather, 1984; Mirels & Garrett, 1971), PE scores seem to be related to referents such as respect for authority, obedience, and antiimagination, but hardly at all to our attitude referents when race is not involved.

In the next study we set out to demonstrate by using a priming technique that the theoretically predicted relations are causal in nature. We designed the experiment to test the notions that an induced increase in the cognitive availability of a single value orientation or attitude will tend to produce an increased endorsement of the corre-

Table 5.2. Intercorrelations of Attitude and Value Scales for Colleges and Total Sample

School	n	Pro–Anti	Pro–HE	Pro–PE	Anti–HE	Anti–PE	He–PE
North							
Iowa State University	173	−.17	.27**	−.23**	−.19	.48**	.01
Providence College	77	.01	.44**	−.28**	−.06	.23*	−.06
Brooklyn College 1	74	−.14	.33**	.10	−.16	.34**	.08
Brooklyn College 2	—[a]	−.09	.52**	.02	−.31*	.57**	−.12
Carnegie-Mellon University	167	−.27**	.48***	−.11	−.36**	.36**	.04
Manhattanville College	67	.13	.40**	−.05	−.09	.42**	.17
South							
University of Delaware	29	−.43*	.40*	−.45*	−.29	.33	−.43*
University of Georgia	87	−.27**	.17	−.24*	−.17	.37**	−.02
Texas A&M	50	−.07	.30*	−.32*	.00	.40**	−.05
Total sample[b]	—[c]	−.16**	.46**	−.14**	−.28**	.40**	.05

Note. Pro = Pro-Black scale, Anti = Ant-Black scale, HE= Humanitarian–Egalitarian Scale, PE = Protestant Ethic Scale

[a] For the Brooklyn College 2 sample, $n = 59$ for Pro–Anti and 41 for all correlations.
[b] These are pooled within group correlations, adjusting for differences in sample means.
[c] Pooled correlations involving HE are based on data from the revised HE scale only (administered to Carnegie-Mellon University, Manhattanville, and Brooklyn College 2 samples), hence $n = 783$ or 765 for pooled correlations not involving HE, and 275 for the HE correlations.
* $p < .05$. ** $p < .01$ (Tests were two-tailed.)

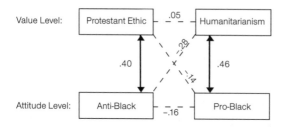

Value Level:

Attitude Level:

FIGURE 5.1. ■ Pooled product–moment correlations between value and attitude scores.

sponding attitude or value, but not of the theoretically unrelated value or attitude.

Study 2

That making one set of cognitions salient can arouse other, mentally related concepts has been shown in recent work in cognition and social cognition, and in the study of context effects in attitude surveys. Current theories of cognition hold that concepts are held in memory in an associative network consisting of clusters of related material. At any given moment each concept in the network has a certain level of activation, and when that activation exceeds a threshold the concept enters consciousness. The two major determinants of the level of activation of a category (its availability or accessibility) are the recency and frequency of its being accessed from memory (Tversky & Kahneman, 1974). Furthermore, the activation process spreads through the associative network so that a concept's activation level is raised by the processing of a related concept (Glass & Holyoak, 1986). For example, Meyer and Schvaneveldt (1976) have demonstrated that response time to a test word is faster when that word is immediately preceded in the test list by a closely related word than it is when the test word is preceded by an unrelated word. This priming process is presumed to operate because knowledge is organized, and activating a concept in one part of that organized structure is presumed to facilitate retrieval of other related concepts.

Researchers interested in the social consequences of cognition have found that increasing the momentary accessibility of information may often influence subsequent social judgments (e.g., Higgins, Rholes, & Jones, 1977; Iyengar, Kinder, Peters, & Krosnick, 1984; Wyer, Bodenhausen, &

Gorman, 1985). Priming can also influence what details are remembered after exposure to a given situation (Pichert & Anderson, 1977; Trabasso, 1982). Dovidio, Evans, and Tyler (1986) demonstrated that priming can facilitate the retrieval of cognitions relevant to racial attitudes. They found that priming subjects with racial categories (White or Black) shortened response times to identify traits that are stereotypically attributed to these groups. It is as if once made accessible, the primed concept acts as a mental filter through which the later events are processed or recalled.

In general terms, beliefs, attitudes, and values facilitate the organization of material in memory. They improve the recall of cognitively relevant material, and they promote the creation of cognitively consistent inferences. Bradburn (1982) and Schuman and Presser (1981) have cited numerous examples of attitude surveys with counterbalanced designs in which early questions are shown to activate a mental context (similar to a prime in the terminology used here) and influence respondents' replies to later questions. As one of the processes underlying context effects, Schuman and Presser described an increase in the availability of responses that results from altering the respondent's mental set.

Rather than viewing the effects of question–ordering as a problem, we made use of them in the current experiment to investigate further the value–attitude connections found in Study 1. We hypothesized that if subjects were first given a single value scale (HE or PE) to fill out and afterwards administered the complete attitude questionnaire, the value scale would act as a prime so that their scores would be raised on the theoretically corresponding attitude scale (Pro- or Anti-Black), but not on the other attitude scale. We also hypothesized that if subjects first filled out a single attitude scale (Pro- or Anti-Black) and subsequently the complete value questionnaire, the attitude scale would act as a prime so that their scores would be raised on the theoretically corresponding value (HE or PE), but not on the other value.

Values have long been thought of as more basic or central than attitudes. In our conceptualization, we retain that notion by viewing values as important cognitive structures with associative connections to many attitudes. The difference between values and attitudes, then, is in terms of the relative number of interconnections with otherwise similar cognitive elements, with values surrounded by and connected to more attitudes than vice versa. Once a particular value–attitude connection is activated, however, there is no reason to expect it to operate any more rapidly or strongly in one direction than in the other. We therefore expected that the attitude prime would activate the relevant value no less than the value prime activated the relevant attitude. (Our cognitive model would lead us to speculate that a value prime would activate *more* attitudes than vice versa, but that is a matter for future research.)

Method

SUBJECTS

Subjects in the experiment were 122 White students (54 men and 68 women) in an introductory psychology course at Brooklyn College. They participated in order to satisfy part of a course requirement. (We excluded from the analysis 59 Black, Hispanic, and Asian students who participated.)

PROCEDURE

Subjects were run in groups of 2 to 9 people. They were seated at individual carrel desks that were widely separated from one another in order to minimize interaction between subjects and provide them with a sense of privacy while they completed the questionnaires. Subjects were assigned to conditions by the random distribution of questionnaire booklets. Because the instructions and procedure were identical for all conditions, more than one condition was run simultaneously during an experimental session. The experimenter was always blind as to the assignment of any given subject, as well as to the conditions being run during the session.

In all six experimental conditions, subjects first completed a questionnaire that acted as the priming manipulation. In the two value prime conditions, one group of subjects completed the HE Scale and another group filled out the PE Scale of the Social Values Questionnaire described in Study 1. In the two attitude prime conditions, subjects filled out either the Pro-Black or the Anti-Black scale of the Racial Attitudes Questionnaire, also described in Study 1. Subjects in the two control conditions completed a filler questionnaire with the same 6-point response format, called the *Survey of Personal Values*. It consisted of 12 innocuous attitude items designed to be unrelated to racial attitudes, humanitarianism, and the Protestant ethic (e.g., "The food we eat has a big effect on the state of our health").

On completion of the priming questionnaire, subjects in the two value prime conditions and half of the control subjects were given the complete Racial Attitudes Questionnaire. Those in the attitude prime conditions and the other half of the control group were given the complete Social Values Questionnaire. Afterwards, subjects were debriefed and then dismissed.

Results — Please explain!

Table 5.3 shows the effect of the Protestant ethic and humanitarianism primes on subjects' racial attitudes. We analyzed the results of this portion of the experiment by using a 2 × 3 mixed analysis of variance (ANOVA), with the three levels of the priming manipulation (humanitarianism, Protestant ethic, and control) as a between-subjects factor and the Pro-Black and Anti-Black scales as a within-subjects factor. The analysis produced a significant, although conceptually meaningless, main effect for the attitudes measure, $F(1, 56) = 4.89$, $p < .05$. This result simply means that subjects tended to agree more with the statements on the Pro-Black Scale than they did with statements on the Anti-Black Scale. Because we made no attempt to equate the strength of the statements when the two scales were constructed, it is difficult to interpret the meaning of this effect. Of more interest is the marginally significant interaction effect of the priming manipulation and the racial

Table 5.3. Effects of Value Scale Priming on Racial Attitudes Scores

Measured attitude	Priming condition		
	HE Scale (*n* = 19)	PE Scale (*n* = 20)	Control (*n* = 20)
Pro-Black			
M	36.79	32.25	33.10
SD	4.13	11.56	6.94
Anti-Black			
M	27.79	34.05	27.70
SD	8.54	7.83	11.05

Note. The higher the score, the more extreme the attitude. HE = Humanitarianism–Egalitarianism; PE = Protestant Ethic.

attitudes scales, $F(2, 56) = 2.80$, $p < .07$, which takes the form that we hypothesized. Subjects responded more favorably to the Pro-Black Scale when they were primed with the humanitarianism statements than when they were primed with PE statements or control items. However, the reverse effect occurred on responses to the Anti-Black Scale, where scores were higher with a PE prime than with an HE or a control prime. Consistent with these findings, a 2 × 2 ANOVA done on the four experimental conditions resulted in a significant interaction effect that supported the hypothesis, $F(1, 37) = 4.82$, $p < .05$.

Furthermore, direct comparison of the experimental conditions with the control conditions suggests that the primed value outlook caused an intensification of the corresponding racial attitude component without affecting the theoretically unrelated racial attitude. The PE prime intensified anti-Black attitude, $F(1, 56) = 4.71$, $p < .05$, whereas the HE prime did not, $F < 1$, ns. Although in the expected direction, the HE prime effect on Pro-Black scores was not significant, $F(1, 56) = 1.98$, $p > .10$. Pro-Black scores were not influenced by the PE prime, $F < 1$, ns.

The part of the experiment designed to test the effect of priming racial attitudes on PE and HE scores also produced hypothesis-confirming results (see Table 5.4). We analyzed the data using a 2 × 3 mixed ANOVA with three levels of the priming manipulation (pro-Black statements, anti-Black statements, and control) as a between-subjects variable and the two value scales as a within-subjects factor. Again the analysis produced a conceptually unimportant main effect between the

value scales, $F(1, 60) = 29.96$, $p < .01$, indicating that subjects had higher scores on HE than on PE.

The relevant finding was the significant interaction, as predicted, between the priming manipulation and the value scale responses, $F(2, 60) = 7.22$, $p < .01$. As Table 5.4 shows, this interaction supported the hypothesized relation. Subjects were more willing to express humanitarian values when primed with pro-Black statements than when primed with anti-Black statements or control items. The reverse effect was found on the responses to the PE Scale, in which scores were higher for subjects who had been exposed to anti-Black statements than for those who had been exposed to pro-Black statements or control items. Also consistent with the hypothesis, a 2 × 2 ANOVA done on the four experimental conditions resulted in a significant interaction effect, $F(1,40) = 11.03$, $p < .01$.

Direct comparison of the experimental and control conditions suggests that the primed racial attitude caused increased agreement with the theoretically corresponding value items without affecting responses to the theoretically unrelated value items. That is, the pro-Black prime strengthened endorsement of HE items, $F(1, 60) = 6.86$, $p < .02$, whereas the anti-Black prime did not, $F < 1$, ns. Similarly, the anti-Black prime increased PE scores, $F(1, 60) = 4.06$, $p < .05$, whereas the pro-Black prime did not, $F < 1$, ns.

To examine our priming hypotheses further, we compared subjects who scored above and below the median on the priming scale. If making the topic of the priming questionnaire salient activates and increases endorsement of the related cognitive dimension, the effect should be stronger for those subjects who are more in agreement with the primed attitude or value. For example, strong agreement with the items on the HE Scale when it was used as the prime should lead to greater endorsement of the Pro-Black Scale items. Weak agreement with the humanitarianism prime should dampen the effect, although it should not eliminate it. Because of the unipolarity of the scales (discussed later in this article), subjects both above and below the median should be affected by the priming manipulation, although the strength of the effect should be greater for those subjects above the median.

We divided the subjects in each of the four experimental conditions into two groups based on whether their scores were above or below the median on the priming questionnaire. We found that

Table 5.4. Effects of Racial Attitude Scale Priming on Value Scores

	Priming condition		
Measured value	Pro-Black Scale (n = 22)	Anti-Black Scale (n = 20)	Control (n = 21)
Humanitarianism			
M	43.00	39.20	37.81
SD	6.45	5.72	7.19
Protestant ethic			
M	33.00	38.05	32.76
SD	10.53	7.50	6.50

Note. The higher the score, the more extreme the value.

in every instance the hypothesized effect of the priming manipulation was stronger for those subjects whose scores were above the median on the prime than for those whose scores were below the median. Differences that were significant when comparing scores of subjects above the median on the prime became nonsignificant when we analyzed data from subjects who scored below the median. (Cell means are presented in Table 5.5.)

More specifically, subjects whose responses to the humanitarianism prime were above the median became significantly more favorable than control subjects on the Pro-Black Scale items, $F(1, 36) = 5.06$, $p < .04$, whereas subjects who scored below the median did not differ significantly from the control subjects, $F < 1$. Similarly, subjects who were above the median on the PE priming questionnaire endorsed the Anti-Black Scale items significantly more than control subjects, $F(1, 37) = 8.19$, $p < .01$, whereas subjects who scored below the median did not, $F < 1$.

When we used the racial attitudes scales as the priming manipulation, we obtained corresponding results. Subjects who were above the median on the pro-Black prime became significantly more willing to endorse items on the HE Scale than did control subjects, $F(1, 40) = 5.15$, $p < .05$. Subjects below the median on the pro-Black prime also tended to increase their endorsement of HE items when compared with control subjects, but the difference was not significant, $F(1, 40) = 3.15$, $p < .09$. Finally, subjects whose responses to the anti-Black prime were above the median had higher PE scores than did control subjects, $F(1, 38) = 6.89$, $p < .02$, whereas subjects below the median did not, $F(1, 38) = 1.74$, ns.

Of course, some portion of the results of the median shift analysis is probably due to the correlations between the scales (e.g., someone who has a high score on the HE Scale is likely to be more pro-Black than the norm to begin with). Although the current research design does not permit an unambiguous removal of the effect of the interscale correlations from the median split analysis, it is clear that the results cannot be fully accounted for by the correlations. This fact is made most evident by the results for the subjects whose scores on the priming questionnaire were *below* the median. If the results were primarily due to the correlations between the scales, scores for subjects who were below the median on the prime should have been *lower* than those of control subjects. However, as Table 5.5 shows, the means for the below-the-median subjects were consistently *higher* than those for the corresponding control subjects (although the levels did not achieve customary levels of significance). Although these results are suggestive, more methodologically satisfying separation of the effects of the prime on subjects above and below the median from the effects of the scale correlations would require additional research.

To summarize then, in every comparison groups above the median on the prime became significantly more favorable toward the hypothesized value or racial attitude than control group subjects, whereas subjects below the median on the priming questionnaire consistently differed (nonsignificantly) in the same direction as the above-the-median subjects. Finally, in no case was there a significant effect of a priming manipulation on any theoretically unrelated value or racial attitude either for subjects above the median or for sub-

Table 5.5. Median Split Comparison of the Effect of the Priming Manipulation

	Priming manipulation				
	Humanitarianism			Protestant ethic	
Measure	Above median	Below median	Control	Above median	Below median
Attitude					
Pro-Black	38.10	35.33	33.10	32.18	32.33
Anti-Black	25.90	29.89	27.70	37.64	29.67
n	10	9	20	11	9
	Pro-Black		Control	Anti-Black	
Value					
Humanitarianism	43.63	42.36	37.81	39.20	39.20
Protestant ethic	32.64	33.36	32.76	39.80	36.30
n	11	11	21	10	10

jects below the median on their respective priming questionnaire, all $Fs < 1$.

Discussion

It appears that the correlations observed in Study 1 between the HE and Pro-Black scales and between the PE and Anti-Black scales do indeed reflect systematic linkages between value and attitude components within two distinct cognitive structures. The results of Study 2 seem rather striking when one considers the weakness of the priming manipulation, which consisted merely of having subjects fill out a brief questionnaire on the concept being primed. Presumably, a manipulation that more strongly advocated the primed concept might have had a greater effect.[6]

However, because the results of priming experiments are often open to alternative explanations based on demand characteristics, we should consider the viability of a demand interpretation of Study 2. Because the priming manipulation consisted of filling out a questionnaire, it may have evoked various motivations when subjects filled out the dependent measure questionnaire.

We believe demand explanations are untenable, because of the several patterns of results that one might argue demand characteristics could produce, none corresponds to the complete pattern of results obtained. One possibility is that the particular racial attitude or value outlook measured by the priming questionnaire might have suggested to subjects that certain responses on the later questionnaire were more "correct" or desired by the experimenter. Because the items on the scales used to measure the effect of the priming manipulation were always mixed, and were not obviously distinguishable as items on separate scales, such a motivation on the part of subjects should have led to greater agreement with items on one scale and greater *disagreement* with items on the other. For example, the HE Scale prime should have led both to stronger endorsement of Pro-Black items and to rejection of Anti-Black statements. The results, however, repeatedly showed an increase in agreement with the items on the scale theoretically connected to the prime and no effect on the other scale. Why the priming manipulation should produce an effect on the items of one of the scales that followed it but not on other items that common sense would say should be related is difficult to explain in terms of demand characteristics.

Another demand-characteristics explanation could be that the priming questionnaire put subjects in an "agree-mode" that affected their responses on the second questionnaire, because the wording of most of the items on the questionnaires was in the same direction. But of course an agree orientation should have produced an increase in the scores obtained on *both* of the scales contained in the second questionnaire, another pattern of results different from those obtained.

For either of the foregoing demand-characteristics explanations to account for the results obtained, subjects would spontaneously have had to become aware that the scrambled items on the second questionnaire were in two categories, accurately assigned the items to the two scales, and correctly identified one group of items as related to the priming questionnaire and the other group as unrelated to it. We consider this a very unlikely scenario, given the nonobviousness of the scale differences.

A further bit of evidence against the foregoing demand interpretations is provided by the median split analysis. That effects were stronger for subjects whose scores on the priming questionnaire were above the median than for those with scores below the median is not easily explained in terms of situational demands. Real or imagined situational pressure to give what might have seemed an experimentally desirable or socially correct response should have been the same regardless of subjects' scores on the priming questionnaire.

---

[6] We should comment on an important difference in the procedures used in Studies 1 and 2, and the effect of that difference on the results. In Study 1 subjects filled out, successively, the *complete* Racial Attitudes Questionnaire (Pro-Black and Anti-Black scales) and the *complete* Social Values Questionnaire (HE and PE scales). Because subjects were exposed to *both* parts of each questionnaire, and because on each questionnaire the items from the two scales were thoroughly mixed, we did not expect priming effects. The arousal of either of the cognitive domains (humanitarian–pro-Black, or Protestant ethic–anti-Black) should have been weakened or cancelled by the simultaneous arousal of the other. The absence of order effects in Study 1 confirms the absence of priming effects. In Study 2, on the other hand, the priming manipulation was designed to increase the cognitive salience of only one of the value–attitude pairs, without arousing the other pair. So, although subjects in both experiments filled out value and attitude questionnaires, differential priming effects were produced only in the second study.

We also believe that the full pattern of results cannot be explained in terms of a need to appear consistent. If, when subjects filled out the second questionnaire, they perceived a demand to appear consistent with their responses on the priming questionnaire, the demand should have been especially strong for those subjects who scored above the median on the prime. Hence, they should have given more extreme responses on the related postpriming scale, as we found. However, similar consistency effects should have been found on the other postpriming scale as well, because the scrambled items were not readily distinguishable. However, contrary to the consistency-demand explanation, subjects above the median on the prime did not show any priming effects on the theoretically unrelated scale. Furthermore, subjects filled out the questionnaires anonymously while seated at desks separated from one another, which should have reduced a need to appear consistent to others.

Another issue relating to the present results has to do with the direction of the priming effects. As we predicted, the priming manipulation consistently produced stronger endorsement of the attitude or value corresponding to the prime, rather than a polarization of responses to the scales. It is important to note that in other instances of priming one would expect the manipulation to produce polarization of responses on a subsequent issue. For example, priming subjects on a controversial topic such as abortion rights might polarize subjects' attitudes toward a political candidate: those favoring abortion rights becoming more favorable toward a candidate who advocates a similar position, and those who oppose abortion becoming more negative toward the candidate (Iyengar et al., 1984). In the present experiment, however, we did not predict polarized responses following the priming manipulation because we believe the dimensions underlying the scales to be unipolar in our society. Unipolarity should be especially likely for the Protestant ethic and humanitarian values. Both are prominent values that are generally endorsed and socially important. The racial attitudes scales were also conceptualized as largely unipolar. The reader will recall, for example, that being low on the Pro-Black Scale is neither conceptually nor empirically equivalent to being high on the Anti-Black Scale. Moreover, with the possible exception of the Anti-Black Scale (which produced a relatively symmetrical distribution), the responses to the scales were generally in line with our unipolarity assumptions. That is, most subjects indicated more agreement than disagreement with the concepts underlying the scales.

Finally, a question arises as to whether the results of the present experiment represent attitude and value *change* in the usual sense of the term. Because we did not measure subjects' attitudes and values again after a lapse of time or in another context, we cannot answer this question with certainty. However, we conjecture that the current results represent a temporary shift in emphasis based on the activation of a group of related cognitions, rather than enduring, internalized attitude change.

One emphasizes in an expression of attitude that part of one's cognitive structure that comes to mind easily, that which is momentarily most accessible. We suspect that if a different set of cognitions related to the attitude were made salient to the subject, the part of the attitude emphasized would shift in that direction. Building on Sherif and Hovland's (1961) concept of a latitude of acceptance, Hass (1981) has argued in favor of defining attitudes as cognitive ranges, rather than as points on a scale. Conceptualizing attitudes as ranges fits with current notions of attitudes as cognitive categories and schemata. An attitude is, of course, a complex cognitive structure comprised of many individual cognitions in association with one another. Those individual cognitions are in many cases also associated with other cognitions that are not considered part of the attitude. Priming an individual with a concept related to an attitude should make salient or accessible the portion of the attitude cognitively associated with the primed concept. As a result, the current point of emphasis will shift toward that part of the attitude most related to the prime. Such shifts are probably temporary, situationally specific, and in effect only so long as the prime is salient. However, it is possible (perhaps likely) that if such value–attitude associations are made frequently and in persuasive or socially reinforcing contexts that strengthen their cognitive integration, the shifts may become more enduring.

General Discussion

We have identified in White college students two contradictory, relatively independent dimensions

Reverse scaled Q's test if acquiescence bias is important influence on subjects

of attitudes toward Blacks, one friendly and the other hostile. We found these conflicting components to be causally linked with two discrete value orientations: a humanitarian–egalitarian outlook apparently creating commitment to racial justice and sympathy for Blacks as the underdog, and the Protestant ethic, with its emphasis on self-reliance and self-discipline, which seems to generate critical perceptions of Blacks. There undoubtedly are many other distinguishable components of racial attitude, including some that are positive. (The MRAI, for example, measures 13 such factors; Brigham et al., 1976; Woodmansee & Cook, 1967.) Also, there likely exist many other value–attitude linkages. However, our purpose has been to focus on a particular sector of this cognitive domain. Within this sector our correlational and experimental findings generally support the conception of two distinct value–attitude structures existing simultaneously within individuals.

Although the data generally conform to this pattern, there are some deviations that should be mentioned. Most notably, as Table 5.2 shows, the expected configuration does not show up consistently in the three southern subsamples. The data obtained from a very small group of University of Delaware students ($n = 29$) deviate sharply from the model. However, results for the larger Georgia and Texas subsamples are more in line with predictions, except for relations between the Pro-Black and the two value scales. We find these exceptions puzzling and can only speculate that because racial segregation in the South was historically more rigid and pervasive than in the North, the kind of beliefs tapped by the Pro-Black items may still strongly reflect traditional local norms or inequality. As a result, the tie to certain general values may be more tenuous than in the North. (Recall that Pro-Black scores in the southern sample are significantly lower than in the northern sample.) In general, the notion of a value–attitude duality may prove to be less descriptive of people in some regions, localities, and socioeconomic groups than in others.[7]

Of course, our interpretation of Studies 1 and 2 assumes that the scales adequately assess the relevant value and attitude constructs. We present data in Study 1 that support this assumption. All of the newly devised instruments are internally consistent and virtually free of social desirability response bias, as measured by the SDS. Also, responses to Pro-Black and Anti-Black items that are keyed in a reverse direction indicate that acquiescence bias is not an important influence on subjects' scores. Additional evidence in support of the construct validity of both attitude scales is provided by (a) correlations between the scales and two subscales of Woodmansee and Cook's MRAI, and (b) comparisons of the mean scores of White and Black samples.

The findings on validity are not conclusive, and do not entirely rule out the possibility that individual differences in candor are a major source of variation in the attitude scores. On the other hand, the fact that the attitude questionnaire was answered anonymously in a group setting suggests that if subjects did withhold their true feelings, their purpose was to enhance their personal self-image of fairness and kindliness toward Blacks as a disadvantaged group. Subjects should, however, have no need to defend such a self-image if they have not in some degree internalized the principle of racial justice.

Moreover, if concealment of one's true feelings is a strong motive behind the questionnaire responses, the effect should be even more apparent on the Anti-Black Scale than on the Pro-Black Scale, because the expression of racial antagonism is probably perceived as more self-revealing than failure to express sympathy. Yet the mean rating assigned to individual Anti-Black items in the northern sample is approximately midway between *agree* and *disagree*. Apparently these subjects are not suppressing critical beliefs about Black people to the extent of rejecting most of the Anti-Black items. Also, if defensiveness is a pervasive influence on responses, it should both elevate Pro-Black scores and depress Anti-Black scores, in which case individual differences in defensiveness would create an inverse correlation between the two. However, the obtained correlation in the northern sample is a low −.12. We conclude that at least in the northern sample, faking of responses is not a serious threat to the validity of the racial attitude scales.

We should also mention that several of our pro-

---

[7]Furthermore, in the absence of relevant empirical data we do not assume that the obtained relation between the Protestant Ethic and Anti-Black scales is generalizable to other racial or ethnic out-groups because there probably is considerable variation in the majority's beliefs about different groups. Some Asian populations in America, for example, are probably seen as positive rather than the negative exemplars of the Protestant ethic values.

and anti-Black items do not directly measure attitude in the usual sense, but instead try to get an attitude inferentially by assessing opinions regarding alleged facts about Black people, as well as other kinds of belief. Our assumption is that these cognitions are likely to have associated with them certain positive and negative affects, such as liking and sympathy or disdain and hostility. The validation data are encouraging in this regard. However, it remains to be determined by further research whether our putative attitudes "behave" like attitudes in the sense of predicting measurable affects and actions in concrete situations.

Another issue relating to the adequacy of the attitude scales has to do with the extent to which important areas of racial sentiment have been left out. On the face of it, two obvious omissions are fear of Black violence and aversion to close interracial contacts. Sears and Allen (1984) have suggested that many Whites acquire deep-rooted racial fears and animosities in their early years and never lose them. These feelings appear to be nurtured by the subjective association of Blacks with crime and social disorder, especially on the part of Whites who live near racial ghettos and feel threatened by their expanding boundaries. (See, for example, Ashmore & Del Boca, 1976; Rieder, 1987.) We are currently in the process of developing a scale to measure racial fear.

However, our present purpose is not to measure all the components of racial attitude, but rather to demonstrate the prevalence of a type of positive attitude and a type of negative attitude toward Blacks, each of which is rooted in a core American value outlook. Our thinking has been influenced by Rokeach's (1973) early experiments on the relation between the values of freedom and equality, on one hand, and civil rights attitude and behavior, on the other hand. Whereas Rokeach focuses on the linkage between beliefs in freedom and equality (particularly the latter) and favorable racial attitude, however, we are concerned with a duality in the general value–racial attitude relation. We do not maintain that all important components of racial attitude are value expressive. On the contrary, we accept Herek's (1986) neofunctionalist position, which calls attention to a range of other psychological functions served by attitudes. For example, Bobo (1983) has shown that an important function of racial prejudice is the protection of vested material interests.

We believe our scales may prove useful in studying the relation between one type of attitudinal conflict and behavior. Rokeach demonstrated that inducing self-awareness of value–attitude inconsistencies can lead to positive change in responses to minorities; and a few other investigators, such as Frey and Gaertner (1986) and McConahay (1986) have assumed that egalitarian beliefs may sometimes inhibit the expression of racial bias. Overall, however, there have been relatively few attempts at exploring this area more fully.

Elsewhere we have proposed a theory about the role of ambivalence as a motivation of extreme behavior toward minority group members (I. Katz, 1981; I. Katz, Wackenhut, & Hass, 1986). The new Pro-Black and Anti-Black scales can be used to investigate the behavioral effects of one kind of ambivalence by measuring the conflicting attitudes directly.

Beyond the conceptual issues we have discussed, there seem to be social implications to the present findings. We note first that the causal relation in the northern sample between totalitarianism and sympathy for Blacks as a deprived group suggests the usefulness of an educational strategy that strengthens the egalitarian outlook and spells out its relation to minority rights. In addition, the observed causal linkage between endorsement of the Protestant ethic and expression of certain negative sentiments about Blacks is intriguing because Protestant ethic values appear to be central in American culture, whereas unfavorable racial attitudes are no longer publicly sanctioned. If indeed some derogatory views about Black people are rooted in an important value outlook of the majority, this fact would help explain their enduring nature. Furthermore, it suggests that communicators who advocate commitment to self-reliance, self-discipline, and work may have the (perhaps unintended) effect of increasing the strength of an anti-Black attitude in their audience even if racial issues are not mentioned. To prevent this outcome, they should make clear in their messages that the use of Protestant ethic standards of evaluation is appropriate only when competitive opportunities and incentives are equal for all players. Finally the apparent independence of the pro-Black–humanitarian cognitive structure and the anti-Black–Protestant ethic structure in the North offers at least a partial explanation of the resistance of certain kinds of anti-Black sentiment to change based on appeals made exclusively to egalitarian motives. Such efforts may strengthen a person's pro-Black attitude without having any effect on his or her anti-Black feelings.

REFERENCES

Allport, G. W. (1954). *The nature of prejudice.* Reading MA: Addison-Wesley.

Ashmore, R. D., & Del Boca, F. K. (1976). Psychological approaches to understanding intergroup conflicts. In P. A. Katz (Ed.), *Towards the elimination of racism* (pp. 73–123). New York: Pergamon Press.

Bobo, L. D. (1983). Whites' opposition to busing: Symbolic racism or realistic group conflict? *Journal of Personality and Social Psychology, 45,* 1196–1210.

Bradburn, N. M. (1982). Question-wording effects in surveys. In R. M. Hogarth (Ed.), *Question framing and response consistency* (pp. 65–76). San Francisco: Jossey-Bass.

Brickman, P., Rabinowitz, V. C., Karuza, J., Jr., Coates, D., Cohen, E., & Kidder, L. (1982). Models of helping and coping. *American Psychologist, 37,* 368–384.

Brigham, J. C., Woodmansee, J. J., & Cook, S. W. (1976). Dimensions of verbal racial attitudes: Interracial marriage and approaches to racial equality. *Journal of Social Issues, 32,* 9–21.

Campbell, A. (1971). *White attitudes toward Black people.* Ann Arbor, MI: Institute for Social Research.

Crosby, F., Bromley, S., & Saxe, L. (1980). Recent unobtrusive studies of Black and White discrimination and prejudice: A literature review. *Psychological Bulletin, 87,* 546–563.

Dovidio, J. F., Evans, N., & Tyler, R. B. (1986). Racial stereotypes: The contents of their cognitive representations. *Journal of Experimental Social Psychology, 22,* 22–37.

Feagin, J. R. (1980). School desegregation: A political economic perspective. In W. S. Stephan & J. R. Feagin (Eds.), *School desegregation: Past, present and future* (pp. 25–50). New York: Plenum Press.

Feather, N. T. (1984). Protestant ethic, conservatism, and values. *Journal of Personality and Social Psychology, 46,* 1132–1141.

Frey, D. L., & Gaertner, S. L. (1986). Helping and the avoidance of inappropriate interracial behavior: A strategy that perpetuates a nonprejudiced self-image. *Journal of Personality and Social Psychology, 50,* 1083–1090.

Glass, A. L., & Holyoak, K. J. (1986). *Cognition* (2nd ed.). New York: Random House.

Greenberg, J. (1978). Equity, equality, and the Protestant ethic: Allocating rewards following fair and unfair competition. *Journal of Experimental Social Psychology, 14,* 217–226.

Hass, R. G. (1981). Presentational strategies and the social expression of attitudes: Impression management within limits. In J. Tedeschi (Ed.), *Impression management theory and social psychological research* (pp. 127–146). New York: Academic Press.

Herek, G. M. (1986). The instrumentality of attitudes: Toward a neo-functional theory. *Journal of Social Issues, 42,* 99–144.

Higgins, E. T., Rholes, W. S., & Jones, C. R. (1977). Category accessibility and impression formation. *Journal of Experimental Social Psychology, 13,* 141–154.

Hsu, F. L. K. (1972). American core values and national character in F. L. K. Hsu (Ed.), *Psychological anthropology* (pp. 241–262). Cambridge, MA: Schenkman.

Iyengar, S., Kinder, D. R., Peters, M. D., & Krosnick, J. A. (1984). The evening news and presidential evaluations. *Journal of Personality and Social Psychology 16,* 778–787.

Jackman, M. R. (1978). General and applied tolerance: Does education increase commitment to racial integration? *American Journal of Applied Science, 22,* 302–324.

Jones, F. C. (1977). *The changing mood in America: Eroding commitment?* Washington, DC: Howard University Press.

Jones, J. M. (1972). *Prejudice and racism.* Reading, MA: Addison-Wesley.

Katz, D. (1968). The functional approach to the study of attitudes. *Public Opinion Quarterly, 24,* 163–204.

Katz, I. (1981). *Stigma: A social psychological analysis.* Hillsdale, NJ: Erlbaum.

Katz, I., Wackenhut, J., & Hass, R. G. (1986). Racial ambivalence, value duality, and behavior. In J. F. Dovidio & S. L. Gaertner (Eds.), *Prejudice, discrimination, and racism* (pp. 35–60). New York: Academic Press.

Kerlinger, F. N. (1984). *Liberalism and conservatism: The nature and structure of social attitudes.* Hillsdale, NJ: Erlbaum.

Lipset, S. M. (1967). *The first new nation.* Garden City, NY: Doubleday.

Lipset, S. M. (1987). Blacks and Jews: How much bias? *Public Opinion, 10,* 4–5, 57–58.

Lipset, S. M., & Schneider, W. (1978). The Bakke case: How would it be decided at the bar of public opinion? *Public Opinion, 1,* 38–44.

MacDonald, A. P. (1972). More on the Protestant ethic. *Journal of Consulting and Clinical Psychology, 39,* 116–122.

McConahay, J. B. (1986). Modern racism, ambivalence, and the Modern Racism Scale. In J. E Dovidio & S. L. Gaertner (Eds.), *Prejudice, discrimination, and racism* (pp. 91–126). New York: Academic Press.

Meyer, D., & Schvaneveldt, R. (1976). Meaning, memory and mental processes. *Science, 192,* 27–33.

Mirels, H., & Garrett, J. (1971). The Protestant ethic as a personality variable. *Journal of Consulting and Clinical Psychology, 36,* 40–44.

Parsons, T. (1960). *Structure and process in modern societies.* New York: Free Press of Glencoe.

Pichert, J. W., & Anderson, R. C. (1977). Taking different perspectives on a story. *Journal of Educational Psychology, 69,* 309–315.

Public Opinion. (1983). Opinion roundup. *Public Opinion, 6,* 27.

Rieder, J. (1987). Inside Howard Beach. *The New Republic, 196,* 17–19.

Rokeach, M. (1973). *The nature of human values.* New York: Free Press.

Rubin, Z., & Peplau, L. A. (1975). Who believes in a just world? *Journal of Social Issues, 81,* 65–89.

Schuman, H. (1969). Free will and determination in public beliefs about race. *Trans-Action, 7,* 44–48.

Schuman, H., & Harding, J. (1963). Sympathetic identification with the underdog. *Public Opinion Quarterly, 27,* 230–241.

Schuman, H., & Presser, S. (1981). *Questions and answers in attitude surveys: Experiments on question form, wording, and content.* New York: Academic Press.

Schuman, H., Steeh, C., & Bobo, L. (1985). *Racial attitudes in America.* Cambridge, MA: Harvard University Press.

Sears, D. O., & Allen, H. M., Jr. (1984). The trajectory of

local desegregation controversies and Whites' opposition to busing. In M. Brewer & N. Miller (Eds.), Groups in contact: The psychology of desegregation (pp. 123–151). New York: Academic Press.

Sherif, M., & Hovland, C. I. (1961). *Social judgment: Assimilation and contrast effects in communication and attitude change*. New Haven: Yale University Press.

Smith, M. B., Bruner, J. S., & White, R. W. (1956). *Opinions and personality*. New York: Wiley.

Smith, T. W., & Sheatsley, P. S. (1984). American attitudes toward race relations. *Public Opinion, 7,* 14–15, 50–53.

Trabasso, T. (1982). The importance of context in understanding discourse. In R. M. Hogarth (Ed.), *Question framing and response consistency* (pp. 77–89). San Francisco: Jossey-Bass.

Tversky, A., & Kahneman, D. (1974). Judgment under uncertainty: Heuristics and biases. *Science, 185,* 1124–1131.

Weber, M. (1958). *The Protestant ethic and the spirit of capitalism* (T. Parsons, Trans.). New York: Scribner (Original work published 1904–1905)

Williams, R. M., Jr. (1979). Change and stability in values and value systems: A sociological perspective. In M. Rokeach (Ed.), *Understanding human values* (pp. 15–46). New York: Free Press.

Woodmansee, J., & Cook, S. W. (1967). Dimensions of verbal racial attitudes: Their identification and measurement. *Journal of Personality and Social Psychology, 48,* 324–338.

Wyer, R. S., Jr., Brodenhausen, G. V., & Gorman, T. F. (1985). Cognitive mediators of reactions to rape. *Journal of Personality and Social Psychology, 48,* 324–338.

Appendix

Attitude and Value Items

Pro-Black	Anti-Black
1. Black people do not have the same employment opportunities that Whites do.	1. The root cause of most of the social and economic ills of Blacks is the weakness and instability of the Black family.
2. It's surprising that Black people do as well as they do, considering all the obstacles they face.	2. Although there are exceptions, Black urban neighborhoods don't seem to have strong community organization or leadership.
3. Too many Blacks still lose out on jobs and promotions because of their skin color.	3. On the whole, Black people don't stress education and training.
4. Most big corporations in America are really interested in treating their Black and White employees equally.[a]	4. Many Black teenagers don't respect themselves or anyone else.
5. Most Blacks are no longer discriminated against.	5. Blacks don't seem to use opportunities to own and operate little shops and businesses.
6. Blacks have more to offer than they have been allowed to show.	6. Very few Black people are just looking for a free ride.[a]
7. The typical urban ghetto public school is not as good as it should be to provide equal opportunities for Blacks.	7. Black children would do better in school if their parents had better attitudes about learning.
8. This country would be better off if it were more willing to assimilate the good things in Black culture.	8. Blacks should take the jobs that are available and then work their way up to better jobs.
9. Sometimes Black job seekers should be given special consideration in hiring.	9. One of the biggest problems for a lot of Blacks is their lack of self-respect.
10. Many Whites show a real lack of understanding of the problems that Blacks face.	10. Most Blacks have the drive and determination to get ahead.[a]

Protestant Ethic	Humanitarianism–Egalitarianism
1. Most people spend too much time in unprofitable amusements.	1. One should be kind to all people.
2. Our society would have fewer problems if people had less leisure time.	2. One should find ways to help others less fortunate than oneself.
3. Money acquired easily is usually spent unwisely.	3. A person should be concerned about the well-being of others.
4. Most people who don't succeed in life are just plain lazy.	4. There should be equality for everyone—because we are all human beings.
5. Anyone who is willing and able to work hard has a good chance of succeeding.	5. Those who an unable to provide for their basic needs should be helped by others.
6. People who fail at a job have usually not tried hard enough.	6. A good society is one in which people feel responsible for one another.
7. Life would have very little meaning if we never had to suffer.	7. Everyone should have an equal chance and an equal say in most things.
8. The person who can approach an unpleasant task with enthusiasm is the person who gets ahead.	8. Acting to protect the rights and interests of other members of the community is a major obligation for all persons.
9. If people work hard enough they are likely to make a good life for themselves.	9. In dealing with criminals the courts should recognize that many are victims of circumstances.
10. I feel uneasy when there is little work for me to do.	10. Prosperous nations have a moral obligation to share some of their wealth with poor nations.
11. A distaste for hard work usually reflects a weakness of character.	

[a]Item scored in reverse.

Category and Stereotype Activation: Is Prejudice Inevitable?

Lorella Lepore and Rupert Brown • University of Kent at Canterbury

Three experiments tested the hypothesis that people high and low in prejudice respond similarly to direct stereotype activation but differently to category activation. Study 1 ($N = 40$) showed that high- and low-prejudice people share the same knowledge of the stereotype of Black people. In Study 2, ($N = 51$) high-prejudice participants formed a more negative and less positive impression of the target person after subliminal priming of the category Blacks than did participants in the no-prime condition. Low-prejudice people tended in the opposite direction. In Study 3 ($N = 45$), both high- and low-prejudice people increased negative ratings when valenced stereotype content was also primed. These findings support a distinction between automatic stereotype activation resulting from direct priming and that consequent upon category activation, implying that the relations among categorization, stereotyping, and prejudice are more flexible than it is often assumed.

A man and a woman, both obviously Italian to judge from their looks and language, are engaged in an apparently confidential conversation that culminates with the man passing the woman an envelope.

Is it romantic love or a mafia-related exchange? Both interpretations are stereotypic, and two hypothetical observers would probably *know* both aspects of the stereotype. However, would both stereotypic interpretations immediately spring to mind once the category *Italian* is activated? It seems unlikely. Rather, an observer with mainly positive beliefs about Italian people would readily think of a romantic gesture, such as a love letter, and one with mainly negative views would just as easily infer an illicit transaction. That is, different aspects of the stereotype would be activated in the two observers.

The present research was concerned with the relation between categorization and stereotyping. In particular, it investigated the automaticity of stereotype activation upon categorization and the role played by people's prejudice level in the occurrence and pattern of such activation.

The Inevitability of Prejudice Argument

A long tradition has conceived of stereotyping and prejudice as an automatic and inevitable consequence of categorization (Allport, 1954; Hamilton, 1981; Tajfel, 1969), which, in turn, has been regarded as an adaptive and functional process

(Brewer, 1988; Bruner, 1957; Fiske & Neuberg, 1990; Rosch, 1978). Specifically, people's' memberships in fundamental categories such as age, gender, and race seem to be attended to automatically (e.g., Brewer, 1988; Bruner, 1957; Fiske & Neuberg, 1990). The associated stereotypes become activated upon perception of the category and influence judgments and behaviors (Hamilton & Sherman, 1994; Hamilton, Sherman, & Ruvolo, 1990; Stangor & Ford, 1992; Stangor & Lange, 1994). Negative group stereotypes can be thought of as the cognitive component of prejudice (Brown, 1995). Thus, prejudice springs from normal cognitive processes and seems to be inevitable. As Billig (1985) summarized this view, "people will be prejudiced so long as they continue to think" (p. 81).

Automatic Stereotype Activation

It is generally assumed that stereotypes are automatically activated upon perception of a category member (e.g., Allport, 1954; Deaux & Lewis, 1984; Fiske & Neuberg, 1990; also see Hilton & von Hippel, 1996; Stangor & Lange, 1994). Often stereotypes are seen as networks of linked attributes variously conceptualized. The representation of the social group results from the associative links between discrete nodes (e.g., Carlston, 1992; Fiske, 1982; Stephan & Stephan, 1993). The traits become associated with the group node (category) through frequency and consistency of activation (e.g., Fazio, Sanbonmatsu, Powell, & Kardes, 1986; Higgins & King, 1981; Stephan & Stephan, 1993). When encountering a category member the group node is activated, and the excitation spreads from it to other connected nodes, the stereotypic characteristics. Are all characteristics *known* to be stereotypic automatically activated? Probably not, since within the representation some links may be stronger than others (Anderson, 1983; Collins & Loftus, 1975; Rumelhart, Hinton, & McClelland, 1986) if they are activated more often. The attributes corresponding to these links are the ones that will be activated automatically (e.g., Bargh, 1984; Posner & Snyder, 1975; Shiffrin & Schneider, 1977; Smith & Lerner, 1986; also see Stangor & Lange, 1994, for a discussion of the sources of associative strength). What links become stronger might vary systematically with a person variable such as prejudice level, as argued later.

The expression *automatic stereotype* activation has been applied to both the direct priming of stereotypic characteristics and the stereotypic responses resulting from priming the category (see Bargh, 1994; Greenwald & Banaji, 1995; von Hippel, Sekaquaptewa, & Vargas, 1995). To specify how stereotypes are elicited upon perception of a category member (or some other cue symbolic of the category), category and stereotype priming should be distinguished. The two modes of stereotype activation can also affect judgments differently. For example, Pratto and Bargh (1991) found that category and stereotype priming had distinct effects on impression formation. This is consistent with their model, in which categories are represented at a level distinct from the concrete attributes associated with them (Andersen & Klatzky, 1987). Neely (1977) and Fazio et al. (1986) proposed similar models in other domains. Ford, Stangor, and Duan (1994) also reported different effects for category and stereotype priming in impression formation, thus supporting the distinction between them.

Stereotype Priming

Automatic stereotype activation is not a consequence of categorization when stereotypic characteristics—with or without category labels—are primed directly. Rather, it is a cause of stereotypic judgments. For example, Banaji, Hardin, and Rothman (1993) found that the applicability (Higgins, 1996) of the primed stereotypic concept to the associated gender category increased ratings of the male targets as aggressive and female targets as dependent.

In a highly influential study, Devine (1989, Experiment 2) primed subconsciously both the category *Blacks* and the stereotype content. High- and low-prejudice people did not differ in their subsequent impression of a target person. This was rated more extremely on the hostility- (and stereotype-) related scales than on the hostility-unrelated scales. Although this study has been quoted widely as demonstrating that high- and low-prejudice people automatically activate the stereotype in the same negative way, it does not actually do so. In fact, both category labels and stereotypic attributes were present in the prime. Thus, whether the strength of association between the category and the traits varies with prejudice level remains an unanswered question. Devine's results sometimes have been explained as being attributable to semantic priming. Many primes had clear negative connotations (e.g., "lazy," "nigger," "welfare," "busing," "ghetto") that could have directly cued hostility (see Greenwald & Banaji, 1995; Hamilton & Sherman, 1994). The absence of differences between high- and low-prejudice people can have another explanation. As with all knowledge, stereotypes are *available* in memory and can be primed, thus becoming accessible *temporarily* (Bargh, 1994; Higgins, 1989). The recent activation of available knowledge results in the well documented assimilation effects on applicable constructs (e.g., Bargh & Pietromonaco, 1982; Erdley & D'Agostino, 1988; Higgins, Bargh, & Lombardi, 1985; Srull & Wyer, 1979, 1980). In Devine's (1989) study, the primed stereotype was applicable only to the hostility- (and stereotype-) related scales. Thus, the hostility ratings increased as an assimilation-type effect, which is likely to occur for all participants. It therefore cannot be inferred that high- and low-prejudice people would *spontaneously* activate the cultural stereotype in this way as an automatic response to a group member (or a symbolic equivalent).

Category Priming

Automatic stereotype activation is an effect of categorization when only the category is primed. Other research that has examined differences between high- and low-prejudice people in automatic processing typically has used category priming. This research makes the implicit assumption that the traits are differentially associated with the category in high- and low-prejudice people, but it presents an ambiguous picture as to how stereotype activation occurs. Gaertner and McLaughlin (1983) found no differences in the attribution of positive and negative traits to the category *Blacks*. The same stereotype activation was present for both high- and low-prejudice people. Locke, MacLeod, and Walker (1994) used a Stroop-like paradigm to activate the category *Aborigines*. Only high-prejudice people demonstrated greater interference in naming the stereotype-related words (compared with the unrelated words). Low-prejudice respondents were unaffected by word stereotypicality, suggesting less responsiveness to category activation. No effect attributable to valence of the words was found. Since our own work was conducted, Wittenbrink, Judd, and Park (1997)

reported two lexical decision studies in which ethnic category primes presented subliminally facilitated responses to "Black" negative and "White" positive stereotypic words. This effect was correlated with prejudice level. Thus, people higher in prejudice showed greater activation of positive in-group and negative out-group stereotypes. Fazio, Jackson, Dunton, and Williams (1995) observed that the automatic evaluation of the category *Blacks* varied from negative to positive, although not reliably with prejudice level.

Studies that have not involved prejudice level do not all show automatic stereotype activation upon categorization. Perdue and Gurtman (1990) and Perdue, Dovidio, Gurtman, and Tyler (1990) found that subliminal in-group primes facilitated responses on positive target words and out-group primes on negative words. However, *semantic* stereotype activation was not demonstrated directly in these studies because the target words were not stereotypical of the categories primed. Gilbert and Hixon (1991) showed that category activation may not result in stereotype activation. Participants under cognitive overload did not increase the number of stereotypic completions on a word fragment task when the assistant presenting the stimuli was Asian. However, they still categorized her correctly.

In summary, a model of automatic stereotype activation is still incomplete (see Bargh, 1994; Stangor & Lange, 1994). Stereotype activation resulting from categorization and its qualification by prejudice level need further investigation. The present studies sought to disentangle the effects of direct stereotype activation and category activation on an impression formation task. This is particularly important because Devine's (1989) study is the only one involving prejudice level directly related to person perception. Different patterns of stereotype activation may be possible for high- and low-prejudice people if category and stereotype priming are separated.

Social Group Representations

To challenge the view of prejudice as inevitable, Devine (1989) distinguished between stereotype knowledge and endorsement (Ashmore & Del Boca, 1981). In her model, differential stereotype endorsement affects only controlled (Neely, 1977; Posner & Snyder, 1975) processes. High- and low-prejudice respondents listed different thoughts about Black people (Devine, 1989, Experiment 3). In contrast, common stereotype knowledge should determine an absence of difference between high- and low-prejudice people in automatic responses. As discussed, Devine (1989, Experiment 2) did not really prove this point because both category and stereotypic content were present in the prime. However, the conceptual argument is considered here. Even though low-prejudice people do not endorse the stereotype, stereotype knowledge is thought to be activated automatically because of its longer history of activation than personal beliefs (Higgins & King, 1981). Thus, low-prejudice people's response to a stimulus evocative of a stereotyped group is nonprejudiced only if the automatic prejudiced reaction can be inhibited. This conclusion still implies that prejudice is inevitable, at least at an automatic level.

In Devine's (1989) model, the divergent stereotypic associations described in our opening vignette are impossible. Smith (1998) noted that Devine's (1989) theory of the automatic activation of stereotype knowledge presents a conceptual problem. In associational models of stereotypes, the links between the group node and associated characteristics usually represent the perceiver's beliefs that the group possesses those attributes (also see Hilton & von Hippel, 1996; Stangor & Lange, 1994). If low- and high-prejudice people's automatic responses are the same, the links (i.e., the beliefs and hence their representations) do not differ. Thus, it is not clear how low-prejudice people's rejection of the negative stereotype is represented cognitively in such a model.

Research has shown that high- and low-prejudice people have *available* to them the full range of stereotypic attributes culturally associated with a given out-group but *endorse* different beliefs about it (Augoustinos, Innes, & Ahrens, 1994; Devine, 1989; Devine & Elliot, 1995). In particular, high-prejudice people endorse more the negative and low-prejudice people the positive stereotypic features (Augoustinos et al., 1994, Experiment 2; Devine & Elliot, 1995). Thus, their evaluations of the group differ, possibly strengthening the links with negative traits for high-prejudice people and positive traits for the low-prejudice within the network (see the model by Stephan & Stephan, 1993). Augoustinos et al. (1994, Experiment 2) provided some evidence that stronger associative links may correspond to such different beliefs within the rep-

resentation. Low-prejudice people were not only more likely to endorse the positive descriptions of Aborigines, but also faster than high-prejudice individuals in doing so. High-prejudice participants endorsed the negative descriptions more and faster than low-prejudice respondents.

Thus, high- and low-prejudice people's representations of the social group may not necessarily differ in terms of *content* (at least for stereotype knowledge) but because stronger *links* may have developed for different characteristics. Some of the research reviewed earlier hints at differences in high- and low-prejudice people's representations of a social group due to associative strength (Locke et al., 1994; Wittenbrink et al., 1997).

As part of knowledge accepted as true (Devine, 1989), beliefs should be activated frequently to process incoming information. The stronger endorsed connections between the group and the frequently activated characteristics should be the ones activated automatically (Bargh, 1984; Higgins & King, 1981; Posner & Snyder, 1975; Stangor & Lange, 1994; Stephan & Stephan, 1993).

If low-prejudice people reject the negative stereotype and high-prejudice people endorse it, the category-negative attribute linkages should be stronger for high-prejudice people. Thus, only high-prejudice people should show automatic activation of the negative stereotypic components. Because low-prejudice people endorse the positive stereotypic features (Augoustinos et al., 1994; Devine & Elliot, 1995), they could traverse their category-positive attributes linkages more frequently, resulting in activation of the positive stereotypic components. This does not exclude another possibility. Because stereotypes of the out-group are mainly negative (e.g., Dovidio, Evans, & Tyler, 1986), low-prejudice people's rejection of the stereotype could mean that all their category–trait pathways are weaker. This would result in less stereotype activation altogether, as some empirical data suggest (Locke et al., 1994).

Overview and General Hypothesis

Our overall aim was to demonstrate that the links among categorization, stereotyping, and prejudice can be somewhat flexible. Accordingly, we hypothesized that if an out-group label or some symbolic equivalent are primed, the resultant stereotype activation and social judgments should diverge, being more negative for the high- and either less evidently stereotypic or more positive for the low-prejudice people. On the other hand, when some valenced stereotype content is primed directly, we predicted similar effects in both groups.

Study 1 assessed whether high- and low-prejudice people have the same knowledge of the cultural stereotype of an ethnic minority. In Study 2, the differential effects of *category* activation on high- and low-prejudice people were tested. Study 3 examined the effects of *stereotype* activation in a conceptual replication of Devine's (1989) priming experiment.

Study 1: Stereotype Knowledge

To attribute differences between high- and low-prejudice people to differential endorsement of stereotypic features, one first has to show that knowledge of the cultural stereotype is common to all. Devine (1989, Experiment 1) and later Augoustinos et al. (1994, Experiment 1) asked participants to list the content of a cultural stereotype. Devine's data on the stereotype of Black people in the United States resulted in 15 categories, of which only 2 were positive characteristics. The proportions of high- and low-prejudice participants listing each category did not differ. The data of Augoustinos et al. on the stereotype of Aborigines in Australia resulted in 19 categories, of which only 2 positive characteristics. The findings were mostly consistent with Devine's, and only 3 of the coding categories were mentioned in different proportions by high- and low-prejudice people. Results of the two studies suggest that knowledge of such cultural stereotypes often is shared widely and does not depend on prejudice level. A subsequent study by Devine and Elliot (1995), using a modification of Katz and Braly's (1933) technique, confirmed these findings.

Consistent with these previous studies, we used a free-response task to ascertain the nature of the cultural stereotype of Black people in the United Kingdom and to explore possible differences between high- and low-prejudice people. Incidentally, we also present a new measure of prejudice suitable for use in a British context. Commonly used prejudice scales (e.g., the Modern Racism Scale of McConahay, Hardee, & Batts, 1981) contain items that are not appropriate in non-American samples.

A New Measure of Prejudice

A new prejudice scale was developed from existing modern and subtle racism measures (e.g., Jacobson, 1985; McConahay et al., 1981; Pettigrew & Meertens, 1995), modified considerably to be suitable for the British context. It is presented in the Appendix. Because the scale consists of 15 items and the responses range from 1 (*strongly disagree*) to 7 (*strongly agree*), the scale range is 15–105, with a midpoint of 60. A high score indicates greater tolerance (i.e., a lower prejudice level).

Extensive pretesting for optimal item selection ensured that the scale had good internal reliability and construct validity. The observed reliabilities in each of the three studies are presented later. Here, we briefly report the results from an independent sample of White British students ($N = 162$) who completed this measure and five other related scales under development for use in the United Kingdom (i.e., old-fashioned racism, aversive racism, national identification, threat to national identity, contact with ethnic minorities). Factor analysis of the prejudice measure revealed that it had a two-factor structure and that, with oblique rotation, these two factors were substantially correlated ($r = .47$). Thus, combining all 15 items into a single scale seemed justified, a decision confirmed by the high internal reliability observed (Cronbach's $\alpha = .85$). The overall mean in this sample was 75.14 ($SD = 13.15$). As evidence for the scale's validity, we report substantial and theoretically meaningful correlations with each of the five other measures: old fashioned, $r = -.76$; aversive, $r = -.65$; identification, $r = -.52$; threat, $r = -.61$; and contact, $r = .41$. ($p < .001$ in each case). Such a pattern of correlations is completely consistent with that reported by other researchers working with similar scales in other cultural contexts (McConahay, 1986; Pettigrew & Meertens, 1995).

Method

Forty White British first-year psychology students took part in the study voluntarily and received course credit. In a class administration, the experimenter distributed the envelopes containing the booklets and orally gave the instructions for each task, instructions that also were repeated in the response booklets. All participants responded anonymously throughout. For the first task, participants were told that materials were needed to set up an experiment on stereotypes and were asked to list words and images evocative of West Indians that were often associated with this group. Participants were also told not to express their personal views but to list positive and negative things that would make most British people think of West Indians. Several blank lines followed in two columns: positive and negative. The second task was introduced as one designed to help researchers better understand stereotypes. Participants were asked to list the content of the cultural stereotype of West Indians. Again, they were told that the researchers were not interested in their personal views. Next, participants filled in the prejudice scale, on the basis of which they were later allocated to high- and low-prejudice groups through a median split.

Results and Discussion

Because both tasks required thinking about the same ethnic category, it seemed more appropriate to code what respondents had listed across tasks. If the same concept was mentioned in different ways, it was ultimately coded only once in that category.

After examining the protocols, the experimenter, unaware of participants' prejudice level, proposed the coding categories. These were explained to two independent judges (also unaware of participants' prejudice level), further discussed, modified, and finally agreed upon. The judges then coded each individual response. Multiple responses in one category were counted only once. One respondent declared that she did not know the stereotype, did not list anything, and was therefore excluded from the analyses.

According to Scott's (1955) agreement coefficient (which corrects for chance agreement), the interjudge reliability was high (.84). Participants were divided into high- ($n = 18$) and low-prejudice ($n = 21$) groups at the median of the prejudice scale (Cronbach's $\alpha = .92$; Ms and SDs for the high- and low-prejudice groups were 57.61 and 11.36 and 81.48 and 9.55, respectively).

Of the 24 categories, only 2 revealed any reliable differences between high- and low-prejudice people: miscellaneous negative, $\chi^2(1, N = 39) =$ 4.13, $p < .05$, and superstitious, $\chi^2(4, N = 39) =$ 3.80, $p < .05$. In both cases, these categories were mentioned more frequently by high- than by low-prejudice people (see Table 6.1).

For the purposes of Studies 2 and 3, it is also worth noting the most consensual features of the Black British stereotype. Apart from the 3 neutral descriptive categories (i.e., physical description, culture, and religion), the attributes more frequently mentioned by both high- and low-prejudice people were as follows: musical, criminal, violent, athletic, lazy, colorful, relaxed, fun loving, and poor. As demonstrated later, these attributes guided our choice of dependent measures in the subsequent experiments.

A 3 × 2 analysis of variance (ANOVA) was run on the totals of positive, negative, and neutral features listed by high- and low-prejudice participants. The only significant effect was a main effect for type of category, $F(2, 74) = 10.90, p < .001$. Both high- and low-prejudice participants listed more negative features than positive and more positive than neutral ($Ms = 4.1, 3.2,$ and 2.3, respectively).

Table 6.1. Proportion of High- and Low-Prejudice People Mentioning Each Coding Category

Category	High prejudice	Low prejudice
Musical	.83	.81
Athletic	.56	.48
Colorful	.44	.52
Fun loving	.33	.38
Loyal	.11	.19
Relaxed	.44	.33
Warm	.11	.19
Miscellaneous positive	.17	.29
Physical description	.72	.43
Culture	.78	.62
Religion	.39	.48
Miscellaneous neutral	.67	.52
Lazy	.39	.52
Violent	.61	.48
Criminal	.72	.76
Poor	.28	.43
Uneducated	.22	.14
Sexist	.17	.24
Rude	.39	.19
Unintegrated	.17	.38
Smelly	.17	.14
Persecuted	.28	.25
Superstitious*	.17	.00
Miscellaneous negative*	.56	.24

*Chi-square significant at $p < .05$.

Respondents did not differ in the mean total number of categories they mentioned.

The results of Study 1 are generally consistent with those obtained in previous studies, showing that the ethnic stereotype is more negative than positive overall and, more important, that high- and low-prejudice people substantially share the same knowledge of such stereotypes (Augoustinos et al., 1994; Devine, 1989; Devine & Elliot, 1995). These findings also indicate that ethnic stereotypes are as much a part of the British cultural fabric as they are in the United States and elsewhere.[1]

However, some findings in these data suggest that although overall knowledge of the stereotype is the same for high- and low-prejudice people, the representation of the group as such might not be. High-prejudice participants listed significantly more negative idiosyncratic features (miscellaneous negative), hinting at an overall more negative representation of the group. They also tended to mention more physical characteristics, such as skin color and shape of the nose or lips, suggesting an overall attention to perceptual differences between Black and White people that could be conducive to categorizing by ethnicity even when other categories are available (see Stangor, Linch, Duan, & Glass, 1992; see also Zarate & Smith, 1990). In summary, high- and low-prejudice people's representations of the group were substantially equivalent in terms of *content*. However, there were indications that the representations may differ in terms of the *linkages* among those contents. This issue was the main focus of Study 2.

Study 2: Differences in Automatic Responses to Category Activation

If knowledge of the cultural stereotype of Black people is available to the same extent for high- and low-prejudice people, how easily is that knowledge, or part of it, activated? As discussed earlier, endorsement could lead to differential strength of association between stereotypic characteristics and group node in high- and low-prejudice people through frequency of activation. Thus, different stereotypic traits should be automatically activated in these two groups upon perception of a category member (or its symbolic equivalent), resulting in divergent stereotypic judgments.

If it can be shown that high- and low-prejudice people differ in their automatic responses to cat-

egory activation, this would suggest that they hold different representations because of their beliefs and despite their common stereotype knowledge.

A parafoveal subliminal priming procedure similar to that used by Bargh and Pietromonaco (1982) and Devine (1989) was employed to reveal the effects of preconscious automaticity, a kind that requires only a triggering stimulus (Bargh, 1989). In this case, the triggering stimuli were category labels and some category-evocative words, but not valenced stereotypic content. The use of such primes should prevent any effect due to purely semantic priming or recent priming of the cultural stereotype (e.g., Higgins et al., 1985). The subsequent judgments should reflect only a preconscious automatic operation (Bargh, 1994). Unlike most priming studies, in which the construct or concept is primed and then measured (but see Bargh, Raymond, Pryer, & Strack, 1995), here the category was primed and the differential activation of the associated stereotype assessed in the subsequent impression-formation task. With such a procedure, any effects are due to spreading activation. Thus, the differential strength of association between the category and traits in high- and low-prejudice people can be revealed in the form of divergent stereotypic judgments.

Other researchers have used a brief ambiguous paragraph for the impression formation task (Srull & Wyer, 1979). However, here the target person was described by behavioral sentences (Hamilton & Gifford, 1976) containing four stereotypic dimensions (two positive and two negative). Thus, the stimulus ambiguity was achieved with a "mixed" description (see Higgins, 1996) comprising evaluatively opposite constructs (Smith, 1989). This kind of description was designed to enable participants to use positive or negative stereotypic constructs differentially in their judgment as divergent automatic associations were predicted. Note that although the specific behaviors were clearly interpretable (each was carefully chosen

---

[1]As further evidence on this point, we note that Britain was the major colonial power in the 19th century and it was largely responsible for the establishment of the slave trade. Britain imported large numbers of Afro-Caribbean people after World War II to meet particular labor shortages. It subsequently enacted a whole sequence of immigration laws designed to restrict the entry of non-White people to the country, and it has had its own share of "race relations" incidents, including several race riots in the 1980s (e.g., Banton, 1983; Reicher, 1986).

to be representative of part of the stereotype), the combination of positive and negative dimensions rendered the overall description of the target person more genuinely ambiguous than proved possible with Srull and Wyer's (1979) type of task.[2] Thus, it should be more sensitive to differential stereotype activation.

Because stronger links are more strongly activated and influence judgments (see Stangor & Lange, 1994), high-prejudice participants in the prime condition should rate the target person more extremely on the negative stereotypic dimensions and less so on the positive dimensions. Low-prejudice people may tend to do the opposite.

Method

Participants. Fifty-one university students took part in the study. They were White British nationals who had agreed to participate when approached by the experimenter on campus. They were paid £2.

Design. The design was a 2 (high vs. low prejudice) × 2 (prime vs. no-prime condition) between subjects. Participants were randomly assigned to the prime or the no-prime condition.

Materials and Procedure. The experiment was conducted using a Macintosh Quadra 650 computer. The height of the computer was adjusted so that the center of the screen was at eye level. The eye-to-screen distance was maintained at 70–80 cm. Participants were tested individually.

Priming Task. The priming phase, described as "Experiment 1," was composed of 100 trials grouped in four blocks. Participants had to respond to a series of scrambled letters, appearing at random locations and intervals on the screen, by pressing a key to indicate if the stimulus was at the left or right of the central fixation dot that preceded it. They were instructed not to lean forward, to look at the center of the screen to facilitate stimulus detection, and to be fast and accurate.

Within each block of trials, the stimulus was presented an equal number of times in four parafoveal positions (2–6° of the visual field). No word began farther away than 6.5 cm from the center of the screen or ended closer than 3.5 cm. In the prime condition, 13 words evocative of the category *Black people* were used. They were category labels themselves and neutral associates of the category, based on free responses in pretesting. The words used were as follows: Blacks, Afro-

Caribbean, West Indians, colored, afro, dreadlocks, Rastafarian, reggae, ethnic, Brixton, Notting Hill,[3] rap, and culture. Each word appeared on the screen for 100 ms and was then masked by a 14-letter string (xqfbzrpmqwhgbx) that stayed on the screen for 100 ms. The intertrial interval varied from 2 to 6.5 s. The first trial of each new block had an intertrial interval of 7.5 s.

Similar parameters have been used repeatedly to ensure the subliminality of such parafoveal priming, confirmed by the results of the recognition and guess conditions (Bargh, Bond, Lombardi, & Tote, 1986; Bargh & Pietromonaco, 1982; Devine, 1989). In the current experiment, the central dot appeared on the screen for 1 s immediately before each presentation, whereas in previous studies the fixation point was visible on the screen at all times. By cuing participants' attention to the center of the screen right before the stimulus came up, it was less likely for the eye to wander around the screen and hence occasionally catch a glimpse of a particular word.

The procedure was the same in the no-prime condition, except that no real words were used as primes. Instead, the mask flashed up on the screen twice, creating the same subjective experience as in the prime condition (a double flashing, according to participants' reports in both conditions).

Neutral words unrelated to the category *Blacks* were used for the 10 practice trials. These were accommodation, methodology, fireplace, notebook, apple, success, orange, tree, stairs, and danger.

Impression Formation Task and Dependent Measures. Immediately after the priming task, the instructions on screen stated that we also were interested in the way people form impressions of others and introduced "Experiment 2." Eight behavioral sentences described a person whose ethnicity was not specified. The participants then rated this target person on a number of trait scales (randomly ordered for each participant). Of the eight sentences, two were descriptive of the construct *athletic* (e.g., "He plays football regularly"), two of the construct *fun loving* (e.g., "He goes to

---

[2] Pretesting showed that Srull and Wyer's (1979) "Donald" paragraph was perceived by our participants in unambiguously negative terms, thus obscuring differences between the prime and no-prime conditions and also not permitting an impression of the person in positive or negative ways.

[3] Brixton and Notting Hill are two well-known areas of London with high concentrations of Afro-Caribbean people.

parties most weekends"), two of the construct *aggressive* (e.g., "He can easily get angry at people who disagree with him"), and two of the construct *unreliable* (e.g., "He cannot be bothered to be on time for meetings and appointments"). These four constructs had been generated spontaneously in pretesting to describe Black people (see Study 1).[4] The selected sentences were chosen from a bigger pool of pretested sentences; they were descriptive of their respective contructs, but not too extremely. The final sentences were pretested further for the impression they conveyed when presented together to ensure that the balance among the four constructs was maintained. This meant that the overall image of the target person was ambiguous yet also contained different stereotypic features that might be accessed more or less easily by high- and low-prejudice participants.

Twenty-one rating scales followed the behavioral sentences. Four traits were descriptive of the dimension *athletic* (i.e., athletic, fit, sporty, and active), six represented the dimension *fun-loving* (i.e., outgoing, fun loving, flamboyant, lively, easy going, and relaxed), five were related to the dimension *unreliable* (i.e., unreliable, irresponsible, careless, disorganized, and lazy), and six were descriptive of the dimension *aggressive* (i.e., aggressive, hostile, dislikable, quarrelsome, quick tempered, and touchy). To demonstrate these constructs' internal coherence, an independent sample ($N = 15$) of respondents was provided with the defining attribute of the construct (e.g., athletic) and asked to rate how much a person who had that attribute also possessed each of the other associated attributes (e.g., fit, sporty, and active) using scales ranging from 1 (*not at all*) to 7 (*extremely*). All individual traits were rated above 4.0 (the scale midpoint), and the composite ratings for each of the four constructs all were significantly greater than 4.0 ($p < .001$ in each case). In the event, we elected to simplify the analysis by combining the four dimensions into two, one positive one negative. All scales ranged from *not at all* (1) to *extremely* (9). Participants therefore had a choice of two positive and two negative stereotypic dimensions on which to judge the target person.

The prejudice scale was presented as an "opinion survey," the last task in the study.[5] Anonymity of the answers and complete freedom to agree or disagree with each item were emphasized.

An extensive individual debriefing then took place. Any observations were recorded, particu-larly whether participants perceived any connection between the tasks (none did). Finally, the experimenter thanked, paid, and dismissed the respondents.

Recognition Condition. Twelve additional participants were run in a recognition condition to check on the awareness of the content of the primes. After the priming task, the experimenter explained that words had been flashed on the screen and that in the next part of the experiment the participant should select one of three words after each trial. The experimenter reminded the participant to look at the center of the screen and not to lean forward; the computer was then made to proceed. A computer-based administration of the prejudice scale followed the 33 recognition trials.

To ensure maximum sensitivity, the recognition test was designed as in Bargh and Pietromonaco (1982, Experiment 2): Instead of choosing the words at the end of the experiment, when the immediate awareness of some words could have worn off, participants had to indicate their choice after each trial when the word had just been presented. More powerfully still, the test was not administered after the impression formation task (see Bargh et al., 1986; Bargh & Pietromonaco, 1982, Experiment 1) but after the priming phase. Each priming word appeared three times in the 39 trials of the recognition test. This gave participants another opportunity to detect the target words because they were presented more than once. After each trial, the target word came up on the screen together with two other words. The distractors were matched in length as much as possible to the

---

[4]Our choice of constructs perhaps deserves some comment. We chose *athletic* and *fun loving* as the two positive constructs because pretesting had indicated that these were both unambiguously positive and could also be captured in behavioral sentences. *Musical* and *colorful*, although mentioned more frequently in Study 1, were less convenient in these respects. Similar considerations applied to *unreliable* (subsumed in the *lazy* category in Study 1). *Aggressive* was chosen rather than *criminal* to provide some comparability with previous work (e.g., Devine, 1989).

[5]For practical reasons, it was not possible to pretest participants in their level of prejudice. However, given that responses to prejudice measures like this presumably are rather stable, it seems unlikely that any of the preceding procedures could have affected the participants' prejudice scores. Moreover, such posttest measurement of prejudice level has been used successfully in several other comparable studies (e.g., Augoustinos et al., 1994; Devine & Elliot, 1995; Locke, MacLeod, & Walker, 1994; Wittenbrink et al., 1997).

target words and were similar to these either in meaning or phonetically. Across the three repetitions, the relative positions of the words was varied. Following each choice, the computer proceeded with the next trial, which was presented after a random interval (2–6.5 s).

Results

Recognition Test and Self-Reports. The presentation of the primes appears to have been subliminal, as intended. Participants in the recognition condition did not score better than chance. The mean proportion correct was .35, which did not differ significantly from the chance value of .33, $t(11) = 0.66$, *ns*. In addition, only 1 participant in the prime condition reported being aware of (one or two) words. This individual was excluded from all subsequent analyses. Given that in total some 2,800 presentations were made, this is a low percentage indeed and indicates that cuing attention to the center of the screen immediately before each trial successfully prevented awareness of the primes.

Prime and No-Prime Conditions. Participants were divided at the median into high- ($n = 25$) and low-prejudice ($n = 25$) groups on the basis of their score on the prejudice scale ($Mdn = 71.5$; Ms and SDs for the high- and low-prejudice groups were 59.10 and 9.85 and 80.28 and 7.29, respectively; $\alpha = .84$).

To simplify the analysis, the 10 scales making up the two positive constructs were combined into a single positive index with good internal reliability ($\alpha = .76$). Similarly, the 11 scales tapping the negative constructs were combined into a single negative index, also with high reliability ($\alpha = .82$). These two indexes were incorporated into the design as a within-subjects variable: 2 (high and low prejudice) x 2 (prime and no-prime condition) × 2 (positive and negative valence). Our hypothesis specified that high-prejudice people would form a more negative and less positive impression and that low-prejudice people would do the reverse in response to the prime. Therefore, the predicted effect of interest was a three-way interaction.

An ANOVA revealed several significant effects: a main effect for valence, $F(1, 46) = 11.40$, $p < .002$, showing that the positive scales had higher ratings than the negative scales ($Ms = 6.70$ and 5.99, respectively) and a Prejudice x Valence interaction, $F(1, 46) = 4.01$, $p < .051$. All of these effects were qualified by the expected three-way

interaction, Condition × Prejudice × Valence, $F(1, 46) = 6.06$, $p < .02$ (see Figure 6.1).

Analysis of the simple effects of priming revealed that the Condition x Valence interaction was significant only for high-prejudice participants, $F(1, 47) = 6.07$, $p < .02$. High-prejudice participants in the prime condition rated the target person more extremely on the negative construct ($Ms = 6.76$ vs. 5.88), $t(46) = 3.43$, $p < .005$ and less extremely on the positive construct ($Ms = 6.31$ vs. 6.88), $t(46) = 2.22$, $p < .025$. Low-prejudice participants increased their ratings on the positive scales ($Ms = 6.98$ vs. 6.54), $t(46) = 1.69$, $p < .05$, but showed no difference on the negative ones ($Ms = 5.65$ vs. 5.73). Simple effects analysis also revealed that the Prejudice x Valence interaction was significant in the prime condition, $F(1, 47) = 10.26$, $p < .002$, but not in the no-prime condition, $F(1, 47) = 0.18$, *ns*. High- and low-prejudice participants did not differ in the absence of prime. When primed, however, high-prejudice participants rated the target person more negatively than did the low-prejudice ($Ms = 6.76$ vs. 5.65), $t(46) = 4.48$, $p < .0005$, and less positively than did low-prejudice participants ($Ms = 6.31$ vs. 6.98), $t(46) = 2.70$, $p < .005$. Note that the direction of the effect of the prime on the positive and negative stereotypic construct was exactly the opposite for high- and low-prejudice people.

Discussion

As predicted, high- and low-prejudice people differed from each other in response to a sublimi-

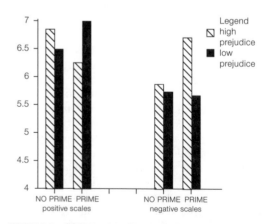

FIGURE 6.1. ■ Differential effects of category activation in high- and low-prejudice participants.

nally presented prime. In particular, high-prejudice participants increased their ratings of the target person on the negative stereotypic dimensions and decreased them on the positive constructs. Low-prejudice participants appeared to be less affected by category activation altogether, although they tended in the opposite direction, showing activation of the positive stereotypic components. Thus, upon category activation the unintentional activation of the stereotype did not occur in an all-or-none fashion (Fiske & Dyer, 1985; Hayes-Roth, 1977) but selectively. One finding deserves some comment. High-prejudice participants' ratings on the positive scales were lower in the prime than in the no-prime condition. This finding, although not predicted, can be explained by considering that most associative models allow for the operation of both excitatory and inhibitory processes (e.g., Carlston, 1992; Stephan & Stephan, 1993). The excitation of the negative stereotypic dimensions might have inhibited the positive ones in these respondents.

By restricting the prime to category labels and neutral associates, semantic priming effects or recency effects were eliminated as explanations of the findings. The preconscious automatic activation of the stereotype proved different for high- and low-prejudice participants. Despite common stereotype knowledge, differential endorsement can make certain stereotypic features more accessible than others. This implies that the strength of association between positive or negative stereotypic traits and category varies in high- and low-prejudice people and therefore so does the resulting mental representation of the group. This pattern of results is completely consistent with the model outlined earlier. As predicted, there seem to be individual differences in the strength of association between the category and various characteristics, resulting, we speculate, from different histories of endorsement of prejudiced (and nonprejudiced) stereotypic beliefs.

Study 3: A Conceptual Replication of Devine (1989)

The differential strength of association between stereotypic characteristics and the group node in high- and low-prejudice people could not be revealed by Devine (1989, Experiment 2) because category and stereotype activation were not distinguished. The results from Study 2 show that automatic category activation alone did elicit differential responses for high- and low-prejudice people. If the absence of differences between high- and low-prejudice people in Devine's study was due to semantic priming or to recency of activation of the available stereotype per se, then including some of the negative stereotype content in the priming stimuli should allow a conceptual replication. At the same time, the effects of category activation can be compared with those of stereotype activation.[6]

The priming stimuli were pretested so that they could be comparable to those used by Devine (1989): Fifty percent of the stereotype-related words she used were negative. In the current study, 6 of the 13 words were negative, and this was the only difference between Studies 3 and 2.

For reasons discussed earlier, in this experiment high- and low-prejudice people should not differ in their response to stereotype activation. Priming effects are observed if the primed structure is applicable to the following judgment (e.g., Higgins, 1989). Both the semantic (Erdley & D'Agostino, 1988; Higgins, Rholes, & Jones, 1977; Neely, 1977) and the evaluative content of the prime (e.g., Bargh, Chaiken, Govender, & Pratto, 1992; Bargh, Chaiken, Raymond, & Hymes, 1996; Greenwald, Klinger, & Liu, 1989) can provide a match with the stimuli in the judgment task. Because the part of the stereotype that is activated by the prime is negative, the prime should be applicable to the negative, but not the positive, stereotypic features. Specifically, we predicted that ratings should increase on the directly applicable negative stereotypic traits in the prime compared with the no-prime condition, but not on the positive traits.

---

[6]A conceptual rather than an exact replication of Devine (1989) was necessary for several reasons. First, use of our behavioral sentences impression formation task allowed direct comparability between Studies 2 and 3 and the effect of category or stereotype activation. Second, an exact replication would have been virtually impossible given the different cultural context. As already noted (see Footnote 2), the impression formation task Devine used was not appropriate for our participants. In addition, the dependent measures she used are not perceived in the same way in the British context. Among the hostility-unrelated scales she used, *conceited, narrow-minded, boring, dependable* (and *kind*) are part of the autostereotype of British people. They therefore cannot be considered neutral or contrasted with the "hostility-related" scales in this case.

Method

Pretesting. Fifty percent of the words in each replication used by Devine (1989) had negative connotations. To achieve a prime comparable to hers, the 24 words of Devine's replications were rated by five American judges for their negativity on a 7-point scale. A slightly larger pool of words ($n = 30$) obtained in pretesting in the British context was rated by five British judges.

Results show that all the negative words used in Devine's (1989) experiment were rated negatively by the American judges ($M = 4.50$) compared to the remaining stereotype-related words ($M = 1.80$). All the negative British words were also rated negatively ($M = 4.75$) compared to the remaining words ($M = 2.78$). The six negative words selected for the current experiment received a mean rating of 5.05 and the remaining priming words 2.86. There was thus a good correspondence between the valence of the primes used in the two experiments.

Participants. Forty-five university students took part in the study. They were White British nationals who had agreed to participate when approached on campus by the experimenter. They were paid £2.

Design. The design was a 2 (high vs. low prejudice) × 2 (prime vs. no-prime condition) between subjects. Participants were randomly assigned to the prime or the no-prime condition.

Materials and Procedure. All materials, parameters, and procedures were as described for Study

2. The only change was in the stimulus words for the prime condition. The experiment was designed with 13 priming words. Three were category labels (i.e., Blacks, West Indians, and Afro-Caribbean), six were negative (i.e., nigger, rude, dirty, crime, unemployed, and drugs), and the remaining four were evocative of the category (i.e., dreadlocks, reggae, Brixton, and ethnic). Apart from the negative words, the primes were the same as those used in Study 2.

Guess Condition. As a check of the immediate awareness of the stimulus words, 8 additional participants were tested in a guess condition. After each presentation in the priming phase, they had to guess what the word was. As for the other conditions, the instructions were not to lean forward and to look at the center of the screen—where a central dot would appear—to facilitate detection, given the random location and timing of the words. Following Bargh and Pietromonaco (1982, Experiment 2) and Devine (1989), the guessing criterion was lowered to be more sensitive to immediate awareness. Participants were told to guess and prompted to do so if they could not come up with anything. The experimenter wrote down each guess.

Results

Guess Condition. The 8 participants in this condition reported during the task and the debriefing that they found it difficult, could just see scrambled letters (the mask), and did not know what the actual words were. However, 1 participant admitted not following instructions and looking off the center of the screen at times. This participant alone had a total of eight correct guesses.

Of the 800 trials, the total number of correct guesses was 16, or 2%. These figures are comparable to those obtained in previous research (e.g., Bargh & Pietromonaco, 1982; Devine, 1989), especially considering that the person who failed to follow instructions accounted for half of the total hits. Excluding this person lowered the hit rate to 1%. A consideration of the remaining guesses revealed that they were not related to Black people or the stereotype associated with them.

Prime and No-Prime Condition. On the basis of the prejudice scale, participants were divided at the median into high-prejudice ($n = 22$) and low-prejudice ($n = 22$) groups ($Mdn = 76.5$; Ms and

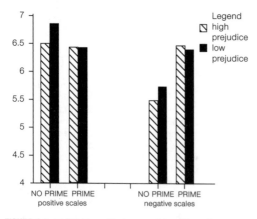

FIGURE 6.2. ■ Priming effects on rating of target person.

*SD*s for the high- and low-prejudice groups were 64.60 and 8.01 and 88.77 and 7.75, respectively; α = .88).[7]

Once again, the two positive and two negative constructs were grouped to simplify the interpretation of the results. The internal reliabilities of these two constructs again were acceptably high (αs = .70 and .80 for the positive and negative scales, respectively). A 2 (high and low prejudice) × 2 (prime and no-prime condition) × 2 (valence) mixed ANOVA was run on the grouped positive and negative scales. No effects due to prejudice level were expected in this case because the negative prime should cancel the differences between high- and low-prejudice people. The predicted effect was thus a two-way interaction, Condition × Valence.

The analysis revealed two significant effects: a main effect for valence, $F(1, 40) = 7.73$, $p < .008$, indicating that, overall, ratings on the positive scales were slightly more extreme than on the negative scales (*M*s = 6.53 vs. 6.01), and the predicted Condition × Valence interaction, $F(1, 40) = 5.09$, $p < .03$. As can be seen from Figure 6.2, both high- and low-prejudice participants did not respond much to the positive scales comparing the prime and no-prime conditions (*M*s = 6.43 and 6.66, respectively), $t(40) = 1.03$, *ns*, but both rated the target person more negatively in the prime than in the no-prime condition (*M*s = 6.33 and 5.70, respectively), $t(40) = 2.86$, $p < .005$.

Although prejudice level did not enter in the significant interaction—the relevant three-way interaction was nonsignificant, $F(1, 40) = 0.04$, $p < .84$—priming effects should be stronger for high-prejudice participants: The ease with which they activate the negative features (see Study 2) should combine with the effects of priming itself, making them more responsive than low-prejudice participants to the applicable negative traits. High-prejudice participants in fact significantly increased their ratings on the negative scales comparing the prime and no-prime conditions, $t(40) = 2.62$, $p < .01$. The same comparison was not significant in the low-prejudice group, $t(40) = 1.30$, $p < .1$.

---

[7]Because of missing responses on the prejudice scale, the prejudice score could not be computed for 1 participant, who was therefore excluded from analysis.

Discussion

The results of Study 3 replicate those obtained by Devine (1989), suggesting that priming negative stereotypic dimensions is sufficient to blur the differences in automatic responses between high- and low-prejudice people. When the stereotype is activated directly, both high- and low-prejudice people increase their ratings on the applicable negative stereotypic traits. Because it is similar for the two groups, stereotype knowledge is available in memory and can be temporarily accessed through priming, leading to the expected assimilation effects (Bargh, 1994; Higgins, 1989). On closer inspection, however, these effects seemed to be a little stronger for high-prejudice participants. This is consistent with the assumption that endorsement has made the negative stereotypic traits more accessible for high-prejudice people. It is also consistent with Higgins's (1996) recent discussion of increased accessibility for specific linkages in various domains. Presumably, the greater activation effect in high-prejudice participants is caused by their having both a chronic and an immediately primed component of stereotype activation; low-prejudice participants have only the primed component. A similar result was obtained by Bargh et al. (1986) and Higgins and Brendl (1995).

Study 3 did not specifically rule out the possibility of semantic priming effects. These results (and those of Devine, 1989) would be the same, whether obtained because of direct semantic priming or because of a more general activation of negative stereotypic components. In either event, what is more important is that the effects of a category and stereotype prime are different. Stereotype knowledge seems to make high- and low-prejudice people indistinguishable only if it is primed directly.

General Discussion

The general aim of the three studies was to assess the possible flexibility of the relations among categorization, stereotyping, and prejudice as opposed to the fixed pathway implicit in some traditional views (Allport, 1954; Hamilton, 1981; Tajfel, 1969). High- and low-prejudice people know the stereotype of Black people in much the same way and to the same extent (Study 1). Because of this, they do not differ in their automatic responses when some negative aspects of the stereotype are activated (primed; Study 3). However, and crucially, high- and low-prejudice people differ in their automatic responses when the category—and not the stereotype per se—is primed (Study 2). In discussing these results, four issues seem to be particularly important.

The Inevitability of Stereotype Activation

The first issue is the inevitability of stereotype activation upon perception of a category member. In the introduction, we identified two meanings of automatic stereotype activation in the literature. Stereotypes can be activated because they are directly primed or because the category is primed. The results of our studies show that category and stereotype activation have different effects on judgments, thus supporting the distinction between the two. In Study 2, high-prejudice participants responded to category activation by enhancing negative stereotypic trait ratings and attenuating the positive. This pattern was quite different for the low-prejudice participants, who showed less responsiveness to the prime and tended in the opposite direction. Only when some stereotypic associates of the category were also primed did these differences between high- and low-prejudice respondents disappear (Study 3). These findings strongly suggest that Devine's (1989) results (of no effect of prejudice level on automatic processes) were due to the presence of both the category and stereotypic associates in the prime. Because the stereotype was directly primed, no inferences can be drawn from that study about how stereotypes are activated upon perception of a category member. By contrast, our Study 2 directly addressed the question of what associations are evoked when encountering a category member. Although other evidence is beginning to accumulate that high- and low-prejudice people may differ in their automatic cognitive processes (Locke et al., 1994; Wittenbrink et al., 1997), differences in stereotype activation resulting from category priming have not been observed in a judgment task before (to our knowledge). The more realistic social judgment context perhaps permits more direct inferences about the consequences of categorization in real life than are warranted with reaction time studies.

Thus, automatic stereotype activation resulting from direct stereotype priming should be distinguished from that consequent upon categorization. Gilbert and Hixon (1991) showed that it is possible to separate empirically category activation from stereotype activation. They achieved this by manipulating a situational variable (the presence or absence of a cognitively distracting task); our results suggest that person variables (e.g., habitual level of prejudice) also may be important in predicting whether and how a stereotype becomes activated consequent on category activation.

Hilton and von Hippel (1996) noted the lack of empirical tests of different accounts of stereotyping. We believe that these data contribute to rectifying that lacuna since they clearly support a differential model of automatic stereotype activation rather than the all-or-none conception implied by some theories (e.g., Devine, 1989; Hayes-Roth, 1977; also see Fiske & Taylor, 1991).

Group Representations

The second issue concerns whether not just knowing the stereotype, but believing it to be true, affects automatic processes. Our findings underline how stereotype knowledge and endorsement both affect the automatic level of processing, but in different ways. Such findings challenge Devine's (1989) suggestion that stereotype knowledge is activated automatically because it has a longer history of activation than personal beliefs. If this were so, no differences should have been found between high- and low-prejudice people in Study 2. The pattern obtained, instead, is best explained by the model outlined in the introduction, which rests on differential stereotype endorsement in high- and low-prejudice people. Stereotypic features believed to be true of the group (endorsed) are presumably the ones activated most often. These endorsed characteristics become more strongly associated with the category (group node) and thus can be activated automatically. Stereotype endorsement then affects judgments when the category is primed. Stereotype knowledge affects judgments when it is primed directly. Because it is available in both groups, stereotype knowledge can be primed, thus eliciting similar assimilation-type effects in high- and low-prejudice people (Study 3).

The studies show that high- and low-prejudice people have different representations of the group.

These representations do not differ in content (Study 1) but in the strength with which the positive and negative attributes are associated with the category label (Study 2). As hypothesized, the activation spreads preferentially to the negative traits for high-prejudice people. At the same time, the lower ratings (compared with the no-prime condition) on the positive stereotypic traits suggest an automatic inhibition of them. Low-prejudice people respond in the opposite direction, demonstrating a significant increase in the positive ratings. These findings can be accommodated easily by current models which incorporate both excitatory and inhibitory mechanisms (Carlston, 1992; Rumelhart & McClelland, 1986; Stephan & Stephan, 1993). The excitation of some nodes results in the inhibition of others. Activation of a category, then, does not make the activation of the associated stereotype inevitable in an all-or-none manner.

An issue for future research is to test further the selective activation observed here. For low-prejudice people in particular, the cultural stereotype could be less central in their representation of the group.

Comparability of This Research Context and That of Devine (1989)

It is worth briefly considering the different social contexts in which this research and that of Devine (1989) were carried out. To be sure, ethnic relations and the associated intergroup stereotypes between Black and White people in Britain in the 1990s are not identical to those between White and Black people in the United States in the 1980s. Is it possible that these contextual differences can explain the pattern of findings of Studies 2 and 3? We believe not.

Such an argument might first contend that negative stereotypes about Black people are not as prevalent in Britain as they have been in the United States. The data from Study 1 and the most cursory historical analysis (see Footnote 1) clearly belie such an assumption. There is every reason to suppose that negative stereotypic images of Black people are as embedded in the British culture as they seem to be in the United States. Second, our measure of prejudice was different from that used by Devine (1989). However, it was based on well-established measures, it had excellent reliability, and it correlated sensibly with theoretically related

measures. Presumably, the problem cannot lie there. Finally, we fail to see how such an argument (based on cultural differences) can explain the similarity of results between Study 3 and Devine's (1989) Experiment 2. If negative stereotypes are not as salient in Britain, why was it possible to prime them so easily (and approximately equally for high- and low-prejudice people) in Study 3? The equivalence of these results with those of Devine seems to argue that, whatever the cultural differences, it is possible to replicate her findings provided that both categorical and stereotypical material are primed directly. Only when the latter are removed (as in Study 2) does one observe the predicted divergence between high- and low-prejudice people.

The Inhibition of Prejudiced Responses

The fourth issue relates to the inhibition of prejudiced responses. Devine (1989) explained the absence of differences between high- and low-prejudice people at an automatic level, arguing that prejudice is like a habit that has to be broken.[8] It requires conscious control, an inhibition of an automatic prejudiced response on the part of low-prejudice people. However, such an interpretation is not easy to reconcile with a functional analysis of stereotypes, which has become of central importance in recent years (e.g., Fiske, 1993; Macrae, Stangor, & Milne, 1994; Snyder & Miene, 1994; Stangor & Lange, 1994). If stereotypes really are functional to save cognitive resources, they should not operate so as to require conscious inhibition of an automatic prejudiced response. Such a process would be taxing for the cognitive system (e.g., Gilbert & Hixon, 1991; Macrae, Milne, & Bodenhausen, 1994).

In fact, our findings contradict the hypothesis of a conscious inhibition of prejudiced responses. Instead of inhibiting an activated stereotype, low-prejudice people may not even access parts of it. Such activation may happen selectively and more strongly for high- than for low-prejudice people (e.g., our Study 2; Locke et al., 1994). The data even provide evidence of activation of positive stereotypic components. Others, too, have discussed

---

[8]Devine herself has also modified her position somewhat from her earlier 1989 article (see Devine & Monteith, 1993). Some low-prejudice people may be further along the process and have effectively broken the prejudice habit.

data inconsistent with the conscious inhibition of an automatic prejudiced response (Fazio et al., 1995; Gilbert & Hixon, 1991). Moreover, high- and low-prejudice people seem to have different beliefs and stereotypic expectancies (weaker for the low-prejudice people) about the behavior of Black people (Vargas & von Hippel, 1993; von Hippel et al., 1995). These findings confirm that low- and high-prejudice people have different representations of the target group. The resulting qualitative differences in automatic processes can be accommodated by an emerging view of stereotypes as theories of how other groups are and act (e.g., von Hippel et al., 1995).

Faced with a member of the stereotyped group or a symbolic equivalent, people seem to react automatically *according to the representation they have in mind*. Thus, conscious inhibition of a prejudiced reaction does not take place; the differences between high- and low-prejudice people appear at an automatic level, supporting the idea of a flexible link between categorization and stereotyping.

A modification of Devine's (1989) model is therefore suggested: It is endorsement, not knowledge, that is likely to shape the representation in memory, strengthening the links between the category label and certain stereotypic features instead of others. Prejudice does not resemble a habit that has to be broken but one that is, for some people, already broken.

REFERENCES

Allport, G. W. (1954). *The nature of prejudice*. Reading, MA: Addison-Wesley.

Andersen, S. M., & Klatzky, R. (1987). Traits and social stereotypes: Levels of categorization in person perception. *Journal of Personality and Social Psychology, 53,* 235–246.

Anderson, J. R. (1983). *The architecture of cognition*. Cambridge, MA: Harvard University Press.

Ashmore, R. D., & Del Boca, F. K. (1981). Conceptual approaches to stereotypes and stereotyping. In D. L. Hamilton (Ed.), *Cognitive processes in stereotyping and intergroup behavior* (pp. 1–35). Hillsdale, NJ: Erlbaum.

Augoustinos, M., Innes, J. M., & Ahrens, C. (1994). Stereotypes and prejudice: The Australian experience. *British Journal of Social Psychology, 33,* 125–141.

Banaji, M. R., Hardin, C., & Rothman, A. J. (1993). Implicit stereotyping in person judgment. *Journal of Personality and Social Psychology, 65,* 272–281.

Banton, M. (1983). The influence of colonial status upon Black-White relations in England, 1948–1958. *Sociology, 17,* 546–559.

Bargh, J. A. (1984). Automatic and conscious processing of social information. In R. S. Wyer, Jr., & T. K. Srull (Eds.),

Handbook of social cognition (Vol. 3, pp. 1–43). Hillsdale, NJ: Erlbaum.

Bargh, J. A. (1989). Conditional automaticity: Varieties of automatic influence in social perception and cognition. In J. S. Uleman & J. A. Bargh (Eds.), *Unintended thought* (pp. 3–51). New York: Guilford Press.

Bargh, J. A. (1994). The four horsemen of automaticity: Awareness, intention, efficiency, and control in social cognition. In R. S. Wyer, Jr. & T. K. Srull (Eds.), *Handbook of social cognition* (Vol. 1, 2nd ed., pp. 1–40). Hillsdale, NJ: Erlbaum.

Bargh, J. A., Bond, R. N., Lombardi, W. J., & Tota, M. E. (1986). The additive nature of chronic and temporary sources of construct accessibility. *Journal of Personality and Social Psychology, 50,* 869–878.

Bargh, J. A., Chaiken, S., Govender, R., & Pratto, F. (1992). The generality of the automatic attitude activation effect. *Journal of Personality and Social Psychology, 62,* 893–912.

Bargh, J. A., Chaiken, S., Raymond, P., & Hymes, C. (1996). The automatic evaluation effect: Unconditional automatic attitude activation with a pronunciation task. *Journal of Experimental Social Psychology, 32,* 104–128.

Bargh, J. A., & Pietromonaco, P. (1982). Automatic information processing and social perception: The influence of trait information presented outside of conscious awareness on impression formation. *Journal of Personality and Social Psychology, 43,* 437–449.

Bargh, J. A., Raymond, P., Pryor, J. B., & Strack, F. (1995). Attractiveness of the underling: An automatic power → sex association and its consequences for sexual harassment and aggression. *Journal of Personality and Social Psychology, 68,* 768–781.

Billig, M. (1985). Prejudice, categorization and particularization: From a perceptual to a rhetorical approach. *European Journal of Social Psychology, 15,* 79–103.

Brewer, M. B. (1988). A dual process model of impression formation. In T. K. Srull & R. S. Wyer, Jr. (Eds.), *Advances in social cognition* (Vol. 1, pp. 1–36). Hillsdale, NJ: Erlbaum.

Brown, R. (1995). *Prejudice: Its social psychology*. Oxford, England: Blackwell.

Bruner, J. S. (1957). On perceptual readiness. *Psychological Review, 64,* 123–152.

Carlston, D. E. (1992). Impression formation and the modular mind: The associated systems theory. In L. L. Martin & A. Tesser (Eds.), *The construction of social judgments* (pp. 301–341). Hillsdale, NJ: Erlbaum.

Collins, A. M., & Loftus, E. F. (1975). A spreading-activation theory of semantic processing. *Psychological Review, 82,* 407–428.

Deaux, K., & Lewis, L. L. (1984). Structure of gender stereotypes: Interrelations among components and gender label. *Journal of Personality and Social Psychology, 46,* 991–1004.

Devine, P. G. (1989). Stereotypes and prejudice: Their automatic and controlled components. *Journal of Personality and Social Psychology, 56,* 5–18.

Devine, P. G., & Elliot, A. J. (1995). Are racial stereotypes *really* fading? The Princeton trilogy revisited. *Personality and Social Psychology Bulletin, 21,* 1139–1150.

Devine. P. G., & Monteith, M. J. (1993). The role of discrepancy-associated affect in prejudice reduction. In D. M.

Mackie & D. L. Hamilton (Eds.), *Affect, cognition, and stereotyping: Interactive processes in group perception* (pp. 317–344). San Diego, CA: Academic Press.

Dovidio, J. E., Evans, N., & Tyler, R. B. (1986). Racial stereotypes: The contents of their cognitive representations. *Journal of Experimental Social Psychology, 22,* 22–37.

Erdley, C. A., & D'Agostino, P. R. (1988). Cognitive and affective components of automatic priming effects. *Journal of Personality and Social Psychology, 54,* 741–747.

Fazio. R. H., Jackson, J. R., Dunton, B. C., & Williams, C. J. (1995). Variability in automatic activation as an unobtrusive measure of racial attitudes: A bona fide pipeline? *Journal of Personality and Social Psychology, 69,* 1013–1027.

Fazio, R. H., Sanbonmatsu, D. M., Powell, M. C., & Kardes, F. R. (1986). On the automatic activation of attitudes. *Journal of Personality and Social Psychology, 50,* 229–238.

Fiske, S. T. (1982). Scheme-triggered affect: Applications to social perception. In M. S. Clark & S. T. Fiske (Eds.), *Affect and cognition* (pp. 55–78). Hillsdale, NJ: Erlbaum.

Fiske, S. T. (1993). Social cognition and social perception. *Annual Review of Psychology, 44,* 155–194.

Fiske, S. T., & Dyer, L. M. (1985). Structure and development of social schemata: Evidence from positive and negative transfer effects. *Journal of Personality and Social Psychology, 48,* 839–852.

Fiske, S. T. & Neuberg, S. L. (1990). A continuum of impression formation, from category-based to individuating processes: Influences of information and motivation on attention and interpretation. *Advances in Experimental Social Psychology, 23,* 1–74.

Fiske, S. T., & Taylor, S. E. (1991). *Social cognition* (2nd ed.). New York: McGraw-Hill.

Ford, T. E., Stangor, C., & Duan, C. (1994). Influence of social category accessibility and category-associated trait accessibility on judgments of individuals. *Social Cognition, 12,* 149–168.

Gaertner, S. L., & McLaughlin, J. P. (1983). Racial stereotypes: Associations and ascriptions of positive and negative characteristics. *Social Psychology Quarterly, 46,* 23–30.

Gilbert, D. T., & Hixon, J. G. (1991). The trouble of thinking: Activation and application of stereotypic beliefs. *Journal of Personality and Social Psychology, 60,* 509–517.

Greenwald, A. G., & Banaji, M. R. (1995). Implicit social cognition: Attitudes, self-esteem, and stereotypes. *Psychological Review, 102,* 4–27.

Greenwald, A. G., Klinger, M. R., & Lui, T. J. (1989). Unconscious processing of dichoptically masked words. *Memory & Cognition, 17,* 35–47.

Hamilton, D. L. (Ed.). (1981). *Cognitive processes in stereotyping and intergroup behavior.* Hillsdale, NJ: Erlbaum.

Hamilton, D. L., & Gifford, R. K. (1976). Illusory correlation in interpersonal perception: A cognitive basis of stereotypic judgment. *Journal of Personality and Social Psychology, 12,* 392–407.

Hamilton, D. L., & Sherman, J. W. (1994). Stereotypes. In R. S. Wyer, Jr. & T. K. Srull (Eds.), *Handbook of social cognition* (Vol. 2, 2nd ed., pp. 1–68). Hillsdale, NJ: Erlbaum.

Hamilton, D. L., Sherman, S. J., & Ruvolo, C. M. (1990). Stereotype-based expectancies: Effects on information processing and social behavior. *Journal of Social Issues, 46,* 35–60.

Hayes-Roth, B. (1977). Evolution of cognitive structure and processes. *Psychological Review, 84,* 260–278.

Higgins, E. T. (1989). Knowledge accessibility and activation: Subjectivity and suffering from unconscious sources. In J. S. Uleman & J. A. Bargh (Eds.), *Unintended thought* (pp. 75–123). New York: Guilford Press.

Higgins, E. T. (1996). Knowledge activation: Accessibility, applicability, and salience. In E. T. Higgins & A. W. Kruglanski (Eds.). *Social psychology: Handbook of basic principles* (pp. 133–168). New York: Guilford Press.

Higgins, E. T., Bargh, J. A., & Lombardi, W. (1985). Nature of priming effects on categorization. *Journal of Experimental Psychology: Learning, Memory, and Cognition, 11,* 59–69.

Higgins, E. T., & Brendl, C. M. (1995). Accessibility and applicability: Some "activation rules" influencing judgment. *Journal of Experimental Social Psychology, 31,* 218–243.

Higgins, E. T., & King, G. (1981). Accessibility of social constructs: Information-processing consequences of individual and contextual variability. In N. Cantor & J. F. Kihlstrom (Eds.), *Personality and social interaction* (pp. 69–121). Hillsdale, NJ: Erlbaum.

Higgins, E. T., Rholes, W. S., & Jones, C. R. (1977). Category accessibility and impression formation. *Journal of Experimental Social Psychology, 13,* 141–154.

Hilton, J. L., & von Hippel, W. (1996). Stereotypes. *Annual Review of Psychology, 47,* 237–271.

Jacobson, C. K. (1985). Resistance to affirmative action: Self-interest or racism? *Journal of Conflict Resolution, 29,* 306–329.

Katz, D., & Braly, K. (1933). Racial stereotypes in one hundred college students. *Journal of Abnormal and Social Psychology, 28,* 280–290.

Locke, V., MacLeod, C., & Walker, I. (1994). Automatic and controlled activation of stereotypes: Individual differences associated with prejudice. *British Journal of Social Psychology, 33,* 29–46.

Macrae, C. N., Milne, A. B., & Bodenhausen, G. V. (1994). Stereotypes as energy-saving devices: A peek inside the cognitive toolbox. *Journal of Personality and Social Psychology, 66,* 37–47.

Macrae, C. N., Stangor, C., & Milne, A. B. (1994). Activating social stereotypes: A functional analysis. *Journal of Experimental Social Psychology, 30,* 370–389.

McConahay, J. B. (1986). Modern racism, ambivalence, and the Modern Racism Scale. In J. F Dovidio & S. L. Gaertner (Eds.), *Prejudice, discrimination and racism* (pp. 91–125). New York: Academic Press.

McConahay, J. B., Hardee, B. B., & Batts, V. (1981). Has racism declined? It depends upon who's asking and what is asked. *Journal of Conflict Resolution, 25,* 563–579.

Neely, J. H. (1977). Semantic priming and retrieval from lexical memory: Roles of inhibitionless spreading activation and limited-capacity attention. *Journal of Experimental Psychology: General, 106,* 226–254.

Perdue, C. W., Dovidio, J. F., Gurtman, M. B., & Tyler, R. B. (1990). Us and them: Social categorization and the process of intergroup bias. *Journal of Personality and Social Psychology, 59,* 475–486.

Perdue, C. W.. & Gurtman, M. B. (1990). Evidence for the automaticity of ageism. *Journal of Experimental Social Psychology, 26,* 199–216.

Pettigrew, T. F., & Meertens, R. W. (1995). Subtle and blatant prejudice in Western Europe. *European Journal of Social Psychology, 25,* 57–75.

Posner, M. I., & Snyder, C. R. R. (1975). Attention and cognitive control. In R. L. Solso (Ed.), *Information processing and cognition: The Loyola Symposium* (pp. 55–85). Hillsdale, NJ: Erlbaum.

Pratto, F., & Bargh, J. A. (1991). Stereotyping based on apparently individuating information: Trait and global components of sex stereotypes under attention overload. *Journal of Experimental Social Psychology, 27,* 26–47.

Reicher, S. D. (1986). Contact, action and racialization: Some British evidence. In M. Hewstone & R. Brown (Eds.), *Contact and conflict in intergroup encounters* (pp. 152–168). Oxford, England: Blackwell.

Rosch, E. (1978). Principles of categorization. In E. Rosch & B. B. Lloyd (Eds.), *Cognition and categorization* (pp. 27–48). Hillsdale, NJ: Erlbaum.

Rumelhart, D. E., Hinton, G. E., & McClelland, J. L. (1986). A general framework for parallel distributed processing. In D. E. Rumelhart, J. L. McClelland, & the PDP Research Group (Eds.), *Parallel distributed processing* (pp. 45–76). Cambridge, MA: MIT Press.

Rumelhart, D. E., & McClelland, J. L. (Eds.) (1986). *Parallel distributed processing* (Vol. 1). Cambridge, MA: MIT Press.

Scott, W. A. (1955). Reliability of content analysis: The case of nominal scale coding. *Public Opinion Quarterly, 19,* 321–325.

Shiffrin, R. M., & Schneider, W. (1977). Controlled and automatic human information processing: Perceptual learning, automatic attending, and a general theory. *Psychological Review, 84,* 127–190.

Smith, E. R. (1989). Procedural efficiency: General and specific components and effects on social judgment. *Journal of Experimental Social Psychology, 25,* 500–523.

Smith, E. R. (1998). Mental representation and memory. In D. Gilbert, S. T. Fiske, & G. Lindzey (Eds.), *Handbook of social psychology.* Boston: McGraw-Hill.

Smith, E. R., & Lerner, M. (1986). Development of automatism of social judgments. *Journal of Personality and Social Psychology, 50,* 246–259.

Snyder, M., & Miene, P. (1994). On the functions of stereotypes and prejudice. In M. P. Zanna & J. M. Olson (Eds.), *The psychology of prejudice: The Ontario Symposium* (Vol. 7, pp. 33–54). Hillsdale, NJ: Erlbaum.

Srull, T. K., & Wyer, R. S., Jr. (1979). The role of category accessibility in the interpretation of information about persons: Some determinants and implications. *Journal of Personality and Social Psychology, 37,* 1660–1672.

Srull, T. K., & Wyer, R. S., Jr. (1980). Category accessibility and social perception: Some implications for the study of person memory and interpersonal judgments. *Journal of Personality and Social Psychology, 38,* 841–856.

Stangor, C., & Ford, T. E. (1992). Accuracy and expectancy-confirming orientations and the development of stereotypes and prejudice. *European Review of Social Psychology, 3,* 57–89. New York: Wiley.

Stangor, C., & Lange, J. E. (1994). Mental representations of social groups: Advances in understanding stereotypes and stereotyping. *Advances in Experimental Social Psychology, 26,* 357–416.

Stangor, C., Linch, L., Duan, C., & Glass, B. (1992). Categorization of individuals on the basis of multiple social features. *Journal of Personality and Social Psychology, 62,* 207–218.

Stephan, W. G., & Stephan, C. W. (1993). Cognition and affect in stereotyping: Parallel interactive networks. In D. M. Mackie & D. L. Hamilton (Eds.), *Affect, cognition, and stereotyping: Interactive processes in group perception* (pp. 111–136). San Diego, CA: Academic Press.

Tajfel, H. (1969). Cognitive aspects of prejudice. *Journal of Social Issues, 23,* 79–97.

Vargas, P., & von Hippel, W. (1993, June). *The role of stereotypes and prejudice in behavioral identification.* Paper presented at the Fifth Annual Meeting of the American Psychological Society, Chicago.

von Hippel, W., Sekaquaptewa, D., & Vargas, P. (1995). On the role of encoding processes in stereotype maintenance. *Advances in Experimental Social Psychology, 27,* 177–254.

Wittenbrink, B., Judd, C. M., & Park, B. (1997). Evidence for racial prejudice at the implicit level and its relationship with questionnaire measures. *Journal of Personality and Social Psychology, 72,* 262–274.

Zarate, M. A., & Smith, E. R. (1990). Person categorization and stereotyping. *Social Cognition, 8,* 161–185.

Appendix

Prejudice Scale

1. It makes sense for minority groups to live in their own neighbourhoods because they share more and get along better than when mixing with Whites. (reversed item)
2. I consider our society to be unfair to Black people.
3. It should be made easier to acquire British citizenship.
4. The number of Black Members of Parliament (MPs) is too low, and political parties should take active steps to increase it.
5. Minority groups are more likely to make progress in the future by being patient and not pushing so hard for change. (reversed item)
6. Given the present high level of unemployment, foreigners should go back to their countries. (reversed item)
7. The rights of immigrants should be *restricted* (1), *left as they are* (4), *extended* (7).
8. If many Black persons moved to my neighbourhood in a short period of time, thus changing its ethnic composition, it would not bother me.
9. If people move to another country they should be allowed to maintain their own traditions.
10. Once minority groups start getting jobs because of their colour, the result is bound to be fewer jobs for Whites. (reversed item)
11. Those immigrants who do not have immigration documents should be sent back to their countries. (reversed item)
12. Some Black people living here who receive support from the state could get along without it if they tried. (reversed item)
13. Suppose that a child of yours had children with a person of very different colour and physical characteristics than your own. If your grandchildren did not physically resemble the people on your side of the family, you would be *very bothered* (1), *not bothered at all* (7).
14. It is unfair to the people of one country if the immigrants take jobs and resources. (reversed item)
15. I would not be concerned if most of my peers at the university were Black.

Note. Items 3, 7, 11, 12, and 13 are from "Subtle and Blatant Prejudice in Western Europe" by T. F. Pettigew and R. W. Meertens, 1995, *European Journal of Social Psychology, 25,* pp. 62–63. Copyright 1995 by John Wiley & Sons. Ltd. Reprinted and adapted by permission. Items 5, 8, and 10 are from "Resistance to Affirmative Action: Self-Interest or Racism?" by C. K. Jacobson, 1985, *Journal of Conflict Resolution, 29,* pp. 312, 314. Copyright 1995 by Sage Publications. Reprinted and adapted by permission.

How do Stereotypes Develop?

One of the difficulties created for those who are interested in preventing stereotyping and prejudice is that they develop so early in children. Of course, this probably isn't very surprising—after all, because stereotypes are part of the culture itself, children naturally learn them quickly. This section concerns research into the development of stereotypes and prejudice.

The first two articles in this section consider how stereotypes might develop through direct observation of the individuals that we end up stereotyping. Women are seen as compassionate and caring in part because they spend a lot of time taking care of children, and the stereotype that Jews were "greedy" seems to have stemmed in part from the fact that their religion allowed them to work in the banking industry (whereas other religions did not). In Reading 7, Eagly and Steffen present a particularly well considered and rigorous analysis of the origins of gender stereotypes based on the argument that these beliefs are, at least in some sense, real, because they closely follow the differential distribution of men and women into given roles in the society. Because women are more likely than men to be the caretakers of children, we end up believing that women are, by nature, compassionate and caring. And because men are more likely to be in positions of power, we tend to think that they are assertive and dominant. Of course, these beliefs ignore the fact that not all women are compassionate, and that not all men are assertive, and they do not of course indicate that there is anything innate or genetic about differences between men and women. Nevertheless, we may not always realize this, and thus differences in social roles may cause us to infer that stereotypes are "real."

Although Eagly and Steffen's social role theory of stereotype development assumes that there is a "kernel of truth" to gender stereotypes, Hamilton and Gifford propose in Reading 8 that stereotypes can result from our perceptions of others, even when there is no truth whatsoever to them, because some stereotypes are simply the result of *illusory correlations*. One type of illusory correlation—an *expectancy-based illusory correlation*—occurs when we use our expectations to make judgments about the frequency of behaviors that have seen. Thus, if we believe that we have seen more women than men driving poorly, it is probably because our expectations (that women are bad drivers) are influencing our perceptions.

Hamilton and Gifford study a second type of illusory correlation, which we might call a *data-based illusory correlation*. Data-based illusory correlations occur because there are naturally occurring differences in both the frequency of positive and negative events, and the size of different groups of people. Hamilton and Gifford proposed a "distinctiveness" explanation for illusory correlations, based on the frequency of observed events, which assumes that the most infrequent behaviors are the most memorable, and thus have the biggest influence on judgments. Illusory correlations have been studied in many research programs, and many different explanations have been proposed for them. Illusory correlations seem to occur particularly when individuals are not processing the provided information very thoroughly; they tend to be diminished when more thorough information processing occurs (Stroessner & Plaks, 1999). In addition to the original distinctiveness explanation proposed by Hamilton and Gifford, data has also been found that supports other explanations for illusory correlations. One idea is that because there is a general tendency to distinguish groups from each other, misperceptions result from this process

(McGarty, Haslam, Turner, & Oakes, 1993). Another approach is based on the idea that larger groups provide more information (because we know more about them) and thus, because they are based on smaller and more variable sample sizes, the judgments made of minority groups will frequently be more extreme (Stroessner & Plaks, 1999).

In an important approach to considering the development of stereotypes, Maass, Salvi, Arcuri, and Semin suggest in Reading 10 that stereotypes develop through the use of language itself. They based their analysis on the Linguistic Category Model, which argues that we may use different levels of language to represent the same event when we describe others, ranging from descriptions that are very general and that imply long-term, stable characteristics of the person (he is dishonest) to those that are very specific and that imply only short-term situational events (he stole a book from the bookstore). In essence, stereotypes represent the more general levels of description. Their interesting paper demonstrates that we are more likely to use higher level categories to describe the positive behaviors of in-groups and the negative behaviors of out-groups, and to use lower levels to describe the negative behaviors of in-groups and the positive behaviors of out-groups. These differential categorizations, called the *linguistic intergroup bias*, contribute to the development of negative stereotypes about others. Indeed, the general idea that we make broad and global attributions for the positive behaviors of in-groups and the negative behaviors of out-groups is a substantial part of stereotyping (Pettigrew, 1979).

Finally, no account of the development of stereotypes would be complete without considering the importance of social identity. As we have seen, a basic cause of stereotypes and prejudice is that, because we want to feel good about ourselves, we value our own groups more than other groups, which leads to in-group favoritism. In Reading 9, Fein and Spencer provide some of the most important available evidence supporting the relationship between prejudice and feeling good about oneself. In their research, they find both that feeling good about ourselves reduces the need to derogate members of out-groups, but also the reverse: that stereotyping others can make us feel better about ourselves.

Discussion Questions

1. List the reasons that you can think of why people develop stereotypes and prejudice. What empirical data, if any, supports these reasons?
2. Eagly and Steffen's social-role theory has been used to explain the development of gender stereotypes. Can it also explain stereotypes about other social groups?
3. What are "illusory correlations," and how, according to Hamilton and Gifford, might they produce stereotypes?
4. Based on your knowledge of social categorization and the functions of stereotypes and prejudice, what techniques might be useful in preventing children from developing them?
5. Many college campuses have programs that celebrate and discuss ethnic diversity. From a social-psychological perspective, what are likely to be the positive and negative outcomes of such programs on intergroup beliefs?

Suggested Readings

Brown, R. (1995). *Prejudice: Its social psychology*. Cambridge, MA: Blackwell. Chapter 5 in this book contains a contemporary review of how children develop stereotypes and prejudice.

Eagly, A. H. (1987). *Sex differences in social behavior: A social-role interpretation*. Hillsdale, NJ: Erlbaum. Eagly expands her social-role theory of stereotypes in this important book.

Hoffman, C., & Hurst, N. (1990). Gender stereotypes: Perception or rationalization? *Journal of Personality and Social Psychology, 58*, 197–208. An interesting empirical demonstration of how the roles that we play can influence stereotypes that others have about us.

Hogg, M. A., & Abrams, D. (1988). *Social identifications: A social psychology of intergroup relations and group processes*. London: Routledge. A theory of stereotyping and prejudice based on social identity theory.

Pettigrew, T. (1979). The ultimate attribution error: Extending Allport's cognitive analysis of prejudice. *Personality and Social Psychology Bulletin, 5*, 461–476. An analysis of the prevalence of biased attributions about the causes of positive and negative behaviors of in-groups and out-groups.

Gender Stereotypes Stem From the Distribution of Women and Men Into Social Roles

Alice H. Eagly and Valerie J. Steffen • Purdue University

According to stereotypic beliefs about the sexes, women are more communal (selfless and concerned with others) and less agentic (self-assertive and motivated to master) than men. These beliefs were hypothesized to stem from perceivers' observations of women and men in differing social roles: (a) Women are more likely than men to hold positions of lower status and authority and (b) women are more likely than men to be homemakers and are less likely to be employed in the paid work force. Experiments 1 and 2 failed to support the hypothesis that observed sex differences in status underlie belief in female communal qualities and male agentic qualities. Experiment 3 supported the hypothesis that observed sex differences in distribution into homemaker and employee occupational roles account for their beliefs. In this experiment, subjects perceived the average woman and man stereotypically. Female and male homemakers were perceived as high in communion and low in agency. Female and male employees were perceived as low in communion and high in agency, although female employees were perceived as even more agentic than their male counterparts. Experiments 4 and 5 examined perceptions that might account for the belief that employed women are especially agentic: (a) A double burden of employment plus family responsibilities did not account for this belief and (b) freedom of choice about being employed accounted for it reasonably well.

Gender stereotypes, like other social stereotypes, reflect perceivers' observations of what people do in daily life. If perceivers often observe a particular group of people engaging in a particular activity, they are likely to believe that the abilities and personality attributes required to carry out that activity are typical of that group of people. For example, if perceivers consistently observe women caring for children, they are likely to believe that characteristics thought to be necessary for child care, such as nurturance and warmth, are typical of women. Because most of people's activities are determined by their various social roles, stereotypes about groups of people should reflect the distribution of these groups into social roles in a society. Furthermore, certain stereotypes may reflect the distribution of groups into broader aspects of social structure such as social class. For example, beliefs about racial differences may be based at least in part on observations that racial groups differ in social class (Feldman, 1972; Smedley & Bayton, 1978; Triandis, 1977).

In applying this social structural analysis to people's beliefs about gender we faced two issues: (a) What is the content of stereotypes about women and men? (b) What are the major differences in the ways that women and men are distributed into sexual roles? Concerning content, we decided to restrict our focus to the beliefs about gender that, by virtue of the frequency with which they have been documented by research amplified in theoretical discussions, appear to be most important. These beliefs concern communal and agentic personal qualities: Perceivers generally assume that men are oriented toward agentic goals and women toward communal goals (e.g., Bem, 1974; Block, 1973; Broverman, Vogel, Broverman, Clarkson, & Rosenkrantz, 1972; Spence & Helmreich, 1978). Following Bakan's (1966) discussion of this distinction, agentic qualities are manifested by self-assertion, self expansion, and the urge to master, whereas communal qualities are manifested by selflessness, concern with others, and a desire to be at one with others. This distinction has been accorded considerable importance in theoretical discussions of gender (Bakan, 1966; Parsons, 1955) and in the development of measures of sex-typed and androgynous personalities (e.g., Bem, 1974; Spence & Helmreich, 1978). Furthermore, these beliefs about gender appear to be cross-culturally general (Williams & Best, 1982).

To examine why women are perceived as communal and men as agentic, we considered two major differences in the distribution of females and males into social roles. The first of these differences is that women are more likely than men to hold positions at low levels in hierarchies of status and authority and are less likely to hold higher level positions. The second difference is that women are more likely than men to be homemakers and are less likely to be employed in the paid work force.

Given the pervasiveness in natural settings of sex differences in status, it seems plausible that gender stereotypes stem from the tendency of perceivers to observe women in lower status roles than men. Such observations would be made in organizational settings in which the positions held by men tend to be higher in status and authority than the positions held by women (e.g., Brown, 1979; England, 1979; Kanter, 1977; Mennerick, 1975). Also, in family settings husbands tend to have an overall power and status advantage over wives (Blood &

Wolfe, 1960; Gillespie, 1971; Scanzoni, 1982). Such differences in the status of men's and women's roles may be determining factors in beliefs about gender.

Another reason for examining status differences is that recent research by Eagly and Wood (1982) demonstrated that the stereotypic beliefs that women are more easily influenced than men are and that men exert influence more easily than do women (e.g., Broverman et al., 1972; Spence & Helmreich, 1978; Taylor, Fiske, Etcoff, & Ruderman, 1978) stem from perceivers' inferences that (a) women occupy lower status positions than men and (b) the lower an individual's status relative to other persons, the more that individual yields to their influence. To extend this analysis to the communal and agentic aspects of gender stereotypes, we hypothesized that people who are higher in status and authority have been observed to behave with less communion (selflessness and concern with others) and more agency (self-assertion and urge to master) than those who have lower status positions. Therefore, perceivers' observations that women occupy lower status positions than men may lead them to believe that women are more communal and less agentic than men.

By a similar logic, the differing distributions of women and men into the roles of homemaker and employee may account for the stereotypic beliefs that women are communal and men are agentic. Because the labor-force participation rates of women (51.2%) and men (77.2%) still differ considerably (U.S. Department of Labor, 1980), perceivers are like to have observed fewer women than men in employee roles and almost exclusively women in the homemaker role. The perception of woman as less agentic and more communal than men would follow if employees have been observed to behave more assertively and masterfully than homemakers as well as less selflessly and supportively toward others. According to this analysis, the stereotypic differences between women and men should parallel the differences that people perceive between homemakers and employees. Some empirical support for this hypothesis is provided by Clifton, McGrath, and Wick's (1976) finding that the communal attributes ordinarily ascribed to women were assigned only to housewives and not to four other categories of women (female athlete, career woman, club woman, and "bunny").

The experiments that we have carried out to test these ideas share several features of design. To minimize demand characteristics stemming from subject's knowledge of our hypotheses, each subject read a description of only one woman or man. In addition, the aspect of social roles presumed to account for gender stereotypes (hierarchical status, or occupation as a homemaker or employee) was varied: (a) In Experiments 1 and 2, which examined hierarchical status, some stimulus persons had high-status job titles and some had low-status job titles, and (b) in Experiment 3, which examined the homemaker–employee distinction, some stimulus persons were homemakers and others were employees. For other stimulus persons, this stereotype-relevant aspect of the social role was omitted: (a) In the status experiments, the job title was omitted, and (b) in the homemaker–employee experiment, designation as a homemaker or employed person was omitted. It was in these experimental conditions, in which the role descriptions were omitted, that subjects should have manifested gender stereotyping. According to our analysis, perceivers view men and women stereotypically in the absence of role information, because under such conditions the attributes ascribed to women and men reflect the differing social roles that underlie the stereotypes. In contrast, the addition of role descriptions to female and male stimulus persons prevents gender-stereotypic judgments if such descriptions (e.g., job titles) provide clear-cut information about the aspect of social roles that ordinarily covaries with sex (e.g., hierarchical status). In the presence of such role information, the covariation of sex and role that is the implicit basis of gender stereotypes is removed, and role would determine perceivers' beliefs about people's attributes. Women and men who have the same role would be perceived equivalently.

Experiments 1 and 2

Method

SUBJECTS

In Experiment 1, 276 females and 218 males participated. Of these subjects, 256 were University of Massachusetts psychology students who participated in a laboratory setting to obtain extra-credit course points. An experimenter randomly

selected the remaining 228 subjects by choosing on repeated occasions every fourth person seated in a University of Massachusetts coffee shop. In Experiment 2, 237 females and 243 males participated. One female and one male experimenter each randomly selected half of the subjects by choosing every fourth person seated in a coffee shop or general library at Purdue University. Especially in Experiment 1, the subjects sampled from the public campus locations included university staff as well as students. In the experiments reported in this article, 80% or more of the persons selected from such locations agreed to participate. Subjects' mean age was 22.30 years in Experiment 1 and 21.81 years in Experiment 2.

PROCEDURE

Each subject read a brief description of an employee (e.g., "Phil Moore is about 35 years old and has been employed for a number of years by a supermarket. He is one of the managers") and rated this stimulus person. The description in Experiment 1 varied according to a $2 \times 3 \times 2$ (female vs. male × high-status job title vs. low-status job title vs. no job title × bank vs. supermarket setting) factorial design. The design of Experiment 2 differed with respect to the setting variable, which had four levels because a medical clinic and a university department of biology were added.

In the laboratory sessions of Experiment 1, a female experimenter administered materials to subjects in groups of about 25. Subjects first indicated their age and sex. To ensure that subjects thought carefully about the stimulus person, the experimenter had them "spend a moment thinking about" the stimulus person (after reading the description) and then write a few sentences about the person. Subjects then responded to the measures described below.

At the public campus locations in both experiments, an experimenter approached each subject by asking her or him to participate in a study on "impressions of other people." After the subject had completed the questionnaire, the experimenter asked her or his age and recorded this information along with the subject's sex.

MANIPULATION OF INDEPENDENT VARIABLES

Sex of Stimulus Person. The stimulus persons were either female or male. Sex was identified by sex-typed names (e.g., Sue Fisher, Phil Moore).

Status of Job Title and Setting of Job. The stimulus persons had either a high-status job title, a low-status job title, or no job title. To provide an internal replication of the design, the stimulus persons were described as employed by a bank or a supermarket and, in Experiment 2, also by a medical clinic or a university department of biology. The high- and low-status job titles for these settings were vice-president and teller, manager and cashier, physician and x-ray technician, and professor and lab technician, respectively.

MEASURING INSTRUMENTS[1]

Beliefs About Stereotypic Attributes. Using 5-point scales, subjects rated the stimulus persons on 18 attributes presented either as per quality characteristics (Experiment 1) or as attributes of on-the-job behavior (Experiment 2). Each on-the-job rating scale was preceded by a question asking how much of the attribute the stimulus person exhibited on the job (e.g., "How competitive do you think this person is on the job?")

Attributes were selected primarily from the Personal Attributes Questionnaire (Spence & Helmreich, 1978) to ensure that they (a) represented gender stereotypes and (b) included both communal and agentic qualities. A factor analysis (varimax orthogonal rotation) of subjects' ratings was performed for each of the experiments in this series. All analyses yielded similar two-factor solutions. One factor, labeled *communal*, accounted for an average of 17.4% of the variance in the five experiments, and another factor, labeled *agentic*, accounted for an average of 23.9% of the variance. Although various other labels have been used by researchers to characterize these dimensions (e.g., expressiveness vs. instrumentality, social orientation vs. task orientation, and femininity vs. masculinity), none provided as close a match to the actual content of the factors as did Bakan's (1966) terms, communion and agency.

The measure of perceived communion was the mean of each subject's ratings on the attributes that (in the five experiments) consistently loaded highly on the communal factor: kind, helpful, understanding, warm, aware of others' feelings, and (in all but Experiment 1, which omitted this attribute) able to devote self to others. The measure of perceived agency was the mean of each subject's

ratings on the attributes that consistently loaded highly on the agentic factor: active, not easily influenced, aggressive, independent, dominant, self-confident, competitive, makes decisions easily, never gives up easily and (in all but Experiment 1, which omitted this scale) stands up well under pressure. These measures had satisfactory internal consistency. The mean values or coefficient alpha (Cronbach, 1951) in the five experiments were .84 for communion and .86 for agency. The findings of all five experiments are presented in terms of these measures. Because few significant effects were obtained on several rating scales not included in these measures, these findings will not be reported.

Inferred Job Status. In the laboratory portion of Experiment 1 and in Experiment 2, subjects estimated (in dollars) the stimulus person's annual salary. In Experiment 2, for stimulus persons who had no job title, subjects also gave their "best guess" concerning the individual's job title. Coders blind to the experimental renditions divided the job titles into (a) a high-status category consisting of jobs that either included an administrative or managerial component or required high-level technical skills and (b) a low-status category of other jobs. Coders agreed on approximately 95% of these relatively objective judgments, and disagreements were resolved by discussion. In the laboratory portion of Experiment 1, subjects also rated the status of the stimulus person's job on a 15-point scale ranging from low status to high status.[2]

Results

The principal data analyses were Sex of Stimulus Person × Status of Job Title × Setting analyses of variance (ANOVAS). Because no significant effects occurred in Experiment 1 for locale in which stimulus materials were administered (coffee shop vs. laboratory), this variable was dropped from the analyses reported here. Also, analyses including subject sex as an additional variable yielded very few differences between female and male subjects

---

[1]For all experiments, measures are listed in the order in which they were administered.

[2]Because this rating-scale measure proved insensitive to differences between conditions, it was not included in additional studies and will not be discussed further.

for any of the experiments in this series.[3] Therefore, this variable was also dropped from all analyses reported in this article. Finally, because analyses including experimenter (female vs. male) as an additional factor yielded very few effects in Experiment 2 (or in Experiments 3 and 5, which also used one experimenter of each sex), this variable was dropped from all reported analyses.

INFERRED JOB STATUS

Salary Estimates. On subjects' estimates of the stimulus persons' salaries, the main effects of sex of stimulus person and status of job title were highly significant for both Experiments 1 and 2.[4] Women were judged to have lower salaries than men: For Experiment 1, $Ms = \$12,154$ versus $\$15,425$, respectively, $F(1, 244) = 27.24, p < .001$, and for Experiment 2, $Ms = \$19,749$ versus $\$23,535$, respectively, $F(1, 449) = 15.29, p < .001$. Consistent with the significant main effects of status—for Experiment 1, $F(2, 244) = 50.58$, and for Experiment 2, $F(2, 449) = 137.28, ps < .001$—persons with high-status job titles were judged to earn considerably more than persons whose job titles were not given, who in turn were judged to earn more than persons with low-status job titles: For Experiment 1, $Ms = \$19,236$ versus $\$11,773, p < .001$, and $\$11,773$ versus $\$10,120, p < .025$; for Experiment 2, $Ms = \$32,057$ versus $\$18,548, p < .001$, and $\$18,548$ versus $\$14,359, p < .001$. The Sex × Status interactions were nonsignificant, $F(2, 244) = 1.64$ and $F(2, 449) = 1.61$.

---

[3]The absence of Sex of Subject × Sex of Stimulus Person interactions is noteworthy in view of research suggesting that in-group members perceive in-groups more favorably and less stereotypically and homogeneously than they perceive outgroups (e.g., Brewer, 1979; Tajfel, 1981; see also Park & Rothbart, 1982, regarding perceptions of women and men). Perhaps this in-group–out-group bias is a manifestation of the self-enhancing tendency in a person perception (e.g., Zuckerman, 1979) and occurs when respondents rate in-group members as they would rate themselves. It is likely that in the present experiments, subjects merely retrieved their concepts of various groups of people (e.g., male bank tellers, employed women, average men) and did not treat themselves as exemplars of the same-sex categories.

[4]Because the variance of subjects' salary estimates was extremely heterogeneous, with larger means associated with larger variances, analyses were performed on the logarithm of the salaries in all experimenting in this series. There was no serious heterogeneity on the other dependent variables in these experiments.

The findings that women were judged to have lower salaries than men, regardless of whether job titles were indicated, suggest that the salary estimates may have functioned largely as a measure of perceived wage discrimination. To provide clear-cut evidence that lower status was associated with women more than with men, the tendency to ascribe lower salaries to women should have been especially strong in conditions omitting job titles, in which the typical status difference was not countered by information that equated women's and men's jobs. Thus the absence of the expected Sex × Status interaction in Experiment 1 led us to include a purer indicator of status, job title guesses, in Experiment 2.

Job Title Guesses. For stimulus persons without job titles in Experiment 2, a greater proportion of subjects' job-title guesses were categorized as high status (vs. low status) for male than for female stimulus persons. High-status job titles were ascribed to 48 men and 30 women, and low-status job titles were ascribed to 30 men and 39 women. A loglinear analysis of the cell frequencies (Bishop, Fienberg, & Holland, 1975; Davis, 1974) revealed a significant likelihood ratio chi-square ($G^2 = 4.82, p < .05$) for the interaction between sex of stimulus person and judged job-title status. Thus the job-title measure of inferred status yielded clear evidence that without knowing job titles, subjects inferred that women held lower status positions than men.

BELIEFS ABOUT STEREOTYPIC ATTRIBUTES

Subjects' mean ratings of the stimulus persons' communion and agency appear in Tables 7.1 and 7.2. On communion, the main effect of sex of stimulus person was marginally significant in Experiment 1 and significant in Experiment 2. Women were perceived as more communal than men: For Experiment 1, $Ms = 3.61$ versus 3.48, respectively, $F(1,472) = 3.71, p < .06$; for Experiment 2, $Ms = 3.53$ versus $3.34, F(1, 456) = 9.95, p < .002$. Consistent with a significant Sex × Status interaction in Experiment 2 only, $F(2, 456) = 3.46, p < .05$, this stronger communal tendency was ascribed to women (vs. men) with low-status or no job titles ($ps < .01$ or smaller) but was nonsignificant with high-status job titles.

On agency, the main effects of sex and status were highly significant in both experiments. Women were perceive as more agentic than men:

TABLE 7.1. Mean Ratings of Stereotypic Attributes of Female and Male Employees Who Varied in Status of Job Title: Experiment 1

Stimulus person	High status	Low status	No title
Female			
Communal	3.55	3.59	3.69
Agentic	3.74	2.63	2.85
Male			
Communal	3.41	3.58	3.48
Agentic	3.52	2.43	2.78

Note. Means are on a 5-point scale; larger numbers indicate greater communion or agency. Cell *n*s ranged from 78 to 85. For communal, *MSe* = 0.54; for agentic, *MSe* = 0.44.

For Experiment 1, Ms = 3.08 versus 2.92, respectively, $F(1,472)$ = 7.80, $p < .005$; for Experiment 2, Ms = 3.53 versus 3.37, $F(1, 456)$ = 9.99, $p < .002$. Consistent with the significant main effects of status—for Experiment 1, $F(2, 472)$ = 121.01, and for experiment 2, $F(2, 456)$ = 21.33, $ps < .001$—persons with high-status job titles were perceived as more agentic than persons whose job titles were not given or persons with low-status job titles: For Experiment 1, Ms = 3.63 versus 2.81 for high-status versus no job title and 3.63 versus 2.53 for high- versus low-status job title, respectively, $ps < .001$; for Experiment 2, Ms = 3.69 versus 3.36, and 3.69 versus 3.30, respectively, $ps < .001$. In Experiment 1, the contrast between the no job title and low-status job title conditions was also significant ($p < .001$).[5]

Discussion

Several aspects of these finding are unfavorable to the hypothesis that the stereotypes of female

TABLE 7.2. Mean Ratings of On-the-Job Behavior of Female and Male Employees Who Varied in Status of Job Title: Experiment 2

Stimulus person	High status	Low status	No title
Female			
Communal	3.48	3.53	3.50
Agentic	3.77	3.37	3.40
Male			
Communal	3.51	3.21	3.30
Agentic	3.61	3.23	3.25

Note. Means are on a 5-point scale; larger numbers indicate greater communion or agency. All cell *n*s = 80. For communal, *MSe* = 0.41; for agentic, *MSe* = 0.34.

communion and male agency stem from having observed women in lower status roles than men. First, our status-difference explanation of gender stereotypes implies that perceptions of lower status persons resemble those of average women and that perceptions of higher status persons resemble those of average men. This expectation was only partly correlated: Persons with low-status job titles were perceived as considerably less agentic than persons with high-status job titles, but there was no difference in communion.

The second and most surprising aspect of the findings that discount the status hypothesis is the counterstereotypic effect that the sex of the stimulus persons had on the ascription of agentic traits. Women were perceived as more agentic than men despite the perceptions that (a) women earn less than men and hold lower status positions and (b) persons in lower status positions are less agentic than persons in higher status positions. Furthermore, women were perceived as more communal than men, even though persons in lower and higher status positions did not differ in perceived communion.

These perceived sex differences were relatively small, despite their statistical significance. The differences were no larger than .19 on a 5-point scale, with an effect size (d) of .30 (Cohen, 1977). Nevertheless, several aspects of the experiments promote confidence in the reliability of the findings. First, the generalizability of the findings across subjects recruited at two universities and by two different methods (subject pool and random sampling at public campus locations) reduces the likelihood that artifacts arose from particular subject populations. Second, the generalizability of the finding across four organizational settings reduces the likelihood that artifacts arose from beliefs about particular work environments. Third, the generalizability of the findings across two different types of ratings (personality traits and on-the-job behavior) reduces the likelihood that artifacts arose from insufficient sensitivity of global trait ratings. Because inferences from job titles to

[5]In Experiments 1 and 2, several effects of employment setting were also obtained on beliefs and on inferred status. Only one of these effects involved the sex of the stimulus persons. Consistent with this Sex × Setting interaction obtained in Experiment 2 on perceived agency ($p < .01$), subjects rated women's behavior as more agentic than men's in the bank and the supermarket ($ps < .01$), as marginally more agentic than men's in the university department of biology ($p < .09$), but not different from men's in the medical clinic.

attributes of on-the-job behavior should be easier and more direct than inferences from job titles to personality traits, the job behavior ratings of Experiment 2 should have maximized the possibility of obtaining any effects of explicit and implicit variation of job status.

Our findings may be more consistent with the hypothesis that distributions of women and men into homemaker and employee roles underlie gender stereotypes. Because all of the stimulus persons presented in Experiments 1 and 2 were described as employed, the relative absence of gender-stereotypic perceptions may reflect the inclusion of this information about occupational role. Therefore, our third experiment tested the hypothesis that gender stereotypes stem from perceivers' observations of the distribution of women and men into the roles of homemaker and employed person. In this experiment, some female and male stimulus persons were described as employees and some as homemakers, and the occupation of others was not indicated.

One implication of the homemaker versus employee explanation of gender stereotypes is that the differences perceived between persons in these two occupational roles parallel the stereotypic differences between women and men. Therefore, homemakers were expected to be perceived as more communal and less agentic than employed persons. It also follows that women and men are perceived stereotypically when their role assignment as homemaker or employee is unknown, because perceivers have observed that more women than men are homemakers and fewer women are employees. Furthermore, the homemaker–employee analysis implies that women and men are perceived similarly if they have the same occupational role, that is, if both are homemakers or both are employees. Yet, consistent with the agency findings of the first two experiments and inconsistent with our social role analysis, we expected that female employees would be perceived as somewhat more agentic than male employees. We were less confident that female employees would be perceived as more communal because of the marginal significance of this finding in Experiment 1.

The design of our third experiment also allowed us to examine two possible explanations of the relatively high agency ratings of employed women. One explanation is that respondents are no longer willing to derogate women on stereotype questionnaires because of changes in attitudes toward women, greater wariness about revealing one's stereotyping, or possibly other causes. This explanation implies that it would be impossible to replicate the stereotypes of women and men obtained by other investigators (e.g., Broverman et al., 1972; Spence & Helmreich, 1978). The inclusion of *average woman* and *average man* cues in our third experiment allowed us to examine this issue.

According to another explanation for the high level of agency ascribed to employed women, subjects believed that women are less likely to be employed than men and therefore inferred that higher standards are applied to women than to men by employers (or by women themselves) when women are selected for jobs. This selection hypothesis implies that people who are thus highly selected (or self-selected) for a role are believed to be more extreme in role-relevant characteristics. If agentic qualities are believed to be relevant to job success, employed women would be perceived as being more agentic than employed men. It also follows that male homemakers would be perceived as being more communal than female homemakers (provided that communal characteristics are believed to be relevant to the homemaker role). The inclusion of homemaker stimulus persons (as well as employees) allowed us to examine these selection considerations.

The greater agency ascribed to employed women (vs. men) is not plausibly explained in terms of a belief that discrimination makes it necessary for female employees to be more qualified than their male counterparts. People are likely to believe that discrimination exists in relation to high-status positions or other male-dominated jobs, for which traditionally there were barriers excluding or discouraging women. However, in Experiments 1 and 2, subjects were found to believe in women's superiority in agentic qualities when low-status as well as high-status job titles were given. It seems unlikely that subjects believed that women face discrimination in obtaining the low-status positions used in our research (e.g., bank teller, supermarket cashier).

Experiment 3

Method

SUBJECTS

A total or 108 females and 132 males participated. One female and one male experimenter each randomly selected half of the subjects by choosing persons seated in a coffee shop or general library at Purdue University. The subjects' mean age was 21.61 years.

PROCEDURE

Each subject read a brief description (e.g., "an average man" or "an average woman who is employed full-time") and rated this stimulus person. The descriptions varied according to a 2 × 3 (female vs. male × employee vs. homemaker vs. no occupational description) factorial design.

MANIPULATION OF INDEPENDENT VARIABLES

Sex of Stimulus Person. The measures described as an average woman or as an average man.

Occupation of Stimulus Person. The stimulus persons were described as employed full time, or as caring for a home and children and not employed outside the home, or no occupational description was provided.

MEASURING INSTRUMENTS

Beliefs About Stereotypic Attributes. The measures described for Experiment 1 were used.

Inferred Likelihood of Employment. For the stimulus persons for whom no occupational description was provided, subjects indicated on an 11-point scale, ranging from 0% chance to 100% chance, the likelihood that the person was employed full-time.

Inferred Job Status. For stimulus persons described as employed full-time, the salary measure described in Experiment 1 was used.

Results

The principal data analyses were Sex of Stimulus Person × Occupation of Stimulus Person ANOVAS.

INFERRED LIKELIHOOD OF EMPLOYMENT AND INFERRED JOB STATUS

Subjects who received no occupational information about the stimulus person inferred that the woman was less likely than the man to be employed full-time (Ms = 56.50% vs. 79.75%, respectively), $F(1, 78) = 30.39$, $p < .001$. Subjects who rated employees ascribed lower salaries to the woman ($M = \$15,615$) than the man ($M = \$21,193$), $F(1, 78) = 13.06$, $p < .001$.

BELIEFS ABOUT STEREOTYPIC ATTRIBUTES

Subjects' mean ratings of communion and agency appear in Table 7.3. On communion, the significant main effects of sex, $F(1, 234) = 13.32, p < .001$, and occupation, $F(2, 234) = 49.08, p < .001$, should be interpreted in the context of a significant Sex × Occupation interaction, $F(2, 234) = 12.34, p < .001$. These effects are best described in terms of the planned contrasts implied by the hypotheses. As expected, homemakers, regardless of their sex, were perceived as more communal than employees ($p < .001$ for female stimulus persons; $p < .005$ for male stimulus persons). In addition, for stimulus persons without occupational descriptions, the traditional gender stereotype of the woman as being more communal than the man was obtained ($p < .001$). The female and male employees were not perceived to differ in communion, nor were the female and male homemakers. The communal tendency of the woman whose occupation was not given was less than that of the female homemaker ($p < .001$) but greater than that of the employed woman ($p < .001$). The communal tendency of the man whose occupation was not given was less than that of the male homemaker ($p < .001$) or of the employed man ($p < .005$).

On agency, the significant main effect of occupation, $F(2, 234) = 21.88, p < .001$, should be interpreted in the context of the significant Sex × Occupation interaction, $F(2, 234) = 10.14, p < .001$. According to the planned contrasts, employees (regardless of their sex) were perceived as more agentic than homemakers ($ps < .001$ for female and male stimulus persons). In addition, for stimulus persons without an occupational description,

TABLE 7.3. Mean Ratings of Stereotypic Attributes of Females and Males Who Varied in Occupation: Experiment 3

Stimulus person	Employee	Homemaker	No occupational description
Female			
Communal	3.31	4.22	3.81
Agentic	3.69	3.02	3.00
Male			
Communal	3.39	4.11	3.03
Agentic	3.40	2.90	3.46

Note. Means are on a 5-point scale; larger numbers indicate greater communion or agency. All cell ns = 40. For communal MSe = 0.33; for agentic, MSe = 0.31.

the traditional gender stereotype of the man as more agentic than the woman was obtained ($p <$ .001). The female employee was perceived as more agentic than the male employee ($p < .025$), whereas the female and the male homemaker were not perceived to differ. The agentic tendency of the woman without an occupational description did not differ from that of the female homemaker but was less than that of the female employee ($p < .001$). The agentic tendency of the man without an occupational description was greater than that of the male homemaker ($p < .001$) but not different from that of the male employee.

These ANOVA findings are generally consistent with the theory that gender stereotypes stem from the observed distribution of women and men into homemaker and employee roles. Therefore, it is worthwhile to examine the correlations between (a) inferred role distributions of the stimulus persons who lacked occupational descriptions and (b) the ascription of gender-stereotypic attributes to them. Overall, the higher the inferred likelihood that the average woman or man was employed, the lower was her or his communion, $r(78) = -.34, p < .01$, and the higher was her or his agency, $r(78) = .41, p < .001$. Yet inferred likelihood of employment should have been a stronger predictor of stereotypic perceptions for the woman than for the man. This differential predictability would be expected because likelihood of employment for the average man was relatively invariant ($SD = 15.61$ for average man vs. 21.31 for average woman), $F(39, 39) = 1.86, p < .05$, no doubt because this likelihood was generally quite high (see the previous subsection of results). For the woman, greater inferred likelihood of employment was associated with slightly less communion, $r(38) = -.19, p < .25$, and greater agency, $r(38) = .43, p < .01$. For the man, the correlations between inferred likelihood of employment and perceived communion, $r(38) = .13$, and agency $r(38) = .01$, were very small and nonsignificant.

Discussion

The findings of Experiment 3 were generally favorable to the hypothesis that a sex difference in the distribution of women and men into homemaker and employee roles underlies the stereotype that women are communal and men are agentic. Two findings confirmed prerequisite conditions for testing this hypothesis: (a) The average woman and man without occupational descriptions were perceived stereotypically (i.e., the woman was perceived as more communal and the man as more agentic), and (b) the average man was judged as considerably more likely than the average woman to be employed.

The correlational analyses relating likelihood of employment to the attributes of the average woman and man provided one test of whether observations of women's and men's differing occupational roles account for stereotypes. The likelihood that the average woman was employed related positively to her agency and negatively (albeit weakly) to her communion. In other words, subjects who reported that women are often employed tended to view women counterstereotypically, and those who reported that women are less often employed (and presumably more often homemakers) tended to view women stereotypically. Comparable findings were not obtained for men, probably because they are generally employees and rarely homemakers in the naturally occurring situations in which subjects had made their previous observations.

The ANOVA findings concerning the attributes of the stimulus persons whose occupations were described reveal even more clearly that social roles underlie gender stereotypes. Subjects believed that, regardless of sex, persons described as homemakers differed from persons described as employees. Female and male homemakers were perceived to be like stereotypic women (high in communion and low in agency), whereas female and male employees were perceived to be like stereotypic men (low in communion and high in agency). Another important aspect of subjects' beliefs about the stimulus persons with occupational descriptions is that the females and males were perceived relatively equivalently once their social role as employee or homemaker was clarified. The only exception to this pattern, and an exception that demands explanation, is the significantly greater perceived agency of employed women compared with employed men.

The comparisons between same-sex persons who differed in occupation were also moderately consistent with our role-distribution theory of gender stereotypes. Because subjects judged that there was roughly a 50–50 chance that the average woman was employed, perceptions of her personal attributes should have fallen between those of the employed women and the female homemaker. Although this expectation was fulfilled (see Table

7.3), the average woman's perceived agency did not differ significantly from that of the homemaker. Because subjects considered it quite likely that the average man was employed, their beliefs about his personal attributes should have been similar to their beliefs about the employed man. This expectation was fulfilled for agency, but the average man was perceived as significantly less communal than the employed man.[6]

Although the findings of this experiment are generally supportive of the idea that perceived sex differences stem from perceivers' observations of women and men in differing occupational roles, they do not explain the tendency for employed women to be perceived as more agentic than employed men.[7] It is noteworthy that this finding was obtained in Experiments 1 and 2 for the stimulus persons without job titles as well as in Experiment 3 for the average employed persons because these stimulus persons were probably thought to have lower status positions if they were female. As demonstrated in Experiments 1 and 2, lower status employees were believed to be less agentic than higher status employees; therefore, any tendency to ascribe lower status to women could tend to counteract any factors making them appear more agentic than men.

Both of the explanations that we introduced earlier for this sex difference in agentic qualities were discounted by the findings from Experiment 3. The idea that subjects would be unwilling to derogate women on stereotype questionnaires was discounted by their perception of the average woman as significantly less agentic than the average man. The other explanation of female employees' greater agency was that categories of people (e.g., women) who are relatively uncommon in a social role (e.g., employee) are believed to be more stringently selected in terms of the requirements of the role than people who commonly occupy the role. This explanation was discounted by the finding that the male homemaker, who is considerably rarer than the female employee, was not perceived to differ from the female homemaker in communion, the quality that subjects believed typical of homemakers.[8]

Yet another explanation of employed women's higher agency is that this perceived gender difference reflects a semantic or response-language difference in the way males and females are judged (e.g., Manis, 1971; Upshaw, 1969) rather than a difference in how they are perceived. If stimulus persons are implicitly compared with same-sex reference groups, this semantic interpretation suggests that female employees are implicitly compared with other females and therefore are judged as very agentic, whereas male employees are implicitly compared with other males and therefore are judged as not especially agentic. This interpretation also suggests that male homemakers are implicitly compared with other males and therefore are judged as very communal, whereas female homemakers are implicitly compared with other females and therefore are not judged as especially communal. Although female employees were perceived as more agentic than male employees, male homemakers were not perceived as more communal than female homemakers. The fact that female and male homemakers were perceived equivalently, then, does not support the explanation that the perceived sex differences are an artifact of differences in the reference group implic-

---

[6]In the interpretation of these findings, subjects' judgments of the probability that the average woman and man are employed should not be treated as exact estimates of the observed distributions of people into employee and homemaker roles. One reason for our caution is that males who are not employed have probably been observed in largely different roles than females who are not employed. Whereas such females are usually homemakers, probably such males are retired or seeking employment. Therefore, the subjects' judgment that there is an 80% chance that the average man is employed does not imply that 20% of men have been observed as homemakers. It also does not imply that the average man's personality attributes would be perceived as between those ascribed to employees and those ascribed to homemakers. Perhaps the low level of communion ascribed to the average man reflects the unfavorably evaluated roles ascribed to the 20% of men not thought to be employed (e.g., being retired, seeking employment).

[7]Other investigators have reported higher perceived agency and competence in females than males, yet in these studies the situation faced by the stimulus person was judged to be especially difficult or demanding for women (Abramson, Goldberg, Greenberg, & Abramson, 1977; Taynor & Deaux, 1973), or the stimulus materials may have implied employment or special competence (Deaux & Lewis, 1984). Also, in Experiment 3 the communal ratings of employed women and men did not differ (although they did differ significantly in Experiment 2 and marginally in Experiment 1). Therefore, only the sex difference in employees' agency appears reliable and consequently requires explanation.

[8]Yet it could be that this selection hypothesis pertains to the employee role (because perceivers know that people are screened for employment) but not to the homemaker role (because perceivers are uncertain about whether people are screened for the occupation of homemaker).

itly used by subjects when rating females and males. Yet so little is known about how people use implicit comparison standards that we cannot be completely certain that such a process has no relevance to our findings.

Because our experiments so consistently revealed that female employees were perceived as more agentic than their male counterparts and because this finding is counterstereotypic and perhaps important, we considered another explanation of the finding. Accordingly, the fact that employed women often balance two demanding roles—homemaker and employee—may account for the relatively high agency ratings of such women. Perceivers may have observed these agentic qualities among the women who experience this potential role overload and role conflict.

To enable us to test this "double-burden" explanation, subjects in a fourth experiment rated the personality attributes of an employed woman or man described as either married or single and as either having or not having children at home. Other subjects rated an employed woman or man whose marital and parental statuses were not described. Should the double-burden explanation of women's greater agency be correct, employed women with family responsibilities, especially involving children, would be regarded as particularly agentic. Family responsibilities would increase the agency ascribed to employed men only if such men did not have wives who typically would carry out the household duties. The single father would fulfill this criterion and, as a consequence, might also be perceived as especially agentic.

Experiment 4

Method

SUBJECTS

A total of 108 females and 135 males participated in groups of about 15 in a laboratory setting to fulfill a psychology course requirement at Purdue University. One female experimenter administered all stimulus materials. Subjects' mean age was 19.33 years.

PROCEDURE

Each subject read a brief description of a full-time employee (e.g., "an average man who is employed full-time, is married, and has no children") and rated this stimulus person. The descriptions varied according to a $2 \times 2 \times 2$ (employed female vs. employed male × married vs. not married × children at home vs. no children at home) factorial design. Two control conditions were provided: a female for whom neither marital nor parental status was provided and a male for whom neither status was provided.

MANIPULATION OF INDEPENDENT VARIABLES

Sex of Stimulus Person. The stimulus persons were described as an average employed woman or an average employed man.

Marital Status of Stimulus Person. The stimulus persons whose marital status was provided were described as married or as not married. For the remaining stimulus persons, no information about marital status was provided.

Parental Status of Stimulus Person. The stimulus persons whose parental status was provided were described as having children at home or not having children. (The unmarried woman or man with children at home was further described as a "single parent," to aid subjects in this potentially ambiguous description). For the remaining stimulus persons, no information about children was provided.

MEASURING INSTRUMENTS

Subjects' beliefs about stereotypic attributes and job status were assessed using measures described in Experiment 1. The subjects also estimated the number of hours that the stimulus person worked per day doing household and family-related work. For stimulus persons whose marital and parental statuses were not provided, subjects used an 11-point rating scale, ranging from 0% to 100% chance, to rate the likelihood that the person was married. On a second, similar scale, the subjects rated the likelihood that the person had children at home.

Results and Discussion

The principal data analyses were Sex of Stimulus Person × Marital Status of Stimulus Person × Parental Status of Stimulus Person ANOVAS, with the error term including the two control conditions, which omitted the information about marital and parental statuses.

INFERENCES ABOUT MARRIAGE, CHILDREN, HOUSEHOLD WORK, AND JOB STATUS

For employees whose marital and parental statuses were omitted, the woman was judged less likely to be married ($M = 54.17\%$) than the man ($M = 76.00\%$), $F(1,47) = 20.50, p < .001$. She was also judged less likely to have children at home than her male counterpart ($Ms = 43.75\%$ versus 66.00%, respectively). $F(1, 47) = 16.22, p < .001$. Thus subjects did not consider it highly likely that the average employed woman faced a double burden of family and employment responsibilities.

Analyses of subjects' estimates of the number of hours per day the employed persons spent doing household and family-related work revealed only one significant effect: Persons with children were judged to do more work than persons without children ($Ms = 4.91$ versus 3.34, respectively), $F(1, 233) = 6.96, p < .01$. Subjects failed to acknowledge that married female employees spend more time on household work than married male employees, even though this sex difference has been well documented in sociological literature on housework (e.g., Hartmann, 1981).

Analyses of subjects' salary estimates replicated the effect of sex obtained in our previous experiments: Women were judged to have lower salaries than men ($Ms = \$18,074$ versus $\$25,055$, respectively), $F(1, 233) = 38.29 \, p < .001$.

BELIEFS ABOUT STEREOTYPIC ATTRIBUTES

Subjects' mean ratings of communion and agency appear in Table 7.4. On communion, the main ef-

fects of marital and parental statuses were both significant. Married employees were judged as being more communal than single employees ($Ms = 3.54$ versus 3.26, respectively), $F(1, 233) = 9.60$, $p < .01$. Employees with children at home were judged as more communal than employees without children at home ($Ms = 3.68$ versus 3.11, respectively), $F(1, 233) = 41.75, p < .001$.[9]

On agency, only the sex effect proved significant: Replicating the three previous experiments, female employees were perceived as more agentic than male employees ($Ms = 3.75$ versus 3.59, respectively), $F(1, 233) = 7.27, p < .01$, calculated on the basis of all 10 conditions.[10] Thus, contrary to the double-burden hypothesis, neither marital nor parental status influenced the agency ascribed to employed women or men.

In view of this nonconfirmation of the double-burden explanation of women's perceived agency and in view of the continued reliability of the finding itself, we considered yet another explanation: Perhaps employed women are considered more agentic than their male counterparts because they are more likely to have chosen to be employed. Because agency evidently typifies employees (per-

---

[9] Consistent with a Sex of Stimulus Person × Parental Status of Stimulus person interaction, $F(1, 233) = 5.86, p < .05$, male employees with children at home were perceived as considerably more communal than male employees without children at home ($Ms = 3.76$ versus 2.97, respectively $p < .001$), whereas female employees with children at home were not perceived as so greatly different ($M = 3.59$) from female employees without children at home ($M = 3.25$), although this difference remained significant for the females ($p < .01$).

[10] For all five role descriptions, the female agency mean was larger than the male mean. Yet this agency sex difference became quite small for the stimulus person for whom marital and parental statuses were not described. However, in this female stimulus-person condition, there were two unusually low agency scores.

TABLE 7.4. Mean Ratings of Stereotypic Attributes of Female and Male Employees Who Varied in Marital and Parental Statuses: Experiment 4

Stimulus person	Married/ children	Married/no children	Single/ children	Single/no children	No description
Female					
Communal	3.77	3.38	3.42	3.11	3.30
Agentic	3.70	3.83	3.91	3.84	3.49
Male					
Communal	3.86	3.10	3.66	2.87	3.40
Agentic	3.59	3.54	3.75	3.60	3.45

Note. Means are on a 5-point scale; larger numbers indicate greater communion or agency. Cell ns ranged from 22 to 27. For communal, $MS_e = 0.37$; for agentic, $MS_e = 0.24$.

haps because most jobs require and reward agentic behavior), observing that women often are employed by choice may have led perceivers to infer that such women are agentic. This explanation of the effects of choice on stereotype formation follows from correspondent inference theory (Jones & Davis, 1965), which suggests that perceivers more often infer that an employee possesses the personal qualities she or he manifests behaviorally if it appears that the employee has freely chosen to work and has not been required to work by virtue of her or his life situation or sex role.

In a test of this freedom-of-choice explanation, subjects in a fifth experiment rated the personal attributes of a female or male employee described as employed by choice or employed out of necessity. Other subjects rated a female or male employee about whom no choice information was provided.

Experiment 5

Method

SUBJECTS

A total of 110 females and 132 males participated. One female and one male experimenter each randomly selected half of the subjects by choosing persons seated in a coffee shop or general library at Purdue University. Subjects' mean age was 20.59 years.

PROCEDURE

Each subject read a brief description of a full-time employee [e.g., "an average woman who is employed full-time and who is employed because she wants to work (and not because she has to work)"] and rated this stimulus person. The descriptions varied according to a 2 × 3 (female vs. male × employed by choice vs. employed out of necessity vs. no choice information) factorial design.

MANIPULATION OF INDEPENDENT VARIABLES

Sex of Stimulus Person. The stimulus persons were described as an average employed woman or an average employed man.

Choice of Stimulus Person to be employed. The stimulus persons were described as employed be-

cause they want to work and not because they have to work or employed because they have to work and not because they want to work, or no information about employment choice was provided.

MEASURING INSTRUMENTS

Subjects' beliefs about stereotypic attributes and job status were assessed with the measures described in Experiment 1. For the stimulus persons about whom no choice information was provided, subjects used an 11-point scale, ranging from 0% to 100% chance, to rate the likelihood that the person worked "because she [he] has to and not because she [he] wants to."

Results

The principal data analyses were Sex of Stimulus Person × Choice of Stimulus Person to Be Employed ANOVAS.

INFERRED LIKELIHOOD OF EMPLOYMENT OUT OF NECESSITY AND INFERRED JOB STATUS

The average employed woman was judged less likely to be employed out of necessity than the average employed man (Ms = 48.75% versus 67.33%, respectively), $F(1, 78)$ = 11.50, $p < .01$. Also, women were judged to have lower salaries than men (Ms = $16,330 versus $23,983, respectively), $F(1, 235)$ = 55.81, $p < .001$. The main effect of the stimulus person's choice to be employed, $F(2, 235)$ = 17.78, $p < .001$, revealed that higher salaries were ascribed to employees working by choice (M = $23,265) or to employees without choice information (M = $21,304) than to employees working out of necessity (M = $15,977, $ps < .001$).

BELIEFS ABOUT STEREOTYPIC ATTRIBUTES

Subjects' mean ratings of communion and agency appear in Table 7.5. On communion, only the main effect of choice proved significant, $F(2, 236)$ = 7.41, $p < .001$: Greater communion was ascribed to employees working by choice (M = 3.43) or employees without choice information (M = 3.35) than to employees working out of necessity (M = 3.10 $ps < .01$ or smaller).

On agency, the main effects of sex and choice

TABLE 7.5. Mean Ratings of Stereotypic Attributes of Female and Male Employees Who Varied in Choice to Be Employed: Experiment 5

Stimulus person	Employed by choice	Employed out of necessity	No choice information
Female			
Communal	3.38	3.23	3.41
Agentic	3.86	2.95	3.80
Male			
Communal	3.45	2.98	3.27
Agentic	3.85	2.66	3.38

Note. Means are on a 5-point scale; larger numbers indicate greater communion or agency. Cell *ns* ranged from 40 to 41. For communal, *MSe* = 0.31; for agentic, *MSe* = 0.27.

were both significant, as was the interaction between these variables. Women were perceived as more agentic than men (*Ms* = 3.54 vs. 3.30, respectively), $F(1, 236) = 12.34, p < .001$. Consistent with the choice main effect, $F(2, 236) = 89.54, p < .001$, employees working by choice were perceived as more agentic than employees without choice information (*Ms* = 3.86 versus 3.59, p < .002, respectively), who in turn were more agentic than employees working out of necessity ($M = 2.80$ $p < .001$). Consistent with the Sex × Choice interaction, $F(2, 236) = 3.46, p < .05$, the tendency for women to be perceived as more agentic than men was significant for employees without choice information ($p < .001$) and employees working out of necessity ($p < .025$) and nonsignificant for employees working by choice. Note also that for women, the agency of the employee working by choice did not differ from that of the employee without choice information, and these two employees were more agentic than the employee working out of necessity ($ps < .001$). For men, the agency of the employee working by choice was greater than that of the employee with no choice information ($p < .001$), and these two employees were more agentic than the employee working out of necessity ($ps < .001$).

These ANOVA findings generally support the hypothesis that employed women are perceived as more agentic than employed men, because women have been observed to exercise greater choice about being employed. Thus it is worthwhile to examine, for employees about whom no choice information was provided, the correlation between freedom of choice and agency. Overall, the more likely an employee was to be regarded as working

out of necessity rather than choice, the lower was her or his agency, $r(78) = -.40, p < .001$. However, this relation was considerably stronger for the female employee, $r(38) = -.55, p < .001$, than the male employee, $r(38) = -.09, ns$.

Discussion

In Experiment 5, the average employed woman was once again rated as more agentic than the average employed man, and the findings of this experiment favored the hypothesis that this sex difference stems from perceivers' observations that women are more likely than men to have chosen to be employed. One of the findings favoring this hypothesis is that the average employed woman was judged as more likely than the average employed man to be working by choice rather than necessity. Furthermore, on a correlational basis, the less likely subjects believed it was that the average employed woman works out of necessity, the more agency they ascribed to her.

Stronger evidence that sex differences in choice to be employed underlie the greater perceived instrumentality of female (vs. male) employees is provided by subjects' beliefs about the agency of employees described as either having or lacking freedom of choice. The choice information strongly affected agency ratings in the expected direction: Regardless of their sex, employees working by choice were perceived as more agentic than employees working out of necessity. Furthermore, perceived agency was similar for the women and men about whom choice information was provided. When employed by choice, the woman and the man did not differ in agency, although when employed out of necessity, the woman was perceived as somewhat more agentic than the man.[11]

In addition, it should be noted that the comparisons between stimulus persons of the same sex are relatively consistent with our freedom-of-choice

---

[11]The meaning or these comparisons is necessarily somewhat ambiguous because the choice information may have had different implications for males than for females. For example, a man employed by choice may be perceived as independently wealthy, whereas a woman employed by choice may be perceived as married and merely in comfortable financial circumstances. Similarly, a woman employed out of necessity may be perceived as single or in especially poor financial circumstances, whereas a man employed out of necessity may be perceived as fairly typical of all men (as suggested by the findings presented above).

hypothesis. Because subjects believed that it was moderately likely that the average employed woman had freedom of choice, her agency should have been perceived as similar to that of the woman employed by choice. As expected, the agency of the average employed woman did not differ from that of the woman employed by choice, and it was greater than that of the woman employed out of necessity. Because subjects believed that it was moderately unlikely that the average employed man had freedom of choice, his agency should have been perceived as lower than that of the man employed by choice. As expected, the agency of the average employed man was lower than that of the man employed by choice although higher than that of the man employed out of necessity.

Even though the communion findings are not relevant to our hypothesis, it should be noted that lack of choice also lowered the stimulus persons' communal tendency. The fact that the effect of choice on communion was weaker than its effect on agency may explain why women's greater freedom of choice did not cause female employees to be perceived as more communal than male employees, as well as more agentic. Consistent with the weak effect of choice on communion, in this series of experiments, nonsignificant tendencies in the female direction were found in the majority of communion comparisons, and in Experiment 2, which had a large number of subjects, the comparison reached significance.

As we noted earlier, the relation between freedom of choice and agency may be attributionally mediated. Because jobs are thought to require agentic behavior, observations that members of a particular group are generally employed by choice may favor the correspondent inference that such people possess agentic personality attributes. It is also possible that employed women's greater freedom of choice implies that they are more qualified because of selection or self-selection in terms of agentic qualities. That is, mainly those women who are agentic have chosen to work or have been specially selected to work (see also Footnote 8). An additional explanation stems from the finding that activities perceived to be voluntary rather than required are associated with more positive affect and higher involvement (Csikszentmihalyi & Figurski, 1982). Therefore, the higher ratings of the agency (and communion) of employees who freely chose to work might be a consequence of the positive affect that has been observed to char-

acterize this major portion of such individuals' lives.

General Discussion

According to our framework, social structure accounts for the content of stereotypes, or more exactly, the observed distribution of groups into various aspects of social structure underlies stereotypes. Although such an explanation may account for stereotypes about other subgroups within societies (e.g., races), we have confined our investigation to gender stereotypes by hypothesizing that the observed distribution of women and men into social roles underlies these stereotypes. In particular, our experiments investigated whether perceivers' beliefs about women and men stem from their previous observations of women and men in differing statuses within work hierarchies and in differing occupational roles. Because the content of gender stereotypes arises from perceivers' observations of people's activities and these activities are determined primarily by social roles, gender stereotypes (operationally defined as beliefs that certain attributes differentiate women and men; see Ashmore & Del Boca, 1981) arise when women and men are observed typically to carry out different social roles.

Any theory of the content of gender stereotypes should account for the major perceived gender differences documented in past research—namely, the agentic qualities ascribed to men and the communal qualities ascribed to women. These differences should be accounted for by one or both of the major differences in the way women and men are distributed into social roles—namely, the concentration of women in lower positions in hierarchies of status and authority, and in the homemaker rather than the employee occupational role. In our research, only the homemaker–employee difference appeared to account for the subjects' beliefs that women are especially communal and men especially agentic. Although status differences did not account for these beliefs, it would be surprising, in view of the importance that sociologists have accorded to hierarchy as a fundamental aspect of social roles (e.g., Blau, 1964; Weber, 1947) if observed status differences did not underlie any beliefs about gender-differentiating traits and behaviors. On the contrary, status differences have been shown to account for the belief that women are more compliant than men (Eagly & Wood, 1982).[12]

In documenting that occupational roles underlie belief in female communal qualities and male agentic qualities, our research has shown that beliefs about women resemble those about homemakers and that beliefs about men resemble those about employed persons. In addition, our research has shown that beliefs about what is typical of homemakers and employees override beliefs about what is typical of women and men, whereas the converse does not occur. Beliefs about what is typical of women and men do not override beliefs about what is typical of homemakers and employees.[13] Instead, except for the greater agency of female employees, women and men were perceived equivalently once their occupational role as homemaker or employee was specified. The underlying reason that occupational role is more important than self in determining beliefs about communal and agentic characteristics is that stereotypes concerning these qualities have become associated with the sexes mainly because sex has been observed to covary with occupational role.

Although the finding that female employees are perceived as more agentic than their male counterparts was initially serendipitous, it is compatible with our social–structural perspective if it is interpreted in terms of perceived choice. The perception that employed women are likely to be employed by choice arises not only from perceivers' observations that women (and not men) are homemakers but also from their belief that women's primary obligation is to the domestic role, a belief documented by public opinion research (e.g., Mason, 1973; Mason, Czajka, & Arber, 1976). Because traditionally the role of homemaker did not include any obligation to seek employment outside the home, employment tends to be regarded as an optional or freely chosen aspect of married women's lives. Therefore, even the perception of employed women as more agentic than employed men reflects previous observations of women's and men's different distributions into (and obligations in relation to) domestic and paid employment roles.

Relation to Research on Cognitive Bases of Stereotyping

Our research has implications for several aspects of stereotyping that have been examined recently in the research literature on social cognition. One highly relevant analysis has treated sex stereotypes as prior probabilities in a Bayesian model (Locksley, Borgida, Brekke, & Hepburn, 1980; Locksley, Hepburn, & Ortiz, 1982). Locksley and her colleagues found perceived sex differences in a target person's assertiveness only when subjects did not have diagnostic, individuating information about the target's previous levels of assertiveness. This information caused the prior probabilities of women's and men's assertiveness to be revised. Similarly, in our research, even extremely general information about a person's employment status caused subjects to revise their estimates of women's and men's communal and agentic qualities.

Our findings, however, highlight the incompleteness of the Bayesian analysis, which does not explain why stereotypes have certain content, even though it does model a process by which past behavior or other characteristics that are believed to predict future behavior override information about sex. To account parsimoniously for the content of gender stereotypes, an investigator must find a behavioral of personal attribute that is diagnostic of the particular set of attributes believed to characterize women and men—namely, the strong communal and weak agentic tendencies ascribed to women and the weak communal and strong agentic tendencies ascribed to men. To explain these beliefs, an attribute must (a) differentiate the sexes and (b) relate to perceived agency and communion in opposite directions. As we have shown, these criteria are fulfilled by the occupational roles of homemaker and employee. Yet we have shown that one's position in hierarchies of status and authority does not meet these requirements.

Although most social cognition research has little power to account for the content of stereo-

---

[12]Indeed, still other aspects of the distribution of men and women in society may affect beliefs about the sexes. For example, Kiesler (1975) suggested that because men outnumber women as successful achievers in many occupations, perceivers tend to evaluate an individual woman's achievements less favorably than an individual man's, even when their products are objectively equal. Perceivers' judgments of an individual's success may thus reflect the probability of success for persons of the individual's gender.

[13]Deaux and Lewis (1984) have also reported that role information is more important than sex in determining beliefs about women and men, although their role descriptions included more than occupational cues (e.g., the masculine role was described as "head of the household, financial provider, a leader, and responsible for household repairs").

types, research on "illusory correlation" (e.g., Hamilton, 1981; Hamilton & Gifford, 1976) pertains to content. It has shown that minority group members may be perceived to have characteristics with low probability of occurrence merely because the group members and such characteristics are both rare and therefore distinctive. In our research women constitute minorities in some social roles (e.g., as high-status employees), as do men in other social roles (e.g., as homemakers). Nevertheless, despite their rarity, such women and men appear to be assigned primarily the attributes that correspond to the roles they occupy.

Our research also relates to the issue of whether there is a basic level of categorization that people commonly use in representing other people and ascribing attributes to them (Brewer, Dull, & Lui, 1981; Cantor & Mischel, 1979; Taylor, 1981). In particular, categorizations at this basic level are hypothesized to maximize the richness, differentiation, and vividness of subjects' perceptions of people. Using such criteria, Cantor and Mischel (1979) concluded that categorization at the level of social roles or "persona" is basic in person perception. It is notable that the research reported in the present article and our earlier research on beliefs about social influence (Eagly & Wood, 1982) point to the importance of categorizations at the level of social roles (i.e., occupation and hierarchical status), which are highly diagnostic of people's traits and abilities. One's sex can be considered less basic than roles because it functions as a cue that, due to its previous association with social roles, provides indirect access to occupation and hierarchical status.

Finally, our framework is not inconsistent with the idea popular in the social cognition literature that stereotypes function as prototypes (e.g., Cantor & Mischel, 1979) or schemata (e.g., Taylor & Crocker, 1981). Our claim that observations of social roles underlie gender stereotypes is not meant to imply that the stimulus person's social role is ordinarily retrieved for perceivers to infer her or his attributes. Instead, perceivers' prototype or schema of a typical woman or man is retrieved, and judgments are made in terms of the personal attributes already associated with it. Because people's activities are determined primarily by their social roles, the prototypes or schemata that perceivers possess of woman and man consist largely of attributes that covary with the role assignments of women and men. Therefore, our

analysis primarily elaborates the process by which stereotypes have acquired particular content rather than the processes that occur when stereotypes are used to make judgments. Yet our analysis includes the important point that the use of gender stereotypes is under the control of cues that carry role information because of the origin of these stereotypes in observed variation in role assignments. Gender stereotypes are not applied when typical role arrangements are invalidated by these cues.

Conclusion

To turn from issues of cognitive mediation toward more general issues addressed in the stereotyping literature, we note that our analysis bears on the classic "kernel-of-truth" question pertaining to the validity of stereotypes. In assuming that stereotypes validly represent the social structure and division of labor in a society, our approach is consistent with that of other investigators who have implicated these factors as the kernel of truth of ethnic stereotypes (Brewer & Campbell, 1976) and gender stereotypes (Williams & Best, 1982). As such, our approach deviates from psychologists' more typical assumptions that stereotypes stem from psychological factors such as perceivers' distortions (e.g., Katz & Braly, 1933; Lippmann, 1922) and biases inherent in perceivers' cognitive processing (e.g., Hamilton, 1979). However the kernel-of-truth question is considerably broader than our social structural hypothesis, and as Brigham (1971), Campbell (1967), and others have noted, there is ample reason to believe that stereotypes both represent and distort reality. Our research, by relating stereotypes to perceived distributions into social roles, provides a promising avenue for addressing the kernel-of-truth question.

This kernel-of-truth issue raises the question of whether the various attributes associated with social roles reflect ingrained personality traits and abilities characteristic of the typical occupants of the roles. In relation to homemaker and employee roles for example, one may wonder whether girls are socialized to acquire communal traits and boys to acquire agentic traits, with the result that women as a group are more suited to perceivers' concept of the homemaker role and men as a group to perceivers' concept of the employee role. Although we believe that socializing agents tend to prepare girls and boys for the social roles that they believe these girls and boys probably occupy as adults

(Eagly, 1983), our theory of stereotypes does not address these issues of how people are prepared for roles and recruited into them. According to our framework, the proximal cause of gender stereotypes is the differing distributions of women and men into social roles, whatever the causation that lies behind these differing distributions.

We also note that our findings have some implications for the issue of gender equality. The gender of "sex role" stereotypes that psychologists have made famous and enshrined in their theories about gender and the methods of gender research appear to be eradicated and even partly reversed by information as general and basic as the fact that the persons being judged are employed. A literal interpretation of our findings suggests that employed women, who constitute about half of American women (U.S. Department of Labor, 1980), are probably not ordinarily perceived in terms of the female stereotype of low agency and high communion, because it is usually quite salient to an employed woman's friends, associates, and family members that she is employed. Yet it is no doubt incorrect to think that employed women escape the traditional female stereotype altogether, because we did not fully understand the conditions under which people apply occupational stereotypes in preference to gender stereotypes. It is very likely that there are contexts in which an employed woman is perceived traditionally, even by people who know that she is employed.

It is also important to note that the stereotypes we obtained of employees do not portray women and men equally. Instead, these stereotypes favor the formerly excluded group: Employed women are perceived as more agentic than employed men (even though women are believed to have lower wages). Yet it should be kept in mind that the source of the extra agency appears to be the belief that women have freely chosen to be employed. Free choice is, of course, absent for many women, a fact acknowledged by our respondents in their estimates of the likelihood that employed women have freedom of choice. Enhanced agency would be ascribed mainly to relatively affluent, married women, because they could most plausibly be regarded as having freely chosen to enter the paid work force.

Another implication of our idea that social structure underlies beliefs about gender is that change in these beliefs probably must await social change. Our theory and findings suggest that gender stereotypes—the beliefs that women in general differ from men in general—will not disappear until people divide social roles equally, that is, until child care and household responsibilities are shared equally by women and men and the responsibility to be employed outside the home is borne equally. Interventions designed to affect ideas about gender through education and exposure to the media (e.g., ensuring that textbooks have nonsexist portrayals of women and men) would, of course, have some impact in terms of our theory because beliefs about the distribution of people into social roles derive from indirect sources such as textbook portrayals as well as from direct experience. Yet daily life provides abundant direct experience with women and men. Therefore, efforts to remove gender stereotypes educationally may have relatively little impact, compared with actual changes in the distribution of the sexes into social roles.

REFERENCES

Abramson, P. R., Goldberg, P. A., Greenberg, J. H., & Abramson, L. M. (1977). The talking platypus phenomenon: Competency ratings as a function of sex and professional status. *Psychology of Women Quarterly, 2,* 114–124.

Ashmore, R. D., & Del Boca, F. K. (1981). Conceptual approaches to stereotypes and stereotyping. In D. Hamilton (Ed.), *Cognitive processes in stereotyping and intergroup behavior* (pp. 1–35). Hllldale, NJ: Erlbaum.

Bakan, D. (1966). *The duality of human existence: An essay on psychology and religion.* Chicago: Rand McNally.

Bem, S. L. (1974). The measurement of psychological androgyny. *Journal of Consulting and Clinical Psychology, 42,* 155–162.

Bishop, Y. M. M., Fienberg, S. E., & Holland, P. W. (1975). *Discrete multivariate analysis: Theory and practice.* Cambridge, MA: MIT Press.

Blau, P. (1964). *Exchange and power in social life.* New York: Wiley.

Block, J. H. (1973). Conceptions or sex roles: Some cross-cultural and longitudinal perspectives. *American Psychologist, 28,* 512–526.

Blood, R. O., Jr., & Wolfe, D. M. (1960). *Husbands and wives: The dynamics of married living.* Glencoe, IL: Free Press.

Brewer, M. B. (1979). In-group bias in the minimal intergroup situation: A cognitive–motivational analysis. *Psychological Bulletin, 6,* 307–324.

Brewer, M. B., & Campbell, D. T. (1976) *Ethnocentrism and intergroup attitudes: East Africa evidence.* New York: Sage.

Brewer, M. B., Dull, V., & Lui, L. (1981). Perceptions of the elderly: Stereotypes as prototypes. *Journal of Personality and Social Psychology, 41,* 656–670.

Brigham, J. (1971). Ethnic stereotypes. *Psychological Bulletin, 76,* 15–38.

Broverman, I. K., Vogel, S. R., Broverman, D. M., Clarkson, F. E., & Rosenkrantz, P. S. (1972). Sex-role stereotypes: A current appraisal . *Journal of Social Issues, 28,* 59–78.

Brown, I. K. (1979). Women and business management. *Signs, 6,* 266–288.

Campbell, D. T. (1967). Stereotypes and the perception of group differences. *American Psychologist, 22,* 817–829.

Cantor, N., & Mischel, W. (1979). Prototypes in person perception. *Advances in Experimental Psychology, 12,* 3–52.

Clifton, A. K., McGrath. D., & Wick, B. (1976). Stereotypes of women: A single category? *Sex Roles 2,* 135–148

Cohen, J. (1977). *Statistical power analysis for the behavioral sciences* (2nd ed.). New York: Academic Press.

Cronbach, L. J. (1951). Coefficient alpha and the internal structure of tests. *Psychometrika, 16,* 297–334.

Csikszentmihalyi, M., & Figurski, T. J. (1982). Self-awareness and aversive experience in everyday life. *Journal of Personality, 50,* 15–28.

Davis, J. A. (1974). Hierarchical models for significance tests in multivariate contingency tables: An exegesis of Goodman's recent papers. In H. L. Costner (Ed.), *Sociological methodology, 1973–1974* (pp. 189–234). San Francisco: Jossey Bass.

Deaux, K., & Lewis, L. L. (1984). The structure of gender stereotypes: Interrelationships among components and gender label. *Journal of Social Psychology, 46,* 991–1004.

Eagly, A. H. (1983). Gender and social influence: A social psychological analysis. *American Psychologist, 38,* 971–981.

Eagly, A. H., & Wood, W. (1982). Inferred sex differences in status as a determinant of gender stereotypes about social influence. *Journal of Personality and Social Psychology, 43,* 915–928.

England, P. (1979). Women and occupational prestige. A case of vacuous sex equality. *Signs, 5,* 252–265.

Feldman, J. M. (1972). Stimulus characteristics and subject prejudice as determinants of stereotype attribution. *Journal of Personality and Social Psychology, 21,* 333–340.

Gillespie, D. L. (1971). Who has the power? The marital struggle. *Journal of Marriage and the Family, 33,* 445–458.

Hamilton, D. L. (1979). A cognitive–attributional analysis of stereotyping. *Advances in Experimental Social Psychology, 12,* 53–84.

Hamilton, D. L. (1981). Illusory correlation as a basis for stereotyping. In D. Hamilton (Ed.), *Cognitive processes in stereotyping and intergroup behavior* (pp. 115–144). Hillsdale, NJ: Erlbaum.

Hamilton, D. L., & Gifford, R. K. (1976). Illusory correlation in interpersonal perception: A cognitive basis of stereotypic judgments. *Journal of Experimental Social Psychology, 12,* 392–407.

Hartmann, H. I. (1981). The family as the focus of gender, class, and political struggle: The example of housework. *Signs, 6,* 366–394.

Jones, E. E., & Davis, K. E. (1965). From acts to dispositions: The attribution process in person perception. *Advances in Experimental Social Psychology, 2,* 219–266.

Kanter, R. M. (1977). *Men and women of the corporation.* New York: Basic Books.

Katz, D., & Braly, K. W. (1933). Racial stereotypes of one hundred college students. *Journal of Abnormal and Social Psychology, 28,* 280–290.

Kiesler, S. D. (1975). Actuarial prejudice toward women and its implications. *Journal of Applied Social Psychology, 5,* 201–216.

Lippmann, W. (1922). *Public Opinion.* New York: Harcourt, Brace.

Locksley, A., Borgida, E., Brekke, N., & Hepburn, C. (1980). Sex stereotypes and social judgement. *Journal of Personality and Social Psychology, 39,* 821–831.

Locksley, A., Hepburn, C., & Ortiz, V. (1982). Social stereotypes and judgments of individuals: An instance of base rate fallacy. *Journal of Experimental Social Psychology, 18,* 23–42.

Manis, M. (1971). Context reflects in communication: Determinants of verbal output and referential decoding. In M. H. Appley (Ed.), *Adaptation-level theory* (pp. 237–255). New York: Academic Press.

Mason, K. O. (1973). Studying change in sex-role definitions via attitude data. *Proceedings of American Statistical Association, Social Statistics Section,* 138–141.

Mason, K. O., Czajka, J. L., & Arber, S. (1976). Change in U.S. women's sex-role attitudes 1964–1974. *American Sociological Review, 41,* 573–596.

Mennerick, L. A. (1975). Organizational structuring of sex roles in a non-stereotypical industry. *Administrative Science Quarterly, 20,* 570–586.

Park, B., & Rothbart, M. (1982). Perception of out-group homogeneity and levels of social categorization: Memory for the subordinate attributes in in-group and out-group members. *Journal of Personality and Social Psychology, 42,* 1051–1068.

Parsons, T. (1955). Family structure and socialization of the child. In T. Parsons & R. F. Bales (Eds.), *Family: Socialization and interaction process* (pp. 35–131). Glencoe, IL: Free Press.

Scanzoni, J. (1982). *Sexual bargaining: Power politics in the American marriage* (2nd ed.). Chicago: University of Chicago Press.

Smedley, J. W., & Bayton, J. A. (1978). Evaluative race–class stereotypes by race and perceived class of subjects. *Journal of Personality and Social Psychology, 36,* 530–535.

Spence, J. T., & Helmreich, R. L. (1978). *Masculinity & femininity: Their psychological dimensions, correlates, & antecedents.* Austin: University of Texas Press.

Tajfel, H. (1981). *Human groups and social categories.* New York: Cambridge University Press.

Taylor, S. E. (1981). A categorization approach to stereotyping. In D. Hamilton (Ed.), *Cognitive processes in stereotyping and intergroup behavior* (pp. 83–114). Hillsdale, NJ: Erlbaum.

Taylor, S. E., & Crocker, J. (1981). Schematic bases of social information processing. In E. T. Higgins, C. P. Herman, & M. P. Zanna (Eds.), *Social cognition: The Ontario symposium* (Vol. 1, pp. 89–134). Hillsdale, NJ: Erlbaum.

Taynor, J., & Deaux, K. (1973). When women are more deserving than men: Equity, attribution, and perceived sex differences. *Journal of Personality and Social Psychology, 28,* 360–367.

Triandis, H. C. (1977). *Interpersonal behavior.* Monterey, CA: Brooks/Cole.

Upshaw, H. S. (1969). The personal reference scale: An approach to social judgment. *Advances in Experimental Social Psychology, 4,* 315–371.

U.S. Department of Labor, Bureau of Labor Statistics. (1980). *Perspectives on working women: A databook* (Bulletin 2080). Washington, DC: Government Printing Office.

Weber, M. (1947). *The theory of social and economic organization.* Glencoe, IL: Free Press.

Williams, J. E., & Best, D. L. (1982). *Measuring sex stereotypes: A thirty-nation study.* Beverly Hills, CA: Sage.

Zuckerman, M. (1979). Attribution of success and failure revisited, or: The motivational bias is alive and well in attribution theory. *Journal of Personality, 47,* 245–287.

Illusory Correlation in Interpersonal Perception: A Cognitive Basis of Stereotypic Judgments

David L. Hamilton and Robert K. Gifford • Yale University

Illusory correlation refers to an erroneous inference about the relationship between two categories of events. One postulated basis for illusory correlation is the co-occurrence of events which are statistically infrequent; i.e., observers overestimate the frequency of co-occurrence of distinctive events. If one group of persons "occurs" less frequently than another and one type of behavior occurs infrequently, then the above hypothesis predicts that observers would overestimate the frequency that that type of behavior was performed by members of that group. This suggested that the differential perception of majority and minority groups could result solely from the cognitive mechanisms involved in processing information about stimulus events that differ in their frequencies of co-occurrence. Results of two experiments testing this line of reasoning provided strong support for the hypothesis. Implications of the experiments for the acquisition of stereotypes are discussed.

Chapman (1967) has introduced the concept of illusory correlation to refer to "the report by observers of a correlation between two classes of events which, in reality, (a) are not correlated, or (b) are correlated to a lesser extent than reported" (p. 151). Most research on this topic has been concerned with illusory correlation as a basis for erroneous reports of relationships between symptoms of patients and performance on psychodiagnostic tests (Chapman & Chapman, 1967, 1969; Golding & Rorer, 1971; Starr & Katkin, 1969). The interest of the present research was in studying illusory correlation in the way persons make judgments about other people. Specifically, the two experiments reported here were designed to explore the possibility that stereotypic

judgments can be acquired on the basis of purely cognitive, information-processing mechanisms.

In Chapman's (1967) original demonstration of illusory correlation, a series of 12 word pairs—constructed by pairing each of four words from one list with each of three words from a second list—was presented to subjects a number of times. Each word pair was shown the same number of times. When subjects were asked to estimate, for each word on the first list, the percentage of occurrences of that word in which it was paired with each word in the second list, certain systematic biases were observed. When there was a strong associative connection between the words (e.g., *lion–tiger, bacon–eggs*), subjects overestimated the frequency of co-occurrence. In addition, one word

if words made sense/a similar, subjects overestimated

161

in each list was longer than the other words, and subjects consistently overestimated the frequency with which those two words have been paired. Chapman hypothesized that this latter finding was due to the distinctiveness of the long words within their respective lists, and that the co-occurrence of distinctive stimuli can result in an overestimation of the frequency with which the two events occurred together. The long words were distinctive only because the other words were short. Thus, distinctiveness is considered here as due to statistical infrequency. The present research explores the implications of the latter finding— illusory correlation based on the co-occurrence of distinctive stimuli—for social perception.

Why would the co-occurrence of distinctive events result in an illusory correlation? It is well established that observers are more attentive to distinctive than to nondistinctive stimuli, and the heightened attention to a distinctive stimulus should result in a greater encoding of that information. Extending this line of reasoning, the co-occurrence of two distinctive events should be particularly salient to an observer, resulting in increased attention to and more effective encoding of the fact that the two events occurred together, thereby increasing the subjective belief that a relationship exists between them.

Experiment 1

Tajfel (1969) has defined stereotyping as "the attribution of general psychological characteristics to large human groups" (pp. 81–82). Thus stereotyping begins with the differential perception of social groups. When a perceiver differentially evaluates two groups, then the particular content associated with those evaluations constitutes the basis for stereotypic perceptions. Traditional conceptions of the development of stereotypes have emphasized the role of learning and motivational processes (cf. Brigham, 1971; Hamilton, 1976). Recently, however, several lines of research indicate that such differential perceptions of groups can develop simply as a consequence of our normal cognitive processes (see Hamilton, 1976, for a discussion of this research). The present research is consistent with this line of investigation.

The first experiment reported here examined whether the differential perception of groups can be based on the way perceivers process information about co-occurring events, and more specifically, on the co-occurrence of distinctive events. The following conceptual parallel will make the rationale underlying the present research more understandable. In the everyday experience of the typical white suburbanite, interaction with blacks, and even observation of them, is a relatively infrequent occurrence. That is, it is a statistically infrequent event and hence is "distinctive" in the sense that that term was used above. Also, since for most varieties of behavior the norm is positive in value, undesirable (nonnormative) behavior is statistically less frequent than desirable behavior and can also be considered distinctive. Given this framework, the implication of Chapman's (1967) finding is that, even if the distribution of desirable and undesirable behavior is the same for both blacks and whites, the pairing of "blackness" with "undesirable behavior" would lead the typical white observer to infer that those two events co-occur more frequently than they actually do. Such an inference would provide the basis for the differential perception of the majority and minority groups, and hence for stereotypic judgments, based solely on characteristics of how persons process information about other people. The first experiment was designed to subject this line of reasoning to experimental test.

Method

Development of Stimulus Materials. A list of 95 behavior descriptions was developed. The behaviors portrayed in these items for the most part were common, everyday behaviors, such as the following: "is rarely late for work," "always talks about himself and his problems," "converses easily with people he does not know well." This list of behavior descriptions was given to 36 undergraduate college students who rated each item in terms of how desirable they considered the behavior to be. The mean rating of each item was considered to be the desirability scale value of the behavior. From this list, 27 moderately desirable and 12 moderately undesirable items were selected for use in the stimulus materials.

In this study we were interested in examining "paired distinctiveness" as a possible basis for stereotypic judgment. Consequently, members of any actual minority group could not be used as stimulus persons, since judgments of such persons would in all likelihood already be biased by previously formed associations. Therefore, a minority group was "manufactured." Of the 39 stimulus persons used in the study, 26 were identified as members of Group A and 13 as members of Group B.

The stimulus materials used in the study consisted of a series of statements, each statement describing a behavior performed by one male person who was either a member of Group A or Group B, e.g., "John, a member of Group A, visited a sick friend in the hospital." The distribution of the 39 sentences according to desirability of the behavior and the group membership was as follows: Group A, desirable: 18; Group A, undesirable, 8; Group B, desirable: 9; Group B, undesirable: 4. It can be seen that two-thirds of the statements described behaviors performed by members of Group A; this was true of sentences describing both desirable and undesirable behaviors. Also, desirable behaviors were more frequent than undesirable behaviors; for both Groups A and B, there was a 9:4 ratio of desirable to undesirable behaviors. Thus, Group B is distinctive by its occurring less frequently than A, as is undesirable behavior also distinctive by its statistical infrequency. The four sentences which describe a member of Group B performing an undesirable act therefore represent instances of the co-occurrence of distinctive events.

In assigning behavior descriptions to the two groups, care was taken to ensure that the mean and variability of the desirability values of the two groups of sentences were essentially equal. In addition, in view of the rating scales to be used (see below), an attempt was made to equate the two groups on the proportion of sentences describing interpersonal as opposed to task-related behaviors.

Instructions and Procedures. Subjects were run in small groups of four to six per session. The experiment was described as being concerned with how people process and retain information that is presented to them visually, and after some expansion on this theme, the instructions indicated that subjects would see a series of slides, each slide showing a single sentence describing a behavior performed by a particular person. A few examples of the kinds of sentences they would see were then shown. The sample sentences presented descriptions of a person performing some behavior but did not include identification of the actor's membership in Group A or Group B (e.g., "Alex tried not to take sides when two of his friends had an argument"). These sample slides were included in order to expose subjects to the kinds of behavior

that they would see in the experimental set of slides. The instructions then continued as follows.

> In the sentences you will see in the actual experiment, the persons described in the statements will be identified by their membership in a certain group. Each person described in the slides is a member of one of two groups which, to keep things simple, will be referred to as Group A or Group B. In collecting behavior descriptions of people for this experiment we tried to draw a random sample from the population. In the real-world population, Group B is a smaller group than is Group A. Consequently statements describing members of Group B occur less frequently in the slides you will see. . . .
> You will be shown a rather large number of statements like the ones you saw a few minutes ago. . . . As the slides are presented, simply read each statement carefully.

Following these instructions the sequence of 39 slides was presented to the subjects. Each slide was presented for a period of 8 seconds.

When the series of slides was completed, subjects were given a booklet containing materials for the three dependent measures.

Trait Ratings. This experiment was primarily interested in illusory correlation as a basis of differential perceptions of groups. One section of the booklet therefore asked subjects to rate the members of Groups A and B on a series of characteristics. The questionnaire consisted of a list of 20 attributes, each attribute accompanied by two 10-point inference scales, one for Group A and one for Group B. In order to guarantee some degree of heterogeneity in the inference scales used, the 20 attributes were selected on the basis of Rosenberg, Nelson, and Vivekananthan's (1968) analysis of the dimensions underlying first impressions. These authors found two dimensions to be both empirically satisfactory and conceptually useful, a Social or interpersonal dimension (e.g., *popular, sociable* vs. *irritable, unhappy*) and an Intellectual or task-related dimension (e.g., *industrious, intelligent* vs. *lazy, foolish*). Six words representing the positive pole and four words representing the negative pole of each of these two dimensions were used in the trait inference task. If "paired distinctiveness" is a basis for stereotypic judgments, then subjects should give less desirable ratings to members of Group B.

Attributions of Group Membership. Another section of the booklet asked the subject to indicate the group membership of the person who had performed each behavior. The 39 behavior descriptions were listed, each statement beginning with the following phase, "A member of Group ____." For each item, the subjects were asked to write letter A or B in the blank space. If the co-occurrence of distinctive events can result in an overestimate of the frequency of those events, there should be a tendency for negative behaviors to be overattributed to members of Group B.

Frequency of Estimates. The last page of the questionnaire booklet told the subjects how many of the statements had described members of Group A and Group B, and asked them to estimate in each case how many of these statements had described *undesirable* behavior. If subjects overestimate the frequency of co-occurrence of the distinctive events, then they should overestimate the number of undesirable behaviors for Group B.

For half of the subjects, the dependent measures occurred in the order described above. The other half of the subjects completed the trait inferences after filling out the group membership attributions. This manipulation provided a check on the effect of completing one dependent measure on the responses to subsequent measures. In all cases the frequency estimates were completed last. (Since the instructions for the frequency estimates measure specifically focused the subjects' attention on the desirability–undesirability variable, it was decided that this should be the last measure completed by all subjects.)

When the subjects had completed the dependent measures, the purpose of the study and the rationale underlying the procedure used were explained.

Subjects. Subjects in the experiment were 20 male and 20 female undergraduate students at a state university in New Haven. Half of the subjects of each sex received the dependent measures in each of the orders described above.

In a task in which stimulus person's name (John, Bill, etc.), group membership (A, B), and the behavior described were all varying, it is possible that some subjects did not attend to the group membership information while viewing the sequence of slides. However, the basic conditions for testing the present hypotheses require that membership in Group B be recognized as having occurred less frequently than membership in Group A in the series of stimulus sentences. On the attributions of group membership task, if a

subject attributed a majority of the behaviors to Group B (which actually occurred one-third of the time), then that subject could not have perceived information about Group B as distinctive due to its infrequency of occurrence, and hence that subject's data do not provide an adequate basis for testing the hypotheses. It was therefore decided to eliminate from the sample any subject who attributed less than half of the behaviors to Group A (the actual majority group). Seven subjects were thereby eliminated from the sample, and the results reported below are based on the remaining 33 subjects. (Analyses based on the total sample yielded very similar results.)

Results

Attributions of Group Membership. On one dependent measure, subjects attributed each behavior description to a member of Group A or a member of Group B. In classifying these data, a 2 x 2 table was constructed in which the rows referred to the evaluation of the behavior (desirable or undesirable) and the columns were defined by the group membership (A or B) assigned by the subject to each behavior description. Each subject's responses to the 39 items were classified according to such a table, and a phi coefficient was calculated from the data for each subject. In the stimulus sentences there was no relationship between behavior desirability and group membership (cf. Table 8.1a). It was hypothesized, however, that subjects would overattribute undesirable behaviors to members of Group B, a tendency that would result in a nonzero correlation. To test this hypothesis, each subject's phi coefficient was converted to a Fisher's Z-score, and a t-test was conducted to determine whether the mean of this distribution was significantly greater than zero. The results of this test supported the hypothesis, $t(32) = 2.57$, $p < .02$. A 2 x 2 (Sex of Subject × Order of Dependent Measure) analysis of these Z-scores indicated that there were no significant effects associated with these variables.

To examine the basis for this illusory correlation, the mean number of desirable and undesirable statements attributed to members of Group A and Group B on this task was determined. These data, shown in Table 8.1b, indicate that subjects tended to overattribute the undesirable behaviors to Group B. This effect is reflected in the conditional probabilities (shown in parentheses) for the

TABLE 8.1. Results of Experiment 1 for Attributions of Group Membership and Frequency Estimates Measures

(a) Distribution of stimulus sentences

Behaviors	Group A	B	
Desirable	18	9	27
Undesirable	8	4	12
	26	13	39

(b) Attributions of group membership means (conditional probabilities in parentheses)

Behaviors	Group assigned by subject A	B	
Desirable	17.52 (.65)	9.48 (.35)	27.00 (1.00)
Undesirable	5.79 (.48)	6.21 (.52)	12.00 (1.00)
	23.31	15.69	39.00

(c) proportion of each sentence type recalled accurately (values expected by chance in parentheses)

Behavior	Group A	B
Desirable	.74 (.60)	.54 (.40)
Undesirable	.55 (.60)	.65 (.40)

d) Frequency estimates means (conditional proportion in parentheses)

Behaviors	Group A	B	
Desirable	17.09 (.66)	7.27 (.56)	24.36
Undesirable	8.91 (.34)	5.73 (.44)	14.64
	26.00 (1.00)	13.00 (1.00)	39.00

assignment of behaviors to Groups A and B, given the desirability value of the behavior. In the stimulus slides, the probability that a statement described a member of Group A was .67, regardless of desirability value (18 of 27 desirable and eight of 12 undesirable behaviors described members of that group). While the probability that a desirable behavior would be attributed to Group A was .65 (slightly less than the correct probability), the comparable probability given an undesirable behavior was only .48. In other words, although only one-third of the undesirable statements described members of Group B, over half of them were attributed to Group B on the group membership attribution task. Thus, the bias was associated with the undesirable statements, and the data support the interpretation that the illusory correlation was based on the overattribution of undesirable behaviors to the smaller group.

Responses on the attributions of group membership task were further examined to determine the accuracy with which subjects recalled the group membership for each sentence type. If, as argued earlier, subjects differentially attend to and encode information contained in infrequently co-occurring stimulus events, then they should be better able to recall accurately group membership in the case of undesirable behaviors performed by members of Group B. Table 8.1c shows the proportion of correct responses for each sentence type. The proportions expected by chance are shown in parentheses. In their attributions of group member-

ship subjects assigned "A" to 60% of the sentences and attributed 40% to Group B. Thus for those behaviors actually performed by Group A stimulus persons (left column of the table) chance responding would yield correct answers in 60% of the cases. Similarly, 40% accuracy would be expected for those behaviors performed by members of Group B. The data in this table illustrate three points: (a) subjects performed above chance level in three of the four cases, (b) the overattribution of undesirable behaviors to Group B, as described above, resulted in below-chance accuracy for undesirable behaviors associated with Group A, and (c) most important, subjects' performance exceeded the chance level by the greatest amount in the case of the infrequently co-occurring stimuli.

Frequency Estimates. Whereas the preceding analyses demonstrated a bias in subjects' attributions of specific behavior instances, the frequency estimates measure was included to determine whether or not an illusory correlation would manifest itself in a subject's overall estimates of the frequency of desirable and undesirable statements characterizing each group. The subject was told that there were 26 statements describing members of Group A, and he was asked how many of those he thought were undesirable. Subtracting the subject's estimate from 26 yielded his estimate of the number of desirable-behavior statements there had been about Group A. A comparable procedure for Group B yielded the subject's estimate for that group. The resulting means are presented in Table

8.1d. The proportions of desirable and undesirable behaviors estimated for each group, based on these means, are shown in parentheses. It can be seen that subjects estimated that a larger proportion of the behaviors describing Group B had been undesirable.

Two statistical analyses were performed on these frequency estimates. Subjects estimated the number of undesirable behaviors for Group A and Group B, and the correct values were 8 and 4, respectively. For each subject, two deviation scores were determined by subtracting these correct values from his corresponding estimates. The resulting means were 0.91 and 1.73, indicating that subjects did tend to overestimate the number of undesirable behaviors for Group B. This difference, however, was not statistically significant. The second analysis consisted of determining a phi coefficient for each subject, based on the 2×2 table constructed from his estimates. A t test of the hypothesis that the mean correlation was greater than zero approached significance, $t(32) = 1.92, p < .10$. A 2×2 analysis of variance showed that neither sex of subject nor order of dependent measures had a significant effect on these data.

Trait Ratings. The findings reported thus far demonstrate that an illusory correlation was established such that subjects perceived a relationship between group membership and behavior desirability. The question of primary interest to the present research is whether this bias would have an effect upon the subjects' perceptions of the two groups.

Subjects rated Group A and Group B on 20 trait scales. Four kinds of inference scales were used: Good Social, Bad Social, Good Intellectual, and Bad Intellectual. Each subject's average rating for Group A and Group B were determined for each scale category, and these data were analyzed in a 2 (Subject Sex) $\times$ 2 (Order of Dependent Measure) $\times$ 2 (Social/Intellectual Scales) $\times$ 2 (Good/Bad Scales) x 2 (Groups A and B) analysis of variance with repeated measures on the last three factors. Of primary interest is the interaction of Good/Bad Scales with Groups, which was highly significant, $F(1,29) = 9.36, p < .01$. The mean ratings of the two groups for each scale category, presented in Table 8.2, indicate that members of Group A were rated as more likely to have desirable properties and less likely to have undesirable characteristics. These findings provide strong support for the primary hypothesis of this experiment, that the differential perception of groups can be based solely on the cognitive mechanisms involved in processing information about pairs of events that differ in their frequencies of co-occurrence.[1]

Discussion

The results of Experiment 1 clearly supported the hypotheses, and are consistent with the interpretation that subjects developed an illusory correlation based on the co-occurrence of distinctive stimulus events and that this bias resulted in the differential perception of the two groups. However, since desirability and frequency of occurrence were confounded in the stimulus materials, other explanations remain plausible.

One possibility is that the present results were due to "mere exposure" effects (Zajonc, 1968): the greater frequency of occurrence of members of Group A might have resulted in the subjects' developing more positive attitudes toward members of that group. The general enhancement in evaluation of members of Group A evidenced in the trait inferences (Table 8.2) clearly would follow from this interpretation. A mere exposure explanation would posit that subjects overresponded to the most frequently occurring class of stimulus items (i.e., members of Group A performing desirable behaviors) and that a bias to do so resulted in a more favorable evaluation of the members of the larger group. Analyses of the Attribution of Group Membership responses, however, indicated that subjects in fact overestimated the frequency with which the distinctive events co-occurred (cf. Table 8.1b), i.e., the bias was associated with the undesirable, not the desirable, statements. Thus the

TABLE 8.2. Mean Trait Ratings for Groups A and B: Experiment 1

Rating scales	Group A	Group B
Good Social	6.66	6.03
Bad Social	4.43	5.63
Good Intellectual	7.16	6.26
Bad Intellectual	4.35	4.98

Note: Ratings were made on 10-point scales.

[1]While there were some significant effects associated with the other factors, they were few in number, do not qualify the primary findings presented here, and hence will not be discussed further.

mere exposure hypothesis would seemingly have difficulty accounting for this result. Nevertheless, the extent to which mere exposure contributed to (at least some of) the findings of this study remain undetermined.

Another possibility is that the statement in the instructions that "Group B is a smaller group than Group A" could have led subjects to infer that Group B was a minority group, and if they believe most minority groups are "less good" than the majority, such a bias could have contributed to the results. However, R. A. Jones et al. (1974) have replicated this study omitting that statement, and report similar findings. Thus it is unlikely that the present results were due to that instructional statement. Nevertheless, any conception the subjects may have had that "smaller groups are less desirable than larger groups" could still have influenced the findings.

Experiment 2

Because of these interpretive problems, a second experiment was undertaken. Since the alternative explanations are tied to evaluation in a manner that the present interpretation is not, a comparative test is straightforward. That is, if the co-occurrence of distinctive events is particularly salient to the observer, then it should be possible to produce a *positive* stereotype of Group B by making desirable behaviors less frequent than undesirable behaviors in the stimulus sequence. The co-occurring distinctivenes explanation would then predict that subjects would have a more *favorable* impression of Group B than of Group A, as well as that they would overestimate the frequency with which those desirable behaviors were performed by members of Group B. The alternative hypotheses, on the other hand, would still predict a more favorable impression of Group A.

Method

The methodology and procedures used in this experiment were essentially the same as those employed in Experiment 1. The major difference was in the distribution of desirable and undesirable behaviors included in the stimulus set, which in this case consisted of 36 statements. Of those 36, 24 described undesirable behaviors, while 12 described desirable behaviors. Also, 24 of the 36

statements characterized members of Group A, with 12 sentences describing members of Group B. However, the distribution of desirable and undesirable behaviors was the same for both groups, one-third of the statements for each group describing desirable behaviors. Thus, a sentence describing a member of Group B performing a *desirable* behavior represented an instance of the co-occurrence of events which were infrequent, and therefore distinctive, within the two information categories.

Two replication sets were used. Due to the limited number of behavior descriptions available within the scale intervals used, two independent sets of statements could not be developed. Instead, the same 36 sentences were used for both sets, with the 12 Group B sentences in Set 1 applied to Group A in Set 2 and the Group B descriptions for Set 2 coming from Group A sentences in Set 1. Thus, two-thirds of the sentences were associated with different group memberships in the two sets. Although not providing independent replications, this strategy did afford some basis for examining the generalizability of results.

The sentences in both stimulus sets were assigned to groups so that the mean desirability values of the behaviors describing the two groups were equal and so that approximately the same proportions of interpersonal and task-related behaviors were contained in each group. As in Experiment 1, each statement presented a man's name, his group membership, and a behavior description. Again, the sentences were presented on slides, and each slide was shown for 8 sec. To avoid the possibility of tapping preexisting conceptions of minority groups, no mention was made in the instructions of the relative sizes of Groups A and B. Other than this omission, the instructions and procedures were the same as those used in Experiment 1.

The same dependent measures were obtained in this experiment, i.e., trait inferences, attributions of group membership, and frequency estimates. Trait inference scales were selected from the same two dimensions (Rosenberg et al., 1968), in this case three attributes from each pole of each dimension being included in the questionnaire. As in Experiment 1, the order of the first two dependent measures was counterbalanced. Finally, a series of postexperimental questions asked subjects what aspects of the stimulus information they focused on during the slide presentation and what strategies they developed for remembering those aspects.

Subjects were 70 female students at a state university in New Haven. Each of the two stimulus sets was presented to 35 subjects, and within those groups approximately half completed the dependent measures in each of the two orders used. As in Experiment 1, subjects who, on the attributions of group membership task, assigned more than half of the sentences to Group B were eliminated from the sample. Seventeen subjects were thereby discarded. Examination of their responses to the post-experimental questions confirmed that most were focusing their attention on other aspects of the stimulus information (e.g., the relationship between types of names and types of behaviors) and *not* on group memberships. The results reported below are based on the reduced sample of 53 subjects. Due to failures to complete one or another of the dependent measures, the number of subjects included in the analyses was 52 for the Group Attribution and Frequency Estimates data and 50 for the Trait Rating data. (Results based on the total sample were generally in the predicted direction but did not achieve statistical significance.)

Results

ATTRIBUTIONS OF GROUP MEMBERSHIPS

The distribution of stimulus sentences by group and behavior desirability is shown in Table 8.3a. Each subject's responses on the group attribution task were tallied to determine the frequency with which desirable and undesirable behaviors were assigned to the two groups, and a phi coefficient was calculated from each subject's frequency table. These coefficients were converted to Fisher's Z-scores and the mean value was determined. In this case it was predicted that this value would be negative, indicating a perceived relationship of Group B with desirable and Group A with undesirable behaviors. The mean was in fact negative and significantly different from zero, $t(51) = -3.04$, $p < .01$. A 2×2 (Replication Sets × Order of Dependent Measure) analysis of variance conducted on these Z-scores yielded no significant effects.

The mean number of desirable and undesirable statements attributed to the two groups is shown in Table 8.3b. The conditional probabilities for the assignment of behaviors to groups again reveal that the bias was associated with the co-occurrence of infrequent events. As in the first experiment, the probability that a statement (desirable or undesirable) described a member of Group A was .67. In the subjects' responses, the probability that an undesirable behavior would be assigned to this group was .65, rather close to the correct value. On the other hand, the probability of a desirable behavior being attributed to Group A was only .49, i.e., over half of these statements were attributed to Group B, despite the fact that only one-third of them was actually associated with that group. Thus the illusory correlation was due to the subject's tendency to overattribute the desirable behaviors to members of Group B.

Data relevant to the accuracy with which group memberships were recalled are presented in Table 8.3c. In their responses on this task subjects again

TABLE 8.3. Results of Experiment 2 for Attributions of Group Membership and Frequency Estimates Measures

(a) Distribution of stimulus sentences

Behaviors	Group A	B	
Desirable	8	4	12
Undesirable	16	8	24
	24	12	36

(b) Attribution of group membership means (conditional probabilities in parentheses)

Behaviors	Group assigned by subject A	B	
Desirable	5.87 (.49)	6.13 (.51)	12.00 (1.00)
Undesirable	15.71 (.65)	8.29 (.35)	24.00 (1.00)
	21.58	14.42	36.00

(c) proportion of each type recalled accurately (values expected by chance in parentheses)

Behaviors	Group A	B
Desirable	.53 (.60)	.59 (.40)
Undesirable	.73 (.60)	.49 (.40)

(d) Frequency estimates means (conditional proportion in parentheses)

Behaviors	Group A	B	
Desirable	8.23 (.34)	6.62 (.55)	14.85
Undesirable	15.77 (.66)	5.38 (.45)	21.15
	24.00 (1.00)	12.00 (1.00)	36.00

attributed 60% of the behaviors to Group A and 40% to Group B, so that chance performance would yield a 60% accuracy rate in those cells referring to Group A statements and 40% accuracy for those behaviors performed by members of Group B. The findings show that (a) subjects' performance exceeded chance expectations for three of the four categories of statements, (b) the only case in which below-chance performance occurred was for desirable behaviors performed by Group A persons, i.e., behaviors which had been overattributed to Group B, and (c) accuracy most exceeded the chance level for desirable behaviors attributed to Group B. Thus, Tables 8.3b and 8.3c show a pattern of results for desirable behaviors remarkably similar to that shown in Table 8.1 for undesirable behaviors, as would be predicted by the present interpretation.

Frequency Estimates. Subjects were told that there had been 24 statements describing members of Group A and 12 describing Group B, and were asked how many statements for each group were highly desirable. For each subject, the correct values (eight and four, respectively) were subtracted from her estimates. The means for these deviation scores were 0.23 and 2.62, and the difference between them was highly significant, $F(1.51) = 8.10$, $p < .01$. Thus, subjects significantly overestimated the number of desirable behaviors performed by members of Group B. These estimates were also used to construct 2×2 frequency tables from which a phi coefficient was calculated for each subject, as in Experiment 1. The mean of these coefficients (converted to Z-scores) was negative and approached being significantly different from zero, $t(.51) = -1.75$, $p < .10$. A 2×2 analysis of variance yielded no significant effects due to either Replication Sets or Order of Dependent Measures.

The means for the frequency estimate data are shown in Table 8.3d. It can be seen that, although only one-third of the statements described desirable behaviors (for each group), subjects on the average estimated that over half of the behaviors associated with Group B were desirable. In contrast the average estimate for Group A was quite accurate.

Trait Ratings. The mean rating on each of the four scale categories (Good Social, Bad Social, Good Intellectual, Bad Intellectual) was determined for each subject. These data were then analyzed by a 2 (Replication Sets) × 2 (Order of Dependent Measures) × 2 (Social/ Intellectual Scales)

TABLE 8.4. Mean Trait Ratings for Groups A and B: Experiment 2

Rating scales	Group A	Group B
Good Social	4.87	6.25
Bad Social	5.98	5.04
Good Intellectual	5.24	5.59
Bad Intellectual	6.12	4.87

Note: Ratings were made on 10-point scales.

× 2 (Good/Bad Scales) × 2 (Groups A and B) analysis of variance with repeated measures on the last three factors. The crucial interaction of Good/Bad Scales with Groups was again highly significant, $F(1,46) = 7.61, p < .01$. The mean ratings of Groups A and B for each scale category are shown in Table 8.4. In marked contrast to Experiment 1, members of Group B were rated more favorably in each case.[2]

Discussion

The findings of Experiment 2 provide strong support for the hypotheses. Subjects again developed an illusory correlation between behavior desirability and group membership, but in this case the bias was reflected in the overattribution of *desirable* behaviors to the minority group. Moreover, the illusory correlation had an influence on the subjects' trait ratings, with Group B receiving significantly more favorable ratings than Group A. These results are quite supportive of the interpretation that the co-occurrence of distinctive stimuli results in an overestimation of the frequency with which that event pair occurred, with consequent effects on the subjects' perceptions of the two groups.

The results of this experiment are most useful in eliminating from plausibility certain competing explanations for the results of Experiment 1. In particular, while the results of the first study could be viewed as due to mere exposure effects, these results directly contradict the predictions of that explanation for Experiment 2. Whereas the mere exposure hypothesis would predict findings similar to Experiment 1, this study yielded results significantly in the opposite direction. Similarly,

---

[2]There were a few other significant effects due to other factors, but in no case did these results suggest a qualification of the primary findings reported here. Hence a complete description of these results is not necessary.

any other interpretation which links evaluation with group size (e.g., a tendency to view any smaller or "minority" group as likely to be "less good" than the majority group) now appears implausible as an explanation for the results of Experiment 1.

General Discussion

Illusory correlation refers to an erroneous inference a person makes about the relationship between two categories of events. The present findings demonstrate that distortions in judgment can result from the cognitive mechanisms involved in processing information about co-occurring events, at least when the various events co-occur with differential frequencies. The consequence in these studies was that two groups of stimulus persons were systematically perceived as being different from each other when no informational basis for such differences was available.

Little is known about the means by which observers develop concepts of relationships between variables, or "subjective correlations," and how biases can enter into that process. The concern here is specifically with the case in which events co-occur with differing frequencies, and the present interpretation emphasizes the salience of distinctive stimuli for the observer. While unusual or infrequent events are themselves distinctive, the *co-occurrence* of two distinctive events presumably would be particularly noticeable, differentially drawing the observer's attention to the fact that these events co-occurred. As the observer's attention is differentially directed to several instances of two "unusual" events "going together," the perception of a relationship between them can develop, providing the basis for the illusory correlation. In the experiments reported here, the increased accuracy in recall of this class of stimuli, as well as the overestimation of its frequency of occurrence, lends support to this interpretation of the processes which produced the observed effects. However, further research will be needed to more definitively determine the cognitive processes underlying these biased judgments.

The present study was conceptualized as an investigation of cognitive bases of stereotype formation, and the results indicate that perceptions of group differences can be based on certain characteristics of the way people process information about others. Obviously, this is not to deny, or even question, the importance of socially learned or culturally transmitted bases of stereotypes, and we are *not* suggesting that present-day stereotypes are due as much to information processing biases as to these learning mechanisms. The findings do indicate, however, that not all stereotyping necessarily originates in the learning and motivational processes emphasized in the stereotype literature; cognitive factors alone can be sufficient to produce differential perceptions of social groups (cf. Hamilton, 1976).

It is also possible that the two processes reinforce each other. If, for example, in our society whites learn through acculturation that blacks have a variety of undesirable characteristics, then they would be less likely to want to have much interaction with blacks. This infrequency of interaction, combined with the salience of the negative information received when some form of undesirable behavior is observed, would provide the basis for a cognitively based illusory correlation that would reinforce the learned stereotypic judgments. The reverse process may also occur. Some subgroups of the population become distinctive in the experience of others due to such arbitrary factors as geographic location (e.g., "Southerners" for those who live outside the South) or population distribution (e.g., one finds relatively few Catholics in small Midwestern towns). Such accidentally-gained distinctiveness, when combined with the distinctiveness of certain categories of behavior, can provide the basis for an illusory correlation such as that reported here. The erroneous inferences and assumptions acquired by this process can then be transmitted to other members of the predominant group, as well as to the next generation, so that what originally had a purely cognitive basis is now learned by others. It wouldn't seem unreasonable that some of our current stereotypes originated in this way. Thus, the two processes underlying illusory correlations are not only complementary but may, in everyday experience, be confounded and mutually reinforcing.

The present findings also have implications for one long-standing issue in the stereotype literature, the "kernel of truth" controversy (cf. Brigham, 1971). This hypothesis asserts that although stereotypes may be gross overgeneralizations, and may even be maintained by defensive processes that serve individual needs, nevertheless there is some "kernel of truth" underlying the elements comprising the stereotypes of any given group. The results of this experiment suggest that while this may be true of some stereotypes, it may not be a *necessary* condition underlying the formation of all stereotypes. There was no actual informational basis for the perceived differences between Groups A and B that were reported by subjects in the present experiment.

REFERENCES

Brigham, J. C. (1971). Ethnic stereotypes. *Psychological Bulletin, 76,* 15–38.

Chapman, L. J. (1967). Illusory correlation in observational report. *Journal of Verbal Learning and Verbal Behavior, 6,* 151–155.

Chapman, L. J., & Chapman, J. P. (1967). Genesis of popular but erroneous psychodiagnostic observations. *Journal of Abnormal Psychology, 72,* 193–204.

Chapman, L. J., & Chapman. J. P. (1969). Illusory correlation as an obstacle to the use of valid psychodiagnostic signs. *Journal of Abnormal Psychology, 74,* 271–280.

Golding, S. L., & Rorer. L. G. (1972). Illusory correlation and subjective judgment. *Journal of Abnormal Psychology, 80,* 249–260.

Hamilton, D. L. (1976). Cognitive biases in the perception of social groups. In J. S. Carroll & J. W. Payne (Eds.), *Cognition and social behavior.* Hillsdale, NJ: Erlbaum.

Jones, E. E., & Davis, K. E. (1965). From acts to dispositions: The attribution process in person perception. In L. Berkowitz (Ed.), *Advances in experimental social psychology* (Vol. 2). New York: Academic Press.

Jones, R. A., Stoll, J., Solernou, J., Noble, A., Fiala, J., & Miller, K. (1974). *Availability and stereotype formation.* Unpublished manuscript, University of Kentucky.

Rosenberg, S., Nelson, C., & Vivekananthan, P. S. (1968). A multidimensional approach to the structure of personality impressions. *Journal of Personality and Social Psychology, 9,* 283–294.

Starr, B. J., & Katkin, E. S. (1969). The clinician as an aberrant actuary: Illusory correlation and the Incomplete Sentence Blank. *Journal of Abnormal Psychology, 74,* 670–675.

Tajfel, H. (1969). Cognitive aspects of prejudice. *Journal of Social Issues, 25,* 79–97.

Zajonc, R. B. (1968). Attitudinal effect of mere exposure. *Journal of Personality and Social Psychology, 9*(2, Pt. 2).

Prejudice as Self-Image Maintenance: Affirming the Self Through Derogating Others

Steven Fein • Williams College
Steven J. Spencer • Hope College

The authors argue that self-image maintenance processes play an important role in stereotyping and prejudice. Three studies demonstrated that when individuals evaluated a member of a stereotyped group, they were less likely to evaluate that person negatively if their self-images had been bolstered through a self-affirmation procedure, and they were more likely to evaluate that person stereotypically if their self-images had been threatened by negative feedback. Moreover, among those individuals whose self-image had been threatened, derogating a stereotyped target mediated an increase in their self-esteem. The authors suggest that stereotyping and prejudice may be a common means to maintain one's self-image, and they discuss the role of self-image-maintenance processes in the context of motivational, socio-cultural, and cognitive approaches to stereotyping and prejudice.

A most striking testament to the social nature of the human psyche is the extent to which the self-concept—that which is the very essence of one's individuality—is integrally linked with interpersonal dynamics. Since the earliest days of the formal discipline of psychology, the significant influences of a number of social factors on the self-concept have been recognized. A central focus of sociocultural and social–cognitive approaches to psychology has concerned the ways in which individuals' self-concepts are defined and refined by the people around them. This is evident in early discussions of the social nature of individuals' self-concepts (Cooley, 1902; Mead, 1934) and of social comparison theory (Festinger, 1954),

and it continues to be evident in more recent work, such as that concerning self-fulfilling prophecies (e.g., Eccles, Jacobs, & Harold, 1990; Rosenthal & Jacobson, 1968; Snyder, 1984) and cultural influences (Abrams, 1994; Cameron & Lalonde, 1994; Cohen & Nisbett, 1994; H. R. Markus & Kitayama, 1991, 1994; Triandis, 1989; Turner, Oakes, Haslam, & McGarty, 1994).

The converse focus—the self-concept's influence on perceptions of and reactions toward others—has been recognized more fully within the last two decades, through, for example, research on self-schemas (H. Markus, 1977; H. Markus & Wurf, 1987), self-verification (Swann, Stein-Seroussi, & Giesler, 1992), self-discrepancies

(Higgins, 1996; Higgins & Tykocinski, 1992), and a host of self-serving biases in individuals' perceptions, judgments, and memories involving the self (e.g., Ditto & Lopez, 1992; Greenwald, 1980; Klein & Kunda, 1992, 1993; Nisbett & Ross, 1980; Ross & Sicoly, 1979; Schlenker, Weigold, & Hallam, 1990).

Particularly within the past decade, research has converged on the role of self-image- and self-esteem-maintenance processes in people's perceptions and reactions regarding others. These approaches, whose roots can be seen in the earlier work of James, Festinger, Heider, Sherif, Tajfel, and others, include research on downward social comparison (Brown, Collins, & Schmidt, 1988; Brown & Gallagher, 1992; Gibbons & Gerrard, 1991; Gibbons & McCoy, 1991; Taylor & Lobel, 1989; Wills, 1981, 1991; Wood & Taylor, 1991), self-evaluation maintenance (Tesser, 1988; Tesser & Cornell, 1991), social identity (Abrams & Hogg, 1988; Brewer, 1993; Crocker, Thompson, McGraw, & Ingerman, 1987; Hogg & Abrams, 1988; Smith, 1993; Turner, 1982), terror management (Greenberg et al., 1992), and self-affirmation (Liu & Steele, 1986; Steele, 1988; Steele & Liu, 1983).

This article examines the role of self-image-maintenance processes in a particular set of reactions and perceptions: those concerning prejudice and negative evaluations of others. More specifically, we examine the thesis that many manifestations of prejudice stem, in part, from the motivation to maintain a feeling of self-worth and self-integrity. That is, self-image threat may lead people to engage in prejudiced evaluations of others. These negative evaluations can, and often do, make people feel better about themselves. Prejudice, therefore, can be self-affirming. By using available stereotypes to justify and act on prejudices, individuals may be able to reclaim for themselves a feeling of mastery and self-worth, often saving themselves from having to confront the real sources of self-image threat.

Several self-image-maintenance processes are described or implied in the existing literature, but the research reported in this article focuses on one in particular: self-affirmation. Steele and his colleagues (e.g., Steele, Spencer, & Lynch, 1993) have argued that people seek to maintain "an image of self-integrity, that is, overall moral and adaptive

adequacy" (p. 885). If an individual experiences a threat to this image, he or she attempts to restore this image by reevaluating and reinterpreting experiences and events in ways that reaffirm the self's integrity and value. Supported by research on self-affirmation effects in cognitive dissonance, Steele et al. (1993) argued that when facing a potential threat, even an important one, people have "the option of leaving the threat unrationalized—that is, accepting the threat without countering it or its implications—and affirming some other important aspect of the self that reinforces one's overall self-adequacy" (p. 885).

We argue that prejudice often serves a self-affirming function for individuals, and providing people with other means of self-affirmation should reduce their desire to make prejudiced evaluations. The link between self-image threats and the use of prejudice should be weakened by providing people with the opportunity to self-affirm, that is, by providing them with information that restores their positive sense of self-integrity. This approach is distinct from many of the classic approaches to stereotyping and prejudice, such as frustration–aggression theory and scapegoating (Dollard, Doob, Miller, Mowrer, & Sears, 1939; Miller & Bugelski, 1948), social identity theory (Tajfel, 1982), and downward social comparison theory (Wills, 1981). We argue that this process of self-affirmation should reduce the desire to make prejudiced evaluations even though it does not release pent-up anger or aggression, as frustration–aggression theory would require; enhance social identity, as social identity theory would require; make self–other comparisons, as downward social comparison theory would require; or confront the threat itself in any way. Only a self-affirmational perspective suggests that restoring a positive sense of self-integrity in this way would result in the decrease of prejudiced evaluations. Of course, this thesis shares many assumptions with these other theoretical positions. Our approach, however, can be seen as extending previous approaches by examining self-image maintenance as both cause and effect of prejudiced evaluations and by integrating these approaches with contemporary views of the self.

Taken together, the studies reported in this article examined both sides of this process: the roles of self-affirmation and self-image threat in influencing the likelihood that individuals will use stereotypes or prejudice and the role of prejudice in helping individuals restore a positive sense of self.

Study 1

In Study 1, we examined the hypothesis that self-affirmation should make participants less likely to evaluate another individual in ways that reflect their prejudice toward the individual's group. Participants in this study were asked to evaluate a target person who apparently was either a member of a group for which there was a readily available negative stereotype or a member of some other outgroup for which there was not a strong available stereotype. Before being exposed to this target person, participants were either self-affirmed or not affirmed. That is, half of the participants completed a task designed to affirm and make salient an important aspect of their self-concepts, and the other half completed a task designed not to affirm any important aspects of their self-concepts.

We believe that many stereotypes and prejudices are such readily available and cognitively justifiable means of self-enhancement that individuals often use their stereotypes and prejudices to self-enhance in the face of everyday vulnerabilities and frustrations (e.g., see Wood & Taylor, 1991). That is, unless other motives are activated, such as a goal of accurate perception (Darley, Fleming, Hilton, & Swann, 1988; Neuberg & Fiske, 1987), accountability (Tetlock, 1983), or social desirability or egalitarian motives (Dovidio & Gaertner, 1991; Monteith, 1993), people may find stereotyping and prejudice to be a reliable and effective way to protect their self-esteem in a frequently threatening world. To the extent, then, that the use of stereotypes and prejudice stems in part from self-image maintenance needs, self-affirmation should make individuals less likely to resort to this use. Study 1 was designed to test this hypothesis.

Method

PARTICIPANTS

Seventy-two introductory psychology students from the University of Michigan participated in this experiment as partial fulfillment of a course requirement.[1]

PROCEDURE

The participants were told that they would participate in two experiments in this session. The first experiment was portrayed as a study of values. The second experiment was portrayed as an investigation of how employees evaluate candidates in the hiring process.

Manipulation of Self-Affirmation. Half of the participants completed a self-affirmation procedure, and half did not. This procedure was a modified version of that used by Steele and Liu (1983; see also Steele, 1988; Tesser & Cornell, 1991) to affirm and make salient an important part of individuals' self-concepts. Participants were given a list of several values (adapted from values characterized by the Allport–Vernon Study of Values), including *business/economics, art/music/ theater, social life/relationships,* and *science/pursuit of knowledge.* Participants in the self-affirmation condition were asked to circle the value that was most important to them personally and then to write a few paragraphs explaining why this value was important to them.[2] In contrast, participants in the no-affirmation condition were asked to circle the value that was least important to them personally and then to write a paragraph explaining why this value might be important to someone else. Steele and his colleagues (e.g., Spencer & Steele, 1990; Steele, 1988) have found that causing participants to think about a value that is personally very important to them is an effective means of producing self-affirmation and that, in the absence of self-image threat, it does not affect participants' state self-esteem.

Evaluation Task. For what we portrayed as the second experiment, participants were placed in individual cubicles and were told that their task was to evaluate an individual who had applied for a job as a personnel manager at a particular organization. The participants were given general information about the responsibilities of a person-

---

[1]Although 72 people participated in the experiment, 18 were excluded because they were Jewish, for reasons that are described in the *Manipulation of target's ethnicity* section. Thus, the data from 54 participants were included in all analyses.

[2]None of our participants wrote paragraphs concerning prejudice or tolerance. Moreover, the effects of the manipulation were not related to which value—business/economics, art/music/theater, social life/relationships, or science/pursuit of knowledge—the participants chose.

positive?
or *who decides what is neg.*

nel manager at this hypothetical organization and were encouraged to try to make an accurate assessment of the candidate's suitability for the job.

All participants next examined information about a fictitious job candidate who was about to graduate from their university. Participants were given the candidate's completed job application to examine. The application contained questions about the candidate's previous work experience, academic and extracurricular skills and interests, and other resume-type information. The completed application was constructed to suggest that the applicant was fairly well qualified for the position but was not necessarily a stellar candidate. Attached to the application was a photograph of the candidate. All of the participants saw virtually the same application and photograph; the variations are noted in the section below. After examining this material, participants watched an 8-min videotape presented as excerpts from the candidate's job interview. All participants saw the same videotape, which featured a fairly neutral performance by the candidate—that is, her responses tended to be adequate but not extremely positive or negative. After watching the excerpts, participants completed a questionnaire about the candidate and her qualifications.

Manipulation of Target's Ethnicity. Although all participants saw the same job interview excerpts, saw the same woman in the photograph attached to the job application, and read the same information about her work experiences, academic record, and other job-relevant information, we included two minor variations in the photograph and three in the application to suggest either that the candidate was Jewish or that she was not Jewish (and probably was Italian).

We used this distinction for several reasons. At the time and place in which this study was conducted, there was a very well known and relatively freely discussed stereotype concerning the "Jewish American princess" (JAP). There was a fairly sizable and salient minority of students at this campus who were Jewish women from New York City and Long Island, New York, and these women were the targets of a number of JAP jokes that spread across campus. In contrast to stereotypes about African Americans, gay men and lesbians, and many other groups, the JAP stereotype was one that many students were willing to discuss quite candidly with many of them openly endorsing it.[3]

Another factor that played a role in our deci-

sion to examine this form of prejudice was that we were able to select a stimulus person who could be considered representative of the Jewish American princess and yet, with a few subtle manipulations, could just as easily be considered representative of a non-Jewish group—one that also was an outgroup to most participants but about which there was no strong negative stereotype or prejudice on this campus. This alternative categorization was of an Italian American woman. Although also a minority on campus, this group was not nearly as salient on campus, and as pilot testing confirmed, there was no strong, consensual stereotype or prejudice on campus concerning this group.

To manipulate the target's ethnic background, we varied the following elements of her application: her name (Julie Goldberg vs. Maria D'Agostino), an extracurricular activity (volunteering for a Jewish or Catholic organization), and her sorority (either of two sororities that shared similar reputations in terms of status, but one of which consisted predominantly of Jewish women and one of which consisted predominantly of non-Jewish women of European, but not Hispanic, descent). All the other information on the application, including all of the job-relevant information, was identical.

In both conditions, the photograph attached to the job application was of the same woman (who was also featured in the videotape). We had chosen a female undergraduate, unknown to the participants, who could be seen either as fitting the prototypic image of a Jewish American princess or as non-Jewish (and probably Italian). The photograph varied slightly, however, so that "Julie" was wearing a necklace featuring the Star of David and had her hair flipped up in back (in a clip that some pilot test students referred to as a JAP clip), whereas "Maria" was wearing a cross and had her hair down. Pilot testing suggested that our manipulation was successful.

This woman appeared in the video wearing a sweater that covered her necklace, and her hair was

---

[3]One of the reasons for this may be that the stereotype is diffused across two types of prejudice: anti-Semitism and sexism. That is, those who endorse the stereotype are protected against being considered anti-Semitic because they are not implicating Jewish men in their derogatory comments or beliefs, and they are protected against being considered sexist because they are not implicating most women. A second reason may be that the targeted group is perceived as being relatively privileged, and thus, disparaging them may not seem as harmful.

Devine!

can't prove the participant endorsed the stereotype

down but brushed in such a way that its length seemed somewhere in between the styles depicted in the two photographs, As indicated above, all participants saw the same 8-min video.

Dependent Measures. Participants rated the candidate in terms of her overall personality and her qualifications for the job. Her personality was assessed by the extent to which participants agreed (on a 7-point scale) that each of the following traits described her: intelligent, insensitive, trustworthy, arrogant, sincere, inconsiderate, friendly, self-centered, down-to-earth, rude, creative, materialistic, motivated, cliquish, ambitious, conceited, happy, vain, warm, superficial. Negative traits were reverse scored. Her job qualifications were assessed by the extent to which participants agreed (on a 7-point scale) with the following statements: "I feel this person would make an excellent candidate for the position in question," "I would likely give this person serious consideration for the position in question," "I would guess that this person is in the top 20% of people interviewed," and "I felt favorably toward this person." Both scales showed good internal reliability (Cronbach's alphas of .93 and .91, respectively). Finally participants were asked to indicate their own and the target's ethnicity and religion.

Results

Recall that our prediction was that when participants were not self-affirmed, they would evaluate the target more negatively when she was portrayed as Jewish than when she was portrayed as Italian, whereas when participants were self-affirmed, this difference would be reduced or eliminated.

The critical measure in this study was participants' ratings of the target's personality across a variety of dimensions. These ratings were subjected to a two-way analysis of variance (ANOVA). The ANOVA revealed that there was no significant main effect for the manipulation of affirmation, $F(1, 50) = 1.8$, $p > .15$, but that there was a significant main effect for the manipulation of the apparent ethnicity of the target, as the target was rated more positively when she appeared to be Italian than when she appeared to be Jewish, $F(1, 50) = 4.9$, $p < .05$. Most importantly, this main effect was qualified by a significant interaction, $F(1, 50) = 8.5$, $p < .01$. As can be seen in Figure 9.1, and consistent with our predictions, not affirmed participants who evaluated the Jewish target were sig-

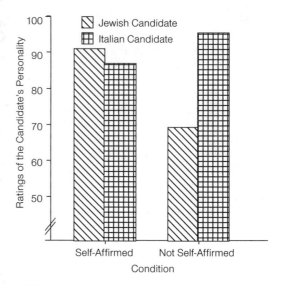

FIGURE 9.1. ■ Rating of candidate's personality as a funtion of self-affirmation condition and ethnicity of the candidate. Higher numbers indicate more favorable evaluations.

nificantly more negative in their evaluations of the target's personality than were participants in all other conditions, $t(50) = 3.7$, $p < .001$. None of the other conditions differed significantly from each other.[4]

Ratings of how qualified the target was for the job in question also were consistent with our predictions. A two-way ANOVA revealed that participants who had not been affirmed tended to rate the target more negatively than did participants who had been affirmed, $F(1, 50) = 4.6$, $p < .05$. The ANOVA revealed further that participants rated the candidate more positively when she was depicted as Italian than when she was depicted as Jewish, $F(1, 50) = 6.3$, $p < .05$. These main effects were qualified, however, by a marginally significant interaction between the two independent variables, $F(1, 50) = 3.0$, $p < .10$. Consistent with our predictions, not affirmed participants evaluated the

---

[4]We used this planned comparison for both dependent measures in this study, as well as a comparable planned comparison for each of the dependent measures in Studies 2 and 3, because it was the most direct test of our theoretically derived hypotheses (see, e.g., Hays, 1981; Keppel, 1973; Rosenthal & Rosnow, 1991; Winer, 1971). For each of these measures, we also conducted the more conservative Newman–Keuls post hoc comparisons. In each case, the Newman–Keuls comparisons indicated the difference tested in the planned comparison to be significant and revealed further that none of the other conditions differed significantly from each other.

qualifications of the candidate more negatively when she was portrayed as Jewish ($M = 14.9$) rather than Italian ($M = 20.6$), whereas affirmed participants did not make this discrimination (Ms = 20.2 and 21.2, respectively). The planned comparison indicated that not affirmed participants who evaluated the Jewish target were significantly more negative in their evaluations of the target's job qualifications than were participants in all other conditions, $t(50) = 3.7, p < .001$. None of the other conditions differed significantly from each other.

Discussion

The results of this study demonstrate that self-affirmation can reduce the likelihood that individuals will derogate members of stereotyped groups. In the absence of self-affirmation, participants' evaluations of the job candidate were biased as a function of her apparent ethnicity. That is, these participants evaluated the target more negatively if she was a member of a stereotyped group than if she was not. Among participants who had been self-affirmed, however, this difference was eliminated.

These results, therefore, highlight the significant role played by the self-concept in prejudice. More specifically, they support the idea that thinking about a self-relevant value, even one completely unrelated to prejudice, can reduce the expression of prejudice. Thinking about a self-relevant value has this effect even though it need not release pent-up anger or aggression, enhance social identity, or involve self–other comparisons, as frustration–aggression theory, social identity theory, and downward social-comparison theory would require.

In a replication of this study, we also examined the potential mediating role of participants' mood in this paradigm with an independent sample of 71 participants. We measured participants' mood using the Mehrabian and Russell (1974) mood scale after the manipulation of self-affirmation but before the participants evaluated the target. The mood scale consists of three subscales, each consisting of six sets of bipolar adjectives. These subscales measure pleasure (e.g., happy–unhappy, pleased–annoyed), arousal (e.g., stimulated–relaxed, excited–calm), and dominance (e.g., controlled–controlling, influential–influenced). Consistent with the findings of Liu and Steele (1986), the manipulation of self-affirmation had no significant effects on any one or any combination of

these subscales (all Fs < 1). Moreover, participants' mood was unrelated to their evaluation of the target's personality, $r(69) = -.120$, ns, or of her qualifications for the job, $r(69) = .04$, ns. Replicating the results of Study 1, not affirmed participants who evaluated the Jewish target rated the target's personality significantly more negatively than did participants in all other cells, $t(67) = 2.4$, $p < .01$. Similarly, not affirmed participants who evaluated the Jewish target tended to rate the target's job qualifications more negatively than did participants in all other cells, $t(67) = 1.8, p < .05$.

The results of these studies suggest that at least part of the negative evaluation of people who are stereotyped may result from people trying to affirm their self-image. To the extent that people's self-images have been buffered by other means of self-affirmation, they should be less drawn to such a strategy. In the absence of such self-affirmation, however, stereotyping and prejudice may provide a mechanism by which people protect or bolster their self-esteem. Stereotyping and prejudice may be reinforced, therefore, because they can make people feel better about themselves.

Study 2

The results of Study 1 suggest that self-affirmation can play an important role in reducing the effects of stereotyping or prejudice on individuals' evaluations of a member of a stereotyped group. In Study 2, we focused on the other side of this self-image maintenance coin by examining whether a self-image threat would exacerbate the effects of stereotyping or prejudice on individuals' evaluations of a member of a stereotyped group.

Study 2 differed from Study 1 in two other important ways, thereby providing a better test of the generalizability of our hypotheses. First, rather than varying the target's apparent ethnicity, in Study 2 we manipulated the target's apparent sexual orientation. Thus, whereas the stereotyped group in Study 1 was contrasted with a nonstereotyped group that was also a distinct minority, the stereotyped group in Study 2 was contrasted with the nonstereotyped majority. Second, rather than measuring participants' general derogation of a target as a function of her membership in a stereotyped group, Study 2 measured participants' stereotyping of an individual as a function of his membership in a stereotyped group.

More specifically, some participants in this study received self-image-threatening information in the form of bogus negative feedback on an intelligence test; the other participants received no such threat. Later, all participants evaluated a target on a series of trait dimensions relevant to popular stereotypes of gay men. The biographical information about the target was manipulated so as to suggest to some of the participants that the target may have been gay and to suggest to the other participants that he was straight (heterosexual). The hypothesis tested in Study 2 was that participants should be more likely to exhibit stereotyping of the (apparently) gay target if they had previously received negative feedback on the intelligence test than if they had not.

Method

PARTICIPANTS

Sixty-one male undergraduates from Williams College participated in this experiment either for extra credit for their introductory psychology course or for the chance to win money in a random drawing.

PROCEDURE

Participants reported to the laboratory individually and completed the tasks in individual rooms containing a desk and a Macintosh computer. Participants first read a sheet of paper containing the cover story, which stated that the study involved a series of different cognitive and social judgment tasks. The first part of the study involved the manipulation of self-relevant feedback (described below). After some filler tasks (e.g., a simple word-stem completion task) designed to preserve the integrity of the cover story, participants completed the social judgment task, in which the participants read information about a male target. The information was designed to suggest either that the target was gay or that he was straight. After rating the target on a series of dimensions, the participants were probed for any suspicions, debriefed thoroughly and thanked for their participation.

Manipulation of Feedback. Half of the participants were assigned randomly to the negative feedback condition, and the other half were assigned to the neutral condition. To the former half, the experimenter introduced the first set of tasks as "a new form of intelligence test that is given on the computer. It measures both verbal and reasoning abilities." To the latter half, the experimenter explained that they had been assigned to a control condition in which they were simply to read the materials contained in a bogus test of intelligence. The experimenter revealed to these participants that the participants in the treatment condition of the study would be told that the test was a real, valid measure of intelligence. In other words, the experimenter told the neutral condition participants the truth. These participants were instructed to refrain from trying hard to answer the questions on the bogus test because many of the questions had no correct answer and because the time limits were unrealistically quick. The experimenter also told them that the computer would present them with bogus scores at the conclusion of the test. To assure the participants that these scores were indeed bogus, the experimenter told them what these scores would be. The experimenter explained that the participants in the treatment condition would be led to believe that the scores were real. The purpose of having the participants in the neutral condition learn this cover story and go through the test was so that they would be exposed to the same test and specific items as the participants in the negative feedback condition, but that the test would have no relevance to their self-image.[5]

All subsequent instructions for the test were presented on the computer. The instructions were presented in a professional-looking design that introduced the intelligence test as "The Reasoning and Verbal Acuity Battery." The instructions explained that the test had been validated in numerous studies throughout the United States and Canada. The test consisted of five parts, each tapping different sets of intellectual skills. The first four parts consisted of analogies, antonyms, sentence completions, and syllogisms. The fifth part was called a "verbal–nonverbal matching test" and involved matching difficult vocabulary words to various pictures; this was a modified version of

---

[5]Consistent with the intent of the manipulation, pilot testing of 36 other participants from the same population revealed that the state self-esteem (as measured by Heatherton & Polivy's [1991] state self-esteem scale) of participants in the neutral condition was not significantly lower than that of participants who were not exposed to the test or cover story ($F < 1$). In addition, the state self-esteem of these participants (in either condition) was significantly higher than that of pilot test participants who were led to believe the test was real (Fs > 6).

the Ammons and Ammons (1962) Quick Test of Intelligence. The instructions to this battery of tests explained that research had shown that this combination of tasks was the ideal, most valid method to measure individuals' general intelligence.

To emphasize the relevance of these intellectual skills, each test within the battery was introduced with an explanation of what it measured. Many of the specific items in these tests were taken from advanced tests used for admission to graduate school or law school. To make the tests seem even more challenging (and thus to help to justify the bogus feedback for the participants in the negative feedback condition), we modified several of the items so that there was no correct answer among the options given. Moreover the time limits for each item were very short (ranging from 10 to 20 s, depending on the test), and a clock showing the seconds ticking away appeared on the screen for each item.

At the conclusion of this battery of tests, the computer program indicated that it was calculating the scores. After 7 s a new screen appeared that indicated the participant's percentile rankings (relative to other college students tested in the United States and Canada) for each test. Each participant received an identical set of scores: 51st percentile for the analogies test, 54th for the antonyms, 56th for the sentence completions, 33rd for the syllogisms, and 38th for the verbal–nonverbal matching. Given the prestige of the college in which this study was conducted and the students' previous scores on tests such as the Scholastic Achievement Test, these scores are extremely disappointing to the students from this population. (See Footnote 5.)

Manipulation of Target's Apparent Sexual Orientation. After administering a series of brief cognitive tasks designed to enhance the integrity of the cover story, the experimenter introduced the "social judgment tasks" by informing the participants that they would read some information about an individual and make some judgments about him or her.

All participants read about a target named Greg, a 31-year-old struggling actor living in the East Village in New York City. The information summarized Greg's ambitions and career struggles and listed some of the many odd jobs that Greg had taken to pay the rent while he pursued his dream. The information continued by detailing a recent event in Greg's life concerning landing "a fairly large part in a serious and rather controversial play

directed by a young director." Participants read that Greg was excited about the play and, in particular, about working with this young director. The director's name was not mentioned, but gender pronouns indicated that the director was a man. The participants read that after the first week of rehearsals, Greg approached the director and asked him whether he wanted to get "a drink or something" with him after that night's rehearsal so that they could talk about his role in some more depth. The story continued for a few paragraphs, summarizing the play's opening and reviews, and it concluded with the information that while continuing to act in the play Greg was writing his own play and had already gotten a commitment from the director to help him with it.

The information about Greg was identical across conditions with the following exceptions. In the first sentence, the participants in the straight-implied condition read that Greg "has been living with his girlfriend, Anne, in a small apartment" for several years. Anne's name was mentioned three more times in subsequent parts of the story about Greg, and there was one additional reference to his "girlfriend." For the gay-implied condition, in the first sentence we replaced the word "girlfriend" with "partner" and dropped reference to Anne. Neither the partner's name nor the partner's gender was specified, and there were no subsequent references to this partner.

Many of the details of the story about Greg (e.g., his living in the East Village, his caring "for a very close and very ill friend for the last 2 months of his friend's life," and his relationship with the director) were included to support the implication in the gay-implied condition that Greg was gay. Because each piece of information by itself very plausibly could describe a straight actor's life, however, we believed that the participants who were introduced immediately to references to Greg's girlfriend would not entertain the idea that Greg was gay.[6]

Dependent Measures. Participants used an 11-

---

[6]An obvious question is why we did not simply state that Greg was gay. Pilot testing of students from this campus revealed quite strongly that many of the participants became suspicious of the purpose of the study if they read that the target was gay. More than half of the participants told the experimenter that they suspected that the study concerned their stereotypes about gay men. When we eliminated any explicit references to Greg's sexuality, our pilot test participants did not raise these suspicions, although most of them did spontaneously entertain the thought that Greg was gay.

point scale ranging from 0 (*not at all*) to 10 (*extremely*) to rate Greg's personality on each of 10 dimensions. Three of these (intelligent, funny, and boring) were included as stereotype-irrelevant fillers. The stereotype-relevant traits included sensitive, assertive/aggressive, considerate, feminine, strong, creative, and passive (see Fein, Cross, & Spencer, 1995; Kite & Deaux, 1987). Assertive/aggressive and strong were reverse-coded so that for each item, higher ratings indicated greater stereotyping. An index of this set of seven traits showed moderate internal reliability (Cronbach's α = .77). It may be worth noting that these traits, when taken out of a stereotyped context, are not necessarily negative and may indeed be rather positive. But to the extent that participants perceived these traits as more descriptive of a target if they thought that the target was gay than if they thought he was straight, this would indicate stereotyping, and the valence of these traits would be debatable.

In addition, participants used the same 11-point scale to indicate the degree to which they would like Greg as a friend and the degree to which their own personality was similar to Greg's. These measures, of course, were less ambiguous in terms of valence: Lower ratings on these two measures clearly indicated more negative feelings toward the target.

Results

Recall that we predicted that if participants read information about a target that implied that he was gay, they would be more likely to evaluate this target consistently with the gay stereotype if they had received threatening, negative feedback about their performance on the intelligence test than if they had not received any threatening feedback. If the information about the target indicated that he was straight, however, the manipulation of feedback should not have had a strong effect on participants' evaluation of the target. The results supported these predictions.

STEREOTYPING

A two-way ANOVA on the ratings of the target on the set of seven stereotype-relevant trait dimensions revealed a significant main effect for the manipulation of feedback, $F(1, 57) = 11.3$, $p < .001$, indicating that participants who had received negative feedback on the intelligence test rated the target more stereotypically (i.e., gave higher rat-

ings on the stereotype-consistent items) than did participants who had not received any feedback. In addition, the ANOVA revealed a significant effect for the manipulation of the target's apparent sexual orientation, $F(1, 57) = 5.3$, $p < .03$, indicating that participants who read information that implied that the target was gay rated him more stereotypically than if they read information suggesting that he was straight. Most importantly, the ANOVA revealed a significant interaction, $F(1, 57) = 4.4$, $p < .05$. As can be seen in Figure 9.2, and consistent with our predictions, participants who had received negative feedback and read information implying that the target was gay rated the target much more stereotypically than did participants in all other conditions, $t(57) = 4.1$, $p < .001$. None of the other conditions differed significantly from each other (see Footnote 4).

Although the stereotype-irrelevant traits were used as filler to make the participants less likely to be suspicious of the intent of our questions, we did conduct an ANOVA on the ratings concerning those traits. The independent variables did not have any significant effects on participants' ratings of the target on any or all of these traits (all $Fs < 1$).

LIKING AND SIMILARITY

The measure of stereotyping yielded results consistent with our predictions. But would self-esteem

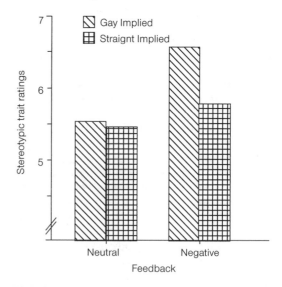

FIGURE 9.2. ■ Rating of target on stereotype-relevant traits as a function of feedback and implied sexual orientation of the target. Higher numbers indicate greater stereotyping.

threat also make participants less willing to indicate that they would like the target as a friend or that their own personality was similar to the target's? To address this question, we conducted an ANOVA on each of these measures.

The ANOVA on participants' ratings of the degree to which they would like the target as a friend revealed a significant main effect for the manipulation of feedback, $F(1, 57) = 5.7$, $p < .03$, indicating that participants who had received negative feedback on the intelligence test rated themselves as less inclined to like the target ($M = 5.81$) than did participants in the neutral condition ($M = 6.87$). The main effect for the manipulation of the information about the target's apparent sexual orientation did not approach significance ($F < 1$), but the interaction between the two variables was significant, $F(1, 57) = 4.1$, $p < .05$. Participants who had received negative feedback on the intelligence test were significantly less inclined to like the target than were those who had not received the feedback, whether or not the target information suggested he was gay, but the interaction reflects the tendency for this difference to be greater in the gay-implied condition ($Ms = 5.48$ vs. 6.98) than in the straight-implied condition ($Ms = 6.11$ vs. 6.75).

The ANOVA on participants' ratings of how similar their own personality was to the target's revealed a significant main effect for the manipulation of feedback, $F(1, 57) = 5.3$, $p < .03$, reflecting the tendency for participants to rate their personality as less similar to the target's if they had received negative feedback on the intelligence test ($M = 4.16$) than if they had received no feedback ($M = 5.33$). The manipulation of information about the target's sexual orientation did not have a significant effect ($F < 1$). More important, the independent variables produced a significant interaction, $F(1, 57) = 4.1$, $p < .05$. Consistent with our predictions, participants were particularly unlikely to rate their personality as similar to the target's if they had received negative feedback and read information implying that the target was gay ($M = 3.94$), $t(57) = 2.3$, $p < .03$. None of the other conditions differed significantly from each other.

Discussion

Consistent with our predictions, participants showed more stereotyping in their evaluations of the target if they had previously received negative feedback about their own performance on an intelligence test. In addition to resulting in greater stereotyping, the negative feedback led participants to psychologically distance themselves from the target if they had reason to suspect that he was gay, by rating themselves as less likely to be friends with or be similar in personality to the target. If the information about the target suggested he was straight, however, the negative feedback had less effect on these measures.

These results support the hypothesis that self-esteem threat can increase individuals' likelihood of exhibiting stereotyping or prejudice toward members of stereotyped groups. Using a different stereotype, a different stereotype comparison condition (i.e., a majority rather than alternative minority group condition), and different dependent measures from those used in Study 1, Study 2 yielded results consistent with the hypothesis that self-image-maintenance processes can play an important moderating role in stereotyping or prejudice.

But does stereotyping or prejudice in response to self-image threat restore an individual's self-esteem? This question was addressed in Study 3.

Study 3

Our view suggests that one motivation for stereotype- or prejudice-based evaluations is that these sorts of evaluations can restore a threatened self-image. Study 3 provides the first complete test of this hypothesis by examining both sides of this process: the role of a threatened self-image in causing participants to derogate a member of a stereotyped group and the role of this derogation in restoring participants' threatened self-image. Thus, an important goal of Study 3 was to provide the first evidence that negative evaluation of a stereotyped target in response to self-image threat mediates increase in self-esteem.

Participants in Study 3 took what they thought was an intelligence test. Unlike in Study 2, all participants in Study 3 were led to believe that the test was real. They received bogus positive or negative feedback.[7] After the feedback, all participants

---

[7]We believed that it would be difficult or impossible to provide performance feedback that would be neutral for most participants, unless, as in Study 2, we did not lead the participants to believe that the test was real. An average score was quite threatening to our participants, and determining how much above average would be neutral for all participants seemed impossible.

completed a questionnaire that measured their state self-esteem. In an ostensibly unrelated experiment that followed, participants evaluated a woman portrayed as Jewish or Italian, as in Study 1. Following this evaluation, participants again completed the state self-esteem questionnaire so that we could monitor changes in their self-esteem.

We predicted that (a) participants who received negative feedback would have lower state self-esteem than participants who received positive feedback, (b) participants who received negative feedback and evaluated the Jewish target would rate the target more negatively than would the participants in the other conditions, (c) participants who received negative feedback and evaluated the Jewish target would exhibit a greater increase in state self-esteem than would participants in the other conditions, and (d) this increase in state self-esteem would be mediated by their evaluations of the target.

Method

PARTICIPANTS

One hundred twenty-six introductory psychology students from the University of Michigan participated in this experiment for partial fulfillment of a course requirement.[8]

PROCEDURE

Overview. Participants reported to the laboratory in pairs and were told that they would be participating in two experiments: an intelligence test and a social interaction. Participants first were given an intelligence test and were given bogus feedback about their performance. They next completed a measure of their state self-esteem (Heatherton & Polivy, 1991) and were asked to indicate their score on the intelligence test, after which they were thanked for their participation, dismissed, and sent to the "social evaluation" experiment, where they were met by a different ex-

perimenter. The social evaluation experiment involved the same procedure as that used in Study 1. That is, participants received information about a job candidate who was depicted as either Jewish or Italian. After evaluating this candidate's personality and job qualifications by using the same measures as those used in Study 1, participants again completed the Heatherton and Polivy measure of state self-esteem, after which they were asked to indicate their own and the target's race and ethnicity. Finally, they were probed for any suspicions, debriefed thoroughly, and thanked for their participation.

Manipulation of Feedback. When participants arrived for what was portrayed as the first experiment, they were told that the study was concerned with a new, improved form of intelligence test. The rationale and instructions were similar to but briefer than those given to the participants in Study 2. The intelligence test used in this study consisted of a longer but less difficult version of one of the tests from the battery of tests used in Study 2: the verbal–nonverbal matching test in which participants tried to match difficult vocabulary words to various pictures. This test was purported to be a very valid test of verbal and nonverbal skills. The experimenter began by giving each participant a pencil and a form commonly used for exams featuring multiple-choice questions that are graded via a computer. The test consisted of three sets of 10 words each.

The test was designed to be difficult and ambiguous enough for students to believe either positive or negative performance feedback. Some of the words were difficult or obscure for the average student (e.g., *capacious, celerity*) and some were easier (*forlorn, imminent*), but all had the feel of the kinds of vocabulary items that are included in college entrance exams, and many were such that participants felt as if they may have known what they meant but could not be sure. Moreover, the match between words and pictures often was not obvious, particularly given the fast pace of the test. Pretests and postexperiment interviews confirmed that participants tended to be unsure of how they were doing during the test and to believe the feedback that was given them.

At the completion of the test, the experimenter took the participants' answers and went into an adjacent room. The door to this room was left open, and the participants could hear what sounded like a Scantron machine grading the tests. The experi-

---

[8]Although 126 participants participated in the experiment, 17 were excluded because they were Jewish, 7 because they were foreign students and, consequently, would have been less likely to be familiar with the stereotype about Jewish American women, 4 because they misidentified the target's ethnicity, and 2 because they did not believe the false feedback about their performance on the intelligence test. Thus, the data from 96 participants were included in all analyses.

menter returned each participant's answer form to him or her. The experimenter explained that a red mark appeared next to each incorrect answer, that the first number on the bottom of the form indicated the number of correct answers, and that the second number indicated the participant's percentile ranking relative to all the other students who had taken the test thus far.

The feedback was, of course, bogus. Half of the participants received positive false feedback about their test performance (i.e., a high score that ostensibly put them in the 93rd percentile for the university), whereas the other half received negative false feedback (i.e., a low score that ostensibly put them in the 47th percentile). Although the 47th percentile is close to the median, pretesting had indicated that participants uniformly found this to be very negative feedback (see also Stein, 1994).

Results and Discussion

Recall that we predicted that if participants had received threatening, negative feedback about their performance on the intelligence test, they would be more likely to derogate the target as a function of her apparent ethnicity than if they had received positive feedback about their performance. We also predicted that derogating the stereotyped target would help restore threatened participants' self-esteem. The results were consistent with these predictions.

EVALUATIONS OF THE TARGET

Participants' ratings of the target's personality were subjected to a two-way ANOVA, which revealed strong support for our predictions. Two significant main effects emerged: Participants who had received negative feedback about their performance on the intelligence test rated the target's personality more negatively than did participants who had received positive feedback, $F(1, 92) = 9.1, p < .05$, and participants who were led to believe that the woman was Jewish rated her qualifications more negatively than did participants who were led to believe that the woman was Italian, $F(1, 92) = 5.2$, $p < .01$. More importantly, these main effects were qualified by a significant interaction between the manipulations of feedback and ethnicity, $F(1, 92) = 7.1, p < .01$. As can be seen in Figure 9.3, participants who had received positive feedback did not evaluate the personality of the target as a func-

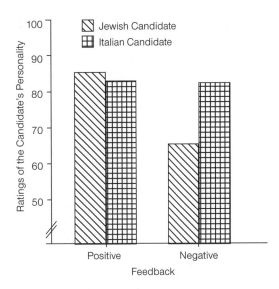

FIGURE 9.3. ■ Rating of candidate's personality as a function of feedback and ethnicity of the candidate. Higher numbers indicate more favorable evaluations.

tion of her apparent ethnicity, whereas participants who had received negative feedback evaluated the qualifications of the target much more negatively if she was portrayed as Jewish than if she was portrayed as Italian. The planned comparison indicated that participants who had received negative feedback and evaluated the Jewish target were significantly more negative in their evaluations of the target's personality than were participants in all other conditions, $t(92) = 4.5, p < .001$. None of the other conditions differed significantly from each other (see Footnote 4).

The ANOVA of the ratings of the target's job qualifications yielded a similar pattern of results. The two main effects were again significant: Participants who had received negative feedback about their performance on the intelligence test rated the target's qualifications more negatively than did participants who had received positive feedback, $F(1, 92) = 3.7, p = .05$, and participants who were led to believe that the woman was Jewish rated her qualifications more negatively than did participants who were led to believe that the woman was Italian, $F(1, 92) = 6.3, p < .05$. Although the interaction was not significant for this measure, $F(1, 92) = 2.3, p < .12$, the pattern of cell means was consistent with our predictions. Participants who had received positive feedback did not evaluate the target very differently as a function of her apparent ethnicity (M_{Jewish} = 18.8 vs. $M_{Italian}$ = 19.7), but participants who had received negative feedback evaluated the qualifications of the target much more negatively if she was portrayed as Jewish (M = 15.3) than if she was portrayed as Italian (M = 19.3). The planned comparison indicated that participants who had received negative feedback and evaluated the Jewish target were significantly more negative in their evaluations of the target's qualifications than were participants in all other conditions, $t(92) = 3.4, p < .001$. None of the other conditions differed significantly from each other.

These results, therefore, provide a conceptual replication of those found in Study 2 and support the generalizability of the findings by demonstrating them in the context of a different stereotype, a different kind of nonstereotyped group, and different dependent measures.

SELF-ESTEEM

In Study 3 we measured participants' state self-esteem at two points: after the feedback manipulation and after they rated the target. The theoretical range for this scale is 20 to 100, with higher numbers indicating higher state self-esteem. As expected, feedback had a significant effect on participants' state self-esteem. Participants who received the positive feedback felt better about themselves (M = 77.5) than did those who received the negative feedback (M = 72.9), $F(1, 94) = 4.4, p < .05$.

The change in state self-esteem from this first measure to the measure taken after participants evaluated the target was also consistent with predictions. The ANOVA revealed a marginally significant interaction between feedback and ethnicity $F(1,92) = 2.7, p = .10$. As can be seen in Figure 9.4, and consistent with our predictions, participants who received negative feedback and evaluated the Jewish target had a significantly greater increase in state self-esteem than did participants in the other conditions, $t(92) = 2.3, p < .05$. None of the other conditions differed significantly from each other on this measure.

These results suggest that the participants who received negative feedback and rated the Jewish woman restored their self-esteem by engaging in negative evaluation of the stereotyped target. We conducted a path analysis to test this reasoning (Baron & Kenny, 1986). Figure 9.5 depicts the results of this analysis. We allowed the planned in-

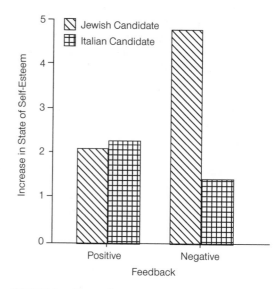

FIGURE 9.4 ■ Change in state self-esteem as a function of feedback and ethnicity of the job candidate. Higher numbers indicate greater increase in state self-esteem.

teraction contrast to predict change in participants' self-esteem. This direct effect was significant, $\beta = .23, t(92) = 2.3, p < .05$. Next we allowed the planned interaction contrast to predict participants' ratings of the target's personality. This path was significant as well, $\beta = .42, t(92) = 4.6, p < .01$. Finally, we allowed the planned interaction contrast and participants' ratings of the target's personality to predict participants' change in state self-esteem. The path from participants' ratings of the target was significant, $\beta = .37, t(92) = 3.5, p < .01$,

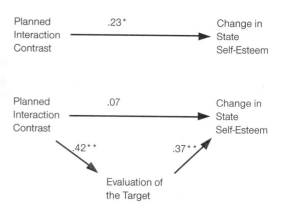

FIGURE 9.5 ■ Change in state self-esteem as mediated by negative evaluations of the job candidate's personality. $*p < .05.$ $**p < .01.$

but the direct effect of the planned interaction contrast on participants' change in self-esteem was no longer significant, $\beta = .07$, $t(92) = 0.7$, $p > .40$. Thus, this path analysis suggests that the direct effect of the manipulations in this experiment on participants' change in state self-esteem was mediated by their evaluations of the stereotyped target's personality. These analyses suggest that the negative feedback led to increased derogation of the Jewish target, which in turn led to increased state self-esteem, rather than suggesting that positive feedback led to a reduced derogation of the Jewish target.

Taken together, these results provide the first demonstration that self-image threats, such as negative feedback, can lead to negative evaluations of a stereotyped target and that these negative evaluations, in turn, can restore people's threatened self-images. Moreover, these findings support our hypothesis that derogating a stereotyped target in response to self-image threat mediates increase in self-esteem. These results, therefore, strongly corroborate the idea that negative evaluations of a stereotyped target may often result from an effort to affirm a threatened self-image.

General Discussion

This set of three studies examined evaluations of a member of a stereotyped group. Study 1 found that participants evaluated an individual target person more negatively if they thought she was a member of a stereotyped group than if they thought she was a member of a nonstereotyped group, but this effect did not occur if the participants' self-images had been bolstered through an affirmation procedure. Study 2 found that receiving self-image-threatening information led participants to evaluate an individual more stereotypically if he appeared to be a member of a stereotyped group. Study 3 demonstrated that receiving self-image-threatening information led participants to negatively evaluate an individual if she appeared to be a member of a stereotyped group, and these negative evaluations in turn were particularly effective in restoring participants' self-esteem. Moreover, the degree to which these participants made negative evaluations of the stereotyped target mediated the restoration of their self-esteem. Taken together this research suggests that a threat to one's positive self-image or a self-affirmation that provides a buffer against self-image threats can moderate negative evaluations of a member of a stereotyped group and that these biased evaluations can in turn affect one's sense of self-worth.

Self-Affirmation and Negative Evaluations of Others

This set of studies highlights the role of self processes in the perceptions of others. Information that threatens perceivers' sense of self-worth leads to the need to restore a positive self-image. Research by Steele and others (Steele, 1988; Steele & Liu, 1983; Steele et al., 1993) has shown that people can restore a threatened self-image in a number of ways, including by drawing on their own self-concept resources or by taking advantage of affirmational opportunities available in the situation. Steele et al. (1993) have suggested, however, that it may be difficult for people to spontaneously draw upon their self-concept resources to affirm their self-image. Therefore, people will often look to the situation to find opportunities to affirm their self-image. The studies presented here demonstrate that stereotyping or derogation of a member of a stereotyped group can provide such situational opportunities to restore a threatened self-image. Because it is likely that people often will encounter others in situations where it is personally and socially acceptable to evaluate them negatively, stereotyping and prejudice may be common reactions to self-image threat. However, when perceivers encounter someone who is a member of a group for which they do not have strong, accessible negative stereotypes, such as the woman in Studies 1 and 3 who was Italian or the man in Study 2 who apparently was straight, stereotyping or derogation is unlikely to be used as a self-affirmational strategy

These studies also suggest that self-affirmation processes may affect a wide range of phenomena. Most of the research on self-affirmation theory has examined how self-affirmation affects cognitive dissonance processes (Steele, 1988; Steele & Liu, 1983; Steele et al., 1993), but some research has suggested that self-affirmation can also influence self-evaluation maintenance (Tesser & Cornell, 1991), learned helplessness reactions (Liu & Steele, 1986), and the academic performance of women and minorities (Steele & Aronson, 1995). The present research, in which self-affirmation affected stereotyping and prejudice, provides further evidence that self-affirmation and self-image maintenance processes have broad applicability to a wide range of important phenomena.

Relations to Other Theories

Our approach emphasizes that stereotyping others is one of several possible self-image-maintenance strategies (Steele, 1988; Tesser & Cornell, 1991). We argue that negatively evaluating others has the potential to restore a positive self-image. Because these evaluations are part of a larger self-system that seeks to maintain an overall image of the self as morally and adaptively adequate, the state of the self-image—specifically, the extent to which it is threatened or affirmed—will influence when people will engage in stereotyping and when that stereotyping will restore a positive self-image. This approach clearly is related to other theories of stereotyping and prejudice, such as frustration–aggression, social identity and downward social comparison. However, there are distinct theoretical differences between our approach and these approaches. In addition, the findings of the current studies support our approach and would not be predicted by these other theories.

In contrast to frustration–aggression theory, which argues that people may displace aggression by derogating others in response to blocked goals and frustrations in their life, our approach emphasizes that threats to the self-image in particular rather than any source of frustration, lead to derogation of others. The results of Study 1 highlight this difference. Consistent with our predictions, we found that self-affirmation reduced participants' tendency to derogate a stereotyped target. It is unclear from frustration–aggression theory how a self-affirmation procedure such as that used in Study 1 would reduce frustration, unless frustration is defined more broadly than it has been in the past.

Social identity theory suggests that people favor their own groups over other groups in an effort to boost their group's status, which in turn boosts their own self-esteem. Although our approach would suggest that favoring one's own group over another group can restore one's self-image, we argue that negatively evaluating a stereotyped target can restore one's self-image even if group evaluations and in-group–out-group comparisons are not made. In the current studies there is no evidence that people are making in-group–out-group evaluations or comparisons. Both the threats and the affirmation were directed at the self, rather than at the group, and the evaluations were always of a single individual. Given that the self-affirmation manipulation in Study 1 was irrelevant to participants' group identity or status, it is unclear how social identity theory could account for the results of this study. Moreover, from a perspective that emphasizes in-group–out-group differences, one might predict that the negative feedback in Study 3 should have caused participants to derogate the Italian candidate because the Italian candidate could be considered an out-group member for most of the participants. In addition, such derogation should have been associated with a greater increase in self-esteem. The results do not support this account.

Downward social comparison theory argues that people make negative evaluations of others to bolster their self-esteem. A more precisely defined conception of downward social comparison, however, might require that social comparisons involve self–other distinctions. Our approach suggests that such self–other distinctions might indeed restore one's self-image, but negative evaluations of stereotyped others that do not involve self–other comparisons should also restore one's self-image. In the current studies there is no evidence that our participants made self–other comparisons when evaluating the targets. Moreover, even if participants made self–other distinctions, downward social comparison theory would predict that the self-image threats should have led to derogation of all other targets, whether or not they appeared to be members of a stereotyped group. The results of our studies do not support such a prediction.

At a theoretical level, therefore, our approach is consistent in many ways with other theories, such as frustration–aggression, social identity, and downward social comparison theory, although there are some important differences. In addition, only our account can explain the set of results found in the current studies.

At an empirical level, several studies have shown that self-image threat can lead to negative evaluations of others (Brown & Gallagher, 1992; Crocker et al., 1987; Gibbons & Gerrard, 1991), and other studies have demonstrated that negative evaluations of others can lead to increased self-esteem (Brickman & Bulman, 1977; Taylor & Lobel, 1989; Wills, 1991; Wood & Taylor, 1991). Our studies differ from these previous studies by demonstrating that when people experience self-image threats, their negative evaluations of stereotyped others can mediate an increase in self-esteem. Furthermore, the current studies are the first to show that thinking about a self-relevant value unrelated to prejudice can lead to a reduction in stereotyping. Thus, the findings of the current studies support our contention that stereotypic evaluations of others can serve a self-image-maintenance function.

In our view, any negative evaluation of others—through downward social comparisons, intergroup discrimination, or stereotyping and prejudice—has the potential to serve a self-image-maintenance function. Because of the prevalence, consensual nature, and potential subtlety of negative stereotypes in particular, stereotyping and prejudice may be an especially common and effective means of self-affirmation.

The Role of Motivation in Stereotyping and Prejudice

Major reviews of the stereotyping and prejudice literature (e.g., Ashmore & Del Boca, 1981; Brewer & Kramer, 1985; Hamilton & Trolier, 1986; Hilton & von Hippel, 1996; Snyder & Miene, 1994; Stroebe & Insko. 1989) acknowledge the role of motivational factors (which may be paired with or subsumed under a personality or psychodynamic approach) as one of the principal perspectives or approaches to the study of stereotyping and prejudice, alone with the sociocultural and cognitive approaches. Typically, however, relatively little empirical evidence beyond research concerning psychodynamic-based constructs and theories from the 1940s and 1950s or intergroup relations and related phenomena (e.g., realistic group conflict and social identity theory) is cited in support of this perspective. The present research, along with recent examinations of the roles of affect and emotion (Esses, Haddock, & Zanna, 1994; Forgas, 1995; Islam & Hewstone, 1993; Mackie & Hamilton, 1993) and inhibition in stereotyping and prejudice (Bodenhausen & Macrae, 1996; Devine, 1989; Devine, Monteith, Zuwerink, & Elliot, 1991; Monteith, 1993), examinations of the functions of stereotyping and prejudice (Snyder & Miene, 1994), examinations of the influence of desired beliefs on person perception (Klein & Kunda, 1992), and examinations of the roles of self-esteem and collective self-esteem in inter-

group perceptions and discrimination (Branscombe & Wann, 1994; Crocker et al., 1987), reflects a burgeoning interest in processes that are relevant to this underdeveloped motivational perspective.

The results of the studies reported in this article suggest that prejudiced perceptions of members of stereotyped groups can, under the appropriate conditions, help perceivers restore a positive self-image. Engaging in stereotyping and prejudice, therefore, can be an attractive way for many individuals to feel better about themselves in the absence of more readily available means of alleviating self-image threats or of affirming oneself. Given the same sociocultural context, and given the same cues and information and information-processing conditions, perceivers who are motivated to restore a feeling of overall self-worth should be more likely than other perceivers to seek out or take advantage of stereotypes.

This is not to suggest, however, that sociocultural and cognitive factors are not also critically important in the processes examined in our studies. Rather, these studies reflect an interplay of each of these factors. This is reflected in the interaction between ethnicity or sexual orientation of the target and the manipulation of self-affirmation (Study 1) or self-esteem threat (Studies 2 and 3). If the need to restore a positive overall sense of self-worth influenced prejudice independently of social-cognitive factors, then the manipulations of self-affirmation and self-threat should have resulted simply in more positive (when self-affirmed) or more negative (when the self was threatened and not affirmed) evaluations of the target individual. Rather, the manipulations of self-affirmation and self-threat significantly influenced participants' evaluations of the target only when they thought she or he was a member of a group for which there was a strong and negative stereotype, but not when they thought the target was not a member of such a group. Furthermore, evaluating the target negatively was associated with greater self-esteem boost in the former but not in the latter condition. Thus, the presence of the stereotype, stemming from sociocultural and cognitive factors, facilitated the process of derogating the target person and restoring self-esteem.

Only after recognizing the interplay among sociocultural, cognitive, and motivational factors can one adequately address the question of why derogating *any* target would not make participants feel better about themselves. In other words, if a threat to perceivers' self-esteem makes them want to restore their self-esteem, why not derogate an Italian woman if she is more available than a Jewish woman? Cognitive and sociocultural factors provide an answer to this question. Within the culture in which Studies 1 and 3 were conducted, there was a strong negative stereotype of Jewish American women but not of Italian American women. The JAP stereotype provided participants with the cognitive basis for perceiving the individual in a negative light. Similarly, the gay man stereotype provided participants in Study 2 with the cognitive basis for perceiving the individual in a stereotypical and negative light. Derogation would seem less justifiable in the absence of the stereotype because participants' judgments would not have been biased by the stereotype. Rather than feel better about themselves, most individuals likely would feel worse if they realized that they had disparaged another person in order to restore their own sense of self-worth (e.g., Devine et al., 1991). Stereotypes, through social-cognitive processes such as assimilation, illusory correlations, and schematic processing, can therefore facilitate self-image maintenance, particularly to the extent that perceivers are not aware of this influence.

The Nature of Stereotyping

Most of the stereotypes that we can think of are predominantly negative. Although they are very different from each other, stereotypes about African Americans, people with disabilities, Latinos, women, Native Americans, older people, gay men, lesbians, and those low in social economic status are similar in that they are primarily negative. The current analysis provides a possible explanation for the predominantly negative character of these stereotypes. Although there are undoubtedly other mechanisms that create and perpetuate negative stereotypes (e.g., illusory correlations, out-group homogeneity, in-group bias, and social roles), our analysis suggests that stereotypes may often take on a negative character because the negativity can help restore people's self-images. When people form stereotypes about a group, they may be more likely to characterize the group in negative terms because such characterizations allow evaluations of the group that can be used for later self-affirmation. Similarly, these stereotypes may be particularly resistant to change because they can make perceivers feel better about themselves.

This analysis emphasizes the important role that motivation can play in stereotyping and prejudice. People may be more likely to stereotype others or engage in prejudicial evaluations to the extent that they are motivated to restore or enhance their self-images. Thus, understanding people's motivations may be critical in determining whether they will stereotype others, how they will stereotype others, and what form these stereotypes will take. Stereotyping and prejudice are clearly an important problem in our society. Our analysis suggests that a complete understanding of these processes, and ways of mitigating them, requires an understanding of the role of the self in people's perceptions of others.

REFERENCES

Abrams, D. (1994). Social self-regulation. *Personality and Social Psychology Bulletin, 20,* 473–483.

Abrams, D., & Hogg, M. A. (1988). Comments on the motivational status of self-esteem in social identity and intergroup discrimination. *European Journal of Social Psychology, 18,* 317–334.

Ammons, R. B., & Ammons, C. H. (1962). The quick test: Provisional manual. *Psychological Reports, 11,* 111–161.

Ashmore, R. D., & Del Boca, E. K. (1981). Conceptual approaches to stereotypes and stereotyping. In D. L. Hamilton (Ed.), *Cognitive processes in stereotyping and intergroup behavior* (pp. 1–35). Hillsdale, NJ: Erlbaum.

Baron, R. M., & Kenny, D. A. (1986). The moderator–mediator variable distinction in social psychological research: Conceptual, strategic, and statistical considerations. *Journal of Personality and Social Psychology, 51,* 1173–1182.

Bodenhausen, G. V., & Macrae, C. N. (1996). The self-regulation of intergroup perception: Mechanisms and consequences of stereotype suppression. In C. N. Macrae, M. Hewstone, & C. Stangor (Eds.), *Foundations of stereotypes and stereotyping* (pp. 227–253). New York: Guilford Press.

Branscombe, N. R., & Wann, D. L. (1994). Collective self-esteem consequences of outgroup derogation when a valued social identity is on trial. *European Journal of Social Psychology, 24,* 641–657.

Brewer, M. B. (1993). Social identity, distinctiveness, and ingroup homogeneity. *Social Cognition, 11,* 150–164.

Brewer, M. B., & Kramer, R. M. (1985). The psychology of intergroup attitudes and behavior. *Annual Review of Psychology, 36,* 219–243.

Brickman, P., & Bulman, R. J. (1977). Pleasure and pain in social comparison. In J. M. Suls & R. L. Miller (Eds.), *Social comparison processes: Theoretical and empirical perspectives* (pp. 149–186). Washington, DC: Hemisphere.

Brown, J. D., Collins, R. L., & Schmidt, G. W. (1988). Self-esteem and direct versus indirect forms of self-enhancement. *Journal of Personality and Social Psychology, 55,* 445–453.

Brown, J. D., & Gallagher, F. M. (1992). Coming to terms

with failure: Private self-enhancement and public self-effacement. *Journal of Experimental Social Psychology, 28,* 3–22.

Cameron, J. E., & Lalonde, R. N. (1994). Self, ethnicity, and social group memberships in two generations of Italian Canadians. *Personality and Social Psychology Bulletin, 20,* 514–520.

Cohen, D., & Nisbett, R. E. (1994). Self-protection and the culture of honor: Explaining Southern violence. *Personality and Social Psychology Bulletin, 24,* 551–567.

Cooley, C. H. (1902). *Human nature and the social order.* New York: Schocken Books.

Crocker, J., Thompson, L. J., McGraw. K. M., & Ingerman, C. (1987). Downward comparison, prejudice, and evaluations of others: Effects of self-esteem and threat. *Journal of Personality and Social Psychology, 52,* 907–916.

Darley, J. M., Fleming, J. H., Hilton, J. L., & Swann, W. B. (1988). Dispelling negative expectancies: The impact of interaction goals and target characteristics on the expectancy confirmation process. *Journal of Experimental Social Psychology, 24,* 19–36.

Devine, P. G. (1989). Stereotypes and prejudice: Their controlled and automatic components. *Journal of Personality and Social Psychology, 56,* 5–18.

Devine, P. G., Monteith, M. J., Zuwerink. J. R., & Elliot, A. J. (1991). Prejudice with and without compunction. *Journal of Personality and Social Psychology, 60,* 817–830.

Ditto, P. H., & Lopez, D. E. (1992). Motivated skepticism: Use of differential decision criteria for preferred and nonpreferred conclusions. *Journal of Personality and Social Psychology, 63,* 568–584.

Dollard, J., Doob, L. W., Miller, N. E., Mowrer, O. H., & Sears, R. R. (1939). *Frustration and aggression.* New Haven, CT: Yale University Press.

Dovidio, J. F., & Gaertner, S. L. (1991). Changes in the expression and assessment of racial prejudice. In H. J. Knopke, R. J. Norrell, & R. W. Rogers (Eds.), *Opening doors: Perspectives on race relations in contemporary America* (pp. 119–148). Tuscaloosa: University of Alabama Press.

Eccles, J. S., Jacobs, J. E., & Harold, R. D. (1990). Gender role stereotypes, expectancy effects, and parents' socialization of gender differences. *Journal of Social Issues, 46,* 183–201.

Esses, V. M., Haddock, G., & Zanna, M. P. (1994). The role of mood in the expression of intergroup stereotypes. In M. P. Zanna & J. M. Olson (Eds.), *The psychology of prejudice: The Ontario Symposium* (Vol. 7, pp. 77–101). Hillsdale, NJ: Erlbaum.

Fein, S., Cross, J. A., & Spencer, S. J. (1995, August). *Self-esteem maintenance, stereotype consistency, and men's prejudice toward gays.* Paper presented at the 103rd Annual Convention of the American Psychological Association, New York.

Festinger, L. (1954). A theory of social comparison processes. *Human Relations, 7,* 117–140.

Forgas, J. P. (1995). Mood and judgment: The affect infusion model (AIM). *Psychological Bulletin, 117,* 39–66.

Gibbons, F. X., & Gerrard, M. (1991). Downward social comparison and coping with threat. In J. M. Suls & T. A. Wills (Eds.), *Social comparison: Theory and research* (pp. 317–345). Hillsdale, NJ: Erlbaum.

Gibbons, F. X., & McCoy, S. B. (1991). Self-esteem, similarity and reaction to active versus passive downward comparison. *Journal of Personality and Social Psychology, 60,* 414–424.

Greenberg, J., Solomon, S., Pyszczynski, T., Rosenblatt, A., Burling, J., Lyon, D., Simon, L., & Pinel, E. (1992). Why do people need self-esteem? Converging evidence that self-esteem serves an anxiety-buffering function. *Journal of Personality and Social Psychology, 63,* 913–922.

Greenwald, A. G. (1980). The totalitarian ego: Fabrication and revision of personal history. *American Psychologist, 35,* 603–618.

Hamilton, D. L., & Trolier, T. K. (1986). Stereotypes and stereotyping: An overview of the cognitive approach. In J. E Dovidio & S. L. Gaertner (Eds.), *Prejudice, discrimination, and racism: Theory and research* (pp. 127–163). Orlando, FL: Academic Press.

Hays, W. L. (1981). *Statistics* (3rd ed.). New York: Holt, Rinehart & Winston.

Heatherton, T. F., & Polivy, J. (1991). Development and validation of a scale for measuring state self-esteem. *Journal of Personality and Social Psychology, 60,* 895–910.

Higgins, E. T. (1996). Emotional experiences: The pains and pleasures of distinct regulatory systems. In R. D. Kavanaugh, B. Zimmerberg, & S. Fein (Eds.), *Emotion: Interdisciplinary perspectives* (pp. 203–241). Mahwah, NJ: Erlbaum.

Higgins, E. T., & Tykocinski, O. (1992). Self-discrepancies and biographical memory: Personality and cognition at the level of psychological situation. *Personality and Social Psychology Bulletin, 18,* 527–535.

Hilton, J. L., & von Hippel, W. H. (1996). Stereotypes. *Annual Review of Psychology, 47,* 237–271.

Hogg, M. A., & Abrams, D. (1988). *Social identifications: A social psychology of intergroup relations and group processes.* London: Routledge.

Islam, M. R., & Hewstone, M. (1993). Dimensions of contact as predictors of intergroup anxiety, perceived out-group variability, and out-group attitude: An integrative model. *Personality and Social Psychology Bulletin, 19,* 700–710.

Keppel, G. (1973). *Design and analysis: A researcher's handbook.* Englewood Cliffs, NJ: Prentice Hall.

Kite, M., & Deaux, K. (1987). Gender belief systems: Homosexuality and the implicit inversion theory. *Psychology of Women Quarterly, 11,* 83–96.

Klein, W. M., & Kunda, Z. (1992). Motivated person perception: Constructing justifications for desired beliefs. *Journal of Experimental Social Psychology, 28,* 145–168.

Klein, W. M., & Kunda, Z. (1993). Maintaining self-serving social comparisons: Biased reconstruction of one's past behaviors. *Personality and Social Psychology Bulletin, 19,* 732–739.

Liu, T. J., & Steele, C. M. (1986). Attributional analysis as self-affirmation. *Journal of Personality and Social Psychology, 51,* 531–540.

Mackie, D. M., & Hamilton, D. L. (Eds.). (1993). *Affect, cognition, and stereotyping: Interactive processes in group perception.* San Diego, CA: Academic Press.

Markus, H. (1977). Self-schemata and processing information about the self. *Journal of Personality and Social Psychology 35,* 63–78.

Markus, H., & Wurf, E. (1987). The dynamic self-concept. *Annual Review of Psychology, 38,* 299–337.

Markus, H. R., & Kitayama, S. (1991). Culture and the self: Implications for cognition, emotion, and motivation. *Psychological Review, 98,* 224–253.

Markus, H. R., & Kitayama, S. (1994). A collective fear of the collective: Implications for selves and theories of selves. *Personality and Social Psychology Bulletin, 20,* 568–579.

Mead, G. H. (1934). *Mind, self, and society.* Chicago: University of Chicago Press.

Mehrabian, A., & Russell, J. (1974). *An approach to environmental psychology.* Cambridge, MA: MIT Press.

Miller, N. E., & Bugelski, R. (1948). The influence of frustrations imposed by the in-group on attitude expressed toward out-group. *Journal of Psychology, 25,* 437–442.

Monteith, M. J. (1993). Self-regulation of prejudiced responses: Implications for progress in prejudice-reduction efforts. *Journal of Personality and Social Psychology, 65,* 469–485.

Neuberg, S. L., & Fiske, S. T. (1987). Motivational influences on impression formation: Outcome dependency, accuracy-driven attention, and individuating processes. *Journal of Personality and Social Psychology, 53,* 431–444.

Nisbett, R. E., & Ross, L. (1980). *Human inference: Strategies and shortcomings of social judgment.* Englewood Cliffs, NJ: Prentice Hall.

Rosenthal, R., & Jacobson, L. (1968). *Pygmalion in the classroom: Teacher expectation and pupils' intellectual development.* New York: Holt, Rinehart & Winston.

Rosenthal, R., & Rosnow, R. L. (1991). *Essentials of behavioral research: Methods and data analysis* (2nd ed.) New York: McGraw-Hill.

Ross, M., & Sicoly, F. (1979). Egocentric biases in availability and attribution. *Journal of Personality and Social Psychology, 37,* 322–336.

Schlenker, B. R., Weigold, M. F., & Hallam. J. R. (1990). Self-serving attributions in social context: Effects of self-esteem and social pressure. *Journal of Personality and Social Psychology, 58,* 855–863.

Smith, E. R. (1993). Social identity and social emotions: Toward new conceptualizations of prejudice. In D. M. Mackie & D. L. Hamilton (Eds.), *Affect, cognition, and stereotyping: Interactive processes in group perception* (pp. 297–315). San Diego. CA: Academic Press.

Snyder, M. (1984). When belief creates reality. In L. Berkowitz (Ed.), *Advances in experimental social psychology* (Vol. 18, pp. 248–306). New York: Academic Press.

Snyder, M., & Miene, P. (1994). On the functions of stereotypes and prejudice. In M. P. Zanna & J. M. Olson (Eds.), *The psychology of prejudice: The Ontario Symposium* (Vol. 7, pp. 33–54). Hillsdale, NJ: Erlbaum.

Spencer, S. J., & Steele, C. M. (1990, May). *The role of self-esteem functioning in IQ estimation.* Paper presented at the 62nd meeting of the Midwestern Psychological Association, Chicago.

Steele, C. M. (1988). The psychology of self-affirmation: Sustaining the integrity of the self. In L. Berkowitz (Ed.), *Advances in experimental social psychology* (Vol. 21, pp. 261–302). New York: Academic Press.

Steele, C. M., & Aronson, J. (1995). Stereotype threat and the intellectual test performance of African Americans. *Journal of Personality and Social Psychology, 69,* 797–811.

Steele, C. M., & Liu, T. J. (1983). Dissonance processes as self-affirmation. *Journal of Personality and Social Psychology, 45,* 5–19.

Steele, C. M., Spencer, S. J., & Lynch, M. (1993). Self-image resilience and dissonance: The role of affirmational resources. *Journal of Personality and Social Psychology, 64,* 885–896.

Stein, K. F. (1994). Complexity of the self-schema and responses to disconfirming feedback. *Cognitive Therapy and Research, 18,* 161–178.

Stroebe, W., & Insko, C. A. (1989). Stereotype, prejudice, and discrimination: Changing conceptions in theory and research. In D. Bar-Tal, C. F. Graumann, A. W. Kruglanski, & W. Stroebe (Eds.), *Stereotyping and prejudice: Changing conceptions* (pp. 3–34). New York: Springer-Verlag.

Swann, W. B., Stein–Seroussi, A., & Giesler, R. B. (1992). Why people self-verify. *Journal of Personality and Social Psychology, 62,* 392–401.

Tajfel, H. (Ed.). (1982). *Social identity and intergroup relations.* Cambridge, England: Cambridge University Press.

Taylor, S. E., & Lobel, M. (1989). Social comparison activity under threat: Downward evaluation and upward contacts. *Psychological Review, 96,* 569–575.

Tesser, A. (1988). Toward a self-evaluation maintenance model of social behavior. In L. Berkowitz (Ed.), *Advances in experimental social psychology* (Vol. 21, pp. 181–227). New York: Academic Press.

Tesser, A., & Cornell, D. P. (1991). On the confluence of self processes. *Journal of Experimental Social Psychology, 27,* 501–526.

Tetlock, P. E. (1983). Accountability and the perseverance of first impressions. *Social Psychology Quarterly, 46,* 285–292.

Triandis, H. C. (1989). The self and social behavior in differing cultural contexts. *Psychological Review, 96,* 506–520.

Turner, J. C. (1982). Toward a cognitive redefinition of the social group. In H. Tajfel (Ed.), *Social identity and intergroup relations.* Cambridge. England: Cambridge University Press.

Turner, J. C., Oakes, P. J., Haslam, S. A., & McGarty, C. (1994). Self and collective: Cognition and social context. *Personality and Social Psychology Bulletin, 20,* 454–463.

Wills, T A. (1981). Downward comparison principles in social psychology. *Psychological Bulletin, 90,* 245–271.

Wills, T. A. (1991). Similarity and self-esteem in downward comparison. In J. M. Suls & T. A. Wills (Eds.), *Social comparison: Theory and research* (pp. 51–78). Hillsdale, NJ: Erlbaum.

Winer, B. J. (1971). *Statistical principles in experimental design* (2nd ed.). New York: McGraw-Hill.

Wood, J. V., & Taylor, K. L. (1991). Serving self-relevant goals through social comparison. In J. M. Suls & T. A. Wills (Eds.), *Social comparison: Theory and research* (pp. 23–50). Hillsdale, NJ: Erlbaum.

Language Use in Intergroup Contexts: The Linguistic Intergroup Bias

Anne Maass and Daniela Salvi • Università di Padova
Luciano Arcuri • Università di Trieste
Gün Semin • University of Sussex

Three experiments examine how the type of language used to describe in-group and out-group behaviors contributes to the transmission and persistence of social stereotypes. Two experiments tested the hypothesis that people encode and communicate desirable in-group and undesirable out-group behaviors more abstractly than undesirable in-group and desirable out-group behaviors. Experiment 1 provided strong support for this hypothesis using a fixed-response scale format controlling for the level of abstractness developed from Semin and Fiedler's (1988a) linguistic category model. Experiment 2 yielded the same results with a free-response format. Experiment 3 demonstrated the important role that abstract versus concrete communication plays in the perpetuation of stereotypes. The implications of these findings and the use of the linguistic category model are discussed for the examination of the self-perpetuating cycle of stereotypes in communication processes.

Since the early social-psychological writings on prejudice and intergroup relations (cf. Allport, 1954), theorists have repeatedly commented on the fact that out-group stereotypes and in-group favoritism are apparently highly resistant to change and are likely to persist across generations. In recent years, various explanations have been tendered to account for the persistence of social stereotypes and intergroup biases. Motivational theories (see Tajfel & Turner 1979; Turner, 1987), on one side, tend to stress the functional role of intergroup bias for self-esteem maintenance. Social-cognitive approaches, on the other side, refer to cognitive principles that contribute to the perpetuation of existing stereotypic beliefs even in the face of disconfirming evidence; among these

principles are the preference for expectancy-confirming information (e.g., Snyder & Swann, 1978), superior recall for expectancy-congruent information regarding groups (Hastie & Kumar, 1979; Howard & Rothbart, 1980; Rothbart, Evans, & Fulero, 1979; Srull, Lichtenstein, & Rothbart, 1985), the existence of highly simplistic schemata about the out-group (Linville, Salovey, & Fischer 1986), the exclusion of atypical group members from the category (Rothbart & Lewis, 1988), and the stereotype-consistent interpretation of ambiguous behavioral episodes (Duncan, 1976; Sagar & Schofield, 1980). For general overviews, see Brewer and Kramer, 1985; Hamilton, 1981; Hamilton & Trolier, 1986; and Dovidio and Gaertner, 1986a.

Surprisingly, the role of language in the maintenance and transmission of stereotypes has largely been ignored in this context (for exceptions, see Van Dijk's work; e.g., Van Dijk, 1984, 1987). Although there is ample evidence that language apparently plays an important role in other domains of human cognition, its contribution to intergroup biases in general and to the persistence of social stereotypes in particular has remained unclear.

In this article, we advance the thesis that, in an intergroup context, language is used in a manner that renders disconfirmation of preexisting ideas about in-group and out-group difficult. Applying a recent psycholinguistic model by Semin and Fiedler (1988a, 1988b; Fiedler & Semin, 1988a, 1988b), we argue that the same behavioral episodes are encoded at different levels of abstraction depending on whether such behaviors have positive or negative connotations and whether they are performed by in-group or out-group members.[1] In particular, we argue that socially desirable in-group behaviors and undesirable out-group behaviors are encoded at a high level of abstraction, whereas socially undesirable in-group behaviors and desirable out-group behaviors are encoded at a low level of abstraction. Considering that information encoded at an abstract level is relatively resistant to disconfirmation and implies high stability over time (Semin & Fiedler, 1988a), our approach may contribute to a better understanding of the persistence of stereotypic beliefs. Thus, we propose a model in which existing intergroup biases produce a biased language use, which in turn contributes to the maintenance of existing biases. We briefly outline Semin and Fiedler's model and subsequently discuss its implications for the intergroup context.

The Linguistic Category Model. Semin and Fiedler's (1988a) linguistic category model distinguishes four linguistic categories that may be used in describing other people (see Table 10.1). The same behavioral episode may be encoded at four different levels of abstraction. At the most concrete level, it may be encoded in terms of descriptive action verbs (DAVs), such as *to call* or *to touch*, that refer to a single, observable event, de-

---

[1]Throughout this article, we use the term *encoding* in a somewhat different and more general way than is usually done by cognitive psychologists. In reference to its original meaning as "translating into a code," we define *encoding* as the translation of language-free (visually presented) information into a linguistic code.

TABLE 10.1. Semin and Fiedler's (1988a) Linguistic Category Model

Level, category, and characteristic features	Examples
I: Descriptive action verb—Objective description of a specific and observable behavior with clear beginning and end; refers to specific situation and specific object; usually does not have positive or negative connotations	Kiss Look Run Visit Call
II: Interpretive action verb—Describes a general class of behaviors (including various possible behavioral acts), but refers to aspecific action with clear beginning and end, to a specific object situation; provides an interpretation beyond the mere description; has positive or negative semantic connotations	Help Offend Inhibit Cheat Threaten
III: State verb—Enduring states (emotional, affective, mental, etc.) beyond specific behaviors or situations; reference to specific object; no clear beginning and end; provides interpretation beyond mere description; does not readily take the progressive form or imperative	Believe Love Admire Desire Envy
IV: Adjectives—Describe highly abstract person dispositions; no object reference or situation reference; highly interpretive, detached from specific behaviors	Honest Impulsive Reliable Helpful Creative

fined by at least one physically invariant feature. At the second level of abstraction are interpretive action verbs (IAVs), such as *to help* or *to cheat*, which are no longer bound to physically invariant features although they preserve the reference to a single behavioral episode. In contrast to DAVs, IAVs such as *to help* describe a general class of behaviors without identifying the specific behavior to which they refer in a given context (e.g., *to help* may refer to such different behaviors as lending money, opening the door, or reviving somebody). State verbs (SVs) describe a psychological state such as hate or desire; they have no direct reference to a specific behavioral episode or to a specific situation, but do refer to a specific object. At the highest level of abstraction are adjectives (ADJ), such as *aggressive* or *creative*, that describe highly abstract dispositions or characteristics of a person. ADJs provide generalizations across specific behavioral events, across situations, and across objects.

The following hypothetical example illustrates

how the same behavioral episode can be encoded at different levels of abstraction. Imagine that Person A is hitting Person B's arm with his fist. This behavioral event may be encoded at a concrete level as "A is punching B," or at a slightly more abstract level as "A is hurting B." Alternatively, one may interpret the scene as "A hates B," or at the highest level of abstraction, one may conclude that "A is aggressive." The codification at a higher or lower level of abstraction may have a number of important implications. An abstract statement such as "A is aggressive" implies great stability over time and generality across settings and interaction partners, suggesting that Person A will behave similarly in the future, in different situations, and with other people. He could also be expected to show related aggressive behaviors such as kicking, spitting, or pulling hair. Obviously, none of these conclusions could be drawn from a description at the concrete level.

In fact, Semin and Fiedler (1988a) have demonstrated that abstract statements as opposed to concrete statements are perceived as less verifiable; they also imply greater temporal stability and are perceived as revealing more about the person and less about the situation than are concrete statements; furthermore, they are perceived more readily as giving rise to disagreement.

Implications for Intergroup Settings. We believe that, as a conceptual framework and methodological tool, the language category model may have a number of interesting implications for intergroup relations and stereotyping. Membership biases are so well documented in the literature on intergroup relations (see Brewer, 1979; Brewer & Kramer, 1985; Hamilton & Trolier, 1986; Tajfel, 1982; Wilder, 1986, for reviews) that a detailed description appears superfluous in this context. This research consistently demonstrates that the mere categorization of people into groups can lead to favoritism toward the in-group and discrimination against the out-group. The tendency to establish a relative superiority of the in-group over the out-group has generally been interpreted in motivational terms. According to social identity theory (Tajfel & Turner, 1979), people strive to enhance the value of their own group relative to the out-group in order to maintain a positive social identity.

Consistent with this general bias, people also tend to hold differential expectancies about the behavior of in-group and out-group members. They expect in-group members to display more desirable and fewer undesirable behaviors than out-group members (Howard & Rothbart, 1980). Furthermore, they are more likely to infer negative dispositions from undesirable out-group behaviors than from undesirable in-group behaviors and are less likely to infer positive dispositions from desirable out-group behaviors than from desirable in-group behaviors (e.g., Taylor & Jaggi, 1974; Pettigrew, 1979; Hewstone & Jaspars, 1984). This suggests that the evidence-to-inference (Rothbart & Park, 1986) or act-to-disposition link is much tighter when a behavior episode confirms preconceived ideas about the actor.

This bias is not as illogical as it may initially appear, considering that stereotypic expectancies make probabilistic rather than deterministic predictions. Assume that members of Group A expect members of an out-group, B, to display socially undesirable behaviors. Obviously they do not expect members of Group B to always behave in socially undesirable ways. Rather, they assume that, compared with the overall average rate of such behaviors, members of Group B have an above-chance probability of engaging in undesirable behaviors and a below chance probability of showing desirable behaviors. Consequently, when members of the out-group do display desirable behaviors, there is no need to revise the general negative conception of out-group members because a probabilistic expectancy explicitly allows for a certain number of instances in which desirable behaviors will occur. According to Wilder (1986), this tendency is particularly pronounced for unexpected behaviors of out-group members, for which is held an Aristotelian view of lawfulness that allows for a great number of exceptions before the general rule has to be revised.

There are at least two ways to reconcile unexpected behaviors (e.g., a generous act of a single member of the Jewish community) with the general conception of the category (e.g., Jews are stingy), namely, the dissociation of the single, atypical member from the category as a whole (Allport's, 1954, refencing principle; see also Rothbart & Lewis, 1988; Weber & Crocker, 1983) and the dissociation of the single act from the group member. It is this second mechanism that is of interest here. Thus, an out-group member's socially desirable behavior may simply be interpreted as a specific instance that is situationally and temporally bound and that is largely unrelated to the actor's more enduring properties, such as his or her inclinations or psychological state. Basically, expectancy-incongruent behavior episodes are treated as exceptions to the rule that can be reconciled through situational and temporal constraints. We believe that this mechanism is reflected in a corresponding linguistic inter-group bias in which unexpected behaviors (desirable out-group and undesirable in-group behaviors) are described in concrete terms without generalizing beyond the given information.

Although people may occasionally hold positive expectancies about out-groups (e.g., embedded in the overall negative stereotype of Jews is the expectancy that Jews will display exceptionally high levels of intelligence), the general tendency to favor one's own group and the specific expectancies about in-group and out-group behaviors will, in most cases, coincide. For such cases, we suspect that when people observe members of their own category performing desirable behavior, they will readily associate those acts with the actors' enduring properties or psychological state, and hence will describe the acts in abstract linguistic terms. A similar tendency should emerge for undesirable out-group behaviors. In contrast, desirable out-group and undesirable in-group behavior are more likely to be encoded as concrete behavioral instances, without abstraction beyond the given information. Such behavioral episodes that are incongruent with the general perception of in-group and out-group and as such are unexpected are treated as the exception that confirms the rule by simply shifting the level of analysis from the general to the specific.

Hypotheses. We predict, therefore, that people will tend to encode (and to communicate) favorable in-group and unfavorable out-group behaviors at a higher level of abstraction than unfavorable in-group and favorable out-group behavior. In particular, the same socially desirable (e.g., altruistic) act will be encoded at a higher level of abstraction when performed by an in-group member than when performed by an out-group member. On the contrary, a socially undesirable (e.g., aggressive) act will be encoded at a higher level of abstraction when performed by an out-group member rather than when performed by an in-group member. These patterns of behavior are termed the *linguistic intergroup bias.*

To test these hypotheses, in the first 2 experiments we exposed members of mutually exclusive social categories to a series of episodes in which members of either the in-group or the out-group performed socially desirable or undesirable behavior. The subject's task was simply to encode the visually presented information. In Experiment 1, four response alternatives were provided, corresponding to the four levels of abstraction in the linguistic category model, from which the subject had to select one (multiple-choice responses). In Experiment 2, subjects were exposed to the same stimulus material, but were instructed to provide a short description of each scene (free description). Thus, Experiment 1 attempted to maximize experimental control and to minimize the likelihood of uncodable responses, whereas Experiment 2 intended to increase the external validity by rendering the subjects' task similar to naturally occurring encoding processes.

Experiment 1

Method

Choice of In-Group Versus Out-Group Category. Because the experiments were conducted in Italy, we tried to identify social groups that represented meaningful categories within the cultural context of that country. Various cities in Italy, most notably Siena, have yearly horse racing competitions called *palio*, in which members of the various sections or quarters of the city (so-called *contrada*) compete against each other. The horse races, which take place in the central square of the city, are public festivals where members and supporters of the various contrada cheer for their teams. Identification with the contrada is remarkably high, partially because of the fact that there is a direct competition between the contrada and partially because of the long historical tradition of the palio. For example, the palio of Ferrara—a small city in northern Italy where the present series of studies was conducted—dates back to 1279. The tradition was interrupted only during short periods in which the city was hit by the Black Plague. Not surprisingly, intergroup hostilities are particularly frequent during the weeks before the palio and may take more or less playful forms, ranging from water balloon fights to reciprocal flag thefts to secretly drugging the other team's horses or donkeys.

Of the eight contrada of Ferrara, we selected two with approximately equal status and comparable probability of winning for the first experiment.[2] Fifty-one subjects (15 women and 36 men) from the contrada San Giorgio ($n = 31$) and San Giacomo ($n = 20$) participated in the experiment. The mean age of subjects was 24.2.

Procedure. Subjects were recruited in the respective clubhouses of the contrada, which, during the weeks before the competition, are regularly frequented by the members of the contrada. A female experimenter visited the clubhouses in the evenings and asked those present to participate in a psycholinguistic study. Of the six contrada (of which two were used for pilot testing, two for Experiment 1, and two for Experiment 2), four were visited only once, whereas two visits on consecutive evenings were necessary for the data collection in the remaining contradas. The overall rate of volunteering (for pilot study Experiment 1, and Experiment 2 combined) was 93%, with only 11 out of 160 subjects refusing to participate in the study. Depending on the number of subjects present, up to 10 subjects were run at the same time. Communication between subjects regarding the study was discouraged until all questionnaires had been completed. Subjects were informed that the episodes were real and had been collected over the past 2 years. The subjects were further informed that each episode referred to different protagonists, but that the protagonists' identities were disguised in the visual representation in order to protect their anonymity.

Members of two contrada were presented with 16 single-frame cartoons in which a member of either their own contrada (in-group) or a competing contrada (out-group) performed a behavior. Half the cartoons portrayed socially desirable behaviors (e.g., helping), and half portrayed undesirable behaviors (e.g., littering). For both behavior types, half the cartoons showed an isolated actor, whereas the other half showed a protagonist interacting with others. Both types of items were included in order to test whether Semin and Fiedler's (1988a) model—originally formulated for interactional verbs—was also applicable to noninteractional episodes such as littering. The

cartoons were further divided into general behaviors such as littering or kicking a dog and palio-specific ones such as stealing each other's flags or drugging the other team's horse. On intuitive grounds, one might suspect that intergroup biases are more likely to surface with palio-specific episodes because they are directly relevant to the categorization. Subjects were provided with four response alternatives, each giving a brief description of the protagonist's behavior in the scene. The four response alternatives corresponded to the different levels of abstraction in the linguistic category model. Subjects were simply asked to select the one that, in their opinion, described the scene best. Thus, the design consisted of a 2 (contrada San Giacomo vs. San Giorgio) × 2 (in-group vs. out-group protagonist) × 2 (desirable vs. undesirable behaviors) × 2 (protagonist alone vs. interacting) × 2 (general vs. palio-specific behaviors) design in which the last three factors represent repeated measures.

Stimulus Materials and Pilot Testing. The episodes were presented in form of visual episodes (cartoons) for two reasons:

1. Compared with written representations, this procedure is language-free and therefore does not bias subsequent encoding due to the initial level of abstraction (see Fiedler & Semin, 1988a, for the impact of prior encoding abstraction on subsequent processing).
2. Compared with other visual representations such as films or videotapes, cartoons allow systematic variations of the protagonist's group membership (in this case, by changing the color of the actor's skin according to the color of his contrada) while holding all other features constant.

To select an appropriate set of episodes, 24 episodes were generated and subjected to an extensive pretest involving 44 subjects from two contrada (subsequently not used in either experiment). Twelve episodes described positive behaviors and 12 described negative behaviors. Within each group, the episodes depicted 3 behaviors that were specific and interactional, 3 that were general and interactional, 3 that were specific and noninteractional, and 3 that were general and noninteractional. The cartoons were produced by a semiprofessional cartoonist in such a way that the protagonist's age and sex remained ambiguous. Approximately half the pilot subjects were

---

[2] Status equality was considered an important prerequisite as the degree of intergroup biases has often been found to vary with group status in previous research (e.g., Deschamps, 1972/1973). Because the present experiments attempted to provide the very first empirical test of the linguistic intergroup hypothesis, we decided to keep potentially moderating variables such as status difference constant.

instructed to select one of four response alternatives, whereas the remaining half provided free descriptions of each episode. Furthermore, half of both subsamples received a version in which the protagonists of all scenes were members of the ingroup, whereas for the remaining subjects, the protagonists were out-group members. In addition to the encoding task, pilot subjects were asked to rate the social desirability of each act on a 5-point scale (ranging from 1 = *very negative* to 5 = *very positive*).

On the basis of the pilot test, the initial pool of cartoons was reduced to 16, according to the following criteria. First, the only episodes included were those judged positively (> 3.5) or negatively (< 2.5), respectively, for both in-group and out-group protagonists. This criterion resulted in the exclusion of various items in which, for example, an undesirable behavior was judged negatively only when performed by an out-group, but was judged neutrally or even slightly positively when performed by an in-group member. Second, episodes were excluded (or, in some cases, modified) whenever the descriptions of the free-response subjects indicated that the scene had been interpreted differently than was intended by the experimenters.

The final series of cartoons consisted of eight socially desirable and eight undesirable behaviors (either interactional or involving an isolated actor and either general or palio-specific) with two items representing each episode type. The protagonist was always identified by the letter *A,* whereas for interactional items the interaction partner was labeled *B*. The episodes were presented in the same randomly determined order for all subjects. The cartoons were bound into booklets containing black and white reproductions of the original drawings. The protagonist's group membership was identified by the color of his shirt, which corresponded to the color of his contrada. As in other sports, each contrada is associated with a particular color combination (applied to the competitors' dress, saddles, flags, watch, bracelets, etc.). These colors, which have remained constant over the centuries (as testified by antique flags) and are therefore well-known not only to those directly involved in the palio but also to the general population of Ferrara, allowed an easy identification of the protagonist's contrada. Thus, group membership was unambiguous and highly salient, as it consti-

tuted the only color in an otherwise black-and-white drawing. Although a misattribution of the protagonist's group membership was highly unlikely, any possibility of error was further reduced by explicitly reminding the subject of the actor's contrada in the formulation of the dependent variable (e.g., "A, member of the contrada San Giacomo. . . . ").

Level of Abstraction: Response Alternatives. Four response alternatives were provided for each episode, corresponding to the four levels of abstraction in the linguistic category model and presented in the same standardized order, starting from the lowest level of abstraction (DAV, IAV, SV, ADJ; e.g., A, a member of the contrada San Giacomo, hits B; hurts B; hates B; is violent). To be included among the response alternatives, a description had to meet the following criteria:

1. It had to be considered an appropriate and valid description of a given scene as based on the independent judgments of two raters.
2. It had to be assigned to the same level of abstraction by two independent raters familiar with the linguistic category model.
3. It had to be sufficiently simple to be comprehensible to all subjects independent of their social class or educational level (unusual or sophisticated expressions were avoided).
4. Finally, items were unacceptable whenever the distribution across response alternatives was grossly uneven, such that one of the four alternatives attracted almost all choices in the pilot study.

Subjects were instructed to view each episode in the booklet and to select the response alternative that, in their opinion, best described the scene. There was no time limit. As in previous research (see Semin & Fiedler, 1988b), the subjects' responses were scored according to the level of abstraction, such that higher values indicated greater abstraction (ranging from 1 = *DAV* to 4 = *ADJ*). Each subject's responses were averaged across the two items representing the same episode type (e.g., desirable, palio-specific, interactional episodes).

Positivity Rating. After completing the encoding task, subjects were asked to view the episodes again and, this time, to rate the positivity or negativity of each behavioral episode on a 5-point scale (ranging from 1 = *very negative* to 5 = *very positive*).

Results

Level of Abstraction. We excluded 3 subjects from the analysis owing to missing data. A preliminary 2 (contrada) × 2 (in-group vs. out-group protagonist) × 2 (desirable vs. undesirable behavior) × 2 (isolated actor vs. interaction) × 2 (general vs. palio-specific behavior) analysis of variance (ANOVA) with repeated measures on the last three variables was conducted in order to test whether the subject's contrada, the episode's interactional character, or the specific reference to the palio would moderate the predicted interaction between the protagonist's group membership and the act's desirability. Because none of these three variables produced any main or interaction effects, we report the results of a simplified two-way ANOVA in which the protagonist's group membership constituted the independent variable and social desirability the repeated measure. Obviously, the dependent variable for this analysis was the mean level of abstraction for all eight desirable and all eight undesirable episodes, respectively. The results confirm the predicted interaction between group membership and social desirability, $F(1,46) = 9.49, p < .01$, which is presented in Table 10.2. As predicted, the same desirable behavior was encoded at a higher level of abstraction when displayed by an in-group member than when displayed by an out-group member, $t(46) = 1.82, p < .05$, one-tailed. Exactly the opposite occurred for socially undesirable episodes, which were encoded at a higher level of abstraction when performed by an out-group member rather than an in-group member, $t(46) = 2.57, p < .01$, one-tailed. A different way to look at these data is to compare the level of abstraction for desirable and undesirable acts within each group. Here the results show that undesirable out-group behaviors were encoded at a higher level of abstraction than were desirable ones, $t(46) = 2.90, p < .01$, one-tailed, whereas there was a nonsignificant trend in the opposite direction when the same behaviors were attributed to in-group members, $t(46) = 1.49, ns$.

Underlying this analysis and the respective coding scheme is the assumption that the four levels of abstraction form a continuum, approximating an interval scale (see also Semin & Fiedler, 1988b). As this assumption may be questioned, we performed a second set of analyses, using as the dependent variable the overall frequency with which

TABLE 10.2. Mean Level of Abstraction as a Function of Group Membership and Social Desirability: Experiment 1

Membership of protagonist	Desirability of behavior	
	Desirable	Undesirable
In-group		
M	2.69	2.51
n	24	24
Out-group		
M	2.47	2.82
n	24	24

Note. Means are based on a 4-point scale, with higher scores indicating higher levels of encoding abstraction.

each linguistic category was selected to describe positive and negative episodes of in-group and out-group protagonists. Separate log-linear analyses were performed for desirable and undesirable episodes in order to investigate the effect of the protagonist's group membership on the use of the linguistic categories (DAV, IAV, SV, ADJ). Both analyses supported the predicted interaction between category membership and level of abstraction, $\chi^2 (3, N = 384) = 7.66, p = .05$, for desirable episodes and $\chi^2 (3, N = 384) = 7.30, p = .06$, for undesirable episodes (see Table 10.3).

For desirable episodes, concrete descriptions (DAVs and IAVs) were used more frequently for out-group than for in-group episodes, whereas abstract descriptions (SVs and ADJs) were used more frequently for in-group than for out-group episodes. Follow-up comparisons between expected and observed frequencies, however, indicated that these differences reached conventional levels of significance only for DAVs and SVs (see Table 10.3). Turning to the undesirable episodes, one sees that an exactly opposite pattern emerged. Here, subjects showed a clear preference for concrete descriptions (DAVs and IAVs) when describing in-group rather than out-group behaviors. At the same time, they tended to describe out-group members more frequently in adjectival or state terms than they did in-group members. Again, actual response frequencies deviated from the expected frequencies only for two of the four categories, namely IAVs and ADJs. Summarizing the results of the log-linear analyses, the frequencies with which each linguistic category was selected as a function of group membership and desirability points, in every case, in the predicted direction. However, comparisons are statistically reli-

TABLE 10.3. Frequency of Linguistic Category as a Function of Group Membership Experiment 1

Episode type and group membership of protagonist	Linguistic category				
	DAV	IAV	SV	ADJ	Total
Desirable					
In-group	27**	56	59**	50	192
Out-group	42**	64	40**	46	192
Undesirable					
In-group	48	56*	31	57**	192
Out-group	40	40*	32	80**	192

Note. DAV = descriptive action verb, IAV = interpretative action verb, SV = state verb, ADJ = adjective.
* p <0.06, one-tailed. ** p <.05, one-tailed.

able only for DAVs and SVs when the episodes are socially desirable and for IAVs and ADJs when the episodes are undesirable.

Results are even clearer when the two lower levels (DAV and IAV combined) and the two higher levels (SV and ADJ combined) of abstraction are considered together. In this case, the protagonist's group membership had a strong impact on the level of abstraction both for desirable, $\chi^2(1, N = 384) = 5.53, p < .05$, and undesirable episodes, $\chi^2(1, N = 384) = 6.03, p < .05$. Desirable in-group behaviors were considerably more likely to be encoded at an abstract level ($n = 109$ out of 192 entries) than at a concrete level ($n = 83$), whereas desirable out-group behaviors were more frequently encoded in concrete terms ($n = 106$) than in abstract terms ($n = 86$). This tendency reversed for undesirable episodes, where concrete descriptions ($n = 104$) outnumbered abstract ones ($n = 88$) when the episodes were attributed to an in-group member. For out-group episodes, abstract descriptions ($n = 112$) were favored over concrete ones ($n = 80$).

Positivity Rating. The positivity ratings were subjected to a 2 (contrada) × 2 (in-group vs. out-group protagonist) × 2 (desirable vs. undesirable behavior) × 2 (isolated actor vs. interaction) × 2 (general vs. palio-specific behavior) ANOVA with repeated measures on the last three variables. Four subjects were excluded owing to missing data. Not surprisingly, in-group behavior were rated more positively ($M = 2.99$) than out-group behavior ($M = 2.74$), $F(1, 40) = 10.33, p < .01$, and desirable behavior were rated more positively ($M = 4.06$) than undesirable behaviors ($M = 1.67$), $F(1,40) = 559.55, p < .01$. Furthermore, interactional episodes were rated more positively ($M = 2.94$) than

those involving single actors ($M = 2.79$), $F(1, 40) = 7.79, p < .01$. Finally, a significant In-group–Out-group × Interactional–Isolated Actor × General–Palio-Specific Behavior interaction indicated that in-group behaviors were rated significantly more positively than identical out-group behaviors only for general and interactional behaviors (3.16 for in-group vs. 2.74 for out-group), $t(40) = 2.02, p < .05$, and for palio-specific behaviors involving single actors (3.18 for in-group vs. 2.58 for out-group), $t(40) = 2.90, p < .05$. For the remaining two types of episodes (general-single actor and specific-interactional), positivity ratings were virtually identical for in-group and out-group.

Correlational Analyses. A somewhat different way to conceptualize our main thesis is in correlational terms. One may predict that, for in-group behaviors, the more socially desirable an action is perceived to be, the higher the average level of abstraction at which it is encoded. The opposite should be expected for out-group behaviors, with desirable actions being encoded at a lower level of abstraction. To test this hypothesis, we obtained correlations between the two dependent variables, using the different episodes (rather than subjects) as the unit of analysis. After excluding subjects with missing responses on either dependent variable, the mean favorability and mean level of encoding abstraction were calculated for each of the 16 episodes. This was done separately for the in-group and out-group conditions. Thus, for each of the 16 episodes, the average positivity rating of the episode was calculated for subjects in the in-group and out-group conditions, as was the respective average abstraction level that each group had selected when encoding the episode. Despite the fact that (as we have reported) out-group episodes had overall been rated less favorably than in-group behavior, the two groups agreed perfectly on the relative evaluation of the episodes. The correlation between the evaluation of the episodes performed by in-group and out-group members was $r(16) = .96, p < .01$. More important, as expected, the more positive an episode ascribed to an out-group member, the lower the average abstraction level at which it was encoded, $r(16) = -.55, p < .05$. For episodes ascribed to in-group members, a reverse trend was observed, with positively evaluated episodes encoded at a higher level of abstraction, $r(16) = .28, ns$. Not surprisingly, correlations for in-group and out-group members differed significantly from each other ($Z = 2.33, p < .01$).

Discussion

The results of the first experiment clearly confirm the hypothesis that people encode undesirable out-group and desirable in-group behavior at a higher level of abstraction than they do desirable out-group and undesirable in-group behaviors. Interestingly, this finding was not modified by any higher-order interaction (see preliminary analysis), suggesting that encoding differences of desirable and undesirable in-group and out-group behaviors occur for general as well as conflict-setting-specific episodes, and for interactional as well as noninteractional episodes. The correlational analysis provides further support for our contention. The more negatively an out-group action is perceived, the higher the level of abstraction at which it is encoded. Interestingly, people show exactly the opposite tendency when observing behavior episodes of in-group members. In this case, the desirable actions tend to be encoded at a slightly higher level of abstraction.

Yet, one may object that the data pattern could possibly be the result of an experimental artifact. It is conceivable that the experimentally provided response alternatives had more extreme evaluative implications at a higher level of abstraction. That is, the selected state verbs and adjectives may have had a more positive connotation than descriptive and interpretative action verbs when the episode referred to a socially desirable act, but a more negative connotation when the episode referred to a socially undesirable act (e.g., *altruistic* may be considered more positive than *to help*, and *aggressive* may be considered more negative than to *hit somebody*). If this was the case, subjects may simply have selected a low level of abstraction for desirable out-group behaviors and a high level of abstraction for undesirable out-group behaviors in an attempt to describe the out-group as negatively as possible.

To test this possibility, we conducted a small follow-up study in which 35 subjects not involved in the palio were asked to rate the positivity or negativity of each response alternative without having been exposed to the cartoons. To avoid an unreasonable demand on the subjects, we created two subsets by randomly assigning one item of each episode type to Set A and the other to Set B. Each subject rated on a 5-point scale (with higher scores indicating higher social desirability) the positivity of 32 sentences (four desirable and four

undesirable episodes with four response alternatives each), which were presented in the same order as in the experiment and in which the names of the contrada had been substituted with *Group X* and *Group Y*. Thus, each subject received a list of 32 sentences (e.g., "A, a member of group X, burns the flag of group Y") and was asked to rate the positivity of each action ("In your opinion, how positive or negative is the behavior or attribute described in this sentence?") A 2 × 2 within-subjects ANOVA with desirability of the episode and low level (DAV, IAV) versus high level (SV, ADJ) of abstraction as variables revealed a main effect for both—$F(1, 34) = 733.10, p < .01$, for desirability and $F(1, 34) = 11.16, p < .01$, for high versus low abstraction—but no interaction. This suggests that response alternatives at a higher level of abstraction (SV and ADJ, $M = 2.92$) were considered more positively than those at a lower level of abstraction (DAV and IAV, $M = 2.78$), but this was true for both desirable and undesirable episodes. This clearly precludes the alternative interpretation that the level of abstraction selected by the subjects in Experiment 1 was mediated by the differential positivity of the response alternatives.

This suggests that people do, in fact, encode undesirable out-group and desirable in-group behaviors at a higher level of abstraction than desirable out-group and undesirable in-group behavior and that this tendency is not simply an experimental artifact. Yet it remains to be demonstrated that group members show the same tendency when freely encoding an observed action. In the interest of experimental control, response alternatives were provided in the first experiment, thereby preventing subjects from generating their own interpretation of the episodes. Besides imposing a specific interpretation of each episode (which may or may not have coincided with the subject's own interpretation), the forced-choice procedure used in Experiment 1 artificially reduced the almost infinite world of alternative interpretations to only four, which in turn may have led to an overestimation of the linguistic intergroup bias: In this experiment, the only possibility of providing differential descriptions of in-group and out-group behaviors was to shift the level of analysis along the linguistic abstractness dimension. In the real world, subjects are free to use alternative and possibly more immediate strategies of language use to distinguish in-group and out-group behaviors. For example, they may simply use different terms within the same linguistic category (e.g., a behavior that is described as "playful" when displayed by an in-group member may be interpreted as "aggressive" when ascribed to an out-group member; see Duncan, 1976; Sagar & Schofield, 1980). It is possible that the linguistic intergroup bias is displayed only in situations in which people are prevented from using other strategies. Therefore, we conducted a second experiment in which subjects were asked to provide free descriptions of each scene.

Experiment 2

Method

In the second experiment, we used a procedure and stimulus material identical to those used in the previous one, with one modification: Rather than selecting a response in a multiple-choice procedure, subjects were asked to briefly describe each scene in their own words. To ensure that the subject of the sentence would refer to the protagonist, a sentence completion task was used, starting with "A member of the contrada S. Maria in Vado [or S. Spirito]."

Subjects. Forty-four subjects from two contrada (Santa Maria in Vado and Santo Spirito) not involved in the pilot study or in Experiment 1 participated in the study. As in Experiment 1, the sample reflected the general sociodemographic characteristics of the contrada, whose members tend to be young (subjects' mean age = 21.1, ranging from 14 to 33) and predominantly male (30 men, 14 women).

Scoring. Responses were scored by two independent raters familiar with Semin and Fiedler's (1988a, 1988b) scoring criteria (interrater reliability, $r = .81$), but blind as to the protagonist's category membership. The original scoring system was modified in three ways: First, nouns functionally identical to adjectives were scored as ADJ (e.g., "he is an altruist," "he is a spy"). Note that the use of nouns instead of adjectives is quite common in the Italian language. Second, sentences with more than one (nonauxiliary) verb or adjective (e.g., "he is happy because he won") received multiple scores, which were then averaged to an overall score. Third, verbs in connection with *always* were coded as ADJ (e.g., "he always hits dogs"). Furthermore, responses in which the sub-

ject of the sentence did not refer to the protagonist were considered uncodable (e.g., "that is okay," "I agree"). Twelve percent of the responses were unclassifiable.[3] Almost half of the subjects ($n = 21$) gave uncodable responses for at least one item, and 10 subjects provided uncodable responses for both items of a given episode type (e.g., socially desirable, palio-specific episodes involving an interaction partner). To avoid an unreasonable subject attrition, the variables interactional-single actor and genetic-palio-specific were collapsed in the analysis. In fact, a separate treatment of these variables appears unnecessary in view of the results of Experiment 1, showing that neither the interactional character of the episode nor its specificity to the palio had any effect on the level of encoding abstraction, and that neither variable interacted with the main factors under investigation (group membership and desirability). Thus, for each subject we calculated one mean score for the socially desirable episodes and one for the undesirable episodes by averaging all codable responses.

Results

Level of Abstraction. As predicted, desirable in-group behaviors were encoded at a higher level of abstraction than desirable out-group behaviors, $t(40, \text{one-tailed}) = 2.62, p < .01$ (see Table 10.4). However, undesirable in-group and out-group behaviors were encoded at virtually the same level of abstraction. Furthermore, episodes involving out-group members were encoded at a higher level of abstraction when they were undesirable than

---

[3]Compared with previous research reporting a 6% rate of unclassifiable responses (see Semin & Fiedler, 1988b), uncodable responses are relatively frequent in this experiment (12%). We suspect that three factors may have contributed to the high rate of unclassifiable responses: (a) The average educational level of our subjects was clearly lower than that of the university students used by Semin and Fiedler. The sentence completion, using the protagonist as the grammatical subject, may require a prior training period for such subjects. (b) The social setting (evening meetings at the clubhouses as opposed to the classroom setting in Semin & Fiedler's study) may have contributed to the subjects' tendency not to follow the experimentally imposed rules closely. (c) Contrary to Semin and Fiedler's subjects, our subjects were personally involved in the experimental task as they were participating in an important competition. Their high level of ego involvement may have facilitated unclassifiable responses in which subjects provided spontaneous reactions to (e.g., "these bastards, I agree") rather than descriptions of the action.

TABLE 10.4. Mean Level of Abstraction as a Function of Group Membership and Social Desirability: Experiment 2

Membership of protagonist	Desirability of behavior	
	Desirable	Undesirable
In-group		
M	2.63	2.75
n	19	19
Out-group		
M	2.38	2.67
n	25	25

Note. Means are based on a 4-point scale, with higher scores indicating higher levels of encoding abstraction.

when they were desirable, $t(40, \text{one-tailed}) = 3.24$, $p < .01$, whereas episodes involving in-group members were encoded in a largely unbiased manner.

Positivity Rating. Four subjects were excluded owing to missing data. In line with Experiment 1, a 2 (in-group vs. out-group membership of the protagonist) x 2 (desirable vs. undesirable behaviors) x 2 (contrada) mixed ANOVA indicated that socially desirable episodes ($M = 3.67$) were rated more positively than undesirable ones ($M = 1.72$), $F(1, 36) = 58.33$, $p < .01$, and that in-group behaviors ($M = 2.93$) were rated more positively than otherwise identical out-group behaviors ($M = 2.53$), $F(1, 36) = 10.61$, $p < .01$.

Discussion

The results of Experiment 2 partially confirm those of the Experiment 1. As in that experiment, subjects tended to encode undesirable out-group behaviors at a higher level of abstraction than desirable ones, even when providing their own interpretation of a behavioral sequence, whereas there was no such bias when encoding in-group behavior. Apparently, the linguistic intergroup bias is much more pronounced for out-group than for in-group actions. This is in line with Wilder's (1986) contention that people tend to apply an Aristotelian view of lawfulness to out-group member but not to in-group members. Rather than revising the perception of the out-group in the face of expectancy-incongruent evidence, people are likely to regard such inconsistencies as single, exceptional episodes largely unrelated to the general rule. In fact, subjects in Experiment 2 shifted their level of analysis to the concrete pole of the abstractness dimension only when encountering

expectancy-incongruent episodes involving out-group members.

The second experiment further suggests that the same desirable episodes were encoded at a higher level of abstraction when performed by an in-group member than when performed by an out-group member. However, contrary to our initial hypothesis and to the findings of the previous experiment, this tendency did not reverse for undesirable behavior. At this point it remains unclear why the results of the second study deviate in this respect from those obtained in Experiment 1.

With this one exception, the findings of the first two experiments provide consistent support for our contention that language may be used in a biased fashion in intergroup settings. Apparently, the encoding of behavioral episodes varies as a function of the protagonist's category membership and the desirability of his or her action. This finding, we believe, may have interesting implications for the interpersonal communication and transmission of stereotypes. Assume that somebody is being observed as he runs into a burning house and returns a few seconds later carrying a small child in his arms. A news reporter may communicate this story at very different levels of abstractions, by simply describing the behavior sequence, by providing an interpretation ("the protagonist saved the child from the flames; he risked his life"), or even by ascribing abstract dispositions to the protagonist, describing him as courageous or as a hero. Our findings suggest that the news reporter may communicate the story at a lower level of abstraction when the protagonist is an out-group member. If this is the case, the news story should provide less information about the protagonist and imply lesser temporal stability than if the same story was communicated at a higher level of abstraction (see Semin & Fiedler, 1988a).

An intriguing aspect of the linguistic category model in our context is the prediction that communications at higher levels of abstraction are more informative about the actor and, in particular, induce the expectation that the actor will display similar behavior or traits in the future. In the preceding example, the description of the protagonist as altruistic should induce a greater expectancy that he or she will engage in similar altruistic acts in the future than would a mere description of the behavior sequence. The same reasoning can be applied to undesirable acts as well. For instance, the sentence "A is a liar" implies greater temporal stability and a greater probability that A will lie in the future than an act-specific description such as "A was lying." Thus, communications at higher levels of abstraction (SV or ADJ) are more likely to produce expectancies about future behavior, which in turn may bias subsequent information processing in a top-down fashion.

In line with the linguistic category model, we predicted a linear trend such that, moving from the lowest to the highest level of abstraction, more information would be revealed about the protagonist. Furthermore, we predicted an increasing expectancy that the act be repeated. To test these hypotheses, we conducted a third experiment in which subjects were asked to rate how much information sentences at different levels of abstraction revealed about the protagonist and how likely subjects thought it was that the protagonist would display the same behavior or trait in the future.

Experiment 3

Method

Twenty subjects not involved in the palio (10 men, 10 women, mean age = 24.2) were asked to read the response alternatives provided in Experiment 1 without having been exposed to the visual representation (cartoons). To prevent motivational problems, the stimulus material was reduced by randomly selecting one item from each pair representing the same episode type (e.g., one desirable, palio-specific, interactional episode). Thus each subject rated 32 sentences (four response alternatives referring to each of the eight episodes). The selected response alternatives were presented in the same order as in Experiment 1. The palio-specific group membership (name of contrada) was substituted by the more general term *Group X* or *Group Y*. The experiment was described as a psycholinguistic study. The instructions were virtually identical to those used by Semin and Fiedler (1988a, Experiment 1). Subjects were asked to rate each sentence on a 5-point scale with regard to two questions: (a) In your opinion, how much information does the phrase reveal about the protagonist, and (b) in your opinion, how likely is it that the same action or attribute will be repeated in the future? Each subject's responses were collapsed across generic versus patio-specific and interactional versus noninteractional ratings in

order to obtain separate scores for how informative (or how stable) each subject considered DAV, IAV, SV, or ADJ sentences describing desirable and undesirable acts.

Results

Information About Protagonist. Two subjects were excluded from this and the subsequent analysis owing to missing data. A 2 (desirable vs. undesirable episodes) × 4 (level of abstraction) repeated measures ANOVA revealed the predicted main effect for level of abstraction, $F(3, 17) = 5.36, p = .01$ (see Table 10.5). A linear trend analysis (Winer, 1971) indicated that, moving from DAV to ADJ, the amount of information about the protagonist increased steadily, $F(1, 51) = 7.51, p < .01$. This effect was modified by an interaction with desirability, $F(3, 17) = 4.32, p < .05$. There was a strong linear increase in informativeness for desirable episodes, $F(1, 51) = 7.06, p < .05$, but not for undesirable ones, $F(1, 51) = 2.82$, *ns*. However, for both desirable and undesirable episodes, the lower levels of abstraction (DAV and IAV combined = 2.78 for desirable episodes and 3.06 for undesirable episodes) were considered less informative about the protagonist than were the higher levels (SV and ADJ combined = 3.38 for desirable episodes and 3.41 for undesirable episodes), $t(17) = 4.56, p < .01$, one-tailed, for desirable episodes, and $t(17) = 2.58, p < .0l$, one-tailed, for undesirable episodes.

Likelihood of Repetition. Similar results emerged for the likelihood of repetition ratings. Again, a 2 (desirable vs. undesirable episodes) × 4 (level of abstraction) repeated measures ANOVA revealed the predicted main effect for level of abstraction, $F(3, 17) = 5.90, p = .01$ (see Table 10.5). On the average, repetition in the future was considered less likely for the lower levels of abstraction (DAV and IAV combined = 3.48) than for the higher levels of abstraction (SV and ADJ combined = 3.84), $t(17) = 2.07, p < .05$, one-tailed. An additional interaction with desirability, $F(3, 17) = 7.77, p < .01$, indicated that perceived likelihood of repetition increased reliably only for undesirable episodes, $F(1, 51) = 6.66, p < .05$, whereas the linear increase was quite weak for desirable episodes, $F(1, 51) = 3.11, p < .09$. In fact, actions encoded at lower levels of abstraction (DAV and IAV combined = 3.12) were perceived as less likely to be displayed again in the future than were those en-

TABLE 10.5. Mean Ratings of Informativeness and Likelihood of Repetition as a Function of Level of Abstraction and Desirability of Episode: Experiment 3

Desirability of episode	Level of abstraction			
	DAV	IAV	SV	ADJ
Information about protagonist				
Desirable				
M	2.51	3.04	3.44	3.31
n	18	18	18	18
Undesirable				
M	3.00	3.13	3.28	3.54
n	18	18	18	18
TOTAL	2.76	3.09	3.36	3.43
Likelihood of repetition				
Desirable				
M	3.79	3.86	3.94	3.89
n	18	18	18	18
Undesirable				
M	3.13	3.11	3.64	3.86
n	18	18	18	18
Total	3.46	3.49	3.79	3.88

Note. DAV = Means are based on 5-point scales, with higher scores indicating greater informativeness and greater likelihood of repetition.

coded at higher levels (SV and ADJ combined = 3.75) only for undesirable episodes, $t(17) = 5.25$, $p < .01$, but not for desirable ones (DAV and IAV combined = 3.83; SV and ADJ combined = 3.92).

Correlational Analyses. To further investigate the effect of linguistic abstraction on perceived informativeness and probability of repetition, first-order and partial correlations were run between these three variables, using single descriptions rather than subjects as unit of analysis. Thus, informativeness and probability of repetition scores were obtained for each of the 32 sentences of the stimulus material by averaging across subjects. Level of abstraction was reliably and positively correlated with both the amount of information provided about the protagonist, $r(32) = .58$, $p < .01$, and the probability of repetition, $r(32) = .35$, $p < .05$. Furthermore, neither correlation disappeared when the third variable was partialed out (correlation between abstraction and informativeness was .61, $p < .01$, when controlling for likelihood of repetition; correlation between abstraction and likelihood of repetition was .42, $p < .05$, when controlling for informativeness). This sug-

gests that level of abstraction has entirely independent effects on perceived informativness and likelihood of repetition. In fact, there is no correlation between these two variables, $r(32) = .02$, *ns.*

Another interesting finding emerges when the two variables are correlated with linguistic abstraction separately for phrases describing desirable and undesirable episodes. Whereas the amount of information about the protagonist increases with increasing level of abstraction for both desirable, $r(16) = .63$, $p < .01$, and undesirable episodes, $r(16) = .53$, $p < .05$, the perceived likelihood of repetition increases with abstraction only for undesirable episodes, $r(16) = .67$, $p < .01$, but not for desirable episodes, $r = .10$, *ns.* This is not completely surprising, considering that our subjects indicated a very high overall probability (3.9 on a 5-point scale) that desirable acts would be repeated in the future, suggesting that the law correlation may at least partially be a function of a restriction of range.

Discussion

The results of the third experiment generally confirm our contention that with increasing level of abstraction the amount of information about the actor and the expectancies of repetition increase in a linear fashion. However, the first trend was more pronounced for desirable episodes and the latter for undesirable episodes. The latter finding is particularly interesting as it suggests that, at least for undesirable actions, abstract information may serve as a schema that induces expectancies about future behaviors, which in turn may guide subsequent information processing. It is also interesting to note that the amount of information a phrase provides about the actor and the probability of the act's being repeated in the future appear to be two completely independent consequences of linguistic abstraction.

General Discussion

Taken together the present experiments provide the first evidence for biased language use in intergroup contexts. In particular, they provide evidence that the same socially desirable behavior is encoded at a higher level of abstraction when performed by an in-group member than when performed by an out-group member. Apparently, desirable in-group behaviors induce generalizations to the actor's character or psychological state, or, in Heider's (1944) terms, a unit formation of actor and act. In contrast, desirable out-group behaviors are more likely to be encoded as concrete behavioral instances without abstraction beyond the given information.

Results are somewhat less consistent with respect to socially undesirable episodes. Here only the first experiment found the predicted reversal, such that out-group behaviors were encoded at a higher level of abstraction than in-group behaviors. One may argue that undesirable behaviors are generally more diagnostic and informative about the protagonist (Ajzen & Fishbein, 1975; Jones & Davis, 1965) and as such may facilitate abstract encoding independent of group membership. Although the exact reasons need to be addressed in future research, the present experiments suggest that intergroup biases in language use may be more pronounced and robust for desirable than for undesirable episodes.

A different way to look at the data is to compare encoding of desirable versus undesirable episodes within in-group and out-group. Here our findings suggest that people encode and communicate behavioral information involving out-group protagonists at a higher level of abstraction when it is undesirable than when it is desirable (Experiments 1 and 2). Interestingly, in-group behaviors were encoded in a largely unbiased fashion. In terms of linguistic abstractness, desirable and undesirable in-group behaviors were treated in an undifferentiated manner, whereas out-group behaviors were strongly polarized. The same pattern also emerged from the correlational analysts (Experiment 1), which found a strong correlation between social desirability and abstractness for out-group episodes: The more negative the action, the higher the level of abstraction at which it was encoded. Although this correlation reversed for episodes involving in-group members, the correlation became considerably weaker. This, again, suggests that the language bias is more pronounced for out-group protagonists.

Implications of the Linguistic Intergroup Bias

Differential language use—as demonstrated in the first two experiments—apparently has a number of important implications that may contribute to

the persistence of stereotypes. There is evidence that once a negative out-group or positive in-group behavior has been communicated in abstract linguistic terms, it influences subsequent information processing of both source and receiver of the communication in various ways. First, linguistically abstract communications are perceived as providing more information about the actor than do concrete ones (Experiment 3; see also Semin & Fiedler, 1988a).

Second, abstract descriptions are perceived as relatively stable over time (Semin & Fiedler, 1988a) and consequently produce the expectation that the (undesirable) action be repeated in the future (Experiment 3).

Third, abstract encoding may have an interesting—yet to be tested—implication: Abstract descriptions may induce a top-down process in which subsequent information processing is guided (and biased) by the initial description. Recently, some evidence for such a top-down process in social judgment tasks has been reported by Fiedler and Semin (1988a). They found that, after having provided an initial abstract description of a person, people tended to produce additional concrete information congruent with their initial description whenever the validity of the initial trait description was challenged. Interestingly, concrete initial descriptions apparently had much less impact on subsequent processing. The idea that abstract encoding will induce a top-down process is also congruent with Arcuri's (1983) finding that information about people coded at the level of adjectives (personality traits) had greater diagnostic power than information coded at a more specific level (verbs expressing behaviors). Thus, abstract descriptions tend to trigger schemata-driven processes in impression formation.

Finally, there is evidence that abstract descriptions are considered less verifiable than concrete ones (Semin & Fiedler, 1988a). It is considerably easier to confirm or disconfirm the occurrence of a concrete behavior than the existence of a trait or psychological state. For instance, a single observation should be sufficient to disconfirm a false concrete statement such as "A hits B," whereas many behavioral instances should be required before an abstract statement such as "A is aggressive" can be disconfirmed. The lack of verifiability should then make abstract statements more resistant to disconfirmation and change. This idea is quite similar to Rothbart's (see Rothbart & John,

1985; Rothbart & Park, 1986) contention that traits differ in their susceptibility to evidence and that many stereotypic beliefs pertain to exactly those traits that are not easily verifiable. Whereas Rothbart and Park's (1986) analysis focuses on inter-trait differences, the present model applies the same basic principle to differences in confirmability between linguistic categories.

Considering this wide range of implications, one can easily envisage a self-perpetuating cycle in which biased language use maintains or even aggravates initial intergroup biases in applied settings. For instance, subtle language biases may occur in the legal system, where witnesses may reveal quite different information by describing the observed sequence of events in more or less abstract terms. As the likelihood of repetition of a criminal act partially determines the severity of the sentence, abstract communications can easily contribute to more severe sentences. In a similar vein, teachers or parents may inadvertently bias cross-generational communication in much the same way as reporters may choose different levels of abstraction depending on whether the protagonist of a given news story shares their own category membership. The first indirect evidence for this contention comes from a recent international research program about the image of Africa in the mass media (involving six European and eight African countries and supported by the Food and Agricultural Organization; see Pugliese, 1988). Besides the highly biased news story selection and the generally negative tone of the coverage, the report complained about a "linguistic stereotype . . . in which phrases referring to Blacks are characterized by the predominance of nouns and the almost complete absence of verbs, at least in the active form, whereas the exact opposite occurs in reference to Westerners, denoted by action verbs" (Pugliese, 1988, p. 57).

Beyond its practical contributions, the present approach may also have some interesting methodological implications. First, the linguistic intergroup bias may represent a subtle source of error in those research paradigms in which an ongoing interaction is encoded. In this case, the judge's description of an action may depend, in predictable fashion, on the social category membership of the interactants. Similar biases may occur for certain content analytical techniques that require the recoding of information. Second, the present approach may provide a useful methodological

tool for the empirical study of racism and intergroup discrimination. As traditional reactive measures of racism have become largely ineffective in tapping more subtle racial and ethnic prejudice (e.g., Crosby, Bromley, & Saxe, 1980; Dovidio & Gaertner, 1986a, 1986b; McConahay, 1986), the study of language use may provide a less obtrusive, alternative method, particularly for intergroup contexts in which the overt expression of prejudice is normatively unacceptable, as in the case of Jews or Blacks.

Open Problems

Considering that this series of studies represents a first attempt to test the linguistic intergroup bias, it is not surprising that various issues remain open to future investigation. First, at this point it is not entirely clear which mechanism triggers the linguistic intergroup bias. In the introduction, we proposed a model in which people hold differential expectancies regarding in-group and out-group behaviors, which in turn determine the language representation of behavioral episodes. Expectancy-congruent observations are translated into abstract language that generalizes from the single act to more enduring properties of the actor. In contrast, expectancy-incongruent observations are described in concrete terms as single, situationally and temporally bound instances.

Alternatively, one may argue from an attributional perspective that our results simply reflect the linguistic expression of latent causal attributions. If one assumes that concrete codings reflect implicit situational attributions and abstract codings reflect implicit dispositional attributions, our results could easily be interpreted as the linguistic manifestation of the well-known group-serving bias (e.g., Hewstone & Jaspars, 1984). We are inclined to reject this hypothesis mainly because the taxonomy proposed by the linguistic category model is not equivalent to the continuum of situational-to-personal causation. Moving from DAVs to ADJs, there is no linear increase in implicit personal causation, and low levels of abstraction do not necessarily imply situational causation. DAVs generally do not imply any causation at all, but simply provide a noncausal description of behavioral information. In fact, that DAVs lack interpretation is one of their defining features.

Differences between the linguistic category model and the attributional model become even clearer when considering the two intermediate levels of abstraction. Moving from IAVs to SVs, we observe an increase in abstraction but a decline in personal causation. Since Brown and Fish's (1983) and Garvey and Caramazza's (1974) pioneering work on implicit causality, various studies involving such diverse languages as Chinese, Italian, Afrikaans, and English have investigated the implicit causality of verbs embedded in subject–verb–object sentences. These studies have generally found that the causality is regularly attributed to the subject when the verb is an IAV, but to the object when the verb is an SV (e.g.. Au, 1986; Brown, & Fish, 1983; Franco, Arcuri, & Cadinu, 1988; Garvey & Caramazza, 1974; Van Kleeck, Hillger, & Brown, 1988; Voster, 1985). Thus, if our subjects mainly had implicit causality on their minds when describing desirable episodes, they should have used IAVs more frequently and SVs less frequently when describing in-group members than when describing out-group members. The results of Experiment 1 clearly contradict this idea (for additional evidence see Arcuri, Maass, & Semin, 1989). This suggests that the linguistic intergroup bias is not simply a function of an implicit group-serving attributional bias and that people may choose abstract versus concrete language representations for reasons other than their attributional implications (e.g., degree of situational or temporal generalization).

Yet another, primarily motivational explanation of the linguistic intergroup bias may be derived from social identity theory. From this perspective, our findings may be interpreted as a subtle strategy of establishing an intergroup difference in favor of one's own group in order to maintain or enhance a distinct and positive social identity. For instance, describing favorable out-group behaviors as single, concrete instances unrelated to the protagonist's enduring properties may represent just one possible strategy of out-group derogation. Contrary to our own account, this explanation does not rely on the mediating role of differential expectancies.

At this point, it remains unclear whether the linguistic intergroup bias observed in the present experiments reflects an attempt to protect one's social identity, whether it is primarily the consequence of differential expectancies, or whether both processes may have contributed. An exact understanding of the underlying mechanism is not just a matter of academic curiosity. Although the

two processes may often coincide, they lead in some cases to exactly opposite predictions. If desire for a positive social identity is at the basis of the linguistic intergroup bias, then such bias should emerge in any intergroup setting in which the in-group–out-group categorization becomes salient. It should be particularly pronounced in situations in which the individual's social identity is at stake, such as after self-esteem threat (Lemyre & Smith, 1985) or when groups are in direct competition (as was the case in our experiments).

Yet if encoding differences are mainly a function of differential expectancies, then predictions vary according to type and specificity of such expectancies. In certain intergroup settings such as the one investigated here, people have negative general views of the out-group, and hence expect out-group members to display more undesirable behaviors and fewer desirable behaviors than in-group members without expecting any specific behavior patterns (see also Howard & Rothbart, 1980). For such cases, predictions derived from a differential expectancy viewpoint will largely coincide with those derived from a social identity perspective. Often, however, expectancies reflect well-defined stereotypes referring to very specific behavior patterns (e.g., Jews are expected to be stingy but not to be unfriendly). For such cases, predictions derived from a differential expectancy perspective deviate from the more general intergroup bias perspective, as, according to the former, biases in language use should occur only for those behaviors that are directly relevant to the stereotype. Furthermore, such stereotypes may occasionally contain positive elements that are in contrast to the overall affective tone of the stereotype, as in the case of the intellectual achievements of Jews. Following a differential expectancy viewpoint, behaviors of Jews that are indicative of intelligence should be encoded at a high level of abstraction because they are expectancy congruent. Yet, non-Jews should prefer concrete language representations if they are mainly concerned with maintaining a positive social identity. There are even cases in which members of mutually exclusive social categories share the same stereotypes. A striking example of these are sex stereotypes that are largely agreed on by male and female subjects (e.g., Deaux, 1976). According to a differential expectancy perspective, both male and female subjects should encode sex role-incongruent behaviors ("feminine" behaviors of male protagonists and "masculine" behaviors of female protagonists) in concrete terms independent of their valence. This is quite in contrast to a social identity perspective, according to which both sexes should encode undesirable in-group and desirable out-group behaviors in concrete terms independent of their stereotypicality.[4]

We believe that, for a better understanding of the exact underlying mechanism, it would be very useful to study the linguistic intergroup bias in situations in which specific expectancies are either experimentally induced or already contained in a well-defined stereotype.

A second problem to be resolved by future research regards the potential impact of a real or imagined audience or communication partner. Similar to previous studies (Semin & Fiedler, 1988b), subjects in our experiments were instructed to provide written descriptions of events without knowing who would receive their message and what that person's social category membership might be. In real settings, people are generally aware of the group membership of their audience and are therefore able to adjust their message accordingly. It is conceivable that the choice of behavioral descriptions will vary not only according to the group membership of sender and protagonist, but also according to the in-group or out-group status of who is expected to receive the communication. A similar argument can be made regarding the interpretation of communications of varying levels of abstraction (see Experiment 3). Here, the implicit subject informativeness and probability of repetition may vary not only according to the level of abstraction, but also according to the sender's category membership. Thus, the communication process may actually be more complex than suggested by our findings.

Although a number of issues remain unresolved at this point, we hope that the present approach will contribute to the understanding of how language—an often neglected aspect of social cognition—contributes to both the interindividual maintenance and the interindividual communication and transmission of stereotypes. It is this latter aspect

that, we believe, distinguishes the present approach from many previous ones, as it shifts the level of analysis from the individual to the medium by which group relations are maintained and negotiated.

REFERENCES

Ajzen, I., & Fishbein, M. A. (1975). Bayesian analysis of attribution processes. *Psychological Bulletin, 82*, 261–277.

Allport, G. W. (1954). *The nature of prejudice.* Reading, MA: Addison-Wesley.

Arcuri, L. (1983). Schemi di persone e potere diagnostico delle infotmazioni [Person schemata and diagnostic power of information). *Giornale Italiano di Psicologia, 10*, 483–500.

Arcuri, L., Maass, A., & Semin, G. (1989). *Linguistic intergroup bias vs. self-serving attributional bias: The role of implicit causality of verbs.* Unpublished manuscript.

Au, T. K. F. (1986). A verb is worth a thousand words: The causes and consequences of interpersonal events implicit in language. *Journal of Memory and Language, 25*, 104–122.

Brewer, M. B. (1979). In-group bias in the minimal intergroup situation: A cognitive–motivational analysis. *Psychological Bulletin, 86*, 307–324.

Brewer, M. B., & Kramer, R. M. (1985). The psychology of intergroup attitudes and behavior. *Annual Review of Psychology, 36*, 219–243.

Brown, R., & Fish, D. (1983). The psychological causality implicit in language. *Cognition, 14*, 237–273.

Crosby, F., Bromley, S., & Saxe, L. (1980). Recent unobtrusive studies of black and white discrimination and prejudice: A literature review. *Psychological Bulletin, 8*, 546–563.

Deaux, K. (1976). *The behavior of women and men.* Monterey, CA: Brooks/Cole.

Deschamps, J.-C. (1972/1973). Imputation de la responsibilité de l'échec (Ou de la réussite) et catégorisation sociale [Attribution of responsibility of failure (or success) and social categorization]. *Bulletin de Psychologie, 26*, 794–806.

Dovidio, J. F., & Gaertner, S. L. (1986a). *Prejudice, discrimination and racism.* Orlando, FL: Academic Press.

Dovidio, J. F., & Gaertner, S. L. (1986b). Prejudice, discrimination, and racism: Historical trends and contemporary approaches. In J. F. Dovidio & S. L. Gaertner (Eds.), *Prejudice, discrimination and racism* (pp. 1–34), Orlando, FL: Academic Press.

Duncan, B. L. (1976). Differential social perception and attribution of intergroup violence: Testing the lower limits of stereotyping of blacks. *Journal of Personality and Social Psychology, 34*, 590–598.

Fiedler, K., & Semin, G. R. (1988a). *Language use and reification of social information: Top-down and bottom-up processing in person cognition.* Unpublished manuscript.

Fiedler, K., & Semin, G. R. (1988b). On the causal information conveyed by different interpersonal verbs: The role of implicit sentence context. *Social Cognition, 6*, 21–39.

Franco, F., Arcuri, L., & Cadinu, M. (1988). *L'attribuzione di causalità nei verbi interpersonali: Una verifica sulla lingua italiana* [Causal attributions implicit in interpersonal verbs: A test in Italian language]. Unpublished manuscript.

---

[4]It is even conceivable that the two processes interact with situational variables such that language use reflects the desire to protect one's social identity whenever groups are in direct competition; however, cognitive expectancy processes may prevail whenever a person judges the behavior of in-group and out-group members from the perspective of an uninvolved observer.

Garvey, C., & Caramazza, A. (1974). Implicit causality in verbs. *Linguistic Inquiry, 5,* 459–464.

Hamilton, D. L. (1981). *Cognitive processes in stereotyping and intergroup behavior.* Hillsdale, NJ: Erlbaum.

Hamilton, D. L., & Trolier, T. K. (1986). Stereotypes and stereotyping: An overview of the cognitive approach. In J. F. Dovidio & S. L. Gaertner (Eds.), *Prejudice, discrimination and racism* (pp. 127–163). Orlando, FL: Academic Press.

Hastie, R., & Kumar, P. A. (1979). Person memory: Personality traits as organizing principles in memory for behavior. *Journal of Personality and Social Psychology, 37,* 25–38.

Heider, F. (1944). Social perception and phenomenal causality. *Psychological Review, 51,* 358–384.

Hewstone, M., & Jaspars, J. M. F. (1984). Social dimensions of attribution. In H. Tajfel (Ed.), *The social dimension: European development in social psychology* (Vol. 2, pp. 379–404). Cambridge, England: Cambridge University Press.

Howard, J., & Rothbart, M. (1980). Social categorization and memory for in-group and out-group behavior. *Journal of Personality and Social Psychology, 38,* 301–310.

Jones, E. E., & Davis, K. E. (1965). From acts to disposition: The attribution process in person perception. In L. Berkowitz (Ed.), *Advances in experimental social psychology.* (Vol. 2, pp. 219–266). New York: Academic Press.

Lemyre, L., & Smith, P. M. (1985). Intergroup discrimination and self-esteem in the minimal group paradigm. *Journal of Personality and Social Psychology, 49,* 660–670.

Linville, P. W., Salovey, P., & Fischer, G. W. (1986). Stereotyping and perceived distributions of social characteristics: An application to ingroup-outgroup perception. In J. E Dovidio & S. L. Gaertner (Eds.), *Prejudice, discrimination and racism* (pp. 1–34). Orlando, FL: Academic Press.

McConahay, J. B. (1986). Modern racism, ambivalence, and the modem racism scale. In J. F. Dovidio & S. L. Gaertner (Eds.), *Prejudice discrimination and racism* (pp. 91–125). Orlando, FL: Academic Press.

Pettigrew, T. F. (1979). The ultimate attribution error: Extending Allport's cognitive analysis of prejudice. *Personality and Social Psychology Bulletin, 5,* 461–476.

Pugliese, C. (1988). Quale immagine? [Which image?]. *Nigrizia, 106,* 56–57.

Rothbart, M., Evans, M., & Fulero, S. (1979). Recall for confirming events: Memory processes and the maintenance of social stereotypes. *Journal of Experimental Social Psychology, 15,* 343–355.

Rothbart, M., & John, O. P. (1985). Social categorization and behavioral episodes: A cognitive analysis of the effects of intergroup contact. *Journal of Social Issues, 41,* 81–104.

Rothbart, M., & Lewis, S. (1988). Inferring category attributes from exemplar attributes: Geometric shapes and social categories. *Journal of Personality and Social Psychology, 55,* 861–871.

Rothbart, M., & Park, B. (1986). On the confirmability and disconfirmability of trait concepts. *Journal of Personality and Social Psychology, 50,* 131–142.

Sagar, H. A., & Schofield, J. W. (1980). Racial and behavioral cues in black and white children's perceptions of ambiguously aggressive acts. *Journal of Personality and Social Psychology, 39,* 590–598.

Semin, G. R., & Fiedler, K. (1988a). The cognitive functions of linguistic categories in describing persons: Social cognition and language. *Journal of Personality and Social Psychology, 54,* 558–568.

Semin, G. R., & Fiedler, K. (1988b). *Relocating attributional phenomenon within a language-cognition interface: The case of actors' and observers' perspectives.* Unpublished manuscript.

Snyder, M., & Swann, W. B. (1978). Hypothesis-testing processes in social interaction. *Journal of Personality and Social Psychology, 36,* 1202–1212.

Srull, T. D., Lichtenstein, M., & Rothbart, M. (1985). Associative storage and retrieval processes in person memory. *Journal of Experimental Psychology: Learning, Memory and Cognition, 11,* 316–345.

Tajfel, H. (1982). Social psychology of intragroup relations. *Annual Review of Psychology, 33,* 1–39.

Tajfel, H., & Turner, J. C. (1979). An integrative theory of intergroup conflict. In W. S. Austin & S. Worchel (Eds.), *The social psychology of intergroup relations* (pp. 33–47). Monterey, CA: Brooks/Cole.

Taylor, D. M., & Jaggi, V. (1974). Ethnocentrism and causal attribution in a South Indian context. *Journal of Cross-Cultural Psychology, 5,* 162–171.

Turner, J. C. (1987). *Rediscovering the social group: A self-categorization theory.* Oxford: Blackwell.

Van Dijk, T. A. (1984). *Prejudice and discourse. An analysis of ethnic prejudice in cognition and conversation.* Amsterdam: Benjamins.

Van Dijk, T. A. (1987). *Communicating racism: Ethnic prejudice in thought and talk.* Newbury Park, CA: Sage.

Van Kleeck, M., Hillger, L., & Brown, R. (1988). Fitting verbal schemas against information variables in attribution. *Social Cognition, 6,* 89–106.

Voster, J. (1985). Implicit causality in language: Evidence from Afrikaans. *South African Journal of Psychology, 15,* 62–67.

Weber, R., & Crocker, J. (1983). Cognitive processes in the revision of stereotypic beliefs. *Journal of Personality and Social Psychology, 45,* 961–977.

Wilder, D. A. (1986). Social categorization: Implications for creation and reduction of intergroup bias. In L. Berkowitz (Ed.), *Advances in experimental social psychology* (Vol. 19, pp. 291–355). New York: Academic Press.

Winer, B. J. (1971). *Statistical principles in experimental design.* New York: McGraw-Hill.

Why Are Stereotypes Maintained Even When They Are Inaccurate?

Stereotypes and prejudice present such great problems for our society in part because they are so difficult to change, once they get started. And the difficulty is that there are many different processes that contribute to stereotype maintenance. We will address the issue of stereotype maintenance in this section by considering both the ways that we process information about social groups and the ways that we behave toward these social groups. Both of these processes produce biases such that our stereotypes and prejudices are likely to be maintained, even in the face of contradictory information.

The first stage in processing information about others involves seeking out and attending to relevant information that will be used to form our opinions about the characteristics of individuals. As we do this, only some of the vast amount of available information is processed, and the rest is ignored. But once stereotypes are developed, they begin to operate as expectations that influence how we seek out and attend to new information. Once information is attended to and selected for processing, the next stage is *encoding*. Encoding involves the interpretation of the information and its storage in memory for later use. Incoming information would not be well understood or easily stored in memory if it was not related to existing information. Rather, incoming information is encoded in terms of existing expectations (in the form of schemas or prototypes). The outcome of this encoding process is that we tend to remember information that confirms our stereotypes better than information that disconfirms them (Fyock & Stangor, 1994).

For instance, in one experiment, Claudia Cohen (Cohen, 1981) showed people a videotape of a woman engaging in some everyday activities at her house. Although they all saw the same video (the woman engaged in a number of activities, including playing the piano, listening to classical music, eating a hamburger, and watching TV), one-half of the participants were told that the woman was a librarian, whereas the other half were told that she was a waitress. After they saw the video, Cohen gave all of the participants a multiple-choice test, asking them to indicate which of the activities they had actually seen. Cohen's results showed that the participants remembered more information consistent with their expectations (for instance, that she watched TV if they though she was a waitress and that she played the piano if they thought she was a librarian) than information that was inconsistent with their expectations. You can see how such a bias would make it difficult to ever change our stereotypes.

Reading 11, by Darley and Gross, is an elegant demonstration of the natural tendency of humans to process new information in a way that confirms and strengthens their existing stereotypes and expectations. Rather than merely demonstrating that people remember information that matches their beliefs, Darley and Gross show how people may actively distort ambiguous information to make it more supportive of their stereotypes—in this case stereotypes about the likely intellectual performance of a child who is described as being of either high or low socioeconomic status. What is perhaps most interesting about their research is the extent to which the ambiguous information that describes the child,

and that does not portray her in either a particularly positive or negative light, nevertheless serves to strengthen and to validate them.

Although information-processing biases, such as those that distort information seeking and memory, can explain in part why stereotypes are resistant to change, *self-fulfilling prophecies* are perhaps even more important causes of stereotype maintenance. Self-fulfilling prophecies occur when our expectations or stereotypes about others lead us to act toward those individuals in a way that causes those stereotypes to actually come true. In their well-known study, Word, Zanna, and Cooper (Reading 12) demonstrate how even well-intentioned European-American college students may behave differently toward European Americans than they do toward African Americans, even when they have no idea they are doing so.

One limitation of the study by Word, Zanna, and Cooper is that it does not show the self-fulfilling prophecy effect directly. Rather, the self-fulfilling prophecy is shown only by having White participants copy the behaviors of the original, Black participants in the second study. On the other hand, in Reading 13, Miller, Rothblum, Felicio, and Brand not only provide an elegant demonstration of self-fulfilling prophecies, but also show how people can learn to prevent them from occurring when they are aware of the expectations that others hold about them. You might also enjoy reading this paper because it deals with a category that—although it is highly stereotyped and poses a problem for many individuals—is not frequently studied.

Discussion Questions

1. What types of information-processing biases contribute to stereotyping and prejudice?
2. How do Darley and Gross propose that stereotypes are maintained, and how do their data support this hypothesis?
3. What are self-fulfilling prophecies? When do they occur, and what effects do they have on people?
4. How and when can individuals prevent self-fulfilling prophecies from influencing how people behave toward them?
5. Consider, from your own perspective, and based on the readings, what it is like (or what you think it might be like) to be a member of a stereotyped group.

Suggested Readings

Fyock, J., & Stangor, C. (1994). The role of memory biases in stereotype maintenance. *British Journal of Social Psychology, 33,* 331–343. A meta-analysis of studies which, when taken together, show the extent to which people tend to preferentially remember information that confirms their stereotypes.

Jussim, L., & Fleming, C. (1996). Self-fulfilling prophecies and the maintenance of social stereotypes: The role of dyadic interactions and social forces. In C. N. Macrae, C. Stangor, & M. Hewstone (Eds.), *Stereotypes and stereotyping* (pp. 161–192). New York: Guilford Press. A current review of self-fulfilling prophecies, stereotypes, and prejudice.

Yzerbyt, V., Schadron, G., Leyens, J., & Rocher, S. (1994). Social judgeability: The impact of meta-informational cues on the use of stereotypes. *Journal of Personality and Social Psychology, 66,* 48–55. A theoretical approach, with supporting data, concerning how, why, and when individuals feel entitled to use their stereotypes to judge others.

Zanna, M. P., & Pack, S. J. (1975). On the self-fulfilling nature of apparent sex differences in behavior. *Journal of Experimental Social Psychology, 11,* 583–591. A classic study demonstrating the power of gender stereotypes to influence women's behavior.

A Hypothesis-Confirming Bias in Labeling Effects

John M. Darley and Paget H. Gross • Princeton University

The present study examines the process leading to the confirmation of a perceiver's expectancies about another when the social label that created the expectancy provides poor or tentative evidence about another's true dispositions or capabilities. One group of subjects was led to believe that a child came from a high socioeconomic background; the other group, that the child came from a low socioeconomic background. Nothing in the socioeconomic data conveyed information directly relevant to the child's ability level, and when asked, both groups of subjects reluctantly rated the child's ability level to be approximately at her grade level. Two other groups received the social-class information and then witnessed a videotape of the child taking an academic test. Although the videotaped performance series was identical for all subjects, those who had information that the child came from a high socioeconomic background rated her abilities well above grade level, whereas those for whom the child was identified as coming from a lower class background rated her abilities as below grade level. Both groups cited evidence from the ability test to support their conflicting conclusions. We interpret these findings as suggesting that some "stereotype" information (e.g., socioeconomic class information) creates not certainties but hypotheses about the stereotyped individual. However, these hypotheses are often tested in a biased fashion that leads to their false confirmation.

The expectancy-confirmation process is an important link in the chain leading from social perception to social action (Darley & Fazio, 1980; Rosenthal & Jacobson, 1968; Snyder & Swann, 1978a). As research has demonstrated, two processes leading to the confirmation of a perceiver's beliefs about another can be identified. The first, called a "behavioral confirmation effect" (Snyder & Swann, 1978b), is consistent with Merton's (1948) description of the "self-fulfilling prophecy." In this process, perceiver's behaviors toward the individual for whom they hold an expectancy channel the course of the interaction such that expect-ancy-confirming behaviors are elicited from the other individual (Rosenthal, 1974; Snyder, Tanke, & Berscheid, 1977). The second process leads to what we may call a "cognitive confirmation effect." We use this term to refer to expectancy-confirmation effects that occur in the absence of any interaction between the perceiver and the target person. In these cases, perceivers simply selectively interpret, attribute, or recall aspects of the target person's actions in ways that are consistent with their expectations (Duncan, 1976; Kelley, 1950; Langer & Abelson, 1974). Thus, perceivers with different expectancies about another may witness an identical action sequence and still emerge with their divergent expectancies "confirmed."

The focus of the present article is on the mediation of cognitive confirmation effects. We suggest that there are at least two different processes that bring about the cognitive confirmation of expectancies. The key to separating these processes lies in recognizing that people distinguish between the kinds of information that create conceptions of other people. Perceivers may define a continuum, one end of which involves information that is seen as a valid and sufficient basis for judgments about another; at the other end is evidence that is seen as a weak or invalid basis for those judgments.

As an example of valid information, consider a teacher who receives the results of a standardized test indicating that a particular pupil has high ability. The expectancies this information creates about the child are assumed to reflect the child's actual capabilities and are probably quite automatically applied. At the other end of the continuum, and of primary interest to this article, is expectancy-creating information that most perceivers would regard as incomplete with respect to an individual's abilities or dispositions. Many of our social stereotypes fall into this category. For example, racial or social-class categories are regarded by most of us as an insufficient evidential basis for conclusive judgments of another's dispositions or capabilities. In this case, we suspect that perceivers are highly resistant to automatically applying their expectancies to a target person. A teacher, for example, would be extremely hesitant to conclude that a black child had low ability unless that child supplied direct behavioral evidence validating the application of the label.

The end of the continuum defining information that is seen as insufficient evidence for social judgments is of interest because we find what appears to be a paradox in the literature dealing with social stereotypes. Some recent investigations of the influence of stereotypes on social judgments have demonstrated a "fading" of stereotypic attributions (e.g., Karlins, Coffman, & Walters, 1969; Locksley, Borgida, Brekke, & Hepburn, 1980). For example, investigators have noted participants' increasing unwillingness to make stereotypic trait ascriptions (Brigham, 1971). Moreover, Quattrone and Jones (1980) demonstrate that although people

may make stereotype-based judgments about a social group, they are unwilling to use category-based information to predict the behavior of any member of that group.

Given this resistance to the utilization of expectancies when the social labels establishing them are not seen as valid guides for judgments, one might expect an elimination of the expectancy-confirmation bias. That is, perceivers would not unjustly assume the truth of a stereotype; they would instead require that evidence substantiating the accuracy of that stereotype be provided. This leads to the prediction that, ultimately, judgments about the target person will reflect the actual evidence produced by his or her behavior, unbiased by the perceivers' initial expectancies. Unfortunately, this conclusion stands in contradiction to the bulk of the self-fulfilling prophecy literature in which one finds that confirmation effects are often produced when racial, ethnic, or other negative social labels are implicated—exactly those cases in which one expects perceivers to refrain from using category-based information (e.g., Foster, Schmidt, & Sabatino, 1976; Rist, 1970; Rosenhan, 1973; Word, Zanna, & Cooper, 1974). We suggest that this apparent contradiction can be resolved if the following two-stage expectancy-confirmation process is assumed: Initially, when perceivers have reason to suspect that the information that establishes an expectancy is not diagnostically valid for determining certain of the target person's dispositions or capabilities, they will refrain from using that information to come to diagnostic conclusions. The expectancies function not as truths about the target person but rather as hypotheses about the likely dispositions of that person. If perceivers were asked for judgments at this point in the process, without any behavioral evidence to confirm their predictions, they would not report evaluations based on their expectancies. They would instead report that either they did not have sufficient information or they would make judgments consistent with normative expectations about the general population.

The second stage occurs when perceivers are given the opportunity to observe the actions of the labeled other. They then can test their hypotheses against relevant behavioral evidence. The initiation of a hypothesis-testing process would seem to be an unbiased approach for deriving a valid basis for judgments about another. If, however, individuals test their hypothesis using a "confirming strategy"—as has often been demonstrated—a tendency to find evidence supporting the hypothesis being tested would be expected (Snyder & Cantor, 1979; Snyder & Swann, 1978b). A number of mechanisms operating in the service of a hypothesis-confirming strategy may contribute to this result. First, the search for evidence may involve selective attention to information that is consistent with expectations and a consequent tendency to recall expectancy-consistent information when making final evaluations (Zadny & Gerard, 1974). Second, a hypothesis-confirming strategy may affect how information attended to during a performance will be weighted. Typically, expectancy-consistent information has inferential impact, whereas inconsistent information has insufficient influence in social-decision tasks (Nisbett & Ross, 1980). In fact, a recent study by Lord, Ross, and Lepper (1979) indicates that even when expectancy-inconsistent information is brought to the attention of the perceiver, it may be regarded as flawed evidence and therefore be given minimal weight in the evaluation process. Third, it is also possible for inconsistent actions to be attributed to situational factors and thereby be attributionally discounted (Regan, Strauss, & Fazio, 1974). Finally, apparently inconsistent behavior may be reinterpreted as a manifestation of positions that are consistent with the initial expectancy (Hayden & Mischel, 1976).

Given the operation of all or these biasing mechanisms, an expectancy-confirmation effect could arise even when the target person's behavior does not objectively confirm the perceiver's expectancies. Nonetheless, the opportunity to observe the diagnostically relevant information is critical to the process because it provides what perceivers consider to be valid evidence, and thus, they can feel that they have made an "unbiased" judgment.

In the present study, we attempted to find evidence of this two-stage expectancy-confirmation process. To do this, perceivers were given information that would induce them to categorize an elementary school child as belonging to a high- or low-socioeconomic status (SES) class (cf. Cooper, Baron, & Lowe, 1975). Consistent with the two-stage model, we predicted that perceivers given only this demographic information about the child would be reluctant to provide label-consistent ability evaluations. Another group of evaluators were given the identical demographic information about the child (high or low SES) and were then shown a performance sequence that provided ability-relevant information about the child. Owing to the hypothesis-confirming bias, it was predicted that these individuals would find evidence in the identical performance sequence to support their opposing hypotheses and would thus report widely different judgments of the child's ability. Moreover, we expected these perceivers to mislocate the source of their evidence from their own expectancies to the "objective" evidence provided by the performance sequence.

Method

As part of a study on "teacher evaluation methods," students viewed a videotape of a fourth-grade female child and were asked to evaluate her academic capabilities. Variation in the videotape determined the four experimental conditions. The first segment provided demographic information about the child and was used to establish either positive or negative expectations for the child's academic potential. Half of the participants viewed a sequence that depicted the child in an urban, low-income area (negative expectancy); the other half were shown the same child in a middle-class, suburban setting (positive expectancy).

Orthogonal to this manipulation was the performance variable. Half of the participants from each expectancy condition were shown a second segment in which the child responded to achievement-test problems (performance). The tape was constructed to be inconsistent and relatively uninformative about the child's abilities. The remaining participants were not shown this segment (no performance).

The design was thus a 2 × 2 factorial one, with two levels of expectancy (positive and negative) and two levels of performance (performance and no performance). In addition, a fifth group of participants viewed the performance tape but were not given prior information about the child's background (performance only). Their evaluations were used to determine if the performance tape was, as intended, an ambiguous display of the child's academic capabilities.

All viewers then completed an evaluation form on which they rated the child's overall achievement and academic skill level. Additional questions about the child's performance and manipulation checks were included. After completing their evaluation form, participants were given a questionnaire designed to probe their suspiciousness about the experiment. Finally, participants were debriefed, thanked, and paid.

Subjects

Seventy (30 male and 40 female) Princeton University undergraduates volunteered for a study on "teacher evaluation and referral" for which they were paid $2.50 for a 1-hour session. Participants were randomly assigned to one of five (four experiments and one control) conditions, with an attempt made to have an equal number of men and women in each condition. None of the students in the study reported having any formal teacher training; two students had informal teaching experience, both at the high school level. Only three of the original subjects were eliminated from the study because of suspiciousness about the experimental procedures.

Instructions

The experimenter introduced herself as a research assistant for a federal agency interested in testing new educational procedures. Students were told that their participation would be useful for determining the reliability of a new evaluation form teachers would use when referring pupils to special programs (these included remedial classes and programs for gifted students). To test the completeness and scorability of the evaluation form, subjects, acting as teachers, were asked to provide an academic evaluation of a selected child on this specially designed form. The experimenter emphasized that all evaluations would be anonymous and confidential and asked participants not to place their names anywhere on the form. She also requested that they replace the form in its envelope and seal it when they were finished. Each participant was further admonished to be as accurate and objective as possible when evaluating their selected pupil.

The research assistant then went on to explain that a videotape file of elementary school children had been prepared for a previous study (numerous videotape reels were on shelves in front of the subject). Participants would be selecting one child

from this sample to observe and evaluate. It was made clear that this "randomly selected sample of children includes some who perform well above their grade level, some who would benefit from remedial programs, and some at all levels between these extremes." To select a child from this file, participants drew a number corresponding to a videotape reel. The experimenter, who had been blind to condition until this point, placed the tape on a television monitor and gave the participant a fact sheet appropriate to the child they selected.

The participant actually selected one of five prepared tapes (corresponding to the four experimental and one control conditions). In all conditions, the child was a nine-year-old female Caucasian named Hannah, who was a fourth grader attending a public elementary school. The information about the child's name, grade, and so forth appeared on the fact sheet and was reiterated in the narrative of the tape.

Demographic Expectancy Manipulation

To establish either positive or negative expectancies about Hannah's ability, participants viewed a tape of Hannah that contained environmental cues indicating either a high or low socioeconomic background. Each tape included 4 minutes devoted to scenes of Hannah playing in a playground (filmed at a distance to prevent clear perception of her physical attractiveness) and 2 minutes devoted to scenes of her neighborhood and school. The tapes were filmed at two different locations.

In the negative-expectancy condition, subjects viewed Hannah playing in a stark fenced-in school yard. The scenes from her neighborhood showed an urban setting of run down two-family homes. The school she attended was depicted as a three-story brick structure set close to the street, with an adjacent asphalt school yard. The fact sheet given to participants included the following information about Hannah's parents: Both parents had only a high school education; her father was employed as a meat packer; her mother was a seamstress who worked at home.

In the positive-expectancy condition, Hannah was seen playing in a tree-lined park. The scenes from the neighborhood showed a suburban setting of five- and six-bedroom homes set on landscaped grounds. Her school was depicted as a sprawling modern structure with adjacent playing fields and a shaded playground. Further, Hannah's fact sheet indicated that both her parents were college graduates. Her father's occupation was listed as an attorney, her mother as a free-lance writer.

The Performance Manipulations

Two groups were asked to evaluate Hannah's academic ability immediately after viewing one or the other expectancy tape (no performance); two other groups were given the opportunity to observe Hannah in a test situation (performance).

Subjects in the performance conditions observed a second 12-minute tape sequence in which Hannah responded to 25 achievement-test problems. This portion of the tape was identical for both performance groups. The problems were modified versions of items selected from an achievement-test battery and included problems from the mathematics computation, mathematics concepts, reading, science, and social studies subtests. The grade level for the problems ranged from the second to the sixth grade. Participants were told that the test included "easy, moderate, and difficult problems." The problems were given orally to Hannah by a male tester who held up the possible solutions on cards. The sequence was filmed from behind the child so the viewer was able to see the cards held by the tester but not Hannah's face.

Hannah's performance was prearranged to present an inconsistent picture if her abilities. She answered both easy and difficult questions correctly as well as incorrectly. She appeared to be fairly verbal, motivated, and attentive on some portions of the tape and unresponsive and distracted on other portions of the tape. The tester provided little feedback about Hannah's performance. After each problem, he recorded Hannah's response and went on to the next problem.

To determine what information the tape provided about Hannah's ability in the absence of a priori expectancies, a group of participants, given the same cover-story as subjects in the other conditions, were shown only the performance tape. These subjects were given no information about the child other than her name, age, grade, address, and the school she attended.

Dependent Measures

After reviewing the tape, participants were given an evaluation form to complete. The form contained the following sections:

Ability Measures. Nine curriculum areas forming three board categories were listed. Included in this section were reading (reading comprehension, reading ability, writing, language ability), mathematics (mathematical concepts, mathematical computation), and liberal arts (science, general knowledge, social studies). Each curriculum area was followed by a scale extending from kindergarten to the sixth-grade, ninth-month grade level, with points labeled at 3-month intervals. Subjects were instructed to indicate the grade level that represented the child's ability in each of these areas. For subsequent analyses, mean ratings of items within these three categories were used, and grade levels were converted to a scale with months represented as fractions of a year (i.e., third grade, sixth month would equal 3.5).

Performance Measures. Participants in the performance conditions were asked to estimate the number of easy, moderate, and difficult problems the child answered correctly and to report the overall grade level of the test administered to the child. In an open-ended question, participants were asked to report the "information they found most useful in determining the child's capabilities."

Supplementary Academic Measures. Twenty traits or skills, followed by exemplars of classroom behaviors characterizing both the positive and negative ends of each of these traits, were listed. Subjects were asked to check the point on a 9-point scale that would best characterize the child on the dimension. Next to each scale, a box labeled "insufficient information" was also provided. Subjects were instructed to check this box rather than a scale value if they felt they had not been given sufficient information to rate the child on a given dimension.

These 20 items were selected to form five clusters: work habits (organization, task orientation, dependability, attention, thoroughness), motivation (involvement, motivation, achievement orientation), sociability (popularity, verbal behavior, cooperation), emotional maturity (confidence, maturity, mood, disposition), and cognitive skill (articulation, creativity, learning capability, logical reasoning). Mean ratings or items within these five categories were used in subsequent analysis.

Manipulation Checks. In the last part of the booklet, subjects were asked to rate the child's "attractiveness" and the "usefulness of socioeconomic information as an indicator of a child's academic ability." The final open-ended question asked subjects to report the child's socioeconomic level.

Suspiciousness Probe. Finally, participants filled out a questionnaire assessing for the agency, "how they had been treated during the experimental session." This was designed to probe their suspiciousness about the experimental procedures and purpose of the study. Following this, participants were thoroughly debriefed and paid.

Results

Ability-Level Ratings

Our primary hypothesis was that expectancy-confirmation effects occur only when perceivers feel they have definitive evidence relevant to their expectations. Specifically, we predicted that subjects who viewed only the positive- or negative-expectancy tape segment (no performance) would show little, if any, signs of expectancy confirmation in their ratings of the child's ability level, whereas subjects who viewed both the expectancy segment and the test segment (performance) would show considerable signs of expectancy confirmation. As a test of this hypothesis, a 2 (positive vs. negative) × 2 (performance vs. no performance) analysis of variance (ANOVA) was performed on ability-level ratings.

As shown in Figure 11.1, the results support our predictions. The ANOVA interaction term was significant for each index: liberal arts, $F(1, 56) = 6.67$, $p < .02$; reading $F(1,56) = 5.73$, $p < .03$; and mathematics $F(1, 56) = 9.87$, $p < .01$. Although a main effect for expectancy emerged for each of the three indexes—liberal arts, $F(1,56) = 19.24$, $p < .01$; reading, $F(1, 56) = 32.98$, $p < .001$; and mathematics, $F(1, 56) = 19.78$, $p < .001$—Newman–Keuls tests revealed that the subjects in the no-performance conditions did not rate the child's ability level as differing much in either direction from the known school grade. On only one of the indexes (liberal arts) did the no-performance–positive-expectancy subjects rate the child significantly higher than the negative-expectancy subjects ($p < .05$). In the two performance conditions, however, positive-expectancy subjects made reliably higher ratings on all three indexes ($p < .05$ in all cases). The fan-shaped interaction of Figure 11.1 is consistent with the hypothesized two-stage confirmation process in which subjects first reserve judg-

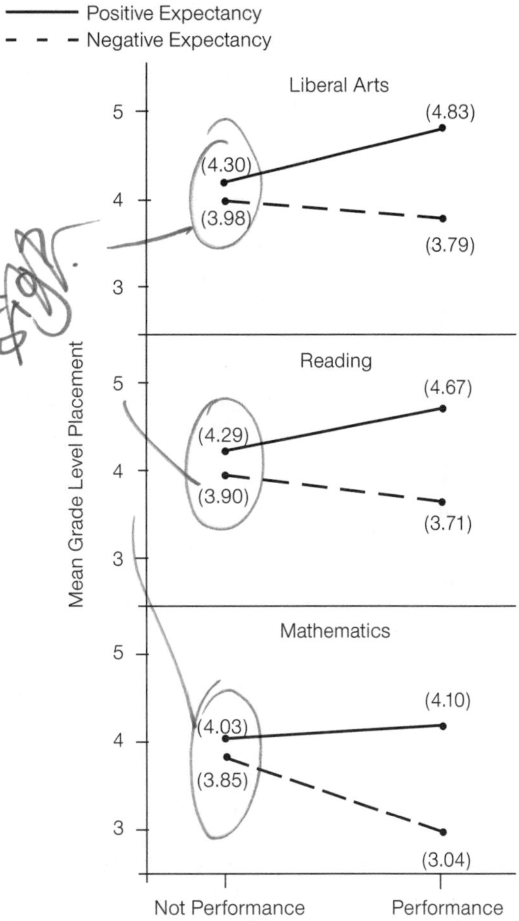

FIGURE 11.1 ■ Mean grade-level placements on the liberal arts, reading, and mathematics indexes for experimental conditions.

ment—if that judgment is based on only demographic indicators—but then allow their judgment about an ability to be biased in the direction of hypothesis confirmation.[1]

Manipulation Checks

The manipulation checks indicate that the above results were not artifactually produced. First, the

[1]We also analyzed this data by pooling across the three ability measures. As one would expect, because this increases the number or observations, the significance levels are improved, although the basic interactional pattern ($p = .002$) remains the same. Again, post hoc comparisons reveal that the two performance conditions are reliably different ($p < .01$), whereas the two no-performance groups do not differ reliably.

expectancy manipulation was as successful for subjects who viewed the child's test performance as for those who did not. Without exception, positive-expectancy subjects reported the child's socioeconomic status as upper middle or upper class, and negative-expectancy subjects reported the child's socioeconomic status as lower middle or lower class. Second, analyses of ratings of the child's attractiveness and the usefulness of socioeconomic information for predicting ability yielded no differences across groups. The latter result is especially important in indicating that those who had seen the child's test performance did not regard the demographic information as any more diagnostic than those who had not seen it. Thus, the greater impact of induced expectancies in the performance conditions was not attributable to greater confidence in an implicit theory of the social-class–ability relation. Moreover, mean ratings of the usefulness of socioeconomic information (for all groups) were just below the midpoint toward the "not useful" end of the scale.

Finally, as can be seen in Table 11.1, ability ratings of the performance-only group indicate that the performance segment was, as intended, an ambiguous display of Hannah's capabilities.

We hoped that evaluations of the child's ability would tend to be variable, reflecting the inconsistencies in the child's performance; however, mean estimates would be expected to fall close to the child's given grade level. As the data in Table 11.1 indicate, ratings on the three curriculum indexes do show considerable variability, and the perceivers do use the child's grade level as an anchor for their judgments. The mathematics ratings were somewhat lower and less variable than the others, indicating that her performance in this area may have been poorer and more consistent.[2] (This will be discussed at a later point.)

Judgments of the Performance

If performance subjects were no less aware of, or impressed by, the relevance of the expectancy information, it follows that they found support for

TABLE 11.1. **Mean Grade-Level Placements on Curriculum Areas by Performance Control Group**

Index	M	Grade level	SD
Liberal arts	4.0	3rd grade, 9th month	.505
Reading	3.8	4th grade	.581
Mathematics	3.5	3rd grade, 6th month	.238

Note. n = 10.

their divergent hypotheses in the child's performance. Measures from the academic evaluation form indicate several ways in which perceivers obtained support for their diverse hypotheses. (All of these were measures of the subjects' perceptions of the performance and therefore were taken only from the groups that witnessed the test sequence. Recall that all of these subjects witnessed the identical performance tape.)

Test Difficulty. Performance on a test is a joint function of the test taker's ability (and other personal factors) and the difficulty of the test. Therefore, one way of justifying a high-ability inference from an inconsistent test performance is to perceive the test as being very difficult. Conversely, one way of rationalizing a low-ability inference from the same performance would be to perceive the test as easy. This happened. Subjects in the positive-expectancy condition rated the test as significantly more difficult (M grade = 4.8) than did those in the negative-expectancy condition (M grade = 3.9), $t(28) = 2.69$, $p < .02$.

Problems Correct. Subjects also estimated the number of problems the child answered correctly within each of the problem categories: very difficult, moderately difficult, and easy.

A repeated measures analysis of variance revealed a marginally reliable tendency for subjects with positive expectancies to estimate that the child correctly answered a higher percentage of problems, $F(1, 28) = 3.94$, $p < .06$. Follow-up analyses revealed that subjects with positive expectancies estimated that the child correctly answered more of the easy (M = 94% vs. 79%) and moderately difficult (M = 69% vs. 53%) problems than did subjects with negative expectancies, $t(28) = 2.55$ and 2.2l, respectively, $ps < .05$. Expectancy did not affect estimates of answers to difficult problems (M = 37% vs. 36%). The overall pattern suggests a bias to report more instances of expectancy-consistent than expectancy-inconsistent test responses.

---

[2]An F_{max} test of the difference between several variances indicates no difference between the variances of the liberal arts and reading indexes. The variances of the mathematics index is, however, significantly different from that of the liberal arts index, $F_{max}(9,91) = 5.92$, $p < .05$, and shows a marginally significant difference from that of the reading index.

Reporting Relevant Behaviors. Subjects had been asked to report, in an open-ended format, the performance information "most relevant for determining the child's capabilities." We expected that subjects anticipating a good performance would report more instances of positive behaviors than those expecting a poor performance. For each subject, we computed a positivity index by subtracting the number of negative instances from the number of positive instances. Consistent with predictions, positive-expectancy subjects reported a significantly greater number of positive behaviors relative to negative ones as being relevant in their judgments than did negative-expectancy subjects, $t(28) = 34.65$, $p < .001$.

To summarize the performance judgments, positive- and negative-expectancy subjects, although agreeing that the performance provided information that was sufficient to estimate the child's capabilities, disagreed on how difficult the test was. How many problems the child answered correctly, and how many of her test behaviors reflected either positively or negatively on her achievement level. On every measure, positive-expectancy subjects made interpretations more favorable to the child than did negative-expectancy subjects.

Supplementary Academic Measures

Information Sufficiency. Recall that subjects reporting on these measures were allowed to check a scale value or a box labeled insufficient information. We believed that the no-performance subjects who had only demographic-based expectancies to rely on would display a greater reluctance to evaluate the child and that this reluctance would lead to more frequent use of the insufficient information answer: A 2 × 2 analysis of variance on these data yielded only a main effect for performance, $F(1, 56) = 12.86$, $p < .001$, such that no-performance subjects chose this option more often (M = 43% of the items) than subjects who viewed the test sequence (*M* = 22% of the items). A one-way analysis of variance, comparing the no-performance, performance, and performance-only conditions yielded a reliable effect, $F(2, 67) = 12.41$, $p < .001$. Moreover, comparing these means (via Duncan's test), we find that the performance-witnessing groups were not significantly different from each other, whereas both were significantly different from the no-performance groups ($p < .01$). Thus, the difference found between perfor-

mance and no-performance groups on the use of the insufficient information option did not seem to depend on the fact that the mere quantity of evidence provided to performance subjects was greater (two tape segments) than that given to no-performance subjects (one tape segment). The performance-only subjects, who also saw only one tape segment, did not differ from performance subjects on this measure. The difference is better attributed to the greater perceived diagnostic utility of the performance segment. Performance subjects apparently felt that the child's test performance provided sufficient diagnostic information on which to base their evaluations.

Trait Measures. A 2 (expectancy) × 2 (performance) analysis of variance was performed on ratings for each of the five trait dimensions. Because participants were given the option of not checking a scale value on these measures, missing values were given a score of 5, which, on a 9-point scale represents the neutral point.[3] These data are presented in Table 11.2.

Consistent with our findings for the curriculum indexes, a significant interaction emerged for the work habits index such that individuals expecting the child to perform well rated her more positively after viewing the performance tape whereas those expecting her to perform poorly rated her more negatively after viewing the performance tape, $F(1, 56) = 5.15$, $p < .03$). The predicted interaction effect was not obtained for the motivation, sociability, emotional maturity, or cognitive skill measures. For each of these measures, we found a main effect for expectancy, with the positive-expectancy groups rating the child significantly higher than the negative-expectancy groups, $F(1, 56) = 6.99$, 4.57, 5.76, and 5.84, respectively, $ps < .05$. In addition, there was a significant effect for performance on the cognitive skill index, with the performance groups showing lower ratings than the no-performance groups, $F(1, 56) = 7.73$, $p < .05$. These data indicate that certain expectancy-con-

---

[3] Analyses of these data require a decision about how to treat the responses of subjects who checked the "not enough information to rate" alternative. The means presented in Table 11.2 are calculated by assigning a score of 5 to missing scale value. This assumes that the nonresponding subjects would have checked the scale midpoint if forced to respond. Another way of dealing with this same issue is to insert the cell-mean score for each such subject. Using this procedure, the pattern of results is essentially unchanged. The same effects emerged as significant.

TABLE 11.2. Mean Ratings on Trait Measures for Experimental Groups

Condition	Dependent measure				
	Work habits	Motivation	Sociability	Maturity	Cognitive skills
Positive, performance	5.21$_a$	5.16$_a$	5.25$_a$	5.31$_{a,b}$	4.73$_a$
Positive, no-performance	4.92$_{a,b}$	5.31$_a$	4.82$_{a,b}$	5.65$_b$	5.55$_b$
Negative, no-performance	5.13$_a$	4.80$_{a,b}$	4.38$_b$	4.67$_a$	4.83$_b$
Negative, performance	4.36$_b$	4.11$_b$	4.58$_{a,b}$	4.77$_{a,b}$	4.12$_a$

Note. n = 15 per condition. The higher the number, the more positive the evaluation. Letter subscripts indicate vertical comparisons of cell means by Duncan's multiple-range test. Means that do not share a common subscript are significantly different from each other at the .05 level.

sistent judgments may not require a two-stage process. Although it may be necessary to provide performance information to obtain judgments of a child's ability level, judgments about other dispositional characteristics may be made without this information.

Discussion

Unlike many previous studies demonstrating expectancy-confirmation effects, the expectancies in the present study were not created by information that most people would regard as definitively establishing their validity. They were not created by objective test results, expert judgments, or other authoritative information. Instead, the expectancies were conveyed by such cues as the child's clothes, the bleakness of the playground on which she played, or the high- or low-status character of her parents' occupations.

We suggested that perceivers would realize that expectancies created by this information do not form a completely valid basis for some of the evaluations they were asked to make. The results indicate that this is so: Perceivers who were given only demographic information about the child demonstrated a resistance to making expectancy-consistent attributions on the ability indexes. Their estimations of the child's ability level tended to cluster closely around the one concrete fact they had at their disposal: the child's grade in school. When given the opportunity to avoid making dispositional attributions altogether, nearly half of the time these perceivers chose that option.

In contrast, a marked expectancy-confirmation effect was evident for those perceivers who evaluated the child after witnessing an ability-relevant performance. Those who believed the child came

from a high socioeconomic class reported that her performance indicated a high ability level, whereas those who believed the child came from a low socioeconomic class reported that the identical performance indicated a substantially lower level of ability.

This pattern of results suggests that when the diagnostic validity of a perceiver's expectations is suspect, expectancies function as hypotheses, and the task of evaluating an individual for whom one has an expectancy is a hypothesis-testing process. Expectancy confirmation, then, does not always result from automatic inference process. Instead, it occurs as the end product of an active process in which perceivers examine the labeled individual's behavior for evidence relevant to their hypothesis.[4]

As is apparent from our data, the hypothesis-testing strategy that perceivers use has a bias (as Snyder & Cantor, 1979, have suggested) toward confirmation of the hypothesis being tested. The literature suggests a number of related mechanisms that can contribute to this effect (see Nisbett & Ross, 1980, for a review). We do have evidence to suggest what some of these mechanisms may have been in our study. First, there seems to be a selective recall of evidence: Perceivers who expected

---

[4] In the experimental paradigm in which expectancy effects are typically demonstrated, perceivers are always provided with the opportunity to observe or interact with the labeled target person. By using this research design, one cannot conclusively determine whether the resulting expectancy effect was due to differential perceptions or the target person, as most researchers suggest, or if subjects had simply based their evaluations on the information provided by the label and had ignored the performance. By including conditions in the present study in which some perceivers are not provided with performance information, it becomes possible to distinguish between expectancy effects arising from a nonobservationally based inference process and those arising from expectancy-guided search processes.

the child to do well reported the child as having answered more easy and more moderately difficult problems correctly than those expecting the child to do poorly. Second, there seems to be a selective weighting of the evidence such that hypothesis-consistent behaviors are regarded as more "typical" of the child's true capabilities. When people were asked to report what evidence they found most useful in determining their evaluations, they reported only those test items on which the child's performance was consistent with their initial expectations. Third, perceivers appeared to develop auxiliary hypotheses that would render apparently inconsistent behavior consistent with their hypotheses. These auxiliary hypotheses did not seem to be revised assessments of the actor but rather assessments of situational factors that could account for discrepancies in the actor's behavior. For instance, we found that persons who expected a good performance decided that the test given to the child was very difficult, a conclusion that would account for instances of otherwise inconsistent poor performance; whereas persons who expected a poor performance reported that the test was easy, which would account for inconsistent good performance. Finally, we found evidence in the open-ended reports of some participants to suggest that the meaning given to the child's behaviors was often consistent with the perceivers' initial hypotheses. For example, a low-SES Hannah was reported to have "difficulty accepting new information," whereas a high-SES Hannah was reported to have the "ability to apply what she knows to unfamiliar problems."

Implicit in this data is the conclusion that perceivers seem to be aware that witnessing a particular test performance does not give them automatic access to an individual's underlying ability. Many other factors, such as luck, task difficulty, or lack of motivation, may intervene (Darley & Goethals, 1980; Weiner et al., 1971). Therefore, the meaning of a person's performance is susceptible to multiple interpretations that can be consistent with, and even supportive of, opposing hypotheses about that person's ability.

Thus far, we have treated information as creating expectancies that are either valid and automatically applied to others or weak and only hypothesis generating. It is more likely that any item of information about a person generates some certainties and some hypotheses, depending on the domain to which is applied. In the present study,

the demographic information seems to have this character of creating both certainties and hypotheses. On the supplemental measures related to school achievement—specifically, on measures of motivation, sociability, and emotional maturity—a simple main effect was obtained such that people who saw the child as coming from a high socioeconomic background judged her more positively, and those who did not see the performance had as extreme ratings as those who did. (But keep in mind that individuals had the opportunity not to rate the child on these measures and that, overall, many more people from the no-performance conditions chose not to rate.) Apparently, some individuals felt that demographic data alone was sufficient evidence on which to base an evaluation of, for example, a child's likely achievement orientation. Thus, the addition of performance information was not necessary for a conclusive judgment in this area. In general, our social categories do trigger expectancies for a constellation of dispositions and behaviors, and for some of these, it may not be necessary to rely on performance evidence to feel certain that one's expectations are accurate.

The Validity of Demographic Evidence

From another perspective, one could ask whether demographic information does not warrant correspondent inferences of ability. Certainly numerous studies show correlations between social class and school performance (Dreger & Miller, 1960; Kennedy, VanDeReit, & White, 1963; Lesser, Fifer, & Clark, 1965). From this perspective, the differential judgments of people who witnessed the same test with different demographically produced expectancies was less evidence of bias than it was of an understanding of the true workings of the world. Two things can be said about this: First, part of the general argument of those concerned with self-fulfilling prophecies is that the present process is exactly how the link between social class and academic performance comes about. Second, the data from our no-performance perceivers indicate that people regard the question of what exists in the world as a separate question from that addressed in the present study. Base-rate information (i.e., estimates of the frequencies with which an attribute or capability level occurs in a social group) represents probabilistic statements about a class of individuals, which may not be applicable to every member of the class. Thus, regardless of what an individual perceives the actual base rates to be, rating any one member of the class requires a higher standard of evidence. When one child's ability is being considered, demographic information does not appear to meet the perceiver's criteria for a valid predictor; performance information, on the other hand, clearly does.

There is yet another way to pose the validity question, and that is to consider the role of demographic evidence when perceivers formulate a working hypothesis. From an information-processing perspective, hypothesis formulation serves a useful function: It allows one to make better use of subsequent evidence. The rub, of course, is that once a hypothesis is formulated, regardless of our judgments of the validity of the evidence on which it is based, our cognitive mechanisms are biased toward its eventual confirmation. Thus, when asking whether these final judgments of the perceiver accurately reflect what exists in the world, we should not obscure an important point: how those judgments come about. To clarify further the "judgmental bias" in the present study does not refer to the indiscriminate use of category-based information, or to the (in)accuracy of final judgments, but to the processes that determine what those judgments will be.

An Alternative Explanation

An alternative explanation for the general pattern of results reported here is possible. The individuals who witnessed only the demographic information may have actually made ability inferences but chose not to report them. Their failure to report their evaluations may have been due to fears that the experimenter would regard the inferences as unjustified. However, in the experiment we minimized the possible cause for this concern by demonstrating to the participants that the responses would be anonymous. The experimenter was not present while the participants filled out the dependent-measures form and did not return until he or she deposited the questionnaire in an anonymity-guaranteeing location. Furthermore, on the final questionnaire, participants were asked if they were sufficiently assured of the anonymity of their responses, and all of them replied affirmatively.

It is, of course, still possible to make a generalized version of the same point: The perceiver's resistance to using the demographic information could, at least in part, be motivated by the awareness that their behavior was under scrutiny by others. This does not necessarily diminish the interest in the phenomenon. In the real world, people who make judgments frequently know their judgments may be public. Teachers classifying students, clinicians diagnosing clients, and employers selecting new personnel are all aware that their actions may be scrutinized by others. Thus, whether this awareness is based on personal knowledge, social pressure, or internalized social desirability concerns, both the processes that bring about those judgments and the consequences in terms of judgmental bias are likely to be the same.

The present study finds results that at first glance seem contradictory to results of some other studies. One thinks particularly of the work of Locksley et al. (1980) and that of Kahneman and Tversky (1973). In the Locksley et al. study, the direction of the interaction appears to be the reverse of that obtained here. A strong stereotype effect in trait ratings is found with category-membership information (gender labels) or when nondiagnostic information accompanies the category label. This stereotype effect disappears with diagnostic information. However, consider the differences in the type of information given to perceivers in the present study and that given to perceivers in the correspondent conditions of the Locksley et al. study. The perceivers in the present study who were reluctant to apply stereotypes (the no-performance conditions) received nondiagnostic case information, as do some in the Locksley et al. study. However, perceivers in the present study observe the child they will rate and are given a fair amount of family data–information that would certainly distinguish the child from others in her social group. The diagnostic information used by Locksley et al. consists of information that could be applied to almost any person and may not have created an individuated impression of the person to be rated. The two conditions, then, are not identical, and comparing them leads us to the following possibility: Stereotype effects persist with information that does not distinguish the target from the target's social category, whereas dilution effects (nonstereotypic judgments) appear when case information successfully creates an individuated impression of the target. Recent studies by Quattrone and Jones (1980) and Locksley, Hepburn, and Oritz (1982) support this conclusion.

In comparing other conditions of the Locksley et al. (1980) and the present study, differences in the type of information given to perceivers produces discrepant results. The diagnostic information given to perceivers in the Locksley et al. study consists of a single behavioral exemplar that confirms or disconfirms a gender-based trait expectancy. A dilution effect is found only with a disconfirming behavior sample. In contrast, the diagnostic test sequence in the present study contains both confirming and disconfirming behavioral evidence. Furthermore, we know from supplementary measures that perceivers found the expectancy-consistent portions more diagnostically informative than the inconsistent portions. Therefore, with a source of multiple information— with many information elements that serve to confirm expectancies—a confirmation effect is not surprising. Had the performance tape in the present study provided only compelling disconfirming evidence, we suspect a dilution effect might have been found here as well.

Discrepancies between this work and that of Kaheman and Tversky (1973) can be addressed as well. In Kahneman and Tversky's studies, individuals are asked to predict a target person's occupational-category membership from a brief personality description. Predictions are overwhelmingly based on the degree to which the personality information "fits" with an occupational stereotype (i.e., a representativeness effect). This appears inconsistent with the stereotype-resisting judgments of the perceivers in our study who received no performance information. However, the demographic information given to our no-performance perceivers, although it does allow for a judgment of fit to a social category, does not provide information for a judgment on an ability dimension. The condition, then, is similar to Kahneman and Tversky's Experiment 3 in which the personality description is uninformative with regard to the target person's profession (i.e., it contains no occupation-relevant personality traits). In their study, occupational-category predictions were essentially random. That is, they were based neither on prior probabilities nor on similarity. This is essentially the same effect we find for no-performance perceivers in the present study. Apparently, the representativeness effect (or an expectancy effect) depends on the provision of information that allows for a similarity match to the categories perceivers are asked to judge.

Further, the no-performance conditions in the present study are not identical to Kahneman and Tversky's (1973) null-description condition. In that condition, subjects are given no information whatsoever about the target—neither individuating information nor category-relevant information. Here a strong base-rate effect emerges. Although this might cause one to predict a strong stereotype effect in the present no-performance conditions, our earlier point about individuating information may explain why it is not obtained. No-performance perceivers may lack relevant case information, but they do have a significant amount of individuating target information; apparently, this significantly alters the framework for prediction.

We might summarize as follows: Representativeness and expectancy effects are found when relevant case data are provided so that individuals can determine the target person's fit to a category. Base-rate effects (and non-observationally based stereotypic judgments) are found when neither case data nor individuating information is given. Finally, assume that three conditions are met: individuating information is given, information about base rates is withheld, and a priori expectancies are not relied on because they may not be applicable to a particular target. Then, without relevant case data, a judgment of fit is precluded, attenuating a representativeness or a biased confirmation effect. In these circumstances, judgments are made at the scale midpoint or the chance level. We find this latter effect in both Kahneman and Tversky's (1973) uninformed condition and in the no-performance conditions of the present study.

A final point is relevant to both of the studies reviewed above. Predicting ability from social-class information may not be equivalent to predicting personality traits from gender labels or occupational membership. The nature of the prediction required (ability rather than personality characteristics) may cause individuals to regard social-class information as at the invalid end of the continuum we have defined. But an individual's gender or occupation, on the other hand, may be regarded as valid information on which to base an inference about personality. Related to this point is that the standards of evidence required for different stereotype confirming judgments may be different. Automatic assumptions about personality may be made from occupation or gender label and thus, stereotype effects are obtained with this information alone, or with minimal additional information. To make judgments of a low-SES child's ability, perceivers require more information and, specifically, criterion-relevant information. Thus, stereotypic judgments are not found with only category or nondiagnostic information but are found only when a sufficient amount of apparently confirming diagnostic information is provided.

Limits to the Conformation Process

The present study finds results consistent with those of many other studies. For instance, Swann and Snyder (1980) found that target individuals labeled as dull witted were still seen as dull witted even after the perceivers had witnessed a sequence in which these target individuals outperformed those labeled as bright, a situation in which a cognitive confirmation effect triumphed over apparently strongly disconfirming evidence. Nonetheless, we suspect that there are limits to the cognitive confirmation process.

We can suggest several variables, some of which we have mentioned, that may determine whether a confirmation or a disconfirmation effect is found. First, there is the clarity of the disconfirming evidence. In the domain of abilities, in spite of the above example, sustained high-level performance is compelling evidence for high ability. I may perceive another as a slow runner, but if I see him or her do several successive 4-minute miles, my expectancy must change. When this occurs, it is possible that a contrast effect will take place in which the significance of the disconfirming behavior will be exaggerated and the initial expectancy reversed. Intuitively, no such unambiguous evidence exists in the personality realm, where even compelling positive behavior can be attributed to negative underlying motives or dispositions. Second, the strength with which the initial expectancy or hypothesis is held may produce conflicting effects. "Strength of expectancy" is an ambiguous phrase. It may refer to one's degree of commitment to an expectancy of a fixed level, or it may refer to the extremity of the expectancy. In the first instance, the stronger the commitment to the expectancy, the more resistant it would be to disconfirmation. However, the more extreme the expectancy, the more evidence there is that potentially disconfirms it. Finally, the perceiver's motivation may play a role. Under certain circumstances, an individual may prefer to see his or her expectancy confirmed; in other situations he or she may have a preference for the disconfirmation of the same expectancy. All of these suggestions, of course, require empirical testing.

A Final Comment

The self-fulfilling prophecy and the expectancy-confirmation effect have been of interest to psychologists partially because of the social policy implications of the research. However, in many of the research studies that document the effect, the specific and limited character of the material that creates the expectancies is lost, and we talk as if any material that creates expectancies is automatically accepted as valid by the perceiver. The image of the perceiver that emerges is one of an individual who takes his or her stereotypes and prejudices for granted and indiscriminately applies them to members of the class he or she has stereotyped without any consideration of the unjustness of such a proceeding. The present study suggests that this is an oversimplification that in turn does some injustice to the perceiver. There are times when perceivers resist regarding their expectancies as truths and instead treat them as hypotheses to be confirmed or disconfirmed by relevant evidence. Perceivers in the present study did not make the error of reporting stereotypic judgments without sufficient evidence to warrant their conclusions. They engaged in an extremely rational strategy of evaluating the behavioral evidence when it was available and refraining from judgment when it was not. It was the strategy perceivers employed to analyze the evidence that led them to regard their hypotheses as confirmed even when the objective evidence did not warrant that conclusion. The error the perceivers make, then, is in assuming that the behavioral evidence they have derived is valid and unbiased. Future research could profitably address the question of the conditions under which this general confirmation strategy can be reversed or eliminated. In the meantime, however, the image of the perceiver as a hypothesis tester is certainly more appealing than that of a stereotype-applying bigot, even though the end result of both processes, sadly enough, may be quite similar.

REFERENCES

Brigham, J. C. (1971). Ethnic stereotypes. *Psychological Bulletin, 76,* 15–38.

Cooper, H. M., Baron, R. M., & Lowe, C. A. (1975). The importance of race and social class information in the formation of expectancies about academic performance. *Journal of Educational Psychology, 67,* 312–319.

Darley, J. M., & Fazio, R. H. (1980). Expectancy confirmation processes arising in the social interaction sequence. *American Psychologist, 35,* 867–881.

Darley, J. M., & Goethals, G. R. (1980). People's analyses of the causes of ability-linked performances. In L. Berkowitz (Ed.), *Advances in experimental social psychology* (Vol. 13). New York: Academic Press.

Dreger, R. M., & Miller, S. K. (1960). Comparative psychological studies of Negroes and whites in the United States. *Psychological Bulletin, 57,* 361–402.

Duncan, B. L. (1976). Differential social perception and attribution of intergroup violence. Testing the lower limits of stereotyping of blacks. *Journal of Personality and Social Psychology, 34,* 590–598.

Foster, G., Schmidt, C., & Sabatino, D. (1976). Teacher expectancies and the label "learning disabilities." *Journal of Learning Disabilities, 9,* 111–114.

Hayden, T., & Mischel, W. (1976). Maintaining trait consistency in the resolution of behavioral inconsistency: The wolf in sheep's clothing? *Journal of Personality, 14,* 109–131.

Kahneman, D., & Tversky, A. (1973). On the psychology of prediction. *Psychological Review, 80,* 237–251.

Karlins, M., Coffman, T. L., & Walters, G. (1969). On the fading of social stereotypes: Studies in three generations of college students. *Journal of Personality and Social Psychology, 13,* 1–16.

Kelley, H. H. (1950). The warm-cold variable in first impressions of persons. *Journal of Personality, 18,* 431–439.

Kennedy, W. A., VanDeReit, V., & White, J. C. (1963). A formative sample of the intelligence and achievement of Negro elementary school children in the southeastern United States. *Monographs of the Society for Research in Child Development, 28,* 13–112.

Langer, E. J., & Abelson, R. P. (1974). A patient by any other name ...: Clinician group differences in labeling bias. *Journal of Consulting and Clinical Psychology, 42,* 4–9.

Lesser, G. S., Fifer, G., & Clark, D. H. (1965). Mental abilities of children from different social class and cultural groups. *Monographs of the Society for Research in Child Development, 30,* 1–115.

Locksley, A., Borgida, E., Brekke, N., & Hepburn, C. (1980). Sex stereotypes and social judgment. *Journal of Personality and Social Psychology, 39,* 821–831.

Locksley, A., Hepburn, C., & Ortiz, V. (1982). Social stereotypes and judgments of individuals: An instance of the base-rate fallacy. *Journal of Experimental Social Psychology, 18,* 23–42.

Lord, C., Ross, L., & Lepper, M. E. (1979). Biased assimilation and attitude polarization: The effects of prior theories on subsequently considered evidence. *Journal of Personality and Social Psychology, 37,* 2098–2109.

Merton, R. K. (1948). The self-fulfilling prophecy. *Antioch Review, 8,* 193–210.

Nisbett, R., & Ross, L. (1980). *Human inference: Strategies and shortcomings of social judgment.* Englewood Cliffs, NJ: Prentice Hall.

Quattrone, G. A., & Jones, E. E. (1980). The perception of variability within in-groups and out-groups: Implications for the law of small numbers. *Journal of Personality and Social Psychology, 38,* 141–152.

Regan, D. T., Strauss, E., & Fazio, R. (1974). Liking and the attribution process. *Journal of Experimental Social Psychology, 10,* 385–397.

Rist, R. C. (1970). Student social class and teacher expectations. The self-fulfilling prophecy in ghetto education. *Harvard Educational Review, 40,* 411–450.

Rosenhan, D. L. (1973). On being sane in insane places. *Science, 179,* 240–258.

Rosenthal, R. (1974). *On the social psychology of self-fulfilling prophecy: Further evidence for Pygmalion effects and their mediating mechanisms.* New York: MSS Modular Publications, Module 53.

Rosenthal, R., & Jacobson, L. (1963). *Pygmalion in the classroom.* New York: Holt, Rinehart & Winston.

Snyder, M., & Cantor, N. (1979). Testing hypotheses about other people: The use of historical knowledge. *Journal of Experimental and Social Psychology, 14,* 148–162.

Snyder, M., & Swann, W. B. (1978a). Behavioral confirmation in social interaction: From social perception to social reality. *Journal of Experimental Social Psychology, 14,* 148–162.

Snyder, M., & Swann, W. B. (1978b). Hypothesis-testing processes in social interaction. *Journal of Personality and Social Psychology, 36,* 1202–1212.

Snyder, M., Tanke, E. D., & Berscheid, E. (1977). Social perception and interpersonal behavior: On the self-fulfilling nature of social stereotypes. *Journal of Personality and Social Psychology, 35,* 656–666.

Swann, W. B., & Snyder, M. (1980). On translating beliefs into action: Theories of ability and their application in an instructional setting. *Journal of Personality and Social Psychology, 6,* 879–888.

Weiner, B., et al. (1971). *Perceiving the causes of success and failure.* Morristown, NJ: General Learning Press.

Word, C. O., Zanna, M. P., & Cooper, J. (1974). The nonverbal mediation of self-fulfilling prophecies in interracial interaction. *Journal of Experimental Social Psychology, 10,* 109–120.

Zadny, J., & Gerard, H. B. (1974). Attributional intentions and information selectivity. *Journal of Experimental Social Psychology, 10,* 34–52.

The Nonverbal Mediation of Self-Fulfilling Prophecies in Interracial Interaction

Carl O. Word, Mark P. Zanna, and Joel Cooper • Princeton University

Two experiments were designed to demonstrate the existence of a self-fulfilling prophecy mediated by nonverbal behavior in an interracial interaction. The results of Experiment 1, which employed naive, white job interviewers and trained white and black job applicants, demonstrated that black applicants received (a) less immediacy, (b) higher rates of speech errors, and (c) shorter amounts of interview time. Experiment 2 employed naive, white applicants and trained white interviewers. In this experiment subject-applicants received behaviors that approximated those given either the black or white applicants in Experiment 1. The main results indicated that subjects treated like the blacks in Experiment 1 were judged to perform less adequately and to be more nervous in the interview situation than subjects treated like the whites. The former subjects also reciprocated with less proximate positions and rated the interviewers as being less adequate and friendly. The implications of these findings for black unemployment were discussed.

Sociologist Robert Merton (1957), by suggesting that an originally false definition of a situation can influence the believer to act in such a way as to bring about that situation, is generally credited with focusing attention on the phenomenon of the self-fulfilling prophecy. The present investigation is concerned with such a phenomenon in face-to-face, dyadic interactions. In this context it is hypothesized that one person's attitudes and expectations about the other person may influence the believer's actions, which in turn, may induce the other person to behave in a way that confirms the original false definition. Interpersonally, this phenomenon has been documented in schools, with teachers' expectations influencing students' performances, and in psychology laboratories, with experimenters' expectations in-fluencing subjects' responses (cf. Rosenthal, 1971).

In the present study attention will be directed toward (1) possible nonverbal mediators of the effect, and (2) the reciprocal performances of the interactants. The focus, in addition, will be on the interaction of black and white Americans with a view toward examining the employment outcomes of job applicants interviewed by whites.

Attitudes and Immediacy

Mehrabian (1968) has recently reported a series of studies linking attitudes toward a target person and the concomitant nonverbal behavior directed toward that person. The results of these studies have consistently found that closer interpersonal distances, more eye contact, more direct shoulder orientation, and more forward lean are a consequence of more positive attitudes toward an addressee. Mehrabian (1969) has considered such nonverbal behaviors in terms if "immediacy" and has defined immediacy "as the extent to which communication behaviors enhance closeness to and nonverbal interaction with another . . . greater immediacy is due to increasing degrees of physical proximity and/or increasing perceptual availability of the communicator to the addressee" (p. 203).

A related series of studies has been conducted by Kleck and his associates (Kleck, 1968; Kleck et al., 1968; Kleck, Ono, & Hastorf, 1966) pursuing Goffman's (1963) observation that normals tend to avoid stigmatized persons. They have begun to document what might be called a nonverbal stigma effect. For example, normal interactants were found to terminate interviews sooner (Kleck et al., 1966) and to exhibit greater motoric inhibition (Kleck, 1968) with a handicapped person (i.e., leg amputee), and to employ greater interaction distances with an epileptic stranger (Kleck et al., 1968). This set of studies, then, also suggests that those persons who possess a personal characteristic which is discrediting in the eyes of others are treated with less immediate behaviors. In addition to such discrediting characteristics as a physical disability or a criminal record, Goffman (1963) includes blackness in a white society as a stigmatizing trait.

Thus, a body of data suggests that (1) attitudes toward an individual are linked with nonverbal behavior emitted toward that individual, and (2) positive attitudes lead to more immediate nonverbal behaviors. Two questions that now arise are concerned with whether such behaviors are (1) decoded or understood by the target and (2) reciprocated.

Decoding and Reciprocating Immediacy

Recent studies suggest that such evaluative, nonverbal behaviors are both decoded and reciprocated. Mehrabian (1967) found friendliness ratings of an interviewer varied as a function of the physical interaction distance, and the immediacy of head and body positions given subjects. Eye

contact has been extensively investigated. Both Kleck and Nuessle (1968) and R. E. Jones and Cooper (1971) found that a high degree of eye contact produced higher evaluations of the communicator and produced more positive evaluations on the part of the subjects than did low eye contact.

Since individuals apparently are able to decode affective components of communications from variations in immediacy behavior, it seems reasonable to expect they would reciprocate such variations. This proposition also has received support. Rosenfeld (1967), for example, found that subjects treated to more smiles and positive head nods did reciprocate with more of each.

Thus individuals apparently decode less immediacy as indicating less friendly behavior and reciprocate with less friendly (i.e., less immediate) behavior of their own. Since individuals seldom are able to monitor their own nonverbal behaviors, they are more likely to attribute the reciprocated immediacy, not to their own, original nonverbal behavior, but instead to some disposition inherent in their cointeractant (cf. E. E. Jones & Nisbett, 1971). With this nonverbal reciprocation, then, a self-fulfilling prophecy is born.

White–Black Interaction in a Job Setting

So far we have been concerned with describing possible mechanisms of interpersonal, self-fulfilling prophecies. The discussion now turns to consider such a process in black–white, dyadic interactions. It has been demonstrated time and again that white Americans have generalized, negative evaluations (e.g., stereotypes) of black Americans. This has been shown most recently in our own subject population by Darley, Lewis, and Glucksberg (1972). Such negative evaluations, of course, represent the kind of attitudes that can initiate an interpersonal, self-fulfilling prophecy. The general hypothesis that the present study sought to investigate, therefore, was that whites interacting with blacks will emit nonverbal behaviors corresponding to negative evaluations and that blacks, in turn, will reciprocate with less immediate behaviors. If the context in which the interaction occurs involves a job interview, with the white interviewing the black, such reciprocated behavior may be interpreted as less adequate performance, thus confirming, in part, the interviewer's original attitude.

These general expectations are operationalized by two subhypotheses: First, black, as compared to white, job applicants will receive less immediate nonverbal communications from white job interviewers; second, recipients of less immediate nonverbal communications, whether black or white, will reciprocate these communications and be judged to perform less adequately in the job interview situation than recipients of more positive nonverbal communications. The first hypothesis was tested in Experiment 1, which employed naive, white job interviewers and trained white and black job applicants; the second in Experiment 2, which used naive, white job applicants and trained white job interviewers who were instructed to emit either immediate or nonimmediate cues.

Experiment 1

Method

OVERVIEW

In the context of a study on group decision-making, white subjects, as representatives of a team in competition with other teams, interviewed both black and white job applicants. The applicants were trained to respond similarly in both the verbal and nonverbal channels. The interview situation itself was arranged to give the subject-interviewers the opportunity to treat their applicants differently without the knowledge (1) that their own behavior was being monitored, or (2) that race of the applicants was the experimental variable.

SUBJECTS (INTERVIEWERS) AND CONFEDERATES (APPLICANTS AND TEAM MEMBERS)

Subject-interviewers were 15 white, Princeton males recruited to participate in a study of group decision-making conducted by Career Services and the Psychology Department. They were informed that the study would last approximately one hour and a half and that they would be paid $2.00 and possibly $5.00 more. One of the subjects was eliminated when he indicated that he was aware of the purpose of the study before the debriefing period. No other subject volunteered this sort of information after intensive probing, leaving an n of 14.

Confederate-applicants were two black and three white high school student volunteers referred by their high counselor. Each was told that the study was concerned with cognitive functioning and that the experimenter was interested in finding how subjects made up their minds when forced to choose between nearly identical job applicants. All confederates in both experiments were naive with respect to the hypotheses. Intensive probing following the experiment indicated that they did not become aware. The three confederates who served as the subject's "team members" and the experimenter were male Princeton volunteers.

PROCEDURE

Upon arrival the subjects entered a room containing two confederate team members, who introduced themselves and acted friendly. Another confederate entered and acted friendly, as well. Then the experimenter entered, handed out written instructions and answered any questions.

The instructions informed subjects that the four people in the room constituted a team; that they were to compete with four other teams in planning a marketing campaign; and that they needed to select another member from four high school applicants. In order to increase incentive and concern, an additional $5.00 was promised to the team which performed best in the competition. Using a supposedly random draw, the subject was chosen to interview the applicants. He was then handed a list of 15 questions which was to serve as the interview material, told he had 45 minutes to interview all four high school students and taken to the interview room where the first confederate-applicant was already seated.

In order to measure the physical distance that the interviewer placed himself from the applicant, the experimenter upon entering the interview room, feigned to discover that there was no chair for the interviewer. Subjects were then asked to wheel in a chair from an adjoining room.

Subjects were led to believe that there would be four interviews so that the race variable would be less apparent to them. In addition, to eliminate any special effect that might occur in the first and last interview, an a priori decision was made not to analyze the data from the first "warm-up" interview and not to have a fourth interview. The "warm-up" job candidate was always white. Half the subjects then interviewed a black followed by a white applicant; the other half interviewed a white then a black candidate. After completion of the third interview, subjects were told that the fourth applicant had called to cancel his appointment. After the third interview, subjects were paid and debriefed.

APPLICANT PERFORMANCE

Confederate-applicants were trained to act in a standard way to all interviewers. First, they devised answers to the 15 questions such that their answers, though not identical, would represent equally qualifying answers. Confederates then rehearsed these answers until two judges rated their performances to be equal. Confederates were also trained to seat themselves, shoulders parallel to the backs of their chairs (10° from vertical) and to make eye contact with the interviewer 50% of the time. A code was devised to signal confederates during their interviews if they deviated from the pose or began to reciprocate the gestures or head nods given them.

DEPENDENT MEASURES

Immediacy Behaviors. Following Mehrabian (1968, 1969), four indices of psychological immediacy were assessed: (1) Physical Distance between interviewer and interviewee; measured in inches; (2) Forward Lean, scored in 10° units, with zero representing the vertical position and positive scores representing the torso leaning toward the confederate; (3) Eye Contact, defined as the proportion of time the subject looked directly at the confederate's eyes; and (4) Shoulder Orientation, scored in units of 10° with zero representing the subject's shoulders parallel to those of the confederate and positive scores indicating a shift in either direction. Two judges[1] placed behind one-way mirrors, scored the immediacy behaviors.

More distance and shoulder angle represent less immediate behaviors while more forward lean and more eye contact represent more immediate behaviors. An index of total immediacy was constructed by summing the four measures, standardized, and weighted according to the regression equation beta weights established by Mehrabian (1969). Final scores of this index represent (−.6) distance + (.3) forward lean + (3) eye contact + (−

.1) shoulder orientation. Positive scores represent more immediate performances.

Related Behaviors. Two related behaviors, which indicate differential evaluations of the applicants (cf. Mehrabian, 1969), were also assessed: (1) interview length indicates the amount of time from the point the subject entered the interview room until he announced the interview was over, in minutes. This measure was taken by the experimenter. (2) Speech Error Rate, scored by two additional judges from audiotapes, represents the sum of (a) sentence changes, (b) repetitions, (c) stutters, (d) sentence incompletions, and (e) intruding, incoherent sounds divided by the length of the interview and averaged over the two judges. Higher scores represent more speech errors per minute.

Results

RELIABILITIES AND ORDER EFFECTS

Reliabilities, obtained by correlating the judges' ratings, ranged from .60 to .90 (see Table 12.1). Preliminary analyses also indicated that there were no effects for the order in which confederate-applicants appeared, so that the results are based on data collapsed across this variable.

IMMEDIACY BEHAVIORS

The results, presented in Table 12.1, indicate that, overall, black job candidates received less immediate behaviors than white applicants ($t = 2.79$; $df = 13$; $p < .02$). On the average, blacks received a negative total immediacy score; whites received a positive one. This overall difference is primarily due to the fact that the white interviewers physically placed themselves further from black than white applicants ($t = 2.36$; $df = 13$; $p < .05$). None of the other indices of immediacy showed reliable differences when considered separately.

RELATED BEHAVIORS

The results for interview length and speech error rate are also present in Table 12.1. Here it can be

---

[1]All judges employed in the present research were Princeton undergraduates. Each worked independently and was naive concerning the hypothesis under investigation. Intensive probing indicated that they did not become aware of the hypothesis.

seen that blacks also received less immediate behaviors. White interviewers spent 25% less time ($t = 3.22$; $df = 13$; $p < .01$) and had higher rates of speech errors ($t = 2.43$; $df = 13$; $p < .05$) with black as compared to white job candidates.

The results of the first experiment provide support for the hypothesis that black, as compared to white, job applicants receive less immediate nonverbal communications from white job interviewers. Indirectly the results also provide support for the conceptualization of blackness as a stigmatizing trait. The differences in time (evidenced by 12 of 14 interviewers), in total immediacy (evidenced by 10 of 14 interviewers), and in speech error rate (evidenced by 11 of 14 interviewers) argues for an extension of the stigma effect obtained by Kleck and his associates to include black Americans.

Experiment 2

Method

OVERVIEW

A second experiment was conducted to ascertain what effect the differences black and white applicants received in Experiment 1 would have on an applicant's job interview performance. In the context of training job interviewers, subject-applicants were interviewed by confederate-interviewers under one of two conditions. In the immediate condition, as compared to the Nonimmediate condition, interviewers (1) sat closer to the applicant, (2) made fewer speech errors per minute, and (3)

roles Reversed

actually took longer to give their interviews. The main dependent measures were concerned with the interview performance of the applicant, both in terms of its judged adequacy for obtaining the job and in terms of its reciprocation of immediacy behaviors.

SUBJECTS (JOB APPLICANTS) AND CONFEDERATES (INTERVIEWERS)

Thirty white male Princeton University students were recruited ostensibly to help Career Services train interviewers for an upcoming summer job operation. No subjects were eliminated from the study, leaving an n of 15 in each condition. The two confederate-interviewers were also white male Princeton students.

PROCEDURE

Upon arrival each subject was given an instruction sheet which informed him that Career Services had contracted with the Psychology Department to train Princeton juniors and seniors in the techniques of job interviewing and that one of the techniques chosen included videotaping interviewers with job applicants for feedback purposes. The subject was then asked to simulate a job applicant, to be honest, and to really compete for the job, so as to give the interviewer real, lifelike practice. To make the simulation more meaningful, subjects were also informed that the applicant chosen from five interviewed that evening would receive an additional $1.50.

Table 12.1. Mean Interviewer Behavior as a Function of Race of Job Applicant; Experiment 1

Behavior	Reliability	Blacks	Whites	t^b	p
Total immediacy[a]	—	−.11	.38	2.79	<.02
Distance	.90	62.29 inches	58.43 inches	2.36	<.05
Forward lean	.68	−8.76 degrees	−6.12 degrees	1.00	n.s.
Eye contact	.80	62.71%	61.46%	<1	n.s.
Shoulder orientation	.60	22.46 degrees	23.08 degrees	<1	n.s.
Related behaviors					
Interview length	—	9.42 min.	12.77 min.	3.22	<.01
Speech error rate	.88	3.54 errors/min.	2.37 errors/min.	2.43	<.05

[a]See text for weighting formula, from Mehrabian (1960).
[b]t test for correlated samples was employed.

Subjects were taken to the interview room and asked to be seated in a large swivel chair, while the Experimenter turned on the camera. The confederate-interviewer then entered, and assumed either an immediate or nonimmediate position which will be described in more detail below. Exactly five minutes into the interviewing in both conditions, a guise was developed whose result was that the experimenter had to reclaim the chair in which the subject was sitting. The subject was then asked to take a folding chair leaning against the wall and to continue the interview. The distance from the interviewer which the subject placed his new chair was one of the study's dependent measures designed to assess reciprocated immediacy.

When the interview ended, the experimenter took the subject to another room where a second investigator, blind as to the condition of the subject, administered self-report scales and answered any questions. Subject was then paid and debriefed.

IMMEDIACY MANIPULATION

As in the Kleck and Nuessle (1968) and the R. E. Jones and Cooper (1971) studies, systematic nonverbal variations were introduced by specifically training confederates. Two confederate-interviewers alternated in the two conditions. In the immediate condition, confederates sat at a chair on the side of a table. In the Nonimmediate condition, confederates sat fully behind the table. The difference in distance from the subject's chair was about four inches, representing the mean difference in distance white interviewers gave black and white applicants in Experiment 1.[2]

In addition, the confederate-interviewers in the Immediate condition were trained to behave as precisely as possible like the subject-interviewer in Experiment 1 had acted toward white applicants. In the Nonimmediate condition, interviewers were trained to act as subject-interviewers had acted toward Blacks in Experiment 1. The factors used to simulate the immediacy behaviors found in the first experiment were speech error rate, length of interview and, as has been previously mentioned, physical distance. Eye contact, shoulder orientation and forward lean did not show significant dif-

ferences in Experiment 1 and thus were held constant in Experiment 2 (with levels set at 50% eye contact, 0° shoulder orientation and 20° forward lean).

DEPENDENT MEASURES

× judges were blind to conditions right?

Three classes of dependent measures were collected: (1) judges' ratings of interview performance; (2) judges' ratings of reciprocated immediacy behaviors; and (3) subjects' ratings of their post-interview mood state and attitudes toward the interviewer.

Applicant Performance. Applicant interview performance and demeanor were rated by a panel of two judges from videotapes of the interviews. The videotapes were recorded at such an angle that judges viewed only the applicant, not the confederate-interviewer. The judges were merely instructed about the type of job subjects were applying for, and were asked to rate (1) the overall adequacy of each subject's performance and (2) each subject's composure on five (0–4) point scales. High scores, averaged over the judges, represent more adequate and more calm, relaxed performances, respectively.

Reciprocal Immediacy Behaviors. Two additional judges, placed behind one-way mirrors as in Experiment 1, recorded subjects' forward lean, eye contact, and shoulder orientation in accordance with the procedures established by Mehrabian (1969). Distance was directly measured after each interview, and represents the distance, in inches, from the middle of the interviewer-confederate's chair to the middle of the subject's chair, after the interruption. Speech errors were scored by another panel of two judges from audiotapes of the interviews, also according to Mehrabian's (1969) procedures. High scores represent more speech errors per minute.

Applicant Mood and Attitude Toward the Interviewer. After the interview, subjects filled out a series of questionnaires designed to assess their mood state and their attitudes toward the interviewer. Following R. E. Jones and Cooper (1971), subjects' moods were expected to vary as a function of immediacy conditions. The mood scale adapted from that study was employed. It consisted of six polar adjectives (e.g., happy–sad) separated by seven-point scales. Subjects were asked to respond to each pair according to "the way you feel about yourself."

---

[2]By having the interviewer sit either behind or at the side of the table, the impact of the four inch difference in distance was intentionally maximized in terms of psychological immediacy.

Two measures of subjects' attitudes toward the interviewer were collected. First, subjects were asked to rate the friendliness of the interviewer on an 11-point scale, with zero representing an "unfriendly" and 10 representing a "friendly" interviewer, respectively. Second, in order to assess subjects' attitudes concerning the adequacy of the interviewer as an individual, they were asked to check the six adjectives best describing their interviewer from a list of 16 drawn from Gough's Adjective Checklist. Final scores represent the number of positive adjectives chosen minus the number of negative adjectives checked.

Results

RELIABILITIES AND INTERVIEWER EFFECTS

Reliabilities, obtained by correlating judges' ratings, ranged from .66 to .86 (see Table 12.2). Preliminary analyses also indicated that there were no effects for interviewers, so that the results presented are based on data collapsed across this variable.

APPLICANT PERFORMANCE

It was predicted from an analysis of the communicative functions of nonimmediacy that applicants would be adversely affected by the receipt of nonimmediate communications. Those effects were expected to manifest themselves in less adequate job-interview performances.

Subjects in the two conditions were rated by two judges from videotapes. The main dependent measure, applicant adequacy for the job, showed striking differences as a function of immediacy conditions (see Table 12.2). Subjects in the Nonimmediate condition were judged significantly less adequate for the job ($F = 7.96$; $df = 1/28$; $p <$

.01). Subjects in the Nonimmediate condition were also judged to be reliably less calm and composed ($F = 16.98$; $df = 1/28$; $p < .001$).

RECIPROCATED IMMEDIACY BEHAVIORS

Following Rosenfeld (1987), among others, it was expected that subjects encountering less immediate communications would reciprocate with less immediate behaviors of their own. This expectation was supported by both the measures of physical distance and speech error rate (see Table 12.2).

Subjects in the Immediate condition, on the average, placed their chairs eight inches closer to the interviewer after their initial chair was removed; subjects in the Nonimmediate conditions placed their chairs four inches further away from their interviewer. The mean difference between the two groups was highly significant ($F = 9.19$; $df = 1/28$; $p < .01$).

As in Experiment 1 mean comparisons for the forward lean, eye contact, and shoulder orientation measures of immediacy did not reach significance. The combination of these measures, using the weighting formula devised by Mehrabian (1969), however, was reliably different (means of −.29 and .29 in the Nonimmediate and Immediate conditions, respectively; $F = 5.44$; $df = 1/28$; $p < .05$).

The rate at which subjects made speech errors also tended to be reciprocated with subjects in the Nonimmediate condition exhibiting a higher rate than subjects in the Immediate condition ($F = 3.40$; $df = 1/28$; $p < .10$).

APPLICANT MOOD AND ATTITUDE TOWARD THE INTERVIEWER

It was expected that subjects receiving less immediate (i.e., less positive) communication would (1)

Table 12.2. Mean Applicant Responses Under Two Conditions of Interviewer Immediacy; Experiment 2

Response	Reliability	Nonimmediate	Immediate	F	P
Applicant performance					
Rated performance	.68	1.44	2.22	7.96	<.01
Rated demeanor	.86	1.62	3.02	16.46	<.001
Immediacy behaviors					
Distance	—	72.78 inches	56.98 inches	9.19	<.01
Speech error rate	.74	5.01 errors/min	3.33 errors/min	3.40	<.10
Self-reported mood and attitudes					
Mood	—	3.77	5.97	1.34	n.s.
Interviewer friendliness	—	4.33	6.60	22.91	<.001
Interviewer adequacy	—	−1.07	1.53	8.64	<.01

feel less positively after their interviews, and (2) hold less positive attitudes toward the interviewer himself. These expectations were only partially supported (see Table 12.2). Although subjects in the Nonimmediate condition reported less positive moods than subjects in the Immediate condition, this difference was not statistically reliable.

Subjects in the less immediate condition did, however, rate their interviewers to be less friendly ($F = 22.91$; $df = 1/28$; $p < .001$) and less adequate overall ($F = 8.64$; $df = 1/28$; $p < .01$) than subjects in the more immediate condition.

Discussion

Results from the two experiments provide clear support for the two hypotheses, and offer inferential evidence for the general notion that self-fulfilling prophecies can and do occur in interracial interactions.

The results of Experiment 1 indicated that black applicants were, in fact, treated to less immediacy than their white counterparts. Goffman's (1963) conception of blackness as a stigmatizing trait in Anglo–American society is, thus, given experimental support—insofar as that classification predicts avoidance behaviors in interactions with normals. These results may also be viewed as extending the stigma effect documented by Kleck and his associates with handicapped persons.

That the differential treatment black and white applicants received in Experiment 1 can influence the performance and attitudes of job candidates was clearly demonstrated in Experiment 2. In that experiment those applicants treated similarly to the way Blacks were treated in Experiment 1, performed less well, reciprocated less immediacy, and found their interviewers to be less adequate. Taken together the two experiments provide evidence for the assertion that nonverbal immediacy cues mediate, in part, the performance of an applicant in a job interview situation. Further, the experiments suggest that the model of a self-fulfilling prophecy, mediated by nonverbal cues, (1) is applicable to this setting, and (2) can account, in part, for the less inadequate performances of black applicants (cf. Sattler, 1970).

Social scientists have often tended to focus their attention for such phenomena as unemployment in black communities on the dispositions of the disinherited. Such an approach has been termed "victim analysis" for its preoccupation with the wounds, defects, and personalities of the victimized as an explanation for social problems (Ryan, 1971). The present results suggest that analyses of black-white interactions, particularly in the area of job-seeking Blacks in white society, might profit if it were assumed that the "problem" of black performance resides not entirely within the Blacks, but rather within the interaction setting itself.

REFERENCES

Darley, J. M., Lewis, L. D., & Glucksberg, S. (1972). *Stereotype persistence and change among college students: One more time.* Unpublished manuscript, Princeton University.

Goffman, E. (1963). *Stigma: Notes on the management of spoiled identity.* Englewood Cliffs, NJ: Prentice-Hall.

Jones, R. E., & Cooper, J. (1971). Mediation of experimenter effects. *Journal of Personality and Social Psychology, 20,* 70–74.

Jones, E. E., & Nisbett, R. E. (1971). The actor and the observer: Divergent perceptions of the causes of behavior. In E. E. Jones, D. E. Kanouse, H. H. Kelley, R. E. Nisbett, S. Valins, & B. Weiner (Eds.), *Attribution: Perceiving the causes of behavior.* New York: General Learning Press.

Kleck, R. E. (1968). Physical stigma and nonverbal cues emitted in face-to-face interactions. *Human Relations, 21,* 19–28.

Kleck, R. E., Buck, P. L., Goller, W. L., London, R. S., Pfeiffer, J. R., & Vukcevic, D. P. (1968) Effects of stigmatizing conditions on the use of personal space. *Psychological Reports, 23,* 111–118.

Kleck, R. E., & Nuessle, W. (1968). Congruence between indicative and communicative functions of eye contact in interpersonal relations. *British Journal of Social and Clinical Psychology, 7,* 241–246.

Kleck, R. E., Ono, H., & Hastorf, A. H. (1966). The effects of physical deviance upon face-to-face interaction. *Human Relations, 19,* 425–436.

Mehrabian, A. (1967). Orientation behaviors and nonverbal attitude communication. *Journal of Communication, 17,* 324–332.

Mehrabian, A. (1968). Inference of attitudes from the posture, orientation, and distance of a communicator. *Journal of Consulting and Clinical Psychology, 32,* 296–308.

Mehrabian, A. (1969). Some referents and measures of nonverbal behavior. *Behavior Research Methods and Instrumentation, 1,* 203–207.

Merton, R. K. (1957). *Social theory and social structure.* New York: Free Press.

Rosenfeld, H. M. (1967). Nonverbal reciprocation of approval: An experimental analysis. *Journal of Experimental and Social Psychology, 3,* 102–111.

Rosenthal, R. (1971). Teacher Expectations. In G. S. Lesser (Ed.), *Psychology and the educational process.* Glenview, IL: Scott, Foresman.

Ryan, W. (1971). *Blaming the victim.* New York: Pantheon.

Sattler, J. (1970). Racial "experimenter effects" in experimentation, testing, interviewing and psychotherapy. *Psychological Bulletin, 73,* 136–160.

Compensating for Stigma: Obese and Nonobese Women's Reactions to Being Visible

Carol T. Miller and Esther D. Rothblum • University of Vermont
Diane Felicio • Goddard College
Pamela Brand • State University of New York at Oswego

The hypothesis that obese women compensate for the prejudice of others was tested by having obese and nonobese women converse by telephone with someone who they believed, correctly or incorrectly, could or could not see them. Partners rated obese women's social skills negatively when the women were visible (thus activating the partners' prejudice) but thought they were not. Obese women rated themselves as more likable and socially skilled than nonobese women did when the women thought they were visible to female partners. Judges' ratings of the women's contribution to the conversation indicated that there were no obvious differences in the impressions created by their verbal or nonverbal behaviors. Results support the hypothesis that obese women who were aware of the need to compensate for their partners' reactions to their appearance were able to do so.

In an article commemorating the 30th anniversary of Marilyn Monroe's death, the *New York Times* speculated that one key to her immortality as a cultural symbol is that she never got fat. Obesity is a condition so stigmatizing that people, especially women, would do almost anything to avoid it (Crandall & Biernat, 1990; DeJong & Kleck, 1986; Rothblum, 1992). Stereotyes about obese people and people with endomorphic (fat) physiques are pervasive (Lerner & Gellert, 1969; Rothblum, Miller, & Garbutt, 1988; Ryckman et al., 1991), and people blame the obese for their condition (Crandall, 1991; Weiner, Perry, & Magnusson, 1988). The reason is likely that our society maintains the belief that body weight is controllable, despite accumulating evidence that it is not (Rodin, Silberstein, & Striegel-Moore, 1984; Stunkard et al., 1986). In a society that prizes physical attractiveness and in which being thin is virtually a prerequisite for being attractive, the obese may face formidable barriers to establishing and maintaining social relationships.

Research has shown that people who have negative expectations about another alter their behavior toward that person in ways that often create a self-fulfilling prophecy (Deaux & Major, 1987; D. T. Miller & Turnbull, 1986). Self-fulfilling prophecies are insidious because the targets of such expectations become caught in a web in which their responses to others' treatment of them can affect how they think about themselves. Crocker and Major (1989) reviewed the many theoretical perspectives that converge to suggest that negative expectations should ultimately have deleterious consequences for the self-esteem of stigmatized people. Moreover, developmental theorists have pointed out that children who are perceived as physically unattractive may have repeated experiences with rejection and discrimination and may therefore have fewer opportunities for social interaction and social skill development. The cumulative effect of expectancy confirmation processes is the development of real, lifelong differences between attractive and unattractive people (Adams, 1977; Jarvie, Lahey, Graziano, & Framer, 1983; Langlois & Stephan, 1981).

The hypothesis that stereotypes can have long-term effects on the social skills of physically unattractive people was tested in a study by Goldman and Lewis (1975), who reported that unattractive college students were evaluated less positively than attractive students by telephone partners who never saw them. Similarly, C. T. Miller, Rothblum, Barbour, Brand, and Felicio (1990) found that obese women who spoke by telephone to another person received lower ratings on social skills and likability from their telephone partners than nonobese women did, even though the partners never saw the women. These findings suggest that the social behaviors of unattractive and overweight people are negatively affected by their experiences with the reactions others have to their appearance.

Other research suggests that this may be too pessimistic a view of the lives of obese women and other stigmatized people. One clue that this view is not the whole story is that stigmatized people, including women, African Americans, obese people, and children with mental retardation, generally do not have low self-esteem (Crocker & Major, 1989). In a recent meta-analysis of the correlates of physical attractiveness, Feingold (1992) reported that self-esteem is not correlated with objective physical attractiveness, although it is correlated with self-rated attractiveness. Beyond the empirical evidence that being a member of a stigmatized group does not lead to lowered self-esteem as would be predicted by expectancy confirmation theories, there are other reasons to suspect that stigmatized people may somehow overcome people's prejudice against them.

Research on self-affirmation or self-enhancement suggests that people in general strive to maintain a positive image of themselves and go to great lengths to do so (Steele, 1988). One strategy they use is to compensate for undesirable traits or behaviors by bolstering or inflating other aspects of themselves. For example, Steele (1975) found that people who were criticized were more willing to volunteer for a worthy cause than people who received no criticism, even if what they were criticized about was irrelevant to volunteering. His explanation for this finding is that criticism threatened self-esteem, and people compensated for this by volunteering. In another experimental demonstration of compensation, Baumeister (1982) found that male students who knew that their partners had negative information about one aspect of their personalities did not try to refute the negative information when asked to describe themselves but did describe themselves positively on personality characteristics unrelated to their alleged shortcoming. An important feature of the self-affirmation process is that, as demonstrated by the experiments just described, individuals need not refute, correct, or deny the characteristic or behavior that threatens self-image. Compensation is flexible, so that the affirmation of qualities or values that are unrelated to the threat can restore self-worth.

Steele (1988) pointed out that membership in a stigmatized group poses two types of threat. Discrimination threatens the welfare of stigmatized people by denying them equal access to resources. Prejudice also threatens self-regard because stigmatized people are aware of the negative expectations others have of them. Research on self-affirmation suggests that stigmatized people, like anybody who faces a threat to self-regard, will try to buttress the integrity of the self by focusing on or bolstering socially desirable aspects of the self. This suggests that obese people will emphasize aspects of themselves other than appearance when they interact in situations in which they believe their weight will be a handicap.

In addition, research on self-verification by Swann and his colleagues indicates that people try to disconfirm information and expectations others have about them that are inconsistent with their self-concepts (see Swann, 1984, for a review). Swann (1984) pointed out that it is not surprising that self-verification often overcomes the effects of expectations, because in many situations the other has only just formed an expectation, but the target of that expectation may have a lifetime of experience with a particular self-concept.

Research on the efforts people make to maintain positive or consistent self-concepts has not been used much to understand stigmatized people. One reason is that the perspective of the stigmatized person has been neglected in prior research. With few exceptions (Crocker, Voelkl, Testa, & Major, 1991; Harris, Milich, Corbitt, Hoover, & Brady, 1992), researchers have been more likely to study stigmatized people as the targets or objects of prejudice than as active participants in social interaction.

In addition, Graham (1992) and Harris et al. (1992) pointed out that researchers rarely study people who are actually stigmatized. In much of the research on confirmation of expectations arising from stereotypes, the targets of the stereotyped expectations were not actually stigmatized people. Rather, they were college students who were randomly assigned to be labeled as members of a stigmatized group. This procedure is ideal for experimental control, but it might miss some important skills and strategies that people who are actually stigmatized have learned or developed to cope with negative expectations.

For example, in an experiment in which White male undergraduates were told that the person with whom they were about to interact had been informed that they were either a homosexual or a mental patient, Farina, Allen, and Saul (1968) reported that one student who thought his partner had been told he was a homosexual became "obviously alarmed" when his partner put his arm around his shoulders to assist him in operating the equipment for the task they were performing. As this example illustrates, in such experiments the supposedly stigmatized students may be confronting for the first time in their lives what it is like to be stigmatized.

In other studies, college women have been randomly assigned to be labeled as a man or a woman (Skrypnek & Snyder, 1982), college women unselected for physical attractiveness have been labeled by way of a photograph that supposedly depicted them as being beautiful or ugly (Snyder, Tanke, & Berscheid, 1977), and White male college students were randomly assigned to interact with an interviewer who had been trained to treat them as other college students had previously be-haved when they interviewed a Black or White confederate (Word, Zanna, & Cooper, 1974). Swann (1984) pointed out that most compelling demonstrations of behavioral confirmation have involved expectancies arising from stereotypes. But one reason these demonstrations produced such dramatic results may be that they involved experimental designs in which nonstigmatized college students played the role of a stigmatized person.

Finally, in many studies of expectancy confirmation, the person who has been assigned to play the role of a stigmatized person is not aware of this fact. This is in sharp contrast to the situations stigmatized people actually confront, in which they are usually well aware that they are members of a stigmatized group and they know or suspect that others will react to them accordingly. Hilton and Darley (1985), who were among the first to recognize the importance of awareness, informed some subjects, but not others, that another person with whom they were going to converse expected them to have a cold personality. The experimenters also manipulated whether the other person actually had been led to believe that the target had a cold personality. Results showed that a self-fulfilling prophecy effect occurred only in the condition in which targets were *unaware* of what had been said about them.

Results of other studies also show that when interacting with a person who was expected to be unfriendly, students compensated by increasing their own friendliness rather than reciprocating their partner's expected chilliness (Bond, 1972; Ickes, Patterson, Rajecki, & Tanford, 1982). People who know they must engage in an interaction with an unpleasant person are highly motivated to avoid unpleasantness, and so compensation will be the preferred strategy provided that there is some hope that the other person will respond to the friendly overture in a positive manner (Curtis & Miller, 1986; D. T. Miller & Turnbull, 1986; Neuberg, Judice, Virdin, & Carrillo, 1993).

Research on self-affirmation, self-verification, the importance of awareness in whether expectations become self-fulfilling prophecies, and the compensatory strategies people use to avert potentially unpleasant social situations suggests that there are a variety of ways in which people in general and stigmatized people in particular might cope with situations in which others have negative expectations about them.

There are also strategies that are uniquely available to members of stigmatized groups. In a review of a large volume of research, Crocker and Major (1989) concluded that members of stigmatized groups have devised strategies to protect themselves from the adverse consequences that stereotyping and prejudice would otherwise have for their self-esteem. People can attribute negative reactions from others to prejudice rather than to their own abilities, traits, or behaviors; they can limit social comparisons to other members of their group rather than comparing themselves with members of more advantaged groups; and they can selectively devalue characteristics on which their group is evaluated negatively.

Research on such self-protective strategies is just beginning, but it has shown that African Americans, women, and obese women attribute feedback received during an experiment to race, gender, and weight, respectively (Baumeister, Kahn, & Tice, 1990; Crocker, Cornwell, & Major, 1993; Crocker et al., 1991). Surveys indicate that obese people believe that weight interferes with their social activities (Rothblum, Brand, Miller, & Oetjen, 1990; Tiggemann & Rothblum, 1988). However, Crocker et al. (1993) suggested that for obese women, unlike other stigmatized people, attribution of negative social feedback to their stigma may not serve to buffer self-esteem, because they blame themselves for being overweight and therefore do not blame others for disliking them.

This suggests that obese people may need other strategies to protect themselves from the consequences of prejudice. Although the present experiment is the first to investigate this issue, studies of the social interactions of physically unattractive people offer some relevant insights. In a study in which college students kept diaries about their social interactions, Reis et al. (1982) found that physical attractiveness was positively correlated with the quality of women's social relationships, that social assertiveness and social competence were also positively correlated with the quality of women's social relationships, but that attractiveness was not correlated with women's social competence and was negatively related to social assertiveness. In interpreting their findings, Reis et al. suggested that attractive and unattractive women establish satisfying social relationships in different ways. Attractive women rely on their looks, and less attractive women learn to be socially assertive.

Similarly, Major and Sherman (1976) found that low-attractive women tended to perform better with a partner in both competitive and noncompetitive cognitive tasks than attractive women. They suggested that attractive women may be accustomed to receiving social rewards as a result of their looks and that unattractive women may feel they have to try harder to compensate for their lack of beauty. Results of a study by Dion and Stein (1978) support this suggestion. Physically attractive and unattractive fifth- and sixth-graders tried to persuade another child to eat a cracker that had been coated with a bitter-tasting substance. Attractive girls were successful with boys, even though they made the fewest influence attempts and were judged by raters as least persistent and forceful. Unattractive girls were not successful with boys or girls but, consistent with Reis and associates' findings, they displayed a relatively assertive persuasive style. They made the most influence attempts overall and were rated as persistent. These might be the rudiments of a repertoire of behaviors that could eventually enable them to compensate for the detrimental effects of stereotypes about attractiveness.

Although compensation could be an important tool in stigmatized people's battle against the adverse consequences of stereotyping, it may also have some detrimental effects on performance and motivation. If stigmatized people are more motivated to perform well if they think the expectations of others will be a barrier to positive social interaction, they may consequently exert less effort when they think stereotypes will not be important. Because stigma creates considerable ambiguity about what explains negative social interactions (Crocker et al., 1991, 1993), stigmatized people may underestimate the effort and skills they would need to exert if their social interactions were uncontaminated by stereotypes and prejudice.

This reasoning suggests an alternative explanation for the findings that unattractive college students (Goldman & Lewis, 1975) and obese women (C. T. Miller et al., 1990) made relatively poor impressions during a telephone conversation even though their raters had no information about their appearance. Results of both studies have been interpreted as support for the view that appearance-related prejudices prevent people deemed unattractive from developing social skills. However, it is also possible that because stigmatized people must learn to compensate for their stigma, they may sometimes fail to recognize that the absence of stigma by itself does not guarantee smooth social relations. If the unattractive and overweight participants in these studies underestimated the level of social skills that nonstigmatized people must use to establish good relations, the relatively poor impressions they created on people who could not see them could result from not using, rather than from not having, the social skills to interact in a likable fashion.

In the present study, the hypothesis that obese women may be able to compensate for prejudice against fat people was tested by having obese and nonobese women participate in a brief telephone conversation with a man or a woman. We manipulated the telephone partners' expectations about the women by varying whether they could see the women on a television monitor during the conversation. Regardless of whether their telephone partners actually could see them, the women were led to believe either that their partners could see them or that their partners could not see them.

The hypothesis that obese women protect themselves or compensate for the effects of others' negative reactions to their weight predicts that the women's beliefs about whether their partners can see them should affect their self-descriptions and behavior. Research on self-affirmation suggests that obese women might affirm their self-worth by emphasizing desirable aspects of themselves other than their appearance. Research on self-verification and the efforts people in general make to disconfirm negative expectations suggests that obese women should also try to behave in a more socially desirable fashion when they think they can be seen than when they think they cannot be seen. If prejudice against fat people constitutes a threat to self-esteem, obese women who believe they are visible to their partners should be motivated to disconfirm negative expectations and/or enhance their self-description.

A corollary of this hypothesis is that obese women who think they are not visible to their partners may create a more negative impression than nonobese women. This follows from the reasoning that the need to compensate may lead stigmatized people to underestimate the social skills required in interactions that are unaffected by stigma. It also follows from previous research in which unattractive students (Goldman & Lewis, 1975) and overweight women (C. T. Miller et al., 1990)

were evaluated relatively negatively when they were not visible to others.

Experiment 1

Method

DESIGN

Obese and nonobese women had a brief telephone conversation with a man or a woman. All the women were videotaped, and both the women and their telephone partners were audiotaped. Telephone partners' expectations about the women were manipulated by allowing half of them to see the women they spoke to on a video monitor (actually visible condition). The remaining partners conversed without seeing the women on the monitor (actually not visible condition). The women's beliefs about whether their appearance could affect their partners' reactions to them were manipulated by telling half of them that their partners could watch their behavior on a monitor (perceived visible condition) and telling the rest that their partners could not see them (perceived not visible condition).

In addition to the conditions just described, we included control groups of obese women and of nonobese women who were audiotaped, but not videotaped, during the conversation. Their telephone partners, half of whom were male and half female, were unable to see the women, and the women knew this. The reason for including these control conditions is that all women in the experimental conditions were videotaped. This was necessary because otherwise the effects of the experimental manipulations of actual and perceived visibility would be confounded with behavioral changes that might result from the videotaping itself (see Wicklund, 1975, for a review of theory and research relevant to this issue).

The women were randomly assigned to all experimental and control conditions, including random assignment to a male or female telephone partner.

SUBJECTS

Women. The women were 77 obese and 78 nonobese women who were recruited for a study of "women's experiences across the life span" through advertisements in local newspapers. The advertisements stated that we needed women with different experiences, including "married, single, divorced, overweight, etc." The women who answered the advertisement were screened by telephone to determine whether they fit our definitions of obesity and nonobesity): Women who were at least 20% more than the midpoint of the weight range for medium build for their height (according to Metropolitan Life Insurance Company, tables) were classified as obese. Those who weighed within 10% of the average weight for their height were classified as nonobese. The telephone interviews followed a standard script, and the questions about the women's weight were embedded in other questions about their age, place of birth, and so on. Each woman received $20 for her participation, which lasted approximately 90 min.

On average, the obese women were somewhat older ($M = 43.7$ years) than the nonobese women ($M = 39.9$ years), $F(1, 155) = 6.62$, $p < .02$, and reported completing fewer years of college than the nonobese women ($Ms = 3.6$ and 4.4, respectively); where 3 = some college education, 4 = completed college, and 5 = some postgraduate education), $F(1, 155) = 14.47$, $p < .0002$.[1] Both obese and nonobese women reported having individual incomes in the $10,000–$20,000 range and household incomes in the $20,000–$30,000 range. All the obese women indicated that they were overweight and, on average they thought that they were 45.8 lb. overweight. Only 50% of the nonobese women thought that the question about how many pounds overweight they were applied to them, and those who answered the question indicated, on average, that they were only 8.8 lb. overweight. Dieting to lose weight was more prevalent among obese (49%) than nonobese (21%) women, $F(1, 149) = 14.34$, $p < .0002$. Scale weight measures obtained at the completion of the experiment indicated that obese women were, on average, 45.5% above the ideal weight for their height according to Metropolitan Life height and weight tables whereas nonobese women, on average, were 2% underweight for their height.

There were 7 obese and 6 nonobese women who attended an experimental session but declined to

participate, and there were an additional 14 experimental sessions in which data could not be collected or had to be discarded. These sessions included 2 in which male telephone partners were unwilling or unable to participate, 7 in which there was equipment failure, 1 session in which the woman and her partner met by accident before the session began, 2 sessions in which the woman appeared to be disoriented, and 2 sessions in which the partner revealed whether the woman was actually visible.

The distribution of obese and nonobese women across experimental and control conditions produced cell sizes (collapsed across telephone partner gender) that ranged from 13 to 17. Within each condition, male and female telephone partners were represented in approximately equal numbers, with the largest difference (7 male and 10 female partners) in the nonobese woman/actually visible/perceived not visible condition.

Telephone Partners. We also recruited, through newspaper advertisements for a study of first impressions, 76 men and 79 women to serve as telephone partners. These people received $10 for their participation, which lasted approximately 1 hr.

The telephone partners' answers to questions they completed at the end of the experiment showed that their mean age was 37.6 years for men and 39.1 years for women. On average, the men had completed four-year college degrees and had individual incomes in the $20,000–$30,000 per year range and household incomes in the $30,000–$40,000 range. The women, on average, had some college education, individual incomes slightly less than $10,000 per year, and household incomes in the $30,000–$40,000 range. In general, both male and female telephone partners perceived themselves to be average weight to slightly overweight. The only significant difference between male and female telephone partners was that males reported significantly higher individual incomes, $F(1, 153) = 20.31$, $p < .0001$.

PROCEDURE

The women were scheduled to arrive at the experiment 15 min before their telephone partners to preclude their meeting by chance before the experiment began. When they arrived, a female experimenter told the women that they would have a telephone conversation with a man or woman

---

[1]The finding that obese women reported fewer years of college than nonobese women is consistent with research showing that obese women receive less parental financial support for higher education (Crandall, 1991).

from the local community. They were asked to permit the experimenter to record them on audiotape and, except for women in the audiotape-only control condition, were also asked to allow the experimenter to videotape them for later analysis.[2] Those assigned to the perceived visible conditions were told that the camera was connected to a monitor in their partner's room so that the partner could see as well as hear them. Those assigned to the perceived not visible conditions were told that they were being recorded for later analysis but that their partner could not see them. Regardless of what the women were told, partners in the actually visible conditions could see the women on a monitor connected to the video camera by a cable. Partners in the actually not visible conditions could not see the women on the monitor.

At the same time, a second female experimenter was preparing the telephone partner for the conversation. The partner was told that he or she would be talking on the telephone with a woman from the local area and that the purpose of the experiment was to study the formation of first impressions.

Before the telephone conversation began, telephone partners in the actually visible conditions watched the woman briefly (for approximately 10 s) on the monitor. The experimenter explained that this was to make certain the equipment was working properly. During this brief period, the woman was instructed to sit quietly while the equipment was being checked. Immediately after this brief exposure to the woman's appearance, the telephone partners completed a conversation rating form on the basis of their expectations of what she would be like, using their first impressions. Telephone partners in the actually not visible conditions were simply asked to complete the conversation rating form, knowing only that the woman with whom they were about to speak was from the local community.

The conversation rating form consisted of items to assess partners' perceptions of how likable, socially skilled, and physically attractive the women were. Each item asked the partner to rate how true a statement was about the woman (1 = *not at all*

true, 5 = *very true*). The phrase "During the conversation, do you think your partner will be . . ." introduced the items, which were randomly ordered. The liking items were "friendly," "nice for you to have as a friend," "likable," "a potentially good co-worker for you," and "able to make a good impression on you." The social skills items were "able to get off to a good start in the conversation," "socially skilled during the conversation," "a good conversationalist," "poised," "competent," "able to put you at ease," "easy for you to talk with," and "able to end the conversation well." The physical attractiveness items were "comfortable with her physical appearance," "physically attractive," and "someone who has a good body." Composite likability, social skills, and physical attractiveness scores were computed by averaging across items.

The same items, reworded so that they referred to self, were included on a rating form the women completed about themselves before the conversation began. For example, in the phrase that introduced the items, *you* was substituted for *your partner*. Each item asked the woman to rate how she thought she would be during the conversation.

The women and their partners were instructed to try to get to know the other person by conversing on the telephone. To protect confidentiality, both parties were instructed to use their first names only or, if they preferred, a fictitious first name. In addition, all telephone partners were told to give a noncommittal answer if the woman asked whether they could see her, regardless of whether they could in fact see her. As mentioned above, only two partners were unable to follow this instruction, and data from these sessions were excluded from all analyses.

The women and their partners were allowed 5 min to converse about whatever they liked. The experimenters were not present during the conversation. After it was over, the experimenters gave both the women and their partners, still seated in their respective rooms, a conversation rating form to complete. These questionnaires were identical to the ones they had completed just before the conversation, except that the questions were in the past tense. Composite scores for likability, social skills, and attractiveness were computed in the same way as for the preconversation ratings.

At this point, the women and their partners were debriefed separately and given the option of erasing any record made of their behavior. During the

---

[2]The present experiment is part of a larger investigation of obese and nonobese women's social skills and social relationships. At the beginning of the experiment, the women filled out a number of questionnaire measures about their social relationships. The results of these measures are reported elsewhere (Miller, Rothblum, Brand, & Felicio, 1995).

debriefing, the women were photographed in a standard full-body shot and were weighed. None of the women voiced any suspicions about the manipulations of actual or perceived visibility to their partners, and none chose to erase recordings of the conversation.

Results

OVERVIEW

We used analysis of covariance (ANCOVA) to examine ratings made by the women and their telephone partners. The covariates in all analyses were the women's age and education, and all means are adjusted for these covariates. The women's weight, their actual visibility to their telephone partners, and perceived visibility to their partners were used as between-subjects factors in all analyses of the experimental conditions. In addition, the audio-tape-only control condition (in which obese and nonobese women conversed without being video-taped) was analyzed separately with ANCOVAs in which the women's weight was the only be-tween-groups factor.

PARTNERS' RATINGS OF THE WOMEN

The hypothesis that telephone partners would ste-reotype obese women predicts an interaction be-tween the women's weight and their actual vis-ibility to their partners. As might be expected, this interaction occurred in partners' ratings of the women's physical attractiveness; preconversation $F(1, 107) = 3.42$, $p = .07$; postconversation $F(1, 108) = 6.66$, $p < .01$.[3]

Simple effects comparisons between partners' postconversation means indicated that partners of obese women gave lower attractiveness ratings than partners of nonobese women in the actually visible condition ($Ms = 3.2$ and 3.7), $F(1, 109) = 6.75$, $p = .01$, but not in the actually not visible condition ($Ms = 3.7$ and 3.5), $F(1, 109) = 0.89$, $p = .35$. In addition, partners of obese women rated them as significantly less attractive when they could see them than when they could not, $F(1, 109) = 6.61$, $p = .01$, whereas actual visibility of nonobese women to their partners had no effect

on partners' postconversation ratings of their at-tractiveness, $F(1, 109) = 1.06$, $p = .31$.

Simple effects tests on preconversation attrac-tiveness ratings showed that partners of obese women who could see them gave significantly lower attractiveness ratings than partners of obese women who could not see them, $F(1, 110) = 3.77$, $p = .05$, whereas nonobese women's visibility to their partners did not affect their attractiveness ratings, $F(1, 110) = 0.18$, $p = .67$. However, in nei-ther visibility condition did partners of obese women make significantly lower ratings of their attractiveness than partners of nonobese women ($Ms = 3.0$ and 3.2, respectively, when partners could see the women; $Ms = 3.3$ and 3.1, respec-tively, when partners could not see the women), $Fs(1, 110) \leq 2.28$, $ps \geq .13$. The fact that partners had stronger reactions to the women's appearance after the conversation was over than before it be-gan may be attributable to the greater amount of exposure partners had to the women's appearance when they completed the postconversation ratings.

These findings suggest that the partners noticed the women's appearance and evaluated the obese women's attractiveness relatively negatively, es-pecially after the conversation was over. Analysis of the partners' perceptions of the women's likabil-ity and social skills indicated that the women's actual visibility to the partners did not by itself re-sult in negative ratings of obese women. There was instead a significant interaction between the women's weight, actual visibility, and perceived visibility on the partners' postconversation ratings of the women's social skills, $F(1, 108) = 4.23$, $p < .04$.

Simple effects F tests revealed that obese women received relatively low ratings on social skill when their partners could see them, but only if the women thought their partners could *not* see them (see Table 13.1). The mean rating by partners of obese women in the actually visible/perceived not visible condition was lower than that by partners of nonobese women in this condition, $F(1, 110) = 4.41$, $p = .04$. The mean partner rating in the obese woman/actually visible/perceived not visible con-dition was also lower than the mean partner rating in the obese woman/actually visible/perceived vis-ible condition, $F(1, 110) = 3.02$, $p = .09$, and in the obese woman/actually not visible/perceived not visible condition, $F(1, 110) = 9.53$, $p = .003$. There were no other significant effects in partners' pre- or postconversation ratings of the women's likabil-ity and social skills.

---

[3]Degrees of freedom differ slightly for different analyses because of missing data and differing software package criteria for inclusion of subjects with missing data.

TABLE 13.1. Partners' Mean Postconversation Ratings of Women's Social Skills

	Actually Visible		Actually Not Visible	
	Perceived Visible	Perceived Not Visible	Perceived Visible	Perceived Not Visible
Obese women	4.2 (13)	3.7 (13)	4.4 (16)	4.5 (15)
Nonobese women	4.1 (17)	4.2 (17)	4.5 (15)	4.2 (14)

Note: Ratings could range from 1 (least favorable) to 5 (most favorable). Means are adjusted for women's age and education. Numbers in parentheses are cell *n*s.

The finding that it was obese women who were unaware that their partners could see them who received relatively low ratings on social skills suggests that obese women may need to use compensatory strategies to overcome the effect of their stigmatized appearance on others' reactions to them. Telephone partner perceptions of obese and nonobese women in the control condition in which the women were audiotaped (but not videotaped) supply some additional insight on this point. In this condition, the women were aware that they were not visible during the conversation to their partners and would not be visible later to other people. It is interesting, therefore, that partners' postconversation ratings of women in the control condition revealed that partners of obese women liked them less ($M = 4.1$) than partners of nonobese women ($M = 4.6$), $F(1, 29) = 5.86$, $p = .02$. Partners of obese and nonobese women in the control condition did not differ in their ratings of the women's social skills (Ms = 4.2 and 4.5, respectively), $F(1, 29) = 2.36$, $p = .13$, or attractiveness (Ms = 3.5 and 3.7, respectively), $F(1, 29) = 1.13$, $p = .30$, although obese women did tend to receive lower ratings on both measures.

Because partners in the control condition did not see the women before the conversation began, we included the partners' preconversation ratings of the women (which were based solely on the information that they were about to speak to a woman from the local area) as a covariate in the ANCOVAs in addition to the women's age and education. This provides a more sensitive test of the impressions created by the women's behavior because it controls for preexisting and theoretically irrelevant individual differences among partners' preconversation impressions.

Finally, we redid all the foregoing analyses of the telephone partner ratings with telephone partner gender included as an additional between-groups factor. There were no significant effects that qualified any of the effects described above, all *p*s > .67.

WOMEN'S SELF-RATINGS

In the control condition, the women's preconversation self-ratings showed that obese women predicted that they would be less likable ($M = 3.5$) than nonobese women did ($M = 3.8$), $F(1, 28) = 4.69$, $p = .04$. This finding is of special interest because the telephone partner ratings discussed above showed that, in the control condition, the telephone partners of obese women did, in fact, like them less than the telephone partners of nonobese women. This suggests that the obese women may have been less motivated to make a good impression when they could not be seen. Prior to the conversation, obese women in the control condition also rated themselves as less attractive ($M = 2.5$) than nonobese women did ($M = 3.6$), $F(1, 30) = 16.43$, $p = .0003$. There were no other significant differences between the ratings made by obese and nonobese women, and telephone partner gender had no significant effects on ratings made by women in the control condition.

The hypothesis that obese women compensate for prejudice against fat people suggests that, in the experimental conditions, obese women should try to be or claim to be more likable and socially skilled when they think they are visible. The expected interaction between the women's weight and perceived visibility was not significant for any of the women's self-ratings. However, inclusion of telephone partner gender in the analysis revealed that the predicted results did occur for women who spoke to female partners. That is, there was a weight by perceived visibility by partner gender interaction for women's pre- and postconversation self-ratings of likability, Fs(1, 104) = 10.33, $p = .002$ (pre), and 4.30, $p = .04$ (post), social skills, Fs(1, 104 = 5.11, $p = .03$ (pre), and 3.23, $p = .08$ (post), and attractiveness, Fs(1, 104) = 5.68, $p = .02$ (pre), and 7.14, $p = .009$ (post).

As seen in Table 13.2, when the women spoke to female telephone partners, self-ratings of obese and nonobese women did not differ when the women thought they could *not* be seen, whereas obese women rated themselves as more likable and socially skilled than nonobese women did when the women thought they *could* be seen by their female partners. These differences between obese and nonobese women's ratings are attributable to two trends. Obese women who thought they were visible tended to inflate their self-ratings (relative to obese women who did not think they were visible), whereas nonobese women tended to deflate their self-ratings when they thought they were visible.

Obese women rated themselves as less physically attractive than nonobese women did, but only when the women thought they were not visible to their female partners. The difference between attractiveness ratings made by women in the perceived visible and perceived not visible conditions was not significant for either obese women or nonobese women.

Obese women who spoke to male partners consistently rated themselves as less physically attractive than nonobese women did. Moreover, obese women who spoke to male partners rated themselves as significantly less physically attractive in the perceived visible condition than in the perceived not visible condition. Otherwise, the ratings of women who spoke to male partners revealed only that nonobese women rated themselves (both before and after the conversation) as more socially skilled in the perceived visible condition than in the perceived not visible condition, and before the conversation began, nonobese women in the perceived visible condition also rated themselves as significantly more socially skilled than obese women in this condition did.

SUMMARY AND DISCUSSION

These findings indicate that the perception of being visible altered what obese and nonobese women said about their behavior and, depending on

Table 13.2: Women's Mean Self-Ratings and Simple Effects Comparisons for Women's Weight and Perceived Visibility, Experiment 1

Condition and Rating	Preconversation Ratings			Postconversation Ratings		
	Perceived Visible	Perceived Not Visible	Effect of Visibility F =	Perceived Visible	Perceived Not Visible	Effect of Visibility F =
Female partners						
Likability						
Obese women	3.9	3.7	1.32	4.5	4.1	3.40*
Nonobese women	3.5	4.1	10.03***	3.8	4.3	5.03**
Effects of weight F =	4.87**	3.73*		9.74***	<1	
Social skills						
Obese women	3.8	3.5	1.28	4.1	4.1	1.60
Nonobese women	3.4	3.6	1.12	3.7	4.1	2.22
Effects of weight F =	3.38*	<1		9.06**	<1	
Attractiveness						
Obese women	2.8	2.5	1.08	3.3	3.0	1.84
Nonobese women	3.1	3.6	2.14	3.3	3.8	2.66
Effects of weight F =	1.67	14.68***		<1	8.14***	
Male partners						
Likability						
Obese women	3.5	3.6	<1	4.1	4.0	<1
Nonobese women	3.7	3.5	1.76	4.1	3.9	<1
Effects of weight F =	2.44	<1		<1	<1	
Social skill						
Obese women	3.4	3.4	<1	4.2	3.9	1.62
Nonobese women	3.7	3.2	6.24***	4.2	3.7	5.55**
Effects of weight F =	3.34	<1		<1	<1	
Attractiveness						
Obese women	2.0	2.7	4.00**	2.4	3.1	5.81**
Nonobese women	3.5	3.5	<1	3.6	3.1	<1
Effect of weight F =	27.66***	5.99**		15.64***	2.11	

Note: Ratings could range from 1 (least favorable) to 5 (most favorable).
* $p < .07$; ** $p < .05$; *** $p < .01$.

whether the partners actually could see the women, also altered how the women were perceived by their partners. This raises the question of what the women did to affect their partners' perceptions of them.

Experiment 2

We examined the women's behavior by asking naive judges to indicate how likable, socially skilled, and attractive they thought the women were after reviewing the audiotapes or the videotapes of the women's contribution to the conversation. We chose this route because there are innumerable specific verbal and nonverbal behaviors that might account for the impressions that the women created on their partners, and the fact that the interaction we studied was not face to face creates difficulties in interpreting many specific variables such as eye gaze and body orientation. Finally, we believed it was more important to determine the general domain (verbal vs. nonverbal) in which the women's behavior may have differed than to measure a large number of behaviors in the hope that some number of them might reveal how the women altered their behavior.

Design and Hypotheses

Having judges evaluate either the audiotapes or the videotapes provides an indication of whether verbal behaviors, such as what the women spoke about, or nonverbal behaviors, such as facial expression, were responsible for the impressions the women created on their partners. An obvious problem with simply comparing ratings based on audiotapes with those based on videotapes is that judges are subject to the same prejudices as everyone else. Ratings made of videotapes are likely to reflect judges' reactions to the women's weight as well as the women's behavior. For this reason, the audiotapes were evaluated under two conditions—one in which judges heard the audiotape of each woman accompanied by the photograph of her taken at the end of the experimental session (audiotape plus photograph condition) and the other in which the audiotapes were not accompanied by a photograph (audiotape-only condition). Including the audiotape plus photograph condition is one way to disentangle the effects of the women's nonverbal behaviors (which can be seen

only in the videotapes) from the effects of their weight (which is visible in both the videotapes and the photographs).

If the content of the women's conversation explains why the women's beliefs about whether they were visible to their telephone partners affected the partners' impressions of them, then judges in the audiotape-only condition should form a more positive impression of the social skills of obese women in the perceived visible condition than in the perceived not visible condition. Similarly, if nonverbal cues were important, obese women in the perceived visible condition should receive more positive ratings than obese women in the perceived not visible condition from judges who see videotapes but not from those who hear audiotapes.

Method

JUDGE RECRUITMENT

We recruited members of eight nonprofit organizations (e.g., parents of children on athletic teams and other school-related parent groups) to supply volunteers from their group to serve as judges. We divided $750 among these volunteers, who participated in order to donate the money to their organization. Organizations heard about the study through word of mouth and contacted us to volunteer.

Mean ages of the organization members were 40.2 years for women ($n = 124$) and 38.0 years for men ($n = 74$). On average, judges reported having some college education.

RATING PROCEDURES

Volunteers from each organization judged the behavior of 20 of the women. These women included 16 women who each represented one cell of our 2 (Women's Weight) × 2 (Perceived Visibility) × 2 (Actual Visibility) × 2 (Partners' Gender) design and 4 women from our 2 (Women's Weight) × 2 (Partners' Gender) audiotape-only control condition. In this way, we were able to have groups of judges evaluate participants who represented one complete replication of the experiment, thereby ensuring that any differences between members of different organizations would not be confounded with any of our experimental manipulations. The women judged by each group were randomly selected within these constraints.

Volunteers from each organization participated in subgroups of five to six judges. These subgroups were randomly assigned to evaluate women representing the same complete replication of the experiment under different conditions. One subgroup judged the women's audiotapes, another judged their videotapes, and a third subgroup judged the women's audiotapes accompanied by their photographs. These rating sessions lasted for approximately 2½ hr. The subgroup assigned to evaluate the videotapes evaluated only 16 women (rather than 20) because the 4 women within a replication who participated in the control conditions were not videotaped.

Judges were not aware of what experimental condition the women and their partners were in and, in fact, were unaware that the recordings were made under different conditions. Judges rated the women and their partners on social skills, likability, and physical attractiveness. The questions used to assess these dimensions were the same ones used to assess the women's and telephone partners' pre- and post-conversation evaluations of each other, and composite scores were computed as in Experiment 1.

These scores were averaged across the judges within a subgroup. Thus, for each woman we obtained an average rating made by five to six judges of her likability, social skill, and physical attractiveness. There were three sets of these scores, one for the audiotape-only condition, one for the audiotape plus photograph condition, and one for the videotape condition. We computed average judge scores for each woman because to use the judges rather than the women as the unit of analysis would inflate the degrees of freedom.

Results

Judges' ratings of women in the experimental conditions were analyzed by a repeated-measures ANCOVA in which the between-subjects factors were the women's weight, perceived visibility, actual visibility, and telephone partner gender; the repeated-measures factor was the condition in which the judges rated the women (audiotape only, audiotape plus photograph, videotape); and the covariates were the women's age and education.

The only theoretically relevant effect in these analyses was an interaction between the women's weight and rating condition on ratings of the women's physical attractiveness, $F(2, 200) = 11.60$, $p < .0001$. Judges rated obese women as

less physically attractive than nonobese women when they saw the women on videotape ($Ms = 2.5$ and 3.3, respectively), $F(1, 112) = 58.42, p < .0001$, when they saw photographs of them ($Ms = 2.8$ and 3.4, respectively), $F(1, 112) = 27.04$, $p < .00001$, and when they listened to but did not see them ($Ms = 3.1$ and 3.4, respectively), $F(1, 112) = 7.72$, $p = .006$. The finding that judges in the audiotape plus photograph and videotape conditions rated obese women as less attractive indicates that judges who saw the women perceived obese women as relatively unattractive. The finding that judges in the audiotape-only condition also perceived obese women they never saw as relatively unattractive replicates our previous study (Miller et al., 1990) in which people who never saw obese women evaluated them relatively negatively.

Judges' ratings of women in the control conditions were analyzed by 2 (Women's Weight) × 2 (Partner Gender) repeated-measures ANCOVAs in which the repeated measure, rating condition, had only two levels (audiotape only and audiotape plus photograph) because women were not videotaped in the control conditions. The only relevant effect was a main effect for the women's weight on judges' attractiveness ratings, $F(1, 21) = 11.99$, $p =.002$. However, the interaction between the women's weight and rating condition approached significance, $F(1, 23) = 3.44$, $p = .08$, and separate analysis of each rating condition revealed that judges in the audiotape plus photograph condition rated obese women as less attractive ($M = 2.8$) than nonobese women ($M = 3.5$), $F(1, 23) = 18.04$, $p = .0003$, whereas judges in the audiotape-only condition did not ($Ms = 3.1$ and 3.3, respectively), $F(1, 23) < 1$.

General Discussion

Partner ratings of the women's attractiveness revealed that the partners noticed the women's appearance and rated obese women as less attractive than nonobese women but, as might be expected, only when the partners actually saw the women. Partner ratings of the women's likability and social skills indicated that obese women received relatively low ratings in two instances. First, obese women received low ratings on social skills in the condition in which the partners' prejudices were activated (because they could see the women) but the women did not know this (because they thought they could not be seen). Second, obese women in the control condition, who knew that they could not be seen by their partners and would not be seen by anyone else (because no video camera was present), were rated as less likable than nonobese women.

One explanation for the finding that the obese women who received low ratings were those who were unaware that their partners could see them is that partners did have stereotypes about obese women but that something occurred in the condition in which the women thought they could be seen that prevented this stereotype from affecting the partners' reactions. We suspect that what blocked the biasing effects of the partners' expectations may have been something that the women did to compensate for the handicap their weight poses for social interactions. This interpretation is consistent with prior research that indicates that physically unattractive women and girls may be more socially assertive (Dion & Stein, 1978; Reis et al., 1982). It is also consistent with evidence that reports about the social relationships of obese and nonobese women made by the women themselves and by people who know them (friends and coworkers) do not reveal any differences between the social relationships of obese and nonobese women (Miller, Rothblum, Brand, & Felicio, 1995). These findings suggest that obese women's compensatory response to the handicap posed by their weight may meet with long-term as well as immediate success.

The finding that obese women in the control condition were liked less by their partners than nonobese women replicates a previous study in which we found that obese women who knew that nobody could observe them during a telephone conversation received lower ratings on social skills and likability than nonobese women, even though the raters never saw the women (Miller et al., 1990). We had previously interpreted results of that study as support for the hypothesis that repeated experiences with rejection reduce the opportunities obese women have to develop social skills. In light of the present data, another explanation for the finding that obese women make a more negative impression than nonobese women when they think they are not visible to others is that compensation, even when effective in overcoming prejudice, may have detrimental effects on the motivation and performance of obese women when they believe their weight will not be a factor in an interaction.

Because stereotyping and discrimination provide an explanation for negative outcomes received by members of stigmatized groups, group members may have difficulty disentangling the effects of stigma from their own contributions to the outcomes they receive (Crocker & Major, 1989; Crocker et al., 1991; Pettigrew, 1979). It is difficult for members of stigmatized groups to know for certain whether others are reacting to what they did or to who they are.

We believe that the possibility that their weight could explain why obese women receive negative social outcomes is likely to have detrimental effects on their behavior in situations where they think their weight is not important—as was the case in the control conditions of the present study and in our previous experiment (C. T. Miller et al., 1990). Because obese women are likely to attribute negative experiences to their weight (Baumeister et al., 1990; Crocker et al., 1993), they may imagine that thin women enjoy positive interpersonal interactions just by virtue of being thin. Consequently, obese women might underestimate the level of effort and social skills needed in situations in which weight is not an issue. Perhaps, then, obese women have acquired social skills comparable to or even better than those of nonobese women, but they may not use them optimally if they believe weight will not be an important influence on those with whom they interact.

The self-ratings of obese and nonobese women revealed that obese women reported being more likable and socially skilled than nonobese women when the women thought they were visible to their female partners. When they thought they were not visible to female partners, and when they spoke to male partners, obese and nonobese women generally did not differ in their self-ratings except that obese women consistently rated themselves as less attractive.

One explanation for these findings is that obese women attempted to be more likable and socially skilled than nonobese women did when they thought they would have to compensate for their partners' negative reaction to seeing that they were obese. Their self-ratings reflected what their intentions and goals for the interaction were. Alternatively, the more positive ratings made by obese women when they thought their partners could see them may indicate an effort to bolster their self-image because their partners' awareness of their appearance constituted a threat to self-esteem. They could not alter their appearance or their partners' reactions to it, but they could emphasize how likable and socially skilled they were by inflating their self-ratings.

That obese women did this when they spoke to women but not when they spoke to men suggests that obese and nonobese women may have had different expectations about how men and women would react to their appearance. Stigmatized people may have stereotypes about the type of person who would stereotype them (Jones et al., 1984), and people who believe they are disliked by others do not try to disconfirm the others' expectations if they think the others' opinion is unlikely to change (Curtis & Miller, 1986). Accordingly, obese women might have had little confidence that they could compensate for the negative reactions they thought males would have to their appearance. In support of this conclusion, there is some research showing that unattractive women are more competitive with men than with women whereas attractive women are relatively noncompetitive with men (Kahn, Hottes, & Davis, 1971; Major & Sherman, 1976). These researchers concluded that unattractive females may feel that they have nothing to gain or lose socially by outperforming a male because he will not be attracted to them in either case, so they might as well maximize their outcomes on the experimental task. In the present study, obese women may have been more motivated when interacting with a woman, whereas nonobese women may have been more motivated when interacting with a man.

The self-ratings of nonobese women are consistent with this view. Nonobese women who thought they were visible to men inflated their self-rated social skills, whereas nonobese women who thought they were visible to women rated themselves relatively negatively on social skills and likability. These ratings could reflect differences in nonobese women's motivation to make a good impression on male and female partners.

The judges' ratings suggest that whatever effects perceived visibility had on obese and nonobese women's intentions, neither the content of what the women said nor the way they spoke to their partners differed sufficiently for the judges to detect any differences between obese and nonobese women in the perceived visible and perceived not visible conditions. Evidently, therefore, differences in the women's behavior that were detected by the telephone partners were more subtle than what topics the women chose to dis-

cuss or whether their facial expressions and other nonverbal cues radiated warmth and friendliness or reserve and withdrawal.

The only difference between obese and nonobese women that the judges did detect was that they rated obese women they saw (in a photograph or on videotape) and obese women they did not see as less physically attractive than nonobese women. Beyond confirming that obese women sometimes make negative impressions on others who are unaware of their weight, these findings cannot explain what obese and nonobese women might have done differently as a consequence of believing they were visible, because this effect occurred regardless of the women's beliefs about their visibility.

The present study has limitations that suggest the need for additional research. The interpretation that can be made of the women's self-ratings is not as clear as it could be, because it is impossible to know whether the ratings reflect the women's intentions with respect to the interaction, an attempt to affirm their self-worth, or some other motivation. Moreover, even if the self-ratings reflect what the women were trying to accomplish during the interaction, the self-ratings do not fully explain how the partners reacted to the women. On the one hand, this is only to be expected, because the partners' ratings are likely to be affected by the partners' stereotypes and interpretations of the women's behavior as well as by what the women actually did. On the other hand, it is difficult to reconcile the finding that obese and nonobese women's self-descriptions in the different perceived visibility conditions depended on their partners' gender but the partners' reports about the women did not. This finding suggests that the social skills ratings made by partners reflect a behavioral change on the part of obese and nonobese women of which the women themselves were unaware. If so, it is consistent with a finding in our previous study, which showed that the self-ratings of obese and nonobese women following a telephone conversation showed no awareness of the fact that obese women had actually made a poorer impression on their partners than nonobese women (C. T. Miller et al., 1990). Nevertheless, there was some correspondence between what the women said they would be like and how their partners perceived them. Obese women in the control condition said they were relatively unlikable, and their partners, who never saw them, agreed.

This study also suffers from the sampling problems that plague virtually all experimental studies. Although we had the advantage of recruiting a noncollege sample, there is no way of knowing whether the obese and nonobese women who participated were particularly troubled or untroubled by social relationships, relative to a representative sample of obese and nonobese women. One advantage of the present sample is that the obese women were far more obese than the typical college sample. As we pointed out earlier, the practice of randomly assigning college students to be labeled temporarily as members of a stigmatized group is ideal for experimental control but not for describing what people do when they must live with the prejudices of others.

In summary, compensating for prejudice against fat people may have both desirable and undesirable effects on the social interactions of obese women. Although they cannot entirely escape the effects of prejudice, the skills and strategies they acquire to mitigate its consequences might make obese women more resilient in the long run. In discussing their finding that less attractive women were more socially assertive than more attractive women, Reis and his colleagues (1982) said, "After having learned to enjoy socializing enhanced in large part by the reactions of others to one's appearance rather than one's social competence, a deficiency endures that becomes consequential once beauty fades and other people no longer provide the spark" (p. 994). The pervasive prejudice that exists against those who do not fit current narrow definitions of beauty and fitness ensures that obese women will have some difficulties to overcome in establishing social relationships but may, in the process, learn how to provide their own spark.

REFERENCES

Adams, G. R. (1977). Physical attractiveness research: Toward a developmental social psychology of beauty. *Human Development, 20,* 217–239.

Baumeister, R. F. (1982). Self-esteem, self-presentation, and future interaction: A dilemma of reputation. *Journal of Personality, 50,* 29–45.

Baumeister, R. F., Kahn, J., & Tice, D. M. (1990). Obesity as a self-handicapping strategy: Personality, selective attribution of problems, and weight loss. *Journal of Social Psychology, 130,* 121–123.

Bond, M. (1972). Effect of an impression set on subsequent behavior. *Journal of Personality and Social Psychology, 24,* 301–305.

Crandall, C. S. (1991). Do heavy-weight students have more difficulty paying for college? *Personality and Social Psychology Bulletin, 17,* 606–611.

Crandall, C. S., & Biernat, M. R. (1990). The ideology of anti-fat attitudes. *Journal of Applied Social Psychology, 24,* 227–243.

Crocker, J., Cornwell, B., & Major, B. (1993). The stigma of overweight: Affective consequences of attributional ambiguity. *Journal of Personality and Social Psychology, 64,* 60–70.

Crocker, J., & Major, B. (1989). Social stigma and self-esteem: The self-protective properties of stigma. *Psychological Review, 96,* 608–630.

Crocker, J., Voelkl, K., Testa, M., & Major, B. (1991). Social stigma: The affective consequences of attributional ambiguity. *Journal of Personality and Social Psychology, 60,* 218–228.

Curtis, R. C., & Miller, K. (1986). Believing another likes or dislikes you: Behaviors making beliefs come true. *Journal of Personality and Social Psychology, 51,* 284–290.

Deaux, K., & Major, B. (1987). Putting gender into context: An integrative model of gender-related behavior. *Psychological Review, 94,* 369–389.

DeJong, W., & Kleck, R. E. (1986). The social psychological effects of overweight. In C. P. Herman, M. P. Zanna, & E. T. Higgins (Eds.), *Physical appearance, stigma, and social behavior: The Ontario Symposium (*Vol. 3). Hillsdale, NJ: Lawrence Erlbaum.

Dion, K. K., & Stein, S. (1978). Physical attractiveness and interpersonal influence. *Journal of Experimental Social Psychology, 14,* 97–108.

Farina, A., Allen, J. G., & Saul, B. (1968). The role of the stigmatized person in affecting social relationships. *Journal of Personality, 36,* 169–182.

Feingold, A. (1992). Good-looking people are not what we think. *Psychological Bulletin, 111,* 304–341.

Goldman, W., & Lewis, P. (1975). Beautiful is good: Evidence that the physically attractive are more socially skillful. *Journal of Experimental Social Psychology, 13,* 125–130.

Graham, S. (1992). "Most of the subjects were White and middle class": Trends in published research on African Americans in selected APA journals, 1970–1989. *American Psychologist, 47,* 629–639.

Harris, M. J., Milich, R., Corbitt E. M., Hoover, D. W., & Brady, M. (1992). Self-fulfilling effects of stigmatizing information on children's social interactions. *Journal of Personality and Social Psychology, 63,* 41–50.

Hilton, J. L., & Darley, J. M. (1985). Constructing other persons: A limit on the effect. *Journal of Experimental and Social Psychology, 21,* 1–18.

Ickes, W., Patterson, M. L., Rajecki, D. W., & Tanford, S. (1982). Behavioral and cognitive consequences of reciprocal versus compensatory responses to reinteraction exchanges. *Social Cognition, 1,* 160–190.

Jarvie, G. J., Lahey, B., Graziano, W., & Framer, E. (1983). Childhood obesity and social stigma: What we know and what we don't know. *Developmental Review, 3,* 237–273.

Jones, E. E., Farina, A., Hastorf, A. H., Marcus, H., Miller, D. T., & Scott R. A. (1984). *Social stigma: The psychology of marked relationships.* New York: W. H. Freeman.

Kahn, A., Hottes, J., & Davis, W. S. (1971). Cooperation and optimal responding in the prisoner's dilemma game: Effects of sex and physical attractiveness. *Journal of Personality and Social Psychology, 17,* 267–279.

Langlois, J. H., & Stephan, C. W. (1981). Beauty and the beast: The role of physical attractiveness in the development of peer relations and social behavior. In S. S. Brehm, S. M. Kassin, & F. X. Gibbons (Eds.), *Developmental social psychology: Theory and research* (pp. 152–168) . New York: Oxford University Press.

Lerner, R. M., & Gellert, E. (1969). Body build identification, preference, and aversion in children. *Developmental Psychology, 5,* 256–262.

Major, B., & Sherman, R. C. (1976). *The effects of physical attractiveness and fear of success on competitive performance in women.* Unpublished manuscript.

Miller, C. T., Rothblum, E. D., Barbour, L., Brand, P. A., & Felicio, D. (1990). Social interactions of obese and nonobese women. *Journal of Personality, 58,* 365–380.

Miller, C. T., Rothblum, E. D., Brand, P. A., & Felicio, D. M. (1995). Do obese women have poorer social relationships than nonobese women? Reports by self, friends, and co-workers. *Journal of Personality, 63,* 65–85.

Miller, D. T., & Turnbull, W. (1986). Expectancies and interpersonal processes. *Annual Review of Psychology, 37,* 233–256.

Neuberg, S. L., Judice, T. N., Virdin, L. M., & Carrillo, M. A. (1993). Perceiver self-presentational goals as moderators of expectancy influences: Ingratiation and the disconfirmation of negative expectancies. *Journal of Personality and Social Psychology, 64,* 409–420.

Pettigrew, T. F. (1979). The ultimate attribution error: Extending Allport's cognitive analysis of prejudice. *Personality and Social Psychology Bulletin, 5,* 461–476.

Reis, H. T., Wheeler, L., Spiegel, W., Kernis, M. H., Wezlek, J., & Perri, M. (1982). Physical attractiveness and social interaction: II. Why does appearance affect social experience? *Journal of Personality and Social Psychology, 43,* 979–996.

Rodin, J., Silberstein, L., & Striegel-Moore, R. (1984). Women and weight: A normative discontent. In T. B. Sonderegger (Ed.), *Nebraska Symposium on Motivation* (Vol. 32, pp. 267–307). Lincoln: University of Nebraska Pres,.

Rothblum, E. D. (1992). The stigma of women's weight: Social and economic realities. *Feminism & Psychology, 2,* 61–73.

Rothblum, E. D., Brand, P. A., Miller, C. T., & Oetjen, H. A. (1990). The relationship between obesity, employment discrimination, and employment-related victimization. *Journal of Vocational Behavior, 37,* 251–266.

Rothblum, E. D., Miller, C. T., & Garbutt B. (1988). Stereotypes of obese female job applicants. *International Journal of Eating Disorders, 7,* 277–283.

Ryckman, R. M., Robbins, M. A., Thornton, B., Kaczor, L. M., Gayton, S. L., & Anderson, C. V. (1991). Public self-consciousness and physique stereotyping. *Personality and Social Psychology Bulletin, 17,* 400–405.

Skrypnek, B. J., & Snyder, M. (1982). On the self-perpetuating nature of stereotypes about men and women. *Journal of Experimental Social Psychology, 18,* 277–291.

Snyder, M., Tanke, E. D., & Berscheid, E. (1977). Social perception and social behavior: On the self-fulfilling nature of social stereotypes. *Journal of Personality and Social Psychology, 35,* 656–666.

Steele, C. M. (1975). Name calling and compliance. *Journal of Personality and Social Psychology, 31,* 361–369.

Steele, C. M. (1988). The psychology of self-affirmation: Sustaining the integrity of the self. In L. Berkowitz (Ed.), *Advances in experimental social psychology* (Vol. 21, pp. 261–302). New York: Academic Press.

Stunkard, A. J., Sorenson, T. I. A., Hanis, C., Teasdale, T. W., Chakraborty, R., Schull, W. H., & Shulsinger, F. (1986). An adoption study of human obesity. *New England Journal of Medicine, 314,* 193–198.

Swann, W. B., Jr. (1984). Quest for accuracy in person perception: A matter of pragmatics. *Psychological Review, 91,* 457–477.

Tiggemann, M., & Rothblum, E. D. (1988). Gender differences in social consequences of perceived overweight in the United States and Australia. *Sex Roles, 18,* 75–86.

Weiner, B., Perry, R. P., & Magnusson, J. (1988). An attributional analysis of reactions to stigmas. *Journal of Personality and Social Psychology, 55,* 738–748.

Wicklund, R. A. (1976). Objective self-awareness. In L. Berkowitz (Ed.), *Advances in experimental social psychology* (Vol. 8, pp. 253–275). New York: Academic Press.

Word, C. O., Zanna, M. P., & Cooper, J. (1974). The nonverbal mediation of self-fulfilling prophecies in interracial interaction. *Journal of Experimental Social Psychology, 10,* 109–120.

When Do We Use Stereotypes and Prejudice?

Stereotypes and prejudice would not create a social problem if we did not use them so frequently in our interactions with others. But these beliefs are problematic exactly because they do influence our judgments of and our behavior toward members of out-groups. And our beliefs often influence our responses to others such that we treat them negatively, or do not treat them as individuals. But stereotypes and prejudice do not always lead to discrimination for all people or at all times, and much is known about the people for and the conditions under which they do and they do not. This is the topic of the readings in this section.

The influence of stereotypes on responses to others is determined by both the characteristics of the situation in which the interaction occurs and the characteristics of the person who is making the judgments. In terms of the social situation, because making judgments about others takes effort, using stereotypes can simplify the process of person perception. Thus social categorization is more likely to occur in situations that demand our cognitive resources, for example, when there is a lot of information about others available to be processed, a lot of different people to learn about, or are other things that need to be done at the same time. Stereotypes and prejudice are more likely to have a negative impact under these conditions.

The research by Bodenhausen, presented in Reading 14, provides a nice empirical demonstration of the general principle that stereotypes come into action when people are not operating to their full capacity. Although this paper does not directly test the hypothesis that more complex situations produce more stereotyping because they tax the cognitive capacity of the perceivers, there are other demonstrations of this effect in the literature (Bodenhausen & Macrae, 1998; Macrae, Milne, & Bodenhausen, 1994).

Just as stereotypes are not used in all situations, not all people use them. For instance, there are differences among individuals in terms of their needs to "structure" or to make sense of their environment. People who have higher needs for structure express more stereotypes and prejudice (Neuberg & Newsom, 1993), both because they are more likely to differentiate in-groups from out-groups and because they make distinctions among members of out-groups in order to help them see their worlds more simply. Furthermore, individuals with greater needs to feel good about themselves (for instance, those who have low self-esteem) also show more prejudice. In Reading 15, Pratto, Sidanius, Stallworth, and Malle study a number of personality variables that have been considered to be predictors of prejudice. In their research they develop still another individual difference measure, known as *social dominance orientation* (SDO), that reflects an underlying characteristic of individuals that relates to prejudice. SDO is an interesting personality variable, both because it differentiates people who are high and low in prejudice toward many different out-groups, but also because it considers how these beliefs relate to people's beliefs about social hierarchy and political attitudes more generally.

Because prejudice is an attitude, we can draw from the important literature in social psychology concerning the conditions under which attitudes influence behavior to understand the conditions under which prejudice will be related to discrimination. One important determinant of the extent to which attitudes predict behavior is the social context in which the behavior occurs. Our beliefs about social groups will influence our behavior only when the norms of the situation do not prevent them from doing so. In one demonstration of this effect, La Piere (1936) sent letters to owners of restaurants in the western United States and asked them if they would serve a Chinese person in their restaurant. During that time, prejudice against Chinese was so strong that most of the restaurant owners who replied to the letter indicated that they would not. Yet when the researcher later showed up at the same restaurants with a Chinese person, almost all of the parties were seated. La Piere argued that this was a case in which the attitude (prejudice) did not predict behavior (discrimination) because the social norms that came into play at the restaurant (for instance, that the party might have been offended and created a scene) made it difficult to act on one's prejudices.

Reading 16, by Gaertner and Dovidio, summarizes an important line of theory and research, based in part on the impact of social norms on behavior, that helps explain how and when racist beliefs produce racial discrimination. These authors argue that in today's Western society, most people (except, perhaps, the most prejudiced of us) try to act in the same way to members of other groups as we do toward members of our own group. We hold these egalitarian attitudes because we feel that this is appropriate (our personal beliefs), but also because the norms of society make it clear that we should. Gaertner and Dovidio argue, however, that this does not mean that racism has disappeared, but rather that it is now more subtle than it was in the past. According to their approach, "aversive racism" is a type of racism that does not involve active hostility toward African Americans on the part of European Americans, but rather represents a feeling of uneasiness or discomfort that makes Whites prefer to avoid contact with Blacks. (You can see that this approach is similar to the "ambivalent" and "modern" approaches to racism discussed earlier.)

Gaertner and Dovidio show how aversive racism interacts with social norms and personal beliefs about discrimination. In short, societal norms against discrimination generally prevent individuals from acting on their negative beliefs and feelings, but discrimination (such as the failure to help others) may still appear when the norms of the situation are more ambiguous and there are other available explanations for the behavior. This chapter presents a number of interesting studies supporting this important theory.

Monteith, Devine, and Zuwerink expand the analysis of the relationship between prejudice and discrimination even farther in their model of prejudice, presented in Reading 17. For one, they explicitly consider the relationship between personal beliefs and behaviors, arguing that even low-prejudice people sometimes act in ways that they do not think are socially appropriate. Furthermore, Monteith and her colleagues make it clear that the outcome of violating one's personal norms is negative affect, at least for low-prejudice individuals.

Discussion Questions

1. How does Bodenhausen demonstrate that cognitive capacity is important in producing stereotyping? Are there real-world situations in which constraints on cognitive capacity might influence stereotyping, prejudice, and discrimination?
2. According to the readings, what kinds of people are likely to be most prejudiced, and why?
3. What are *aversive racism* and *modern racism*, and how do they differ from traditional racism?
4. According to Monteith and her colleagues, how do high- and low-prejudice individuals differ in their beliefs, feelings, and behaviors about people from other groups?

Suggested Readings

Bodenhausen, G. V., & Macrae, C. N. (1998). Stereotype activation and inhibition. In R.S. Wyer, Jr. (Ed.), *Advances in social cognition* (Vol. 11, pp. 1–52). Mahwah, NJ: Erlbaum. A general theory of the impact of stereotypes on judgments and behavior.

LaPiere, R. T. (1936). Type rationalization of group antipathy. *Social Forces, 15,* 232–237. A field study demonstrating how social norms can determine when prejudice relates to discrimination.

Macrae, C. N., Milne, A. B., & Bodenhausen, G. V. (1994). Stereotypes as energy-saving devices: A peek inside the cognitive toolbox. *Journal of Personality and Social Psychology, 66,* 37–47. An elegant demonstration of how stereotypes are used to help process information.

Neuberg, S. L., & Newsom, J. T. (1993). Personal need for structure: Individual differences in the desire for simple structure. *Journal of Personality and Social Psychology, 65,* 113–131. Another individual difference variable that predicts stereotyping.

Stereotypes as Judgmental Heuristics: Evidence of Circadian Variations in Discrimination

Galen V. Bodenhausen • Michigan State University

The question of when people rely on stereotypic preconceptions in judging others was investigated in two studies. As a person's motivation or ability to process information systematically is diminished, the person may rely to on increasing extent on stereotypes, when available, as a way of simplifying the task of generating a response. It was hypothesized that circadian variations in arousal levels would be related to social perceivers' propensity to stereotype others by virtue of their effects on motivation and processing capacity. In support of this hypothesis, subjects exhibited stereotypic biases in their judgments to a much greater extent when the judgments were rendered at a nonoptimal time of day (i.e., in the morning for "night people" and in the evening for "morning people"). In Study One, this pattern was found in probability judgments concerning personal characteristics; in Study Two, the pattern was obtained in perceptions of guilt in allegations of student misbehavior. Results generalized over a range of different types of social stereotypes and suggest that biological processes should be considered in attempts to conceptualize the determinants of stereotyping.

When do people rely on their stereotypic beliefs in forming impressions of and making judgments about other people? This question is at the heart of many recent investigations of stereotyping and discrimination. Bodenhausen and Wyer (1985) proposed that stereotypes can be viewed as judgmental heuristics that are sometimes used to simplify the cognitive tasks confronted by the social perceiver. Whether we respond to others based on general beliefs about their group or a thoughtful analysis of each person's unique attributes depends to a large extent on whether stereotypic beliefs provide an easy, seemingly relevant basis for responding and whether a quick

and less effortful response is necessary or desirable (Chaiken, Liberman, & Eagly, 1989). Stereotypic responses may predominate unless the social perceiver has sufficient momentary ability and motivation to engage in effortful, systematic thought. Motivational factors include personal involvement (Erber & Fiske, 1984) and incentives for accuracy (Neuberg & Fiske, 1987). Factors that limit ability to process information systematically include distraction (Petty, Wells, & Brock, 1976), information overload (Rothbart, Fulero, Jensen, Howard, & Birrell, 1978), and task complexity (Bodenhausen & Lichtenstein, 1987).

The present research examined the intriguing possibility that there are regular patterns of variation in the social perceiver's motivation and information processing capacities that produce what might be characterized as circadian rhythms in social perception. It has been well established that there are significant time-of-day effects in many types of human performance (Blake, 1967; Colquhoun, 1971; Freeman & Hovland, 1934). These effects have been attributed to variations in circadian arousal levels affecting the capacity and efficiency of working memory (Folkard, Wever, & Wildgruber, 1983) as well as to more general notions of fatigue or alertness. For many tasks, performance peaks at a certain level of circadian arousal, and this peak occurs at a fairly regular point in the day.

Several studies suggest that there are considerable inter-individual differences in the time of day at which one reaches one's peak, or acrophase (Horne & Östberg, 1977; Pátkai, 1971). The notion of "morning people" and "night people" suggests that there are two clusters of individuals who tend to reach their functional peak either earlier or later in the day. In order to explore this possibility, Horne and Östberg (1976) devised a self-assessment questionnaire to measure this individual difference. The measure, called the Morningness–Eveningness Questionnaire (MEQ), has since been utilized fairly extensively and has been shown to have predictive validity and other desirable psychometric properties (Smith, Reilly, & Midkiff, 1989).

If people are more likely to rely on stereotypic preconceptions in making judgments when they are not particularly motivated or are less cognitively able to consider carefully the relevant evidence at hand, and if cognitive capabilities and motivation fluctuate as a function of time of day, it follows that reliance on stereotypes in the judgment process should also vary as a function of time of day, other things being equal. Stereotypic responses should be least likely during acrophase. Because some people show a pattern of matutinal acrophase, they should be least likely to exhibit symptoms of stereotyping during the morning. Others characteristically show a vespertine acrophase, so they should be least likely to show stereotype-based discrimination during the evening. These predictions were investigated in two studies, using two different judgment tasks and several different social stereotypes.

Study 1

The first study examined the impact of common social stereotypes on performance in a probability estimation task. Specifically, materials used by Tversky and Kahneman (1983) to demonstrate the conjunction fallacy in probability judgment were adopted. The conjunction fallacy refers to the erroneous belief that the joint probability of two events is greater than the probability of either of the constituent events separately. It is theoretically linked to the operation of the representativeness heuristic (Kahneman & Tversky, 1972). When people use this heuristic, they make probability estimates based on the apparent similarity of the event or entity being judged to a representative stereotype. People show a strong tendency to believe that the conjunction of a representative (stereotypic) and an unrepresentative element is more probable than the probability of the unrepresentative element in isolation.

In this study, I tested students on a probability estimation task at either 9 a.m. or 8 p.m. It was expected that morning people would be more prone to rely on simple stereotypes and commit the conjunction fallacy in the evening, whereas evening people would be more likely to commit the conjunction fallacy in the morning.

Method

SUBJECTS AND DESIGN

Fifty-nine undergraduate psychology students were recruited for a study of human judgment. They received course credit. Subjects were randomly assigned to report to the testing location at either 9 a.m. or 8 p.m. in groups of approximately 15. Show-up rates were in excess of 80% for all sessions and did not differ as a function of time of day.

Subjects completed the MEQ and were categorized as either morning-types or evening-types on the basis of a median split of their scores. Thus, the research design was a 2 (time of day: 9 a.m. vs. 8 p.m.) × 2 (personality type: morning vs. evening) between-subjects factorial design.

MATERIALS AND PROCEDURE

Subjects were given a booklet in which they were asked to read a description of one of two people,

Bill or Linda, and make judgments about the person's characteristics. The descriptions were taken verbatim from Tversky and Kahneman (1983). Bill was described in terms representative of common stereotypes about accountants. Linda was described as possessing traits stereotypically ascribed to feminists. After reading the description, subjects were asked to choose which of two statements about the target was more likely to be true. One of these statements consisted of a conjunction of a representative (stereotypic) label and an unrepresentative characteristic (e.g., "Bill is an accountant who plays jazz for a hobby") while the other was the unrepresentative characteristic in isolation. Choice of the conjunction constitutes the conjunction fallacy.

Having completed the probability judgment task, subjects were given the MEQ as part of an ostensibly unrelated study and then were debriefed.

Results and Discussion

The results were collapsed across the two target cases (i.e., Bill and Linda). The conjunction fallacy occurred with high probability under all of the experimental conditions. However, the expected pattern was obtained: 94% of subjects with "morning" personalities committed the conjunction fallacy during an evening experimental session ($n = 16$), while only 71% did so in the morning ($n = 14$). Conversely, subjects with "evening" personalities were more likely to commit this fallacy during a morning experimental session (92%, $n = 12$) than during the evening (70%, $n = 17$). In an analysis of error rates, the interaction of personality type and time of testing was significant, $F(1, 55) = 4.55$, $p < .05$. There were no other significant effects.

These results support the idea that people process information in a more heuristic fashion during times of the day at which they are not at their "peak" level of circadian arousal. Specifically, subjects relied more on representative stereotypes about feminists and accountants (rather than applying a straightforward rule of logic) when there was a mismatch between their acrophase and the time of testing.

Study 2

In the second study, subjects were asked to consider cases of alleged misbehavior by college stu-

dents and to determine the probability of the accused students' guilt. Sometimes the students were identified as members of particular social groups, and they were accused of committing offenses that were consistent with stereotypes of these groups. In other conditions, the cases involved students who had been accused of involvement in the exact same offenses but who had not been identified as members of a stereotyped group. Subjects were expected to rely more on guilt-implying stereotypic beliefs when asked to make guilt judgments at nonoptimal times of day.

Method

SUBJECTS AND DESIGN

Subjects were 189 undergraduate students recruited from psychology classes; they received course credit. Subjects were randomly assigned to experimental sessions held at 9 a.m., 3 p.m., or 8 p.m. They were classified as morning or evening types by a median split of MEQ scores. Participants considered a case involving either a stereotyped or a nonstereotyped student defendant, also randomly determined. Thus, the basic design of the experiment was a 3 (time of testing: 9 a.m., 3 p.m., or 8 p.m.) × 2 (personality type: morning vs. evening) × 2 (stereotype activation: present vs. absent) between-subjects factorial design.

MATERIALS AND PROCEDURE

The study was presented as an investigation of legal socialization in the college environment. Specifically, subjects were told that they would read about the alleged misconduct of other college students and would be asked to "provide feedback" about these cases. Three different cases were constructed. One involved a student accused of cheating on an exam, one a student who allegedly physically attacked his roommate, and one a student who allegedly sold drugs. Each of these offenses was matched to a stereotyped group that had been shown (via pretesting in the same subject population) to be associated, however unfairly, with these offenses. Specifically, athletes were seen as more likely to be cheaters, Hispanics as more likely to be physically aggressive, and African-Americans as more likely to sell drugs.

A small set of evidence was provided about each case (approximately 4 to 5 relevant pieces of information) in the form of a written prose summary. This evidence was identical for stereotypic and nonstereotypic offenders. Some evidence pointed toward guilt, but no conclusive proof was forthcoming. Stereotype activation was accomplished in two different ways. For the cheating case, a sentence identifying the defendant as a "well-known athletic star on campus" was either included or was not. In the other two cases, stereotypes were activated by manipulating the defendant's name. In the assault case, the student defendant was named either "Robert Garner" or "Roberto Garcia." In the drug dealing case, the student defendant was named either "Mark Washburn" or "Marcus Washington." Pretesting confirmed that students inferred Garcia, but not Garner, to be Hispanic, and Washington, but not Washburn, to be African-American.

Following presentation of the case evidence, subjects were asked to indicate the likelihood of the student's guilt on an 11-point scale (0 = extremely unlikely to 10 = extremely likely). They were also asked to rate the seriousness of the alleged offense on an 11-point scale ranging from 0 (completely trivial) to 10 (extremely serious). Then they were asked some filler questions that reflected the alleged purpose of the study. Finally, subjects were debriefed.

Results and Discussion

An initial analysis of subjects' guilt judgments included the three case replications as a factor in the analytic model. There was a theoretically uninteresting main effect such that guilt was seen as most likely in the cheating case ($M = 7.14$), moderately likely in the assault case ($M = 5.65$), and least likely in the drug dealing case ($M = 4.61$). As there were no interactions of this replication factor with the other independent variables (all $ps > .35$), the results were collapsed across this variable for ease of presentation.

Mean ratings of the defendant's likelihood of guilt as a function of stereotype activation, time of testing, and personality type are presented in Table 14.1. The expected interaction of stereotype activation, time of testing, and personality type was significant, $F(2, 177) = 3.49, p < .05$. No other effects were significant in the overall analysis. Supplementary analyses confirmed that, as expected, morning types perceived stereotyped targets to be more likely to be guilty in the afternoon

TABLE 14.1. Mean Ratings of Perceived Guilt Likelihood of Student Defendants as a Function of Time of Day, Personality Type, and Stereotype Activation

	Time of Day		
	9 a.m	3 p.m.	8 p.m.
Morning Types			
Stereotype	4.92 (13)	6.67 (18)	6.50 (16)
No Stereotype	5.39 (13)	5.61 (18)	5.79 (14)
Evening Types			
Stereotype	6.79 (19)	5.13 (16)	5.60 (15)
No Stereotype	5.05 (19)	5.67 (15)	6.45 (13)

Note. Cell sizes are indicated in parentheses.

and evening than the morning, $F(1, 44) = 5.16, p < .05$. For evening types, perceptions of the stereotyped targets' guilt were significantly greater in the morning than in the afternoon or evening, $F(1, 47) = 4.39, p < .05$. Perceptions of the nonstereotyped defendants were not affected by time of testing, $ps > .25$.[1]

These results bolster our confidence in the proposition that stereotypes are more likely to be relied on in judgmental tasks that occur at nonoptimal times of day. Using a different type of task and three different social stereotypes, the implications of the first study were supported quite nicely.

General Discussion

The results obtained in these studies have a number of interesting implications. First and foremost, they support the view that stereotypes function as judgmental heuristics and, as such, are likely to be more influential under circumstances in which people are less motivated or less able to engage in more systematic and careful judgment strategies (Bodenhausen & Lichtenstein, 1987; Chaiken et al., 1989). Morning people, who reach their functional peak early in the day, were more likely to fall back on stereotypic responses in the afternoon and evening, while evening people, who reach their functional peak later in the day, showed a greater tendency toward stereotypic responses in the morning. These results suggest that regular variations in arousal levels may play a role in determining the types of information-processing strategies that

---

[1]A similar pattern of results obtained for the seriousness judgment. Details are available from the author.

are adopted by social perceivers. These results also highlight the potential value that may accrue from considering the role of time and temporal cycles in studies of social cognition. McGrath and Kelly (1986) have argued that time has been a neglected variable in social psychological research, one that might be exploited in numerous ways. One way, exemplified in the present research, is to use temporal cycles as a methodological tool to examine basic theoretical issues. Broadbent, Broadbent, and Jones (1989) also employed this strategy. They were able to resolve some conflicting results in research on basic attentional processes by examining the impact of time of day on task performance. Although circadian variations were explored in the present research primarily as a way of testing specific theoretical claims about the effects of processing resources on social judgment strategies, the more general possibility of regular circadian variations in social perception is an intriguing issue that deserves further exploration.

Consideration of the role of circadian variations in arousal levels on social judgment is particularly interesting because it represents a conflux of biological, cognitive, and social processes. As such, it may provide one small step toward an integrated theoretical account of human thought and action that exploits important developments in several subdisciplines. As the motivational and ability factors that affect social information processing strategies become more well specified, the role of basic biological processes will doubtlessly become increasingly recognized.

REFERENCES

Blake, M. J. F. (1967). Time of day effects on performance in a range of tasks. *Psychonomic Science, 9,* 349–350.

Bodenhausen, G. V., & Lichtenstein, M. (1987). Social stereotypes and information-processing strategies: The impact of task complexity. *Journal of Personality and Social Psychology, 52,* 871–880.

Bodenhausen, G. V., & Wyer, R. S. (1985). Effects of stereotypes on decision making and information-processing strategies. *Journal of Personality and Social Psychology, 48,* 267–282.

Broadbent, D. E., Broadbent, M. H. P., & Jones, J. L. (1989). Time of day as an instrument for the analysis of attention. *European Journal of Cognitive Psychology, 1,* 69–94.

Chaiken, S., Liberman, A., & Eagly, A. (1989). Heuristic and systematic information processing within and beyond the persuasion context. In J. Uleman & J. Bargh (Eds.), *Unintended thought* (pp. 212–252). New York: Guilford.

Colquhoun, W. P. (1971). Circadian variations in mental efficiency. In W. P. Colquhoun (Ed.), *Biological rhythms and human performance*. London: Academic Press.

Erber, R., & Fiske, S. T. (1984). Outcome dependency and attention to inconsistent information. *Journal of Personality and Social Psychology, 17,* 709–726.

Folkard, S., Wever, R. A., & Wildgruber, C. M. (1983). Multi-oscillatory control of circadian rhythms in human performance. *Nature, 305,* 223–226.

Freeman, G., & Hovland, C. (1934). Diurnal variation in performance and related physiological processes. *Psychological Bulletin, 31,* 777–799.

Horne, J. A., & Östberg, O. (1976). A self-assessment questionnaire to determine morningness-eveningness in human circadian rhythms. *International Journal of Chronobiology, 4,* 97–110.

Horne, J. A., & Östberg, O. (1977). Individual differences in human circadian rhythms. *Biological Psychology, 5,* 179–190.

Kahneman, D., & Tversky, A. (1972). Subjective probability: A judgment of representativeness. *Cognitive Psychology, 3,* 430–454.

McGrath, J. E., & Kelly, J. R. (1986). *Time and human interaction: Toward a social psychology of time.* New York: Guilford.

Neuberg, S. L., & Fiske, S. T. (1987). Motivational influences on impression formation: Outcome dependency, accuracy-driven attention, and individuating processes. *Journal of Personality and Social Psychology, 53,* 431–444.

Pátkai, P. (1971). Interindividual differences in diurnal variation in alertness, performance, and adrenaline excretion. *Acta Psychologica Scandinavica, 81,* 35–46.

Petty, R. E., Wells, G. L., & Brock, T. C. (1976). Distraction can enhance or reduce yielding to propaganda: Thought disruption versus effort justification. *Journal of Personality and Social Psychology, 24,* 874–884.

Rothbart. M., Fulero, S., Jensen, C., Howard. J., & Birrell, P. (1978). From individual to group impressions: Availability heuristics in stereotype formation. *Journal of Experimental Social Psychology, 14,* 237–255.

Smith, C. S., Reilly, C., & Midkiff, K. (1989). Evolution of three circadian rhythm questionnaires with suggestions for an improved measure of morningness. *Journal of Applied Psychology, 74,* 728–738.

Tversky, A., & Kahneman, D. (1983). Extensional versus intuitive reasoning: The conjunction fallacy in probability judgment. *Psychological Review, 90,* 293–315.

Social Dominance Orientation: A Personality Variable Predicting Social and Political Attitudes

Felicia Pratto, Jim Sidanius, Lisa M. Stallworth, and Bertram F. Malle • University of California at Los Angles

Social dominance orientation (SDO), one's degree of preference for inequality among social groups, is introduced. On the basis of social dominance theory, it is shown that (a) men are more social dominance-oriented than women, (b) high-SDO people seek hierarchy-enhancing professional roles and low-SDO people seek hierarchy-attenuating roles, (c) SDO was related to beliefs in a large number of social and political ideologies that support group-based hierarchy (e.g., meritocracy and racism) and to support for policies that have implications for intergroup relations (e.g., war, civil rights, and social programs), including new policies. SDO was distinguished from interpersonal dominance, conservatism, and authoritarianism. SDO was negatively correlated with empathy, tolerance, communality, and altruism. The ramifications of SDO in social context are discussed.

Group conflict and group-based inequality are pervasive in human existence. Currently, every continent is enduring some form of ethnic conflict, from the verbal debate over multiculturalism in the United States and Canada to civil war in Liberia and Bosnia. Other conflicts between groups are ancient: the European persecution of Jews, "Holy Wars" waged by Christians and Muslims around the Mediterranean, imperialism in South America, and anti-Black racism in northern Africa and elsewhere. Regardless of the intensity of the conflict, the participants justify their behavior to others by appealing to historical injustices, previous territorial boundaries, religious prohibitions, genetic and cultural theories of in-group superiority, or other such ideologies.

Prompted by the ubiquitous nature of group-based prejudice and oppression, we developed social dominance theory (see Pratto, in press; Sidanius, 1993; Sidanius & Pratto, 1993a); the theory postulates that societies minimize group conflict by creating consensus on ideologies that promote the superiority of one group over others (set also Sidanius, Pratto, Martin, & Stallworth, 1991). Ideologies that promote or maintain group inequality are the tools that legitimize discrimination. To work smoothly, these ideologies must be widely accepted within a society, appearing as self-apparent truths; hence we call them *hierarchy-legitimizing myths.*[1] By contributing to consensual or normalized group-based inequality, legitimizing myths help to stabilize oppression. That is, they

259

minimize conflict among groups by indicating how individuals and social institutions should allocate things of positive or negative social value, such as jobs, gold, blankets, government appointments, prison terms, and disease. For example, the ideology of anti-Black racism has been instantiated in personal acts of discrimination, but also in institutional discrimination against African-Americans by banks, public transit authorities, schools, churches, marriage laws, and the penal system. Social Darwinism and meritocracy are examples of other ideologies that imply that some people are not as "good" as others and therefore should be allocated less positive social value than others.

Thus far, we have given examples of legitimizing myths that enhance or maintain the degree of social inequality. Other ideologies may serve to attenuate the amount of inequality. For example, the "universal rights of man" and the view summarized by "all humans are God's children" are inclusive, egalitarian ideologies that explicitly do not divide persons into categories or groups. To the extent that such ideologies are widely shared, there should be less group inequality. There are, then, two varieties of legitimizing myths: hierarchy-enhancing legitimizing myths, which promote greater degrees of social inequality, and hierarchy-attenuating legitimizing myths, which promote greater social equality.

Social Dominance Orientation

Given our theoretical postulate that acceptance of legitimizing myths has significant influence on the degree of inequality in societies, it is quite important to understand the factors that lead to the acceptance or rejection of ideologies that promote or attenuate inequality. Social dominance theory postulates that a significant factor is an individual-difference variable called *social dominance orientation* (SDO), or the extent to which one desires that one's in-group dominate and be superior to out-groups. We consider SDO to be a general

attitudinal orientation toward intergroup relations, reflecting whether one generally prefers such relations to be equal, versus hierarchical, that is, ordered along a superior–inferior dimension. The theory postulates that people who are more social-dominance oriented will tend to favor hierarchy-enhancing ideologies and policies, whereas those lower on SDO will tend to favor hierarchy-attenuating ideologies and policies. SDO is thus the central individual-difference variable that predicts a person's acceptance or rejection of numerous ideologies and policies relevant to group relations.

Another way that individuals' levels of SDO may influence their contribution to social equality or inequality is in the kinds of social roles they take on, particularly, roles that either enhance or attenuate inequality. We thus predict that those who are higher on SDO will become members of institutions and choose roles that maintain or increase social inequality, whereas those who are lower on SDO will belong to institutions and choose roles that reduce inequality.

The purpose of the present research was to demonstrate that individual variation in SDO exists and to show that this construct behaves according to the theory outlined above. Specifically, our goals were (a) to develop a measure of SDO that is internally and temporally reliable, (b) to show that SDO is related to the attitudinal and social role variables specified by social dominance theory (predictive validity), (c) to show that the measure is not redundant with other attitude predictors and standard personality variables (discriminant validity), and (d) to show that SDO serves as an orientation in shaping new attitudes.

Hypotheses

The first set of hypotheses we tested was derived from social dominance theory and concerned those variables to which SDO should strongly relate, termed *predictive validity*. The second set of hypotheses, termed *discriminant validity*, states either that SDO should be independent of other variables or that SDO should have predictive value in addition to the effects of these other variables. We also hypothesized that SDO should relate moderately to certain other personality variables, from which SDO is conceptually distinct. The third set of hypotheses we tested concerns SDO's power to predict new social attitudes.

---

[1]The term *myth* is meant to imply that everyone in the society perceives these ideologies as explanations for how the world is—not that they are false (or true). Social dominance theory is meant only to describe the social and psychological processes that act on these ideologies not to ascertain whether these ideologies are true, fair, moral, or reasonable.

Predictive Validity

GENDER

The world over, men and women hold different roles with regard to the maintenance of hierarchy. Ubiquitously, men serve as military leaders and hold leadership roles in religious, social, political, and cultural spheres (e.g., Brown, 1991, pp. 110, 137). Moreover, men hold more hierarchy-enhancing attitudes, such as support for ethnic prejudice, racism, capitalism, and right-wing political parties, than do women (e.g., Avery, 1988; Eisler & Loye, 1983; Ekehammar & Sidanius, 1982; Shapiro & Mahajan, 1986; Sidanius & Ekehammar, 1980; see review by Sidanius, Cling, & Pratto, 1991). On the basis of these general societal patterns, we have predicted and shown that, on average, men are more social dominance-oriented than women (see Pratto, Sidanius, & Stallworth, 1993; Sidanius, Pratto, & Bobo, 1996). We tested this hypothesis with the measure of SDO developed in the present research.

LEGITIMIZING MYTHS

Ethnic Prejudice. One of the major kinds of ideology concerning relative group status is ethnic prejudice. In the United States, the most longstanding and widely disseminated version of ethnic prejudice is anti-Black racism. Therefore, we predicted that SDO would be strongly related to anti-Black racism in the present U.S. samples. In the United States, a theoretical and empirical debate about how best to measure anti-Black racism has been conducted for some time (e.g., see Bobo, 1983; McConahay, 1986; Sears, 1988; Sniderman & Tetlock, 1986a, 1986b). Social dominance theory merely postulates that SDO should predict whatever ideologies are potent within the culture at the time of measurement. From our theoretical viewpoint, it does not matter whether the basis for racism is fairness (e.g., Kluegel & Smith, 1986), genetic or biblical racial inferiority theories, symbolic racism (e.g., Sears, 1988), or family pathology (e.g., Moynihan, 1965). Any potent ideology that describes groups as unequal and has policy implications is a legitimizing myth and should, therefore, correlate with SDO. During the period the present research was conducted, our subjects' country was engaged in a war against Iraq, so we also measured anti-Arab racism and expected it to correlate with SDO.

Nationalism. A more general kind of in-group prejudice that can occur in nation-states is nationalism, chauvinism, or patriotism. Kosterman and Feshbach (1989) suggested that procountry feelings (patriotism) can be distinguished from comparative prejudice, that is, that one's country is better than other countries (nationalism), and as such should dominate other countries (chauvinism). Even so, all three reflect attitudinal bias in favor of the national in-group, and thus we postulated that patriotism, nationalism, and chauvinism would all be significantly related to SDO.

Cultural Elitism. All societies share the idea that one of the defining features of those who belong to their society (are part of the in-group, or are considered by them to be human) is that they are "cultured." In some societies, including English and American society, an elitist ideology built on the cultured–not cultured distinction postulates that the elite class has "culture" not shared by middle- and working-class people and is therefore more deserving of the "finer things in life." We term this legitimizing myth *cultural elitism*, and we expected it to correlate with SDO as well.

Sexism. We believe that antifemale sexism is a ubiquitous legitimizing myth, although, as with ethnic prejudice, the content basis of sexist ideology varies widely with religion, cultural history, and technology. In the present U.S. samples, we used scales that assess sexism as the extent to which people believe men and women are "naturally" different and should have different work roles outside and inside the home (Benson & Vincent, 1980; Rombough & Ventimiglia, 1981) and the extent to which people believe that women rather than men can be blamed for unwanted sexual advances such as rape and sexual harassment (Burt, 1980). We predicted that all of these would be positively correlated with SDO, even controlling for subject sex.

Political-Economic Conservatism. Political-economic conservatism is associated with support for capitalism versus socialism (e.g., Eysenck, 1971). Given that capitalism implies that some people and businesses should thrive, while those who are less "competitive" should not, we consider political-economic conservatism to be a hierarchy-enhancing legitimizing myth that should positively correlate with SDO (see also Sidanius & Pratto, 1993b). Other policies supported by conservatives, such as that women should stay home with children and that the USSR must be kept in its place, divide people into groups "deserving" different treatment, so we feel conservatism generally can be viewed as a legitimizing myth. In fact, Wilson's extensive work on the body of attitudes that make up conservatism shows that a preference for hierarchical social relationships is one of conservatism's many dimensions (Wilson, 1973, p. 22).

Noblesse Oblige. A hierarchy-attenuating ideology that exists in many cultures is that those with more resources should share them with those who have fewer resources (e.g., the Marxist maxim, "From each according to his [sic] ability, to each according to his need," and the potlatch custom of the Kwakiutl). The English-American version is called *noblesse oblige*, which we expected to be negatively correlated with SDO.

Meritocracy. Another hierarchy-enhancing ideology is that wealth and other social values are already distributed appropriately, based on the deservingness of the recipients. The Protestant work ethic and just world theory are examples of meritocratic ideologies, so we administered standard measures of belief in the Protestant work ethic and belief in a just world and predicted that they would be positively correlated with SDO. In the United States, attributions for poverty due to laziness or to some other inherent fault in the poor are predicated on the idea that equal opportunity is available to all (Kluegel & Smith, 1986), so we wrote an equal opportunity scale and predicted that it would correlate positively with SDO.

SOCIAL POLICY ATTITUDES

According to social dominance theory, individuals who are social dominance oriented will favor social practices that maintain or exacerbate inequality among groups and will oppose social practices that reduce group inequality. The particular social policies that correlate with SDO may vary from society to society, but we predicted that SDO would relate to support for, or opposition to, the following policies in U.S. samples.

Social Welfare, Civil Rights, and Environmental Policies. We expected SDO to correlate with opposition to social policies that would reduce inequality between U.S. nationals and foreigners or immigrants, rich and middle class or poor, men and women, ethnic groups, heterosexuals and homosexuals, and humans versus other species. As such, we measured our subjects' attitudes toward

a variety of government social programs, racial and sexual discrimination laws, gay and lesbian rights, domination of foreigners, and environmental policies. In several samples we also assessed attitudes toward "interracial dating" and "interracial marriage," because miscegenation has been central to the U.S. racial policy debate.

Military Policy. Because the military is a symbol of nationalism and can be one of the chief means of domination of one nation over others, we expected SDO to correlate positively with expressed support for military programs and actions.

Punitive Policies. Despite its stated creed to enact equality before the law, the U.S. criminal justice system shows class and ethnic bias at all levels from arrest to plea bargaining to sentencing (e.g., Bienen, Alan, Denno, Allison, & Mills, 1988; General Accounting Office, 1990; Kleck, 1981; Nickerson, Mayo, & Smith, 1986; Paternoster, 1983; Radelet & Pierce, 1985; Reiman, 1990; Sidanius, 1988). As one example, in a review of 1,804 homicide cases in South Carolina, Paternoster (1983) found that in cases where Blacks killed Whites, rather than other Blacks, prosecutors were 40 times more likely to request the death penalty. For this reason, we expected support for "law and order" or punitive policies, particularly the death penalty, to be positively related to SDO (see also Mitchell, 1993; Sidanius, Liu, Pratto, & Shaw, 1994).

Discriminant Validity

INTERPERSONAL DOMINANCE

SDO, or preference for unequal relationships among categories of people, is conceptually distinguishable from the common personality conception of interpersonal dominance, which concerns the extent to which individuals like to be in charge and are efficacious. For example, people who score high on the California Personality Inventory (CPI) Dominance scale are confident, assertive, dominant, and task oriented, whereas people who score low are unassuming and nonforceful (Gough, 1987, p. 6). People who score high on the Jackson Personality Research Form (JPRF) Dominance scale attempt to control their environments and influence or direct other people; they are forceful, decisive, authoritative, and domineering (Jackson, 1965). We tested this theoretical distinction between social and task or interpersonal dominance by using the CPI and JPRF Dominance subscales in several samples reported here. We predicted that SDO would not correlate with these two measures.

AUTHORITARIANISM

There is clearly some theoretical similarity in the effects of social dominance theory's SDO construct and authoritarian personality theory's authoritarian construct (see Adorno, Frenkel-Brunswik, Levinson, & Sanford, 1950). High-SDO people and authoritarian personalities are theorized to be relatively conservative, racist, ethnocentric, and prejudiced, and they would show little empathy for lower status others. Our conception of SDO, however, differs from classical authoritarianism in several respects. First, classical authoritarian theorists viewed authoritarianism as an aberrant and pathological condition and is a form of ego-defense against feelings of inadequacy and vulnerability (see also Frenkel-Brunswik, 1948, 1949). SDO, however, is not conceived of in clinical terms, as an aberrant personality type, or as a form of ego-defense. Rather, SDO is conceived as a "normal" human propensity on which people vary. Second, authoritarian personality theory emphasized the sources of authoritarianism as springing from psychodynamic processes. Specifically, Adorno et al. (1950) postulated that strict and harsh parental styles would provoke conflicts between the child and parents that would be "unresolved." As a way of resolving these, the child as an adult would submit to authorities and be intolerant of those who would not. In contrast, we theorize that such a personal history is unnecessary to developing a relatively high SDO tendency. Rather, both temperament and socialization probably influence one's level of SDO. Third and most important, whereas authoritarianism is primarily conceived as a desire for individual dominance resulting from experiences with authority figures, SDO is regarded as the desire that some categories of people dominate others. Because the two constructs are defined differently, measurements of each should not be highly correlated.

Given that authoritarianism should predict many of the same variables we postulate SDO should predict, it is important for us to show that SDO has explanatory value in addition to authoritarianism. We tested the "marginal utility" of the SDO construct by testing whether correlations between SDO and support for legitimizing myths and policies are significant after partialing out authoritarianism.

CONSERVATISM

Political-economic conservatism serves as a legitimizing myth in our theory, and thus we expect it to correlate positively with SDO. Conservatism is also a well-known robust predictor of social and political attitudes (e.g., Eysenck & Wilson, 1978; Wilson, 1973). To show that SDO has utility in addition to political-economic conservatism, we tested whether SDO substantially correlated with social attitudes after partialing out conservatism.

STANDARD PERSONALITY VARIABLES

Because we think our concept of SDO is a yet unstudied personality dimension, we expected it to be independent of other standard personality variables such as self-esteem and the Big-Five personality dimensions: Extraversion, Agreeableness, Openness, Neuroticism, and Conscientiousness (see Costa & MacRae, 1985; John, 1990, for reviews).

EMPATHY, ALTRUISM, COMMUNALITY, AND TOLERANCE

People who are highly empathic with others would seem to be less prejudiced and discriminatory against out-groups. Thus, it is reasonable to expect a general concern for other people to be negatively correlated with SDO. Similarly, any general prosocial orientation might mitigate prejudiced feelings and behaviors toward out-group members, so altruism should be negatively correlated with SDO. Furthermore, people who are quite inclusive in their definitions of what constitutes an in-group should be less able to discriminate against out-groups, so we expected communality to be negatively correlated with SDO. And finally, because tolerance is the antithesis of prejudice, we might expect that a general measure of tolerance would be negatively correlated with a general desire for in-group superiority. We used Davis' (1983) multidimensional empathy scale, Super and Nevill's (1985) altruism subscale, the Personal Attribute Questionnaire (PAQ) Communality scale (Spence, Helmreich, & Stapp, 1974), and the Jackson Personality Inventory (JPI) Tolerance scale (Jackson, 1976) to test these hypotheses. If SDO has merit as a new personality variable, none of these correlations should be very high.

Present Research

Overview

We examined data from 13 samples to test the predictive and discriminant validity and reliability of our measure of SDO. Our logic in using this large number of samples is to examine statistically significant results that are reliable across samples. We organized the results by topic, but we report the results in each sample so that the reader can see the magnitude of effects in each sample and the stability of the results across samples. At the end of the Results section, we provide a summary of the results in the form of meta-analyses.

DATA COLLECTION

Generally, subjects were college students who participated in a study called "Social Attitudes" for partial course credit. All of their responses were anonymous and confidential, and they completed batteries of self-administered questionnaires. Subjects in Samples 2, 3b, 5, 6, 8, 9, and 13 spent about 1 hr in our laboratory completing the questionnaires. The experimenter described the study as designed to measure students' social attitudes and personal preferences. Subjects in Samples 1 and 13 completed the SDO scale after participating in unrelated experiments, and subjects in the remaining samples completed the SDO scale and follow-up scales in two consecutive mass-testing sessions normally conducted on subject pool participants. All subjects completed a demographic background sheet and our 14-item SDO scale intermixed with related items, a Nationalism scale based on Kosterman and Feshbach's (1989) measure, along with other attitude or experience measures, each having their own instructions and response scales. We also administered some standard personality or attitude scales according to the instructions of their authors. In several samples we also administered ideological (legitimizing myths) or policy attitude items on a questionnaire entitled "Policy Issues Questionnaire."

MEASURES

SDO. In previous archival studies, we measured proxies for SDO using items dealing with equality from the National Election Study or the S6 Conservatism scale (see Sidanius, 1976). In developing the present measure of SDO, we tested over 70 items whose content we felt related to SDO or to constructs one can define as separate but that might be considered adjacent to SDO (e.g., nationalism and prestige-striving), following Loevinger's (1957) suggestion about scale construction. However, on the basis of our desire to develop a simple, unidimensional scale that is balanced, we selected 14 items from this extensive questionnaire as the SDO scale. The selected items concerned the belief that some people are inherently superior or inferior to others and approval of unequal group relationships (see items in Appendix A). The 14-item SDO scale was balanced in that half the items indicated approval of inequality and half indicated approval of equality (see items in Appendix A). We assume that these items tap a latent construct and so we are interested in the relationships between the scale mean and other measures rather than relationships between individual SDO items and other measures.

SDO is an attitudinal orientation, so instructions read, "Which of the following objects or statements do you have a positive or negative feeling towards? Beside each object or statement, place a number from '1' to '7' which represents the degree of your positive or negative feeling." The scale was labeled *very positive* (7), *positive* (6), *slightly positive* (5), *neither positive nor negative* (4), *slightly-negative* (3), *negative* (2), and *very negative* (1).

The order of the SDO items and the filler items differed among Form A, completed by Samples 1, 2, 3, and 4; Form B, completed by Samples 5, 6, 7, 8, and 12; and Form C, completed by Samples 9, 10, and 11. The format and instructions for the three forms were identical, and we saw no evidence that results pertinent to reliability or validity issues differed across the questionnaire form. Subsequent to the present research, we have used just the 14 items on a questionnaire and found reliability coefficients of .90 and predictive validity results similar to those reported below.

Political-Economic Conservatism. Some of the standard scales assessing political-economic conservatism actually measure individuals' support for particular social policies (e.g., the C-scale, Wilson & Patterson, 1968). Because we wished to measure political-economic conservatism separately from policy attitudes, and because we wanted to use a measure that should not vary with time and place, we used a self-identified liberal-conservative measure in all samples. On the demographic background sheet, the political-economic conservatism question read, "Use one of the following numbers to indicate your political views in the accompanying categories." Below these instructions was a scale labeled *very liberal* (1), *liberal* (2), *slightly liberal* (3), *middle of the road* (4), *slightly conservative* (5), *conservative* (6), and *very conservative* (7) and a blank next to each type of issue: "foreign policy issues," "economic issues," and "social issues." Political-economic conservatism was the mean of self-ratings on these three items.

Authoritarianism. Authoritarianism research has been fraught with measurement difficulties. After surveying the authoritarianism measurement literature, we decided to administer two rather different measures of authoritarianism, both of which are balanced: the Right Wing Authoritarian (RWA) scale by Altemeyer (1981) and Goertzel's (1987) bipolar personality measure. Goertzel (1987) intended his adjective checklist to measure the personality rather than the ideological aspect of authoritarianism, but did show that it correlates with attitudes toward policies falling along toughness and consistency dimensions. Altemeyer's (1981) scale is the only other internally reliable measure of authoritarianism that is close to the original conception of authoritarianism, including conventionalism, authoritarian submission, and authoritarian aggression (see Duckitt, 1989, for a review).

Original Legitimizing Myths and Policy Attitudes. The consent form and instructions informed subjects that their opinions and preferences toward a variety of ideas, kinds of people, events, and so forth would be measured. On our "Policy Issues Questionnaire" we included items from various legitimizing myth or policy attitude scales. Items from each scale were interspersed throughout the questionnaire. Next to each item was a 1–7 scale, and the instructions read, "Which of the following objects, events, or statements do you have a positive or negative feeling towards? Please indicate your feelings by circling the appropriate

number alongside each item. Use one of the following responses. Remember, your first reaction is best. Work as quickly as you can." The scale points were labeled *very negative* (1), *negative* (2), *slightly negative* (3), *uncertain* or *neutral* (4), *slightly positive* (5), *positive* (6), and *very positive* (7).

Items from the original legitimizing myths and policy attitude scales were selected for their content and for their internal reliability across samples. These scales are shown in Appendix B. Several personality measures were used as well; these are described in the Method section.

Method

SUBJECTS

Although our 1,952 subjects were college students, they represent some diversity in terms of sex, ethnicity, and income groups, coming from public and private universities in California. Demographic information about the samples is shown in Table 15.1.

SAMPLES AND PROCEDURES

Sample 1 (spring 1990) consisted of 98 University of California at Berkeley undergraduates who completed the CPI Dominance, Flexibility, and Capacity for Status subscales (Gough, 1987), the JPRF Dominance subscale (Jackson, 1965), the JPI Tolerance subscale (Jackson, 1976), and the Rosenberg (1965) Self-Esteem Scale (RSE).

Sample 2 (fall and winter 1990–1991) consisted of 463 San Jose State University (SJSU) undergraduates who completed the CPI and JPRF Dominance subscales; Mirels and Garrett's (1971) Protestant Work Ethic Scale; the Just World Scale (Rubin & Peplau, 1975); the four-factor Interpersonal Reactivity Index (IRI), which measures empathy (Davis, 1983); a number of policy attitude measures; and some demographic descriptors.

Sample 3a (September, 1990) consisted of 81 Stanford University undergraduates who completed the SDO scale as part of a mass-testing session. Sample 3b included 57 subjects from the same population who participated in a study in our lab in December, 1990, during which they completed the SDO scale again and a number of attitude and personality measures. The overlap of

Table 15.1. Description of Samples

Measure	Sample													
	1	2	3a	3b	4	5	6	7	8	9	10	11	12	13
	Age and gender breakdown													
n	98	463	81	57	190	144	49	224	115	97	231	100	135	46
Age range	17–34	15–56	17–21	17–21		17–35	17–23		17–59	17–36				
% men	50	47		51	47	49	69	50	40	33	54		59	100
% women	50	53		49	53	51	31	50	60	67	46		41	0
	Ethnic breakdown													
% Euro-American	48	38		58	38	53	59	49	29	19	67		50	52
% Asian-American	23	40		16	40	24	24	25	51	45	22		33	33
% Hispanic	13	8		4	8	10	15	10	14	17	4		10	11
% Black	15	5		14	5	8	2	6	2	10	4		4	0
% Arab-American	1	2		6	2	0	0	1	3	8	1		1	4
	Family Income													
Under 20K		12			10	21	6		17	19				
20–30K		9			8	16	6		13	15				
30–40K		11			5	12	8		13	17				
40–55K		17			10	8	10		15	12				
55–70K		20			10	19	10		17	15				
70–100K		14			21	14	19		13	9				
100–150K		8			15	6	19		5	2				
150–200K		5			13	3	11		2	3				
200K+		5			8	1	11		5	6				

Note. Missing numbers indicate that information was not available. Samples 4, 7, 10–13 are probably similar in age distribution and range to Sample 3. Income was self-reported annual family income in thousands of dollars.

these two samples (*N* = 25 with complete data) was used to assess the cross-time reliability of SDO.

Sample 4 (January, 1991) consisted of 190 Stanford University undergraduates who completed the SDO scale and an attitude scale about the Iraq war assessing environmental concerns in the war, anti-Arab racism, willingness to sacrifice for the war, willingness to restrict civil liberties for the war effort, and support for the use of military force by the United States against Iraq.

Sample 5 (fall 1991) consisted of 144 SJSU undergraduates who completed the RSE (Rosenberg, 1965), the Rombough and Ventimiglia (1981) Tri-Dimensional Sexism Scale, the Sexist Attitudes Toward Women Scale (Benson & Vincent, 1980), the Rape Myths Scale (Burt, 1980), the Altruism subscale from the Values Scale (Super & Nevill, 1985), and the IRI (Davis, 1983). We also measured policy attitudes toward gay rights, women's equality policies, militarism, punitiveness, racial policies, and environmental policies. In addition, we measured ideologies such as anti-Black racism, elitism, patriotism, belief in

equal opportunity, and opposition to miscegenation.

Sample 6 (September, 1991) consisted of 49 Stanford undergraduates who completed the same measures as subjects in Sample 5.

Sample 7 (September, 1991) consisted of 224 Stanford undergraduates who completed a battery of personality questions, including Malle and Horowitz's (1994) bipolar descriptions of Factors I (Extraversion), II (Agreeableness), IV (Neuroticism), and V (Conscientiousness) of the Big-Five personality dimensions (see John, 1990, for a review). A few weeks later, in the 3 days including and following the day Clarence Thomas was confirmed to the Supreme Court, those subjects who had given their prior permission were telephoned and asked four questions about their opinions regarding this Supreme Court nomination. In all, 149 subjects were reached by telephone, and the response rate was 100%.

Sample 8 (February, 1992) consisted of 115 Stanford undergraduates who completed the PAQ (Spence et al., 1974), CPI Dominance scale (Gough, 1987), JPRF Dominance scale (Jackson,

1965), JPI Tolerance scale (Jackson, 1976), IRI (Davis, 1983), RSE (Rosenberg, 1965), a post-Iraq war attitude survey, a general war attitude survey, and a number of other policy attitude measures similar to those in Sample 5.

Sample 9 (April, 1992) consisted of 97 SJSU undergraduates. They completed the CPI and JPW Dominance subscales; the JPI Tolerance subscale; the IRI; the Protestant Work Ethic Scale; all 19 of the authoritarian bipolar adjective choices (Goertzel, 1987); Altemeyer's (1981) 30-item RWA Scale; John, Donahue, and Kentle's (1992) Big-Five Personality Inventory; the PAQ; McConahay's (1986) Modern Racism Scale; and Katz and Hass' (1988) Pro-Black, Anti-Black, and Humanitarian-Egalitarian Scales. They also completed a number of policy attitude items similar to those for Sample 5.

Sample 10 (March, 1992) consisted of 231 Stanford undergraduates who completed the SDO scale. Two weeks later, 176 of these subjects completed a comprehensive survey about their ideologies and general attitudes about the death penalty and their attitude about the execution of Robert Alton Harris, who was executed by the state of California the day before the survey was administered.

Sample 11 (March, 1991) consisted of 100 Stanford University undergraduates who completed the SDO scale and a battery of other questionnaires including Snyder's (1974) self-monitoring scales; Fenigstein, Scheier, and Buss' (1975) Self-Consciousness scales; and Malle and Horowitz' (1994) bipolar adjective versions of Factors I and IV of the Big-Five personality dimensions.

Sample 12 (January, 1992) included 139 Stanford undergraduates who completed the SDO scale in a mass-testing session. Of these, 70 also completed Malle and Horowitz' (1994) measures of Factors I and IV.

Sample 13 included 46 undergraduate men at Stanford during 1990–1991 who were selected to be in an experiment on the basis of having either extremely high or low SDO scores in Samples 3, 4, and 11. They participated in the experiment between 6 weeks and 8 months after their first testing and completed the SDO scale again.

Results

We first present the internal and temporal reliability of our SDO scale. We then examine whether this measure related to the ideological, policy attitude, and hierarchy role variables predicted by social dominance theory. We show that SDO was either independent of other personality variables with which it might be confused or that it predicted the attitudinal outcomes over and above the effects of these other variables. We also show that it was not redundant with other personality measures. Finally, we show that SDO predicted new social and political attitudes. To summarize the results across samples, we report simple averages of the internal reliability coefficients across samples and averaged correlations across samples using Fisher's z-to-r transformation.

RELIABILITY OF THE SDO MEASURE

Unidimensionality. We conducted two kinds of analyses to confirm that the 14 SDO items assessed a single construct. First, within each sample, principal-components analyses of the 14 SDO items showed that a single dimension captured the bulk of the variance in these items. That is, there was a precipitous drop between the values of the first and second eigenvalues in every sample. Second, we subjected our largest sample, Sample 2 (N = 446 with complete data on all SDO items) to confirmatory factor analysis. Using maximum-likelihood estimation, we tested a model in which all 14 items were driven by a single latent construct. Each item had a statistically significant relationship to the latent factor ($ps < .0001$). By freeing only 3 of 91 possible off-diagonal elements of the θ_δ, matrix,[2] we obtained a satisfactory χ^2/df ratio of 2.89 (e.g., Carmines & McIver, 1981), suggesting that our data are consistent with a model in which a single dimension underlies responses to all the items. Thus, the 14 items appear to measure a unitary construct.

Internal Reliability. Item statistics showed that the 14-item SDO scale showed good internal reliability across all samples, averaging $\alpha = .83$ (see internal reliability coefficients and item statistics by sample in Table 15.2). Item analyses also showed that all items were highly correlated with the remainder of the scale in every sample. The average lowest item-total correlation across samples was .31 and the average highest item–total correlation across samples was .63. Item 7 had the

---

[2]The freed elements of the matrix corresponded to Items 8 and 9, Items 2 and 4, and Items 10 and 11 in Appendix A.

TABLE 15.2. Coefficient Alphas, Correlation With Subject Gender, and Average Item Means and Variances by Sample for 14-Item Social Dominance Orientation Scale

Measure	Sample												
	1	2	3a	3b	4	5	6	7	8	9	10	11	12
α	.85	.83	.84	.85	.84	.81	.84	.89	.82	.80	.83	.81	.83
r_{pbi}	.29**	.27**	.32**	.31*	.32**	.11	.36*	.28*	.27**	.03	.30**	—	.26**
M	2.44	2.74	2.55	2.31	2.59	2.97	2.50	2.59	3.02	3.12	3.13	2.91	2.60
Variance	0.14	0.22	0.18	0.17	0.21	0.40	0.24	0.23	0.18	0.36	0.66	0.27	0.23

Note. Positive correlations with gender indicate that men were higher than women.
  * $p < .05$. ** $p < .01$.

lowest item-total correlation in 4 of 12 independent samples ($Z = 3.52$, $p < .001$). Item 9 had the highest item-total correlation in 3 samples ($Z = 2.40$, $p < .01$). No other items were either the most or least correlated across samples in numbers that differed from chance using a binomial test.

Stability of SDO Measure Over Time. We measured the stability of scores on our scale over time in two samples. Twenty-five of the subjects in Sample 3 were tested on SDO twice at a 3-month interval. Their SDO scores substantially correlated from Time 1 to Time 2 ($r = .81$, $p < .01$). The mean difference from Time 1 to Time 2 was 0.09 on a 7-point scale, which did not differ reliably from zero ($t < 1$). In contrast, the Time 1–Time 2 correlation for the 10-item RSE was .50.

Sample 13 consisted of 46 of the highest and lowest scoring men on the SDO scale from Samples 3, 4, and 11, who completed that scale again some months later. The correlation in this sample from Time 1 to Time 2 was .84 ($p < .001$), and the mean difference in scores from Time 1 to Time 2 was essentially zero ($M = 0.03$, $t < 1$; for the high group, $M = -0.03$ and for the low group, $M = 0.09$). All of the subjects first classified as "high" or "low" on SDO met this criterion again in the second testing. The near-zero mean changes within both groups are particularly telling because one could have expected at least some regression toward the mean. Thus, even in different testing contexts, our SDO measure appears highly stable in the short term.

PREDICTIVE MEASURES

Gender Differences. The gender difference we expected showed in all but two samples; men were higher on SDO than women (see point-biserial correlations in Table 15.2).

SDO and Hierarchy Role. A question on the demographic background questionnaire asked subjects in what sector of the economy they intended to work after graduation. There were 20 career choices provided. Theoretically, we define those whose work is primarily aimed at protecting, serving, or benefiting elite members of society more than oppressed members of society "hierarchy-enhancing." Those whose work benefits the oppressed more than elites we define as "hierarchy-attenuating." As such, we classified subjects as (a) hierarchy enhancers (those intending careers in law, law enforcement, politics, and business); (b) "middlers" who would not obviously attenuate or enhance inequality through their professional work, such as science and sales; or (c) hierarchy attenuators (those intending to be in such professions as social work or counseling; see also Sidanius, Pratto, Martin, & Stallworth, 1991). We predicted that hierarchy enhancers would have higher SDO levels than hierarchy attenuators, and that middlers' SDO levels would fall somewhere between the other two. Sample 2 was large enough to test this hypothesis; we also combined Samples 5, 6, 8, and 9 to replicate the test. Because more women tend to go into hierarchy-attenuating careers, and because we know that SDO exhibits a gender difference, we also included subject sex as an independent variable along with hierarchy role. SDO was the outcome variable in simultaneous regression-style analyses of variance (ANOVAs) with planned contrasts. In Sample 2, the results were as expected: Those who intended to work in hierarchy-attenuating professions had lower SDO levels ($M = 2.28$) than did middlers ($M = 2.72$), $F(1, 432) = 5.49$, $p < .05$, and also lower levels than those intending to work in hierarchy-enhancing professions ($M = 2.88$), $F(1, 432) = 10.21$, $p < .01$. Men also had higher SDO levels ($M = 3.03$) than women ($M = 2.51$), $F(1, 432) = 36.86$, $p < .001$. In the merged sample, hierarchy attenuators again had lower SDO levels ($M = 2.64$) than hierarchy enhancers ($M = 3.09$), $F(1, 378) = 5.01$, $p < .05$. Middlers' SDO levels were in the middle ($M = 2.94$) and were not distinguishable from those of either enhancers or attenuators. Again, men ($M = 3.07$) had higher SDO levels than women ($M = 2.90$), $F(1, 378) = 3.72$, $p = .05$. Results from both these large samples indicate that intended hierarchy attenuators did indeed have lower SDO levels than intended hierarchy enhancers, even after controlling for subjects' sex.

SDO and Hierarchy-Legitimizing Myths. We hypothesized that SDO should be related to any social or political ideology that helps legitimize group-based inequality.

Ideologies. The three-item index of self-described political ideology had good internal reliability, averaging $\alpha = .78$ across samples (see Table 15.3). SDO correlated positively and significantly with political-economic conservatism in 7 of 8 samples, averaging $r = .38$; conservatives were higher on SDO than liberals (see Table 15.3). The

scales measuring meritocratic ideologies, the Protestant Work Ethic and Just World Scales, had fairly low internal reliabilities in all samples, considering that they are 19- and 20-item scales, respectively (see Table 15.3). In a Stanford sample (Sample 3b), but not in two samples from SJSU (Samples 2 and 9), the Protestant Work Ethic Scale and Just World Scale had significant positive correlations with SDO (see Table 15.3). This suggested to us that variations in the cultural background of these samples may affect the ideologies known to and accepted by them. Results from our demographic questionnaire showed that compared with Stanford, SJSU tends to have more first-generation American, more Catholic, and fewer Euro-American students.

The other legitimizing myth scales that we constructed fared better (see items for all other scales Appendix B). The nationalism, patriotism, cultural elitism, and equal opportunity measures all had good internal reliability and were positively correlated with SDO (rs ranged from .22 to .67), with

Table 15.3. Coefficient Alphas of Legitimizing Myth Scales and Correlations With Social Dominance Orientation Sample

Measure	No. of items	Sample 2 ($n = 408$)	Sample 3b ($n = 57$)	Sample 4	Sample 5 ($n = 144$)	Sample 6 ($n = 49$)	Sample 8 ($n = 115$)	Sample 9 ($n = 95$)	Sample 10 ($n = 156$)
				Coefficient α					
Political-economic conservatism	3	.69	.83	.89ᵃ	.80	.71	.80	.72	.78
Protestant Work Ethic	19	.68	.75					.73	
Just World	20	.55	.42						
Nationalism	6	.75	.88	.80ᵃ	.68	.86	.78	.66	.62
Patriotism	12				.83	.89		.80	
Cultural elitism	7				.67	.78		.59	
Equal opportunity	6				.65	.76		.49	
Noblesse oblige	6	.58	.80	.69ᵃ	.65	.73	.56	.72	.54
Anti-Black racism	5	.68	.77		.70	.74	.60	.77	
				Correlations					
Political-economic conservatism		.26**	.28*	.44**ᵇ	.11	.72**	.24*	.17*	.55**
Protestant Work Ethic		-.03	.33*					.03	
Just World		.09	.43**						
Nationalism		.52**	.41**	.53**ᵇ	.43**	.67**	.51**	.47**	.72**
Patriotism					.43**	.65**		.22*	
Cultural elitism					.51**	.23		.44**	
Equal opportunity					.51**	.51**		.34**	
Noblesse oblige		-.39**	-.54**	-.43**ᵇ	-.60**		-.69**	-.50**	-.72**
Anti-Black racism		.57**	.42**		.49**	.61**	.65**	.52**	

ᵃ$n = 180$. ᵇ$n = 90$.
* $p < .05$. ** $p < .01$.

only one exception (see Table 15.3). These correlations showed that the more subjects tended to prefer group dominance in general, the more nationalistic and patriotic they were (average rs = .51 and .45, respectively) and the more they subscribed to cultural elitism (average r = .40) and equal opportunity ideologies (average r = .46). As predicted, the noblesse oblige scale was strongly negatively correlated with SDO in every sample, ranging from –.39 to –.69 (see Table 15.3). In Samples 1, 3a, and 7 (not shown in Table 15.3), SDO correlated –.47, –.56, and –.67 with noblesse oblige (ps < .01), for an overall average correlation of –.54.

Ethnic prejudice. SDO was strongly correlated with our anti-Black racism measure in every sample, ranging from .42 to .65 and averaging .55 (see Table 15.3). In Sample 4, we also measured anti-Arab racism (a = .73), which correlated with SDO (r = .22, p < .05). In Sample 9, we administered McConahay's (1986) seven-item Modern Racism Scale (α = .79), which correlated .53 with SDO. Katz and Hass' (1988) 10-item Pro-Black Scale (α = .68) was negatively correlated with SDO (r = –.38, p < .01), and their 10-item Anti-Black Scale (α = .62) was positively correlated with SDO (r = .30, p < .01). These results, using rather different racism measures, are consistent with the idea that generalized preference for group dominance drives belief in culturally specific forms of ethnic prejudice.

Sexism. We assessed antifemale sexism in Samples 5 and 6 with several measures, all of which proved to be internally reliable. These measures were highly correlated with SDO (rs ranging from .34 to .63; see Table 15.4). Across both samples and all sexism measures, the average correlation was .47. Partial correlations controlling for gender with SDO were also reliable and of

about the same magnitude. For this reason, the large correlations between SDO and sexism cannot be attributed to gender differences on SDO or sexism measures.

In summary, all of the measured ideologies (hierarchy-legitimizing myths) except the Protestant Work Ethic Scale and Belief in a Just World Scale were reliably correlated with SDO in the expected directions across virtually all samples. SDO was most strongly related with ideologies concerning group prejudice against other nations, ethnic groups, and women.

SDO and Policy Attitudes. We hypothesized that SDO would predict support for social policies with implications for the distribution of social value among groups. We assessed attitudes toward chauvinist policies (United States dominating other national groups), law and order policies, military programs, gay rights, women's rights, social programs generally, racial policies, and environmental policies in most of our samples (see coefficient alphas in Table 15.5).

Support for chauvinist policies and law and order policies were positively correlated with SDO in almost all samples, averaging .34 and .28, respectively. Support for military programs was positively correlated with SDO in all samples, averaging .44. Support for gay rights, women's rights, social welfare programs, ameliorative racial policy, miscegenation, and environmental policy were significantly negatively related to SDO in all but three cases (see Table 15.5). These relationships were of about the same magnitudes as the policy attitudes described above. We assessed political party preference by having subjects rate themselves from *strong Democrat* (1) through *independent* (4) to *strong Republican* (7) and *others.* Excluding "others," Republican political party preference correlated positively and significantly with SDO in six

Table 15.4. Coefficient Alphas of Sexism Scales and Correlations With Social Dominance Orientation Within Samples

Measure	No. of items	Coefficient α		Correlations	
		Sample 5	Sample 6	Sample 5	Sample 6
Rombough & Ventimiglia sexism	20	.90	.94	.44**	.54**
Sex differences	5	.68	.65	.38**	.56**
Internal (household) labor	10	.89	.94	.34**	.63**
External (paid) labor	6	.78	.85	.45**	.36*
Sexist Attitudes Toward Women	40	.91	.94	.46**	.55**
Rape Myths	10	.84	.75	.46**	.40**

* p < .05. ** p < .01.

Table 15.5. Coefficient Alphas of Policy Scales, Correlations With Social Dominance Orientation, and Partial Correlations Controlling for Conservatism, Across Samples

Policy scale	No. of items	Sample						
		2 (n = 455)	3b (n = 50)	4	5 (n = 129)	6 (n = 37)	8 (n =100)	9 (n = 89)
		Coefficient α						
Chauvinism	8			.73		.73		.58
Law and order	4	.64	.71		.59	.77^a	.67	.77^b
Military programs	3	.67^a	.75		.73	.67		.59
Gay & lesbian rights	2	.82	.91		.85	.86		.83
Women's rights	4	.63	.72		.69	.63	.80^c	.74
Social programs	10	.78	.77		.79	.86	.66^c	.81^d
Racial policy	7	.71	.81		.68	.72	.60^c	.77
Miscegeny	2	.96	.97		.93	.94	.91	.87
Environmental policies	5				.71	.80		.76
		Correlations of social dominance orientation and policy items						
Chauvinism					.37**	.49**		.14
Law and order		.08	.23*		.30**	.59**	.24*	.19
Military programs		.33**	.27*		.33**	.70**		.47**
Gay and lesbian rights		−.32**	−.50**		−.29**	−.55**		−.17
Women's rights		−.42**	−.32**		−.39**	−.34*	−.52**	−.42**
Social programs		−.50**	−.31**		−.29**	−.70**	−.55**	−.39**
Racial policy		−.42**	−.46**		−.23**	−.62**	−.54**	−.34**
Miscegeny		−.31**	−.15		−.30**	−.31*	−.25*	−.18
Environmental policies					−.27**	−.40**		−.47**
Republican party preference		.15**	.25*		.24**	.45**	.33**	.27*
		Partial correlations removing political-economic conservatism						
Chauvinism					.40**	.16		.06
Law and order		−.02	.15		.29***	.31*	.25***	.15
Military programs		.16***	.18		.31***	.40**		.46***
Gay & lesbian rights		−.28***	−.32**		−.29***	−.14		−.15
Women's rights		−.38**	−.31**		−.35***	−.27*	−.46***	−.40***
Social programs		−.30***	−.27*		−.30***	−.49**	−.50***	−.37***
Racial policy		−.33***	−.30**		−.22***	−.38**	−.49***	−.31***
Miscegeny		−.28***	−.19		−.31***	−.08	−.23**	−.17*
Environmental policies					−.27***	−.31*		−.46***

^{a} Three items. ^{b} Two items. ^{c} Six items. ^{d} Seven items.
* p < .05. ** p < .01. *** p < .001.

out of six samples, averaging .28 (see Table 15.5).

In addition to support for military programs, we expected support for military action including war to be positively related to SDO. We tested this hypothesis by surveying attitudes toward war in general and specific attitudes toward the war against Iraq fought by the United States and other nations at the time of data collection. In fall 1990, while Iraq was occupying Kuwait and the United States was amassing troops near Iraq, data from Sample 2 were collected, including a single war

policy item, "Going to war to maintain low oil prices." This item correlated .30 with SDO ($p <$ .01). In January, 1991, when the United States and allies had just begun bombing Iraq, we administered a balanced scale concerning war and related attitudes to Sample 4. A reliable ($\alpha = .85$) tight-item pro-war scale correlated .51 with SDO ($p <$ .01). One year later, we asked Sample 8 about their attitudes toward the Iraq war. The resulting Iraq War Attitudes scale was reliable ($\alpha = .85$) and correlated .29 with SDO ($p < .01$).

Does SDO, then, unconditionally predict support for war, or only war for certain purposes? We attempted to answer this question by designing a General War Attitudes scale including two kinds of items, namely, Wars of Dominance, which we expected to relate positively to SDO, and Wars for Humanitarian Reasons, which we did not expect to relate positively to SDO. This scale was administered to Sample 8 in January, 1992. Factor analysis confirmed that these were two independent dimensions. The Wars of Dominance scale (eight items) was reliable ($\alpha = .82$) and correlated positively with SDO ($r = .31, p < .01$). The Humanitarian Wars scale (six items)[3] was also reliable ($\alpha = .73$) and correlated negatively with SDO ($r = -.41, p < .01$), so SDO is not merely antipacifism. The Wars of Dominance scale was positively correlated with support for the Iraq war ($r = .63, p < .001$), but the Humanitarian Wars scale was uncorrelated with support for the Iraq war ($r = .07$). These results suggest that SDO does not predict support for war unconditionally; rather, SDO predisposes people to endorse group dominance ideologies, thus facilitating support for wars of dominance.

DISCRIMINANT VALIDITY

We expected SDO to correlate with political-economic conservatism, and indeed it did. However, to show that SDO has utility as a predictor of policy attitudes over and above political economic conservatism, we computed the correlations between SDO and the policy attitudes reported above after partialing out political-economic conservatism. Of the 41 significant zero-order correlations between SDO and policy attitudes in Table 15.5, only 5 become nonsignificant when political-economic conservatism is partialed out.[4] A few of the very high zero-order correlations were reduced substantially, but many more partial correlations were almost the same as the zero-order correlations (see Table 15.5). Across all the samples, then, there was no consistent evidence that political-economic conservatism could replace SDO as a predictor of the policy attitudes we assessed.

In Sample 9, we assessed another rival predictor of policy attitudes, namely authoritarianism, using two measures. Altemeyer's 30-item RWA

scale had good internal reliability ($\alpha = .78$); Goertzel's measure was adequate for a bipolar scale ($\alpha = .53$). Both measures of authoritarianism correlated with political-economic conservatism ($r = .31$ for RWA, $r = .29$ for the Goertzel measure, both $ps < .01$), confirming their validity. Neither, however, correlated strongly with SDO. RWA correlated $.14 (ns)$ with SDO, and the Goertzel measure correlated $.18$ with SDO ($p < .10$). Correcting these correlations for attenuation yielded slightly higher correlations ($r^* = .18, p < .05$ for RWA; $r^* = .28, p < .01$ for the Goertzel measure).

We also computed partial correlations between SDO and the policy attitudes, partialing the two authoritarianism measures and political-economic conservatism. In Sample 9, all the policies that showed significant zero-order correlations with SDO also had significant correlations with SDO, partialing out the effects of political-economic conservatism, RWA, and the Goertzel measure. Both authoritarianism measures showed substantial zero-order correlations with attitudes that were not as highly correlated with SDO in this sample: gay rights ($r = -.51$ for RWA, $r = -.31$ for the Goertzel measure, $ps < .01$) and chauvinistic policies ($r = .38$ for RWA, $p < .01$, $r = .25$ for the Goertzel measure, $p < .05$). As Peterson, Doty, and Winter (1993) showed recently authoritarianism still predicts social attitudes, particularly those relevant to untraditional sexual practices and prejudice against foreigners.

Because authoritarian personality theory (Adorno et al., 1950) also postulates that authoritarianism should predict ethnocentrism, racism, nationalism, and conservatism, we tested whether SDO would still predict belief in these legitimizing myths, controlling for authoritarianism. All the reliable zero order correlations between SDO and ideological measures were reliable after controlling for RWA and the Goertzel measure, except for the correlation with political-economic conservatism. The correlation between SDO and political-economic conservatism, partialing RWA, was $.13 (p = .11)$. Partialing the Goertzel measure, the correlation between SDO and political-economic conservatism was $.16 (p = .07)$, and partialing both measures, the correlation was $.13 (p = .11)$. Although the relationship between SDO and conservatism may be explained by their joint relationship to authoritarianism, the relationships between SDO and racism and nationalism cannot.

---

[3] Two unreliable items were eliminated from the scale.

[4] One other correlation actually became significant because partial correlations use one-tailed tests.

Dominance and Self-Esteem. Conservatism and authoritarianism were the only rival variables we identified as predictors of social and political attitudes, and the analyses above show that SDO substantially related to such attitudes, even when controlling for political-economic conservatism and for authoritarianism. To show a different kind of discriminant validity, we tested whether SDO correlated with other personality measures. If any of these were large, we would then be obliged to test the partial correlations with the social and political attitudes discussed above.

Only once did SDO correlate with the CPI and JPRF Dominance subscales across five samples (see Table 15.6). On average, CPI Dominance correlated .03 with SDO, and JPRF Dominance correlated −.006. These results clearly indicate that SDO is independent of interpersonal dominance. In Sample 1, SDO was also unrelated to CPI Flexibility ($r = .06$) and Capacity for Status ($r = .05$). For the most part, SDO was also uncorrelated with self-esteem in Samples 1 through 9, averaging −.08 (see Table 15.6).

Other Personality Measures. We used data collected by other researchers at Stanford during mass testing sessions to further investigate the discriminant validity of SDO. SDO was uncorrelated with all the self-monitoring and self-consciousness scales in Sample 11. In Samples 7, 9, 11, and 12, SDO correlated −.06, −.11, .08, and −.19, respectively, with Extraversion; none of these correlations differed reliably from zero. SDO correlated −.02, .13, −.08, and .21 in those samples, respec-

tively, with Neuroticism; none of these differed reliably from zero. SDO correlated −.03 with Agreeableness in Sample 7 and −.41 ($p < .01$) in Sample 9. SDO correlated −.04 and −.14 with Conscientiousness in Samples 7 and 9, neither of which differed reliably from zero. SDO correlated −.28 with Openness ($p < .01$) in Sample 9. These data do not suggest that SDO is redundant with any of the Big-Five dimensions and strongly imply that SDO is independent of Extraversion and Neuroticism. Across this set of correlations, there was also no evidence that SDO is related to the positively valued personality dimensions (e.g., Extraversion and Calmness) as opposed to the negative dimensions (e.g., Introversion and Neuroticism).

CONVERGENT VALIDITY

Empathy, Altruism, and Communality. We expected that feelings of closeness and kindness toward others should mitigate desire to dominate other groups, so empathy, altruism, and communality should correlate negatively with SDO. We first tested whether different varieties of empathy were negatively related to SDO using Davis' (1983) IRI. The Concern for Others subscale was significantly negatively correlated with SDO in every sample (rs ranged from −.40 to −.53 and averaged −.46; see Table 15.7). High dominance-oriented people expressed less concern for others than did low dominance-oriented people. The patterns of correlations between SDO and the other

TABLE 15.6. Coefficient Alphas of Interpersonal Dominance and Self-Esteem and Correlations With Social Orientation Within Samples

Measure	No. of items	\multicolumn{9}{Sample}
		1 ($n = 98$)	2 ($n = 403$)	3a ($n = 80$)	3b ($n = 57$)	4 ($n = 90$)	5 ($n = 144$)	6 ($n = 56$)	8 ($n = 115$)	9 ($n = 95$)
		Coefficient α								
CPI Dominance	35	.82	.79		.79				.71	.71
JPRF Dominance	19	.81	.81		.74				.73	.69
Rosenberg Self-Esteem	10	.87	.87	.88	.88	.90	.87	.85	.84	.83
		Correlations								
CPI Dominance		−.11	−.03		−.17				.24**	.20
JPRF Dominance		−.04	.13**		−.17				.01	.04
Rosenberg Self-Esteem		−.09	−.18	.09	.01	.16	−.23**	−.01	−.29**	−.14*

Note. CPI = California Psychological Inventory; JPRF = Jackson Personality Research Form.
* $p < .05$. ** $p < .01$.

TABLE 15.7. Coefficient Alphas of Empathy, Altruism, and PAQ Subscales and Correlations With Social Dominance Orientation

Measure	No. of items	Sample 2 (n =403)	Sample 3b (n = 57)	Sample 5 (n = 144)	Sample 6 (n = 56)	Sample 8 (n = 115)	Sample 9 (n = 95)
				Coefficient α			
Empathy	28	.76	.72	.77	.75	.75	.73
Concern	7	.73	.77	.66	.75	.69	.68
Distress	7	.71	.70	.67	.74	.61	.52
Perspective-taking	7	.64	.78	.74	.84	.71	.58
Fantasy	7	.71	.79	.70	.72	.70	.64
Altruism	5			.87	.87		
PAQ Communality	23					.76	.78
PAQ Agency	28					.80	.80
				Correlations			
Empathy		−.40**	−.21	−.26**	−.36*	−.38**	−.24*
Concern		−.45**	−.51**	−.47**	−.41**	−.53**	−.40**
Distress		−.03	−.11	.10	−.16	.22**	.21*
Perspective-taking		−.30**	.05	−.20*	−.16	−.39**	−.15
Fantasy		−.23**	.01	−.06	−.25*	−.21*	−.23*
Altruism				−.32**	−.24*		
PAQ Communality						−.42**	−.24*
PAQ Agency						−.10	−.08

Note. PAQ = Personal Attributes Questionnaire
* $p < .05$. ** $p < .01$.

subscales were not as consistent across samples, but when they were significant, all correlations were negative (see Table 15.7). The total Empathy scale was negatively correlated with SDO in 5 of 6 samples (averaging $r = -.31$), but not as highly as the Concern for Others subscale. We conclude that concern for others is the form of empathy that precludes the desire to dominate other groups.

As one might expect, altruism was correlated with the Concern for Others subscale in Samples 5 and 6 ($ps < .001$) and was negatively correlated with SDO (see Table 15.7). Communality was negatively correlated with SDO in Samples 8 and 9 (see Table 15.7). In addition, Katz and Hass' (1988) 10-item Humanitarian-Egalitarian Scale correlated negatively with SDO ($\alpha = .80$, $r = -.34$, $p < .01$) in Sample 9; this scale includes altruistic, inclusive, and egalitarian items.

The constellation of qualities including communality, emotional empathy, and altruism has been termed "linking" and is stereotypically associated with the female sex (e.g., Eisler & Loye, 1983). However, it is important to note that SDO's correlations with communality, altruism, and concern for others were significant even after controlling for sex. Thus, gender differences alone are not responsible for the correlations between SDO

and communality, altruism, and concern for others. Lest high levels of dominance orientation be confused with agency, it is important to emphasize that there was no correlation between SDO and the PAQ Agency scale in Samples 8 and 9 (see Table 15.7).

Tolerance. SDO was negatively related to the JPI Tolerance subscale ($rs = -.27, -.36,$ and $-.27$, all $ps < .01$ in Samples 1, 8, and 9, respectively), despite the low reliabilities of the Tolerance subscale, which has a true-false response format (.53,[5] .59, and .18, respectively). When corrected for attenuation, the correlations were −.40, −.52, and −.71, respectively ($ps < .001$), but these may be considered "overcorrected" because of the low reliability coefficients of the Tolerance scale. The average correlation between SDO and Tolerance was −.30.

SDO AS AN ORIENTATION: PREDICTING NEW ATTITUDES

According to social dominance theory, one of SDO's most significant functions is orienting

---

[5]By accident, only the 10 false-coded items in the scale were administered to Sample 1.

people toward or away from new social attitudes. Therefore, we tested whether SDO predicted beliefs in new legitimizing myths and support for new policies. Unfolding public events provided three opportunities to test attitudes toward "new" policies, some of which had rather novel legitimizations provided for them.

Iraq War. War making is an extreme act of discrimination against an out-group; enemy out-group members are routinely starved, raped, killed, maimed, or made ill during war. Given that, we expect that arguments given in support of war would serve as legitimizing myths and thus should relate to SDO. We tested this hypothesis looking at U.S. policy in the aftermath of the Iraqi invasion of Kuwait in 1990. Pundits seemed to feel the White House gave several different reasons for U.S. policy at the time, so this was an opportune occasion to examine the operation of new legitimizing myths. National random-sample opinion polls showed significant fluidity of attitudes about appropriate policy up until the United States began bombing Iraq on January 16, 1991. For example, the *Los Angeles Times* poll showed that merely 38% of the public favored going to war against Iraq on November 14, 1990, but that once U.S. troops had begun bombing, 81% of the public on January 17–18, 1991, and on February 15–17, 1991, approved of the war. Even just before and after the bombing began, there were dramatic

shifts in opinion; from January 8–12, 1991, 39% felt that economic sanctions against Iraq should be used without resorting to war, but on January 17–18, 1991, 72% of the public believed President Bush had given enough time for economic sanctions to work. The outcome of the present study was, then, by no means certain.

During the third week of January, 1991, subjects in Sample 4 completed an Iraq War Attitudes survey. We asked subjects how willing they would be to make sacrifices for war (as opposed to making sacrifices to prevent wars), whether they favored suspending certain civil liberties and invoking the draft during war, and whether they favored military action against Iraq. We also measured a new "legitimizing myth," namely, that Iraq should be stopped because of the environmental damage that it was inflicting on the Gulf. This idea was brought up because the Iraqi leader, Saddam Hussein, had threatened to burn all of Kuwait's oil if Iraq was bombed, and the recent 20th anniversary of Earth Day had put environmental concerns on the public's mind. SDO was positively and significantly correlated with each of these attitude dimensions (see Table 15.8). Higher SDO levels were associated with favoring military action against Iraq, favoring suspension of civil liberties for the war, a willingness to make sacrifices for the war effort, and a nationalistic view of environmental problems associated with the war.

TABLE 15.8. Coefficient Alphas and Correlations of Social Dominance Orientation With New Attitudes

Scale or item	No. of items	Coefficient α	Correlation with social dominance orientation
Sample 4			
Favors military action by U.S.	5	.78	.48**
Willing to make sacrifices for war	4	.56	.45**
Favors suspending liberties for war	4	.51	.45**
Concerned about environment in war	4	.57	.28**
Sample 7			
Favors appointing a Black person			−.20*
Favors appointing a conservative			.32***
Favored Clarence Thomas' confirmation			.22**
Believed Anita Hills' testimony			−.26***
Sample 10			
Specific deterrence	3	.70	.35**
Favored executing Harris	2	.96	.36**
Painful executions	8	.86	.42**
Belief in retribution	5	.74	.51**

* p < .05. ** p < .01. *** p < .001.

Clarence Thomas' Nomination to the Supreme Court. Political appointments can also be considered policies that have implications for intergroup relations, and also can be legitimized; therefore, their relationship to SDO is of theoretical concern. The second new attitude that we assessed was support for Clarence Thomas' appointment to the Supreme Court. This appointment was related to a number of long-standing legitimizing myths, including conservatism, meritocracy, racism, and sexism, shown above to relate to SDO. Thomas, widely considered a Black conservative, was nominated to replace Thurgood Marshall, a Black former civil rights lawyer, who announced his intention to retire. President Bush nominated Thomas to the Supreme Court in the spring of 1991, and the Senate Judiciary Committee held hearings on this nomination in the spring and fall. Just before the vote to confirm Thomas was scheduled, a news story broke that two of Thomas' former subordinates had accused him of sexual harassment. One of these persons, Anita Hill, was called to testify before the Judiciary Committee, and the proceedings received much publicity including gavel-to-gavel television and radio coverage. After an entire weekend of testimony solely about the sexual harassment charge, the Judiciary Committee voted to confirm Thomas on October 15, 1991.[6]

We telephoned 149 of the 173 (86%) subjects in Sample 7 (who had completed the SDO scale in late September) on that day or on the following 2 days and asked them four attitudinal questions about Thomas and Hill. They responded to statements on 7-point scales where 1 meant *strongly disagree* and 7 meant *strongly agree*. The statements were (a) "after Thurgood Marshall's retirement from the Supreme Court, it was good that George Bush appointed a Black person to the Court," (b) "after Thurgood Marshall's retirement from the Supreme Court, it was good that George Bush appointed a conservative to the Court," (c) "If I were in the Senate, I would have voted in favor of Clarence Thomas' confirmation to the Supreme Court," and (d) "Anita Hill was telling the truth in claiming that Clarence Thomas sexually harassed her." We found that SDO significantly predicted opposition to nominating a Black to the Supreme Court, support for nominating a conservative to the court, support for Clarence Thomas,

and disbelief of Anita Hill's testimony (see correlations in Table 15.8).

Death Penalty. Elsewhere, we have argued that SDO should also be related to support of legal institutions that are discriminatory or inegalitarian in their effects (Sidanius, 1993; Sidanius, Liu, Pratto, & Shaw, 1994). Mitchell (1993) showed that SDO is related to ideologies that legitimize the use of the death penalty, such as the belief in legal retribution or the belief that the death penalty has a deterrent effect on crime. We assessed SDO in March, 1992, in Sample 10; 2 weeks later, we administered an extensive survey about death penalty ideologies and about the execution of Robert Alton Harris, who was executed by the state of California the day before the subjects were surveyed. Belief that executions have a specific deterrent effect, support for Harris' execution, support of painful executions, and belief in retribution were positively correlated with SDO (see Table 15.8).

Summary

To provide a summary of the correlations with SDO, we used Fisher's z-to-r formula to average the correlations across samples (e.g., Rosenthal, 1986, p. 27). To test the average statistical significance of the correlation coefficients, we computed standard normal (Z) scores corresponding to each correlation coeffecient using the large-sample formula $Z = r \times (N)^{\frac{1}{2}}$. The total of the Z scores across samples divided by the square root of the number of samples can be compared with the standard normal distribution to test the null hypothesis that the pattern of correlations obtained over samples occurred because of chance associations between SDO and the variable in question.[7]

On average, subject sex correlated .26 with SDO ($Z = 9.92$, $p < .001$). Thus, the data were consistent with our prediction that men will be higher on SDO than women.

In terms of discriminant validity, over five samples, the average correlation between SDO and CPI Dominance was .03 and the average correlation between SDO and JPRF Dominance was −.01. Over nine samples, the average correlation between SDO and RSE was −.08. Averaged over

---

[6]Because of the time delay between Washington, DC, and California, Californians heard this news as they awoke.

[7]A Z statistic with smaller variance could also have been computed by using the sample variance to weight the Z from each sample, which would cause all the *p* values given below to be smaller.

Table 15.9. Average Correlations and Significance Tests Across Samples Between Social Dominance Orientation and Personality Variables, Ideologies, and Policy Attitudes

Measure	Mean r	n	Z
Personality variables			
Concern for others	−.46	6	−8.92
Communality	−.33	2	−4.84
Tolerance	−.30	3	−5.31
Altruism	−.28	2	−3.98
Ideologies			
Anti-Black racism	.55	6	15.05
Noblesse oblige	−.57	10	20.30
Nationalism	.54	8	15.96
Sexism	.47	12	14.91
Equal opportunities	.46	3	7.51
Patriotism	.45	3	6.84
Cultural elitism	.40	3	6.94
Political-economic conservatism	.38	8	10.26
Just World	.27	2	3.58
Protestant Work Ethic	.11	3	1.25
Policy attitudes			
Social programs	−.47	6	−12.74
Racial policy	−.44	6	−11.74
Women's rights	−.40	6	−11.52
Military programs	.44	5	−10.12
Gay & lesbian rights	−.37	5	−8.79
Environmental programs	−.38	3	−6.16
Chauvinism	.34	3	5.34
Miscegeny	−.25	6	−7.36
Republican party preference	.28	6	7.08
Law and order	.28	6	6.38

Note. All Zs were significant at $p < .0001$ except for Just World ($p = .0002$) and Protestant Work Ethic ($p = .10$). The mean r was computed using Fisher's z; n denotes number of samples.

four samples, SDO correlated −.03 with Extraversion and .10 with Neuroticism. Clearly SDO is independent of all of these constructs. As expected, SDO had moderate negative correlations with concern for others, communality, tolerance, and altruism (see average correlations in Table 15.9). The averaged correlations were clearly different from zero, but they were not high enough that they indicate redundancy between these measures and SDO either, given that they ranged from −.28 for altruism to −.46 for concern for others.

SDO strongly and consistently related to belief in a number of hierarchy-legitimizing myths, most strongly to anti-Black racism and nationalism. SDO also was strongly negatively related to a hi-

erarchy-attenuating ideology, noblesse oblige. SDO correlated consistently positively with beliefs in sexism, equal opportunities, patriotism, cultural elitism, conservatism, and a Just World. The Protestant Work Ethic was the only legitimizing ideology that we did not find to relate to SDO reliably over samples (see Table 15.9).

Finally, SDO showed strong consistent correlations with scales assessing opposition to social programs, racial policies, and women's rights, and with support for military programs. SDO was also consistently correlated with opposition to gay and lesbian rights, environmental programs, and miscegeny and was consistently correlated with support for U.S. chauvinism, law-and-order policies, and Republican party identification (see Table 15.9). SDO also predicted attitudes toward new political events, including the 1991 war against Iraq, Clarence Thomas as a Supreme Court Justice, and a state execution. Those aspiring to hierarchy-enhancing careers had higher SDO scores than those aspiring to hierarchy-attenuating careers. Thus, we have provided substantial evidence that SDO (a) can be measured reliably, (b) is stable over time, (c) is higher among men than among women, (d) is higher among those who support hierarchy-enhancing ideologies and is lower among those who support hierarchy-attenuating ideologies, (e) is higher among those who support hierarchy-enhancing policies and lower among those who support hierarchy-attenuating policies, (f) is higher among those who choose hierarchy-enhancing social roles and lower among those who choose hierarchy-attenuating social roles, and (g) serves to orient new social and political attitudes.

Discussion

On the basis of social dominance theory, we postulated that there is an important individual difference in general preference for group domination, which we call *social dominance orientation*. As its definition and name implies, SDO may best be considered a general *social-attitudinal orientation* or implicit value relevant to intergroup relations. Some of our data inform us that there may be a significant relationship between one's orientation toward other persons in general and one's orientation toward other groups. People who are highly empathic (specifically, concerned with others' well-being) and to a lesser extent, those who feel interdependent or communal with others, tend to prefer egalitarian relationships among groups. Given that SDO predisposes people to believe in legitimizing myths and discriminatory policies, this would seem to make them less likely to believe in ideologies that relegate certain persons to "inferior" categories and to policies that disadvantage certain groups systematically. The recent work being done on interdependence (e.g., Depret & Fiske, 1993; Markus & Kitayama, 1991) may end up being quite informative about how to mitigate intergroup discrimination.

We might note that we came to postulate the existence of SDO not by thinking about "personality" in the traditional, individualistic sense, but by thinking about how group-based human social life is and the considerable data generated by researchers of political attitudes. We consider individual differences on SDO to be important not for showing the uniqueness of each person, nor for enabling us to classify persons into taxonomies. Rather, our finding of individual variation on SDO is central to our postulation of a dynamic model of human oppression in which different kinds of people (e.g., with high or low SDO) play different roles (e.g., enhance or attenuate inequality) and have different effects on each other (e.g., in how much they discriminate in the allocation of resources).

Despite significant variations in the degree of oppression from one society to another, it seems to us that many societies share the basic social-psychological elements that contribute to inequality: socially shared myths that define "superior group" and "inferior group" and that attempt to justify this distinction and the policies that "should" follow from it. As such, we postulate that individual variation on SDO could be reliably measured in many other societies and would show the same pattern of relationships to ideologies, policy attitudes, and hierarchy role as those shown here. Some of our previous research showed that group-dominance orientation significantly correlated with support for military programs, capitalism (Sidanius & Pratto, 1993b), racism, and sexism (Sidanius, Devereux, & Pratto, 1992; Sidanius & Pratto, 1993a) in Sweden, a much more egalitarian country than the United States, and showed the same gender difference in Australia, Sweden, Russia, and the United States (see Sidanius, Pratto, & Brief, 1993). In the future, we hope to examine whether SDO relates to rather different kinds of legitimizing myths that exist in very different cultural contexts, such as anti-Semitism in Poland, xenophobia in Japan, or fatalism in China.

Another kind of research endeavor that could further show the dynamic link between SDO and societal oppression would use SDO to predict attitudes toward new ideologies or policies. We expect that even when societies undergo substantial change, as with mass migration, technological innovation, or dramatic changes in borders or political leadership, such changes will be accepted only to the extent that they are satisfactorily legitimized and meet the public's level of desire for social dominance. Hence, the operation of SDO in the invention of new legitimizations and processes that assort persons into hierarchy roles may inform studies of political and social change.

SDO and Social Class

Several political psychologists and sociologists have postulated or investigated the relationship between social class and conservatism, racism, or authoritarianism, with Lipset (1960) postulating that the working class is more authoritarian, and Stacey and Green (1968, 1971) and many others presenting evidence to the contrary. We have made no predictions concerning whether SDO should be correlated with social class in either direction; instead we suspect that SDO's relationship to these variables may vary as a function of hierarchy-group membership, which in some societies would be designated by class and in others by racial group, caste, and so forth. We tested for correlations between SDO and class in the present samples, and we found no statistically significant relationships between SDO and respondents' social class or family income category. Although there was substantial heterogeneity in these samples on these variables for the respondents' families of origin, the education level in these samples is clearly restricted. In contrast, in a random survey of the Los Angeles area, Sidanius et al. (1996) found statistically significant and monotonic decreases in scores from an abbreviated SDO scale with increasing family income level and increasing respondent's education level. With the data now in hand, we cannot say whether social classes differ on SDO.

Authoritarianism Reconsidered

In the sample in which we assessed SDO and authoritarianism, the correlations between two measures of authoritarianism and SDO were weak. However, because SDO predicts many of the social attitudes conceptually associated with authoritarianism (e.g., ethnocentrism, punitiveness, and conservatism), a more thorough comparison of these constructs is warranted. To begin with, there is little theoretical consensus on the construct of authoritarianism. The original and some contemporary researchers have described authoritarianism as a multifaceted construct; for example, Heaven (1985) suggested that authoritarianism is part achievement motivation, part dominance, part conventionalism, part militarism, part punitiveness, and part ethnocentrism. Although we think that the tendency for these constructs to covary is extremely important, calling this compendium *authoritarianism* is conceptually unsatisfying. It is neither a clear definition of a unitary construct nor a theory of why the separate constructs covary. In our view, punitiveness, ethnocentrism, conservatism, and sometimes conventionalism can function as legitimizing myths. Because legitimizing myths tend to be correlated with SDO, they are often spuriously correlated with one another. Thus, it is entirely possible that SDO underlies these correlations. By separately defining the presumably causative value orientation (SDO) and ideological stances (legitimizing myths and policy attitudes) and using distinct measures of the constructs, we have avoided the conceptual problem of describing an individual tendency as a set of correlations (see also Duckitt, 1989).

Other definitions of *authoritarianism* have avoided the compendium problem by radically restricting the meaning of the term. Ray (1976) postulated that part of authoritarianism is leadership desire or directiveness. That SDO did not significantly correlate with two robust measures of interpersonal dominance or with CPI Capacity for Status or PAQ Agency suggests that SDO cannot be interpreted as leadership desire. On this dimension, SDO and authoritarianism are distinct.

There is a new view of authoritarianism that we see as complementary to SDO, namely, Duckitt's (1989) description of authoritarianism as the desire for individuals to submit to authority figures within the in-group. The three classical dimensions of authoritarianism that covary empirically—submitting to in-group conventions, submitting to in-group authorities, and desiring to punish members who do not submit to in-group norms and authorities (Altemeyer, 1981)—all concern the relation of the individual to the group. Thus, in Duckitt's view, authoritarianism is primarily an intragroup phenomenon concerning individuals' or groups' attitudes about what the relationship between individuals and their in-groups should be. By comparison, SDO concerns individuals' attitudes about what kind of relationship should exist between in-groups and out-groups, which is an intergroup phenomenon.

SDO Versus Political-Economic Conservatism

The other well-known individual predictor of social and political attitudes is political-economic conservatism. The power of political-economic conservatism to predict social and political attitudes and candidate preference is far too robust to refute. In fact, we postulate that political-economic conservatism is a prototypic legitimizing myth: an ideology that separates people into groups and suggests that some groups should be accorded more positive social value (e.g., tax breaks, funds for schools, and access to health care), whereas other groups should be allocated more negative social value (e.g., prison terms, censorship, and layoffs).

Our analysis of conservatism as a legitimizing myth can explain why, in many previous studies, conservatism was correlated with racism (e.g., Dator, 1969; Levinson, 1950; Sidanius & Ekehammar, 1979; Stone & Buss, 1976). We believe political-economic conservatism and racism are spuriously correlated and that both are "driven" by SDO. In fact, recent studies have shown that there was no significant residual correlation between political-economic conservatism and racism once SDO was controlled (see Sidanius & Pratto, 1993a, 1993b; Sidanius et al., 1992).

We believe SDO has significant power to predict policy attitudes over and above political-economic conservatism. In the present study, virtually all partial correlations between policy attitudes and SDO, controlling for political-economic conservatism, were reliable. Part of the advantage SDO may have over political-economic conservatism is that SDO is an attitudinal orientation rather than a policy doctrine and therefore does not require expertise or deliberate application. That is, to formulate a policy attitude consistent with one's political ideology, one must have a thorough understanding of that ideology and think through or know how it "should" apply to the acceptance of new policy initiatives. In contrast, one's SDO level will provide a gut reaction to new policy initiatives that imply changes in intergroup relations, essentially "I like it" or "I don't like it." In other words, we expect SDO to be a better predictor of group relevant social and political attitudes than political-economic conservatism among nonideologues, whenever thoughtful ideological reasoning is not engaged, and for new social attitudes.

The present results can be compared with Wilson's (e.g., 1973) extensive work on conservatism as an attitudinal orientation, rather than as an ideology. Wilson found that conservatism was a convenient label for describing the dimension underlying a similar constellation of ideological beliefs and policy attitudes to those we have shown to relate to SDO: racism, nationalism, ethnocentrism, militarism, law and order, and proestablishment politics. Conceptually, our definition of SDO differs from Wilson's conservatism in that we have not included fundamentalist religiosity, antihedonism, or strict morality as part of SDO. Our supposition is that those beliefs are particularly Western legitimizing myths that happen to be held by people who make distinctions between superior and inferior or deserving and undeserving people in a Calvinist vein, but that they would not necessarily be related to SDO in all cultural contexts. Likewise, it seems that forms of ethnic prejudice other than anti-Black racism would be more powerfully related to SDO in certain other cultural contexts. The comparison between SDO and attitudinal conservatism highlights that our measure of SDO is relatively independent of particular cultural beliefs or policies. That is, our items do not specify which groups of people are referred to (with the exception of nations) because we felt that a general orientation toward groups could predict attitudes toward specific groups or specific group-relevant policies.

We modified our SDO scale so that it related to our conceptual definition more strongly by making each item refer only to the generic concept *group*. We compared the 14-item scale in Appendix A with this new scale in a sample of 199 Stanford students. We administered the 14-item SDO scale ($\alpha = .88$) and a brief policy attitude survey with a 1 (*very negative*) to 7 (*very positive*) response format. Four weeks later, we administered the balanced 16-item SDO scale shown in

Appendix C ($\alpha = .91$). The two scales correlated .75 with one another ($p < .01$), comparable with the cross-time reliability correlation of the 14-item SDO scale. Both SDO scales correlated significantly with the policy attitudes in the directions expected and to very similar degrees. The 14- and 16-item SDO scales correlated, respectively, with attitudes toward affirmative action (rs = $-.34$, $-.44$), civil rights ($-.51$, $-.59$), gay rights ($-.36$, $-.32$), the military ($.40$, $.39$), decreased immigration ($.37$, $.41$), equal pay for women ($-.38$, $-.29$), and the death penalty ($.40$, $.34$), all ps < .01. We also tested an abbreviated scale consisting of Items 1, 3, 4, 7, 10, 12, 13, and 14 in Appendix C ($\alpha = .86$), which correlated in nearly the same magnitudes with the policy items above. We administered the 16-item SDO scale to another sample of 245 Stanford students along with the Rombough and Ventimiglia (1981) sexism scale. In this second sample, the 16-item scale was internally reliable ($\alpha = .91$) and correlated .51 ($p < .01$) with the sexism scale and .26 with subject sex ($p < .01$). The abbreviated (8-item) version of this scale was internally reliable ($\alpha = .86$) and correlated .47 with sexism ($p < .01$) and .26 with subject sex ($p < .01$). The 16-item scale (and its 8-item abbreviated form) has slightly more face validity than the 14-item SDO scale, and it seems to have similar properties.

SDO and the Dynamics of Oppression

Our present focus on SDO is not meant to imply that all phenomena related to prejudice and group conflict can be solely understood or reduced to individual differences. In fact, social dominance theory implies that SDO and other individual variables must be considered within their social context, because individual variables and social-structural variables have a dynamic relationship.

For example, our data suggest that empathy with other persons may be a significant attenuator of SDO. However, concern for others (particularly out-group members) is not just a fixed individual propensity, but instead seems likely to be influenced by social structures and policies. Social structures and policies that prevent the formation of close relationships and empathy between high- and low-status persons (e.g., economically or legally enforced segregation, language barriers, publishing biases), would seem to discourage empathy between groups and the formation of a common identity. These factors, along with the desire for group-based status and the presumption of status or privilege, may also give rise to SDO. An important enterprise for future research is to investigate the social contextual factors that contribute to SDO and to inequality in general.

As a causal variable, we believe SDO is pertinent to the dynamics of group conflict and institutional discrimination. In the remainder of our discussion, we focus on these ramifications.

SDO and Group Discrimination

Social dominance theory states that SDO should predict prejudice and discrimination against out-groups; social identity theory (e.g., Tajfel & Turner, 1986) implies that emotional affiliation or identification with one's in-group should do the same. Social identity theory posits out-group denigration as a device for maintaining positive social identity; social dominance theory posits it as a device to maintain superior group status. In a minimal groups experiment, SDO and in-group identification each predicted degree of out-group discrimination (Sidanius, Pratto, & Mitchell, 1994). However, these effects were not independent—those who were high on SDO and on in-group identification were even more discriminatory against a minimal out-group. Crocker and Luhtanen (1990) found a parallel interaction in another experiment: People who strongly affiliated with their in-groups and whose group status was threatened especially denigrated out-groups. We consider their results to be consistent with both theories in that both group identification and group status needs motivated greater discrimination. Levin and Sidanius (1993) found a similar interaction between SDO and group status; high-SDO subjects who belonged to artificially high-status groups especially denigrated out-group members. High group status and group-status threat may work similarly in these studies because high-status groups, having the most status to lose, may experience the most threat when confronted by possible loss of status. Understanding the circumstances under which people have high levels of in-group identification, high group status, and high SDO, then, appears to be important for understanding when discrimination is likely to be especially severe. Some of our other research has addressed the question of when these three predictors of discrimination will co-occur.

Because SDO is the desire for one's group to dominate others, SDO should have a differential relationship to in-group identification depending on the group's level of social status. Sidanius, Pratto, and Rabinowitz (1994) documented that SDO and in-group identification were more positively correlated in higher status than in lower status groups. Using various ethnic identification measures, we showed that the covariance between ethnic identification and SDO was statistically significant and positive within a high-status group (i.e., Euro-Americans), whereas this relationship was statistically significant and negative within a low-status group (Hispanics and African-Americans).

These experimental and correlational findings suggest that high-status groups will be the most discriminatory against out-groups because their members are most likely to have both high SDO levels and high levels of in-group identification. It is important to remember that these two variables, in experimental studies, interact to cause extremely severe out-group discrimination. In total, these results support social dominance theory's contention that higher status groups will tend to be more in-group serving than lower status groups. That is, higher status groups are more discriminatory against out-groups than lower status groups, and the aggregate affect of this asymmetry is not equal groups in conflict, but the maintenance of hierarchical group relations (see Sidanius & Pratto, 1993a).

SDO and Social Role

By performing organizational roles, individuals greatly expand their capacity for group discrimination because collective institutions can often allocate resources or costs on a far larger scale than individuals can. Therefore, institutional discrimination is one of the major contributors to the creation and maintenance of social inequalities and social hierarchy (e.g., Feagin & Feagin, 1978). The individual organizational member, however, is not insignificant. An organization's members help an institution perform its hierarchy role by endorsing legitimizing myths and adapting their SDO levels to the institution's norms. Several processes may contribute to a match between individuals and institutions. There is mounting evidence that people seek roles in an institution compatible with their SDO levels and ideological beliefs. The present research showed two replications of this relationship between SDO and aspired hierarchy role. A previous study showed the same relationship between aspired hierarchy role and belief in legitimizing myths (Sidanius, Pratto, Martin, & Stallworth, 1991). In another study, police recruits were found to have significantly higher SDO levels and related attitudes than public defenders (Sidanius, Liu, Pratto, & Shaw, 1994). Self-selection into roles based on hierarchy-relevant ideologies may be a contributing factor to institutional discrimination.

An institution also reinforces and contributes to the match between individuals' attitudes and institutional hierarchy role. For example, White police academy recruits became increasingly more negative toward Blacks during their first 18 months as police (Teahan, 1975). Also, the initial racial attitudes of intended hierarchy enhancers resisted the usual liberalizing influence of college the longer they stayed in college (Sidanius, Pratto, Martin, & Stallworth, 1991). Any number of socialization or social influence processes may have caused such effects. Hierarchy-enhancing behaviors or attitudes may even be rewarded by hierarchy-enhancing institutions. One study of campus police officers showed that those who were most successful in their careers, as evidenced by several measures such as superior's evaluations and salary increases, tended to score higher on measures of racism and ethnocentrism (Leitner & Sedlacek, 1976). More recently, in a study of the Los Angeles Police Department, the Christopher Commission (1991) found that those police officers with the highest number of civilian complaints for brutality and excessive force received unusually positive performance evaluations from their supervising officers. In addition, these supervisor evaluations "were uniformly optimistic about the officers' progress and prospects on the force" (Christopher et al., 1991, p. 41).

Apparently, individuals and institutions reinforce each other's hierarchy-enhancing tendencies, which we believe makes their discriminatory behaviors powerful and difficult to change. More research on the detailed processes by which individuals and institutions reinforce one another's prejudices may be useful to those seeking to reduce institutional discrimination.

To summarize, the present research indicates that SDO, the desire for group dominance, is a significant predictor of social and political attitudes pertaining to intergroup relations and also of hierarchy roles. Social dominance theory suggests that the confluence of this individual-difference variable and a number of social factors including lack of common identity, high in-group status, and social role, contributes to the oppression of social groups.

REFERENCES

Adorno, T. W., Frenkel-Brunswik, E., Levinson, D. J., & Sanford, R. N. (1950). *The authoritarian personality.* New York: Norton.

Altemeyer, B. (1981). *Right-wing authoritarianism.* Manitoba: University of Manitoba Press.

Avery, P. G. (1988). Political tolerance among adolescents. *Theory and Research in Social Education, 16,* 183–201.

Benson, P. L., & Vincent, S. (1980). Development and validation of the sexist attitudes toward women scale. *Psychology of Women Quarterly, 5,* 276–291.

Bienen, L., Alan, N., Denno, D. W, Allison, P. D., & Mills, D. L. (1988). The reimposition of capital punishment in New Jersey: The role of prosecutorial discretion. *Rutgers Law Review* (Fall).

Bobo, L. (1983). Whites' opposition to busing: Symbolic racism or realistic group conflict? *Journal of Personality and Social Psychology, 45,* 1196–1210.

Brown, D. E. (1991). *Human universals.* New York: McGraw-Hill.

Burt, M. R. (1980). Cultural myths and supports for rape. *Journal of Personality and Social Psychology, 38,* 217–230.

Carmines, E. G., & McIver, J. D. (1981). Analyzing models with unobserved variables: Analysis of covariance structures. In G. W Bohinstedt & E. F. Borgatta (Eds.), *Social measurement: Current issues* (pp. 65–115). Beverly Hills, CA: Sage.

Christopher, W., Arguellas, J. A., Anderson, R. A., Barnes, W. R., Estrada, L. F., Kantor, M., Mosk, R. M., Ordin, A. S., Slaughter, J. B., & Tranquada, R. E. (1991). *Report of the Independent Commission on the Los Angeles Police Department.* Suite 1910, 400 South Hope Street, Los Angeles, CA 90071–2899.

Costa, P. T., & MacRae, R. R. (1985). *The NEO Personality Inventory Manual.* Odessa, FL: Psychological Assessment Resources.

Crocker, J., & Luhtanen, R. (1990). Collective self-esteem and in-group bias. *Journal of Personality and Social Psychology, 58,* 60–67.

Dator, J. A. (1969). What's left of the economic theory of discrimination? In S. Shulman & W. Darity, Jr. (Eds.), *The question of discrimination: Racial inequality in the U.S. labor market* (pp. 335–374). Middletown, CT: Wesleyan University Press.

Davis, M. H. (1983). Measuring individual differences in empathy: Evidence for a multidimensional approach. *Journal of Personality and Social Psychology, 44,* 113–126.

Depret, E. F., & Fiske, S. T. (1993). Social cognition and power: Some cognitive consequences of social structure as a source of control deprivation. In G. Weary, F. Gleicher, & K. L. Marsh (Eds.), *Control motivation and social cognition* (pp. 176–202). New York: Springer Verlag.

Duckitt, J. (1989). Authoritarianism and group identification: A new view of an old construct. *Political Psychology, 10,* 63–84.

Eisler, R., & Loye, D. (1983). The "failure" of liberalism: A reassessment of ideology from a feminine-masculine perspective. *Political Psychology, 4,* 375–391.

Ekehammar, B., & Sidanius, J. (1982). Sex differences in socio-political ideology: A replication and extension. *British Journal of Social Psychology, 21,* 249–257.

Eysenck, H. J. (1971). Social attitudes and social class. *British Journal of Social and Clinical Psychology 10,* 210–212.

Eysenck, H. J., & Wilson, O. D. (1978). *The psychological basis of ideology.* Baltimore, MD: University Park Press.

Feagin, J. R., & Feagin, C. B. (1978). *Discrimination American style: Institutional racism and sexism.* Malabar, FL: Krieger.

Fenigstein, A., Scheier, M. F., & Buss, A. H. (1975). Public and private self-consciousness: Assessment and theory. *Journal of Consulting and Clinical Psychology, 43,* 522–527.

Frenkel-Brunswik, E. (1948). A study of prejudice in children. *Human Relations, 1,* 295–306.

Frenkel-Brunswik, E. (1949). Intolerance of ambiguity as an emotional and perceptual variable. *Journal of Personality, 18,* 108–143.

General Accounting Office. (1990). *Death penalty sentencing: Research indicates pattern of racial disparities.* United States General Accounting Office, Report to Senate and House Committees on the Judiciary (GAO/GGD-90-57). Washington, DC: Government Printing Office.

Goertzel, T. G. (1987). Authoritarianism of personality and political attitudes. *Journal of Social Psychology, 127,* 7–18.

Gough, H. (1987). *California Psychological Inventory: Administrator's guide.* Palo Alto, CA: Consulting Psychologists Press.

Heaven, P. C. L. (1985). Construction and validation of a measure of authoritarian personality. *Journal of Personality Assessment, 49,* 545–551.

Jackson, D. N. (1965). *Personality Research Form.* Goshen, NY: Research Psychologists Press.

Jackson, D. N. (1976). *Jackson Personality Inventory.* Goshen, NY: Research Psychologists Press.

John, O. P. (1990). The Big Five factor taxonomy: Dimensions of personality in the natural language and in questionnaires. In L. A. Pervin (Ed.), *Handbook of personality psychology: Theory and research* (pp. 66–100). Hillsdale, NJ: Erlbaum.

John, O. P., Donahue, E., & Kentle, R. L. (1992). *The Big Five Inventory: Versions 4a and 54.* Technical Report, Institute of Personality Assessment and Research.

Katz, I., & Hass, R. G. (1988). Racial ambivalence and American value conflict: Correlational and priming studies of dual cognitive structures. *Journal of Personality and Social Psychology, 55,* 893–905.

Kleck, G. (1981). Racial discrimination in criminal sentencing: A critical evaluation of the evidence with additional evidence on the death penalty. *American Sociological Review, 46,* 783–805.

Kluegel, J. R., & Smith, P. M. (1986). *Beliefs about inequality: Americans' views of what is and what ought to be.* Hawthorne, NY: Aldine de Gruyter.

Kosterman, R., & Feshbach, S. (1989). Toward a measure of patriotic and nationalistic attitudes. *Political Psychology, 10,* 257–274.

Leitner, D. W., & Sedlacek, W. E. (1976). Characteristics of successful campus police officers. *Journal of College Student Personnel, 17,* 304–308.

Levin, S. L., & Sidanius, J. (1993). *Intergroup biases of a function of social dominance orientation and in-group status.* Unpublished manuscript, University of California at Los Angeles.

Levinson, D. J. (1950). Politico-economic ideology and group memberships in relation to ethnocentrism. In T. Adorno, E. Frenkel-Brunswik, D. J. Levinson, & R. N. Sanford (Eds.), *The authoritarian personality* (pp. 151–207). New York: Norton.

Lipset, S. M. (1960). *Political man.* London: Heinemann.

Loevinger, J. (1957). Objective tests as instrument of psychological theory. *Psychological Reports,* Monograph Supplement 9.

Malle, B. F., & Horowitz, L. M. (1994). *The puzzle of negative self-views. An explanation using the schema concept.* Unpublished manuscript. Stanford University.

Markus, H. R., & Kitayama, S. (1991). Culture and the self: Implications for cognition, emotion, and motivation. *Psychological Review, 98,* 224–253.

McConahay, J. B. (1986). Modern racism, ambivalence, and the modern racism scale. In J. F. Dovidio & S. L. Gaertner (Eds.), *Prejudice, discrimination, and racism* (pp. 91–125). San Diego, CA: Academic Press.

Mirels, H. L., & Garrett, J. B. (1971). The Protestant ethic as a personality variable. *Journal of Consulting and Clinical Psychology, 36,* 40–44.

Mitchell, M. (1993). *Attitudes towards the death penalty and use of executions: A social dominance perspective.* Unpublished dissertation, Department of Psychology, University of California at Los Angeles.

Moynihan, D. P. (1965). *The Negro family: The case for national action.* Washington, DC: Office of Policy Planning and Research, U.S. Department of Labor.

Nickerson, S., Mayo, C., & Smith, A. (1986). Racism in the courtroom. In J. E Dovidio & S. L. Gaertner (Eds.), *Prejudice, discrimination, and racism* (pp. 255–278). San Diego, CA: Academic Press.

Paternoster, R. (1983). Race of victim and location of crime: The decision to seek the death penalty in South Carolina. *Journal of Criminal Law and Criminology, 74,* 754–785.

Peterson, B. E., Doty, R. M., & Winter, D. G. (1993). Authoritarianism and attitudes towards contemporary social issues. *Personality and Social Psychology Bulletin, 19,* 174–184.

Pratto, F. (1996). Sexual politics: The gender gap in the bedroom and the cabinet. In D. M. Buss & N. Malamuth (Eds.), *Sex, power and conflict: Evolutionary and feminist perspectives.* New York: Oxford University Press.

Pratto, F., Sidanius, J., & Stallworth, L. M. (1993). Sexual selection and the sexual and ethnic basis of social hierarchy. In L. Ellis (Ed.), *Social stratification and socioeconomic inequality: A comparative biosocial analysis* (pp. 111–137). New York: Praeger.

Radelet, M. L., & Pierce, G. L. (1985). Race and prosecutorial discretion in homicide cases. *Law and Society Review, 19,* 587–621.

Ray, J. (1976). Do authoritarians hold authoritarian attitudes? *Human Relations, 29,* 307–325.

Reiman, J. (1990). *The rich get richer and the poor get prison: Ideology, class, and criminal justice.* New York: Macmillan.

Rombough, S., & Ventimiglia, J. C. (1981). Sexism: A tridimensional phenomenon. *Sex Roles, 7,* 747–755.

Rosenberg, M. (1965). *Society and the adolescent self image.* Princeton, NJ: Princeton University Press.

Rosenthal, R. (1986). *Meta-analytic procedures for social research.* Beverly Hills, CA: Sage.

Rubin, Z., & Peplau, L. A. (1975). Who believes in a just world? *Journal of Social Issues, 31,* 265–289.

Sears, D. O. (1988). Symbolic racism. In P. A. Katz & D. A. Taylor (Eds.), *Eliminating racism: Profiles in controversy* (pp. 53–84). New York: Plenum.

Shapiro, R. Y, & Mahajan, H. (1986). Gender differences in policy preferences: A summary of trends from the 1960s to the 1980s. *Public Opinion Quarterly, 50,* 42–61.

Sidanius, J. (1976). *Further tests of a Swedish Scale of Conservatism.* Reports from the Department of Psychology, University of Stockholm, Supplement 36.

Sidanius, J. (1988). Race and sentence severity: The case of American justice. *Journal of Black Studies, 18,* 273–281.

Sidanius, J. (1993). The psychology of group conflict and the dynamics of oppression: A social dominance perspective. In W. McGuire & S. Iyengar (Eds.), *Current approaches to political psychology* (pp. 183–219). Durham, NC: Duke University Press.

Sidanius, J., Cling, B. J., & Pratto, F. (1991). Ranking and linking behavior as a function of sex and gender: An exploration of alternative explanations. *Journal of Social Issues, 17,* 131–149.

Sidanius, J., Devereux, E., & Pratto, F. (1992). A comparison of symbolic racism theory and social dominance theory as explanations for racial policy attitudes. *Journal of Social Psychology, 132,* 377–395.

Sidanius, J., & Ekehammar, B. (1979). Political socialization: A multivariate analysis of Swedish political attitude and preference data. *European Journal of Social Psychology, 9,* 265–279.

Sidanius, J., & Ekehammar, B. (1980). Sex-related differences in socio-political ideology. *Scandinavian Journal of Psychology, 21,* 17–26.

Sidanius, J., Liu, J., Pratto, F., & Shaw, J. (1994). Social dominance orientation, hierarchy-attenuation and hierarchy-enhancers: Social dominance theory and the criminal justice system. *Journal of Applied Social Psychology, 24,* 338–366.

Sidanius, J., & Pratto, F. (1993a). The dynamics of social dominance and the inevitability of oppression. In P. Sniderman & P. E. Tetlock (Eds.), *Prejudice, politics, and race in America today* (pp. 173–211). Stanford, CA: Stanford University Press.

Sidanius, J., & Pratto, F. (1993b). Racism and support of free-market capitalism: A cross-cultural analysis. *Political Psychology, 14,* 383–403.

Sidanius, J., Pratto, F., & Bobo, L. (1996). Racism, concervatism, affirmative action, and intellectual sophisti-cation: A matter of principled conservatism or group dominance? *Journal of Personality and Social Psychology, 70,* 476–490.

Sidanius, J., Pratto, F., & Brief, D. (1993). *Group dominance and the political psychology of gender: A cross-cultural comparison.* Unpublished manuscript, University of California at Los Angeles.

Sidanius, J., Pratto, F., Martin, M., & Stallworth, L. M. (1991). Consensual racism and career track: Some implications of social dominance theory. *Political Psychology, 12,* 691–720.

Sidanius, J., Pratto, F., & Mitchell, M. (1994). In-group identification, social dominance orientation, and differential intergroup social allocation. *Journal of Social Psychology, 131,* 151–167.

Sidanius, J., Pratto, F., & Rabinowitz, J. (1994). Gender, ethnic status, and ideological asymmetry: Social dominance interpretation. *Journal of Cross-Cultural Psychology, 25,* 194–216.

Sniderman, P. M., & Tetlock, P. E. (1986a). Reflections on American racism. *Journal of Social Issues, 42,* 173–188.

Sniderman, P. M., & Tetlock, P. E. (1986b). Symbolic racism: Problems of motive attribution in political analysis. *Journal of Social Issues, 42,* 129–150.

Snyder, M. (1974). The self-monitoring of expressive behavior. *Journal of Personality and Social Psychology, 10,* 526–537.

Spence, J. T, Helmreich, P., & Stapp, J. (1974). The personal attributes questionnaire: A measure of sex role stereotypes and masculinity-femininity. *JSAS Catalog of Selected Documents in Psychology, 4,* 1–42.

Stacey, B. G., & Green, R. T. (1968). The psychological bases of political allegiance among white-collar males. *British Journal of Social and Clinical Psychology, 7,* 45–60.

Stacey, B. G., & Green, R. T. (1971). Working-class conservatism: A review and an empirical study. *British Journal of Social and Clinical Psychology, 10,* 10–26.

Stone, W. F., & Russ, R. C. (1976). Machiavellianism as tough-mindedness. *Journal of Social Psychology, 98,* 213–220.

Super, D. E., & Nevill, D. D. (1985). *The values scale.* Palo Alto, CA: Consulting Psychologists Press.

Tajfel, H., & Turner, J. C. C. (1986). The social identity theory of intergroup behavior. In S. Worchel & W. G. Austin (Eds.), *Psychology of intergroup relations* (pp. 7–24). Chicago: Nelson-Hall.

Teahan, J. E. (1975). A longitudinal study of attitude shifts among Black and White police officers. *Journal of Social Issues, 31,* 47–56.

Wilson, G. D. (Ed.). (1973). *The psychology of conservatism.* San Diego, CA: Academic Press.

Wilson, G. D., & Patterson, J. R. (1968). A new measure of conservatism. *British Journal of Social and Clinical Psychology, 1,* 264–269.

Appendix A

Items on the Social Dominance Orientation Scale

1. Some groups of people are simply not the equals of others.
2. Some people are just more worthy than others.
3. This country would be better off if we cared less about how equal all people were.
4. Some people are just more deserving than others.
5. It is not a problem if some people have more of a chance in life than others.
6. Some people are just inferior to others.
7. To get ahead in life, it is sometimes necessary to step on others.
8. Increased economic equality.
9. Increased social equality.
10. Equality.
11. If people were treated more equally we would have fewer problems in this country.
12. In an ideal world, all nations would be equal.
13. We should try to treat one another as equals as much as possible. (All humans should be treated equally.)
14. It is important that we treat other countries as equals.

All items were measured on a *very negative* (1) to *very positive* (7) scale. Items 8–14 were reverse-coded. The version of Item 13 in parentheses was used in Samples 5–12. The order of items differed from above and across samples.

Appendix B

Items Used on Scales

Samples 2, 3b, 4, 5, 6, 8, 9: Items Comprising the Original Legitimizing Myths Scales

Anti-Black Racism Scale
 A Black president.[a]
 Racial integration.[a]
 White superiority.
 Blacks are inherently inferior.
 Civil rights activists.[a]

Anti-Arab Racism Scale
 Most of the terrorists in the world today are Arabs.
 Historically, Arabs have made important contributions to world culture.[a]
 Iraqis have little appreciation for democratic values.
 People of the Muslim religion tend to be fanatical.
 Muslims value peace and love.[a]

Cultural Elitism Scale
 The poor cannot appreciate fine art and music.
 No amount of education can make up for the wrong breeding.
 Qualifications and not personality should determine whether a candidate gets votes.
 The ideal world is run by those who are most capable.
 Western civilization has brought more progress than all other cultural traditions.

Someone who treats other people poorly but is very good at his job should be promoted.
 Great art is not meant for the common folk.

Equal Opportunity Scale
 In America, every person has an equal chance to rise up and prosper.
 Lower wages for women and ethnic minorities simply reflect lower skill and education levels.
 America is the "land of opportunity."
 Salaries are usually reflective of education, which in turn is reflective of intelligence and ambition.
 Affirmative Action prevents the more qualified from attaining positions.
 Potential to do well should not be sufficient for admission to any program. Only those with proven competence in that field should be allowed.

Patriotism Scale
 Flag burning should be illegal.
 In American public schools, every day should begin with the Pledge of Allegiance.
 I supported the United States' actions in Iraq.
 Patriotism is the most important qualification for a politician.
 I believe in mandatory military service by all citizens of the United States in the armed forces.

It was disloyal for people to question the President during the Iraq war.

With few exceptions, the American government does a good and honest job.

Other countries should be happy to have American intervention and influence.

I am proud to be an American.

Congressman who voted against the war should be removed from office.

The United States suffers when patriotism wanes.

Patriots are the ones who have made this country great.

Nationalism Scale

In view of America's moral and material superiority it is only right that we should have the biggest say in deciding United Nations policy.

This country must continue to lead the "Free World."

We should do anything necessary to increase the power of our country, even if it means war.

Sometimes it is necessary for our country to make war on other countries for their own good.

The important thing for the U.S. foreign aid program is to see to it that the U.S. wins a political advantage.

Generally, the more influence America has on other nations, the better off they are.

Noblesse Oblige Scale—Form A

As a country's wealth increases, more of its resources should be channeled to the poor.

The more money one makes, the greater proportion of that money should be paid in taxes.

Those with more resources have more obligations toward their fellow human beings.

Giving to others usually benefits the givers as well.

The man with two coats in his closet should give one away.

Extra food on the table belongs to those who are hungry.

Noblesse Oblige Scale—Form B

As a country's wealth increases, more of its resources should be channeled to the poor.

Giving to others usually benefits the givers as well.

Those with more resources have more obligations toward their fellow human beings.

It is beneficial to all to spend money on the public sector such as education, housing and health care.

Those who are well off can't be expected to take care of everyone else.[a]

Social charities just create dependency.[a]

Samples 2, 3b, 5, 6, 8, 9: Items on the Policy Scales

Law and Order Policies
Death penalty for drug kingpins.
Death penalty.
Prisoner's rights.[a,b,c]
Longer prison sentences.[d]

Gay Rights
Gay or lesbian marriage.
Gay and lesbian rights.

Women's Rights
Guaranteed job security after maternity leave.
Stiffer penalties for wife beating.[c]
Equal pay for women.
More women judges.

Social Programs
Government sponsored health care.
Better support for the homeless.
More support for early education.[c,d]
Free school lunches.[c,d]
Low income housing.[c,d]
Arresting the homeless.[a,c]
Guaranteed jobs for all.
Reduced benefits for the unemployed.[a]
Greater aid to poor kids.
Increased taxation of the rich.

Racial Policy
Racial quotas.
Affirmative action.
School busing.[c]
Civil rights.
Helping minorities get a better education.
Government helping minorities get better housing.
Government has no business helping any particular ethnic group in the job market.[a]

Military Programs
Decreased defense spending.[a]
Strategic Defense Initiative.
B-2 (Stealth) bomber.
Going to war.[e]

Environmental Policies
Drilling for oil off the California coast.[a]
Government-mandated recycling programs.
Taxing environmental polluters to pay for superfund clean ups.
More government involvement on clean air and water.

Drilling for oil under the Arctic National Wildlife Refuge.*

Chauvinism Scale
Central Intelligence Agency (CIA).
English as the official language.
Decreased immigration to the U.S.
National security.
American way of life.
No welfare for new immigrants.
America first.
America as world's policeman.

Sample 4: Iraq War Scales (January, 1991)

Favors Military Action by (U.S.)
The U.S. really had no choice but to use military force against Iraq.
The U.S. should not be using military force against Iraq.*
Saddam Hussein must be stopped by any means necessary—including nuclear weapons.
The U.N. coalition should not participate in any military action that will kill civilians no matter how few.ª
The U.N. coalition should cease bombing Iraq and offer to negotiate.*

Willing to Make Sacrifices for War
It would be worth our country's having a lower standard of living to maintain world peace.*
I would be willing to pay double the current prices of gasoline to avoid similar conflicts over oil in the future.*
I am willing to risk my life to help with the war effort in the Persian Gulf.
I'd be willing to pay higher taxes to finance the war in the Gulf.

Favors Suspending Liberties for War
President Bush should be given whatever power he needs to conduct war.
Sometimes political leaders must be unencumbered by legislatures so that they can govern effectively.
It is appropriate to reinstitute the military draft to help with the conflict with Iraq.
Military censorship of the press is appropriate in times of war.

Concerned About Environment in War
Iraq should be held entirely responsible for cleaning up the oil spills in the Persian Gulf.
The U.S. is partly to blame for the environmental damage to the Persian Gulf region.ª

Potential environmental damage should have been considered in the decision to go to war.*

Sample 8: Post-War Pro-Iraq War Items (February, 1992)

The U.S. had no choice but to begin bombing Iraq on January 16, 1991.
The U.S. should have tried political and economic pressure for a longer time before bombing Iraq.*
Bombing the cities of Iraq was justified.
The President went to war to increase his popularity.*
The U.S. could have prevented more civilian casualties in Iraq.*
The Gulf War wasn't worth the human cost.*
The U.N. Coalition really taught Hussein a lesson.
We should spend as much money and effort on solving domestic problems as we did on the Iraq war.*
Once there was 250,000 U.S. troops in the Persian Gulf region, it would have been embarrassing not to "use" them in war.
President Bush should not have set a date for Iraqi withdrawal from Kuwait.*
Strict control of the press coverage of the Iraq war was necessary.
If we understood the Iraqis better, we might have been able to avoid the war.*
In all, the press reports we received about the war were fair and impartial.
The military response to Iraq's invasion of Kuwait will probably discourage others from invading countries.
The Gulf War wasn't worth the environmental cost.*

Wars of Dominance
To insure our influence is felt in that nation.
To protect our economic interests.
To protect our citizens being held hostage.
For U.S. national security purposes.
To restore a freely elected government which had been overthrown by a military coup.
To keep an enemy from acquiring chemical or nuclear weapons.
If we started disarming, it would only lead to more war.
A U.S. Military presence helps maintain peace.

Humanitarian Wars
To ensure that human rights were respected in that country.
To ensure that emergency food supplies could reach civilians.

To protect unarmed civilians from battles.

Ultimatums usually lead to war, rather than diplomatic solutions.

By selling arms to other countries, we increase the likelihood of war.

War should always be considered a last resort.

Sample 10: Items on Death Penalty Survey

Favored Executing Harris

I felt that Robert Alton Harris' death sentence should have been commuted to life in prison without possibility of parole.[a]

I felt that Robert Alton Harris should have been executed.

Believes in Specific Deterrence

If not executed, murderers will commit more crimes in the future.

We don't need the death penalty to insure that a murderer never repeats his crime.[a]

If not executed, a murderer will be on the street in a few years.

Support for Painful Executions

Murderers should suffer when they are executed.

I might support the use of burning alive to execute those who commit the most heinous crimes.

If people have to be executed, they should be executed in the most painless way possible.[a]

The electric chair should be quick and painless.[a]

Executions should be as bloodless as possible.[a]

The crime problem has gotten so bad that maybe we should bring back public hangings.

We should use more graphic forms of executions (such as a firing squad).

When using the electric chair for executions, the voltage should be applied slowly so the criminal suffers before dying.

Belief in Retribution

Society does not have the right to get revenge for murder.[a]

For a terrible crime, there should be a terrible punishment.

Even the worst criminal should be considered for mercy.[a]

Those who hurt others deserve to be hurt in return.

Punishment should fit the crime.

Note. Response scale for all items was *strongly disagree* (1) to *strongly agree* (7) except for the nationalism, anti-Black racism, and chauvinism items, which were *very negative* (1) to *very positive* (7). The instructions for the Wars scales were to indicate how much the subject agreed or disagreed that his or her country would be justified in using military force (for the items beginning with "to" or "for") or agreement or disagreement with support for military use of force in general (for items that are complete sentences).
[a]Item was reverse-coded. [b]Item was omitted in Sample 6. [c]Item was omitted in Sample 8. [d]Item was omitted in Sample 9. [e]Item was omitted in Sample 2.

Appendix C

Items on the 16-Item Dominance Orientation Scale

1. Some groups of people are simply inferior to other groups.
2. In getting what you want, it is sometimes necessary to use force against other groups.
3. It's OK if some groups have more of a chance in life than others.
4. To get ahead in life, it is sometimes necessary to step on other groups.
5. If certain groups stayed in their place, we would have fewer problems.
6. It's probably a good thing that certain groups are at the top and other groups are at the bottom.
7. Inferior groups should stay in their place.
8. Sometimes other groups must be kept in their place.
9. It would be good if groups could be equal.
10. Group equality should be our ideal.
11. All groups should be given an equal chance in life.
12. We should do what we can to equalize conditions for different groups.
13. Increased social equality.
14. We would have fewer problems if we treated people more equally.
15. We should strive to make incomes as equal as possible.
16. No one group should dominate in society.

Items 9–16 should be reverse-coded. The response scale was *very negative* (1) to *very positive* (7).

The Aversive Form of Racism

Samuel L. Gaertner • University of Delaware
John F. Dovidio • Colgate University

Introduction

The results of several recent surveys indicate that white America's racial attitudes have become substantially more tolerant and liberal over the past few decades (Campbell, 1971; Greeley & Sheatsley, 1971; *Newsweek*; 1979, Taylor, Sheatsley, & Greeley, 1978). Other evidence, however, suggests that although the old-fashioned, "red-necked" form of bigotry is less prevalent, prejudice continues to exist in more subtle, more indirect, and less overtly negative forms (Crosby, Bromley, & Saxe, 1980; Gaertner, 1976; Gaertner & Dovidio, 1981; Katz, 1981; McConahay & Hough, 1976; Sears & Allen, 1984). The present chapter, like that of Katz, Wackenhut, and Hass (1986), proposes that the fundamental nature of white America's current attitudes toward blacks is complex and conflicted. Consistent with this assumption, Katz and his colleagues have accumulated evidence supporting Myrdal's (1944) conclusions that the attitudes of many whites toward blacks and other minorities are neither uniformly negative nor totally favorable, but rather are ambivalent.

The aversive racism perspective assumes that given the historically racist American culture and human cognitive mechanisms for processing categorical information, racist feelings and beliefs among white Americans are generally the rule rather than the exception. We use the term *aversive racism* (also see Kovel, 1970) to describe the type of racial attitude that we believe characterizes many white Americans who possess strong egalitarian values. In contrast to aversive racism is the more traditional, dominative form of racism (Kovel, 1970). The *dominative racist,* who exhibits the more "red-necked" form of discrimination, is the "type who acts out bigoted beliefs—he represents the open flame of racial hatred" (Kovel, 1970, p. 54). Aversive racists, in comparison, sympathize with the victims of past injustice; support public policies that, in principle, promote racial equality and ameliorate the consequences of racism; identify more generally with a liberal political agenda; regard themselves as nonprejudiced and nondiscriminatory; but, almost unavoidably, possess negative feelings and beliefs about blacks. Because of the importance of the egalitarian value system to aversive racists' self-concept, these negative feelings and associated beliefs are typically excluded from awareness. When a situation or event threatens to make the negative portion of their attitude salient, aversive racists are motivated to repudiate or dissociate these feelings from their self-image, and they vigorously try to avoid acting wrongly on the basis of these feelings. In these situations, aversive racists may overreact and amplify their positive behavior in ways that would reaffirm their egalitarian convictions and their apparently nonracist attitudes. In other situations, however, the underlying negative portions of their attitudes are expressed, but in subtle, rationalizable ways.

In our view, aversive racism represents a particular type of ambivalence in which the conflict is between feelings and beliefs associated with a sincerely egalitarian value system and unacknowledged negative feelings and beliefs about blacks. Although our position is very much aligned with that of Katz and his colleagues (1986), we do not assume the widespread existence of genuinely problack, favorable components of whites' racial attitudes that are independent of egalitarian values. Sympathy without additional feelings of friendship or respect does not in our view represent a truly positive racial attitude. Nevertheless, aversive racists' inability to acknowledge their negative racial feelings and their apparent rejection of negative racial stereotypes, together with their sympathetic feelings toward victims of injustice, convince them that their racial attitudes are largely positive, and certainly not prejudiced.

In terms of etiology, aversive racism is conceived to be an adaptation resulting from an assimilation of an egalitarian value system with (1) feelings and beliefs derived from historical and contemporary culturally racist contexts, and (2) impressions derived from human cognitive mechanisms that contribute to the development of stereotypes and prejudice (see Hamilton, 1981; Hamilton & Troilier, 1986). The aversive racism perspective assumes that cognitive biases in information processing and the historically racist culture of the United States lead most white Americans to develop beliefs and feelings that result in antipathy toward blacks and other minorities. Because of traditional cultural values, however, most whites also have convictions concerning fairness, justice, and racial equality. The existence both of almost unavoidable racial biases and the desire to be egalitarian forms the basis of the ambivalence that aversive racists experience. While we believe that the prevalence of the old-fashioned red-neck form of racism may have declined since the 1930s, we also believe that it would be a mistake to assume that this old-fashioned form is no longer a significant social force in the United States. Indeed, not all racists are ambivalent.

The negative affect that aversive racists have for blacks is not hostility or hate, instead, this negativity involves discomfort, uneasiness, disgust, and sometimes fear, which tend to motivate avoidance rather than intentionally destructive behaviors. There are a variety of different sources that we believe contribute to the negative content of the aversive racist's attitude. This negativity may be partially due to the affective connotations of black-ness and whiteness per se. *White* is considered good and active, whereas *black* is considered bad and passive (Williams, 1964; Williams, Tucker, & Dunham, 1971). Differences in the physical appearance of blacks and whites may also provide bases for differential responses. From an anthropological perspective, Margaret Mead proposes that although people must "be taught to hate, the appreciation and fear of difference is everywhere," (Mead & Baldwin, 1971, p. 28). From a psychological perspective, biasing effects of mere categorization into an ingroup and an outgroup have been empirically demonstrated and are thoroughly reviewed by Brewer (1979) and more recently by Stephan (1985). People behave more positively toward ingroup than toward outgroup members (e.g., Billig & Tajfel, 1973); they also evaluate ingroup members more favorably and associate more desirable personal and physical characteristics to ingroup than to outgroup members (e.g., Doise et al., 1972). Furthermore, greater belief similarity is attributed to members of the ingroup than to members of the outgroup (Stein, Hardyck, & Smith, 1965). Assumptions of belief similarity or dissimilarity can, in turn, mediate interracial attraction (Rokeach & Mezei, 1966). Also, because our society provides greater opportunity for intraracial than interracial contact, the "mere exposure effect" (Zajonc, 1968)—that familiarity promotes liking—could contribute to whites' more positive attitudes toward whites than toward blacks.

In addition, motivational factors can operate on these and other bases to promote and maintain racial biases. At the individual level, needs for self-esteem and superior status are frequently hypothesized to be among the major causes and perpetuators of prejudice and racial discrimination (Allport, 1954; Ashmore & Del Boca, 1976; Harding, Proshansky, Kutner, & Chein, 1969; Tajfel & Turner, 1979). At the societal level, economic competition that threatens to alter the traditionally subordinate status of blacks relative to whites fosters discrimination of whites against blacks (Wilson, 1980). The theory of internal colonization (Hechter, 1975), for example, proposes that the powerful majority group is motivated to ensure its advantages by initiating policies that perpetuate the existing stratification system. Given that traditional social structures have given privileges to whites, practices that threaten deprivation of that advantaged status, particularly when they involve the preferential treatment of blacks, may create negative affect even among people who in principle support ameliorative programs such as affimative action.

The attempt to maintain a nonprejudiced self-image can, in itself, also increase disaffection for blacks because interracial interactions become characterized by anxiety or uneasiness. Rather than being relaxed and spontaneous, aversive racists may have to guard vigilantly even an unwitting transgression that could be attributed by themselves or by others to racial antipathy. Thus interracial interactions may arouse negative affect that can become associated directly with blacks.

Social and cultural factors also contribute to aversive racists' negative feelings toward blacks. Black culture in the United States emphasizes values that are not always consistent with the tenets of white culture's Protestant ethic (see Jones & Block, 1984). Thus, belief or value dissimilarity also fosters disaffection. Furthermore, the context of socialization directly influences feelings and beliefs about racial differences. In the United States, traditional cultural stereotypes characterize blacks as lazy, ignorant, and superstitious; they portray whites, in contrast, as ambitious, intelligent, and industrious (Karlins, Coffman, & Walters, 1969). In our culture, blacks are frequently associated with poverty, crime, illegitimacy, and welfare. For example, in the 1950s and 1960s blacks on television "had minor roles and were rarely portrayed as powerful or prestigious" (Liebert, Sprafkin, & Davidson, 1982, p. 161). Even in the 1970s, when blacks were no longer generally characterized less favorably in the media than were whites, blacks were more likely to appear on television as poor, employed in service occupations, and involved in murders and other criminal activities (U.S. Commission on Civil Rights, 1977, 1979). These portrayals of blacks in the media and the culture more generally which associate blacks with roles and values that have negative connotations for whites may contribute to the development of negative affect toward blacks.

From a sociological perspective, the structure of society tends to perpetuate prejudice and discrimination. Specifically, the institutional racism framework proposes that, through the process of internal colonization, beliefs about relative status and power become embedded in social roles and norms (see Feagin & Feagin, 1978). These beliefs, in turn, help to maintain the social, educational, political, and economic advantages that whites have over blacks. Whites currently have advantages relative to blacks in most important aspects of American life: infant mortality, standard of living, educational achievement, socioeconomic status, and life expectancy (see Chapters 1 and 10). Thus, even if people genuinely attempt to reject the socially less desirable stereotypes and characterizations of blacks, it may be difficult for even the most well-intentioned white persons to escape the development of negative beliefs concerning blacks and to avoid feelings of superiority and relative good fortune over the fact that they are white rather than black and are culturally advantaged rather than disadvantaged (also see Ryan, 1971). These impressions, however, are not rooted in the traditional, old-fashioned bigoted belief that white superiority results from innate racial differences. Instead, these impressions of superiority, and accompanying feelings of sympathy, reflect historical and contemporary realities, which aversive racists believe result from racist traditions and practices. Nevertheless, the issue of white superiority characterizes whites' perceptions of the relationship between blacks and whites and may continue to play a role in the forces of oppression.

While we have identified many cognitive, motivational, and sociocultural factors that can contribute to the formation and maintenance of prejudice, the list is by no means exhaustive. Many other processes (e.g., illusory correlation, polarization and schema complexity) are discussed in other chapters in the present volume and are well documented in the literature. Nevertheless, in a nation founded on the principle that "all men [sic] are created equal," there are strong forces that promote racial equality. Norms of fairness and equality have had great social, political, and moral impact on the history of the United States. The prevalence of these egalitarian norms has been clearly documented in experimental (e.g., Sigall & Page, 1971) and survey (e.g., Schuman & Harding, 1964) research. And, of course, because of the civil rights legislation of the 1960s, it is no longer merely immoral to discriminate against blacks; it is also illegal. Thus, due to contradictory influences that operate on the levels of both the individual and the culture, most whites in the United States experience an "American dilemma" (Myrdal, 1944). This chapter, then, is about people who have developed a value system that maintains it is wrong to discriminate against a person because of his or her race, who reject the content of racial stereotypes, who attempt to dissociate negative feelings and beliefs about blacks from their self-concepts, but who nonetheless cannot entirely escape cultural and cognitive forces.

Aversive Racism: Derivation of Hypotheses and Empirical Tests

Our formulation of aversive racism enables the derivation of predictions concerning when egalitarian values and negative racial attitudes will each be observable. Because aversive racists are very concerned about their egalitarian self-images, they are strongly motivated in interracial contexts to avoid acting in recognizably unfavorable or normatively inappropriate ways. Indeed, if the fear of acting inappropriately in interracial contexts is a salient concern of many whites, then racial discrimination would be most likely to occur when normative structure within the situation is weak, ambiguous, or conflicting. Under these conditions, the concepts of right and wrong are less applicable, and the more negative components of aversive racists' attitudes may be more clearly observable. Here, blacks may be treated unfavorably or in a manner that disadvantages them, yet whites can be spared the recognition that they behaved inappropriately. When the normative structure of a situation is salient, however, racial discrimination would not then be expected. That is, in situations in which norms prescribing appropriate behavior are clear and unambiguous, blacks would not be treated less favorably than would whites because wrongdoing would be obvious and would more clearly challenge the nonprejudiced self-image. Nevertheless, even when normative guidelines are clear, aversive racists may unwittingly search for ostensibly nonracial factors that could justify a negative response to blacks. These nonracial factors, and not race, are then used to rationalize unfavorable actions. Negative racial attitudes can therefore be expressed indirectly, while whites perceive themselves as nondiscriminating and nonprejudiced.

Interracial Behavior: The Influence of Normative Structure

Because of the conflict and ambivalence that aversive racists experience, we hypothesize that nega-

tive racial affect is expressed subtly and indirectly in interactions involving blacks. Thus racial discrimination among aversive racists may typically go unrecognized because it usually occurs in situations in which there is a lack of normative structure defining appropriate action or under circumstances that allow an unfavorable response to be rationalized by attributing its cause to some factor other than race. When norms indicating appropriate behavior are clear, and rationalization is not possible, deviations from these guidelines during interactions with blacks could readily be attributed to racial bias; here, we hypothesize that aversive racists would be unlikely to discriminate against blacks. Given the high salience of race and racially symbolic issues on questionnaires designed to measure racial prejudice, as well as aversive racists' vigilance and sensitivity to these issues, effective questionnaire measures of aversive racism, in our opinion, would be difficult if not impossible to develop. (See, however, McConahay's [1986] work on the Modern Racism Scale). Instead, our strategy for assessing the usefulness of including aversive racism within a typology of racial attitudes relies heavily on the degree of discriminatory behavior observed in specially constructed situations of varying normative structure. In some of this research, we preselected subjects from among the highest and lowest prejudice-scoring undergraduates, based on an 11-item scale, which was composed of traditional and modern racism items and correlated highly with portions of Woodmansee and Cook's (1967) inventory.[1] Because even the highest prejudice-scoring students on a university campus are usually not dominative racists, we did not expect to obtain main effects or interactions involving prejudice scores.

---

[1] Respondents to the 11-item prejudice questionnaire were asked to indicate their agreement or disagreement (on 5-point scales) to the following statements: (1) Busing elementary school children to schools in other parts of the city actually helps their education; (2) Negroes shouldn't push themselves where they are not wanted; (3) Most blacks on welfare could get along without it if they really tried; (4) These days it seems as though government officials pay more attention to requests from black citizens than from white citizens; (5) Manual labor and menial jobs seem to fit the Negro mentality and ability more than skilled or responsible work; (6) Generally, blacks are not overbearing and disagreeable when they are in positions of responsibility and power; (7) Innately, blacks are as intelligent as whites; (8) I consider the present social system to be fundamentally unjust to the black person; (9) A hotel

The evidence that we have accumulated in support of the aversive racism framework draws heavily from experiments addressing the willingness of whites to act prosocially toward black and white people in need of assistance. We have used prosocial behavior as a dependent measure in our work for both practical and theoretical reasons. Pragmatically, helping behavior provides an index that is sensitive to both race (e.g., Crosby et al., 1980) and attraction (see Piliavin, Dovidio, Gaertner, & Clark, 1981). Theoretically, the Kerner Commission's investigation of the causes of civil disorders suggests that white America's responsibility for racial unrest may reside largely in its inability to recognize and understand institutional racism and in its lack of positive response to the needs of minorities. Thus, the culpability of whites may currently lie primarily in their reluctance to help those who are oppressed by institutional racism. Resistance to affirmative action, for example, may partially be attributable to an unwillingness to personally bear the costs associated with helping blacks and other historically disadvantaged minorities.

The first study, which initiated our interest in aversive racism, was a field experiment that examined the likelihood of black and white persons eliciting prosocial behavior from Liberal and Conservative Party members residing in Brooklyn, New York (Gaertner, 1973). Using a method devised earlier by Gaertner and Bickman (1971), Liberal and Conservative households received apparent wrong-number telephone calls that quickly developed into requests for assistance. The callers, who were clearly identifiable from their dialects as being black or white, explained that their car was disabled and that they were attempting to reach a service garage from a public phone along the parkway. The callers further claimed that they had no more change to make another call and asked the subject to help by calling the garage. If the subject refused to help or hung up after the caller

owner ought to have the right to decide for himself whether he is going to rent rooms to Negro guests; 10) Even though we will all adopt racial integration sooner or later, the people of each community should be allowed to decide when they are ready for it; (11) I would probably feel somewhat self-conscious dancing with a black person in a public place. This scale correlates highly ($r = .83$) with three subscales of the Woodmansee and Cook (1967) Inventory of Verbal Racial Attitudes: (a) Ease of Interracial Contacts, (b) Derogatory Beliefs, and (c) Private Rights.

explained that he or she had no more change, a "not helping" response was recorded. If the subject hung up prior to learning that the motorist had no more change, the response was considered to be a "premature hang-up." Based on previous findings relating political ideology to authoritarianism, ethnocentrism, and racial prejudice, the major prediction was easily and directly derived: The extent to which black callers would be helped less frequently than white callers would be greater among Conservative than among Liberal Party members.

The results, excluding consideration of premature hang-up responses, indicated that Conservatives were significantly less helpful to blacks than to whites (65% vs. 92%), whereas Liberals helped blacks and whites about equally (75% vs. 85%). In terms of helping, therefore, Liberals seemed relatively well-intentioned. Surprisingly, though, Liberals hung up prematurely more frequently on blacks than on whites (19% vs. 3%), whereas Conservatives did not discriminate in this way (8% vs. 5%). Liberals discriminated against the black male in particular in this regard. That is, Liberals hung up prematurely on black and white male callers 28% and 10% of the time, respectively.

While this study was in progress, other Liberal and Conservative Party members were interviewed about what they believed that they would do if they received a wrong-number call from a black or a white motorist. In virtually every case, participants indicated that they would help and that they would do so without regard to the person's race. These people genuinely seemed to believe that race would not influence their behavior under such circumstances. Nevertheless, the finding that Liberals did not discriminate against blacks once they recognized that help was needed but hung up prematurely more frequently on blacks than on whites suggested the importance of normative structure on the interracial behavior of liberal, well-intentioned people.

Specifically, when social responsibility norms, norms that people should help others who are in need (Berkowitz & Daniels, 1963), were made salient by the plight of the victim or by a full description of the motorist's need, Liberals did not discriminate against blacks. Failure to offer assistance to a black person once the necessity for help has been recognized would violate prescriptions for appropriate behavior and could be attributed to racial antipathy. Discrimination did occur, though, before the motorist's need became clear and when it was not inappropriate to terminate the conversation with a wrong-number caller. That is, at the point where the caller simply explained that he or she reached the wrong number, there were no guidelines for appropriate action; after explaining that the caller reached the wrong number, the question of hanging up or continuing the conversation has no prescribed answer. Because we did not have control over whether or not subjects heard the entire plea for help from the motorist or hung up prematurely, it is of course possible that there were other reasons besides normative structure that could explain the pattern of results. In subsequent research, therefore, we systematically manipulated the salience of normative guidelines.

As a further test of the role of normative structure on the interracial behavior of whites, another experiment (Frey & Gaertner, 1986) varied the clarity of normative structure regarding the appropriateness of delivering assistance to black and white partners on an experimental anagram task. As suggested by the results of the Liberal–Conservative study, we expected that whites would be less helpful to blacks than to whites only in situations in which the failure to help would not violate normative guidelines. When normative guidelines indicate that the failure to help would be clearly inappropriate, it was predicted that discrimination against blacks would be unlikely to occur because not helping a black person would be less rationalizable and would more likely be attributed to bigoted intent.

Normative appropriateness for helping was varied by manipulating the causal locus (internal vs. external) of the recipient's need and the source of the request for help (recipient vs. observer). With respect to the locus of need, Schopler and Matthews (1965) suggest that someone who is dependent because of moral weakness or personal choice does not raise the salience of social responsibility norms relative to victims of unavoidable circumstances. Considering the source of the request for aid, Enzle and Harvey (1977) concluded that, because a request for help from a third party influences a potential benefactor's normative beliefs about the appropriateness of helping, more help is given when a request for assistance is issued by a disinterested third party than by the potential recipient.

In our experiment, the need of the potential recipient, who was a black or a white fellow student working on an experimental task, was either self-induced by a failure to work hard (internal cause) or due to the unusual difficulty of the assignment (external cause). Female subjects subsequently received a request for aid that originated either from the potential recipient or from a third-party observer. They then had an opportunity to help by providing the other student with Scrabble letters to complete a task and bonus points to earn a prize. The dependent measures were whether or not the subject helped, the number of letters given, the utility value of these letters, and the number of bonus points awarded. Because either the external locus of need or the third-party request for assistance could increase the salience of social responsibility norms, the aversive racism framework expected that black recipients would be helped less than whites only in the condition in which the recipient did not work hard and personally made the request for assistance.

The results supported our prediction (see Table 16.1). They indicated that subjects helped blacks significantly less than they helped whites only in the internal need–recipient request condition. When the locus of need was external (i.e., due to task difficulty), or the request originated from a third party, or both, there was no significant effect of race on helping. Thus when social responsibility norms were salient, racial bias in helping did not exist. Only when the deservingness of the victim was questionable, rendering the failure to help more justifiable and rationalizable, were blacks disadvantaged relative to whites. Consistent with our framework, the normative structure of the situation played a critical role in determining the prosocial behavior of whites toward blacks.

In another experiment, we examined interracial help-seeking rather than help-giving (Dovidio & Gaertner, 1983b). Help-seeking is of particular interest because obtaining help involves acknowledging the relative superiority of the potential donor (Wills, 1983). Given the traditional role relationship in which blacks have been subordinate to and dependent on whites, it was assumed that whites would experience discomfort at the possibility of being subordinated to a black person (Dovidio & Gaertner, 1981) and, therefore, they would be motivated to avoid reversals of the traditional status relationship. If, however, the avoidance of subordinate status and dependency involves violating normative guidelines, we hypothesized that whites would be forced to ac-

Table 16.1. Helping Behavior toward Blacks and Whites as a Function of Locus of Need and Source of Request

	Internal locus				External locus			
	Recipient asks		Third-party asks		Recipient asks		Third-party asks	
	Black recipient	White recipient	Black recipient	White recipient	Black recipient	White recipient	Black recipient	White recipient
Help	33%	73.3%	73.3%	60%	93.3%	100%	93%	66.7%
Number of letters	1.47	4.67	4.60	4.20	9.87	7.67	10.60	7.20
Mean utility value	1.25	3.81	3.10	3.27	9.24	7.35	9.21	6.06
Bonus credit	27.80	37.13	30.07	30.60	43.27	43.40	40.80	38.47
Appropriateness of helping	3.60	4.73	4.80	4.27	6.22	6.40	6.33	5.87

Note. From Frey & Gaertner, 1986. Copyright 1986 by the American Psychological Association. Reprinted by permission of the publisher.

cept such a reversal so as to avoid acting inappropriately.

In this study, high- or low-prejudice-scoring white males were presented with one of two situations in which they could continue to work alone on a task described as involving abstract cognitive ability or they could obtain aid from a black or white partner whom they knew was available to help. In one condition, the partner volunteered assistance and the subject had to choose whether to *accept* or *refuse* the unsolicited offer. Our assumption that refusing assistance that is spontaneously offered would be regarded as normatively inappropriate was supported in two separate pilot surveys of student opinion. Therefore, in this condition we expected generally that subjects would accept spontaneously offered assistance at least as frequently from a black partner as from a white partner. In the other situation, subjects were aware that the partner was available to help, but they had to decide whether or not to *ask* for assistance. Our surveys indicated that the appropriateness of soliciting aid in this situation is unclear. Thus, here we predicted that subjects would *solicit* help less frequently from a black partner than from a white partner, given that the reversal of the traditional role relationship with blacks could be avoided without clearly violating normative guidelines.

The obtained interaction between race of the partner and the type of offer supported our hypotheses. Regardless of the prejudice score of the subject, white college students who received the spontaneous offer of assistance accepted help more often from a black partner than from a white partner (80% vs. 55%). In the conditions in which assistance had to be actively solicited, however, subjects asked for help less frequently from black than

from white partners (40% vs. 60%)—even though they reported that blacks were equally capable and equally willing to help as were whites. Thus, whites avoided subordinate status and dependency with blacks, but only when they could avoid the relationship without violating normative guidelines.

In summary, the results of these experiments involving diverse experimental manipulations provide consistent support for a basic proposition of the aversive racism framework. When norms for appropriate behavior are well-defined, white subjects do not discriminate against blacks; when norms are ambiguous or conflicting, rendering the concepts of right and wrong less applicable, both low- and high-prejudice-scoring subjects exhibit racial bias. It is possible, however, that even when normative guidelines are clear, other nonracial factors lead even well-intentioned people to discriminate against blacks. In the following section, we consider this implication of the aversive racism perspective.

Interracial Behavior: The Salience of Nonracial Factors

Another proposition of the aversive racist perspective is that even when normative guidelines are relatively clear, aversive racists are sensitive to nonracial factors that can justify, rationalize, or legitimize behavior that more generally disadvantages blacks relative to whites. In particular, we propose an indirect attitudinal process that operates differentially as a function of another person's race to enhance the salience and potency of *non-race-related* elements in a situation that would justify or rationalize a negative response even if a white person were involved (Gaertner & Dovidio, 1977).

Because of the increased salience of these non-racial factors in interracial situations, whites may discriminate against blacks and still perceive themselves as being nonprejudiced and egalitarian: They can attribute the reasons for their behavior to factors other than race. For example, children have been bused for a variety of reasons to public and private schools for many years without substantial vocal opposition from parents. When busing became a tool to implement desegregation, however, there was strong opposition. This protest often was not about desegregation per se but about the nonracial element—busing. Thus, people may discriminate against blacks while maintaining a nondiscriminating self-concept.

To examine the proposed indirect attitudinal process, we conducted a study (Dovidio & Gaertner, 1981) that examined factors that potentially contribute to resistance to affirmative action. Even though whites may try to avoid circumstances in which they are subordinate to or dependent on minorities (as in our previously described study), affirmative action increases the likelihood that whites will be involved in situations in which they are subordinate to black supervisors or in which whites may perceive that they are disadvantaged relative to black candidates for hiring, advanced training, or promotion. Although recent protests by whites regarding affirmative action seem to express mainly the concern that *qualified* whites will be disadvantaged relative to *less qualified* blacks (Regents of the University of California v. Bakke, 1978), it is possible that the reversal of the traditional role relationship, in which whites occupied positions of superior status, represents the primary threat to whites. Here, beliefs about the superior status of whites may continue to play a role in the forces of oppression. The purpose of this study was to investigate the possibility that the generally articulated issue of relative competence is a rationalization in which a nonracial factor, competence, is used by whites to object to affirmative action programs that increase the likelihood that they will be subordinated to blacks. Specifically, the experiment investigated the manner in which racial attitudes affect the prosocial orientation of whites as they enter supervisory and subordinate role relationships with blacks and whites of high and low ability.

High- and low-prejudice-scoring male college students were introduced to a black or white male confederate who was presented as either the subject's supervisor or subordinate. In addition, the confederate was described as being either higher or lower than the subject in an intellectual ability that was relevant to their dyad's task. After these manipulations of status and ability, but before the experimental task began, the confederate accidentally knocked a container of pencils to the floor. This situation provided the subject with an opportunity to offer assistance which was not absolutely necessary but which could connote affiliative and friendly feelings. If it is relative ability and not a reversal of the traditional status relationship that underlies resistance to affirmative action, then subjects would be expected to be more helpful to higher- than to lower-ability black supervisors. If, however, subordinate status is the major factor, then whites would be expected to respond in a less helpful manner toward black supervisors than toward black subordinates, regardless of ability.

The results indicate that relative status, rather than relative ability, was the primary determinant of both high- and low-prejudice-scoring subjects' helping behavior toward blacks. A Race × Role interaction was obtained: Black supervisors were helped less than black subordinates (58% vs. 83%), whereas white supervisors were helped somewhat more than white subordinates (54% vs. 41%). Relative ability, in contrast, did not affect prosocial behavior toward blacks. Regardless of status, high- and low-ability blacks were helped equally often (70% each); whereas high-ability white partners were helped more frequently than were low-ability white partners (67% vs. 29%). Thus, ability, not status, was instrumental in determining helping toward whites, but status, not ability, was the major factor influencing prosocial behavior toward blacks. Given that there were no significant effects involving subjects' degree of prejudice, it seems that even well-intentioned whites will respond relatively negatively to a black supervisor compared to a black subordinate, *regardless* of apparent qualifications.

How could people in this experiment rationalize responding negatively to a competent black supervisor? Subjects' postexperimental evaluations of their partners revealed that their behaviors may have been mediated by perceptions of *relative* intelligence (competence). Specifically, although subjects' ratings indicated that they accepted high-ability white partners as being somewhat more intelligent than themselves, the ratings revealed that they described even high-ability black part-ners as significantly less intelligent than them-selves. It therefore appears that although whites may accept that a black person is intelligent on an absolute dimension, they are reluctant or unable to recognize that a black person is higher or equal in intelligence compared to themselves. If subjects believed that black partners were relatively less intelligent than themselves, irrespective of their introduced ability, it is not surprising that their prosocial behavior was not affected by the com-petence of black partners. Furthermore, if whites misperceive the competence of blacks relative to their own ability, then resistance to being subor-dinated to blacks may appear quite legitimate to the protestors. Insufficient competence, not race, becomes the apparent rationale for resisting the reversal of the traditional role relationship. Simi-larly, deficiencies in prerequisite qualifications (relative to one's own), not racial antipathy, be-come the dominant articulated theme for protest-ing special admissions policies for minorities. Thus, although racist traditions may have initially produced social inequities, many whites, truly believing that they are nonprejudiced and nondiscriminating, may presently be participating in the continued restriction of opportunities for blacks and other minorities by opposing programs that threaten their own advantaged status and by misperceiving the relative competence of those who have traditionally occupied lower-status po-sitions. Although not the specific focus of this chapter, this last experiment was replicated (Dovidio & Gaertner, 1983a) using gender rather than race as a social category with traditionally demarcated role relationships. An identical pattern of results was obtained in response to women as was obtained in response to blacks.

In another experiment, we investigated the in-fluence of the hypothesized indirect attitudinal process in a situation in which an individual's de-cision to help or not to help could have signifi-cant, immediate consequences for a person in need of emergency assistance. In this experiment (Gaertner & Dovidio, 1977), high- and low-preju-dice-scoring college women heard an unambigu-ous emergency involving a black or a white fe-male victim. Subjects were led to believe that they were participating in an extrasensory perception (ESP) experiment in which they would try to re-ceive telepathic messages from a sender who was located in a cubicle across the hallway and whom

they could hear through an intercom system. Os-tensibly to determine the relationship between physiological reactions and ESP receptivity, sub-jects were wired with biotelemetry equipment that monitored their heartrates. The race of the sender, who would later become the victim of the emer-gency, was manipulated by her dialect and also by the picture on her ID card, which was exchanged with the subject at the beginning of the study. Half of the participants in the experiment were informed that they would be the only receiver, whereas the others were told that there were two other receiv-ers, each located in a separate cubicle across the hallway from the sender. Additional ID cards in-dicated that the other receivers (who were not ac-tually present) were white and female. After sev-eral trials of the ESP task passed uneventfully, the sender interrupted the procedure and explained that a stack of chairs piled up to the ceiling of her cu-bicle looked as if they were about to fall. In a few moments the emergency occurred. The sound of chairs crashing to the door was accompanied by the victim's screams: "They're falling on me!"

The presence of other bystanders was introduced in this study to provide a non-race-related factor that could allow a bystander to justify or rational-ize a failure to intervene. In Darley and Latané's (1968) classic experiment, it was discovered that the mere belief that other bystanders are capable of helping affects the likelihood that a bystander will intervene. When a person is alone, all of the responsibility for helping is focused on this one bystander. Under these conditions, the probabil-ity of this bystander intervening is quite high. As the number of bystanders is increased, though, each bystander becomes more likely to believe that one of the other bystanders will intervene or al-ready has intervened, and each bystander's share of the responsibility for helping is decreased. Con-sequently, the likelihood that each person will in-tervene is reduced.

We predicted that the belief that other bystand-ers are present would have a greater inhibiting ef-fect on the subject's response when the emergency involved a black victim than when it involved a white victim. Failure to help a black person in this situation could be justified or rationalized by the belief that the victim is being helped by someone else. Bystanders believing themselves to be the sole witness, however, were not expected to discrimi-nate against black victims relative to white vic-tims because any search for non-race-related factors to rationalize a failure to intervene would not be as successful as when subjects believed that other people were available to help. When alone, the failure to help a black victim could be more readily attributed to bigoted intent. Even relatively high-prejudice-scoring college students were expected to help without regard for the victim's race when they were the sole bystander. Although many of these relatively high-prejudice-scoring people (compared to other college students) may have awareness of their negative racial feelings, we believe that they would not regard themselves as particularly bigoted, and certainly not bigoted enough to be unresponsive to an emergency solely because of the victim's race.

As predicted, the results revealed a significant interaction involving the victim's race and whether or not bystanders thought that other people were available to intervene. Bystanders who thought that they were the only witness helped black victims somewhat more often than they helped white victims (94% vs. 81%). Subjects aware of the presence of other bystanders, however, helped black victims much less frequently than they helped white victims (38% vs. 75%). No main effects or interactions involving subjects' prejudice scores were obtained. Thus, the opportunity to diffuse responsibility for intervening, an apparently nonracial factor, had greater salience and potency among both low- and high-prejudice-scoring subjects when the victim was black than when she was white.

An added feature of this experiment was the monitoring of subjects' heartrates (using biotelemetry equipment) before and just after the emergency occurred. Paralleling the helping behavior findings, subjects who believed that they were the only witness to the emergency showed slightly more heartrate escalation when the accident occurred to a black victim than when it occurred to a white victim (Means = +14.52 vs. +11.39 beats per minute). Bystanders who believed that they were alone appeared equally concerned, both behaviorally and psychophysiologically, about the black and white victims. Subjects who thought that other bystanders were capable of intervening, however, showed lower levels of arousal with black than with white victims (Means = +2.40 vs. +10.84 beats per minute). These subjects thus showed much less evidence of personal concern, in terms of both physiological response and helping behavior, for black victims than for white victims.

As predicted, the results of this experiment indicated that the presence of other bystanders—a nonracial element in an emergency involving a black or white victim—differentially influenced the reactions of both low- and high-prejudice-scoring subjects. This pattern of results supports the hypothesis that when a racially biased response can be rationalized or attributed to factors other than race even well-intentioned people will discriminate, probably unintentionally, against blacks in a situation of deep consequence to the victim. Yet, the subtlety by which motivational factors alter the cognitive and emotional experience of the situation permits the continued maintenance of a nondiscriminating image among these people.

In other research on emergency helping behavior, we found that the face-to-face presence of other bystanders (actually confederates) who uniformly remained inactive and did not intervene had a greater inhibiting effect on white bystanders when the victim was black than when the victim was white (Gaertner, 1975; Gaertner, Dovidio, & Johnson, 1982). Bystanders who believed that they were the only witness, however, again helped black victims somewhat more frequently than white victims. We hypothesize that subjects who were with the inactive bystanders were concerned about deviate status in the group. This normative pressure not to intervene had greater salience and potency when the victim was black than when the victim was white.

It is possible that bystanders' differential responsiveness to the race of the victim represents a prowhite rather than an antiblack bias. That is, favorable feelings toward a person of one's own race may motivate a person to resist forces to diffuse responsibility or to conform to the uniform behavior of a group. On the basis of a review of research in the minimal intergroup situation, Brewer (1979) concludes that intergroup bias, which may provide a general foundation for interracial bias to develop, often reflects a pro-ingroup rather than an anti-outgroup orientation. Some additional research addressed this issue of separate ingroup and outgroup biases.

An experiment by Faranda and Gaertner (1979) investigated the extent to which high- and low-authoritarian-scoring white college students playing the role of jurors would follow a judge's instruction to ignore inadmissible prosecution testimony that was damaging to a black or white defendant. Participants in this study were presented with a court transcript of a fictitious criminal case in which the defendant was accused of murdering a storekeeper and the storekeeper's grandchild while committing a robbery. Subjects receiving a description of the trial in one condition were presented with the prosecution's evidence, which pilot research had indicated was weak. Subjects in a second condition were presented with the same weak prosecution case plus an extremely damaging statement introduced by the prosecution that indicated that the defendant confessed about the crimes to a third party. The defense attorney objected to this statement as hearsay because the prosecution was not able to produce the third party in court. Sustaining the motion by the defense, the judge instructed the jurors to ignore this inadmissible evidence.

Both high- and low-authoritarian subjects discriminated against black defendants relative to white defendants in their handling of the inadmissible testimony, but they did so in different ways. In their ratings of certainty of guilt (see Figure 16.1), high authoritarian subjects did not ignore the inadmissible testimony when the victim was black. As indicated in Figure 16.1, they were more certain of the black defendant's guilt when they were exposed to the inadmissible evidence than when they were not presented with this testimony. For the white defendant, however, high authoritarian subjects followed the judge's instructions perfectly: Ratings of the certainty of the white defendant's guilt were equal across the two conditions. High authoritarian subjects thus showed an anti-outgroup bias. Low authoritarian subjects, in contrast, followed the judge's instructions about ignoring the inadmissible testimony when the victim was black. They were equally uncertain of his guilt in both conditions. Low authoritarians, however, were biased *in favor* of white defendants when inadmissible evidence was presented. That is, low authoritarian subjects were less certain of the white defendant's guilt when the inadmissible evidence was presented than when it was omitted. These subjects later reported that they were angry with the prosecution for trying unfairly to introduce this hearsay testimony. They did not express this anger, however, when the defendant was black. Thus, low authoritarian subjects demonstrated a pro-ingroup bias. It is important to note that both the anti-outgroup bias of high authoritarian subjects and the pro-ingroup orientation of low authoritarians disadvantage blacks relative to whites. The question we examine in the next section is how the relative bias is reflected in expressions of racial attitudes.

Belief Systems Within Contemporary Racial Attitudes: Attributions and Associations

The implication of aversive racism for contemporary racial attitudes is rather straightforward. We hypothesize that because most whites want to see themselves as fair, just, and egalitarian, they will not directly express their prejudice against blacks. Expressing negative attitudes or endorsing overtly prejudiced statements would obviously challenge a person's egalitarian self-image. Thus, we propose that prejudice and stereotyped belief systems, like discrimination, still exist but that the contemporary forms are more subtle and less overtly negative than their more traditional ancestors.

On the basis of our assumptions about the type of ambivalence that aversive racists experience, we have conducted several experiments to determine the content of contemporary stereotypes among college students. In contrast to previous research (e.g., Woodmansee & Cook, 1967) that directly assessed attitudes toward blacks and assumed a favorable–unfavorable continuum of feelings, we have attempted to measure independently both negative *and* positive beliefs and feelings about blacks *relative* to whites.

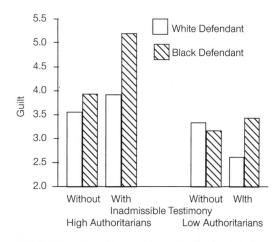

FIGURE 16.1 ■ The effects of incriminating inadmissible evidence on high- and low-authoritarian subjects' ratings of the guilt of black and white defendants.

With the assumption that a stereotype is a collection of associations that link a target group to a set of descriptive characteristics, Gaertner and McLaughlin (1983, Studies 1 and 2) engaged high- and low-prejudice-scoring white subjects in a task patterned after Meyer and Schvaneveldt's (1971, 1976) lexical decision procedure. This procedure yields a measure of associative strength between two words, based on the time that it takes subjects to decide if two strings of letters are both words. Meyer and Schvaneveldt (1971, 1976) report that highly associated word pairs (e.g., Doctor–Nurse) produce faster reaction times than do unassociated word pairs (e.g., Doctor–Butter).

In our research, the words "blacks" and "whites" were paired with negative (lazy, stupid, welfare) and positive (ambitious, smart, clean) words. It was hypothesized that if white people's characterizations of whites are more positive than are their characterizations of blacks, then subjects would be expected to make more rapid decisions about positive characteristics when they are paired with *whites* than when they are paired with *blacks*. Furthermore, if contemporary stereotypes are actually antiblack, then *blacks* paired with negative attributes would yield faster reaction times than would *whites* paired with these same words. This lexical decision task offers a less reactive approach than do adjective checklists to the study of stereotyping. Subjects are not directly asked to endorse the appropriateness of a specific word-pair combination, but only to indicate whether or not members of the pair are both words.

The results, which are shown in Figure 16.2, demonstrate the predicted interaction between the evaluative nature of the stereotype-related word and the racial category word. White subjects responded reliably faster when positive traits were paired with *whites* than when they were paired with *blacks*. Both high- and low-prejudice-scoring subjects, however, responded as quickly to *whites* paired with negative attributes as to *blacks* paired with negative attributes. A second experiment that substituted the word *negroes* for *blacks* replicated this pattern of results. These findings, then, are quite consistent with the results of our rating scale studies (discussed later). Specifically, the data indicate that white college students, irrespective of prejudice score, differentially associate positive, but not negative, stereotypic characteristics to whites and blacks.

Another reaction time experiment (Dovidio,

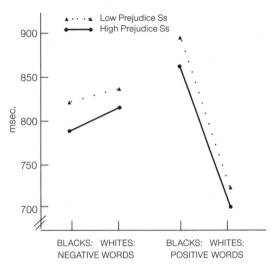

FIGURE 16.2 ■ Reaction times to positive and negative words paired with "blacks" and "whites." (From Gaertner & McLaughlin, 1983.)

Evans, & Tyler, 1984) was conducted to broaden our sample of evaluative words and subject populations and to provide a conceptual replication of our previous work. Specifically, we used words that have been demonstrated to be evaluatively positive or negative (Dovidio & Gaertner, 1981, 1983a), but which are not part of traditional racial stereotypes. In this study, we used a modification of Rosch's (1975a, 1975b) priming technique. In Rosch's method, a cue, or "prime" (e.g., fruit), is presented and provides some information about an upcoming test stimulus (e.g., orange, apricot). Rosch's (1975a, 1975b) results indicate that reaction times to typical instances (e.g., orange, apricot) are significantly facilitated after the category name prime, whereas decisions about atypical instances (e.g., date, prune) are facilitated much less.

In this study, the racial categories black and white were presented as primes, and positive and negative evaluative words were presented as test stimuli. The positive traits were good, responsible, trustworthy, kind, and important; the negative traits were bad, irresponsible, untrustworthy, cruel, and unimportant. Subjects were asked to indicate (by pressing a response key) whether the test word characteristic could "ever be true" of the prime category or was "always false." Despite the differences in stimuli and procedure from those used in our previous reaction time experiment, the results were remarkably similar. In particular, a Prime Type × Trait Type interaction was obtained: Subjects responded more quickly to positive evaluative traits following a prime of *white* than following a prime of *black* ($Ms = 767$ vs. 908 msec), but for negative traits there was no significant difference ($Ms = 891$ vs. 885 msec). Thus, racial category labels influence information processing in systematic ways.

Our reaction-time experiments provide consistent evidence across two different experimental procedures, subject populations, and sets of characteristics that contemporary stereotypes involve differential association of positively valued characteristics to whites but not negatively valued traits to blacks. How does this pattern translate into expressed racial attitudes? We performed additional self-report studies that addressed this question.

One of our rating scale experiments (Gaertner & McLaughlin, 1983, Study 3) provided separate groups of white subjects with six-point semantic differential-type rating scales in which either two positive (e.g., Smart–Not Stupid) or two negative (e.g., Unambitious–Lazy) traditionally stereotypic items were presented as anchors. Each of the negative scales represented a negative-to-less-negative dimension, and each of the positive scales reflected a positive-to-less-positive dimension. Using either the positive or the negative rating scales, subjects were asked to complete the phrase, "Blacks relative to whites are_____." Then subjects, using the same scales, were asked to complete the phrase, "Whites relative to blacks are _____." It was expected that if negative attributes are not differentially ascribed to blacks and whites, then ratings on the scales with negative traits as anchors would be quite similar when subjects responded to "blacks relative to whites" as when they responded to "whites relative to blacks." Furthermore, if positive traits are differentially ascribed to the racial groups, then the ratings of "whites relative to blacks" should be closer to the more positive end of the scale than with the ratings of "blacks relative to whites." This pattern is precisely what occurred. Blacks were not evaluated as more lazy, stupid, or dirty than were whites on the negative trait scales. Whites, however, were regarded as more ambitious, smart, and clean relative to blacks on the positive trait scales.

In a subsequent study (Dovidio, 1984), we broadened our sample of evaluative words. We used the words from our priming experiment that were evaluatively positive or negative, but which were not associated with traditional cultural stereotypes. Subjects were asked to indicate on seven-point scales how well each characteristic describes the typical black (or white) person. Consistent with our previous research, there was no significant difference as a function of race for the mean negative ratings, but there was a significant effect for the mean positive responses. Although the typical black person was not rated more negatively than the typical white person ($Ms = 3.30$ vs. 3.28), the typical white person was rated more positively than the typical black person ($Ms = 4.48$ vs. 4.23).

The results of our two rating-scale studies and our two reaction-time experiments converge on similar conclusions. White college students, at least those from primarily northern populations, do not readily express antiblack sentiments and do not appear to have strong antiblack associations. They do, however, exhibit a racially based ingroup bias. Our subjects consistently rated whites more favorably than blacks, and they had stronger positive associations with whites than with blacks. Thus, even though our subject samples appear to be quite liberal and egalitarian on traditional prejudice scales (Dovidio, Tannenbaum, & Ellyson, 1984), racial bias is still evident in their responses. Consistent with our assumptions about racism among well-intentioned people, prejudice is expressed indirectly and in a way that is not recognizably antiblack.

Discussion

In general, the results of several different types of experiments conducted since 1970 have produced consistent support for our aversive racism framework. Specifically, the behavioral findings (presented in the first two subsections) and the findings concerning subjects' associations and beliefs (presented in the third subsection) yield similar conclusions: Prejudiced thinking and discrimination still exist, but the contemporary forms are more subtle, more indirect, and less overtly negative than are more traditional forms. Furthermore, the contemporary form of prejudice is expressed in ways that protect and perpetuate a nonprejudiced, nondiscriminating self-image.

In terms of interracial behavior, the presence or absence of norms governing appropriate behavior is a critical factor mediating the expression of prejudice. When norms are clear, bias is unlikely to occur; when norms are ambiguous or conflicting, discrimination is often exhibited. Regarding the expression of racial attitudes and stereotypes, people do not appear to associate negative traits more strongly with blacks than with whites, an act that would likely appear bigoted. Whites do, however, consistently ascribe more positive characteristics to whites than to blacks. In addition, even when norms are clear, whites continue to be more sensitive to ostensibly nonracial factors that could permit them to rationalize a negative response toward blacks. Specifically, we propose that in situations involving blacks, an indirect attitudinal process operates to increase the salience and potency of factors that can substitute for the issue of race in justifying negative behavior. These nonracial factors may be related to characteristics of the situation (e.g., the presence of other bystanders who could share responsibility for helping) or may refer to personal or cultural values (e.g., perceptions of equity or justice). We do not mean, however, that contemporary white Americans are hypocritical; rather, they are victims of cultural forces and cognitive processes that continue to promote prejudice and racism.

We believe that aversive racism, although it represents a subtle form of racism, is a particularly insidious type. One reason that old-fashioned racism has shown a significant decline in recent years may be that, because it is direct and obvious, it may be susceptible to conventional techniques of attitude change and to social and legal pressures. It is unlikely, however, that aversive racism can be alleviated by such direct methods. Attempts to educate people to accept egalitarian ideals would have little impact on aversive racists; aversive racists already believe that they are egalitarian, nonprejudiced, and nondiscriminating. In fact, whenever aversive racists consciously monitor their behavior in interracial situations, they react in ways that consistently reinforce their egalitarian self-images. Techniques directed at revealing the negative components of aversive racists' attitudes would probably only produce reverse discrimination (Dutton & Lake, 1973) or a token reaction (Dutton & Lennox, 1974) that would permit aversive racists to deny their antiblack feelings. Introducing clear, salient norms into interracial situations would be an effective way of controlling discrimination, but it would probably not have long-term, generalizable consequences. Because of the salient external justification for their actions, aversive racists would not necessarily internalize the principles

involved in their interracial behavior. Thus, like a virus that mutates into new forms, old-fashioned prejudice seems to have evolved into a new type that is, at least temporarily, resistant to traditional attitude-change remedies that emphasize the evils of prejudice as a means of eliminating racism.

REFERENCES

Allport, G. W. (1954). *The nature of prejudice.* Cambridge, MA: Addison-Wesley.

Ashmore, R. D., & Del Boca, F. K. (1976). Psychological approaches to understanding intergroup conflict. In P. Katz (Ed.), *Toward the elimination of racism* (pp. 73–123). New York: Pergamon Press.

Berkowitz, L., & Daniels, L. R. (1963). Responsibility and dependency, *Journal of Abnormal and Social Psychology, 66*, 429–436.

Billig, M., & Tajfel, H. (1973). Social categorization and similarity in intergroup behavior. *European Journal of Social Psychology, 3*, 27–52.

Brewer, M. B. (1979). In-group bias in the minimal intergroup situation: A cognitive-motivational analysis. *Psychological Bulletin, 76*, 15–38.

Campbell, A. (1971). *White attitudes toward black people.* Ann Arbor: Institute for Social Research.

Crosby, F., Bromley, S., & Saxe, L. (1980). Recent unobtrusive studies of black and white discrimination and prejudice: A literature review. *Psychological Bulletin, 87*, 546–563.

Darley, J. M., & Latané, B. (1968). Bystander intervention in emergencies: Diffusion of responsibility. *Journal of Personality and Social Psychology, 8*, 377–383.

Doise, W., Csepeli, G., Dann, H., Gouge, C., Larsen, K., & Ostell, A. (1972). An experimental investigation into the formation of intergroup relations. *European Journal of Social Psychology, 2*, 202–204.

Dovidio, J. F. (1984). *Attributions of positive and negative characteristics to blacks and whites.* Unpublished manuscript, Colgate University, Department of Psychology, Hamilton, NY.

Dovidio, J. F., Evans, N., & Tyler, R. (1984). *Racial stereotypes as prototypes.* Unpublished manuscript, Colgate University, Department of Psychology, Hamilton, NY.

Dovidio, J. F., & Gaertner, S. L. (1981). The effects of race, status, and ability on helping behavior. *Social Psychology Quarterly, 44*, 192–203.

Dovidio, J. F., & Gaertner, S. L. (1983a). The effects of sex, status, and ability on helping behavior. *Journal of Applied Social Psychology, 13*, 191–205.

Dovidio, J. F., & Gaertner, S. L. (1983b). Race, normative structure, and help-seeking. In B. M. DePaulo, A. Nadler, & J. D. Fisher (Eds.), *New directions in helping, Volume 2, Help-seeking* (pp. 285–302). New York: Academic Press.

Dovidio, J. F., Tannenbaum, S., & Ellyson, S. L. (1984, April). *The irrationality of prejudice: Logical reasoning about blacks and whites.* Paper presented at the annual meeting of the Eastern Psychological Association, Baltimore, MD.

Dutton, D. G., & Lake, R. A. (1973). Threat of own prejudice and reverse discrimination in interracial situations. *Journal of Personality and Social Psychology, 28*, 94–100.

Dutton, D. G., & Lennox, V. L. (1974). Effect of prior "token" compliance on subsequent interracial behavior. *Journal of Personality and Social Psychology, 29,* 65–71.

Enzle, M. E., & Harvey, M. D. (1977). Effects of a third-party requester's surveillance and recipient awareness of request on helping. *Personality and Social Psychology Bulletin, 3,* 421–424.

Faranda, J. A., & Gaertner, S. L. (1979, April). *The effect of inadmissible evidence introduced by the prosecution and the defense, and the defendant's race on the verdicts of high and low authoritarians.* Paper presented at the annual meeting of the Eastern Psychological Association, New York.

Feagin, J. R., & Feagin, L. B. (1978). *Discrimination American style: Institutional racism and sexism.* Englewood Cliffs, NJ: Prentice-Hall.

Frey, D., & Gaertner, S. L. (1986). Helping and the avoidance of inappropriate interracial behavior: A strategy that can perpetuate a non-prejudiced self-image. *Journal of Personality and Social Psychology, 50,* 1083–1090.

Gaertner, S. L. (1973). Helping behavior and discrimination among liberals and conservatives. *Journal of Personality and Social Psychology, 25,* 335–341.

Gaertner, S. L. (1975). The role of racial attitudes in helping behavior. *Journal of Social Psychology, 97,* 95–101.

Gaertner, S. L. (1976). Nonreactive measures in racial attitude research: A focus on "Liberals." In P. Katz (Ed.), *Toward the elimination of racism* (pp. 183–211). New York: Pergamon Press.

Gaertner, S. L., & Bickman, L. (1971). Effects of race on the elicitation of helping behavior: The wrong number technique. *Journal of Personality and Social Psychology, 20,* 218–222.

Gaertner, S. L., & Dovidio, J. F. (1977). The subtlety of white racism, arousal, and helping behavior. *Journal of Personality and Social Psychology, 35,* 691–707.

Gaertner, S. L., & Dovidio, J. F. (1981). Racism among the well-intentioned. In E. G. Clausen & J. Bermingham (Eds.), *Pluralism, racism, and public policy: The search for equality* (pp. 208–222). Boston: G. K. Hall.

Gaertner, S. L., Dovidio, J. F., & Johnson, G. (1982). Race of victim, non-responsive bystanders, and helping behavior. *Journal of Social Psychology, 117,* 69–77.

Gaertner, S. L., & McLaughlin, J. P. (1983). Racial stereotypes: Associations and ascriptions of positive and negative characteristics. *Social Psychology Quarterly, 46,* 23–30.

Greeley, A. M., & Sheatsley, P. B. (1971). Attitudes toward racial integration. *Scientific American, 225,* 13–19.

Hamilton, D. L. (Ed.). (1981). *Cognitive processes in stereotyping and intergroup behavior.* Hillsdale, NJ: Erlbaum.

Hamilton, D. L., & Trolier, T. (1986). Stereotypes and stereotyping: An overview of the cognitive approach. In J. F. Dovidio & S. L. Gaertner (Eds.), *Prejudice, Discrimination and Racism* (pp. 127–164). Orlando: Academic Press.

Harding, J., Proshansky, H., Kutner, B., & Chein, I. (1969). Prejudice and ethnic relations. In G. Lindzey & E. Aronson (Eds.), *The handbook of social psychology.* Second edition, Volume 5 (pp. 1–76). Reading, MA: Addison-Wesley.

Hechter, M. (1975). *Internal colonialism.* Berkeley: University of California Press.

Jones, J. M., & Block, C. B. (1984). Black cultural perspectives. *The Clinical Psychologist, 37,* 58–62.

Karlins, M., Coffman, T. L., & Walters, G. (1969). On the fading of social stereotypes: Studies in three generations

of college students. *Journal of Personality and Social Psychology, 13,* 1–16.

Katz, I. (1981). *Stigma: A social psychological analysis.* Hillsdale, NJ: Erlbaum.

Kovel, J. (1970). *White racism: A psychohistory.* New York: Pantheon.

Liebert, R. M., Sprafkin, J. N., & Davidson, E. S. (1982). *The early window: Effects of television on children and youth* (2nd ed.). New York: Pergamon Press.

McConahay, J. B., & Hough, J. C. (1976). Symbolic racism. *Journal of Social Issues, 32,* 23–45.

Mead, M., & Baldwin, J. (1971). *A rap on race.* New York: J. B. Lippincott.

Meyer, D. E., & Schvaneveldt, R. W. (1971). Facilitation in recognizing pairs of words: Evidence of dependence between retrieval operations. *Journal of Experimental Psychology, 90,* 227–234.

Meyer, D. E., & Schvaneveldt, R. W. (1976). Meaning, memory structure, and mental processes. *Science, 192,* 27–33.

Myrdal, G. (1944). *An American dilemma.* New York: Harper.

Newsweek. (1979, February 26).

Piliavin, J. A., Dovidio, J. F., Gaertner, S. L., & Clark, R. D. III (1981). *Emergency intervention.* New York: Academic Press.

Regents of the University of California v. Bakke (1978). *U. S. Law Weekly, 46,* 4896.

Rokeach, M., & Mezei, L. (1966). Race and shared belief as factors in social choice. *Science, 151,* 167–172.

Rosch, E. (1975a). Cognitive reference points. *Cognitive Psychology, 7,* 532–547.

Rosch, E. (1975b). Cognitive representations of semantic categories. *Journal of Experimental Psychology: General, 104,* 192–233.

Ryan, W. (1971). *Blaming the victim.* New York: Pantheon.

Schopler, J., & Matthews, M. (1965). The influence of perceived causal locus of partner's dependence on the use of interpersonal power. *Journal of Personality and Social Psychology, 2,* 247–254.

Schuman, H., & Harding, J. (1964). Prejudice and the norm of rationality. *Sociometry, 27,* 353–371.

Sears, D. O., & Allen, H. M., Jr. (1984). The trajectory of local desegregation controversies and whites' opposition to busing. In N. Miller & M. B. Brewer (Eds.), *Groups in contact: The psychology of desegregation* (pp. 123–151). New York: Academic Press.

Sigall, H., & Page, R. (1971). Current stereotypes: A little fading, a little faking. *Journal of Personality and Social Psychology, 18,* 247–255.

Stein, D. D., Hardyck, J. A., & Smith, M. B. (1965). Race and belief: An open and shut case. *Journal of Personality and Social Psychology, 1,* 281–299.

Stephan, W. G. (1985). Intergroup relations. In G. Lindzey & E. Aronson (Eds.), *The handbook of social psychology* (3rd ed., pp. 599–658). New York: Random House.

Tajfel, H., & Turner, J. (1979). An integrative theory of intergroup conflict. In W. G. Austin & S. Worchel (Eds.), *The social psychology of intergroup relations* (pp. 33–47). Monterey, CA: Brooks/Cole.

Taylor, D. G., Sheatsley, P. B., & Greeley, A. M. (1978). Attitudes toward racial integration. *Scientific American, 238,* 42–49.

United States Commission on Civil Rights. (1977). *Window dressing on the set: Women and minorities in television.*

Washington, D.C.: U.S. Government Printing Office.

United States Commission on Civil Rights. (1979). *Window dressing on the set: An update*. Washington, D.C.: U.S. Government Printing Office.

Williams, J. E. (1964). Connotations of color names among Negroes and Caucasians. *Perceptual and Motor Skills, 18,* 721–731.

Williams, J. E., Tucker, R. D., & Dunham, F. Y. (1971). Changes in the connotations of color names among Negroes and Caucasians. *Journal of Personality and Social Psychology, 19,* 222–228.

Wills, T. A. (1983). Social comparison in coping and help-seeking. In B. M. DePaulo, A. Nadler, & J. D. Fisher (Eds.), *New directions in helping, Volume 2,* Help-seeking (pp. 109–141). New York: Academic Press.

Wilson, W. J. (1980). *The declining significance of race* (2nd ed.). Chicago: University of Chicago Press.

Woodmansee, J. J., & Cook, S. W. (1967). Dimensions of verbal racial attitudes: Their identification and measurement. *Journal of Personality and Social Psychology, 7,* 240–250.

Zajonc, R. B. (1968). Attitudinal effects of mere exposure. *Journal of Personality and Social Psychology, 9,* 1–27.

Self-Directed Versus Other-Directed Affect as a Consequence of Prejudice-Related Discrepancies

Margo J. Monteith, Patricia G. Devine, and Julia R. Zuwerink
• University of Wisconsin–Madison

Personal standards for responding toward gay males and affective reactions to discrepancies were examined for low prejudiced (LP) and high prejudiced (HP) Ss in 2 studies. These standards and discrepancies involved responses varying in controllability and acceptability. Results indicated that LP Ss experienced negative self-directed affect in connection with transgressions from their nonprejudiced and well-internalized standards, regardless of the type of response. HP Ss' personal standards were quite nonprejudiced and well internalized for relatively controllable and unacceptable prejudiced responses. Nevertheless, HP Ss' transgressions from their standards produced negative affect directed toward others but not toward the self, regardless of the type of response. The findings supported Higgins's (1987) argument that the standpoint of standards determines affective reactions to discrepancies. Apparently, LP Ss' standards are based on the *own* standpoint, but HP Ss' standards are based on the *other* standpoint.

Recent research suggests that prejudice reduction can be conceptualized as a process in which eliminating one's prejudiced responses is gradual, rather than all or none (Devine, 1989; Devine, Monteith, Zuwerink, & Elliot, 1991; Monteith, 1992). That is, the personal decision to adopt nonprejudiced beliefs will not be followed immediately by the elimination of all types of prejudiced responses because automatic, stereotype-consistent responses persist (but see Gilbert & Hixon, 1991). These stereotype-consistent responses can be supplanted only if they are inhibited and then replaced with responses based on

internalized, nonprejudiced beliefs. Thus, we have argued that the change process involves at least three steps (see Devine & Monteith, 1993): (a) establishing nonprejudiced standards based on one's personal beliefs for how one ought to respond, (b) internalizing those standards by linking them to the self-concept, defining them as important, and feeling committed to them, and (c) learning how to inhibit stereotypic responses so as to respond consistently with one's personal standards.

Empirical findings supporting this analysis have optimistic implications concerning low prejudiced individuals' potential for making progress in the prejudice-reduction process.[1] Specifically, Devine et al. (1991) found that low prejudiced individuals reported nonprejudiced standards for how they should feel toward members of stereotyped groups in various contact situations, and these standards were highly internalized. Even so, these subjects reported that their actual feelings toward stereotyped group members are sometimes more prejudiced than their personal standards suggested was appropriate. Such discrepancies between their actual responses and their personal standards gave rise to feelings of compunction (e.g., guilt and self-criticism). These findings suggest that low prejudiced individuals have completed the initial two steps of the change process, but face the difficult task of mastering the final step of inhibiting spontaneous stereotypic responses.

A second line of research provides reason to believe that low prejudiced individuals can master this final step. In particular, Monteith (1992) found that when low prejudiced subjects believed they had violated their nonprejudiced personal standards, several self-regulatory processes (e.g., feelings of compunction, heightened self-focus, and slowing of responses) aimed at avoiding future discrepant responses were instigated. Moreover, after the engagement of this regulatory cycle, subjects were effective at inhibiting stereotypic responses; in a subsequent situation they responded on the basis of their nonprejudiced beliefs. Therefore, discrepancies from well-internalized nonprejudiced standards appear to facilitate individuals' efforts to learn how to inhibit stereotypic responses so that belief-based responses can be provided. Theoretically, then, if low prejudiced individuals monitor their responses so as to detect discrepancies, they can make progress in learning to eliminate their prejudicelike responses.

In contrast, we have found little reason for optimism about high prejudiced subjects' potential involvement at any step in the prejudice-reduction process. For example, Devine et al. (1991) found that high prejudiced subjects' personal standards for responding to stereotyped group members permitted moderate degrees of prejudice, were not well internalized, and appeared to be derived from prevailing societal norms rather than from personal

moral standards. Like low prejudiced subjects, high prejudiced subjects reported that they sometimes manifested responses that were more prejudiced than their personal standards permitted. However, their discrepancies were associated only with global discomfort (e.g., bothered and threatened) and not with high levels of self-directed negative affect. Furthermore, their discrepancies appeared neither to instigate self-regulatory processes nor to reduce the likelihood of providing prejudiced responses on an occasion following a discrepancy experience (Monteith, 1992).

This research suggests that there are important differences in the nature of the discrepancies experienced by low and high prejudiced individuals. These differences can be illuminated with reference to Higgins's (1987) self-discrepancy theory. In Higgins' terms, both low and high prejudiced people appear to be prone to *actual:ought* discrepancies: By their own assessment, their actual responses are more prejudiced than they ought to be. However, standards for how one ought to respond can be derived from the own personal standpoint or from the standpoint of significant other (e.g., friends, relatives, and societal norms). Higgins's theory posits that discrepancies from standards involving different standpoints lead to different emotional reactions. Specifically, ought discrepancies involving the own standpoint lead to feelings of self-disappointment and self-criticism, whereas ought discrepancies involving the other standpoint produce feelings of threat and potentially resentment (Higgins, 1987).

Within this framework, Devine et al.'s (1991) results suggest that low prejudiced individuals' personal standards are based on the own standpoint. When their actual responses were discrepant from their personal standards, they felt guilty and self-critical. In contrast, high prejudiced individuals' actual responses appear to violate personal standards that are based on others' conceptions of their duties or obligations for responding, because their discrepancies led to general feelings of discomfort and threat.

The present research extends Devine et al.'s (1991) work by comparing low and high prejudiced subjects' standards, discrepancies, and discrepancy-associated affect across different types of responses toward stereotyped groups. That is, Devine et al.'s research concerned only feeling-related responses (e.g., feeling uncomfortable sitting next to a gay male on a bus). Yet two other

---

[1] *Low prejudiced* is used to denote individuals whose personal beliefs, according to standard measures of prejudice, are nonprejudiced. High prejudiced individuals' personal beliefs permit greater levels of prejudice.

important response domains include people's thoughts and behaviors. These three response domains can be construed as differing in at least two important ways. First, they generally differ in the degree of control they afford. For the most part, feelings are the least controllable and behaviors are the most controllable (cf. Logan, 1989). Second, although exceptions likely exist, prejudiced behaviors generally are less acceptable than prejudiced feelings and thoughts. Only behaviors are outwardly discriminatory, and society has established laws and social norms that underscore the unacceptable nature of prejudiced behaviors.

The fact that prejudiced behaviors are overt, unacceptable, and controllable makes the behavioral domain particularly interesting. As far as low prejudiced subjects are concerned, because they have already internalized nonprejudiced standards based on the own standpoint for relatively uncontrollable feelings (Devine et al., 1991), they would also be expected to have such standards in the behavioral domain. The more interesting possibilities, however, concern high prejudiced people. Given the relatively overt and controllable nature of prejudiced behavior, coupled with existing social norms prohibiting their expression, there is reason to believe that high prejudiced people may at least have established nonprejudiced standards for behaviors. Whether these standards are based on their own standpoint or that of others (e.g., society) is an open question, the answer to which could have important implications. If high prejudiced subjects have established nonprejudiced standards based on the own standpoint for their behaviors, tactics for encouraging them to generalize such beliefs to other types of responses (e.g., more acceptable and less controllable feelings) might be devised.

The suggestion that high prejudiced individuals may have internalized nonprejudiced standards based on the own standpoint for unacceptable and controllable behavior seems reasonable, given the nature of their more general views on equality. Specifically, many prejudiced theorists have argued that most Americans—presumably including high prejudiced individuals—personally endorse general egalitarian ideals (e.g., Dovidio & Gaertner, 1991; Gaertner & Dovidio, 1986; McConahay, 1986; Myrdal, 1944; Rokeach, 1973). Although such ideals are inconsistent with prejudiced standards and responses, people apparently can use various strategies to disregard the incon-

sistency. For example, people might rationalize or justify their prejudiced reactions (McConahay, 1986), exclude them from awareness (Gaertner & Dovidio, 1986), or simply fail to confront the inconsistency (see Rokeach, 1973). Although these strategies may be successfully applied in the face of relatively acceptable and uncontrollable prejudiced feelings and thoughts toward stereotyped groups, their application might be less successful in the case of clearly unacceptable and controllable prejudiced behaviors. The inconsistency between egalitarian ideals and engaging in prejudiced behaviors is likely to be extremely salient and observable by the self and others. Thus, even high prejudiced individuals may have established internalized, nonprejudiced standards based on the own standpoint for their behaviors. To the extent that our high prejudiced subjects have established such behavioral standards, we would expect them to feel guilt and self-criticism when their actual behavior is more prejudiced than their standards permit. On the other hand, if their standards are based-on the other standpoint, then we would expect these subjects to feel threatened and uncomfortable as a result of discrepancies (thus replicating Devine et al., 1991).

Examining the various response domains has an additional implication that is related specifically to the controllability of the responses: People may be more prone to discrepancies in the less controllable response domains. Assuming that, in general, feelings are the least controllable type of response and behaviors are the most controllable (cf. Logan, 1989), individuals should be most prone to discrepancies in the feeling domain. This result should be observed for both high and low prejudiced subjects.

We conducted a pilot study to identify feeling, thought, and behavioral responses that would be appropriate for use in the main studies. Specifically, we identified particular feeling-related responses that were evaluated as less controllable and more acceptable than particular thought-related responses, and behavior-related responses that were evaluated as more controllable and less acceptable than the thought-related responses.[2] In Study 1 we examined subjects' personal standards

---

[2] We recognize that in reality a particular feeling, for example, may be more controllable and less acceptable than a particular thought. Thus, we do not want to claim that the results to be presented generalize to all feelings, thoughts, and behaviors.

and their perceptions of society's standards in the behavioral domain. The central aim was to determine whether high prejudiced subjects' behavioral standards were fairly nonprejudiced and, most important, were not established merely on the basis of societal norms. In Study 2 we investigated the magnitude of discrepancies from personal standards and the relation between discrepancies and affect in each of the response domains.

Pilot Study

Method

Subjects were 55 female and 39 male heterosexual introductory psychology students participating for extra credit.[3] The design was a 2 (prejudice: low vs. high) × 3 (response type: feelings vs. thoughts vs. behaviors) × 3 (type of judgment: acceptability vs. intention vs. responsibility) mixed model factorial design. Prejudice was the only between subjects factor. The order of the sorting tasks that subjects completed was counterbalanced but had no significant effects in the initial analyses. Thus, we collapsed across this variable in the reported analyses.

Twenty-one scenarios were generated, each describing a different situation in which a male target person had a negative response toward a gay male. The negative response was either a *feeling* (6 scenarios), a *thought* (6 scenarios), or a *behavior* (9 scenarios). Subjects, participating in groups of 6–12, were seated at different tables and were assured that their responses would be anonymous. Index cards numbered 1–11 were evenly spaced across the table to demarcate the categories for the sorting task. Subjects sorted the 21 cards into categories three times, each time making a different type of judgment. A shuffled set of the 21 index cards was provided for each sorting.

Before completing each sorting, subjects were asked to read the cards and to think about the tar-

gets' responses in terms of the relevant judgment to be made. They were instructed to use as few or as many of the categories as they thought were appropriate and were told that each category could be used multiple times. The judgments concerned how acceptable and intentional the target's response was (1 = *completely unacceptable/unintentional*, 11 = *completely acceptable/intentional*), and how responsible the target was for his response (1 = *not at all*, 11 = *completely*). Subjects were asked to rely on their personal opinions or beliefs, not on what others would think, when doing the task.

After the sorting tasks, the participants completed the Heterosexual Attitudes Toward Homosexuals (HATH) questionnaire (Larsen, Reed, & Hoffman, 1980). This questionnaire served as the measure of prejudice in each study we report. Subjects rated each of the 20 HATH items on a 5-point Likert-type scale ranging from *strongly agree* (1) to *strongly disagree* (5). Responses then were summed, after reverse scoring when necessary, so that scores could range from 20 (*low prejudice*) to 100 (*high prejudice*). For the pilot study, 48 subjects were identified as relatively low prejudiced (HATH range = 25–51) and 46 as relatively high prejudiced (HATH range = 52–98). The mean HATH score was 53.78 (*SD* = 18.67). Male participants tended to have higher HATH scores than female participants, $r(94) = .27, p < .05$.

Selection of Stimulus Materials and Analyses

We considered the category number into which each of the scenarios was placed to be a rating of acceptability, intent, and responsibility. The intent and responsibility ratings for each scenario were averaged together to form a measure of perceived control. Then we examined the acceptability and perceived-control ratings to select four each of the feeling, thought, and behavior scenarios. We chose feeling scenarios that were rated as relatively high in acceptability and low in controllability, thought scenarios with relatively moderate ratings on both dimensions, and behavior scenarios that were rated as relatively low on acceptability and high on controllability.

The acceptability and control ratings for the selected scenarios were then examined statistically to ensure that differences between the response types were reliable. Several indices were formed

---

Nevertheless, for ease of presentation, we refer to each class of responses only by noting the appropriate response domain (e.g., "feeling responses" are used rather than "feeling responses evaluated as uncontrollable and acceptable, relative to the thought and behavioral responses used in the present research").

[3] In addition, one woman and one man were not heterosexual, so their data were not used.

for these analyses. An *Acceptability* index for the feelings was formed by averaging subjects' ratings of the four feeling response scenarios (Cronbach's $\alpha = .89$). Similarly, Acceptability indices were formed for the selected thought and behavioral responses (Cronbach's αs = .81 and .88, respectively). Finally, the perceived control ratings were averaged together to form separate *Control* indices for feelings (Cronbach's $\alpha = .87$), thoughts (Cronbach's $\alpha = .85$), and behaviors (Cronbach's $\alpha = .86$).

The Acceptability and Control indices were analyzed using separate 2 (prejudice: low vs. high) × 3 (response type: feelings vs. thoughts vs. behaviors) mixed model analyses of variance (ANOVAs). For both indices, the response type main effect was significant. Subjects evaluated the negative behaviors toward gay males as least acceptable ($M = 3.08$), followed by negative thoughts ($M = 5.10$) and negative feelings ($M = 7.02$), $F(2, 184) = 139.70$, $p < .001$. For the Control index, feelings were evaluated as least controllable ($M = 4.74$), followed by thoughts ($M = 6.52$) and behaviors ($M = 8.77$), $F(2, 184) = 239.84$, $p < .001$. Thus, we successfully identified feeling, thought, and behavioral scenarios that differed reliably in their perceived acceptability and controllability.

The analyses additionally revealed prejudice main effects on both the Acceptability, $F(1, 92) = 66.82$, $p < .001$, and the Control, $F(1, 92) = 13.21$, $p < .001$, indices. Overall, low prejudiced subjects found the responses less acceptable ($M = 3.84$) and more controllable ($M = 7.33$) than did the high prejudiced subjects (Ms = 6.35 and 6.39, respectively).

Study 1

The primary interest in Study 1 was whether high prejudiced subjects' personal standards for behaving could be distinguished from their perceptions' of society's standards for how one should behave toward gay males. The strategy used by Devine et al. (1991, Study 3) for examining feeling-related standards was used to investigate this question. We measured the degree of prejudice manifested both in low and high prejudiced subjects' personal standards for behaviors and in their perceptions of society's standards for behaviors directed toward gay males. Subjects also indicated the degree to which they had internalized their personal stan-

dards and society's standards and how obligated they felt to respond consistently with each of these standards.

Devine et al.'s (1991) conclusion that high prejudiced subjects' feeling-related standards were derived from prevailing societal norms was based on several findings. First, the location of their personal standards corresponded with the location of their perceptions of society's standards (i.e., the two standards permitted the same degree of prejudice). Second, even though their personal standards were more internalized than their perceptions of society's standards, these subjects had internalized societal standards to a greater degree than low prejudiced subjects. Finally, high prejudiced subjects felt the same degree of obligation to respond consistently with societal standards as with their personal standards. Thus, if the present findings are similar to Devine et al.'s results, high prejudiced subjects' behavioral standards could well be derived from prevailing societal norms. However, significant differences among the location, internalization, and obligation ratings for high prejudiced subjects' personal standards compared with society's standards would suggest that their standards were not simply based on societal norms.

Method

SUBJECTS

Several hundred introductory psychology students completed the HATH scale (Larsen et al., 1980) as a part of a larger survey. Those scoring relatively low or high in prejudice were identified as eligible participants. A total of 62 heterosexual individuals were randomly selected and recruited. This sample included an approximately equal number of men and women who were relatively low (range = 25–45) or high (range = 67–95) in prejudice ($M = 54.07$, $SD = 21.81$). Steps were taken to ensure that the experimenter was blind to subjects' prejudice level.

DESIGN

The design was a 2 (prejudice: low vs. high) × 2 (standard type: personal vs. society) × 2 (standard order: society-personal vs. personal-society) × 2 (gender: male vs. female) mixed model factorial. Standard type was the only within-subject variable.

MATERIALS AND PROCEDURE

Subjects participated in small groups, and the experimenter emphasized that subjects' anonymity would be ensured by having them place their completed questionnaire in a large envelope at the end of the session. This questionnaire had the same format and instructions used by Devine et al. (1991, Study 3). The initial instructions alerted subjects to the socially sensitive nature of the issues being investigated and underscored the importance of responding openly and honestly. Subjects were also told to keep in mind that the research concerned reactions to gay males only.

There were two main sections in the questionnaire: One included the items relevant to subjects' personal standards, and the other included the items about society's standards. Separate instructions were provided for each section, and before completing the second section, subjects were informed that their responses might or might not be consistent with their previous responses. After all subjects in the session had completed the questionnaire, they were debriefed and thanked for participating.

Personal Standards. Subjects were instructed to consider how they should respond in each of four situations and to base their responses on their own personal standards rather than on what others might think or expect. The four behavioral scenarios involved informing a gay couple in a bar that "gays aren't welcome here," "leaving a restaurant to eat elsewhere" after discovering the waiter was gay, muttering "watch where you're going, queers" after a gay couple who were absorbed with each other accidently bumped into you, and "writing the word 'faggot' over a bunch of pink triangles" painted on the sidewalk (the triangles were specified as a representation of gay pride, presumably leftover from a recent gay rights march).

After reading each scenario, subjects completed a rating using a scale ranging from *strongly disagree* (1) to *strongly agree* (7). For two of the situations, subjects rated the degree to which they believed they should have the negative response in the situation described. For the remaining two scenarios, subjects rated the degree to which they believed they should not have the negative response. The four personal should ratings were averaged, after reverse scoring the should not items, to form a *Personal Should index* (Cronbach's α = .87).

The same three internalization questions used by Devine et al. (1991) were then asked in connection with subjects' personal standards. Subjects indicated how important and how central to their self-concept they felt it was to respond consistently with their standards and how committed they were to trying to respond consistently with their personal standards. Subjects' responses to these three items were averaged to form a *Personal Standard Internalization index* (Cronbach's α = .88). A fourth question concerned how obligated they felt to responding consistently with their personal standards. All questions were answered using 7-point scales ranging from *not at all* (1) to *very* (7).

Society's Standards. In this section, subjects were asked to base their responses on the norms that society sets up for how people should behave toward gay males and to think about what society as a whole would consider a socially desirable response (rather than what they personally thought was desirable). Subjects then indicated on scales ranging from *strongly disagree* (1) to *strongly agree* (7) how they believed society would say they should respond in the same four behavioral situations. A *Society Should index* was formed by averaging the four ratings (Cronbach's α = .91).

Subjects then completed the same additional four ratings (i.e., importance, commitment, etc.) described previously with regard to their personal standards. The phrasing of the questions was altered so that the focus was on society's standards. A *Society Standard Internalization index* was formed by averaging subjects' ratings for the importance, commitment, and centrality measures (Cronbach's α = .84).

Results and Discussion

Mixed model ANOVAs involving all of the factors were initially performed on each dependent measure. Standard order was associated with a significant effect on only one measure. For all other measures, we collapsed across this variable.

PERSONAL STANDARD AND SOCIETY STANDARD MEASURES

The ANOVA revealed a significant main effect for prejudice, $F(1, 54)= 23.90$, $p < .001$, which was qualified by a significant Prejudice × Standard Type interaction, $F(1,54) = 4.44$, $p < .04$. As shown in the top row of Table 17.1, low prejudiced subjects' personal standards were less prejudiced than those of the high prejudiced subjects. Low prejudiced subjects also perceived society as permitting lower levels of prejudice than did high prejudiced subjects. The interaction resulted because high prejudiced subjects' perceptions of society's standards were more similar to their own personal standards than was the case for low prejudiced subjects.

Nevertheless, the personal standard versus society standard comparison for high prejudiced subjects was significant. Furthermore, the correlation between these subjects' personal standards and their perception of society's standards was not significant, $r(29) = .26$, ns. These findings suggest that, unlike Devine et al.'s (1991) findings for feeling-related standards, the location of high prejudiced subjects' personal standards did not appear to be based entirely on their perceptions of societal norms. Instead, their personal standards permitted significantly less prejudice than their perceptions of society's standards.

The overall ANOVA on subjects' should standards revealed additional effects, none of which qualify the theoretically relevant effects. A main effect for standard order was obtained, $F(1, 54) = 10.11$, $p < .002$, which was qualified by a significant Standard Type × Standard Order interaction, $F(1,54) = 8.26, p < .006$. Subjects' ratings of society's standards were more prejudiced when they reported their personal standards first ($M = 3.60$), compared with when their personal standards were reported second ($M = 2.32$). However, standard order had little effect on subjects' ratings of their personal standards (personal standards reported first, $M = 2.07$; reported second, $M = 1.85$). A significant Standard Type × Gender interaction also was found, $F(1, 54) = 6.45$, $p < .01$. The difference between the reports of society's standards and personal standards was larger for female subjects ($M = 3.18$ and 1.72, respectively) than for male subjects ($M = 2.74$ and 2.21, respectively).

INTERNALIZATION INDICES

The ANOVA performed on the internalization indices revealed a significant main effect for prejudice, $F(1,54) = 4.85$, $p < .03$, and for standard type, $F(1, 58) = 88.98$, $p < .001$. These effects were qualified by a significant Prejudice × Standard

TABLE 17.1. Mean Ratings of Personal and Society Behavior Standards as a Function of Prejudice Level: Study 1

Standard	Low prejudice		High prejudice	
	Society	Personal	Society	Personal
Should	2.58$_{b,A}$	1.19$_{a,A}$	3.35$_{b,B}$	2.73$_{a,B}$
Internalization	3.16$_{a,A}$	5.91$_{b,B}$	3.25$_{a,A}$	4.58$_{b,A}$
Obligation	2.53$_{a,A}$	5.32$_{b,A}$	2.66$_{a,A}$	4.51$_{b,A}$

Note. For each dependent measure, two types of mean comparisons were performed. First, the society and personal ratings were compared within each prejudice level. Different lowercase subscripts indicate that this comparison was significant ($p < .05$ at least, by relevant tests of simple main effects). Second, the effect of prejudice was examined, first with respect to society ratings and next with respect to personal ratings. For each of these dependent measures, cell means at different levels of prejudice with different uppercase subscripts are significantly different from each other ($p < .05$ at least, by Fisher's least significant difference tests).

Type interaction, $F(1, 58) = 10.86$, $p < .002$. As shown in the second row of Table 17.1, whereas low prejudiced subjects reported considerably greater internalization of their personal compared with society's standards, this difference was much smaller for high prejudiced subjects. The results of the a priori comparisons revealed several notable significant differences. First, both low and high prejudiced subjects had internalized their personal standards to a greater degree than society's standards. Second, in contrast to Devine et al.'s (1991) findings concerning the feeling domain, high prejudiced subjects had not internalized society's standards for behaving to a greater degree than had low prejudiced subjects. Finally, although high prejudiced subjects' personal behavioral standards appeared to be better internalized than societal standards, their personal standards were still not as well internalized as those of the low prejudiced subjects.

OBLIGATION

The only significant effect found in the analysis of the obligation data was a main effect for standard type, $F(1, 58) = 88.98, p < .001$. Overall, subjects felt more obligated to respond consistently with their personal standards ($M = 4.91$) than with society's standards ($M = 2.59$). Although the Standard Type × Prejudice interaction was not significant, $F(1, 58) = 2.81$, $p < .10$, a priori comparisons were performed and are summarized in the third row of Table 17.1. Most important, in contrast to Devine et al. (1991), high prejudiced subjects felt significantly more obligated to respond consistently with their personal standards than with society's standards. Also, low prejudiced subjects felt only marginally ($p < .07$) more obligated to respond consistently with their personal standards than did high prejudiced subjects.

Altogether, the results suggest that high prejudiced subjects' personal standards for behavior toward gay males were not based exclusively on the standpoint of prevailing societal norms. The two types of standards could be distinguished in terms of the location, internalization, and obligation measures. Moreover, high prejudiced subjects' personal standards for behaving were significantly less prejudiced than their perceptions of society's standards and involved greater levels of internalization and obligation. Given these findings, one may be tempted to conclude that these high prejudiced subjects have established relatively nonprejudiced behavioral standards based on the own standpoint. However, standards derived from the other standpoint may be based either on societal norms or standards of specific others (Higgins, 1987). The findings from Study 1 do not rule out the possibility that high prejudiced subjects' behavioral standards are based on those of specific others, such as friends or relatives. By focusing on the affective consequences of discrepancies from these standards, Study 2 should help determine whether these standards are based on the own or other standpoint.

Study 2

Subjects reported their personal standards for responding to gay males in various feeling-, thought-, and behavior-related situations, and they reported how they actually would respond in these situations. Subjects also indicated their feelings about the match between their personal standards and their actual responses. This procedure allowed us to address several new issues.

First, we compared the affective consequences of discrepancies for the three response types. Extending Devine et al.'s (1991) findings, all subjects should experience general discomfort when their actual responses are more prejudiced than their personal standards permit, regardless of response type. Additional more specific affective reactions to discrepancies should depend on

whether subjects' standards are based on the own or the other standpoint. Because low prejudiced subjects' standards are based on the own standpoint in the most acceptable and least controllable domain of feelings (Devine et al., 1991), we expected the same to be true in the thought and behavioral domains. Thus, we expected that their discrepancies in all response domains would produce negative self-directed affect (i.e., guilt). In contrast, the only domain in which high prejudiced subjects may have established standards based on the own standpoint is that of behavior. The experience of guilt in connection with behavior discrepancies would strongly suggest that these subjects' standards were based on the own standpoint. To the extent that feelings of guilt are not associated with behavioral discrepancies, we explored whether the affect experienced is consistent with discrepancies from the other standpoint. Specifically, Higgins (1987) suggested that conflict involving one's actual responses and personal standards based on the standpoint of others can produce resentment toward others. The presence of resentment-related feelings would provide strong support for the idea that high prejudiced subjects' standards are based on the standpoint of others.

We addressed two other issues in Study 2. One concerned the location of subjects' standards in the feeling, thought, and behavioral domains. Given that the prejudiced behaviors used in the present research were judged to be quite unacceptable and controllable, high prejudiced subjects' behavioral standards were expected to be significantly less prejudiced than their feeling- and thought-related standards. Replicating and extending the findings of Devine et al. (1991), we expected low prejudiced subjects to report nonprejudiced standards for all three response types. The second issue concerned subjects' proneness to discrepancies in the three response domains. Logan's analysis of controllability (Logan, 1989) and our own pilot data suggest that both high and low prejudiced subjects should be most prone to discrepancies in the feeling domain, followed by the thought and then the behavioral domain.

Method

SUBJECTS

The subjects were recruited in one of two ways. First, 178 heterosexual students from an introductory psychology class participated in exchange for extra credit. These participants' prejudice levels were assessed using the HATH scale, which they completed after they responded to the experimental questionnaire. Second, to obtain an approximately equal number of men and women with various levels of prejudice, an additional 121 subjects were recruited after a pretesting session in which several hundred introductory psychology students completed the HATH scale as part of a larger survey. Heterosexual respondents in the lower (scores = 20 – 46), middle (scores = 47 – 73), and upper (scores = 74 – 100) range of the HATH distribution were selected at random, contacted by phone, and asked to participate. (For the sample of subjects who participated in Study 2, HATH score M = 57.02, SD = 20.20.) The experimenter conducting the sessions was different from the recruiter and was kept blind to subjects' prejudice level. Data from two subjects were discarded because they did not follow instructions.

MATERIALS AND PROCEDURE

Subjects participated in mixed gender and mixed prejudice-level groups ranging from 12 to approximately 45 individuals. Anonymity was ensured using the same procedure as in Study 1. Each subject was randomly assigned to complete one of three questionnaires (i.e., regarding feeling, thought, or behavioral discrepancies). The format and instructions were identical for the three questionnaires and followed the format used in previous research (see Devine et al., 1991, for additional details). After they completed all measures, subjects were debriefed and thanked for participating.

Should, Would, Discrepancy, and Affect Measures. The initial instructions were identical to those used in Study 1 and were followed by a three-section questionnaire. The first section constituted the should measure. The instructions and the 7-point scales on which subjects recorded their responses were the same as those used in Study 1 for the Personal Standards index. The four personal should ratings (for feelings, thoughts, or behaviors, depending on condition) were averaged to form a *Total Should index* (Cronbach's α = .86). The second section of the questionnaire constituted the would measure and assessed how subjects believed they actually would respond in the same four situations. The instructions emphasized that

the subjects' actual would ratings may or may not be consistent with their personal should ratings. Subjects then considered each of the four scenarios again and indicated the degree to which they would (or would not) have the particular negative response described. The would rating scales were identical to the should rating scales. A *Total World index* was computed by averaging the four would ratings after reverse scoring when necessary (Cronbach's α = .84). In addition, a Discrepancy index (Total-d) was calculated by subtracting subjects' should rating from their would rating for each scenario and summing the discrepancies across the four situations (Cronbach's α = .66).

The third section of the questionnaire contained the affect measure. Subjects indicated the degree to which each of 35 affect items described their feelings about how well their actual (would) responses matched their personal (should) standards. Ratings were made on a scale ranging from *does not apply* (1) to *applies very much* (7). The particular affect items used are specified in the Results section. After the affect ratings, subjects were reminded that three of the ratings they made concerned negative affect directed toward others (i.e., angry at others, irritated at others, and disgusted with others). Then, if they had indicated that they felt at least somewhat negative toward others on these items, they were asked to explain toward whom these negative feelings were directed.

Feeling, Thought, and Behavior Scenarios. All scenarios (chosen on the basis of the results of the pilot study) included sufficient detail to allow the subjects to fully imagine themselves in the situations described. The four feeling scenarios involved feeling uncomfortable that a job interviewer was a gay man, irritated that the topic on a talk show concerned gay males, uneasy about going to work after discovering that a co-worker is a gay man, and upset that a gay male couple moved in next door. The four thought scenarios involved thinking "typical job for a gay," upon seeing a hairstylist who happened to be homosexual; "that guy must be gay," upon seeing a "rather effeminate" waiter; "homosexuals are disgusting," after seeing an advertisement for an annual gay and lesbian dance; and "gays must have some personality quirk that causes them to be gay," after spotting a newspaper article concerning gay rights in America. The four behavioral scenarios were the same as those used in Study 1.

Results and Discussion

OVERVIEW OF ANALYSES

The data were analyzed using hierarchical regression. Gender was coded so that male = −1 and female = 1, and the response type variable was represented using orthogonal contrast coding.[4] Both Total-d and prejudice level were continuous variables. Main effects were assessed simultaneously to test the significance of the unique portion of variance attributable to each variable. The increment in R^2 for each interaction was assessed at the step when the interaction term was entered into the regression equation. Power polynomial analyses were also performed to test for a curvilinear relation between prejudice and the dependent measures. Thus, the quadratic aspect of prejudice was entered into the regression equation after the linear component was entered, and each interaction term involving the quadratic aspect of prejudice was entered after the appropriate term involving the linear component was entered. The effect for the quadratic aspect of prejudice was assessed only after the linear main effect was assessed; the same was true for the interaction terms. Results including the quadratic component of prejudice are reported when significant.

TOTAL SHOULD AND TOTAL WOULD SCORES

A hierarchical regression analysis using gender, prejudice, response type, and all interaction terms to predict subjects' Total Should scores was performed. The increment in R^2 attributable to gender was significant, $F(1, 263) = 7.20$, $p < .008$ (B = −.159), indicating that the men's personal standards were more prejudiced than the women's standards. The increment in R^2 also was significant for prejudice, $F(1, 263) = 223.43$, $p < .001$ (B = .044), and for response type, $F(2, 263) = 34.65$, $p < .001$ (feelings Y = 2.57, thoughts Y = 2.88, behaviors Y = 1.71). However, these main effects

---

[4]The two codes used to represent each response type were 1 and −1 for feelings, 0 and 2 for thoughts, and −1 and −1 for behaviors. Initially, effects for response type were tested by entering the two codes simultaneously. If this omnibus test resulted in a significant increment in the squared multiple correlation, the difference between feelings and behavior was then tested by computing the t value associated with the first code. Other comparisons between the response type levels were then conducted by reanalyzing the data and varying the response type to which the various codes were assigned.

were qualified by an interaction between prejudice and response type, $F(2, 261) = 8.41$, $p < .001$. As shown in the top row of Table 17.2, the difference between low and high prejudiced subjects' personal standards was considerably smaller for the behaviors than for either the feelings or the thoughts. It is important to note that the high prejudiced subjects' personal standards for behaviors were considerably less prejudiced than their standards for thoughts of feelings. It does appear, therefore, that these subjects had established relatively nonprejudiced standards regarding behaviors toward gay males. However, additional analyses performed separately within each domain revealed significant effects for prejudice. Thus, in all three domains, low prejudice subjects' personal standards were still less prejudiced than those of high prejudiced subjects.

The analysis of subjects' Total Would scores revealed a significant increment in R^2 due to prejudice, $F(1, 263) = 257.50$, $p < .001$ (B = .051), as well as a significant increment due to the quadratic aspect of prejudice, $F(1, 262) = 9.46$, $p < .002$. The curvilinear relation was such that subjects' Total Would scores increased with prejudice, but leveled off at very high levels of prejudice. The main effect for response type also was significant, $F(2, 262) = 107.48$, $p < .001$ (feelings Y = 3.73, thoughts Y = 4.34, behaviors Y = 2.16). In addition, the Prejudice × Response Type interaction added a significant increment in R^2, $F(2, 260) = 5.68$, $p < .004$. As shown in the bottom row of Table 17.2, the difference between low and high prejudiced subjects' Total Would scores was less pronounced for the behaviors than for the feelings and thoughts.

DISCREPANCY SCORES

Out of the 297 usable cases, 10% had negative Total-d scores (i.e., their woulds were less prejudiced than their shoulds indicated was appropriate). Because our central theoretical interest concerned subjects' reactions to positive discrepancies, these data were not included in the primary analyses and are summarized instead in a later subsection. Of the 268 remaining cases, 22% had a Total-d score of 0 (such that their actual responses, overall, were consistent with their personal standards). The percentages of subjects with 0 discrepancies for the feeling, thought, and behavioral response types were 20%, 5%, and 45%,

TABLE 17.2. Predicted Values for Total Should and Total Would Ratings as a Function of Prejudice Level and Response Type: Study 2

Rating	Feeling response		Thought response		Behavior response	
	LP	HP	LP	HP	LP	HP
Total should	1.53	3.61	1.82	3.93	1.16	2.24
Total would	2.43	5.04	3.31	5.37	1.37	2.93

Note. For each dependent measure, comparisons between low and high prejudiced subjects within each domain were performed. The effect for prejudice was significant in every case ($p < .05$ at least). LP = low prejudice; HP = high prejudice.

respectively. The other 78% of the subjects reported positive Total-d scores (indicating their actual responses were more prejudiced than their standards permitted).

The regression analysis performed on subjects' Total-d scores revealed a significant main effect for prejudice, $F(1, 263) = 5.78$, $p < .02$ (B = .029) and a significant increment in R^2 attributable to the quadratic aspect of prejudice, $F(1, 262) = 20.24$, $p < .001$. Total-d scores increased as prejudice increased, but decreased slightly at high levels of prejudice. A marginally significant interaction between gender and prejudice also was found for the Total-d scores, $F(1, 257) = 3.74$, $p < .054$. This interaction was such that the difference between low and high prejudiced subjects' Total-d scores for men (Ys = 3.76 and 4.69, respectively) was smaller than the difference for women (Ys 3.47 and 6.25, respectively).

Of particular interest was whether subjects' Total-d scores would differ across the three response types such that subjects would be most prone to discrepancies in the least controllable (feeling) domain. As expected, the response type main effect was significant, $F(2, 262) = 26.96$, $p < .001$. Specific comparisons revealed that Total-d scores were significantly smaller in the most controllable behavioral response domain (Y = 1.81), compared with feelings (Y = 4.66) and thoughts (Y = 5.99, ps < .001). In contrast with our expectations, Total-d scores for thoughts were actually significantly larger than for feelings ($p < .05$), even though thoughts are presumably easier to control (Logan, 1989).

One possible explanation for this last effect, given the imagination technique used, is that it is simply easier to imagine having a stereotypic thought than a prejudiced feeling. It could be ar-

gued that the thoughts were more concrete than the diffuse types of feelings (e.g., uneasy and bothered) that the subjects imagined. Perhaps with more concrete or personally relevant feeling scenarios (e.g., discovering a friend was a gay male, having a gay male friend make a sexual advance), discrepancies would be larger.[5] Alternatively, and perhaps more theoretically interesting, is the possibility that our subjects did not have a lot of personal contact with gay males but still had well-learned stereotypic representations of them (e.g., through media and discussions with others), making the cognitive component of the stereotype highly accessible. Despite this departure from expectations, one clear finding was that feeling- and thought-related discrepancies were much larger than behavior-related discrepancies.

CONSTRUCTION OF AFFECT INDICES

A principal-axis factor analysis performed on the 35 affect items yielded a solution that was nearly identical to the solution obtained by Devine et al. (1991). On the basis of the results, five separate affect indices were created by averaging the ratings of items included in the index. The indices constructed were as follows: *Negself* (angry at myself, guilty, annoyed with myself, disgusted with myself, regretful, shameful, and self-critical), *Negother* (angry at others, irritated at others, and disgusted with others), *Discomfort* (Fearful, uneasy, embarrassed, bothered, tense, threatened, and uncomfortable), *Positive* (friendly, happy, energetic, optimistic, content, and good), and *Depressed* (low, depressed, sad, helpless, anxious, and frustrated). Separate hierarchical regression analyses were performed on each affect index, using gender, prejudice, response type, Total-d, and all possible interactions as the predictor variables. Significant effects are reported in Table 17.3.

Discomfort and Negself. Our prediction was that the magnitude of subjects' discrepancies would be positively related to their level of discomfort, regardless of prejudice level and response domain. As expected, larger Total-d scores were associated with greater discomfort than were smaller Total-d scores. Consistent with Devine et al.'s (1991) results, we also found that, overall, subjects higher in prejudice experienced greater discomfort than did subjects lower in prejudice. Although this prejudice main effect is open to various explanations, one possibility is that high preju-

TABLE 17.3. Significant Results of Hierarchical Regression Analyses Performed on the Affect Indices: Study 2

Affect index	df	F	p<	B
Discomfort				
Total-d	1,262	24.84	.001	.009
Prejudice	1,262	4.70	.03	.102
Negself				
Total-d	1,262	25.66	.001	.084
Prejudice	1,262	7.16	.008	−.009
Total-d × Prejudice	1,261	20.50	.001	
Positive				
Total-d	1,261	12.48	.001	−.087
Prejudice[a]	1,261	3.72	.05	
Total-d × Prejudice[a]	1,259	7.11	.008	
Negother				
Prejudice[a]	1,261	5.90	.02	
Total-d × Prejudice	1,260	6.80	.01	
Depressed				
Total-d	1,262	12.78	.001	.059

[a]The significant effect noted involves the quadratic aspect of prejudice.

diced subjects experienced discomfort because they were required to think about gay males throughout the experiment.

Of particular interest in the present research was whether low and high prejudiced subjects would differ in their reported Negself feelings as a function response type as well as discrepancy magnitude. For low prejudiced subjects, Negself feelings were expected to increase as Total-d increased for all types of responses. Furthermore, if high prejudiced subjects' relatively nonprejudiced behavioral standards were based on the own standpoint, Negself should increase as Total-d scores for the behaviors increase. This three-way interaction among Total-d, prejudice, and response type was not significant, $F(2, 255) = 2.19$, ns. Instead, the regression analysis revealed significant main effects for both Total-d and prejudice (see Table 17.3), and these effects were qualified only by a significant Prejudice × Total-d interaction. Replicating Devine et al.'s (1991) findings, low prejudiced subjects with larger discrepancies reported greater Negself feelings (Y = 3. 19) than those with smaller discrepancies (Y = 1.65); this difference was much smaller for high prejudiced subjects (small Total-d, Y = 1.79; large Total-d, Y = 2.02).[6]

Additional analyses were performed to examine the effects of our predictor variables on Negself and Discomfort, independent of the correlation between the two indices. The hierarchical regression analysis in which Negself was partialed out

of Discomfort indicated that the main effect for Total-d remained significant, $F(1, 261) = 7.69$, $p < .01$, B =.052. Furthermore, the Prejudice × Total-d interaction remained significant when Discomfort was partialed out of Negself, $F(1, 260) = 18.60$, $p < .001$.

In sum, even though high prejudiced subjects' personal standards for the behaviors were significantly less prejudiced than their standards for feelings and thoughts, the degree of compunction experienced in association with their behavioral discrepancies was not particularly high. Because restricted power possibly could have precluded the detection of a significant three-way interaction, analyses that were more specific to examining high prejudiced subjects' affective reactions to their discrepancies were performed. First, an analysis involving only subjects assigned to the behavioral response type revealed that the Prejudice × Total-d interaction remained significant, $F(1, 77) = 7.38$, $p < .01$. Second, we examined whether high prejudiced subjects experienced greater Negself feelings in association with behavioral than feeling or thought discrepancies. This analysis did not reveal a significant Response Type × Total-d interaction, $F < 1$. Together, these analyses provide further evidence that high prejudiced subjects experienced little compunction as a result of their discrepancies, even concerning responses for which their standards were relatively nonprejudiced and well internalized. The theoretical implication is that high prejudiced subjects' behavioral standards did not involve the own standpoint.

Negother. If high prejudiced subjects' standards are based on the other standpoint, then one might expect to find that their discrepancies are associated with negative feelings directed toward others, in addition to global discomfort. In the analysis of the Negother index, a significant effect for the quadratic aspect of prejudice was found, which again was qualified by a significant interaction between prejudice and Total-d. In this case, high prejudiced subjects with large discrepancy scores experienced greater Negother feelings (Y = 3.54)

---

[5]We thank an anonymous reviewer for making this suggestion.

[6] This interaction was further qualified by a marginally significant Total-d × Prejudice × Gender interaction, $F(1, 246) = 3.80$, $p = .052$. The nature of this interaction was such that the effects of Total-d on Negself feelings was somewhat stronger for low prejudiced female subjects than for their male counterparts.

than those with small discrepancy scores (Y = 2.57). However, there was little difference between low prejudiced subjects' Negother feelings when they had large (Y = 2.62) compared with small discrepancy scores (Y = 2.94). Thus, rather than directing negative affect inward as a result of their discrepancies, the high prejudiced subjects appeared to externalize their negative feelings by becoming angry, irritated, and disgusted with other people. These Negother feelings were qualitatively distinct from general Discomfort-related feelings, as the Total-d × Prejudice interaction remained significant when Discomfort was partialed from Negother, $F(1, 259) = 11.65$, $p < .001$. Theoretically, the nature of the Prejudice × Total-d interaction provides further evidence that high prejudiced subjects' standards involved the other standpoint. That is, Higgins (1987) maintains that discrepancies from standards involving the other standpoint produce resentment, due to the anticipation of negative sanctions from others, in addition to more global discomfort.

To investigate toward whom subjects' Negother feelings were directed, we content analyzed the explanations provided by subjects who scored greater than 1 on the Negother index (N = 204). The percentages of low, moderate, and high prejudiced subjects scoring greater than 1 were 72%, 72%, and 84%, respectively. Two independent judges, blind to subjects' prejudice level, coded each protocol into one of four categories. Two of the categories were of theoretical interest: (a) statements indicating that subjects were feeling negative toward people who are prejudiced toward gays or who perpetuate negative stereotypes about gays and (b) statements indicating that subjects were feeling negative toward gays. A third category consisted of miscellaneous statements (20% of the protocols). Unfortunately, 29% of the subjects (distributed approximately equally among prejudice levels) failed to provide any explanation of the target of their negative feelings. These protocols were coded in a "no response" category. The two coders disagreed on only 10 cases, which were resolved by a third judge.

Examination of these data revealed interesting differences between low and high prejudiced subjects. Whereas 56.9% of the low prejudiced subjects' protocols were in Category 1 (feeling negative toward those who are prejudiced), only 5.3% of the high prejudiced subjects' protocols were in this category. In contrast, the percentage of low

prejudiced subjects' protocols fitting in Category 2 (feeling negative toward gays) was only 6.2%, compared with 44% of the high prejudiced subjects' protocols. The moderately prejudiced subjects' protocols were approximately evenly split between the two categories, with 21.9% indicating anger at gay males and 17.2% indicating anger at people who are prejudiced toward gay males.

Additional analyses indicated that high prejudiced subjects' proclivity to experience Negother feelings directed toward gays, rather than some other target, was related to the magnitude of their Total-d score. Specifically, we computed the point-biserial correlation between statements falling in this category as opposed to any of the other categories and their Total-d scores. A significant correlation was found, $r(73) = .26$, $p < .025$, indicating that as Total-d increased, high prejudiced subjects were more likely to direct their anger toward gay males.

There are a number of possible explanations for the finding that gay males are the targets of high prejudiced subjects' Negother feelings. For example, the high prejudiced subjects may have construed gay males as the cause of their threatening predicament (e.g., without gay males, discrepancies would not arise). Second, high prejudiced subjects may have felt aggressive toward those upon whom their personal standards were based, but displaced their feelings onto gay males. Finally, the procedure itself most likely increased the accessibility of gay males by referring frequently to the group.

In sum, the Negother findings indicated that discrepancy experiences among high prejudiced people may be associated with an affective reaction more specific than just diffuse discomfort. In contrast with low prejudiced subjects, whose negative affect was directed inward (i.e., guilt), high prejudiced subjects' negative affect appeared to be directed outward (i.e., negative feelings toward others).

Positive. The quadratic aspect of prejudice was significant in the analysis of the Positive index, so the power polynomial results are reported (see Table 17.3). In addition to this effect for prejudice, a significant effect for Total-d was found. These main effects were qualified by an interaction between the quadratic component of prejudice and Total-d. Replicating Devine et al.'s (1991) findings, the basic form of this interaction was that low prejudiced subjects with large discrepancies felt considerably less positive (Y = 2.95) than those with small discrepancies (Y = 4.46); however, little difference was observed between high prejudiced subjects with large (Y = 3.18) as compared with small discrepancy scores (Y = 3.70).

Depressed. Replicating Devine et al. (1991), a significant main effect for Total-d was found on the depressed index. Increases in Total-d scores were associated with heightened feelings of depression.

ANALYSES OF NEGATIVE DISCREPANCY DATA

The theoretical interest in the present research centered on instances in which subjects' actual responses either matched or were more prejudiced than their personal standards. However it may also be instructive to examine data from subjects whose actual responses were less prejudiced than their personal standards.

The 31 negative discrepancy scores could reflect subject errors, or true discrepancies, or both. If they reflect true discrepancies, one would expect negative discrepancies to be most common in the behavioral domain. That is, laws and social norms are most likely to deter one from behaving in a manner that is as prejudiced as one's standards. In addition, negative discrepancies should be most common among high prejudiced subjects because, compared with low prejudiced subjects, their standards do permit fairly prejudiced responses. Analyses of the data revealed that negative discrepancies were far more common for the behaviors (n = 20) than for the feelings (n = 7) and thoughts (n = 4). Furthermore, the HATH scores of the negative discrepancy subjects were high (M = 68.97, SD = 16.44). Thus, the negative discrepancy data consisted mostly of moderately to highly prejudiced subjects. In fact, only three of the subjects would be classified as low in prejudice, using the bottom third of the HATH distribution (i.e., scores between 20 and 46) as the criterion.

If the standards of high prejudiced subjects with negative discrepancies involve the other standpoint (as appears to be the case for high prejudiced subjects with 0 and positive discrepancies), their discrepancies should be associated with Discomfort and Negother feelings. For example, realizing that "I cannot behave as prejudiced as my friends maintain I ought to behave" constitutes an actual–own versus ought–other discrepancy, and thus should give rise to feelings of threat, fear, and resentment

(see Higgins, 1987). To examine this possibility, we included the quadratic aspect of Total-d in analyses involving the negative discrepancy data along with the 0 and positive discrepancy data. The reasoning was that for both Discomfort and Negother, an interaction between prejudice and the quadratic aspect of Total-d should be found if the high prejudiced subjects' negative discrepancies were from standards involving the other standpoint. More specifically, low prejudiced subjects should show steady increases in Discomfort as Total-d increases. However, high prejudiced subjects with either large positive or negative discrepancies should experience high levels of discomfort, relative to high prejudiced subjects with small positive discrepancies. The same would be expected for the Negother index, except that no relation necessarily should be found between low prejudiced subjects' Total-d scores and their Negother feelings.

The results for the Discomfort index revealed significant main effects for Total-d, $F(1, 295) = 12.79, p < .001$ (B = .058) and prejudice, $F(1, 295) = 10.97, p < .001$ (B = .013), and a significant effect for the quadratic aspect of Total-d, $F(1, 294) = 3.88, p < .05$. In addition, the interaction between prejudice and the quadratic aspect of Total-d was significant, $F(1, 292) = 3.71. p < .05$. Further examination of the findings indicated that high levels of discomfort were experienced by high prejudiced subjects with either large positive or negative discrepancies, relative to high prejudiced subjects with 0 or small positive discrepancy scores. For low prejudiced subjects, Discomfort increased steadily as Total-d increased. Analysis of the Negother index revealed that the interaction between prejudice and the quadratic aspect of Total-d was the only significant effect, $F(1, 292) = 9.39, p < .002$. For high prejudiced subjects, the pattern of the Negother results was identical to the findings on the Discomfort index. In contrast, low prejudiced subjects with moderate discrepancy scores experienced slightly greater Negother affect, relative to those with smaller and larger dis-

---

[7]Explanations provided by subjects with negative discrepancy scores concerning the targets of their anger were content analyzed. We found that 29.16% of the subjects reported feeling negative toward gay males and 4.16% felt negative toward people who are prejudiced toward gay males. We coded 37.5% of the protocols as miscellaneous, and the remaining 29.16% of the subjects failed to indicate the targets of their anger.

crepancy scores.[7]

These findings indicate that negative discrepancies, which were experienced almost exclusively by moderately to highly prejudiced subjects, entail the violation of standards involving the other standpoint. Consistent with this interpretation, inclusion of the negative discrepancy data in an analysis of the Negself index neither attenuated the significance of the Prejudice × Total-d interaction nor changed the pattern of this interaction.[8] Altogether, the findings suggest that some fairly high prejudiced individuals monitor their behaviors to produce responses that are less prejudiced than their personal standards permit. Such discrepancies foster discomfort as well as negative affect directed toward others, just as do high prejudiced subjects' positive discrepancies.

General Discussion

The results of the present studies both replicate and extend Devine et al.'s (1991) research by looking at personal standards and the affective consequences of discrepancies from those standards in a number of response domains. Whereas Devine et al. examined responses in the feeling domain only, the present research also examined responses in thought and behavioral domains. Low prejudiced subjects reported nonprejudiced personal standards in all response domains. In contrast, the location of high prejudiced subjects' personal standards depended on the response domain. In comparison with feeling and thought standards, they reported relatively nonprejudiced standards only for the relatively overt and controllable behavioral responses. Even so, their standards for behavioral responses were neither as nonprejudiced nor as well internalized as those of the low prejudiced subjects.

Further replicating and extending Devine et al. (1991), discrepancies from personal standards for the low prejudiced subjects led to not only feelings of global discomfort, but also to more specific negative affect directed toward the self (e.g., guilt and self-criticism). As expected, this pattern was true across all response domains. Perhaps the most intriguing finding of the present work concerns high prejudiced subjects' reactions to discrepancies. First, consistent with Devine et al. is the finding that high prejudiced subjects experienced global discomfort in connection with their

discrepancies. However, in contrast to our previous findings, they also reported a more specific type of negative affect, one that was directed at others. Thus, rather than feeling guilty and self-critical (directing the negative affect inward) like the low prejudiced subjects, high prejudiced subjects felt angry, irritated, and disgusted with others (directing the negative affect outward). Finally, it is important to note that the pattern of affect experienced by these subjects was the same in all response domains. So, even for the relatively unacceptable and controllable behaviors, high prejudiced subjects show little evidence of having established and internalized nonprejudiced standards based on the own standpoint.

The distinct types of negative affect experienced by low and high prejudiced subjects in association with their discrepancies are consistent with the notion that their personal standards involve different standpoints. Following Higgins's (1987) self-discrepancy theory, it appears that low prejudiced subjects' standards involve the own standpoint, so that guilt and self-criticism arise when they are transgressed. High prejudiced subjects' standards appear to involve the standpoint of significant others and how these others believe they should respond, so that anger at others is experienced when the standard is transgressed.

Future Research

It will be important to examine systematically the consequences of the affect experienced by low and high prejudiced people. Initial research concerning this issue has encouraging implications for low prejudiced subjects' efforts to overcome prejudice. For example, Monteith (1992) demonstrated that feelings of guilt and self-criticism following a prejudice-relevant discrepancy experience can actually facilitate low prejudiced people's prejudice-reduction efforts. However, the results of the present study have less encouraging implications for prejudice reduction among high prejudiced individuals. That is, these subjects' feelings of negativity directed toward others after discrepancy

---

[8]Subjects' personal standards, actual responses, discrepancy scores, positive affect, and depressed affect were all reanalyzed using the negative discrepancy data in addition to the 0 and positive discrepancy data. Virtually no differences were found between the results of these analyses and those reported in this article.

experiences could have the unfortunate outcome of fueling or escalating prejudice. Such other-directed negative affect, then, could decrease the likelihood that high prejudiced people will enter into the prejudice-reduction process.

Nevertheless, there is room for optimism about the potential for change among high prejudiced people. To encourage them to establish and internalize nonprejudiced standards based on the own standpoint, those promoting change may need to emphasize explicitly the fundamental conflict between endorsing egalitarianism and simultaneously holding prejudiced standards. Indeed, Rokeach (1973) argued that change can be brought about by encouraging individuals to confront the inconsistency between their self-conception as fair, tolerant, unselfish, and democratic and their prejudiced values and/or attitudes. According to Rokeach, realizing this inconsistency gives rise to self-dissatisfaction, which in turn motivates cognitive and behavioral change. If Rokeach's method can be applied in a supportive and nonthreatening manner, negative self-directed (rather than other-directed) affect should result from the realization of the contradiction. This affect, then, may provide the motivation among high prejudiced people to reconsider their standards and the impetus for initiating the prejudice-reduction process.

However, the effectiveness of Rokeach's (1973) method rests on two assumptions: (a) that egalitarian values and ideals are self-defining and (b) that these values are more self-defining than specific prejudiced attitudes. To the extent that these assumptions are true for an individual, Rokeach's method may indeed produce change (i.e., a reduction of prejudiced attitudes so as to maintain one's egalitarian self-conception). However, these assumptions may not hold true for all people. In particular, we argue that the veracity of Rokeach's second assumption is likely to depend on the specific function (i.e., psychological need) served by the prejudiced attitude (D. Katz, 1960; Smith, Bruner, & White, 1956; see also Herek, 1986, 1987).

Rokeach's (1973) self-confrontation technique might be particularly well suited for reducing prejudice when prejudiced attitudes serve an instrumental function.[9] Rather than being tied to the self-concept, such attitudes are based on the costs and benefits that are directly or potentially derived from the attitude object (Abelson & Prentice, 1989). Thus, the nature of the conflict between an attitude that serves an instrumental function and one's more general egalitarian self-conception favors revision of the more specific attitude to be consistent with the global self-image.

When prejudiced attitudes serve a symbolic function, however, Rokeach's (1973) technique may be less effective. Because such attitudes are used as a means of expressing and/or protecting one's sense of self they are by definition self-relevant (i.e., self-defining). Thus, with regard to prejudiced attitudes serving a symbolic function, Rokeach's method brings two aspects of one's self-concept into conflict. Resolving such an inconsistency (i.e., changing either aspect) would require substantial change and reorganization of the self-concept as a whole. In general, people resist such changes (Greenwald, 1980; Markus & Kunda, 1986; Markus & Wurf, 1987; Swann, 1990). Consequently, rather than dealing with the conflict by changing the prejudiced attitude, people may be more likely to find alternative ways to cope with the conflict (e.g., repress it or rationalize it away).

Another important issue for future research concerns whether people will spontaneously bring their standards to mind and compare them with their prejudiced responses in the "real world." The method used in the present research has little potential for answering this question, because we required subjects to compare their responses with their personal standards. Other research, however, has indicated that at least low prejudiced subjects spontaneously compare their prejudice-related responses with their personal standards when they actually engage in behaviors (rather than imagining behaviors) that violate those standards (Monteith, 1992). Additional research aimed at systematically investigating factors that may affect the likelihood of such comparisons is needed. Situational factors such as who one is with, how many distractions there are, how much time is available for reflection, and so forth, are likely to affect whether actual responses are compared with

---

[9]For the purposes of this general discussion, we have chosen to use the dichotomy between instrumental and symbolic functions (Abelson & Prentice, 1989; Herek, 1986, 1987) rather than discuss each of the functions that have been described by Katz (1960) and Smith et al. (1956). It should be understood that within this dichotomy, symbolic attitudes are presumed "to meet needs for value expression, social adjustment and ego defense, for example, while instrumental attitudes may serve object appraisal, knowledge, and utilitarian functions" (Herek, 1987, p. 286).

personal standards. The salience and severity of the transgression also may affect the likelihood of such comparisons. Finally, the accessibility of one's standards should be important: The more accessible one's standards, the more likely one will be to bring them to mind and compare them with one's actual responses.

A final issue for future research concerns the need for longitudinal data to test directly our assumptions regarding the prejudice-reduction process. There is no evidence, for example, that the low prejudiced subjects in this research were, at some previous point, higher in prejudice. Likewise, there is no evidence that low prejudiced individuals without discrepancies did at one time experience discrepancies between their standards and their actual responses. Thus, to fully test and validate our assumptions, longitudinal data are needed.

Conclusions

Although the present research focused on gay males as the stereotyped group, the theoretical rationale for the research maintains that the findings and their implications should hold for other groups for which well-learned stereotypes exist. That is, to the extent that the stereotype is well learned, spontaneous stereotype activation may result in prejudiced responses that conflict with one's personal standards (Devine, 1989; Klinger & Beal, 1992). Supporting this reasoning, the general pattern of results reported herein have also been found when prejudice-related discrepancies concerned Black people (Devine et al., 1991; Zuwerink, Devine, & Cook, 1992) and women (Pressly & Devine, 1992). Thus, regardless of the stereotyped group, the completion of the prejudice-reduction process appears to require learning to inhibit the spontaneous influence of stereotypes.

In sum, the findings across a number of studies suggest that people who abjure prejudiced beliefs but still experience some difficulty inhibiting (especially their less controllable) stereotype-based responses, are truly struggling to achieve change. Experienced failures in their efforts to learn to control their stereotype-based responses threaten their nonprejudiced self-conceptions and thus arouse compunction. We argue, as did Rokeach (1973), that this self-dissatisfaction serves to motivate further efforts to change (see Monteith,

1992). Unfortunately our data suggest that realizing discrepancies between standards and actual responses is not likely to have this facilitating effect on prejudice reduction for high prejudiced individuals. It may, in fact, only escalate intolerance of the target group. Thus, despite the measure of progress that both society and some individuals have made in overcoming prejudice, the enduring challenge is to devise effective strategies for encouraging prejudice reduction among high prejudiced people.

REFERENCES

Abelson, R. P., & Prentice, D. A. (1989). Beliefs as possessions: A functional perspective. In A. R. Pratkanis, S. J. Breckler, & A. G. Greenwald (Eds.), *Attitude structure and function* (pp. 361–381). Hillsdale, NJ: Erlbaum.

Devine, P. G. (1989). Stereotypes and prejudice: Their automatic and controlled components. *Journal of Personality and Social Psychology, 56,* 5–18.

Devine, P. G., & Monteith, M. J. (1993). The role of discrepancy-associated affect in prejudice reduction. In D. M. Mackie & D. L. Hamilton (Eds.), *Affect, cognition, and stereotyping: Interactive processes in intergroup perception* (pp. 317–344). San Diego, CA: Academic Press.

Devine, P. G., Monteith, M. J., Zuwerink, J. R., & Elliot, A. J. (1991). Prejudice with and without compunction. *Journal of Personality and Social Psychology, 60,* 817–830.

Dovidio, J. F., & Gaertner, S. L. (1991). Changes in the nature and assessment of racial prejudice. In H. Knopke, J. Norrell, & R. Rogers (Eds.), *Opening doors: An appraisal of race relations in contemporary America* (pp. 201–241). Tuscaloosa, AL: University of Alabama Press.

Gaertner, S. L., & Dovidio, J. F. (1986). The aversive form of racism. In J. F. Dovidio & S. L. Gaertner (Eds.), *Prejudice, discrimination, and racism* (pp. 61–89). San Diego, CA: Academic Press.

Gilbert, D., & Hixon, J. G. (1991). The trouble with thinking: Activation and application of stereotypic beliefs. *Journal of Personality and Social Psychology, 60,* 509–517.

Greenwald, A. G. (1980). The totalitarian ego: Fabrication and revision of personal history. *American Psychologist, 35,* 603–618.

Herek, G. M. (1986). The instrumentality of attitudes: Toward a neo-functional theory. *Journal of Social Issues, 42,* 99–114.

Herek, G. M. (1987). Can functions be measured? A new perspective on the functional approach to attitudes. *Social Psychology Quarterly, 50,* 285–303.

Higgins, E. T. (1987). Self-discrepancy theory: A theory relating self and affect. *Psychological Review, 94,* 319–340.

Katz, D. (1960). The functional approach to the study of attitudes. *Public Opinion Quarterly, 24,* 163–204.

Klinger, M. R., & Beal, P. M. (1992, April). *Conscious and unconscious effects of stereotype activation.* Paper presented at the meeting of the Midwestern Psychological Association, Chicago.

Larsen, K. S., Reed, M., & Hoffman, S. (1980). Attitudes of heterosexuals toward homosexuality: A Likert-type scale and construct validity, *Journal of Sex Research, 16,* 245–257.

Logan, G. D. (1989). Automaticity and cognitive control. In J. S. Uleman & J. A. Bargh (Eds.), *Unintended thought* (pp. 52–74). New York: Guilford Press.

Markus, H., & Kunda, Z. (1986). Stability and malleability of self-concept. *Journal of Personality and Social Psychology, 51,* 858–886.

Markus, H., & Wurf, E. (1987). The dynamic self-concept: A social psychological perspective. *Annual Review of Psychology, 38,* 299–337.

McConahay, J. G. (1986). Modern racism, ambivalence, and the modern racism scale. In J. F. Dovidio & S. L. Gaertner (Eds.), *Prejudice, discrimination, and racism* (pp. 91–125). San Diego, CA: Academic Press.

Monteith, M. J. (1992). *Self-regulation of stereotypic responses: Implications for prejudice reduction efforts.* Unpublished doctoral dissertation, University of Wisconsin—Madison.

Myrdal, G. (1944). *An American dilemma.* New York: Harper & Row.

Pressly, S. L., & Devine, P. G. (1992, April). *Sex, sexism, and compunction: Group membership or internalization of standards?* Paper presented at the meeting of the Midwestern Psychological Association, Chicago.

Rokeach, M. (1973). *The nature of human values.* New York: Free Press.

Smith, M. B., Bruner, J. S., & White, R. W. (1956). *Opinions and personality.* New York: Wiley.

Swann, W. B. (1990). To be adored or to be known? The interplay of self-enhancement and self-verification. In E. T. Higgins & R. M. Sorrentino (Eds.), *Handbook of motivation and cognition: Vol. 2* (pp. 408–448). New York: Guilford Press.

Zuwerink, J. R., Devine, P. G., & Cook, D. (1992, April). *Prejudice with and without compunction: A replication in Arkansas.* Paper presented at the meeting of the Midwestern Psychological Association, Chicago.

The Impact of Stereotypes and Prejudice

There would be no particular reason to worry about stereotypes and prejudice if those beliefs didn't have a negative impact on the people who are stereotyped and who are the targets of prejudice. But stereotyping and prejudice may limit the opportunities of individuals to work to their full potential, both because direct discrimination prevents individuals from gaining access to resources, such as housing and jobs, and because relationships that occur across racial boundaries may be more anxiety provoking and thus less productive (Devine, Evett & Vasquez-Suson, 1996; Stephan & Stephan, 1985). The readings in this section consider how stereotypes and prejudice affect people. Interestingly, we'll see that it is not only the stereotypes held by others that have an impact, but that stereotypes about one's own groups are just as important.

One of the most common outcomes of social categorization is perceived out-group homogeneity: the tendency to see all members of out-groups as similar and interchangeable people, rather than as separate individuals. There is a substantial literature on the conditions under which such perceptions do or do not occur (Ostrom & Sedikides, 1992). In Reading 18, Simon and Brown provide an important demonstration of both the occurrence of out-group homogeneity and the conditions under which the reverse (perceived in-group homogeneity) can be found. Their analysis is important particularly because it shows how cognitive processes (the tendency to categorize others) and motivation processes (needs for social identity) interact to influence social categorization and social perception.

Fiske, Bersoff, Borgida, Deaux, and Heilman were asked by the American

Psychological Association to provide a brief to the U.S. Supreme Court, which was considering a case in which a woman claimed that she had been denied a partnership in a prestigious accounting firm because she had been stereotyped. Reading 19 summarizes the case and reviews the wide variety of empirical data from the social-psychological literature used to support the claims of Ann Hopkins that she had been the victim of stereotyping. In addition to providing an example of the potential negative outcomes of stereotypes on the lives of individuals, the trial also represents an important and groundbreaking use of social-psychological research to inform public policy. Furthermore, the case points out how difficult it is to make clear claims about the impact of stereotypes in any given situation. Just because stereotypes *could* be influencing decisions does not mean that they actually were (the "mixed motive" problem in legal terms). Yet in the end the Supreme Court was convinced by the argument, and this decision was influenced in part by the social-psychological research that underscored it.

In Reading 20, Crocker, Voelkl, Testa, and Major present an important analysis of the influence of stereotypes, based on attribution theory, concerning the positive and negative outcomes of being the target of prejudice. The idea is that individuals who expect to be stereotyped are always in a state of uncertainty, known as *attributional ambiguity*, because they cannot be sure whether the behaviors of members of other groups are based on their own qualities (such as their skills or knowledge), or on the basis of stereotypes and prejudice about them. This ambiguity can be problematic, for instance, if individuals always assume that negative

behaviors from others were caused by discrimination. Crocker and her colleagues present a theoretical analysis of attributional ambiguity and demonstrate that attributing negative outcomes to discrimination can have short-term positive consequences. But you can imagine that in the long run, making attributions to discrimination might not necessarily be so positive.

Although it is perhaps not that surprising that stereotypes and prejudice can influence our relationships with others, it is perhaps even more interesting that the stereotypes that we hold about our own groups can be just as damaging. Steele and Aronson were interested in understanding the large differences in academic performance across racial groups on standardized tests and in grades and persistence in high school and college. African-American students are more likely to drop out of college than are European-American students, and they also receive poorer grades than would be expected given their performance on academic tests such as the SAT. Although such differences had traditionally been explained in terms of different skills, socialization, or interest in school-related topics, Steele and Aronson argue in Reading 21 that stereotypes about academic skills held about one's own group are also important. Steele and Aronson demonstrate that *stereotype vulnerability,* even when created with a very simple experimental manipulation, can have a profound influence on performance. Perhaps most notably, it is the individuals who are most concerned about doing well in academics who, although they may be highly prepared and competent to perform well, are nevertheless likely to be most harmed by stereotype vulnerability.

Discussion Questions

1. What is perceived out-group homogeneity, and why does it occur? In what cases and for what reasons does perceived in-group homogeneity occur instead?
2. What research empirical findings did Susan Fiske and her colleagues use to document that stereotypes influenced the partnership decision of Ann Hopkins in their brief to the U.S. Supreme Court?
3. What is attributional ambiguity, and how might it influence the behavior of members of groups that are stereotyped?
4. How do members of groups that are likely to be stereotyped respond to attributional ambiguity, and what are the positive and negative consequences of these responses?
5. What is stereotype vulnerability, and how does it influence the academic performance of individuals from stereotyped groups. How do you think it might be alleviated?

Suggested Readings

Crocker, J., Major, B., & Steele, C. (1998). Social stigma. In D. Gilbert, S. T. Fiske, & G. Lindzey (Eds.), *Handbook of social psychology* (4th ed., Vol. 2, pp. 504–553). Boston: McGraw Hill. A contemporary review of the impact of stereotypes on members of stereotyped groups.

Devine, P. G., Evett, S. R., & Vasquez-Suson, K. A. (1996). Exploring the interpersonal dynamics of group contact. In R. M. Sorrentino & E. T. Higgins (Eds.), *Handbook of motivation and cognition: The interpersonal context* (Vol. 3, pp. 423–464). New York: Guilford. A review of how and when interactions between members of different social groups produce problems.

Ostrom, T. M., & Sedikides, C. (1992). Out-group homogeneity effects in natural and minimal groups. *Psychological Bulletin, 112,* 536–552. A review of the conditions under which perceived outgroup homogeneity does and does not occur.

Stephan, W. G., & Stephan, C. W. (1985). Intergroup anxiety. *Journal of Social Issues, 41,* 157–175. A theory about how anxiety impairs social interactions among individuals from different social groups.

Swim, J. T., & Stangor, C. (1998). *Prejudice from the target's perspective.* Santa Barbara, CA: Academic Press. This book presents a series of chapters containing theoretical and empirical approaches to understanding the influence of prejudice on individuals.

READING 18

Perceived Intragroup Homogeneity in Minority-Majority Contexts

Bernd Simon • Universität Münster
Rupert Brown • University of Kent

An experiment was conducted to examine how the factors *relative in-group size* and *relative out-group size* (i.e., minority vs. nonminority) affect the perception of in-group and out-group homogeneity. On the basis of social identity theory, we hypothesized that (a) members of minorities would perceive the in-group as more homogeneous than the out-group, whereas members of nonminorities would perceive the reverse; (b) this effect would be strongest on dimensions most strongly correlated with the social categorization; and (c) members of minorities would identify more strongly with their in-group than would members of nonminorities. One hundred ninety-two 13- to 15-year-old children participated in the experiment. On the presumed basis of a perceptual task, approximately half were randomly allocated to minimal social categories, which differed in perceived size relative to an out-group (which also differed in perceived size). They were asked to estimate the homogeneity of the two groups on a number of dimensional attributes. The remaining (control) subjects gave similar estimates under identical conditions, except that they were not allocated to a category. The data confirmed all but the second hypothesis, which was only partially supported. The results were interpreted in line with our theoretical analysis in terms of social identification processes. By analyses of the control conditions, where the differential homogeneity effects did not occur, we were able to rule out an alternative explanation simply in terms of an inverse relation between group size and perceived group homogeneity. Also, explanations in terms of rating extremity and in-group favoritism could be rendered improbable.

This study is concerned with the effects of social categorization on the perceived similarity or homogeneity within the out-group and the in-group.

Tajfel (1969) claimed that when people assume a consistent and predictable relation (biserial correlation) between a categorization and the variation of stimuli on a continuous dimension, "there will be a tendency to exaggerate the differences on that dimension between items which fall into distinct classes, and to minimize these differences within each of the classes" (Tajfel, 1969, p. 83). In other words, social categorization processes will result in an accentuation of intergroup differences and of intragroup similarities (Tajfel & Wilkes, 1963). For references to earlier and recent evidence confirming these accentuation principles, see Tajfel (1982).

However, the results of several studies suggest that the accentuation of intragroup similarities might be an asymmetrical phenomenon leading to greater perceived homogeneity within the out-group than within the in-group (*out-group homogeneity hypothesis*; e.g., Linville & Jones, 1980; Quattrone & Jones, 1980). On the theoretical explanations of this asymmetry that have been most frequently put forward (see Quattrone & Jones, 1980; Wilder, 1984), one argument states that the differential perception of homogeneity is due to people's motivation to increase predictability regarding the out-group and to assert their own individuality and free themselves from constraining expectations simultaneously. Another line of reasoning focuses on differential experiences with in-group and out-group. For example, people can be expected to interact with in-group members more frequently and in a greater variety of contexts than with out-group members. Hence, they are likely to know more in-group members and to develop more differentiated judgments about them. Finally, it was suggested that out-group homogeneity could be interpreted in terms of evaluative discrimination or in-group favoritism.

However, Jones, Wood, and Quattrone (1981) indicated that the perceived variability within a group hardly depends in any simple way on the number of group members known personally (also see Malpass & Kravitz, 1969) or on the evaluative preference for that group. These results throw doubt on the last two explanations just listed. Moreover, the evidence concerning the out-group homogeneity hypothesis resulted either from a situation in which a *majority* in-group was confronted with a *minority* out-group (e.g., Hamilton & Bishop, 1976; Linville & Jones, 1980; Malpass & Kravitz, 1969) or from a situation in which neither the in-group nor the out-group was in an explicit majority or minority position, thus implying that the in-group and the out-group were numerically equivalent (e.g., Jones et al., 1981; Park & Rothbart, 1982; Philo, 1979, Experiment 4; Quattrone & Jones, 1980; Wilder, 1984).

Contrary to these findings, one study—the only one we know of—claims to have found evidence for greater perceived in-group homogeneity relative to perceived out-group homogeneity. Stephan (1977) presented empirical data indicating that members of three different ethnic groups (Blacks, Chicanos, and Anglos) perceive their own group as less differentiated. Given the preceding discussion, an interesting feature of this study, although

not highlighted by Stephan himself, is that two of the groups that participated in his study (Blacks and Chicanos) can be classified as minorities.

Research suggests that the structural variable *relative group size* is an important characteristic of the intergroup situation that influences the perception, behavior, or both of group members (see Gerard & Hoyt, 1974; Kanter, 1977; Moscovici & Paicheler, 1978; Sachdev & Bourhis, 1984; Taylor, 1981). Accordingly, we hypothesize that the minority status of the in-group also influences the differential perception of in-group compared to out-group homogeneity. Our theoretical reasoning is based on social identity theory (Tajfel, 1978; Tajfel & Turner, 1979; Turner, 1982), which we will briefly sketch.

The key concept of social identity theory is *social identity*, which is defined as "that *part* of an individual's self-concept which derives from his knowledge of his membership of a social group (or groups) together with the value and emotional significance attached to that membership" (Tajfel, 1978, p. 63). Furthermore, the theory posits that each individual strives to achieve a positive social identity. That implies social comparison processes between the in-group and salient out-groups aiming at the establishment of positive distinctiveness of the in-group compared with other groups. The well-established phenomenon of in-group bias, for example, is interpreted as an outcome of this search for distinctiveness (see Brewer, 1979; Brown, Tajfel, & Turner, 1980; Turner, 1981).

We now turn to the psychological implications of membership in a minority group. There is some indication that being in a minority group poses a threat to a person's self-esteem (see Festinger, 1954, pp. 136–137; Gerard, 1985, p. 174; Sachdev & Bourhis, 1984, p. 39). We assume that minority members are motivated to counteract that threat by accentuating their positive social identity. Discrimination against a relevant out-group is one means to achieve that goal (Sachdev & Bourhis, 1984). For example, Gerard and Hoyt (1974) reported that the smaller the in-group, the more favorably an author of an essay allegedly belonging to the in-group was evaluated relative to an out-group author. This finding strongly supports our assumption.

However, we argue that people belonging to a minority group will also try to strengthen their positive social identity by still another means. Perceiving more intragroup similarity (i.e., homogeneity) within the in-group than within the out-group, especially regarding comparison dimensions strongly correlated with the social categorization (Tajfel, 1959; Wilder, 1984), should enhance the perceived entitativity (Campbell, 1958) or groupness of the in-group compared to that of the out-group. This differential ascription of groupness to in-group and out-group, indicating that the former is construed more in terms of a group than is the latter, is supposed to highlight the superiority of the in-group regarding the extent of social support and solidarity it offers its members (see Allen, 1985, pp. 230–231). Thus, comparatively greater groupness of the in-group should contribute to the accentuation of one's positive social identity. Let us reiterate here that in accordance with social identity theory, which attaches central importance to social comparison processes, we stress the comparative perception of groupness or homogeneity, that is, the degree of perceived in-group homogeneity in relation to the degree of perceived out-group homogeneity. Consequently, we predict that minority members perceive more in-group than out-group homogeneity at the expense of the degree of individuality allowed for in-group compared to out-group members.

Like all group members, members of nonminorities also strive for positive social identity, for example by discriminating against an out-group (e.g., Sachdev & Bourhis, 1984). However, in contrast to minority members, the former do not have to cope additionally with the kind of threat already specified. Being more positive about their self-esteem, nonminority members are motivated less to perceive comparatively greater groupness of the in-group than to demonstrate the great extent of individuality possible within the in-group in contrast to the uniformity within the out-group. Thus, they free themselves from constraining expectations while increasing the predictability concerning the out-group (Quattrone & Jones, 1980). Hence, we predict that nonminority members perceive more out-group than in-group homogeneity.

Before summarizing our hypotheses, we need to make two anticipatory comments on our experimental design. First, one could argue that smaller samples per se will generally be perceived as more homogeneous than will larger ones. The predictions we have made would also be suggested by such a relation. In order to demonstrate that the

minority or nonminority status of the in-group is the decisive factor that produces the expected effects, we also varied the minority/nonminority status of the out-group. If our hypothesis is correct, this factor should have no effect on the perception of comparative group homogeneity. Additionally, our study included control conditions in which outside observers belonging to no groups were asked to provide some estimates of the homogeneity of groups that were of the same sizes as the groups judged by actual group members in the experimental conditions. In this manner, we could examine the validity of an alternative explanation simply in terms of an inverse relation between group size and perceived group homogeneity. Second, because we used minimal groups within and between which no face-to-face interaction had ever taken place (Tajfel, Billig, Bundy, & Flament, 1971), the argument—often marshalled to support the out-group homogeneity hypothesis—that discrepancies between perceived in-group and out-group homogeneity are due to differential experiences with in-group and out-group members can hardly be relevant to our study.

To summarize: Group members generally strive for positive social identity, which, for example, can be achieved by discrimination against an out-group. Because of threatened self-esteem, minority members are motivated to accentuate further their positive social identity with the aid of a perceptual bias favoring in-group above out-group homogeneity. Conversely, because they can rely on a more secure self-esteem, nonminority members emphasize the individuality within the in-group by contrasting it with the uniformity within the out-group. Hence, in their eyes, out-group homogeneity will exceed in-group homogeneity. Moreover, as a consequence of the greater importance attached to their social identity by minority members, we expect them to identify more strongly with their in-group than will members of nonminorities. In conclusion, our theoretical analysis leads to the following hypotheses:

1. *In-group homogeneity hypothesis*: (a) Members of nonminorities will perceive the out-group as more homogeneous than they will perceive the in-group, whereas members of minorities will perceive more homogeneity within the in-group than within the out-group; (b) the minority/nonminority status of the out-group will not influence the perception of comparative in-

group and out-group homogeneity; (c) the degree of intragroup homogeneity perceived by an outside observer belonging to no group will not be influenced by the minority/nonminority status of the respective groups.

2. *Correlation hypothesis*: We expect the effect predicted in Hypothesis 1(a) to be strongest on comparison dimensions most strongly correlated with the social categorization.

3. *Identification hypothesis*: Members of minorities will identify more strongly with their in-group than will members of nonminorities.

Method

Subjects

One hundred ninety-two male and female school-children, ages 13 to 15, from a secondary school in Canterbury participated in the experiment, which was run in two identical sessions. The interval between the sessions was about 15 min.

Design

The first two hypotheses were tested by using a 2 × 2 × 2 factorial design with two between-subjects factors, relative in-group size (nonminority vs. minority) and relative out-group size (nonminority vs. minority), and one within-subjects factor, stimulus group (in-group vs. outgroup). Parallel to the experimental conditions, the control conditions yielded an analogous 2 × 2 × 2 factorial design: Relative Size of the Blue Group (nonminority vs. minority) × Relative Size of the Green Group (nonminority vs. minority) × Stimulus Group (blue group vs. green group, repeated measure). In the control conditions, the subjects were not allocated to one of the two stimulus groups. Thus, there was no categorization into in-group and out-group.

To test Hypothesis 3, we used a two-factor design with the same between-subjects factors described. The control conditions, of course, are of no relevance to the third hypothesis.

Procedure

Each testing session began with our randomly allocating the participants to the experimental and control conditions. Those in the latter group were taken to a second room on the alleged grounds that technical problems prevented all the children from being in the same room. Thereafter, the experimental and control conditions were run simultaneously in these separate rooms. In each room, subjects were further randomly allocated to the different cells of the factorial design, thus permitting all treatments to be run simultaneously.

The procedure adopted was a variant of the minimal group paradigm (Tajfel et al., 1971). A categorization into groups was effected by using a perceptual task. Subjects were given information about the sizes of the groups and also about some additional attributes alleged to be associated with the dimension of categorization. Subjects were then asked to provide some estimates of the homogeneity of the groups on the original dimension of classification and these other attributes.

Experimental Conditions. The experiment was introduced as being concerned with the relation between color perception and personality. At first, subjects viewed 16 slides varying in background color (5 clearly blue, 5 clearly green, and 6 an ambiguous mixture of blue and green) and in the number of red dots on them (ranging from 24 to 86). After the subjects had estimated the background color of and the number of dots on each slide, they had to answer two other questions: "Suppose you have won £100 [$200] in a lottery. How much money would you spend on traveling?" and "imagine you traveled with three other English people to a large city in a foreign country. How would you feel being surrounded by so many people who are different from you?"

Although primarily intended as a filler task, the second question was also used to draw the subjects' attention to the emotional implications of being in a minority group. The classification into groups was then carried out. The experimenter announced that the subjects would be assigned to one of two groups, called the blue group and the green group, according to which background color they had recognized better in the previous perception task. He emphasized that it would not be better to belong to one or the other of those two groups. Then a cover story was presented stating that a person's being a member of the blue or the green group would also relate to some of his or her other characteristics. For example, the blue group was said to make errors in estimating the number of dots especially on the blue slides, whereas the green group would make errors especially on the green slides ("*many* scientists have *proved* that . . ."). Furthermore, it was indicated that both groups might also differ as to the amount of money they would spend on traveling, that is, the blue group would spend less money than would the green group, although as yet that relation had not been proven ("a *few* scientists *believe* that . . ."). In this way, three attributes were associated with the groups: one by definition (color perception), one highly correlated (dot estimation), and one less well correlated (use of money). In the dependent measures (to be explained), a fourth attribute was also added (ability at schoolwork), but no information was given as to the correlation of this attribute with the original categorization. Subsequently, each subject was given a booklet, the first page of which indicated his or her own group membership and how many people were in each group. Additionally, the number of people not belonging to any group was given. However, those people were not referred to as a third group. Instead, the experimenter stated that there were some who could not be allocated to any group because they did not recognize one color better than the other and therefore they would be of no importance to the present experiment. This artifice was necessary to create a condition in which both in-group and out-group were allegedly in a minority position. Of course, the booklets were prepared in advance so that all four combinations of the two two-level between-subjects factors could be run simultaneously:

1. *Nonminority in-group and nonminority out-group:* 26 people in the in-group and 26 people in the out-group; 4 people belonged to no group.
2. *Nonminority (majority) in-group and minority out-group:* 48 people in the in-group and 4 people in the out-group; 4 people belonged to no group.
3. *Minority in-group and nonminority (majority) out-group:* 4 people in the in-group and 48 people in the out-group; 4 people belonged to no group.
4. *Minority in-group and minority out-group:* 4 people in the in-group and 4 people in the out-group; 48 people belonged to no group.

Control Conditions. Subjects assigned to these conditions were not categorized into groups at any stage of the procedure. They were presented the same stimulus material as were their classmates in the experimental conditions (i.e., slides and the two additional questions), but they were not asked to estimate the color of the slides or the number of dots. They had to answer only the second filler question. Then they were told the same cover story about the relation between color perception and personality as were the subjects in the experimental conditions. The booklet, however, although otherwise identical to those in the experimental conditions, did not refer to an in-group or an out-group but to people who allegedly had been divided into a blue group and a green group in a "real" experiment conducted previously. The absolute numbers given in the booklet to create the four combinations of the between-subjects factors were identical with those in the respective experimental conditions. Of course, no reference to own group membership was contained in the booklets. The rationale provided for the questions in the booklets was the experimenter's interest in people's ability to make judgments about those for whom one has little information.

Dependent Measures

Subjects were asked to rate the two stimulus groups on four dimensions: (a) color perception (CP), that is, how good members of each group were at recognizing the colors (*very good at recognizing blue* to *very good at recognizing green*), (b) dot estimation (DE), or how many errors members of each group made (*no errors* to *many errors*), (c) use of money (UM), or how much of the £100 members of each group would spend on traveling (*£0* to *£100*), and (d) schoolwork (SW), or how good members of each group were at schoolwork (*not good at all* to *very good*).

On each dimension, two ratings were required for each stimulus group. The subjects had to mark those two scale values that they thought would bracket the values for all individual members of the respective group (i.e., the perceived range of the distribution of the members along the quantitative dimension). This range score is seen as the most appropriate measure for perceived group homogeneity (see Jones et al., 1981; Simon, 1985).

The ratings for the two stimulus groups were made on different pages of the booklet. The respective order was counterbalanced, as was own group category (blue vs. green in-group). To reinforce the manipulations of group size, on each page subjects had to fill in the number of people in the particular group and, except in the control conditions, indicate whether it was their own group or the other group. In addition, they were asked how much they believed in relations between group membership and performance in the dot-estimation task or the way a person spends his or her money.[1] Subjects in the experimental conditions were also asked how much they saw themselves as belonging to their in-group.[2] All ratings were made on continuous 100-mm lines. Finally, we added an open-ended question as to the perceived purpose of the study to detect any suspicion of the deception used in the experiment.

A debriefing for all participants followed the second session.

Results

We included in the final analysis only those subjects who correctly endorsed the manipulation regarding the size of the stimulus groups and, except in the control conditions, own group membership (group category) in the booklet. In addition, the data of 2 subjects in the experimental conditions were deleted because they had indicated that they were color-blind and hence not able to do the perception task properly. In the control conditions, 2 subjects had obviously not understood how to use the response scales. Their data were also excluded from the analysis. Subjects' responses to the last question in the booklet did not reflect any suspicion regarding the cover story or the other manipulations (size of the stimulus groups, own group membership).

In all, 23 subjects were excluded from the analyses, and there was no indication that these were not randomly distributed over the conditions. The final sample size was 98 in the experimental conditions (23 to 26 per cell) and 71 in the control conditions (17 to 18 per cell).

[1]The precise wordings of these questions were as follows: "How much do you believe that the blue group makes errors in estimating the number of dots especially on the blue slides, whereas the green group makes errors especially on the green slides?" (*Not at all. . .very much*) and "How much do you believe that the blue group in general would spend less of the £100 on traveling than the green group would spend?" (*Not at all . . . very much*).

[2]The precise wording of this question was as follows: "How much do you agree? I am a person who sees myself as belonging to the blue (green) group." (*Not at all . . . very much*).

Color of the group labels did not influence the significant effects found in the experimental conditions ($F < 1.81$, *ns*, for the respective interactions with group label, i.e., blue vs. green in-group). Presentation order of stimulus groups also did not affect any of the results relevant to our hypotheses, as preliminary analyses of variance (ANOVAS) revealed. Hence, both factors were ignored in the main analysis.

In-Group Homogeneity Hypothesis

A $2 \times 2 \times 2$ multivariate analysis of variance (MANOVA) was performed on the range scores for all dimensions (CP, DE, UM, SW) with the SPSS-X(2) statistical package. In accordance with the in-group homogeneity hypothesis, we predicted a relative In-Group Size × Stimulus Group interaction effect for the experimental conditions. For the second between-subjects factor (relative out-group size), we did not expect such an interaction effect. Moreover, no effects were predicted for the control conditions.

Table 18.1 presents the mean range scores and standard deviations from the experimental conditions together with all significant effects observed in the MANOVA.

On the multivariate level, our prediction was clearly confirmed, as the highly significant predicted interaction effect for the experimental conditions reveals, $F(4, 91) = 4.83, p \leq .001$. On the univariate level, the predicted interaction effect was significant on the CP dimension, $F(1, 94) = 7.23$, $p < .01$, and on the SW dimension, $F(1, 94) = 6.91$, $p < .01$. On both dimensions (see Figure 18.1), the minority in-group was perceived as more homogeneous than was the out-group; for the CP dimension, $M(\text{in}) = 39.6, M(\text{out}) = 43.9, t(94) = -1.98, p < .05$, and for the SW dimension, $M(\text{in}) = 40.0, M(\text{out}) = 45.9, t(94) = -2.97, p < .01$; one-tailed. The greater perceived out-group homogeneity in the nonminority in-group condition reached the .05 level of significance only on the CP dimension, $M(\text{in}) = 44.1, M(\text{out}) = 40.0, t(94) = 1.89, p < .05$, one-tailed. However, it was nonsignificant on the SW dimension, $M(\text{in}) = 41.5$, $M(\text{out}) = 39.9, t(94) = .81$, one-tailed.

Although the order of the in-group and out-group ranges on the DE dimension was as expected (see Table 18.1), that interaction effect remained only suggestive, $F(1, 94) = 2.91, p < .1$. On the UM dimension, the predicted effect was far from

TABLE 18.1. Mean Range Ratings for In-Group and Out-Group in Experimental Conditions

	Relative out-group size							
	CP		DE		UM		SW	
Relative in-group size	*M*	*SD*	*M*	*SD*	*M*	*SD*	*M*	*SD*
				Nonminority				
Nonminority (*n* = 24)								
In-group range	39.9	21.6	34.7	14.2	44.3	13.8	45.5	23.6
Out-group range	41.6	21.4	32.6	15.8	39.9	14.8	44.7	22.7
Minority (*n* = 23)								
In-group range	43.8	16.2	35.5	19.8	49.0	19.8	41.7	23.7
Out-group range	48.0	19.5	38.6	19.7	47.0	19.1	45.6	20.7
				Minority				
Nonminority (*n* = 25)								
In-group range	48.1_a	21.3	41.9	16.1	41.8	15.6	37.6	19.5
Out-group range	38.4_b	23.5	39.5	20.5	36.8	15.5	35.3	16.5
Minority (*n* = 26)								
In-group range	35.9	21.6	37.0	13.7	42.3	11.5	38.6_a	19.3
Out-group range	40.2	18.9	40.5	15.7	40.3	19.0	46.3_b	22.9
MS_e (between subjects)	736.7		450.1		415.8		803.8	
MS_e (within subjects)	115.2		130.5		117.4		96.4	

Note. CP = color perception, DE = dot estimation, UM = use of money, SW = schoolwork. Range scores for in-group and out-group with different subscripts (per dimension and per cell) differ at the .05 level of significance or better in planned comparisons using one-tailed *t* tests based on mean square error (within subjects). Significant MANOVA effects (multivariate): Relative out-group size, $F(4,91) = 2.54$, $p < .05$. Relative In-group Size (RIS) x Stimulus Group (SG), $F(4,91) = 4.83$, $p \leq .001$. Significant MANOVA effects (univariate); SG, (UM) $F(1, 94) = 4.68$, $p < .05$. RIS x SG: (CP) $F(1, 94) = 7.23$, $p < .01$; (SW) $F(1, 94) = 6.91$, $p \leq .01$. All other multivariate and univariate effects were nonsignificant.

significance, $F(1, 94) = 0.81$, *ns*. Finally, relative out-group size, as predicted, had no influence on the comparative estimates of in-group versus out-group homogeneity. All effects that included this factor were nonsignificant except one, which, however, did not involve the within-subjects factor: On the multivariate level, relative out-group size yielded a main effect, $F(4, 91) = 2.54$, $p < .05$, whereas none of the corresponding univariate effects was significant.

Turning to the control conditions (see Table 18.2), on the whole our predictions were also corroborated. In that design, no multivariate interaction effect—in fact, no multivariate effect at all—reached an acceptable level of statistical significance. On the univariate level, the within-subjects factor *stimulus group* interacted significantly with a between-subjects factor just once, namely with the relative size of the green group on the CP dimension, $F(1, 67) = 4.06$, $p < .05$. That unexpected interaction effect was due mainly to that condition in which the green group was in a minority position facing the blue group, which was a majority. The green group was then perceived as more homogeneous than the blue group. But as seen in Table 18.2, there is no consistent tendency for a minority group to be perceived as more homogeneous than the majority it is confronted with. Hence, the alternative explanation for the findings in the experimental conditions in terms of a minority effect per se can be ruled out. Furthermore, one significant effect that did not involve the within-subjects factor emerged in the control conditions: The two between-subjects factors interacted significantly on the CP dimension, $F(1, 67) = 6.92$, $p < .05$. This interaction effect indicated that subjects in the nonminority blue-group/nonminority green-group condition and especially those in the minority blue-group/minority green-group condition generally rated both groups more homogeneous than did subjects in the other two conditions.

Finally, within both experimental and control conditions, the within-subjects factor *stimulus group* yielded a weak main effect significant only at the univariate level. On the UM dimension, the out-group was perceived as significantly more homogeneous than the in-group, $F(1,94) = 4.68$, $p < .05$. More inexplicable is the main effect for stimulus group on that dimension for the control

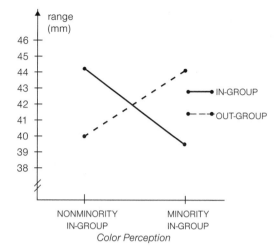

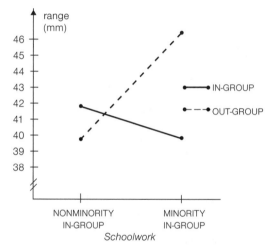

FIGURE 18.1 ■ Perceived homogeneity of in-group and out-group on two dimensions as a function of the minority/nonminority status of the in-group.

conditions, $F(1, 67) = 4.33, p < .05$: The blue group was perceived as more homogeneous than the green group on the UM dimension.

Correlation Hypothesis

The cover story explicitly offered three comparison dimensions (CP, DE, and UM) and further suggested to the subjects that those were differentially correlated with the social categorization. A manipulation check confirmed that the subjects did actually believe more strongly that their being a member of the blue or green group would be re-

lated to their performance in the dot-estimation task than they believed that their group membership would be related to the way they would spend their money; belief scores were $M(DE) = 49.1$, $M(UM) = 44.3, t(97) = 1.95, p < .05$, one-tailed. Originally we expected the reversal toward in-group homogeneity primarily on the CP and the DE dimensions. On the UM dimension, such an effect, if it occurred at all, should be rather weak. The highly significant effect on the CP dimension ($p < .01$, see Table 18.1) is in accordance with our expectation. However, contrary to our hypothesis, the predicted effect on the DE dimension remained merely suggestive, although the order of the means was as expected ($p < .1$). Also expectedly, the respective effect was far from significance on the UM dimension, which was least strongly correlated with the social categorization. On the fourth dimension (SW), minority in-group subjects perceived significantly less homogeneity within the out-group than within the in-group. This finding is especially remarkable as no information was previously given regarding the correlation between this dimension and the categorization.

Identification Hypothesis

Analysis of the identification measure yielded a significant main effect for the factor *relative in-group size*, clearly supporting our third hypothesis: Subjects assigned to a minority group identified more strongly with their in-group than did subjects allegedly belonging to a nonminority; for the minority in-group condition, $M = 63.8$, and for the nonminority in-group condition, $M = 49.1$, $F(1, 94) = 8.52, p < .005$; see Table 18.3. No other effect was statistically significant.

Further Analyses: Homogeneity, Favorability, and Extremity

Each range rating consisted of two individual ratings. The averaged means of the two ratings made by each subject are presented in Table 18.4. Three-way ANOVAS yielded four significant effects: In accordance with the information presented to them in the cover story, subjects differentiated between in-group and out-group on the CP and UM dimensions; main effects for the within-subjects factor were $F(1, 94) = 48.86, p < .001$, and $F(1, 94) = 126.24, p < .001$, for the CP and UM dimension, respectively. On the value-loaded SW dimension,

TABLE 18.2. Mean Range Ratings for Blue Group and Green Group in Control Conditions

| | Relative green-group size | | | | | | | |
| | CP | | DE | | UM | | SW | |
Relative blue-group size	M	SD	M	SD	M	SD	M	SD
Nonminority								
Nonminority ($n = 18$)								
Blue-group range	39.9	16.8	42.9	19.2	33.5	10.4	42.3	17.6
Green-group range	41.2	16.2	40.9	17.1	35.6	9.6	41.6	17.8
Minority ($n = 17$)								
Blue-group range	46.3	15.3	34.4	16.4	31.8$_a$	18.3	42.0$_a$	19.1
Green-group range	45.6	16.7	37.1	18.6	38.5$_b$	18.3	46.8$_b$	22.8
Minority								
Nonminority ($n = 18$)								
Blue-group range	54.7$_a$	15.8	43.9	17.4	39.3	14.1	37.9	18.0
Green-group range	43.1$_b$	19.8	46.7	21.2	43.1	13.5	41.4	18.4
Minority ($n = 18$)								
Blue-group range	38.3	12.7	42.8	20.2	34.7	20.4	41.7	24.3
Green-group range	35.6	13.6	44.8	20.6	36.6	20.7	42.5	23.3
MS_e (between subjects)	386.4		592.6		414.8		755.8	
MS_e (within subjects)	125.0		123.9		107.3		69.3	

Note. CP = color perception, DE = dot estimation, UM = use of money, SW = schoolwork. Range scores for blue group and green group with different subscripts (per dimension and per cell) differ at the .05 level of significance or better in planned comparisons using one-tailed *t* tests based on mean square error (within subjects). Significant MANOVA effects (univariate): Relative Blue-Group Size x Relative Green Group Size (RGS), (CP) $F(1,67) = 6.92$, $p < .05$. Stimulus group (SG), (UM) $F(1,67) = 4.33$, $p < .05$. RGS x SG, (CP) $F(1,67) = 4.06$, $p < .05$. All other multivariate and univariate effects were nonsignificant.

the ratings were biased in favor of the in-group; the main effect for the within-subjects factor was $F(1, 94) = 5.61$, $p < .05$. Finally, relative in-group size interacted significantly with the within-subjects factor on the UM dimension, $F(1, 94) = 4.65$, $p < .05$.

Because the anchoring of the DE and SW dimensions, unlike that of the CP and UM dimensions, implicated an evaluation of in-group and out-group in terms of bad or good performance in the

TABLE 18.3. Mean Identification Scores

| | Relative in-group size | |
Relative out-group size	Nonminority	Minority
Nonminority		
M	48.9	67.4
SD	26.2	24.7
n	24	23
Minority		
M	49.4	60.5
SD	27.0	22.7
n	25	26

Note. The higher the score, the stronger the identification with the in-group. Significant ANOVA effects: Relative in-group size, $F(1.94) = 8.52$, $p < .005$. All other effects were nonsignificant. Mean square error = 632.8.

dot-estimation task and in schoolwork, there could be a confound of favorability and perceived homogeneity. In fact, as reported on the SW dimension, subjects evaluated the in-group significantly more favorably than the out-group. Although, as seen in Table 18.4, this bias increased slightly when the in-group was a minority, the respective interaction was nonsignificant, $F(1, 94) < 1$. Analyses of covariance (ANCOVAS) using the range rating as dependent variable and the mean rating as covariate were performed for the DE and SW dimensions. The significant two-way interaction between relative in-group size and stimulus group (in-group vs. out-group) on the SW dimension found in our main analysis was replicated in the ANCOVA, $F(1, 93) = 6.96$, $p \le .01$. Also, on the DE dimension this interaction effect, which was only suggestive in the main analysis, now reached statistical significance, $F(1, 93) = 4.59$, $p < .05$.

Furthermore, it might be suggested that rating extremity would tend to be associated with increased perceived homogeneity as a result of the restrictions imposed by the scale endpoints (see Jones et al., 1981). The distance from the mean rating to the midpoint of the scale was used as an extremity measure. Then ANCOVAS using the

TABLE 18.4. Mean Ratings for In-Group and Out-Group in Experimental Conditions

Relative in-group size	Relative out-group size							
	CP		DE		UM		SW	
	M	SD	M	SD	M	SD	M	SD
	Nonminority							
Nonminority (n = 24)								
In-group	44.4	13.2	50.6	14.8	40.6	17.6	52.2	8.6
Out-group	57.4	11.6	49.5	14.0	65.6	12.1	49.9	8.8
Minority (n = 23)								
In-group	40.1	15.9	45.4	14.3	47.7	16.7	53.4	13.9
Out-group	58.5	17.0	52.5	14.6	60.8	16.8	49.1	11.9
	Minority							
Nonminority (n = 25)								
In-group	39.9	10.8	49.7	13.0	38.0	12.0	52.8	8.4
Out-group	59.9	15.3	47.1	13.5	63.8	10.6	49.5	13.1
Minority (n = 26)								
In-group	43.5	16.6	52.7	14.1	37.1	12.8	53.7	14.4
Out-group	58.8	12.2	53.5	15.6	58.5	16.2	48.7	11.4

Note. The lower (higher) the scores on the CP and the UM dimensions, the closer the ratings to that endpoint of the scale alleged to be typical for the in-group (out-group). The higher the scores on the DE and the SW dimensions, the more favorable the evaluations.

range rating as dependent variable and the extremity measure as covariate were performed for all four dimensions. The significant two-way interactions between relative in-group size and stimulus group (in-group vs. out-group) on the CP and SW dimensions found in our main analysis were replicated in the ANCOVAS, $F(1, 93) = 5.44, p < .05$, and $F(1, 93) = 4.83, p < .05$, respectively, and so was the main effect for stimulus group on the UM dimension, $F(1, 93) = 4.48, p < .05$. Again, the predicted interaction effect on the DE dimension, which was only suggestive in the main analysis, now reached statistical significance, $F(1, 93) = 4.29, p < .05$. In sum, we can conclude that differences in perceived homogeneity are no artifact of differences in rating extremity or favorability.

Discussion

Our experiment was designed mainly to demonstrate the influence of the minority status of the in-group on the differential perception of in-group compared to out-group homogeneity and thus to qualify the usual finding of greater perceived homogeneity in the out-group.

Our main hypothesis (in-group homogeneity hypothesis) was clearly confirmed at the multivariate level. On the univariate level, the predicted

interaction effect also reached an acceptable level of statistical significance for two of four comparison dimensions (CP and SW), whereas on the third dimension (DE) the effect remained merely suggestive. On the CP and the SW dimensions, subjects in the minority in-group conditions perceived greater homogeneity among in-group members than among out-group members. Those subjects allegedly belonging to nonminorities, however, either perceived greater homogeneity among the out-group members than among the in-group members (CP dimension) or perceived no homogeneity differential at all (SW dimension). For the remaining comparison dimension (UM dimension), the traditional finding of greater perceived out-group homogeneity was replicated irrespective of the experimental condition.

Two arguments can be advanced against an alternative explanation of our main results in terms of an inverse relation between group size and perceived group homogeneity (i.e., in terms of a minority effect per se). First, assuming such a relation, one would expect not only the minority/ nonminority status of the in-group but also that of the out-group to influence the discrepancy between perceived in-group and out-group homogeneity. However, the latter influence was nonsignificant on all four dimensions. Second, the subjects in the control conditions did not show a consistent ten-

dency to perceive a minority group as more homogeneous than the majority it was confronted
with. On the other hand, one might possibly query
the validity of our control conditions on the
grounds of low interest or low attention among
the control subjects, given the fact that they did
not belong to any group themselves. However, the
means of the two individual ratings given by each
control subject for each stimulus group strongly
suggest that these subjects were not inattentive to
the task: In full accordance with the cover story,
they differentiated between the blue group and the
green group. That is, the blue group was clearly
believed to recognize the color blue better and the
color green worse than the green group did and to
spend less money on traveling than the latter, CP
dimension: M(blue) = 37.4, M(green) = 60.4, $t(70)$
= 8.72, $p < .001$; UM dimension: M(blue) = 38.2,
M(green) = 60.2, $t(70) = 9.72, p < .001$; one-tailed.
Furthermore, less interested or inattentive control
subjects might be expected to show greater variability in their responses than might the experimental subjects. In fact, as inspection of the cell
standard deviations in Tables 18.1 and 18.2 reveals,
this was not the case. The overall pattern of variances in the two conditions was very similar with,
if anything, the control subjects showing slightly
less variability. In sum, there is good reason to
assume the control conditions to be valid and to
rule out the alternative explanation of the perception or comparative in-group homogeneity.

Other researchers reported evidence indicating
that there exists no systematic relation between
the perception of group homogeneity and the
evaluation of the groups concerned (Jones et al.,
1981; Park & Rothbart, 1982). That is in accordance with both the evidence from the ANCOVAS
controlling for favorability and our finding that
the in-group homogeneity hypothesis was corroborated not only with regard to a value-loaded dimension (SW) but also with regard to the CP dimension, whose endpoints were alleged to be
equally valued by the experimenter (see Method
section). Hence, the findings concerning comparative group homogeneity cannot be explained as
mere side effects of in-group favoritism or evaluative discrimination against the out-group.

Moreover, the reported differences in perceived
homogeneity are not likely to be due to corresponding differences in the extremity of the ratings, as
we have shown earlier.

The correlation hypothesis was only partially

confirmed. On the dimension (CP) most strongly
correlated with the social categorization, a strong
reversal toward in-group homogeneity emerged,
whereas, as expected, such an effect was not found
on the least strongly correlated dimension (UM).
However, given the fact that a strong correlation
between the original categorization and dot estimation should have been suggested in the cover
story, the merely suggestive interaction effect on
the DE dimension disappointed our expectation.
The anchoring of the dimension might account for
this disappointing result. Whereas the subjects
were told that the blue group would make errors
in estimating the number of dots especially on the
blue slides and the green group especially on the
green slides, the DE dimension was anchored by
no errors and *many errors*, not differentiating between blue and green background color of the
slides. But because no correlation between group
membership and absolute amount of errors was
alleged by the experimenter, the DE dimension
might have been badly adapted for our purpose.

On the other hand, it is interesting that the predicted effect of in-group homogeneity did reach
statistical significance on the SW dimension even
though that dimension was added to the booklet
without ever being previously mentioned in the
cover story. But why should the effect emerge on
this dimension considering the lack of information concerning its correlation with the original
categorization? An answer to this question can be
given fully in agreement with social identity theory.
The SW dimension is obviously value loaded,
clearly more so than any other comparison dimension available to the subjects in our study. Group
members' belief in a correlation between the SW
dimension and the categorization into in-group and
out-group (implying superiority of the in-group)
can easily be explained as originating from their
search for a positive-social identity. As reported
earlier, the mean ratings on the SW dimension were
indeed biased in favor of the in-group, thus indicating that subjects believed in such a correlation
despite the absence of any pertinent information.

As predicted in the identification hypothesis,
minority members laid particular stress on their
group membership. Clearly, they identified more
strongly with their in-group than did members of
nonminorities. Simultaneously, they assumed
greater in-group than out-group homogeneity in
contrast to nonminority members. This pattern of
results strongly suggests that in accordance with

our theoretical model, social identity is the crucial variable mediating between the social context of the intergroup situation and the resulting social perception or behavior.

Having demonstrated the necessity to qualify the out-group homogeneity hypothesis, our data also point to a direction of research on group processes that deserves more attention in the future. Just as stereotyping the out-group can lead to its homogenization, in-group homogeneity might be considered an outcome of self-stereotyping processes (Brown & Turner, 1981, pp. 38–42; Turner, 1982). The study reported here further suggests that research on such processes might be of particular interest in minority-majority contexts (also see Mugny, 1982).

REFERENCES

Allen, V. L. (1985). Infra-group, intra-group and inter-group: Constructing levels of organisation in social influence. In S. Moscovici, G. Mugny, & E. van Avermaet (Eds.), *Perspectives on minority influence* (pp. 217–238). Cambridge, England: Cambridge University Press.

Brewer, M. B. (1979). In-group bias in the minimal intergroup situation: A cognitive-motivational analysis. *Psychological Bulletin, 86,* 307–324.

Brown, R. J., & Turner, J. C. (1981). Interpersonal and intergroup behavior. In J. C. Turner & H. Giles (Eds.), *Intergroup behaviour* (pp. 33–65). Oxford, England: Blackwell.

Brown, R. J., Tajfel, H., & Turner, J. C. (1980). Minimal group situations and intergroup discrimination: Comments on the paper by Aschenbrenner and Schaefer. *European Journal of Social Psychology, 10,* 399–414.

Campbell, D. T. (1958). Common fate, similarity and other indices of the status of aggregates of persons as social entities. *Behavioural Science, 3,* 14–25.

Festinger, L. (1954). A theory of social comparison processes. *Human Relations, 7,* 117–140.

Gerard, H. (1985). When and how the minority prevails. In S. Mascovici, G. Mugny, & E. van Avermaet (Eds.), *Perspectives on minority influence* (pp. 171–186). Cambridge, England: Cambridge University Press.

Gerard, H., & Hoyt, M. F. (1974). Distinctiveness of social categorization and attitude toward in-group members. *Journal of Personality and Social Psychology, 29,* 836–842.

Hamilton, D. L., & Bishop, G. D. (1976). Attitudinal and behavioral effects of initial integration of white suburban neighborhoods. *Journal of Social Issues, 32(2),* 47–67.

Jones, E. E., Wood, G. C., & Quattrone, G. A. (1981). Perceived variability of personal characteristics in in-groups and out-groups: The role of knowledge and evaluation. *Personality and Social Psychology Bulletin, 7(3),* 523–528.

Kanter, R. M. (1977). Some effects of proportions on group life: Skewed sex ratios and responses to token women. *American Journal of Sociology, 82(5),* 965–990.

Linville, P. W., & Jones, E. E. (1980). Polarized appraisals of out-group members. *Journal of Personality and Social Psychology, 38,* 689–703.

Malpass, R. S., & Kravitz, J. (1969). Recognition for faces of own and other race. *Journal of Personality and Social Psychology, 13,* 330–334.

Moscovici, S., & Paicheler, G. (1978). Social comparison and social recognition: Two complementary processes of identification. In H. Tajfel (Ed.), *Differentiation between social groups* (pp. 251–266). London: Academic Press.

Mugny, G. (1982). *The power of minorities.* London: Academic Press.

Park, B., & Rothbart, M. (1982). Perception of out-group homogeneity and levels of social categorization: Memory for the subordinate attributes of in-group and out-group members. *Journal of Personality and Social Psychology, 42,* 1051–1068.

Philo, N. (1979). *Social categorization and the accentuation of intragroup similarities.* Unpublished doctoral dissertation, University of Bristol, United Kingdom.

Quattrone, G. A., & Jones, E. E. (1980). The perception of variability within in-groups and out-groups: Implications for the law of small numbers. *Journal of Personality and Social Psychology, 38,* 141–152.

Sachdev, I., & Bourhis, R. Y. (1984). Minimal majorities and minorities. *European Journal of Social Psychology, 14,* 35–52.

Simon, B. (1985). *Stereotyping and homogenization of in-group and out-group in majority-minority contexts.* Unpublished master's thesis, University of Münster, Federal Republic of Germany.

Stephan, W. G. (1977). Cognitive differentiation in intergroup perception. *Sociometry, 40,* 50–58.

Tajfel, H. (1959). Quantitative judgement in social perception. *British Journal of Psychology 50,* 16–29.

Tajfel, H. (1969). Cognitive aspects of prejudice. *Journal of Social Issues, 25,* 79–97.

Tajfel, H. (Ed.). (1978). *Differentiation between social groups.* London: Academic Press.

Tajfel, H. (1982). Social psychology of intergroup relations. *Annual Review of Psychology, 33,* 1–39.

Tajfel, H., Billig, M. G., Bundy, R. P., & Flament, C. (1971). Social categorization and intergroup behaviour. *European Journal of Social Psychology, 1,* 149–178.

Tajfel, H., & Turner, J. C. (1979). An integrative theory of intergroup conflict. In W. G. Austin & S. Worchel (Eds.), *The social psychology of intergroup relations* (pp. 33–47). Monterey, CA: Brooks/Cole.

Tajfel, H., & Wilkes, A. L. (1963). Classification and quantitative judgement. *British Journal of Psychology, 54,* 101–114.

Taylor, S. E. (1981). A categorization approach to stereotyping. In D. L. Hamilton (Ed.), *Cognitive processes in stereotyping and intergroup behaviour* (pp. 83–114). Hillsdale, NJ: Erlbaum.

Turner, J. C. (1981). The experimental social psychology of intergroup behaviour. In J. C. Turner & H. Giles (Eds.), *Intergroup behaviour* (pp. 66–101). Oxford, England: Blackwell.

Turner, J. C. (1982). Towards a cognitive redefinition of the social group. In H. Tajfel (Ed.), *Social identity and intergroup relations* (pp. 15–40). Cambridge, England: Cambridge University Press.

Wilder, D. A. (1984). Predictions of belief homogeneity and similarity following social categorization. *British Journal of Social Psychology, 23,* 323–333.

Social Science Research on Trial: Use of Sex Stereotyping Research in *Price Waterhouse v. Hopkins*

Susan T. Fiske • University of Massachusetts at Amherst
Donald N. Bersoff • Hahnemann University and Villanova Law School
Eugene Borgida • University of Minnesota
Kay Deaux • City University of New York Graduate Center
Madeline E. Heilman • New York University

The first Supreme Court case to use psychological research on sex stereotyping was Price Waterhouse v. Hopkins. The case was decided in May 1989 and remanded to Judge Gerhard Gesell, who rendered his final decision in May 1990. In this case, a social psychological expert testified to the antecedent conditions, indicators, consequences, and remedies of stereotyping, on the basis of recent cognitive approaches to stereotyping. The testimony was cited in decisions reached in the trial and appeals courts, as well as in the Supreme Court's review. The American Psychological Association filed an amicus curiae brief supporting the validity of the field of stereotyping and the general methods used by the expert. Such legal application provides further lessons for psychological research on stereotyping.

"The firm of Price Waterhouse refused to make Ann Hopkins a partner. Gender-based stereotyping played a role in this decision" (*Hopkins v. Price Waterhouse*, 1990, p. 1). Thus concluded federal district court Judge Gerhard Gesell in his May 1990 opinion that followed the United States Supreme Court landmark decision in the same sex discrimination case (*Price Waterhouse v. Hopkins*, 1989).[1] The case is unique because it represents the first use of psychological evidence about sex stereotyping by the Supreme Court. Previous sex discrimination litigation has used only statistical approaches. Moreover, social science evidence has played a significant role in race discrimination

cases in the Supreme Court since *Brown v. Board of Education* (1954), but such evidence had not before been used in sex discrimination cases. Originally filed in 1984, *Hopkins v. Price Waterhouse* was the first suit to be brought under a new ruling that partnership decisions qualify for protection under Title VII of the 1964 Civil Rights Act (*Hishon v. King & Spaulding*, 1984). *Hopkins v. Price Waterhouse* was eventually heard by the Supreme Court, was decided by the Court in May 1989, and was remanded to Judge Gesell, who rendered his final decision in May 1990 to comport with the new rules developed by the nation's highest court for such cases. The federal court of appeals affirmed Judge Gesell's opinion in December 1990. Testimony about the psychology of stereotyping played a crucial role at each stage of the litigation as it made its way through the judicial process. The American Psychological Association (APA) submitted to the Supreme Court an amicus curiae brief (which follows this article). As we will discuss later, the brief had a significant impact on that Court's final decision.

The relevant psychological literature was heavily cited in Judge Gesell's original decision (*Hopkins v. Price Waterhouse,* 1985), and the testimony about the psychology of stereotyping was cited at all levels of the appeal and review process, including the Supreme Court's decision and the subsequent remand. Moreover, the APA brief clearly contributed to the Supreme Court's opinion regarding the credibility of this area of research. Now that the case has been decided, it is appropriate to describe and evaluate both the role of psychology in this process and what the drafters of the amicus brief learned about our field as a result.

Factual Background of the Hopkins Case

In 1982, it seemed that Ann Hopkins had established her credentials as a top-notch performer at Price Waterhouse (PW), one of the nation's big-eight accounting firms: She had more billable hours than any other person proposed for partner that year, she had brought in business worth $25 million, her clients praised her, and her supporters recommended her as driven, hard working, and exacting. She was the only woman of 88 candidates proposed that year; of 662 partners at PW, only 7 were women.

Instead of being promoted for her accomplishments, her candidacy was put on hold, and she was not proposed for partner the following year.

---

[1]The position of the names of the parties often changes in a case citation as it goes through trial, appeal, and review process. In this case, Ann Hopkins was the original plaintiff in the federal district (trial) court and Price Waterhouse (PW) was the defendant. Hopkins won at trial; PW then appealed to the intermediate federal appellate court (an appellant's name appears first at this level). After it again lost, PW petitioned the U.S. Supreme Court to review the case. As petitioner, PW's name again appears first. Regardless of the sequence of the names of the parties in this article, the authors are referring to the same underlying case.

Hopkins alleged that she was denied partnership because of her gender. Price Waterhouse countered that she was not admitted because she had interpersonal skills problems. According to some evaluators, this "lady partner candidate" was "macho," she "overcompensated for being a woman," and she needed a "course at charm school." A sympathetic colleague advised that she would improve her chances if she would "walk more femininely, talk more femininely, dress more femininely, wear make-up, have her hair styled, and wear jewelry" (*Hopkins v. Price Waterhouse,* 1985, p. 1117). Instead, Hopkins took the firm to court. In 1982, she filed a complaint in the federal district court of the District of Columbia, alleging a violation of Title VII of the 1964 Civil Rights Act.

She had a strong case in many respects, but her attorneys, Douglas Huron and James Heller, still needed to demonstrate that these stereotypic remarks might account for discriminatory decision making. Huron and Heller had heard about attorney Sarah Burns's novel construction of a prior sex discrimination case, using current research on sex stereotyping, particularly cognitive categorization theories (e.g., Allport, 1954; Ashmore & DelBoca, 1981; Hamilton, 1979; Tajfel, 1972; Taylor, 1981; for a review of subsequent contributions, see Fiske & Taylor, 1991, chap. 4, 5). Although that case had been settled before trial, the deposition by social psychologist Susan T. Fiske was viewed by the plaintiff's attorneys as contributing to a favorable outcome for their client. Huron and Heller asked Fiske to testify about the psychology of stereotyping, with particular reference to the facts of the case. When they described their evidence of stereotyping, Fiske agreed, because, in her opinion, the case so closely fit the literature on sex stereotyping. Moreover, it seemed an excellent test of the utility of social psychological theories and research.

Fiske's testimony in the original *Hopkins v. Price Waterhouse* case drew on both laboratory and field research to describe antecedent conditions that encourage stereotyping, indicators that reveal stereotyping, consequences of stereotyping for out-groups, and feasible remedies to prevent the intrusion of stereotyping into decision making. Specifically, she testified first that stereotyping is most likely to intrude when the target is an isolated, one- or few-of-a-kind individual in an otherwise homogeneous environment. The person's solo or near-solo status makes the unusual category more likely to be a salient factor in decision making (e.g., Crocker & McGraw, 1982; Heilman, 1980; Kanter, 1977; McArthur & Post, 1977; Spangler, Gordon, & Pipkin, 1978; S. E. Taylor, 1981; Wolman & Frank, 1975; for recent reviews, see Fiske & Taylor, 1991, chap. 7; Mullen, 1991; Pettigrew & Martin, 1987). Ann Hopkins qualified as a near-solo in the organization. Stereotyping is also likely to intrude when members of a previously omitted group move into a job that is nontraditional for their group. This is certainly true for women who are senior managers and partners in the big-eight accounting firms. The maximum percentage of women partners in a big-eight firm as of 1989 was 5.6%; PW had the lowest with 2% (Berg, 1988). As of May 1990, PW had 27 female partners out of 900 total, or 3% (Lewin, 1990).

Another antecedent condition concerns the perceived lack of fit between the person's category and occupation (Heilman, 1983). The attributes desirable in a manager—aggressive, competitive, driven, tough, and masterly—are not attributes typically expected of women (e.g., Heilman, Block, Martell, & Simon, 1989; Schein, 1973, 1975). Women who behave in those managerial ways are often disliked (e.g., Brown & Geis, 1984; Costrich, Feinstein, Kidder, Marecek, & Pascale, 1975; Deaux & Lewis, 1983, 1984; Hagen & Kahn, 1975; Heilman et al., 1989; for a recent meta-analytic review, see Eagly, Makhijani, & Klonsky, 1992) and create dissatisfaction among their subordinates (Petty & Lee, 1975; Rousell, 1974).

The testimony also addressed antecedents regarding the information environment. Stereotyping is most likely when evaluative criteria are ambiguous (for reviews, see Arvey, 1979; Kanter, 1977; Nieva & Gutek, 1980; as a general principle of schema use, see Fiske & Neuberg, 1990; Fiske & Taylor, 1991, chap. 4, 5; Markus & Zajonc, 1985; Nisbett & Ross, 1980). Moreover, when information about the individual is ambiguous, it is most open to interpretation (e.g., J. M. Darley & Gross, 1983; Heilman, 1984; Heilman, Martell, & Simon, 1988; Locksley, Borgida, Brekke, & Hepburn, 1980, Study 2; Pheterson, Kiesler, & Goldberg, 1971; Rasinski, Crocker, & Hastie, 1985; for reviews, see Arvey, 1979; Nieva & Gutek, 1980; Tosi & Einbender, 1985). Stereotypes provide structure and meaning and they shape per-

ceptions most when the data themselves are open to multiple interpretations, as suggested by research on the cognitive bases of stereotyping (see Fiske & Taylor, 1991, chap. 4, 5, for a review). For example, a "counting" decision—based on millions of business dollars—is relatively immune to stereotypic biases. However, subjective judgments of interpersonal skills and collegiality are quite vulnerable to stereotypic biases. Cognitive models of stereotyping attest to the effects of well-developed expectancies and stereotypes on the interpretation of ambiguous information. This is not to say that decision makers should not use subjective criteria, merely that one must be alert to the possibility of stereotyping in their application.

The testimony also indicated that the symptoms or indicators of cognitive processes that give rise to stereotyping are straightforward: categorical responding such as unnecessarily labeling and evaluating someone according to gender. In Ann Hopkin's case, people commented that her behavior was evaluated differently "because it's a woman doing it," and they suggested that she "overcompensated for being a woman" (for reviews, see Allport, 1954; Brewer, 1988; Deaux & Kite, 1984; Fiske & Neuberg, 1990; Fiske & Taylor, 1991, chap. 4; Tajfel, 1969).

Another symptom of category-based judgment is evaluating people's credentials along dimensions narrowly relevant to their group's stereotype. For example, the sex role appropriateness of Ann Hopkin's social skills, instead of her business-generating abilities, became the primary dimension along which she was evaluated.

Selective perception and interpretation are also indicators of stereotyping. Hopkin's detractors saw her as an aggressive woman and therefore abrasive and difficult, but her supporters and her clients saw her simply as a determined go-getter (for a gender-relevant example, see Taylor, Fiske, Etcoff, & Ruderman, 1978; as a general process in stereotyping, see reviews by Fiske & Taylor, 1991, chap. 4; Hamilton, 1979, 1981; Higgins & Bargh, 1987; Markus & Zajonc, 1985; Nisbett & Ross, 1980, chap. 2, 8).

Finally, stereotyping is also indicated by extreme, polarized evaluations based on limited evidence. For example, some acquaintances claimed that Hopkins was "universally disliked," which was demonstrably not true (e.g., Kanter, 1977; Taylor, 1981; Wolman & Frank, 1975; for a review, see Mullen, 1991). The testimony dealt with other examples, but these examples illustrate the sense of the argument.

The testimony also noted that the consequences of such stereotyping are obvious. Evaluations are based on category membership, not individual merit (for reviews, see Arvey & Campion, 1982; Heilman, 1983; Nieva & Gutek, 1980; Olian, Schwab, & Haberfeld, 1988; D. N. Ruble & Ruble, 1982; T. L. Ruble, Cohen, & Ruble, 1984; Terborg, 1977). Negative attributes are exaggerated (Kanter, 1977; Linville, 1982; Linville & Jones, 1980; Taylor, 1981; Taylor et al., 1978), and positive ones can be discounted (Deaux, 1976; Deaux & Emswiller, 1974; Feather & Simon, 1975; Feldman-Summers & Kiesler, 1974; Frieze, Fisher, Hanusa, McHugh, & Valle, 1978; Garland & Price, 1977; Hansen & O'Leary, 1983; Heilman & Guzzo, 1978; Heilman & Stopeck, 1985a, 1985b; Nicholls, 1975; Pazy, 1986; Pence, Pendleton, Dobbins, & Sgro, 1982). Furthermore, there are clear constraints on the permissible behavior of the stereotyped person (e.g., Bartol & Butterfield, 1976; Brown & Geis, 1984; Costrich et al., 1975; S. Darley, 1976; Jago & Vroom, 1982; Kristal, Sanders, Spence, & Helmreich, 1975; Wiley & Eskilson, 1982).

Regarding possible remedies, Fiske asserted that stereotyping is controllable (Fiske, 1989a; Fiske & Neuberg, 1990), and people are commonly aware that it is inappropriate. Consequently, adequate information undermines stereotyping (e.g., Deaux & Lewis, 1984; Dipboye & Wiley, 1977; Fiske, Neuberg, Beattie, & Milberg, 1987; Heilman, 1984; Heilman & Martell, 1986; Heilman et al., 1988; Locksley et al., 1980; Pheterson et al., 1971; Renwick & Tosi, 1978; Rasinski et al., 1985; Swim, Borgida, Maruyama, & Myers, 1989). In the PW partnership process, the opinions of people with limited hearsay information were given equal weight with the opinions of people who had more intensive contact. Wider distribution of information about the candidate's performance would have provided a better basis for decisions. More careful weighting of comments by the level of the person's knowledge would have improved overall judgments about performance.

At a minimum, PW had no policy prohibiting sex discrimination (age and health were noted as impermissible reasons for excluding someone from partnership, but race and sex were not even mentioned). If a policy exists, at least some people will be motivated to comply with it, and it helps to es-tablish counterstereotypic norms. Consistent with this failure to establish organizational norms emphasizing fairness, overt expressions of prejudice were not discouraged at PW. One partner commented that he did not see why they kept proposing women as partners, when women were not even suited to being senior managers. It was significant that no one rebuked him. In effect, the organizational climate can encourage or at least allow stereotypic judgments to go unchecked. Alternatively, it can actively discourage such processes from influencing decision making. As recent research indicates, motivational incentives force people to pay closer attention to their own possible biases (e.g., Erber & Fiske, 1984; Howard-Pitney, Borgida, & Omoto, 1986; Kruglanski & Freund, 1983; Tetlock, 1983; for a review, see Fiske & Neuberg, 1990; Fiske & Taylor, 1991, chap. 5). For example, interdependence research would suggest putting people on teams of mixed compositions, as well as making bonuses for partners and managers contingent on their ability to recruit and nurture subordinates from underrepresented groups. Thus, Fiske argued, these are solvable problems, and PW had not responsibly monitored its own decision making.

Judge Gesell's Response to the Psychological Testimony

The preceding is an organized outline of the testimony, approximately as it was presented on the stand. Judge Gerhard Gesell (the son of the late, noted developmental psychologist Arnold Gesell) was extremely interactive, directing the sequence of the testimony, asking many questions, and at times demanding that the expert speak in plain English, rather than in psychological jargon.

For example, Judge Gesell was properly impatient with the roundabout way an academic makes a point, and he was openly critical of overly theoretical discussions. The attorneys and the expert had planned a rambling walk through the field of stereotyping, working uphill to the final viewpoint, the way one might in an academic talk or in a journal article, but Judge Gesell preferred that rules of evidence control the testimony:

The Witness: There are general stereotypes of what people particularly expect men to be like and typically expect women to be like. People typically expect women to be strong on the social dimensions. Women are generally expected to be more tender and understanding and concerned about other people, and soft.

The Court: You say that people who have dealt with women expect that? People who have dealt with women in the business context expect that or are you talking about people out on the farm?

The Witness: Well, I would—

The Court: I mean we have got to talk about people dealing with people in a business context. Does that lady have an opinion that she is going to offer in this case?

Mr. Huron: Yes, sir.

The Court: Why doesn't she give me her opinion? and then tell me what she bases it on.

Mr. Huron: Fine. We were trying to—

The Court: And if we did that then I think I would have a better understanding of where you are getting.

Mr. Huron: Dr. Fiske, have you examined whether stereotyping was occurring at Price Waterhouse; I am talking about sex role stereotyping, at the time and in connection with Ann Hopkins' proposal for partnership which began in August '82 until she was placed on hold in March of 1983?

The Witness: I have examined evidence related to that.

Mr. Huron: Have you formed an opinion as to whether or not stereotyping was occurring?

The Witness: Yes, I have.

Mr. Huron: And what is your opinion?

The Witness: I am confident that stereotyping played a role in the decision about Ann Hopkins.

The Court: Well, now, what kind of role and how confident? Are you able to say that you are confident within a reasonable degree of certainty in your discipline?

The Witness: Yes, I would say so, given—

The Court: All right. That is what I want to know. And then you said it played some part. What part? I don't know how you would express it in your discipline percentage wise or how you would express it, but minor, major, middle? I don't know what the terminology is.

The Witness: Well, in lay language I would say it played a major determining role.

The Court: A major determining role, with reasonable certainty?

The Witness: Yes.

The Court: All right. (*Price Waterhouse v. Hopkins*, 1989, pp. 543–545)

Judge Gesell ultimately ruled that an "employer that treats [a] woman with [an] assertive personality in a different manner than if she had been a man is guilty of sex discrimination" (*Hopkins v. Price Waterhouse*, 1985, p. 1119). He described the firm's decision-making process as "tainted by sexually biased evaluations" (p. 1120). With regard to Fiske's testimony, he noted that "a far more subtle process [than the usual discriminatory intent] is involved when one who is in a distinct minority may be viewed differently by the majority because the individual deviates from an artificial standardized profile" (p. 1118). He went on to say that the firm's "partnership evaluation system permitted negative comments tainted by stereotyping to defeat her candidacy, despite clear indications that the evaluations were tainted by discriminatory stereotyping" (p. 1118). In a footnote, he added,

> Common sense is confirmed by the literature on the problem of sex stereotyping which suggests that making evaluators aware of the risks of biased evaluations and inquiring as to whether the generalizations are supported by concrete incidents can be effective in eliminating or minimizing stereotyping. (p. 1120, note 15)

The Court of Appeals Decision

Price Waterhouse appealed Judge Gesell's decision, and the written record of the trial was reviewed by a three-judge panel of the U.S. Court of Appeals for the District of Columbia. Price Waterhouse argued that the social psychology testimony was "sheer speculation" of "no evidentiary value" (*Price Waterhouse v. Hopkins,* 1987, p. 467).

The majority on the appeals court disagreed, ruling that "partners at Price Waterhouse often evaluated female candidates in terms of their sex . . . the partnership selection process at Price Waterhouse was impermissibly infected by stereotypical attitudes towards female candidates" (*Price*

Waterhouse v. Hopkins, 1987, p. 468). Specifically regarding the testimony, the appeals court stated that

> "convergent indicators of stereotyping" . . . taken together provided Dr. Fiske a sufficient basis from which to draw her conclusions that Hopkins was a victim of stereotyping. To the extent Price Waterhouse believes Dr. Fiske lacked necessary information, the firm is in fact quarreling with her field of expertise and the methodology it employs. (p. 467)

However, the sole dissenting appeals judge described Fiske as someone "purporting to be an expert" (*Price Waterhouse v. Hopkins*, 1987, p. 477) in the field and protested "the remarkable intuitions of Dr. Fiske" (p. 478). His dissent implied that the argument was about the accuracy of perceptions of Hopkins's personality, not the stereotypic manner in which those perceptions were cast. For example, he argued "To an expert of Dr. Fiske's qualifications, it seems plain that no woman could *be* overbearing, arrogant, or abrasive: any observations to that effect would necessarily be discounted as the product of stereotyping" (p. 477). He noted that without information about the so-called truth of the matter, "Dr. Fiske's expertise rose to the occasion. Her arts enabled her to detect sex stereotyping based largely on the 'intensity of the negative reaction'" (p. 477).

Issues in the Supreme Court

Because they lost at the appellate court level, PW asked the Supreme Court to review the case. Review by the nation's highest court is discretionary. It agrees to hear only about 150 of the 3,000 cases it is asked to review each year. But because the appellate court decisions in *Hopkins* and in similar cases had been in conflict, the Supreme Court accepted this case for review. The central legal issues that made this case ripe for review concerned the proper allocation of the burden of proof between the employer and employee, as well as the proper standard of proof required to support allegations of discrimination in what are called *mixed-motive cases*, cases in which the refusal to hire or promote is based on both legitimate and illegitimate reasons. The burden- and standard-of-proof issues are irrelevant to this article, but some discussion of the nature of mixed-motive cases is

necessary to understand the context of social science evidence in this case.

Essentially, the mixed-motive issue asks whether it is permissible to refuse to hire or promote someone on the basis of membership in a protected category (e.g., sex, race, age) if the person also has actual areas of significant incompetence. In effect, one might argue that if people have *real* performance problems, it does not matter if they lose a job or promotion partly because of their race or gender. One might argue that the ultimate outcome is the same in either case, whether the grounds were stereotyping or performance. However, this argument would imply that one can only identify discrimination when the person is otherwise perfect. Most employees are not perfect, having records that, if closely examined, could indicate flaws. Is it permissible then to discriminate against the vast majority of people who are genuinely flawed in some important way? This question is identified in discrimination cases as the mixed-motive issue; it formed the basis of PW's petition to the Supreme Court.

The mixed-motive issue has important practical consequences. Can one discriminate against someone who has genuine problems, or do the targets of such discrimination have to prove that they were so exemplary that they would have been guaranteed the position if discrimination were absent? The mixed-motive question asks whether all else has to be above reproach for a person to prove discrimination. Alternatively, one could argue that decision makers can never use discriminatory motives in personnel judgments, even in the case of someone with known shortcomings. In this case, the defense was that if Ann Hopkins had actual interpersonal skills problems, she could not also be a victim of discrimination. The Supreme Court thought this a sufficiently important point of employment discrimination law that it ought to be resolved.

The APA Amicus Curiae Brief

The APA decided to enter the case for two reasons. First, the crucial finding of discrimination in this case, as characterized by the court of appeals, was grounded on direct evidence that the employer's selection process "was impermissibly infected by stereotypical attitudes toward female candidates" (*Price Waterhouse v. Hopkins*, 1987,

p. 468). As a result, the parties were forced to focus some of their attention on the issue of sex stereotypes. However, they lacked the necessary social science background to present the issue of stereotyping in an empirically based, legally relevant manner. Second, PW consistently disparaged Fiske's testimony by criticizing the methodology and the concepts she used in arriving at her expert opinion that PW discriminated against Hopkins on the basis of sex. APA informed the Court that the methodology and literature Fiske used were consonant with generally accepted research practice. APA was careful not to support Fiske personally as an expert witness or as a researcher. Thus, as a good amicus should, APA addressed an issue (the psychology of stereotyping, as relevant to this case) that the parties did not have adequate space, time, or expertise to discuss.

Price Waterhouse had conceded that the partners' negative comments "might conceivably be taken as indicating that stereotypical thinking was sometimes present 'in the air' at Price Waterhouse" (*Brief for Petitioner PW,* 1988, p. 48), but throughout their briefs they disparaged the psychology of stereotyping. They placed the term *expert* in quotation marks, in a belated effort to discredit the validity of research on stereotyping. In addition, they placed the term *sex stereotyping* within quotation marks, falsely implying that it is an unaccepted neologism, and they characterized as an *amorphous proposition* the appeals court finding that the employer discriminated against Ms. Hopkins because of "stereotypical attitudes" (p. 15). They claimed that the finding was derived from "intuitions about unconscious sexism—discernible only through an 'expert' judgment" (p. 17). In addition to labeling Fiske's opinion as "gossamer evidence" and "intuitively divined" (p. 45), PW claimed that Fiske's conclusions were faulty because she never met Hopkins and only reviewed the partners' evaluations of her. Price Waterhouse accused the lower courts of basing a finding of intentional discrimination on a "chain of intuitive hunches about 'unconscious' sexism" which "were, in turn, magically transformed into evidentiary 'facts' by a shift in the burden of persuasion" (p. 44).

The APA's intent in its brief was to disabuse the Court of the notion that sex stereotyping was not an identifiable and legally cognizable source of sex discrimination prohibited by Title VII, and to inform the court of the scientific validity of the methods and literature used in Fiske's testimony. Moreover, the goal of the brief was to represent the research literature as understood by the researchers who provided the material. The implications of the assessment did favor a particular side of the case, and the amicus used the facts of the case to illustrate the relevance of the sex-stereotyping literature, when appropriate. If the implications of the literature had instead favored PW, in the judgment of the researchers, that perspective would have been presented.

The APA's amicus curiae brief was drafted by a panel of social and industrial/organizational psychologists—Eugene Borgida, Kay Deaux, Susan Fiske, and Madeline Heilman—and the final product was compiled, integrated, and rewritten by then-APA-counsel Donald Bersoff: The brief argued for the validity of the field of stereotyping in general, and sex-stereotyping research in particular. The brief noted, first, that empirical research on sex stereotyping has been conducted over many decades and is generally accepted in the scientific community; second, that stereotyping can create discriminatory consequences for stereotyped groups; third, that some conditions that promote stereotyping were present in the firm's work setting; and finally that the firm took no effective steps to reduce discriminatory stereotyping, although such methods were available.

Oral Arguments and the Court's Decision

On October 31, 1988, the Supreme Court heard oral arguments in *Price Waterhouse v. Hopkins.* Kathryn Oberly argued the case for PW, James Heller for Hopkins. The two lawyers had each presented about a minute of their 30-minute prepared statements when they were interrupted and peppered with questions by the justices for the remainder of their allotted times.

On May 1, 1989, the Court handed down its decision. The vote was six to three. Justice Brennan delivered the opinion, in which Justices Blackmun, Marshall, and Stevens joined; Justices White and O'Connor filed concurring opinions. Justice Kennedy filed a dissenting opinion, in which Justices Rehnquist and Scalia joined. The Court found in favor of Hopkins on the mixed-motive issue and in favor of PW on the standard-of-proof issue. That is, in mixed-motive cases, it is not permissible for employers to use discriminatory criteria, and they (not the plaintiff) must bear the burden of persuading the trier of fact that their decision would have been the same if no impermissible discrimination had taken place. However, the court also said that PW had been held to too high a standard of proof (i.e., clear and convincing evidence) and that Judge Gesell should review the facts to see whether it could win under a less stringent (preponderance of evidence) standard. In all, it was viewed primarily as a victory for Hopkins, although the case was returned to Judge Gesell so that he could decide whether PW was liable under the lower standard of proof.

APA contributed to making explicit, for the first time in any Title VII case, that sex stereotyping was a form of sex discrimination.[2] The Court's plurality specifically criticized PW's placement of the phrase sex stereotyping in quotation marks. The plurality said, "such conduct seems to us an insinuation that such stereotyping was not present in this case or that it lacks legal relevance. We reject both possibilities" (*Price Waterhouse v. Hopkins*, 1989, p. 1791). The plurality went on to endorse the importance of sex stereotyping: "In forbidding employers to discriminate against individuals because of their sex, Congress intended to strike at the entire spectrum of disparate treatment of men and women resulting from sex stereotypes" (p. 1791 , quoting *Los Angeles Dept. of Water & Power v. Manhart,* 1978, p. 707). More specifically, APA had argued that sex-stereotypic prescriptive demands to be feminine simultaneous with job-specific demands to be aggressive place women in a double-bind situation; this was apparently convincing to the court in their framing of Hopkins's dilemma as a "Catch 22."

The Court did not dismiss Fiske's expert testimony on grounds cited by PW that she did not personally interview Hopkins. In characterizing this criticism as scientifically naive and irrelevant, APA stated that PW confused the work of research psychologists such as Fiske with that of clinical psychologists who use interviews and other assessment devices to diagnose a patient. The issue in Fiske's testimony was the presence of discriminatory stereotyping at PW, not the mental status of Hopkins. The proper focus, therefore, was on the conduct of PW partners, reflected in the stereotypic phrasing and content of their evaluations.

Fiske brought precisely that focus when she evaluated the conditions at PW that evoke stereotyping and the nature of the comments by its partners in light of the research literature on stereotyping. The plurality agreed and refused to countenance the PW derogation of Fiske's testimony. The Court said,

> We are not inclined to accept petitioner's belated and unsubstantiated characterization of Dr. Fiske's testimony as "gossamer evidence" based only on her "intuitive hunches" and her detection of stereotyping as "intuitively divined." Nor are we inclined to accept the dissent's dismissive attitude toward Dr. Fiske's field of study and toward her own professional integrity. (*Price Waterhouse v. Hopkins*, 1989, p. 1793)

Instead, they said,

> Indeed, we are tempted to say that Dr. Fiske's expert testimony was merely icing on Hopkins' cake. It takes no special training to discern sex stereotyping in a description of an aggressive female employee as requiring "a course at charm school." Nor . . . does it require expertise in psychology to know that, if an employee's flawed "interpersonal skills" can be corrected by a soft-hued suit or a new shade of lipstick, perhaps it is the employee's sex and not her interpersonal skills that has drawn the criticism. (*Price Waterhouse v. Hopkins*, 1989, p. 1793)

One can interpret this comment in various ways: as dismissive, saying that the social science testimony was all common sense; as merely taking the social psychological expertise for granted; or as suggesting that one does not necessarily require expert witnesses to identify stereotyping when the evidence is egregious.

Finally, in response to the argument that Ann Hopkins might really be an obnoxious person, as described by some acquaintances, the Court agreed with Judge Gesell that,

> The reactions of at least some of the partners were reactions to her as a *woman* manager. Where an evaluation is based on a subjective assessment of a person's strengths and weaknesses, it is simply not true that each evaluator will focus on, or even mention, the same weaknesses. Thus, even if we knew that Hopkins had "personality problems," this would not tell us that the partners who cast their evaluations of Hopkins in sex-based terms would have criticized her as sharply (or criticized her at all) if she had been a man. It is not our job to review the evidence and decide that negative

---

[2] For a review of the impact of other social science amicus curiae briefs, see Acker (1990).

reactions to Hopkins were based on reality; our perception of Hopkins' character is irrelevant. We sit not to determine whether Ms. Hopkins is nice, but to decide whether the partners reacted negatively to her personality because she is a woman. (*Price Waterhouse v. Hopkins, 1989,* pp. 1794–1795)

One could not have asked for a better understanding of the psychology of stereotyping. The Supreme Court concluded,

> In the specific context of sex stereotyping, an employer who acts on the basis of a belief that a woman cannot be aggressive, or that she must not be, has acted on the basis of gender. . . . We are beyond the day when an employer could evaluate employees by assuming or insisting that they matched the stereotype associated with their group. . . . An employer who objects to aggressiveness in women but whose positions require this trait places women in an intolerable Catch 22: out of a job if they behave aggressively and out of a job if they don't. Title VII lifts women out of this bind. (pp. 1790–1791)

The State of the Field, as Revealed by the Amicus Process

Strengths

It is important to give credit where credit is due. In considering material for the brief, we were impressed with the advances made and knowledge accumulated during the past decade or so. Indeed, we gave the most weight to that material. Social scientists (and especially psychologists) have contributed significantly to an understanding of the nature and operation of stereotypes. Areas in which increments in knowledge are most pronounced include (a) the nature of categorization processes, including the development of subtypes; (b) conditions that encourage stereotyping; and (c) the influence of stereotypes or performance evaluation and causal explanation (Deaux, 1985; Deaux & Kite, 1994). The work on stereotyping is an excellent example of basic research that can have practical impact, both in analyzing the current situation and in suggesting future courses of action.

The cognitive categorization approaches to stereotyping are particularly well suited to courtroom use. That is, the cognitive approach by definition concentrates on people's thoughts, not on their feelings, which means the type of evidence one examines is highly compatible with the kinds of evidence available in the courtroom. We do not have to undertake a speculative analysis of an individual's authoritarian personality or of an entire culture's stance toward diversity; the cognitive analysis is more straightforward.

Moreover, laboratory research has some special virtues for training experts in this kind of endeavor. Beginning with the antecedents of stereotyping, laboratory researchers are well suited to analyze the situation, looking for factors that encourage or discourage stereotyping. Training in experimental methods teaches one to divide a social situation into its critical components. In conducting laboratory research, one learns to isolate and manipulate the significant situational factors. Moreover, the same compatibility holds in examining the indicators of stereotyping. First, psychological researchers, particularly those with a cognitive bent, are used to dealing with the written record, hard evidence of people's judgmental processes. Second, evidence suggesting how people categorize another person and evidence pointing to the attributes considered important in decision making are indicators that are often apparent in the written record. When a person labels another person, the written record or reports of conversations provide evidence that is similar to the responses of subjects in a laboratory experiment. Turning to the consequences of stereotyping, there, too, laboratory researchers are well suited to identify sensitive measures and interpret the meaning of a pattern of response. Finally, in suggesting remedies, many laboratory researchers have built their research programs around finding ways to undercut stereotyping. Experimenters are trained to deepen their understanding of an effect by making it come and go through various interventions. Laboratory scientists often assume that the interventions may be effectively translated into the organizational mold. For example, Fiske's research on interdependence and stereotyping has been heavily influenced by the kinds of structural features that operate in organizations and might usefully generalize to those contexts. This type of laboratory research on basic processes then converges with field research on real-world effects of interventions.

Weaknesses

More work is needed, for both theoretical and practical reasons. There is still a need to test more laboratory findings in field settings and to use such findings to revise current theories. In turn, the key dynamics in field settings need to be incorporated systematically into laboratory experiments.

A critical issue for managers as well as attorneys is how to minimize the use of stereotypes. The psychological literature is strong in showing how pervasive stereotypes are, in demonstrating the myriad conditions that promote them, and in showing how resistant they can be to new information. Relatively few research programs explore the conditions that discourage stereotyping. Psychologists need to work further to discover when stereotypes do and when they do not operate. Such efforts might investigate deterrent strategies, the influence of observers or models on stereotyping, and the broader contexts that may emphasize or minimize stereotypes. These issues, all raised by the *Hopkins* case, have not been addressed adequately on an empirical basis.

Specific questions of cognitive process are also raised by this case. For example, how are two or more stereotypic categories combined (e.g., manager and woman)? What are the circumstances under which people use alternative subtypes (e.g., aggressive career woman) and more general categories (e.g., women)? The case specifically raises the issue of whether Hopkins was considered an exemplar of "aggressive career woman" or simply as a deviant from both categories, "woman" and "manager." The continuing debate on perceivers' use of category prototypes versus exemplars is relevant here (see Fiske & Taylor, 1991, chap. 4, for a review).

Perhaps the central issue raised by this case is the distinction between descriptive and prescriptive aspects of stereotypes. This issue is particularly relevant to gender stereotyping, but it arises in other contexts as well. Although it is routinely accepted that sex stereotypes have both descriptive and normative components (e.g., Terborg, 1977), research has been focused primarily on the descriptive component. It has been concentrated on the following four issues: the attributes that constitute sex stereotypes; the processes by which they are ascribed to men and women; the consequences of such ascriptions on expectations, attributions, and evaluations; and the conditions that regulate their occurrence. Underlying this research is a working assumption that if psychologists can determine how and when stereotypic attributes are used to characterize an individual man or woman,

differential treatment can be averted.

The *Hopkins* case forces a reexamination of that assumption. Hopkins was acknowledged as competent, committed, hard working, and effective. The extent of her accomplishments was not the main point of contention, her talents were not denied (although they may have been underrated), and the attributes considered part of the male stereotyped "competency cluster" were accepted. In short, in terms of work-relevant attributes, she did not appear to suffer the ills of a traditional stereotyped description (e.g., passive, weak, indecisive), and yet she was a victim of sex stereotyping. Why? Despite her work-related competence (or perhaps because of it), she was seen as behaving in ways that are considered inappropriate for women. She met certain expectations, but not others, and she was expected to meet both.

The prescriptive aspects of sex stereotypes (i.e., the behaviors deemed respectively suitable for men and women) are clearly important. Nevertheless, in reviewing the literature for the brief, we found surprisingly little attention focused on this issue. Although there is evidence demonstrating that behaving out of sex role has unfavorable consequences and that women and men who violate the "shoulds" of the sex-stereotypic prescription are found to be objectionable, few attempts have been made to systematically explore this larger phenomenon of prescriptive stereotyping. Even fewer attempts have been made to address the question of how to prevent or remedy it. The interventions may be of a different sort than those targeting descriptive aspects of stereotyping. Here the dynamics are likely to involve motivational and affective factors as well as cognitive ones.

How Complete Does the Database Have to Be?

In her testimony, Fiske based her assertions regarding the role of stereotyping on a well-established and thriving literature. Her assessment was grounded in decades of research. Moreover, the use of such "social framework" testimony is likely to continue in various areas of psychology (Goodman & Croyle, 1989). How broad and deep does the database have to be for psychologists to render expert opinions? A crucial concern emerges about the adequacy of scientific databases as social science is increasingly used in the legal system. The number of APA-sponsored briefs has increased, and their influence has been examined (Acker, 1990; Roesch, Golding, Hans, & Repucci, 1991). The increased use of social science data in law, whether to address legislative or adjudicative matters, has generated important conceptual frameworks and evaluative criteria based on peer review standards for evaluating the scientific adequacy of the database in question (e.g., Monahan & Walker, 1988).

Issues about the quality of the database, which also pertain to the use of social science evidence in the *Hopkins* case, have long been debated with regard to research on eyewitness identification (Kassin, Ellsworth, & Smith, 1989; Loftus, 1983; McCloskey & Egeth, 1983). More recently, this issue has emerged as central to the debate regarding the role of APA's amicus curiae brief in death penalty cases, most notably *Lockhart v. McCree*, 1986 (see Bersoff, 1987). Again, the adequacy of the scientific database was at the heart of the controversy. Elliott (1991) took issue with APA's *Lockhart* amicus position that "that stability and convergence of the findings over three decades lends impressive support to their validity" (Bersoff, 1987, p. 68). Elliott was quite critical of the database and argued that the team of experts assembled at APA may have exaggerated the conclusiveness of the database in order to have an impact on legal policy. Ellsworth (1991) strongly rebutted Elliott's criticisms of the research database and argued that the database was adequate by generally accepted peer review standards, that convergent validity was established in this research domain, and that Elliott's claim (i.e., scientific authority was overstated) was unfounded. Most important, Ellsworth argued that "to keep silent until our understanding is perfect is to keep silent forever" (p. 277). The team that developed the amicus position in the *Hopkins* case would strongly endorse Ellsworth's perspective. The amicus experts' favorable assessment of the sufficiency of the scientific database in the *Hopkins* case, as in *Lockhart*, was determined by the convergent validity of the scientific research literature.

The Interplay Between Research and Testimony

A critic might argue that researchers who have contributed to a particular literature should not testify as experts or contribute to amicus briefs because they have a stake in the validity of that literature, and they might overlook the rough spots or misrepresent the degree of consensus in the state of the research. These ethical issues have been a concern from the outset of the expert testimony, in the drafting of the amicus brief, and in the composition of this article.

Regarding the testimony of involved experts, it is difficult to imagine who is more qualified to testify than someone whose primary activity is to conduct research on the topic at hand. Certainly, perennial expert witnesses who conduct little research are not more credible than occasional expert witnesses whose primary identity lies in science. The main motivations for scientists to be involved in such expert testimony are to get well-established research literatures into the relevant legal settings and to receive feedback about the utility of their work. As researchers apply their expertise to legal issues, further research and greater expertise is inspired. Such a cycle must commence with a well-developed research area before it can be exported, but the point is that intellectual involvement of experts ultimately strengthens both research and its application to law.[3]

There are, of course, several safeguards against deliberately or inadvertently misleading legal applications. First, there is the conscience of the individual researcher. This can only be known in the privacy of one's own thoughts, but ultimately there must be some degree of trust in the honor of our colleagues. One's reputation as a scientist is far more important than one's winning any one case. Without peer credibility, a scientist cannot carry on the requisite professional activities that enable his or her continued career.

Another potential criticism of such legal application comes not from misrepresentation of the literature, but in application to a particular setting. The role of expert testimony, whether psychological, medical, statistical, engineering, or whatever, is to discuss a research literature, not to define or

---

[3]As concrete examples of the benefits to research, we know of one meta-analysis that cited *Hopkins* as demonstrating some relevant dimensions for analysis (Eagly, Makhijani, & Klonsky, 1992) and one archival study of solo status and performance evaluations apparently inspired by *Hopkins* (Sackett, DuBois, & Noe, 1991). Moreover, in our own work, one research program has been heavily influenced by *Hopkins* (Fiske, 1989a, 1989b), and one literature review has described the *Hopkins* case as marking "a rite of passage for research on gender stereotypes" (Deaux & Kite, 1994).

address the legal issues involved. The trier of fact (judge or jury) makes the legal decision. The role of the testimony is to be helpful to the trier of fact by providing information about an area of human behavior that might not be familiar. Specifically, expert testimony (a) represents the state of knowledge in the relevant field and (b) applies it to the facts of the particular case. Certainly, there are issues of expert judgment and informed opinion at both stages of the process. But why is the psychology of stereotyping ultimately any different from other areas of admissible expertise? We would argue that there are no fundamental differences that prevent stereotyping researchers from qualifying as experts, representing the database, and applying their knowledge to a particular case.

Within an adversarial system, another safeguard is the alternative view posed by the actual or potential opposing expert, by the judge's neutral expert (a strategy sometimes used for statistical testimony), and by the actual or prospective opposing briefs. The whole premise of an adversarial system is that the most veridical evidence, scientific or otherwise, is the most convincing. Although adversarial safeguards on expert testimony and amicus briefs are not perfect, it is a premise of the legal system that distortion of the data will come out, one way or another.

Turning more specifically to the selection of the amicus drafters, deliberate efforts were made to represent a cross section of expertise and opinion. The APA Legal Affairs Office approved the final composition of the group. Fiske was included because of her work on stereotyping and her intimate knowledge of the case; Deaux was included for her expertise about stereotyping based on gender per se; Heilman was included because of her knowledge of gender stereotyping in work contexts; and Borgida was included for his knowledge of forensic psychology and because his published work has taken a devil's advocate position on some issues in gender stereotyping. All four have published extensively in the relevant areas, have held editorial positions on journals, and have been competitively funded for their research in these areas. Thus, the institutional controls (APA) and the orientations of the individual researchers both worked to assure a balanced perspective on the literature.

One might argue that the amicus drafters, once chosen, were then driven by politics. However, expertise about the effects of stereotyping is not necessarily less neutral than expertise about the

effects of a bullet to the brain. Medical experts can have political or self-serving motivations just as easily; they would fail to qualify if it could be shown that they were primarily motivated to push a policy agenda (e.g., gun control) or to become famous (through involvement in a notorious case despite private misgivings). Yet, one might argue, the researchers representing the psychology of stereotyping are somehow less neutral because they may be potential victims of stereotypes themselves and so are not necessarily neutral. By this argument, female scientists studying gender stereotypes have reduced credibility. As this argument implies, it would be like asking someone who lives in a neighborhood with a high crime rate to serve as an expert on the effects of fatal bullet wounds. Clearly, if such a person had scientific expertise in the topic, as established by peer review and reputation, the person's private life would not be relevant. Obviously, this hypothetical expert would not be called in to testify as an expert against a spouse's murderer, but neither is the stereotyping expert called in to testify in a personal grievance. Careful methods, convincing data, reasonable argument, and debate among peers are the bulwark against bias in science. Careful methods, convincing data, reasonable argument, and debate among peers all protect against bias by experts testifying and drafting amicus briefs.

We are not arguing that the database is perfect or that as researchers we are indifferent to the topics we study or their policy implications. Nor are we arguing that expert opinions may not differ. We are arguing that psychologists' considered and self-critical judgments as researchers were reflected in the use of psychological expertise at trial and in the amicus process in this case.

Conclusions

It is an extraordinary opportunity to have psychological research, in an area so well established and thriving, be confronted by some of the most prominent legal minds in the country. We think psychology came out rather well, on the whole. But we also think, as psychologists, that we have our work cut out for us. To enhance our credibility, we must continue to test our theories in a range of laboratory and field settings. We must attend to those factors in the real world that demand research attention: How can decision makers best guard against the incursions of stereotypic judgments and consequent discrimination? How can people control their stereotypic thinking? What situational and organizational factors influence stereotyping? What are appropriate remedies? Psychology is well equipped to take on these challenges. Meanwhile, the role of expert testimony and amicus briefs is to educate and to bring the pertinent research to the attention of the trier of fact, and then let the courts decide.

REFERENCES

Acker, J. R. (1990). Social science in Supreme Court cases and briefs: The actual and potential contribution of social scientists as *amici curiae*. *Law and Human Behavior, 14,* 225–242.

Allport, G. W. (1954). *The nature of prejudice*. Reading, MA: Addison-Wesley.

Arvey, R. D. (1979). Unfair discrimination in the employment interview: Legal and psychological aspects. *Psychological Bulletin, 86,* 736–765.

Arvey, R. D., & Campion, J. E. (1982). The employment interview: A summary and review of recent research. *Personnel Psychology, 35,* 281–322.

Ashmore, R. D., & Del Boca, F. K. (1981). Conceptual approaches to stereotypes and stereotyping. In D. L. Hamilton (Ed.), *Cognitive processes in stereotyping and intergroup behavior* (pp. 1–36). Hillsdale, NJ: Erlbaum.

Bartol, K. M., & Butterfield, D. A. (1976). Sex effects in evaluating leaders. *Journal of Applied Psychology, 61,* 446–454.

Berg. E. N. (1988, July). The Big Eight: Still a male bastion. *New York Times: Business Day,* pp. 1, 37.

Bersoff, D. N. (1987). Social science data and the Supreme Court. *American Psychologist, 42,* 52–68.

Brewer, M. B. (1988). A dual process model of impression formation. In T. K. Srull & R. S. Wyer, Jr. (Eds.), *Advances in social cognition* (Vol. 1, pp. 1–36). Hillsdale, NJ: Erlbaum.

Brief for petitioner Price Waterhouse. (1988, January). Petition for a writ of certiorari to the United States Court of Appeals for the District of Columbia Circuit.

Brown v. Board of Education, 347 U.S. 483 (1954).

Brown, V., & Geis, F. L. (1984). Turning lead into gold: Evaluations of men and women leaders and the alchemy of social consensus. *Journal of Personality and Social Psychology, 16,* 811–824.

Costrich, N., Feinstein, J., Kidder, L., Marecek, J., & Pascale, L. (1975). When stereotypes hurt: Three studies of penalties for sex-role reversals. *Journal of Experimental Social Psychology, 11,* 520–530.

Crocker, J., & McGraw, K. M. (1982). What's good for the goose is not good for the gander: Solo status as an obstacle to occupational achievement for males and females. *American Behavioral Scientist, 27,* 357–369.

Darley, J. M., & Gross, P. H. (1983). A hypothesis-confirming bias in labeling effects. *Journal of Personality and Social Psychology, 44,* 20–33.

Darley. S. (1976). Big-time careers for the little woman: A dual-role dilemma. *Journal of Social Issues, 32,* 85–98.

Deaux, K. (1976). *The behavior of women and men.* Monterey, CA: Brooks/Cole.

Deaux, K. (1985). Sex and gender. *Annual Review of Psychology, 36,* 49–81.

Deaux. K., & Emswiller, T. (1974). Explanation of successful performance on sex-linked tasks: What is skill for the male is luck for the female. *Journal of Personality and Social Psychology, 29,* 80–85.

Deaux, K., & Kite, M. E. (1994). Gender stereotypes. In F. Denmark & M. Paludi (Eds.), *Handbook on the psychology of women* (pp. 107–139). New York: Greenwood Press.

Deaux. K., & Lewis, L. L. (1983). Components of gender stereotypes. *Psychological Documents, 13,* 25.

Deaux. K., & Lewis, L. L. (1984). The structure of gender stereotypes: Interrelationships among components and gender label. *Journal of Personality and Social Psychology, 16,* 991–1004.

Dipboye, R. L., & Wiley, J. W. (1977). Reactions of college recruiters to interviewer sex and self-presentation style. *Journal of Vocational Behavior, 10,* 1–12.

Eagly, A. H., Makhijani, M. G., & Klonsky, B. G. (1992). Gender and the evaluation of leaders: A meta-analysis. *Psychological Bulletin, 111,* 3–22.

Elliott, R. (1991). Social science data and the APA: The *Lockhart* brief as a case in point. *Law and Human Behavior, 15,* 59–76.

Ellsworth, P. C. (1991). To tell what we know, or wait for Godot? *Law and Human Behavior, 15,* 77–90.

Erber R., & Fiske, S. T. (1984). Outcome dependency and attention to inconsistent information. *Journal of Personality and Social Psychology, 17,* 709–726.

Feather, N. T., & Simon, J. G. (1975). Reactions to male and female success and failure in sex-linked occupations: Impressions of personality, causal attributions and perceived likelihood of different consequence. *Journal of Personality and Social Psychology, 31,* 20–31.

Feldman-Summers, S., & Kiesler, S. B. (1974). Those who are number two try harder: The effect of sex on attributions of causality. *Journal of Personality and Social Psychology, 30,* 846–855.

Fiske, S. T. (1989a). Examining the role of intent: Toward understanding its role in stereotyping and prejudice. In J. S. Uleman & J. A. Bargh (Eds.), *Unintended thought* (pp. 253–283). New York: Guilford.

Fiske, S. T. (1989b, August). *Interdependence and stereotyping: From the laboratory to the Supreme Court (and back).* Invited address given at the 97th Annual Convention of the American Psychological Association, New Orleans.

Fiske, S. T., & Neuberg, S. L. (1990). A continuum of impression formation, from category-based to individuating process: Influences of information and motivation on attention and interpretation. In M. P. Zanna (Ed.), *Advances in experimental social psychology* (Vol. 23, pp. 1–74). San Diego, CA: Academic Press.

Fiske, S. T,. Neuberg, S. L, Beattie, A. E., & Milberg, S. J. (1987). Category-based and attribute-based reactions to others: Some informational conditions of stereotyping and individuating processes. *Journal of Experimental Social Psychology, 23,* 399–427.

Fiske, S. T., & Taylor, S. E. (1991). *Social cognition* (2nd ed.). New York: McGraw-Hill.

Frieze, I. H., Fisher, J. R., Hanusa, B. H., McHugh, M. C., & Valle, V. A. (1978). Attributions of the causes of success and failure as internal and external barriers to achievement. In J. L. Sherman & F. L. Denmark (Eds.), *The psychology of women: Future directions in research* (pp. 519–552). New York: Psychological Dimensions.

Garland, H., & Price, K. H. (1977). Attitudes toward women in management and attributions for their success and failure in a managerial position. *Journal of Applied Psychology, 59,* 705–711.

Goodman, J., & Croyle, R. T. (1989). Social framework testimony in employment discrimination cases. *Behavioral Sciences and the Law, 7,* 227–241.

Hagen, R. L., & Kahn, A. (1975). Discrimination against competent women. *Journal of Applied Social Psychology, 5,* 362–376.

Hamilton, D. L. (1979). A cognitive-attributional analysis of stereotyping. In L. Berkowitz (Ed.), *Advances in experimental social psychology* (Vol. 12, pp. 53–84). San Diego, CA: Academic Press.

Hamilton, D. L. (1981). Stereotyping and intergroup behavior. Some thoughts on the cognitive approach. In D. L. Hamilton (Ed.), *Cognitive processes in stereotyping and intergroup behavior* (pp. 333–353). Hillsdale, NJ: Erlbaum.

Hansen, R. D., & O'Leary, V. E. (1983). Actresses and actors: The effects of sex on causal attributions. *Basic and Applied Social Psychology, 4,* 209–230.

Heilman, M. E. (1980). The impact of situational factors on personnel decisions concerning women: Varying the sex composition of the applicant pool. *Organizational Behavior and Human Performance, 26,* 386–395.

Heilman, M. E. (1983). Sex bias in work settings: The lack of fit model. *Research in Organizational Behavior, 5,* 269–298.

Heilman, M. E. (1984). Information as a deterrent against sex discrimination: The effects of applicant sex and information type on preliminary employment decisions. *Organizational Behavior and Human Performance, 113,* 174–186.

Heilman, M. E., Block, C. J., Martell, R. F., & Simon, M. C. (1989). Has anything changed? Current characterizations of men, women, and managers. *Journal of Applied Psychology, 71,* 935–942.

Heilman, M. E., & Guzzo, R. A. (1978). The perceived cause of work success as a mediator of sex discrimination in organizations. *Organizational Behavior and Human Performance, 21,* 346–357.

Heilman, M. E., & Martell, R. F. (1986). Exposure to successful women: Antidote to sex discrimination in applicant screening decisions? *Organizational Behavior and Human Decision Processes, 37,* 376–390.

Heilman, M. E., Martell, R., & Simon, M. (1988). The vagaries of bias: Conditions regulating the undervaluation, equivalimation, and overvaluation of female job applicants. *Organizational Behavior and Human Performance, 41,* 98-110.

Heilman, M. E., & Stopeck, M. M. (1985a). Attractiveness and corporate success. Different causal attributions for males and females. *Journal of Applied Psychology, 70,* 379–388.

Heilman, M. E., & Stopeck, M. H. (1985b). Being attractive, advantage or disadvantage? Performance-based evaluations and recommended personnel actions as a function of appearance, sex, and job type. *Organizational Behavior and Human Decision Processes, 35,* 202–215.

Higgins, E. T., & Bargh, J. A. (1987). Social cognition and social perception. In M. R. Rosenzweig & L. W. Porter (Eds.), *Annual review of psychology* (Vol. 38, pp. 369–425). Palo Alto, CA: Annual Review.

Hishon v. King & Spaulding, 467 U.S. 69 (1984).

Hopkins v. Price Waterhouse, 618 F Supp. 1109 (D. D.C. 1985).

Hopkins v. Price Waterhouse, No. 84-3040, slip op. (D. D.C. May 14, 1990) (on remand).

Howard-Pitney, B., Borgida, E., & Omoto, A. M. (1986). Personal involvement: An examination of processing differences. *Social Cognition, 4,* 39–57.

Jago, A. G., & Vroom, V. H. (1982). Sex differences in the incidents and evaluations of participative leader behavior. *Journal of Applied Psychology, 67,* 776–783.

Kanter, R. (1977). *Men and women of the corporation.* New York: Basic Books.

Kassin, S. M., Ellsworth, P. C., & Smith, V. L. (1989). The "general acceptance" of psychological research on eyewitness testimony: A survey of the experts. *American Psychologist, 44,* 1089–1098.

Kristal, J., Sanders, D., Spence, J. T., & Helmreich, R. (1975). Inferences about the femininity of competent women and their implications for likability. *Sex Roles, 1,* 33–41.

Kruglanski, A. W., & Freund, T. (1983). The freezing and unfreezing of lay-inferences: Effects of impressional primacy, ethnic stereotyping, and numerical anchoring. *Journal of Experimental Social Psychology, 19,* 448–468.

Lewin, T. (1990, May 16). Partnership in firm awarded to victim of sex bias. *New York Times,* pp. Al, A20.

Linville, P. W. (1982). The complexity–extremity effect and age-based stereotyping. *Journal of Personality and Social Psychology, 12,* 193–211.

Linville, P. W., & Jones, E. E. (1980). Polarized appraisals of out-group members. *Journal of Personality and Social Psychology, 38,* 689–703.

Locksley, A., Borgida, E., Brekke, N., & Hepburn, C. (1980). Sex stereotypes and social judgment. *Journal of Personality and Social Psychology, 39,* 821–831.

Loftus, E. F. (1983). Silence is not golden. *American Psychologist, 38,* 564–572.

Los Angeles Department of Water & Power v. Manhart, 434 U.S. 702, 707 n.13 (1978).

Markus, H., & Zajonc, R. B. (1985). The cognitive perspective in social psychology. In G. Lindzey & E. Aronson (Eds.), *Handbook of social psychology* (3rd ed., Vol. 1, pp. 137–230). New York: Random House.

McArthur, L., & Post, D. (1977). Figural emphasis and person perception. *Journal of Experimental Social Psychology, 13,* 520–535.

McCloskey, M., & Egeth, H. E. (1983). Eyewitness identification: What can a psychologist tell a jury? *American Psychologist, 38,* 550–563.

Monahan, J., & Walker, L. (1988). Social science research in law. *American Psychologist, 43,* 465–472.

Mullen, B. (1991). Group composition, salience, and cognitive representations: The phenomenology of being in a group. *Journal of Experimental Social Psychology, 27,* 297–323.

Nicholls, J. G. (1975). Causal attributions and other achievement-related cognitions: Effects of task outcome, attainment value and sex. *Journal of Personality and Social Psychology, 31,* 379–389.

Nieva, V. F., & Gutek, B. A. (1980). Sex effects on evaluation. *Academy of Management Review, 5,* 267–276.

Nisbett, R., & Ross, L. (1980). *Human inference: Strategies and shortcomings of social judgment.* Englewood Cliffs, NJ: Prentice-Hall.

Olian, J. D., Schwab, D. P., & Haberfeld, Y. (1988). The impact of applicant gender compared to qualifications on hiring recommendations. *Organizational Behavior and Human Decision Processes, 41,* 180–195.

Pazy, A. (1986). The persistence of pro-male bias despite identical information regarding causes of success. *Organizational Behavior and Human Decision Processes, 38,* 366–377.

Pence, E. C., Pendleton, W. C., Dobbins, G. H., & Sgro, J. A. (1982). Effects of causal explanations and sex variables on recommendations for corrective actions following employee failure. *Organizational Behavior and Human Performance, 29,* 227–240.

Pettigrew, T. F., & Martin, J. (1987). Shaping the organizational context for Black American inclusion. *Journal of Social Issues, 13,* 41–78.

Petty, M. M., & Lee, G. K. (1975). Moderating effects of sex of supervisor and subordinate on relationships between supervisor behavior and subordinate satisfaction. *Journal of Applied Psychology, 60,* 624–628.

Pheterson, G. I., Kiesler, S., & Goldberg, P. A. (1971). Evaluation of the performance of women as a function of their sex, achievement, and personal history. *Journal of Personality and Social Psychology, 19,* 114–118.

Price Waterhouse v. Hopkins, 825 F.2d 458 (D.C. Cir. 1987).

Price Waterhouse v. Hopkins, 109 S. Ct. 1775 (1989).

Rasinski, K. A., Crocker, J., & Hastie, R. (1985). Another look at sex stereotypes and social judgment: An analysis of the social perceiver's use of subjective probabilities. *Journal of Personality and Social Psychology, 19,* 317–326.

Renwick, P. A., & Tosi, H. (1978). The effects of sex, marital status, and educational background on selection decisions. *Academy of Management Journal, 21,* 93–103.

Roesch, R., Golding, S. L., Hans. V. P., & Repucci, N. D. (1991). Social science and the courts: The role of amicus curiae briefs. *Law and Human Behavior, 15,* 1–12.

Rousell, C. (1974). Relationship of sex of department head to department climate. *Administrative Science Quarterly, 19,* 211–220.

Ruble, D. N., & Ruble, T. L. (1982). Sex stereotypes. In A. G. Miller (Ed.), *In the eye of the beholder: Contemporary issues in stereotyping* (pp. 188–252). New York: Praeger.

Ruble, T. L., Cohen, R., & Ruble, D. N. (1984). Sex stereotypes: Occupational barriers for women. *American Behavioral Scientist, 27,* 339–356.

Sackett, P. R., DuBois, C. L. Z., & Noe, A. W. (1991). Tokenism in performance evaluations: The effects of work group representation on male-female and White-Black differences in performance ratings. *Journal of Applied Psychology, 76,* 263–267.

Schein, V. E. (1973). The relationship between sex-role stereotypes and requisite management characteristics. *Journal of Applied Psychology, 57,* 95–100.

Schein, V. E. (1975). Relationships between sex-role stereotypes and requisite management characteristics among female managers. *Journal of Applied Psychology, 60,* 340–344.

Spangler, E., Gordon, M. A., & Pipkin, R. M. (1978). Token women: An empirical test of the Kanter hypothesis. *American Journal of Sociology, 84,* 160–170.

Swim, J., Borgida, E., Maruyama, G., & Myers, D. G. (1989). Joan McKay versus John McKay: Do gender stereotypes bias evaluations? *Psychological Bulletin, 105,* 409–429.

Tajfel, H. (1969). Cognitive aspects of prejudice. *Journal of Social Issues, 25,* 79–97.

Tajfel, H. (1972). La categorisation social [Social categorization]. In S. Moscovici (Ed.), *Introduction a la psychologie sociale* (Vol. 1, pp. 272–302). Paris: Larousse.

Taylor, S. E. (1981). A categorization approach to stereotyping. In D. L. Hamilton (Ed.), *Cognitive processes in stereotyping and intergroup behavior* (pp. 88–114). Hillsdale, NJ: Erlbaum.

Taylor, S. E., Fiske, S. T., Etcoff, N. L., & Ruderman, A. J. (1978). Categorical bases of person memory and stereotyping. *Journal of Personality and Social Psychology, 36,* 778–793.

Terborg, J. R. (1977). Women in management: A research review. *Journal of Applied Psychology, 62,* 647–664.

Tetlock. P. E. (1983). Accountability and complexity of thought. *Journal of Personality and Social Psychology, 45,* 74–83.

Tosi, H. L., & Einbender, S. W. (1985). The effects of the type and amount of information in sex discrimination on research: A meta-analysis. *Academy of Management Journal, 28,* 712–723.

Wiley, M. G., & Eskilson, A. (1982). Coping in the corporation: Sex role constraints. *Journal of Applied Social Psychology, 12,* 1–11.

Wolman, C., & Frank, H. (1975). The solo woman in a professional peer group. *American Journal of Orthopsychiatry, 45,* 164–171.

Social Stigma: The Affective Consequences of Attributional Ambiguity

Jennifer Crocker, Kristin Voelkl, Maria Testa, and Brenda Major • State University of New York at Buffalo

Two experiments investigated the hypothesis that the stigmatized can protect self-esteem by attributing negative feedback to prejudice. Fifty-nine women participated in the 1st experiment. Women who received negative feedback from a prejudiced evaluator attributed the feedback to his prejudice and reported less depressed effects than women who received negative feedback from a nonprejudiced evaluator. In the 2nd experiment, 38 Black and 45 White students received interpersonal feedback from a White evaluator, who either could see them or could not. Compared with Whites, Blacks were more likely to attribute negative feedback to prejudice than positive feedback and were more likely to attribute both types of feedback to prejudice when they could be seen by the other student. Being seen by the evaluator buffered the self-esteem of Blacks from negative feedback but hurt the self-esteem of Blacks who received positive feedback.

A great deal of research conducted over the past decades has demonstrated that many social groups are stigmatized in American society. For example, people hold negative stereotypes about Blacks (Brigham, 1974; Hartsough & Fontana, 1970; Karlins, Coffman, & Walters, 1969; Samuels, 1973) and women (Broverman, Vogel, Broverman, Clarkson, & Rosenkrantz, 1972; Heilbrun, 1976; Rosenkrantz, Vogel, Bee, Broverman, & Broverman, 1968), although most people do not characterize these groups in uniformly negative terms (cf. Eagley & Mladinik, 1989; Gaertner & Dovidio, 1986; Katz, Wackenhut, & Hass, 1986). Furthermore, it is well documented that members of these groups are relatively disadvantaged in American society, in terms of either economic or interpersonal outcomes. For example, Blacks of both sexes have fewer eco-

nomic opportunities that do Whites (U.S. Department of Labor, 1978). Obstacles to occupational achievement for Blacks and ethnic minorities at various stages of the employment process have been documented (cf. Braddock & McPartland, 1987). Blacks also have more negative interpersonal outcomes when interacting with the White majority group than do Whites (see Crosby, Bromley, and Saxe, 1980, for a review). Similarly, interpersonal as well as institutional barriers to women's economic advancement are well documented (e.g., Hoiberg, 1982; Kanter, 1977; O'Leary, 1975; Riger & Galligan, 1980; Treiman & Hartman, 1981). Full-time working women typically earn only about 59% of what men earn, in part because the majority of working women are concentrated in female-dominated occupations that earn less than comparable male-dominated occu-

353

pations (Treiman & Hartman, 1981). Women working in more prestigious, male-dominated occupations also face a number of interpersonal barriers (cf. Kanter, 1977), which contribute to the striking underrepresentation of women at the higher ranks of these occupations.

Our concern in this article is with the consequences of prejudice and discrimination for the global personal self-esteem of members of these groups. Self-esteem is widely recognized as a central aspect of psychological functioning (cf. Taylor & Brown, 1988; Wylie, 1979, for reviews) and is strongly related to many other variables, including general satisfaction with one's life (Diener, 1984). Several social psychological theories predict that prejudice and discrimination against members of stigmatized groups will result in lowered self-esteem and diminished self-concept for the stigmatized. For example, the symbolic interactionist perspective (cf. Cooley, 1956; Mead, 1934) posits that the self-concept develops through interactions with others and is a reflection of those others' appraisals of oneself. According to this perspective, members of stigmatized and oppressed groups who are aware that they are regarded negatively by others should incorporate those negative attitudes into the self-concept and consequently should be lower in self-esteem (see Crocker & Major, 1989, for a more extensive discussion).

Research and theory on self-fulfilling prophecies are also consistent with the prediction that social stigma leads to low self-esteem. Self-fulfilling prophecies occur when a perceiver acts on initially false beliefs in such a way that those beliefs come to be confirmed by the behavior of the target (Merton, 1948). Considerable research on self-fulfilling prophecies has documented that targets often come to behave in ways that are consistent with the expectations of others and may alter their self-concept because of this behavior (see Darley & Fazio, 1980; Deaux & Major, 1987; Jones, 1986; Miller & Turnbull, 1986, for reviews). According to this perspective, perceivers who hold negative stereotypes about stigmatized groups may alter their behavior toward members of those groups, so that the stigmatized come to behave and ultimately to see themselves in a manner consistent with those negative stereotypes (cf. Fazio, Effrein, & Falender, 1981). In contrast to the symbolic interactionist perspective, the self-fulfilling prophecy perspective does not require that stigmatized people be aware of the negative attitudes

of others toward their group for those negative attitudes to affect their self-esteem.

Several other theories are also compatible with the prediction that social stigma has negative effects on self-esteem, including theories of efficacy-based self-esteem (Gecas & Schwalbe, 1983), equity theory (Walster, Walster, & Berscheid, 1978), social exchange theory (Thibaut & Kelley, 1959), social comparison theory (Festinger, 1954), and social identity theory (Tajfel & Turner, 1986). This prediction has been widely accepted by social psychologists, to the point that it has been assumed to be true (e.g., Allport, 1954). For example, Cartwright (1950) argued that "the Groups to which a person belongs serve as primary determiners of his self-esteem. To a considerable extent, personal feelings of worth depend on the social evaluation of the group with which a person is identified. Self-hatred and feelings of worthlessness tend to arise from membership in underprivileged or outcast groups." (p. 440) In a similar vein, Erik Erikson wrote, "There is ample evidence of 'inferiority' feelings and of morbid self-hate in all minority groups" (1956, p. 155). Allport (1954) noted that "group oppression may destroy the integrity of the ego entirely, and reverse its normal pride, and create a groveling self-image" (p. 152).

Despite the strong theoretical support for such a prediction, evidence that members of stigmatized groups have lower self-esteem than the non-stigmatized is remarkably scarce (see Crocker & Major, 1989, for a review). For example, a host of studies conclude that Blacks have levels of global personal self-esteem equal to or higher than that of Whites (see Hoelter, 1982; Porter & Washington, 1979; Rosenberg, 1979; Rosenberg & Simmons, 1972; and Wylie, 1979, for reviews of the literature). Similarly, two major reviews of the literature conclude that women do not have lower self-esteem than do men (Maccoby & Jacklin, 1974; Wylie, 1979). Thus, these data contradict predictions derived from the symbolic interactionist and self-fulfilling prophecy literatures.

How are we to account for this discrepancy between theory and data? Recently, Crocker and Major (1989) proposed that several mechanisms buffer the self-esteem of members of stigmatized or oppressed groups from the prejudice of others. One such mechanism is attributing negative feedback or relatively poor outcomes to the prejudiced attitudes of others toward their group. Wright (1960) and others have noted that the stigmatized may assume that their stigma affects all of the behaviors of those who interact with them (see also Kleck and Strenta, 1980). In Kelley's (1972) terms, stigmatized people may follow the discounting principle by attributing negative outcomes not to their level of deservingness, but to an alternative cause: prejudice against their group. Thus, they may discount the negative outcomes and protect their self-esteem.

The hypothesis that attributions for positive and negative outcomes mediate affective reactions to those outcomes is consistent with several theoretical approaches to emotional response (cf. Abramson, Seligman, & Teasdale, 1978; Scheier & Carver, 1988; Weiner, 1980, 1982, 1985, 1986; Weiner, Russell, & Lerman, 1978, 1979), as well as with empirical evidence (cf. MacFarland & Ross, 1982). Both the reformulated helplessness theory of Abramson et al. (1978) and Weiner's attributional analysis of emotion (Weiner, 1985, 1986) deal explicitly with the implications for self-esteem of causal attributions for positive and negative outcomes. Internal attributions for negative outcomes, and external attributions for positive outcomes, are proposed to result in lowered self-esteem. Empirical research is generally consistent with this prediction (e.g., Brewin & Furnham, 1986; Crocker, Alloy, & Kayne, 1988; Tennen & Herzberger, 1987; Weiner et al., 1978, 1979).

Because prejudice against one's group is an external attribution for negative outcomes, this attribution should protect the self-esteem of stigmatized people. Evidence for this self-protective function of attributing negative outcomes to prejudice is provided by studies in which women or members of minority groups received negative feedback or poor outcomes from an evaluator who might have been prejudiced against them (see Dion, 1986, for a review). In one study, female subjects received negative feedback from an evaluator. Following receipt of the feedback, those subjects who believed that they had been discriminated against were higher in self-esteem than were those who did not believe that they had been discriminated against (Dion, 1975; see also Dion & Earn, 1975).

The results of this internal analysis are consistent with the hypothesis that people who are initially high in self-esteem are more likely to attribute negative outcomes to prejudice against their group. More direct evidence for the self-protective function of making attributions to prejudice would be provided by a study in which the perception of prejudice or discrimination was manipulated, rather than simply measured. The studies described in this article addressed this issue by manipulated causal attributions.

Of course, members of stigmatized groups do not receive uniformly negative outcomes or feedback from members of the majority group. At times, the stigmatized may received especially positive feedback or outcomes from the nonstigmatized (Katz, 1981). Causal attributions for these positive events may also have implications for self-esteem. According to Kelley's (1972) augmentation principle, when one can view positive feedback as occurring in spite of prejudice against one's group one should be particularly likely to attribute the positive outcomes to one's high level of skill, ability, or deservingness. Just this pattern was observed in a study by Major, Carrington, and Carnevale (1984). In their study, attractive and unattractive college students wrote an essay, which was evaluated positively by a (bogus) opposite-sex peer, who the subjects believed either could see them or could not see them. The subjects believed that the evaluator was currently unattached and was looking for someone to become involved with. Hence, he or she could have had ulterior reasons for their evaluating their essay positively. Consistent with Kelley's (1972) augmenting principle, unattractive subjects were more likely to believe that the positive evaluation was due to the high quality of their essays when they could be seen by the evaluator than when they could not be seen. Attractive subjects, on the other hand, appeared to discount the positive feedback. They were less likely to attribute the positive evaluation to the quality of their essay when they could be seen than when they could not be seen by the evaluator (see also Sigall & Michela, 1976). On the basis of Kelley's augmenting principle, then, we might predict that the stigmatized will have higher self-esteem when they receive positive feedback from an evaluator they believe is prejudiced in relation to when they receive positive feedback from an evaluator they do not believe is prejudiced.

A second response the stigmatized might show when they receive positive feedback is to discount it. That is, although the stigmatized may sometimes feel that others are prejudiced against them and that to receive positive feedback they must overcome this prejudice, they may also sometimes believe they receive favorable treatment because of their stigma. Specifically, if the stigmatized believe that others are being nice to them or evaluating their work positively out of sympathy for their condition or fear of appearing prejudiced, then positive outcomes should not enhance, and may even decrease, self-esteem.

Recent evidence on the nature of attitudes toward some stigmatized groups supports this possibility. Research on attitudes toward the physically handicapped indicates that people are ambivalent. Their feelings of revulsion and disgust are mixed with feelings of sympathy and concern (cf. Katz, 1981). Furthermore, research on responses to the handicapped indicates that people often behave more positively than the handicapped than toward the nonhandicapped (cf. Kleck, Ono, & Hastorf, 1966). Similarly, attitudes toward Blacks tend to be ambivalent: Negative attitudes are again mixed with feelings of sympathy and concern (cf. Gaertner & Dovidio, 1986; Katz et al., 1986). Again, research indicated that White subjects sometimes respond more favorably to Blacks who are in need (Gaertner & Dovidio, 1977) or evaluate them more positively than similar White targets (Linville & Jones, 1980).

These positive responses toward the stigmatized might reflect either genuine feelings of sympathy and concern or a desire to avoid the appearance of being prejudiced. Most people think of themselves as nonprejudiced and egalitarian, supporting equal rights for Blacks (cf. Gaertner & Dovidio, 1986) as well as for other stigmatized groups (cd. Katz et al., 1986). To avoid appearing prejudiced, either to themselves or to others, people may respond in exaggeratedly positive ways toward the stigmatized under certain circumstances (cf. Gaertner & Dovidio, 1986; Katz, 1981, Katz et al., 1986).

Because of this ambivalence, the stigmatized may be placed in a situation of attributional ambiguity. Positive responses from others might indicate that others think they are genuinely deserving (for example, because their work is good or because they are truly liked), they might indicate feelings of sympathy or they might indicate a desire to avoid appearing prejudiced. When positive responses can be attributed to one's deservingness, self-esteem should increase. However, when they are attributed to others' feeling sorry for one's plight, self-esteem should not increase and may even decrease.

Whether the stigmatized augment or discount positive feedback may vary from group to group. That is, it may seem plausible to members of some stigmatized groups that the nonstigmatized would respond positively to them out of pity or to avoid appearing prejudiced, whereas these attributions might seem quite unlikely to members of other stigmatized groups. Support for this notion has been provided in a study of evaluations of Black, handicapped, and nonstigmatized people (Carver, Glass, & Katz, 1977). In that study, subjects evaluated an interviewer either in a bogus pipeline condition, in which subjects believed the researchers could access their true feelings by assessing their physiological responses, or in a control condition. The results showed that the handicapped interviewer was rated more positively than the nonstigmatized interviewer in both conditions, suggesting that subjects had genuinely positive reactions to the handicapped target, perhaps out of sympathy for his plight. The Black interviewer, however, was rated more positively than the nonstigmatized interviewer in the control condition but more negatively in the bogus pipeline condition, suggesting that the positive evaluations of the Black in the control condition were due to social desirability or self-presentation concerns.

Thus, for members of some stigmatized groups, the possibility that others will respond positively out of sympathy or to avoid appearing prejudiced is quite real. Members of those groups might be aware of that possibility and adjust their attributions for positive feedback accordingly.

To address these issues, we conducted two experiments in which members of a stigmatized group received either positive or negative feedback from an evaluator, whom they either did or did not have reason to suspect was prejudiced. In the first study, female subjects received either a positive or a negative evaluation of an essay they had written by a man whom they either believed was prejudiced against women or was not prejudiced. Attributions for the feedback, self-esteem, and mood were then assessed. We predicted that the women would discount negative feedback from the prejudiced evaluator and that this would buffer their sell-esteem and affect. We predicted that in the positive feedback condition, the women might either augment or discount the feedback.

Experiment 1

Method

Subjects. Fifty-nine women from introductory psychology classes participated in the study in exchange for experimental credit. Fifty-one of the subjects had participated in a group-testing session held early in the semester at which they filled out the Rosenberg Self-Esteem Scale (Rosenberg, 1965), used as a pretest measure.

Procedure. Subjects participated individually. They were instructed, by means of tape, that the experiment involved attitude assessment and that "we [were] interested in what kinds of attitudes college students hold, in how they express and defend those attitudes, and in how they respond to other people's attitudes." Subjects were led to believe that they would be writing an essay expressing their opinion on a current topic, which would be critiqued by a second subject, seated in a different room in the laboratory (who was actually fictitious). Subjects were first asked to complete an attitude survey. The 25-item survey asked about subjects' altitudes toward a variety of current issues, including drugs, national defense, and homosexuality. Five items on the survey assessed subjects' attitudes regarding women's roles in society. Subjects were to indicate their attitude using a 5-point scale (ranging from *strongly disagree* to *strongly agree*) for each statement. In addition, subjects were asked to indicate their age and sex, but not their name, on the survey. Subjects were given 10 min to complete the attitude survey.

After subjects had completed the survey, the experimenter returned to collect the questionnaire and to explain the essay task. All subjects were assigned to write about why homosexuals should or should not be given equal rights. They were instructed to be as persuasive as possible and to try to convince others of the correctness of their views.

After 10 min had elapsed, a second set of tape-recorded instructions announced the end of the writing period and explained the critiquing phase of the experiment. The experimenter explained (on the tape) that each subject would evaluate the other person's essay for clarity, quality of argument, and persuasiveness. Subjects were told to evaluate the essays objectively rather than to criticize the other person's point of view. They were told to be honest with each other and that their identities would never be revealed to each other. Subjects were led to believe that each of them would have the chance to critique the other's essay; however, for the third session, the "other" (fictional) subject would evaluate the (actual) subject's essay.

After the taped instructions ended, the experimenter entered the room with the survey ostensi-

bly completed by the other subject. Subjects were asked if they would mind sharing their attitude questionnaire with the other subject; all agreed. The experimenter then gave the subject the completed survey, explaining that the other subject had agreed to share his questionnaire. The experimenter also collected the subject's essay, ostensibly to give it to the other subject, and left so the subject could peruse the completed survey. Information written on the questionnaire indicated that the other subject was an 18-year-old man. Responses to the attitude items on the questionnaire were identical in all conditions, with the exception of the five items assessing attitudes toward women. Subjects in the prejudiced evaluator condition received a questionnaire on which the other subject had indicated agreement with the statements that women should avoid fields like engineering because they lack mathematical ability (*agree*); that women benefit more from divorce than men do because they receive child support and alimony (*strongly agree*); and that women, who are less serious about their jobs, take jobs away from men with families to support (*strongly agree*). The other subject also indicated disagreement with the statements that husband and wives should share housework if they both work full-time (*disagree*), and that women and men should receive equal pay for work that is similar (*disagree*). In the nonprejudiced evaluator conditions, the experimenter expressed liberal views on these issues.

Four items on the attitude survey concerned gay rights and related issues. To control the perceived agreement of the evaluator with the subject on these issues, in all conditions the evaluator's survey indicated that he held moderately liberal views on these issues. He agreed that homosexuals should have equal rights like everyone else and disagreed with the statements that we should crack down on homosexuals to deter the spread of antiimmunodeficiency syndrome (AIDS), that children with AIDS should not be allowed to go to schools where they can infect other children, and that AIDS testing of government and military employees should be mandatory.

After a few minutes, the subject heard the other subject's voice (actually prerecorded) over the audio system. In the positive feedback conditions, the other subject indicated that he thought the essay was clear and persuasive and that the arguments were well presented. In the negative feedback condition, the other subject stated that the essay was weak, that many arguments were ignored, and that it was not persuasive.

Subjects were told that before they critiqued the other student's essay, it was important to control for their current mood state, so they would he asked to complete an additional questionnaire, which actually contained the dependent measures. Subjects completed the Rosenberg Self-Esteem Scale and a short mood scale and rated the other subject on six 7-point scales: Unfair, Sincere, Cold, Snobby, Intelligent, and Pleasant. They answered several items assessing their attributions for the other subject's evaluation of their essay, including the extent to which their partner's evaluation was due to his attitudes toward women. Manipulation checks were also included. Subjects were then fully debriefed regarding the purpose of the study, and any suspicions regarding the study were assessed.

Materials. The mood scale consisted of four items from each of three subscales or the Multiple Affect Adjective Check List (MAACL; Zuckerman & Lubin, 1965), which have been used as a short mood scale in previous research (Testa & Major, 1990). The MAACL and each of its subscales have good internal consistency and low test–retest reliability, as would be expected of a measure of transient mood (Zuckerman & Lubin, 1965). The four Hostility items were angry, cruel, agreeable, and cooperative; the Anxiety items were fearful, worried, secure, and calm; and the Depression items were blue, discouraged, fine, and active (for each subscale, the last two items were reverse scored).

The Rosenberg Self-Esteem Scale is a 10-item measure of global personal self-esteem. It has high internal consistency and good test–retest reliability (.80) over a 6-week period. The Rosenberg scale is widely used as a measure of general self-esteem, not specific to particular domains of life. It contains items such as, "I feel I am a person of worth, at least on an equal basis with others," and "I often feel like a failure."

Results

The data were analyzed using 2 (prejudiced or nonprejudiced evaluator) × 2 (positive or negative feedback) analyses of variance (ANOVAS).

Manipulation Checks. To determine whether subjects had perceived the feedback correctly, they were asked how their partner had evaluated their work. There was a strong main effect for feedback,

$F(1, 55) = 142.83, p < .001$, indicating that subjects in the positive condition thought their essay had been evaluated more positively ($M = 6.23$) than did negative feedback subjects ($M = 2.68$). No other main effects or interactions were significant on this measure.

Attributions. Subjects were asked the extent to which they believed the evaluation they received was the result of their partner's attitude toward women. ANOVA on this item revealed a significant Evaluator Prejudice × Feedback interaction, $F(1, 55) = 3.46, p < .02$. Simple effect tests (cf. Winer, 1971) revealed that consistent with our predictions, in the negative feedback conditions, the evaluation was significantly more likely to be attributed to the evaluator's attitudes toward women if he had expressed attitudes against women's changing roles in society ($M = 4.15$) than if he had expressed liberal attitudes ($M = 2.33, p < .05$). In the positive feedback conditions, the evaluation was equally likely to be attributed to his attitudes toward women, regardless of whether the evaluator expressed favorable ($M = 3.15$) or unfavorable ($M = 3.11, ns$) attitudes toward women's changing roles.

Mood. The four items within each mood scale were averaged. The three model subscales were analyzed independently, using a 2 × 2 ANOVA. Analysis of the Depression subscale revealed an interaction, $F(1, 54) = 3.89, p < .056$. Simple main effect tests indicated that those subjects who received negative feedback experienced more depressed affect if the evaluator had favorable attitudes toward women's nontraditional roles ($M = 11.53$) than if he had unfavorable attitudes ($M = 8.54, p < .05$). When the feedback was positive, subjects experienced the same level of depressive affect regardless of whether the evaluator had favorable or unfavorable attitudes toward women's changing roles ($Ms = 8.77$ and 9.59, respectively, ns).

There was a main effect of feedback on hostility, $F(1,54) = 16.59$, so that subjects who received negative feedback were more hostile ($M = 9.64$) than were those who received positive feedback ($M = 6.23$). There were no additional significant main effective interactions on the Hostility measure or on the Anxiety measure.

Self-esteem. Scores on the Rosenberg Self-Esteem Scale were analyzed by subtracting pretest scores from the posttest scores and performing an ANOVA on the change scores. The analysis revealed a nonsignificant interaction, $F(1,46) = 1.53$,

$p = .22$. Although this interaction was nonsignificant, the pattern of means was in the predicted direction. Specifically, self-esteem tended to drop when negative feedback was received from a nonprejudiced evaluator and rose in all other conditions.

Ratings of the Evaluator. Ratings of the evaluator on the positive items were reverse scored, so that for all items, higher scores indicated a more negative rating of the other subject. The individual scales were highly correlated (*rs* ranged from .35 to .67), so the scores were summed across all six items.[1] An ANOVA on this summed score revealed a main effect of feedback, so that the evaluator was rated more negatively in the negative feedback conditions ($M = 18.71$) than in the positive feedback conditions ($M = 10.94$), $F(1,54) = 28.66$, $p < .01$. No other effects reached statistical significance on this measure.

Discussion

The results of this study provide preliminary support for our hypothesis that attributing negative outcomes to the prejudice of others has self-protective consequences. Subjects appeared to use the discounting principle and attributed negative feedback from a prejudiced evaluator to the evaluator's prejudice. They also experienced less depressed affect after receipt of negative feedback, if they had previously learned that the evaluator has negative attitudes toward women. The effects of evaluator prejudice on mood appeared to be specific to depression. Although subjects reported more hostility and were more likely to derogate the evaluator following the receipt of negative feedback than of positive feedback, this effect was not moderated by the evaluator's attitudes toward women. Thus, all subjects who received negative feedback apparently felt angry, but only those who could not attribute the feedback to prejudice internalized the feedback.

Results on the self-esteem measure, although in the predicted direction, were not significant, perhaps because the pretest was taken far in advance (from 2 to 10 weeks) of the posttest and in a different testing context (a large group taking a large number of tests vs. individual subjects taking a small number of tests), and because pretest scores were not available for several of the subjects. Alternatively, the nonsignificant results on the self-

esteem scale may be substantively meaningful. That is, perhaps the self-esteem of women is not as vulnerable to feedback from male evaluators (whether prejudiced or not) as we hypothesized.

The results in the positive feedback conditions showed no support for either the augmenting or the discounting hypothesis. Although nonsignificant, the trend was in the direction of discounting of positive feedback: Subjects had nonsignificantly lower depressed affect and higher self-esteem when they received positive feedback from an evaluator who was not prejudiced, as compared with an evaluator who was prejudiced.

Experiment 2

Experiment 2 was conducted to further explore attributions and affective reactions to positive and negative feedback with a different stigmatized group. Black college students received either positive or negative interpersonal feedback from a White peer. Similar to the study by Major et al. (1984), described earlier, the Black subjects believed that the White evaluator either could see them or could not see them and hence was unaware of their race. We predicted that when they received negative feedback and could be seen by the evaluator, the Black students would attribute the feedback to prejudice. Consequently, their self-esteem would not suffer, as compared with when they could not be seen by the evaluator, and could not attribute the negative feedback to prejudice. Again, predictions under conditions of positive feedback were less clear. If subjects use the augmenting principle, then they should have higher self-esteem when the evaluator can see them, because they believe that they received the feedback in spite of their race. If they are aware that the nonstigmatized sometimes evaluate Blacks positively out of self-presentational concerns, however, they might discount positive feedback. In this case, we predicted that they would not have higher and might even have lower self-esteem when they could be seen by the evaluator, because they would feel that they had received the feedback because of their race, not in spite of it.

Method

Subjects. Thirty-eight Black and 45 White students participated in the study. Fifty of the 83 sub-

---

[1] Negative items (unfair, cold, and snobby) were reverse scored.

jects participated in partial fulfillment of a requirement for their introductory psychology course; the remaining subjects were recruited through an advertisement in the campus newspaper and were paid $5 for their participation.

Procedure. Subjects were scheduled to participate alone. On arrival at the experiment, subjects were met by a White, female experimenter who told them that another student had arrived a bit early and was already seated in an adjacent room (the other subject was fictional). Subjects were then led into the experimental room, which was equipped with one-way mirrors and a table. On entering the room, subjects were seated at the table and were asked to sign a consent form.

The experimenter then explained that the study concerned friendship development and was designed to investigate why people make friends and the problems they may have in developing friendships. Subjects were told that some students would be paired with another student of the same race and others would be paired with a student of another race. All subjects were then informed that they had been randomly selected to be paired with a White student, who was already seated in an adjacent room. In all cases, the fictitious student was said to be the same sex as the subject.

Subjects were then asked to fill out the Rosenberg Self-Esteem Scale (1965), which was said to be related to and predictive of friendship development. Then subjects were asked to fill out a self-description form that included questions about the subjects' likes and dislikes, strengths and weaknesses, and personal qualities. Subjects were told that their answers to these questions would be shown to the other student, who would use this information to determine whether the two of them could become friends.

At this point, depending on random assignment to one or two conditions, subjects were either told that the blinds covering the one-way mirror would be raised so the other student would be able to see them or that they would be left down so the other student could not see them. The explanation for the blinds up condition was that being able to see another person helps in the acquaintance process. In the blinds down condition, the experimenter explained that the blinds would be left down because first impressions could often be affected by appearances. Once the subject had answered the questions on the self-description form, the experimenter left to show it to the other subject. Before

leaving, the experimenter told the subject to relax for a few minutes and that they would learn the other student's reactions soon.

The experimenter returned to the room with either a very favorable or a very unfavorable response from the other subject. The feedback form indicated the (bogus) student's sex (which was the same as that of the subject) and race (which was always White). The form also showed the (bogus) student's answers to questions about how much they would like to be in a small class with the subject, work closely at a job with the subject, and be roommates with the subject. As the questions became increasingly intimate, the (bogus) student's answers became increasingly positive or negative.

After subjects received and read the feedback, they completed some additional questionnaires, including a second version of the Rosenberg Self-Esteem Scale. The Rosenberg scale was embedded within the questions from the Janis-Field Feelings of Inadequacy Scale (Janis & Field, 1959), and the response scale was altered to match the response format of the Janis-Field, to disguise the fact that subjects were completing the Rosenberg scale for a second time.

After the self-esteem scale, subjects completed measures of positive and negative mood taken from MacFarland and Ross (1982). On the basis of a factor analysis reported by MacFarland and Ross, the Positive Mood scale included 17 items (satisfied, pleased, delighted, joyful, content, happy, good, composed, hopeful, optimistic, thankful, grateful, excited, lively, exhilarated, energetic, and refreshed). The Negative Mood scale included 29 items (disappointed, dissatisfied, displeased, discouraged, downhearted, discontent, sad, depressed, blue, troubled, gloomy, frustrated, upset, hopeless, pessimistic, worried, unsafe, fearful, insecure, panicked, helpless, angry, mad, disgusted, vindictive, calm, relaxed, safe, and secure); ratings on the last four items were reverse scored. Subjects were asked to rate the extent to which each item "represents how you feel right now" on a scale ranging from *not at all* (1) to *extremely* (11).

Subjects were then asked to indicate the degree to which various factors had influenced the other student's response to them, including the subject's sex, race, and religion, the subject's personality, and the other student's racism. They also indicated the degree to which they had been discriminated against by the other student. Subjects also rated the extent to which the other student was sincere, cold, fair, snobby, intelligent, pleasant, and racist. Finally, as manipulation checks, subjects were asked to indicate the race and sex of the other subject, the degree to which the other subject had liked them, and whether the other subject could see them. All ratings were made on scales ranging from *not at all* (1) to *very much* (5). Subjects were then fully debriefed about the nature of the study, were probed for suspicion, and were asked not to discuss the study with anyone else who might participate.

Results

The data were analyzed with 2 (race of subject: Black or White) × 2 (feedback: positive or negative) × 2 (visibility: blinds up or blinds down) ANOVAS.

Manipulation Checks. All subjects correctly identified the race of the other student as White. Seventy-seven of 83 (92.7%) correctly identified whether the other subject could see them. An ANOVA on this latter item revealed only a main effect of whether the blinds were up or down, $F(1,75) = 176.54, p < .0001$. No other main effects or interactions were significant on this measure. Analysis of the degree to which subjects believed the other student liked them revealed a main effect of feedback $F(1,75) = 452.66, p < .0001$, so that subjects in the positive feedback condition thought the evaluator liked them more ($M = 4.26$) than did subjects in the negative feedback conditions ($M = 1.31$). No other main effects or interactions were significant on this measure.

Attributions of Feedback. Subjects indicated the extent to which they felt the other's response to them was due to their race, the other's racism, and the other's discrimination. These items are conceptually similar and form an index of attributions to racism with acceptable internal consistency (Cronbach's alpha = .76). Consequently, they were combined into a single measure, with a possible range from 3 to 15, with higher numbers indicating more attribution to prejudice.

An ANOVA performed on this composite attribution measure revealed a main effect of subjects's race, so that Black students attributed the feedback more to prejudice ($M = 6.58$) than did White students ($M = 4.89$, $F(1,74) = 11.30, p < .002$. There was also a main effect of feedback when they received negative feedback ($M = 6.93$) than when they received positive feedback ($M = 4.53$), $F(1,$

TABLE 20.1. Attributions to Prejudice as a Function of Race of Subject, Feedback, and Visibility

| | Visibility | | | |
| | Black | | White | |
Feedback	Seen	Unseen	Seen	Unseen
Positive	5.62	3.40	4.70	4.40
Negative	9.58	7.70	5.63	4.81

Note. Means fall on a scale ranging from *not at all due to prejudice* (3) to *very much due to prejudice* (15).

74) $= 22.90, p < .0001$, and a main effect of visibility, indicating that subjects made greater attributions to prejudice when they thought the other student could see them ($M = 6.39$) than when they thought the other student could not see them ($M = 5.08$), $F(1, 74) = 6.77, p < .02$. The feedback main effect was qualified by an interaction with race $F(1, 74) = 16.25, p < .0001$, and the visibility main effect was qualified by a nonsignificant interaction with race, $F(1, 74) = 2.22, p < .14$. The three-way interaction between race, feedback, and visibility was not significant, $F(1,74) = 0.06, p > .80$. Table 20.1 contains means for these interactions. To interpret the interactions, we analyzed the data separately for Blacks and Whites.[2] For Blacks, the effects of feedback, $F(1,36) = 24.12, p < .0001$, and visibility, $F(1, 36) = 5.97, p < .02$ were highly significant. For Whites, neither the effect of feedback, $F(1, 38) = 1,42, p > .24$, nor the effect of visibility, $F(1,38) = 0.97, p > .33$, reached statistical significance, although the reader should bear in mind that the Race × Visibility interaction did not reach statistical significance.

Subjects also indicated the extent to which they thought the other student's reaction to them was due to the subject's personality. Analysis of this item revealed a man effect of feedback, $F(1,74) = 5.71, p < .02$, so that subjects indicated the feedback was due to their own personality more when the feedback was positive ($M = 3.73$) than when it was negative ($M = 3.19$). There was also a Race × Visibility interaction, $F(1, 74) = 7.96, p < .007$, which indicated that Black subjects were more likely to attribute the feedback to their personality

---

[2]The items assessing attributions to racism and discrimination may have been confusing to White subjects who received feedback from a White evaluator. Hence, we expected that White subjects might show greater variance on these items, which in fact they did. This greater variance among Whites could obscure effects obtained for Black subjects. As a result, we analyzed this item separately for Black and White subjects.

when they could not be seen ($M = 3.80$) than when they could be seen ($M = 2.89$, $p < .05$), whereas this effect was nonsignificant and in the opposite direction for White subjects ($Ms = 3.40$ and 3.75 in the blinds down and blinds up conditions, respectively). The three-way interaction between race, visibility, and feedback was not significant, indicating that Black students were more likely to attribute both positive and negative feedback to their personality when the blinds were down.

Self-Esteem. Preliminary analyses indicated that pretest self-esteem was a significant predictor of posttest self-esteem; however, the strength of this relationship varied substantially between conditions of the experiment, violating the assumptions of analysis of covariance. Consequently, self-esteem following receipt of the feedback was analyzed by standardizing scores on the pretest and posttest measures of self-esteem (because the two measures used different response scales), then subtracting pretest and posttest scores.[3] The resulting means indicate change in self-esteem (expressed in standard deviation units); higher numbers indicate an increase in self-esteem. An ANOVA performed on this measure revealed that only the three-way interaction between race, feedback, and visibility was significant $F(1, 73) = 4.37$, $p < .04$. Table 20.2 contains the means for this interaction. To interpret this interaction, we analyzed the data for Black and White subjects separately. For White subjects, the Feedback × Visibility interaction was not significant ($p > .60$), but for Black subjects, the interaction was significant, $F(1, 35) = 6.20$, $p < .02$. Further analysis of this interaction for Black and White subjects indicated that the visibility of the subject had a significant effect in the positive feedback condition ($p > .10$). The direction of the means suggested that having the blinds up tended to protect the self-esteem of Black students following negative feedback, in relation to the blinds down conditions.

Ratings of the Other Subject. Subjects rated the extent to which the other subject was cold, unfair, snobby, sincere, intelligent, and pleasant. Ratings on the positive items were reverse scored, and the ratings were then averaged to provide an index of evaluations of the other subject, with higher numbers indicating more negative evaluations. The index was internally consistent, as indicated by Cronbach's alpha (.94). An ANOVA on this index revealed a main effect of feedback, $F(1,74) = 160.15$, $p < .0001$, and a Feedback × Race inter-

action, $F(1,74) = 4.37$, $p < .04$. Although all students rated the other subject significantly more negatively after negative feedback than after positive feedback, this effect was more pronounced for Black subjects ($Ms = 1.46$ and 3.58 for positive and negative feedback, respectively) than for White subjects ($Ms = 1.62$ and 3.14, respectively).

Subjects also indicated the extent to which they thought the other subject was racist.[4] An ANOVA on this item revealed marginally significant main effect of subject race, $F(1, 75) = 3.52$, $p < .07$, so that Black subjects thought the other subject was more racist ($M = 1.97$) than did White subjects ($M = 1.59$). There was also a main effect of feedback, $F(1, 75) = 41.25$, $p < .0001$, so that subjects thought the evaluator was more racist after negative feedback ($M = 2.43$) than after positive feedback ($M = 1.13$). These main effects were qualified by a Race × Feedback interaction, $F(1, 75) = 4.00$, $p < .05$, which indicated that Black students were significantly more likely to rate the evaluator as racist after negative feedback ($M = 2.82$) than positive feedback ($M = 1.13$, $p < .05$), whereas White students were less likely to show this effect ($Ms = $

---

[3]We recognize that there are many problems with using difference scores as dependent measures. Consequently, we also conducted an analysis in which we corrected posttest self-esteem scores for pretest self-esteem by regressing posttest self-esteem on pretest self-esteem separately within condition and computing a corrected self-esteem score by multiplying pretest self-esteem by the unstandardized regression weight (B) obtained in the regression equation for that condition and subtracting this quantity from posttest self-esteem. Analysis of variance with race, feedback, and visibility as between-subjects variables was then conducted on this corrected self-esteem score. The analysis revealed a very similar pattern of results to that obtained with different scores, with one notable exception. There was a significant interaction between visibility and race, $F(1,73) = 5.51$, $p < .022$, indicating that the visibility manipulation affected the self-esteem of Black subjects, but not Whites. For Black subjects, self-esteem was higher when the blinds were down ($M = .30$) than when they were up ($M = -.28$, $p < .05$). This interaction was qualified by a three-way interaction between race, visibility, and feedback, which indicated that the visibility manipulation significantly affected the self-esteem of Blacks after positive feedback, but not after negative feedback, $F(1,73) = 4.31$, $F < .04$, as we found in the analysis of difference scores.

[4]Because this item involves a trait attribution to the evaluator rather than an attribution for a specific outcome, it is conceptually distinct from the attribution to prejudice items described earlier. Furthermore, correlational analyses indicated that this item was not strongly correlated with the attribution items (rs ranging from .10 to .28). Consequently, this item was analyzed separately.

1.15 and 2.03 for positive and negative feedback, respectively, *ns*).

Positive Mood. The positive mood items from MacFarland and Ross (1982) formed an internally consistent index, as indicated by Cronbach's alpha (.94). The positive mood items were summed to create an index of positive mood with a possible range from 17 to 187. An ANOVA on this index revealed a main effect of feedback, indicating that subjects in the positive feedback conditions experienced more positive mood (*M* = 123.41) than did subjects in the negative feedback conditions (*M* = 100.91), $F(1, 72) = 12.25$, $p < .0008$. This main effect was qualified by a Race × Feedback interaction, $F(1,72) = 3.93, p < .05$. The interaction indicated that White subjects experienced less positive mood after negative feedback (*M* = 89.38) than did Black subjects (*M* = 112.35, $p < .05$), although the two groups of subjects did not differ in their responses to positive feedback (*M*s = 122.7 and 122. 12 for White and Black subjects, respectively). There was also a marginally significant Race × Visibility interaction, $F(1,72) = 2.71, p < .10$, which indicated that Black subjects tended to experience more positive mood when the blinds were down (*M* = 125.44) than when they were up (*M* = 109.03), whereas White subjects tended to experience more positive mood when the blinds were up (*M* = 109.44) than when they were down (*M* = 104.63).

Negative Mood. When the appropriate items were reverse scored, the negative mood items formed an internally consistent index (Chronbach's alpha = .96). An ANOVA performed on the negative mood index revealed two main effects. Blacks subjects experienced less negative mood (*M* = 79.30) than did White subjects (*M* = 99.06), $F(1,72) = 4.14, p < .05$, and overall, subjects experienced more negative mood after negative feedback (*M* = 105.05) than after positive feedback (*M* = 73.31), $F(1, 72) = 10.68, p < .002$.

Discussion

Data from the attribution items indicated that Black subjects were more likely than White subjects to attribute the feedback they received to prejudice when they received negative rather than positive feedback and when the evaluator could see them, hence was aware of their race, than when they were not seen. Black students were also somewhat less likely to believe that the feedback was due to their

Table 20.2. Changes in Self-Esteem as a Function of Race of Subject. Valence of Feedback, and Visibility of Subject

	Role of subject			
	Black		White	
Feedback	Seen	Unseen	Seen	Unseen
Positive	−0.50	0.40	0.38	0.04
Negative	0.06	−0.47	0.07	−0.03

personality if they could be seen by the evaluator than if the evaluator was blind to their race. Thus, from these data, Black students apparently tend to discount interpersonal feedback from White evaluators, especially when they know that the White evaluator can see them, hence is aware of their race.[5] In contrast, the attributions of White subjects were not significantly affected by either the valence of the feedback or whether the evaluator could see them.

These data support our hypothesis that Black students exist in a state of attributional ambiguity regarding the causes of the feedback, both positive and negative, they receive from their White peers. Only when positive feedback was received from a White evaluator who was unaware of their race did Black students indicate that the feedback was not at all due to prejudice. Note that the Black students indicted some uncertainty regarding whether the feedback they received was due to prejudice. Even when they were most likely to

_____

[5]We assumed that when the blinds were up, subjects believed that the other subject was aware of their race and when the blinds were down, they believed the other subject was unaware of their race. Unfortunately, we neglected to include a manipulation check on this assumption. It is possible, because subjects were told that the study concerned race, that all subjects believed the other subject knew their race. If this is true, the visibility manipulation must have manipulated some other conceptual variable. A logical candidate would be objective self-awareness, because when the blinds were up, subjects faced a one-way mirror. According to this view, when the blinds were up, Black subjects focused on their race, which was salient, and therefore made greater attributions to prejudice. However, we think it is unlikely that the effects of visibility manipulation can be entirely explained by objective self-awareness. First, we know of no evidence that when Blacks are objectively self-aware, they make more attributions to prejudice or racism. Second, objective self-awareness leads to more internal attributions, whereas racism constitutes an external attribution. Furthermore, contrary to the predictions of objective self-awareness theory, Black students made less, not more attributions to their personality in the blinds up conditions.

364 ■ Stereotypes and Prejudice

indicate that prejudice contributed to the feedback they received (in the negative feedback, blinds up condition), the mean attribution to prejudice was 9.58, on a scale with a midpoint of 9. Thus, receiving negative feedback, or being evaluated when one's race is known to the evaluator, apparently raises the possibility that prejudice was a factor in the evaluation but by no means exclusively demonstrates that it was a factor, in the view of our subjects. (Of course, the moderate responses on this scale may reflect a reluctance to accuse someone of prejudice, rather than the opinion that they are not prejudiced.)

This attributional ambiguity appears to have self-protective consequences for Blacks who received negative feedback. They reported more positive affect after negative feedback than did White subjects. Self-esteem also was protected by attributional strategy: When Black students received negative feedback and could be seen by the evaluator, they were less likely to attribute the feedback to prejudice, and their self-esteem did not suffer. In contrast, when the evaluator could see them, the Black students were somewhat less likely to attribute the feedback to prejudice, and their self-esteem tended to drop after negative feedback. Neither of these effects of visibility in the negative feedback condition reached statistical significance, however, perhaps because of the high level of attributions to prejudice in the negative feedback conditions, regardless of whether the subject thought he or she was visible to the evaluator.

Of particular interest were the reactions of Black students to positive feedback from the White evaluator. We hypothesized that Black students could either use an augmenting strategy, and feel particularly good after positive feedback when the evaluator knew their race, or Black students could use a discounting strategy. The data provided clear evidence that Black students discounted the positive feedback, but only when they knew the evaluator was aware of their race. Indeed, when the blinds were down, hence the evaluator did not know their race, Black subjects tended to believe the positive feedback had nothing to do with their race, racism, or discrimination. Across these three items, the means for black students on the attributions to prejudice items (3.40) was close to the endpoint of the scale (3.0), indicating that the Black students thought the feedback was not at all due to discrimination in this condition.

This attributional ambiguity created when Black students received positive feedback and the blinds were up appeared to hurt, rather than buffer, self-esteem. Indeed, the self-esteem of Black students felt when they received positive feedback with the blinds up but increased when they received positive feedback with the blinds down.

This pattern of results suggests that the stigmatized may be particularly sensitive to the motives underlying the positive feedback they receive. Blacks may be aware that Whites often respond more positively toward them because they are Black, as recent data show (cf. Carver et al., 1977; Gaertner & Dovidio, 1977; Linville & Jones, 1980). For the stigmatized, positive feedback may have positive consequences for self-esteem only when they are certain the feedback reflects their deservingness, rather than some special consideration or a fear of appearing prejudiced on the part of the nonstigmatized. Consequently, Blacks may sometimes prefer social transactions in which their race is not know to others.

The results of this study indicate that the valence of the feedback received from another student and the visibility of the subjects to the evaluator had stronger effects on Black students than on White students. This pattern was true for the attributions subjects make regarding the feedback for self-esteem, for positive mood, and for ratings of the evaluator. In interpreting this pattern, keep in mind that the race of the evaluator was always White, so the Black students were always evaluated by someone of a different race, whereas White students were always evaluated by someone of the same race. The interracial quality of the interaction may have made the Black students particularly concerned about the feedback overall, because it was a same-race context. The effects of race of subject and the interracial nature of the interaction cannot be disentangled in the design of this study. However, because Black students on predominantly White college campuses and Blacks in general in predominantly White settings are more likely to be evaluated by Whites than are Whites by Blacks, the conditions of this study reflect the circumstances that are both objectively more common and theoretically most interesting. At present, however, it is not clear whether this pattern of results characterizes only the responses of this stigmatized interacting with the nonstigmatized or whether they characterize any intergroup interaction.

General Discussion

These studies provided the clearest evidence to date that the stigmatized will attribute negative outcomes to prejudice against their group when such an attribution is plausible (e.g., when they know that the evaluator has negative attitudes toward their group and when the evaluator is aware of their group membership). This discounting of negative feedback appears to have self-protective consequences for the stigmatized.

However, neither of these studies provided evidence that the stigmatized tend to augment positive feedback from a prejudiced evaluator. Indeed, Experiment 2 suggested that the stigmatized may be suspicious of the motives underlying positive feedback and that if they believe such feedback is due to racism, their self-esteem will suffer. This pattern of results appears to be inconsistent with the work of Sigall and Michela (1976) and that of Major et al. (1984), which showed that unattractive subjects tended to augment positive feedback from an opposite-sex evaluator. Although these results are apparently inconsistent, we believe they reflect the same underlying process—that is, that evaluations from others are discounted when one has a reason to suspect the evaluator has ulterior motives. In the Major et al. and Sigall and Michela studies, subjects who were unattractive had no reason to suspect that the evaluator, who was interested in finding someone to date, would evaluate their work more positively for that reason. Why would an opposite-sex evaluator evaluate an essay positively to get a date with an unattractive subject? The attractive subjects, on the other hand, did have reason to suspect the motives of the evaluator, and they discounted the positive feedback. In our studies, White subjects had no particular reasons to suspect the motives of the evaluator, whereas Black subjects had at least two: The evaluator might give negative feedback because he or she was prejudiced or might give positive feedback because he or she wished to avoid appearing prejudiced. Thus, positive feedback may raise and negative feedback may lower self-esteem only when one believes an evaluator has no ulterior motives for giving the feedback. Blacks students are in double jeopardy in this regard, for White evaluators could have ulterior motives for giving them either positive or negative feedback.

Although there are a number of similarities in the results of these two studies, there are some interesting differences as well. First, the results appear to be considerably stronger for Black subjects than for women. Second, women did not show the same vulnerability to positive feedback by a prejudiced evaluator that Blacks showed. It is difficult to identify the sources of these differences, because the studies varied in their methodology as well as in the groups that were studied. However, these differences may reveal meaningful differences between stigmatized groups. As we noted in the introduction, evidence provided by Carver et al. (1977) suggests that Blacks may have good reason to suspect that positive feedback from Whites is not genuine and reflects self-presentational concerns. Women, on the other hand, may not be as mistrustful of positive feedback from men. Not all stigmatizing conditions are the same either from the point of view of stigmatizer or from the point of view of the stigmatized.

Several implications of this analysis deserve mention. First, members of stigmatized groups who generally believe that they are discriminated against or that others are racist should be more likely to attribute negative feedback to prejudice and therefore may be higher in self-esteem. This prediction is contrary to the predictions of the *looking-glass* perspective, which suggests that believing that others are prejudiced against one's group should result in lower self-esteem. However, the belief that one is discriminated against may undermine the value of positive feedback if positive feedback is also discounted. Thus, the self-protective consequences of believing that others are prejudiced may depend on whether one receives predominantly negative or positive outcomes from the nonstigmatized.

A second implication of our analysis is that the stigmatized may sometimes attempt to manage their interactions to encourage or discourage particular attributions for their outcomes. For example, when they anticipate negative outcomes, the stigmatized may choose to reveal their stigmatizing condition to an evaluator, to provide an excuse for the anticipated failure (cf. Snyder et al.,1983). In contrast, when positive outcomes are anticipated, the stigmatized may prefer that evaluators be blind to their stigmatized condition, to avoid any ambiguity regarding the reasons for their outcomes.

Third, we hypothesize that the attributional ambiguity in which the stigmatized exist may have unanticipated negative consequences. Specifically, attributional ambiguity should make it relatively difficult for the stigmatized to predict their future outcomes and select tasks of appropriate difficulty.[6] Not knowing whether negative outcomes reflect a low level of ability or prejudice against one's group may interfere with accurately assessing one's own skills or abilities, hence choosing future endeavors that are suitable to one's skills.

Conclusions

Most research on social stigma has been devoted to understanding the reactions of the nonstigmatized to the stigmatized, including the beliefs, attitudes, and stereotypes the nonstigmatized hold. Relatively little research has focused on the subjective experience of members of stigmatized groups. Understanding the consequences of social stigma requires an understanding of the phenomenology of being stigmatized. We propose that the subjective experiences of the stigmatized and their behavioral responses to stigma may directly depend on the attributions they make for their outcomes, in particular on whether those outcomes are attributed to their deservingness or to prejudice against their group.

REFERENCES

Abramson, L. Y., Seligman, M. E. P., & Teasdale, J. (1978). Learned helplessness in humans: Critique and reformulation. *Journal of Abnormal Psychology, 87,* 49–74.

Allport, G. (1954). *The nature of prejudice.* Reading, MA: Addison-Wesley.

Braddock, J. H., II, & McPartland, J. M. (1987). How minorities continue to be excluded from equal employment opportunities: Research on labor market and institutional barriers. *Journal of Social Issues, 43,* 1013–1020.

Brewin, C. R., & Furnham, A. (1986). Attributional versus preattributional variables in self-esteem and depression: A comparison and test of learned helplessness theory. *Journal of Personality and Social Psychology, 50,* 1013–1020.

Brigham, J. C. (1974). Views of Black and White children concerning the distribution of personality characteristics. *Journal of Personality, 42,* 144–158.

Broverman, I. K., Vogel, S. R., Broverman, D. M., Clarkson, F. E., & Rosenkrantz, P. S. (1972). Sex stereotypes: A current appraisal. *Journal of Social Issues, 28,* 59–79.

Cartwright, D. (1950). Emotional dimensions of group life. In M. I. Raymert (Ed.), *Feelings and emotions* (pp. 419–447). New York: McGraw-Hill.

Carver, C. S., Glass, D. C., & Katz, I. (1977). Favorable evaluations of Blacks and the handicapped: Positive prejudice, unconscious denial, or social desirability? *Journal of Applied Social Psychology, 8,* 97–106.

Cooley, C. H. (1956). *Human nature and the social order.* New York: Free Press.

Crocker, J., Alloy, L. B., & Kayne, N. T. (1988). Attributional style, depression, and perception of consensus for events. *Journal of Personality and Social Psychology, 54,* 840–846.

Crocker, J., & Major, B. (1989). Social stigma and self-esteem. The self-protective properties of stigma. *Psychological Review, 96,* 608–630.

Crosby, F., Bromley, S., and Saxe, L. (1980). Recent nonobtrusive studies of Black and White discrimination and prejudice: A literature review. *Psychological Bulletin, 87,* 546–563.

Darley, J. M., & Fazio, R. H. (1980). Expectancy confirmation processes arising in the social interaction sequence. *American Psychologist, 35,* 867–881.

Deaux, K. K., & Major, B. (1987). Putting gender into context: An integrative model of gender-related behavior. *Psychological Review, 94,* 369–389.

Diener, E. (1984). Subjective well-being. *Psychological Bulletin, 95,* 542–575.

Dion, K. L. (1975). Women's reactions to discrimination from members of the opposite sex. *Journal of Research in Personality, 9,* 369–389.

Dion, K. L. (1986). Responses to perceived discrimination and relative deprivation. In J. M. Olson, C. P. Herman, & M. P. Zanna (Eds.), *Relative deprivation and social comparison: The Ontario Symposium* (Vol. 4, pp. 159–179). Hillsdale, NJ: Erlbaum.

Dion, K. L., & Earn, B. M. (1975). The phenomenology of being a target of prejudice. *Journal of Personality and Social Psychology, 32,* 944–950.

Eagly, A. H., & Mladinic, A. (1989). Gender stereotypes and attitudes toward women and men. *Personality and Social Psychology Bulletin, 15,* 543–558.

Erikson, E. (1956). The problem of ego-identity. *Journal of the American Psychoanalytic Association, 4,* 56–121.

Fazio, R. H., Effrein, E. A., & Falender, V. J. (1981). Self-perceptions following social interactions. *Journal of Personality and Social Psychology, 41,* 232–242.

Festinger, L. (1954). A theory of social comparison processes. *Human Relations, 7,* 71–81.

Gaertner, S. L., & Dovidio, J. F. (1977). The subtlety of White racism, arousal, and helping behavior. *Journal of Personality and Social Psychology, 35,* 691–707.

Gaertner, S. L., & Dovidio, J. F. (1986). The aversive form of racism. In J. F. Dovidio & S. L. Gaertner (Ed.), *Prejudice, discrimination, and racism* (pp. 61–90). San Diego, CA: Academic Press.

Gecas, V., & Schwalbe, M. L. (1983). Beyond the looking-glass self: Social structure and efficacy-based self-esteem. *Social Psychology Quarterly, 46,* 77–88.

Hartsough, W. R., & Fontana, A. F. (1970). Persistence of ethnic stereotypes and the relative importance of positive and negative stereotyping for association preferences. *Psychological Reports, 27,* 723–731.

Heilbrun, A. B., Jr. (1976). Measurement of masculine and feminine sex role identities as independent dimensions. *Journal of Consulting and Clinical Psychology, 44,* 183–190.

Hoelter, J. W. (1982). Factorial invariance and self-esteem: Reassessing race and sex differences. *Social Forces, 61,* 834–846.

---

[6]We are grateful to Russell Fazio for this suggestion.

Hoiberg, A. (1982). *Women and the world of work.* New York: Plenum.

Janis, J. L., & Field, P. B. (1959). Sex differences and personality factors related to persuasibility. In C. I. Hovland & J. L. Janis (Eds.), *Personality and persuasibility* (pp. 56–68). New Haven, CT: Yale University.

Jones, E. E. (1986). Interpreting interpersonal behavior: The effects of expectancies. *Science, 234,* 41–46.

Kanter, R. M. (1977). Some effects of proportions on group life: Skewed sex ratios and responses to token women. *American Journal of Sociology, 83,* 965–990.

Karlins, M., Coffman, T. L., & Walters, G. (1969). On the fading of social stereotypes: Studies in three generations of college students. *Journal of Personality and Social Psychology, 13,* 1–16.

Katz, I. (1981). *Stigma: A social psychological analysis.* Hillsdale, NJ: Erlbaum.

Katz, I., Wackenhut, J., & Hass, R. G. (1986). Racial ambivalence, value duality and behavior. In J. F. Dovidio & S. L. Gaertner (Eds.), *Prejudice, discrimination, and racism* (pp. 35–60). San Diego, CA: Academic Press.

Kelley, H. H. (1972). Causal schemata and the attribution process. In E. E. Jones, D. E., Kanouse, H. H. Kelley, R. E. Nisbett, S. Valins, & B. Weiner (Eds.), *Attribution: Perceiving the causes of behavior* (pp. 151–176). Morristown, NJ: General Learning Press.

Kleck, R. L., Ono, H., & Hastorf, A. H. (1966). The effects of physical deviance upon face-to-face interaction. *Human Relations, 19,* 425–436.

Kleck, R. E., & Strenta, A. (1980). Perceptions of the impact of negative valued physical characteristics on social interaction. *Journal of Personality and Social Psychology, 39,* 861–873.

Linville, P., & Jones, E. E. (1980). Polarized appraisals of out-group members. *Journal of Personality and Social Psychology, 38,* 689–703.

Maccoby, E. F., & Jacklin, C. N. (1974). *The psychology of sex differences.* Stanford, CA: Stanford University Press.

MacFarland, C., & Ross, M. (1982). Impact of causal attributions on affective reactions to success and failure. *Journal of Personality and Social Psychology Bulletin, 43,* 937–946.

Major, B., Carrington, P. I., & Carnevale, P. (1984). Physical attractiveness and self-esteem: Attributions for praise from an other-sex evaluator. *Personality and Social Psychology Bulletin, 10,* 43–50.

Mead, G. H. (1934). *Mind, self, and society.* Chicago: University of Chicago Press.

Merton, R. K. (1948). The self-fulfilling prophecy. *Antioch Review, 8,* 193–210.

Miller, C. T., & Turnbull, W. (1986). Expectancies and interpersonal processes. In M. R. Rosenweig & L. W. Porter (Eds.), *Annual Review of Psychology* (Vol. 37, pp. 233–256). Palo Alto, CA: Annual Review.

O'Leary, V. (1975). Some attitudinal barriers to occupational aspirations in women. *Psychological Bulletin, 81,* 809–816.

Porter, J. R., & Washington, R. E. (1979). Black identity and self-esteem: A review of studies of Black self-concept, 1968–1978. *Annual Review of Sociology, 5,* 53–74.

Riger, S., & Galligan, P. (1980). Women in management: An exploration of competing paradigms. *American Psychologist, 35,* 902–910.

Rosenberg, M. (1965). *Society and the adolescent self-image.* Princeton, NJ: Princeton University Press.

Rosenberg, M. (1979). *Conceiving the self.* New York: Basic Books.

Rosenberg, M., & Simmons, R. G. (1972). *Black and White self-esteem: The urban school child.* Washington, DC: American Sociological Association.

Rosenkrantz, P., Vogel, S.. Bee. H., Broverman, L., & Broverman, D. M. (1968). Sex role stereotypes and self-concepts in college students. *Journal of Consulting and Clinical Psychology, 32,* 287–295.

Samuels, F. (1973). *Group Images.* New Haven, CT: College & University Press.

Scheier, M. F., & Carver, C. S. (1988). A model of behavioral self-regulation: Translating intention into action. In L. Berkowitz (Ed.), *Advances on Experimental Social Psychology* (Vol. 20, pp. 303–346). San Diego, CA: Academic Press.

Sigall, H., & Michela, J. (1976). I'll bet you say that to all the girls: Physical attractiveness and reaction to praise. *Journal of Personality, 11,* 611–626.

Snyder, C. R., Higgins, R., & Stuckey, R. (1983). Excuses: Masquerades in search of grace. In W. Austin & S. Worchel (Eds.), *The social psychology of intergroup relations* (pp. 7–24). Monterey, CA: Brooks/Cole.

Tajfel, H., & Turner, J. C. (1986). The social identity theory of intergroup behavior. In W. Austin & S. Worchel (Eds.), *The social psychology on intergroup relations* (pp. 7–24). Monterey, CA: Brooks/Cole.

Taylor, S. E., & Brown, J. (1988). Illusion and well-being: Some social psychological contributions to a theory of mental health. *Psychological Bulletin, 103,* 193–210.

Tennen, H., & Herzberger, S. (1987). Depression, self-esteem, and the absence of self-protective attributional biases. *Journal of Personality and Social Psychology, 52,* 72–80.

Testa, M., & Major, B. (1990). The impact of social comparison after failure: The moderating effects of perceived control. *Basic and Applied Social Psychology, 11,* 205–218.

Thibaut, J. W., & Kelley, H. H. (1959). *The social psychology of groups.* New York: Wiley.

Treiman, D. J., & Hartman, H. I. (1981). *Women, work, and wages: Equal pay for jobs of equal value.* Washington, DC: National Academy Press.

U.S. Department of Labor. (1978). Income and earnings differentials between Black and White Americans (Report No. TF-6-95-0). Washington. DC: U.S. Government Printing Office.

Walster, E., Walster, G. W., & Berscheid, E. (1978). *Equity: Theory and research.* Boston: Allyn & Bacon.

Weiner, B. (1980). *Human motivation.* New York: Holt, Rinehart & Winston.

Weiner, B. (1982). The emotional consequences of causal attributions. In M. Clark & S. T. Fiske (Eds), *Affect and cognition: The Seventeenth Annual Carnegie Symposium on Cognition.* Hillsdale, NJ: Erlbaum.

Weiner, B. (1985). An attributional theory of achievement motivation and emotion. *Psychological Review, 92,* 548–573.

Weiner, B. (1986). Attribution emotion and action. In R. M. Sorrentino & E. T. Higgins (Eds.), *Handbook of motivation and cognition* (pp. 281–312). New York: Guilford Press.

Weiner, B., Russell, D., & Lerman, D. (1978). Affective consequences or causal ascriptions. In J. H. Harvey, W. J. Ickes,

& R. F. Kidd (Eds.), *New directions in attribution research* (Vol. 2, pp. 59–90). Hillsdale, NJ: Erlbaum.

Weiner, B., Russell, D., & Lerman, D. (1979). The cognition–emotion process in achievement-related contests. *Journal of Personality and Social Psychology, 37,* 1211–1220.

Winer, B. J. (1971). *Statistical principles in experimental design* (2nd ed.). New York: McGraw-Hill.

Wright, B. (1960). *Physical disability: A psychological approach.* New York: Harper.

Wylie, R. (1979). *The self-concept* (Vol. 2). Lincoln: University of Nebraska Press.

Zuckerman. M., & Lubin, B. (1965). *Manual for the Multiple Affect Adjective Check List.* San Diego, CA: Educational and Industrial Testing Service.

Stereotype Threat and the Intellectual Test Performance of African Americans

Claude M. Steele • Stanford University
Joshua Aronson • University of Texas, Austin

Stereotype threat is being at risk of confirming, as self-characteristic, a negative stereotype about one's group. Studies 1 and 2 varied the stereotype vulnerability of Black participants taking a difficult verbal test by varying whether or not their performance was ostensibly diagnostic of ability, and thus, whether or not they were at risk of fulfilling the racial stereotype about their intellectual ability. Reflecting the pressure of this vulnerability, Blacks underperformed in relation to Whites in the ability-diagnostic condition but not in the nondiagnostic condition (with Scholastic Aptitude Tests controlled). Study 3 validated that ability-diagnosticity cognitively activated the racial stereotype in these participants and motivated them not to conform to it, or to be judged by it. Study 4 showed that mere salience of the stereotype could impair Blacks' performance even when the test was not ability diagnostic. The role of stereotype vulnerability in the standardized test performance of ability-stigmatized groups is discussed.

Not long ago, in explaining his career-long preoccupation with the American Jewish experience, the novelist Philip Roth said that it was not Jewish culture or religion per se that fascinated him, it was what he called the Jewish "predicament." This is an apt term for the perspective taken in the present research. It focuses on a social-psychological predicament that can arise from widely-known negative stereotypes about one's group. It is this: the existence of such a stereotype means that anything one does or any of one's features that conform to it make the stereotype more plausible as a self-characterization in the eyes of others, and perhaps even in one's own eyes. We call this predicament *stereotype threat* and argue that it is experienced, essentially, as a self-evaluative threat. In form, it is a predicament that can beset the members of any group about whom negative

stereotypes exist. Consider the stereotypes elicited by the terms *yuppie, feminist, liberal,* or *White male.* Their prevalence in society raises the possibility for potential targets that the stereotype is true of them and, also, that other people will see them that way. When the allegations of the stereotype are importantly negative, this predicament may be self-threatening enough to have disruptive effects of its own.

The present research examined the role these processes play in the intellectual test performance of African Americans. Our reasoning is this: whenever African American students perform an explicitly scholastic or intellectual task, they face the threat of confirming or being judged by a negative societal stereotype—a suspicion—about their group's intellectual ability and competence. This threat is not borne by people not stereotyped in this way. And the self-threat it causes—through a variety of mechanisms—may interfere with the intellectual functioning of these students, particularly during standardized tests. This is the principal hypothesis examined in the present research. But as this threat persists over time, it may have the further effect of pressuring these students to protectively disidentify with achievement in school and related intellectual domains. That is, it may pressure the person to define or redefine the self-concept such that school achievement is neither a basis of self-evaluation nor a personal identity. This protects the person against the self-evaluative threat posed by the stereotype, but may have the byproduct of diminishing interest, motivation, and, ultimately, achievement in the domain (Steele, 1992).

The anxiety of knowing that one is a potential target of prejudice and stereotypes has been much discussed: in classic social science (e.g., Allport, 1954; Goffman, 1963), popular books (e.g., Carter, 1991) and essays as, for example, S. Steele's (1990) treatment of what he called *racial vulnerability*. In this last analysis, S. Steele made a connection between this experience and the school life of African Americans that has similarities to our own. He argued that after a lifetime of exposure to society's negative images of their ability, these students are likely to internalize an "inferiority anxiety"—a state that can be aroused by a variety of race-related cues in the environment. This anxiety, in turn, can lead them to blame others for their troubles (for example, White racism), to underutilize available opportunities and to generally form a victim's identity. These adaptations, in turn, the argument goes, translate into poor life success.

The present theory and research do not focus on the internalization of inferiority images or their consequences. Instead they focus on the immediate situational threat that derives from the broad dissemination of negative stereotypes about one's group—the threat of possibly being judged and treated stereotypically, or of possibly self-fulfilling such a stereotype. This threat can befall anyone with a group identity about which some negative stereotype exists, and for the person to be threatened in this way, he need not even believe the stereotype. He need only know that it stands as a hypothesis about him in situations where the stereotype is relevant. We focused on the stereotype threat of African Americans in intellectual and

scholastic domains to provide a compelling test of the theory and because the theory, should it be supported in this context for this group, would have relevance to an important set of outcomes.

Gaps in school achievement and retention rates between White and Black Americans at all levels of schooling have been strikingly persistent in American society (e.g., Steele, 1992). Well publicized at the kindergarten through 12th grade level, recent statistics show that they persist even at the college level where, for example, the national dropout rate for Black college students (the percentage who do not complete college within a 6-year window of time) is 70% compared to 42% for White Americans (American Council on Education, 1990). Even among those who graduate, their grades average two thirds of a letter grade lower than those of graduating Whites (e.g., Nettles, 1988). It has been most common to understand such problems as stemming largely from the socioeconomic disadvantage, segregation, and discrimination that African Americans have endured and continue to endure in this society, a set of conditions that, among other things, could produce racial gaps in achievement by undermining preparation for school.

Some evidence, however, questions the sufficiency of these explanations. It comes from the sizable literature examining racial bias in standardized testing. This work, involving hundreds of studies over several decades, generally shows that standardized tests predict subsequent school achievement as well for Black students as for White students (e.g., Cleary, Humphreys, Kendrick, & Wesman, 1975; Linn, 1973; Stanley, 1971). The slope of the lines regressing subsequent school achievement on entry-level standardized test scores is essentially the same for both groups. But embedded in this literature is another fact: At every level of preparation as measured by a standardized test—for example, the Scholastic Aptitude Test (SAT)—Black students with that score have poorer subsequent achievement—GPA, retention rates, time to graduation, and so on—than White students with that score (Jensen, 1980). This is variously known as the overprediction or underachievement phenomenon, because it indicates that, relative to Whites with the same score, standardized tests actually overpredict the achievement that Blacks will realize. Most important for our purposes, this evidence suggests that Black–White achievement gaps are not due solely to group differences in preparation. Blacks achieve less well than Whites even when they have the same preparation, and even when that preparation is at a very high level. Could this underachievement in some part reflect the stereotype threat that is a chronic feature of these students' schooling environments?

Research from the early 1960s—largely that of Irwin Katz and his colleagues (e.g., Katz, 1964) on how desegregation affected the intellectual performance of Black students—shows the sizable influence on Black intellectual performance of factors that can be interpreted as manipulations of stereotype threat. Katz, Roberts and Robinson (1965), for example, found that Black participants performed better on an IQ subtest when it was presented as a test of eye-hand coordination—a nonevaluative and thus threat-negating test representation—than when it was said to be a test of intelligence. Katz, Epps, and Axelson (1964) found that Black students performed better on an IQ test when they believed their performance would be compared to other Blacks as opposed to Whites. But as evidence that bears on our hypothesis, this literature has several limitations. Much of the research was conducted in an era when American race relations were different in important ways than they are now. Thus, without their being replicated, the extent to which these findings reflect enduring processes of stereotype threat as opposed to the racial dynamics of a specific historical era is not clear. Also, this research seldomly used White control groups. Thus it is difficult to know the extent to which some of the critical effects were mediated by the stereotype threat of Black students as opposed to processes experienced by any students.

Other research supports the present hypothesis by showing that factors akin to stereotype threat—that is, other factors that add self-evaluative threat to test taking or intellectual performance—are capable of disrupting that performance. The presence of observers or coactors, for example, can interfere with performance on mental tasks (e.g., Geen, 1985; Seta, 1982). Being a "token" member of a group—the sole representative of a social category—can inhibit one's memory for what is said during a group discussion (Lord & Saenz, 1985; Lord, Saenz, & Godfrey, 1987). Conditions that increase the importance of performing well—prizes, competition, and audience approval—have all been shown to impair performance of even motor skills (e.g., Baumeister, 1984). The stereotype threat hypothesis shares with these approaches

that performance suffers when the situation redirects attention needed to perform a task onto some other concern—in the case of stereotype threat, concern with the significance of one's performance in light of a devaluing stereotype.

For African American students, the act of taking a test purported to measure intellectual ability may be enough to induce this threat. But we assume that this is most likely to happen when the test is also frustrating. It is frustration that makes the stereotype—as an allegation of inability—relevant to their performance and thus raises the possibility that they have an inability linked to their race. This is not to argue that the stereotype is necessarily believed; only that, in the face of frustration with the test, it becomes more plausible as a self-characterization and thereby more threatening to the self. Thus for Black students who care about the skills being tested—that is, those who are identified with these skills in the sense of their self-regard being somewhat tied to having them—the stereotype loads the testing with an extra degree of self-threat, a degree not borne by people not stereotyped in this way. This additional threat, in turn, may interfere with their performance in a variety of ways: by causing an arousal that reduces the ranges of cues participants are able to use (e.g., Easterbrook, 1959), or by diverting attention onto task-irrelevant worries (e.g., Sarason, 1972; Wine, 1971), by causing an interfering self-consciousness (e.g., Baumeister, 1984), or overcautiousness (Geen, 1985). Or, through the ability-indicting interpretation it poses for test frustration, it could foster low performance expectations that would cause participants to withdraw effort (e.g., Bandura, 1977, 1985). Depending on the situation, several of these processes may be involved simultaneously or in alternation. Through these mechanisms, then, stereotype threat might be expected to undermine the standardized test performance of Black participants relative to White participants who, in this situation, do not suffer this added threat.

Study 1

Accordingly, Black and White college students in this experiment were given a 30-min test composed of items from the verbal Graduate Record Examination (GRE) that were difficult enough to be at the limits of most participants' skills. In the stereotype-threat condition, the test was described as diagnostic of intellectual ability, thus making the racial stereotype about intellectual ability relevant to Black participants' performance and establishing for them the threat of fulfilling it. In the nonstereotype-threat condition, the same test was described simply as a laboratory problem-solving task that was nondiagnostic of ability, presumably this would make the racial stereotype about ability irrelevant to Black participants' performance and thus preempt any threat of fulfilling it. Finally, a second nondiagnostic condition was included which exhorted participants to view the difficult test as a challenge. For practical reasons we were interested in whether stressing the challenge inherent in a difficult test might further increase participants' motivation and performance over what would occur in the nondiagnostic condition. The primary dependent measure in this experiment was participants' performance on the test adjusted for the influence of individual differences in skill level (operationalized as participants' verbal SAT scores).

We predicted that Black participants would underperform relative to Whites in the diagnostic condition where there was stereotype threat, but not in the two nondiagnostic conditions—the non-diagnostic-only condition and the non-diagnostic-plus-challenge condition—where this threat was presumably reduced. In the non-diagnostic-challenge condition, we also expected the additional motivation to boost the performance of both Black and White participants above that observed in the non-diagnostic-only condition. Several additional measures were included to assess the effectiveness of the manipulation and possible mediating states.

Method

DESIGN AND PARTICIPANTS

This experiment took the form of a 2×3 factorial design. The factors were race of the participant, Black or White, and a test description factor in which the test was presented as either diagnostic of intellectual ability (the diagnostic condition), as a laboratory tool for studying problem solving (the non-diagnostic only condition), or as both a problem-solving tool and a challenge (the non-diagnostic-challenge condition). Test performance was the primary dependent measure. We recruited 117 male and female, Black and White Stanford

undergraduates through campus advertisements which offered $10.00 for 1 hr of participation. The data from 3 participants were excluded from the analysis because they failed to provide their verbal SAT scores. This left a total of 114 participants randomly as signed to the three experimental conditions with the exception that we ensured an equal number of participants per condition.

PROCEDURE

Participants who signed up for the experiment were contacted by telephone prior to their experimental participation and asked to provide their verbal and quantitative SAT scores, to rate their enjoyment of verbally oriented classes, and to provide background information (e.g., year in school, major, etc.). When participants arrived at the laboratory the experimenter (a White man) explained that for the next 30 min they would work on a set of verbal problems in a format identical to the SAT exam, and end by answering some questions about their experience.

The participant was then given a page that stated the purpose of the study, described the procedure for answering questions, stressed the importance of indicating guessed answers (by a check), described the test as very difficult and that they should expect not to get many of the questions correct, and told them that they would be given feedback on their performance at the end of the session. We included the information about test difficulty to, as much as possible, equate participants' performance expectations across the conditions. And, by acknowledging the difficulty of the test, we wanted to reduce the possibility that participants would see the test as a miscalculation of their skills and perhaps reduce their effort. This description was the same for all conditions with the exception of several key phrases that comprised the experimental manipulation.

Participants in the diagnostic condition were told that the study was concerned with "various personal factors involved in performance on problems requiring reading and verbal reasoning abilities." They were further informed that after the test, feedback would be provided which "may be helpful to you by familiarizing you with some of your strengths and weaknesses" in verbal problem solving. As noted, participants in all conditions were told that they should not expect to get many items correct, and in the diagnostic condition, this test difficulty was justified as a means of providing a "genuine test of your verbal abilities and limitations so that we might better understand the factors involved in both." Participants were asked to give a strong effort in order to "help us in our analysis of your verbal ability."

In the non-diagnostic-only and non-diagnostic challenge conditions, the description of the study made no reference to verbal ability. Instead, participants were told that the purpose of the research was to better understand the "psychological factors involved in solving verbal problems. . . ." These participants too were told that they would receive performance feedback, but it was justified as a means of familiarizing them "with the kinds of problems that appear on tests [they] may encounter in the future." In the non-diagnostic-only condition, the difficulty of the test was justified in terms of a research focus on difficult verbal problems and in the non-diagnostic-challenge condition it was justified as an attempt to provide "even highly verbal people with a mental challenge. . . ." Last, participants in both conditions were asked to give a genuine effort in order to "help us in our analysis of the problem solving process." As the experimenter left them to work on the test, to further differentiate the conditions, participants in the non-diagnostic-only condition were asked to try hard "even though we're not going to evaluate your ability." Participants in the non-diagnostic-challenge condition were asked to "please take this challenge seriously even though we will not be evaluating your ability."

DEPENDENT MEASURES

The primary dependent measure was participants' performance on 30 verbal items, 27 of which were difficult items taken from GRE study guides (only 30% of earlier samples had gotten these items correct) and 3 difficult anagram problems. Both the total number correct and an accuracy index of the number correct over the number attempted were analyzed.

Participants next completed an 18-item self-report measure of their current thoughts relating to academic competence and personal worth (e.g., "I feel confident about my abilities" "I feel self-conscious" "I feel as smart as others," etc.). These were measured on 5-point scales anchored by the phrases *not at all* (1) and *extremely* (5). Participants also completed a 12-item measure of cogni-

tive interference frequently used in test anxiety research (Sarason, 1980) on which they indicated the frequency of several distracting thoughts during the exam (e.g., "I wondered what the experimenter would think of me," "I thought about how poorly I was doing" "I thought about the difficulty of the problems," etc.) by putting a number from 1 (*never*) to 5 (*very often*) next to each statement. Participants then rated how difficult and biased they considered the test on 15-point scales anchored by the labels *not at all* (1) and *extremely* (15). Next, participants evaluated their own performance by estimating the number of problems they correctly solved, and by comparing their own performance to that of the average Stanford student on a 15-point scale with the end points *much worse* (1) and *much better* (15). Finally, as a check on the manipulation, participants responded to the question:

> The purpose of this experiment was to: (a) provide a genuine test of my abilities in order to examine personal factors involved in verbal ability; (b) provide a challenging test in order to examine factors involved in solving verbal problems; (c) present you with unfamiliar verbal problems to measure verbal learning.

Participants were asked to circle the appropriate response.

Results

Because there were no main or interactive effects of gender on verbal test performance or the self-report measures, we collapsed over this factor in all analyses.

MANIPULATION CHECK

Chi-square analyses performed on participants' responses to the postexperimental question about the purpose of the study revealed only an effect of condition, $\chi^2 (2) = 43.18$, $p < .001$. Participants were more likely to believe the purpose of the experiment was to evaluate their abilities in the diagnostic condition (65%) than in the nondiagnostic condition (3%), or the challenge condition (11%).

TEST PERFORMANCE

The ANCOVA on the number of items participants got correct, using their self-reported SAT scores

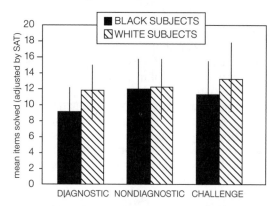

FIGURE 21.1. ■ Mean test performance Study 1.

as the covariate (Black mean = 592, White mean = 632) revealed a significant condition main effect, $F(2, 107) = 4.74, p < .02$, with participants in the non-diagnostic-challenge condition performing higher than participants in the non-diagnostic-only and diagnostic conditions, respectively, and a significant race main effect $F(1, 107) = 5.22, p < .03$, with White participants performing higher than Black participants.[1] The race-by-condition interaction did not reach conventional significance ($p < .19$). The adjusted condition means are presented in Figure 21.1.

If making the test diagnostic of ability depresses the performance of Black students through stereotype threat, then their performance should be lower in the diagnostic condition than in either the non-diagnostic-only or non-diagnostic-challenge conditions which presumably lessened stereotype threat, and it should be lower than that of Whites in the diagnostic condition. Bonferroni contrasts[2] with SATs as a covariate supported this reasoning by showing that Black participants in the diagnostic condition performed significantly worse than Black participants in either the nondiagnostic condition, $t(107) = 2.88, p < .01$, or the challenge condition, $t(107) = 2.63, p < .01$, as well as significantly worse than White participants in the diagnostic condition $t(107) = 2.64, p < .01$.

But, as noted, the interaction testing the differential effect of test diagnosticity on Black and White participants did not reach significance. This may have happened however, because an incidental pattern of means—Whites slightly outperforming Blacks in the nondiagnostic-challenge condition—undermined the overall interaction effect. To pursue a more sensitive test, we constructed a weighted contrast that compared the size of the race effect in the diagnostic condition with that in the nondiagnostic condition and assigned weights of zero to the White and Black non-diagnostic-challenge conditions. This analysis (including the use of SATs as a covariate) reached marginal significance, $F(1, 107) = 3.27, p < .08$. In sum, then, the hypothesis was supported by the pattern of contrasts, but when tested over the whole design, reached only marginal significance.

ACCURACY

An ANCOVA on accuracy, the proportion correct of the number attempted, with SATs as the covariate, found that neither condition main effect nor the interaction reached significance, although there was a marginally significant tendency for Black participants to evidence less accuracy, $p < .10$. This tendency was primarily due to Black participants in the diagnostic condition who had the lowest adjusted mean accuracy of any group in the experiment, .420. The adjusted means for the White diagnostic, White non-diagnostic-only White non-diagnostic-challenge, Black non-diagnostic-only, and Black diagnostic-challenge conditions were, .519, .518, .561, .546, and .490, respectively. Bonferroni tests revealed that Black participants in the diagnostic condition were reliably less accurate than Black participants in the non-diagnostic-only condition and White participants in the diagnostic condition, $t(107) = 2.64, p < .01$, and $t(107) = 2.13, p < .05$, respectively.

No condition or interaction effects reached significance for the number of items completed or the number of guesses participants recorded on the test (all $Fs < 1$). The overall means for these two measures were 22.9 and 4.1, respectively.

Self-Report Measures. There were no signifi-

---

[1]Because we did not warn participants to avoid guessing in these experiments, we do not report the performance results in terms of the index used by Educational Testing Service, which includes a correction for guessing. This correction involves subtracting from the number correct, the number wrong adjusted for the number of response options for each wrong item and dividing this by the number of items on the test. Because 27 of our 30 items had the same number of response options (5), this correction amounts to adjusting the number correct almost invariably by the same number. All analyses are the same regardless of the index used.

[2] All comparisons of adjusted means reported hereafter used the Bonferroni procedure.

cant condition effects on the self-report measure of academic competence and personal worth or on the self-report measure of disruptive thoughts and feelings during the test. Analysis of participants' responses to the question about test bias yielded a main effect of race, $F(1, 107) = 10.47$, $p < .001$. Black participants in all conditions thought the test was more biased than White participants.

Perceived Performance. Participants' estimates of how many problems they solved correctly and of how they compared to other participants both showed significant condition main effects, $F(2, 106) = 7.91$, $p < .001$, and $F(2, 107) = 3.17$, $p < .05$, respectively. Performance estimates were higher in the non-diagnostic-only condition ($M = 11.81$) than in either the diagnostic ($M = 9.20$) or non-diagnostic-challenge conditions ($M = 8.15$). Bonferroni tests showed that Black participants in the diagnostic condition ($M = 4.89$) saw their relative performance as poorer than Black participants in the non-diagnostic-only condition ($M = 6.54$), $t(107) = 2.81$, $p < .01$, and than Black participants in the nondiagnostic-challenge condition ($M = 6.30$), $t(107) = 2.40$, $p < .02$, while test description had no effect on the ratings of White participants. The overall mean was 5.86.

Discussion

With SAT differences statistically controlled, Black participants performed worse than White participants when the test was presented as a measure of their ability, but improved dramatically, matching the performance of Whites, when the test was presented as less reflective of ability. Nonetheless, the race-by-diagnosticity interaction testing this relationship reached only marginal significance, and then, only when participants from the non-diagnostic-challenge condition were excluded from the analysis. Thus there remained some question as to the reliability of this interaction.

We had also reasoned that stereotype threat might undermine performance by increasing interfering thoughts during the test. But the conditions affected neither self-evaluative thoughts nor thoughts about the self in the immediate situation (Sarason, 1980). Thus to further test the reliability of the predicted interaction and explore the mediation of the stereotype threat effect, we conducted a second experiment.

Study 2

We argued that the effect of stereotype threat on performance is mediated by an apprehension over possibly conforming to the negative group stereotype. Could this apprehension be detected as a higher level of general anxiety among stereotype-threatened participants? To test this possibility, participants in all conditions completed a version of the Spielberger State Anxiety Inventory (STAI) immediately after the test. This scale has been successfully used in other research to detect anxiety induced by evaluation apprehension (e.g., Geen, 1985). We also measured the amount of time they spent on each test item to learn whether greater anxiety was associated with more time spent answering items.

Method

PARTICIPANTS

Twenty Black and 20 White Stanford female undergraduates were randomly assigned (with the exception of attaining equal cell sizes) to either the diagnostic or the nondiagnostic conditions as described in Study 1, yielding 10 participants per condition. Female participants were used in this experiment because, due to other research going on, we had considerably easier access to Black female undergraduates than to Black male undergraduates. This decision was justified by the finding of no gender differences in the first study or, as it turned out, in any of the subsequent studies reported in this article—all of which used both men and women.

PROCEDURE

This experiment used the same test used in Study 1, with several exceptions; the final three anagram problems were deleted and the test period was reduced from 30 to 25 min. Also, the test was presented on a Macintosh computer (LCII). Participants controlled with the mouse how long each item or item component was on the screen and could, at their own pace, access whatever item material they wanted to see. The computer recorded the amount of time the items or item components were on the screen as well as the number of referrals between item components (as in the reading comprehension items)—in addition to re-cording participants' answers.

Following the exam, participants completed the STAI and the cognitive interference measure de-scribed for Study 1. Also, on 11-point scales (with end-points *not at all* and *extremely*) participants indicated the extent to which they guessed when having difficulty, expended effort on the test, per-sisted on problems, limited their time on problems, read problems more than once, became frustrated and gave up, and felt that the test was biased.

Results and Discussion

The ANCOVA performed on the number of items correctly solved yielded a significant main effect of race, $F(1, 35) = 10.04$, $p < .01$, qualified by a significant Race × Test Description interaction, $F(1, 35) = 8.07$, $p < .01$. The mean SAT score for Black participants was 603 and for White partici-pants 655. The adjusted means are presented in Figure 21.2. Planned contrasts on the adjusted scores revealed that, as predicted, Blacks in the diagnostic condition performed significantly worse than Blacks in the nondiagnostic condition $t(35) = 2.38$, $p < .02$, than Whites in the diagnostic con-dition $t(35) = 3.75$, $p < .001$, and than Whites in the nondiagnostic condition $t(35) = 2.34$, $p < .025$.

For accuracy—the number correct over the num-ber attempted—a similar pattern emerged: Blacks in the diagnostic condition had lower accuracy ($M = .392$) than Blacks in the nondiagnostic condi-tion ($M = .490$) or than Whites in either the diag-nostic condition ($M = .485$) or the nondiagnostic condition ($M = .435$). The diagnosticity-by-race

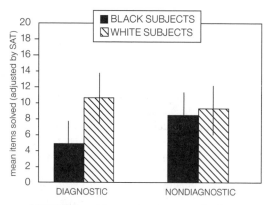

FIGURE 21.2. ■ Mean test performance Study 2.

interaction testing this pattern reached signifi-cance, $F(1, 35) = 4.18$, $p < .05$. But the planned contrasts of the Black diagnostic condition against the other conditions did not reach conventional significance, although its contrasts with the Black nondiagnostic and White diagnostic conditions were marginally significant, with ps of .06 and .09 respectively.

Blacks completed fewer items than Whites, $F(1, 35) = 9.35$, $p < .01$, and participants in the diag-nostic conditions tended to complete fewer items than those in the nondiagnostic conditions, $F(1, 35) = 3.69$, $p < .07$. The overall interaction did not reach significance. But planned contrasts revealed that Black participants in the diagnostic condition finished fewer items ($M = 12.38$) than Blacks in the nondiagnostic condition ($M = 18.53$), $t(35) = 2.50$, $p < .02$; than Whites in the diagnostic condi-tion ($M = 20.93$), $t(35) = 3.39$, $p < .01$; and than Whites in the nondiagnostic condition ($M = 21.45$), $t(35) = 3.60$, $p < .01$.

These results establish the reliability of the diagnosticity-by-race interaction for test perfor-mance that was marginally significant in Study 1. They also reveal another dimension of the effect of stereotype threat. Black participants in the di-agnostic condition completed fewer test items than participants in the other conditions. Test diagnosticity impaired the rate, as well as the ac-curacy of their work. This is precisely the impair-ment caused by evaluative pressures such as evalu-ation apprehension, test anxiety, and competitive pressure (e.g., Baumeister, 1984). But one might ask why this did not happen in the near-identical Study 1. Several factors may be relevant. First, the most involved test items—reading comprehension items that took several steps to answer—came first in the test. And second, the test lasted 25 min in the present experiment whereas it lasted 30 min in the first experiment. Assuming, then, that stereo-type threat slowed the pace of Black participants in the diagnostic conditions of both experiments, this 5-min difference in test period may have made it harder for these participants in the present ex-periment to get past the early, involved items and onto the more quickly answered items at the end of the test, a possibility that may also explain the generally lower scores in this experiment.

This view is reinforced by the ANCOVA (with SATs as a covariate) on the average time spent on each of the first five test items—the minimum number of items that all participants in all conditions answered. A marginal effect of test presentation emerged, $F(1, 35) = 3.52$, $p < .07$, but planned comparisons showed that Black participants in the diagnostic condition tended to be slower than participants in the other conditions. On average they spent 94 s answering each of these items in contrast to 71 for Black participants in the nondiagnostic condition, $t(35) = 2.39$, $p < .05$; 73 s for Whites in the diagnostic condition, $t(35) = 2.12$, $p < .05$, and 71 s for Whites in the nondiagnostic condition, $t(35) = 2.37$, $p < .05$. Like other forms of evaluative pressure, stereotype threat causes an impairment of both accuracy and speed of performance.

No differences were found on any of the remaining measures, including self-reported effort, cognitive interference, or anxiety. These measures may have been insensitive, or too delayed. Nonetheless, we lack an important kind of evidence. We have not shown that test diagnosticity causes in Black participants a specific apprehension about fulfilling the negative group stereotype about their ability—the apprehension that we argue disrupts their test performance. To examine this issue we conducted a third experiment.

Study 3

Taking an intellectually diagnostic test and experiencing some frustration with it, we have assumed, is enough to cause stereotype threat for Black participants. In testing this reasoning, the present experiment examines several specific propositions.

First, if taking or expecting to take a difficult, intellectually diagnostic test makes Black participants feel threatened by a specifically racial stereotype, then it might be expected to activate that stereotype in their thinking and information processing. That is, the racial stereotype, and perhaps also the self-doubts associated with it, should be more cognitively activated for these participants than for Black participants in the nondiagnostic condition or for White participants in either condition (e.g., Dovidio, Evans, & Tyler, 1986; Devine, 1989; Higgins, 1989). Accordingly, in testing whether test diagnosticity arouses this state, the present experiment measured the effect of conditions on the activation of this stereotype and of related self-doubts about ability.

Second, if test diagnosticity makes Black participants apprehensive about fulfilling and being judged by the racial stereotype, then these participants, more than participants in the other conditions, might be motivated to disassociate themselves from the stereotype. Brent Staples, an African American editorialist for the *New York Times*, offers an example of this in his recent autobiography, *Parallel Time*. He describes beginning graduate school at the University of Chicago and finding that as he walked the streets of Hyde Park he made people uncomfortable. They grouped more closely when he walked by, and some even crossed the street to avoid him. He eventually realized that in that urban context, dressed as a student, he was being perceived through the lens of a race-class stereotype as a potentially menacing Black man. To deflect this perception he learned a trick; he would whistle Vivaldi. It worked. Upon hearing him do this, people around him visibly relaxed and he felt out of suspicion. If it is apprehension about being judged in light of the racial stereotype that interferes with the performance of Black participants in the diagnostic condition, then these participants, like Staples, might be motivated to deflect such a perception by showing that the broader racial stereotype is not applicable to them. To test this possibility, the present experiment measured the effect of conditions on participants' stated preferences for such things as activities and styles of music, some of which were stereotypic of African Americans.

Third, by adding to the normal evaluative risks of test performance the further risk of self-validating the racial stereotype, the diagnostic condition should also make Black participants more apprehensive about their test performance. The present experiment measured this apprehension as the degree to which participants self-handicapped their expected performance, that is, endorsed excuses for poor performance before the test.

The experiment took the form of a 2×3 design in which the race of participants (African American or White) was crossed with diagnostic, nondiagnostic, and control conditions. The diagnostic and nondiagnostic conditions were the same as those described for Study 2, while in the control condition participants completed the critical dependent measures without expecting to take a test of any sort. In the experimental conditions, the dependent measures were administered immediately after the diagnosticity instructions and just before the test was ostensibly to be taken. These included measures of stereotype activation, stereotype avoidance, and, as a measure of general performance apprehension, participants' willingness to self-handicap. Participants in this experiment never took the test. The measures of stereotype activation and stereotype avoidance, we felt, could activate the racial stereotype and stereotype threat among Black participants in both the diagnostic and nondiagnostic conditions, making performance results difficult to interpret.

If test diagnosticity threatens Black participants with a specifically racial stereotype, then Black participants in the diagnostic condition, more than participants in the other conditions, should show greater cognitive activation of the stereotype and ability-related self-doubts, greater motivation to disassociate themselves from the stereotype, and greater performance apprehension as indicated by the endorsement of self-handicapping excuses.

Method

PARTICIPANTS

Thirty-five Black (9 male, 26 female) and 33 White (20 male, 13 female) Stanford undergraduates were randomly assigned to either a diagnostic, nondiagnostic, or control condition, yielding from 10 to 12 participants per experimental group.

PROCEDURE

A White male experimenter gave a booklet to participants as they arrived that explained that the study was examining the relationship between two types of cognitive processes: lexical access processing (LAP) and higher verbal reasoning (HVR). They me told that they would be asked to complete two tasks, one of which measured LAP— "the visual and recognition processing of words— and the other of which measured HVR— "abstract reasoning about the meaning of words." Test diagnosticity was manipulated as in Study 1 with the following written instructions to further differentiate the conditions:

> *Diagnostic*: Because we want an accurate measure of your ability in these domains, we want to ask you to try as hard as you can to perform well on these tasks. At the end of the study, we can give you feedback which may be helpful by pointing out your strengths and weaknesses.
> *Nondiagnostic*: Even though we are not evaluating your ability on these tasks, we want to ask

you to try as hard as you can to perform well on these tasks. If you want to know more about your LAP and HVR performance, we can give you feedback at the end of the study.

Finally, participants were shown one sample item from the LAP (an item of the same sort as used in the fragment completion task) and three sample items from the HVR—difficult verbal GRE problems. The purpose of the HVR sample items was to alert participants to the difficulty of the test and the possibility of poor performance, thus occasioning the relevance of the racial stereotype in the diagnostic condition.

Participants in the control condition arrived at the laboratory to find a note on the door from the experimenter apologizing for not being present. The note instructed them to complete a set of measures lying on the desk in an envelope with the participant's name on it. The envelope contained the LAP word fragment measure and the stereotype avoidance measure (described below) with detailed instructions. No mention of verbal ability evaluation was made.

MEASURES

Stereotype Activation. Participants first performed a word-fragment completion task, introduced as the "LAP task," versions of which have been shown to measure the cognitive activation of constructs that are either recently primed or self-generated (Gilbert & Hixon, 1991; Tulving, Schacter, & Stark, 1982). The task was made up of 80 word fragments with missing letters specified as blank spaces (e.g., _ _ C E). Twelve of these fragments had as one possible solution a word reflecting either a race-related construct or an image associated with African Americans. The list was generated by having a group of 40 undergraduates (White students from the introductory psychology pool) generate a set of words that reflected the image of African Americans. From these lists, the research team identified the 12 most common constructs (e.g., lower class, minority) and selected single words to represent those constructs on the task. For example, the word "race" was used to represent the construct "concerned with race" on the task. Then, for each of the words placed on the task, at least two letter spaces were omitted and the word was checked again to determine whether other, non-stereotype-related associations to the word stem were possible. Leaving at least two letter spaces blank in each word fragment greatly unconstrains the number of word completions possible for each fragment when compared to leaving only one letter space blank. This reduces the chance of ceiling effects in which virtually all participants would think of the race-related fragment completion. The complete list was as follows: _ _ C E (RACE); L A _ _ (LAZY); _ _ A C K (BLACK); _ _ OR (POOR); C L _ S _ (CLASS); B R _ _ _ _ _ (BROTHER); _ _ _ T E (WHITE); M I _ _ _ _ _ _ (MINORITY); W E L _ _ _ _ (WELFARE); C O _ _ _ (COLOR); T O_ _ _(TOKEN).

We included a fairly high number (12) of target fragments so that if ceiling or floor effects occurred on some fragments it would be less likely to damage the sensitivity of the overall measure. To reduce the chance that participants would become aware of the racial nature of the target fragments they were spaced with at least three filler items between them, and there were only two target fragments per page in the task booklet. Participants were instructed to work quickly, spending no more than 15 s on each item.

Self-Doubt Activation. Seven word fragments reflecting self-doubts about competence and ability were included in the 80-item LAP task: L O_ _ _ (LOSER); D U _ _ (DUMB); S H A _ _ (SHAME); _ _ _ E R I O R (INFERIOR); F L_ _ _ (FLUNK); _ A R D (HARD); W _ _ K (WEAK). These were generated by the research team, and again included at least two blank letter spaces in each fragment. As with the racial fragments, these were separated from one another (and from the racial fragments) by at least three filler items.

Stereotype Avoidance. This measure asked participants to rate their preferences for a variety of activities and to rate the self-descriptiveness of various personality traits, some of which were associated with images of African Americans and African American life. Participants in the diagnostic and nondiagnostic conditions were told that these ratings were taken to give us a better understanding of the underpinnings of LAP and HVR processes. Control participants were told that these measures were being taken to assess the typical interests and personality traits of Stanford undergraduates. The measure contained 57 items asking participants to rate the extent to which they enjoyed a number of activities (e.g., pleasure reading, socializing, shopping, traveling etc.), types of music (e.g., jazz, rap music, classical music), sports

(e.g., baseball, basketball, boxing), and finally, how they saw themselves standing on various personality dimensions (e.g., extroverted, organized, humorous, etc.). All ratings were made on 7-point Likert scales with 1 indicating the lowest preference or degree of trait descriptiveness. Some of these activities and traits were stereotypic of African Americans. For an item to be selected as stereotypic, 65% of our pretest sample of 40 White participants had to have generated the item when asked to list activities and traits they believed to be stereotypic of African Americans. In the activities category, the stereotype-relevant items were: "How much do you enjoy sports?" and "How much do you enjoy being a lazy 'couch potato'?" The stereotype-relevant music preference item was *rap music*; the stereotype-relevant sports preference item was *basketball*; and the stereotype-relevant trait ratings were *lazy* and *aggressive/belligerent*.

Participants also completed a brief demographic questionnaire (asking their age, gender, major, etc.) just before they expected to begin the test. As another measure of participants' motivation to distance themselves from the stereotype, the second item of this questionnaire gave them the option of recording their race. We reasoned that participants who wanted to avoid having their performance viewed through the lens of a racial stereotype would be less willing to indicate their race.

Self-Handicapping Measures. This measure just preceded the demographic questionnaire. The directions stated "as you know, student life is sometimes stressful, and we may not always get enough sleep, etc. Such things can affect cognitive functioning, so it will be necessary to ask how prepared you feel." Participants then indicated the number of hours they slept the night before in addition to responding on 7-point scales (with 7 being the higher rating on these dimensions) to the following questions: "How able to focus do you feel?;" "How much stress have you been under lately?;" "How tricky/unfair do you typically find standardized tests?"

Results

STEREOTYPE ACTIVATION

A 2 (race) × 3 (condition: diagnostic, nondiagnostic, or control) ANCOVA (with verbal SAT as the covariate: Black mean = 581, White mean = 650) was performed on the number of target word fragments filled in with stereotypic completions. This analysis yielded significant main effects for both race, $F(1, 61) = 13.77$, $p < .001$, and for experimental condition, $F(2, 61) = 5.90$, $p < .005$. These main effects, however, were qualified by a significant Race × Condition interaction, $F(2, 61) = 3.30$, $p < .05$. Figure 21.3 shows that as expected, the diagnostic condition significantly increased the number of race-related completions of Black participants but not of White participants. Black participants in the diagnostic condition produced more race-related completions ($M = 3.70$) than Black participants in the nondiagnostic condition ($M = 2.10$), $t(61) = 3.53$, $p < .001$, or for that matter, more than participants in any of other conditions, all $ps < .05$.

SELF-DOUBT ACTIVATION

It did the same for their self doubts. The number of self-doubt-related completions of self-doubt target fragments were submitted to an ANCOVA (as described above) yielding a main effect of experimental condition, $F(2, 61) = 4.33$, $p < .02$, and a Race × Condition interaction, $F(2, 61) = 3.34$, $p < .05$. As Figure 21.3 shows, Black participants in the diagnostic condition, as predicted, generated the most self-doubt-related completions, significantly more than Black participants in the nondiagnostic condition, $t(61) = 3.52$, $p < .001$, and more than participants in any of the other conditions as well, all $ps < .05$.

STEREOTYPE AVOIDANCE

The six preference and stereotype items described above were summed to form an index of stereotype avoidance that ranged from 6 to 42 with 6 indicating high avoidance and 42 indicating low avoidance (Cronbach's alpha = .65). When these scores were submitted to the ANCOVA they yielded a significant effect of condition, $F(2, 61) = 4.73$, $p < .02$, and a significant Race × Condition interaction, $F(2, 61) = 4.14$, $p < .03$. As can be seen in Figure 21.3, Black participants in the diagnostic condition were the most avoidant of conforming to stereotypic images of African Americans ($M = 20.80$), more so than Black participants in the nondiagnostic condition ($M = 29.80$), $t(61) = 3.61$, $p < .001$, and/or White participants in either condition, all $ps < .05$.

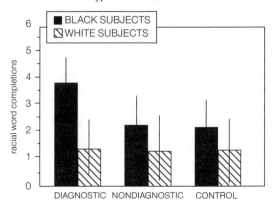

Stereotype Activation Measure

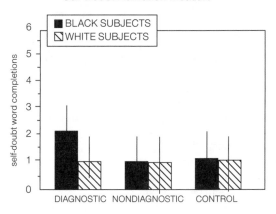

Self-Doubt Activation Measure

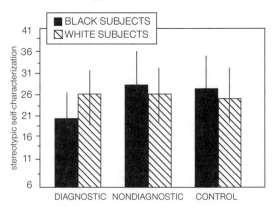

Stereotype Avoidance Measure

FIGURE 21.3. ■ Indicators of stereotype threat.

INDICATING RACE

Did the ability diagnosticity of the test affect participants' tendency to indicate their race on the demographic questionnaire? Among Black participants in the diagnostic condition, only 25% would indicate their race on the questionnaire, whereas 100% of the participants in each of the other conditions would do so. Using a 0/1 conversion of the response frequencies (with 0 = refusal to indicate race and 1 = indication of race) the standard ANCOVA performed on this measure revealed a marginally significant effect of race, $F(1, 61) = 3.86, p < .06$, a significant effect of condition, $F(1 2.61) = 3.40, p < .04$, and a significant Race × Condition interaction, $F(1, 61) = 6.60, p < .01$, all due, of course, to the unique unwillingness of Black participants in the diagnostic condition to indicate their race.

SELF-HANDICAPPING

Four measures assessed participants' desire to claim impediments to performance. Because participants in the control conditions did not complete this measure, these responses were submitted to separate 2 (race) × 2 (diagnosticity) ANCOVAs. Cell means are presented in Table 21.1. Framing the verbal tasks as diagnostic of ability had significant effects on three of the four measures. For the number of hours of sleep, the ANCOVA yielded a significant effect of race, $F(1, 39) = 8.22, p < .01$, and a significant effect of condition, $F(1, 39) 6.53, p < .02$. These effects were qualified by a significant Race × Condition interaction, $F(1, 39) = 4.1, p < .01$. For participants' ratings of their ability to focus, a similar

TABLE 21.1. Self-Handicapping Responses in Study 3

Measure	Diagnostic		Nondiagnostic	
	Blacks ($n = 12$)	Whites ($n = 11$)	Blacks ($n = 11$)	Whites ($n = 10$)
Hours of sleep	5.10$_a$	7.48$_b$	7.05$_b$	7.70$_b$
Ability to focus	4.03$_a$	5.88$_b$	5.85$_b$	6.16$_b$
Current stress	5.51$_a$	5.24$_a$	5.00$_a$	5.02$_a$
Tests unfair	5.46$_a$	2.78$_b$	3.14$_b$	2.04$_b$

Note. Means not sharing a common subscript differ at the .01 level according to Bonferroni procedure. Means sharing a common subscript do not differ.

result emerged: main effects of race, $F(1, 39) = 7.26, p < .02$, and condition, $F(1, 39) = 10.67, p < .01$, and a significant qualifying interaction, $F(1, 39) = 5.73, p < .03$. And finally, the same pattern of effects emerged for participants' ratings of how tricky or unfair they generally find standardized tests to be: a race main effect, $F(1, 39) = 13.24, p < .001$, a condition main effect, $F(1, 39) = 13.42, p < .001$, and a marginally significant, qualifying interaction, $F(1, 39) = 3.58, p < .07$. No significant effects emerged on participants' ratings of their current stress.

Discussion

We had assumed that presenting an intellectual test as diagnostic of ability would arouse a sense of stereotype threat in Black participants. The present results dramatically support this assumption. Compared to participants in the other conditions—that is, Blacks in the nondiagnostic condition and Whites in either condition—Black participants expecting to take a difficult, ability-diagnostic test showed significantly greater cognitive activation of stereotypes about Blacks, greater cognitive activation of concerns about their ability, a greater tendency to avoid racially stereotypic preferences, a greater tendency to make advance excuses for their performance, and finally, a greater reluctance to have their racial identity linked to their performance even in the pedestrian way of recording it on their questionnaires. Clearly the diagnostic instructions caused these participants to experience a strong apprehension, a distinct sense of stereotype threat.

So far, then, we have shown that representing a difficult test as diagnostic of ability can undermine the performance of Black participants, and that it can cause in them a distinct sense of being under threat of judgment by a racial stereotype. This manipulation of stereotype threat—in terms of test diagnosticity—is important because it establishes the generality of the effect to a broad range of real-life situations.

But two questions remain. The first is whether stereotype threat itself—in the absence of the test being explicitly diagnostic of ability—is sufficient to disrupt the performance of these participants on a difficult test. That is, we do not know whether mere activation of the stereotype in the test situation—without the test being explicitly diagnostic of ability—would be enough to cause such effects. A second question is whether the disruptive effect of the diagnosticity manipulation was in fact mediated by the stereotype threat it caused. Showing first that test diagnosticity disrupts Black participants' performance and then, separately, that it causes in these participants to be threatened by the stereotype, does not prove that the effect of test diagnosticity on performance was mediated by the stereotype threat it caused. The performance effect could have been mediated by some other effect of the diagnosticity manipulation. We conducted a fourth experiment to address these questions, and thereby, to test the replicability of the stereotype threat effect under different conditions.

Study 4

This experiment again crossed a manipulation of stereotype threat with the race of participants in a 2 × 2 design with test performance as the chief dependent measure. We addressed the first question above by representing the test in this experiment as nondiagnostic of ability. If stereotype threat then depressed Black participants' performance, we would know that stereotype threat is sufficient to cause this effect even when the test is not represented as diagnostic of ability. We addressed the second question by taking from Study 3 a dependent measure of stereotype threat that had been significantly affected by the diagnosticity manipulation, and manipulating that variable as an independent variable in the present experiment. If this manipulation then affects Black participants' performance, we would know that at least one aspect of the stereotype threat caused by the diagnosticity manipulation was able to impair performance. This would mean that the effect of that manipulation on performance was, or could have been, mediated by the stereotype threat it caused.

The variable that we manipulated in the present study was whether or not participants were required to list their race before taking the test. Recall that in Study 3, 75% of the Black participants in the diagnostic condition refused to record their race on the questionnaire when given the option, whereas all of the participants in the other conditions did. On the assumption that this was a sign of their stereotype avoidance, we reasoned that having participants record their race just prior to the test should prime the racial stereotype about

ability for Black participants, and thus make them stereotype threatened. If this threat alone is sufficient to impair their performance, then, with SATs covaried, these participants should perform worse than White participants in this condition.

In the non-stereotype-threat conditions, the demographic questionnaire simply omitted the item requesting participants' race and, otherwise, followed the nondiagnostic procedures of Studies 1 and 2. Without raising the specters of ability or race-relevant evaluation, we expected Black participants in this condition to experience no stereotype threat and to perform (adjusted for SATs) on par with White participants.

Method

DESIGN AND PARTICIPANTS

This experiment took the form of a 2 × 2 design in which participants' race was crossed with whether or not they recorded their ethnicity on a preliminary questionnaire. Twenty-four Black (6 male, 18 female) and 23 White (11 male, 12 female) Stanford undergraduates were randomly assigned to either the race-prime condition or the no-race-prime condition. Data from two Black participants were discarded because they arrived with suspicions about the racial nature of the study. One White student failed to provide her SAT score and was discarded from data analyses. These participants were replaced to bring the number of participants in each of the four conditions to 11.

PROCEDURE

The procedure closely paralleled that of the nondiagnostic conditions in Studies 1 and 2. After explaining the purpose and format of the test, the experimenter (White man) randomly assigned the participant to the race-prime or no-race-prime condition by drawing a brief questionnaire (labeled "personal information") from a shuffled stack. This questionnaire comprised the experimental manipulation. It was identical for all participants—asking them to provide their age, year in school, major, number of siblings, and parents' education—except that in the race-prime condition the final item asked participants to indicate their race. Because this questionnaire was given to the participant immediately prior to the test the experimenter remained blind to the participant's condition throughout the pretest interaction. After ensuring that the participant had completed the questionnaire, the experimenter started the test and left the room. Twenty-five minutes later he returned, collected the test, and gave the participant a dependent measure questionnaire.

DEPENDENT MEASURES

This experiment used the same 25-min test used in Study 2, but in this experiment it was administered on paper. During the test, participants marked their guesses, and after the test, they indicated on 11-point scales (with end points *not at all* and *extremely*) the extent to which they guessed when they were having difficulty, expended effort on the test, persisted on problems, limited their time on problems, read problems more than once, became frustrated and gave up, and felt that the test was biased.

Participants also completed a questionnaire aimed at measuring their stereotype threat, by expressing their agreement on 7-point scales (with endpoints *strongly disagree* and *strongly agree*) with each of eight statements (e.g., "Some people feel I have less verbal ability because of my race," "The test may have been easier for people of my race," "The experimenter expected me to do poorly because of my race," "In English classes people of my race often face biased evaluations," "My race does not affect people's perception of my verbal ability").

As a measure of academic identification, nine further items explored the effect of conditions on participants' perceptions of the importance of verbal and math skills to their education and intended career (e.g., "verbal skills will be important to my career," "I am a verbally oriented person," "I feel that math is important to me," etc.). Participants responded to these items on 11-point scales with end-points labeled *not at all* and *extremely*.

Results

TEST PERFORMANCE

A 2 (race) × 2 (race prime vs. no race prime) ANCOVA on test performance with self-reported SATs as a covariate (Black mean = 591, White mean = 643) revealed a strong condition interaction in the predicted direction. As Figure 21.4 shows, Blacks in the race-prime condition per-

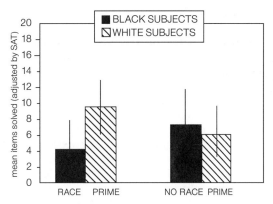

FIGURE 21.4. ■ Mean test performance Study 4.

formed worse than virtually all of the other groups, yet in the no-race-prime condition their performance equaled that of Whites, $F(1, 39) = 7.82$, $p < .01$. Planned contrasts on these adjusted scores revealed that, as predicted, Blacks in the race-prime condition performed significantly worse than Blacks in the no-race-prime condition, $t(39) = 2.43$, $p < .02$, and significantly worse than Whites in the race-prime condition, $t(39) = 2.87$, $p < .01$. Black participants in the race-prime condition performed worse than Whites in the no-race-prime condition, but not significantly so. Nonetheless, the comparison pitting the Black race-prime condition against the three remaining conditions was highly significant, $F(1, 39) = 8.15$, $p < .01$.

ACCURACY

The ANCOVA for this index—the percent correct of the items attempted for each participant—with participants' SATs as the covariate revealed a significant tendency for participants in the race-prime condition to have poorer accuracy, $F(1, 39) = 4.07$, $p = .05$. The adjusted means for the Black and White participants in the race-prime condition were .402 and .438 respectively, while those for the Black and White participants in the no-race-prime condition were .541 and .520 respectively. Condition contrasts did not reach significance, although the difference between the Black participants in the race-prime and no-race-prime conditions was marginally significant, $p < .08$. Again, these data suggest that lessened accuracy is part of the process through which stereotype threat impairs performance.

NUMBER OF ITEMS COMPLETED

An ANCOVA (again with SATs removed as a covariate) revealed only a significant Race × Race Prime interaction for the number of test items participants completed, $F(1, 39)$ 12.13, $p < .01$. In the race-prime condition Blacks completed fewer items than Whites, $t(39) = 3.83$, $p < .001$. The adjusted means were 11.58 and 20.15 respectively. In the no-race-prime condition, however, Blacks and Whites answered roughly the same number of problems. The adjusted means were 15.32 and 13.03, respectively.

PERFORMANCE-RELEVANT MEASURES

Although participants' postexam ratings revealed no differences in the degree to which they thought they guessed on the test ($F < 1$), the ANCOVA performed on the actual number of guesses participants indicated on their test sheet revealed a Race × Race Prime interaction, $F(1, 39) = 5.56$, $p < .03$. Black participants made fewer guesses when race was primed ($M = 1.99$) than when it was not ($M = 2.74$), whereas White participants tended to guess more when race was primed ($M = 4.23$) than when it was not ($M = 1.58$). No significant condition effects emerged for participants' self-reported effort where, on an 11-point scale with 11 indicating *extremely hard* work, the overall mean was 8.84.

Participants' estimates of how well they had performed, taken after the test, showed no condition effects (the overall mean was 7.4 items). Neither were there condition effects on participants' ratings (made during the postexperimental debriefing) of how much having to indicate their ethnicity bothered them during the test (or *would* have bothered them in the case of participants in the no-race-prime condition). The overall mean was 3.31 on an 11-point scale for which 11 indicated the most distraction. Participants often stated in postexperimental interviews that they found recording their race unnoteworthy because they had to do it so often in everyday life. Of the items bearing on participants' experience taking the test, only one effect emerged: Black participants reported reading test items more than once to a greater degree than did White participants, $F(1, 39) = 8.62$, $p < .01$.

STEREOTYPE THREAT AND ACADEMIC IDENTIFICATION MEASURES

A MANOVA of the stereotype threat scale revealed that Black participants felt more stereotype threat than White participants, $F(9, 31) = 8.80$, $p < .01$. No other effects reached significance. Analyses of participants' responses to questions regarding the personal importance of math, verbal skills and athletics revealed that Black participants reported valuing sports less than Whites, $F(1, 39) = 4.11$, $p < .05$. As in Study 3, this result may reflect Black participants distancing themselves from the stereotype of the academically untalented Black athlete. Correlations between participants' numerical performance estimates and their ratings of the importance of sports, showed that for Blacks, the worse they believed they performed, the more they devalued sports—in the no-race-prime condition ($r = .56$), and particularly in the race-prime condition ($r = .70$).

Discussion

Priming racial identity depressed Black participants' performance on a difficult verbal test even when the test was not presented as diagnostic of intellectual ability. It did this, we assume, by directly making the stereotype mentally available and thus creating the self-threatening predicament that their performance could prove the stereotype self-characteristic. In Studies 1, 2 and 3, the stereotype was evoked indirectly by describing the test as diagnostic of an ability to which it was relevant. What this experiment shows is that mere cognitive availability of the racial stereotype is enough to depress Black participants' intellectual performance, and that this is so even when the test is presented as not diagnostic of intelligence. Also— because we know from Study 3 that the diagnosticity manipulation strongly affects participants' willingness to record their race—this finding shows that the performance-depressing effect of the diagnosticity manipulation in the earlier experiments was, or could have been, mediated by the effect of that manipulation on stereotype threat—as opposed to some other aspect of the manipulation.

Still, we had expected Black participants in the race-prime condition to show more stereotype threat (as measured by the stereotype threat and stereotype avoidance measures) than Black participants in the no-race-prime condition—reflecting the effect of the manipulation. Instead, while Blacks showed more stereotype threat than Whites, Blacks in the race-prime condition showed no more stereotype threat than Blacks in the no-race-prime condition. Nor did these groups differ on the identification measures. This may have happened for several reasons. These measures came after the test in this experiment, not before it as in Study 3. Thus, after experiencing the difficult, frustrating exam, all Black participants may have been somewhat stereotype threatened and stereotype avoidant (more so than the White participants) regardless of their condition. Also, the lack of a condition difference between Black participants on the stereotype threat and identification items may have occurred because these items asked participants to respond in reference to settings (e.g., English classes) and attitudes (e.g., about how one's race is generally regarded) that are beyond their immediate experience in the experiment.

Compared to participants in the other conditions, Black participants in the race-prime condition did not report expending less effort on the test; they were not more disturbed at having to list their race; and they did not guess more than other participants. Also, Black participants in both conditions reread the test items more than White participants. Such findings do not fit the idea that these participants underperformed because they withdrew effort from the experiment.

To establish the replicability of the race-prime effect and to explore the possible mediational role of anxiety, we conducted a two-condition experiment which randomly assigned only Black participants to either the race-prime or no-race-prime conditions described in Study 4. We also administered the test on computer to enable a measure of the time participants spent on the items, and gave participants an anxiety measure at the end of the experiment. Replicating Study 4, race-prime participants got significantly fewer items correct ($M = 4.4$) than no-race-prime participants ($M = 7.7$), $t(18) = 2.34$, $p < .04$; they were marginally less accurate ($M = .334$) than no-race-prime participants ($M = .395$), $p = .10$; and they answered fewer items ($M = 13.2$) than no-race-prime participants ($M = 20.1$), $t(18) = 2.89$, $p < .01$. Race-prime participants spent more time on the first five test items (the number which all participants completed) (M

$= 79$ s) than no-race-prime participants ($M = 61$s), $t(18) = 2.27$, $p < .04$, and they were significantly more anxious than no-race-prime participants, $t(18) = 2.34$, $p < .04$. The means on the STAI were 48.5 and 40.5 respectively, on a scale that ranged from 20 (indicating *low anxiety*) to 80 (*extreme anxiety*). These results show that a race prime reliably depresses Black participants' performance on this difficult exam, and that it causes reactions that could be a response to stereotype threat—namely, an anxiety-based perseveration on especially the early test items, items that, as reading comprehension items, required multiple steps.

General Discussion

The existence of a negative stereotype about a group to which one belongs, we have argued, means that in situations where the stereotype is applicable, one is at risk of confirming it as a self-characterization, both to one's self and to others who know the stereotype. This is what is meant by stereotype threat. And when the stereotype involved demeans something as important as intellectual ability, this threat can be disruptive enough, we hypothesize, to impair intellectual performance.

In support of this reasoning, the present experiments show that making African American participants vulnerable to judgment by negative stereotypes about their group's intellectual ability depressed their standardized test performance relative to White participants, while conditions designed to alleviate this threat, improved their performance, equating the two groups once their differences in SATs were controlled. Studies 1 and 2 produced this pattern by varying whether or not the test was represented as diagnostic of intellectual ability—a procedure that varied stereotype threat by varying the relevance of the stereotype about Blacks' ability to their performance. Study 3 provided direct evidence that this manipulation aroused stereotype threat in Black participants by showing that it activated the racial stereotype and stereotype-related self-doubts in their thinking, that it led them to distance themselves from African American stereotypes. Study 4 showed that merely recording their race—presumably by making the stereotype salient—was enough to impair Black participants' performance even when the test was not diagnostic of ability. Taken together these experiments show that stereotype threat—established by quite subtle instructional differences—can impair the intellectual test performance of Black students, and that lifting it can dramatically improve that performance.

Mediation: How Stereotype Threat Impairs Performance

Study 3 offers clear evidence of what being stereotype threatened is like—as well as demonstrating that the mere prospect of a difficult, ability-diagnostic test was enough to do this to our sample of African American participants. But how precisely did this state of self-threat impair performance, through what mechanism or set of mechanisms did the impairment occur?

There are a number of possibilities: distraction, narrowed attention, anxiety, self-consciousness, withdrawal of effort, over-effort, and so on (e.g., Baumeister, 1984). In fact, several such mechanisms may be involved simultaneously, or different mechanisms may be involved under different conditions. For example, if the test were long enough to solidly engender low performance expectations, then withdrawal of effort might play a bigger mediational role than, say, anxiety, which might be more important with a shorter test. Such complexities notwithstanding, our findings offer some insight into how the present effects were mediated.

Our best assessment is that stereotype threat caused an inefficiency of processing much like that caused by other evaluative pressures. Stereotype-threatened participants spent more time doing fewer items more inaccurately—probably as a result of alternating their attention between trying to answer the items and trying to assess the self-significance of their frustration. This form of debilitation—reduced speed and accuracy—has been shown as a reaction to evaluation apprehension (e.g., Geen, 1985); test anxiety (e.g., Wine, 1971; Sarason, 1972); the presence of an audience (e.g., Bond, 1982); and competition (Baumeister, 1984). Several findings, by suggesting that stereotype-threatened participants were both motivated and inefficient, point in this direction. They reported expending as much effort as other participants. In those studies that included the requisite measures—Study 2 and the replication study reported with Study 4—they actually spent more time per

item. They did not guess more than non-stereotype-threatened participants, and, as Black participants did generally, they reported rereading the items more. Also, as noted, these participants were strong students, and almost certainly identified with the material on the test. They may even have been more anxious. Stereotype threat increased Black participants' anxiety in the replication study, although not significantly in Study 2. Together then, these findings suggest that stereotype threat led participants to try hard but with impaired efficiency.

Still, we note that lower expectations may have also been involved, especially in real-life occurrences of stereotype threat. As performance falters under stereotype threat, and as the stereotype frames that faltering as a sign of a group-based inferiority, the individual's expectations about his or her ability and performance may drop—presumably faster than they would if the stereotype were not there to credit the inability interpretation. And lower expectations, as the literature has long emphasized (e.g., Bandura, 1977, 1986; Carver, Blaney, & Scheier, 1979; Pyszczynski & Greenberg, 1983) can further undermine performance by undermining motivation and effort. It is precisely a process of stereotype threat fostering low expectations in a domain that we suggest leads eventually to disidentification with the domain. We assume that this process did not get very far in the present research because the tests were short, and because our participants, as highly identified students, were unlikely to give up on these tests—as their self-reports tell us. But we do assume that lower expectations can play a role in mediating stereotype threat effects.

There is, however, strong evidence against one kind of expectancy mediation. This is the idea that lowered performance or self-efficacy expectations alone mediated the effects of stereotype threat. Conceivably, the stereotype threat treatments got Black participants to expect that they would perform poorly on the test—presumably by getting them to accept the image of themselves inherent in the racial stereotype. The stereotype threat condition did activate participants' self-doubts. This lower expectation, then, outside of any experience these participants may have had with the test itself, and outside of any apprehension they may have had about self-confirming the stereotype may have directly weakened their motivation and performance. Of course it would be important to show that stereotype threat effects are mediated in African American students by expectations implicit in the stereotype, expectations powerful enough to more or less automatically cause their underperformance.

But there are several reasons to doubt this view. For one thing, it isn't clear that our stereotype threat manipulations led Black participants to accept lower expectations and then to follow them unrevisedly to lower performance. For example, they resisted the self-applicability of the stereotype. But most important, as noted, it is almost certain that any expectation formed prior to the test would be superseded by the participants' actual experience with the test items; rising with success and falling with frustration. In fact, another experiment in our lab offered direct evidence of this by showing that expectations manipulated before the test had no effect on performance. Its procedure followed, in all conditions, that of the standard diagnostic condition used in Studies 1 and 2—with the exception that it directly manipulated efficacy and performance expectations before participants took the test. After being told that the test was ability diagnostic, and just before taking the test, the experimenter (an Asian woman) asked participants what their SAT scores were. After hearing the score, in the positive expectation condition, she commented that the participant should have little trouble with the test. In the negative expectation condition, this comment indicated that the participant would have trouble with the test, and nothing was said in a no-expectation condition. Both White and Black participants were run in all three expectation conditions. While the experiment replicated the standard effect of Whites outperforming Blacks under these stereotype threat conditions (participants' SATs were again used as a covariate) $F(1, 32) = 5.12, p < .03$, this personalized expectation manipulation had no effect on the performance of either group. For Blacks, the means were 4.32, 6.38, and 6.55, for the positive, negative and no-expectations conditions, respectively and for Whites, for the same conditions, they were 8.24, 9.25, and 11.23, respectively. Thus in an experiment that was sensitive enough to replicate the standard stereotype threat effect expectations explicitly manipulated before the test had no effect on performance. They are unlikely, then, to have been the medium through which stereotype threat affected performance in this research.

Finally, participants in all conditions of these experiments were given low performance expectations by telling them that they should expect to get few items correct due to the difficulty of the test. Importantly, this instruction did not depress the performance of participants in the non-stereotype-threat conditions. Thus it is not likely that a low performance expectation, implied by the stereotype, would have been powerful enough, by itself, to lower performance among these participants when a direct manipulation of the expectation could not.

The Emerging Picture of Stereotype Threat

In the social psychological literature there are other constructs that address the experience of potential victims of stereotypes. For clarity's sake, we briefly compare the construct of stereotype threat to these.

"TOKEN" STATUS AND COGNITIVE FUNCTIONING

Lord & Saenz (1985) have shown that token status in a group—that is, being the token minority in a group that is otherwise homogeneous—can cause deficits in cognitive functioning and memory, presumably as an outgrowth of the self-consciousness it causes. Although probably in the same family of effects as stereotype threat, token status would be expected to disrupt cognitive functioning even when the token individual is not targeted by a performance-relevant stereotype, as with, for example, a White man in a group of women solving math problems. Nor do stereotype threat effects require token status, as was shown in the present experiments. In real life, of course, these two processes may often co-occur, as for the Black in an otherwise non-Black classroom. They are nonetheless, distinct processes.

ATTRIBUTIONAL AMBIGUITY

Another important theory, and now extensive program of research by Crocker and Major (e.g., Crocker & Major, 1989; Crocker, Voelkl, Testa, & Major, 1991) examined how people contend with the self-evaluative implications of having a stigmatized identity. Both their theory and ours focus on the psychology of contending with social devaluation and differ most clearly in which aspect of this psychology they attend to. The work of Crocker and Major focused on the implications of this psychology for self-esteem maintenance (for example, the strategies available for protecting self-esteem against stigmatized status) and we have focused on its implications for intellectual performance. There is also a conceptual difference. Attributional ambiguity refers to the confusion a potential target of prejudice might have over whether or not he is being treated prejudicially. Stereotype threat, of course, refers to his apprehension over confirming or eliciting the judgment that the stereotype is self-characteristic. Again, the two processes can co-occur—as for the woman who gets cut from the math team, for example—but are distinct.

THE EARLIER RESEARCH OF THE KATZ GROUP

We also note that stereotype threat may explain the earlier findings of Katz and his colleagues. They found in the 1960s that the intellectual performance of Black participants rose and fell with conditions that seemed to vary in stereotype threat—for example, whether the test was represented as a test of intelligence or as one of psychomotor skill. A stereotype threat interpretation of these findings was foiled, however, by the lack of White participant control groups. Thus, the finding that manipulations very similar to Katz's depressed Black participants' performance while not depressing White participants' performance makes stereotype threat a parsimonious account of all these findings.

TEST DIFFICULTY AND RACIAL DIFFERENCES IN STANDARDIZED TEST PERFORMANCE

The test used in these experiments is quite difficult, as the low performance scores indicate. As we argued it may have to be at least somewhat demanding for stereotype threat to be occasioned. But acknowledging this parameter raises a question: Does stereotype threat significantly undermine the performance of Black students on the SAT? And if it does, is it appropriate to use the SAT as the standard for equating Black and White participants on skill level within our experiments? The answer to the first question has to be that it depends on how much frustration is experienced on the SAT. If the student perceives that a significant portion of the test is within his or her competence, it may preempt or override stereotype threat

by proving the stereotype inapplicable. When the student cannot gain this perception, however, the group stereotype becomes relevant as an explanation and may undermine performance. Thus we surmise that over the entire range of Black student test takers, stereotype threat causes a significant depression of scores

And, of course, this point holds more generally. An important implication of this research is that stereotype threat is an underappreciated source of classic deficits in standardized test performance (e.g., IQ) suffered by Blacks and other stereotype-threatened groups such as those of lower socioeconomic status and women in mathematics (Herrnstein, 1973; Jensen, 1969, 1980; Spencer, Steele, & Quinn, 1999). In addition to whatever environmental or genetic endowments a person brings to the testing situation, this research shows that this situation is not group-neutral—not even, quite possibly, when the tests and test content have been accommodated to the test-taker's background. The problem is that stereotypes afoot in the larger society establish a predicament in the testing situation—aside from test content—that still has the power to undermine standardized test performance, and we suspect, contribute powerfully to the pattern of group differences that have characterized these tests since their inception.

But, for several reasons, we doubt that this possibility compromises the interpretation of the present findings. First, it is unlikely that stereotype threat had much differential effect on the SATs of our Black and White participants since both groups, as highly selected students, are not likely to have experienced very great frustration on these tests. Second, even if our Black participants' SATs were more depressed in this way, using such depressed scores as a covariate in the present analyses would only adjust Black performance more in the direction of reducing the Black–White difference in the stereotype threat conditions. Thus, while a self-threateningly difficult test is probably a necessary condition for stereotype threat, and while stereotype threat may commonly depress the standardized test performance of Black test takers, these facts are not likely to have compromised the present results.

In conclusion, our focus in this research has been on how social context and group identity come together to mediate an important behavior. This approach is Lewinian; it is also hopeful. Compared to viewing the problem of Black underachievement as rooted in something about the group or its societal conditions, this analysis uncovers a social psychological predicament of race, rife in the standardized testing situation, that is amenable to change—as we hope our manipulations have illustrated.

REFERENCES

Allport, G. (1954). *The nature of prejudice.* New York: Addison-Wesley.

American Council on Education. (1990). *Minorities in higher education.* Washington, DC: Office of Minority Concerns.

Bandura, A. (1977). Self-efficacy: Toward a unifying theory of behavioral change. *Psychological Review, 84,* 191–215.

Bandura, A. (1986). Fearful expectations and avoidant actions as coeffects of perceived self-inefficacy. *American Psychologist, 41,* 1389–1391.

Baumeister, R. F. (1984). Choking under pressure: Self-consciousness and paradoxical effects of incentives on skillful performance. *Journal of Personality and Social Psychology, 16,* 610–620.

Bond, C. F. (1982). Social facilitation: A self-presentational view. *Journal of Personality and Social Psychology, 42,* 1042–1050.

Carter, S. L. (1991). *Reflections of an affirmative action baby.* New York: Basic Books.

Carver, C. S., Blaney, P. H., & Scheier, M. F. (1979). Reassertion and giving up: The interactive role of self-directed attention and outcome expectancy. *Journal of Personality and Social Psychology, 37,* 1859–1870.

Cleary, T A., Humphreys, L. G., Kendrick, S. A., & Wesman, A. (1975). Educational uses of tests with disadvantaged students. *American Psychologist, 30,* 15–41.

Crocker, J., & Major, B. (1989). Social stigma and self-esteem: The self-protective properties of stigma. *Psychological Review 96,* 608–630.

Crocker, J., Voelkl, K., Testa, M., & Major, B. (1991). Social stigma: The affective consequences of attributional ambiguity. *Journal of Personality and Social Psychology, 60,* 218–228.

Devine, P. G. (1989). Stereotypes and prejudice: Their automatic and controlled components. *Journal of Personality and Social Psychology, 56,* 5–18.

Dovidio, J. F., Evans, N., & Tyler, R. B. (1986). Racial stereotypes: The contents of their cognitive representations. *Journal of Experimental Social Psychology, 22,* 22–37.

Easterbrook, J. A. (1959). The effect of emotion on cue utilization and the organization of behavior. *Psychological Review, 66,* 183–201.

Geen, R. G. (1985). Evaluation apprehension and response withholding in solution of anagrams. *Personality and Individual Differences, 6,* 293–298.

Geen, R. G. (1991). Social motivation. *Annual Review of Psychology, 42,* 377–399.

Gilbert, D. T. & Hixon, J. G. (1991). The trouble of thinking: Activation and application of stereotypic beliefs. *Journal of Personality and Social Psychology, 60,* 509–517.

Goffman, I. (1963). *Stigma.* New York: Simon & Shuster, Inc.

Herrnstein, R. (1973). *IQ in the meritocracy.* Boston: Little Brown.

Higgins, E. T. (1989). Knowledge accessibility and activation: Subjectivity and suffering from unconscious sources. In J. S. Uleman & J. A. Bargh (Eds.), *Unintended thoughts* (pp. 75–123). New York: Guilford.

Jensen, A. R. (1969). How much can we boost IQ and scholastic achievement? *Harvard Educational Review, 39,* 1–123.

Jensen, A. R. (1980). *Bias in mental testing.* New York: Free Press.

Katz, I. (1964). Review of evidence relating to effects of desegregation on the intellectual performance of Negroes. *American Psychologist, 19,* 381–399.

Katz, I., Epps, E. G., & Axelson, L. J. (1964). Effect upon Negro digit symbol performance of comparison with Whites and with other Negroes. *Journal of Abnormal and Social Psychology, 69,* 963–970.

Katz, I., Roberts, S. O., & Robinson, J. M. (1965). Effects of task difficulty, race of administrator, and instructions on digit-symbol performance of Negroes. *Journal of Personality and Social Psychology, 2,* 53–59.

Linn, R. L. (1973). Fair test use in selection. *Review of Educational Research, 13,* 139–161.

Lord, C. G., & Saenz, D. S. (1985). Memory deficits and memory surfeits: Differential cognitive consequences of tokenism for tokens and observers. *Journal of Personality and Social Psychology, 19,* 918–926.

Lord, C. G., Saenz, D. S., & Godfrey, D. K. (1987). Effects of perceived scrutiny on participant memory for social interactions. *Journal of Experimental Social Psychology, 23,* 498–517.

Nettles, M. T. (1988). *Toward undergraduate student equality in American higher education.* New York: Greenwood.

Pyszczynski, T., & Greenberg, J. (1983). Determinants of reduction in effort as a strategy for coping with anticipated failure. *Journal of Research in Personality, 17,* 412–422.

Sarason, I. G. (1972). Experimental approaches to test anxiety: Attention and the uses of information. In C. D. Spielberger (Ed.), *Anxiety: Current trends in theory and research* (Vol. 2). New York: Academic Press.

Seta, J. J. (1982). The impact of coactors' comparison processes on task performance. *Journal of Personality and Social Psychology, 12,* 281–291.

Spencer, S., & Steele, C., & Quinn, D. (1999). Stereotype threat and women's math performance. *Journal of Experimental Social Psychology, 35,* 4–28.

Stanley, J. C. (1971). Predicting college success of the educationally disadvantaged. *Science, 171,* 640–647.

Steele, C. M. (1992, April). Race and the schooling of black Americans. *The Atlantic Monthly.*

Steele, S. (1990). *The content of our character.* New York: St. Martin's Press.

Tulving, E., Schacter, D. L., & Stark, H. A. (1982). Priming effects in word-fragment completion are independent of recognition memory. *Journal of Experimental Psychology: Learning, Memory and Cognition, 8,* 336–342.

Wine, J. (1971). Test anxiety and direction of attention. *Psychological Bulletin, 76,* 92–104.

Improving Intergroup Perceptions and Behavior

Given that stereotypes and prejudice form such an important part of our individual psychology, and indeed of society as a whole, we might despair at the prospect of ever being able to change them. And such despair would not necessarily be out of place. Stereotypes are hard to change, both because they are supported by the informational and behavioral biases that we have already discussed, and also because they are reinforced by the society as a whole. Furthermore, stereotypes persist in part because we are frequently not even aware that we are using them, making it impossible to correct for them. Nevertheless, as we will see in the readings in this section, several research programs have been able to create changes in intergroup beliefs, at least in some situations, and this change can in some cases be relatively long-lasting.

The most common approach to changing stereotypes is to provide people with information about the characteristics of the stereotyped groups by having them interact with each other. This is known as the *contact hypothesis,* and the idea is that our stereotypes will be dispelled once we get a chance to learn about individuals from groups with which we are not familiar. There is a voluminous amount of research on using contact to change stereotypes, in both laboratory and field experiments, and it is well reviewed in Reading 22, by Hewstone. Hewstone organizes his article around the different theories of stereotype change, and you can see that each of these theoretical approaches has been tested in both laboratory and field studies. Although there are some differences of opinion among researchers, analyses of the impact of busing on intergroup attitudes generally finds that, at least over the long run, intergroup contact does improve intergroup attitudes (Schofield, 1991).

Hewstone's careful analysis of different approaches to contact helps make it clear why the contact hypothesis is not always supported. For one, the situations in which the contact occurs are not always set up in a manner that allows the individuals to really get to know each other, and in some cases the situation may even promote intergroup hostility. Furthermore, in some cases there is at least some truth to stereotypes, and contact may therefore amplify rather than dispel them. Hewstone concludes in the end that each of these theories of intergroup contact has potential for explaining the conditions under which contact produces stereotype change, and yet that each also has some limitations.

Perhaps the most important difficulty in using contact to change stereotypes and prejudice is that the changes do not generalize from the individuals who we meet to the group as a whole. Reading 23, by Rothbart and John, provides a theoretical analysis of this difficulty. In their innovative approach to considering stereotype change through contact, they explicitly consider the situations in which generalization from the individual to the group is likely to take place—specifically when we learn about the other as an individual, and yet that individual is prototypical of the group as a whole.

Reading 24, by Gaertner, Mann, Dovidio, Murrell, and Pomare, studies a particular type of intergroup contact: situations in which the members of the different groups are cooperating with each other. Cooperative and interdependent contact (Aronson, Blaney, Stephan, Sikes, & Snapp, 1978) appears to be the most effective method of producing stereotype change through contact, and Gaertner and his colleagues attempt to understand exactly why this is. They propose a *recategorization* theory

of prejudice reduction that suggests that cooperation creates conditions under which we begin to see members of the in-group and the out-group as one broader group. In recategorization, social categorization changes from a perception of two groups ("us" and "them") to a perception of only one group ("we"). This research confirms that working cooperatively with another group is effective in making attitudes toward that group more positive, and demonstrates that this change occurs as a result of recategorization.

Because contact is not always successful in producing stereotype change, other approaches to changing stereotypes and prejudice have also been proposed. One idea is to attempt to get people to avoid thinking about each other in terms of their group memberships at all, and to focus only on their individual features instead. This approach is known as the *colorblind perspective*. However, it turns out that people's group memberships are important to them, and as a result, group membership is not so easily ignored. Indeed, most analyses have suggested that ignoring group memberships entirely is not particularly effective. Still another avenue is through education—we may at least in some cases be able to teach people that their beliefs are incorrect, or at least that it is not appropriate to use them. Indeed, the norms of the society itself do change over time, and stereotypes and prejudice will follow these changes.

Overall, improvements in intergroup relations are probably more likely to occur in situations of relative peace and prosperity, when members of the different groups do not feel particularly threatened by each other. And in many cases, these changes can be produced through changes in social policy, such as the equal rights and affirmative action laws in the United States, which can and have produced changes in stereotypes and prejudice over time.

Discussion Questions

1. What cognitive and motivational processes make it so difficult to change stereotypes?
2. Why is it so difficult to change stereotypes and prejudice through contact? Under which conditions is contact effective?
3. What is *recategorization*, and how does it reduce stereotyping and prejudice?
4. What are some alternatives to using contact to change stereotypes and prejudice? Which approaches seem, in your opinion, to be most likely to be effective?

Suggested Readings

Aronson, E., Blaney, N., Stephan, C., Sikes, J., & Snapp, M. (1978). *The jigsaw class-room.* Beverly Hills, CA: Sage. A review of the effectiveness of the jigsaw technique in improving relationships among individuals from different groups.

Miller, N., & Brewer, M. B. (1984). *Groups in contact: The psychology of desegregation.* Orlando, FL: Academic Press. A thorough analysis of when and how intergroup contact, including busing of children, changes stereotypes.

Schofield, J. (1991). School desegregation and intergroup relations: A review of the literature. In G. Grant (Ed.), *Review of research in education* (Vol. 17, pp. 335–409). Washington, DC: American Educational Research Association. An analysis of the effectiveness of various programs designed to improve racial attitudes in schools.

Weber, R., & Crocker, J. (1983). Cognitive processes in the revision of stereotypic beliefs. *Journal of Personality and Social Psychology, 45,* 961–977. A test of the subtyping, bookkeeping, and conversion models of stereotype change.

Contact and Categorization: Social Psychological Interventions to Change Intergroup Relations

Miles Hewstone • University of Cadiff

Since wars begin in the minds of men, it is in the minds of men that the defences of peace must be constructed.

—UNESCO Motto

One of the most powerful journalistic images of 1994 was of the atrocities committed in the African state of Rwanda, leaving hundreds of thousands dead or brutally injured. Remarkably, the conflict between Hutu and Tutsi is some four centuries old and seemingly intractable. When members of the two groups were asked how they viewed each other, their responses were particularly pessimistic: "Asked whether the characteristics could be changed by training and upbringing, both groups answered that only very limited changes could be made; the qualities were inherent" (Tajfel, 1978, p. 85).[1]

This example gives a flavor of how difficult it may sometimes be to change strongly held stereotypes. Not least, because there is often extensive social support for stereotypes, most evident in the form of power relations, mass media representations, and social norms (Pettigrew, 1981). Yet, because stereotypical perceptions of out-groups are often negative and homogeneous, rationalizing

discrimination and making cooperative intergroup interaction less likely, there is widespread agreement about the need for interventions that can bring about stereotype change. The aim of this chapter is not to review all the available evidence from an array of potential interventions (see Duckitt, 1992; Fisher, 1990; Stephan, 1985; Wilder, 1986b). Instead, I begin by highlighting some of the issues that should be raised at the outset of any review, and I then identify four main themes around which this chapter is organized.

The first point to clarify is the present focus on *social psychological* interventions and their impact on *intergroup relations*. There are, of course, alternative kinds of interventions whose impact is directed at different kinds of outcomes. For example, some more sociological interventions are aimed at structural conditions (e.g., affirmative action programs directed at differential rates of employment in ethnic groups); whereas other more educational interventions target specifically educational outcomes (e.g., academic achievement). These interventions will only be included in this

_____

[1]The quotation is taken by Tajfel from a book by Mason (1970), based on anthropological work in Rwanda by Maquet (1961).

chapter insofar as they influence intergroup relations, which they frequently do (see Schofield, 1989, 1991).

The second point to clarify is that the title of this chapter refers to *intergroup relations*, including behavior but especially perceptions, and not exclusively to stereotypes. This title reflects the diversity of measures found across studies—including racial attitudes, social distance scales, and sociometric measures—although studies that measure stereotypes will be highlighted. Furthermore, intergroup relations includes perceptions of in-group as well as out-group (although most work deals mainly with the latter), because theoretical analyses of intergroup discrimination have emphasized that it is often driven by a pro-in-group rather than an anti-out-group orientation (see Brewer, 1979). From the social identity theory perspective (e.g., Hogg & Abrams, 1988; Tajfel, 1978; Tajfel & Turner, 1979) that has stimulated most of the work reviewed here, the most appropriate and effective interventions may be those that affect in-group perceptions, although the consequences to out-group members may be no less pernicious when they are disadvantaged in this more subtle way (e.g., Mummendey & Schreiber, 1983) than when they are treated with open disparagement, hostility, or aggression.

In writing this chapter for this particular book, I have used four general themes to organize the large number of studies and perspectives. First, since a much-lamented failure of many interventions is that they do not "generalize," I begin by considering types of generalization that could serve as outcome measures in research and then relate the studies reviewed back to these criteria. An underlying goal of the chapter is to identify which, if any, types of generalization are achieved by which interventions. Second, I accentuate the most promising *theoretical* perspectives in this area. To take the topic of school desegregation as an example, several authors have argued that the lack of adequate theory is partly responsible for an inconclusive literature (e.g., Cohen, 1975; St. John, 1975; Schofield, 1978).

Third, I select studies that specify more exactly the *process* underlying effects. To this end, I prefer experiments to surveys, and especially studies that have successfully specified the mediational of moderational effects of key variables (see Baron

& Kenny, 1986). Unfortunately, many surveys in this area suffer from various design flaws, especially when only able to evaluate ongoing programs in a relatively reactive way (see Schofield, 1991). Where the results of experiments and good surveys converge, of course, we can have more faith in the underlying theoretical model supported (Campbell & Fiske, 1959). Fourth, and finally, the title of this chapter is selected to convey two main interventions that emerge from a broad literature: those aimed at encouraging contact between members of opposed groups, and those directed at altering the structure of social categorizations underlying situations of intergroup conflict. I argue that these interventions—and the variants contained within each—are distinct but complementary, and that the next thrust of research in this area should actively seek to integrate them.

Thus this chapter begins by looking at the goal—generalized change in intergroup relations—and then considers what I view as the two most important means of achieving this.

The Nature of Generalized Change

Before planning and evaluating any intervention, one should of course clarify the desired outcomes. In a recent theoretical analysis, Brewer and Miller (1988) argued for a distinction between three types of generalization, any of which a successful intervention might seek to achieve. They also made several useful predictions about the type of intergroup interaction likely to be associated with each type of generalization, and they pointed to some of the dangers associated with each approach to improving intergroup relations. I will refer to these predictions as I evaluate each major intervention in turn.

The first type of generalization, "change in attitudes toward the social category," is the classic outcome variable in this area—generalization from a target individual to the out-group as a whole. Evidence of this effect is quite rare (Amir, 1969, 1976). Brewer and Miller (1988) argue that this type of generalization is most likely to be effected by *category-based* interaction, in which a given in-group member responds to out-group members as interchangeable representatives of a fairly homogeneous category. Brewer and Miller see two main problems with this type of interaction. First, positive contact must be contrived, so that generalized change is in the desired direction; such change may not be easy to engender, and the contact may be constrained and superficial. Second, the distinctiveness of the out-group social category may be reinforced during the course of interaction, thus maintaining in-group/out-group distinctions in the long run.

The second type of generalization, "increased complexity of intergroup perceptions," refers to an increase in the perceived variability of the out-group. Although perceived group variability has become a central area of research on stereotyping and intergroup relations (e.g., Park, Judd, & Ryan, 1991; see Ryan, Park, & Judd, 1996), we shall see that it has only very recently been incorporated as an outcome measure of stereotype change. Brewer and Miller suggest that "differentiated" interaction is most likely to accomplish increased complexity (or perceived variability) of an out-group, whereby perceivers recognize distinctions among members of a given category who are still subtyped within the larger superordinate category. The danger is that the formation of subtypes may prevent change in the perceived characteristics of the group as a whole (stereotypes).

The third type of generalization, "decategorization," refers to change in the perceived usefulness, or meaningfulness, of a social category for identifying and classifying new individuals. Brewer and Miller suggest that this form of generalization is most likely to be realized by a final type of interaction, "personalization," in which an in-group member responds to out-group individuals in terms of their relationship to self, such that self–other comparisons are made across category boundaries. Although this form of generalization may be important in some circumstances, as when group identities are quite weak and recently formed, it seems less likely to be realistic in the context of established identities, intensified by wider social and political factors.

The remainder of this chapter applies the foregoing analysis of change to an evaluation of interventions based on engineering contact between groups, and on changing the structure of social categorizations in intergroup settings. For each separate intervention, I deal with theory, research, and critique, moving toward an integration that could potentially result in all three kinds of generalization.

The Contact Hypothesis: Getting Together . . . but How?

The more we get together, together, together
The more we get together, the happier we'll be
'Cause your friends are my friends
And my friends are your friends
The more we get together, the happier we'll be.
—Traditional Song

The "contact hypothesis" refers to the simple idea that contact between members of different groups will improve relations between them. This view has been the basis of many social policy decisions advocating racial integration in North American schools, housing projects, the armed forces and so on. Allport (1954/1979) acknowledged, however, that contact could increase as well as decrease prejudice and stereotyping. He emphasized the "nature of contact" and saw that its effect would depend on the kinds of people and situations involved. I will not provide a comprehensive review of contact research here (see Amir, 1969, 1976; McClendon, 1974; Riordan, 1978). Instead, I will summarize its main points, its evaluation to date, and its main limitation, opening up the way to a more detailed analysis of recent theoretical developments and research.

Perhaps the major achievement of research on the contact hypothesis was to distill Allport's initial long list of potentially relevant factors down to the few main conditions that should be satisfied to bring about positive intergroup contact. Thus Cook (1962, 1978) predicted that less derogatory out-group attitudes would result when individuals had personal contact with members of a disliked group, but under conditions of equal status, stereotype disconfirmation, cooperation, high "acquaintance potential" and "equalitarian norms." Thus, Cook focused pragmatically on structural features of the interaction situation, that could potentially be manipulated or controlled. After contact under these conditions, people did tend to report more favorable evaluations of the individual out-group members they had come to know. But an increasing number of variables was added to this list, leading to criticisms that the contact hypothesis was now subject to so many qualifications that it had lost its initial value and appeal (Pettigrew, 1986). As Stephan (1987) pointed out, the long list of conditions considered important in creating contact situations with potential for positive outcomes made researchers realize that there are many ways in which contact can lead to negative consequences. In addition, the elaborate creation of harmonious interpersonal relations was so obviously artificial when considered against the external realities of residential segregation, widespread discrimination, and numerous intergroup inequalities (see Hewstone & Brown, 1986).

Extensive assessments of the contact hypothesis yield a complex picture, hardly surprising given the predominance of relatively uncontrolled field studies over laboratory experiments, and the wide range of applied interventions (educational settings, armed services, workplace, and housing projects). The difficulties involved in evaluating the contact hypothesis are well illustrated with the topic of racial desegregation of U.S. schools, the success or failure of which is still fiercely debated (e.g., Cook, 1979, 1985; Gerard, 1983; Schofield, 1991; Stephan, 1978). First, there have been a large number of outcome measures. Evaluations of school desegregation have ranged from short-term, individual measures (e.g., the achievement and self-esteem of minority children) to long-term, societal measures (e.g., the chances that Blacks will subsequently work in integrated settings, or will live in integrated neighborhoods; see Braddock, 1985; Greenblatt & Willie, 1980). Second, many school settings were merely "desegregated" (members of two previously segregated groups were physically copresent) rather than "integrated" (two groups mixed under conditions conducive to positive outcomes; Pettigrew, 1973; Schofield, 1991). Thus, evaluations of school desegregation tend to speak to the effects of mere contact, if even that, rather than to the effects of contact under the conditions specified by Cook and others. Third, Schofield (1991) has argued that contact *theory* did not fundamentally influence the conduct of much empirical work on school desegregation, although when it did, results were generally promising (e.g., Cook, 1978; Schofield, 1979; Schofield & Sagar, 1977).

Thus, research on the contact hypothesis has moved from the optimism based on early studies (e.g., Deutsch & Collins, 1951; Wilner, Walkley, & Cook, 1955; see Cook, 1985) to the pessimism eloquently expressed by Rothbart and John (1993): "The contact hypothesis brings to mind T. H. Huxley's remark about the tragedy that occurs when 'a lovely idea is assaulted by a gang of ugly facts'" (p. 42). A central aspect of this pessimism,

to some authors *the* main shortcoming of the contact hypothesis (Hewstone & Brown, 1986), is the failure to generalize positive attitudes promoted by the contact experience ("specific attitude change") to include other members of the out-group not actually present in the contact situation ("generalized change in out-group attitudes").

The remainder of this section deals with recent theory-based approaches to contact that achieve different kinds of generalization, and shows how a cognitive approach can provide a deeper understanding of the processes underlying stereotype change in intergroup contact. These three approaches give rise to a clearer and more critical understanding of what is accomplished by interventions based on the contact hypothesis.

Contact as "Personalization"

The rationale that Cook (1978) developed for the conditions he felt would induce successful contact derived from a theory of interpersonal attraction: Contact between members of different groups allows individuals to discover that they have, after all, many similar values and attitudes (e.g., Byrne, 1969; Newcomb, 1961; Rokeach, 1960). Thus Triandis (1988, p. 47), for example, argued that the goal of intergroup contact "should be to create in the shortest possible time the largest number of . . . 'successful interpersonal relationships.'" Brewer and Miller's (1984) model of personalized contact also takes an interpersonal perspective.

THEORY

To reduce the salience of category memberships, Brewer and Miller (1984, 1988) argued that contact should be "differentiated" (allowing for distinctions to be made among out-group members) but moreover "personalized" (allowing for perceptions of the uniqueness of out-group members). More recently, Miller and Harrington (1990) have suggested that changes in the perception of self and of in-group members, as well as perceptions of out-group members, are important. They view decategorized intergroup interaction (differentiation and personalization) as "mutual and reciprocal": Personalized interaction with a member of the out-group results both in personalization of self and other, and in differentiation of self from in-group, and of the out-group member from the out-group.

The goal then is a more interpersonally oriented and "non-category-based" form of responding that allows members to "attend to information that replaces category identity as the most useful basis for classifying each other" (Brewer & Miller, 1984, p. 288). With the process of personalization, members attend only to information that is relevant to the self and is not correlated with membership. In personalized contact, category identity should no longer be the sole or major determinant of how members of different groups respond to one another. It is assumed that repeated interpersonal contact of this kind disconfirms the negative stereotype of members of disliked out-groups who are seen as similar to the self. Brewer and Miller contend that the ideal approach to inter-group contact involves personalized interactions that are "more likely to generalize to new situations because extended and frequent utilization of alternative information featured in interactions undermines the availability and usefulness of category identity as a basis for future interactions, with the same or different individuals" (pp. 288–289). This kind of contact, they maintain, will bring about the third type of generalization—decategorization. Frequent individuation of out-group members will result in the category being seen as less "useful" and, thus, being used less often.

RESEARCH

Brewer, Miller, and their colleagues have investigated their model in a series of experimental studies (see Bettencourt, Brewer, Rogers-Croak, & Miller, 1992; Miller, Brewer, & Edwards, 1985). The basic paradigm in these studies follows a three-phase sequence. In the first phase, subjects are arbitrarily divided into two ad hoc groups. To bolster identification with the group, members spend time working together on a task, make evaluations of their own and the other group's product, and receive feedback indicating that the out-group was biased in its evaluations. In the second phase, previously isolated groups are brought together to form two heterogeneous teams comprised of members of each group. At this stage, the independent variables are manipulated. Brewer and Miller propose two general conditions necessary to realize positive outcomes from cooperative interventions: (1) that the nature of the cooperative interaction promotes an *interpersonal* rather than a *task* orientation toward fellow team members; and (2) that

the basis for assignment to team membership (or to roles within teams) is perceived to be independent of category memberships. In a final phase, all subjects view a videotaped interaction of alleged members of both groups with whom they have not interacted. Evaluations of these groups serve as the primary measure of generalized attitude change.

The studies confirmed the hypothesized effects of personalized contact. Under conditions of both interteam cooperation and competition, groups that adopted an interpersonal focus displayed significantly less favoritism toward the videotaped groups than did subjects in either the task focus conditions, or subjects who were given no instructional manipulation. Confirming the proposed role of individuation, subjects differentiated among the out-group members more in the interpersonal conditions, and there was a strong correlation between perceived similarity of out-group members (to each other) and the degree of bias shown toward members of the videotaped teams.

One of the most important potential benefits of Brewer and Miller's model is in further improving cooperative learning techniques, which have been enthusiastically introduced into multiethnic classrooms with encouraging results. These techniques were a response to the fact that traditional classroom instruction methods permitted little contact between students (including those from different groups) that was not simply superficial (Slavin, 1985). Yet, while many of these carefully structured techniques have proved positive in improving dyadic relationships, they have not generally had an impact on perceptions of the group as a whole (for reviews see Aronson, Blaney, Stephan, Sikes, & Snapp, 1978; Aronson & Gonzalez, 1988; Johnson & Johnson, 1982, 1989, 1992; Sharan, 1990; Slavin, 1985). Miller and Harrington (1992) show how key principles from their work impact on cooperative learning; these include "minimization of the salience of social categories when forming teams and during group process" and "provision of opportunities for personalization of team members." In fact, although a number of the models of cooperative learning appear superficially similar, Miller and Harrington point to subtle differences (e.g., whether a competitive interteam reward structure is imposed on the classroom; see DeVries, Edwards, & Slavin, 1978) that do affect outcomes.

Miller and Davidson-Podgorny's (1987)

thoughtful review and meta-analysis of cooperative learning studies isolates some of the key strengths and shortcomings of each technique. They point out that rules for assignment of students to subgroups are generally not explicit in the techniques, and they show that three of the variables highlighted by their theoretical model and laboratory work do moderate the impact of cooperative learning on social relations. Specifically, the effect of cooperative learning is more positive when tasks require interdependence, when pupils are randomly assigned to roles, and when there are equal proportions of minority and White students on a team.

CRITIQUE

Notwithstanding the support gleaned from several elegant studies, there are several grounds on which the personalized model of contact can be criticized. First, although decategorization does appear to have been achieved in the laboratory studies, it remains to be seen whether the "usefulness" of evaluatively laden social categories can be reduced in this way (but see Warring, Johnson, Maruyama, & Johnson, 1985).

Second, although the model seems to accomplish one form of generalization (decategorization), Brewer and Miller concede that the conditions that promote personalization will impede generalization of contact effects to the out-group as a whole (Brewer, 1988; Brewer & Miller, 1988). This is consistent with the paradox noted by Rose (1981), that intimate relationships may generalize over a wide range of situations, but not over different persons. Miller and Harrington (1992) acknowledge that the video rating used in the third phase of their paradigm is designed to test whether new out-group members are interacted with as individuals, rather than to assess generalized attitudes toward the out-group.

Third, interpretation of the results as pure effects of personalization is problematic. Because members wore large identification badges denoting initial group membership, it could be argued that categories remained salient throughout the experiment. Additionally, it is not clear whether the experimental inductions created a purely personalized form of contact, as the authors argue, since decategorization is a joint function of both differentiation, which is considered category-based, and personalization, which involves only self–other considerations and comparisons. In other words, categorizations appear to have been maintained, not erased.

Finally, the personalization strategy is based on the view that decreasing the salience of group boundaries is likely to reduce intergroup bias. Yet, as Schofield (1991) has pointed out, this conclusion is at odds with her own and others' evaluations of schools that have adopted a "color-blind" perspective. Encouraging the suppression of race or ethnicity by all those involved in a desegregated school may actually increase category salience (Saharso, 1989; Schofield, 1986). This is an interesting parallel to the cognitive experimental work showing that consciously trying not to think about something (including a stereotype) may increase the frequency with which one thinks about it (and make one more stereotypic in judgments and behavior; Wegner, 1989; see Bodenhausen & Macrae, 1996). Thus, personalization seems to avoid the important issue highlighted by Schofield (1991), of how cultural diversity can be acknowledged, even encouraged, without worsening intergroup relations. Since membership of ethnic and other kinds of groups often provides a source of desired social identity (Tajfel, 1978), it would be impractical as well as undesirable for all parties concerned to ignore distinctive memberships (see Rist, 1979; Schofield & McGivern, 1979).

Intergroup Contact and Mutual Intergroup Differentiation

Hewstone and Brown (1986) put forward a theoretical perspective on contact, which diverges sharply from personalization, although both are derived from social identity. Hewstone and Brown argue, first, that contact should be "intergroup" not "interpersonal"; and second, that an appropriate model of intergroup contact should be based on "mutual intergroup differentiation."

THEORY

Regarding intergroup contact, Hewstone and Brown (1986) contend (based on Brown & Turner, 1981) that the contact hypothesis is based theoretically on interpersonal relations, focuses in practice on improving interpersonal relations, and that the failure to effect a generalized change of out-group attitudes can be attributed to this interpersonal perspective. To be successful in changing out-group evaluations, they argue that

> favourable contact with an out-group member *must* be defined as an inter*group* encounter. A weak association between the contact-partner and the out-group (i.e., if the target is an *a*typical out-group member) will define the contact situation as an interpersonal, rather than an intergroup, encounter. . . . Somewhat paradoxically, this means making the group affiliations *more* salient and not less and ensuring that in some way the participants in the contact encounters see each other as representatives of their groups. (p. 18)

In the light of subsequent studies (to be discussed), this position appears now to be overstated. However, I still argue that group affiliation, social categorization, should be evident in the contact situations, although not necessarily made "more salient" as originally argued. In addition, I now follow Stephenson's (1981) suggestion that Tajfel's (1978) distinction between interpersonal and intergroup forms of interaction should be restated as two orthogonal dimensions. In certain contexts it is possible to make both personal and social identity highly salient, and thus an interaction might be both highly personalized and categorized (see the preceding interpretation of Brewer and Miller's research).

In view of this clarification of our earlier position, and some misunderstandings of it, it is important to emphasize what intergroup contact should, and should not, be like. First, it is not always necessary for multiple members to be present, and two individuals acting as group representatives also constitute intergroup behavior. In fact, it has been found that having three members of each group present led to less competitive and more cooperative behavior than did a condition in which two individuals opposed each other as group representatives (Insko et al., 1987; cf. team composition in Bettencourt et al., 1992; Miller et al., 1985). Second, intergroup contact should not be confused with "category-based assignment" (Miller et al., 1985), which is a strategy more akin to tokenism. Third, Miller and Harrington (1992) argue *as if* people will behave in ways that enhance the in-group's image relative to the out-group *whenever* social categories are salient features of situational identity. In fact, although social categorization can be a sufficient condition for intergroup discrimination, this is by no means a universal response, and can be extinguished by

feedback concerning how other members of the in- and out-group respond (Locksley, Ortiz, & Hepburn, 1980) or by ensuring that the in-group and out-group are rated on independent dimensions (Mummendey & Schreiber, 1983). Finally, it is worth pointing out that Hewstone and Brown are neither alone nor the first to argue for "intergroup" contact. Similar ideas were suggested many years ago by Chein, Cook, and Harding (1948) and Lewin and Grabbe (1945; see Van Oudenhoven, Groenewoud, & Hewstone, 1995).

Regarding mutual intergroup differentiation, Hewstone and Brown (1986) recommended encouraging groups to recognize mutual superiorities and inferiorities, and to accord equal values to dimensions favoring each group (for similar ideas, see Tajfel, 1981; Turner, 1981; Van Knippenberg, 1984). Mutual intergroup differentiation would be reflected in positive in-group and out-group stereotypes (see D. M. Taylor & Simard, 1979). Again, this recommendation is consistent with other prescriptions for intergroup harmony (Berry, 1984; Schofield, 1986; Stephan & Stephan, 1984).

RESEARCH

There is now considerable support for the view that out-group attitudes are generalized when memberships are clear in the contact situation. Wilder (1984, Exp. 1) systematically varied the typicality of the out-group college member in a simulated intergroup contact situation. The nature of the contact was also varied in line with traditional theorizing on contact. Thus, the contact person behaved either in a pleasant and supportive way toward the real participants, or in a less pleasant and more critical fashion. The interaction took place over a cooperative task. Wilder predicted that only in the combined conditions, in which the interaction was pleasant and the partner could be seen as typical of her college, would ratings of the out-group college become more favorable. Wilder's results were exactly in line with his prediction.

Wilder's research also highlighted a potential problem associated with the manipulation of typicality. Although his first study reported change in out-group attitudes, there was little evidence that the contact manipulation affected stereotypes of the out-group. As Wilder noted, if stereotypes are negative, then "typical" out-group members need to have some negative characteristics, but then how can we ensure positive change in out-group perception? He suggested that the key to this dilemma may lie in the specific stereotypes the out-group members exhibit in the contact setting (Wilder, 1984, 1986a). Some beliefs about the out-group directly implicate the in-group (e.g., "They think they're better than us"), whereas other beliefs do not (e.g., "they're lazy"). Wilder (1984, Exp. 2) showed that contact with a typical out-group member can improve intergroup relations when the out-group member's typicality is based on characteristics that do *not* involve negative actions directed at the in-group. Finally, Wilder (1984, Exp. 3) demonstrated that the more positive evaluation of the out-group following contact with the typical member could be interpreted in terms of ease of generalization. Subjects judged the typical out-group member's personality and behavior to be more indicative of how others in the out-group would act in the same setting.

These findings were replicated and extended in a recent study by Vivian, Brown, and Hewstone (1995). In a cooperative work situation, British subjects were led to believe that their German partner (a confederate) was either typical or atypical of his national group (Germans), which was alleged to be either more or less homogeneous than other national groups within the European Community. Presumably, contact with a typical member from a relatively homogeneous group is construed as more of an intergroup encounter than is contact with atypical members of heterogeneous groups. Although there was no difference between conditions in rating German partners (who were viewed positively as a function of cooperation), only in the typicality (and especially typicality–homogeneity) conditions was this person explicitly associated with the German out-group as a whole, leading to most positive ratings of the out-group as a whole. The effects of perceived typicality were not, however, universally positive in this study. Contact with a typical member also gave rise to some more negative evaluations of the out-group (on stereotype-confirming traits such as materialistic and boring) than did contact with atypical members. Thus, while a categorized form of contact may have some benefits, there may also be certain risks associated with this strategy (to be discussed).

In a second study, Vivian, Hewstone, and Brown (in press) found that dimensions of membership

salience *moderated* the impact of traditional contact variables on European students' generalized attitudes toward a European out-group. There was evidence that different salience variables (typicality, references to nationality, perceived out-group homogeneity) each moderated the effects of at least one contact variable (amount, intimacy, and interdependence of contact). Typicality, especially, moderated the effects of contact variables in a manner consistent with the intergroup model of contact. Thus, the amount of contact and the intimacy of contact were more likely to be associated with a positive view of the out-group *if* an out-group target was perceived as typical of his or her national group.

The final study supporting intergroup contact predicted that attitudes toward out-group members who did not participate in the cooperative setting would be more favorable if social categories were made salient than if the interaction were decategorized (Van Oudenhoven et al., 1995). We found that referring explicitly to the ethnic background of a Turkish partner helped to transfer Dutch students' favorable attitude with respect to a Turkish partner to Turks in general. As in Vivian et al. (1995, Exp. 2), cooperative interaction had a positive effect on ratings of the out-group partner in all conditions, but this was only transferred to the out-group as a whole when the contact was "intergroup."

Taken together, these studies provide support for the intergroup contact model. They show that encountered members of the out-group need to be perceived as having out-group membership as an attribute, that the associative link between individual members and the out-group as a whole cannot be broken altogether, or any change of attitude will not generalize beyond those particular individuals.

There has been less empirical work on mutual intergroup differentiation. Brown and colleagues have, however, supported the idea that in work groups, group differences should be emphasized on dimensions that are accorded equal value, and that a division of labor between groups should permit mutual positive differentiation. In this way, cooperative contact need not threaten one's social identity. Again, the emphasis placed on distinctive memberships directly contradicts that of Brewer and Miller, who argue that group divisions should not be correlated with group membership. In a pair of studies, Brown and colleagues have shown that cooperative encounters involving a division of labor along group lines produce the most favorable responses to members of an out-group (Brown & Wade, 1987; Deschamps & Brown, 1983). Thus, attitudes towards the out-group were friendliest when the groups' roles were clearly defined, and least friendly when their respective roles were ambiguous.

To the extent that our model encourages the recognition of diversity rather than assimilation as a guiding social value, it can be thought of as a more pluralistic model of intergroup relations. It is therefore consistent with those scholars who contend that, in multiethnic societies, the cultural identity of each group should be maintained and positive relations between the groups valued (e.g., Berry, 1984; Berry, Kalin, & Taylor, 1977; Van Oudenhoven & Willemsen, 1989).

CRITIQUE

Although intergroup contact can boast greater success in realising generalized change in out-group attitudes, it is not without its dangers and critics (see Harrington & Miller, 1992; Miller & Harrington, 1992b). First, as noted in the case of Wilder's (1984) research, successfully manipulating typicality may involve manipulating negativity. As the research by Vivian and colleagues (1995) indicated, an intergroup form of contact may produce negative as well as positive generalized change. Thus the basic conditions for successful contact, specified by Allport (1954/1979), Cook (1978) and others, must be met when group memberships are explicit, or made salient.

Second, intergroup contact may have a negative effect on intergroup relations via its effect on intergroup anxiety (Stephan & Stephan, 1985). In principle, contact should reduce anxiety, as it has been shown to among White pupils vis-à-vis Black pupils in some desegregated schools (Collins & Noblit, 1977; Noblit & Collins, 1981; Schofield, 1981). But in cases of real intergroup conflict, an overemphasis on group memberships may increase intergroup anxiety, thereby mitigating against the desired generalization of positive out-group attitudes. Exactly this process was demonstrated by Islam and Hewstone (1993a). In a correlational study of contact between Hindu and Muslim religious groups in Bangladesh, they found that intergroup contact was positively associated with anxiety, which in turn was negatively associated with

perceived out-group variability and out-group attitudes. These findings are consistent with the suggestions that anxiety narrows the focus of attention, leading to the treatment of out-group members less as individuals and more as equivalent members of a category (Stephan & Stephan, 1985). Anxiety can also weaken the impact of stereotype-disconfirming information (Wilder, 1993a, 1993b; Wilder & Shapiro, 1989). Thus, to the extent that intergroup contact brings about an increase in anxiety, it will worsen, not improve, intergroup relations.

Notwithstanding these valid criticisms of the intergroup contact model, its emphasis on typicality is also shared by cognitive analyses of stereotype change, which approach the issue of contact from a quite different theoretical background. These approaches are now considered. The studies reported in the following section can arguably also be seen as relating to the intergroup contact model (Hewstone & Brown, 1986; Vivian et al., in press).

A Cognitive Analysis of Contact: The Impact of Stereotype-Disconfirming Information

Recent approaches to the contact hypothesis have, rather than addressing Allport's and Cook's (1978) dimensions separately, proposed that they share an impact on the ways people process stereotype-relevant, and especially stereotype-disconfirming, information. This focus on information processing is the hallmark of cognitive analyses of intergroup relations.

THEORY

Rothbart and John's (1985) cognitive analysis of intergroup contact is based on principles of categorization. If we accept that objects, or exemplars, differ in the degree to which they are viewed as prototypical examples of a category (what Barsalou, 1987, calls "graded structure"), then we should accept that it is the *goodness of fit* to the stereotype, and not just a few defining features, that determines whether a person becomes associated with a given category. Rothbart and Lewis (1988) showed that as prototypicality increased, the degree of inference from member to group increased. From this view, disconfirming attributes are most likely to become associated with the stereotype if they belong to an individual who is otherwise a very good fit to the category.

Rothbart and John's (1985) view implies that the more a particular episode disconfirms a stereotypic category of which it is an instance, the more likely it is to be associated with a different, possibly counterstereotypic, category. This process enhances the tendency of stereotypic beliefs to confirm themselves. Thus individuating information can "release" an exemplar from the attributes of a superordinate category, and at the same time render the stereotype immune from the attributes of the exemplar. Somewhat counterintuitively, stereotype-disconfirming information should therefore be linked to typical out-group members (see also Wilder, 1986a), a view that is consistent with Hewstone and Brown's (1986) idea that categories should be maintained in contact settings. Unless this is the case, people tend to react to stereotype-disconfirming information not with generalization, but with what Allport (1954/1979) called "re-fencing." The "special case" is excluded and the category held intact (see also Williams, 1964).

RESEARCH

Rothbart and John's (1985) prototype model has received support from experimental studies investigating three cognitive models of stereotype change: "bookkeeping," "conversion," and "subtyping" (Weber & Crocker, 1983). The bookkeeping model (Rothbart, 1981) proposes a gradual modification of stereotypes by the additive influence of each piece of disconfirming information. Any single piece of disconfirming information elicits only a minor change in the stereotype; major change occurs gradually and only after the perceiver has accumulated many disconfirming instances that deviate systematically from the stereotype. The conversion model (Rothbart, 1981) envisages a radical change in response to dramatic disconfirming information, but no change in response to minor disconfirming information. Finally, the subtyping model of stereotype change views stereotypes as hierarchical structures, in which discriminations can be created in response to disconfirming information (Ashmore, 1981; Brewer, Dull, & Lui, 1981; Taylor, 1981). This process leads to the formation of subtypes, which constitute exceptions, unrepresentative of the group as a whole. One serious consequence of subtyping is that it may insulate the superordinate stereotype from change (Weber-Kollmann, 1985).

These models were tested in a series of studies that compared stereotype change in response to disconfirming information that was either "dispersed" across several group members (each of whom slightly disconfirms the stereotype), or "concentrated" in a small number of highly disconfirming members. Weber and Crocker (1983) found that stereotypes of occupational groups (librarians and lawyers) changed more when the disconfirming information was dispersed than when it was concentrated, but only under large-sample conditions (30 vs. 6 members). They also showed that disconfirmers with high representativeness (e.g., White, middle-class, high-earning lawyers) were more successful at bringing about stereotype change than were disconfirmers with low representativeness (e.g., Black lawyers). Overall, Weber and Crocker provided strongest support for subtyping, some support for bookkeeping, and none for conversion. Generally, stereotype-disconfirming information had greater impact on perceptions of the group as a whole (generalization) when it was associated with a group member who was perceived as typical of the group.

The results from a series of studies by Hewstone and colleagues also strongly support the subtyping model (although there is some scattered support for the other models; for a review see Hewstone, 1994). These more recent studies have specified the cognitive processes underlying stereotype change. Johnston and Hewstone (1992) showed, first, that weak disconfirming members (in the dispersed condition) were rated more typical than strong disconfirming members (in the concentrated condition). Moreover, this perceived typicality was the only dependent measure that *mediated* the relatively weaker stereotyping in the dispersed condition. This mediating role of perceived typicality has also been demonstrated in three other independent studies, generalizing across manipulations, subject groups, and target groups (Hantzi, 1995; Hewstone, Hassebrauck, Wirth, & Waenke, 1995; Maurer, Park, & Rothbart, 1995).

A "prototype subtyping" model seems to provide the best account of how stereotypes change in response to dispersed or concentrated patterns of disconfirming information. Stereotype change is generally effected via the perceived typicality, or goodness of fit, of mild disconfirmers in the dispersed condition; it is generally impeded by the atypicality, or badness of fit, of strong discon-firmers in the concentrated condition. Desforges et al. (1991) tested the hypothesis that contact af-fects attitudes, in part, by eliciting a more positive portrait of the typical group member. They found that changes in portraits of the typical mental pa-tient were significantly correlated with changes in attitudes (see also Werth & Lord, 1992).

Some doubt remains, however, as to whether the formation of subtypes results in change, iner-tia, or active preservation of a stereotype (Hamilton & Sherman, 1994). Subtyping may lead to change when subtypes become sufficiently strong that they weaken and ultimately dissolve the stereotype (Pettigrew, 1981; Rothbart & John, 1985). But subtyping may simply limit generalization, result-ing in inertia, if there is little overlap between a subtype, which contains some disconfirming in-formation, and the global stereotype (e.g., Devine & Baker's [1991] example of "businessman Black" vs. "Blacks").

The third possible outcome of subtyping high-lights the active, purposive nature of subtyping. According to this view, perceivers may deliber-ately subcategorize members who disconfirm the stereotype *for the purpose of* preserving the ge-neric stereotype (Weber & Crocker, 1983). For example, women whose behavior disconfirms the superordinate-level gender stereotype may be sub-typed as lesbians or macho women (Costrich, Feinstein, Kidder, Maracek, & Pascale, 1975; Deaux & Lewis, 1984; Jackson & Cash, 1985). This active preservation of the stereotype clearly impedes change, but may be even more pernicious. Taylor (1981) has argued that subtyping may strengthen the overall stereotype since, as the num-ber of subtypes within it increases, any behavior per-formed by a member of the group can be fitted to at least one subtype. Hewstone, Macrae, Griffiths, Milne, and Brown (1994) reported results consis-tent with the view that subtyping is associated with active preservation of the stereotype. Stereotyp-ing was stronger in two- vs, one-subtype condi-tions, when subtypes were based on disconfirming information. Hence, where contact allows, or worse, facilitates subtyping, generalized change in out-group attitudes will tend to be blocked.

CRITIQUE

Perhaps the most general and valid criticism of this cognitive research is that it more or less ig-

nores affective change. Yet, Dovidio and colleagues (Chapter 9, this volume) raise an interesting issue about the relationship between cognitive and af-fective change. To the extent that cognitive and affective stereotypes operate independently, such ways of reducing prejudice and discrimination may be limited: Change in the cognitive component may have no impact on the affective component. Besides, some of the interventions that do work (e.g., cooperation) may actually provoke affective changes (e.g., anxiety, self-esteem) that have con-sequences for the processing of stereotypic infor-mation, but which are at present untapped. More speculatively, following Fiske's (1982) idea that affect is stored with a schema and is cued by cat-egorization, research should attend to which para-digms and interventions might achieve a change in these "affective tags" and other aspects of af-fective responding, in addition to cognitive mea-sures of stereotyping.

A second, general criticism concerns the para-digm used in much, but not all, of this research. The concentrated–dispersed paradigm confounds several properties (see Hewstone et al., 1994), deals with processing of presented disconfirming infor-mation that perceivers may not actively seek out (Johnston & Macrae, 1994), and should not lead us to ignore alternative manipulations of the pat-tern of presented information (e.g., how informa-tion is organized *within* stimulus persons; White & Zsambok, 1994). Despite these reproaches, the cognitive approach has contributed significantly to our understanding of the processes underlying stereotype change, demonstrating the mediating role of typicality.

Summary and Conclusions

The simple contact hypothesis is, in terms of atti-tude theory, both appealing and naive. It is appeal-ing because, compared with attitudes based on secondhand information, attitudes based on direct experience are relatively strong, held more confi-dently, brought to mind more easily, and are more resistant to change. They should therefore predict subsequent behavior more accurately (Fazio, 1990). All this is desirable *if* contact is positive and leads to positive attitude change. But the con-tact hypothesis is naive, because it represents an inappropriate selection of target beliefs to be changed (i.e., trying to change attitudes toward groups as a whole by changing beliefs about particular members of the group; Fishhein & Ajzen, 1975).

The three approaches reviewed in this section all receive substantial empirical support. We now know which variables to manipulate in order to bring about either personalization or intergroup contact; and we know that perceived typicality plays a mediating role and intergroup contact a moderating role, in changing intergroup perceptions. There is also evidence that personalized, decategorized contact can achieve one form of generalization (decategorization), whereas intergroup contact can accomplish another form (generalized change of out-group attitudes). I will defer integration of these approaches until the end of the chapter, when I attempt to pull all three approaches together with those reviewed in the next section and ask, not "which of these approaches to use," but "when to use which of these approaches."

Cook (1985) relates how one of the factors that drew him to study the contact hypothesis was that he had "grown up in the South and had many opportunities to observe and experience *a type of interracial contact that had left prejudice untouched*" (p. 452, italics added). We have, I would argue, made progress in terms of learning what contact to provide, how to provide it, and what is likely to change. We have also learned to be careful, especially with surveys, to check that a substantial amount of contact has actually taken place (e.g., Hamilton & Bishop, 1976) and not been avoided or replaced by resegregation (e.g., Sagar & Schofield, 1984).

If anything, I am more not less sanguine when I try to answer a question we (Hewstone & Brown, 1986) raised in 1986: Is any positive contact better than none? First, prolonged isolation may reduce the likelihood of future intergroup contact, and the continued assumption of belief dissimilarity will likely reinforce the boundary between groups (Allen & Wilder, 1975). Second, Sagar and Schofield (1984) noted one rather subtle positive change in peer relations, even among students in more highly *re*segregated schools: There had been a reduction in the "almost automatic fear" with which many students, especially Whites, responded to members of the other race. According to the authors, the experience of "simple conflict-free exposure" served a fear-reducing function, even if it did not go as far as generalized change of out-group attitudes. Third, especially through cooperative learning techniques, cross-ethnic friendships do develop and access is gained to friendship networks, which can be a major source of increasing cross-friendship friendships (Miller & Harrington, 1992; Slavin, 1985). In turn, these social relations may affect minority students' academic achievement, and access to desegregated networks can help them to obtain better employment (Braddock & McPartland, 1987; Pettigrew, 1967; Schofield, 1991). Against a background of extensive racial segregation in housing, these effects are of no little significance. Indeed, consistent with the theoretical analysis of change provided by Brewer and Miller (1988), we should acknowledge the importance, and the consequences, of various forms of generalization, and not focus solely on the one type that may be hardest to realize.

Categorization: Changing Cognitive Representations of "Us" and "Them"

I against my brother.
I and my brother against my cousin.
I, my brother and our cousin against the foreigner.
—Bedouin Proverb

The two interventions reviewed in this section start from the same premise as Brewer and Miller (1984), that since social categorization is the cause of discrimination, an improvement in intergroup relations must be brought about by reducing the salience of existing social categories. These interventions try to achieve this, however, not by eliminating categorization, but by altering which categorizations are used (see also Wilder, 1986b). Specifically, they attempt to structure a definition of group categorization in ways that reduce intergroup bias and conflict (Gaertner, Dovidio, Anastasio, Bachman, & Rust, 1993).

Like two of the recent approaches to contact, both interventions are inspired theoretically by social identity theory (Tajfel, 1978) and, more recently, self-categorization theory (e.g., Oakes, Haslam, & Turner, 1994; Turner, 1987). These perspectives emphasize that we all typically belong to several social categories and therefore may have a series of social identifications, one of which is salient at any given time. Self-categorization theory develops the earlier social identity perspective by arguing that self can be conceived on a number of levels of inclusiveness (e.g., me as an individual, me as a group member, me as a human being). The level at which the self is defined determines how one relates to others, including members of the same group. Thus self-categorization theory addresses self- as well as other stereotyping, in-group- and out-group stereotyping, and emphasizes that individuals ascribe to themselves characteristics associated with their in-group. From this perspective, attempts to change intergroup perceptions should look more closely than they have done at how interventions might change both in-group and out-group perceptions. The two interventions reviewed in this section—crossed categorization and common in-group identity—do just this.

Crosscutting Social Categorization

Most realistic contexts involve several categorizations, some of which coincide and some of which tend to cut across each other. This means that some people who belong to an individual's membership group according to one categorization simultaneously belong to a different group according to a second categorization. A simple idea lies behind the crossed-categorization intervention. When category boundaries are crosscutting versus converging, competing bases for in-group/out-group categorization should reduce the importance of any *one* category and force the perceiver to classify other individuals on *multiple* dimensions at the same time (Miller & Brewer, 1986).

THEORY

Proponents of different theories differ somewhat in their predictions concerning discrimination in favor of, or against, each of the four possible target groups created by crossing two dimensions, A/B and X/Y, and in how they see crossed categorization working (for a review see Hewstone, Islam, & Judd, 1993). There are two main theoretical positions.

According to Doise's (1978) "category differentiation model," single and simple categorization leads to two cognitive processes: an accentuation of both the differences between categories (an "interclass effect") and similarities within categories (an "intraclass effect"; see Tajfel, 1959). In contrast, the crossing of two categorizations leads to "convergence" between the categories (weakening the interclass effect) and "divergence" within

each category (weakening the intraclass effect). Thus, for example, the accentuation of perceived similarities within one category (e.g., A) will be counteracted by a simultaneously aroused accentuation of perceived differences, because category A contains two different subgroups according to another (e.g., X/Y) categorization (Vanbeselaere, 1991). As a result of these processes, intergroup discrimination based on the A/B categorization can be reduced or even eliminated.

In contrast to Doise's purely cognitive model, an account of crossed-categorization phenomena based on social identity theory (e.g., Tajfel & Turner, 1979) argues that social categorization arouses self-evaluative social comparison processes whereby individuals strive to obtain a positive self-esteem. Brown and Turner (1979) hypothesized that the motivation to create positive differences between in-group and out-group(s), stemming from the need for a positive social identity, persists in a situation of crossed categorizations and leads to an additive combination of tendencies to discriminate. All out-groups will be discriminated against (relative to the double in-group), provided that both categorizations are of equal relevance to social identity, but discrimination will be stronger toward out-groups differing on two rather than on only one dimension.

A further theoretical development was necessary to take account of the fact that outside the laboratory, categorizations tend to be of unequal psychological significance, connoting differences in status, numerosity, and power. Brewer, Ho, Lee, and Miller (1987) suggested four alternative models in cases of unequal category salience:

1. *Category dominance*: A single categorization will dominate, and categorization based on the subordinate category distinction will be ignored.
2. *Additivity*: Both category distinctions are attended to, and are combined additively to from a categorization judgment.
3. *Category conjunction*: A target individual is only classified as an "in-group" member when he or she shares category membership with the subject on all available category distinctions, and all other combinations are classified as "out-groups."
4. *Hierarchical ordering*: The effects of one category distinction are dependent on prior categorization on the other dimension (thus in-group/out-group differentiation on a second

category distinction would be greater for a target person classified as an in-group member on the first dimension, than for a target classified as an out-group member on the first dimension).

A review of the relevant research indicates partial support for each of the models, but only a qualified success for the intervention.

RESEARCH

Deschamps and Doise (1978), in the first experimental study, showed that intergroup discrimination could be reduced by crossing gender (a strong categorization) with red/blue (a weak, experimentally created categorization). This study was criticized by Brown and Turner (1979), however, for not using categories of equal psychological significance (which could surely not "cancel each other out," the putative process according to the category differentiation model). Yet, the main finding was replicated by Vanbeselaere (1987). Using two artificial categories and improved methodology, he found bias was reduced, not eliminated, in the crossed-categorization conditions, on specific and general evaluations (see also Brown & Turner, 1979; Rehm, Lilli, & Van Eimeren, 1988; Vanbeselaere, 1991). Diehl (1989, 1990) also used two artificially created categorizations of equal psychological significance, but reported that subjects in a crossed-categorization condition discriminate against the totally different group, but not against a partly overlapping group.

Taken together, these and other studies have not yet distinguished between category-differentiation and social-identity predictions, but have fairly consistently shown the strongest discrimination against the double out-group, which is attenuated in the case of the two crossed conditions (e.g., Brown & Turner, 1979; Deschamps & Doise, 1978; Vanbeselaere, 1987). Although interpretable in terms of reduced category salience (see Messick & Mackie, 1989; Stephan, 1985; Wilder, 1986b), such studies do still constitute "intergroup" situations, because categories are not ignored when crossed (see Arcuri, 1982; Brewer, 1968; Vanbeselaere, 1987).

There has also been support for each of the four models specified by Brewer and colleagues (1987), which sometimes make similar predictions to the two earlier perspectives (see Hewstone et al., 1993). In specific circumstances, there is evidence

for category dominance (e.g., Hewstone et al., 1983; Islam & Hewstone, 1993b, Exp. 2), additive (e.g., Brewer, 1968), category-conjunction (e.g., Rogers, Miller, & Hennigan, 1981) and hierarchical-ordering (e.g., Brewer et al., 1987) effects. Hewstone and colleagues (1993) therefore suggest that further research should pay closer attention to when (i.e., the situations in which) and how (i.e., the processes by which) each model might operate. In the context of a general discussion of how to improve intergroup relations, the category-dominance model seems crucial. Both category-differentiation and social-identity perspectives are severely limited by their focus on crossed categorizations of equal psychological significance. Outside the laboratory, one categorization tends to be primary whenever research relies on real social categorizations that have historical, cultural, socioeconomic and affective significance. Thus, the category dominance model appears to reflect reality in multigroup societies (e.g., race in South Africa or the United States, religion in Northern Ireland or Bangladesh, and language in Belgium or Quebec).

The idea of crossing social categories has considerable appeal and may underlie other socialpsychological interventions. As we saw in the previous section, Miller and colleagues manipulated decategorized contact by placing members of different groups on the same team. Thus, the results of their studies could be seen in terms of crossed categorization (e.g., out-group members of one's team are out-group on the original categorization but in-group on the team categorization). Indeed, Marcus-Newhall, Miller, Holtz, and Brewer (1993) made explicit the importance of crossed categorization (role assignment) in their paradigm. They reported that, compared with converging-category assignment, crosscutting categories and role assignments decrease perceptions of similarity within categories and increase perceptions of similarity across categories. This supports Doise's (1978) category-differentiation account of the underlying process. Marcus-Newhall and colleagues were even able to show that an index of perceived similarity (based on decreased similarity between individuals within the same category and increased similarity between individuals from different categories) *mediated* the effect of role assignment on bias. But there was no generalization beyond the team setting to out-group perception in general.

Crossed categorization may also be usefully incorporated into applied settings. Schofield (1991) discusses evidence that crosscutting ties can improve peer relations in desegregated schools (Schofield & McGivern, 1979) and speculates that the creation of crosscutting ties may help to account for the positive impact of cooperative-learning teams on intergroup relations (e.g., the "Jigsaw Classroom" created by Aronson et al., 1978). Finally, Duckitt (1992) refers to the understated and undeveloped role of social scientists in designing constitutions and political systems to reduce or channel interethnic conflicts (e.g., Horowitz, 1985), which may seek to reinforce crossed, rather than converging, categorizations.

CRITIQUE

A first criticism concerning this intervention concerns the lack of clarity about exactly what effect it achieves. A recent meta-analysis of crossed-categorization studies by Migdal, Hewstone, and Mullen (1995) concluded that crossed categorization does not achieve a notable reduction in the magnitude of intergroup bias observed under simple categorization conditions. Why, then, do many studies on crossed categorization appear to "work," in the sense that they yield significant results. The answer, we believe, lies both in the creation of the double out-group condition and in the frequent failure to compare bias in simple and crossed conditions within the same study (an exception is Brown & Turner, 1979, but they failed to find discrimination in the simple categorization conditions).

First, what most studies show, and most models predict, is greatest bias toward the double out-group. But from this we should not conclude that crossed categorization "reduces" intergroup bias, only that it can help to reduce bias against existing double (or multiple) out-groups. Of course, outside the laboratory, multiple categorization is the rule, rather than the exception, and the double out-group response found in crossed-categorization studies is consistent with Brewer and Campbell's (1976) discussion of increased discrimination in situations of "converging boundaries," in which multiple intergroup differences coincide. Thus, perhaps crossed categorization should be more accurately presented as a technique for reducing bias against out-groups characterized by converging boundaries (by no means a rare occurrence outside the laboratory; see Pettigrew's, 1981, discussion of "double jeopardy").

Second, the processes underlying crossed-categorization effects are far from clear, and there is evidence consistent with several explanations (including the reduction of original categorization salience, the self-esteem conferring function of social identity, and category differentiation; see Hewstone et al., 1993). Future work must be more process oriented and might include factors such as attention paid to different categorizations and perceived homogeneity of in- and out-groups (see Smith, 1992). One interesting possibility is that crossed-categorization effects may be mediated by perceptions of a common in-group identity (see the following discussion of work by Gaertner et al.).

Third, future research should be guided by a more detailed consideration of the change likely to be associated with crossed categorization. At present, there is little evidence that crossed categorization achieves any reduction in discrimination compared with simple categorization. Moreover, given that crossing categories should, at least, make perceivers aware that the out-group consists of different subgroups, this intervention should—logically—be associated with the second type of generalization, differentiation. Tajfel (1982) explicitly mentioned the hypothesis that crossed categorizations break down the perceived homogeneity of the out-group, yet there is little evidence for this effect (but see Marcus-Newhall et al., 1993).

Finally, given that category dominance is probably the norm when real, conflicting groups are studied, it may prove impossible to weaken discrimination by crossing multiple categorizations (e.g., Hewstone et al., 1993, Exp. 2). Yet, if crossed categorization can *force* continual realignments among individuals and categories via extended interactions on the basis of multiple categorizations at different points in time (Miller & Brewer, 1986), then it should be a significant component of many interventions to reduce intergroup discrimination.

Common In-Group Identity

In Sherif's (1966) famous summer camp studies, an initial attempt to reduce intergroup conflict involved bringing boys from two opposing groups into contact in pleasant surroundings. It resulted in further hostile exchanges (see also Diab, 1970; Sherif & Sherif, 1965). Sherif concluded that there needed to be some positive and functional interdependence between groups before conflict between them would abate. He created these conditions in the form of superordinate goals, goals that neither group could attain on its own and that superseded other goals each group might have had. Sherif also reported that a single superordinate goal was not sufficient to reduce intergroup conflict; a series of cumulative superordinate goals was required (see also Wilder & Thompson, 1980). A recent theoretical perspective developed by Gaertner and colleagues (1993) has built on Sherif's work emphasizing goals, to argue that it is ultimately group members' *cognitive representations* of the situation that are the critical variable mediating a reduction in intergroup bias.

THEORY

The "common in-group identity" model argues that bias can be reduced by factors that transform members' perceptions of group boundaries from "us" and "them" to a more inclusive "we." Indeed, there is evidence that manipulation of the pronouns *we* and *they* can differentially influence intergroup perception and behavior (Perdue, Dovidio, Gurtman, & Tyler, 1990; see Maass & Arcuri, 1996). Gaertner and colleagues argue that several features specified by the contact hypothesis are effective, in part, because they contribute to the development of a common in-group identity.

Although Gaertner et al. acknowledge that several factors influence intergroup bias and conflict, they still regard the cognitive representations of the situation as the critical mediating variable. Whereas a representation of the situation as one involving two groups is thought to maintain or enhance intergroup biases, decategorized (i.e., separate individuals) or recategorized (i.e., common in-group identity) representations are expected to reduce tension, albeit in different ways. Decategorization reduces bias through a process that moves initial in-group members away from the self and toward out-group members; thus former in-group members are seen less positively and as more evaluatively similar to out-group members. Recategorization, in contrast, should reduce bias by increasing the attractiveness of former out-group members, once they are included within the superordinate group structure.

RESEARCH

Two main experimental studies support the common in-group identity model (for a discussion of more indirect support see Gaertner et al., 1993). The first study used a two-step procedure whereby previously isolated problem-solving groups were brought together under different conditions (Gaertner, Mann, Murrell, & Dovidio, 1989). By varying the structural arrangements (i.e., integrated, segregated, or separate seating patterns), the nature of interdependence among participants, and the identifying labels given to participants (new group name, original group names, individual names), the experiment was designed to induce a "one-group," "two-groups," or "separate-individuals" representation of the intergroup situation. As predicted, subjects in one-group and separate-individuals conditions showed lower levels of intergroup bias than subjects in the two-groups condition (which maintained the salience of intergroup boundaries). Furthermore, the positive effects associated with the two former conditions were apparently controlled by different mechanisms, as specified earlier. In the one-group condition, bias was reduced primarily by increased attraction to former out-group members; in the separate-individuals condition, bias was reduced by decreased attraction to former in-group members.

The second study (Gaertner, Mann, Dovidio, Murrell, & Pomare, 1990) tested the prediction that intergroup cooperation reduces bias, at least partly, because it decreases the salience of the intergroup boundary. The results confirmed the hypothesis that a one-group representation would produce lower levels of bias than a two-groups representation. Gaertner and colleagues also provided definitive *mediational* evidence that cooperation affected bias via cognitive representations of social categorization. Consistent with the common in-group identity model, the one-group representation was the only significant predictor of out-group member evaluations; moreover, the significant effect for interdependence (cooperation vs competition) effectively disappeared once the one-group representation was controlled for.

Gaertner and colleagues also conducted a field study of factors related to the contact hypothesis in a multiethnic high school (Gaertner, Rust, Dovidio, Bachman, & Anastasio, 1994). They reported that the effect of perceptions of interdependence on out-group bias was partially mediated by perceptions that the school body was "one group" (positive relation) and "different groups" (negative relation). The evidence of mediation was, however, much weaker, and the data could be seen to give more support to Sherif's model, whereby goal relations have a direct effect on bias (see Vivian et al., in press). Nonetheless, like the other interventions reviewed, the common in-group identity model has considerable intuitive appeal in applied settings (e.g., Schofield & McGivern, 1979; Slavin, 1985).

CRITIQUE

The first and most obvious criticism of this approach is that it may not be realistic. Can the recategorization process and the creation of a superordinate group identity overcome powerful ethnic and racial categorizations on more than a temporary basis? Gaertner and colleagues' strategy is open to the same criticisms leveled at Sherif's method of inducing superordinate goals. When Sherif finally introduced superordinate goals, the conflict was to all intents and purposes over (Billig, 1976; Tajfel, 1978). Success by this method is achieved by fusing together the two groups. Thus, it can be argued that the situation is no longer an intergroup one at all.

Second, the common in-group identity strategy is analogous to those forms of assimilation that supposedly work by blurring and ultimately merging identities into a single, broader superordinate identity (Duckitt, 1992), a model of intergroup relations that is now fairly uniformly rejected (e.g., Berry, 1984; van Oudenhoven & Willemsen, 1989). As Turner (1981) argued, cooperative interdependence is not, and should not be, incompatible with psychological distinctiveness for each separate group. Thus, a more successful strategy in practice seems likely to involve a superordinate identity *and* distinctive subgroup identities (e.g., Brown & Wade, 1987; Deschamps & Brown, 1983).

Third, it is nor clear what kind of generalization, and to what extent, is actually realized by this intervention. The reported reduction in bias suggests a decrease in the use of the original category (i.e., decategorization), but there are no measures of generalized change in out-group attitudes. In fact, Gaertner and colleagues propose that "*generalization* will be maximized when the salience of the initial group identities are [*sic*] main-

tained, but *within a context* of a salient superordinate common in-group identity" (1993, p. 6, italics in original). This statement invites an integration of the common in-group identity approach and the intergroup model of contact (see next section). Of course, whether it will be possible to make dual memberships simultaneously salient is an empirical question, but here integration with the crossed-categorization approach is suggested. Despite these criticisms, the common in-group identity approach is exemplary in its theoretical grounding and its methodological sophistication; it surely has a role to play in any integrated model of changing intergroup relations.

Summary and Conclusions

Interventions that manipulate social categorizations have yielded an array of supportive data. They have also reminded researchers that a change in intergroup perceptions could mean a change in perceptions of the in-group as well as the out-group. These interventions may best be viewed as "contact-enhancing" manipulations that can reduce the likelihood of applying old categorizations, can perhaps also increase the complexity of out-group perceptions, but which cannot necessarily achieve a change in generalized out-group attitudes. They may, however, when paired with cooperation that results in success, be equally important in providing undeniable evidence that members of two previously antagonistic groups can work together. Extreme care must be exercised to ensure that a realignment of categorization does not redirect conflict elsewhere. Intergroup conflict is not resolved when the presence of a new, extreme out-group leads to a previously moderate out-group being assimilated to the in-group (see Wilder & Thompson, 1988).

An Integration

Everybody has won and all must have prizes.
—Lewis Carroll (*Alice in Wonderland*)

The research reviewed in this chapter indicates that different interventions bring about different kinds of changes, and never bring about all three kinds of change in one study (see Table 22.1 for an overview).

Personalized contact (Brewer & Miller, 1984) can effect both more differentiated out-group per-

TABLE 22.1. Changing Intergroup Perceptions: A Summary of the Impact of Different Interventions

Type generalization	Intervention	Exemplary research	Process(es)
Change in attitudes toward the social category	Intergroup contact	Wilder (1984)	Only contact with typical members of the out-group leads to a change in perceptions of the group as a whole.
		Johnston & Hewstone (1992)	Perceived typicality of dis-confirming group members *mediates* stereotype change.
		Vivian et al. (in press)	Intergroup contact *moderates* intergroup bias (generalized perceptions of in-group vs. out-group).
Increased complexity of intergroup perceptions	Decategorized contact (differentiation/ personalization)	Bettencourt et al. (1992)	Personalized contact leads to greater out-group differentiation, which is (negatively) correlated with bias.
	Crossed categorization	Marcus-Newhall et al. (1993)	Perceived out-group homogeneity *mediates* bias.
Decategorization	Decategorized contact	Bettencourt et al. (1992)	Personalized contact leads to less biased perceptions of individual members of out-group versus in-group.
	Common in-group identity	Gaertner et al. (1993)	Cognitive representations of "one group" *mediate* biased perceptions of individual members of out-group versus in-group.

ception and a decrease in the extent to which a category is used (decategorization; e.g., Bettencourt et al., 1992). Intergroup contact (Hewstone & Brown, 1986) and contact with pro-totypical out-group members (Rothbart & John, 1985), can realize change in out-group attitudes (and this fact is acknowledged by other perspectives; Brewer, 1988; Gaertner et al., 1993). Yet, by encouraging group distinctiveness, we may risk increasing intergroup anxiety and tendencies to bias. This tension between the merits of emphasizing membership, on the one hand, and either individuality or common identity, on the other, represent what is perhaps the central issue on the field (Vivian et al., in press). Crossed categorization (Deschamps & Doise, 1978) seems best suited to achieving a change in the complexity of intergroup perception, and this can reduce bias

(Marcus-Newhall et al., 1993), whereas common in-group identity (Gaertner et al., 1993) can effect decategorization (and possibly, over time, differentiation, too).

If we take the view that ultimately all three types of generalization are desirable, we should then want to plan interventions that can achieve all three outcomes. Some support for this kind of integration already exists. For example, personalized contact does seem to include some degree of category maintenance, and a revised model of intergroup contact now accepts that interpersonal and intergroup aspects of contact can and should be manipulated orthogonally. Cook's (1978, 1984) work, for example, shows how the category-based and personalization approaches can come together. He successfully brought about generalization by both making categorization salient *and* creating positive interpersonal encounters. In his 1978 study, White subjects experienced pleasant, cooperative interracial contact with Black individuals. When their well-liked Black coworker gave an account of the discrimination he experienced (*as a Black*), Cook then ensured that another White participant advocated desegregation and racial equality. This was done in such a way that the White subjects understood how the adoption of egalitarian social policies would make it less likely that their new Black friends would encounter prejudice and discrimination. Thus peer-group support served as a "cognitive booster" for generalization, from favorable interpersonal contact to positive attitudes toward the group as a whole. As Pettigrew and Martin (1987) concluded, Cook "achieves generalization to blacks as a group *by deliberately making group categorization salient*" (p. 68, italics added). The results of the study by Van Oudenhoven and colleagues (1995) can be interpreted in the same way.

The next question that arises concerns the order in which we should try to achieve the different kinds of change, because they seem to be linked to different interventions and difficult, if not impossible, to realize simultaneously. Given three types of generalization, there are at least six different orders we could investigate (in fact, many more possibilities, since there are at least four main types of intervention). How should we do this? The simple answer is that we do not know, but must find out. The prejudice and out-group derogation that make such interventions necessary are unlikely to be reduced by one-off interventions, and are more likely to require a graduated series of interactions involving a variety of manipulations.

It may be useful to speculate on a few possibilities that seem to merit research. First, given the acknowledged danger of fomenting intergroup conflict by maintaining or emphasizing category memberships, we should perhaps initially try to establish positive interpersonal relations (especially when intergroup relations are divisive), only later seeking to manipulate typicality. Although Van Oudenhoven and colleagues (1995) found no difference between two conditions that introduced categorization at the beginning or middle of a cooperative interaction, they suggested that gradual introduction of ethnic categorization may be more effective in generalizing out-group attitudes under more threatening circumstances (when anxiety may be high; Wilder, 1993a, 1993b).

An alternative view, of course, is that typicality should be clear from the outset, while trying to reduce category-based processing. Here research could be guided by the graded-structure approach to social categories (Barsalou, 1987) and research on the nature of stereotypic traits (Rothbart & Park, 1986). We should try to identify those stereotype-confirming traits that convey no more than the required degree of typicality to mediate stereotype change, and those disconfirming traits that are actually susceptible to change and likely to effect desired change in other traits.

A second issue concerns how to achieve both generalized change in out-group attitudes and a change in intergroup complexity. One line of reasoning suggests that we should try to change variability first, and in this way "unfreeze" cognitions (Kruglanski, 1989; Lewin, 1948). Conversely, it can he argued that a change in cognitive representation may make change more difficult to achieve. By increasing the variability of a stereotype when inconsistent group members are encountered, social perceivers can maintain the stereotype's central tendency (see Srull, 1981). Indirect support for this view comes from research showing that subtypes consisting of stereotype-disconfirming members were associated with active preservation of the stereotype (Hewstone et al., 1994).

A potential resolution to this problem is offered by new research. Maurer, Park, and Rothbart (1995) distinguished between "subtyping" (distinguishing between stereotype-confirming and disconfirming individuals) and "subgrouping" (instructions to divide group members into multiple groups). They predicted and found that the principle consequence of subtyping was preservation of the stereotype, whereas the principle consequence of subgrouping was greater perceived variability and less stereotypic perceptions of the group. Thus attempts to induce changes in perceived variability should be based on subgrouping, not subtyping.

Conclusions

Not only are we using the tools of persuasion, but we've got to use tools of coercion. Not only is this thing a process of education, but it is also a process of legislation.
— Martin Luther King, Jr.

People of comfortable circumstance live peacefully together and those afflicted by poverty do not.

—John Kenneth Galbraith

In his wide-ranging analysis of prejudice, Duckitt (1992) argues for a multilevel approach. He identifies three causal processes that establish and maintain prejudice, and proposes that change at each level would be required to effect a significant reduction in prejudice: (1) the level of social structure and intergroup relations; (2) the level of social influences to which individuals are exposed; and (3) the level of individual susceptibility. This chapter has focused on two broad interventions—contact and categorization—that address the first and second levels, but ignore the third. This can be justified on the grounds that prejudice is primarily a social, and not an individual, problem, but still it could be argued that these interventions leave untouched the problem of institutionalized discrimination, which is the core of the problem (Pettigrew, 1986).

To get at the underlying, social structural causes of prejudice, higher level interventions will surely be required, as implied by the quotations at the beginning of this section. Yet, notwithstanding the importance of legal, educational, and politico-economic factors, there remains a role for social psychology, because it is often individuals' subjective representations of these factors that guide perceptions and behavior. More pragmatically, since it is not in our gift, as social psychologists, to change the social structure, I argue that our time and efforts are better spent in continuing to work as we do. But in so doing, we should try to b e more innovative and less reactive than we have been in the past, as in the case of evaluating school desegregation (see Cook, 1985). For example, schools in South Africa are currently being desegregated, and they surely have much to learn from the North American experience, but innovative, theory-driven programs should first be put into place there and then evaluated.

I have argued throughout for the importance of *theory*, and the value of good, testable theory is exemplified in the diverse interventions that have sprung from Tajfel's social identity theory. I have proposed that each of the main interventions reviewed can help to change intergroup relations in particular circumstances, but that an integrated approach is likely to be most effective. If we accept that there are different types of change to achieve, and that different interventions may realize different types of change, then our future interventions will need to be more complex to be more successful.

REFERENCES

Allen, V. L., & Wilder, D. A., (1975). Categorization, belief similarity, and intergroup discrimination. *Journal of Personality and Social Psychology, 32,* 971–977.

Allport, G. W. (1979). *The nature of prejudice.* Cambridge/ Reading, MA: Addison-Wesley. (Original work published 1954)

Amir, Y. (1969). Contact hypothesis in ethnic relations. *Psychological Bulletin, 71,* 319–342.

Amir, Y. (1976). The role of intergroup contact in change of prejudice and ethnic relations. In P. A. Katz (Ed.), *Towards the elimination of racism* (pp. 245–308). Elmsford, NY: Pergamon Press.

Arcuri, L. (1982). Three patterns of social categorization in attribution memory. *European Journal of Social Psychology, 11,* 271–282.

Aronson, E., Blaney, N., Stephan, C., Sikes, J., & Snapp, M. (1978). *The jigsaw classroom.* Newbury Park, CA: Sage.

Aronson, E., & Gonzalez, A. (1988). Desegregation, jigsaw, and the Mexican American experience. In P. A. Katz & D. A. Taylor (Eds.), *Eliminating racism: Profiles in controversy* (pp. 301–314). New York: Plenum Press.

Ashmore, R. D. (1981). Sex stereotypes and implicit personality theory. In D. L. Hamilton (Ed.), *Cognitive processes in stereotyping and intergroup relations* (pp. 37–81). Hillsdale, NJ: Erlbaum.

Baron, R. M., & Kenny, D. A. (1986). The moderator–mediator variable distinction in social psychological research: Conceptual, strategic, and statistical considerations. *Journal of Personality and Social Psychology, 51,* 1173–1182.

Barsalou, L. W. (1984). Cultural relations in plural societies: Alternatives to segregation and their sociopsychological implications. In N. Miller & M. B. Brewer (Eds.), *Groups in contact: The psychology of desegregation* (pp. 11–27). San Diego: Academic Press.

Berry, J. W., Kalin, R., & Taylor, D. M. (1977). *Multiculturalism and ethnic attitudes in Canada.* Ottawa: Ministry of Supply and Services.

Bettencourt, B. A., Brewer, M. B., Rogers-Croak, M., & Miller, N. (1992). Cooperation and the reduction of intergroup bias: The role of reward structure and social orientation. *Journal of Experimental Social Psychology, 28,* 301–319.

Billig, M. (1976). *Social psychology and intergroup relations.* London: Academic Press.

Bodenhausen, G., & Macrae, C. (1996). The self-regulation of intergroup perception: Mechanisms and consequences of stereotype suppression. In C. N. Macrae, C. Stangor, & M. Hewstone (Eds.), *Stereotypes and Stereotyping* (pp. 227–253). New York: Guilford Press.

Braddock, J. H., II. (1985). School desegregation and black assimilation. *Journal of Social Issues, 41,* 9–22.

Braddock, J. H., II, & McPartland, J. (1987). How minorities continue to be excluded from equal employment opportunities: Research on labor marker and institutional barriers. *Journal of Social Issues, 43,* 5–39.

Brewer, M. B. (1968). Determinants of social distance among East African tribal groups. *Journal of Personality and Social Psychology, 10,* 279–289.

Brewer, M. B. (1979). In-group bias in the minimal intergroup situation: A cognitive–motivational analysis. *Psychological Bulletin, 86,* 307–334.

Brewer, M. B. (1988). A dual process model of impression formation. In T. K. Srull & R. S. Wyer (Eds.), *Advances in social cognition* (Vol. 1, pp. 1–36). Hillsdale, NJ: Erlbaum.

Brewer, M. B., & Campbell, D. T. (1976). *Ethnocentrism and intergroup attitudes: East African evidence.* New York: Halstead Press.

Brewer, M. B., Dull, V., & Lui, L. (1981). Perceptions of the elderly: Stereotypes as prototypes. *Journal of Personality and Social Psychology, 41,* 656–670.

Brewer, M. B., Ho, H. K., Lee, J. Y., & Miller, N. (1987). Social identity and social distance among Hong Kong schoolchildren. *Personality and Social Psychology Bulletin, 13,* 156–165.

Brewer, M. B., & Miller, N. (1984). Beyond the contact hypothesis: Theoretical perspectives on desegregation. In N. Miller & M. B. Brewer (Eds.), *Groups in contact: The psychology of desegregation* (pp. 281–302). Orlando, FL.: Academic Press.

Brewer, M. B., & Miller, N. (1988). Contact and cooperation: When do they work? In P. Katz & D. Taylor (Eds.), *Eliminating racism: Means and controversies* (pp. 315–326). New York: Plenum Press.

Brown, R. J., & Turner, J. C. (1979). The criss-cross categorization effect in intergroup discrimination. *British Journal of Social and Clinical Psychology, 18,* 371–383.

Brown, R. J., & Turner, J. C. (1981). Interpersonal and intergroup behaviour. In J. Turner & H. Giles (Eds.), *Intergroup behavior* (pp. 33–65). Oxford: Blackwell.

Brown, R. J., & Wade, G. S. (1987). Superordinate goals and intergroup behavior: The effects of role ambiguity and status on intergroup attitudes and task performance. *European Journal of Social Psychology, 17,* 131–142.

Byrne, D. (1969). Attitudes and attraction. In L. Berkowitz (Ed.), *Advances in experimental social psychology* (Vol. 4, pp. 35–89). New York: Academic Press.

Campbell, D. T., & Fiske, D. W. (1959). Convergent and discriminant validation by the multitrait-multimatrix method. *Psychological Bulletin, 56,* 81–105.

Chein, I., Cook, S. W., & Harding, J. (1948). The field of action research. *American Psychologist, 3,* 43–50.

Cohen, E. (1975). The effects of desegregation on race relations. *Law and Contemporary Problems, 39,* 271–299.

Collins, T. W, & Noblit, G. W. (1977). *Crossover high.* Unpublished manuscript, Memphis State University, Memphis, TN.

Cook, S. W. (1962). The systematic analysis of socially significant events: A strategy for social research. *Journal of Social Issues, 18,* 66–84.

Cook, S. W. (1978). Interpersonal and attitudinal outcomes in cooperating interracial groups. *Journal of Research and Development in Education, 12,* 97–113.

Cook, S. W. (1979). Social science and school desegregation: Did we mislead the Supreme Court? *Personality and Social Psychology Bulletin, 5,* 420–437.

Cook, S. W. (1984). Cooperative interaction in multiethnic contexts. In N. Miller & M. B. Brewer (Eds.), *Groups in contact: The psychology of desegregation* (pp. 156–186). New York: Academic Press.

Cook, S. W. (1985). Experimenting on social issues: The case of school desegregation. *American Psychologist, 40,* 452–460.

Costrich, N., Feinstein, J., Kidder, L., Maracek, J., & Pascale, L. (1975). When stereotypes hurt: Three studies of penalties for sex-role reversals. *Journal of Experimental Social Psychology, 11,* 520–530.

Deaux, K., & Lewis, L. L. (1984). The structure of gender stereotypes: Interrelationships among components and gender label. *Journal of Personality and Social Psychology, 46,* 991–1104.

Deschamps, J.-C., & Brown, R. (1983). Superordinate goals and intergroup conflict. *British Journal of Social Psychology, 22,* 189–195.

Deschamps, J.-C., & Doise, W. (1978). Crossed category memberships in inter-group relations. In H. Tajfel (Ed.), *Differentiation between social groups* (pp. 141–158). Cambridge, UK: Cambridge University Press.

Desforges, D. M., Lord, C. G., Ramsey, S. L., Mason, J. A., Van Leeuwen, M. D., & Lepper, M. R. (1991). Effects of structured cooperative contact on changing negative attitudes toward stigmatized social groups. *Journal of Personality and Social Psychology, 60,* 531–544.

Deutsch, M., & Collins, M. E. (1951). *Interracial housing: A psychological evaluation of a social experiment.* Minneapolis: University of Minnesota Press.

Devine, P. G., & Baker, S. M. (1991). Measurement of racial stereotype subtyping. *Personality and Social Psychology Bulletin, 17,* 44–50.

DeVries, D., Edwards, K., & Slavin, R. (1978). Biracial learning teams and race relations in the classroom: Four field experiments in Teams-Games-Tournament. *Journal of Educational Psychology, 70,* 356–362.

Diab, L. N. (1970). A study of intragroup and intergroup relations among experimentally produced small groups. *Genetic Psychology Monographs, 82,* 49–82.

Diel, M. (1989). Dichotomie und Diskriminierung: Die Auswirkungen von Kreuzkategorisierungen auf die Diskriminierung im Paradigma der minimalen Gruppen [Dichotomy and discrimination: The effect of crossed categorizations on discrimination in the minimal group paradigm]. *Zeitschrift für Sozialpsychologie, 20,* 92–102.

Diehl, M. (1990). The minimal group paradigm: Theoretical explanations and empirical findings. In W. Stroebe & M. Hewstone (Eds.), *European review of social psychology* (Vol. 1, pp. 263–292). Chichester, UK: Wiley.

Doise, W. (1978). *Groups and individuals: Explanations in social psychology.* Cambridge, UK: Cambridge University Press.

Duckitt, J. (1992). *The social psychology of prejudice.* New York: Praeger.

Fazio, R. H. (1990). Multiple processes by which attitudes guide behavior: The MODE model as an integrative framework. In M. P. Zanna (Ed.), *Advances in experimental social psychology* (Vol. 23, pp. 75–109). New York: Academic Press.

Fishbein, M., & Ajzen, I. (1975). *Belief, attitude, intention and behavior: An introduction to theory and research.* Reading, MA: Addison-Wesley.

Fisher, R. J. (1990). *The social psychology of intergroup and international conflict resolution*. New York: Springer-Verlag.

Fiske, S. T. (1982). Schema-triggered affect: Applications to social perception. In M. S. Clark & S. T. Fiske (Eds.), *Affect and cognition: The 17th Annual Carnegie Symposium* (pp. 55–77). Hillsdale, NJ: Erlbaum.

Gaertner, S. L., Dovidio, J. F., Anastasio, P A., Bachman, B. A., & Rust, M. C. (1993). The common ingroup identity model: Recategorization and the reduction of intergroup bias. In W. Stroebe & M. Hewstone (Eds.), *European review of social psychology* (Vol. 4, pp. 1–26). Chichester, UK: Wiley.

Gaertner, S. L., Mann, J. A., Dovidio, J. F., Murrell, A. J., & Pomare, M. (1990). How does cooperation reduce intergroup bias? *Journal of Personality and Social Psychology, 59*, 692–704.

Gaertner, S. L., Mann, J., Murrell, A., & Dovidio, J. F. (1989). Reducing intergroup bias: The benefits of recategorization. *Journal of Personality and Social Psychology, 57*, 239–249.

Gaertner, S. L., Rust, M. C., Dovidio, J. F., Bachman, B. A., & Anastasio, P. A. (1994). The contact hypothesis: The role of common ingroup identity on reducing intergroup bias. *Small Group Research, 25*, 244–249.

Gerard, H. B. (1983). School desegregation: The social science role. *American Psychologist, 38*, 869–877.

Greenblatt, S. L., & Willie, C. V. (1980). The serendipitous effects of school desegregation. In W. G. Stephan & J. Feagin (Eds.), *School desegregration* (pp. 51–66). New York: Plenum Press.

Hamilton, D. L., & Bishop, G. D. (1976). Attitudinal and behavioral effects of initial integration of white suburban neighbourhoods. *Journal of Social Issues, 32*, 47–67.

Hamilton, D. L., & Sherman, J. W. (1994). Stereotypes. In R. S. Wyer & T. K. Srull (Eds.), *Handbook of social cognition* (2nd ed., Vol. 2, pp. 1–68). Hillsdale, NJ: Erlbaum.

Hantzi, A. (1995). Change in stereotypic perceptions of familiar and unfamiliar groups: The pervasiveness of the subtyping model. *British Journal of Social Psychology, 34*, 463–477.

Harrington, H. J., & Miller, N. (1992). Research and theory in intergroup relations: Issues of consensus and controversy. In J. Lynch, M. Modgil, & S. Modgil (Eds.), *Cultural diversity in the schools: Consensus and controversy* (pp. 159–178). London: Palmer Press.

Hewstone, M. (1994). Revision and change of stereotypic beliefs: In search of the elusive subtyping model. In W. Stroebe & M. Hewstone (Eds.), *European review of social psychology* (Vol. 5, pp. 69–109). Chichester, UK: Wiley.

Hewstone, M., & Brown, R. J. (1986). Contact is not enough: An intergroup perspective on the "contact hypothesis." In M. Hewstone & R. J. Brown (Eds.), *Contact and conflict in intergroup encounters* (pp. 1–44). Oxford: Blackwell.

Hewstone, M., Hassebrauck, M., Wirth, A., & Waenke, M. (1995). *Mediation of stereotype change via perceived typicality of disconfirmers*. Unpublished manuscript, University of Wales, Cardiff, and University of Mannheim.

Hewstone, M., Islam, M. R., & Judd, C. M. (1993). Models of crossed categorization and intergroup relations. *Journal of Personality and Social Psychology, 64*, 779–793.

Hewstone, M., Macrae, C. N., Griffiths, R., Milne, A., & Brown, R. (1994). Cognitive models of stereotype change: (5) Measurement, development, and consequences of subtyping. *Journal of Experimental Social Psychology, 30*, 505–526.

Hogg, M. A., & Abrams, D. (1988). *Social identifications: A social psychology of intergroup relations and group processes*. London: Routledge.

Horowitz, D. (1985). *Ethnic groups in conflict*. Berkeley: University of California Press.

Insko, C. A., Pinkley, R. L., Hoyle, R. H., Dalton, R., Hong, G., Slim, R., Landry, P., Holton, B., Ruffin, P. F., & Thibaut, J. (1987). Individual–group discontinuity: The role of intergroup contact. *Journal of Experimental Social Psychology, 23*, 250–267.

Islam, M. R., & Hewstone, M. (1993a). Dimensions of contact as predictors of intergroup anxiety, perceived out-group variability, and out-group attitude: An integrative model. *Personality and Social Psychology Bulletin, 19*, 700–710.

Islam, M. R., & Hewstone, M. (1993b). Intergroup attributions and affective consequences in majority and minority groups. *Journal of Personality and Social Psychology, 64*, 936–950.

Jackson, L. A., & Cash, T. F. (1985). Components of gender stereotypes: Their implications for inferences on stereotypic and nonstereotypic dimensions. *Personality and Social Psychology Bulletin, 11*, 326–344.

Johnson, D. W., & Johnson, R. T. (1989). *Cooperation and competition: Theory and research*. Edina, MI: Interaction.

Johnson, D. W., & Johnson, R. T. (1992). Positive interdependence: Key to effective cooperation. In R. Hertz-Lazarowitz & N. Miller (Eds.), *Interaction in cooperative groups: The theoretical anatomy of group learning* (pp. 174–199). Cambridge, UK: Cambridge University Press.

Johnston, L., & Hewstone, M. (1992). Cognitive models of stereotype change: (3) Subtyping and the perceived typicality of disconfirming group members. *Journal of Experimental Social Psychology, 28*, 360–386.

Johnston, L., & Macrae, C. N. (1994). Changing social stereotypes: The case of the information seeker. *European Journal of Social Psychology, 14*, 581–592.

Kruglanski, A. W. (1989). *Lay epistemics and human knowledge: Cognitive and motivational bases*. New York: Plenum Press.

Lewin, K. (1948). *Resolving social conflict*. New York: Harper.

Lewin, K., & Grabbe, P. (1945). Conduct, knowledge, and acceptance of new values. *Journal of Social Issues, 2*, 53–64.

Locksley, A., Ortiz, V., & Hepburn, C. (1980). Social categorization and discriminatory behavior: Extinguishing the minimal intergroup discrimination effect. *Journal of Personality and Social Psychology, 39*, 773–783.

Maass, A., & Arcuri, L. (1996). Language and stereotyping. In C. N. Macrae, C. Stangor, & M. Hewstone (Eds.), *Stereotypes and stereotyping* (pp. 193–226). New York: Guilford Press.

Maquet, J. J. (1961). *The premise of inequality in Rwanda*. Oxford: Oxford University Press.

Marcus-Newhall, A., Miller, N., Holtz, R., & Brewer, M. B. (1993). Cross-cutting category membership with role assignment: A means of reducing intergroup bias. *British Journal of Social Psychology, 32*, 125–146.

Mason, P. (1970). *Race relations*. Oxford: Oxford University Press.

Maurer, K. L., Park, B., & Rothbart, M. (1995). Subtyping versus subgrouping processes in stereotype representation.

Journal of Personality and Social Psychology, 69, 812–824.

McClendon, M. J. (1974). Interracial contact and the reduction of prejudice. *Sociological Focus, 7,* 47–65.

Messick, D. M., & Mackie, D. M. (1989). Intergroup relations. *Annual Review of Psychology, 33,* 45–81.

Migdal, M., Hewstone, M., & Mullen, B. (1995). *The impact of crossed categorization on intergroup discrimination: A meta-analysis.* Unpublished manuscript, University of Syracuse and University of Wales, Cardiff.

Miller, N., & Brewer, M. B. (1986). Social categorization theory and team learning procedures. In K. S. Feldman (Ed.), *The social psychology of education* (pp. 172–198). Cambridge, UK: Cambridge University Press.

Miller, N., Brewer, M. B., & Edwards, K. (1985). Cooperative interaction in desegregated settings: A laboratory analogue. *Journal of Social Issues, 41,* 63–81.

Miller, N., & Davidson-Podgorny, G. (1987). Theoretical models of intergroup relations and the use of cooperative teams as an intervention for desegregated settings. In C. Hendrick (Ed.), *Group processes and intergroup relations* (pp. 41–67). Beverly Hills, CA: Sage.

Miller, N., & Harrington, H. J. (1990). A model of social category salience for intergroup relations: Empirical tests of relevant variables. In P. Drenth, J. Sergeant, & R. Takens (Eds.), *European perspectives in psychology* (Vol. 3, pp. 205–220). Chichester, UK: Wiley.

Miller N., & Harrington, H. J. (1992). Social categorization and intergroup acceptance: Principles for the design and development of cooperative learning teams. In K. Hertz-Lazarowitz & N. Miller (Eds.), *Interaction in cooperative groups: The theoretical anatomy of group learning* (pp. 203–227). Cambridge, UK: Cambridge University Press.

Mummedey, A., & Schreiber, H.-J. (1983). Better or just different? Positive social identity by discrimination against or by differentiation from outgroups. *European Journal of Social Psychology, 13,* 389–397.

Newcomb, T. M. (1961). *The acquaintance process.* New York: Holt, Rinehart & Winston.

Noblit, G. W., & Collins, T. W. (1981). Gui bono? White students in a desegregated high school. *Urban Review, 13,* 205–216.

Oakes, P. J., Haslam, A., & Turner, J. C. (1994). *Stereotyping and social reality.* Oxford: Blackwell.

Park, B., Judd, C. M., & Ryan, C. S. (1991). Social categorization and the representation of variability information. In W. Stroebe & M. Hewstone (Eds.), *European review of social psychology* (Vol. 2, pp. 211–246). Chichester, UK: Wiley.

Perdue, C. W., Dovidio, J. F., Gurtman, M. B., & Tyler, R. B. (1990). "Us" and "Them": Social categorization and the process of intergroup bias. *Journal of Personality and Social Psychology, 59,* 475–486.

Pettigrew, T. F. (1967). Social evaluation theory: Convergences and applications. In D. Levine (Ed.), *Nebraska symposium on motivation* (Vol. 15, pp. 241–311). Lincoln: University of Nebraska Press.

Pettigrew, T. F. (1973). The case for the racial integration of the schools. In O. Duff (Ed.), *Report on the future of school desegregation in the United States* (pp. 52–93). Pittsburgh: University of Pittsburgh, Consultative Resource Center on School Desegregation and Conflict.

Pettigrew, T. F. (1981). Extending the stereotype concept. In

D. L. Hamilton (Ed.), *Cognitive processes in stereotyping and intergroup behavior* (pp. 301–331). Hillsdale, NJ: Erlbaum.

Pettigrew, T. F. (1986). The intergroup contact hypothesis reconsidered. In M. Hewstone & R. Brown (Eds.), *Contact and conflict in intergroup encounters* (pp. 169–195). New York: Blackwell.

Pettigrew, T. F., & Martin, J. (1987). Shaping the organizational context for black American inclusion. *Journal of Social Issues, 43,* 41–78.

Rehm, J., Lilli, W., & Van Eimeren, B. (1988). Reduced intergroup differentiation as a result of self-categorization in overlapping categories: A quasi-experiment. *European Journal of Social Psychology, 18,* 375–379.

Riordan, C. (1978). Equal status interracial contact: A review and revision of the concept. *International Journal of Intercultural Relations, 2,* 161–185.

Rist, R. C. (1979). *Desegregated schools: Appraisals of an American experiment.* New York: Academic Press.

Rogers, M., Miller, N., & Hennigan, K. (1981). Cooperative games as an intervention to promote cross-racial acceptance. *American Education Research Journal, 18,* 513–516.

Rokeach, M. (Ed.). (1960). *The open and closed mind.* New York: Basic Books.

Rose, T. L. (1981). Cognitive and dyadic processes in intergroup contact. In D. L. Hamilton (Ed.), *Cognitive processes in stereotyping and intergroup behavior* (pp. 259–302). Hillsdale, NJ: Erlbaum.

Rothbart, M. (1981). Memory processes and social beliefs. In D. L. Hamilton (Ed.), *Cognitive processes in stereotyping and intergroup behavior* (pp. 145–181). Hillsdale, NJ: Erlbaum.

Rothbart, M., & John, O. P. (1985). Social categorization and behavioral episodes: A cognitive analysis of the effects of intergroup contact. *Journal of Social Issues, 41,* 81–104.

Rothbart, M., & John, O. P. (1993). Intergroup relations and stereotype change: A social-cognitive analysis and some longitudinal findings. In P. M. Sniderman, P. E. Tetlock, & E. G. Carmines (Eds.), *Prejudice, politics and the American dilemma* (pp. 32–58). Stanford, CA: Stanford University Press.

Rothbart, M., & Lewis, S. (1988). Inferring category attributes from exemplar attributes: Geometric shapes and social categories. *Journal of Personality and Social Psychology, 55,* 861–872.

Rothbart, M., & Park, B. (1986). On the confirmability and disconfirmability of trait concepts. *Journal of Personality and Social Psychology, 50,* 131–141.

Ryan, C., Park, B., & Judd, C. (1996). Assessing stereotype accuracy: Implications for understanding the stereotyping process. In C. N. Macrae, C. Stangor, & M. Hewstone (Eds.), *Stereotypes and stereotyping* (pp. 121–157). New York: Guilford Press.

Sagar, H. A., & Schofield, J. W. (1984). Integrating the desegregated school: Problems and possibilities. In M. Maehr & D. Bartz (Eds.), *Advances in motivation and achievement: A research manual* (pp. 203–242). Greenwich, CT: JAI Press.

Saharso, S. (1989). Ethnic identity and the paradox of equality. In J. P. van Oudenhoven & T. M. Willemsen (Eds.), *Ethnic minorities: Social psychological perspectives* (pp. 97–114). Amsterdam: Swets & Zeitlinger.

Schofield, J. W. (1978). School desegregation and intergroup attitudes. In D. Bar-Tal & L. Saxe (Eds.), *Social psychology of education: Theory and research* (pp. 330–363). Washington, DC: Halsted Press.

Schofield, J. W. (1979). The impact of positively structured contact on inter-group behaviour: Does it last under adverse conditions? *Social Psychology Quarterly, 42,* 280–284.

Schofield, J. W. (1981). Uncharted territory: Desegregation and organizational innovation. *The Urban Review, 13,* 227–242.

Schofield, J. W. (1986). Causes and consequences of the colorblind perspective. In J. E Dovidio & S. L. Gaertner (Eds.), *Prejudice, discrimination, and racism* (pp. 231–254). Orlando, FL: Academic Press.

Schofield, J. W. (1989). *Black and white in school: Trust, tension, or tolerance?* New York: Teachers College Press.

Schofield, J. W. (1991). School desegregation and intergroup relations: A review of the literature. In G. Grant (Ed.), *Review of research in education* (Vol. 17, pp. 335–409). Washington, DC: American Educational Research Association.

Schofield, J. W., & McGivern, E. (1979). Changing interracial bonds in a desegregated school. In R. G. Blumberg & W. J. Roye (Eds.), *Interracial bonds* (pp. 106–119). New York: General Hall.

Schofield, J. W., & Sagar, H. A. (1977). Peer interaction patterns in an integrated middle school. *Sociometry, 40,* 130–138.

Sharan, S. (Ed.). (1990). *Cooperative learning: Theory and research.* New York: Praeger.

Sherif, M. (1966). *Group conflict and cooperation.* London: Routledge & Kegan Paul.

Sherif, M., & Sherif, C. W. (1965). Research on intergroup relations. In O. Klineberg & R. Christie (Eds.), *Perspectives in social psychology.* New York: Holt, Rinehart & Winston.

Slavin, R. E. (1985). Cooperative learning: Applying contact theory in desegregated schools. *Journal of Social Issues, 41,* 45–62.

Smith, E. R. (1992). The role of exemplars in social judgment. In L. L. Martin & A. Tesser (Eds.), *The construction of social judgments* (pp. 107–132). Hillsdale, NJ: Erlbaum.

Srull, T. K. (1981). Person memory: Some tests of associative storage and retrieval models. *Journal of Experimental Psychology: Human Learning and Memory, 7,* 440–463.

St. John, N. H. (1975). *School desegregation: Outcomes for children.* New York: Wiley.

Stephan, W. G. (1978). School desegregation: An evaluation of predictions made in *Brown v. Board of Education. Psychological Bulletin, 85,* 217–218.

Stephan, W. G. (1985). Intergroup relations. In G. Lindzey & E. Aronson (Eds.), *Handbook of social psychology* (3rd ed., Vol. 2, pp. 599–658). New York: Random House.

Stephan, W. G. (1987). The contact hypothesis in intergroup relations. In C. Hendrick (Ed.), *Group processes and intergroup relations: Review of personality and social psychology* (Vol. 9, pp. 13–40). Newbury Park, CA: Sage.

Stephan, W. G., & Stephan, C. W. (1984). The role of ignorance in intergroup relations. In N. Miller, & M. B. Brewer (Eds.), *Group in contact: The psychology of desegregation* (pp. 229–255). New York: Academic Press.

Stephen, W. G., & Stephan, C. W. (1985). Intergroup anxiety. *Journal of Social Issues, 41,* 157–175.

Stephenson, G. M. (1981). Intergroup bargaining and negotiation. In J. C. Turner & H. Giles (Eds.), *Intergroup behavior* (pp. 168–198). Oxford: Blackwell.

Tajfel, H. (1959). Quantitative judgment in social perception. *British Journal of Psychology, 50,* 16–29.

Tajfel, H. (Ed.). (1978). *Differentiation between social groups.* London: Academic Press.

Tajfel, H. (1981). Social stereotypes and social groups. In J. C. Turner & H. Giles (Eds.), *Intergroup behaviour* (pp. 144–167). Oxford: Blackwell.

Tajfel, H. (1982). Social psychology of intergroup relations. *Annual Review of Psychology, 33,* 1–39.

Tajfel, H., & Turner, J. C. (1979). An integrative theory of intergroup conflict. In W. C. Austin & S. Worchel (Eds.), *The social psychology of intergroup relations* (pp. 33–47). Monterey, CA: Brooks/Cole.

Taylor, D. M., & Simard, L. (1979). Ethnic identity and intergroup relations. In D. J. Lee (Ed.), *Emerging ethnic boundaries.* Ottawa: University of Ottawa Press.

Taylor, S. E. (1981). A categorization approach to stereotyping. In D. L. Hamilton (Ed.), *Cognitive processes in stereotyping and intergroup behavior* (pp. 83–114). Hillsdale, NJ: Erlbaum.

Triandis, H. C. (1988). The future of pluralism revisited. In P. A. Katz & D. A. Taylor (Eds.), *Eliminating racism: Profiles in controversy* (pp. 31–50). New York: Plenum Press.

Turner, J. C. (1981). The experimental social psychology of intergroup behavior. In J. C. Turner & H. Giles (Eds.), *Intergroup behaviour* (pp. 1–32). Oxford: Blackwell.

Turner, J. C. (1987). *Rediscovering the social group: A self-categorization theory.* Cambridge, UK: Cambridge University Press.

Vanbeselaere, N. (1987). The effect of dichotomous and crossed social categorizations upon intergroup discrimination. *European Journal of Social Psychology, 17,* 143–156.

Vanbeselaere, N. (1991). The different effects of simple and crossed categorizations: A result of the category differentiation process or of differential category salience? In W. Stroebe & M. Hewstone (Eds.), *European review of social psychology* (Vol. 2, pp. 247–278). Chichester, UK: Wiley.

Van Knippenberg, A. (1984). Intergroup differences in group perceptions. In H. Tajfel (Ed.), *The social dimension: European developments in social psychology* (Vol. 2, pp. 560–578). Cambridge, UK: Cambridge University Press.

Van Oudenhoven, J. P., Groenewoud, J. T., & Hewstone, M. (1995). Cooperation, ethnic salience and generalization of interethnic attitudes. *European Journal of Social Psychology, 25,* 1–13.

Van Oudenhoven, J. P., & Willemsen, T. M. (Eds.). (1989). *Ethnic minorities: Social psychological perspectives.* Amsterdam: Swets & Zeitlinger.

Vivian, J., Brown, R., & Hewstone, M. (1995). *Changing attitudes through intergroup contact: The effects of group membership salience.* Manuscript under review.

Vivian, J., Hewstone, M., & Brown, R. J. (in press). Intergroup contact: Theoretical and empirical developments. In R. Ben-Ari & Y. Rich (Eds.), *Understanding and enhancing education for diverse students: An international perspective.* Ramat Gan, Israel: Bar-Ilan University Press.

Warring, D., Johnson, D. W., Maruyama, G., & Johnson, R. (1985). Impact of different types of cooperative learning on cross-ethnic and cross-sex relationships. *Journal of Educational Psychology, 77,* 53–59.

Weber, R., & Crocker, J. (1983). Cognitive processes in the revision of stereotypic beliefs. *Journal of Personality and Social Psychology, 45,* 961–977.

Weber-Kollmann, R. (1985). *Subtyping: The development and consequences of differentiated categories for stereotyped groups*. Unpublished doctoral dissertation, Northwestern University, Evanston, IL.

Wegner, D. M. (1989). *White bears and other unwanted thoughts: Suppression, obsession, and the psychology of mental control*. New York: Viking Press.

Werth, J. L., & Lord, C. G. (1992). Previous conceptions of the typical group member and the contact hypothesis. *Basic and Applied Social Psychology 13*, 351–369.

White, R. M., & Zsambok, C. (1994). Biases in memory for and use of inconsistent beliefs in stereotyping. *British Journal of Social Psychology, 33*, 243–258.

Wilder, D. A. (1984). Intergroup contact: The typical member and the exception to the rule. *Journal of Experimental Social Psychology, 20*, 177–194.

Wilder, D. A. (1986a). Cognitive factors affecting the success of intergroup contact. In S. Worchel & W. G. Austin (Eds.), *Psychology of intergroup relations* (pp. 49–66). Chicago: Nelson-Hall.

Wilder, D. A. (1986b). Social categorization: Implications for creation and reduction of intergroup bias. In L. Berkowitz (Ed.), *Advances in experimental social psychology* (Vol. 19, 293–355). New York: Academic Press.

Wilder, D. A. (1993a). Freezing intergroup evaluations: Anxiety fosters resistance to counterstereotypic information. In M. A. Hogg & D. Abrams (Eds.), *Group motivation: Social psychological perspectives* (pp. 68–86). Hemel Hempstead, UK: Havester Wheatsheaf.

Wilder, D. A. (1993b). The role of anxiety in facilitating stereotypic judgment of outgroup behavior. In D. M. Mackie & D. L. Hamilton (Eds.), *Affect, cognition, and stereotyping: Interactive processes in group perception* (pp. 87–109). San Diego: Academic Press.

Wilder, D. A., & Shapiro, P. N. (1989). Role of competition-induced anxiety in limiting the beneficial impact of positive behavior by an out-group member. *Journal of Personality and Social Psychology, 56*, 60–69.

Wilder, D. A., & Thompson, J. G. (1980). Intergroup contact with independent manipulations of ingroup and outgroup interaction. *Journal of Personality and Social Psychology, 38*, 589–603.

Wilder, D. A., & Thompson, J. E. (1988). Assimilation and contrast effects in the judgement of groups. *Journal of Personality and Social Psychology, 54*, 62–73.

Williams, R. M. (1964). *Strangers next door: Ethnic relations in American communities*. Englewood Cliffs, NJ: Prentice-Hall.

Wilner, D. M., Walkley, R., & Cook, S. W. (1955). *Human relations in interracial housing: A study of the contact hypothesis*. Minneapolis: University of Minnesota Press.

READING 23

Social Categorization and Behavioral Episodes: A Cognitive Analysis of the Effects of Intergroup Contact

Myron Rothbart and Oliver P. John • University of Oregon

The effects of intergroup contact on stereotypic beliefs, it is argued, depend upon (1) the potential susceptibility of those beliefs to disconfirming information and the degree to which the contact setting "allows" for disconfirming events, and (2) the degree to which disconfirming events are generalized from specific group members to the group as a whole. To account for the generalization of attributes from a sample to a population, we present a cognitive-processing model. The model assumes that impressions of groups are most heavily influenced by the attributes of those members most strongly associated with the group label. In order for group stereotypes to change, then, disconfirming information must be associated with the group labels. However, a number of powerful cognitive processes work against this association. As a consequence, we predict that stereotype change will be relatively rare under "normal" circumstances but may occur when disconfirming information is encountered under circumstances that activate the group label (e.g., when disconfirming attributes are associated with otherwise typical group members).

In an influential article summarizing the voluminous literature on intergroup contact, Amir (1976) wrote:

Despite a substantial amount of research on ethnic contact, our theoretical understanding of what contact involves as a potential agent of change and what are the underlying processes is still very limited. . . . The lack of basic theory is also exemplified in the little interaction between studies in ethnic contact and general theories of attitude formation and change, or theories in other psychological fields such as perception. . . . (p. 289)

In this paper, we attempt to address Amir's concern. We present a preliminary theoretical model that may account for the effects of intergroup contact on stability and change in intergroup perception. We consider the process of stereotype change produced through contact with individual group members an example of the general cognitive process by which attributes of category members modify category attributes. As we shall argue later, this issue is complex and involves basic questions about the nature of categorization processes. More generally, we propose a two-phase model in which disconfirmation will occur when (1) the stereotypic beliefs themselves are susceptible to disconfirmation and the intergroup contact provides experiences that disconfirm the stereotype,

419

and (2) those experiences become associated with the superordinate stereotypic category. The second phase requires a detailed examination of categorization processes.

To convey what is new about our model, it may be useful to consider it in the context of a traditional approach to the effects of intergroup contact. The traditional approach characterizes intergroup perception as a process of "autistic hostility" (cf. Newcomb, 1947), that is, a self-amplifying cycle of antagonism, separation, and unrealistically negative attributions. Intergroup hostility leads to avoidance, which in turn leads *both* to more extreme negative perceptions and to an inability to test those perceptions against reality.

Since avoidance and separation enable extant (negative) perceptions to remain unchallenged, contact exposes those unrealistically extreme perceptions to disconfirming evidence. It is assumed that experiences with individuals who disconfirm the negative stereotype generalize to the group as a whole through the process of "stimulus generalization" (cf. Cook, 1970). In short, the traditional approach seems to make three major assumptions: (a) initial perceptions are unrealistic and potentially disconfirmable, (b) contact provides the evidence necessary to disconfirm these unrealistic beliefs and (c) the disconfirming attributes of members generalize to the group as a whole.

However, each of these three major assumptions, while plausible, seriously underestimates the complexity of the processes of belief change. In contrast to these assumptions, we argue that (a) stereotype beliefs differ dramatically in their susceptibility to disconfirmation; (b) intergroup contact may either disconfirm *or* corroborate existing stereotypes, depending upon the nature of the intergroup contact; and (c) even when contact with individual members does disconfirm the group stereotype, cognitive processes basic to underlying category-exemplar relations may isolate those instances from the group stereotype. Among these three assumptions, the second, concerning the nature of the intergroup contact, has already been carefully examined (e.g., Amir, 1976; Cook, 1984a,b), and a number of aspects of intergroup contact, such as "equal status," "intimate contact," and "cooperative atmosphere," have been proposed to characterize the type of contact that leads to favorable attitude change. Although we do not disagree with these interpretations, we share Amir's concern that these types of contact have not been

closely tied to the basic psychological processes implicated in belief change. At the end of our paper, we will attempt to relate the types of intergroup contact more closely to the processes of belief change outlined in our model.

The Potential Disconfirmability of Stereotypic Beliefs

In general, we propose that belief change can be induced by direct personal experiences as well as by indirectly obtained information. This distinction implies that changes in stereotypic beliefs about groups may come from two sources: (a) direct contact with members, and (b) indirect "atmosphere" effects. Atmosphere effects mean general, nonspecific changes in laws, social norms, and expectancies, as well as images promulgated by parents, peers, gatekeepers, and the media. Very roughly, they are what Sarnoff, Katz, and McClintock (1954) have referred to as changes produced by the application of social rewards and punishments. The rewards and punishments involved may be quite subtle, however, amounting to little more than alterations in the media's portrayal of a particular group (e.g., the dramatic change in the media's coverage of Mainland China after President Nixon announced his trip to that country). Atmosphere effects may change people's attitudes and beliefs without any direct contact with group members. Although a number of possible explanations exist for such atmosphere effects, including sheer repetition and familiarity (e.g., Hasher, Goldstein, & Toppino, 1977), we will focus here on effects of direct contact on stereotype change.

If a contact episode is to create belief change, it must first provide information that differs from the observer's initial beliefs. According to the present model, such a discrepancy will occur only if both the stereotypic belief is potentially susceptible to disconfirmation *and* the contact provides disconfirming information. Figure 23.1 lists three characteristics of social beliefs that define their susceptibility to disconfirmation and should, therefore, influence the probability of stereotype change following direct contact with group members.

Rothbart and Park (1986) have argued that at least three dimensions affect the disconfirmability of trait attributions: (1) the clarity and specificity of the relation between a trait and observable be-

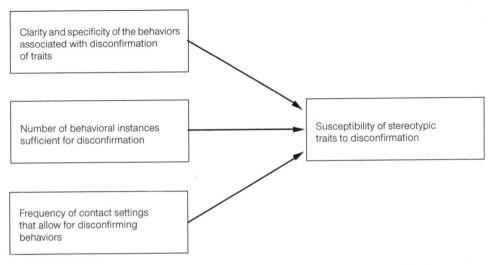

FIGURE 23.1 ■ Factors influencing the susceptibility of stereotypic traits to disconfirmation.

havior, (2) the number of behavioral observations necessary to establish or disconfirm whether a trait applies to a person or group, and (3) the number of occasions that allow for confirming and/or disconfirming behaviors. In Rothbart and Park's (1986) study, judges rated 150 trait terms on these three dimensions, as well as the frequency and social desirability (favorability) of these terms. Each of the three dimensions is now examined in more detail.

Clarity of Concept-Exemplar Relations

Traits differ in the degree to which they imply clear behavioral referents. We may be very clear about the behaviors that would confirm or disconfirm the belief that a person is messy, neat, quiet, or talkative, but the behaviors that confirm or disconfirm sly, treacherous, devious, or suspicious are less clear. Traits denoting easily observable behaviors are expected to be amenable to disconfirmation, whereas traits for which it is difficult to specify disconfirming behaviors may be quite resistant to change. It is interesting that groups in conflict are particularly prone to ascribe to each other such traits as untrustworthy and devious, which were the traits that Rothbart and Park (1986) found to have the least clear behavioral implications, and are therefore probably the least likely to be disconfirmed.

Criterion for Trait Inferences

A second dimension potentially related to the disconfirmability of trait concepts is the number of relevant observations required to establish or disconfirm the belief that a group can be described by a particular trait. Strong correlations were obtained between the favorability of a trait and the number of instances required for its confirmation ($r = .71$) and disconfirmation ($r = -.70$). In particular, the more *unfavorable* the trait, the fewer the number of instances required for confirmation and the *greater* the number of instances necessary for disconfirmation. Thus, favorable traits are difficult to acquire but easy to lose, whereas unfavorable traits are easy to acquire but difficult to lose. This finding suggests that unfavorable characteristics, once acquired as part of the stereotype, may be difficult to lose in part because of the large number of observations necessary for their disconfirmation, particularly when the frequency of intergroup contact is low.

Frequency of Occasions Allowing for Disconfirming Behaviors

This dimension reflects both the properties of social situations and the properties of trait concepts. Friendliness or talkativeness refer to behaviors that can be expressed in most social settings, whereas traits such as brave, heroic, or cowardly may never find occasion for expression across an individual's lifetime. In our view, the frequency dimension is of considerable importance, since even if trait-behavior links are clear as for heroic, the opportunities for engaging in heroic behavior are few. Rothbart and Park (1986) found a low but significant correlation between the favorability of a trait and the number of occasions available for disconfirmation, suggesting that more occasions are available for disconfirming favorable than unfavorable traits, in turn implying that unfavorable stereotypes resist change more than favorable stereotypes.

This dimension has particular importance for understanding the effects of intergroup contact. In the Rothbart and Park research, global frequency ratings were obtained across "typical" situations, yet different settings elicit different behaviors. Heroism and cowardice would be more prevalent in wartime, for example, than during dinner with friends (unless, of course, one is dining with Clint Eastwood or Charles Bronson). Highly structured role relationships (e.g., employer to employee) are not as likely to yield information on generosity, trustworthiness, or warmth than less-structured relationships (e.g., between friends). For this reason, it is extremely important to categorize contact situations in terms of the traits that might find expression.

In a recent study on the perception of intergroup contact episodes (John & Rothbart, in preparation) we asked students to describe situations in which they had interacted with a member of an outgroup (e.g., *Blacks, Asians, Fraternity Members, Lesbians*).[1] The students first described the contact setting on 32 situation feature scales (such as formal vs. informal, intimate vs. casual, pleasant vs. unpleasant), and then they rated whether that situation had provided them with information about a number of traits of the outgroup member. In an analysis of more than 300 such descriptions of contact episodes, we found that in informal (compared to formal) situations the outgroup members were described as showing more extroverted, loud, and impulsive behaviors; in intimate (compared to casual) contact situations they appeared more intelligent, scientifically minded, and artistic. In other words, characteristics of the contact situation were correlated with the observation of particular kinds of behaviors. Thus, impressions of groups may depend, at least to some extent, on the

situations in which one samples that group's behavior. In our study, subjects who interacted with Asians (who are generally regarded as quiet and introverted) at a dance party rated them as louder and as more impulsive than after interacting with them in a more formal setting. Thus, for subjects' perceptions of Asians, informal contact provided information disconfirming the stereotype. In contrast, observations of fraternity members in the same kind of informal situation confirmed the traditional stereotype about that group's social behavior. Thus, although some contact settings may permit the expression of a wide array of behaviors, we cannot assume that the same kind of setting will always permit the observation of disconfirming behaviors for all kinds of groups; rather, one's sample of disconfirming information depends on both the behaviors elicited by the situation and the nature of the observer's prior stereotypic beliefs.

Another subtle issue in the perception of outgroup behavior in typical contact settings derives from the so-called "fundamental attribution error" (Ross, 1977). In intergroup relations based on unequal power, such as men and women or whites and blacks, the less powerful group is often described as devious, sly, cunning, or shrewd. Considering minority groups' relative lack or power to satisfy physical and psychological needs, it is not surprising that their goals will often be achieved circuitously rather than directly. Ruthless aggression, for example, may be effective when used by white male corporate executives, but this "strategy" is typically not available to women or to blacks of either sex and, if used, is less likely to be successful. Thus behaviors encoded by the dominant group as devious or cunning appear to be behaviors *elicited* by powerlessness, rather than inherent characteristics of the minority group.

We have argued that not all traits are equally disconfirmable, and that contact settings vary in the degree to which they permit the observation of disconfirming behaviors. One way, therefore, to understand *which* contact settings are most likely to promote stereotype change is to classify settings in terms of their potential for eliciting confirming and disconfirming behaviors. Contact set-

---

[1]Throughout this paper, we use capitalized italics to refer to group or category names, such as the categories *Asian, Fraternity Member*, and *Bird*, whereas the attributes of specific members of a group or category appear in standard print.

tings may influence stereotype change in a variety of other ways—for example, by making the ingroup–outgroup distinction salient and by activating interactional goals that direct people's attention to disconfirming information. These variables will be discussed in the framework of a cognitive model of belief change, which will now be presented. The final section will consider how these variables relate to differences among settings and to the categories of intergroup contact suggested by Amir (1976) and Cook (1984b).

Processing Information About Groups and Group Members

The two traditional assumptions examined in the first part of this paper concern (a) whether the stereotypic concepts are amenable to disconfirmation and (b) whether the nature of a contact setting permits the observation of disconfirming information. Another general issue is whether information disconfirming a group stereotype obtained through contact with a *sample* of group members generalizes to the group as a whole. In our view, such generalization cannot be taken for granted, and in fact can probably be assumed *not* to occur. Similarly, Cook (1984b) finds that generalization of attitude change from a sample to a population does not always occur; he argues for the introduction of "a sort of 'cognitive booster' for generalization from . . . individuals to . . . groups" (Cook, 1984b, p. 20). A recent elaborate study on the effects of integrating women into the Marine Corps concludes that "men are not harassing the women they know in their groups, but rather are harassing women in general, those they do not know personally. . . . Women are generally accepted in their groups as individuals; change in esteem for women as a class has not yet occurred" (Royle, 1983, p. 113). In an attempt to discover why generalization from individuals to the group is so difficult to achieve, we will now examine some of the processes governing category-exemplar relations.

To understand how disconfirming exemplars of a category are integrated into or isolated from that category, it is necessary to consider the dynamic relation between the attributes of a category and the attributes of category members. Thinkers as diverse as Lippman (1922/1961) and Piaget (1952/1963) have noted that our existing concepts (categories, beliefs, or stereotypes) structure the perception of events relevant to these concepts. The process of assimilation, through selective encoding of the stimulus event, increases the "goodness-of-fit" between a category and its members. But Piaget noted that categories also accommodate the attributes of category members, implying that at some point the attributes of category members different from, or incompatible with, the category are no longer "assimilated" but serve to reconstruct the category itself.

This interaction between a category and its members is a fundamentally important, albeit complex process. Many of Piaget's examples come from the perception of the physical world, where discrepancies between an expected and an observed event are often clear and unambiguous, But, as discussed earlier, social beliefs can be notoriously fuzzy and difficult to disconfirm. Moreover, social beliefs are typically complex; even when exceptions are clearly perceived, they may be functionally isolated from the relevant category. Freud's compartmentalization (Freud, 1961), Abelson's differentiation (Abelson, 1959), and Allport's refencing (Allport, 1954) all describe mechanisms that serve to protect beliefs from disconfirming information by dividing a category into functionally isolated components.

Matching Category and Individual Members: A Prototype View

Our current model assumes that the perceiver derives the attributes of a particular social category by integrating those episodes from memory that he or she most strongly associates with (i.e., retrieves via) that category (cf. Hintzman, 1984, for a prototype model based on retrieval of individual episodes). For example, if a subject is asked to describe the characteristics of *Sorority Women*, it is assumed that activation of the category *Sorority Women* leads our subject to retrieve instances of specific sorority women, whose attributes are then integrated into a single impression. Two points require clarification. First, an episode is considered to be any specific event that has left a trace in memory; there could be many episodes for a given person, and many individuals could be included in a single episode. Second, we do not make any precise claims as to the nature of the weighting rule used to integrate individual episodes into a composite judgment; however, following findings in other domains of categorization (Anderson, 1980; Posner, 1974), we assume that episodes most representative of the category will receive greater weight than will unrepresentative episodes. Obviously, the characteristics of the weighting rule are important, but this issue need not be resolved here.

Since the attributes of a category are derived from the attributes of the episodes already associated with that category, a fundamental question arises as to *which* episodes are likely to become associated with a particular social category. We answer this question as follows: The likelihood of a new episode becoming associated with any given category is a function of the goodness-of-fit between that category and the episode. Once again, the question of exactly how this match is computed (i.e., whether it is the number of features in common or some weighting of the centrality of the common features) has not been resolved. It should be noted, however, that this similarity matching principle presupposes a prototype view of categories, rather than one based on defining features, and this assumption has important implications for social categorization.

Consider, for example, some social categories that would become associated with a hypothetical black male, John Smith, who is a highly educated, famous biochemist: *Blacks, Men, Scientists.* In terms of defining attributes, this person's dark skin and negroid features should make him strongly associated with the category *Black Person* but, for an observer holding traditional stereotypes about blacks, the overall fit to this category is poor, given the presence of the attributes "highly educated" and "biochemist" (assuming that the traditional stereotype of blacks does not include these attributes). Thus, for this observer, John Smith is more prototypic of the category *Scientist* than of the category *Black Person*, and we would expect the former category to be more strongly associated with this episode than the latter category. Logically, of course, the attributes of John Smith represent an intersection of the categories *Blacks* and *Scientists*, but the model assumes that the two categories, because they are not themselves associated, are treated as functionally independent.

Although physical characteristics, such as skin color or primary sex characteristics, logically constitute the basis for deciding whether an individual belongs to the category *Blacks* or *Women*, these characteristics may only be necessary but not sufficient attributes for category membership. Rosch

(e.g., 1978), Smith and Medin (1981), and others have argued that categories of natural objects do not conform to the classical Aristotelian model, which assumes the existence of defining attributes. According to the Aristotelian model, objects either do or do not belong to a particular category, and those that do belong are all equally "good" members of the category.

Objects differ, however, in the degree to which they are viewed as prototypical examples of a category. For example, robins and eagles are highly prototypical exemplars of the *Bird* category because their attributes correspond to our beliefs about what "birds in general" are like. Penguins, however, although technically birds, do not seem to really belong because of the many attributes they do not share with other birds (e.g., swimming and diving, rather than flying and sitting in trees).

By extension, individual blacks may differ as to how prototypical they are as examples of *Black People*. What would be the criteria for determining the goodness-of-fit of an individual to a social category such as *Blacks*? We suspect prototypicality for that group is not strongly related to variations in "defining" attributes, such as skin color, but rather to stereotypic attributes already associated with the category. This means, of course, that "typical" blacks are the ones most likely to be associated with that category, and thus when we think of *Blacks,* we tend to think of the typical members of the category, rather than of the individuals who are inconsistent with that category's attributes.

This reasoning is supported by cognitive research on attribute listing and category name-production tasks (Gernsbacher, 1985), which suggests that "bad" examples of natural object categories are not stored under the category node (or are difficult to retrieve under that node). Thus, when people are asked to imagine an "animal" or to list the characteristic attributes of that category, they do so by imagining some particular category member of high prototypicality, such as a dog, rather than a spider or a mole (Anderson, 1980; Posner, 1974).

In summary, we assume that pairing an individual with a social category is determined by the degree to which the individual's attributes match those of the category rather than by the logical set-inclusion relations between the category and its members. If this assumption is true, our model has general implications for hypothesis testing and belief change because it implies a mechanism by which disconfirming exemplars can be isolated from the stereotypic category. More specifically, the model rejects the assumption that social categories represent the "node" under which *all relevant* (i.e., confirming and disconfirming) exemplars are stored. That is, rather than assuming that all relevant blacks, Jews, and women are stored under the category nodes *Blacks, Jews,* and *Women,* respectively, this model suggests that the category nodes *Blacks, Jews,* and *Women* mainly store stereotypically "good" examples of those categories; bad examples tend to be stored under alternative category labels.

The above assumptions, if correct, have extraordinary implications for social perception. These assumptions reintroduce, in effect, the ultimate form of the stimulus error: a person who is in reality a *Black* may not be mentally represented as a *Black*; a person who is in reality a *Woman* may not be mentally represented as a *Woman*. Even though we are tempted to think that the defining features of the category *Blacks and Women* are relatively unambiguous, the model states that it is the overall goodness-of-fit to the stereotype, and not just a few defining features, that determines whether a person (or episode) becomes associated with a given category.

Typicality and the Impact of Disconfirming Attributes

We argue that two general factors determine which particular social category becomes associated with a given episode. One determinant, already discussed as the goodness-of-fit principle, is the "strength of activation" of a category produced by the episode itself. A second determinant, which we label *exogenous*, refers to the strength of activation of a category produced by the social context. This second source of activation has been studied in priming research, and will be discussed later.

Given that goodness-of-fit (or typicality) determines the episode-category match, we can make the following general prediction: The more a particular episode disconfirms a stereotypic category of which it is an instance, the more likely it is to be associated with a different, possibly counterstereotypic category. In the example cited earlier, John Smith, a black biochemist, was more strongly associated with the category *Scientist* than with

the category *Black*. This prediction implies that when people are asked to judge the characteristics of *Blacks*, John Smith is unlikely to be retrieved as an example of that category, just as a penguin is unlikely to be retrieved as an example of *Bird*; consequently, John Smith's attributes are unlikely to influence people's judgments about the general category of *Blacks*. Notice that John Smith's attributes are not lost, and that they are retrievable from a category that does fit his attributes more closely, namely *Scientist*. As stated earlier, the prediction of interest is that the *more* disconfirming (or atypical) a member is of a category, the *less* likely it is that the person will be associated with that category. It is apparent that this process enhances the tendency of stereotypic beliefs to confirm themselves.

However, the model also specifies how disconfirming events can become associated with the category. Since we have argued that it is the *overall* goodness-of-fit between an episode and a category that contributes to the strength of association, disconfirming attributes can become associated with the stereotype if they belong to an individual who otherwise is a very good fit to the category. Support for this prediction comes from a study by Weber and Crocker (1983, Experiment 3), who presented subjects with information about a sample of corporate lawyers; a portion of that information was disconfirming of the general stereotype of corporate lawyers (e.g., frequently wearing ill-fitting clothes, having difficulty analyzing problems and developing logical conclusions). Weber and Crocker, however, paired the disconfirming information in two different ways: if it was paired with lawyers who were otherwise good examples of the category (e.g., those described as white, married, and rich), it was more likely to affect subjects' beliefs about corporate lawyers in general than if the same information was paired with bad (atypical) members of the category (e.g., those black, single, and poor).

Thus, although the current model may seem to predict stability rather than change in people's stereotypic beliefs, it does predict change when disconfirming information is embedded in an episode that otherwise represents a good fit to the stereotypic category. Perhaps this good fit is one of the "cognitive boosters" sought by Cook. This cognitive mechanism may also explain why individuals like Martin Luther King, Jr., are unlikely to be retrieved as examples of *Blacks*—they would be seen as too different on too many features traditionally associated with blacks. In summary, then, we would expect that fraternity jocks who happen to support the nuclear freeze movement, and sorority queens who work diligently for women's and minority rights, would be the type of persons most likely to change the stereotype that fraternity and sorority members are politically conservative.

Familiarity with an Individual and Level of Categorization

Until now we have been discussing the kind of social category that an observer would "choose" to associate with a person about whom he or she may know rather little. In a sense, the choice is between *domains* of category, such as gender, occupation, ethnicity, etc. Would the same processes be apparent if we considered the effects of increasing amounts of information about a single individual? Before answering this question, it may be useful to consider a distinction offered by Rosch (1978).

Category systems can be conceived as having both a vertical and a horizontal dimension (Rosch, 1978). The vertical dimension refers to the level of inclusiveness of the category (e.g., *Politician* vs. *Democrat* vs. *Democratic Presidential Candidate*, or *European* vs. *Italian* vs. *Sicilian*), and the horizontal dimension refers to the domain of category (e.g., occupation, nation, race, gender). In the domain of social categories, horizontal categorization seems particularly relevant for understanding how a given person initially becomes associated with a category. Vertical categorization is particularly helpful for conceptualizing changes in the "level of categorization" used when increasing amounts of more specific information become available about an individual person. Since one of the major effects of intergroup contact is an increase in the *amount* of information about a given individual, it is critical to know whether that information is capable of altering perceptions of the attributes of the general social category.

As we view it, the same basic processes operate in vertical as in horizontal categorization, except that with additional individuating information about a particular individual, the perceiver will shift from superordinate to more subordinate levels of categorization (i.e., it becomes more useful to think of Mary Jones as a *Female Nurse* than as

a *Woman*). This prediction is in accord with Rosch's view that, up to a point, lower levels of categorization are more useful than higher levels.

However, the category eventually used to represent the person in memory depends on the compatibility between the initial categorization and subsequent information. To the degree that additional subordinate information shows a good fit with the initial superordinate categorization (as *Nurse* does for *Woman*), the initial superordinate categorization will be strengthened. However, if the more specific information shows a poor match to the superordinate category (for example, if we learn that Mary Jones is a *Mechanical Engineer*), then the superordinate, stereotypic association will be weakened, leaving the more specific category (*Mechanical Engineer*) as relatively strong and the superordinate category (*Woman*) as relatively weak. Once again, the appearance of disconfirming attributes within the same stimulus person can result in isolation from the perceiver's stereotypic category.

This prediction is interesting for a number of reasons. First, it allows for the possibility that individuating information can "release" the exemplar from the attributes of the superordinate category (cf. Locksley, Borgida, Brekke, & Hepburn, 1980; Locksley, Hepburn, & Ortiz, 1982), and at the same time renders the stereotype immune from the attributes of the exemplar. Second, it can account for some of the dynamic changes in the importance of particular attributes in perceptions of people. For example, when a white (who is unfamiliar with blacks) first meets a black person, "blackness" (an attribute associated with a superordinate category) may be the most salient feature, and the one that becomes most strongly associated with relevant behavioral episodes. With increasing familiarity, the black person becomes "individuated" and is encoded under more specific categories (*Artist, Scientist, Extrovert,* etc.), with "blackness" losing its salience.[2] The interesting implication, however, is that as the person loses his or her "blackness" s/he is less likely to be stored under the category *Black People*, and his/her counter-stereotypic attributes may therefore become isolated from the stereotypic category.

[2] One of us (MR) had an experience with a southern colleague at a conference, who expressed less than flattering sentiments toward *Blacks*: when MR asked him about his obviously intelligent and scholarly co-author, who was black, he responded. "I never think of him as black!"

Some experimental evidence lends at least indirect support to these conjectures. Since one of the important differences between ingroup and outgroup observers is the amount of information they have available about group members, differences in the way ingroup and outgroup observers categorize group members is relevant to our argument. Park and Rothbart (1982) examined the "levels of categorization" used by subjects when making judgments about ingroup and outgroup members. In their second experiment, men and women were asked to make predictions about groups described by both gender and occupational categories, such as *Female Physics Majors* or *Male Dance Majors*. When the two categories conflicted with the cultural stereotype (as in these examples), it was hypothesized that opposite-sex judges (outgroup members) would be more likely to base their predictions on gender (superordinate category) than on occupational (subordinate category) information, whereas same-sex judges (ingroup members) would be more likely to rely on occupational than on gender information (i.e., subordinate rather than superordinate categories). As predicted, women viewed female physics majors primarily as physics majors, whereas men viewed them primarily as women. Similarly, men viewed male dance majors primarily as dance majors whereas women viewed them primarily as men. Subjects thus used different levels of categorization when making judgments about groups, and one predictor of these choices was the subject's status as an ingroup or outgroup member.

Whereas this experiment focused on the *use* of categorical information, Park & Rothbart's fourth experiment investigated the level at which information about a stimulus person is *encoded*. In this study, men and women were given news-storylike information about a male or female stimulus person, including a description of the person's occupation. Two days later, subjects' memory of the person's sex and occupation was assessed, using both free and cued recall. Paralleling the results of the earlier experiment, the more specific category (occupation) was recalled less well by outgroup than by ingroup members.

We began this section with the argument that, for most purposes, *Nurse* will be seen as more informative or predictive of behavior than the superordinate category *Woman*. More important, however, we suggested that when the subordinate category is consistent with the superordinate category, encoding by the superordinate category is probably strengthened or at least not weakened. However, when the subordinate category contradicts the superordinate category (as *Mechanical Engineer* "contradicts" *Woman*), encoding by the superordinate category is weakened, and the perceiver more strongly associates the person to the subordinate than to the superordinate category. In summary, we have argued in this section that (a) contact and familiarity permit a more differentiated encoding of a stimulus person, and (b) this very process of individuation serves to insulate the attributes associated with the category from those of the individual. This process leads to the unhappy prediction that inferences from the individual to the group should *decline* with increasing familiarity with that individual, particularly when the individual is perceived as atypical of the group. Once again, the processes of categorization may isolate disconfirming instances from the superordinate category.

Exogenous Sources of Category Activation

Earlier we stated that the likelihood of a given category being paired with a behavioral episode is a joint function of the strength of association between the episode and that category, and the independent activation of that category from "exogenous" sources. Such exogenous factors include the distinctiveness of a contrasting environment (e.g., when visiting a foreign country, it is difficult not to attribute people's actions to their national character), competitive group interactions (in which the category divisions between ingroup and outgroup are paramount), or other contextual factors activating particular categories. Similarly, the recent work on priming of social categories (Bargh & Pietromonaco, 1982; Higgins & King, 1981; Higgins, King, & Mavin, 1982; Srull & Wyer, 1979; Srull & Wyer, 1980) has emphasized the importance of exogenous events in activating social categories. Thus we will now discuss some of the ways in which contact settings and/or goals during intergroup contact activate particular categories.

Distinctiveness and Salience. Categories related to perceptually distinct aspects of a setting are likely to be activated, and may then serve as "magnets" for causal attributions. For example, a visitor to a foreign country, such as Germany, becomes very much aware of the "German-ness" of the environment. The category *German* becomes very salient (or activated), at least during the initial phase of a visit. Research by Taylor and her colleagues (Taylor, 1981) on the perception of a single woman in a group of men, or a single black in a group of whites, suggests that distinctive attributes disproportionately influence observers' causal judgments. In our view this may occur because these "solo" individuals activate the category that defines their uniqueness (i.e., their "femaleness" or blackness), increasing the likelihood that this category will be associated with behavioral episodes.

It is not difficult to see that settings that reinforce the ingroup–outgroup dimensions, such as those based on competition for limited resources, almost continually activate the outgroup category. In a series of experiments, Brewer and Miller (1983) found that contact between ingroup and outgroup did not lead to attitude change toward *specific* outgroup members if the nature of the contact reinforced the dimension along which the groups differed. Brewer and Miller created interacting groups using the minimal-group procedure developed by Tajfel (1970), in which an arbitrary dimension (under- or over-estimating dots) served as the basis for mutually exclusive categorization. Once ingroups and outgroups were established, the researchers created intergroup contact of either a cooperative or a competitive nature. Most importantly, Brewer and Miller introduced several types of cooperative interaction. For example, the basis for selecting members for intergroup contact was either connected with, or independent of, the original basis for categorization. According to their prediction, cooperation was more likely to lead to favorable attitude change toward specific outgroup members when the selection procedure was independent of the initial basis of categorization.[3] According to Brewer and Miller,

> cooperation will not have a significant or lasting impact on intergroup perceptions as long as the social category membership of those on a cooperating team remains a salient or distinctive feature of the setting. (p. 3)

In slightly different terms, as long as the setting reinforces the activation of the outgroup category, it is unlikely that individual group members will be perceived (and treated) as anything other than members of the outgroup category. In principle, this could be quite desirable, since cooperative behavior associated with an outgroup should lead to attitude change, but it is not clear from the Brewer and Miller report whether the behavior of the outgroup members was perceived unambiguously as favorable; in short, assimilation to the more negative outgroup category was possible in this context. In light of Brewer and Miller's findings, however, it is interesting that attempts to redress social inequality by a quota system use a procedure in which the basis for intergroup contact is *totally* correlated with category membership—hardly an optimal strategy for promoting intergroup harmony, although it might be desirable as a means for redistributing resources.

Category Accessibility. Individual differences in category accessibility are another source of exogenous activation. Higgins and King (1981) report stable individual differences in the accessibility of trait categories in describing others. Trait concepts and social categories are quite similar in many aspects, and we would expect that the accessibility of social categories also differ from one individual to another. The classic research by Allport and Kramer (1946) on the difference between high and low anti-Semitic subjects in their recognition of Jewish faces assumed that the category *Jewish* was more meaningful, salient, or accessible for prejudiced than for nonprejudiced subjects. The predilection for government officials to use the concepts of Marxism, communism, and terrorism rather than the concepts of nationalism or national character as explanations for revolutionary movements testifies to the pervasiveness of differences in category accessibility.

Priming and Self-Confirmatory Expectations. The priming literature has other relevance for our model. If a social category has already been activated by an exogenous source, the threshold of activation necessary for associating that category with a relevant episode should decrease correspondingly. Since the likelihood of association between a category and an episode is proportional to the *total* activation of the category, from both episodic and exogenous sources, it follows that as activation from the exogenous source increases, the amount of activation from the episode itself

---

[3]Once again, it is important to distinguish between inferences about the sample and the population. The effects of contact mentioned here pertain only to the sample, a finding which we (and Brewer and Miller) ascribe to the specific members being perceived along dimensions unrelated to the outgroup category.

(i.e., the goodness-of-fit) required to associate the episode and the category is reduced. This process implies that when a stereotypic category is already activated by context, less evidence from the behavioral episode is required to represent that episode in a stereotypic manner. This mechanism explains the process of *assimilation*, in which an ambiguous stimulus is interpreted in accord with an already primed category. It should be noted, then, that priming a stereotypic category can have very different effects on stereotype change, depending on whether or not the behavioral episode is ambiguous. Until now, it has been assumed that disconfirming episodes are *unambiguously* disconfirming. However, if the event is ambiguous and subject to alternative interpretations, the category priming will structure the interpretation of the event in a way that is consistent with that category, and thus will serve to corroborate, rather than disconfirm the stereotype.

Interactional Goals. An important exogenous source of activation that influences the level of vertical categorization is the *goals* of the observer. One of Rosch's most important contributions is her finding that categories at some levels of abstraction are more useful than categories at other levels. Rosch (1978) also pointed out, however, that the level at which categorization is particularly useful depends upon the perceiver's experience or expertise, as well as on the context in which the categorization is made.

The specificity of the category used depends upon the nature and goals of the intergroup contact. If, as men, we interact with a woman with the goal of collaborating on a chapter, we would be highly attentive to her creativity, verbal fluency, reliability, and other attributes relevant to that goal. Although the original encoding category may have been *Woman*, it may soon become *Psychologist* or *Fluent Writer* or *Creative Person*. However, the transition from global to differentiating categories may also be influenced by the match between the category and the individual's behavior during the contact episode. That is, the more the interaction elicits behaviors highly stereotypic of the original category, the more that category is reinforced, making it unlikely that more differentiating categories are invoked. For example, a sexist male professor may well *elicit* sex-stereotypic behavior from a female graduate student, thus reinforcing his initial gender categorization. Thus, the processes that affect category differentiation cannot

be conveniently separated from the characteristics of the individual, the goals of the observer, and the setting in which the interaction takes place.

Cognitive approaches to intergroup perception are frequently criticized for neglecting the social settings and goals of social interaction. One way in which social context affects stereotyping is by influencing the kinds of categories activated and the level of categorization used (cf. Higgins & McCann, 1984). Although Rothbart and Park's (1982) Experiments 2 and 4 suggested that outgroup members (e.g., men) are unlikely to encode a stimulus person's (e.g., a woman's) subordinate attributes, their subjects had no goals *vis-a-vis* that person, and the social context was that of a psychology experiment. As we stated before, we would fully expect that a male who had to collaborate with a female on an important academic assignment would not fail to encode his partner's intellectual interest and characteristics, a view wholly consistent with the work of Locksley and her colleagues (1980, 1982) on the power of individuating information.

Contact settings may elicit vastly different interactional goals. For example, settings in which there are large power differences among the interactants do not usually require the person of greater power to encode the subordinate attributes of those of lesser power, whereas it is adaptive for powerless individuals to discriminate among the powerful (e.g., professors tend to know less about students than students do about professors). Within traditional subcultures, the same power relationships may extend to differences between men and women. Even aside from power differences, different interactional goals encourage encoding at different levels; we use different categories when approaching people to sign a political petition than we do in deciding with whom we might enjoy dinner, hiking, or love-making.

Figure 23.2 provides a schematic overview of the factors included in pairing disconfirming information with a stereotypic category, and illustrates both endogenous and exogenous sources of category activation.

How Do Disconfirming Instances Alter the Stereotype?

Since we have argued that (1) repeated contact and increasing familiarity lead to a "recoding" of the individual in more specific, differentiated, and id-

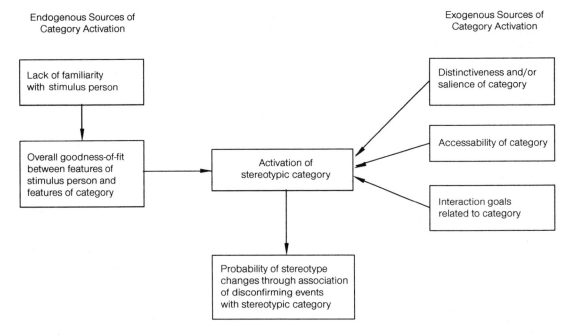

FIGURE 23.2 ■ Factors influencing the probability of associating the attributes of a specific individual with those of the stereotypic category. It is assumed that there are two sources of category activation (association)—endogenous and exogenous—and that the degree of familiarity with a particular individual reduces the overall goodness-of-fit between the individual and the category.

iosyncratic terms, and (2) such recoding is likely to prevent the characteristics of that person from generalizing to those of the category, we must return to the critical question: How does contact lead to stereotype change?

Assuming that the other necessary conditions for disconfirmation outlined in Figures 23.1 and 23.2 have been met (i.e., stereotypic beliefs are disconfirmable, settings allow for disconfirming behaviors, disconfirming information originates from otherwise typical members), we suspect that the process of disconfirmation involves both a change in the kinds of episodes associated with the general (stereotypic) category *and* a concomitant shift toward the use of more specific categories in encoding the stimulus person. In other words, a decrease in the predictive utility of the superordinate category leads to the use of more differentiated and predictive categories. Suppose, for example, a person stereotypes women as passive, and then repeatedly encounters assertive women under the conditions optimal for change outlined above. Eventually, episodes involving assertive women become attached to the superordinate category *Women*. At that point the

category *Women* is represented by a node attached to numerous assertive episodes as well as the earlier passive episodes. When then asked about the characteristics of women, a person holding the stereotype should answer so that the perceived "average" shifts toward the assertive end; at the same time, the variance should increase (assuming the original passive episodes have not been forgotten). The increase in perceived within-group variability implies that membership in the category *Women* is less predictive of passive versus assertive behaviors than it used to be; if the person wishes to make judgments related to passivity, he or she must use information that is more differentiating than gender, such as occupation, college major, membership in social organizations, or specific personality characteristics.

Taylor.(1981) and Weber and Crocker (1983) have argued that the accumulation of such disconfirming information should lead to the formation of a *subtype* of women that differentiates assertive women from women in general. We do not disagree with that position, but in our view continual subtyping should effectively lead to the dissolution of the stereotype. To the degree that the category *Women* no longer predicts passivity, intuitiveness, and so on, this lack of predictability should eventually lead people to rely on information more specific than gender when making predictions about behavior; the more frequent use of such specific categories is equivalent to a loss in meaning of the broader stereotypic category.

This somewhat optimistic analysis of the abolition of superordinate stereotypes has to be qualified by two considerations. First, it assumes that there is little predictive value to the stereotype when in fact there may be some degree of predictive utility. Second, even if the incidence of a stereotypic trait (e.g., passivity) is no greater for women than for men, there will be some women who are passive, and it is likely that these few, albeit nonrepresentative, cases may disproportionately reinforce the stereotype. Both these concerns are problems of psychological inertia and reflect the self-perpetuating nature of prior beliefs (Peterson & DuCharme, 1967; Ross, 1977; Rothbart, 1981). To the degree that social norms and settings elicit even slight amounts of stereotypic behavior from a group, an existing stereotype might persist, if for no other reason than that people may be insensitive to small changes in contingencies. There is good evidence for the "feature-positive" effect (Fazio, Sherman, & Herr, 1982), which indicates that people are disproportionately sensitive to the presence rather than the absence of events.

With our position now qualified, what is the prognosis for stereotype change? Although we would like to be optimistic about the possibility of change, it seems more realistic to conclude that the conditions leading to change through contact are quite restricted. Even Cook (1984a), one of the researchers most optimistic about the ameliorative effects of intergroup contact, lists five conditions necessary for favorable attitude change: (1) equal status in the contact setting, (2) personal attributes that disconfirm the stereotype, (3) mutual interdependence, (4) a setting that promotes individual (rather than categorical) perception, and (5) a contact setting that promotes egalitarian norms. However, if one considers the typical contact settings in which, say, blacks and whites interact, it seems that most violate all of Cook's conditions necessary for favorable attitude change. In other words, in a society where there is enormous social inequality between groups and many behavioral differences associated with that inequality, it

is extremely difficult to satisfy, under normal conditions, either Cook's five criteria or the conditions outlined here.

Previous Analyses of Intergroup Contact and the Current Model

The five conditions suggested by Cook (1984a) as necessary for attitude change fit reasonably well with our model. Equal status, stereotype-disconfirming attributes of outgroup members, and interdependence are all likely to promote episodes that disconfirm a group stereotype. Although this may be less true for Cook's dimension of mutual interdependence (e.g., Brewer & Miller, 1983), negative images of outgroups are more likely to be contradicted under conditions of interdependence rather than independence. Cook's fourth requirement, that the setting promote individual rather than categorical perception, will, according to our view, release the individual from the group stereotype, and should lead to favorable attitudes toward that individual. However, there still is the troublesome question, as Cook acknowledged, about whether or not attitude change generalizes from the individual to the group. Finally, the requirement that the setting promote egalitarian norms relates to change promoted through atmosphere effects rather than through direct, belief-disconfirming information.

Amir (1976, p. 288) lists eight factors thought to promote favorable attitude change, many of which overlap with Cook's five variables. Again, most are factors that increase the likelihood of stereotype-disconfirming information (particularly for outgroup stereotypes based on differences in power or status).

Conclusions

Our model has several implications about stereotype change. First, the model emphasizes the difficulty of producing stereotype change by positing that (a) many stereotypic beliefs resist disconfirmation, (b) most typical contact situations do not provide disconfirming information, and (c) disconfirming episodes tend to be associated only weakly with the stereotypic category, but more strongly with alternative categories of which they are more typical.

Second, it emphasizes the difficulty of producing stereotype change by extensive contact with a few individuals, since the process of increasing individuation decreases the likelihood of associating the individual with the stereotypic category. This process can explain the often autonomous relationship between category attributes and the attributes of individual category members.

Third, the model is consistent with evidence about the use of different categorical levels by ingroup and outgroup members.

Fourth, since the model recognizes the predictive utility associated with different categorical levels, it can account for the initial strength and—with increasing contact and familiarity—the ultimate fading of distinctive attributes, such as skin color, ethnic origin, and religion.

Fifth, consistent with recent experimental findings, the model helps define settings in which contact is most likely to lead to attitude change. In particular, these are settings that (a) permit the observation of disconfirming behaviors, (b) keep the ingroup-outgroup distinction salient, and (c) foster goals that require the encoding of subordinate attributes of outgroup members.

Finally, our theoretical analysis may help resolve a dispute over interpersonal versus intergroup determinants of social behavior. Brown and Turner (1981) criticize the contact hypothesis on the grounds that it constitutes an interpersonal approach to an intergroup problem. They argue that intergroup behavior cannot be understood as a simple extension of interpersonal processes. They consider attempts to modify intergroup perception and behavior through interpersonal techniques as implied, for example, by the contact hypothesis (and by research on belief similarity), misguided, since the factors that influence intergroup processes remain in effect even after attitudes and beliefs regarding particular individuals have changed. Although we agree with many of Brown and Turner's (1981) ideas, the distinction between interpersonal and intergroup behavior is not as absolute as they suggest; in fact, the distinction rests precisely on the question of whether particular individuals are viewed in individualistic terms or as members of broad social categories. We have tried to define the conditions under which persons are encoded in terms of broad categories or along more specific, idiosyncratic dimensions. This difference in the "level of categorization" used to encode individuals is, in fact, an important psycho-

logical phenomenon. Simply declaring that one level is irrelevant to the analysis of the other is not sufficient.

In summary, we have argued that impressions of groups are heavily influenced by the attributes of those group members most strongly associated with the group label. If stereotypic impressions are to change, disconfirming information must become associated with the group label. But, as we have argued, a number of cognitive processes work against such an association. Probably our central point is that the objectively verifiable attributes of a person (such as gender or race) are the ones a perceiver uses to mentally represent that person. Thus, in American society, a particular woman engineer of any race may be more strongly associated with the category *Engineers* than with *Women*, and a particular black scientist may be more strongly associated with *Scientists* than with *Blacks*. In order to achieve changes in stereotypic beliefs, it is necessary to attach the disconfirming attributes to the *superordinate* category label, instead of the more natural subordinate category.

This mechanism must have been known to Sojourner Truth, a former black slave and feminist, who spoke to a convention on women's rights in 1851. Sojourner Truth presented herself as a woman who did not fit society's image of women. Since she knew she would be thought of as a black rather than as a woman, it was necessary for her to continually remind the audience that she was a member of the latter category as well as of the former:

> That man over there says that women need to be helped into carriages, and lifted over ditches, and to have the best place everywhere. Nobody ever helps me into carriages, or over mud-puddles, or gives me any best place! And ain't I a woman? Look at me! Look at my arm! I have ploughed and planted, and gathered into barns, and no man could head me! And ain't I a woman? I could work as much and eat as much as a man—when I could get it—and bear the lash as well! And ain't I a woman? (Schneir, 1972, pp. 94–95)

Sojourner Truth recognized that stereotypes about women would change when people realized that powerful qualities such as her own should be associated with the category *Women*, and she also realized that people would be more likely to consider her as a black rather than a woman. By continually activating the category *Women*, she implicitly recognized the importance of associating attributes with the appropriate social category, and used a technique that, in accord with the arguments of this paper, may have some success in modifying stereotypic beliefs.

REFERENCES

Abelson, R. P. (1959). Modes of resolution of belief dilemmas. *Journal of Conflict Resolution, 3,* 343–352.

Allport, G. W. (1954). *The nature of prejudice.* Cambridge. MA: Addison-Wesley.

Allport, G. W., & Kramer, B. M. (1946). Some roots of prejudice. *Journal of Psychology, 22,* 9–39.

Amir, Y. (1976). The role of intergroup contact in change of prejudice and ethnic relations. In P. Katz (Ed.), *Towards the elimination of racism* (pp. 245–308). New York: Pergammon Press.

Anderson, J. R. (1980). *Cognitive psychology: Its implications.* San Francisco, CA: Freeman.

Bargh, J. A., & Pietromonaco. P. (1982). Automatic information processing and social perception: The influence of trait information presented outside of conscious awareness on impression formation. *Journal of Personality and Social Psychology, 43,* 437–449.

Brewer, M. B., & Miller, N. (1983). *Social categorization and intergroup acceptance.* Paper presented at Society of Experimental Social Psychologists, Pittsburgh, PA.

Brown, R. J., & Turner, J. C. (1981). Interpersonal and intergroup behaviour. In J. C. Turner & H. Giles (Eds.), *Intergroup behavior* (pp.13–65). Chicago. IL: University of Chicago Press.

Cook, S. W. (1970). Motives in a conceptual analysis of attitude-related behavior. In W. J. Arnold and D. Levine (Eds.), *Nebraska symposium on motivation, 1969* (pp. 179–235). Lincoln, NE: University of Nebraska Press.

Cook, S. W. (1984a). The 1954 social science statement and school desegregation: A reply to Gerard. *American Psychologist, 39,* 819–832.

Cook, S. W. (1984b). Experimenting on social issues: The case of school desegregation. Paper presented at 92nd annual convention of the American Psychological Association, Toronto.

Fazio, R. H, Sherman, S. J., & Herr, P. M. (1982). The feature-positive effect in the self-perception process: Does not doing matter as much as doing? *Journal of Personality and Social Psychology, 42,* 404–411.

Freud, S. (1961). *The interpretation of dreams.* NY: Science Editions.

Gernsbacher, M. A. (1985). *Comparing principles of category structure.* Department of Psychology, University of Oregon. Eugene, OR.

Hasher, L., Goldstein, D., & Toppino, T. (1977). Frequency and the conference of referential validity. *Journal of Verbal Learning and Verbal Behavior, 16,* 107–112.

Higgins, E. T., & King, G. (1981). Accessibility of social constructs: Information-processing consequences of individual and contextual variability. In N. Cantor & J. F. Kihlstrom (Eds.), *Personality, cognition, and social interaction* (pp. 69–121). Hillsdale, NJ: Erlbaum.

Higgins, E. T., King, G., & Mavin, G. H. (1982). Individual

construct accessibility and subjective impressions and recall. *Journal of Personality and Social Psychology, 43,* 35–47.

Higgins, E. T., & McCann, C. D. (1984). Social encoding and subsequent attitudes, impressions, and memory: "Context-driven" and motivational aspects of processing. *Journal of Personality and Social Psychology, 47,* 26–39.

Hintzman, D. (1984). "Schema abstraction" in a multiple-trace memory model. *University of Oregon Cognitive Science Program Technical Report No. 84–1.*

John, O. P., & Rothbart, M. (in preparation). *An empirical assessment of the dimensions of intergroup contact.* Department of Psychology, University of Oregon, Eugene, OR.

Lippmann, W. (1961). *Public opinion.* New York: Macmillan. (Original work published 1922)

Locksley, A., Borgida, E., Brekke, N,. & Hepburn, C. (1980). Sex stereotypes and social judgment. *Journal of Personality and Social Psychology, 9,* 821–831.

Locksley, A., Hepburn, C., & Ortiz, V. (1982). Social stereotypes and judgments of individuals: An instance of the base-rate fallacy. *Journal of Experimental Social Psychology, 18,* 23–42.

Newcomb, T. M. (1947). Autistic hostility and social reality. *Human Relations, 1,* 69–86.

Park, B., & Rothbart, M. (1982). Perception of out-group homogeneity and levels of social categorization: Memory for the subordinate attributes of in-group and out-group members. *Journal of Personality and Social Psychology, 42(6),* 1051–1068.

Peterson, C. R., & DuCharme, W. M. (1967). A primacy effect in subjective probability revision. *Journal of Experimental Psychology, 73,* 61–65.

Piaget, J. (1963). *The origins of intelligence in children.* New York: W. W. Norton. (Original work published 1952)

Posner, M. I. (1974). *Cognition: An introduction.* Glenview, IL: Scott Foresman.

Rosch, E. (1978). Principles of categorization. In E. Rosch & B. Lloyd (Eds.), *Cognition and categorization* (pp. 27–48). Hillsdale, NJ: Erlbaum.

Ross, L. (1977). The intuitive psychologist and his shortcomings: Distortions in the attribution process. In L. Berkowitz (Ed.), *Advances in experimental social psychology,* Vol. 10 (pp.173–262). New York: Academic Press.

Rothbart, M. (1981). Memory processes and social beliefs. In D. L. Hamilton (Ed.), *Cognitive processes in stereotyping and intergroup behavior* (pp. 145–181). Hillsdale. NJ: Erlbaum.

Rothbart, M. & Park, B. (1986). On the confirmability and disconfirmability of trait concepts. *Journal of Personality and Social Psychology, 50,* 131–142.

Royle, M. H. (1983). *Factors affecting the integration of women into Marine Corps units.* Ph.D. dissertation. Claremont Graduate School, Claremont, CA.

Sarnoff, I., Katz, D., & McClintock. C. (1954). The motivational basis of attribute change. *Journal of Abnormal and Social Psychology, 49,* 115–124.

Schneir, M. (Ed.). (1972). *Feminism: The essential historical writings.* New York: Random House.

Smith, E. E., & Medin, D. L. (1981). *Categories and concepts.* Cambridge, MA: Harvard University Press.

Srull, T. K., & Wyer, R. S., Jr. (1979). The role of category accessibility in the interpretation of information about persons: Some determinants and implications. *Journal of Personality and Social Psychology, 38,* 1660–1672.

Srull, T. K., & Wyer, R. S., Jr. (1980). Category accessibility and social perception: Some implications for the study of person memory and interpersonal judgments. *Journal of Personality and Social Psychology, 38,* 841–856.

Tajfel, H. (1970). Experiments in intergroup discrimination. *Scientific American, 223,* 96–102.

Taylor, S. E. (1981). The interface of cognitive and social psychology. In J. H. Harvey (Ed.), *Cognition, social behavior, and the environment* (pp. 189–211). Hillsdale, NJ: Erlbaum.

Weber, R., & Crocker, J. (1983). Cognitive processes in the revision of stereotypic beliefs. *Journal of Personality and Social Psychology, 45,* 961–977.

How Does Cooperation Reduce Intergroup Bias?

Samuel L. Gaertner • University of Delaware
Jeffrey A. Mann • Wheaton College
John F. Dovidio • Colgate University
Audrey J. Murrell • University of Pittsburgh
Marina Pomare • University of Delaware

This experiment examined the hypothesis derived from the social categorization perspective that intergroup cooperation reduces bias by transforming members' cognitive representations of the aggregate from 2 groups to 1 group. Two 3-person groups experienced intergroup contact under conditions that varied (a) members' representations of the aggregate as 1 group or 2 groups (without involving cooperation) and (b) the presence or absence of intergroup cooperation. As expected, in the absence of cooperation, bias was lower among Ss induced to conceive of the 6 participants as 1 group rather than as 2 groups. Also as predicted, among Ss in the 2-groups condition, intergroup cooperation increased the strength of the 1-group representation and decreased bias. Multiple regression mediation analysis revealed, as expected, that members' representations mediated bias and that the 1-group representation primarily increased the attractiveness of former outgroup members.

Despite substantial documentation that intergroup cooperative interaction reduces bias (Allport, 1954; Aronson, Blaney, Stephan, Sikes, & Snapp, 1978; Cook, 1985; Deutsch, 1973; Johnson, Johnson, & Maruyama, 1983; Sherif, Harvey, White, Hood, & Sherif, 1954; Slavin, 1985; Worchel, 1979), it is not clear how cooperation achieves this effect. One basic issue involves the psychological processes that mediate this change. A second issue concerns which specific aspects of intergroup cooperation (e.g., interaction, common goals, and common fate), as well as what other general features of the contact situation (e.g., equal status between the groups, equalitarian norms, opportunities to learn stereotype-inconsistent information; see Cook, 1985), are necessary and sufficient to reduce intergroup bias. The present research addressed primarily the first issue: How does cooperative interaction reduce bias?

The classic functional relations perspective by Sherif et al. (1954) views cooperative interdependence as a direct mediator of attitudinal and behavioral changes. However, several additional explanations have been proposed (see Brewer & Miller, 1984; Miller & Davidson-Podgorny, 1987; Worchel 1979, 1986). For example, cooperation may induce greater intergroup acceptance as a result of dissonance reduction serving to justify this type of interaction with the other group; as a result of the positive, reinforcing consequences of mutual cooperation (Lott & Lott, 1965); or as the result of increases in knowledge about the other group, which reduces intergroup anxiety (Stephan & Stephan, 1984). An additional model that may account for the effects of cooperation is based on Tajfel's (1969) and Tajfel and Turner's (1979) work on social categorization and social identity theory. This model proposes that intergroup cooperation promotes intergroup acceptance because it reduces the cognitive salience of the intergroup boundary (set also Wilder, 1986). A recent position proposed by Brewer and Miller is aligned with the categorization model; this position proposes in addition that when intergroup cooperative interaction permits members' attention to focus on one another's personal qualities, it contributes to the development of personalized rather than categorized interactions and thereby to reduced bias (see also Miller & Brewer, 1986; Miller, Brewer, & Edwards, 1985). Also Neuberg and Fiske (1987) have shown more generally that cooperative interdependence increases motivation to form more individuated impressions.

Within the framework of the social categorization model, the present study examined the hypothesis that intergroup cooperation reduces bias, at least partially, because intergroup cooperation reduces the salience of the intergroup boundary. Specifically we proposed that intergroup cooperation induces the members to conceive of themselves as one (superordinate) group rather than as two separate groups, thereby transforming their categorized representations from *us* and *them* to a more inclusive *we* (see Brown & Turner, 1981; Campbell, 1958; Doise, 1978; Feshbach & Singer, 1957; Hornstein, 1976; Turner, 1981; Worchel, Axsom, Ferris, Samaha, & Schweitzer, 1978). Indeed, Sherif and Sherif (1969, pp. 268–269) acknowledged the potential that intergroup cooperation has toward facilitating the development of a common superordinate entity. This possibility, however, was conceived by Sherif and Sherif to represent the very gradual development of a highly structured superordinate group, rather than the immediate creation of a social entity that may only exist more ephemerally within the perceptions of one or more of its members.

Assuming that intergroup cooperation may initially transform members' cognitive representations from two groups to one group, how might this change reduce bias? The process by which a revised one-group representation could reduce intergroup bias rests theoretically on two related conclusions of Brewer's (1979) analysis of the origins of intergroup bias and on propositions underlying social identity theory (Tajfel & Turner, 1979) and self-categorization theory (Turner 1985; Turner, Hogg, Oakes, Reicher, & Wetherell, 1987; see also Hogg & Abrams, 1988). First, intergroup bias frequently takes the form of in-group enhancement rather than out-group devaluation (see Rosenbaum & Holtz, 1985, for a different perspective). Second, group formation brings in-group members closer to the self, but the distance between the self and out-group (or non-in-group) members remains relatively unchanged. Consequently, circumstances that induce the memberships to adopt a one-group representation can extend the cognitive and motivational processes that brought original in-group members closer to the self and thereby enhance attitudes toward the former out-group members.

This reasoning is supported in an earlier study (Gaertner, Mann, Murrell, & Dovidio, 1989), in which the members of two 3-person groups were induced to conceive of the total 6-person aggregate as one group, two groups, or as six separate individuals (i.e., no groups). As expected, the one-group and the separate-individuals conditions each had lower levels of intergroup bias than did the two-groups control condition (which maintained the salience of the intergroup boundary). Furthermore, supportive of Brewer's (1979) analysis as well as self-categorization theory (Turner, 1985; Turner et al., 1987), these recategorized conditions reduced bias in different ways. In the one-group condition, bias was reduced primarily by increasing the attractiveness of former out-group members, whereas in the separate-individuals condition, bias was reduced primarily by decreasing the attractiveness of former in-group members. Thus, as specified by Turner et al.'s self-categorization theory, "the attractiveness of an individual is not constant, but varies with in-group membership" (p. 60). Consequently, to the extent that the proposed changes in members' conceptual representations from two groups to one group mediate the causal relation between intergroup cooperation and reduced intergroup bias, bias should diminish primarily because of the development of more positive attitudes toward former out-group members.

The present study was designed to assess the

efficacy of the proposed recategorization model. Most likely, intergroup cooperation reduces bias by means of several different pathways, only one of which involves transforming the memberships' representations of the aggregate. By tracking the status of subjects' cognitive representations of the memberships in the present study, we investigated whether the proposed cognitive changes played a role in reducing intergroup bias.

To examine the hypothesis that the causal relation between intergroup cooperation and reduced intergroup bias is mediated (at least partially) by members' transformed representations of the aggregate from two groups to one group, we initially mated two separate 3-person laboratory groups and then brought these groups into contact under circumstances designed to vary (a) the members' representations of the aggregate as either one group or two groups and (b) the presence or absence of intergroup cooperative interaction.

Members' representations of the aggregate were manipulated by exposing them to a set of systematically varied features (not involving cooperation), which in concert were expected to influence their conceptual representations of the memberships as one group or two groups (e.g., see Gaertner et al, 1989). For example, we varied whether the two groups sat at a single table in an alternating seating pattern or at two separate tables (see also Ryen, 1974) and whether they were assigned a new single name to represent both groups or maintained their earlier selected, separate group names, as well as other features.

Intergroup cooperation is a complex process that usually involves several features, including interaction, common problems or goals, and common fate between the memberships. Brewer's (1979) review noted that the introduction of a cooperative intergroup reward structure alone, without intergroup interaction, is not sufficient to eliminate intergroup bias. Also, when intergroup cooperation has been operationalized in natural settings (see Johnson et al., 1983; Sherif et al., 1954; and Slavin, 1985), it specifically involves the opportunity for interaction, common goals, and common fate between the memberships. Therefore, to manipulate intergroup cooperation in the current experiment, we varied the presence or absence of all three features simultaneously. In the cooperation condition, there was an opportunity for interaction between the memberships during the joint development of a single solution to a common problem while the groups shared a common fate that turned on the effectiveness of their joint solution. In the no-cooperation condition, both groups together (in either the one-group or two-groups conditions) listened to a tape recording of some other group's discussion and then, as individuals and without interdependence, rated the effectiveness of the recorded group's discussion.

Although an assessment of which specific features of intergroup cooperation are necessary and sufficient to reduce bias would be an important undertaking, this was not the goal of the current study. Rather, in the context of varying (in an all or none manner) the three major features of intergroup cooperation, this study began to address our primary question, which involved the psychological processes that mediate the relationship between intergroup cooperation and reduced bias. The no-cooperation/two-groups condition (which emphasized the two-groups categorization) is especially pertinent because of its partial structural similarity to Tajfel, Billig, Bundy, and Flament's (1971) minimal intergroup situation, except that in the present study all participants met face to face, following an initial period of in-group interaction. In Tajfel et al.'s work, members were isolated from each other, and intergroup bias resulted exclusively from the simple categorization of two groups. Tajfel et al.'s two groups, like our own, existed in the absence of explicit competition, interaction, a common problem, or common fate between the memberships. Thus, with circumstances similar in these ways to Tajfel et al.'s to serve as the no-cooperation baseline, the current study examined the consequences of introducing the major features of intergroup cooperation. The dependent variables included measures of subjects' representations of the aggregate (e.g., "Does it [the aggregate] feel like one group, two groups or separate individuals?"), of how cooperative were all 6 participants, and of evaluative ratings of in-group and out-group members.

The experimental design and the results of two comparisons permits a test of the hypothesis that a one-group representation mediates the causal relation between intergroup cooperation and reduced intergroup bias. In particular, one assumption of the present research was that there is a causal link between a one-group representation and reduced bias, even in the absence of cooperative interaction. Thus, within only the no-cooperation conditions of the present study, bias should be lower in the one-group than in the two-groups condition. In addition, if cooperation transforms members' representations from two groups to one group, then within only the two-groups representation conditions comparisons involving the no-cooperation and cooperation conditions should indicate that the introduction of intergroup cooperation results in an increase in the extent to which the aggregate feels like one group (e.g., an increase on a scale ranging from 1 to 7 that measured how much the aggregate feels like one group) and a decrease in intergroup bias. Furthermore, we predicted that this reduction in bias, which is mediated by changes in members' representations, would occur primarily because attitudes toward former outgroup members become more positive. In addition, the major hypothesis that a one-group representation mediates the causal relation between intergroup cooperation and reduced intergroup bias was evaluated with the multiple regression mediation approach suggested by Baron and Kenny (1986) and Judd and Kenny (1981).

Method

Subjects

Four hundred seventy-four students (234 men and 240 women) enrolled in the general psychology course participated in partial fulfillment of their research-readings or participation requirement. Testing the subjects in same-sex groups of 6 people per session, our intention was to assign 10 groups of men and 10 groups of women to each of the 4 experimental cells. In error, only 9 groups of men were assigned to the cooperation/one-group cell; therefore only 79 six-person groups were run.

Procedure

Subgroup Formation. In each session, two 3-person groups were assigned ostensibly to two different experiments located in different areas within the laboratory complex. Each group was unaware of the other group's existence. Greeted by different experimenters, members of each group were assigned one of three different color-coded identity tags reserved for each person (purple, yellow and brown; or green, orange, and red) as they were led to their designated laboratory As they entered, the experimenter asked each person to

attach these identification tags to their clothing and to sit according to their color-coded identity, which was matched by a color-coded placemat on the group's table. Each room was also equipped with a visible video camera and microphone. Tape-recorded instructions explained that the study involved the examination of group decision-making processes and that we would be videotaping their group interaction as they attempted to reach consensus to the winter survival problem (Johnson & Johnson, 1975). Members of each group were first asked to create a name for their group and to record it on their special group consensus form as well as on their personal identity tags. Following the 3-person group discussion focused on the winter survival problem, subjects were informed of their subsequent contact with the other group, which would take place soon in a larger room within the laboratory complex.

Cooperation Manipulation. Overall, three aspects of inter group cooperation were varied simultaneously: interaction, a common problem requiring a consensus solution, and common fate. In the no-cooperation condition, none of these features were present. Instead, the members of both groups were brought together and exposed to a tape-recorded discussion of two other groups reaching consensus on the winter survival problem. Following exposure to the 6-min recording, each participant recorded an evaluation of the effectiveness of the prerecorded group's solution. In the cooperation condition, all three features of cooperation were present. Specifically, the two groups were interdependent in that they discussed the winter survival problem and reached a single consensus solution that if effective (in terms of an absolute standard determined by the experimenters) would qualify the 6 participants for entry into a lottery at the end of the semester during which they could share a $60 prize (i.e., $10 per person). No feedback about the group's effectiveness was given during the experimental session.

Representation Manipulation (One Group vs. Two Groups). The goal of the representation manipulation was to vary the subjects' cognitive representations of the 6 participants as either one group or as two separate groups; it was very similar operationally to Gaertner et al. (1989). To induce these groups to have a one-group representation of the aggregate during contact (independent of the presence or absence of cooperative interaction), the members of both groups were seated in same colored chairs at a single hexagonal table in an integrated seating pattern (ABABAB). Subsequent instructions emphasized their common identity as students at the same university and instructed them all to wear the same available T-shirts displaying the name of their university. Also, an experimenter assigned the members of both groups a new single name to represent all 6 people and instructed them to replace the name of their original 3-person group written on their personal identity tags with this new name. The experimenter announced, ostensibly for the TV recording, that the _____ (3-person group name) and the _____ (3-person group name) had merged to form the STARS (new 6-person group name), which members were also asked to use on all subsequent experimental forms. Also, the two visible TV cameras were each directed at all 6 people during the contact period. In addition, all participants were asked to hold on to a rope placed in the center of the table, ostensibly to keep all participants within camera range. Last, because in the cooperation conditions, the derived consensus solution would function as a tangible product to represent all 6 participants, subjects in the no-cooperation one-group condition were instructed to estimate (based on observations of others' nonverbal reactions) the 6 current participants' average evaluative rating of the prerecorded group's solution. Thus, each subject in the no-cooperation one-group condition derived a single rating to represent all 6 participants but without cooperative interaction or interdependence as in the cooperation/one-group condition.

In the two-groups condition, the members of each 3-person group sat at different tables (36 in. apart) in a segregated seating pattern (AAABBB), in different colored chairs (one group used red chairs; the other group used yellow chairs), during exposure to instructions that did not mention their common university identity or require them to wear university T-shirts. Also, each group maintained their separate 3-person group names on their identity tags throughout, and the experimenter announced the session using the names of both groups without mention of any merger. Also in the two-groups condition, the 6 participants did not hold on to a rope, nor did they estimate an average of the other participants' ratings of the group's interaction. Instead, each participant in the no-cooperation/two-groups condition separately recorded his or her own evaluation of the effectiveness of the prerecorded group's discussion. Finally, each of the two TV cameras was aimed at a different 3-person group throughout.

Measures. Following the experimental manipulations, the participants were given a postexperimental questionnaire containing items which asked about (a) their conceptual representations of the aggregate ("Which description best characterizes your impression of all of you currently participating in this experiment? It felt most like one group, two groups, or separate individuals"), as well as to what extent, *not at all* (1) *to very much* (7), it felt like each of these representations (after Gaertner et al., 1989); (b) their rating of how much it felt like they were cooperating and competing with each other during the contact period; and (c) their evaluative ratings (1–7) of each participant (except for themselves) regarding how much they liked each of the others, as well as their ratings of each person's honesty, cooperativeness, and similarity to themselves. Separate in-group and out-group ratings were constructed for each person and then averaged for each 6-person group. Thus ratings of in-group and out-group members were based on rating by individuals of individuals from which group-level evaluations were constructed.

Results

Because of the possible interdependence among the 6 participants per session, the unit of analysis throughout all statistical analyses was the group mean for each 6-person group ($n = 79$) rather than each individual's ratings.

Efficacy of the Experimental Manipulations

When asked to select the representation (one group, two groups, or separate individuals) that best characterized their impressions of the aggregate, sizable percentages of subjects within each 6-person group in the one-group and two-groups conditions selected the alternative most appropriate to their treatment condition (see Table 24.1). Separate 2 (representation) × 2 (cooperation) × 2 (sex of subject) analyses of variance (ANOVAS) conducted on the average percentage of subjects per group ($n = 79$) selecting the one-group and two-groups alternatives each yielded main effects for the representation and cooperation manipulations and no effect for sex of subject. Supportive

TABLE 24.1. Effects of Cooperation and Representation on Members' Impressions of the Interaction

Impression	No cooperation		Cooperation	
	Two groups (n=20)	One group (n=20)	Two groups (n=20)	One group (n=19)
Members' representations				
Percentage				
One group	15.8_a	39.7_b	48.3_{bc}	66.7_c
Two groups	75.0_a	47.8_b	47.5_{bc}	28.9_c
Separate individuals	9.0_a	12.5_b	4.2_{bc}	4.4_c
Mean rating (1–7)				
One group	2.7_a	3.9_b	4.4_{bc}	5.1_c
Two groups	5.1_a	3.5_b	3.3_b	2.3_c
Separate individuals	2.8_a	2.5_a	1.7_b	1.7_b
We were cooperating	4.6_a	4.7_a	5.8_b	5.9_b
We were competing	2.2_a	2.2_a	2.2_a	1.7_b

Note. Means with different subscripts within a row are reliably ($p < .05$) different than one another according to Tukey's honestly significant difference method.

of the efficacy of the representation manipulation, greater percentages of subjects in the one-group condition (52.8%) selected the one-group alternative in relation to those in the two groups condition (32.1%), $F(1, 71) = 16.03$, $p < .001$. Correspondingly, greater percentages of participants in the two-groups condition selected the two-groups alternative (61.25%) than did subjects in the one-group condition (38.63%), $F(1,71) = 21.40$, $p < .001$. In addition, the efficacy of the representation manipulation was supported by similar ANOVAS conducted on subjects' separate ratings of the extent (1–7) to which the aggregate felt like one group and two groups. As indicated in Table 24.1, subjects in the one-group, in relation to the two-groups, condition saw the aggregate more as one group, $F(1, 71) = 26.30$, $p < .001$, and less as two groups, $F(1, 71) = 67.98$, $p < .001$.

The efficacy of the cooperation manipulation was evaluated by additional 2 (representation) × 2 (cooperation) × 2 (sex) ANOVAS on subjects' ratings (1–7) of the levels of cooperation during the contact period. As expected, subjects in the cooperation condition rated the participants as more cooperative ($M = 5.86$) than did participants in the no-cooperation condition ($M = 4.63$, $F(1, 71) = 139.25$, $p < .001$). Parallel but substantially weaker effects were obtained for subjects' rating of competition within the cooperation ($M = 1.98$) and no-cooperation ($M = 2.20$) conditions, $F(1, 71) = 4.34$, $p < .04$. Thus, subjects' ratings of the contact pe-

riod supported the efficacy of the representation and cooperation manipulations.

Does Cooperation Transform Members' Representations?

If subjects' representations of the aggregate mediate the causal relationship between intergroup cooperation and intergroup bias, then each of the ANOVAS involving the measures of subjects' representations should have also yielded main effects for the manipulation of cooperation. Indeed, in addition to the effects for representation, each of the analyses reported earlier did obtain main effects for cooperation. For example, supportive of the idea that intergroup cooperation transforms members' conceptual representations of the aggregate from two groups to one group, the separate ANOVA involving the average percentages of subjects selecting the one-group alternative (as opposed to two groups or separate individuals) yielded a main effect for cooperation, $F(1, 71) = 31.40$, $p < .001$. As expected, when the groups cooperated, higher percentages of subjects indicated that the aggregate felt like one group (57%) in relation to when the opportunity for cooperation was not available (28%). Corresponding effects were obtained for the percentages of subjects selecting the two-groups alternative, $F(1, 71) = 21.44$, $p < .001$. Also, main effects for cooperation were obtained on the (1–7) measures of the extent to which the aggregate felt like one group, $F(1,71) = 67.66$, $p < .001$, and two groups, $F(1,71) = 93.90, p <.001$. As indicated in Table 24.1, subjects in the cooperation condition, in relation to the no-cooperation condition, saw the aggregate more as one group and less as two groups.

Although not specifically expected, main effects for cooperation also were obtained for the percentages of subjects selecting the separate-individuals alternative, $F(1, 72) = 4.39, p < .04$, and for subjects' ratings of the extent (1–7) to which the aggregate felt like separate individuals, $F(1, 71) = 29.34, p < .001$. Within the cooperation condition, somewhat smaller percentages of subjects selected the separate-individuals representation and rated it more weakly than did subjects in the no-cooperation condition (4.3% vs. 10.8%, respectively and 1.71 vs. 2.63). Thus, although the cooperation manipulation affected subjects' impressions regarding the separate-individuals possibility this particular representation was less common and weaker than the alternative representations (see Table 24.1).

How Does Cooperation Reduce Intergroup Bias?

The measures of intergroup bias involved subjects' ratings (1–7) of in-group and out-group members' likability, cooperativeness, honesty, and similarity to the self. The internal consistency for these ratings by each group was high, as indicated by Cronbach's alpha (in-group = .89; out-group = .93). Multivariate comparisons involving these four ratings were conducted in accordance with the predictions derived from the hypothesis that a one-group representation would mediate the causal relation between intergroup cooperation and reduced bias. Separate indexes for in-group and out-group members consisting of the mean of these four evaluative ratings (Table 24.2) also were calculated to illustrate more clearly the pattern of findings associated with the multivariate effects.[1]

A major assumption of the present research was that there is a causal link between a one-group representation and reduced bias, even in the absence of cooperative interaction. Thus, considering only the no-cooperation conditions of the present study ($n = 40$ groups), if subjects' representations of the

aggregate were transformed as expected, bias would be lower in the one-group than in the two-groups condition.

First, as expected within the no-cooperation conditions, subjects receiving the one-group manipulation selected the one-group alternative more frequently, 39.7% versus 15.8%, $F(1, 36) = 21.38$, $p <.001$, and rated (on scales ranging from 1 to 7) the aggregate more strongly as one group than did subjects receiving the two-group manipulation, $F(1, 36) = 9.84, p < .003$.

Second, to determine whether the representation manipulation affected intergroup bias in the absence of cooperative interaction, we conducted a 2 (representation) × 2 (sex) × 2 (in-group, out-group) multivariate analysis of variance (MANOVA), with repeated measures on the in-group, out-group variable, on the four evaluative ratings within only the no-cooperation condition. The results of this analysis revealed the expected Representation × In-group, Out-group interaction, $F(4, 33) = 2.55, p = .058$, each of the four univariate effects reached statistical significance at least at the .02 probability level. In this and subsequent analyses of bias, there were no effects involving subjects' sex. Examination of the evaluative in-

Table 24.2. Effects of Cooperation and Representation on Measures of Intergroup Bias

Measure	No cooperation		Cooperation	
	Two groups	One group	Two groups	One group
Like				
In-group	5.38	5.12	5.62	5.53
Out-group	4.48	4.75	5.19	5.27
Bias	0.90	0.36	0.43	0.26
Honest				
In-group	5.89	5.49	6.17	5.97
Out-group	4.98	5.15	6.08	6.01
Bias	0.90	0.35	0.08	−0.04
Cooperative				
In-group	5.93	5.44	5.88	5.96
Out-group	5.09	5.13	5.66	5.87
Bias	0.84	0.31	0.22	0.09
Similar to me				
In-group	4.64	4.23	4.85	4.92
Out-group	3.95	4.05	4.41	4.74
Bias	0.69	0.18	0.44	0.18
Average				
Index $_{in-group}$	5.46	5.07	5.63	5.59
Index $_{out-group}$	4.63	4.77	5.33	5.47
Bias	0.83	0.30	0.30	0.12

[1]Comparable univariate analyses involving these indexes yielded similar findings to those reported at the multivariate level.

dexes composing the bias measure, calculated to illustrate the pattern of the multivariate effects (see Table 24.2), indicated that bias (i.e., $Index_{IN} - Index_{OUT}$) in the no-cooperation/one-group condition (.30) was lower than in the no-cooperation/two-groups condition (.83). Although these findings were consistent with expectations, closer examination revealed that bias was reduced here because out-group members were evaluated more favorably (.14) in the one-group condition ($Index_{OUT}$ = 4.77) than in the two-groups condition ($Index_{OUT}$ = 4.63), which was expected, and also because in-group members were regarded less favorably (−.39) in the one-group condition ($Index_{IN}$ = 5.07) than in the two-groups condition ($Index_{IN}$ = 5.46). Thus, the between-groups comparisons suggest that there is a causal relationship between the representation manipulation and intergroup bias in the absence of cooperative interaction.[2]

A second hypothesis was that if cooperation influences members' representations of the aggregate, then within only the two-groups condition, cooperation would transform members' representations from two groups to one group and consequently would reduce bias. Within only the two-groups conditions ($n = 40$ groups), the results of a series of planned comparisons between the no-cooperation and cooperation conditions supported these expectations.

First, 2 (cooperation) × 2 (sex) ANOVAS conducted on measures of subjects' representations within only the two-groups conditions revealed the expected main effects for cooperation. For example, the average percentage of subjects selecting the one-group representation was greater for the cooperation (48.3%) than for the no-cooperation (15.8%) condition, $F(1, 36) = 22.7, p = .001$. Similarly, the extent (as measured on a scale ranging from 1 to 7) to which the aggregate felt that one group was greater in the cooperation condition ($M = 4.44$) than in the no-cooperation condition ($M = 2.72$), $F(1, 36) = 38.03, p < .001$. Measures of the two-groups representation corroborated this pattern of findings.

Second, in terms of whether cooperation reduces bias, the results of a 2 (cooperation) × 2 (sex) × 2 (in-group, out-group) MANOVA with repeated measures on the in-group/out-group variable, which was performed on the four evaluative ratings within just the two-groups conditions yielded the expected Cooperation × In-group/Out-group interaction, $F(4, 33) = 4.82, p < .004$. The evalua-

tive indexes for in-group and out-group members (see Table 24.2), within just the two-groups conditions, indicated that indeed, intergroup bias ($IndexIN - Index_{OUT}$) was lower in the cooperation/two-groups condition (.83) than the no-cooperation/two-groups condition (.83). Furthermore, the pattern of change responsible for lower bias that was due to intergroup cooperation here was consistent with our expectations. That is, although in-group members were regarded slightly more favorably (.17) in the cooperation ($Index_{IN} = 5.63$) versus no-cooperation ($Index_{IN} = 5.46$) conditions, the change for out-group members (.70) was even greater ($Index_{OUT} = 5.33$ vs. 4.63, respectively). Given the pattern of these means, the Cooperation × In-group/Out-group interaction effect within just these two-groups representation conditions (mentioned previously) indicated that change sustained by out-group members was, as expected, reliably greater than the change for in-group members.[3]

The between-treatments analyses were strongly supportive of the predictions derived from the model that proposes that the relationship between intergroup cooperation and reduced intergroup bias is mediated by transformations in members' representations of the aggregate from two groups to one group.

Multiple Regression Mediation Approach

Further evidence more directly supportive of the proposed model is offered by the multiple regres-

---

[2]Furthermore, correlational analyses within these no-cooperation conditions involving subjects' representational ratings (1–7) further suggest that the one-group representation related to intergroup bias as expected. The more strongly subjects indicated that the aggregate felt like one group, the lower the bias, $r(38) = -.5134, p < .001$, and the higher the rating of out-group members, $r(38) = .5070, p < .001$. The ratings of the one-group representation did not relate to the evaluation of in-group members, $r(38) = .0336, ns$. In general, then, the patterns of relationships between representation and bias in the no-cooperation condition supported our hypothesis that representations of the aggregate, in the absence of cooperation, could influence intergroup bias.

[3] Furthermore, correlational analyses involving subjects' representational ratings, ranging from *not at all* (1) to *very much* (7), and intergroup evaluations again suggested support for the proposed relationship between a one-group representation and intergroup bias. The more strongly subjects rated the aggregate as one group, the lower the bias, $r(38) = -.6085, p < .001$, and the higher the rating of out-group members, $r(38) = .7776, p < .001$. Also, ratings of the one-group representation did not relate to the evaluation of in-group members, $r(38) = .2292, p < .15$.

sion mediation approach suggested by Baron and Kenny (1986) and Judd and Kenny (1981). The multiple regression mediation analysis (a form of path analysis) requires that a series of regression equations be estimated. In one equation, the dependent variable, for example, bias (Index_{IN}– Index_{OUT}) regressed on the independent variables (e.g., cooperation and representation) should demonstrate that the independent variable(s) affect the dependent variable; this of course would be similar to main effects for cooperation and representation on bias in an overall ANOVA between-treatments approach. In other equations, each of the potential mediators (i.e., the extent, ranging from 1 to 7, to which the aggregate felt like one group, two groups or separate individuals and the degree of perceived cooperativeness or competitiveness during the contact period) that are regressed on the independent variables should indicate that the independent variable(s) also affect one or more of the potential mediators. These effects were reported earlier in the between-treatments analyses. Finally, and most advantageously, another equation in which the dependent variable (e.g., bias) is regressed on the independent variables together with the set of potential mediators should indicate that at least one of the potential mediators affects the dependent variable over and above the influence of the other variables. Also in this last equation, the effect of the independent variable(s) should be weaker than in the initial equation because if there was perfect mediation, the independent variable(s) would have no effect beyond the association between the mediator and the dependent variable.

This multiple regression mediation approach was particularly useful for the current research because it permitted an estimate of any independent effects of the different representations of the aggregate; thus it more directly examined portions of the proposed model than would be possible with the between-treatments approach alone. For example, it is possible that, contrary to the details of our theoretical view the only representation that mediates intergroup attitudes is the degree to which the memberships categorize themselves as two groups. Once the categorized representation is degraded, bias may be reduced regardless of whether the two-groups categorization is replaced by some other representation (e.g., as one group or as separate individuals). Our earlier work, however, indicated that different residual representa-

tions reduced bias in different ways (Gaertner et al., 1989). Therefore, because we expected the ratings of the one-group and separate-individuals representations to relate differently to feelings toward in-group and out-group members, we conducted a separate mediation analysis for each of three relevant dependent variables—bias (Index_{IN-OUT}, see Figure 24.1), Index_{IN}, and Index_{OUT}—to more fully examine the processes by which different representations might reduce bias. Statistically reliable relationships beyond the .05 level are indicated by the bolder arrows connecting these variables.

As indicated in Figure 24.1, when entered by themselves, the independent variables of representation and cooperation (see left column of Figure 24.1) had standardized beta weights of .35 ($p <$ .001) and –.36 ($p < .005$) with the degree of bias (Index_{IN-OUT}, represented in the oval to the right). These results paralleled the main effects for these variables obtained in an overall between-treatments analysis.[4] Also, these independent variables each relate to several of the potential mediators (see center column). For example, cooperation is related to the ratings of one group (beta = .63),

---

[4]An overall 2 (representation) x 2 (cooperation) × 2 (sex) × 2 (in-group, out-group) multivariate analysis of variance (MANOVA) with repeated measures on the in-group/out-group variable was performed on the four evaluative ratings. This overall analysis yielded both a Representation × In-group/Out-group interaction, $F(4, 68) = 3.25, p < .017$, as well as a Cooperation × In-group/Out-group $F(4, 68) = 7.26, p < .001$, interaction. Bias ($\text{Index}_{IN} - \text{Index}_{OUT}$) was lower in the one-group condition (5.32 –.11 = .21) than in the two-groups condition (5.54 – 4.98 = .56); also, bias was lower in the cooperation condition (5.61 – 5.40 = .21) than in the no-cooperation condition (5.26 – 4.70 = .56). Examination of these means revealed that the reduced bias in the one-group condition, in relation to the two-group condition, was attributable both to a more positive attitude toward out-group members (.13) as well as to a less positive attitude toward in-group members (–.22). However, the reduced bias associated with the cooperation condition, in relation to the no-cooperation condition, was due primarily to the greater enhancement of attitudes toward out-group members (.70) than toward in-group members (.30). Given the pattern of means involved in these comparisons, the Cooperation × In-group/Out-group MANOVA interaction reported in this note, indicated that this positive change toward out-group members was reliably more substantial than the change toward in-group members. Although not directly related to the framework that initiated the research, this MANOVA also yielded a main effect (across both in-group and out-group ratings) for cooperation, $F(4, 68) = 11.44, p < .001$. Overall, the evaluative ratings were higher for both in-group and out-group members in the cooperation ($M = 5.51$) than in the no-cooperation (4.98) condition. No other effects were obtained.

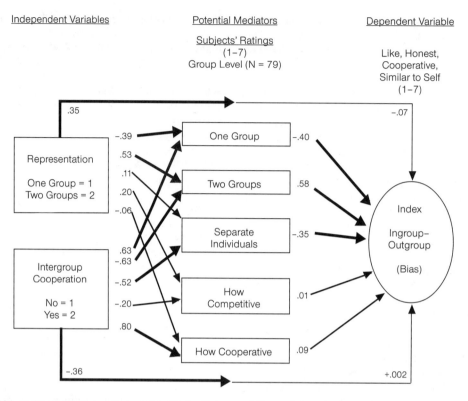

FIGURE 24.1. ■ The mediation analysis of the effects of representation and cooperation on intergroup bias. (Bold arrows indicate that $p < .05$.)

two groups (beta $= -.63$), and also to subjects' ratings of cooperation (beta $= .80$). Also, in the last equation, when the manipulations of representation and cooperation were entered into the regression equation together with subjects' ratings of one group, two groups, separate individuals, cooperation, and competition (adjusted $R^2 = .434$), each of the ratings of subjects' representations of the aggregate were predictive of intergroup bias. Specifically, the betas for one group, two groups, and separate individuals with bias were $-.40$, $.58$ and $-.35$, respectively. Consistent with our earlier work, both the one-group and separate-individuals representations were negatively associated with intergroup bias, in contrast to the positive association for the two-groups representation. Also, as we would expect if mediation had been occurring, when all variables were entered together into the last equation, the independent variables of representation (beta $= -.07$) and cooperation (beta $= .002$) no longer related reliably to intergroup bias.

Also note that in the current experiment, the

ratings of cooperation and competition did not appear to relate independently to bias once the representation ratings were controlled. Nevertheless, their effects might have been suppressed by one or more of the other variables because of potential multicollinearity. As would be expected by our hypothesis, the ratings (1–7) of cooperation and one group were reliably related $r(77) = .685$, $p < .001$. Supplemental analyses for the last equation suggested that when bias was regressed on the full set of other variables, the betas for the one-group and cooperation ratings were correlated negatively but weakly, $r(71) = -.277$, $p < .05$.[5] However, the tolerance of the one-group and cooperative ratings (tolerance $= .249$ and $.280$, respectively) suggested that their beta weights were not so influenced by the set of other variables as to be wholly determined by them.

The additional mediation analyses for the ratings of in-group members only indicated that in the last equation, the ratings of the separate-individuals representation (beta $= -.43$) and two groups representation (beta = .53) related to in-group ratings (adjusted R^2 = .307). The less subjects felt like separate individuals and the more they felt like two groups, the more positively they evaluated original in-group members. However, in the last equation in the mediation analyses involving only the ratings of out-group members (adjusted R^2 = .533), only the ratings of one group (beta = .58) related reliably to the out-group ratings. As expected, the more subjects felt like they were one group, the more positive were their ratings of original out-group members.

In terms of the full design of the experiment, the regression analyses indicated that the manipulations of representation and cooperation each influenced members' representations of the aggregate, which in turn were the major factors that influenced attitudes toward in-group and out-group members. However, a more specific test of the proposed model involved the effects of cooperation when it was the sole potential contributor to variation in members' representations. Therefore, another set of multiple regression mediation analyses were conducted involving only subjects (i.e., groups) in the two-groups conditions ($n = 40$), so that the effects of cooperation alone could be assessed. Thus, these analyses excluded the representation manipulation and were again conducted separately for the three relevant dependent variables: bias ($Index_{IN-OUT}$, $Index_{IN}$, and $Index_{OUT}$).[6] When only the independent variable of cooperation was considered, the results—despite the reduction in sample size—continued to demonstrate the importance of subjects' representations of the aggregate as mediators of the causal relation between intergroup cooperation and bias.

As indicated by Figure 24.2, when bias was regressed (in the last equation) on all of the other variables (adjusted R^2 = .48), only the two-groups (beta = .72) and the separate-individuals (beta = −.44) representation ratings influenced bias. The more the aggregate felt like two groups and the less it felt like separate individuals, the higher was the degree of bias. Thus, when the representation manipulation was omitted, the ratings of the one-group representation (beta = −.13) did not relate independently to bias (although the simple correlation between the one-group representation ratings and bias was reliable, $r(38) = -.6085, p < .001$. However, the additional regression analyses involving the separate components of bias, namely, the evaluations of in-group and out-group members separately, more specifically clarify the special role of the one-group representation as it mediates the relationship between intergroup cooperation and reduced bias.

When the evaluations of former in-group members were considered separately and regressed on all of the other variables in the last equation (adjusted R^2 = .10), only the two-groups (beta = .61) and the separate-individuals (beta = −.54) representation ratings were predictors of the evaluations of in-group members. Thus, attitudes toward in-group members are not influenced primarily by the one-group representation.

The separate regression analyses involving the evaluations of out-group members, however, revealed (see Figure 24.3) that when the out-group evaluations were regressed (in the last equation) on the full set of other variables (adjusted R^2 = .58), only the ratings of the one-group representation (beta = .47) reliably and independently influenced these ratings of out-group members. As expected, the greater the extent to which the aggregate felt like one group, the more positive were the evaluations of out-group members. Thus, although the one-group representation did not independently affect bias or the ratings of in-group members, it was the only reliable determinant of the attitudes toward out-group members.

---

[5]The notion of a correlation between betas can be somewhat confusing because it is not obvious how we could obtain a correlation involving only a single pair of values. The meaning of this statistic should be understood in terms of a correlation between an infinitely large set of estimated beta pairs, each based on one of an infinitely large number of (fixed-effects) replications of the present experiment. Each replication generates a somewhat different value for the dependent variable (i.e., bias) and thereby results in different estimates for these two betas. The correlation between these infinite number of beta pairs can be estimated (see Finn, 1974, p. 100); it is this estimate that is reported.

[6]For just the two-groups conditions, we hypothesized that cooperation would reduce bias primarily by changing subjects' representations from the baseline of two groups to one group. Thus, because the one-group representation was theoretically presumed to decrease the distance between the self and out-group member we anticipated that reduced bias in the two-groups conditions would be due more strongly to changes in the evaluations of out-group members than to changes involving in-group members. Consistent with this reasoning, in the two-groups conditions, reductions in bias ($Index_{IN-OUT}$) when correlated more highly, $t(37) = 3.03, p < .01$, with more positive ratings of out-group members, $r(38) = -.72, p < .001$, than they were with less positive ratings of in-group members, $r(38) = .37, p < .009$.

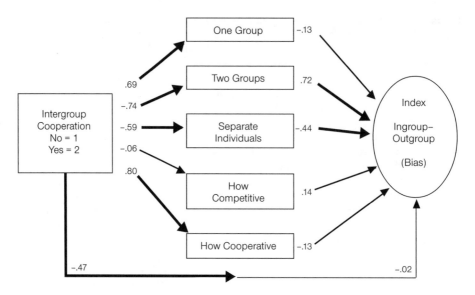

FIGURE 24.2 ■ The mediation analysis (for the two-groups conditions only) of the effects of cooperation on intergroup bias. (*n* = 40. Bold arrows indicate that *p* < .05.)

Discussion

Overall, the results offer convergent support for the social categorization approach and the hypothesis that the causal relation between intergroup cooperation and reduced bias is mediated by transformations in members' cognitive representations of the aggregate. Specifically, cooperation degraded the two-groups representation and induced the memberships to recategorize themselves primarily as one larger group. Also, the more strongly the aggregate was regarded as one group, the more highly out-group members were evaluated, a consequence that contributed substantially to the reduction of intergroup bias.

The multiple regression mediation analyses on the full experimental design (see Figure 24.1), in which cooperation and the additional features constituting the representation manipulation could both contribute to the induction of a one-group representation, suggested that the one-group representation ratings could relate independently to changes in bias, as well as to the evaluations of out-group members. These circumstances presented by the full design may be structurally comparable to some natural settings in which intergroup cooperation is accompanied by other features, which according to the elaborated version of contact hypothesis (Allport, 1954; Brewer

& Miller, 1984; Cook, 1978; Pettigrew, 1971; Stephan, 1987), have the potential for influencing the results of the contact experience. Perhaps some of these features (e.g., equal-status contact, the opportunity for more intimate encounters, and equalitarian norms) affect the quality of the contact experience because they further contribute to transformations of members' categorized representations (Brewer & Miller). From our perspective, some of these features may also further encourage the development of a one-group representation.

In the regression analyses when the representation manipulation was omitted (i.e., considering only the two-groups-representation conditions; see Figures 24.2 and 24.3), the one-group representation did not independently affect bias per se, but rather exerted its influence primarily by enhancing the evaluations of outgroup members. This pattern, however, is consistent with the proposed model. To the extent that cooperation reduced bias by transforming members' representations from two groups to one group, bias was reduced primarily because attitudes toward former out-group members became more positive. With the revised one-group representation induced by cooperation, former out-group members were regarded as generally more likable, cooperative, honest, and similar to the self. These results are supportive of

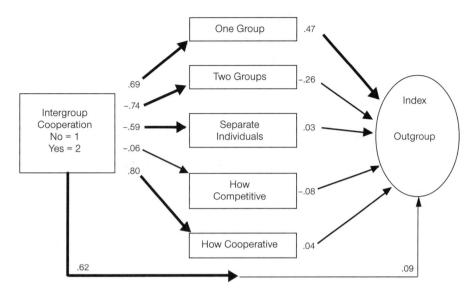

FIGURE 24.3 ■ The mediation analysis (for the two-groups conditions only) of the effects of cooperation on the evaluation of out-group members. (*n* = 40. Bold arrows indicate that *p* < .05.)

Turner's (1985) theory of self-categorization and Brewer's (1979) conclusion that group formation primarily brings in-group members closer to the self.

The presence of cooperation distinctly altered subjects' representations of the memberships and also the pattern of in-group and out-group attitudes. With cooperation, the one-group representation dominated subjects' impressions in the one-group (66.7%) and the two-groups (48.3%) conditions (see Table 24.1); whereas without cooperation, subjects selected this representation only 39.7% and 15.8% of the time, respectively[7]. In relation to the set of other features intended to influence subjects' representations, cooperation sharply increased the percentages of subjects selecting the one-group alternative in both the one-group and especially in the two-groups conditions. Also, intergroup bias was lower with cooperation. This finding also was somewhat more noteworthy in the two-groups conditions. Furthermore, the reduced bias associated with cooperation was attributable primarily to the development of more positive attitudes toward former out-group members. Overall, the pattern of these findings is supportive of the proposed model.

Unexpectedly, cooperation also decreased the extent to which subjects endorsed the Separate-Individuals representation, albeit from weak to barely negligible (see Table 24.1 and Figures 24.1 and 24.2). Thus, although subjects did not frequently choose the separate-individuals representation to characterize themselves (i.e., it was only selected 7.5% of the time overall, and subjects did not rate it strongly on the scale ranging from *not at all* (1) to *very much* (7), *M* = 2.16), cooperation, nevertheless, still further reduced the strength of this impression. In retrospect, this change for the separate-individuals representation was reasonable, if indeed cooperation emphasizes one's state of belonging to the superordinate entity. This finding is important to our theoretical framework because the mediation analyses indicated that higher ratings of separate individuals was associated with lower levels of intergroup bias and with decreased attraction to former in-group members. These latter findings are consistent with our previous work

---

[7]Despite the weakness of the one-group representation when it was induced by factors other than cooperation, the reduced bias was due partially to the enhanced attitude toward out-group members as well as to less positive attitudes toward in-group members. The reason that attitudes toward in-group members were less positive in the one-group condition than in the two-groups condition in the absence of cooperation may be related to Wilder's (1986) suggestion that the salience of a specific outgroup (as would be the case in our two-groups condition) can increase favorable regard for in-group members.

(Gaertner et al., 1989), with Brewer's (1979) analysis, and with Turner's (1985) self-categorization theory.[8]

In general, the results offer support for the model that initiated the research. Nevertheless, we do not believe that intergroup cooperation reduces bias solely by modifying members' representations of the aggregate. Statistically, the regression analyses, which suggested that there was no independent causal relation between the cooperation treatment variable (or ratings of cooperation) with bias, can be misleading. For example, to the extent that there may be collinearity between the ratings of cooperation and representation measures, the statistical power associated with these variables may be reduced. Discussing the potential problems caused by collinearity, Judd and Kenny (1981, p. 607) indicate, "We may conclude that a particular variable in a causal chain exerts no effect upon the next variable simply because of poor power."

Furthermore, within the experimental design, the variety of processes by which cooperation could have reduced bias might not have been fully represented. For example, in the current study, the effects of cooperation were compared with a control condition involving no cooperation, rather than with competition. Indeed, the design was intended to assess the effects of introducing intergroup cooperation per se, rather than the effects of removing intergroup competition. In Sherif et al.'s (1954) study, a series of intergroup cooperative encounters produced harmony among groups with a history of competitiveness and hostility toward the other. By contrast, in the current study, one cooperative episode reduced mild levels of largely pro-

---

[8] The regression analyses (see Figures 24.1 and 24.2), however, suggest that as cooperation decreases the salience of a separate-individuals representation, it contributes to an increase in intergroup bias. Although these findings were unexpected, they are consistent with a theoretical framework that emphasizes the mediating role played by members' representations of the aggregate. Paradoxically, to the extent that intergroup cooperation induces a one-group representation, it can contribute to reduced bias, whereas, to the extent that cooperation decreases the separate-individuals representation, it can increase intergroup bias. This result suggests that the specific effect of cooperation on bias depends on the pattern of representations induced by cooperation and, more specifically, by relative strength of the different residual representations. The findings indicate that intergroup cooperation degrades the two-group representation and most strongly increases the salience of a one-group representation. Consequently, cooperation generally reduces bias.

in-group bias produced primarily by social categorization per se without prior history of competitive or hostile relations between the groups. Worchel et al. (1978) showed that the degree of bias reduced by intergroup cooperation is dependent on the nature of the earlier relationship between groups (i.e., whether they were cooperative, competitive, or independent) as well as by the degree of success achieved by the cooperative venture. Therefore, the relative strength of the different processes by which cooperation can reduce bias may also vary differentially depending on the circumstances. Finally, the present study was designed primarily to examine the efficacy of the proposed theoretical model and not to test its effectiveness in relation to each of the other models. Therefore, for example, we did not include a success/failure manipulation, which would have more directly provided an opportunity to test reinforcement theory.

Although members' representations are probably not the only mediators of the relation between cooperation and intergroup bias, it is clear from this study that although the other major theories are not disproved, the other explanations would have difficulty explaining the reported findings without including members' representations in the causal chain. In particular, the lower bias obtained between the one-group condition and the two-groups condition without cooperation would be problematic for the other positions. During intergroup contact without cooperation in this study, there is little reason to believe that subjects in the one-group condition in relation to the two groups condition engaged in behavior that created a state of imbalance to be rectified, gained more knowledge about the other group or its members, or experienced greater levels of positive reinforcement. Also, the degree to which members' conceived of themselves as separate individuals did not differ for these conditions; therefore it is unlikely that subjects had more individuated or personalized impressions of out-group members in the one-group than in the two-groups conditions. However, these conditions differed in terms of the extent to which the manipulations transformed members' representations from two groups to one group. In addition, these results weaken the possibility that in the cooperation condition, reduced bias (the final dependent variable in the regression analysis) preceded the transformations in members' representations (the proposed mediators). Indeed, in the no-cooperation condition, in which the direction of causality was more certain because of the elimination of interaction, changes in members' representations most plausibly preceded changes in bias.

Intergroup cooperation increased the extent to which subjects adopted a one-group representation, and intergroup cooperation also decreased intergroup bias. However, which features of the cooperation treatment were most responsible or necessary and sufficient to produce these effects? Compared with the no-cooperation condition, participants in the cooperation condition interacted with one another, worked together toward a common goal, and shared the same fate regarding the outcome of the joint venture. Certainly, each of these features was involved when Sherif and Sherif's (1969) groups of summer campers cooperated in their search for leaks to the camp's water supply and during their attempts to get the food truck started. Similarly, each of these features is involved in cooperative team-learning interventions which have positive effects on intergroup behavior (Johnson et al., 1983; Slavin, 1985).

Also, intergroup cooperation that permits each group to work separately but to have equally important and complementary roles toward achieving a superordinate objective may be especially effective at reducing bias (Brown & Wade, 1987; Deschamps & Brown, 1983). For example, when group affiliation is meaningful to members' self-identities, intergroup cooperation that allows each group to make favorable and distinctive intergroup comparisons may permit the memberships to develop mutual respect for one another without threatening their own positive group identities (Deschamps & Brown, 1983; see also Hewstone & Brown, 1986). This position is not necessarily incompatible with our own. Previously, we suggested that the acceptance of a common in-group identity may not necessarily require subgroups to forsake their earlier categorizations entirely (Gaertner et al., 1989). Within the context of a more inclusive superordinate group representation, the salience of these subgroup identities may enable the enhanced appreciation for out-group members to generalize beyond those directly involved in the cooperative effort. We would expect, however that the extent of these changes would be mediated more by the strength of the superordinate group representation than by the extent to which the subgroups were salient.

Although researchers are learning more about the relationship between intergroup cooperation and intergroup bias, a major obstacle faces those wishing to apply this knowledge. As noted by Worchel (1979, 1986), it is often difficult to inspire cooperation among connecting groups. However, it is our hope that we could identify alternative strategies for reducing intergroup bias if we could more precisely understand how cooperation reduces bias, which specific aspects of cooperative interaction are most critical, and why the other features specified by the elaborated contact hypothesis are beneficial. The current work, for example, suggests that there may be some value in trying to transform members' categorized representations of one another. In some contexts, this may be more feasible than directly inducing intergroup cooperation or orchestrating equal-status contact. Modifying members' representations even slightly may encourage the initiation of more constructive and cooperative intergroup relations.

REFERENCES

Allport, G. W. (1954). *The nature of prejudice.* Cambridge, MA: Addison-Wesley.

Aronson, E., Blaney, N., Stephan, C., Sikes, J., & Snapp, M. (1978). *The jigsaw classroom.* Beverly Hills, CA: Sage.

Baron, R. M., & Kenny, D. A. (1986). The moderator-mediator variable distinction in social psychological research: Conceptual, strategic, and statistical considerations. *Journal of Personality and Social Psychology, 51,* 1173–1182.

Brewer, M. B. (1979). In-group bias in the minimal intergroup situation: A cognitive–motivational analysis. *Psychological Bulletin, 86,* 307–324.

Brewer, M. B., & Miller, N. (1984). Beyond the contact hypothesis: Theoretical perspectives on desegregation. In N. Miller & M. B. Brewer (Eds.), *Groups in contact: The psychology of desegregation* (pp. 281–302). San Diego, CA: Academic Press.

Brown, R. J., & Turner, J. C. (1981). Interpersonal and intergroup behavior. In J. C. Turner & H. Giles (Eds.), *Intergroup behavior* (pp. 33-64). Chicago: The University of Chicago Press.

Brown, R., & Wade, G. (1987). Superordinate goals and intergroup behaviour: The effect of role ambiguity and status on intergroup attitudes and task performance. *European Journal of Social Psychology, 17,* 131–142.

Campbell, D. T. (1958). Common fate, similarity and other indices of the status of aggregates of persons as social entities. *Behavioral Science, 3,* 14–25.

Cook, S. W. (1978). Interpersonal and attitudinal outcomes in cooperating interracial groups. *Journal of Research and Development in Education, 12,* 97–113.

Cook, S. W. (1985). Cooperative interaction in multiethnic contexts. In N. Miller a M. B. Brewer (Eds.), *Groups in contact: The psychology of desegregation* (pp. 281–302). San Diego, CA: Academic Press.

Deschamps, J. C., & Brown, R. (1983). Superordinate goals

and intergroup conflict. *British Journal of Social Psychology, 22,* 189–195.

Deutsch, M. (1973). *The resolution of social conflict.* New Haven, CT: Yale University Press.

Doise, W. (1978). *Groups and individuals: Explanations in social psychology.* Cambridge, England: Cambridge University Press.

Feshbach, S., & Singer, R. (1957). The effects of personal and shared threats upon social prejudice. *Journal of Abnormal and Social Psychology, 54,* 411–416.

Finn, J. D. (1974). *A general model for multivariate analysis.* New York: Holt, Rinehart & Winston.

Gaertner, S. L., Mann, J., Murrell, A., & Dovidio, J. F. (1989). Reducing intergroup bias: The benefits of recategorization. *Journal of Personality and Social Psychology, 57,* 239–249.

Hewstone, M., & Brown, R. J. (1986). Contact is not enough: An intergroup perspective on the "contact hypothesis." In M. Hewstone and R. Brown (Eds.), *Contact and conflict in intergroup encounters* (pp. 1–44). Oxford, England: Basil Blackwell.

Hogg, M. A., & Abrams, D. (1988). *Social identifications: A social psychology of intergroup relations and group processes.* London: Routledge & Kegan Paul.

Hornstein, H. A. (1976). *Cruelty and kindness: A new look at aggression and altruism.* Englewood Cliffs, NJ: Prentice-Hall.

Johnson, D. W., & Johnson, F. P. (1975). *Joining together: Group theory and group skills.*

Johnson, D. W., Johnson, R., and Maruyama, G. (1983). Interdependence and interpersonal attraction among heterogeneous and homogeneous individuals: A theoretical formulation and a meta-analysis of the research. *Review of Educational Research, 55,* 5–54.

Judd, C. M., & Kenny, D. A. (1981). Process analysis: Estimating mediation in evaluation research. *Evaluation Research, 5,* 602–619.

Lott, A. J., & Lott, B. E. (1965). Group cohesiveness as interpersonal attraction: A review of relationships with antecedent and consequent variables. *Psychological Bulletin, 64,* 259–309.

Miller, N., & Brewer, M. B. (1986). Categorization effects on ingroup and outgroup perception. In J. F. Dovidio & S. L. Gaertner (Eds.), *Prejudice, discrimination and racism* (pp. 209–230). San Diego CA: Academic Press.

Miller, N., Brewer, M. B., & Edwards, K. (1985). Cooperative interaction in desegregated settings: A laboratory analog. *Journal of Social Issues, 11,* 63–75.

Miller, N., & Davidson-Podgorny, G. (1987). Theoretical models of intergroup relations and the use of cooperative teams as an intervention for desegregated settings. In C. Hendrick (Ed.), Group processes and intergroup relations. *Review of Personality and Social Psychology, 9,* 41–67.

Neuberg, S. L., & Fiske, S. T. (1987). Motivational influences on impression formation: Outcome dependency, accuracy-driven attention, and individuating processes. *Journal of Personality and Social Psychology, 53,* 431–444.

Pettigrew, T. F. (1971). *Racially separate or together.* New York: McGraw-Hill.

Rosenbaum, M. E., &Holtz, R. (1985, August). *The minimal intergroup discrimination effect: Out-group derogation, not in-group favorability.* Paper presented at the 93rd Annual Convention of the American Psychological Association, Los Angeles.

Ryen, A. (1974, September). *Cognitive and behavioral consequences of group membership.* Paper presented at the 82nd Annual Convention of the American Psychological Association, New Orleans, LA.

Sherif, M., Harvey, O. J., White, B. J., Hood, W. R., & Sherif, C. (1954). *Experimental study of positive and negative intergroup attitudes between experimentally produced groups: Robbers Cave experiment.* Norman, OK: University of Oklahoma.

Sherif, M., & Sherif, C. W. (1969). *Social Psychology.* New York: Harper & Row.

Slavin, R. E. (1985). Cooperative learning: Applying contact theory in desegregated schools. In W. G. Stephan & J. C Brigham (Eds.), Intergroup contact. *Journal of Social Issues, 41,* 45–62.

Stephan, W. G. (1987). The contact hypothesis in intergroup relations. In C. Hendrick (Ed.), Group processes and intergroup relations. *Review of Personality and Social Psychology, 9,* 41–67.

Stephan, W. G., & Stephan, C. W. (1984). The role of ignorance in intergroup relations. In N. Miller & M. B. Brewer (Eds.), *Groups in contact: The psychology of desegregation* (pp 229–257). San Diego, CA: Academic Press.

Tajfel, H. (1969). Cognitive aspects of prejudice. *Journal of Social Issues, 25,* 79.

Tajfel, H., Billig, M. G., Bundy, R. F., & Flament, C. (1971). Social categorization and intergroup behavior. *European Journal of Social Psychology, 1,* 149–177.

Tajfel, H., & Turner, J. C. (1979). An integrative theory of intergroup conflict. In W. G. Austin & S. Worchel (Eds.), *The social psychology of intergroup relations.* Monterey, CA: Brooks/Cole.

Turner, J. C. (1981). The experimental social psychology of intergroup behavior. In J. C. Turner & H. Giles (Eds.), *Intergroup behavior* (pp. 66–101). Chicago: The University of Chicago Press.

Turner, J. C. (1985). Social categorization and the self-concept: A social cognitive theory of group behavior. In E. J. Lawler (Ed.), *Advances in group processes* (Vol. 2, pp. 77–122). Greenwich, CT: JAI Press.

Turner, J. C., Hogg, M. A., Oakes, P. J., Reicher, S. D., & Wetherell, M. S. (1987). *Rediscovering the social group: A self-categorization theory.* Oxford. England: Basil Blackwell.

Wilder, D. A. (1986). Social categorization: Implications for creation and reduction of intergroup bias. In L. Berkowitz (Ed.), *Advances in experimental social psychology, 19,* 291–355.

Worchel, S. (1979). Cooperation and the reduction of intergroup conflict: Some determining factors. In W. G. Austin & S. Worchel (Eds.), *The social psychology of intergroup relations.* Monterey, CA: Brooks/Cole.

Worchel, S. (1986). The role of cooperation in reducing intergroup contact. In S. Worchel & W. G. Austin (Eds.), *Psychology of intergroup relations* (2nd ed., pp. 288–304). Chicago: Nelson-Hall.

Worchel, S, Axsom, D., Ferris, F. ,Samaha, C., & Schweitzer, S. (1978). Factors determining the effect of intergroup cooperation on intergroup attraction. *Journal of Conflict Resolution, 22,* 428–439.

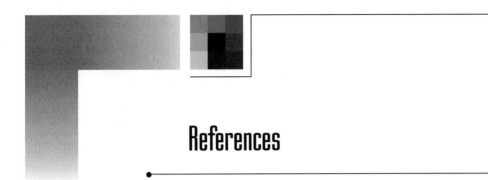

References

Aboud, F. E. (1988). *Children and prejudice.* New York: Basil Blackwell.

Aboud, F. E., & Doyle, A. (1996). Parental and peer influences on children's racial attitudes. *International Journal of Intercultural Relations, 28,* 161–170.

Albert, A. A., & Porter, J. R. (1983). Age patterns in the development of children's gender-role stereotypes. *Sex Roles, 9,* 59-67.

Allport, G. W. (1954). *The nature of prejudice.* Reading, MA: Addison-Wesley.

Amir, Y. (1969). Contact hypothesis in ethnic relations. *Psychological Bulletin, 71,* 319–342.

Aronson, E., Blaney, N., Stephan, C., Sikes, J., & Snapp, M. (1978). *The Jig-Saw Classroom.* London: Sage.

Asch, S. E. (1952). *Social psychology.* Engelewood Cliffs: Prentice-Hall.

Ashmore, R. D., & DelBoca, F. K. (1981). Conceptual approaches to stereotypes and stereotyping. In D. L. Hamilton (Ed.), *Cognitive processes in stereotyping and intergroup behavior* (pp. 1–35). Hillsdale, NJ: Erlbaum.

Ashmore, R. D., & DelBoca, F. K. (1976). Psychological approaches to understanding intergroup conflict. In P. A. Katz (Ed.), *Towards the elimination of racism* (pp. 1–35). New York: Pergamon.

Ashton, M., & Esses, V. (1999). Stereotype accuracy: Estimating the academic performance of ethnic groups. *Personality and Social Psychology Bulletin, 25,* 225–236.

Banaji, M. R., & Hardin, C. D. (1996). Automatic stereotyping. *Psychological Science, 7,* 136–141.

Bargh, J. (1994). The four horsemen of automaticity: Awareness, intention, efficiency, and control in social cognition. In R. Wyer & T. Srull (Eds.), *Handbook of social cognition* (Vol. 1, pp. 1–41). Hillsdale, NJ: Erlbaum.

Bargh, J. (Ed.). (1999). *The cognitive monster: The case against the controllability of automatic stereotype effects.* New York: Guilford.

Bar-Tal, D. (1997). Formation and change of ethnic and national stereotypes: An integrative model. *International Journal of Intercultural Relations, 21,* 491–523.

Bar-Tal, Y. (1989). Can leaders change followers' stereotypes? In D. Bar-Tal, C. F. Grauman, A. W. Kruglanski, & W. Stroebe (Eds.), *Stereotyping and prejudice: Changing conceptions* (pp. 225–242). New York: Springer-Verlag.

Baumeister, R., & Leary, M. (1995). The need to belong: Desire for interpersonal attachments as a fundamental human motivation. *Psychological Bulletin, 117,* 497–529.

Bem, S. L. (1981). Gender schema theory: A cognitive account of sex typing. *Psychological Review, 88,* 354–364.

Bodenhausen, G. V. (1990). Stereotypes as judgmental heuristics: Evidence of circadian variations in discrimination. *Psychological Science, 1,* 319–322.

Bodenhausen, G. V., & Lichtenstein, M. (1987). Social stereotypes and information processing strategies: The impact of task complexity. *Journal of Personality and Social Psychology, 52,* 871–880.

Bodenhausen, G. V., & Macrae, C. N. (1998). Stereotype activation and inhibition. In R. Wyer (Ed.), *Advances in Social Cognition* (Vol. 11, pp. 1–52). Mahwah, NJ: Erlbaum.

Bodenhausen, G. V., Schwarz, N., Bless, H., & Wanke, M. (1995). Effects of atypical exemplars on racial beliefs: Enlightened racism or generalized appraisals? *Journal of Experimental Social Psychology, 31,* 48–63.

Brewer, M. B. (1979). In-group bias in the minimal intergroup situation: A cognitive–motivational analysis. *Psychological Bulletin, 86,* 307–324.

Brewer, M., & Miller, N. (1984). Beyond the contact hypothesis: Theoretical perspectives on desegregation. In N. Miller & M. Brewer (Eds.), *Groups in contact: The psychology of desegregation* (pp. 281–302). Orlando, FL: Academic Press.

Brewer, M. B. (1988). A dual process model of impression formation. In T. K. Srull & R. S. Wyer (Eds.), *Advances in social cognition* (Vol. 1, pp. 1–36). Hillsdale, NJ: Erlbaum.

Brewer, M. B., Dull, L., & Lui, L. (1981). Perceptions of the elderly: Stereotypes as prototypes. *Journal of Personality and Social Psychology, 41,* 656–670.

Brodt, S. E., & Ross, L. D. (1998). The role of stereotyping in overconfident social prediction. *Social Cognition, 16,* 225–252.

Brown, R. (1995). *Prejudice: Its social psychology.* Cambridge, MA: Blackwell.

Cadinu, M. R., & Rothbart, M. (1996). Self-anchoring and differentiation processes in the minimal group setting. *Journal of Personality and Social Psychology, 70,* 661–677.

Cantor, N., & Mischel, W. (1977). Traits as prototypes: Effects on recognition memory. *Journal of Personality and Social Psychology, 35,* 38–48.

Clark, K., & Clark, M. (1947). Racial identification and preference in Negro children. In E. Maccoby, T. Newcomb, & E. Hartley (Eds.), *Readings in social psychology* (pp. 602–611). New York: Holt, Rinehart & Winston.

Clarke, R. B., & Campbell, D. T. (1955). A demonstration of bias in estimates of Negro ability. *Journal of Abnormal & Social Psychology, 51*, 585–588.

Cohen, C. E. (1981). Person categories and social perception: Testing some boundaries of the processing effects of prior knowledge. *Journal of Personality and Social Psychology, 40*, 441–452.

Cook, S. W. (1978). Interpersonal and attitudinal outcomes in cooperating interracial groups. *Journal of Research in Developmental Education, 12*, 97–113.

Cook, S. W. (1984). Cooperative interaction in multiethnic contexts. In N. Miller & M. B. Brewer (Eds.), *Groups in contact*. New York: Academic Press.

Cota, A. A., & Dion, K. L. (1986). Salience of gender and sex composition of ad hoc groups: An experimental test of distinctiveness theory. *Journal of Personality and Social Psychology, 50*, 770–776.

Crandall, C., & Biernat, M. (1990). The ideology of anti-fat attitudes. *Journal of Applied Social Psychology, 20*, 227–243.

Crocker, J., & Major, B. (1989). Social stigma and self-esteem: The self-protective properties of stigma. *Psychological Review, 96*, 608–630.

Crocker, J., Major, B., & Steele, C. (1998). Social stigma. In D. Gilbert, S. T. Fiske, & G. Lindzey (Eds.), *Handbook of social psychology* (4th ed., Vol. 2, pp. 504–553). Boston: McGraw Hill.

Crosby, F., Bromley, S., & Saxe, L. (1980). Recent unobtrusive studies of black and white discrimation and prejudice: A literature review. *Psychological Bulletin, 87*, 546–563.

Darley, J. M., & Fazio, R. H. (1980). Expectancy confirmation processes arising in the social interaction sequence. *American Psychologist, 35*, 867–881.

Deaux, K., Reid, A., Mizrahi, K., & Ethier, K. A. (1996). Parameters of social identity. *Journal of Personality and Social Psychology, 68*, 280–291.

Deaux, K., & Major, B. (1987). Putting gender into context: An interactive model of gender-related behavior. *Psychological Review, 94*, 369–389.

DePaulo, B. M., & Coleman, L. M. (1986). Talking to children, foreigners, and retarded adults. *Journal of Personality and Social Psychology, 51*, 945–959.

Devine, P. G. (1989). Stereotypes and prejudice: Their automatic and controlled components. *Journal of Personality and Social Psychology, 56*, 5–18.

Devine, P. G., & Baker, S. M. (1991). Measurement of racial stereotype subtyping. *Personality and Social Psychology Bulletin, 17*, 44–50.

Devine, P. G., Evett, S. R., & Vasquez-Suson, K. A. (1996). Exploring the interpersonal dynamics of group contact. In R. M. Sorrentino & E. T. Higgins (Eds.), *Handbook of motivation and cognition: The interpersonal context* (Vol. 3, pp. 423–464). New York: Guilford.

Diehl, M. (1990). The minimal group paradigm. *European Review of Social Psychology, 1*, 263–292.

Dovidio, J., Evans, N., & Tyler, R. (1986). Racial stereotypes: The contents of their cognitive representations. *Journal of Experimental Social Psychology, 22*, 22–37.

Dovidio, J. F., Brigham, J. C., Johnson, B. T., & Gaertner, S. L. (1996). Stereotyping, prejudice, and discrimination: Another look. In C. N. Macrae, C. Stangor, & M. Hewstone (Eds.), *Stereotypes and stereotyping* (pp. 276–322). New York: Guilford.

Duncan, B. L. (1976). Differential social perception and attribution of intergroup violence: Testing the lower limits of stereotyping of blacks. *Journal of Personality and Social Psychology, 34*, 590–598.

Eagly, A. H. (1987). *Sex differences in social behavior: A social-role interpretation*. Hillsdale, NJ: Erlbaum.

Eagly, A. H., & Mladinic, A. (1989). Gender stereotypes and attitudes toward women and men. *Personality and Social Psychology Bulletin, 15*, 543–558.

Eagly, A. H., & Steffen, V. J. (1984). Gender stereotypes stem from the distribution of women and men into social roles. *Journal of Personality and Social Psychology, 46*, 735–754.

Epstein, R., & Komorita, S. S. (1966). Prejudice among Negro children as related to parental ethnocentrism. *Journal of Personality and Social Psychology, 4*, 643–647.

Farina, A., Gliha, D., Boudreau, L. A., Allen, J. G., & Sherman, M. (1971). Mental illness and the impact of believing others know about it. *Journal of Abnormal Psychology, 77*, 1–5.

Farina, A., Sherman, M., & Allen, J. G. (1968). Role of physical abnormalities in interpersonal perception and behavior. *Journal of Abnormal Psychology*.

Fazio, R., Jackson, J., Dunton, B., & Williams, C. (1995). Variability in automatic activation as an unobtrusive measure of racial attitudes: A Bona Fide pipeline? *Journal of Personality and Social Psychology, 69*, 1013–1027.

Fein, S., & Spencer, S. J. (1997). Prejudice as self-image maintenance: Affirming the self through derogating others. *Journal of Personality and Social Psychology, 73*, 31–44.

Fiedler, K. (1991). Heuristics and biases in theory formation: On the cognitive processes of those concerned with cognitive processes. *Theory & Psychology, 1*, 407–430.

Fiske, S. T. (1982). Schema-triggered affect: Applications to social perception. In M. S. Clark & S. T. Fiske (Eds.), *Affect and cognition: The 17th Annual Carnegie Symposium on Cognition* (pp. 55–78). Hillsdale, NJ: Erlbaum.

Fiske, S. T. (1989). Examining the role of intent: Toward understanding its role in stereotyping and prejudice. In J. S. Uleman & J. A. Bargh (Eds.), *Unintended thought* (pp. 253–286). New York: Guilford.

Fiske, S. T. (1998). Stereotyping, prejudice and discrimination. In D. T. Gilbert, S. T. Fiske, & G. Lindzey (Eds.), *Handbook of social psychology* (4th ed., Vol. 2, pp. 357–414). New York: McGraw Hill.

Fiske, S. T., Bersoff, D. N., Borgida, E., Deaux, K., & Heilman, M. E. (1991). Social science research on trial: The use of sex stereotyping research in Price Waterhouse vs. Hopkins. *American Psychologist, 46*, 1049–1060.

Fiske, S. T., & Neuberg, S. L. (1990). A continuum of impression formation, from category based to individuating processes: Influences of information and motivation on attention and interpretation. In M. P. Zanna (Ed.), *Advances in Experimental Social Psychology* (Vol. 23, pp. 1–74). New York: Academic Press.

Ford, T. E., & Stangor, C. (1992). The role of diagnosticity in stereotype formation: Perceiving group means and variances. *Journal of Personality and Social Psychology, 63*, 356–367.

Fyock, J., & Stangor, C. (1994). The role of memory biases in stereotype maintenance. *British Journal of Social Psychology, 33*, 331–343.

Gaertner, S. L., & Dovidio, J. F. (1986). *Prejudice, discrimination, and racism*. Orlando, FL: Academic Press.

Gaertner, S. L., & McLaughlin, J. P. (1983). Changing not fading: Racial stereotypes revealed by a non-reactive, reaction time measure. *Social Psychology Quarterly, 46*, 23–30.

Gaertner, S. L., Rust, M. C., Dovidio, J. F., Bachman, B. A., & Anastasio, P. (1994). The contact hypothesis: The role of a common ingroup identity on reducing intergroup bias. *Small Group Research, 25*, 224–249.

Gardner, R. C. (1973). Ethnic stereotypes: The traditional approach, a new look. *Canadian Psychologist, 14*, 133–148.

Gardner, R. C. (1994). Stereotypes as consensual beliefs. In M. P. Zanna & J. M. Olson (Eds.), *The psychology of prejudice: The Ontario symposium (Vol. 7)* (pp. 1–31). Hillsdale, NJ: Erlbaum.

Gilbert, G. M. (1951). Stereotype persistence and change among college students. *Journal of Abnormal and Social Psychology, 46*, 245–254.

Glick, P., & Fiske, S. (1996). The Ambivalent Sexism Inventory: Differentiating hostile and benevolent sexism. *Journal of Personality and Social Psychology, 70*, 491–512.

Glick, P., Zion, C., & Nelson, C. (1988). What mediates sex discrimination in hiring decisions? *Journal of Personality & Social Psychology, 55*, 178–186.

Greenwald, A. G., & Schuh, E. S. (1994). An ethnic bias in scientific citations. *European Journal of Social Psychology, 24*, 623–639.

Hamilton, D. L., Dugan, P. M., & Trolier, T. K. (1985). The formation of stereotypic beliefs: Further evidence for distinctiveness-based illusory correlations. *Journal of Personality and Social Psychology, 48*, 5–17.

Hamilton, D. L., & Gifford, R. K. (1976). Illusory correlation in interpersonal perception: A cognitive basis of stereotypic judgments. *Journal of Experimental Social Psychology, 12*, 392–407.

Hamilton, D. L., & Sherman, J. W. (1994). Stereotypes. In R. S. Wyer & T. K. Srull (Eds.), *Handbook of social cognition* (Vol. 2, pp. 1–68). Hillsdale, NJ: Erlbaum.

Hamilton, D. L., & Sherman, S. J. (1996). Perceiving individuals and groups. *Psychological Review, 103*, 336–355.

Harasty, A. S. (1997). The interpersonal nature of social stereotypes: Differential discussion patterns about in-groups and out-groups. *Personality and Social Psychology Bulletin, 23*, 270–284.

Haslam, S. A., Oakes, P. J., Reynolds, K. J., & Turner, J. C. (1999). Social identity salience and the emergence of stereotype consensus. *Personality and Social Psychology Bulletin, 25*, 809–818.

Haslam, S. A., Turner, J., Oakes, P., Reynolds, K., Eggins, R., Nolan, M., & Tweedie, J. (1998). When do stereotypes become really consensual? Investigating the group-based dynamics of the consensualization process. *European Journal of Social Psychology, 28*, 755–776.

Haslam, S. A., Oakes, P. J., McGarty, C., Turner, J. C., Reynolds, K. J., & Eggins, R. A. (1996). Stereotyping and social influence: The mediation of stereotype applicability and sharedness by the views of ingroup and outgroup members. *British Journal of Social Psychology, 35,* 369–397.

Herek, G. M. (1987). Can functions be measured? A new perspective on the functional approach to attitudes. *Social Psychology Quarterly, 50*, 285–303.

Hewstone, M. (1996). Contact and categorization: Social psychological interventions to change intergroup relations. In C. N. Macrae, C. Stangor, & M. Hewstone (Eds.), *Stereotypes and stereotyping* (pp. 323–368). New York: Guilford.

Hewstone, M., & Brown, R. (1986). Contact is not enough: An intergroup perspective on the 'Contact Hypothesis'. In M. Hewstone & R. J. Brown (Eds.), *Contact and conflict in intergroup encounters* (pp. 1–44). London: Basil-Blackwell.

Hilton, J. L., & Darley, J. M. (1985). Constructing other persons: A limit on the effect. *Journal of Experimental Social Psychology, 21*, 1–18.

Hoffman, C., & Hurst, N. (1990). Gender stereotypes: Perception or rationalization? *Journal of Personality and Social Psychology, 58*, 197–208.

Hogg, M. A., & Abrams, D. (1988). *Social identifications: A social psychology of intergroup relations and group processes*. London: Routledge.

Hogg, M. A., & Abrams, D. (1990). Social motivation, self-esteem and social identity. In D. Abrams & M. A. Hogg (Eds.), *Social identity theory: Constructive and critical advances* (pp. 28–47). New York: Springer-Verlag.

Howard, J. W., & Rothbart, M. (1980). Social categorization and memory for in- group and out-group behavior. *Journal of Personality and Social Psychology, 38*, 310.

Jackson, S. E., & Ruderman, M. N. (Eds.). (1995). *Diversity in work teams: Research paradigms for a changing workplace*. Washington, DC: American Psychological Association.

Jetten, J., Spears, R., & Manstead, A. S. R. (1996). Intergroup norms and intergroup discrimination: Distinctive self-categorization and social identity effects. *Journal of personality and Social Psychology, 71*, 1222–1233.

Johnston, L., & Macrae, C. N. (1994). Changing social stereotypes: The case of the information seeker. *European Journal of Social Psychology, 24*, 237–266.

Jones, J. M. (1996). *Prejudice and racism*. Boston: McGraw-Hill.

Judd, C. M., & Park, B. (1988). Outgroup homogeneity: Judgments of variability at the individual and group levels. *Journal of Personality and Social Psychology, 54*, 778–788.

Judd, C. M., Ryan, C. S., & Park, B. (1991). Accuracy in the judgment of in-group and out-group variability. *Journal of Personality and Social Psychology, 61*, 366–379.

Jussim, L. (1989). Teacher expectations: Self-fulfilling prophecies, perceptual biases, and accuracy. *Journal of Personality and Social Psychology, 57*, 469–480.

Jussim, L. (1991). Social perception and social reality: A reflection-construction model. *Psychological Review, 98*, 54–73.

Jussim, L. & Fleming, C. (1996). Self-fulfilling prophecies and the maintenance of social stereotypes: The role of dyadic interactions and social forces. In C. N. Macrae, C. Stangor, & M. Hewstone (Eds.), *Stereotypes and stereotyping* (pp. 161–192). New York: Guilford.

Jussim, L., Lee, Y., & McCauley, R. (1995). *Accuracy and inaccuracy in stereotyping*. Washington, DC: American Psychological Association.

Kanter, R. M. (1977). Some effects of proportions on group life: Skewed sex ratios and responses to token women. *American Journal of Sociology, 82*, 965–990.

Karlins, M., Coffman, T., & Walters, G. (1969). On the fading of social stereotypes: Studies in three generations of college students. *Journal of Personality and Social Psychology, 13*, 1–16.

Katz, D., & Braly, K. W. (1933). Racial stereotypes of one hundred college students. *Journal of Abnormal and Social Psychology, 28*, 280–290.

Katz, I., & Hass, R. G. (1988). Racial ambivalence and American value conflict: Correlational and priming studies of dual cognitive structures. *Journal of Personality and Social Psychology, 55*, 893–905.

Kleck, R., Ono, H., & Hastorf, A. H. (1966). The effects of physical deviance upon face-to-face interactions. *Human Relations, 19*, 425–436.

Kunda, Z., & Thagard, P. (1996). Forming impressions from stereotypes, traits and behaviors: A parallel constraint satisfaction theory. *Psychological Review, 103,* 284–308.

La Piere, R. T. (1936). Type rationalization of group antipathy. *Social Forces, 15,* 232–237.

Lemyre, L., & Smith, P. M. (1985). Intergroup discrimination and self-esteem in the minimal group paradigm. *Journal of Personality and Social Psychology, 49*, 660–670.

Lepore, L., & Brown, R. (1997). Category and stereotype activation: Is prejudice inevitable? *Journal of Personality and Social Psychology, 72*, 275–287.

Liben, L. S., & Signorella, M. L. (1980). Gender-related schemata and constructive memory in children. *Child Development, 51*, 11–18.

Linville, P. W., Salovey, P., & Fischer, G. W. (1986). Stereotyping and perceived distributions of social characteristics: An application to ingroup-outgroup perception. In J. F. Dovidio & S. L. Gaertner (Eds.), *Prejudice, discrimination and racism* (pp. 165–208). Orlando, FL: Academic Press.

Maass, A., & Arcuri, L. (1996). Language and stereotyping. In C. N. Macrae, C. Stangor, & M. Hewstone (Eds.), *Stereotypes and stereotyping* (pp. 193–226). New York: Guilford.

Maass, A., Salvi, D., Arcuri, L., & Semin, G. (1989). Language use in intergroup contexts: The linguistic intergroup bias. *Journal of Personality and Social Psychology, 57,* 981–993.

Mackie, D. M., Hamilton, D. L., Susskind, J., & Rosselli, F. (1996). Social psychological foundations of stereotype formation. In C. N. Macrae, C. Stangor, & M. Hewstone (Eds.), *Stereotypes and stereotyping* (pp. 41–78). New York: Guilford.

Macrae, C. N., Hewstone, M., & Griffiths, R. J. (1993). Processing load and memory for stereotype-based information. *European Journal of Social Psychology, 23*, 77–87.

Macrae, C. N., Milne, A. B., & Bodenhausen, G. V. (1994). Stereotypes as energy-saving devices: A peek inside the cognitive toolbox. *Journal of Personality and Social Psychology, 66*, 37–47.

Madon, S., Jussim, L., Keiper, S., Eccles, J., Smith, A., & Palumbo, P. (1998). The accuracy and power of sex, social class, and ethnic stereotypes: A naturalistic study in person perception. *Personality & Social Psychology Bulletin, 24*, 1304–1318.

Martin, C. L., & Halverson, C. F., Jr. (1981). A schematic processing model of sex typing and stereotyping in children. *Child Development, 52*, 1119–1134.

McArthur, L. Z., & Baron, R. M. (1983). Toward an ecological theory of social cognition. *Psychological Review, 90*, 215–238.

McCauley, C., & Stitt, C. L. (1978). An individual and quantitative measure of stereotypes. *Journal of Personality and Social Psychology, 36*, 929–940.

McConahay, J. B. (1986). Modern racism, ambivalence, and the modern racism scale. In S. Gaertner & J. Dovidio (Eds.), *Prejudice, discrimination, and racism* (pp. 91–126). Orlando, FL: Academic Press.

Merton, R. (1948). The self-fulfilling prophecy. *Antioch Review, 8*, 193–210.

Miller, C. T., Clarke, R. T., Malcarne, V. L., Lobato, D., & et al. (1991). Expectations and social interactions of children with and without mental retardation. *Journal of Special Education, 24*, 454–472.

Miller, C. T., Rothblum, E. D., Felicio, D., & Brand, P. (1995). Compensating for stigma: Obese and nonobese women's reactions to being visible. *Personality and Social Psychology Bulletin, 21*, 1093–1106.

Miller, D. T., & Turnbull, W. (1986). Expectancies and interpersonal processes. *Annual Review of Psychology, 37*, 233–256.

Miller, N., Brewer, M., & Edwards, K. (1985). Cooperative interaction in desegregated settings: A laboratory analogue. *Journal of Social Issues, 41*, 63–81.

Monteith, M. J., Devine, P. G., & Zuwerink, J. R. (1993). Self-directed versus other-directed affect as a consequence of prejudice-related discrepancies. *Journal of Personality and Social Psychology, 64*, 198–210.

Mullen, B., & Johnson, C. (1990). Distinctiveness-based illusory correlations and stereotyping: A meta-analytic integration. *British Journal of Social Psychology, 29*, 11–28.

Neuberg, S. L. (1989). The goal of forming accurate impressions during social interactions: Attenuating the impact of negative expectancies. *Journal of Personality and Social Psychology, 56*, 374–386.

Neuberg, S. L., & Fiske, S. T. (1987). Motivational influences on impression formation: Outcome dependency, accuracy-driven attention, and individuating processes. *Journal of Personality and Social Psychology, 53*, 431–444.

Neuberg, S. L., & Newsom, J. T. (1993). Personal need for structure: Individual differences in the desire for simple structure. *Journal of Personality and Social Psychology, 65*, 113–131.

Oakes, P., & Turner, J. (1980). Social categorization and intergroup behaviour: Does minimal intergroup discrimination make social identity more positive. *European Journal of Social Psychology, 10*, 295–301.

Oakes, P., & Turner, J. (1990). Is limited information processing capacity the cause of social stereotyping? *European Review of Social Psychology, 1*, 111–135.

Oakes, P. J., Turner, J. C., & Haslam, S. A. (1991). Perceiving people as group members: The role of fit in the salience of social categorizations. *British Journal of Social Psychology, 30*, 125–144.

Ostrom, T. M., & Sedikides, C. (1992). Out-group homogeneity effects in natural and minimal groups. *Psychological Bulletin, 112*, 536–552.

Park, B., & Judd, C. M. (1990). Measures and models of perceived group variability. *Journal of Personality and Social Psychology, 59*, 173–191.

Park, B., Judd, C. M., & Ryan, C. S. (1991). Social categorization and the representation of variability information. *European Review of Social Psychology, 2*, 221–245.

Park, B., & Rothbart, M. (1982). Perception of out-group homogeneity and levels of social categorization: Memory for the subordinate attributes of in-group and out-group members. *Journal of Personality and Social Psychology, 42*, 1051–1068.

Park, B., Ryan, C. S., & Judd, C. M. (1992). Role of meaningful subgroups in explaining differences in perceived variability for in-groups and out-groups. *Journal of Personality and Social Psychology, 63*, 553–567.

Perdue, C. W., Dovidio, J. F., Gurtman, M. B., & Tyler, R. B. (1990). Us and them: Social categorization and the process of intergroup bias. *Journal of Personality and Social Psychology, 59*, 475–486.

Perdue, C. W., & Gurtman, M. B. (1990). Evidence for the automaticity of ageism. *Journal of Experimental Social Psychology, 26*, 199–216.

Pettigrew, T. (1979). The ulitmate attribution error: Extending Allport's cognitive analysis of prejudice. *Personality and Social Psychology Bulletin, 5*, 461–476.

Pinel, E. (1999). Stigma-consciousness: The psychological legacy of social stereotypes. *Journal of Personality and Social Psychology, 76*, 114–128.

Pryor, J. B., Reeder, G. D., & McManus, J. A. (1991). Fear and loathing in the workplace: Reactions to AIDS-infected co-workers. *Personality and Social Psychology Bulletin, 17*, 133–139.

Rosenthal, R., & Jacobson, L. (1966). Teachers' expectancies: Determinants of pupils IQ gains. *Psychological Reports, 19*, 115–118.

Rothbart, M., Davis-Stitt, C., & Hill, J. (1997). Effects of arbitrarily placed category boundaries on similarity judgments. *Journal of Experimental Social Psychology, 33*, 122–145.

Rothbart, M., & John, O. P. (1985). Social categorization and behavioral episodes: A cognitive analysis of the effects of intergroup contact. *Journal of Social Issues, 41*, 81–104.

Rubin, M., & Hewstone, M. (1998). Social identity theory's self-esteem hypothesis: A review and some suggestions for clarification. *Personality and Social Psychology Review, 2*, 40–62.

Ruble, D., & Martin, C. (1998). Gender development. In W. Damon (Ed.), *Handbook of child psychology,* (5th ed., pp. 933–1016). New York: Wiley.

Ruscher, J. B., Hammer, E. Y., & Hammer, E. D. (1996). Forming shared impressions through conversation: An adaptation of the continuum model. *Personality and Social Psychology Bulletin, 22*, 705–720.

Sagar, H. A., & Schofield, J. W. (1980). Racial and behavioral cues in black and white children's perception of ambiguously aggressive acts. *Journal of Personality and Social Psychology, 39*, 590–598.

Schaller, M. (1992). In-group favoritism and statistical reasoning in social inference: Implications for formation and maintenance of group stereotypes. *Journal of Personality and Social Psychology, 63*, 61–74.

Schaller, M., & Latané, B. (1996). Dynamic social impact and the evolution of social representations: A natural history of stereotypes. *Journal of Communication, 46*, 64–77.

Schofield, J. (1991). School desegregation and intergroup relations: A review of the literature. In G. Grant (Ed.), *Review of research in education* (Vol. 17, pp. 335–409). Washington, DC: American Educational Research Association.

Secord, P. F., Bevan, W., & Katz, B. (1956). The Negro stereotype and perceptual accentuation. *Journal of Abnormal and Social Psychology, 53*, 78–83.

Sigall, H., & Page, R. (1971). Current stereotypes: A little fading, a little faking. *Journal of Personality & Social Psychology, 18*, 247–255.

Simon, B., & Brown, R. J. (1987). Perceived intragroup homogeneity in minority-majority contexts. *Journal of Personality and Social Psychology, 53*, 703–711.

Simon, B., & Hamilton, D. L. (1994). Self-stereotyping and social context: The effects of relative in-group size and in-group status. *Journal of Personality and Social Psychology, 66*, 699–711.

Smith, E. R., & Henry, S. (1996). An in-group becomes part of the self: Response time evidence. *Personality & Social Psychology Bulletin, 22*(6). 635–642.

Smith, E. R., & Zarate, M. A. (1990). Exemplar and prototype use in social categorization. *Social Cognition, 8*, 243–262.

Snyder, M. (1981). On the self-perpetuating nature of social stereotypes. In D. L. Hamilton (Ed.), *Cognitive processes in stereotyping and intergroup behavior* (pp. 183–212). Hillsdale, NJ: Erlbaum.

Snyder, M., & Uranowitz, S. W. (1978). Reconstructing the past: Some cognitive consequences of person perception. *Journal of Personality and Social Psychology, 36*, 941–950.

Stangor, C. (1995). Content and application inaccuracy in social stereotyping. In Y. T. Lee, L. J. Jussim, & C. R. McCauley (Eds.), *Stereotype accuracy: Toward appreciating group differences* (pp. 275–292). Washington, DC: American Psychological Association.

Stangor, C., & Lange, J. (1994). Mental representations of social groups: Advances in conceptualizing stereotypes and stereotyping. *Advances in Experimental Social Psychology, 26*, 357–416.

Stangor, C., Lynch, L., Duan, C., & Glass, B. (1992). Categorization of individuals on the basis of multiple social features. *Journal of Personality and Social Psychology, 62*, 207–218.

Stangor, C., & Ruble, D. N. (1989). Differential influences of gender schemata and gender constancy on children's information processing and behavior. *Social Cognition, 7*, 353–372.

Stangor, C., & Schaller, M. (1996). Stereotypes as individual and collective representations. In C. N. Macrae, C. Stangor, & M. Hewstone (Eds.), *Stereotypes and stereotyping* (pp. 3–40). New York: Guilford.

Steele, C. M., & Aronson, J. (1994). Contending with a stereotype: African-American intellectual test performance and stereotype vulnerability. *Journal of Personality and Social Psychology, 69*, 797–811.

Stephan, W. (1987). The contact hypothesis in intergroup relations. In C. Hendrick (Ed.), *Group processes and intergroup relations: Review of personality and social psychology* (Vol. 9, pp. 13–40). Newbury Park, CA: Sage.

Stephan, W. G. (1978). School desegregation: An evaluation of predictions made in Brown versus the Board of Education. *Psychological Bulletin, 85*, 217–238.

Stephan, W. G. (1985). Intergroup relations. In G. Lindzey & E. Aronson (Eds.), *Handbook of social psychology* (pp. 599–658). New York: Random House.

Stephan, W. G., & Stephan, C. W. (1985). Intergroup anxiety. *Journal of Social Issues, 41*, 157–175.

Stroebe, W., & Insko, C. A. (1989). Stereotypes, prejudice and discrimination: Changing conceptions in theory and research. In D. Bar-Tal, C. F. Graumann, A. W. Kruglanski, & W. Stroebe (Eds.), *Stereotyping and prejudice: Changing conceptions* (pp. 3–34). New York and London: Springer-Verlag.

Stroessner, S. J., & Plaks, J. E. (1999). Illusory correlation and stereotype formation: Tracing the arc of research over two decades. In G. Moscowitz (Ed.), *Future directions in social cognition.* Mahwah, NJ: Erlbaum.

Swann, W. B., & Hill, C. A. (1982). When our identities are mistaken: Reaffirming self-conceptions through social interaction. *Journal of Personality and Social Psychology, 43,* 59–66.

Swim, J., Aikin, K., Hall, W., & Hunter, B. A. (1995). Sexism and racism: Old-fashioned and modern prejudices. *Journal of Personality and Social Psychology, 68,* 199–214.

Swim, J. K. (1994). Perceived versus meta-analytic effect sizes: An assessment of the accuracy of gender stereotypes. *Journal of Personality and Social Psychology, 66,* 21–36.

Swim, J. T., & Stangor, C. (1998). *Prejudice from the target's perspective.* Santa Barbara, CA: Academic Press.

Tajfel, H. (1970). Experiments in intergroup discrimination. *Scientific American, 223,* 96–102.

Tajfel, H. (1978). *Differentiation between social groups: Studies in the social psychology of intergroup relations.* London: Academic Press.

Tajfel, H., Billig, M., Bundy, R., & Flament, C. (1971). Social categorization and intergroup behavior. *European Journal of Social Psychology, 1,* 149–178.

Tajfel, H., & Wilkes, A. L. (1963). Classification and quantitative judgment. *British Journal of Psychology, 54,* 101–114.

Taylor, D. M., & Jaggi, V. (1974). Ethnocentrism and causal attribution in a South Indian context. *Journal of Cross-Cultural Psychology, 5,* 162–171.

Taylor, M. C. (1979). Race, sex, and the expression of self-fulfilling prophecies in a laboratory teaching situation. *Journal of Personality and Social Psychology, 37,* 897–912.

Taylor, S. E., & Crocker, J. (1981). Schematic bases of social information processing. In E. T. Higgins, C. P. Herman, & M. P. Zanna (Eds.), *Social cognition: The Ontario symposium* (Vol. 1, pp. 89–134). Hillsdale, NJ: Erlbaum.

Taylor, S. E., & Fiske, S. T. (1978). Salience, attention and attribution: Top of the head phenomena. *Advances in Experimental Social Psychology, 11,* 249–288.

Taylor, S. E., Fiske, S. T., Etcoff, N. L., & Ruderman, A. J. (1978). Categorical and contextual bases of person memory and stereotyping. *Journal of Personality and Social Psychology, 36,* 778–793.

Trope, Y., & Thompson, E. (1997). Looking for truth in all the wrong places? Asymmetric search of individuating information about stereotyped group members. *Journal of Personality and Social Psychology, 73,* 229–241.

Turner, J. C. (1975). Social comparison and social identity: Some prospects for intergroup behavior. *European Journal of Social Psychology, 5,* 5–34.

Turner, J. C. (1987). *Rediscovering the social group: A self-categorization theory.* Oxford: Basil Blackwell.

Ugwuegbu, D. C. (1979). Racial and evidential factors in juror attribution of legal responsibility. *Journal of Experimental Social Psychology, 15,* 133–146.

Van Knippenberg, A., & Dijksterhuis, A. (1996). A posteriori stereotype activation: The preservation of stereotypes through memory distortion. *Social Cognition, 14,* 21–54.

Van Knippenberg, A., van Twuyver, M., & Pepels, J. (1994). Factors affecting social categorization processes in memory. *British Journal of Social Psychology, 33,* 419–431.

von Hippel, W., Sekaquaptewa, D., & Vargas, P. (1997). The linguistic intergroup bias as an implicit indicator of prejudice. *Journal of Experimental Social Psycology, 33*(5), 490–509.

Weber, R., & Crocker, J. (1983). Cognitive processes in the revision of stereotypic beliefs. *Journal of Personality and Social Psychology, 45,* 961–977.

Wittenbrink, B., Judd, C., & Park, B. (1997). Evidence for racial prejudice at the implicit level and its relationship with questionnaire measures. *Journal of Personality and Social Psychology, 72,* 262–274.

Worchel, S., & Rothgerber, H. (1996). Changing the stereotype of the stereotype: Emphasizing the side of group perceptions. In R. Spears, N. Oakes, N. Ellemers, & S. A. Haslam (Eds.), *The social psychology of stereotyping and group life* (pp. 72–93). Oxford: Basil Blackwell.

Word, C. O., Zanna, M. P., & Cooper, J. (1974). The nonverbal mediation of self-fulfilling prophecies in interracial interaction. *Journal of Experimental Social Psychology, 10,* 109–120.

Zanna, M. P., & Pack, S. J. (1975). On the self-fulfilling nature of apparent sex differences in behavior. *Journal of Experimental Social Psychology, 11,* 583–591.

Appendix: How to Read a Journal Article in Social Psychology

Christian H. Jordan and Mark P. Zanna • University of Waterloo

How to Read a Journal Article in Social Psychology

When approaching a journal article for the first time, and often on subsequent occasions, most people try to digest it as they would any piece of prose. They start at the beginning and read word for word, until eventually they arrive at the end, perhaps a little bewildered, but with a vague sense of relief. This is not an altogether terrible strategy; journal articles do have a logical structure that lends itself to this sort of reading. There are, however, more efficient approaches–approaches that enable you, a student of social psychology, to cut through peripheral details, avoid sophisticated statistics with which you may not be familiar, and focus on the central ideas in an article. Arming yourself with a little foreknowledge of what is contained in journal articles, as well as some practical advice on how to read them, should help you read journal articles more effectively. If this sounds tempting, read on.

Journal articles offer a window into the inner workings of social psychology. They document how social psychologists formulate hypotheses, design empirical studies, analyze the observations they collect, and interpret their results. Journal articles also serve an invaluable archival function: They contain the full store of common and cumulative knowledge of social psychology. Having documentation of past research allows researchers to build on past findings and advance our understanding of social behavior, without pursuing avenues of investigation that have already been explored. Perhaps most importantly, a research study is never complete until its results have been shared with others, colleagues and students alike. Journal articles are a primary means of communicating research findings. As such, they can be genuinely exciting and interesting to read.

That last claim may have caught you off guard. For beginning readers, journal articles may seem anything but interesting and exciting. They may, on the contrary, appear daunting and esoteric, laden with jargon and obscured by menacing statistics. Recognizing this fact, we hope to arm you, through this paper, with the basic information you will need to read journal articles with a greater sense of comfort and perspective.

Social psychologists study many fascinating topics, ranging from prejudice and discrimination, to culture, persuasion, liking and love, conformity and obedience, aggression, and the self. In our daily lives, these are issues we often struggle to understand. Social psychologists present systematic observations of, as well as a wealth of ideas about, such issues in journal articles. It would be a shame if the fascination and intrigue these topics have were lost in their translation into journal publications. We don't think they are, and by the end of this paper, hopefully you won't either.

Journal articles come in a variety of forms, including research reports, review articles, and theoretical articles. Put briefly, a *research report* is a formal presentation of an original research study, or series of studies. A *review article* is an evaluative survey of previously published work, usually organized by a guiding theory or point of view. The author of a review article summarizes previous investigations of a circumscribed problem, comments on what progress has been made toward its resolution, and suggests areas of the problem that require further study. A *theoretical article* also evaluates past research, but focuses on the development of theories used to explain empirical findings. Here, the author may present a new theory to explain a set of findings, or may compare and contrast a set of competing theories, suggesting why one theory might be the superior one.

This paper focuses primarily on how to read research reports, for several reasons. First, the bulk of published literature in social psychology consists of research reports. Second, the summaries presented in review articles, and the ideas set forth in theoretical articles, are built on findings presented in research reports. To get a deep understanding of how research is done in social psychology, fluency in reading original research reports is essential. Moreover, theoretical articles frequently report new studies that pit one theory against another, or test a novel prediction derived from a new theory. In order to appraise the validity of such theoretical contentions, a grounded understanding of basic findings is invaluable. Finally, most research reports are written in a standard format that is likely unfamiliar to new readers. The format of review and theoretical articles is less standardized, and more like that of textbooks and other scholarly writings, with which most readers are familiar. This is not to suggest that such articles are easier to read and comprehend than research reports; they can be quite challenging indeed. It is simply the case that, because more rules apply to the writing of research reports, more guidelines can be offered on how to read them.

The Anatomy of Research Reports

Most research reports in social psychology, and in psychology in general, are written in a standard format prescribed by the American Psychological Association (1994). This is a great boon to both readers and writers. It allows writers to present their ideas and findings in a clear, systematic manner. Consequently, as a reader, once you understand this format, you will not be on completely foreign ground when you approach a new research report— regardless of its specific content. You will know where in the paper particular information is found, making it easier to locate. No matter what your reasons for reading a research report, a firm understanding of the format in which they are written will ease your task. We discuss the format of research reports next, with some practical suggestions on how to read them. Later, we discuss how this format reflects the process of scientific investigation, illustrating how research reports have a coherent narrative structure.

TITLE AND ABSTRACT

Though you can't judge a book by its cover, you can learn a lot about a research report simply by reading its title. The title presents a concise statement of the theoretical issues investigated, and/or the variables that were studied. For example, the following title was taken almost at random from a prestigious journal in social psychology: "Sad and guilty? Affective influences on the explanation of conflict in close relationships" (Forgas, 1994, p.

56). Just by reading the title, it can be inferred that the study investigated how emotional states change the way people explain conflict in close relationships. It also suggests that when feeling sad, people accept more personal blame for such conflicts (i.e., feel more guilty).

The abstract is also an invaluable source of information. It is a brief synopsis of the study, and packs a lot of information into 150 words or less. The abstract contains information about the problem that was investigated, how it was investigated, the major findings of the study, and hints at the theoretical and practical implications of the findings. Thus, the abstract is a useful summary of the research that provides the gist of the investigation. Reading this outline first can be very helpful, because it tells you where the report is going, and gives you a useful framework for organizing information contained in the article.

The title and abstract of a research report are like a movie preview. A movie preview highlights the important aspects of a movie's plot, and provides just enough information for one to decide whether to watch the whole movie. Just so with titles and abstracts; they highlight the key features of a research report to allow you to decide if you want to read the whole paper. And just as with movie previews, they do not give the whole story. Reading just the title and abstract is never enough to fully understand a research report.

INTRODUCTION

A research report has four main sections: introduction, method, results, and discussion. Though it is not explicitly labeled, the introduction begins the main body of a research report. Here, the researchers set the stage for the study. They present the problem under investigation, and state why it was important to study. By providing a brief review of past research and theory relevant to the central issue of investigation, the researchers place the study in an historical context and suggest how the study advances knowledge of the problem. Beginning with broad theoretical and practical considerations, the researchers delineate the rationale that led them to the specific set of hypotheses tested in the study. They also describe how they decided on their research strategy (e.g., why they chose an experiment or a correlational study).

The introduction generally begins with a broad consideration of the problem investigated. Here, the researchers want to illustrate that the problem they studied is a real problem about which people should care. If the researchers are studying prejudice, they may cite statistics that suggest discrimination is prevalent, or describe specific cases of discrimination. Such information helps illustrate why the research is both practically and theoretically meaningful, and why you should bother reading about it. Such discussions are often quite interesting and useful. They can help you decide for yourself if the research has merit. But they may not be essential for understanding the study at hand. Read the introduction carefully, but choose judiciously what to focus on and remember. To understand a study, what you really need to understand is what the researchers' hypotheses were, and how they were derived from theory, informal observation, or intuition. Other background information may be intriguing, but may not be critical to understand what the researchers did and why they did it.

While reading the introduction, try answering these questions: What problem was studied, and why? How does this study relate to, and go beyond, past investigations of the problem? How did the researchers derive their hypotheses? What questions do the researchers hope to answer with this study?

METHOD

In the method section, the researchers translate their hypotheses into a set of specific, testable questions. Here, the researchers introduce the main characters of the study—the subjects or participants—describing their characteristics (gender, age, etc.) and how many of them were involved. Then, they describe the materials (or apparatus), such as any questionnaires or special equipment, used in the study. Finally, they describe chronologically the procedures of the study; that is, how the study was conducted. Often, an overview of the research design will begin the method section. This overview provides a broad outline of the design, alerting you to what you should attend.

The method is presented in great detail so that other researchers can recreate the study to confirm (or question) its results. This degree of detail is normally not necessary to understand a study, so don't get bogged down trying to memorize the particulars of the procedures. Focus on how the independent variables were manipulated (or measured) and how the dependent variables were measured.

Measuring variables adequately is not always an easy matter. Many of the variables psychologists are interested in cannot be directly observed, so they must be inferred from participants' behavior. Happiness, for example, cannot be directly observed. Thus, researchers interested in how being happy influences people's judgments must infer happiness (or its absence) from their behavior—perhaps by asking people how happy they are, and judging their degree of happiness from their responses; perhaps by studying people's facial expressions for signs of happiness, such as smiling. Think about the measures researchers use while reading the method section. Do they adequately reflect or capture the concepts they are meant to measure? If a measure seems odd, consider carefully how the researchers justify its use.

Oftentimes in social psychology, getting there is half the fun. In other words, how a result is obtained can be just as interesting as the result itself. Social psychologists often strive to have participants behave in a natural, spontaneous manner, while controlling enough of their environment to pinpoint the causes of their behavior. Sometimes, the major contribution of a research report is its presentation of a novel method of investigation. When this is the case, the method will be discussed in some detail in the introduction.

Participants in social psychology studies are intelligent and inquisitive people who are responsive to what happens around them. Because of this, they are not always initially told the true purpose of a study. If they were told, they might not act naturally. Thus, researchers frequently need to be creative, presenting a credible rationale for complying with procedures, without revealing the study's purpose. This rationale is known as a *cover story*, and is often an elaborate scenario. While reading the method section, try putting yourself in the shoes of a participant in the study, and ask yourself if the instructions given to participants seem sensible, realistic, and engaging. Imagining what it was like to be in the study will also help you remember the study's procedure, and aid you in interpreting the study's results.

While reading the method section, try answering these questions: How were the hypotheses translated into testable questions? How were the variables of interest manipulated and/or measured? Did the measures used adequately reflect the variables of interest? For example, is self-reported income an adequate measure of social class? Why or why not?

RESULTS

The results section describes how the observations collected were analyzed to determine whether the original hypotheses were supported. Here, the data (observations of behavior) are described, and statistical tests are presented. Because of this, the results section is often intimidating to readers who have little or no training in statistics. Wading through complex and unfamiliar statistical analyses is understandably confusing and frustrating. As a result, many students are tempted to skip over reading this section. We advise you not to do so. Empirical findings are the foundation of any science and results sections are where such findings are presented.

Take heart. Even the most prestigious researchers were once in your shoes and sympathize with you. Though space in psychology journals is limited, researchers try to strike a balance between the need to be clear and the need to be brief in describing their results. In an influential paper on how to write good research reports, Bem (1987) offered this advice to researchers:

> No matter how technical or abstruse your article is in its particulars, intelligent nonpsychologists with no expertise in statistics or experimental design should be able to comprehend the broad outlines of what you did and why. They should understand in general terms what was learned. (p. 74)

Generally speaking, social psychologists try to practice this advice.

Most statistical analyses presented in research reports test specific hypotheses. Often, each analysis presented is preceded by a reminder of the hypothesis it is meant to test. After an analysis is presented, researchers usually provide a narrative description of the result in plain English. When the hypothesis tested by a statistical analysis is not explicitly stated, you can usually determine the hypothesis that was tested by reading this narrative description of the result, and referring back to the introduction to locate an hypothesis that corresponds to that result. After even the most complex statistical analysis, there will be a written description of what the result means conceptually. Turn your attention to these descriptions. Focus on the conceptual meaning of research findings, not on the mechanics of how they were obtained (unless you're comfortable with statistics).

Aside from statistical tests and narrative descriptions of results, results sections also frequently contain tables and graphs. These are efficient summaries of data. Even if you are not familiar with statistics, look closely at tables and graphs, and pay attention to the means or correlations presented in them. Researchers always include written descriptions of the pertinent aspects of tables and graphs. While reading these descriptions, check the tables and graphs to make sure what the researchers say accurately reflects their data. If they say there was a difference between two groups on a particular dependent measure, look at the means in the table that correspond to those two groups, and see if the means do differ as described. Occasionally, results seem to become stronger in their narrative description than an examination of the data would warrant.

Statistics *can* be misused. When they are, results are difficult to interpret. Having said this, a lack of statistical knowledge should not make you overly cautious while reading results sections. Though not a perfect antidote, journal articles undergo extensive review by professional researchers before publication. Thus, most misapplications of statistics are caught and corrected before an article is published. So, if you are unfamiliar with statistics, you can be reasonably confident that findings are accurately reported.

While reading the results section, try answering these questions: Did the researchers provide evidence that any independent variable manipulations were effective? For example, if testing for behavioral differences between happy and sad participants, did the researchers demonstrate that one group was in fact happier than the other? What were the major findings of the study? Were the researchers' original hypotheses supported by their observations? If not, look in the discussion section for how the researchers explain the findings that were obtained.

DISCUSSION

The discussion section frequently opens with a summary of what the study found, and an evaluation of whether the findings supported the original hypotheses. Here, the researchers evaluate the theoretical and practical implications of their results. This can be particularly interesting when the results did not work out exactly as the researchers anticipated. When such is the case, consider the researchers' explanations carefully, and see if they seem plausible to you. Often, researchers will also report any aspects of their study that limit their interpretation of its results, and suggest further research that could overcome these limitations to provide a better understanding of the problem under investigation.

Some readers find it useful to read the first few paragraphs of the discussion section before reading any other part of a research report. Like the abstract, these few paragraphs usually contain all of the main ideas of a research report: What the hypotheses were, the major findings and whether they supported the original hypotheses, and how the findings relate to past research and theory. Having this information before reading a research report can guide your reading, allowing you to focus on the specific details you need to complete your understanding of a study. The description of the results, for example, will alert you to the major variables that were studied. If they are unfamiliar to you, you can pay special attention to how they are defined in the introduction, and how they are operationalized in the method section.

After you have finished reading an article, it can also be helpful to reread the first few paragraphs of the discussion and the abstract. As noted, these two passages present highly distilled summaries of the major ideas in a research report. Just as they can help guide your reading of a report, they can also help you consolidate your understanding of a report once you have finished reading it. They provide a check on whether you have understood the main points of a report, and offer a succinct digest of the research in the authors' own words.

While reading the discussion section, try answering these questions: What conclusions can be drawn from the study? What new information does the study provide about the problem under investigation? Does the study help resolve the problem? What are the practical and theoretical implications of the study's findings? Did the results contradict past research findings? If so, how do the researchers explain this discrepancy?

Some Notes on Reports of Multiple Studies

Up to this point, we have implicitly assumed that a research report describes just one study. It is also quite common, however, for a research report to describe a series of studies of the same problem in a single article. When such is the case, each study reported will have the same basic structure (introduction, method, results, and discussion sections) that we have outlined, with the notable exception that sometimes the results and discussion section for each study are combined. Combined "results and discussion" sections contain the same information that separate results and discussion sections normally contain. Sometimes, the authors present all their results first, and only then discuss the implications of these results, just as they would in separate results and discussion sections. Other times, however, the authors alternate between describing results and discussing their implications, as each result is presented. In either case, you should be on the lookout for the same information, as outlined above in our consideration of separate results and discussion sections.

Reports including multiple studies also differ from single study reports in that they include more general introduction and discussion sections. The general introduction, which begins the main body of a research report, is similar in essence to the introduction of a single study report. In both cases, the researchers describe the problem investigated and its practical and theoretical significance. They also demonstrate how they derived their hypotheses, and explain how their research relates to past investigations of the problem. In contrast, the separate introductions to each individual study in reports of multiple studies are usually quite brief, and focus more specifically on the logic and rationale of each particular study presented. Such introductions generally describe the methods used in the particular study, outlining how they answer questions that have not been adequately addressed by past research, including studies reported earlier in the same article.

General discussion sections parallel discussions of single studies, except on a somewhat grander scale. They present all of the information contained in discussions of single studies, but consider the implications of all the studies presented together. A general discussion section brings the main ideas of a research program into bold relief. It typically begins with a concise summary of a research program's main findings, their relation to the original hypotheses, and their practical and theoretical implications. Thus, the summaries that begin general discussion sections are counterparts of the summaries that begin discussion sections of single study reports. Each presents a digest of the research presented in an article that can serve as both an organizing framework (when read first), and as a check on how well you have understood the main points of an article (when read last).

Research Reporting as Story Telling

A research report tells the story of how a researcher or group of researchers investigated a specific problem. Thus, a research report has a linear, narrative structure with a beginning, middle, and end. In his paper on writing research reports, Bem noted that a research report:

> ...is shaped like an hourglass. It begins with broad general statements, progressively narrows down to the specifics of [the] study, and then broadens out again to more general considerations. (1987, p. 175)

This format roughly mirrors the process of scientific investigation, wherein researchers do the following: (1) start with a broad idea from which they formulate a narrower set of hypotheses, informed by past empirical findings (introduction); (2) design a specific set of concrete operations to test these hypotheses (method); (3) analyze the observations collected in this way, and decide if they support the original hypotheses (results); and (4) explore the broader theoretical and practical implications of the findings, and consider how they contribute to an understanding of the problem under investigation (discussion). Though these stages are somewhat arbitrary distinctions—research actually proceeds in a number of different ways—they help elucidate the inner logic of research reports.

While reading a research report, keep this linear structure in mind. Though it is difficult to remember a series of seemingly disjointed facts, when these facts are joined together in a logical, narrative structure, they become easier to comprehend and recall. Thus, always remember that a research report tells a story. It will help you to organize the information you read, and remember it later.

Describing research reports as stories is not just a convenient metaphor. Research reports are stories. Stories can be said to consist of two components: A telling of what happened, and an explanation of why it happened. It is tempting to view science as an endeavor that simply catalogues facts, but nothing is further from the truth. The goal of science, social psychology included, is to *explain* facts, to explain *why* what happened happened. Social psychology is built on the dynamic interplay of discovery and justification, the dialogue between systematic observation of relations and their theoretical explanation. Though research reports do present novel facts based on systematic observation, these facts are presented in the service of ideas. Facts in isolation are trivia. Facts tied together by an explanatory theory are science. Therein lies the story. To really understand what researchers have to say, you need consider how their explanations relate to their findings.

The Rest of the Story

> There is really no such thing as research. There is only search, more search, keep on searching. (Bowering, 1988, p. 95)

Once you have read through a research report, and understand the researchers' findings and their explanations of them, the story does not end there. There is more than one interpretation for any set of findings. Different researchers often explain the same set of facts in different ways.

Let's take a moment to dispel a nasty rumor. The rumor is this: Researchers present their studies in a dispassionate manner, intending only to inform readers of their findings and their interpretation of those findings. In truth, researchers aim not only to inform readers, but also to *persuade* them (Sternberg, 1995). Researchers want to convince you their ideas are right. There is never only one explanation for a set of findings. Certainly, some explanations are better than others; some fit the available data better, are more parsimonious, or require fewer questionable assumptions. The point here is that researchers are very passionate about their ideas, and want you to believe them. It's up to you to decide if you want to buy their ideas or not.

Let's compare social psychologists to salesclerks. Both social psychologists and salesclerks want to sell you something; either their ideas, or their wares. You need to decide if you want to buy what they're selling or not—and there are potentially negative consequences for either decision. If you let a sales clerk dazzle you with a sales pitch, without thinking about it carefully, you might end up buying a substandard product that you don't really need. After having done this a few times, people tend to become cynical, steeling themselves against any and all sales pitches. This too is dangerous. If you are overly critical of sales pitches, you could end up foregoing genuinely useful products. Thus, by analogy, when you are too critical in your reading of research reports, you might dismiss, out of hand, some genuinely useful ideas—ideas that can help shed light on why people behave the way they do.

This discussion raises the important question of how critical one should be while reading a research report. In part, this will depend on why one is reading the report. If you are reading it simply to learn what the researchers have to say about a particular issue, for example, then there is usually no need to be overly critical. If you want to use the research as a basis for planning a new study, then you should be more critical. As you develop an understanding of psychological theory and research methods, you will also develop an ability to criticize research on many different levels. And *any* piece of research can be criticized at some level. As Jacob Cohen put it, "A successful piece of research doesn't conclusively settle an issue, it just makes some theoretical proposition to some degree more likely" (1990, p. 1311). Thus, as a consumer of research reports, you have to strike a delicate balance between being overly critical and overly accepting.

While reading a research report, at least initially, try to suspend your disbelief. Try to understand the researchers' story; that is, try to understand the facts—the findings and how they were obtained—and the suggested explanation of those facts—the researchers' interpretation of the findings and what they mean. Take the research to task only after you feel you understand what the authors are trying to say.

Research reports serve not only an important archival function, documenting research and its findings, but also an invaluable stimulus function. They can excite other researchers to join the investigation of a particular issue, or to apply new methods or theory to a different, perhaps novel, issue. It is this stimulus function that Elliot Aronson, an eminent social psychologist, referred to when he admitted that, in publishing a study, he hopes his colleagues will "look at it, be stimulated by it, be provoked by it, annoyed by it, and then go ahead and do it better.... That's the exciting thing about science; it progresses by people taking off on one another's work" (1995, p. 5). Science is indeed a cumulative enterprise, and each new study builds on what has (or, sometimes, has not) gone before it. In this way, research articles keep social psychology vibrant.

A study can inspire new research in a number of different ways, such as: (1) it can lead one to conduct a better test of the hypotheses, trying to rule out alternative explanations of the findings; (2) it can lead one to explore the limits of the findings, to see how widely applicable they are, perhaps exploring situations to which they do not apply; (3) it can lead one to test the implications of the findings, furthering scientific investigation of the phenomenon; (4) it can inspire one to apply the findings, or a novel methodology, to a different area of investigation; and (5) it can provoke one to test the findings in the context of a specific real world problem, to see if they can shed light on it. All of these are excellent extensions of the original research, and there are, undoubtedly, other ways that research findings can spur new investigations.

The problem with being too critical, too soon, while reading research reports is that the only further research one may be willing to attempt is research of the first type: Redoing a study better. Sometimes this is desirable, particularly in the early stages of investigating a particular issue, when the findings are novel and perhaps unexpected. But redoing a reasonably compelling study, without extending it in any way, does little to advance our understanding of human behavior. Although the new study might be "better," it will not be "perfect," so *it* would have to be run again, and again, likely never reaching a stage where it is beyond criticism. At some point, researchers have to decide that the evidence is compelling enough to warrant investigation of the last four types. It is these types of studies that most advance our knowledge of social behavior. As you read more research reports, you will become more comfortable deciding when a study is "good enough" to move beyond it. This is a somewhat subjective judgment, and should be made carefully.

When social psychologists write up a research report for publication, it is because they believe they have something new and exciting to communicate about social behavior. Most research reports that are submitted for publication are rejected. Thus, the reports that are eventually published are deemed pertinent not only by the researchers who wrote them, but also by the reviewers and editors of the journals in which they are published. These people, at least, believe the research reports they write and publish have something important and interesting to say. Sometimes, you'll disagree; not all journal articles are created equal, after all. But we recommend that you, at least initially, give these well-meaning social psychologists the benefit of the doubt. Look for what they're excited about. Try to understand the authors' story, and see where it leads you.

Author Notes

Preparation of this paper was facilitated by a Natural Sciences and Engineering Research Council of Canada doctoral fellowship to Christian H. Jordan. Thanks to Roy Baumeister, Arie Kruglanski, Ziva Kunda, John Levine, Geoff MacDonald, Richard Moreland, Ian Newby-Clark, Steve Spencer, and Adam Zanna for their insightful comments on, and appraisals of, various drafts of this paper. Thanks also to Arie Kruglanski and four anonymous editors of volumes in the series, Key Readings in Social Psychology for their helpful critiques of an initial outline of this paper. Correspondence concerning this article should be addressed to Christian H. Jordan, Department of Psychology, University of Waterloo, Waterloo, Ontario, Canada N2L 3G1. Electronic mail can be sent to chjordan@watarts.uwaterloo.ca.

REFERENCES

American Psychological Association (1994). *Publication manual* (4th ed.). Washington, D.C.

Aronson, E. (1995). Research in social psychology as a leap of faith. In E. Aronson (Ed.), *Readings about the social animal* (7th ed., pp. 3–9). New York: W. H. Freeman and Company.

Bem, D. J. (1987). Writing the empirical journal article. In M. P. Zanna & J. M. Darley (Eds.), *The compleat academic: A practical guide for the beginning social scientist* (pp. 171–201). New York: Random House.

Bowering, G. (1988). *Errata.* Red Deer, Alta.: Red Deer College Press.

Cohen, J. (1990). Things I have learned (so far). *American Psychologist, 45,* 1304–1312.

Forgas, J. P. (1994). Sad and guilty? Affective influences on the explanation of conflict in close relationships. *Journal of Personality and Social Psychology, 66,* 56–68.

Sternberg, R. J. (1995). *The psychologist's companion: A guide to scientific writing for students and researchers* (3rd ed.). Cambridge: Cambridge University Press.

Author Index

A

Abelson, R. P., 60, *62*, 66, *81*, 212, *225*, 320, *321*, 423, *433*
Aboud, F. E., 10, 57, *63, 451*
Abrams, Dominic, 4, 75, *77*, 172, 173, *188, 189*, 395, *415, 453*
Abramson, L. M., 151n.7, *159*
Abramson, P. R., 151n.7, *159*, 355, *366*
Acker, J. R., 348, *350*
Ackerman, N. W., 24, *47*
Adams, G. R., 235, *248*
Adorno, T., 263, 272, *282*
Ahrens, C., 122, *134*
Aikin, K., 84
Ajzen, I., 204, *207*, 405, *414*
Alan, N., 262, *282*
Albert, A. A., 14, *451*
Allen, H. M., Jr., 115, *116–117, 303*
Allen, J. G., 100, 236, 289, *248, 452*
Allen, V. L., 328, *337*, 405, *413*
Allison, P. D., 262, *282*
Alloy, L. B., 355, *366*
Allport, F. H., 65, *77*
Allport, Gordon W., 4, 8, 15, 30, 46–47, *47*, 51, 53, *61, 62*, 68, 69, 73, *77*, 102, *116*, 119, 120, 131, *134*, 191, 193, *207*, 290, *302*, 339, 340, *350*, 354, *366*, 370, *389*, 396, 402, *413*, 423, 428, *433*, 435, 436, *449, 451*
Altemeyer, P. G., 265, 267, 272, 279, *282*
Amir, Y., 15, 395, 396, *413*, 419, 420, 423, 431, *433, 451*
Ammons, C. H., 178–179, *188*
Ammons, R. B., 178–179, *188*
Anastasio, P. A., 405, 409, *414–415*
Anderson, C. V., *249*
Andersen, S. M., 120, *134*
Anderson, J. R., 120, *134*
Anderson, N., 56, *61*
Anderson, R. A., *282*
Anderson, R. C., 108, *116*
Anglin, J., 68, *77*
Apfelbaum, E., 60, *61*
Arber, S., 157, *160*
Arcuri, Luciano, 14, 69, *80*, 204, 206, *207*, 407, 409, *413, 454*
Arguellas, J. A., *282*
Aronson, E., 392, 398, 408, *413*, 435, *449*, 464, *451*
Aronson, Joshua, 1, 7, 70, *81*, 185, *190*, 324, *455*
Arvey, R. D., 340, 341, *350*
Asch, S. E., 5, 56, 56, *61*, 65, *77, 451*

Ashley-Montagu, M. F., 30, *47*
Ashmore, R. D., 5, 10, 74, *77*, 87, 95, *98, 116*, 121, *134*, 156, *159*, 187, *188*, 290, *302*, 339, *350*, 403, *413, 451*
Ashton, M., 12, *451*
Atkins, R. D., *47*,
Au, T. K. F., 206, *207*
Augoustinos, M., 122, 123, 125, *134*
Austin, G. A., 53, *61*
Avery, P. G., 261, *282*
Axelson, L. J., 371, *389*
Axson, D., 436, *450*

B

Bachman, B. A., 15, 405, 409, *414–415, 453*
Bakan, D., 143, 145, *159*
Baker, S. M., 3, 68, *77, 78*, 404, *414, 452*
Baldwin, J., 290, *303*
Banaji, M. R., 9, 10, *80*, 120, 121, *134, 135, 451*
Bandura, A., 371, 386, *389*
Banton, M., *134*
Barbour, L., 235, *249*
Bargh, J., 6, 9, 11, 120, 121, 122, 125, 126, 127, 129, 130, 131, *134, 135, 136*, 340, *351*, 427, *433, 451*
Barnes, W. R., *282*
Barnett, E. V., 53, *62*
Baron, R. M., 5, 184, *188*, 214, *225*, 395, 438, *449, 454*
Barsalou, L. W., 71, *77*, 402, 412, *413*
Bar-Tal, D., 10, *451*
Bar-Tal, Y., 15, 16, 72, *77, 451*
Bartlett, F. C., 50, *61*, 66, *77*
Bartol, K. M., 341, *350*
Batts, V., 88, *99*, 123, *135*
Baumeister, R. F., 4, 235,237, 246, *248*, 371, 376, 386, *389, 451*
Bayton, J. A., 142, *160*
Beall, P., 88, 96, 97, *98*, 321, *322*
Beattie, A. E., 341, 350
Bee, H., 353, *367*
Bell, J., 69, *78*
Belmore, S. M., 65, *78*
Bem, D. J., 461, 463, *466*
Bem, S. L., 5, 66, 70, 72, *78*, 143, *159, 451*
Benson, P. L., 261, 266, *282*
Berg, E. N., *350*
Berger, P., 59, *61*
Berkowitz, L., *302*

Bernstein, S., 66
Berry, B., 45, *47*
Berry, J. W., 400, 402, 410, *413*
Berscheid, E., 212, *225*, 236, *249*, 354, *366, 367*
Bersoff, Donald N., 7, 323–324, 348, *350, 452*
Best, D. L., 143, 158, *160*
Bettencourt, B. A., 398, 400, 411, *413*
Bevan, W., 11, 54, *62, 455*
Bickman, L., 293, *303*
Bienen, L., 262, *282*
Biernat, M., 1, 234, *248, 452*
Billig, M., 4, 54, 59, *61, 63*, 120, *134*, 290, *302*, 328, *337*, 410, *413*, 437, *450, 456*
Birrell, P., 57, 62, 254, *258*
Bishop, G. D., 327, *337*, 405, *415*
Bishop, Y. M., 146, *159*
Black, J. B., 49, *61*
Black, P., *47*
Blake, M. J. F., 255, *258*
Blaney, N., 392, 398, *413*, 435, *449, 451*
Blaney, P. H., 386, *389*
Blau, J. H., 156, *159*
Bless, H., 6, *451*
Block, C. B., 291, *303*
Block, C. J., 340, *351*
Blood, J. H., 143, *159*
Bobo, L., 96, *99*, 102, 115, *116*, 282, 261, *284*
Bodenhausen, Galen V., 4, 6, 11, 67, 71, 74, *78*, 98, *99*, 108, *117*, 187, *188*, 251–252, 254, 257, *258*, 399, *413, 451, 454*
Bogardus, E. S., 35, *47*
Bond, C. F., *389*
Bond, M., 236, *248*
Bond, R. N., 126, *134*
Borden, R. J., *78*
Borgida, Eugene, 7, 157, *160*, 213, *225*, 323–324, 340, 341, 344,, 349, *351, 352*, 426, *433, 452*
Boster, J. S., 68, 72, *78*
Boudreau, L. A., *452*
Bourhis, R. Y., 76, *81*, 327, 328, *337*
Bower, C. H., 49, *61*
Bowering, G., 463, *466*
Boyes-Bream, P., 49, *62*
Bradburn, N. M., 108, *116*
Braddock, J. H., *366*, 397, 405, *413*
Brady, M., 236, *248*
Braly, K. W., 7, 8, 65, 72, 77, *80*, 86, 87–90, 91t, 92–93, 93t, 95–97, 123, *135*, 158, *160*, 454
Brand, Pamela, 15, 210, 235, 237, 246, *249*, 454
Branscombe, N. R., 187, *188*
Braumeister, R. F., *248*
Brehm, S. S., 95, *98*
Brekke, N., 157, *160*, 212, *225*, 340, *351*, 426, *433*
Brendl, C. M., 131, *135*
Brewer, M. B., 1, 2, 3, 5, 13, 15, 16, 55, *61*, 70, 71, *78*, 120, *134*, 158, *159*, 173, 187, *188*, 191, 193, *207*, 290, 298, *302*, 327, *337*, 340, *350*, 395–396, 397, 398, 399, 400, 401, 403, 405, 406, 407, 408, 410, 411 *413, 414–415*, 428, 431, *433*, 436, 437, 446, 447–448, *449, 451, 454*
Brewin, C. R., 355, *366*
Brickman, P., 102, *116*, 186, *188*, 212, *225*
Brief, D., 278, *284*
Brigham, I., 158, *159, 452*

Brigham, J. C., 71, *78*, 97, *98*, 101, 104, 114, *116*, 162, 170, *171*, 353, *366*
Broadbent, D. E., 258, *258*
Broadbent, M. H. P., 258, *258*
Brock, T., 254, *258*
Brodt, S. E., 4, *451*
Bromley, S., 10, 97, *98*, 102, *116*, 205, *207*, 289, *302*, 353, *366, 452*
Broverman, D. M., 143, 148, *159* 353, *366, 367*
Broverman, I. K., 143, 148, *159*, 353, *366, 367*
Brown, I. K., 143, *159*
Brown, J. D., 75, *78*, 173, 186, *188–189*, 354, *366*
Brown, Rupert, 10, 12, 15, 16t, 65, 66, 71, *79*, 84, *134*, 206, *207, 208*, 323, 327, 337, *337*, 397, 399–400, 401, 402, 403, 404, 405, 406, 407, 408, 410, 411, *413, 414, 415, 417*, 430, *433*, 436, 449, *449–450, 451*, 453, 454, 455
Brown, V., 340, 341, *350*
Brown, W. E., 261, *282*
Bruner, J. S., 49, 50, 52, 53, 58, *61*, 66, *78*, 102, *117*, 120, *134*, 320, *322*
Brunswik, E., 58, *61*
Buck, P. L., *233*
Bugelski, R., 173, *190*
Bulman, R. J., 186, *188*
Bundy, R. P., 4, 55, *63*, 328, *337*, 437, *450, 456*
Burling, J., *189*
Burt, M. R., 266, *282*
Buss, A. H., 267, 279, *283*
Buss, A. R., 60, *61*
Butterfield, D. A., 341, *350*
Byrne, D., 397, *414*

C
Cadinu, M. R., 13, 206, *207, 451*
Cameron, J. E., 172, *189*
Campbell, A., 101, *116*, 289, *302*
Campbell, B. H., *62*
Campbell, D. T., 7, 51, 53, *61*, 158, *159*, 328, *337*, 395, 408, *414*, 436, *449, 452*
Cantor, N., 11, 49, 56, 57, *61*, 158, *160*, 214, 220, *225, 451*
Caramazza, A., 206, *208*
Carlston, D. E., 120, 129, 133, *134*
Carmines, E. G., 267, *282*
Carnevale, P., 355, *366, 367*
Carrillo, M. A., 236, *249*
Carrington, P. I., 355, *366, 367*
Carter, S. L., 370, *389*
Cartwright, D., 354, *366*
Carver, C. S., 355, 356, 364, *366, 367*, 386, *389*
Cash, T. F., 404, *415*
Chaiken, S., 71, *78*, 129, *134*, 254, 257, *258*
Chakraborty, R., *249*
Champion, J. E., 341, *350*
Chapman, J. P., 161, *171*
Chapman, L. J., 58, *61*, 161–162, *171*
Chein, I., 73, *79*, 290, *303*, 400, *414*
Christopher, W., 281, *282*
Cialdini, R. B., 75, *78*
Clark, D. H., 221, *225*
Clark, K., 10, *452*
Clark, M., 10, *452*

Clark, M. S., *78*
Clark, R. D., 293, *303*
Clarke, R. B., 7, *452*
Clarke, R. T., 11, *454*
Clarkson, F. E., 143, *159*, 353, *366*
Cleary, T. A., 370, *389*
Cling, B. J., 261, *284*
Coates, D., *116*
Coffman, T., 8, 87, *98*, 213, *225*, 291, *303*, 353, *366*, *367*, *454*
Cohen, Claudia E., 209–210, *452*
Cohen, D., 172, *189*
Cohen, E., *116*, 395, *414*
Cohen, F. X., 42, *47*,
Cohen, Jacob, *160*, 464
Cohen, R., 341, *352*
Cohn, N., 59, *61*
Coleman, L. M., 11, *452*
Coller, W. L., *233*
Collins, A. M., 67, 71, *78*, 120, *134*
Collins, M. E., 397, *414*
Collins, R. L., 75, *78*, 173, *189*
Collins, T. W., 402, *416*
Colquhoun. W. P., 255, *258*
Commins, B., 60, *61*
Cook, D., 91, *99*, 321, *322*
Cook, S. W., 15, 16, 101, 104, 114, *116*, *117*, 292, 299, *304*, 396, 397, 400, 402, 405, 411, 412, 413, *414*, *418*, 420, 423, 425, 431, *433*, 435, 446, *449*, *452*
Cooley, C. H., 172, *189*, 354, *366*
Cooper, Joel, 14, 210, 213, *225*, 227, 231, *233*, *456*
Cooper, H. M., 214, *225*, 236, *249*
Corbitt, E. M., 236, *248*
Cornell, D. P., 173, 174, 185, 186, *190*
Cornwell, B., 237, *248*
Costa, P. T., 263, *282*
Costrich, N., 340, 341, *350*, 404, *414*
Cota, A. A., 5, *452*
Craik, F. I. M., 57, *61*
Crandall, C. S., 1, 69, *78*, 234, *248*, *452*
Crane, M., 66, *80*
Crocker, Jennifer, 1, 5, 6, 7, 65, 66, 70, 72, 76, *78*, *80*, *81*, *82*, *116*, 173, 186, *189*, 193, *208*, 235, 236, 237, 246, *248*, 281, *282*, 324, 340, *350*, *352*, 354, 355, *366*, 403, 404, *417*, 425, 430, *434*, *452*, *456*
Cronbach, L. J., *160*
Crosby, F., 10, 84, 97, *98*, 101, 205, *207*, 289, 293, *302*, 353, *366*, *452*
Cross, J. A., 180, *189*
Crowne, D. P., 76, *78*
Croyle, R. T., 347, *351*
Csepeli, G., *302*
Csikszentmihalyi, M., 156, *160*
Curtis, R. C., 236, 247, *248*
Czajka, J. L., 157, *160*

D

D'Agostino, P. R., 121, 129
Dahlke, O. H., *47*,
Dalton, R., *415*
D'Andrade, R. G., 72, *78*

Daniels, L. R., 293, *302*
Dann, H., *302*
Darley, John M., 14, 174, *189*, 210, 212, 221, *225*, 227, *233*, 236, *248*, 297, *302*, 340, 341, *350, 354, *366*, *452*, *453*
Dator, J. A., *282*
Davidon, R. S., 51, *61*
Davidson, E. S., 291, *303*
Davidson-Podgorny, G, 398–399, *416*, 435, *450*
Davie, M. R., 42, 44, *47*
Davis, J. A., 146, *160*
Davis, K. E., 154, *160*, *171*, 204, *208*
Davis, M. H., 265, 266, 267, *282*
Davis, W. S., 247, *248*
Davis-Stitt, C., 12, *455*
Deaux, Kay, 1, 4, 7, 13, 120, *134*, 151n.7, 157n.12, *160*, 180, *189*, 206, *207*, 234, *248*, 323–324, 340, 341, 344, 346, 349, *350*, 354, *366*, 404, *414*, *452*
DeJong, W., 234, *248*
Del Boca, F. K., 5, 10, 74, *77*, 87, 95, 115, *116*, 121, *134*, 156, *159*, 187, *188*, 290, *302*, 339, *350*, *451*
Denno, D. W., 262, *282*
DePaulo, B. M., 11, *452*
Depret, E. F., 278, *282*
Deschamps, J.-C., 60, *61*, 195n, *207*, 402, 407, 410, 411, *414*, 449, *449–450*
Desforges, D. M., 404, *414*
Deutsch, M., 397, *414*, 435, *450*
Devereux, E., 278, *284*
Devine, Patricia G., 3, 8, 9, 68, 77, *78*, 83–84, 87–89, 91, 94, 95, 96, 97, 98, *98*, *99* 120–121, 122, 123, 125, 129, 130, 132–134, *134–135*, 187, 188, *189*, 253, 305, 306, 307, 309, 310, 311–312, 315, 316, 317–318, 319, 321, *321, 322*, 323, 377, *389*, 404, *414*, *452*, *454*
DeVinney, L. C., 69, *81*
DeVries, D., 398
Diab, L. N., 409, *414*
Dickson, L., 27, *47*
Diel, M., *414*
Diehl, M., 13, 67, 74, *78*, 407, *414*, *452*
Diener, E., 356, *366*
Dijksterhuis, A., 14, *456*
Dion, K. K., 237, 246, *248*
Dion, K. L., 5, 355, *366*, *452*
Dipboye, R. L., 341, *350*
Ditto, P. H., 173, *189*
Dixon, R., 69, *78*
Dobbins, G. H., 341, *352*
Doise, W., 52, 58, *61, 290, *302*, 406, 407, 411, *414*, 436, *450*
Dollard, J., 173, *189*
Donahue, E., 267, *283*
Doob, L. W., 44, *47*, 173, *189*
Doty, R. M., 76, *78*, 272, *283*
Dovidio, John F., 1, 6, 9, 15, 67, 71, 74, 77, *78*, 87, 91–93, 95, 96, 97, *98*, 108, *116*, 122, *135*, 174, *189*, 191, *207*, 252–253, 289, 293, 294, 295, 296, 297, 298, 300, 301, *302*, *303*, 307, *321*, 353, 356, 364, *366*, 377, *389*, 392, 404, 405, 409, *414–415*, *416*, 436, *450*, *452*, *453*, *455*
Doyle, A., 10, *451*
Dreger, R. M., 221, *225*
Driscoll, D. M., 65, *79*
Duan, C., 3, 65, 71, 74, *81*, 120, 125, *135*, *136*, 455

DuBois, C. L. Z., *352*
DuCharme, W. M., 431, *433*
Duckitt, J., 265, 279, *282*, 394, 408, *414*
Dugan, P. M., 11, *453*
Dull, L., 1, *451*
Dull, V., 158, *159*, 403, *414*
Duncan, B. L., 11, 13–14, 60, *61*, 191, 200, *207*, 212, 225, 452
Dunham, F. Y., 290, *304*
Dunton, B., 9, 121, *135*, 452
Dutton, D. G., 302, *303*
Duveen, G., 68, *78*
Dyer, H. S., 23, *47*,
Dyer, L. M., 129, *135*

E

Eagly, Alice H., 1, 7, 9, 70, 71, *78*, 139, 143, 156–157, 158–159, *160*, 254, *258*, 340, *350*, *366*, 452
Earn, B. M., 355, *366*
Easterbrook, J. A., 371, *389*
Eccles, J., 71, *79*, 172, *189*, 454
Edwards, K., 15, 398, *414–415*, 436, *450*, 454
Effrein, E. A., 354, *366*
Egeth, H. E., 348, *351*
Eggins, R. A., *453*
Einbender, S. W., 340, *352*
Eiser, J. R., 52, 58, *61*
Eisler, R., 261, 274, *283*
Ekehammar, B., 261, 279, *283*, 284
Elliot, Andrew J., 83–84, 97, *98*, 122, 123, 125, *134*, 187, *189*, 305, *321*
Elliot, R., 348, *350*
Ellsworth, P C., 348, *350*, *351*
Ellyson, S. L., 301, *302*
Emswiller, T., 341, *350*
England, P., 143, *160*
Enzle, M. E., 294, *303*
Epps, E. G., 371, *389*
Epstein, R., 10, 68, *78*, 452
Erber, R., 254, *258*, 350
Erdley, C. A., 121, 129, *135*
Erhlich, H. J., 73, 75, *78*, 87, 98, *98*
Erikson, Erik, 354, *366*
Eskilson, A., 341, *352*
Esses, V. M., 12, 187, *189*, 451
Estrada, L. F., *282*
Etcoff, N. L., , 2, 57, *63*, 143, *160*, 340, *352*, 456
Ethier, K. A., 452
Evans, M., 191, *208*
Evans, N., 6, 67, *78*, 87, *98*, 108, *116*, 122, *135*, 300, *302*, 377, *389*, 452
Evett, S. R., 323, 452
Eysenck, H. J., 261, 263, *283*

F

Fagot, B. I., 68, *78*
Falander, 354, *366*
Faranda, J. A., 298, *303*
Farina, A., 1, 236, *248*, 452
Farr, R. M., 68, *78*

Fazio, R. H., , 9, 10, 14, 71, 120, 121, 134, *135*, 212, 214, 225, 354, *366*, 404, *414*, 431, *433*, 452
Feagin, C. B., 281, *283*, 291, *303*
Feagin, J. R., 100, *116*, 281, *283, 291, 303*
Feather, N. T., 102, 105, 107, *116*, 341, *350*
Fein, Steven, 4, 13, 140, 180, *189*, 452
Feingold, A., 235, *248*
Feinstein, J., 340, *350*, 404, *414*
Feldman, J. M., 142, *160*
Feldman-Summers, S., 341, *350*
Felicio, Diane, 15, 210, 235, 246, *249*, 454
Fenigstein, A., 267, *283*
Ferris, F., 436, *450*
Feshbach, S., 261, 264, *283*, 436, *450*
Festinger, L., 54–55, *61*, 172, *189*, 173, *189*, 327, *337*, 354, 366
Fiala, J., *171*
Fiedler, K, 11, 192, 193, 195, 196, 197, 200, 201, 202, 204, 207, *207, 208*, 452
Field, P. B., *367*
Fienberg, S. E., 146, *159*
Fifer, G., 221, *225*
Figurski, T. J., 156, *160*
Findlay, J. C., 65, *79*
Fischer, G. W., 12, 67, *80*, 191, *208*, 454
Fish, D., 206, *207*
Fishbein, M. A., 204, *207*, 405, *414*
Fisher, J. R., 341, *350*
Fisher, R. J., 394, *414*
Fishman, J. A., 54, *61*, 68, 73, 74, *78*
Fiske, D. W., 395, *414*
Fiske, Susan T., 2, 3, 5, 7, 8, 11, 12, 57, *63*, 65, 66, 70, 73, *78–79*, 84, 120, 132, 133, *135*, 143, *160*, *190*, 254, *258*, 278, *282*, 323–324, 339, 340, 341, 342, 343, 344, 345, 346, 347, 349, *350*, *352*, 404, *414*, 436, *450*, 452, 453, 454, 456
Flament, C., 4, 55, *63*, 328, *337*, 437, *450*, 456
Fleming, C., 14, 15, 65, 70, *80* , 453
Fleming, J. H., 174, *189*
Flowerman, S., 69, *81*
Folkard, S., 255, *258*
Fontana, A. F., 353, *366*
Ford, T. E., , 9, 12, 70, 73, 74, 75, 77, *79*, 81, 120, *135, 136*, 452
Forgas, Joseph P., 49, 56, 60, *61*, 65, 73, 74, *81*, 187, *189*, 458–459, 466
Foster, G., 213, *225*
Fox-Cardamone, D. L., 75, *79*
Framer, E., 235, *248*
Franco, F., 206, *207*
Frank, H., 340, *352*
Freeman, G., 255, *258*
Freeman, S., *78*
French, J., 36, *47*
Frenkel-Brunswick, E., 263, *282*, *283*
Freud, Sigmund, 30, *47*, 423, *433*
Freund, T., 74, *80*, 88, 98, *98*, 341, *351*
Frey, D., 294, *303*
Frey, D. L., 115, *116*
Friendly, M. L., 56, *61–62*
Frieze, I. H., 341, *350*
Fulero, S., 57, *62*, 191, *208*, 254, *258*
Furnham, A., 355, *366*
Fyock, J., , 14, 65, 66, 67, *79*, 209, *452–453*

G

Gaertner, Samuel L., 1, 10, 15, 71, *78*, 87, 91–92, 95, 96, 97, *98*, 115, *116*, 121, *135*, 174, *189*, 191, 205, *207*, 252–253, 289, 293, 294, 295, 296, 297, 298, 300, 301, *302*, *303*, 307, *321*, 353, 356, 364, *366*, 392, 405, 409, 410, 411, *414–415*, 436, 437, 438, 447–448, 449, *450*, *452*, *453*
Gallagher, E. M., 173, 186, *188–189*
Galligan, P., 353, *366*, *367*
Gangestad, S., 53, *62*
Garbutt, B., 234, *249*
Gardner, R. C., 7, 8–9, 64, 65, 72, 73, 74, *79*, 97, *98*, *453*
Garland, H., 341, *351*
Garrett, J., 102, 105, 107, *116* , 265, *283*
Garvey, C., 206, *208*
Gayton, S. L., *249*
Gecas, V., 354, *366*
Geen, R. G., 371, 375, 386, *389*
Geis, F. L., 340, *350*
Gellert, E., 234, *249*
Gerard, H. B., 76, *62*, *79*, 214, *225*, 397, *415*
Gernsbacher, M. A., 424, *433*
Gerrard, M., 173, 186, *189*
Gerta, E., *47*
Gibbons, F. X., 173, 186, *189*
Giesler, R. B., 172, *190*
Gifford, Robert K., 11, 57, 58, *62*, 65, 66, 70, *79*, 125, *135*, 140, 157–158, *160*, *453*
Gilbert, D. T., 67, *79*, 121, 132, 133, *135*, 305, *321*, 378, *389*
Gilbert, G. M., 8, *47*, 87, 88, 90, 92–93, 95, *98*, 134, *453*
Giles, H., 69, *79*
Gillespie, D. L., 143, *160*
Glass, A. L., 108, *116*
Glass, B., 3, 71, *81*, 125, *136*, *455*
Glass, D. C., 356, *366*
Glick, P., 11, 84, *453*
Gliha, D., *452*
Glucksberg, S., 56, 227, *233*
Godfrey, D. K., 371, *389*
Goertzel, T. G., 265, 272, *283*
Goethals, G. R., 221, *225*
Goffman, E., 227, 233, *233*
Goffman, I., 370, *389*
Goldberg, P. A., 151n.7, *159*, 340, *352*
Golding, S. L., 161, *171*, 348, *352*
Goldman, W., 235, 237, 238, *248*
Goldstein, D., 420, *433*
Gonzalez, A., 398, *413*
Goodman, C. C., 52, *62*
Goodman, J., 347, *351*
Goodnow, J. J., *62*
Gorbspe, F. H., 72, *79*
Gordon, M. A., 340, *352*
Gorkin, L., 88, *99*
Gorman, T. F., 108, *117*
Gough, C., *302*
Gough, H., 265, 266, *283*
Govender, R. 129, *134*
Grabbe, P., 400, *415*
Graham, S., 236, *248*
Graumann, C. E., 75, *79*
Gray, W. D., 49, *62*
Graziano, W., 235, *248*
Greeley, A. M., 289, *303*

Green, R. T., 278, *284*
Greenberg, J., 69, 75, *79*, *81*, 102, *116*, 151n.7, *159*, 173, *189*, 386, *389*
Greenblatt, S. L., *415*
Greenwald, A. G., 12, 120, 121, 129, *135*, 173, *189*, 321, *321*, *453*
Griffiths, R. J., 4, 404, *415*, *454*
Groenewoud, J. T., 400, *417*
Grosovsky, E. A., 66, *80*
Gross, Paget H., 210, 340, *350*
Guitterez, F., 69, *82*
Gurtman, M. B., 6, 10, 121, *135*, 409, *416*, *455*
Gutek, B. A.,340, 341, *351*
Guzzo, R. A., 341, *351*

H

Haber, R. N., 50, *62*
Haberfield, Y., 341, *352*
Haddock, G., 187, *189*
Hagen, R. L., 340, *351*
Hall, W., 84, *456*
Hallam, J. R., 173, *190*
Halverson, C. F., Jr., 14, *454*
Hamilton, David L., 5, 10, 11, 12, 57, 58, 60, *62*, 65, 66, 70, *79*, 119, 120, 121, 125, 131, *135*, 140, 157–158, *160*, 162, 170, *171*, 187, *189*, 191, *193*, 290, *303*, 327, *337*, 339, 340, *351*, 404, 405, *415*, *454*, *455*
Hammer, E. D., 6, *455*
Hammer, E. Y., 6, *455*
Hanis, C., *249*
Hans, V. P., , 348, *352*
Hansen, R. D., 341, *351*
Hantzi, A., 403, *415*
Hanusa, B. H., 341, *350*
Harasty, A. S., 7, *453*
Hardee, B. B., 88, *99*, 123, *135*
Hardin, C. D., 9, 10, 120, *134*, *451*
Harding, J., 73, *79*, *116*, 290, 291, *303*, 400, *414*
Hardyck, J. A., 290, *303*
Harold, R. D., 172, *189*
Harré, R., 55, *62*
Harrington, H. J., 397, 398, 399, 400, 402, 405, *415*, *416*
Harris, M. J., 236, *248*
Hartley, E. L., 35, *47*, 71, *79*
Hartman, H. I., 353, 354, *367*
Hartman, P., 69, 75, *79*
Hartmann, H. I., *160*
Hartsough, W. R., 353, *366*
Harvey, M. D., 294, *303*
Harvey, O. J., 435, *450*
Hasher, L., 420, *433*
Haslam, S. A., 5, 6, 7, 77, *80*, 172, *190*, 405, *416*, *453*, *454*
Hass, R. Glen, , 8, 84, 113, 115, *116*, 267, 274, *283*, 289, 353, *367*, *454*
Hassebrauck, M., 403, *415*
Hastie, R., 57, *62*, 66, *80*, 191, *208*, 340, *352*
Hastorf, A. H., 1, 227, *233*, *248*, 356, *367*, *454*
Hayakawa, S. I., 76, *79*
Hayden, T., 214, *225*
Hayes-Roth, B., 129, 132, *135*
Hays, W. L., *189*
Heatherton, T. F., 182, *189*

Heaven, P. C. L., 279, *283*
Hechter, M., *303*
Heider, F., 53, 60, *62*, 73, *79*, 204, *208*
Heilbrun, A. B., Jr., 353, *366*
Heilman, Madeline E., 7, 323–324, 340, 341, 344, 349, *351*, *452*
Helmreich, P., 263, *284*
Helmreich, R. L., 70, *81*, 143, 145, 148, *160*, 341, *351*
Hennigan, K., 407, *416*
Hepburn, C., 66, *80*, 157, *160*, 213, 222, *225*, 340, *351*, 400, *415*, 426, *433*
Hepworth, J. T., 76, *79*
Herek, G. M., 1, 102, 115, *116*, 320, *321*, *453*
Herr, P. M., 431, *433*
Herrstein, R., 388, *389*
Hershenson, M., 50, *62*
Hertzberger, S., 355, *367*
Herzlich, C., 60, *61*
Hewstone, Miles, 4, 13, 15–16, 60, *62*, 65, 66, 70, 71, *79*, 187, *189*, 193, 205, *208*, 391–392, 397, 399–400, 401, 402, 403, 404, 405, 406, 407, 408, 411, 412, *415*, *417*, 449, *450*, *453*, *454*, *455*
Higgins, E. T., 71, 77, *79*, *80*, 98, *98*, 108, *116*, 120, 121, 122, 125, 129, 130, 131, *135*, 172–179, *189*, 306, 312, 317, *321*, 340, *351*, 377, *389*, 427, 428, 429, *433*
Higgins, R., *367*
Hill, C. A., 76, *79*, *456*
Hill, J., 12, 15, *455*
Hillger, L., 206, *208*
Hilton, J. L., 14, 120, 122, 132, *135*, 174, 187, *189*, 236, *248*, *453*
Hinkle, S., 75, *79*
Hinton, G. E., 120, *136*
Hintzman, D., 423, *433*
Hixon, J. G., 67, *79*, 121, 132, 133, 134, *135*, 305, *321*, 378, *389*
Ho, H. K.,406, *414*
Hochstrasser, M., 66, *80*
Hoelter, J. W., 354, *366*
Hoffman, C., 7, 70, *79*, *453*
Hoffman, S., *321*
Hogg, Michael A., 4, 75, 77, 173, *188, 189*, 395, *415*, 436, *450, 453*
Hoiberg, A., 353, *367*
Holland, P. W., 146, *159*
Holton, B., *415*
Holtz, R., 407, *415*, 436, *450*
Holyoak, K. J., 108, *116*
Hong, G., *415*
Hood, W. R., 435, *450*
Hoover, D. W., 236, *248*
Horne, J. A., 255, *258*
Hornstein, H. A., 436, *450*
Horowitz, D., 408, *415*
Horowitz, L. M., 266, 267, *283*
Horwitz, M., 55, *62*
Hottes, J., 247, *248*
Hough, J. C., *303*
Hovland, C. I., 76, *79*, *258*
Howard, J. W., 4, 57, *62*, 191, 193, 206, *208*, 254, *258*, *453*
Howard-Pitney, B., 341, *351*
Howland, C. I., 113, *117*
Hoyle, R. H., *415*

Hoyt, M. E., 76, *79*
Hoyt, M. F., 327, *337*
Hsu, F. L. K., 100, 102, *116*
Hubbard, M. L., 65, *78*
Humphrey, G., *47*
Humphrey, N. D., *47*
Humphreys, L. G., 370, *389*
Hunter, B. A., 84, *456*
Hurst, N., 7, 70, *79*, *453*
Husband, C., 69, 75, *79*
Hymes, C., 129, *134*

I

Ickes, W., 236, *248*
Imbert, L., 66, *80*
Ingerman, C., 173, *189*
Innes, J. M., 122, *134*
Insko, C. A., 10, 187, *190*, 400, *415*, 455–456
Isaacs, Susan, 36, *47*
Islam, M. R., 187, *189*, 402, 406, 407, *415*
Iyengar, S., 108, 113, *116*

J

Jacklin, C. N., 354, *367*
Jackman, M. R., 100, *116*
Jackson, D. N., 262, 263–264, 265, 266–267, *283*
Jackson, J. R., 121, *135*, *452*
Jackson, L. A., 404, *415*
Jackson, S. E., 1, 9, *453*
Jacobs, J., 71, *79*, 172, *189*
Jacobson, C. K., 123, *135*
Jacobson, L., 14, 172, *190*, 212, *225*, *455*
Jaggi, V., 4, 60, *63*, 193, *208*, *456*
Jago, A. G., 341, *351*
Jahoda, M., 24, *47*, 52, *63*
Jamieson, D. W., 88, 98, *98*
Janis, I. L., *367*
Jarvie, G. J., 235 *248*
Jaspars, J., 60, *62*, 193, 205, *208*
Jensen, A. R., *389*
Jensen, C., 57, *62*, 254, *258*
Jetten, J., 4, 13, 98, *99*, *453*
John, Oliver P., 16, 71, *81*, 205, *208*, 263, 267, *283*, 392, 397, 402, 403, 404, 411, *416*, 422, *433*, *455*
Johnson, B. T., *452*
Johnson, C., 11, 69, 71, *80*, 298, *303*, *454*
Johnson, D. M., 49, *62*
Johnson, D. W., 398, 399, *417*, 435, 437, 438, 449, *450*
Johnson, R. T., 398, 399, *415*, *417*, 435, 438, *450*
Johnston, L., 13, 15, 65, *79–80*, 403, 404, *415*, *453*
Jonas, K., 67, 74, *78*
Jones, C. R., 108, *116*, 129, *135*
Jones, E. E., 154, *160*, *171*, 204, *208*, 213, 222, *225*, 227, *233*, 247, *248*, 327, 328, 330, 336, *337*, 341, *351*, 354, 356, 364, *367*
Jones, E. G., *62*
Jones, F. C., *116*
Jones, J. L., 258, *258*
Jones, J. M., 1, *98*, *98*, 100, *116*, 291, *303, 453*
Jones, R. A., 167, *171*
Jones, R. E., 227, 231, *233*

Jost, J. T., 73, *80*
Judice, T. N., 236, *249*
Judd, C. M., , 7, 9, 12, 67, 77, *80*, 121, *136*, 396, *415*, *416*, 438, 448, *450*, *453*, *454*, *455*, *456*
Jussim, L., , 4, 7, 14, 15, 65, 70, *80*, *453*, *454*

K

Kaczor, L., *249*
Kahn, A., 247, *248*, 340, *351*
Kahn, J., 237, *248*
Kahnemann, D., 57, *63*, 108, *117*, 222, 223, 225, 255, 256, *258*
Kalin, R., 402, *413*
Kanter, R. M., 5, 143, *160*, 327, *337*, 340, 340, 341, *351*, 353, 354, *367*, *454*
Kantor, M., *282*
Kardes, F. R., 120, *135*
Karlins, M., 8, 87, 88, 89, 90, 92, 93, 95, *98*, 213, *225*, 291, *303*, *367*, *454*
Karuza, J. Jr., *116*
Kassim, S. M., 95, *98*, 348, *351*
Katkin, E. S., 161, *171*
Katz, B., 11, 54, *62*, *455*
Katz, D., 7, 8, 65, 72, 77, *80*, 86, 87–90, 91t, 92–93, 93t, 95–97, *98*, 102, *116*, 123, *135*, 158, *160*,
Katz, D., 320, *321*, 420, *433*, *454*
Katz, Irwin, 8, 84, 101, 115, *116*, 267, 274, *283*, 289, 290, *303*, 353, 355, 356, *366*, *367*, 371, *389*, *454*
Katz, P. A., 72, *80*
Kayne, N. T., 355, *366*
Keiper, S., *454*
Kelley, H. H., 212, *225*, 354, 355, *367*
Kelly, George A., 53, *62*
Kelly, H. H., 73, *80*
Kelly, J. R., 258, *258*
Kendrick, S. A., 370, *389*
Kennedy, W. A., 221, *225*
Kenny, D. A., 184, *188*, 395, *413*, 438, 448, *449*, *450*
Kentle, R. L., 267, *283*
Keppel, G., *189*
Kerlinger, F. N., 102, *116*
Kernis, M. H., *249*
Kidder, L., *116*, 340, *350*, 404, *414*
Kiernan, V. G., 59, *62*
Kiesler, S. B., *350*
Kiesler, S. D., 157n.12, *160*, 340, 341, *352*
Kinder, D. R., 90, *99*, 108, *116*
King, G., 71, *79*, 98, *98*, 120, 122, *135*, 427, 428, *433*
Kirby, D. M., 65, 72, *79*
Kirkland, S., *79*
Kitayama, S., 172, *189–190*, 278, *283*
Kite, M., 180, *189*, 340, 346, *350*
Klatzky, R., 120, *134*
Kleck, G., 262, *283*
Kleck, R. E., 1, 227, 230, 231, 233, *233*, 234, *248*, 355, *367*, *454*
Kleck, R. L., , 356, *367*
Klein, W. M., 173, 187, *189*
Klinger, M., 88, 96, 98, *98*, 129, *135*, 321, *321*
Klonsky, B. G., 78,340, *350*
Kluckhohn, C., 58, *62*
Klugel, J R., 261, 262, *283*

Komorita, S. S., 10, 68, *78*, *452*
Kosterman, R., 261, 264, *283*
Kovel, J., 289, *303*
Kramer, B. M., 428, *433*
Kramer, R. M., 173, 187, *188*, 191, 193, *207*
Krauss, R. M., 49, 60, *62*
Kravitz, J., 329, *337*
Kristal, J., 341, *351*
Krosnick, J. A., 108, *116*
Kruglanski, A. W., 73, 74, *80*, 88, 98, *98*, 341, *351*, 412, *415*
Kumar, P. A., 57, *62*, 191, *208*
Kunda, Z., 6, 173, 187, *189*, 320, *322*, *454*
Kutner, B., 43, *47*, 79, 290, *303*

L

LaFarge, J., *47*
Lahey, B., 235, *248*
Lake, R. A., 302, *302*
Lalonde, R. N., 97, *98*, 172, *189*
Landry, P., *415*
Lange, J., 5, 6, 65, 70, 71, 72, *81*, 120, 121, 122, 126, 133, *136*, *455*
Langer, E. J., 66, *80*, 212, *225*
Langlois, J. H., 235, *249*
La Piere, R. T., 42–43, *47*, 252, *454*
Larsen, K., *302*, 309, *321*
Latane, B., 6–7, 297, *302*, *455*
La Violette, F., 76, *80*
Leary, M., 4, *451*
Lee, A. M., *47*
Lee, G. K., 340, *352*
Lee, I. Y., 406, *414*
Lee, Y., 4, *453*
Leinbach, M. D., 68, *78*
Leitner, D. W., 282, *283*
Lemyre, L., 13, 206, *208*, *454*
Lennox, V. L., 302, *303*
Lent, R. H., 53, *62*
Lepore, Lorella, 12, 84, *454*
Lepper, M. E., 214, *225*
Lepper, M. R., 71, *414*
Lerner, M., 120, *136*
Lerner, M. J., 74, *80*
Lerner, R. M., 234, *249*
Lerman, D., 355, *367*, *368*
Lesser, G. S., 221, 225
Levin, S., 281, 282, *283*
Levine, J. M., 77, *80*, *81*
Levinson, D. G., 263, *282*
Levinson, D. J., 279, *283*
Lewicki, P., 67, *80*
Lewin, Kurt, 34, 36, *47*, 400, 412, *415*
Lewin, T., 340, *351*
Lewis, L. L., 120, *134*, 151n.7, 157n.12, *160*, 340, 341, *350*, 402, *414*
Lewis, P., 235, 237, 238, *248*
Lewis, S., 70, *81*, 191, 193, *208*, 404, *416*
Liben, L. S., 10, 14, 227, *233*, *454*
Liberman, A., 254, *258*
Lichtenstein, M., 11, 71, *78*, 191, *208*, 254, 257, *258*, *451*
Liebert, R. M., 291, *303*
Lilli, W., 51, *62*, 407, *416*

Linch, L., 125, *136*
Linn, R. L., 370, *389*
Linville, P. W., 12, 67, 72, 67, 72, *79*, *80*, 191, *208*, 327, *337*, 341, *351*, 356, 364, *367*, *454*
Lippit, R., 36, *47*
Lippman, Walter, 6, 64, *80*, 158, *160*, 423, *433*
Lipset, 100, 102, *116*, 278, *283*
Liu, J., 262, 282, *284*
Liu, T. J., 129, 173, 174, 177, 185, *189, 190*
Lloyd, B. B., 49, 60, *62*, 68, *78*
Lobato, D., 11, *454*
Lobel, M., 173, 186, *190*
Locke, V., 121, 122, 132, 133, *135*
Lockhart, R. S., 57, *61*
Locksley, A., 66, *80*, 157, *160*, 213, 222, 223, *225,* 340, 341, *351*, 400, *415*, 426, 429, *433*
Lockwood, J., 60, 61
Loevinger, J., 264, *283*
Loftus, E. E., 67, 71, *78*, 120, *134*, 348, *351*
Logan, G. D., 307, 312, *322*
Lohman, J. D., *47*
Lombardi, W., 121, 126, *134*, *135*
London, R. S., *233*
Loomis, J., 69, *82*
Lopez, D. E., 173, *189*
Lord, C. G., 71, *80*, 214, *225*, 371, 387, *389*, 404, *414*, *417*
Lott, A. J., 66, *80*, *450*
Lott, B. E., *450*
Lowe, C. A. 214, *225*
Loye, D., 261, 274, *283*
Lubin, B., *368*
Luckman, T., 59, *61*
Luhtanen, R., 75, 76, *78*, *80*, 281, 282, *282*
Lui, L., 1, *135*, 158, *159*, 403, *414*, *451*
Lundberg, A., 27, *47*
Lynch, C., 3, 71, *81*
Lynch, L., *455*
Lynch, M., 173, *190*
Lyon, D., *79*, *189*

M

Maass, Anne, 14, 69, *80*, 140, 206, *207*, 409, *454*
Maccoby, E. F., 354, *367*
MacDonald, A. P., 102, *116*
Mackie, D. M., 10, 52, 70, 71, 75, *80*, 187, *189*, 407, *415*, *454*
MacLeod, C. 121, *135*
Macrae, C. N., 4, 13, 15, 65, 74, *78*, *79*, 98, *99*, 132, *135*, 187, *188*, 252, 399, 404, *415*, *451*, *453*, *454*
MacRae, R. R., 263, *282*
Madon, S., 4, *454*
Magnusson, J., 234, *249*
Mahajan, H., 261, *284*
Major, Brenda, 1, 7, 72, *78*, 234, 235, 236, 237, 246, 247, *248, 249, 324*, 354, 355, 365, *366, 367*, 387–388, *452*
Makhijani, M. G., *78*, 340, *350*
Malcarne, V. L., 11, *454*
Malle, Bertram F., 252, 266, 267, *283*
Malpass, R. S., 327, *337*
Manis, M., 151, *160*
Mann, J., 436, *450*

Mann, J. A., 409, *415*
Mann, Jeffrey F., 60, *62*, 392
Manstead, A. S. R., 4, *453*
Maquet, J. J., *415*
Marchand, B., 51, *62*
Maracek, J., 340, *350*, 404, *414*
Marcus-Newhall, A., 407, 408, 411, *415*
Markus, H., 65, 66, 71, *80*, 172, *189*, 248, 320, 322, 340, *351*
Markus, H. R., 172, *189–190*, 278, *283*
Marlowe, D., 76, *78*
Martell, R. F., 340, 341, *351*
Martin, C. L., 10, 14, 77, *80*, *454*, 455
Martin, J., 340, *352*, 412, *416*
Martin, M., 259, 268, 282, *284*
Maruyama, G., 341, *352*, 399, *417*, 435, *450*
Mason, J. K., *414*
Mason, K. O., 157, *160*
Mason, P. *415*
Massing, P. E., 43, *47*
Matthews, M., 294, *303*
Maurer, K. L., 403, 412, *415*
Mavin, G. H., 427, *433*
Mayo, C., 262, *283*
Mazelan, P. M., 74, *80*
McArthur, L. Z., 5, 66, *80*, 340, *351, 454*
McCann, C. D., 429, *433*
McCauley, C., 7, 74, 77, *80*, 97, *99*, *454*
McCauley, R., 4, *453*
McClelland, J. L., 120, 132, *136*
McClendon, M. J., 396, *415*
McClintock, C., 420, *433*
McCloskey, M., 348, *351*
McConahay, J. B., 8, 84, 88, 90, *99*, 100, 115, *116*, 123, *135*, 205, *208*, 261, 267, *283*, 289, 292, *303*, 307, *322*, *454*
McCoy, S. B., 173, *189*
McDougall, W., 65, *80*
McFarland, C., 355, 363, *367*
McGarty, C., 172, *189*, *453*
McGarth, D., 143, *160*
McGarth, J. E., 258, *258*
McGivern, E., 399, 408, 410, *415*, *416–417*
McGraw, K. M., 173, *189*, 340, *350*
McHugh, M. C., 341, *350*
McIver, J. D., 267, *282*
McLaughlin, J. P., 10, 97, 121, *135*, 300, 301, *303*, *453*
McManus, J. A., 1, *455*
McMillan, D., 65, 66, 67, *81*
McPartland, J. M., *366*, 405, *413*
Mead, G. H., 172, *190*, 354, *367*
Mead, M., 290, *303*
Medin, D. L., 424, *433*
Meertens, R. W., 123, *136*
Mehrabian, A., 177, *190*, 226, 227, 229, 231, 232, *233*
Mennerick, L. A., 143, *160*
Merton, Robert, 14, 226, *233*, 354, *367*, *454*
Mervis, C. B., 49, 50, 56, *62*
Messick, D. M., 407, *415*
Mezei, L., 290, *303*
Meyer, D., 108, *116*, 300, *303*
Michela, J., 365, *367*
Midkiff, K., 255, *258*
Miene, P., 73, *81*, 133, *136*, 187, *190*

Migdal, H., 408, *415*
Milgram, S., 74, *80*
Milich, R., 236, *248*
Millberg, S. J., 341, *350*
Miller, Carol T., 11, 15, 210, 234, 235, 236, 237, 238, 246, 247, *249*, 354, *367*, *454*
Miller, D. T., 14, 74, 234, 236, *248*, *249*, *454*
Miller, K., *171*, *248*
Miller, N., 15, 16, 395–396, 397, 398–399, 400, 401, 402, 405, 406, 407, 408, 410, *413*, *414–415*, *416*, 428, 431, *433*, 435, 436, 446, *449–450*, *451*, *454*
Miller, N. E., 173, *189, 190*
Miller, S. K., 221, *225*
Mills, C. J., 67, *80*
Mills, D. L., 262, *282*
Milne, A. B., 98, *99*, 133, *135*, 253, 404, *415*, *454*
Mirels, H., 102, 105, 107, *116*, 265, *283*
Mischel, W., 11, 49, 55, 57, *61*, 158, *160*, 214, *225*, *451*
Mitchell, M., 262, 281, *283*, 284
Mizrahi, K., *452*
Mladinic, A., 1, 9, *452*
Monahan, J., 348, *351*
Monteith, Marso J., 8, 10, 12, 91, 96, 87, 98, *98*, *99*, *134–135*, 174, 187, *189*, *190*, 253, 305, 306
Monteith, Marson J., 319, 321, *321*, *322*, *454*
Moreno, J. L., *47*
Morrow, A., 36, *47*
Moscovia, S., *62*
Moscovici, S., 49, 51, 55, 60, 65, 68, *78*, *80*, 327, *337*
Mosk, R. M., *282*
Mossop, M. R., 58, *61*
Mowrer, O. H., 173, *189*
Moynihan, D. P., 261, *283*
Mugny, G., 337, *337*
Mullen, B., 11, 69, *80*, 340, *351*, 408, *415*, *454*
Mummendy, A., 395, 400, *415*, *416*
Murray, A. H., *47*
Murrell, Audrey J., 392, 409, *415*, 436, *450*
Myers, D. G., 341, *352*
Myrdal, Gunnar, 42, *47*, 74, *80*, 291, *303*, 307, *322*

N
Neely, J. H., 120, 121, 129, *135*
Nelson, C., 11, 163, *171*, *453*
Nelvill, D. D., *284*
Nero, A. M., 97, *98*
Nettles, M. T., 370, *389*
Neuberg, S. L., 3, 15, 70, 73, 74, *79*, *80*, 120, *135*, *190*, 236, *249*, 252, 254, *258*, 340, 341, *350*, 436, *450*, *452*, *454*
Newcomb, T. M., 397, *415*, *416*, 420, *433*
Newsom, J. T., 74, *80*, 252, *454*
Nicholls, J. G., 341, *351*
Nickerson, S., 262, *283*
Nieva V. F., 340, 341, *351*
Nisbett, R. E., 172, *189*, 214, 220 *225*, 227, *233*, 340, *351*
Noble, A., *171*
Noblit, G. W., 402, *414*, *416*
Noe, A. W., *352*
Nolan, M., *453*
Noseworthy, C. M., 66, *80*
Nuessle, W., 227, 231, *233*

O
Oakes, P. J., 4, 5, 6, 13, 71, 74, 77, *80*, 172, *190*, 405, *416*, 436, *450*, *453*, *454*
O'Boyle, C., 68
O'Brien, M., 65, 66, 70, *81*
Oetjen, H. A., 237, *249*
O'Leary, V. E., 341, *351*, 353, *367*
Olian, J. D., 341, *352*
Omoto, A. M., 341, *351*
Ono, H., 1, 227, *233*, *454*
Ordin, A. S., *282*
Ortiz, V., 157, *160*, 222, *225*, 400, *415*, 426, *433*
Osgood, C. E., 51, *62*
Östberg, O., 255, *258*
Ostell, A., *302*
Ostrom, T. M., 12, 323, *454*

P
Pack, S. J., 14, *456*
Page, R., 9, 84, 97, *99*, 291, *303*, *455*
Paicheler, G., 327, *337*
Palmore, E. B., 69, *80*
Palumbo, P., *454*
Park, B., 7, 9, 12, 66, 67, 77, *80*, 92, 93, *99*, 121, *136*, *160*, 193, 205, *208*, 327, 336, *337*, 396, 403, 412, *415*, *416*, 420–421, 422, 427, 429, *433*, *453*, *454*, *455*, *456*
Parsons, T., 102, *116*, 143, *160*
Pasaderos, Y., 69, *80*
Pascale, L., 340, *350*, 404, *414*
Paternoster, R., *283*
Pátkai, P., 255, 262, *258*
Patterson, J. R., *284*
Patterson, M. L., 236, *248*
Pavelchak, M. A., 66, *79*
Pazy, A., 341, *352*
Pence, F. C., 341, *352*
Pendleton, W. C., 341, *352*
Pepels, J., 4, *456*
Peplau, L. A., 106, *116*, 265, *284*
Perdue, C. W., 6, 10, 121, 409, *416*, *455*
Perri, M., *249*
Perry, R. P., 234, *249*
Peters, M. D., 108, *116*
Peterson, C. R., 431, *433*
Petterson, B. E., 75, *78*, *135*, 272, *283*
Pettigrew, T., 53, *62*, 70, 75, *80–81*, 123, *136*, 140, 193, *208*, 246, *249*, 340, *352*, 394, 396, 397, 404, 405, 408, 412, 413, *416*, 446, *450*, *455*
Petty, M. M., 340, *352*
Petty, R. E., 254, *258*
Pfeiffer, J. R., *233*
Pheterson, G. I., 340, 341, *352*
Pipkin, R. M., 340, *352*
Philo, N. 327, *337*
Piaget, Jean, 38, *47*, 52, *62*, 423, *433*
Pichert, J. W., 108, *116*
Pierce, G. L., 262, *283*
Pietromanoco, P., 121, 125, 126, 130, *134*, 427, 433
Piliavin, J. A., 293, *303*
Pinel, E., 5, *189*, *455*
Pinkley, R. L., *415*
Plaks, J. E., 140, *456*

Polivy, J., 182, *189*
Pomare, Marina, 392, 409, *415*
Porter, J. R., 14, 354, *367, 451*
Posner, M. I., 120, 121, 122, *136*, 424, *433*
Post, D., 340, *351*
Post, D. L., 66, *80*
Postman, L. 46–47
Potter, M. C., 50, *61*
Powell, M. C., 120, *135*
Pratkanis, A. R., 88, *99*
Pratto, Felicia, 120, 129, *134, 136*, 252, 259, 261, 262, 268, 278, 279, 281, 282, *283, 284*
Prentice, D. A., 320, *321*
Presser, S., 108, *116*
Pressly, S. L., 321, *322*
Price, K. H., 341, *351*
Proshansky, H., 73, *79*, 290, *303*
Pryor, J. B., 1, 125, *134, 455*
Pugliese, C., 205, *208*
Pyszczynski, T., 69, 75, *79, 81, 189*, 386, *389*

Q

Quattrone, G. A., 213, 222, *225*, 327, 328, *337*

R

Rabbie, J. M., 55, *62*
Rabinowitz, J., 281, *284*
Rabinowitz, V. C., *116*
Radelet, M. L., 262, *283*
Rajecki, D. W., 236, *248*
Ramsey, S. L., *414*
Rasinski, K. A., 340, 341, *352*
Ray, J., 279, *283*
Raymond, P., 125, 129, *134*
Reagan, D. T., 214, *225*
Reeder, G. D., 1, *455*
Rehm, I., 407, *416*
Reicher, S., *81, 136*, 436, *450*
Reid, A., *452*
Rieder, J., 115, *116*
Reiman, J., 262, *283*
Reis, H. T., 237, 246, 248, *249*
Reilly, C., 255, *258*
Remple, J. K., 88, *99*
Repucci, N. D., *352*
Resnick, L. B., 77, *80, 81*
Renwick, P. A., 341, *352*
Reynolds, K. J., 6, *453*
Rholes, W. S., 108, *116*, 129, *135*
Riger, S., 353, *367*
Riordan, C., 396, *416*
Rist, R. C., 213, *225*, 399, *416*
Robbins, M. A., *249*
Roberts, S. O., 371, *389*
Robinson, J. M., 371, *389*
Rodin, J., 234, *249*
Rodrigues, J. S., 52, 61
Roesch, R., 348, *352*
Rogers, M., 407, *416*
Rogers-Croak, M., 398, *413*
Rokeach, M., 102, 115, *116*, 290, *303*, 307, 320, 321, *322*, 397, *416*

Rombough, S., 261, 266, 267, 280, *283*
Rorer, L. G., 161, *171*
Rosch, E., 49, 50, 55, 60, *62*, 120, *136*, 300, *303*, 426, 429, *433*
Rose, A., *47*
Rose, T. L., 65, *79, 416*
Rosenbaum, M. E., 436, *450*
Rosenberg, M., 265, *284*, 354, *367*
Rosenberg, S., 56, *62*, 163, *171,*
Rosenblatt, A., *79, 189*
Rosenfeld, H. M., 227, 232, *233*
Rosenhan, D. L., 213, *225*
Rosenkrantz, P. S., 143, *159*, 353, *366, 367*
Rosenthal, R., 14, 172, *190*, 212, *225, 284, 455*
Rosnow, R. L., *190*
Ross, L., 4, 173, *190*, 214, 220, *225* 340, *351*, 422, 431, *433, 451*
Ross, M., 173, *190*, 355, *367*
Rosselli, F., 10, 70, *454*
Rothbart, Myron, 4, 12, 13, 16, 57–58, *62*, 65, 70, 71, *81*, 92, 93, *99, 160*, 191, 193, 205, 206, *208*, 254, *258*, 327, 336, *337*, 392, 397, 402, 403, 404, 411, 412, *415, 416*, 420–421, 422, 427, 429, 431, *433 , 451*, 453, 455
Rothblum, Esther D., 15, 234, 235, 237, 246, 249, *454*
Rothgerber, H., 15, *456*
Rothman, A. J., 120, *134*
Rousell, C., 340, *352*
Royle, M. H., 423, *433*
Rubin, M., 13, *455*
Rubin, Z., 106, *116*, 265, *284*
Ruble, D. N., 10, 14, 341, *352, 455*
Ruble, T. L., 341, *352*
Ruderman, A. J., 2, 57, *63*, 340, *352, 456*
Ruderman, M. N., 1, *453*
Ruffin, P. F., *415*
Rumelhart, D. E., 120, 133, *136*
Ruscher, J. B., 6, 7, *455*
Russ, R. C., *284*
Russell, D., 355, *367, 368*
Russell, J., 177, *190*
Rust, M. C., 15, 405, 409, *414–415, 453*
Ruvolo, C. M., 120, *135*
Ryan, C. S., 7, 12, 396, *416, 453, 455*
Ryan, R., 233, *233*
Ryan, W., 74, *81*, 291, *303*
Ryckman, R. M., 234, *249*
Ryen, A., 437, *450*

S

Sabatino, D., 213, *225*
Sachdev, I., 76, *81*, 327, 328, *337*
Sackett, P. R., *352*
Saenger, G., 42, *47*, 69, *81*
Saenz, D. S., 371, 387, *389*
Sagar, H. A., 11, 13–14, 191, 200, *208*, 397, 405, *416, 417, 455*
Saharason, S., 399, *416*
Saint-Jacques, B., 69, *79*
Sakalli, N., 69, *78*
Salovey, Peter, 12, 67, *80*, 191, *208, 454*
Salvi, Daniela, 140, *454*
Samaha, C., 436, *450*

Sammuelson, B., *47*
Samuels, F., 353, *367*
Sanbonmatsu, D. M., 120, *135*
Sanders, D., 341, *351*
Sanford, R. N., 263, *282*
Sapir, E., 76, *81*
Sarason, I. G., 371, 373, 386, *389*
Sarnoff, I., 420, *433*
Sattler, J. 233, *233*
Saul, B., 236, *248*
Saxe, L., 10, 97, *98*, 101, *116*, 205, *207*, 289, *302*, 353, *366*, *367*, *452*
Scanzoni, J., 143, *160*
Schacter, D. L., 378, *389*
Schaller, Marc, 6–7, 65, 66, 70, *81*, *455*
Schank, R. C., 60, *62*, 66, *81*
Scheier, M. F., 267, *283*, 355, *367*, 386, *389*
Schein, V. E., 340, *352*
Schiffhauer, K., L., 69, *78*
Schlenker, R. B, 173, *190*
Schmidt, C., 213, *225*
Schmidt, G. W., 75, *78*, 173, *189*
Schneider, W., 100, 102, *116*, 120
Schofield, J. W., 11, 13–14, 191, 200, *208*, 391–392, 395, 397, 399, 400, 402, 405, 408, 410, *416–417*, *455*
Schopler, J., 294, *303*
Schreiber, J-H., 395, 400, *416*
Schuh, E. S., 12, *453*
Schull, W. H., *249*
Schuman, H., 96, 98, *99*, 100, 101, 102, 105, 108, *116*, *303*
Schvaneveldt, R., 108, *116*, 300, *303*
Schwab, D. P., 341, *352*
Schwabe, M. L., 354, *366*, *367*
Schwartz, I., 75, *78*, *451*
Schwarz, N., 6
Schweitzer, S., 436, *450*
Scott, R. A., *248*
Scott, W. A., 124, *136*
Sears, D. O., 90, *99*, 100, 115, *116–117*, 261, *284*, 289, *303*
Sears, R., 76, *79*
Sears, R. R., 173, *189*
Secord, P. F., 11, *62*, *455*
Sedikides, C., 12, 323, *454*
Sedlacek, W. E., 282, *283*
Sedlak, A., 56, *62*
Segal, M., 74, *80*
Sekaquaptewa, D., 14, 120, *136*, *456*
Seligman, M. E. P., 355, *366*, *367*
Selltiz, C., 36
Semin, Gün, 140, 192, 193, 195, 196, 197, 200, 201, 204, 106, 207, *207*, *208*, *454*
Seta, J. J., 371, *389*
Severson, A. L., 42, *47*
Sgro, J. A. 341, *352*
Shapiro, P. A., 402, *418*
Shapiro, R. Y., 261, *284*
Sharan, S., 398, *417*
Shaw, J., 262, 282, *284*
Sheatsley, P. S., 100, 101, 102, 289, *303*
Sherif, C. W., 34, 35, *47*, 409, *417*, 435, 436, 499, *450*
Sherif, M., 34, 35, *47*, *81*, 113, *117*, 408–409, 410, *417, 435, 436, 437, 448, 449, 450*
Sherman, J. W., 5, 65, 70, *79, 135*, 404, *415*, *453*

Sherman, M., *452*
Sherman, R. C., 237, 247, *249*
Sherman, S. J., 11 88, *99* 120, 121, *135*, 431, *433, 453*
Shiffrin, R. M., 120
Shulsinger, F., *249*
Sicoly, F., 173, *190*
Sidali, M., 66, *80*
Sidanius, Jim, 252, 259, 261, 262, 264, 268, 278, 279, 281, 282, *283*, *284*
Signorella, M. L., 10, 14, *454*
Sigall, H., 9, 84, 97, *99*, 291, *303*, 355, 365, *367, 455*
Sikes, J., 392, 398, *413*, 435, *449, 451*
Silberstein, L., 234, *249*
Silvert, K. H., 76, *80*
Simard, L., 400, *417*
Simmons, R. G., 354, *367*
Simon, Bernd, 12, 324, 330, *337, 455*
Simon, J. G., 341, *350*
Simon, L., *189*
Simon, M. C., 340, *351*
Singer, R., 436, *450*
Skrypenk, B. J., 236, *249*
Slaughter, J. B., *282*
Slavin, R. E., 398, 405, 410, *414, 417*, 435, 437, 449, *450*
Slim, K., *415*
Sloane, L. R., *78*
Smedley, J. W., 142, *160*
Smith, A., *283, 454*
Smith, C. S., 255, *258*
Smith, E. E., 424, *433, 455*
Smith, E. R., 6, 67, *81*, 120, 122, 125, *136*, 173, *190*, 408, *417*
Smith, M. B., 102, *117*, 290, *303*, 320, *322*
Smith, P. M., (1985), 13, 206, *208*, 261, 262, *283, 454*
Smith, T. W., 100, 101, *117*
Smith, V. L., 348, *351*
Snapp, M., 392, 398, *413*, 435, *449, 451*
Sniderman, P. M., 261, *284*
Snyder, C. R. R., 121, 122, *136, 367*
Snyder, M., 14, 53, *62*, 65, 73, *81*, 133, *136*, 172, 187, *190*, 191, *208*, 212, 214, 220, 223, *225*, 236, *249*, 267, *284*, *455*
Soja, M., 69, *82*
Solernou, J., *171*
Solomon, S., 75, *79, 81, 189*
Sorenson, T. I. A., *249*
Spangler, E., 340, *352*
Sprafkin, J. N., 291, *303*
Spears, R., 4, *453*
Spence, J. T., 70, *81*, 143, *160*, 263, 266, *284*, 341, *351*
Spencer, Steven J., , 4, 13, 70, 71, *81*, 140, 173, 174, 180, *189, 190*, 388, *389, 452*
Spiegel, W., *249*
Spoerl, D. T., 35, *47*
Srull, T. K., 67, *81*, 121, 125, 126, *136*, 191, *208*, 412, *417*, 427, *433, 434*
Stacey, B. G., 278, *284*
Stallworth, Lisa M., 252, 259, *259*, 261, 268, 282, *283*, *284*
Stallybrass, O., 57, *62*
Stangor, Charles, 1, 3, 5, 6–7, 9, 11, 12, 14, 65, 66, 67, 70, 71, 72, 73, 74, 77, *79, 80, 81*, 120, 121, 122, 125, 126, 133, *135*, *136*, 209, 452–453, *455*
Stanley, J. C., *389*
Stapp, J., 70, *81*, 263, *284*
Stark, H. A., 378, *389*

Starr, B. J., 161, *171*
Starr, S. A., 69, *81*
Steeh, C., 96, *99*, 100, *116*
Steele, Claude M., 1, 7, 70, 71, 75, *81*, 173, 174, 177, 185, 186, *189*, *190*, 235, *249*, 324, 370, 388, *389*, *452*, *455*
Steele, S., 370, *389*
Steffen, Valerie, 7, 139, *452*
Stein, D. D., 290, *303*
Stein, K. F., *190*
Stein, S., 237, 246, *248*
Stein-Seroussi, A., 172, *190*
Stephan, C. W., 15–16, 68, 72, *81*, 120, 122, 129, 132, *136*, 235, *249*, 323, 392, 398, 400, 402, *413*, *417*, 435, 436, *449–450*, *451*, *455*
Stephan, W. G., 15, *62*, 68, 72, *81*, 120, 122, 129, 132, *136*, *303, 323*, 327, *337*, 394, 396–397, 400, 402, 407, *417*, 436, *450, 455*
Stephanson, G. M., 400, *417*
Sternberg, R. J., 464, *466*
Stetler, H. G., 42, *47*
Stinton, J., 69, *81*
Stitt, C. L., 7, 74, 77, *80*, 97, *99, 454*
St. John, N. H., 385, *417*
Stoll, J., *171*
Stone, W. F., 279, *284*
Stopeck, M. H., 341, *351*
Stouffer, S. A., 69, *48, 81*
Strachey, C., 33, *48*
Strack, F., 125, *134*
Strauss, E., 214, *225*
Strenta, A., 355, *367*
Striegel-Moore, E., 234, *249*
Stroebe, W., 10, 52, *61*, 187, *190, 455–456*
Stroessner, S. J., 65, *79*, 140, *456*
Strong, D., 42, *48*
Stuckey, R., *367*
Stunkard, A. J., 234, *249*
Suchman, E. A., 69, *81*
Suci, C. J., 51, *62*
Sumner, G. A., 59, *62*
Super, D. E., *284*
Susskind, J., 10, *454*
Swann, W. B., 15, *62*, 172, 174, *189*, *190*, 191, *208*, 212, 214, 223, *225*, 235–236, *249*, 320, *322*, *456*
Swim, J., 84, *456*
Swim, J. K., 7, *456*
Swim, J. T., 1, 341, *352*, *456*

T

Tajfel, Henri, , 4, 12, 13, 50, 51, 52, 53, 54, 55, 59, 60, *62–63*, 65, 68, 71, 73, 74, *81*, 131, *136*, *160*, 162, *171*, 173, *190*, 191, 193, *208*, 281, *284*, 290, *302*, *303*, 326, 327, 328, 329, *337*, 339, 340, *352*, 354, *367*, 394, 395, 399, 400, 405, 406, 408, 410, 413, *417*, 428, *434*, 436, 437, *450, 456*
Tannenbaum, P. H., 51, *62*
Tannenbaum, S., 301, *302*
Tanford, S., 236, *248*
Tanke, E. D., 212, *225*, 236, *249*
Taylor, D. G., *303*
Taylor, D. M., (1974) , 4, 57, 60, *62, 63*, 193, *208*, 400, 402, 403, *413*, *417*, *456*
Taylor, K. L., 173, 186, *190*

Taylor, L. A., 75, *79*
Taylor, M. C., 15, *456*
Taylor, Shelley E., 2, 3, 5, 6, 57, *63*, 65, 66, *79*, *81*, 132, *135*, 143, 158, *160*, 173, 186, *190*, 329, *337*, 339, 340, 341, 347, *350*, *352*, 354, *367, 417*, 428, 430, *434*, *456*
Taynor, J., *160*
Teahan, J. E., 282, *284*
Teasdale, T. W., *249*
Teasley, S. D., 77, *81*
Tennen, H., 355, *367*
Terborg, J. R., 341, 347, *352*
Tesser, A., 75, *81*, 173, 174, 185, 186, *190*
Testa, Maria, 72, *78*, 236, *248*, 324, *367*, 387, *389*
Tetlock, P. E., 174, *190*, 261, *284*, 341, *352*
Thagard, P., 6, *454*
Tice, D. M., 237, *248*
Tiggemann, M., 237, *249*
Thibaut, J. W., 354, *367*, *415*
Thomas, K., 58, 59, *63*, 74, *81*
Thompson, E., 13, 69, *78*, *456*
Thompson, J. E., 410, *418*
Thompson, J. G., 409, *418*
Thompson, L. J., 173, *189*
Thorne, A., *78*
Thorton, B., *249*
Toppino, T., 420, *433*
Tosi, H. L., 340, 341, *352*
Tote, M. E., 126, *134*
Trabasso, T., 108, *117*
Transquada, R. E., *282*
Treiman, D. J., 353, 354, *367*
Triandis, H., 142, *160*, 172, *190*, 397, *417*
Trolier, T. K., 11, 187, *189*, 191, 193, *208*, *453*
Trope, Y., 13, *456*
Tucker, R. D., 290, *304*
Tulving, E., 378, *389*
Turnbull, W., 14, 234, 236, *249, 354, 367, 454*
Turner, J. C., 4, 5, 6, 13, *63*, 71, 72, 73, 74, 75, 76, 77, *80*, 82, 172, 173, *190*, 193, *208*, 280, 281, *284*, 290, 303, 327, 337, *337, 354, 367*, 399, 400, 405, 406, 407, 408, 410, *414, 416, 417*, 432, *433*, 436, 446–448, *449, 450, 453, 454, 456*
Turner, T. J., 49, 52, 55, 59, 60, 191, *208*
Tversky, A., 57, *63*, 108, *117*, 222, 223, *225*, 255, 256, *258*
Tweedie, J., *453*
Tykocinski, O., 172–173, *189*
Tyler, K. B., 409, *416*
Tyler, R. B., 6, 67, *78*, 87, 98, *116*, 121, 122, *135*, 300, *302*, 377, *389*, *452*, *455*
Tyrrell, D. J., 67, *80*

U

Ugwuegbu, D. C., 11, *456*
Upshaw, H. S., 151, *160*
Uranowitz, S. W., 14, *455*

V

Valle, V. A., 341, *350*
Vanbeselaere, N., 406, 407, *417*
VanDeReit, V., 221, *225*
Van der Plight, J., 58, *61*
van Dijk, T. A., 69, 75, 82, 192, *208*

Van Eimeren, B., 407, *416*
Van Kleeck, M. 206, *208*
van Knippenberg, A., 4, 14, 400, *417*, *456*
Van Leeuwen, M. D., *414*
Van Oudenhoven, J. P., 400, 401, 402, 410, 412, *417*
van Twuyver, M., 4, *456*
Vargas, P., 14, 120, 134, *136*, *456*
Vasquez-Suson, K. A., 323, *452*
Veeder, M., *79*
Ventimiglia, J. C., 261, 266, 280, *283*
Villamin, A., 72, *79*
Vincent, S., 261, 266, *282*
Virdin, L. M., 236, *249*
Vivekananthan, P. S., 163, *171*
Vivian, J., 401, 402, 410, 411, *417*
Voelkl, Kristin, 72, *78*, 236, *248*, 324, 387, *389*
Vogel, S. R., 143, *159*, 353, *366*, *367*
von Hippel, W., 14, 120, 122, 132, 134, *135*, *136*, 187, *189*, *456*
Voster, J., *208*
Vroom, V. H., 341, *351*
Vukcevic, D. P., *233*

W
Wachenhut, J., 115, *116*, 289, 353, *367*
Wade, C. S., 402, 410, *414*
Wade, G., 449, *449*
Waenke, M., 403, *415*
Walker, L., 121, 348, *351*
Walker, M. R., *78*
Walkley, R., 397, *418*
Walster, E., 354, 367
Walster, G. W., 354, 367
Walters, C., 291, *303*
Walters, G., 8, 87, *98*, 213, *225*, 353, *367*, *368*, *454*
Wanke, M., 6, *451*
Wann, D. L., 187, *188*
Warring, D., *417*
Warrington, D., 399, *417*
Washington, R. E., 354, *367, 368*
Wax, S. L., 21, *48*
Weber, M., 102, *117*, 156, *160*
Weber, R., 15, 65, 70, *82*, 193, *208*, 403, 404, *417*, 425, 430, 432, *434*, *456*
Weber-Kollman, R., 403, *417*
Wegner, D. M., 77, *82*, 399, *417*
Weigle, R., 69, *82*
Weigold, M. F., 173, *190*
Weil, A.-M., 38
Wells, G. L., 254, *258*
Wells, H. G., 30, *48*
Weiner, B., 221, *225*, 234, *249*, 355, *367*
Werth, J. L., 404, *417*
Wesman, A., 370, *389*
West, S. G., 76, *79*
Wetherell, M. S., 436, *450*
Wever, R. A., 255, *258*
Wezlek, J., *249*
Wheeler, L., *249*
Wicklund, R. A., *249*
Wicks, B. 143, *160*
White, B. J., 435, *450*
White, J. C. A., 221, *225*

White, R. M., *417*
White, R. W., 102, *117*, 320, *322*
Wilder, D. A., 193, 201, *208*, 327, 328, *337*, 394, 400–401, 402, 403, 404, 405, 407, 409, 410, *413*, *417*, *418*, 436, *450*
Wildgruber, C. M., 255, *258*
Wiley, J. W., 341, *350*, *352*
Wilkes, A. L., 12, 51, *63, 326, 337*, *456*
Wilkins, C., 43, *47*
Wilkins, G., 55, *62*
Willemsen, T. M., 402, 410, *417*
Williams, C., 9, *452*
Williams, C. J., 121, *135*
Williams, J. E., 143, 158, *160*, 290, *304*
Williams, R. M., Jr., 23, *48*, 69, *81*, 102, *117, 403*, *418*
Willie, C. V., 397, *415*
Wilner, D. M., 397, *418*
Wills, T. A., 75, *82*, 173, 186, *190*, 294, *304*
Wine, J., 371, 386, *389*
Winer, B. J., *190*, 202, *208*, 368
Winter, D. G., 76, *78*, 272, *283*
Wintermantel, M., 75, *79*
Wilson, C. C., 69, *82*
Wilson, G. D., 262, 263, *284*
Wilson, O. D., 280, *283*
Wilson, W. J., 290, *304*
Wirth, A., 403, *415*
Wittenbrink, B., 9, 10, 121, 122, 132, *136*, *456*
Wittgenstein, L., 50, *63*
Wolfe, D. M., 143, *159*
Wolman, C., 340, *352*
Wood, G. C., 327, *337*
Wood, J. V., 173, 186, *190*
Wood, W., 143, 156–157, 158, *160*
Woodmansee, J., 101, 104, 114, *116*, *117*, 292, 299, *304*
Worchel, S., 15, 435, 436, 449, *450, 456*
Word, Carl O., 14, 210, 213, *225*, 236, *249*, *456*
Wormer, M. H., 36, *48*
Wright, B., 354–355, *368*
Wurf, E., 172, *189*, 320, *322*
Wyer, R. S., Jr., *81*, 108, *117*, 121, 125, 126, *136*, 254, *258*, 427, *433, 434*
Wyler, R. S., 67
Wylie, R., 354, *368*

Y
Yarrow, P. R., 43, *47*
Young, M. Y., 97, *98*

Z
Zadeh, L. A., 50, *63*
Zadny, J., 214, *225*
Zajonc, R., 51, 52, *63*, 65, 66, *80*, 163, *171*, 290, *304*, 340, *351*
Zalk, S. R., 72, *80*
Zanna, Mark P., 14, 88, 98, *98*, *99*, 187, *189*, 210, 213, *225*, 236, *249*, *456*
Zárate, M. A., 6, 67, *81*, 125, *136*, 455
Zimet, S., 69, *82*
Zion, C., 11, *453*
Zsambok, C., 404, *417*
Zukerman, M., *160*, *368*
Zuwerink, Julia R., 8, 91, 97, *98*, *99*, 187, *189*, 253, 305, 321, *321*, *322*, 454

Subject Index

A

A Modern Utopia, 34
Abelson. R. P., 423
Abramson, L. Y., 355
Abstract, research report,459
Abstraction:
    linguistic intergroup bias, 194, 196–205, 197t, 201t, 203t
    stereotype maintenance, 192–193, 206
Accentuation, 12, 54, 74
Accessibility:
    of category, 5, 428
    of constructs, 71
    memory activation, 108
Accuracy, of stereotypes, 7, 28
Achieved status, 32
Additivity, categorization, 406
Adolescents, learned prejudices/stereotypes, 10–11
Affect and emotion:
    stereotype change, 404
    stereotype role, 187
Affect indices, personal standards study, 315–318, 316t
"Affective tags," 404
African Americans:
    discrimination against, 363
    educational achievement of, 370–371
    measuring prejudice against, 83–84, 86–98, 103–113
    nonverbal behavior toward, 227–233, 230t, 232t
    stereotypes about, 88–89, 91t, 91–98, 94t, 101, 102–103
Agency, gender stereotypes, 142–144, 147, 149–152, 149t, 154–157, 159
"Agree mode," 112
Agreeableness, personality variable, 263
Allen, J. G., 236
Allport, Gordon W., 17–18, 354, 396, 402, 403, 423, 428
Altemeyer, B., 265, 267
Altruism, SDO 263, 273–274
"American dilemma," 291
Amir, Y., 419, 420, 423, 431
Ammons, C. H., 178–179
Ammons, R. B., 178–179
Anthropomorphism, 52
Anti-Black racism, SDO, 260, 261, 285
Anti-Black scale, 100, 103–105, 105t, 106–107, 107t, 108f, 114, 118, 267
    value priming, 109–113, 110t
Anti-Semitism, history of, 59
Antifeminism, 33

Antilocution, 25, 26, 39, 40, 42
Arcuri, Luciano, 140
Aronson, Elliot, 464
Aronson, Joshua, 324
Ascribed status, 32
Assimilation, 429
Assistance, aversive racism study, 293–294, 295t
Atmosphere effects, stereotype change,420–421
Attitudes:
    formation of, 36
    role in prejudice, 24–25, 252
Attractiveness, 235
Attribution, 358, 361t, 361–362
Attribution theory, 60, 324, 354–356
Attributional ambiguity, 324, 363–364, 365–366, 387–388
Augmenting principle, 355
Authoritarianism, SDO, 263, 265, 272, 278–279
"Autistic hostility," 420
Automatic stereotype activation, 120–123, 125–129, 128f, 133–134
Availability:
    memory activation, 108
    stereotypes, 121
Aversive racism, 252–253, 289–292, 301–302
    interracial behavior, 292–299
Avoidance, 25, 39
Awareness, 236
Axelson, L. J., 371

B

Bakan, D., 143, *159*
Barbour, L., 235
Bargh, J. A., 127–128, 130
Baron, R. M., 438
Baumeister, R. F., 235
Bayesian analysis, 157
Behavioral conformation effect, 14–15, 212
Beliefs, role in prejudice, 24–25
Bem, D. J., 461, 463
Bersoff, Donald N., 323–324
Bias, 13–14, 66
Bias reduction, cognitive representations, 440–449, 441t, 444f, 446f, 447f
Big-Five personality Inventory, 266, 267, 273
Blood, segregation of, 42
Bodenhausen, Galen V., 251–252, 254, *258*

Note: f =figures, t=tables

Bogardus, E. S., 35
  social distance scale of, 18, 35
Bookkeeping model, stereotype change, 403
Borgida, Eugene, 323–324
Bradburn, N. M., 108
Braly, K. W., 86, 87–90, 91t, 92–93, 93t, 95–97, 123
Brand, Pamela, 210, 235
Brewer, M. B., 290, 298, 395–399, 400, 401–402, 403, 404, 406, 407, 428, 436, 437, 447–448
Broadbent, D. E., 258
Broadbent, M. H. P., 258
Brown, Rupert, 84, 323, 432
Burns, Sarah, 339
Buss, A. H., 267

C
California Personality Inventory (CPI), SDO, 262, 265, 266, 267, 273
Campbell, D. T., 408
Carnevale, P., 355
Carrington, P. I., 355
Carver, C. S., 365
Caste system, Indian, 23
Categorization:
  automatic, 6, 119–121
  characteristics of, 27–28
  function of, 4, 18–19, 49–50
  nature of, 423–425
  origins, 2–3, 50
  types of, 50–51
Category-based assignment, 400
Category-based interactions, change, 395–396
Category conjunction, 406
Category differentiation model, 406, 407
Category dominance, 406, 408
"Causal nexus," 60
Causality, linguistic intergroup bias, 206
Chapman, L. J., 161–162
Chauvinism scale, SDO study, 287
Checklist approach:
  direct measurement, 8, 9, 83
  racial discrimination, 86, 87
Chein, I., 400
Children:
  in-group formation, 31–32, 38
  learned prejudices/stereotypes, 10
  social category formation, 52
Chinese, discrimination against, 43
Circadian rhythms, impact on judgement, 254–258
Civil rights, SDO, 262
Clarity, trait disconfirmation, 421, 421f
Clifton, A. K., 143
Cognition:
  social categories, 323
  values' role in, 52
Cognitive booster, 412, 425
Cognitive confirmation effect, 212–213
Cognitive egocentrism, 52
Cognitive representations, 6f, 6–7, 409. See also Mental representations
  bias reduction, 440–449, 441t, 444f, 446f, 447f
  mediation role, 436–438, 440–441, 441t

Cohen, Claudia, 209–210
Cohen, Jacob, 464
Collective action, social stereotypes, 58–60
Collective self-esteem, 75–76
Collectivist view point, 36, 68
Colorblind perspective, 392
Common-in-group identity, 409, 410, 411t
Communal goals, gender stereotypes, 142–144, 149, 149t, 156–157
Communalism, 102
Communication:
  bias maintenance, 14
  of prejudices/stereotypes, 10–11
Compartmentalization, 423
Compensation, social strategy, 235, 237
Complexity, intergroup perceptions, 396
Compunction, 306
Concentric loyalties, 37f, 37–38
"Conformation strategy," 214
Conformism, 36
Conjunction fallacy, circadian rhythms study, 255–256
Conscientiousness, personality variable, 263
"Consciousness of kind," 26, 31
Consensual stereotypes, 68, 70, 77
Conservatism:
  SDO, 261–262, 263, 264–265, 272, 279
  value orientation, 102
Conservatives, aversive racism study, 293
"Contact enhancing" interventions, 410
Contact episodes, disconfirmation, 421f, 421–422
Contact hypothesis, 15–16, 391–392, 396–397, 435, 446
Contact settings, disconfirmation, 422–423, 428, 429
Contrada, 194
Conversion model, stereotype change, 403
Cook, S. W., 292, 396, 397, 400, 402, 405, 411, 412, 423, 425, 431
Cooper, Joel, 210, 227, 231
Cooperative atmosphere, stereotype change, 420
Cooperative contact, 392
Correlation hypothesis, in-group homogeneity, 329, 333, 334t, 336
Cover story, research report, 460
Crocker, Jennifer, 235, 237, 324, 354, 403, 425, 430
Cultural elitism, SDO, 261, 285
Cultural norms, collective stereotypes, 69–70, 71–73
Cultural stereotypes, 6–7
Culture:
  social categorization, 49–50
  stereotype formation, 65, 68–70, 77

D
Darley John M., 210, 227, 236, 297
Data-based illusory correlations, 140
Davidson-Podgorny, G., 398–399
Death penalty, SDO study, 276, 288
Deaux, Kay, 323–324
Decategorization, 396, 399, 405, 409, 411t
Deduction, category type, 50, 51
Deductive bias, social categories, 51
Deductive judgements, 74
Demographic information, validity of, 221–222
Depressed affect index, 315, 316t, 318

Derogatory Beliefs subscale, 104–105, 114
Deschamps, J. C., 407
Desforges, D. M., 404
Desirable behavior:
    illusory correlation, 167–170, 168t, 169t
    linguistic bias, 193–194, 197–200, 198t, 201–204
Devine, Patricia G., 83–84, 88–89, 94, 95, 96, 120–121, 123, 125, 129, 130, 131, 133, 134, 253, 306, 309, 310, 311–312, 315, 316, 317–318, 319
Differentiation:
    information processing, 423
    personalization, 397–398
    social stereotypes, 59
Dion, K. K., 237
Direct measurement, 8–9
Directed thinking, 29
Disconfirmation, stereotypes, 402–404, 419–423, 421f
Discomfort affect index, 315–316, 316t, 318
Discrepancy index, 313, 314–315
Discriminant validity, SDO, 260, 262–263, 272–273
Discrimination, 11–12, 25–26, 39, 40–43
    definition of, 40–41
    impact of, 323–324
Discussion section, research report, 459, 461–462
Dissociation, atypical group members, 193
Doise, W., 406, 407
Dominance orientation scale, 288
"Dominant," 7
Dominative racists, 289
Donahue, E., 267
Doty, R. M., 272
"Double burder," 152, 153
Dovidio, John F., 252–253, 404
Downward social comparison theory, 173, 186, 187
Duckitt, J., 279, 408, 413

E
Eagly, Alice H., 139–140, 143, *160*
Ease in Interracial Contacts subscale, 104, 114
Education:
    discrimination in, 42
    stereotype change, 72, 392
Educational achievement, White vs. Black, 370–371
Efficacy-based self–esteem theory, 354
Egalitarianism:
    aversive racism, 289–292
    beliefs, 307
    ideology, 260
Egocentrism, 52
Elliot, Andrew J., 83–84
Elliot, R., 348
Ellsworth, P. C., 348
Emotions, attributional theory of, 355
Empathy, SDO 263, 273–274
Empirical research, concept of, 1
Employment, gender stereotypes, 143–157, 147t, 149t, 153t, 155t
Encoding:
    definition of, 209
    disconfirmation studies, 427, 430
    linguistic bias, 192, 194, 197, 198, 198, 200–201, 203–205
Endorsement, of stereotypes, 121–122, 123, 132–133

Environmental policies, SDO, 262, 270, 286–287
Epps, E. G., 371
Equal status, stereotype change, 420
Erikson, Erik, 354
Erroneous generalization, 26
Ethnic prejudice:
    definition of, 22
    ingredients of, 21, 26
    SDO, 261, 270
Ethnophaulism, 69
Evidence, conflict with, 28–29
Exclusion, atypical group members, 191, 193
Exemplars, 6, 18, 66, 67–68
Expectancy-based illusory correlations, 140
Expectancy confirmation, 235, 236
Expectancy-confirmation bias, 213, 214
Expectancy-confirmation effect, 214, 220, 224
Expectancy-confirmation process, African Americans, 212–214
Expectancy-congruent information, 191, 205
Expectancy-incongruent information, 193–194, 205
Expectations:
    role of, 15, 209–210, 224
    study of, 214–220, 217f, 218t, 220t
Extermination, 26, 39
Extraversion, personality variable, 263
Eye contact:
    immediacy behavior, 229, 231
    nonverbal behavior, 227

F
Fading stereotypes, 89, 213
Family, in-group, 37, 39
Family resemblance," social category, 50
Faranda, J. A., 298
Farina, A., 236
Feedback:
    augmenting principle, 355, 365
    discounting of, 355–356
    self-image study, 181–185, 183f, 184f
Fein, Steven, 141
Felicio, Diane, 210, 235
Fenigstein, A,., 267
Fiedler, K., 193, 195, 200, 202, 204
Fiske, Susan T., 339–341, 343, 344, 345, 346, 347, 349, 303, 436
Forgas, Joseph P., 18
Forward lean, immediacy behavior, 229, 231
Freud, Sigmund, 30, 423
Frustration-aggression theory, 173, 186
Functionalism, stereotype formation, 73–76, 133–134
Fundamental attribution error, 422
"Fuzzy sets," 50

G
Gaertner, Samuel L., 91–92, 95, 252–253, 298, 300, 409, 410, 438
Gay rights, SDO study, 286
Gays:
    prejudice-related discrepancies studies, 308–319
    stereotyping of, 177–188, 180f

Gender: *See also* Sex
  automatic stereotype activation, 120
  origin of, stereotypes, 139, 142–144
  SDO, 261, 268
Gender roles, collective stereotypes, 70
General War Attitudes scale, 271, 272
Generalized change:
  integrated approach, 410–413
  types of, 395–396
Genocide, 43
"Gentlemen's agreement," 40, 41–42
Gerard, H., 327, 397
Gesell, Gerhard, 338–339, 341–342, 345
Ghetto system, 23
Gifford, Robert K., 140
Gilbert, D. T., 132
Gilbert, G. M., 88, 92–93, 95
Gluckberg, S., 227
Goertzel, T. G., 265, 272
Goffman, E., 227, 233
Goldman, W., 235
Goodness of fit, 402, 423, 424, 425
Gough's Adjective Checklist, 323
Grabbe, P., 400
Graduate Record Exam verbal test, 371, 373
Graham, S., 236
Green, R. T., 278
Griffiths, R., 404
Gross, Paget H., 210
Ground, principle of, 31
Group categorization, stereotype change, 405–410
Group discrimination, SDO study, 281
Group-esteem, 75
Group membership, illusory correlations, 163–164, 165–166, 165t, 168–169, 168t
Group norm theory, of prejudice, 35–36
Group prototypes, 66, 67
Group schemas, 66–67
Group size, homogeneity study, 326, 327
Groupness, 328
Groups, processing information about, 423–431

H
Habitual open-mindedness, 29
Hamilton, David L., 140
Harding, J., 400
Harrington, H. J., 397, 398, 399, 400
Harris, M. J., 236
Hass, R. Glen., 84, 274
"Hate-prejudice," 30, 31, 39
Heatherton, T. F., 182
Heaven, P C. L., 279
Heilman, Madeline E., 323–324
Heller, James, 339
Helplessness theory, 355
Help-seeking, aversive racism study, 294–295
Hepburn, C., 222
Heterosexual Attitudes Toward Homosexuals (HATH) questionnaire, 308
Heterosexual Attitudes Toward Homosexuals (HATH) scale, 309, 313, 318

Hewstone, Miles, 391–392, 397, 399–400, 401, 402, 403, 404, 407, 408
Hierarchical ordering, 406–407
Hierarchical status, gender stereotypes, 144
Hierarchy, SDO study, 268
Hierarchy-attenuating myths, SDO, 260
Hierarchy-legitimizing myths, SDO, 259–260, 265, 269, 272
Higgins, E. T., 306, 312, 317, 319, 428
Higher verbal reasoning (HVR), 378, 379
Hilton, J. L., 132, 236
Hitler, Adolf, 26, 36, 43
Hixon, J. G., 132
Holtz, R., 407
Homemaker, gender stereotypes, 143–144, 148, 149t, 151, 156
Homogeneity, perception of, 326–329, 331–337
Hopkins, Ann, 324, 338, 339–341, 345–346
Horne, J. A., 255
Horowitz, L. M., 266, 267
Hostility, 26, 37
Housing, discrimination in, 41–42
Hoyt, M. F., 327
Human beings, separation of, 26–27
Humanitarian orientation, as value prime, 109–110, 110t, 113
Humanitarian-egalitarian orientation, racial attitudes, 102, 103, 106, 113–116
Humanitarian-Egalitarian (HE) scale, 100, 102, 106–108, 107t, 108f, 118, 267, 274
Huron, Douglas, 339, 342
Hypothesis-confirming strategies, 214, 220–221
Hypothesis testing, social categories, 53

I
Identification hypothesis, in-group homogeneity, 329, 333, 334t, 336–337
Ideologies, SDO study, 269–270
"Ideologized positions," 54
Illusory correlations, 11, 58, 140, 157–158, 161–171
Immediacy, definition of, 227
Immediate condition, 230–233
Immediate nonverbal communication, job interview study, 228–230
Immigration, hostility toward, 33
Impression formation, 126–127
In-group:
  nature of, 31–32, 290
  formation of, 31–39, 37f
  positive evaluation of, 55, 290
  transience of, 33–34
In-group favoritism, language bias, 191
In-group favoritism, social category, 4, 12–13, 18
In group homogeneity hypothesis, 328–329, 331–333, 332t, 334t, 335–336
Indirect change, 16
Indirect measurement, 8, 9–10
Individualism, 102
Individuals, stereotype formation, 65–66, 70–71, 76–77
Individuation, 3–4
Induction, category type, 50–51
Inductive bias, social categories, 51
Inductive judgements, 74

"Inferiority anxiety," 370
"Information highway," 69
Information processing, 254–255
Information processing bias, 210
Information search, bias in, 14–15
Institutional racism, 291, 293
Interdependent contact, 392
Intergroup bias, reduction of, 435–438
Intergroup contact, cognitive analysis of, 402–404, 405, 411t, 419–433, 421f, 430f
Intergroup contact:
  generalized change, 399–401, 402
  social categorization model, 431–432
  traditional assumptions, 420
Intergroup cooperation, 436–438, 440–449, 441t, 444f, 446f, 447f
Intergroup relations, 394–395
Internal colonization, 290
Interpersonal dominance, SDO, 262–263, 273
Interpersonal Reactivity Index (IRI), SDO study, 265, 273
Interpretation, bias in, 14–15
Interracial behavior:
  nonracial factors, 295–299
  social norms, 292–295
Interview length, job interview study, 229, 230, 231
Intimate contact, stereotype change, 420
Iraq War, SDO study, 275, 287
Islam, M. K., 402,

J
Jackson Personality Inventory (JPI), SDO, 263–264, 267, 274
Jackson Personality Research Form (JPRF), SDO, 262, 265, 266, 273, 276
Janis-Field Feelings of Inadequacy scale, 360
Jewish American princess," stereotype of, 175
Jewish "predicament," 369
Jews, stereotypes of, 139
John, Oliver P., 267, 392
Jones, E. E., 213, 222, 327
Jones, J. L., 258
Jones, R. E., 227, 231
Journal articles, how to read, 457–465
Judd, C. M., 438, 448
Judgement, circadian rhythms study, 256–257, 257t
Just World Scale, 106, 265, 269, 270
Justification:
  process of, 74
  social stereotypes, 59, 60

K
Kahneman, D., 222, 223, 255, 256
Karlins, M., 88–89, 93, 95
Katz, D., 86, 87–90, 91t, 92–93, 93t, 95–97, 123, 420
Katz, Irwin, 84, 274, 371, 388
Kelley, H. H., 355
Kelly, J. R., 258
Kenny, D. A., 438, 448
Kentle, R. L., 267
"Kernel of truth," stereotypes, 7, 28, 158
King, G., 428

Kleck, R. E., 227, 230, 231, 233
Kramer, B. M., 428

L
La Piere, R. T., 252
Labels, cultural stereotypes, 68, 74–75
Lamb, Charles, 20
Language, stereotype formation, 68–69, 140, 191–207
Latané, B., 297
"Late bloomers," 14–15
Lawfulness, 193, 201
Lepore, Lorella, 84
Lepper, M. E., 214
Level of categorization, disconfirmation, 426, 427, 429
Lewin, Kurt, 34, 400
Lewis, L. S., 227
Lewis, P., 235
Lewis, S., 402
Lexical access promising (LAP), 378
Liberalism, value orientation, 102
Liberals, aversive racism study, 293
Linguistic Category Model, 140, 192–194, 193t, 202
Linguistic intergroup bias, 14, 140, 194–200, 197t, 198t, 204–207
Lippman, Walter, 6, 64, 423
Lipset, S. M., 278
Lockhart v. McCree, 348
Locksley, A., 222, 223, 429
Logan, G. D., 312
Lord, C., 214
"Love-prejudice," 30, 39
Lui, T. J., 174, 177
Lynching, ethnic violence, 44–45

M
Maass, Anne, 140
Macrae, C. N., 404
Major, Brenda, 235, 237, 324, 354, 355, 365
Malle, Bertram F., 252, 266, 267
Marcus-Newhall, A., 407
Marginality, 35
Marital status, gender stereotypes, 152–154, 153t
Marlowe-Crowne Social Desirability Scale (SDS), 104, 105–106
Martin, J., 412
"Master race," 33
Matthews, M., 294
McClintock, C. 420
McFarland, C., 360, 363
McGrath, D., 143, *160*
McGrath, J. E., 258
McLaughlin, J. P., 300
Mead, Margaret, 290
Measurements, types of, 8–10
Media:
  collective stereotypes, 69
  communication of prejudices/stereotypes, 10
  racial stereotypes, 291
Medin, D. L., 424
Mehrabian, A., 177, 226–227, 229, 231, 232

Mehrabian-Russell Mood Scale, 177
Memory
    activation determinants, 106
    bias in, 14, 58, 66
Men, gender stereotypes of, 139, 142–159
Mental representations, 65, 71. *See also* Cognitive
    representaions
Meritocracy, SDO, 260, 262
Merton, Robert K., 212, 226
"Meta-contrast," 74
Method section, research report, 459–460
Meyer, D., 108
Michela, J., 365
Migdal, M., 408
Military policy, SDO, 262, 270–272, 286
Miller, Carol T., 210, 235
Miller, N., 395–399, 400, 401, 405, 407, 428, 436
Milne, A., 404
Minimal intergroup effect, 13, 18
Minority groups:
    self-esteem in, 327
    stereotypes of, 140
Misconceptions, 23
Mitchell, M., 276
Mixed motive case, stereotypes, 344–345
"Modern racism," 84
Modern Racism Scale, 8, 88, 90–91, 267, 292
"Modern sexism," 84
Monteith, Marso J., 253, 306, 319
Mood, attribution studies, 358, 363
"Morning people," 254, 255, 256, 257
Morningness-Eveningness Questionnaire (MEQ), 255, 256
Motivation:
    social categories, 323
    stereotyping, 73–74
Motivational theories, stereotypes, 191, 290
Mullen, B., 408
Multifactor Racial Attitude Inventory (MRAI), 101, 104, 114
Multiple Affect Adjective Check List (MAACL), 358
Multiple studies, in research reports, 462–463
Mutual intergroup differentiation, 401–402

N

Nation, as in-group, 34, 34f, 38
National Election Study, 264
National Opinion Research Center (NORC), racial attitudes,
    101, 102
Nationalism, SDO, 261, 264, 286
Nature or Prejudice, The, 17
Negative mood scale, 360
Negother affect index, 315, 316t, 316–317, 318
Negself affect index, 315–316, 316t, 319
Neuberg, S. L., 436
Neural networks, 6
Neuroticism, personality variable, 263
"Night people," 254, 255, 256, 257
Noblesse oblige, SDO, 262, 286
Nonimediate condition, 230–233
Nonverbal behavior:
    decoding, 227
    description of, 226–227
    reciprocation of, 226, 227–228, 231, 232

self-fulfilling prophecies, 226–230, 233
Nuessle, W., 227, 231
"Nurturant," 7

O

Obesity:
    compensation strategies, 235, 238–248, 242t, 243t
    self-protected strategies, 237, 238
    stigmatized condition, 234
Obligation, 311–312
Occupational discrimination, 42
One World, 37, 38
Open-ended approach, direct measurement, 9
Openness, personality variable, 263
Oppression, SDO study, 280–281
Ortiz, V., 222
Östberg, O., 255
Ought discrepancies, 306
Out-group:
    creation of, 36–37, 59
    homogeneity, 12
    generalized change, 400–401
    language bias, 191, 203–204
    rejection of, 39
    social category, 4, 30, 290
Overcategorization, 17, 23
Overdetermined, prejudices/stereotypes, 10
Overgeneralization, 7, 30

P

"Paired distinctiveness," 162
Paired words, aversive racism study, 299–301, 300f
Palio, 194
Parallel Time, 377
Parental status, gender stereotypes, 152–154, 153t
Parents, communication of prejudices/stereotypes, 10
Park, B., 92, 93, 420–421, 422, 427, 429
Patriotism scale, 285–286
Peers, communication of prejudices/stereotypes, 10–11
Percentage approach, direct measurement, 8–9
Perceptual accentuation, 12, 54
Person prototypes, 56–57
Personal Attribute Questionnaire (PAQ), SDO, 263, 266, 267
Personal beliefs:
    assessment of, 90, 91
    racial prejudice, 83–84, 87–89
Personal Should index, 310
Personal Standard Internalization index, 310, 313
Personal values
    as categories, 29–30
    and prejudice, 30, 102–105
Personality, predictors of prejudice, 252
Personality variables, standard, 263
Personalization, bias reduction, 3–4, 397–399, 405, 410–411,
    436
Peterson, B. E., 272
Pettigrew, T. F., 412
Physical attacks, prejudice, 26, 39, 43–45
Physical distance, immediacy behavior, 229, 231, 232
Physically handicapped, attitudes toward, 355
Piaget, J., 423

"Pictures in the head," 64
Pietromonaco, P., 127–128, 130
Policy Issues Questionnaire, 264
"Polite prejudice," 26
Polivy, J., 182
Positive affect index, 315, 316t, 317–318
Positive mood scale, 360
Pratto, Felicia, 252
Predictive validity, SDO, 260, 261–262
Preferences, social categories, 52
Prejudice:
    acting out, 25–26
    assessment of, 90–91
    contrasted with stereotypes, 8
    definitions of, 1, 18, 22–23, 24
    development theories, 139–141
    group norm theory, 35–36
    inevitability of, 119–120, 132
    maintenance process, 413
    measurement of, 8–10
    model of, 253
    nature of, 20–21
    origin of, 10–11
    relationship to stereotypes, 74
    reversibility test, 23
    study of, 1, 17
    term, 21–22
    theories of, 84
Prejudice. See also Ethnic prejudice
Prejudice reduction process, 305–306, 321
Prejudice Scale, 123, 127, 137
Presser, S., 108
Price Waterhouse v. Hopkins, 338–339, 341–346, 328
Priming
    concept of, 9, 84,
    of categories, 121, 427, 428–429
    Prejudice Scale, 128f, 128, 129, 130f, 130–131
    stereotypes, 120–121
Priming techniques, racial attitudes, 107, 108–113, 109t, 110t,
    111t
Princeton trilogy studies, 86–87, 91, 92–93, 95, 96, 97
    short comings of, 88–89
Pro-Black scale, 100, 103–105, 105t, 106–107, 107t, 108f,
    114, 118, 267
    value priming, 109t, 109–113, 110t
Protestant ethic:
    racial attitudes, 102–103, 105, 115, 291
    as value prime, 109–110, 110t, 113
Protestant Work Ethic (PE) scale, 100, 102, 105–108, 107t,
    108f, 118
    value priming, 109t, 109–112
    SDO study, 265, 267, 269, 270
Protocols of the Elders of Zion, 59
Prototypes, 6, 18, 49, 50, 57, 158, 423–424 . See also Group
    protoypes
Prototype subtyping, model, stereotype change, 403–404
Public Opinion, 6, 102
Punitive policies, SDO, 262, 288

Q
Quattrone, G. A., 213, 222, 327
Quick Test of Intelligence, 178–179

R
Race, automatic stereotype activation, 120–122, 125–129
Racial ambivalence, 100–103, 113–116
Racial attitudes, priming techniques, 107, 108–113, 109t, 110t,
    111t
Racial Attitudes Questionnaire, 109
Racial discrimination, 86
Racial epithets, 40
Racial policy, SDO study, 286
Racial segregation, 18
Racial vulnerability, 370
"Range of tolerable behavior," 36
Rape Myths scale, SDO study, 266
Rationalization, 25
Ray, J., 279
Re-fencing devise, 29, 193, 403, 423
"Readily applicable," values 51
Reasoning and Verbal Acuity Battery, 178
Recategorization model, 436–437
Recategorization, stereotype change, 409–410
Recency, memory activation, 108
Reciprocal behavior, nonverbal, 226–228, 231
Recoding, process of, 429–430
Reference group, 34–35
"Refusniks," 93
Reis, H. T., 237
Relabeling, 72
Religious epithets, 40
Research report
    description of, 458
    function of, 464–465
    how to read, 458–465
    sections of, 459
Results section, research reports, 459, 460–461
Review article, description of, 458
Rewards and punishment, stereotype change, 420
Rewards, in-group, 31
Right Wing Authoritarian (RWA) scale, 265, 267, 272
Riots, ethnic conflict, 44–45
Roberts, S. O., 371
Robinson, J. M., 371
Rokeach, M., 320, 321
Rombough, S., 280
Rosch, E., 300, 429
Rosenberg Self-Esteem scale, 358, 360
Rosenfeld, H. M., 227, 232
Ross, L., 214
Ross, M., 360, 363
Roth, Philip, 369
Rothbart, Myron, 92, 93, 392, 397, 402, 403, 420–421, 422,
    427, 429
Rothbaum, Esther D., 210, 235
Rumor, role of, 46–47
Russel, J., 177

S
Sagar, H. A., 405
Salience, of category, 5, 40, 57, 327–328
Salvi, Daniela, 140
Sarnoff, I., 420
Saul, B., 236
Scapegoating, 173

Schaller, Mark, 18
Scheier, M. F., 267
Schemas, 18, 404. See also Group schemas
Schemata, 6, 50, 57
"Schemata effects," 57
Schofield, J. W., 397, 399, 405, 408
Schopler, J., 294
Schuman, H., 100–102, 108
Schvaneveldt, R., 108
Scripts:
    behavioral, 66
    social categorization, 49
Segregation, form of discrimination, 41
Self-affirmation:
    stereotype function, 173–177, 176f, 185–186, 187
    stigmatized persons, 235, 236, 238
Self-categorization theory, 405–406, 436, 446–448
Self-concept, 60, 172
    theories about, 354
Self-discrepancies, 172–173
Self-discrepancies theory, 306
Self-esteem:
    and attractiveness, 235
    attribution studies, 358–359, 362, 363t
  and dominance, 273
    impact of prejudice on, 354
    maintenance, 173, 186, 191
    minority groups, 327, 328
    stereotype function, 75–76, 181–182, 184f, 184–185, 186, 290
    stereotype origin, 140–141, 187
Self-esteem threat, 206, 238
Self-evaluation maintenance, 173
Self-fulfilling prophecy, 14–15, 172, 210, 212, 213, 224, 428–429
Self-fulfilling prophecy:
    nonverbal behavior, 226–227, 233
    stigmatized persons, 234–236, 354
Self-hate, 34
Self-image maintenance, 172, 173, 187, 188
Self-image threat, 173–174, 178–181, 180t, 181–184, 183f, 186, 187–188
Self-integrity, 173
Self-interest, change and, 29
Self-presentation, 9, 10, 84
Self-report methods, problem with, 84
Self-schemas, 172
Self-threat, 370–371
Self-valuation, stereotype function, 75–76
Self-verification, 172, 235–236, 238
Semantic priming, 120–121
Semantic stereotype activation, 121
Semin, Gün, 140, 192, 193, 195, 200, 202, 204
Sex, in-group, 32–33
Sex stereotypes:
    expectancy perspective, 206–207
    Hopkins case, 339–341, 344–346
Sex. See also Gender
Sexism, 8
    SDO, 261, 270
Sexist Attitudes Toward Women scale, SDO study, 266
Sherif, C., 436, 449
Sherif, M., 408–409, 410, 436, 448, 449

Sherman, R. C., 237
Shoulder orientation, immediacy behavior, 229, 231
Sidanius, Jim, 252, 278
Sigall, H., 365
Simon, Bernd, 323
Slurs, racial/religious, 68–69, 74
Smith, E. E., 424
Snyder, M., 224, 267
Social acceptance, stereotype function, 76
Social attitudes, SDO predictability, 260, 274–276, 277t
Social attribution theory, 60
Social categories:
    activation of, 1–4, 18
    crosscutting, 406–408, 411, 411t
    homogeneity perception of, 323, 326–329, 331–337
    maintenance of, 52–54
    modes of, 51
    outcomes of, 11–13, 18
    role of, 49–50
Social categorization model, 431–432, 436
Social causality, social stereotypes, 59
Social class, SDO, 278
Social cognition, stereotypes, 157–158, 191
Social comparison process, social identity, 54–55, 328
Social comparison theory, 172, 354
Social Darwinism, SDO, 260
Social distance, 35
Social dominance orientation (SDO), 252, 259–260
Social dominance orientation (SDO) scale, , 273t, 274t, 275t, 277t, 285–288
Social dominance orientation (SDO) scale, 264, 285–288, 267–277, 266t, 268t, 269t, 270t, 271t
Social exchange theory, 354
"Social facilitation," of violence, 44
Social identity:
    categorization, 4, 54–56
    definition of, 327
    minority groups, 327–328
    stereotype formation, 140–141, 173
Social identity theory, 173, 186, 193, 206, 327–328, 354, 405, 406, 407, 413, 436
    psychological interventions, 395
Social judgement, 213
    memory activation, 108
Social norms:
    behavioral impact, 252
    collective stereotypes, 69–70
Social policy attitudes, SDO, 262, 270–272
Social programs, SDO study, 286
Social psychological interventions, 394–395
"Social reality," 65
Social relationships, physical attractiveness, 237
Social representation, 49
Social responsibility norms, aversive racism study, 294
Social role:
    SDO study, 281–282
    theories, of stereotypes, 140, 142–159
Social stereotypes, function of, 59–60, 191
Social Value Questionnaire, 109
Social welfare, SDO, 262
Society Should index, 310
Society Standard Internalized index, 310, 311, 311t
Speech error rate, job interview study, 229, 230, 231, 232

Spencer, Steven J., 141
Spielberger State Anxiety Inventory (SSAI), 375
Spinoza, Baruch, 30
Spontaneous categorization, 2
Stacey, R. G., 278
Stallworth, Lisa M., 252
Stangor, Charles, 18
Staples, Brent, 377
Statistics, research report, 461
Steele, Claude M., 173, 174, 177, 185, 235, 324
Steele, S., 370
Steffen, Valerie, 139–140
Stein, S., 237
Stephan, W. G., 290, 327
Stephenson, G. M., 400
Stereotype activation, 108, 120, 378–380
    circadian rhythms study, 257
Stereotype threat, 369–371, 384–389
Stereotype threat studies, 371–385, 374f, 376t, 380f, 381t, 383f
Stereotype vulnerability, 324, 369
Stereotype, term, 5
Stereotypes
    accuracy of, 7–8
    attempts to change, 15–16, 391–392
    categorization, 5–6
    cognitive aspects of, 57–58
    collective formation, 64–65, 68–70, 77
    complexity of, 251–252
    conditions necessary for change, 431
    definition of, 1, 57, 162
    dehumanizing, 75
    development theories, 139–141
    endorsement of, 121–122, 123
    individual formation of, 64–68
    maintenance of, 13–15, 58, 209–210
    measurement of, 8–10, 90
    motivational factors, 187, 191
    normative aspects of, 57, 58
    origin of, 10–11, 17
    structural needs for, 252
    study of, 1, 17, 64–65
Stereotyping, 1, 50
    automaticity of, 119–123, 125–129, 132, 133–134
Stigma, dual threats, 235
Stigmatized person:
    attributional theory, 354–356
    self–esteem, 235, 354
    lack of research on, 236
    nonverbal behavior toward, 227
"Stimulus generalization," 420
Story telling, research reports, 463
Strength of activation, disconfirmation, 425
Subgrouping, 412
Subtype, disconfirmation, 430–431
Subtyping model, stereotype change, 403–404, 412
Subtyping, process of, 3
Superordinate categories, disconfirmation, 426, 431, 432, 436
Survey of Personal Values, 109
Swann, W. B., 224, 235, 236
Symbolic interactive perspective, self–concept, 354
Symbolic racism, 100
Symbols, 37

T
Tajfel, Henri, 18, 162, 326, 400, 408, 413, 428, 436, 437
Taylor, Shelly E., 428, 430
Terror management, 173
Testa, Maria, 324
Testing outcomes, White vs. Black, 370–371, 388–389
Theoretical article, description of, 458
Thomas, Clarence, 276
Title, research report, 458–459
Token" role, 5, 371, 387
Tolerance, SDO study, 274
Total Should index, 313, 314, 315t
Total Would index, 313, 314, 315t
Trait inferences, criterion for, 421, 421f
Traits:
    African Americans, 89, 90–95, 91t, 94t
    direct measurement, 9
    disconfirmation of, 420–421, 421f
    expectancy study, 219, 220t, 222
    illusory correlations, 163, 166, 166t, 169, 169t
    social categorization, 56, 72, 120, 124t, 124–125, 127
Tri-Dimensional Sexism Scale, SDO study, 266
Triandis, H. C., 397
Turner, J. C., 406, 407, 410, 432, 436, 447–448
Tversky, A, 222, 223, 255, 256

U
Undesirable behavior:
    illusory correlation, 162–167, 165t, 166t
    linguistic bias, 193, 194, 197, 198t, 199, 201–204
United Nation, discrimination definition, 40–41

V
Value prime, racial attitudes, 109–113, 109t, 110t, 111t
Values:
    and racial ambivalence, 102, 115
    role of, 108
    social categorization, 18, 23–24, 49, 51–54, 58
Vanbeselaere, N., 407
Van Oudenhoven, J. P., 412
Ventimiglia, J. C., 280
Verbal rejection, out–groups, 39–40, 44
Victim analysis," 233
Violence, 26, 43–45
Vivian, J., 401, 402
Voekl, Kristin, 324
von Hippel, W., 132

W
War of the sexes," 33
Warfare, SDO scale, 287–288
Wax, S. L., 21
Weber, R., 403, 425, 430
Weiner, B., 355
Wells, H. G., 34
Wicks, B., 143
Wilder, 400–401, 402, 403
Wilson, G. D., 262, 280
Winter, D. G., 272
Witchcraft, persecution of, 58–59

Women:
  discrimination against, 353–354
  gender stereotypes of, 139, 142–159
Women's rights, SDO, 286
Wood, G. C., 327
Wood, W., 143, *160*
Woodmansee, J. J., 292
Worchel, S., 449

Word, Carl O., 210
Wyer, R. S., 254, *258*

Y
Youth, hate crimes, 44

Z
Zanna, Mark P., 210
Zuwerink, Julia R., 253